2/01

 St. Louis Community College

Forest Park
Florissant Valley
Meramec

Instructional Resources
St. Louis, Missouri

Software and
Internet Law

Software and Internet Law

Mark A. Lemley

Professor of Law
University of California at Berkeley

Peter S. Menell

Professor of Law
University of California at Berkeley

Robert P. Merges

Wilson, Sonsini, Goodrich, and Rosati
Professor of Law and Technology
University of California at Berkeley

Pamela Samuelson

Professor of Law
University of California at Berkeley

ASPEN LAW & BUSINESS
A Division of Aspen Publishers, Inc.
Gaithersburg   New York

Permissions
Aspen Law & Business
A Division of Aspen Publishers, Inc.
1185 Avenue of the Americas
New York, N Y 10036

Printed in the United States of America

ISBN 0-7355-1312-0

1   2   3   4   5   6   7   8   9   0

Library of Congress Cataloging-in-Publication Data

Software and internet law / Mark A. Lemley ... [et al.].
    p. cm.
  Includes index.
  ISBN 0-7355-1312-0
    1. Copyright—Computer programs—United States. 2. Software protection—Law and legislation—United States. 3. Internet industry—Law and legislation—United States. I. Lemley, Mark A., 1966-

KF3024.C6 S617 2000
343.7309'944—dc21

00-022064

About Aspen Law & Business
Legal Education Division

With a dedication to preserving and strengthening the long-standing tradition of publishing excellence in legal education, Aspen Law & Business continues to provide the highest quality teaching and learning resources for today's law school community. Careful development, meticulous editing, and an unmatched responsiveness to the evolving needs of today's discerning educators combine in the creation of our outstanding casebooks, coursebooks, textbooks, and study aids.

ASPEN LAW & BUSINESS
A Division of Aspen Publishers, Inc.
A Wolters Kluwer Company
www.aspenpublishers.com

For Rose, as ever.
M.A.L.

For Ralph, Nancy, Devon, Carol and Jeffery;
and Claire, Dylan and Noah
P.S.M.

For Jo, Robbie and James
R.P.M.

For Bob, who has made so many
things possible.
P.S.

Summary of Contents

Contents

I

SOFTWARE LAW   47

1

Trade Secret Protection   49

2

Copyright Law   97

8 · *International Protection of Computer Technology* · 643

Ⅱ   *INTERNET LAW*   *773*

9   *Jurisdiction and Choice of Law*   *775*

10   *Intellectual Property in Cyberspace*   *799*

≣ Content Regulation ≣ 921

Internet Governance   *1069*

Preface

The goal of this book is to provide students with a comprehensive treatment of the law of computer software, with a focus on intellectual property, licensing, and antitrust law. We also aim to provide a template for the study of the fast-developing field of Internet law. By their very nature, software and especially Internet law will change rapidly. Our goal, therefore, is not to freeze the development of the law at one particular point in time, but to provide a base of fundamental principles and issues on which subsequent developments will build. Those subsequent developments will be reflected in future supplements to this book and, perhaps more important, in our Web site, http://www.law.berkeley.edu/bclt/pubs/swbook. We encourage those who use this book to refer to the Web site for up-to-date developments before planning their course of study.

Lawyers play many significant roles in servicing the software industry and Internet-using firms. They often draft or review license agreements for acquiring software or other information products. They may monitor ongoing licensing arrangements. They sometimes draft or negotiate agreements for the custom development of software to be performed by other firms. They may conduct intellectual property audits to enable their clients to understand better how to protect the firm's overall intellectual capital. Lawyers also help design electronic ordering systems or review Web sites to ensure that no illegal content is posted there. They may provide assessments about legal or policy developments likely to affect their clients. And when necessary, they litigate claims or otherwise work to settle disputes between their clients and other firms. To play these multiple roles successfully, lawyers need a considerable understanding of the law, how it has been applied in the past, and how it is evolving.

While this understanding can be obtained by taking a standard curriculum in intellectual property, antitrust, contract, and tort law—perhaps with some constitutional or criminal law mixed in—there are several reasons why studying software and Internet law in one course may offer a better framework for providing sound advice to information technology (IT) clients. The most obvious reason to study software and Internet law as a special course is that the practice of law in this field often requires the kind of integrative thinking that this book facilitates. A software entrepreneur may develop an innovative user interface and ask her lawyer: "Should I patent it? Can I copyright it? How else might I protect the look and feel?" Such questions may be easier to answer when the lawyer has studied intellectual property law as it has specifically been applied to software.

There are, however, at least three other reasons to study software and Internet law. While a course on these subjects is useful because it covers cases that involve the application of different kinds of laws to computers, software, or the Internet, a course of this sort will, more importantly, raise fundamental questions about the adequacy of existing laws to adapt to the challenges posed by computer software and the Internet. Computer software was the first digital subject matter to raise such challenges, and several chapters (Chapters 2 on copyright, 3 on patent, and 5 on sui generis laws) address them. (However, as will become apparent in Chapter 9, those challenges are not confined to software.) Why does software pose challenges for the law? The answer lies in the very nature of software. It is a utilitarian text. Copyright law has a long history of protecting literary and artistic works but not utilitarian works. Patent and trade secrecy laws have a long history of protecting utilitarian works but not writings or innovations embodied in textual form. Given the traditional bounds of both copyright and patent law, the hybrid nature of computer programs has made it difficult to integrate this new subject matter into the existing intellectual property regimes.

Another reason to study software and Internet law is that economic considerations, especially those deriving from network effects, complicate the application of existing laws to these industries. When the value of a product depends critically on its compatibility with other products, the absolute character of traditional intellectual property rights can block access to networks, thereby creating particularly serious impediments to competition and new challenges for antitrust law. In addition, firms need to plan their development and marketing strategies with network effects in mind. This may mean planning to give away some software or other digital products or services in order to establish market share, build brand, and take advantage of network effects. See Carl Shapiro & Hal Varian, Information Rules (1998).

Also, the needs of these emerging industries are bringing about legal developments that once might have seemed unlikely or unthinkable. In the 1970s and 1980s, it might have seemed absurd to think that firms could use licensing agreements to distribute mass-marketed information products. Developers of computer software started using "shrinkwrap" licenses for this purpose (that is, putting inside a box of packaged software a document that states, among other things, that the purchaser of the software is a licensee and his or her uses of the software are restricted in certain ways and that the purchaser's opening the package or installing the software constitutes the user's agreement to the terms of the "license"). Yet the ubiquity of such licenses in the software marketplace has paved the way for an increased use of licensing as a means to control distribution of commercially valuable information in other venues and has led to proposals for laws to validate mass-market licensing agreements. New laws of this sort can best be understood in the information industry context out of which they arose.

A book of this magnitude would not be possible without the assistance of many people. We would like to thank Ryan Garcia, Inez Gonzalez, Peter Huang, Kurt Opsahl, Chris Ridder, John Sasson, Jason Schultz, Leah Theriault, and Larry Trask, for their work on the book, and Dan Burk, Susan Friwald, Michael Froomkin, Paul Heald, Dawn Nunziato, David Post and several anonymous reviewers for their comments on earlier drafts.

Mark A. Lemley
Peter S. Menell
Robert P. Merges
Pamela Samuelson

Berkeley, California
March 2000

Acknowledgments

We acknowledge the copyright owners of the following images and excerpts used in this volume with their permission (this list does not include works by the authors of this book):

Maureen O'Rourke, Fencing Cyberspace, 82 Minn. L. Rev. 609 (1998).

Jane Kaufman Winn, The Emerging Law of Electronic Commerce.

J. Bradford De Long & A. Michael Froomkin, The Next Economy, in Internet Publishing and Beyond: The Economics of Digital Information and Intellectual Property (D. Hurley ed., 1998).

David Johnson & David Post, And How Shall the Net Be Governed? A Meditation on the Relative Virtues of Decentralized, Emergent Law, in Coordinating the Internet (Brian Kahin & James Keller, eds., 1997).

Bernadine Trompenaars, IVIR Report.

Dennis Karjala, The Protection of Operating Software Under Japanese Law, 12 Eur. Intell. Prop. Rev. 359 (1998).

Thomas M. Jorde & David Teece, Innovation, Cooperation, and Antitrust, 4 High Tech. L.J. 1 (1989).

League for Programming Freedom, Is This the Future of Programming?, Dr. Dobb's J., Nov. 1990, at 56, reprinted courtesy of Dr. Dobb's Journal (http://www.ddj.com). All rights reserved.

Ward S. Bowman Jr., Patent and Antitrust Law (1973), reprinted by permission of the University of Chicago Press.

Vance Brown, The Incompatibility of Copyright and Computer Software: An Economic Evaluation and Proposal for a Marketplace Solution, 66 N.C. L. Rev. 977 (1988). Copyright 1988 by the North Carolina Law Review Association. Reprinted with permission.

Lauren Fisher Kellner, Trade Dress Protection for Computer User Interface "Look and Feel", 61 U. Chi. L. Rev. 1011 (1994).

Michael Meurer, Price Discrimination, Personal Use and Piracy, 45 Buff. L.
    Rev. 845 (1997).
Andrea Migdal, Shrinkwrap Licenses Abroad, Journal of Internet Law (1999).

Note: We have selectively omitted citations and footnotes from cases without the use of ellipses or other indications. All footnotes are numbered consecutively within each chapter, except that footnotes in cases and other excerpts correspond to the actual footnote numbers in the published reports.

Many of the problems in this text are taken from actual cases. However, in many instances we have altered the facts of the case. In most cases we have also altered the names of the parties involved. In a few cases, however, particularly in the trademark and antitrust chapters, we felt that it was important to the problem to use the name of a product or company with which the reader would be familiar. Readers should understand that the problems are hypothetical in nature and that we do not intend them to represent the actual facts of any case or situation.

Software and
Internet Law

Introduction to Computer Technology, Network Economics, and Intellectual Property Law

Computer software and Internet commerce are among the fastest growing and most promising industries in the United States. A recent government report notes that more than half of U.S. nonfarm industries either produce information technology (IT) directly or invest in and use information technology products and services. U.S. Commerce Department, The Emerging Digital Economy II (1999). The information technology sector of the U.S. economy represented 8 percent of gross domestic product (GDP) in 1999, accounting for more than $700 billion. Computer software accounted for $200 billion of this total. The IT sector of the U.S. economy has steadily increased its share of the GDP in the 1990s and shows no sign of slowing down. These patterns can be seen throughout the global economy. A World Gone Soft: A Survey of the Software Industry, The Economist (May 25, 1996).

While firms such as Intel, Microsoft, Compaq, IBM, Cisco, AOL, and Amazon.com attract much of the attention in the IT marketplace, the IT industries touch almost all aspects of the modern economy. For example, traditional manufacturing firms, such as General Motors, make significant use of computers, computer software, and computer networks in their businesses. Automobile manufacturers use CAD (computer-aided design) software to design new vehicles, CAM (computer-aided manufacturing) software to assemble these designs, and digital networks to purchase component parts and to distribute vehicles to customers. Few businesses, government agencies, schools, or other organizations operate today without extensive use of computer technology and digital networks. An increasingly wide array of companies— whether they sell information, cars, or anything else—use digital networks, principally the Internet, to market products and transact business. While it is easy to scoff at estimates of the potential growth of global electronic commerce because they seem like (and probably are) rank guesswork, electronic commerce

1

has surpassed what once seemed like exaggerated estimates. The Emerging Digital Economy II report notes that in 1997 "private analysts forecast that the value of Internet retailing could reach $7 billion by 2000—a level surpassed by nearly 50 per cent in 1998." While the popular press has mainly concentrated on the growth of Internet business-to-consumer companies, such as Amazon.com, many industry experts believe that business-to-business ecommerce will be larger and have more far-reaching implications for the U.S. economy. Internet technology makes possible great efficiencies in the ways businesses are structured, distribute product and service information, and conduct transactions. The extent of these possibilities are just beginning to emerge.

This chapter describes the early history of computing in Section A. It explains how computers work in very basic terms in Section B, and introduces the principal models of software engineering in Section C. Section D discusses the distinctive economics of computer software and network markets. Finally, Section E offers an overview of the principal intellectual property laws protecting computer technology. Subsequent chapters address these legal regimes in greater detail.

Readers with a strong understanding of how computers work and how programs are written should feel comfortable in skipping or skimming Sections A through C. They should read the balance of the chapter in detail, however, because the economics of computer software and the intellectual property background may be unfamiliar—and will be important in the chapters to come.

Students who do not have a strong background in computer technology should review Sections A through C at this time. For those students, a brief note on methodology in this chapter is in order. Our goal in providing information about the computer industry is to offer students essential background on how computer software works and how markets for computer software function. We do not intend this introduction to provide a complete understanding of the field. In our summaries below, we reference a number of excellent sources providing detailed background. The reader who is interested in more detail than we can possibly provide here should seek out these sources.

A. THE EARLY HISTORY OF COMPUTERS

This Section introduces the reader to the early history of computer hardware and software. The purpose of this Section is to describe the enormous changes that occurred in the early days of the computer industry in order to provide context for the discussions that will follow. This Section does not describe events up to the present day. More recent developments (including the growth of the Internet) are discussed in the sections that follow, and in later chapters, where modern technological developments often present new legal issues.

Following the invention of the abacus approximately 5,000 years ago, the field of computing machines did not develop significantly until the eighteenth century. Leonardo da Vinci (1425-1519) sketched some designs for mechanical adding machines. Blaise Pascal (1623-1662) invented and built the "Pascaline," a sophisticated mechanical device for counting. Although not commercially successful because of its cost and delicate construction, the counting-wheel design served as the basis for most mechanical calculators until the 1960s. At the turn of the nineteenth century, Joseph-Marie Jaquard (1752-1834) introduced a new loom technology that used punched cards to control the movement of needles, thread, and fabric to create distinctive patterns through a binary mechanical automation technology. In the mid-nineteenth century, Charles Babbage envisioned mechanical devices (the Difference Engine and the Analytical Engine) to perform arithmetic operations. His designs, involving thousands of gears, proved impractical. One of his students, Lady Ada August Lovelace, proposed the use of punched cards to automate the operation of such devices.

Toward the end of the nineteenth century, a U.S. Census Bureau agent named Herman Hollerith developed a punched-card tabulating machine to automate the census. Drawing on the use of "punched photography" by railroads (to encrypt passengers' hair and eye color on tickets), Hollerith proposed the encoding of census data for each person on a separate card that could be tabulated mechanically. After developing this technology for the Census Bureau, he formed the Tabulating Machine Company in 1896 to serve the growing demand for office machinery, such as typewriters, record-keeping systems, and adding machines. The company grew through the expansion of its business and merger with other office supply companies, and in 1924 Thomas J. Watson, the company's general manager, changed the company's name to International Business Machines Corporation (IBM). By the late 1920s, IBM was the fourth largest office machine supplier in the world, behind Remington-Rand, National Cash Register (NCR), and Burroughs Adding Machine Company. IBM made numerous improvements to tabulating technology during the 1920s and 1930s and eventually developed a machine that could compare cards, a significant innovation that enabled machines to perform simple logic (if—then) operations.

1. Computer Hardware

The critical breakthrough defining modern computers was the harnessing of electrical impulses to process information. In 1939, Professor John Vincent Atanasoff, with the help of his graduate student, Clifford Berry, developed the first electronic calculating machine. This computer could solve relatively complicated physics computations. Atanasoff and Berry built a more sophisticated version, the ABC (Atanasoff Berry Computer), in 1942. Shortly thereafter, driven in part by wartime demand for computing technology, Professor Howard Aiken, funded in substantial part by IBM, developed a massive electromechanical computer (MARK I). This machine contained three-fourths of a million parts, hundreds of miles of wire, and was 51 feet long, 8 feet high, and 2 feet deep. It could perform three additions a second and one multiplication every six seconds. Although it used an electric motor and a serial collection of electromechanical calculators, the MARK I was in many respects similar to the design of Babbage's analytical engine.

At about this same time, Dr. John Mauchly persuaded the U.S. Army to fund the development of a new computing device to compute trajectory tables to improve the targeting of ordnance. Mauchly envisioned using vacuum tubes rather than mechanical relays to store binary information. In collaboration with J. Presper Eckert, Jr., a young electrical engineer, Mauchly completed the electronic numerical integrator and computer (ENIAC) in 1946. This computer occupied 15,000 square feet, weighed 30 tons, and contained 18,000 vacuum tubes. It operated in decimal (rather than binary) format and therefore needed 10 vacuum tubes to represent a single digit. The ENIAC could perform over 80 additions or 8 multiplication operations per second.

The flexibility provided by programmability greatly enhanced the utility of computers. In the early 1950s, Mauchly and Eckert developed the first commercially viable electronic computer, the universal automatic computer (UNIVAC I) for Remington-Rand Corporation. Limitations on electronic technology, however, constrained the computing power of the first generation of computers. Vacuum tubes, which were bulky, failed frequently, consumed large amounts of energy, and generated substantial heat. This first generation of computers was programmed in binary code (zeros and ones), which could be understood by only a few specialists. IBM introduced its first commercial computer, the IBM 650, in 1954. IBM made incremental improvements to this technology and emerged as the market leader.

Because computers use binary electronic switches to store and process information, the great challenge for the computer industry was to reduce the size of these switches. The second generation of computers replaced vacuum tubes with transistors, which were smaller, required less power, and ran without generating significant heat. This and other innovations in data storage technology made computers smaller, faster, and more reliable. The first scientific computer using transistors was the IBM 7090. A second important innovation of this era was the development of high-level computer languages, which enabled computer specialists to write programs using coded instructions that resemble human language. The IBM 705, introduced in 1959, used the FORTRAN language processor. This model became the standard machine for large-scale data processing companies. Notwithstanding these innovations, computers of this generation remained complex and expensive because circuits had to be wired by hand.

The development of integrated circuits enabled computer manufacturers to incorporate many transistors within the layers of semiconductor material. The greater computing power and efficiency of computers brought the cost of data processing services within the reach of an increasing number of businesses. Many businesses contracted with companies specializing in data processing services, and a few acquired their own computers. IBM's 360 series of mainframe computers emerged during this period as the market leader. These machines used a single machine language. As businesses upgraded their equipment within the 360 series, they could continue to use the same computer programs. This increased the benefit of owning a computer (rather than outsourcing data processing) and expanded the mainframe market. This larger market generated greater demand for computer programmers and spawned new companies to provide computer-related services. An independent software industry began to emerge.

The 1960s and 1970s also witnessed the implementation of time-sharing and telecommunication technologies, which enable multiple users to access a computer from remote terminals. In addition, computers developed during this period could handle multiple tasks simultaneously (parallel processing and multiprogramming).

In 1965, the Digital Equipment Corporation (DEC) introduced the first minicomputer, the PDP-8 (programmed data processor). This machine was substantially smaller and about one-fourth the price of mainframe computers. Minicomputers substantially widened the market for computers and computer programmers. Domestic consumers purchased 260 minicomputers and 5,350 mainframes in 1965. Minicomputer unit sales surpassed mainframe unit sales by 1974. By the 1970s, computers incorporated "semiconductor chips" no larger than a human fingernail and containing more than 100,000 transistors. As chip technology advanced, the size of computers decreased while their computing power increased. Semiconductor chips today can hold many millions of transistors. For the past two decades, the memory capacity of a semiconductor chip has doubled approximately every 18 months.

In the early 1970s, Intel Corporation developed the microprocessor, a chip that contains the entire control unit of a computer. Very large scale integration (VLSI) technology led to the development of the microcomputer. Originally oriented toward computer hobbyists, microcomputers came to dominate the computer industry by the mid-1980s. With its Apple II computer system, which included a keyboard, monitor, floppy disk drive, and operating system, Apple Computer vastly expanded the market for computers. Microcomputer unit sales surpassed minicomputer unit sales in 1976, their second year of production. By 1986, sales of microcomputers (costing less than $1,000) reached approximately 4 million units and produced revenues of almost $12 billion, giving microcomputers the largest share of computer industry revenues.

The rapid growth of the microcomputer sector of the industry spurred the emergence of independent software vendors (ISVs) who developed mass-marketed programs for this growing market of versatile machines. Microcomputer owners were anxious to experiment with different programs. The cost of developing software for these machines was relatively low, product cycles were short, and there was constant pressure to upgrade products.

IBM entered the microcomputer market in 1981 with its PC (personal computer) product. The IBM PC utilized an Intel microprocessor (16-bit 8088 chip) and an operating system, PC-DOS (disk operating system), licensed from

Microsoft, then a fledgling company. Microsoft's MS-DOS is a single-tasking, single-user operating system with a command-line interface. Like other operating systems, MS-DOS oversees operations such as disk input and output, video support, keyboard control, and many internal functions related to program execution and file maintenance.

IBM's strong trademark in the business computer industry as well as its vast distribution network for computers enabled IBM to rapidly attract customers for its PC product. Many ISVs and hardware manufacturers developed and marketed software and peripheral products to run on the IBM PC. IBM actively encouraged ISVs and the makers of peripheral equipment (e.g., printers and monitors) to develop products for the PC. While promoting an "open architecture" with regard to these sectors of the industry, IBM included a specialized chip (BIOS)[1] for transferring data within the PC that hindered other original equipment manufacturers (OEMs) from offering fully compatible computer systems. This enabled IBM to charge premium prices for its PC product.

The rapid success of the IBM PC spurred ISVs to develop a wide range of programs to run on the IBM PC, including word processing, database, and spreadsheet software. For example, Lotus Corporation developed a version of the spreadsheet Visicalc (originally designed to run on the Apple II) to run on the IBM PC platform. Within a year of its introduction, Lotus 1-2-3 eclipsed Visicalc and became the spreadsheet market leader. Its success led to the label "killer app" to designate an application program of such widespread popularity that it spurs sales of a hardware/operating system platform. This reinforced the importance of owning an IBM PC, thereby adding further to the value of IBM's trademark in the microcomputer market. The powerful IBM trademark and the growing availability of software designed to run on the IBM/Microsoft platform catapulted IBM to a dominant position in the early microcomputer marketplace and greatly encouraged the dissemination of microcomputers. It also made Microsoft and Intel well-recognized trademarks in the microcomputer industry.

Microsoft and Intel retained rights to market their products to other OEMs in the computer industry. Because of the availability of software designed to run on the IBM PC platform, other OEMs sought to develop computer systems that could run the growing supply of IBM-compatible software. Although Microsoft's MS-DOS operating system could be licensed in the marketplace, IBM refused to license its BIOS chip. As a result, other OEMs could not fully emulate the internal operations of the IBM PC readily, and some software designed for the IBM PC did not operate satisfactorily on the computer systems of other OEMs. As a result, consumers strongly favored IBM PCs. Other computer companies had little choice but to offer IBM PC compatibility in order to compete effectively in the microcomputer marketplace. Computer manufacturers that developed their own platform did not fare well.

---

1. The BIOS chip is the set of essential software routines that test hardware at startup, start the operating system, and support transfer of data among hardware devices. It is typically stored in read-only memory (ROM) so that it can be executed when the computer is turned on. The BIOS is usually invisible to computer users.

With the exception of Apple Computer, which maintained a niche in the marketplace, no serious alternative to the IBM PC/MS DOS platform survived.

By 1984, Compaq developed a BIOS chip that successfully ran software developed for the IBM PC. Later that year, Phoenix Technologies Ltd. developed a fully IBM PC-compatible ROM BIOS, which it licensed to a broad range of OEMs. Other OEMs entered the market for IBM PC-compatible computer systems. As consumers became increasingly confident that software application programs designed for the IBM PC would run on the computer systems of other OEMs, these PC "clone" computers eroded IBM's dominance of the marketplace by offering lower prices, wider selection, and additional features.

By 1986, numerous OEMs competed in the IBM-compatible/MS-DOS marketplace and IBM's hold on the market had significantly loosened. The broad range of software available for the IBM-compatible/MS-DOS platform enabled MS-DOS to emerge as the de facto operating system standard in the industry by the late 1980s.

At about the same time, Microsoft began developing the Windows operating system platform incorporating a graphical user interface. The Windows platform was backward-compatible with MS-DOS (i.e., applications designed to operate in the MS-DOS environment could run on the Windows platform as well). Most MS-DOS users as well as new computer users migrated to the Windows platform, which has been the dominant platform since the mid-1990s.

2. Computer Software

During the 1940s and 1950s, hardware and software innovation were integrated. The development of computer software was a highly specialized field of scientific research done by academic, government, and government-funded commercial research laboratories. Those who worked with computers had significant scientific and technical expertise. The computer languages and techniques for developing programs were just being created and tested. Computers had relatively narrow use in scientific, military, and space applications. Each computer was unique, and programming was specialized for each machine.

IBM became and remained the dominant force in the commercial computer industry from the 1950s until the early 1980s. During the 1950s and 1960s, IBM and other mainframe manufacturers (e.g., Burroughs, Raytheon, RCA, Honeywell, General Electric, Remington Rand) bundled operating system and application software with hardware for the same price, commonly through a leasing arrangement. During the early stages of the industry, this bundling arrangement made economic sense because there were relatively few computer applications and the hardware manufacturers were able to support these uses of their systems.

As the industry developed, manufacturers encouraged their customers to share software among themselves through software-sharing institutions. IBM formed and supported a user group named SHARE, which served as a clearinghouse for programming information and software for computer users. SHARE distributed software programs, including libraries of subroutines, algorithms published in technical journals, computer code published in text-books and, in some instances, programs written to solve problems in specific areas. Those companies contributing to the software-sharing "bank" were entitled to borrow the works of others. But as computers became increasingly powerful, versatile, and affordable, the sharing model began to break down. Those companies making substantial investments in software development were less willing to share these innovations with others. In addition, computer technology was diffusing from government and scientific uses to commercial applications.

Specialty software supply houses, such as Applied Data Research, Inc. (incorporated in 1959), emerged to provide customized and general-purpose software in direct competition with the hardware manufac-turers. Offering specialized services on a contract basis, this early software industry competed with the bundled (and, hence, unpriced) software pro-grams provided by mainframe manufacturers through mainframe sales and leases.

The advent of less expensive minicomputers as well as the growing versatility and computing power of mainframes spurred the independent software industry. By 1965, there were approximately 40 to 50 independent software suppliers. F. Fisher, J. McKie, & R. Mancke, IBM and the U.S. Data Processing Industry: An Economic History 322 (1983). Applied Data Research introduced Autoflow, a flowchart program, which was the first internationally marketed computer program. International Computer Programs, Inc. (ICP) published catalogs of software programs. The independent software industry grew quickly. There were almost 3,000 vendors by 1968. In 1969, contract programming produced revenues of $600 million; software products generated another $20-25 million. *Id.* at 323. Nonetheless, this accounted for less than 10 percent of the amount spent for programming; the remainder was spent on programmers working in-house.

Founded in 1959, Computer Sciences Corporation (CSC) became a successful software company during the mainframe era. CSC began its business by designing, developing, and implementing software systems for computer manufacturers. Over the course of the 1960s, its computer programming business branched out to serve large companies outside of the computer industry and federal, state, and local government agencies. During this same period, CSC increasingly shifted its focus toward the development of software products. It developed a range of products generally directed to business uses, including tax, accounting, and personnel management software.

IBM's increasing dominance of the computer industry led to antitrust scrutiny by the federal government. In addition, the costs of software develop-ment within IBM increased dramatically, and there was increasing pressure within the company to price software separately. Following the lodging of the government's antitrust complaint in 1969, IBM voluntarily unbundled its hardware from application programs effective in January 1970. This event greatly expanded the business opportunities for independent software vendors. By 1975, there were over 1,000 software firms in the United States offering more than 3,000 products.

The introduction of the microcomputer in the mid- to late 1970s dramatically changed the software industry. The proliferation of minicomputers fostered the growth of ISVs and a shift away from custom programming and support services toward pre-packaged software products. With relatively small investments, computer programmers could develop software for the growing numbers of microcomputer users. Beginning in the late 1970s, ISVs began selling through retail and other channels pre-packaged (i.e., non-customized) software products for use on microcomputers. Wordstar, Visicalc, and other independently developed software products dominated the early microcomputer software marketplace.

As noted in the discussion of computer hardware, Lotus Corporation developed a version of the spreadsheet Visicalc to run on the IBM PC platform. The powerful IBM trademark and the growing availability of software designed to run on the IBM/MS-DOS platform catapulted IBM to a dominant position in the early microcomputer marketplace and greatly encouraged the dissemination of microcomputers. These factors stimulated rapid growth in the software industry.

By the late 1980s, Microsoft had emerged as a dominant force in the computer industry. Its MS-DOS operating system was installed on the majority of microcomputers and its Windows graphical user interface platform was gaining acceptance in the higher end of the microcomputer marketplace. By 1991, Microsoft's operating systems were installed on almost 90 percent of microcomputers in the world. Building upon this success, Microsoft began bundling its office software products into an office suite of products: Microsoft Word word processing software, Microsoft Excel spreadsheet software, Microsoft Access database software, and Microsoft PowerPoint presentation software. This marketing strategy has enabled it to become the leading seller in each of these product categories.

B. AN INTRODUCTION TO COMPUTER TECHNOLOGY

Virtually unknown 50 years ago, computers literally surround most Americans in their daily lives today. In their most easily recognized form, mainframe and minicomputers can be found in most businesses, government offices, and schools. Microcomputers can be found on most business and home desktops for use in word processing, information storage, entertainment games, and electronic shopping. Less commonly recognized, computers can also be found in many home appliances, hand-held organizers, telecommunication devices, automobile dashboards, and elevators, among other places.

1.   Computer Hardware

Computers use a binary base. By setting electrical switches to "on" (electrical current is flowing) or "off" (current is not flowing), early computers could create a single "bit" of information. That piece of information is read as either a 1 ("on") or a 0 ("off"). By translating information into a series of such 1s and 0s, computers could perform mathematical operations.

The first computing machines did not utilize computer "programs" in a form that we would recognize today. These machines were in essence a series of hard-wired circuits constructed to perform one particular computational task. That is, the mathematical function performed by the computer was determined by the physical arrangement and structure of the circuits. The computers had to be rewired in order to perform a different function. These machines were comprised solely of what we call today "hardware"—the physical circuits that make up the machine.

During the late 1940s, scientists developed the first machines that could store and use encoded instructions or programs. This set of innovations dramatically increased the flexibility and usefulness of computers. Users could perform a variety of computational tasks without having to rewire the basic hardware of the computer. Instead, they could simply direct the computer to perform one of the functions that it had stored in its memory. The actual computer in these programmable or "universal" machines is the central processing unit (CPU). The CPU has two principal components: an arithmetic logic unit (ALU), which performs a basic set of primitive functions such as addition and multiplication, and a control unit, which directs the flow of electric signals within the computer. In essence, a computer processes data by performing controlled sequences of primitive functions. As computers grew more powerful and the tasks they performed grew more complex, computer scientists relied on increasingly complex sets of instructions that are executed automatically by the computer. These sets of instructions, known as computer programs, are the focus of most of this book.

The basic hardware of a modern microcomputer system includes a CPU, internal memory storage, disk drives or other devices for physically transferring data and programs into and out of the internal memory, and telephone or network interconnections for linking the computer with other computers. The internal memory of the computer typically features three types of information storage: random access memory (RAM), read-only memory (ROM), and data storage memory (disk space). Data can be input into RAM, erased, or altered. RAM chips serve two information storage functions: they act as temporary storage devices for programs and data currently running on the computer, and they also serve as permanent memory for data or programs. A ROM chip has information permanently embedded in the architecture of the chip, and that information can only be read (not altered) by the computer. ROM chips are used primarily to direct certain basic operating functions of the computer.

Computer engineers design the programming capability of a computer to suit the user's needs. By building more of the desired functions directly into the wiring of the computer, they can achieve more efficient processing for certain applications. Such pre-designed computers are known as "special purpose computers" because they are designed to perform only certain specific tasks. Their greater speed comes at a cost of less flexibility—that is, less ability to run a wide range of programs. This technological trade-off harks back to the early days of computer technology, when all programs were hard-wired into the computer.

Advances in computer technology have made greater efficiencies of processing possible without the need to hard-wire the computer. Most modern computers, particularly personal computers, are "general-purpose computers" that feature a high degree of programming flexibility. When a user has only a few computing needs or desires high-speed processing, however, she may still prefer to rely heavily on internal programming.

Besides the internal memory and processing chips, computers are composed of input and output devices (sometimes referred to as I/O devices) and peripherals. These devices control the transfer of information into and out of a computer. Early programmers "input" information into a computer by changing the physical structure of its circuits, or (in more sophisticated models) by using "punch cards," which allowed computer users to write data for the computer in the form of holes punched in special note cards and then to feed that data into the computer in the form of stacks of such cards. Most modern computers use the typewriter keyboard as their primary input device, allowing users to enter data into the computer by typing it. The typewriter keyboard has been supplemented with other input devices, including the computer "mouse," the telephone line, and microphones coupled with voice recognition software.

The output devices of computers have also changed. Computers originally communicated data to humans in the form of lights that turned on or off, representing the bits of data produced by some computer operation. Advances in computer outputs include the development of the printer, the introduction of television-like computer monitors and screen displays, and telephone and cable output that can "send" data to a remote location.

2. Computer Software

Computer programs are the instructions that allow general-purpose computers to be many different types of machines. When a computer is running a video game, the computer *is* a video game machine. When it executes program instructions to enable users to write letters or reports, the computer *is* a word processing machine. When it carries out a programmed search for data in a large repository of information, the computer *is* an information retrieval machine. Programs can also be written for special-purpose hardware (e.g., the semiconductor chip that monitors the functioning of your toaster) when this will best achieve the developer's objectives.

Computer programs that operate on a single machine fall into two basic categories: operating systems programs and applications programs. Operating system programs manage the internal functions of the computer. They coordinate the reading and writing of data between the internal memory, the CPU, and the external devices (e.g., disk drives, keyboard, and printer); perform basic housekeeping functions of the computer system; and facilitate use of application programs. In essence, the operating system prepares the computer to execute the application programs and serves as an intermediary between the application program and the hardware of the computer. An applications program can order the deletion of a file, but, generally, the operating system actually carries through the details of this function.

Every computer needs an operating system to direct its functions and to manage other software that is run on the computer. Computers do not need, and many do not have, more than one operating system. Because the operating system controls the interactions between the user, the software, and the computer itself, an applications program must be compatible with a particular operating system if it is to interoperate with that program and run on a computer using that operating system. This compatibility requirement means that the designers of operating systems have some degree of control over the applications programs that will work with that operating system. Although the specifications of applications programming interfaces (APIs) are sometimes published freely, often they are licensed from an operating system program developer. Microsoft, for example, licenses its APIs for its operating system programs to applications developers. An alternative way to get access to APIs is through a laborious process of reverse engineering the program (about which more in Chapter 2).

Operating systems may control the execution of instructions in the central processing unit of the computer, but they generally do not perform specific tasks of interest to end users. Applications programs enable users to accomplish specific tasks with computers. Bookkeeping, statistical and financial analysis, word processing, and video game programs are among the many types of application programs available today.

Application programs are often developed to run on particular operating systems. The task of adapting an application program designed to run on one operating system to run on another operating system is often technically complex, time-consuming, and costly. In recent years, software developers have developed programs that run on more than one operating system. In addition, translator programs have been developed to allow users to move files from one application program to another. Nonetheless, the problem of compatibility between applications programs and operating systems remains a major concern in the computer software industry. There is some hope that the Java programming language (about which more in Section C) will enable programmers to write a program once and have it run on many machines.

The line between operating systems and application programs, while sharp in particular instances, may blur when programs once distributed as applications programs are integrated into an operating systems program. Microsoft, for example, has integrated a number of "add-on" features (such as compression software and even rudimentary word processing) into its operating system over time. By selling a bundled product that includes both an operating system and certain applications, Microsoft arguably provides more value to consumers but also eliminates a competitive market for such add-on products. Microsoft's decision to make its Internet Explorer Web browsing software an integrated part of the Windows operating system contributed to the U.S. Justice Department's decision to charge Microsoft with antitrust violations in the late 1990s. (We discuss this suit in more detail in Chapter 7.)

3. Computer Networks

Early computers were self-contained machines. Data could be input into them (usually laboriously by punch card), and after the computer processed the data, output would be produced. But the data never left the physical environs of the single computer. To move data from one computer to another, one had to take the output of one computer and transport it physically to and then input it into the new computer. Even when input and output became somewhat more efficient—for example, by use of magnetic storage media such as "floppy disks" —the necessity for a physical transfer remained.

Computer engineers recognized early on that great benefits would flow from the networking of computers. Networking has been around in specialized computing environments since the late 1960s, but it was not until the 1990s that the Internet afforded easy widespread access to large computer networks. As of June 1999, more than 171 million people around the world had Internet access and 37 percent of the U.S. population had Internet access at home or at work.

Networking technology allows computers to communicate with each other. This communication capability enables dispersed computer users to exchange information—for example, by electronic mail (email). It also reduces the time and cost of transferring information regardless of the physical location of computers. Networked computing also allows computers—and people—to work together to achieve certain tasks that would take much longer to do alone.

Networking computers requires some basic technologies. First, some form of hardware must connect the two computers, either physically or virtually. If the computers are physically close to one another, this can be accomplished by stringing a cable between them. If the computers are physically separated by great distances, networking requires that they be connected either via telephone lines or by some form of wireless communication. Long-distance connections require some form of hardware to convert digital computer data into a form that can be transferred over the telephone lines or "narrowcast" over the airwaves. One common type of hardware that enables telephone transmissions of digital data is a modem. Modems take digital computer data, convert it to analog (sound) form for transfer over telephone lines, and then reconvert it to digital form. Networking software (and sometimes hardware components as well) is required to enable computers to communicate with each other. When one computer sends data, the other must be able to process it. Interoperability issues thus arise in the context of computer networking design. The development of standard protocols for exchanging information has fostered the growth of networking.

Local Area Networks. Many organizations find it useful to develop local area networks (LANs) to link a number of computers so that members of the organization can share information and information resources. LANs provide all of the communications advantages described above: they enable employees to communicate by email, to send files to one another, and to share computing resources. In addition, LANs have made possible a form of specialization or division of labor among computers. Because the computers in a LAN are linked together in real time, it is possible to store files in a single central location and allow any computer to access them at any time. Rather than requiring each computer to be self-sufficient, certain (generally more powerful) computers can be designated as central "servers" where files or programs are located. Individual "client" computers in the network can call up the files or programs on an as-needed basis. Because the server machines are generally faster and more powerful than ordinary computers, LANs offer not only centralized access but also quicker processing time.

LANs also facilitate group projects. "Workgroups" can add to or change the same document simultaneously over the network. This is a particular advantage for companies (e.g., sales companies, airlines, hotels) that rely on large information databases that must be regularly updated. Documents or databases that previously had to be changed by one central programmer can now be altered instantaneously to reflect current information. Because the workgroup is organized on the computer network rather than by the physical sharing of documents, LAN workgroups also contribute to a more flexible organizational structure.

The mass corporate movement towards LANs has important legal implications as well. Information that used to reside on a single computer is now accessible to dozens or hundreds of computers, many of them physically remote from the actual location of the data. LAN administrators must worry about limiting access to their networks, guaranteeing the security of their data, implementing version control on revised documents, and monitoring access to certain "controlled" data (particularly applications software licensed for limited uses from third parties).

Other kinds of private networks also exist. Anyone with a computer and a modem can connect to private dial-up networks. Such dial-up connections normally take place over the telephone lines between individual computers and one or more central "host" computers operated by the private network administrator. Some are operated by information providers who allow people to sign on to the network and download information of particular interest to them. Others may serve as communications forums for people interested in particular topics. Individuals dial into the host computer and communicate with each other through the host, either in real time or by leaving email messages.

Large-Scale Public Networks. In the mid-1960s, researchers working for the Department of Defense's Advanced Research Project Agency (ARPA) began working on the problem of connecting its computers scattered around the United States at various universities and research laboratories to enhance memory storage and time-sharing capabilities. An important design objective of this system was that it not be vulnerable to breaking down in the event of a nuclear attack or other widespread disruption of telecommunications systems. It was initially believed that this would require 136 separate communication lines (17 computers $\times$ 16 $\div$ 2). These lines would be expensive, and the cost would grow geometrically as more computers were added to the network.

At about that time, researchers at Rand Corporation and the National Physical Laboratory in England independently developed the concept of "store-and-forward packet switching" which avoided the problem of having to connect independently each node of a network to each other node. Packet switching technology, using techniques similar to those developed in the telegraph industry, allows multiple messages to flow through a common "backbone" line by transmitting information in smaller packets that contain the address of the destination. Large messages are broken into streams of packets that are sent as individual items into the network. Switching nodes pass the messages along and the receiving computer reconstitutes the full message. Such a system minimizes the risk that the entire system could crash by allowing information to travel along a variety of paths.

In 1970, the ARPANET successfully implemented packet switching technology in a four-node network. The ARPANET grew to more than 20 sites by 1971 and to over 200 sites by 1981. The ARPANET paved the way for the Internet, an international collection of *inter*connected computer *net*works based on an open technical standard known as Transmission Control Protocol/Internet Protocol (TCP/IP). Computers implementing this protocol may connect to the Internet.

By 1996, more that 9 million host computers were connected to the Internet, and it is projected that this number will exceed 200 million by the year 2000. Computer users may gain access to the Internet through Internet service providers (ISPs) such as America Online (AOL), Microsoft Network (MSN), and Netcom; university and library connections; corporate and non-profit portals; and government nodes. Thus, the Internet is a largely decentralized system utilizing a common communication backbone.

Until recently, the Internet has been governed primarily by InterNIC (NSFnet Internet Network Information Center), a consortium involving the National Science Foundation, AT&T, General Atomics, and Network Solutions, Inc. (NSI). NSI has had principal authority to register Internet names and addresses, what have come to be known as "domain names." Domain names are represented in a hierarchical format: server.organization.type —e.g., www.whitehouse.gov. In 1999, the assigning of domain names was opened up to a range of entities operating under the authority of the Internet Corporation for Assigned Names and Numbers (ICANN).

In 1990, Tim Berners-Lee, a researcher at CERN, a European particle physics laboratory, developed the World Wide Web (WWW or Web), a widespread means by which users of the Internet could share databases. The WWW makes accessible to Internet users hypertext documents residing on HTTP (hypertext transfer protocol) servers throughout the world. These Web pages, identified by uniform resource locators (URLs), such as www.whitehouse.gov, are written in HTML (hypertext markup language). Codes embedded in Web pages can instantly access other documents on the World Wide Web. They may also activate embedded software programs and audiovisual images. The Web became a mass media phenomenon with the development of "Web browser" programs that permit personal computers to access a wide variety of files from Web sites. The Web has also become the transaction medium for most electronic commerce.

Users of the Internet can locate Web sites of interest in a number of ways. They can often find on-line merchants, educational and government entities, and companies by using trade and organization names, such as "Microsoft.com," "law.berkeley.edu," and "uspto.gov." They can also "surf" the Internet with the assistance of various "search engines," such as Yahoo, Altavista, and Infoseek. These search engines look for keywords in domain names, actual text on Web pages, and metatags—HTML code created by a Web page developed to attract search engines looking for particular keywords. Search engines will then rank Web sites from all over the Web according to various algorithms designed to arrange indexed materials. Web users may create "bookmarks" on their computers in order to access their favorite Web sites quickly.

As computing has shifted in the 1990s from a stand-alone activity to one conducted increasingly over networks, the way computers function has changed as well. It no longer makes sense to talk about how *a* computer functions. Most computers used in business, and many used in the home, do not operate in self-contained fashion. Computer programs are distributed across LANs and over the Internet, and over the Internet more and more programs are distributed in pieces on an as-needed basis. We discuss this change and its implications for computer law in more detail in the sections that follow.

The Internet has also changed the way commerce is conducted. Virtually everyone was caught off guard by the speed with which the millions of people using the Internet began to use it to buy things. The development of such "ecommerce" poses important new challenges for the legal and technological framework of the Internet. We discuss those challenges in detail in Chapter 9.

C. HOW SOFTWARE IS MADE

Software development has evolved from a significantly hardware-constrained activity to a highly flexible and sophisticated field of engineering. This section briefly summarizes the principal methods involved in modern software development. We note, however, that the proliferation of a wide range of computers—from mainframes to desktop units to a host of embedded systems—has spawned a great range of programming methods. Although many of the stages can be found in other programming contexts, we focus here upon the methods used in the development of relatively complex commercial operating systems and application programs.

Software development is an inherently functional enterprise. Software provides the instructions that enable a computer to perform tasks that serve the users' needs. Software can control anything from the relatively simple operation of a clock to the highly complex operation of an airplane. Whereas the programs that operate a wristwatch may have 1,000 instructions, modern spreadsheet and word processing programs have well over a million lines of instructions or code. In order to make computers more effective and easy to use, software can become extraordinarily complex in design and implementation. To a large extent, software engineering has become an applied science of mastering complexity. The engineering nature of the discipline is discussed in detail in Pamela Samuelson, Randall Davis, Mitchell D. Kapor, & J.H. Reichman, A Manifesto Concerning the Legal Protection of Computer Programs, 94 Colum. L. Rev. 2308, 2327-2329 (1994) [hereinafter Manifesto].

1.4.3 Constructing Programs Is an Industrial Design Process

Once one understands that programs are machines that happen to have been constructed in the medium of text, it becomes easier to understand that writing programs is an industrial design process akin to the design of physical machines. Each stage of the development process requires industrial design work: from identifying the constraints under which the program will operate, to listing the tasks to be performed (i.e., determining what behavior it should have), to deciding what component parts to utilize to bring about this behavior (which in the case of software includes algorithms and data structures), to integrating the component utilitarian elements in an efficient way.

A substantial amount of skilled effort of program development goes into the design and implementation of behavior. Designing behavior involves a skilled effort to decompose the overall, complex task (e.g., word processing) into a set of simpler subtasks requiring simpler behaviors (e.g., deleting a character). Constructing the interaction of these subtasks to produce useful behaviors (e.g., deciding whether the "delete word" command should be implemented as a sequence of delete character commands) also requires design skill. Knowing how and where to break up a complicated task and how to get the simpler components to work together is, in itself, an important form of the engineering design skill of programmers.

The goal of a programmer designing software is to achieve functional results in an efficient way. While there may be elements of individual style present in program design, even those style elements concern issues of industrial design, e.g., the choice of one or another programming technique or the clarity (or obscurity) of the functional purpose of a portion of the program. . . .

At the same time, others have characterized programming, particularly in its earlier days, as akin to an art form. Certainly it is true that while the ultimate goal of computer programming is the design of a functional work, programming has historically been less routinized than most engineering disciplines, and much computer programming has involved "reinventing the wheel."[2] We discuss some of the reasons for that, and modern ways of dealing with it, in the sections that follow.

Software development has traditionally been described as a multistage process often analogized to a waterfall.[3] See generally Stephen R. Schach, Classical and Object-Oriented Software Engineering with UML and C++ (4th ed. 1999); Ben Schneiderman, Designing the User Interface: Strategies for Effective Human-Computer Interaction (3d ed. 1998); Grady Booch, Object-Oriented Analysis and Design with Applications (2d ed. 1994); Ian Somerville, Software Engineering (4th ed. 1992). All software development processes begin with a clear definition of the problem to be solved or task to be automated. The process begins with the identification of the goals of the users and the constraints of the hardware system. This stage is followed by the development of a system and software design. A user interface will also be designed to serve the needs of the target audience for the software product. After the software has been structured and an interface designed, programmers implement the design, test its performance and reliability, and fine-tune the system. In addition, many software products require ongoing maintenance and updating to correct errors and enhance their capabilities.

Although the waterfall model implies a linear flow, modern software engineering typically has an iterative quality with many feedback loops along the development and use life cycle. That is, programming does not occur from the top down, with ideas being turned into algorithms and thence into code. Rather, the development of lower-level program components can influence the design of higher-level components and can even cause the programmer to rethink the goals of the program itself. One might think of this as bottom-up programming. As the authors of the Manifesto note:

Innovation in software development is typically incremental. Programmers commonly adopt software design elements—ideas about how to do particular

---

2. The Manifesto observes that "[t]ypically, a programmer writes every line of code afresh, no matter how large the program is, or how common its tasks. To perceive the impact of this lack of standard building blocks, imagine trying to design an entire car in complete detail, down to the last fastener, without being able to assume the existence of any standard parts at all (not even nuts, bolts or screws)." As its authors observe, "[t]his is not a desirable state of affairs." Manifesto, supra at 2322.

3. Other programming paradigms include the rapid prototyping model, exploratory programming, formal transformation, and system assembly from reusable components.

things in software—by looking around for examples or remembering what worked in other programs. These elements are sometimes adopted wholesale, but often they are adapted to a new context or set of tasks. In this way, programmers both contribute to and benefit from a cumulative innovation process. While innovation in program design occasionally rises to the level of invention, most often it does not. Rather, it is the product of the skilled use of know-how to solve industrial design tasks. . . .

The technical community has recognized the cumulative and incremental nature of software development, and has welcomed efforts to direct the process of software development away from the custom-crafting that typified its early stages and toward a more methodical, engineering approach. The creation of a software engineering discipline reflects an awareness that program development requires skilled effort and applied know-how comparable to other engineering disciplines.

The products of software engineering almost invariably contain admixtures of old and new elements. The innovation in such programs may lie in the manner in which the known elements have been combined in a new and efficient manner. Or it may come from combining some new elements with well-known elements in order to achieve the same result in a new way. When we speak of programs as "industrial compilations of applied know-how," it is in recognition of the frequency with which software engineering involves the reuse of known elements. Use of skilled efforts to construct programs brings about cumulative, incremental innovation characteristic of engineering disciplines. A well-designed program is thus akin to the work of a talented engineer whose skilled efforts in applying know-how, accumulated from years of experience and training, yields a successful design for a bridge or other useful product.

Manifesto at 2330-32.

However programs are designed and written, a fundamental fact about computer programs is that they are functional. They are designed to carry out certain tasks and bring about certain behaviors. Consequently, programs are judged largely on how well they perform the tasks they have been programmed to accomplish. Because the computer instructions serve no function other than to accomplish the defined tasks, the overriding concern in designing a program is to meet the users' needs in the most efficient manner.

The concept of efficiency in this context is broad. "Efficiency" may mean one or more of the following: (1) code efficiency—maximizing the processing speed; (2) memory efficiency—using solution techniques and addressing methods to minimize the amount of memory needed to accomplish the desired tasks; (3) input/output efficiency—maximizing the quality and speed of information transmission between the computer and the user or external hardware devices (such as keyboards and printers); (4) stability—the program must be easy to maintain, upgrade, and adapt to new hardware platforms; and (5) usability—the ease of use by the intended audience. The software engineering field strives to develop methods for improving the efficiency and reliability of programs in a cost-effective manner.

The subsections that follow describe typical processes for designing software at different levels of abstraction, from high-level ideas down through the actual writing of program code.

1. Requirements Analysis and Program Specification

At the conceptual level, software development is comprised of several tasks. Of most importance, the design team must identify the goals of the design process. For example, in developing software to provide banking services through an automated teller machine (ATM), the design team will map out the necessary data, the desired functionality, and hardware and security constraints. They might develop tables or flowcharts to understand the flow of information needed to accomplish the various transactions. As another example, in developing software to run a law office, the designers must identify the various tasks that the computer program should handle—for example, billing clients, filing documents, ordering supplies, preparing budgets, and filing court documents. The design team would typically interview the prospective users of the software system about their needs and desires, study the way information flows in a law office, and develop a schematic representation of the tasks to be programmed. This abstract representation of tasks maps data inputs and outputs and assesses the hardware requirements for possible systems.

Writing an application program is a complex and iterative process. While some programs are small and relatively simple to write, most modern programs involve thousands and even millions of lines of computer code. They may be written not by a single person but by teams of programmers working together over the course of months or years.

Partly to facilitate collaborative work within teams, programmers sometimes develop a flowchart to depict the logical structure of the program. This will not just show what the program is supposed to do but also how it will carry out the desired tasks. A sample flowchart for a computer program is reproduced as Figure 1.

We should emphasize, however, that flow charts are merely conceptual aids, and are by no means a necessary part of programming.

2. Software Design

Processes for designing software systems have undergone significant changes over the past four decades as computer hardware has become more powerful and versatile and the problems sought to be addressed have become more complex. Managing the complexity of large-scale software projects—for example, computer operating systems, avionics (programs to fly large commercial airplanes), robotics, spacecraft simulation, telecommunications, air traffic control—entails significant technological creativity. Programmers have traditionally sought to divide complex problems into component parts and to solve each component separately. This procedure-oriented, "functional decomposition," or "top down" methodology served as the dominant paradigm for software design through at least the mid-1980s, and it continues to be widely used in solving some classes of problems. The programmer begins with a general description of the functions that a program is to perform. The

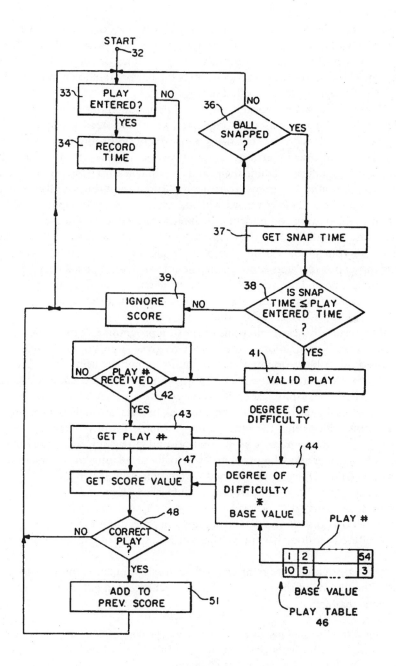

FIGURE 1
Flowchart from a software patent drawing.

programmer then outlines the program, specifying data structures and algorithms to be used. Such outlines are frequently expressed as flowcharts showing the relationship among the various modules or subroutines of the program. These modules are then separately further broken down until the full logic of the program can be spelled out.

While conceptually logical, the classical design methodology has become increasingly problematic as the complexity, scale, and need for updating of software projects has grown. The many parts of very large software systems often interact in a multitude of intricate and subtle ways. Classical top-down designs often require significant redundancies and are difficult to evolve. Programmers must typically build programs from scratch, often requiring re-invention of many components. This contrasts with other engineering disciplines, which typically reuse existing components. Such reuse can reduce design, testing, and other costs. In addition, top-down procedural techniques typically define data structures in one place. Various subroutines refer back to this single location. While this approach offers some efficiencies, it can lead to problems when the program is updated or revised. Whenever a data structure is revised, all subroutines or modules drawing upon that data structure must be suitably altered as well, which can cause a domino effect.

As a result of these limitations of classical programming methodologies, which tend to become more acute as systems grow large, computer scientists developed the "object-oriented" paradigm. Programmers using this paradigm design software by structuring relationships among independent "objects," each of which represents a physical entity in the real world. Each object stores both data representing attributes of the physical objects as well as procedures representing actions that the physical object can perform. Whereas the traditional top-down program is structured around processing of data, object-oriented programs model a problem by actually simulating the interaction of physical entities. Objects are grouped within hierarchical structures. Higher-level classes "inherit" the attributes of subclasses. Object-oriented systems simplify complexity by "encapsulating" the internal data structures and procedures within objects. The data structures and procedures of particular objects can be altered without having to affect other aspects of the larger software system.

Object-oriented programming reflects basic human learning processes. Grady Booch, one of the pioneers of the object-oriented paradigm, offers the following analogy:

> [W]ith just a few minutes of orientation, an experienced pilot can step into a multi-engine jet aircraft he or she has never flown before, and safely fly the vehicle. Having recognized the properties common to all such aircraft, such as the functioning of the rudder, ailerons, and throttle, the pilot primarily needs to learn what properties are unique to that particular aircraft. If the pilot already knows how to fly a given aircraft, it is far easier to know how to fly a similar one.[4]

---

4. Grady Booch, Object-Oriented Design with Applications 12 (1991).

Thus, a programmer starting with an object-oriented program that simulates a basic aircraft can simulate the behavior of a more sophisticated aircraft, such as a fighter jet, by adding additional features, behaviors, and processes of the more advanced plane. The programmer would not need to begin the software design process from scratch.[5]

The above example illustrates some of the ways in which object-oriented design systems economize on programming time and cost. Such designs are more readily adaptable to changes in data structures and new variables than are the traditional top-down approaches. The adaptability of object-oriented software programs substantially reduces the risk that a large investment in software design will be lost if new parameters or features need to be added to a program. Moreover, object-oriented designs tend to yield smaller systems through the reuse of common mechanisms, which reduces the complexity of the software design and the cost of writing code. See Mark A. Lemley & David W. O'Brien, Encouraging Software Reuse, 49 Stan. L. Rev. 255, 259-268 (1997). This reuse of "chunks" of computer code is not only valuable because it saves the cost of rewriting the code, but because it permits a particular software "object" to be refined and debugged and then reused in a variety of different programs. This reuse of software objects by different firms may enhance software compatibility, decrease programming costs, and even improve the safety and reliability of software (since mission-critical software will not have to be written from scratch for each new product, but can use code that has already been tested and proven to work). As a result of these advantages, object-oriented methodologies have increasingly become the norm in designing highly complex computer programs.

3. User Interface Design

As computers have become more versatile and available to a broader and often less technically trained range of users, software development has increasingly focused upon tailoring the program to the particular goals and knowledge base of the intended users. See generally Ben Schneiderman, Designing the User Interface: Strategies for Effective Human-Computer Interaction (3d ed. 1998). The design of computer program user interfaces draws upon the field of computer-human interaction (CHI), a sub-field of a more general field of "human factors" analysis that aims to understand how human beings process information so that products can be better designed to enhance usability. Human factors analysis brings together insights from the fields of education, graphic art, industrial design, industrial management, computer science, mechanical engineering, psychology, artificial intelligence,

---

5. See Barkan, Software Litigation in the Year 2000: The Effect of Object-Oriented Design Methodologies on Traditional Software Jurisprudence, 7 High Tech. L.J. 315 (1992); Smith, Abstraction, Filtration, and Comparison in Computer Copyright Infringement: An Explanation and Update for the Object-Oriented Paradigm, 26 AIPLA Q.J. 1 (1998).

linguistics, information science, and sociology. Recognizing the many ways that the study of human factors can aid computer system design, the computer industry has taken a particularly strong interest in the effort to synthesize and expand this learning.

The field of computer-human interaction has profoundly changed the way in which application programs are both conceptualized and written. The field has identified five human factor goals that programmers should strive to achieve in designing application programs: (1) minimize learning time, (2) maximize speed of performance, (3) minimize rate of user errors, (4) maximize user satisfaction, and (5) maximize users' retention of knowledge over time.

Application programmers attempt to achieve these objectives in designing computer-human interfaces. As a result, many of their design choices are guided by principles of human factor analysis that have evolved over years of empirical research. Among the design issues that have been studied are: the choice among command-based programs, menu-driven programs, and natural language programs; menu design; windowing versus scrolling; the choice of abbreviations and command names; the layout and scheme of graphical interfaces; the color and highlighting of video displays; the consistency of user interfaces; and the design of direct manipulation interfaces. To aid in the implementation of these ideas, many firms engaged in application program development have compiled computer-interface guidelines and criteria to guide their programmers. Apple Computer, which introduced the first commercially successful graphical user interface, developed the following guidelines for user-friendly software design:

1. *Metaphors*—the interface should embody plain, simple metaphors for accomplishing tasks with audio and visual effects to support the metaphor.

2. *Direct Manipulation*—the interface should allow users to directly manipulate items or actions on the screen, rather than indirectly through abstract commands.

3. *See and Point*—the interface should allow the user to effect action by a see-and-point mechanism that is intuitive, rather than by a remember-and-type mechanism that can be intimidating, too abstract or unnatural.

4. *Consistency*—the symbols and mechanisms for accomplishing tasks should be consistent across all application programs through a consistent interface.

5. *WYSIWYG (What You See Is What You Get)*—the interface should present the information on the screen to the user in exactly the form that it will come out on the printer, removing the need to type in abstract formatting commands or to make mental calculations to envision how the screen translates to paper.[6]

These principles—and the basic concept of graphical user interfaces—are in widespread use in the software industry and can be seen in most application programming and web-based user environments.

---

6. Written submission of Apple Computer, Inc., U.S. Copyright Office Public Hearing on Registration and Deposit of Computer Screen Displays 5-6 (Sept. 4, 1987).

4. Generating Computer Code

After designing computer systems, including the user interface, a software engineer engages in a series of steps to translate the design into binary code (representing open and closed circuits) that is actually "readable" by computers. While it is possible to write programs directly into machine-level language, most programming is done in higher-level languages that use abbreviations and short words to convey the action the program will need to carry out. Well-known programming languages include FORTRAN, COBOL, and PASCAL. Special languages, such as C++, Ada, Smalltalk, Object Pascal, and Java, have been developed more recently to implement object-oriented designs. These programming languages, which can be readily understood by skilled programmers, are often referred to as "source code."

Figure 2 contains the source code version of a simple program written in PASCAL for determining and listing in five columns any number of prime numbers. PASCAL is a high-level programming language, and, as you can see, it is relatively easy to comprehend. For example, the statement "Go to 40" instructs the computer to skip intervening steps and execute the instruction at line 40. But it is a specialized language all the same, and (because the programmer is writing for a computer audience) its rules must be followed precisely. "Execute line 40 now" may mean the same thing to a human reader as "Go to 40," but it may be incomprehensible to a computer.

Traditionally, source code was written by computer programmers who had learned one of the specialized computer languages described above. Increasingly, however, the process of writing source code has itself become automated. Computer programmers can now "write" code with the help of a computer "wizard" that translates higher-level design concepts directly into code. Having a computer help write source code can be faster and more efficient than writing it by hand; it can also help prevent programmers from making mistakes that will interfere with the program. As more and more code is written with computer assistance, similarities in actual program code become less meaningful as evidence of copying. This will become important when we consider copyright law in Chapter 2.

In order to be executable by the central processing unit of a computer, source code must be transformed into a machine-executable form. This is generally accomplished by using a special purpose computer program known as a "compiler" to process source code instructions into "object code," the binary code that is processed by the computer. In this machine language, a single 0 or 1 represents the absence or presence of an electrical charge. Each binary digit is referred to as a "bit." These electrical signals processed by a CPU will determine which functions of the CPU will be executed in what order. Computers do not process program instructions one bit at a time. Rather, they process standard lengths of bits. A "word" is the set of characters that occupies one storage location and is treated by the computer circuits as a unit and transported as such. Until the mid-1980s, most computers acted upon words of eight bits,

```
Program PrimeNum (Input, Output);
    {
• • • • • • • • • • • • • • • • • • • • • • • • • • • • • • • • • • • • • • • • • • • •
WRITTEN BY:        Vance F. Brown
DATE:              April 5, 1988
PROGRAM PURPOSE: This program allows user to enter the desired number of prime numbers
to be ascertained. The program then lists the prime numbers (starting with the prime number 2) in
numerical order in five columns.  DEFINITION OF PRIME NUMBER:  A number is prime if it
is not evenly divisible by any number other than itself and 1.
• • • • • • • • • • • • • • • • • • • • • • • • • • • • • • • • • • • • • • • • • • • •
    }
    Var {for variable function explanation, see below}
          num, count, primes, times, divisor: Integer; check: Boolean;
    Begin {of program}
          {***** initialize variables *****}
    num : = 2; {the primenumber candidate}
    count : = 0; {number of prime numbers found}
    times : = 0; {number of columns before a carriage return}
    {***** ask user how many prime numbers to list *****}
    write ('How many prime numbers do you want to find?'):
    read (primes);
    writeln;
    writeln;   {carriage returns}
    writeln;
repeat {until the number of primes is found}
    check : = false;  {initialize: assume first that number is not
                                            prime}
    divisor : = 2;    {first number to be divided into candidate}
    divisor : = succ(divisor);  {first number to be divided into candidate}
    {***** loop to determine if numbr is prime *****}
    while (divisor < num) and (not check) do begin

      check : = num mod divisor = 0; {the remainder after dividing
                                            divisor into num}
      divisor := succ(divsor);      {increment divisor}
      end; {of while loop}

    {***** if a prime number, then display it *****}
    If not check then begin
      write (num:10);
      count : = succ(count);  {increment number of primes
                                            found}
      times : = succ(times);  {increment column number}

    {***** column adjustment, once five numbers displayed,
    carriage return*****}
      if times = 5 then begin
            writeln; {carriage return}
            times : = 0; {start counter for column number over}
        end; {of column adjustment if statement)}
      end; {of display of if prime number statement}
    num : = succ(num); {next candidate for prime number}
    until count = primes; {once the number of primes entered by user is
                                    found, the program ends}
end.  {of program}
```

FIGURE 2
Source code in PASCAL, by Vance Brown.

known as a "byte" (e.g., "01101001"). More recently computers have been designed to act on words of 16, 32, or 64 bits. Figure 3 contains 24 of 1,674 lines of the object code derived from the PASCAL program in Figure 2.

Obviously, high-level programming languages are more compact than machine language, as well as easier for humans to decipher. This results from the fact that the representation of complex information as either a 1 or a 0 requires an enormous number of 1s and 0s.

Because of the difficulty of using and deciphering object code, program-mers developed an intermediate-level language referred to as "assembly language" to facilitate the translation of higher-level languages to object code. Assembly language uses abbreviated alphanumeric symbols such as "ADC," which means "add with carry." For older models of Apple computers, ADC translates to "01101001" in object code. An assembly program or assembler

11101001	01111001	00101100	10010000	10010000	11001101	10101011
01000011	01101111	01110000	01111001	01110010	01101001	01100111
01101000	01110100	00100000	00101000	01000011	00101001	00100000
00110001	00111001	00111000	00110101	00100000	01000010	01001111
01010010	01001100	01000001	01000100	01000100	00100000	01001001
01101110	01100011	00000010	00000100	00000000	10110001	01010111
00000000	00111100	00110011	00000000	00000000	00000000	00000000
00000000	00000000	00000000	00000000	00000000	00000000	00000000
00000000	00000000	00000000	00000000	00000000	00000000	00000000
00000000	00000000	00000000	00000000	00000000	00000000	00000000
00000000	00000000	00000000	00000000	00000000	00000000	00000000
00000000	00000000	00000000	00000000	00000000	00000000	00000000
00000000	00010100	01000100	01100101	01100110	01100001	01110101
01101100	01110100	00100000	01100100	01101001	01110111	01110000
01101100	01100001	01111001	00100000	01101101	01101111	01100100
01100101	01010000	00011001	00000001	11111111	11111111	00001111
00000111	00000111	01110000	00001111	00000111	00000111	01110000
00001110	00000111	00000111	01001111	00101110	10001010	00100111
00001010	11100100	11111001	01110100	00001110	01000011	00101110
10001010	00000111	01010000	11101000	11011000	00001000	01011000
11111110	11001100	01110101	11110011	11111000	11000011	01111010
00000000	11111111	01111011	00001000	00000000	00011111	11000111
00000110	00010010	00000000	001101110	00000000	00101110	11000110
00000110	10010100	00000001	00000000	10111110	00100000	00000000

FIGURE 3
Object code in PASCAL, by Vance Brown.

translates assembly language into object code. Figure 4 contains 29 of 7,330 lines of assembly code produced by "disassembling" the object code. Like object code and unlike higher-level languages, assembly language is specific to a particular computer system.

5. Software Validation and Maintenance

Although this discussion may suggest that programming is a linear process, it is in fact typically an iterative process. Program design often occurs in a series of "feedback loops" in which each stage of the process influences all of the others. Thus, a software engineer may develop a design for a program and then write some code to implement it, but in the process of writing the code, the engineer may discover logical problems with the design that require rethinking the program's basic structure. Often, individual modules or components of a software program will be tested and refined before integrating the various components into a full working version.

Before a software program enters service or the marketplace, the software design team runs the program through a suite of tests selected to ensure that the program operates properly and achieves the objectives set out in the requirement and specification stages of the process. After the various systems within the program are operating properly, the team conducts alpha (acceptance) testing. "Alpha testing" involves running the software with actual data (rather than simulated data) from the intended user. For products that are to be marketed widely, software vendors typically run a further level of testing (commonly referred to "beta testing") in which the program is provided on a limited basis to a range of target customers who agree to use the program and report problems. Beta testing may also identify features that users desire that were not initially included in the program. Based upon this input and further internal testing, the vendor typically makes some further refinements before releasing the product into the commercial marketplace.

All complex software programs have a range of errors (commonly referred to as "bugs"), and the validation stage can be one of the more challenging phases of the software life cycle. Because of the importance of reaching the market quickly, the design team is often under tremendous pressure to complete this phase.

Following the release of a product, software enters the last and what is often the longest phase of its life cycle: maintenance. Computer software users place great significance on a software vendor's ability to correct, improve, and adapt software products and services. Indeed, consumers are often wary of buying the first version of a new software product because it may be "buggy." The planning for maintenance begins early in the process with the documentation of the computer program. Most companies put out a series of "updates" or new releases of their programs to address maintenance problems and to enhance the program's functionality.

Some computer bugs may not manifest themselves until the product has been in use for a long time. The year 2000 (Y2K) problem is to a large extent a

```
L05CF:     PUSH      AX              ;05CF  50
           PUSH      CX              ;05D0  51
           MOV       CL,4            ;05D1  B1 04
           SHR       AX,CL           ;05D3  D3 E8
           ADD       BX,AX           ;05D5  03 D8
           POP       CX              ;05D7  59
           POP       AX              ;05D8  58
           AND       AX,0F           ;05D9  25 0F 00
           RET_NEAR                  ;05DC  C3
                                     ;L05DD    L062A  CC
L05DD:     CMP       BX,DX           ;05DD  3B DA
           JNZ       L05E3           ;05DF  75 02
           CMP       AX,CX           ;05E1  3B C1
                                     L05E3     L05DF CJ
L05E3:     RET_NEAR                  ;05E3  C3
                                     ;L05E4  L0656 CC
L05E4:     ADD       AX,CX           ;05E4  03 C1
           ADD       BX,CX           ;05E6  03 DA
           JMP       SHORTL05CF  ;05E8    EB E5
                                     L05EA    L0625 CC
L05EA:     MOV       AX,ES:[DI+4] ;05EA   26 8B 45 04
           MOV       BX,ES:[DI+6] ;05EE   26 8B 5D 06
           PUSH      AX              ;05F2  50
           OR        AX,BX           ;05F3  0B C3
           POP       AX              ;05F5  58
           RET_NEAR                  ;05F6  C3
```

FIGURE 4
Assembly code, by Vance Brown.

massive and pervasive bug that will have repercussions for computer users well into the future. Software vendors' reputations depend significantly on their ability to support their products and users once they are in the marketplace.

COMMENTS AND QUESTIONS

1. Compare the process of writing a computer program to the following activities: writing a novel, writing a poem, writing a symphony, writing a cookbook, preparing a map, designing a building, engineering a bridge, or inventing a new process for manufacturing steel. In what ways is computer programming similar to and different from these creative activities?

2. Is it possible to identify the "most significant" part of a computer program? Is it the idea for the program? The flowchart that structures the program? The source code that implements it? Which of these activities, if any, can be called the "heart" of programming?

D. THE ECONOMICS OF COMPUTER SOFTWARE AND NETWORK MARKETS

The software industry produces a wide variety of services and products, including operating systems, applications programs, custom programs, embedded systems, and data processing services. Some hardware systems manufacturers, such as Sun Microsystems, develop both operating systems and application software for their systems. There are also many small, independent firms that specialize in aspects of software services and product development. In recent years, a few firms, most notably Microsoft Corporation, have emerged as major forces in the computer software market. As its operating system platforms have become widely adopted, Microsoft has vertically integrated its operations through the development of application programs, and, more recently, electronic commerce product lines. Other software vendors, such as Intuit and Oracle, have concentrated on specific applications program markets, although these companies sometimes extend their product lines as advances in technology open up possibilities for new market niches that may be worth exploiting (e.g., money management software may become useful for managing personal banking as the technology and other developments enable the evolution of this online service). Another major market is for client-server and network management software. Significant players in this market include Novell, Sun Microsystems, and Microsoft.

Software markets evolve rapidly, driven in large part by the rapid pace of technological innovation in computer hardware. New versions of a mass-market software product often appear within a year after the initial release. Indeed, some consumers deliberately delay their purchases of early products and wait for more advanced (and more error-free) versions. Further, the rapid pace of innovation in software products means that the entire structure of the market can change in a very short period of time. At a broader level, new product markets themselves are constantly being created and destroyed as new classes of products become possible and as old software becomes useless or swallowed up into an operating system or another application program.

The rapid pace of software innovation has at least two implications for the law. First, software producers expect obsolescence. They must be prepared either to recover their fixed costs early, before their product is overrun in the marketplace, or to build some sort of long-term, multigeneration relationship with consumers. In either case, they may not need intellectual property protection for their programs beyond the short to medium term (three to ten years). Second, the legal system risks being behind the times unless it evolves rapidly in response to market developments. This is particularly true in antitrust law, where the often-ponderous machinery of antitrust enforcement may not swing into operation until the competitive threat has passed or it is too late to remedy the problem. For similar reasons, intellectual property protection that takes a long time to acquire and enforce tends to provide little effective protection for cutting-edge technologies.

This section discusses two economic concepts of particular relevance to computer software and Internet markets: (1) public goods; and (2) network effects. We then illustrate the operation of the concepts in discussing business strategy and platform competition in the microcomputer industry.

1. Public Goods

All markets for products embodying intellectual property exhibit an externality commonly referred to as the "public goods" problem. Public goods have two distinguishing features: (1) nonexcludability (it is difficult to prevent those who do not pay for the good from consuming it); and (2) nonrivalrous competition (additional consumers of the good do not deplete the supply of the good available to others). Military defense is a classic example of a public goods —it benefits all who are defended, whether they pay for the privilege or not. The result of the public goods problem is well-recognized: the private market will undersupply public goods because producers cannot reap the marginal value of their investment in providing such goods.

The computer software market presents an example of this public goods problem. Given how easily and inexpensively computer users may copy computer programs in digital form, vendors have tremendous difficulty excluding non-purchasers from the benefits of innovative computer programs once they are made commercially available. Programs written in object code and stored in ROM can be readily copied by inserting the chip into a laboratory device and downloading the information onto another chip or printing it on paper. Moreover, one person's use of the information does not detract from any other person's use of that same information, since the information can be copied without affecting the original. Since the authors and creators of computer software cannot reap the marginal value of their efforts, economic theory suggests that in the absence of other incentives to innovate, they will undersupply technological advances in computer software.

The public goods problem is a familiar one to anyone who has studied intellectual property, since it underlies the economic incentive theory of intellectual property. For a more detailed discussion of public goods in the context of intellectual property, see Peter S. Menell, Intellectual Property: General Theories, *in* Encyclopedia of Law and Economics (forthcoming 2000).

2. Network Effects

The second potential source of market failure in the computer software market arises from the presence of network externalities. Network externalities exist in markets for products for which the utility or satisfaction that a consumer derives from the product increases with the number of other consumers of the product. The telephone is a classic example of a product for which there are network externalities. The benefits to a person from owning a telephone are a function of the number of other people owning telephones connected to the same telephone network; the more people on the network, the more people each person can call and receive calls from. Another classic network externality flows from standardization. In this case, the value of learning a particular standard (say, how to use a certain word-processing program) depends on how many other people use that standard. Consider the prevalence of a "normal" typewriter keyboard. Because almost all English language typewriters feature the same keyboard configuration, commonly referred to as "QWERTY," typists need learn only one keyboard system.

Network externalities also inhere in product standards that allow for the interchangeability of complementary products. Examples of products for which this type of network externality is important are video cassette recorders, CD players, and computer operating systems. As discussed above, general-purpose computer operating systems allow consumers to use a variety of application software programs on the same system-unit hardware. The only requirement is that the application program be coded to work on the operating system embedded in the general computer system. Thus, the operating system serves as a "compatibility nexus" for a particular computer network. Application software producers will develop more programs for systems that are widely used; hardware producers will develop more configurations of disk drives, memory, and other features for popular operating systems. In general, the benefits of a larger computer operating system network include a wider variety of application software that can run on that operating system, lower search costs for consumers seeking particular application programs that run on that operating system, reduced retraining costs, greater labor mobility, and wider availability of compatible hardware configurations and peripherals. See generally Peter S. Menell, An Analysis of the Scope of Copyright Protection for Application Programs, 41 Stan. L. Rev. 1045 (1989).

Similarly, the greater the standardization of computer-human interfaces for particular application programs, such as word processing or spreadsheets, the easier it will be for computer users to employ their skills in different working environments. Computer users also want the computer-human interface to be as easy to use as possible—that is, "user friendly." In part, user friendliness is a function of what the user has already learned: things that are familiar tend to be easier to use. More generally, user friendliness is determined by the extent to which the design is tailored to achieve human factor goals—such as maximizing performance speed, minimizing learning time, minimizing rate of errors, and maximizing retention over time.

Standardization can occur by way of market processes, whereby subsequent entrants to a market adopt the standard of an existing firm. This has been referred to as "bandwagon standardization." See Joseph Farrell, Standardization and Intellectual Property, 30 Jurimetrics J. 35, 41 (1989). In the computer industry, firms often foster this process by freely licensing the use of a standard and publishing design and interoperability specifications. The UNIX operating system is an example of an open standard promoted by certain private companies, such as Sun Microsystems. It suffers, however, from the lack of strong sponsorship. Various incompatible versions of UNIX have proliferated over the years, eroding some of the network benefits.

Alternatively, standardization can occur through formal processes, such as government standard-setting and joint development of industry standards by a number of firms. This top-down approach to standard-setting has been common in the telecommunications industry, at least until recently. Regulatory agencies, in consultation with the affected companies, set standards for connecting peripheral devices (including computers) to telephone lines. Only devices that comply with these publicly available standards will operate over the telephone lines.

Finally, industries characterized by strong network externalities will sometimes develop de facto standards, even though neither the companies in the industry nor the government has made any effort to settle on a particular standard or ensure interoperability. The Windows operating system offers a prime example. Microsoft has not "opened" its operating system to competitors. Nonetheless, once the Microsoft operating system reached a certain critical mass of users, the size of its user base began to make it more attractive for other developers to write programs for the Windows platforms. More applications programmers wrote programs to run on Windows because of the large user base; more users adopted the Microsoft system in part because of all the programs being written for it. This positive feedback effect enabled Windows to become the de facto industry standard. In 1999, Windows had close to a 90 percent share of the personal computer operating system market, despite the closed nature of the system and despite the availability of several arguably superior competing systems. For a discussion of these alternative forms of standardization in network markets, see Mark A. Lemley, Antitrust and the Internet Standardization Problem, 28 Conn. L. Rev. 1041 (1996).

An important economic consideration in markets with significant network externalities is whether firms will have the correct incentives to adopt compatible products, thereby enlarging existing networks. Economists have demonstrated that firms might prefer to adopt noncompatible product standards even though their adoption of compatible products would increase net social welfare. See Michael L. Katz & Carl Shapiro, Network Externalities, Competition, and Compatibility, 75 Am. Econ. Rev. 424, 435 (May 1985). The explanation for this behavior is that by adopting a compatible standard, a firm enlarges the size of a network that comprises both the adopter's product and its rivals' products. This will have the effect of increasing the desirability of the rivals' products to consumers, thereby reducing the adopter's market share (although of a larger market) relative to what it would have been had the firm adopted a non-compatible product standard. Although this effect by no means implies that subsequent market entrants will never adopt a compatible operating system or computer-user interface, it does suggest that incentives to adopt compatible standards might be suboptimal.

While a widely adopted product standard can offer important benefits to consumers and firms, it can also "trap" the industry in an obsolete or inferior standard. In essence, the installed base built on the old standard—reflected in durable goods and human capital (training) specific to the old standard—can create an inertia that makes it much more difficult for any one producer to break away from that standard by introducing a non-compatible product, even if the new standard offers a significant technological improvement over the current standard. See Joseph Farrell & Garth Saloner, Standardization, Compatibility, and Innovation, 16 Rand J. Econ. 70 (1985). In this way, network externalities can retard innovation and slow or prevent adoption of improved product standards. This problem is particularly significant in industries that develop rapidly, such as the computer industry. Rapid changes make the adoption of standards (formal or informal) a hazardous enterprise.

A frequently cited example of standard stagnation is the persistence of the standard QWERTY typewriter keyboard despite the availability of a better key configuration. United States Navy studies and typing speed world records indicated that the Dvorak Simplex Keyboard, a typewriter key configuration patented in 1932 by August Dvorak and W.L. Dealey, was significantly more efficient than the QWERTY system. Adoption of the better standard may have been effectively stymied by "switching costs"—the costs of converting or replacing QWERTY keyboards and retraining those who use this system.[7] Because of the fear that national standards would exacerbate the inertia problem, the National Bureau of Standards declined to set interface standards for computers in the early 1970s. Subsequent developments proved that a wise decision.

Nonetheless, standards are essential in many contexts. While the U.S. government did not adopt computer interface standards in the 1970s, the hardware industry had to develop de facto standards in order to allow computers and peripheral devices to communicate with each other. The software industry faced similar problems in ensuring compatibility between operating systems and applications programs in the 1980s, and the network industry faces the same problem today. In each case, the problem goes away if one company controls the market for both goods, as AT&T did in the telephone industry until 1984. If AT&T is the only company to sell both telephone services and telephones, there is unlikely to be a problem in ensuring that your telephone works with your phone line. But this form of standardization comes at the expense of competition. Controlling standards and compatibility in dynamic industries is one of the most vexing policy problems in the computer and telecommunications industries. Yet sometimes advances in technology can aid in solving these problems.

The economics of network markets suggests a range of business strategies that take advantage of network effects. See generally Carl Shapiro & Hal R. Varian, Information Rules (1999). Network markets are inherently "tippy." Given the large payoff to becoming a de facto industry standard, it behooves firms to invest heavily in strategies to attract adopters. Once these customers make investments in installing a product, learning its attributes, and developing data bases, they become locked into the product. This affords the product

---

7. This story has been challenged on its factual merits, however. See S.J. Liebowitz & Stephen E. Margolis, The Fable of the Keys, 33 J.L. & Econ. 1 (1990).

sponsor substantial latitude to charge higher prices, bundle the platform with other products, and exercise some degree of control over innovation and competition in related markets. The history of the microcomputer illustrates the importance of understanding these lessons and the challenges that network markets pose for policymakers, judges, business decision-makers, and lawyers. For a comprehensive discussion of the legal significance of network effects, see Mark A. Lemley & David McGowan, Legal Implications of Network Economic Effects, 86 Cal. L. Rev. 479 (1998).

3. Platform Competition in the Computer Industry

Early entrants into the microcomputer market followed the "single vendor" model of the mainframe and minicomputer markets. Osborne, Apple, Kaypro, and others developed operating systems unique to their computers, which they packaged with application software and marketed as complete systems. These computer systems were not compatible. This enabled these vendors to control markets for software and peripheral equipment for their computer systems, but it had the disadvantage of segmenting the market for application programs.

Similarly, IBM declined to license the leading operating system for Intel 8080 chips, Digital Research Incorporated's CP/M (control program/monitor) operating system. Instead, IBM licensed a new operating system (DOS) from Microsoft Corporation, a young company that had attracted some attention for having developed a version of the BASIC computer language for early microcomputers. Even IBM's use of Microsoft's DOS platform, however, was not completely open to the industry because IBM refused to license its BIOS chip. Due to IBM's strong trademark and marketing network, this decision led to the rapid demise of the CP/M platform and hurt those OEMs that had built their microcomputers upon the CP/M platform.

Building on the name recognition flowing from its association with the IBM PC, Microsoft selected a business model aimed at developing and promoting relationships with a broad range of microcomputer companies, the OEM and ISVs. This model encouraged compatibility of hardware and software products in the industry and enabled software vendors to reach a much larger market for their products: the many computer systems operating on the MS-DOS platform.

As its operating system market grew, Microsoft appreciated the fundamental importance of compatibility in microcomputer markets. In the words of one of its senior executives,

> [c]onsumers value compatibility. Compatibility makes computers easier to learn and leads to a plethora of applications. Microsoft understood in the early 1980s that the potential of personal computers would not be unleashed until the industry provided a broad set of compatible hardware and software products. To help bring

that about, Microsoft developed and promoted an important part of the standard personal computer architecture—a set of operating systems.[8]

Microsoft's business strategy came to encompass four principal elements all directed toward promoting the widespread adoption of the Microsoft operating system platform: (a) encouraging the development of application programs to run on an evolving Microsoft platform; (b) building an intellectual property portfolio to protect its operating system platform; (c) developing long-term relationships with OEMs to promote Microsoft's operating system platforms while preventing direct competition in the platform market and discouraging adoption of competing operating systems; and (d) evolving the operating system platform in a way that was backward-compatible (so as not to strand the existing base of computer users who had developed programs and data bases for prior operating system) while incorporating enhanced functionality made possible by advances in microprocessor, other hardware, and software technology. In particular, Microsoft began developing a graphical user interface OS and various network support products (LAN and Windows NT).

Microsoft understood well the lessons of network economics. It successfully registered its trademarks and invested heavily in advertising them and in expanding its network. The company used pricing, contractual, and bundling strategies to lock consumers into its products while discouraging adoption of competing products. For example, it offered its operating system to OEMs at relatively low prices in contracts that required the OEMs to pay a royalty for every system sold, whether or not they actually installed a Microsoft operating system. Because many microcomputer buyers preferred the Microsoft platform in order to run the large stock of software that was available, OEMs had little incentive to offer competing operating systems. These "per processor" agreements made the marginal cost of installing Microsoft's operating system zero. In the 1990s, Microsoft successfully leveraged its market power into other markets as well. It bundled its application programs for office use (Word, Excel, Access, Powerpoint) into its Office suite. As the World Wide Web became popular, Microsoft integrated its Internet browser (Microsoft Explorer) directly into Windows. These practices took effective advantage of the economics of network markets and expanded Microsoft's dominance throughout the software domain.

Although Microsoft's dominance of the microcomputer industry remains strong, technological developments continue to reshape the competitive landscape. In the mid-1990s, Sun Microsystems introduced Java, which Sun describes as "a standardized application programming environment that affords software developers the opportunity to create and distribute a single version of programming code that is capable of operating on many different, otherwise incompatible systems platforms." See Mark A. Lemley & David McGowan, Could Java Change Everything? The Competitive Propriety of a Proprietary Standard, 43 Antitrust Bull. 715 (1998). Thus described, Java offers the promise of platform-independent computing, the equivalent of a standardized "meta"-

---

8. Direct testimony of Paul Maritz, group vice president for platforms and applications, ¶127, United States v. Microsoft Corp., No. 98-1232, U.S.D.C. DC (public version).

operating system that would allow both consumers and programmers to choose operating systems free of the constraints of network effects. Java may reduce the opportunity cost incurred by those using platforms other than the market standard, thereby facilitating transition among platforms and alleviating concerns that Microsoft can exploit its installed base of users and programmers.

A "standardized application programming environment" sounds to many like an operating system: a good for which applications may be written and that coordinates the computer's functions. The difference is in the meta-operating system characteristic Sun ascribes to Java technology—it is billed as the operating system whose job it is to allow any operating system to function with applications written for any other operating system (or possibly without any system other than Java in mind), so long as both the operating system and the application are themselves compatible with Java. Java may represent the realization of the long-sought platform-independent competitive horizon. Ironically, this platform-independent world would be brought to us by a proprietary program to which Sun owns the intellectual property rights.

Sun faced the problem all companies who want to compete in a network market must deal with: its Java product is new and therefore lacks an installed base. Java has achieved rapid, widespread, and growing acceptance in the software community. Hundreds of thousands of programmers are writing Java code, and some companies are even designing hardware products optimized for Java. Like Microsoft, Sun has sought to follow the lessons of network economics by promoting adoption of its product through advertising, education, competitive pricing, and widespread licensing.

In addition to the Java platform, a grassroots effort among programmers has attracted attention to the open source Linux operating system. Linux was developed from the UNIX operating system, an operating system platform initially developed by AT&T that became fragmented as many companies developed different, incompatible versions. What distinguishes the Linux code from the many other versions of UNIX is that its principal developer and chief promoter, Linus Torvalds, has committed to maintaining Linux as an open standard. Linux has developed a loyal following within the academic world. The size of its network has grown sufficiently large that some commercial software vendors have begun writing programs that run on the Linux platform. At this writing, it remains to be seen whether either Java or Linux will offer significant competition to the Microsoft operating system.

COMMENTS AND QUESTIONS

1.   Does intellectual property protection for products featuring network externalities increase or decrease the likelihood that firms will seek to develop proprietary standards? For an argument that the problem of market power is exacerbated by the availability of intellectual property protection for many of the potential standards in a network market, see Mark A. Lemley & David McGowan, Could Java Change Everything? The Competitive Propriety of a Proprietary Standard, 43 Antitrust Bull. 715 (1998).

2. How should the presence of network externalities with regard to computer software affect the analysis of intellectual property protection? Of what relevance are network externalities to the scope of copyright, patent, or trademark protection? Should the network externalities of operating systems be treated in the same manner as network externalities of user interfaces? See Peter S. Menell, An Epitaph for Traditional Copyright Protection of Network Features of Computer Software, 43 Antitrust Bull. 651 (1998).

3. The development of Java in particular blurs the line between computer operating systems and Internet-related applications programs. In so doing, it raises the possibility of private ownership of the protocols that govern the Internet. Right now, the Internet is built on a fundamentally open architecture, as Jane Winn explains:

> The National Research Council has noted that the Internet is now "open" in at least the following four senses. It is open to users because it does not force users into closed groups or deny access to any sectors of society but instead permits universal connectivity, like the telephone system. It is open to service providers because it provides an open and accessible environment for competing commercial and intellectual interests. For example, competitive access for information providers is permitted. It is open to network providers because any network provider can meet the necessary requirements to attach and become a part of the aggregate of interconnected networks. It is open to change because it continually permits the introduction to new applications and services. It is not limited to only one application, as in television. It also permits the introduction of new technologies as they become available.

Jane Kaufman Winn, Open Systems, Free Markets, and Regulation of Commerce, 72 Tul. L. Rev. 1177 (1998). It is certainly possible, however, to imagine part or all of the Internet protocols being proprietary. Suppose Microsoft develops a privately owned extension to HTML, the basic markup language used to encode information on the Web. If that extension were to become a standard among Web developers, Microsoft would control access to the Internet—at least for anyone who wanted to use that protocol.

We discuss the long-running debate between open and closed systems in several places throughout this book.

E. OVERVIEW OF INTELLECTUAL PROPERTY PROTECTION FOR COMPUTER SOFTWARE

Information technology industries rely heavily on intellectual property law to protect their products and other assets. For this reason, this book provides considerable coverage of intellectual property issues. Chapter 1 demonstrates how trade secrecy law can be used to protect some valuable aspects of software and other information technologies. Chapter 2 considers the extent to which copyright law provides protection to computer programs. Chapter 3 traces the evolution of patent protection for software innovations. Chapter 4 explores the supplemental protection that may be available to information technology firms from trademark law. In addition, Chapter 5 considers some sui generis forms of legal protection that have been considered or adopted to protect certain information technology products (e.g., semiconductor chip designs and databases) for which existing intellectual property regimes may provide inadequate protection. Chapter 8 also provides an overview of some differences in the intellectual property rules applicable to computer software and other information technology innovations in the international market.

While computer software may have been the first digital information product to rely crucially on intellectual property laws, other digital information products rely heavily on intellectual property protection as well. Hence, in Part II, Chapters 10 and 11 will consider a range of digital intellectual property issues that arise in the context of the Internet and the World Wide Web.

Because so much of this book emphasizes intellectual property law and because information technology developers need to develop complex strategies built up as multiple forms of legal protection, this chapter provides a brief overview of the specific forms of intellectual property law. This may be helpful before the reader delves into the book's detailed consideration of how each mode of protection may be used to protect some aspects of software or other information technology products or services.

Intellectual property law comprises a diverse array of state and federal legal regimes. Under state law, intellectual work can be protected through contract law, trade secrecy protection, and trademark protection. Under federal law, intellectual work can be protected by patent law, copyright law, and trademark/trade dress protection under the Lanham Act. These regimes interact in a number of ways, and the subject matter of these various modes of legal protection overlap. For example, both trade secret law and patent protection cover technological advances. Although federal intellectual property protection has primacy, federal law does not preempt state trade secret law, which leaves both bodies of law to operate in tandem.[9] By contrast, copyright protection does not extend to "any idea, procedure, process, system, method of operation, concept, principle, or discovery," so as not to undermine the role of the patent law (which erects a higher threshold for the protection of functional works). 17 U.S.C. §102(b).

1. Trade Secret Law

Software developers and other information technology firms often rely on trade secret law to protect valuable information. The source code forms of

---

9. See Kewanee Oil Co. v. Bicron Corp., 416 U.S. 470 (1974) (patent law does not preempt trade secret law); H.R. Rep. No. 1476, 94th Cong., 2d Sess. 132 (1976) (legislative history of §301 of the Copyright Act stating that trade secret law would remain unaffected by the Act so long as it contains elements different from copyright infringement); Warrington Assocs. v. Real-Time Eng'g Sys., 522 F. Supp. 367, 368-369 (N.D. Ill. 1981) (trade secret not preempted by Copyright Act).

programs and other internal design documentation, for example, are often locked up in secure places and held as trade secrets. Trade secret law protects against the misappropriation of such commercially valuable secret information by unfair or commercially unreasonable means, whether done by competitors or anyone else.

Every state protects trade secrets through either common law or statutory regimes. In 1979, the National Conference of Commissioners on Uniform State Laws promulgated the Uniform Trade Secrets Act (UTSA), which has since been enacted by 40 states and the District of Columbia. The Act prohibits the actual or threatened misappropriation of a trade secret. The UTSA defines a "trade secret" broadly as

> information, including a formula, pattern, compilation, program, device, method, technique, or process, that:
> (i) derives independent economic value, actual or potential, from not being generally known to, and not being readily ascertainable by proper means by, other persons who can obtain economic value from its disclosure or use, and
> (ii) is the subject of efforts that are reasonable under the circumstances to maintain its secrecy.

U.T.S.A. §4. Trade secrets have potentially unlimited duration. As the law's name suggests, information must be a secret if it is to be protected by this law. However, only relative and not absolute secrecy is required. The owner of a trade secret must take reasonable steps to maintain this secrecy. Although trade secrets are often licensed to other firms, the "reasonable steps to maintain secrecy" requirement can generally be satisfied by provisions in the license agreement requiring the licensee to limit access to and use of the trade secret information. In addition, licensees will be under a nondisclosure obligation if the circumstances of the disclosure of a secret give rise to an understanding that the information must be carefully protected. Trade secrets have no definite term of protection, but they will be protected only as long as they are secret. Once a trade secret is disclosed, the legal protection dissipates.

Courts will generally find misappropriation of trade secrets in two circumstances: (1) when a person uses theft or other improper means (e.g., bribery of employees) to acquire the secrets, or (2) where someone uses or discloses the secrets in violation of a confidential relationship. Trade secret laws do not protect against independent discovery or invention of the same information. Nor do they prevent competitors from reverse engineering a lawfully obtained product in order to discern the secrets it might contain. Successful plaintiffs in trade secret cases are entitled to recover damages attributable to the misappropriation of the secret and in some cases to an injunction against use or further disclosure of the secret. However, injunctions may be limited in duration to the time it would have taken a competitor to independently develop the secret or otherwise discover it by fair means.

2. Copyright Law

Software developers and other information technology firms also routinely rely on copyright law. Copyright law protects object code versions of computer programs against exact copying. This law also provides significant protection to other aspects of programs—for example, nonfunctional design elements of user interfaces. There is some debate, as Chapter 2 illustrates, about how far copyright protection extends to the structure and organization of programs.

Unlike trade secrecy law, copyright protection is governed exclusively by federal law, and infringement suits may only be brought in federal courts in the United States. The Constitution provides Congress with the power to "promote the progress of science and [the] useful arts, by securing for limited times to authors . . . the exclusive right in their . . . writings." Congress has used this power to provide protection to "original works of authorship" that have been "fixed in a tangible medium of expression," including computer programs, photographs, paintings, sculptures, musical compositions, dramatic plays, and sound recordings. To qualify for copyright protection, a work must be "original" in the sense that it represents an author's intellectual creation, but it need not be particularly inventive. Works made by employees in the course of their employment are deemed the work of the employer for purposes of copyright ownership.

Copyrights exist from the moment that a work is fixed in a tangible medium of expression. Until legislation was passed in 1998 extending the duration of copyrights by 20 years, protection existed upon the creation of the work and lasted for the life of the author plus 50 years, or 75 years in the case of entity authors. 17 U.S.C. §302. The owner of a copyright has the exclusive right to make copies of his work, prepare derivative works, distribute his works, and perform and display his works in public. 17 U.S.C. §106.

The "useful article" doctrine and the idea/expression dichotomy limit the scope of copyright law so as not to undermine the patent law's protection of functional inventions. The useful article doctrine allows copyright protection for expressive features of "pictorial, graphic, and sculptural works" only to the extent that such features "can be identified separately from, and are capable of existing independently of, the utilitarian aspects of the article." 17 U.S.C. §101 (definition of pictorial, graphic, and sculptural works). The idea/expression dichotomy excludes from copyright protection

> any idea, procedure, process, system, method of operation, concept, principle, or discovery regardless of the form in which it is described, explained, illustrated, or embodied in such work.

17 U.S.C. §102(b). In Baker v. Selden, 101 U.S. 99 (1879), the holder of a copyright in a book describing a particular system of bookkeeping sought to prevent others from using that method (and the forms described). The Supreme Court held that methods and forms needed to use such methods are not

copyrightable. The Court enunciated the idea/expression limitation on copyright protection:

> To give to the author of the book an exclusive property in the art described therein, when no examination of its novelty has ever been officially made, would be a surprise and a fraud upon the public. That is the province of letters-patent, not of copyright. The claim to an invention or discovery of an art or manufacture must be subjected to the examination of the Patent Office before an exclusive right therein can be obtained; and it can only be secured by a patent from the government.

101 U.S. at 104.

The fundamental purpose underlying U.S. copyright law is to promote the creation and dissemination of knowledge. Some authors and artists may be unwilling to invest the time and effort involved in producing a new work of authorship if they know that others can simply copy their work. The cheaper and easier it is to make multiple copies, the greater the potential market failure. Copyright law ameliorates this problem by allowing the copyright owner to capture a significant part of the commercial value (if any) of her work for a limited period of time. One way that copyright encourages the dissemination of new works of authorship is to enable subsequent authors and artists to "build on" the works of their predecessors, either by using the unprotectable ideas conveyed in existing works or by drawing upon works in the public domain (whether because the copyright term has expired, the work is ineligible for copyright protection, or the author dedicated the work to the public domain).

Although not required to obtain copyright protection, software developers may register a claim of copyright with the U.S. Copyright Office, and there are some advantages to doing so. A registration certificate generally constitutes prima facie evidence of the validity of the copyright and of the claim of the registrant to be the owner of the copyright. Second, prompt registration is necessary to qualify for an award of attorney fees or statutory damages under U.S. law. Third, a registration certificate is a necessary precondition for U.S. authors to bring infringement actions in U.S. courts. However, registration is not a precondition for a work to be protected by copyright law. Instead, copyright subsists automatically in original works of authorship from the time they are first created. The duration of a copyright now extends for the life of an individual author plus 70 years (or 95 years from first publication when works are produced by corporations).

Unlike patent law, copyright law protects against only the copying of works, and not making, using, or selling works. Hence, copyright law does not prevent others who independently develop a work from competing with the first inventor. In addition, copyright protection is moderated by the fair use doctrine, which allows others to make limited use of a work for teaching, research, and other purposes. 17 U.S.C. §107.

3. Patent Law

Patents have long been used to protect computer hardware systems and are increasingly used to protect software innovations, such as algorithms and data structures, as well as methods of doing business in the electronic environment. Chapters 3 and 8 show that the United States and other nations differ in their approaches to patent protections for computer software.

Patents are granted to inventors who meet several substantive and procedural requirements. First, the invention must fall within the class of patentable subject matter. Generally, this means it cannot be a purely mental discovery or a law of nature. Second, the resulting product or process must be useful. It must also be novel and be more than an obvious advance over the prior art. A patent is awarded in the United States to the first to invent, not the first to file, a patent claim, as is common in other countries. A patent gives the patentee the exclusive right to use or license the patented product or process in the United States for 20 years from the date the patent application was filed. A patent is not automatically awarded. Rather, the Patent Office requires its examiners to carefully scrutinize the application and make a judgment about whether the patent should be issued. Many applications are disapproved, and others are approved only after significant narrowing of the patent claims.

If the Patent Office grants an inventor a patent, the patent is published, so that everyone else can learn what the inventor has made and how to make it. The inventor gets the right to prevent anyone else in the United States from making, using, or selling a product or process covered by the "claims" of the patent (the portion of the patent defining the invention) while it is in force. If another party does make, use, or sell the patented invention during the term of this exclusive right, the patent owner (called the patentee) is entitled to sue them for infringement of the patent. If the patentee proves that the defendant is in fact infringing the patented invention, the patentee can obtain an injunction against the infringer and damages for past infringement. A patentee can also prevent others from importing infringing works into the United States.

Under 35 U.S.C. §§171-173, an inventor may obtain a design patent for "any new, original and ornamental design for an article of manufacture." In order to receive protection, the inventor must establish that the design is novel, nonobvious, and ornamental, which means reflecting aesthetic skill and artistic conception. If a design is primarily functional rather than ornamental or is dictated by functional considerations, then it is not eligible for a design patent. Design patents are valid for a term of 14 years from the date of issuance.

4. Trademark Law

Trademark law protects words, symbols, and other indicia that serve to identify the source of goods or services against confusingly similar uses in commerce. Examples of protectable trademarks include corporate and product names (e.g., Apple Computer, Inc., and iMac as a name of a computer made by Apple), logos (e.g., the cube-like shape that signifies Sun Microsystem's products), slogans (e.g., "Intel inside"), and product configurations (e.g., nonfunctional aspects of computer keyboard layouts) as long as the significance of the symbol lies principally in designating the origin of goods or services. The word, symbol, or indicia cannot be merely a description of the good itself, or a generic term for a class of goods or services.[10] Further, the identifying mark must not be a functional element of the product itself, but must principally serve an identifying purpose. Functionality in the context of trademark law means that there is no competitive necessity for other market participants to use the same or a very similar designation in order to compete effectively in the market. In addition, trademark owners forfeit their rights by licensing their mark to others without controlling and monitoring the nature and quality of the goods or services with which the mark is used. Finally, trademark protection is directly tied to the use of the mark to identify goods or services in commerce. Under U.S. law, trademarks do not expire on any particular date; they continue in force until "abandoned" by their owner. In some countries, however, as Chapter 8 explains, trademark rights arise by virtue of registration and may expire unless renewed in a timely fashion.

While state common law and statutory law may offer significant protection to trademarks in the United States, the most significant source of trademark protection on a national basis is that conferred under the federal trademark law known as the Lanham Act, 15 U.S.C. §§1051 et seq. This Act establishes a procedure by which federal officials examine trademark registration applications and issue trademark registrations that confer significant benefits upon the registrants. However, federal trademark registration is not necessary to obtain trademark protection. A trademark owner who believes that another is using the same or a similar mark to identify competing goods can bring suit for trademark infringement under state law. The ultimate question in trademark litigation is whether consumers are likely to be confused if two different firms are using the same or similar marks in the marketplace. If so, the trademark owner is entitled to an injunction against the confusing use, damages for past infringement, and in some cases the seizure and destruction of infringing goods.

In recent years, the Lanham Act has been amended to provide federal protection to highly distinctive marks (generally those that are famous) against "dilution" of the good will associated with the mark. A number of state trademark dilution laws also exist. Trademark dilution laws protect trademarks against uses of trademarks even when consumers are unlikely to be confused by the coexistence of the marks in commerce. Dilution laws protect against uses that would cause a blurring of the distinctiveness of the mark (e.g., IBM for

---

10. "Genericide" occurs when consumers associate a trademark with a general product category rather than a designation of source. Prominent examples of trademarks that became generic include thermos, escalator, and linoleum. The "x86" designation has been deemed generic as a way of denoting microprocessors, which explains in part why the latest version of the Intel microprocessor was dubbed "Pentium" rather than "586."

automobiles) or tarnishment (e.g., Lotus as a name for a pornographic book-store).

5.   Sui Generis Laws

Proposals for sui generis intellectual property legislation for software and other information technology products have arisen periodically in legal and policy circles. Generally, the rationale is that existing intellectual property systems did not provide sufficient protection to promote adequate levels of investment in the development of this technology. Sometimes the argument is reversed—that existing intellectual property statutes provide too much protection, or at least the wrong kind of protection.

Although sui generis proposals for software have not taken hold in the United States, this country has adopted a sui generis form of legal protection for semiconductor chip designs. As this book goes to press, the United States is also considering adoption of a sui generis form of legal protection for collections of information that may not meet copyright standards. The European Union has already enacted such a law. Chapter 5 will discuss these laws and proposals.

6.   Contract Law

Traditional contract law provides an important framework for protecting the intellectual work embodied in software products. Contract law establishes the rules for enforcing the bargains of contracting parties. It can be used to structure a wide range of software transactions and relationships, including service contracts for the design and implementation of software systems or programs on a client's computer, sales of software products, and lease agreements. In general, the Uniform Commercial Code governs contracts for goods, while common law and other state statutes govern service contracts. Contracts governing the disclosure of information, rights to use technology, and rights to make copies of a work fall into the latter category. At this writing, a proposed statute (the Uniform Computer Information Transactions Act, or UCITA) would govern transactions in "computer information" and would fundamentally expand the role of contract in protecting software and digital information.

I

SOFTWARE PROTECTION

Part I deals largely with the legal protection of computer software. Most of the chapters concern intellectual property protection for computer software, both in the United States and abroad. Other chapters deal with closely related subjects: the use of contracts and licenses to create alternative forms of protection for software, and the limits that antitrust law places on both intellectual property and contract protection.

The law of computer software is still evolving, though some clear patterns have emerged in the last decade. Part I approaches intellectual property protection in roughly chronological order, beginning with early efforts to protect computer programs as trade secrets. It traces the rise (and partial fall) of copyright law as a primary means of protecting the code and structure of computer programs. Part I then considers the more recent application of both patent and trademark law to protect various aspects of computer programs. Finally, after tracing this chronological development, Chapter 5 explores whether software would be better served by some sui generis form of intellectual property protection. Subsequent chapters explore recent trends toward "protecting" computer programs through contract law, the internationalization of software IP law, and the limits that antitrust law imposes on the software industry.

Because new cases are being decided and statutes created all the time in this field, the picture this book offers of computer software protection will necessarily be incomplete. But a number of principles in this field now seem well settled, and this Part explores those principles.

1

Trade Secret Protection

In the early days of computing, computer companies often bundled software "free" with the hardware they sold to customers to encourage them to buy and use the hardware. Other groups, especially in the government and academia, provided software for free because they were not motivated by profit. As the demand for computing grew, purchasers increasingly had specific needs that could only be filled with customized computer programs. While many companies developed these custom programs in-house, increasingly specialized software development firms realized that many companies needed the same basic sorts of data-processing programs. These firms undertook to develop more general-purpose software that could be sold to multiple clients. As programs became marketable commodities, rather than services provided to a particular client, the need for some sort of intellectual property protection became clear.

Today, the main contours of legal protection for computer technology are relatively clear. Copyright law protects computer software, and it is generally acknowledged that it is not acceptable behavior to make multiple copies of someone else's software without permission, with important exceptions and qualifications discussed later. Patent law protects computer hardware and new processes or "structures" embodied in computer software. But in the late 1970s and early 1980s, things were very different. Whether copyright protected computer programs at all was an open question, debated by the federal Commission on New Technological Uses of Copyright (CONTU)[1] and not finally resolved until the enactment of the

---

1. Final Report of the National Commission on New Technological Uses of Copyrighted Works (U.S. Gov't Printing Office 1978).

1980 Amendments to the Copyright Act. During this period, and even after the 1980 Amendments, courts disagreed over such fundamental issues as the copyrightability of object code and whether copyright protected computer programs against nonliteral infringement.

At the same time, a similar debate was raging in the federal courts over the patentability of computer software. The Supreme Court had held computer programs unpatentable in the 1972 decision of Gottschalk v. Benson, 409 U.S. 63 (1972), and it did not reopen the door *Gottschalk* closed until 1981. Even after 1981, the patentability of "pure" computer software was open to dispute. The issue was sufficiently clouded in 1994, for example, that the Federal Circuit took In re Alappat en banc in an attempt to clarify the standards for issuing software patents. 33 F.3d 1526 (Fed. Cir. 1994) (en banc). It was not until 1998 that the Federal Circuit unambiguously permitted patents on "pure" software. While software patents appear to be here to stay, their status has been uncertain until quite recently.

Against this backdrop, it was important for software vendors in the 1970s and early 1980s to establish their rights vis-à-vis users. One way for vendors to prevent users from freely copying their computer programs was to claim a program as a trade secret. Trade secrecy was a particularly viable alternative in the early days of the computer industry, because most computer software was customized and sold to a limited number of customers, generally large companies, rather than distributed in the mass market. Trade secrets have also been important in the computer industry as a means of protecting projects under development from being taken by departing employees.

As a mass market in software products became a reality, it became clear that software would need more legal protection than trade secrecy alone could provide. However, commercial software vendors did not abandon trade secrecy, even as they began to rely increasingly on copyright and patent protection. In part, this was due to the uncertainty described above, and in part, it is because trade secrecy offers some advantages to vendors that copyright and patent protection alone do not provide. This chapter explores the benefits and limitations of trade secret law as a form of legal protection for computer systems, and investigates the further challenges Internet distribution models pose for trade secret protection.

Today, every one of the 50 states protects trade secrets in one form or another. Improper use or disclosure of a trade secret is generally a common law tort. In this century, the principal document setting forth the law of trade secrets was the Restatement of Torts, published in 1939. Sections 757 and 758 of the Restatement set forth basic principles of trade secret law, which were quickly adopted by courts in most states. Those sections (and accompanying comments) are reproduced in the statutory appendix, which the reader is encouraged to review now. The Restatement protected as a trade secret any information "used in one's business" which gives its owner "an opportunity to obtain an advantage over competitors who do not know or use it," so long as the information was in fact a secret. Restatement §757, comment *b.*

When the Restatement (Second) of Torts was published in 1979, the authors made the decision not to include sections 757 and 758 on the grounds that the law of trade secrets had developed into an independent body of law that no longer relied on general principles of tort law. The influence of the original Restatement remained, however, because it had been adopted by so many courts. The main principles of the Restatement of Torts relating to trade secrets have been adopted in the Restatement (Third) of Unfair Competition, published in 1994.

Beginning in 1979, the National Conference of Commissioners on Uniform State Laws promulgated a model state statute, the Uniform Trade Secrets Act, which differed in some respects from the common law. This Act has now been enacted (in one form or another) by 41 states and the District of Columbia. Because of its importance, we reproduce its primary provisions here.

Uniform Trade Secrets Act, with 1985 Amendments

§1. Definitions

As used in this [Act], unless the context requires otherwise:

(1) "Improper means" includes theft, bribery, misrepresentation, breach or inducement of a breach of a duty to maintain secrecy, or espionage through electronic or other means;

(2) "Misappropriation" means:

(i) acquisition of a trade secret of another by a person who knows or has reason to know that the trade secret was acquired by improper means; or

(ii) disclosure or use of a trade secret of another without express or implied consent by a person who

(A) used improper means to acquire knowledge of the trade secret; or

(B) at the time of disclosure or use, knew or had reason to know that his knowledge of the trade secret was

(I) derived from or through a person who had utilized improper means to acquire it;

(II) acquired under circumstances giving rise to a duty to maintain its secrecy or limit its use; or

(III) derived from or through a person who owed a duty to the person seeking relief to maintain its secrecy or limit its use; or

(C) before a material change of his [or her] position, knew or had reason to know that it was a trade secret and that knowledge of it had been acquired by accident or mistake. . . .

(4) "Trade secret" means information, including a formula, pattern, compilation, program, device, method, technique, or process, that:

(i) derives independent economic value, actual or potential, from not being generally known to, and not being readily ascertainable[2] by proper means by, other persons who can obtain economic value from its disclosure or use, and

(ii) is the subject of efforts that are reasonable under the circumstances to maintain its secrecy.

COMMENTS AND QUESTIONS

While there once was a question as to the availability of copyright and/or patent protection for computer technology, there is no longer. In view of this fact, to what extent should hardware and software manufacturers be able to rely on trade secret protection? Are there disadvantages to trade secret law as a means of protection for innovations in computer technology? On this point, see the Final Report of the Commission on New Technological Uses of Copyright (1978), at 34-35 [hereinafter CONTU Final Report]:

Although many proprietors feel secure when using trade secrecy, there are several problems they must face with respect to its use in protecting programs. Because secrecy is paramount, it is inappropriate for protecting works that contain the secret and are designed to be widely distributed. Although this matters little in the case of unique programs prepared for large commercial customers, it substantially precludes the use of trade secrecy with respect to programs sold in multiple copies over the counter to small businesses, schools, consumers and hobbyists. Protection is lost when the secret is disclosed, without regard to the circumstances surrounding the disclosure. The lack of uniform national law in this area may also be perceived by proprietors as reducing the utility of this method of protection.

From the user's standpoint, there are additional drawbacks. Users must cover the seller's expenses associated with maintaining a secure system through increased prices. Their freedom to do business in an unencumbered way is reduced, since they may need to enter into elaborate nondisclosure contracts with employees and third parties who have access to the secrets and to limit that access to a very small number of people. Since secrets are by definition known to only a few people, there is necessarily a reduced flow of information in the marketplace, which hinders the ability of potential buyers to make comparisons and hence leads to higher prices.

Experts in the computer industry state that a further problem with respect to trade secrecy is that there is much human effort wasted when people do for themselves that which others have already done but are keeping secret.

In his dissent to the CONTU Report, Commissioner Hersey speculated (correctly, as it turns out) that permitting copyright protection for com-

---

2. Some states, including California, do not include the "readily ascertainable" language in the definition of "trade secret." See Cal. Civ. Code §3426.1.—EDS.

puter programs would not stop companies from relying on trade secret protection as well.

Does it make sense to permit both copyright and trade secret to protect the same works?

A. THE SECRECY REQUIREMENT

Even at a very early stage in the history of computer law, there was no serious question that computer hardware and software *could* be protected by the trade secrets laws. See, e.g., University Computing Co. v. Lykes-Youngstown Corp., 504 F.2d 518 (5th Cir. 1974) (plaintiff's computer system was a protectable trade secret). Cases such as *Lykes-Youngstown* involved a fairly typical trade secrets situation—people with access to a secret program still under development attempting to use or sell their own product based in part on the program. See also Cybertek Computer Products v. Whitfield, 203 U.S.P.Q. 1020 (Cal. Super. 1977).

Rivendell Forest Products v. Georgia-Pacific Corp.
United States District Court for the District of Colorado
824 F. Supp. 961 (D. Colo. 1993)

FINESILVER, Chief Judge.

This is a case involving alleged misappropriations of trade secrets. This matter comes before the Court on the motion for summary judgment filed by the defendants, Georgia-Pacific Corporation and Timothy L. Cornwell (collectively, "Georgia-Pacific") and the subsequent cross-motion for summary judgment by the plaintiff, Rivendell Forest Products, Ltd. ("Rivendell"). Jurisdiction is based on 28 U.S.C.A. §1332 (West 1992). The parties have fully briefed the matter.

For the reasons stated below, Georgia-Pacific's motion is GRANTED and Rivendell's is DENIED.

I. Background

Plaintiff Rivendell, now out of business, was a reload wholesaler in the lumber industry. It purchased milled lumber from Canadian mills and had that lumber shipped to and unloaded at any of about ten lumber yards it leased. Defendant Timothy Cornwell went to work for Rivendell in January 1987 and worked there until March 1990. While at Rivendell, Cornwell supervised employees using Rivendell's price quoting screen (the "Quote Screen") to quote prices to customers. He had no involvement in the development of the Quote Screen program's software. By using the Quote Screen, Rivendell was able to instantaneously quote to customers lumber prices, including freight, thereby allowing Rivendell to become more efficient in handling customer inquiries and eliminating the need for time-consuming manual calculations. Rivendell claims the "Quote Screen" system allowed it to be 20 to 30 times faster and to generate two to three times more sales, giving it a huge advantage over competitors, like Georgia-Pacific, who were still using much slower manual systems. Apparently in part to protect the Quote Screen system, Rivendell asked all employees to sign a confidentiality agreement in 1988 and Rivendell claims all employees did so. Rivendell further advised its employees that the business practices of Rivendell were trade secrets.

Defendant Georgia-Pacific is a supplier and wholesaler of lumber and lumber products. After Cornwell left Rivendell in March 1990, Georgia-Pacific hired Cornwell as marketing manager of Canadian lumber for Georgia-Pacific's distribution division. Rivendell alleges that soon after Cornwell arrived at Georgia-Pacific, he helped them to develop a "Quick Quote" system that borrowed heavily from trade secrets embodied in Rivendell's own Quote Screen. Rivendell alleges that shortly after Cornwell began work at Georgia-Pacific, he received an orientation from Georgia-Pacific employees Ken Porter and Dean Johnson. During the orientation, Cornwell was shown a demonstration of Georgia-Pacific's Noranda computer program. He allegedly stated he had a much better program, went to his office, and returned with a far more sophisticated program. Porter recalled in his deposition that the name "Rivendell" was mentioned in connection with the program. Rivendell cites this as both a clear violation of the confidentiality agreement Cornwell signed with Rivendell and evidence of a misappropriation of trade secrets.

Rivendell brought this suit two years after Cornwell left its employment, alleging tortious interference with contract, breach of contract, and theft of trade secrets. Rivendell alleges that while Cornwell worked for Rivendell, he had access to and gained knowledge of its highly sophisticated and customized computer software system. After reading a description of Georgia-Pacific's "Quick Quote" system, L.G. Broderick, Rivendell's former owner and chief executive officer, claimed the two systems were "virtually identical." . . .

III. Misappropriation of Trade Secrets

Georgia-Pacific does not dispute that trade secrets may exist in the implementation or expression, that is, in the computer source code, of Rivendell's Quote Screen software. The questions we must address, then, are whether either Georgia-Pacific copied Rivendell's source code, or Rivendell's Quote Screen contained a protectible combination of concepts or ideas used by Georgia-Pacific. Rivendell has adduced no facts tending to show that Georgia-Pacific copied its source code. Rather, Rivendell relies on the inference that Georgia-Pacific must have misappropriated the trade secret it defines as the Quote Screen's unique method of integrating various concepts and ideas, even though those concepts and ideas were already in existence in the computerization of the lumber industry. . . .

In a letter to Georgia-Pacific's counsel, Rivendell's counsel outlined what Rivendell considered its trade secrets. Behind the Quote Screen, Rivendell stated, were several databases:

1. Customer master file—all information on the customer
2. All current credit information on the customer
3. All current sales prices on all inventory items at all distribution facilities
4. "Real-time" inventories on all items at all distribution facilities
5. "Real-time" delivery status on all inventory "in transit" or on order with mills
6. Current lowest truck transportation rates and mileage from all distribution facilities to the thousands of known customer or prospective customer destinations
7. Bundle sizes of each item at all distribution facilities
8. Weight per MBF of all items, at all yards, by specie and dryness

Furthermore, interacting with these databases was software which made the following calculations:

1. Automatic board footage conversions
2. Automatic calculation of the dollar value per item, per thickness/width, and on entire inquiry
3. Automatic calculation of FOB yard delivered customer destination prices
4. Automatic calculation of weights per bundle, per thickness/width, and on entire inquiry
5. Automatic calculation of inventory availability by item
6. Automatic calculation of real dollar premium or discount to list price being offered by or to customer

Georgia-Pacific claims all of the concepts and ideas (e.g., the databases and functions performed) claimed by Rivendell as its trade secrets were known to and collectively already used by Georgia-Pacific before the alleged misappropriation and before Cornwell was hired. In particular, prior to Cornwell's hiring, two other divisions of Georgia-Pacific were using computer systems that, between them, performed nearly all the functions identified by Rivendell as constituting its trade secrets. Moreover, Georgia-Pacific has provided an exhibit showing that its Quick Quote system has in common with Rivendell's Quote Screen only two attributes: display of bundle sizes and calculation of board-footage conversions.

Bundle size is a constant set by the supplying mill; board-footage calculations are standard industry calculations necessary for selling lumber. Rivendell does not dispute Georgia-Pacific's assertion that both functions are "functional constraints of the lumber industry." Accordingly, neither function is a trade secret in and of itself. Georgia-Pacific concludes that the concepts and ideas embodied in Rivendell's Quote Screen were well known throughout the lumber industry and in particular by Georgia-Pacific. In any event, Georgia-Pacific claims, its own Quick Quote system used only two, unprotectable functions.

Rivendell's responses to this argument are generally unpersuasive. Rivendell first places great weight on Georgia-Pacific's failure to show that Georgia-Pacific's allegedly similar, publicly available systems were ever seen by Cornwell prior to developing the Quick Quote system. There is no relevance to such information. Where a defendant claims that a so-called "trade secret" is in fact public knowledge, it makes no difference whether the defendant obtained that knowledge from the plaintiff, the defendant's own information, or the public library. Rivendell next asks rhetorically why, if Georgia-Pacific had such computer capability, it had to hire Cornwell to "develop[ ] a new computer system." Such rhetorical questions do little to advance Rivendell's burden of going forward on summary judgment. Rivendell also states, incorrectly, that Georgia-Pacific's Quick Quote has more than two similar functions. Regardless, it is clear that protection could not be extended merely to the publicly available functions or elements of Rivendell's Quote Screen. Finally, Rivendell states that Georgia-Pacific has misunderstood Rivendell's trade secret claim, and that the trade secret is Rivendell's software, while the concepts and ideas embodied in the software are merely what makes it so important and valuable to Rivendell.

This argument puts us back where we began. Much of the confusion in Rivendell's arguments stems from the fact that when it argues for the existence of a trade secret, it points generally to its software, secure in the knowledge that some part of that software, whether or not appropriated by Georgia-Pacific, contains a trade secret. By contrast, when Rivendell argues that Georgia-Pacific has used its trade secrets, unable to claim the software has been copied or otherwise compromised, Rivendell focuses broadly on the concepts and ideas contained in the software.

But the concepts and ideas are not protectible, and by declaring its trade secret to be its software, Rivendell makes the unsupportable, contradictory suggestion that Georgia-Pacific appropriated its source code. However, Rivendell has long admitted and does not now deny that Georgia-Pacific did not copy its source code. Furthermore, Rivendell's expert examined the parties' source codes, display screens, file layouts, and detailed program designs without rendering an opinion as to any similarity between the programs. Fortunately, Rivendell ultimately returns to its true claim: the combination of these concepts and their integration into a single, workable and highly sophisticated computer software package is its trade secret. Georgia-Pacific's existing systems were not so expertly integrated as Rivendell's, and thus did Georgia-Pacific come to require the services of Cornwell.

In the terminology of trade secret law, Rivendell appears to be claiming not that Georgia-Pacific misappropriated its concepts and ideas, which are not protectible anyway, but their integration or implementation. Although Rivendell at times inconsistently disputes whether trade secret law contains such a distinction, the case law, including cases cited by Rivendell, is replete with it. . . .

The Tenth Circuit in Kodekey Electronics, Inc. v. Mechanex Corporation, 486 F.2d 449 (10th Cir. 1973) noted that "'novelty and invention are not requisite for a trade secret as they are for patentability. . . . The protection is merely against breach of faith and reprehensible means of learning anothers [sic] secret.'" *Id.* at 455, quoting Restatement of Torts §757, comment b at 6-7. When we say that Rivendell must show some special, protectible attribute of its combination of commonly available concepts and ideas, then, we are not saying that it must show them to be novel, but rather it must point to some justification for their secrecy. It would make little sense to allow individuals to throw veils of secrecy around the most common things, all in an attempt to establish their claim to a trade secret and then to prohibit others from appropriating their "secret." But "simply to assert a trade secret resides in some combination of otherwise known data is not sufficient, as the combination itself must be delineated with some particularity in establishing its trade secret status." Jostens, Inc. v. National Computer Systems, Inc., et al., 318 N.W.2d 691, 699 (Minn. 1982).

It is here that Rivendell fails to bear its summary judgment burden of designating specific facts showing genuine issues for trial on any element challenged by the motion. Its conclusory allegations that it holds a secret method of combining concepts and ideas for computerization of the lumber business, without more, do not establish issues of fact sufficient to defeat summary judgment. Rivendell offers no facts to suggest either that it had a protectible methodology for implementing the combination of concepts and ideas; that Georgia-Pacific appropriated any protected implementing methodology, rather than the unprotectible elements or functions common to both programs; or that Georgia-Pacific's resulting program is similar to Rivendell's in protected particulars. Rivendell makes only bare, unsupported allegations on every point, yet even these bare allegations are refuted with specificity by Georgia-Pacific.

B. Unauthorized Use of a Trade Secret

. . . Trade secret misappropriation can be established despite the lack of any copying or physical appropriation. Knowledge attained while working for the holder of the trade secret or memory alone are sufficient.

However, contrary to what Rivendell told its employees, business practices hold at best a tenuous claim to being trade secrets. In Fishing Concepts v. Ross, et al., 226 U.S.P.Q. (BNA) 692, 695, 1985 WL 1549 (D. Minn. 1985), for example, the Court held that concepts regarding how to market Canadian fishing lodges were not trade secrets but merely "sound business practices." By Rivendell's failure either to make a claim that Cornwell physically appropriated Rivendell's source code; that he held in his mind Rivendell's source code and later gave it to Georgia-Pacific; that he relayed to Georgia-Pacific some relatively novel method of combining commonly known concepts; or that Georgia-Pacific ended up with a very similar system, Rivendell is unable to establish any more than that Cornwell took to Georgia-Pacific his knowledge that certain databases and business techniques lend themselves to speedy customer service. We could not hold as valid an agreement that absolutely prohibited a person from carrying on his or her career by taking generalized business knowledge from job to job. For these reasons and the reasoning we employed to find Rivendell failed to make out a claim for the existence of a trade secret, we find that nothing protectible was used. . . .

Rivendell Forest Products v. Georgia-Pacific Corp.
United States Court of Appeals for the Tenth Circuit
28 F.3d 1042 (10th Cir. 1994)

SETH, Circuit Judge.

. . . This computer software system in issue, Rivendell asserts, took it nine years to develop at a cost of nearly a million dollars. Mr. Cornwell worked for Rivendell in this development, knew it well, and had a significant role although he was not a computer expert. While working for Rivendell he was contacted by an executive of G.P., and two months thereafter was hired by G.P. with a job description to develop a new computer software system for G.P. This new system had become necessary with the decision by G.P. to consolidate its entire Distribution Division which consisted of about 100 distribution centers. G.P. had no need before the consolidation decision for such a new system, and there had been none in place. After the decision to consolidate G.P. contacted Cornwell and he was offered the task to develop a system quickly to permit the consolidation.

Rivendell's system was the only one Cornwell had been familiar with, and was the only one then in the industry which could provide immediate answers on all aspects of the customers' needs. He was not a computer expert, as mentioned, but immediately after being hired by G.P. he went to work on a computer system for G.P. This system was very soon developed, and it was for all practical purposes the same as the one at Rivendell.

. . . [I]n our view, the basic issue was and is whether the computer system of Rivendell was a "trade secret" appropriated by G.P. As mentioned, the authorities hold that what constitutes a trade secret and whether one exists, as claimed, is an issue of fact. Whether Rivendell's computer system was a "trade secret" was sought to be resolved in the summary judgment proceedings. . . .

. . . This issue as to whether there was a trade secret was complicated by the trial court's method for its factual examination of the asserted trade secret. The court required that the software system be examined bit by bit with the further requirement that Rivendell demonstrate protectability of its elements or some of them rather than the protectability of the software system as a whole. The trial court at page 11 of its order states the basic analysis it applied: "Without a showing that the two systems are similar in some protectable particular, there is no such clarity in Rivendell's claim." The authorities recognize that a trade secret such as the one here claimed can consist of a combination of elements which are in the public domain. This was held originally in Imperial Chemical Indus., Ltd. v. Nat'l Distillers & Chemical Corp., 342 F.2d 737 (2d Cir.). The same court again considered the issue in Integrated Cash Management Serv., Inc. v. Digital Transactions, Inc., 920 F.2d 171 (2d Cir.), and in substance adopted the following quotation from *Imperial Chemical Industries* that the case was covered by the operation of

> the general principle that a trade secret can exist in a combination of characteristics and components, each of which, by itself, is in the public domain, but the unified process, design and operation of which, in unique combination, affords a competitive advantage and is a protectable secret.

(Citations omitted.) See also Cybertek Computer Products, Inc. v. Whitfield, 203 U.S.P.Q. (BNA) 1020 (Cal. Super. Ct.).

The trial court also did not apply the doctrine described as follows in *Kodekey*, again:

> "Novelty and invention are not requisite for a trade secret as they are for patentability . . . (here a discussion of patent law). . . . The protection is merely against breach of faith and reprehensible means of learning anothers secret."

. . . We must disagree with the trial court's first statement above that Rivendell had not shown it had a protectable methodology. In our view, the record demonstrates that such a methodology implementing the combination of concepts and ideas was shown. The record establishes the production by Rivendell's software system of immediate final pricing by the integration of the many computations as to size of lumber, type of lumber, location of the lumber, size of bundles, freight charges, time of delivery, and other factors to permit the immediate quotation of a total price. This was a basic factual demonstration of the integration obtained by the software, and it was a total package for immediate use. It was the only system in the industry which could accomplish this. G.P. had nothing comparable before the Defendant Cornwell was hired away from Rivendell. At best

G.P. had a scattering of unrelated elements in the 100+ offices, and had no need for an integrated system until it decided to consolidate its offices. The evidence as to the quick development (four months) after Cornwell went to work for G.P. with the affidavits that the G.P. employees used Cornwell's ideas and the fact that Cornwell had never seen G.P.'s scattered systems before he developed G.P.'s Quick Quote integrated system were important because they demonstrated that he and G.P. relied entirely on Rivendell's system. He was not a computer expert at Rivendell or G.P. The position of G.P. and apparently of the trial court was that throughout G.P.'s large organization with many offices there could be found separately the elements of the Rivendell system. But the fact remained and the testimony of Gary Mote, a G.P. employee, showed there was no prior interest in G.P. to develop a new system. The company decision to integrate its many offices led to the hiring of Cornwell for the purpose of developing a new system; from the fact that the G.P. system was almost identical, the conclusion could well be reached at a trial that G.P. appropriated Rivendell's system.

The trial court in the above quotation refers to unprotected elements or functions, and so would examine the separate elements rather than the combination. We hold that the doctrine has been established that a trade secret can include a system where the elements are in the public domain, but there has been accomplished an effective, successful and valuable integration of the public domain elements and the trade secret gave the claimant a competitive advantage which is protected from misappropriation. . . .

The case must be REVERSED and REMANDED for further proceedings consistent with this opinion.

IT IS SO ORDERED.

COMMENTS AND QUESTIONS

1. Which opinion is more persuasive? Should Rivendell be entitled to protect the basic concepts of organizing a price quote against misappropriation by others? On the one hand, the District Court is surely correct that if Rivendell's ideas are not in fact secret, Georgia-Pacific is free to copy them. On the other hand, the Court of Appeals points out that basic concepts are protectable under trade secret law in certain combinations, if those combinations are not generally known in the industry. On this issue, compare Integrated Cash Mgmt. Serv. v. Digital Transactions, Inc., 920 F.2d 171 (2d Cir. 1990) (the combination of publicly known utility programs into a specific arrangement is protectable as a trade secret) with Comprehensive Technologies, Inc. v. Software Artisans, Inc., 3 F.3d 730 (4th Cir. 1993) (combination of known elements did not qualify as a trade secret where the particular combination was logically required and common in the industry). Cf. Vermont Microsystems Inc. v. Autodesk Inc., 88

F.3d 142 (2d Cir. 1996) (shading algorithm could be protected as a trade secret even though other developers had independently created similar algorithms, because defendant got value from using plaintiff's algorithm).

A related problem has to do with the identification of the trade secret before trial. The appellate court in *Rivendell* took a very flexible approach toward identifying exactly what constituted a trade secret. Other courts, by contrast, have refused to let plaintiffs simply identify the program containing the trade secret. They have demanded a detailed listing of what the plaintiff claims as a trade secret and why. See, e.g., ECT Int'l v. Zwerlein, 594 N.W.2d 479 (Wis. Ct. App. 1999); Cal. Code Civ. Proc. §2019(d) (requiring disclosure of a "trade secrets list" before trial).

2. Note the interaction between the definition of "trade secret" and the question of misappropriation. Like copyright law, trade secret law enters a gray area when what is alleged is not literal copying but similarity of general concepts. While such concepts may sometimes be protected, the case for misappropriation is usually not as clear as when computer code has been literally copied. We discuss this issue in more detail in Section C.

3. Suppose that Rivendell had widely sold its program to lumber companies but required each of its purchasers to keep the program confidential. Can Rivendell protect the basic ideas behind its program as trade secrets? Does your answer differ if what Rivendell seeks to protect is its literal object code? Does it matter that Rivendell's "basic ideas" are not contained in unintelligible 1s and 0s? That they may in fact be obvious to anyone using the program?

A closely related question involves attempts by the owners of information to "contract around" the requirement of secrecy. If the parties agree to treat a piece of information as secret, is the licensee bound not to use or disclose the information under contract principles regardless of whether it is in fact in the public domain? We discuss this issue in more detail in Chapter 7.

B. DISCLOSURE OF TRADE SECRETS

While it was established early on that the secret elements of a computer program could be protected from misappropriation, computer companies that wanted to protect their intellectual property still had a problem. It is a fundamental principle of trade secret law that the thing protected must remain a secret. If the secret is disclosed to the public, protection is forever lost. Computer companies did not want to keep their hardware or software "secret"—they wanted to sell it![3] An influential early case held that they could do both. Key to this conclusion is the fact that software developers generally distribute their programs only in object code

---

3. Of course, some computer code is written for internal use only, and that code can be protected as a secret fairly easily, since it need not leave the company.

form and keep the source code and the design documentation as trade secrets, licensing them only rarely and only under agreements of confidentiality.

Data General Corp. v. Digital Computer Controls, Inc.
Delaware Court of Chancery
297 A.2d 433 (Del. Ch. 1971), aff'd, 297 A.2d 437 (Del. S. Ct. 1972)

MARVEL, Vice Chancellor:

Data General Corporation seeks an order preliminarily enjoining the defendant Digital Computer Controls from making use of claimed trade secrets allegedly contained in design drawings which accompany certain sales of plaintiff's Nova 1200 computer, defendant having acquired such a computer with accompanying drawings from one of plaintiff's customers. This is the decision of the Court on plaintiff's motion for a preliminary injunction as well as on defendants' cross-motion for summary judgment of dismissal of the present action.

The relevant facts thus far adduced are as follows: During the past several years plaintiff has developed and marketed successfully small general-purpose computers to which they have given the name Nova, a large part of plaintiff's research and development budget for the past several years having been allocated to the development of such small computers, which, the parties agree, are the only ones of their type presently being profitably marketed, there having been no device on the market comparable to plaintiff's machines until defendant's entry on the scene.

When a sale of a Nova 1200 computer is made, plaintiff makes available at no extra cost to those customers who wish to do their own maintenance the design or logic drawings of the device sold, in this case a Nova 1200 computer. Such type of maintenance has been found to be desired by some customers in order to avoid periods of unproductive delay while waiting for repairs to be made by plaintiff's trained personnel.

Design drawings made available to customers are furnished subject to the terms of a non-disclosure clause contained in a paper which accompanies a purchase agreement. Furthermore, all drawings bear a legend to the effect that they contain proprietary information of the plaintiff which is not to be used by a purchaser for manufacturing purposes. However, the Nova 1200 is not patented, and its design drawings have not been copyrighted.

In April, 1971, the defendant Ackley, the president of Digital, purchased for his company from a customer of Data General, namely Mini-Computer Systems, Inc., a Nova 1200 computer which the latter had earlier acquired from plaintiff. Although the exact circumstances surrounding such sale are not entirely clear on the present record, the corporate defendant's president, in consummating such purchase, acquired a set of design drawings of the Nova 1200, said drawings having been furnished to MiniComputer by the plaintiff in order to facilitate maintenance by the former of its Nova 1200's. The corporate defendant thereafter proceeded to use such design drawings as a pattern for the construction of a competing machine which it is now about to market, the corporate defendant's president conceding that only minor changes have been made in the basic design of plaintiff's device in the course of the development of defendant's comparable computer.

I.

[The court held that plaintiff's trade secret claims are not preempted by the federal intellectual property or antitrust laws.]

II.

Defendants' other arguments are accordingly based on the law of trade secrets. Thus, in order for the plaintiff to establish its right to relief here, it must demonstrate (1) the existence of a trade secret and that the corporate defendant has either (2) received the information within the confines of a confidential relationship and proposes to misuse the information in violation of such relationship, or (3) that the corporate defendant improperly received the information in question in such a manner that its confidential nature should have been known to it and that it nonetheless proposes to misuse such information.

Trade secrets have been defined in Restatement, Torts §757, comment b. as follows:

> A trade secret may consist of any formula, pattern, device or compilation of information which is used in one's business, and which gives him an opportunity to obtain an advantage over competitors who do not know or use it.

Defendants insist, however, that plaintiff has not maintained that degree of secrecy which will preserve its right to relief, either by publicly selling an article alleged to contain a trade secret, or by failing to restrict access to the design drawings for its device, arguing that matters of common knowledge in an industry may not be claimed as trade secrets.

It has been recognized in similar cases that even though an unpatented article, device or machine has been sold to the public, and is therefore subject to examination and copying by anyone, the manner of making the article, device or machine may yet constitute a trade secret until such a copy has in fact been made, Schulenburg v. Signatrol, Inc., 33 Ill.2d 379, 212 N.E.2d 865, and Tabor v. Hoffman, N.Y., 118 N.Y. 30, 23 N.E. 12.

Defendants contend, however, that the issuance by plaintiff of copies of design drawings to its customers was made without safeguards designed properly to maintain the secrecy requisite to the existence of a trade secret. In other words, it is contended that plaintiff's attempts to maintain secrecy merely consisted of (1) not giving copies of the design drawings to those customers who did not need them for maintenance of their computer, (2) obtaining agreements not to disclose the information from those customers who were given copies of the drawings, and (3) printing a legend on the drawings which contained the allegedly confidential information which identified the drawing as proprietary information, the use of which was restricted. Plaintiff argues, however, that disclosure of the design drawings to purchasers of the computer is necessary properly to maintain its device, that such disclosure was required by the very nature of the machine, and that reasonable steps were taken to preserve the secrecy of the material released. I conclude at this preliminary stage of the case that it cannot be held as a matter of law that such precautions were inadequate, a factual dispute as to the adequacy of such precautions having clearly been raised. Defendants' motion for summary judgment must accordingly be denied.

Finally, I am satisfied that if plaintiff were to prevail at final hearing, it would only be entitled to injunctive relief during that undetermined period of time which would be required for defendants substantially to reproduce to plaintiff's device without its accompanying drawings. Such period of time would, on the present record, vary according to the number of man hours devoted to so-called reverse engineering. Thus, the granting of a preliminary injunction at this juncture would grant plaintiff all the relief it might hope ultimately to obtain after final hearing. Compare Thomas C. Marshall, Inc. v. Holiday Inn, Inc., 40 Del.Ch. 77, 174 A.2d 27. In addition, while plaintiff has presented evidence of its attempts to preserve the secrecy of the alleged secrets it now seeks to have protected by injunction, it has not adduced sufficient evidence to establish that likelihood of ultimate success on final hearing which would entitle it to the issuance of a preliminary injunction.

On notice, an order may be presented denying defendants' motion for summary judgment as well as plaintiff's motion for a preliminary injunction, which order shall also include a provision that all drawings issued by the corporate defendant in connection with the sale of its Nova-type computer contain a restrictive legend of the type now set forth on plaintiff's drawings here in issue.

COMMENTS AND QUESTIONS

1. For background on Data General and the development of the Nova computer, see Tracy Kidder, The Soul of a New Machine (1981).

2. The plaintiff in *Data General* sold over 500 Nova computers to the general public. Each purchaser who requested one got a copy of the "confidential" design drawings. Why are these drawings still considered a secret? Does widespread disclosure compromise the secrecy claim at some point, even though all disclosures are made under an agreement of confidentiality? This issue arises frequently today in the software industry.

As computers have become ubiquitous in business and quite common in the home, the numbers of "secret" programs in circulation may be counted in the millions rather than in the hundreds. *Data General* implicitly concludes that even a relatively widespread disclosure to customers does not compromise the secrecy of the computer design. For cases addressing this issue in the context of computer software, compare Management Science of Am. v. Cyborg Sys., Inc., 1977-1 Trade Cas. (CCH) ¶61,472 (N.D. Ill. 1977) (distribution of 600 copies of a program under a confidentiality agreement did not destroy secrecy) with Young Dental Mfg. Co. v. Q3 Special Prods., Inc., 891 F. Supp. 1345 (E.D. Mo. 1995) (characterizing as "completely frivolous" plaintiff's claim that its publicly sold software was a trade secret).

As we shall see, customers who buy a product on the open market are entitled to break it apart to see how it works. This process is called "reverse engineering" the product. Trade secret law does not protect owners against legitimate purchasers who discover the secret through reverse engineering. But does the possibility that a product might be reverse engineered foreclose *any* trade secret protection? At least one court has said no. In Data General Corp. v. Grumman Systems Support Corp., 825 F. Supp. 340, 359 (D. Mass. 1993), the court upheld a jury's verdict that Grumman had misappropriated trade secrets contained in object code form in Data General's computer program, despite the fact that many copies of the program had been sold on the open market. The court reasoned: "With the exception of those who lawfully licensed or unlawfully misappropriated MV/ADEX, Data General enjoyed the exclusive use of MV/ADEX. Even those who obtained MV/ADEX and were able to *use* MV/ADEX were unable to discover its trade secrets because MV/ADEX was distributed only in its object code form, which is essentially unintelligible to humans." The court noted that Data General took significant steps to preserve the secrecy of MV/ADEX, requiring that all users of the program sign licenses agreeing not to disclose the program to third parties.

The *Data General* cases suggest that reasonable efforts to protect the secrecy of an idea contained in a commercial product—such as locks, black boxes, or the use of unreadable code—may suffice to maintain trade secret protection even after the product itself is widely circulated. Does this result make sense? For a different approach, see Videotronics v. Bend Electronics, 564 F. Supp. 1471, 1476 (D. Nev. 1983) (software cannot be a trade secret if it is publicly distributed and can be readily copied).

3. One way in which computer software cases may be distinguished from other trade secret cases has to do with the nature of what is being distributed. While a particular computer program may be widely distributed, in fact all that is sold to the consumer is a disk containing object code, which is virtually impossible for humans to read without machine assistance.[4] Because of this, computer software is in some sense unlike a

---

4. To be sure, it is possible to reverse-engineer object code in some cases to create a kind of rough estimate of what must have been in the original source code. The process, however, is

physical product whose design is evident to the casual observer. Even after it is publicly distributed, object code is meaningless to the casual observer. Only a complex process of reverse engineering (sometimes called "disassembly" or "decompilation") can enable the user to decipher the source code that was originally written for the program.

Should it matter that a computer program is distributed only in object code form? Consider the following case, in which the defendant was accused of misappropriating a computer program in object code form.

> The source code can and does qualify as a trade secret. . . .
>
> Whether the object code is a trade secret is a more difficult question.[4] Atkinson first contends that the object code cannot be a trade secret because it does not derive independent economic value from its secrecy, and therefore fails the first definitional requirement of a trade secret. This argument has no merit. Trandes generates most of its revenues by providing computer services. . . . Armed with a copy of the object code, an individual would have the means to offer much the same engineering services as Trandes. . . .
>
> Atkinson next argues that the object code cannot be a trade secret because Trandes did not keep it secret. . . . Atkinson asserts that the Tunnel System has been widely disclosed as a mass-marketed product and that its existence and its abilities are not secret. [The court concluded that the object code remained secret because it had only been distributed to two customers, and both of them signed licenses agreeing to keep the program a secret].

Trandes Corp. v. Guy F. Atkinson Co., 996 F.2d 655, 663-664 (4th Cir. 1993). Consider the court's footnote. Can object code be a trade secret, if it can easily be duplicated (whether or not the copier understands what he is copying)? Is the plaintiff in this case really trying to leverage copyright protection out of a trade secret claim?

Why might a company want to maintain both its source code and its object code as a secret?

Some companies may want to distribute not only their object code but also their source code. For example, if a company is in the business of selling software components for reuse by others, it needs to transfer not just the executable code, but at least that portion of the source code that will permit the buyer to build a truly inter-operable component. *See* Mark A. Lemley & David W. O'Brien, Encouraging Software Reuse, 49 Stan. L. Rev. 255, 271-272 (1997). Still other companies distribute their source

---

demanding and time-consuming even for expert programmers. See, e.g., Andrew Johnson-Laird, Reverse Engineering of Software: Separating Legal Mythology from Actual Technology, 5 Software L.J. 331, 342-343 (1992) ("[d]eciphering computer-executable programs is extremely tedious and error-prone").

4. This case presents an unusual set of facts. In the ordinary case, the owner of trade secret computer software will maintain the secrecy of the source code but freely distribute the object code. See, e.g., Q-Co Indus. v. Hoffman, 625 F. Supp. 608, 617 (S.D.N.Y. 1985) (program secret where source code secret, even though object code not secret). In such cases, the owner of the software cannot claim trade secret protection for the object code because its disclosure to the public destroyed its secrecy. In this case, however, Trandes maintained the secrecy of the source code *and* the object code, as we explain below.

code in order to encourage users to help them improve it. Trade secret protection is much harder to obtain if the source code is freely transferred.

4. Trade secrets may be publicly disclosed (through publication or the sale of a product) by someone other than the trade secret owner. Commonly, this occurs when someone other than the owner has independently developed or discovered the secret. Call the first trade secret "owner" *A*, and the independent developer *B*. *A* has no control over what *B* does with her independent discovery; if she chooses to disclose the secret, she defeats not only her rights to trade secret protection, but *A*'s rights as well.

Suppose that *B* had not developed the secret independently of *A* but in fact had stolen it from *A*. What happens if *B* publishes the secret—can *A* still protect it? If so, what happens to *C*, who begins using the secret after reading the publication? This issue was addressed in Religious Technology Center v. Lerma, 908 F. Supp. 1362 (E.D. Va. 1995). In that case, the Church of Scientology sued (among others) The Washington Post, which had quoted from part of the church's confidential "scriptures." The court concluded that the fact that the scriptures were posted on a Usenet newsgroup for 10 days defeated any claim of trade secrecy:

> [For 10 days, the documents] remained potentially available to the millions of Internet users around the world.
>
> As other courts who have dealt with similar issues have observed, "posting works to the Internet makes them generally known" at least to the relevant people interested in the news group. Once a trade secret is posted on the Internet, it is effectively part of the public domain, impossible to retrieve. Although the person who originally posted a trade secret on the Internet may be liable for trade secret misappropriation, the party who merely down loads Internet information cannot be liable for misappropriation because there is no misconduct involved in interacting with the Internet.

Id. 908 F. Supp. at 1368. See also American Red Cross v. Palm Beach Blood Bank Inc., 143 F.3d 1407 (11th Cir. 1998) (holding that a donor list could not be a trade secret because the plaintiff posted it on a computer bulletin board, destroying its confidentiality).

PROBLEM

Problem 1-1. Microsoft Corp.'s Windows 95 operating system has become an industry standard for personal computer operating systems. Microsoft sells several million copies of Windows 95 each year; there are estimated to be upwards of 25 million copies in circulation worldwide. Further, Windows 95 is normally "pre-installed" on most new personal computers, so that PC purchasers automatically purchase the operating system as well. Assuming that Microsoft has taken reasonable efforts to require both hardware manufacturers and end users to keep the program confidential, is

> Microsoft entitled to protect Windows 95 as a trade secret? What efforts would be "reasonable" under these circumstances?

C. MISAPPROPRIATION

Misappropriation of trade secrets can occur in one of two ways: where the defendant acquires the trade secret through improper means, such as by theft or some forms of espionage; and where the defendant uses or discloses the trade secret in breach of a confidential relationship, usually but not necessarily involving a contractual agreement limiting the use of the secret. The legal issues concerning misappropriation are well established in the general law of trade secrets; thus we do not cover them in detail here. For a good summary with a focus on cases in the computer industry, see Gale R. Peterson, Trade Secrets in an Information Age, 32 Hous. L. Rev. 385 (1995). However, there are certain problems that arise specifically in the context of computer software.

Comprehensive Technologies International, Inc. v. Software Artisans, Inc.
United States Court of Appeals for the Fourth Circuit
3 F.3d 730 (4th Cir. 1993)

WILLIAMS, Circuit Judge:

Comprehensive Technologies International, Inc. (CTI), brought this action for copyright infringement against former employees Dean Hawkes, Igor A. Filippides, Randall L. Sterba, Richard T. Hennig, and David R. Bixler (the Defendant employees). CTI also named as defendants Alvan S. Bixler and Software Artisans, Inc. (SA), a corporation formed by Alvan Bixler and several of the Defendant employees shortly after their departure from CTI. CTI contended that "Transend," a computer program developed by the Defendants, infringed upon the copyrights CTI held in its "Claims Express" and "EDI Link" computer programs. CTI appended numerous state law causes of action, including trade secret misappropriation, breach of confidentiality, and breach of contract. CTI also alleged that Hawkes breached his covenant not to compete with CTI by performing services for SA, soliciting CTI's customers, and hiring CTI's former employees. After a bench trial, the district court entered judgment for the Defendants on all counts.

CTI now appeals. . . .

With regard to CTI's copyright infringement and trade secret misappropriation claims, we affirm the judgment for the Defendants. We agree, however, with CTI's contention that Hawkes's covenant not to compete is enforceable. We therefore vacate the judgment for Hawkes on CTI's claim for breach of contract, and remand for the district court to determine whether Hawkes has breached his covenant not to compete. . . .

I. Factual Background

CTI, a California corporation with its principal place of business in Chantilly, Virginia, is engaged in defense related services. CTI was founded in 1980 by Celestino Beltran, who at the time of trial served as CTI's president, chief executive officer, and chairman of the board of directors. By 1988 Beltran was hoping to diversify CTI's operations into newly emerging technologies. At that time, Beltran's next door neighbor, Alvan Bixler, worked for the Electronic Data Interchange Association (EDIA). Electronic data interchange, or EDI, is the computer-to-computer transmission of business transactions in proprietary or standard formats. After discussing EDI with Alvan Bixler and conducting his own research on the subject, Beltran concluded that EDI technology presented substantial growth potential in the small business market.

With the approval of his board of directors, Beltran established a Software Products Group and designated Dean Hawkes to lead it. Hawkes was given the responsibility to design, develop, test, and market software that would enable clients to process and transmit data through EDI technology. CTI selected Igor Filippides as the Software Products Group's Acting Vice President for Sales and gave him primary responsibility for marketing the software. Other members of the Software Products Group included Sterba, Hennig, and David Bixler, who together wrote the actual software. To boost the marketability of its products, CTI obtained an agreement from EDIA to assist CTI in the development of its software. Pursuant to that agreement, Alvan Bixler collaborated with CTI as a consultant on EDI technology.

Each of the Defendant employees except Hawkes signed CTI's standard Confidentiality and Proprietary Information Agreement. Under the Agreement, each employee agreed not to disclose or use, directly or indirectly, during his employment and for three years thereafter any confidential, proprietary, or software-related information belonging to CTI. The Agreement specifically identified the Claims Express and EDI Link projects as confidential. Although Hawkes did not sign a Confidentiality and Proprietary Information Agreement, he did sign an Employment Agreement that contained similar but more restrictive provisions. In addition to promising confidentiality, Hawkes agreed that during the term of his employment he would not compete with CTI, solicit CTI's customers, or employ CTI's current or former employees.

The Software Products Group undertook to develop two software packages for personal computers. The first, Claims Express, is an electronic medical billing system. Claims Express transmits information that conforms to two specific insurance claims forms, the "HFCA 1500" and the "UB 82." The program has been successfully marketed. CTI's second software package, EDI Link, is not specific to the health care industry. It is designed to permit users to create generic forms, enter data on the forms electronically, test that data for errors, and store both the forms and the data on a computer. Although CTI expended substantial effort on EDI Link, at the time of trial the program had not been completed and had never been sold or marketed. Trial testimony indicated that between 35 and 85 percent of the program had been completed.

In February 1991, all of the Defendant employees left CTI. Hawkes executed a formal Termination Agreement with CTI. In that Agreement, Hawkes agreed to rescind his Employment Agreement in return for $50,000 and more than $20,000 worth of equipment. Hawkes also agreed that he would not disclose or use CTI's confidential information, and that, for a period of one year following his departure, he would not (1) compete with CTI, (2) solicit CTI's customers, or (3) hire CTI's employees.

In April 1991, the Defendants incorporated Software Artisans, Inc., located in Fairfax, Virginia. By July 1991, SA had developed and begun to market its own program called Transend. According to its User's Manual, Transend creates a "paperless office environment" by enabling its users to process business forms on a computer. Transend is similar to Claims Express and EDI Link in that it is designed to prepare forms for transmission by EDI. Transend permits the user to input data, check the data for errors, and prepare the data for transmission by EDI. . . .

III.

. . . In denying CTI's claim for trade secret misappropriation, the district court found that CTI did not possess any trade secrets and that, even if CTI did possess trade secrets, the Defendants had not misappropriated them. The court found no evidence that CTI's purported trade secrets— the organization of Claims Express and EDI Link, the database access techniques of the two programs, and the unique identifiers of the two programs—derived independent economic value from not being generally known or were not readily ascertainable by proper means. Consequently, the court concluded that CTI's purported trade secrets failed to satisfy all of the elements necessary to prove a trade secret. The district court also concluded that the Defendants did not "copy" any trade secrets, implying that Defendants did not "use" or otherwise misappropriate them. . . .

CTI reads the district court's opinion as ruling as a matter of law that the organization of a database, its database access techniques, and its unique identifiers could not constitute trade secrets because each of their composite elements was in the public domain. CTI argues vociferously (and correctly) that although a trade secret cannot subsist in information in the public domain, it can subsist in a *combination* of such information, as long as the combination is itself secret. According to CTI, each of its alleged trade secrets is just such a combination of publicly available information.

In making this argument, CTI misreads the district court's opinion. The district court did not rule that unique combinations or arrangements of publicly available information cannot receive protection as trade secrets. Rather, the district court held that CTI failed to present any evidence that its database organization, its access techniques, and its identifiers were not themselves publicly available. The court specifically found that the arrangement and interaction of the functions of Claims Express and EDI Link were "common to all computer programs of this type." Information that is generally known cannot qualify as a trade secret. Consequently, the district court did not misapply the law; it simply found insufficient evidence to support CTI's claim. The district court correctly concluded that CTI failed to prove that the organization, database access techniques, and identifiers of CTI's software constituted trade secrets.

Even if CTI had demonstrated that these items constituted trade secrets, CTI has not convinced us that the district court clearly erred in finding that the Defendants did not misappropriate any of CTI's alleged trade secrets. CTI points to the short development time and the complete lack of design documentation for Transend as strong circumstantial evidence of misappropriation. Although this evidence does raise some suspicions, Defendants provided a colorable explanation for the absence of design documentation. First, Defendant's expert, Dr. Rotenstreich, testified that it was not atypical for small software companies to neglect to prepare extensive design documentation. Second, Sterba testified that he and the others disliked the amount of paperwork involved in documenting their designs, that they preferred to use a "whiteboard" for their design work, and that they placed much of the information that would ordinarily appear in design documentation in the code itself. In light of this testimony, CTI's circumstantial evidence is not enough to convince us that the district court clearly erred in finding that the Defendants did not copy (or "use") any of CTI's alleged trade secret information.

We find instructive the Fifth Circuit's decision in Plains Cotton Cooperative Ass'n v. Goodpasture Computer Service, 807 F.2d 1256 (5th Cir. 1987):

> [T]he trade secrets allegedly involved here are particular implementations of software functions. . . . [T]he misuse of these implementations can occur only through copying the particular software designs on a sufficiently specific level. . . . [The trade secrets] are matters of design, where *the issue of misuse boils down to evidence of copying*. If no copying occurred on any level, appellant cannot demonstrate that appellees misused the trade secrets they allegedly possessed. . . .

> . . . If appellees did not in any way "copy" any part of appellant's pro-
> tected idea or expression, then appellant cannot demonstrate trade secret
> misappropriation any more than it can show copyright infringement.

(Emphasis added). As the district court noted, CTI produced insufficient
evidence that Transend copied any unique designs or functions of either
Claims Express or EDI Link. Without proof of copying at the functional
(or ideational) level, CTI has not proved that Defendants "used" and
thereby misappropriated any of its trade secret information. The district
court correctly concluded that the Defendants did not misappropriate any
trade secret information belonging to CTI.

COMMENTS AND QUESTIONS

1. Compare the result in Integrated Cash Mgmt. Serv. v. Digital
Transactions, Inc., 920 F.2d 171 (2d Cir. 1990):

> As discussed above, the district court properly found a cognizable trade
> secret in the manner in which ICM combined various non-secret utility pro-
> grams to create its software product. The court further found that the defen-
> dants made use of this information in designing similar software. Newlin and
> Vafa "ma[de] use of information learned while at ICM concerning which
> functions and relationships among the modules would and would not work in
> the generic program." Contrary to defendants-appellants' suggestion, the
> court's statement that Vafa "was certainly capable of writing the source code
> in his own right" does not contradict the finding that Vafa and Newlin, in
> fact, used ICM's trade secrets. ICM is, therefore, entitled to injunctive relief.

Id. at 174-175. Is this result consistent with *CTI*? With *Plains Cotton*? In
particular, consider the role of circumstantial evidence of misappropriation.
Should the court in *CTI* have presumed misappropriation from the defendants' short product development time? From their failure to produce a
"paper trail" documenting their software development efforts? On the
other hand, should the court presume independent development if there is
no evidence the defendants took documents or disks with them when they
left? What incentives would each presumption create for strategic behavior
on the part of parties who might be involved in litigation?

2. In both *CTI* and *ICM*, the alleged trade secret at issue was not
the source or object code of the computer program itself, but certain high-
level design features of the program (its "architecture"). Suppose that,
rather than using what they had learned of the architecture of the program
while employed by the company, ICM's former employees had copied the
object code of the program altogether. (Leave aside for the moment
questions of copyright infringement and consider only the trade secrets
issue.) Would they be liable for misappropriating the trade secrets contained in the program architecture on the grounds that copying the pro-

gram in its entirety necessarily copied the architecture? Or would the fact that the object code was publicly disclosed protect them from liability? How would the courts in *Trandes* and the *Data General* cases answer this question? Does the answer suggest a problem with relying on trade secrecy to protect computer programs?

3. Employees inevitably learn a great deal about a business while on the job. They may learn the trade secrets of their employer, but they may also learn basic information such as how many people it takes to make a product, who is likely to buy the product, where to advertise, etc. Further, employees develop personal relationships with vendors, customers, and others that are immensely useful in business. For this reason, many employers would like to prevent their employees from competing against them at all. Such employers often ask their employees to sign noncompetition agreements, which prevent the employee from competing with his former employer for customers for a set period of time. *Comprehensive Technologies* involved such an agreement. Despite finding (above) that the employees took no trade secrets, the court enforced an agreement signed by one of the employees, Dean Hawkes. The agreement provided that for a period of 12 months after he left CTI, Hawkes would not

> engage directly or indirectly in any business within the United States (financially as an investor or lender or as an employee, director, officer, partner, independent contractor, consultant or owner or in any other capacity calling for the rendition of personal services or acts of management, operation or control) which is in competition with the business of CTI. For purposes of this Agreement, the "business of CTI" shall be defined as the design, development, marketing, and sales of CLAIMS EXPRESS and EDI LINK type PC-based software with the same functionality and methodology. . . .

The court stated the general legal standard governing covenants not to compete:

> Virginia has established a three-part test for assessing the reasonableness of restrictive employment covenants. Under the test, the court must ask the following questions:
>
> > (1) Is the restraint, from the standpoint of the employer, reasonable in the sense that it is no greater than is necessary to protect the employer in some legitimate business interest?
> > (2) From the standpoint of the employee, is the restraint reasonable in the sense that it is not unduly harsh and oppressive in curtailing his legitimate efforts to earn a livelihood?
> > (3) Is the restraint reasonable from the standpoint of a sound public policy?

Blue Ridge Anesthesia & Critical Care, Inc. v. Gidick, 239 Va. 369, 389 S.E.2d 467, 469 (Va. 1990). If a covenant not to compete meets each of these standards of reasonableness, it must be enforced. As a general rule, however, the Virginia courts do not look favorably upon covenants not to compete, and will strictly construe them against the employer. The employer bears the burden of demonstrating that the restraint is reasonable.

Id. at 738. The court found that Hawkes' agreement, which prevented him from competing with CTI anywhere in the United States, was reasonable because CTI had offices, clients, or prospects in many (though not all) states throughout the country. Further, the court noted that

> . . . As the individual primarily responsible for the design, development, marketing and sale of CTI's software, Hawkes became intimately familiar with every aspect of CTI's operation, and necessarily acquired information that he could use to compete with CTI in the marketplace. When an employee has access to confidential and trade secret information crucial to the success of the employer's business, the employer has a strong interest in enforcing a covenant not to compete because other legal remedies often prove inadequate. It will often be difficult, if not impossible, to prove that a competing employee has misappropriated trade secret information belonging to his former employer. *Eden Hannon*, 914 F.2d 556 at 561 (applying Virginia law). On the facts of this case, we conclude that the scope of the employment restrictions is no broader than necessary to protect CTI's legitimate business interests.

Id. at 739. There seems to be no question in the court's mind that none of the defendants misappropriated any CTI trade secrets, infringed any copyrights, or otherwise "took" anything belonging to CTI in starting Software Artisans. Why didn't that dispose of the case? What social purpose is served by enjoining former employees from pursuing their livelihood? Shouldn't the mobility and liberty of individuals be the paramount consideration, as California courts have suggested? See Diodes, Inc. v. Franzen, 260 Cal. App. 2d 244 (1968). One author has suggested that there is a more practical economic motivation for precluding such noncompetition agreements. She argues that the relative success of California's Silicon Valley compared to Boston's Route 128 is directly attributable to the prevalence of noncompetition agreements in Route 128 companies, which prevented the free movement of employees and therefore discouraged start-up companies. *See* Annalee Saxenian, Regional Advantage: Culture and Competition in Silicon Valley and Route 128 (1994).

Some courts have limited the enforcement of noncompetition agreements to situations where trade secrets are likely to be used or disclosed if an employee is allowed to compete. The New York Court of Appeals, for example, took the following view:

> Undoubtedly judicial disfavor of these covenants is provoked by "powerful considerations of public policy which militate against sanctioning the loss of a man's livelihood" (Purchasing Assoc. v. Weitz . . .). Indeed, our economy is premised on the competition engendered by the uninhibited flow of services, talent and ideas. Therefore, no restrictions should fetter an employee's right to apply to his own best advantage the skills and knowledge acquired by the

overall experience of his previous employment. This includes those techniques which are but "skillful variations of general processes known to the particular trade" (Restatement, Agency 2d, §396, Comment b; see, also, Customer List —as Trade Secret-Factors, Ann., 28 ALR3d 7).

Of course, the courts must also recognize the legitimate interest an employer has in safeguarding that which has made his business successful and to protect himself against deliberate surreptitious commercial piracy. Thus restrictive covenants will be enforceable to the extent necessary to prevent the disclosure or use of trade secrets or confidential customer information (e.g., Lepel High Frequency Labs. v. Capita, 278 NY 661; Carpenter & Hughes v. De Joseph, 10 NY2d 925). In addition injunctive relief may be available where an employee's services are unique or extraordinary and the covenant is reasonable (e.g., Lumley v. Wagner, 42 Eng Rep 687; Frederick Bros. Artists Corp. v. Yates, 271 App Div 69, *aff'd* 296 NY 820). This latter principle has been interpreted to reach agreements between members of the learned professions (e.g., Karpinski v. Ingrasci, 28 NY2d 45).

Reed Roberts Assoc. v. Strauman, 40 N.Y.2d 303, 353 N.E.2d 590 (N.Y. Ct. App. 1976).

Other states, notably California, have an even more restrictive rule. For example, Cal. Bus. & Prof. Code sec. 16600 provides that "every contract by which anyone is restrained from engaging in a lawful profession . . . is to that extent void." California courts have interpreted this statute to bar noncompetition agreements in employee contracts but to permit such agreements if they are ancillary to the sale of a business, so long as the terms of the agreement are "reasonable." See Monogram Indus., Inc. v. SAR Indus., Inc., 64 Cal. App. 3d 692, 134 Cal. Rptr. 714, 718 (1976). Further, while California courts will not enforce a noncompetition agreement, they will prevent departing employees from using or disclosing their former employer's trade secrets. See State Farm Mutual Automobile Ins. Co. v. Dempster, 344 P.2d 821 (Cal. App. 1959); Gordon v. Landau, 49 Cal. 2d 690, 321 P.2d 456 (Cal. 1958).

Note on Federal Criminal Liability for Trade Secret Misappropriation[5]

Prior to the passage of the Economic Espionage Act of 1996, there was only a single very limited federal statute that directly prohibited the misappropriation of a trade secret.[6] When confronted with an allegation

---

5. This section is adapted from James H.A. Pooley et al., Understanding the Economic Espionage Act of 1996, 5 Tex. Intell. Prop. L.J. 177 (1997).

6. 18 U.S.C. §1905, which provides for misdemeanor criminal sanctions for the unauthorized disclosure of government information, including trade secrets, by a government employee. In the only reported decision under this section, the court in United States v. Wallington, 889 F.2d 573 (5th Cir. 1989), upheld the defendant's conviction for running background checks on several people whom a friend of the defendant suspected of drug dealing. However, because this section provides for misdemeanor sanctions, was only very infrequently prosecuted, and is limited in scope, it is of little importance in this area.

that an individual had misappropriated a valuable trade secret, federal prosecutors were forced to turn to a number of federal statutes that were clearly not designed to cover trade secrets. In particular, prosecutors attempted to use the depression-era Interstate Transportation of Stolen Property Act (ITSP),[7] and the wire fraud[8] and mail fraud[9] statutes. However, a recent court decision severely curtails the use of ITSP, and the use of the mail and wire fraud statutes has always been limited because the theft often does not involve the use of mail or wires. In addition, since a thief often merely copies information and does not necessarily "defraud" the victim permanently of the data, prosecutions are further limited.

The ITSP provides, in pertinent part, as follows:

> Whoever transports, transmits, or transfers in interstate or foreign commerce any goods, wares, merchandise, securities or money, of the value of $5,000 or more, knowing the same to have been stolen, converted or taken by fraud . . .
> Shall be fined not more than $10,000 or imprisoned not more than ten years, or both.

This statute was enacted by Congress in 1934 to fill an enforcement gap in the National Motor Vehicle Theft Act, 18 U.S.C. §2312. Both statutes were intended to aid the states in their detection and punishment of criminals who sought to evade state authorities by fleeing in stolen vehicles or with stolen property over state lines. However, since ITSP was drafted at a time when information did not have the economic value it has today and at a time when information could not be quickly copied and instantaneously transmitted to any location in the world, it is not particularly well suited to deal with the theft of intangible property such as trade secrets. Moreover, in light of United States v. Brown, 925 F.3d 1301 (10th Cir. 1991), it is uncertain whether ITSP can be used to charge a person with theft of trade secrets where no tangible property was transferred across state lines. *Brown*

---

7. 18 U.S.C. §§2314-2315. For cases relying on the ITSP, see, e.g., United States v. Riggs, 739 F. Supp. 414 (N.D. Ill. 1990) (interstate transfer of an intangible computer text file); United States v. Bottone, 365 F.2d 389 (2d Cir. 1966) (interstate transfer of photographs of secret drug manufacturing processes); United States v. Seagraves, 265 F.2d 876 (3d Cir. 1959) (interstate transfer of geophysical maps); United States v. Greenwald, 479 F.2d 320 (6th Cir. 1973) (interstate transfer of a chemical formula); and United States v. Belmont, 715 F.2d 459 (9th Cir. 1983) (interstate sales of videotape cassettes of copyrighted motion pictures that had been copied "off the air"). But cf. United States v. Brown, 925 F.2d 1301 (10th Cir. 1991) (holding that a computer program does not meet the "goods, wares, merchandise" language of §2314, relying on Dowling v. United States, 473 U.S. 207 (1985)).

8. 18 U.S.C. §1343. For cases applying the wire fraud statute, see Carpenter v. United States, 479 U.S. 1016 (1987) (confidential business information); United States v. Cherif, 943 F.2d 692 (7th Cir. 1991) (confidential banking information); United States v. Seidlitz, 589 F.2d 152, 160 (4th Cir. 1978); *cert. denied*, 441 U.S. 922 (1980) (stolen computer source code); and United States v. Riggs, 739 F. Supp. 414 (N.D. Ill. 1990) (network configuration information stolen intrastate, but transferred interstate after theft).

9. 18 U.S.C. §1341. For cases applying the mail fraud statute, see United States v. Cherif, 913 F.2d 692 (7th Cir. 1991); United States v. Mendelson, 896 F.2d 1183 (9th Cir. 1990).

casts serious doubt on whether the phrase "goods, wares and merchandise" contained in section 2314 covers intangible property.

The grand jury indicted Brown for violating section 2314 by transporting computer programs, software, and source code interstate from Georgia to New Mexico. Brown moved to dismiss the indictment, arguing that under United States v. Dowling, 473 U.S. 207 (1985), the government failed to allege that he transferred in interstate commerce "physical goods, wares [or] merchandise" within the meaning of section 2314. The government admitted that it would not be able to prove that the defendant made a copy of the source code using, for example, the company's hard disk or that the defendant had in his possession any tangible property belonging to the company. The trial court ruled that the source code by itself "is not the type of property which is contemplated . . . within the language of the statute, goods, wares or merchandise."

The appellate court agreed, citing *Dowling*. In *Dowling*, the defendant was convicted of violating section 2314 following his interstate distribution of bootleg Elvis Presley records. The Supreme Court reversed the conviction and held that it was not Congress's intention that ITSP function as a criminalization of copyright infringement. The Supreme Court emphasized that its decision did not deal with a situation in which the initial procurement was accomplished by theft or fraud and that the courts have never required that the items stolen and transported remain in entirely unaltered form. The Court emphasized, however, that:

> these cases and others prosecuted under §2314 have always involved physical "goods, wares [or] merchandise" that have themselves been "stolen, converted or taken by fraud." This basic element comports with the common-sense meaning of the statutory language: by requiring that the "goods, wares [or] merchandise" be "the same" as those "stolen, converted or taken by fraud" the provision seems clearly to contemplate a physical identity between the items unlawfully obtained and those eventually transported, and hence some prior physical taking of the subject goods.

Id. at 216. The *Brown* court, quoting this language, held that "[p]urely intellectual property" such as the source code appropriated by the defendants is not the type of property covered by section 2314: "It can be represented physically, such as through writing on a page, but the underlying, intellectual property itself, remains intangible" and thus "cannot constitute goods, wares, merchandise which have been stolen, converted or taken within the meaning of sections 2314 or 2315." *Id.* at 1307-1308. The *Brown* court also stated that the United States v. Riggs, 739 F. Supp. 414 (N.D. Ill. 1990), decision was in error in light of the Supreme Court's decision in *Dowling*.

In *Riggs*, defendants Robert J. Riggs and Craig Neidorf were indicted for wire fraud and interstate transportation of stolen goods. According to the indictment and pleadings, in 1988 Riggs gained unauthorized access to the Southern Bell Data Network (SBDN) and eventually to a sensitive portion of the computer that contained proprietary Southern Bell files, including the enhanced 911 (E911) file, which is a universal service for handling emergency calls in a municipality and surrounding unincorporated areas. Riggs downloaded a copy of the E911 text file to his home computer, located in Atlanta. He then made available a copy of the file to a friend, Craig Neidorf, who was the co-editor of a computer hacker newsletter known as "Phrack." Neidorf downloaded the copy to his computer in his room at his fraternity house at the University of Missouri. After making various revisions to remove all references to Southern Bell from the text file, Neidorf published it in an issue of Phrack. Riggs and Neidorf were charged with two counts of wire fraud, 13 U.S.C. §1343, two counts of the interstate transportation of stolen property, 18 U.S.C. §2314, and three counts of violating the Computer Fraud and Abuse Act of 1986, 18 U.S.C. §1030(a)(6).

Neidorf challenged the indictment by arguing that the computerized text file could not be considered "goods, wares, [or] merchandise" under section 2314 because that section should be narrowly read and was never meant to cover the theft of intangible computer data. The *Riggs* trial judge rejected defendant's "disingenuous" argument that he merely transferred electronic impulses across state lines. The court reasoned that in this case "the information in the E911 text file was accessible at Neidorf's computer terminal in Missouri before he transferred it. . . . The mere fact that the information actually crossed state lines via computer-generated electronic impulses does not defeat a charge under section 2314." The court then framed the issue as not whether electronic impulses are "goods, wares or merchandise" within the meaning of section 2314, but "whether the proprietary information contained in Southern Bell's E911 text file constitutes a 'good, ware or merchandise' within the purview of the statute." Not surprisingly, after presenting the issue in this manner, the court held that "Neidorf's transfer of that information across state lines would clearly constitute the transfer of 'goods, wares, or merchandise' within the meaning of section 2314. This court sees no reason to hold differently simply because Neidorf stored the information inside computers instead of printing it out on paper." In either case, the information is in a transferable, accessible, even salable form. The court was thus unwilling to read a "tangibility requirement" into the definition of "goods, wares or merchandise."

An analysis of the two decisions strongly suggests that *Brown* and not *Riggs* was correctly decided. In particular, if the *Riggs* rationale was followed, it would lead to some clearly unintended results. Specifically, the *Riggs* court opined that it was not necessary to resolve whether or not the E911 file constitutes goods, wares or merchandise, since the defendant and others had the ability to "access the information in viewable form from a reliable storage place which also makes the information tangible, transferable, salable and, in this court's opinion brings it within the definition of 'goods, wares, or merchandise' under section 2314." Here, the *Riggs* court was arguably elevating form over substance. In other words, there is no doubt that defendants Riggs and Neidorf misappropriated the computerized text file. However, section 2314 is not directed towards the act of theft, but to criminalizing interstate *transfer* of stolen goods, wares, or merchandise. The computer text file was transmitted across interstate lines by Riggs in the form of electronic signals and only became tangible property when the electronic signals were printed on paper. Thus the court in *Riggs* did not address the real issue—whether purely intangible property is goods, wares, or merchandise—but instead determined that the acts of the defendants should be covered by section 2314 because, logically, most types of stolen intangible property should not be treated differently from stolen tangible property. If this reasoning were applied to *all* intangible property, it would lead to results clearly not foreseen nor intended by Congress. For example, accessing a computer from out of state would necessarily involve the transfer of property across state lines—there would be no difference, in other words, between "access" and "transfer." Further, section 2314 would apply under certain circumstances to the interstate transportation of patent-infringing goods. In other words, if a person "steals" an invention that is protected by a patent and then ships in interstate commerce an article manufactured in accord with the stolen patented specifications, he or she could be successfully prosecuted under section 2314 according to the reasoning of the *Riggs* court. Congress surely did not intend to criminalize patent infringement through the back door.

If in fact the *Brown* decision was correctly decided and therefore followed by other circuits, federal prosecutors are prevented from charging a person with a violation of section 2314 for transporting in interstate commerce a valuable trade secret if no tangible property was also stolen. The *Brown* decision limits the use by prosecutors of section 2314 to those situations in which a defendant illegally misappropriates a tangible item containing an intangible component. For example, a defendant can be prosecuted for violating section 2314 if the trade secret is written on paper that belongs to the victim and is misappropriated by the defendant. The *Brown* court suggested that stealing this piece of paper violates section 2314, even where the value of the paper is insignificant and is almost wholly derived from the intangible component.[10] However, in an in-

---

10. *Brown*, 925 F.2d at 1307-1308 n.14, citing United States v. Stegora, 849 F.2d 291, 292 (8th Cir. 1988). Further, in United States v. Seagraves, 265 F.2d 876 (3d Cir. 1959) and United States v. Lester, 282 F.2d 750 (3d Cir. 1960), which arose out of a common factual background involving the theft of geophysical maps from Gulf Oil that were then sold and transported in interstate commerce, the courts affirmed the defendants' convictions under section 2314. The defendants argued that in many instances the original maps were not transported, but rather copies, made on the victim's own copying equipment with the victim's supplies, were what were actually transported in interstate commerce. In fact, many of the original maps were never removed from the premises of Gulf Oil. Thus, according to the defendants, no "goods, wares or merchandise" were stolen by the defendants and transported in interstate commerce. *Lester*, 282 F.2d at 755. The court rejected this argument and instead focused on the market value of the maps, which was almost wholly derived from the intangible information contained on them. Citing Black's Law Dictionary, the court in *Seagraves* stated that "[t]he term 'goods, wares or merchandise' is a general and comprehensive designation of

creasingly electronic environment where a thief can transmit the stolen trade secret anywhere in the world electronically, without misappropriating any tangible property owned by the victim, the scope of section 2314 arguably fails to protect against the most serious kinds of theft. Further, there seems to be no good reason why the law should treat two defendants who both misappropriate equally valuable trade secrets differently merely because one of the defendants misappropriated the trade secret, for example, using a computer diskette belonging to the victim. These shortcomings of section 2314 underlie Congress's decision to enact the Economic Espionage Act of 1996 (EEA), 18 U.S.C. §1831 et seq.

The structure of the EEA reflects its rather disparate origins, and the confusion that surrounded major changes made in the last days of the 1996 congressional session. The EEA contains a definition "trade secret" that is taken with only minor modifications from the definition in the Uniform Trade Secrets Act. At the same time, the sections defining "misappropriation" are entirely new and have no parallels in existing trade secrets law.

The sine qua non of an action under the EEA is the existence of a "trade secret." Section 1839(3) defines that term as follows:

> (3) the term "trade secret" means all forms and types of financial, business, scientific, technical, economic or engineering information, including patterns, plans, compilations, program devices, formulas, designs, prototypes, methods, techniques, processes, procedures, programs, or codes, whether tangible or intangible, and whether or how stored, compiled, or memorialized physically, electronically, graphically, photographically, or in writing if
>
> > (A) the owner thereof has taken reasonable measures to keep such information secret; and
> >
> > (B) the information derives independent economic value, actual or potential, from not being generally known to, and not being readily ascertainable through proper means by the public.

---

such personal property or chattels as are ordinarily a subject of commerce." *Seagraves,* 265 F.2d at 880. Since there was evidence that there was a market for the copies of the maps, the maps, including the copies, must be goods, wares, or merchandise within the meaning of section 2314. Thus, in these cases, unlike *Brown,* the defendants misappropriated both the intangible and tangible components, which happened to be embodied in the same object, i.e., the copies of the stolen map. See also Hancock v. Decker, 379 F.2d 552 (5th Cir. 1967) (court, citing section 2314, upheld defendant's state court conviction for theft of computer programs worth $5 million that he copied using his employer's copying machine and paper worth almost nothing). But see United States v. Bottone, 365 F.2d 389 (2d Cir. 1966) (the interstate transfer of copies of secret drug manufacturing processes violate section 2314); United States v. Gallo, 599 F. Supp. 241, 245 (W.D.N.Y. 1984) ("The law of this circuit is that intangible rights can be the basis of prosecution under 18 U.S.C. §2314"); United States v. Gilboe, 684 F.2d 235 (2d Cir. 1982) (electronic transfer of funds fraudulently obtained is a violation of §2314); United States v. Steerwell Leisure Corp., Inc., 598 F. Supp. 171, 174 (W.D.N.Y. 1984) ("Judge Friendly's opinion for the Second Circuit in United States v. Bottone stated in no uncertain terms that intangible rights embodied in tangible objects which are not themselves stolen can be the basis of a prosecution under 18 U.S.C. §2314"); and United States v. Sam Goody, 506 F. Supp. 380, 389 (E.D.N.Y. 1980) (intangible aggregation of sounds embodied on a tangible medium is a good, ware, or merchandise within the purview of section 2314).

This definition, which was added late in the congressional session,[11] gener-ally tracks the definition of "trade secrets" in the Uniform Act. However, there are some differences between the language of the two statutes.

First, the list of potential types of secrets is much more expansive in the EEA than in the Uniform Act, though it has been narrowed somewhat from earlier versions of the statute.[12] It is not clear why Congress chose to expand upon the representative list in the Uniform Act. Because of the expansive interpretation already given to the Uniform Act definition,[13] it is likely that the EEA will apply to all of the same types of information that qualify as trade secrets under the current civil standard. This in itself may be surprising to some; state criminal trade secrets statutes are frequently more limited in scope than their civil counterparts. For example, the Cali-fornia criminal trade secrets statute, Cal. Penal Code §499c, until recently applied only to the theft of scientific or technical information.

Second, the EEA expressly extends the definition of "trade secrets" to encompass information in any form, "whether tangible or intangible, and whether or how stored, compiled, or memorialized physically, electroni-cally, graphically, photographically, or in writing." The references to intangible information and the "whether or how" language strongly suggest that not only information stored in electronic form but also infor-mation "stored" only in an individual's memory, can be the subject of a prosecution for trade secrets theft.

Sections 1831(a) and 1832(a) contain identical language regarding acts of misappropriation. They punish a specified individual who:

> (1) steals, or without authorization appropriates, takes, carries away, or conceals, or by fraud, artifice or deception obtains a trade secret;
> (2) without authorization copies, duplicates, sketches, draws, photo-graphs, downloads, uploads, alters, destroys, photocopies, replicates, trans-mits, delivers, sends, mails, communicates, or conveys a trade secret;
> (3) receives, buys, or possesses a trade secret, knowing the same to have been stolen or appropriated, obtained, or converted without authorization. . . .

These provisions are in some respects significantly broader than corre-sponding civil trade secrets laws such as the Uniform Act.

Section (a)(1) lists a number of means of improper acquisition of a trade secret. In general, the provisions in this section seem to track the

---

11. See Legislation Addressing Trade Secret Theft, Computer Break-ins Passed by Congress, 1 Elec. Info. Pol'y & L. Rep. 599 (Oct. 4, 1996) [hereinafter Legislation Passed] (change from "proprietary economic information" to "trade secrets" added only in the final version of the bill, after conference committee).

12. See Legislation Passed, supra note 11, at 599 (terms "data," "tools," "mechanisms," "compounds," and "commercial strategies" removed from earlier version of the Senate bill).

13. See, e.g., Religious Technology Center v. Lerma, 908 F. Supp. 1362, 1368-1369 (E.D. Va. 1995) (religious scriptures); Thermodyne Food Serv. Prods. v. McDonald's Corp., 940 F. Supp. 1300 (N.D. Ill. 1996) (interrelationship of publicly known elements); Allen v. Johar, Inc., 823 S.W.2d 824 (Ark. 1992) (customer lists); ABBA Rubber Co. v. Seaquist, 286 Cal. Rptr. 518 (Cal. Ct. App. 1991) (customer lists); Restatement (Third) Unfair Computer L. §39, cmt.

"improper means" of acquisition punished in civil cases. In particular, the references to stealing, concealment, fraud, artifice, and deception are reminiscent of the civil law's prohibition against both illegal and "immoral" business conduct. However, the provision also makes it a crime to appropriate or take a secret without authorization from the trade secret owner. These terms might be thought to encompass the sort of lawful business espionage that has long been permitted by civil trade secrets law—conduct on the order of observing a competitor's property from across the street. There is some suggestion in the legislative history that the EEA is not intended to inhibit robust competition.[14] While this might be enough to declare broad categories of competitive intelligence-gathering proper and therefore lawful, the ambiguity of some of the terms in section (a)(1) is troubling.

Broader still is section (2), which gives the trade secret owner the right to control a whole host of activities on the order of duplication, transportation, or destruction of a trade secret. This provision encompasses more than its civil counterparts. Section (2) is not by its terms limited to secrets acquired by "improper means" like those listed in section (1). Even legally acquired secrets can be misappropriated under the EEA if they are analyzed or duplicated in one of the ways listed in section (2). The civil law does prohibit some such uses of a lawfully acquired trade secret, but limits its reach to disclosure or use of a secret in violation of a confidential relationship. By contrast, there is no requirement of such a confidential relationship in the EEA. So long as the requirements of secrecy are satisfied, the trade secret owner is apparently entitled to seek the aid of the Justice Department in preventing the world from engaging in any of the enumerated acts in section (2), even if the secret is contained in a product that the defendant lawfully acquired.[15] As a result, the EEA effectively implies a confidential relationship between the trade secret owner and the world at large, something trade secrets law has never before attempted and an indication that Congress believes trade secrets law is based in property theory, not tort or contract. Further, some of the specific provisions in section (2), such as the prohibition against altering or destroying a trade secret, are outside the normal reach of trade secrets law.[16] While these prohibitions might seem to apply to physical vandals and computer hackers as well as to more traditional types of trade secret defendants, the requirement of section 1832 that the defendant act "with intent to convert a trade secret" arguably incorporates the criminal law relating to conversion. This

14. S. Rep., 142 Cong. Rec. S12212 ("Other companies can and must have the ability to determine the elements of a trade secret through their own inventiveness, creativity and hard work. . . . [P]arallel development of a trade secret cannot and should not constitute a violation of this statute.").

15. See H.R. Rep. 104-788 ("The concept of control also includes the mere possession of the information, regardless of the manner by which the non-owner gained possession of the information.").

16. "Destroying" a secret might mean "destroying its value by publishing it to the world," in which case civil law does provide a remedy. Alternatively, it might mean the physical destruction of valuable information, which is not covered by the Uniform Act.

would preclude prosecution of those who act for noneconomic motives, such as the defendant in United States v. LaMacchia.[17] For this reason, the EEA may be of limited use in many cases involving computer hackers.

COMMENTS AND QUESTIONS

1. In addition to the application of the new federal statute to the computer industry, criminal trade secret cases in the industry have been brought in a number of states. Many of these cases arose in Silicon Valley. Prominent criminal trade secrets prosecutions in the computer industry involved senior officials, at Symantec, who were charged with stealing trade secrets from Borland and Avant!, which allegedly stole trade secrets from rival Cadence.

PROBLEM

Problem 1-2. Software Incorporated (SI), the developer of application software, possesses a valid trade secret on the proprietary computer code in its CALCUTEC program and has taken reasonable steps to protect its secrecy. Q, a disgruntled employee of USER Inc., a licensee of the CALCUTEC program, wrongfully makes the proprietary code widely available by posting it on BBS, an electronic bulletin board service, from which it can be easily copied. SI learns of this unauthorized disclosure within a few weeks and notifies BBS. BBS promptly removes CALCUTEC and posts a notice of the unauthorized disclosure of CALCUTEC on the bulletin board but not before Software Distributors, Inc., among other companies, downloads the program and distributes it. Software Distributors sells CALCUTEC, without designation of source or copyright, to TECH Corp.

- What actions does SI have against Q, USER, BBS, and Software Distributors, and TECH?
- What difficulties might SI encounter in maintaining such an action?
- Does "wrongful publication" of the CALCUTEC code on the BBS negate its status as a secret, thereby placing it in the public domain?
- What does this problem suggest about the viability of trade secret as a means for protecting widely distributed software products?

---

17. 871 F. Supp. 535 (D. Mass. 1994) (holding that criminal copyright statute did not apply to electronic bulletin board owner who posted infringing computer software without receiving any financial benefit). In response to the decision in *LaMacchia*, Congress passed the No Electronic Theft Act in 1997, 17 U.S.C. §506. That Act made it a felony to willfully infringe a copyright if copies of significant value were made, even if the infringement was not undertaken for commercial gain.

D. REVERSE ENGINEERING

One issue requires special attention in the computer context: reverse engineering.

Reverse engineering of a legally obtained product to discover the trade secrets it contains is legal under the Uniform Trade Secrets Act. The Commissioners' Comment to section 1 of the Act provides

> Proper means include: . . .
>   2. Discovery by "reverse engineering", that is, by starting with the known product and working backward to find the method by which it was developed. The acquisition of the known product must, of course, also be by a fair and honest means, such as purchase of the item on the open market for reverse engineering to be lawful. . . .

COMMENTS AND QUESTIONS

1. Why is reverse engineering lawful? If, as the Commissioners suggested, one purpose of trade secrets law is to promote standards of commercial ethics, doesn't there seem to be something wrong with taking apart a competitor's product in order to figure out how to copy it—or, in some cases, how to render it useless? Does reverse engineering benefit only those competitors who are not smart enough to develop ideas or products for themselves?

In the computer context, reverse engineering arguably serves a very important commercial purpose. Decompilation of a computer program may be a necessary first step in analyzing it. As the Manifesto authors explain,

> [m]ost copyrighted works reveal their contents to anyone seeking to read them, which makes it unnecessary to reproduce the texts to get access to the ideas, techniques, methods and information they contain. By contrast, the unprotectable elements embodied in computer programs can only be discerned by decompilation. If decompilation is forbidden, software developers could use copyright law to get de facto monopolies on functional process and systems embodied in programs that have not met patent standards.

Pamela Samuelson et al., A Manifesto Concerning the Legal Protection of Computer Programs, 94 Colum. L. Rev. 2308, 2390 n.329 (1994).

A more general argument for permitting reverse engineering law may be that it serves to differentiate trade secret law from patent law. As we shall see, patent law grants stronger protection than trade secret law (including protection against reverse engineering), but only if the patent holder meets relatively stringent standards. Reverse engineering may be a legal rule designed to weaken trade secret protection relative to patent protection. Can you think of reasons why we would want to weaken trade secret protection? On this point, see Kewanee Oil Co. v. Bicron Corp., 416 U.S. 470 (1974), in which the Court held that the defense of reverse engineering in trade secrets law was an important part of what allowed patents and trade secrets to coexist.

2. Reverse engineering of computer software is not easy. Software is generally found in object code form. To reverse engineer it, experts often try a process generally known as "decompilation"—that is, the attempt to translate the 1s and 0s into some form of assembly language and then into readable source code. This process is expensive and time-consuming and can produce imperfect results. See, e.g., Andrew Johnson-Laird, Reverse Engineering of Software: Separating Legal Mythology from Actual Technology, 5 Software L.J. 331, 342-343 (1992). Further, as we see in the next chapter, reverse engineering a computer program almost always involves making one or more intermediate copies of that program, which might be illegal under the copyright laws. Does the difficulty (both technical and legal) of reverse engineering a computer program from object code affect the balance of rights that *Kewanee*, supra, considered so important?

An alternative means of reverse engineering a computer program is called "black box" analysis. In this process, the analyst does not try to take the software apart to see how it works. Rather, she tests the software by feeding it instructions or commands to see what comes out. While the code of the program cannot be discovered using black box analysis, it is sometimes possible to puzzle out the logical structure of the program by feeding it the right data.

Technicon Data Systems Corp. v. Curtis 1000 Inc.
Delaware Court of Chancery
224 U.S.P.Q. 286 (Del. Ch. 1984)

BERGER, Vice Chancellor

Technicon Data Systems Corp. ("Technicon") brought this action to enjoin Curtis 1000, Inc. ("Curtis") from misappropriating plaintiff's computer trade secrets. On June 7, 1984, Technicon's application for a temporary restraining order was denied and on July 2, 1984, Curtis' motion to stay this action in favor of a subsequently filed federal action also was denied. This is the decision, following extensive expedited discovery, briefing and oral argument, on plaintiff's motion for a preliminary injunction.

The Technicon product that forms the basis of this lawsuit is called the Medical Information System ("MIS"), a computerized system for the storage, transmittal and display of hospital data. The MIS consists of a non-Technicon mainframe host computer connected to numerous video matrix terminals ("VMTs") located throughout the hospital. A person using the VMT, which includes a display screen, keyboard and electronic lightpen, is able to give instructions and input and retrieve data stored in the host computer. For example, a physician is able to prescribe medication for his patient by finding the appropriate medicine on a display on the screen and pointing the lightpen at the medicine selected. The information is transmitted to the host computer and, depending upon the instructions given by the physician, the prescription may be printed out at the pharmacist's VMT and the appropriate nursing station VMT.

Technicon contends that a portion of the computer technology which enables the host computer and VMTs to communicate with each other (the communications interface) is proprietary trade secret information improperly obtained and used to develop defendant's MSI 1000 system. The MSI 1000 consists of a printed circuit board and an emulation program that were designed to enable an IBM personal computer ("IBM PC") to be connected to the MIS host computer and function as a Technicon VMT. Plaintiff contends that, among other things, the non-standard control and function codes, the characters used to begin and end data transmissions, the combination of error checking and acknowledgment messages used and the data screen coordinates and lightpen codes are trade secrets.

Technicon argues that the evidence presented at this preliminary stage establishes that the individuals who developed defendant's MSI 1000 obtained these trade secrets from confidential schematics and other written materials and from their improper manipulation of operating MISs at various hospitals.

At the TRO stage of this litigation, plaintiff argued that Kurt Lawrence ("Lawrence") had misappropriated a Technicon emulation program allegedly used to develop the MSI 1000. Now that the record has been significantly expanded, the focus has shifted to George Bridgmon ("Bridgmon") and John Cline ("Cline"). Bridgmon and Lawrence are former Technicon employees who set up independent computer businesses in the summers of 1982 and 1983 respectively and merged their two companies to form Medsoft, Inc. ("Medsoft") early in 1984. Bridgmon worked for Technicon from 1975 to 1979 assisting in the installation of the MIS at several hospitals. Immediately prior to his departure in July, 1979, Bridgmon had been assigned to Jewish Hospital of St. Louis. Bridgmon left Technicon to become the Vice President in charge of Jewish Hospital's newly installed MIS.

Bridgmon had access to numerous Technicon manuals both during his tenure with Technicon and while supervising the operation of the MIS as an employee of Jewish Hospital. Bridgmon knew that Technicon considered many of its technical manuals confidential and that the contracts between Technicon and its MIS customers contained confidentiality provisions. In addition, Bridgmon executed a confidentiality agreement while employed by Technicon and, while employed by Jewish Hospital, executed one of the hospital's contracts with Technicon on behalf of the hospital.

In the spring of 1983, Bridgmon, then working as a private consultant primarily for hospitals using the MIS, decided to develop an interface which would allow a microcomputer such as the IBM PC to emulate the Technicon VMT. By that time, Technicon had been working on a physicians' office system for almost one year. Using a Convergent Technology microcomputer (the "CT"), Technicon was developing a system whereby a doctor would be able to computerize his office records and also use his CT as a remote VMT capable of interfacing with the hospital's host computer. Lawrence had been working on an aspect of this project for Technicon since July, 1982. In early 1983, at about the same time that he decided to develop the VMT interface, Bridgmon attended a demonstration by Lawrence of Technicon's prototype of its physicians' office system. This meeting apparently marks the beginning of the Bridgmon/Lawrence association that eventually led to the formation of Medsoft.

After unsuccessfully attempting to recruit two Technicon employees to design the VMT interface for him, Bridgmon contacted General Technology Corporation to work on the project. At his first meeting with General Technology in September, 1983, Bridgmon met Cline, an electrical engineer who was a consultant to the company. When Cline and Bridgmon met again a few weeks later, Cline told Bridgmon that he would need access to an operational MIS in order to develop and later test an interface board.

Following these first two meetings, but before Bridgmon and Cline had decided to go forward with the project, Bridgmon sent Cline several pages of schematics which Bridgmon described as Zentec schematics. Zentec manufactures VMTs for Technicon using a modification of standard Zentec equipment. Pursuant to Zentec's manufacturing agreement with Technicon, Zentec is obligated to maintain the confidentiality of the schematics and other technical information relating to the VMT. The schematics that Bridgmon sent to Cline in the fall of 1983 were not diagrams of the standard Zentec product. Rather, they were schematics for Technicon VMT lightpen option.

The evidence indicates only two sources from which Bridgmon could have obtained these diagrams. He could have taken them from the Technicon T4201 Theory of Operation & Maintenance Manual, copies of which were provided to Jewish Hospital during the time Bridgmon was working there and distributed through Bridgmon's wife, who also was working at the hospital. Alternatively, and according to Bridgmon's testimony, the schematics were obtained directly from Zentec. Bridgmon says that, while employed by Jewish Hospital to oversee the MIS, he decided that the MIS maintenance should be performed by the hospital rather than Technicon. In the fall of 1980, Bridgmon claims to have called up the maintenance and repair department at Zentec, explained to Zentec that Jewish Hospital was using the Technicon system and was setting up a repair facility for that system and asked for "whatever information was freely available" for the VMT and its lightpen.

As a result of that phone call and other similar requests made during the period from September, 1980 through May, 1982, Bridgmon received packets of information from Zentec including the schematics he later gave to Cline. Bridgmon says that none of the diagrams or other documents contained any proprietary notice and that Bridgmon had no reason to think that the information provided was confidential. The schematics produced by Cline during discovery do not contain any proprietary notice other than the confidential stamp used in the course of the litigation.

Although defendant contends that Cline never used the schematics provided by Bridgmon, Cline testified that he studied the schematics, highlighted different portions of the circuitry shown on the diagrams and identified an error in one of those circuits. Cline's admissions, together with plaintiff's evidence that the schematics would have been helpful in deciphering the communications interface, make it reasonable to conclude that Cline used the schematics in developing the MSI 1000.

The record indicates that the majority of the developmental work was accomplished by using operating MISs. During the fall of 1983, while Bridgmon and Cline were discussing the interface project, Bridgmon was acting as a consultant at Presbyterian Hospital in Albuquerque, New Mexico. Without the hospital's permission, Bridgmon and Cline tapped into Presbyterian's MIS after normal working hours for the purpose of deciphering certain aspects of the communications interface between the VMT and the host computer. By sending a known instruction through the VMT and studying the electronic impulses transmitted by the VMT for the particular function chosen, Bridgmon and Cline claim to have discovered the function codes and other alleged Technicon trade secrets necessary to create the MSI 1000 circuit board and emulation program. This procedure was described by a non-party witness as, essentially, a wiretap and is the cornerstone of what defendant claims was an accepted and proper method of reverse engineering.

Bridgmon and Cline did not perform all of their work at Presbyterian Hospital. In March, 1984 they started working at Methodist Hospital of Indiana. Cline testified that they did not remain at Presbyterian Hospital because he was told that it "did not wish to cooperate." . . .

More recently, Bridgmon and Cline have continued the development and testing of their interface project at the University of California at Irvine Medical Center ("UCI"). UCI hired Bridgmon in April, 1984, to help oversee the installation of the MIS there. Cline and Bridgmon, who were not authorized by UCI to use its facilities for this purpose, worked in the evenings on further development of their interface project. At UCI, as they did at Presbyterian and Methodist Hospitals, Bridgmon and Cline tapped into the MIS to monitor and trap information being communicated between the VMT and the host computer.

Finally, Bridgmon and Cline have been testing their system at the National Institutes of Health ("NIH") with the express permission of NIH. However, Bridgmon and Cline have been authorized only to demonstrate the MSI 1000, not to develop it. Dr. Lewis, the Associate Director for Information Systems at the Clinical Center of NIH, testified that it is not part of the MSI 1000 demonstration for the Technicon VMT and IBM PC both to be connected to the host computer at the same time. Thus, from the present record, it does not appear that NIH has authorized Bridgmon or Cline to use their wiretap to intercept transmissions between the VMT and the host computer.

[Medsoft, in association with Curtis, began marketing the MSI 1000 interface software and took 55 orders for software.]

Curtis argues that the function and control codes and other aspects of the MIS communications interface claimed by Technicon to be trade secrets are both readily ascertainable by proper means and have not been the subject of reasonable efforts to maintain their secrecy.

The record evidence supports the conclusion, at this preliminary stage, that the MIS communications interface, as a whole, is not readily ascertainable by proper means. Even assuming for the moment that the wiretap method of intercepting transmissions used by Bridgmon and Cline is a proper means of obtaining the information, by their own testimony Bridgmon and Cline devoted more than 2,000 man hours to this project. Moreover, Dr. Lewis testified that, as of a few weeks ago, the MSI 1000 still is unable to fully emulate the Technicon VMT. Although only a portion of the time spent on this project was devoted to deciphering Technicon's alleged trade secrets, the evidence indicates that the alleged "reverse engineering" done by Bridgmon and Cline was a time consuming process. Defendant's expert witness, Ronald Hutchins, confirms this conclusion. Hutchins' affidavit states that the documents produced by Bridgmon and Cline show that they "spent a considerable amount of effort" before they were able to decipher two of the non-standard control and function codes used in the Technicon MIS. On this record, I conclude that the alleged trade secrets are not "readily ascertainable." See Electro-craft Corp. v. Controlled Motion, Inc., Minn. Supr., 332 N.W.2d 890 (1983).

Defendant stresses that electronic signals representing the binary system of "ones" and "zeros" are the basic and well known method of transmitting computer data. They say that the electronic signals intercepted by Bridgmon and Cline cannot be deemed trade secrets since anyone knowledgeable in the industry would be familiar with the communication method used by Technicon. By analogy, defendant is saying that because everyone knows that the combination to a safe consists of three numbers, the numbers that will open Technicon's safe are not secret. Perhaps this is an oversimplification, but it points out the fallacy in defendant's argument.

As to the second part of the definition of a "trade secret," I find that plaintiff probably will be able to establish at trial that it made reasonable efforts, under the circumstances, to maintain the secrecy of the communications interface. Technicon employees were required to execute confidentiality agreements; the contracts between Technicon and hospitals using the MIS included confidentiality provisions; those Technicon manuals which contain schematics and other technical information about the communications interface are marked confidential at the beginning of the manual; and Zentec, the manufacturer of the VMT, is under a written obligation to maintain the confidentiality of Technicon's system. . . .

The next issue is whether Technicon's trade secrets were misappropriated. Defendant acknowledges that Bridgmon gave Cline several pages of schematics for the lightpen option and that Bridgmon and Cline tapped into operating MISs to derive the information needed to develop the MSI 1000. Thus, if either the schematics or the information derived from the wiretap were obtained by improper means, Technicon will be able to establish misappropriation under 6 Del. C. §2001(2).

Plaintiff contends that Bridgmon's description of the manner in which he obtained the schematics should not be believed. Plaintiff points to a Zentec official's affidavit as evidence that Zentec has maintained the confidentiality of Technicon's trade secrets and would not have sent the schematics to Bridgmon. Alternatively, plaintiff says that it would make no sense for Zentec to send Bridgmon only a partial set of schematics as loose sheets without any cover letter. For these reasons, Technicon argues that Bridgmon must have obtained the schematics he gave to Cline from the T4201 Theory of Operation Maintenance Manual which bears a proprietary notice on the inside of the cover.

Although the evidence, when weighed after trial, may support this conclusion, I accept Bridgmon's version of how he obtained those documents for present purposes. In doing so, however, I do not accept Bridgmon's conclusion that he had no reason to know that the schematics were confidential. By Bridgmon's account, before obtaining any information from Zentec, he explained that Jewish Hospital was using a Technicon MIS and needed technical data with which to set up an in-house repair facility for the Technicon equipment. In subsequent telephone calls, Bridgmon states that he obtained additional information from Zentec after explaining that he had been given similar documents in the past. In other words, Bridgmon obtained Technicon data from Zentec not as a member of the general public but as a representative of a hospital authorized to receive that information directly from Technicon.

By virtue of his former association with Technicon and his later affiliation with Jewish Hospital, Bridgmon knew that he had a duty to maintain the confidentiality of Technicon's trade secrets both as an individual (pursuant to his own confidentiality agreement) and as a representative of Jewish Hospital (pursuant to the hospital's contract with Technicon containing confidentiality provisions). Bridgmon also knew that the Technicon user manuals, several of which he helped to prepare, did not contain schematics and other technical data relating to the communications interface. Thus, he had reason to know that the documents he obtained from Zentec were not similar to those manuals which Bridgmon claimed were not treated as confidential by Technicon. Based upon this evidence, I find that Bridgmon acquired the schematics from Zentec "under circumstances giving rise to a duty to maintain [their] secrecy or limit [their] use. . . ." 6 Del. C. §2001(2)b.2.B.

Defendant contends that the method by which Bridgmon and Cline intercepted and deciphered data transmissions between the VMT and the host computer is a well recognized method of reverse engineering and is not actionable. Reverse engineering is the process by which a finished product is broken down into its component parts or otherwise analyzed to determine the manner in which the product was created. Plaintiff agrees with the general proposition that trade secrets may be legitimately discovered through reverse engineering. However plaintiff argues that the MIS communications interface has never been made available to the public and, thus, could not be reverse engineered by proper means.

Technicon does not sell its software or documentation to its customers. Under its contracts, Technicon licenses its software and technical data to the customer for the customer's use subject to confidentiality provisions contained in the contracts. Even customer modifications to Technicon's software are covered by Technicon's confidentiality provisions. For example, several years after NIH contracted with Technicon to obtain the MIS, NIH acquired a perpetual software license from Technicon. The parties contemplated that NIH would be modifying the licensed Technicon software for specific programs needed by NIH. Pursuant to contract modification No. 44, NIH agreed, among other things, that any enhancements or modifications to Technicon's software which retain or reveal any of Technicon's software shall continue to be subject to the non-disclosure provisions of the original agreement. Technicon maintains that this type of non-disclosure requirement prohibits anyone from tapping into the MIS at least where, as here, the purpose of the electronic interception is to develop a competing system for commercial use. In other words, Technicon says that its communications interface is not subject to being reverse engineered by any method because that aspect of the MIS is not in the public domain.

The parties cited numerous cases addressing the question of whether a particular product had been reverse engineered and whether a process or product is a trade secret. However, these cases are not helpful on the issue of whether a product may be the subject of reverse engineering.

Although this legal issue may become significant at a later stage of this proceeding, at this point it is not dispositive because even if the communications interface is subject to reverse engineering, Bridgmon and Cline used improper means to perform this task. Their work at both Presbyterian Hospital and UCI was not authorized and cannot be reasonably viewed as consistent with the consulting agreements pursuant to which Bridgmon was given access to the facilities. At Methodist Hospital, Bridgmon and Cline were given permission to use the MIS but the evidence indicates that that permission was given pursuant to a misrepresentation made by Bridgmon as to the stage of completion of his project.

Based upon this preliminary determination that plaintiff has established a likelihood of establishing that Bridgmon misappropriated trade
secrets, it follows that Technicon is likely to establish that defendant, also,
misappropriated trade secrets. At the very least, as a result of the discovery
taken to date, Curtis knows or has reason to know that the MSI 1000 was
developed, in part, using trade secrets "derived from or through a person
who had utilized improper means to acquire [them]; . . . acquired under
circumstances giving rise to a duty to maintain [their] secrecy or limit
[their] use; or . . . derived from or through a person who owed a duty to
[Technicon] to maintain [their] secrecy or limit [their] use. . . ." 6 Del. C.
§2001(2)b.2.

Even if plaintiff establishes misappropriation, defendant contends that
plaintiff should not obtain relief because plaintiff's alleged anti-competitive
practices constitute unclean hands. Defendant's unclean hands defense
does not appear to be supported by the facts or law and, thus, does not
alter my conclusion that plaintiff has demonstrated a likelihood of success
on the merits. Defendant alleges that Technicon's use of non-standard
communications requiring the use of only Technicon VMTs and printers
with the MIS constitutes a per se illegal tying arrangement in violation of
federal antitrust laws. There is no evidence that Technicon requires its MIS
customers to purchase Technicon printers or VMTs. As a practical matter,
because of incompatible technology, those purchases may be necessary.
However, the authorities cited by defendant do not support the proposition that technologically interrelated products constitute a per se unlawful
tying arrangement.

The decision in Foremost Pro Color, Inc. v. Eastman Kodak Co., 703
F.2d 534 (9th Cir. 1983) specifically rejected such a claim on facts similar
to those at issue here. In *Foremost*, Kodak's new line of cameras, film,
photographic paper and chemicals were alleged to constitute a per se
unlawful tying arrangement because they are incompatible with competitors' products. The court noted that, when a company introduces new
technology, it often produces related accessories which are only compatible
with the new product. Since there is no immediate competition in the
newly developed product market, the technological tie cannot foreclose
competition. The court held that:

> [The] development and introduction of a system of technologically in-
> terrelated products is not sufficient alone to establish a per se unlawful tying
> arrangement even if the new products are incompatible with the products
> then offered by the competition and effective use of any one of the new prod-
> ucts necessitates purchase of some or all of the others.

Id. at 543.

At this point, the evidence establishes that when Technicon developed
the MIS it, like Kodak, was introducing new technology. There being no
comparable computer system on the market, it follows that there was
nothing with which the MIS could have been made compatible.

COMMENTS AND QUESTIONS

1. What did the defendants in *Technicon* do wrong? Isn't this a classic case of "black box" reverse engineering? Obviously, the court was influenced both by its belief that the defendants illegally obtained schematics of the Technicon emulation software and the fact that the defendants conducted their testing surreptitiously and without the permission of the hospitals that employed them.

But could the defendants have reverse engineered the Technicon software under *any* circumstances without fear of liability? Suppose that they had not acquired the schematics from any source but instead had relied solely on the "black box" approach of dialing into the MIS computer and sending known data through the Technicon emulation software. Further, suppose that they had done this with the knowledge and permission of their employer. Would the court's decision have been different? Does the court's description of "black box" analysis as "wiretapping" suggest that it would be impermissible under any circumstances?

2. Consider the defendant's suggestion that Technicon's refusal to allow reverse engineering to achieve compatibility with their emulation software was anticompetitive. Is this a legitimate reason to permit the defendants to use secret information they could not otherwise obtain? In United States Golf Ass'n v. St. Andrews Systems, 749 F.2d 1028 (3d Cir. 1984), the U.S.G.A. sued the defendant for copying its formula for handicapping golf scores and implementing it in a commercial product. Because the formula was not a secret, the court decided the case on the related grounds of misappropriation of ideas. But its final paragraphs are instructive:

> The public acceptance of the U.S.G.A.'s handicap formula stems from the golfing public's desire to have a uniform system of quantifying recent performances in a way that will allow equitable competition among golfers of differing abilities. The U.S.G.A., in furtherance of its role as the governing body of amateur golf, has provided such a system and, in the absence of a better system, the public has apparently accepted it. Under this state of affairs, the emergence of a single standard becomes largely a function of the need for uniformity. To require Data-Max to use a different formula would effectively destroy its ability to provide a handicapping service, since the U.S.G.A. formula is widely accepted by the golfing public. The purpose of a handicap is comparison between golfers, and handicaps based on different formulas cannot be readily compared.
>
> Because the U.S.G.A. formula is the equivalent of an "industry standard" for the golfing public, preventing other handicap providers from using it would effectively give the U.S.G.A. a national monopoly on the golf handicapping business. Where such a monopoly is unnecessary to protect the basic incentive for the production of the idea or information involved, we do not believe that the creator's interest in its idea or information justifies such an extensive restraint on competition. This case provides a good example of why such a restraint would harm the golfing public. Data-Max has expended time

and creative energy in devising its own products and services. It has not only created the program used to calculate handicaps by computer, but has devised a handicapping service which improves on that provided by the U.S.G.A., at least to the extent that Data-Max provides a golfer with a fresh handicap faster than the U.S.G.A. does. In addition, the U.S.G.A. has not been completely deprived of the opportunity to be compensated for its "good will" in connection with the handicap formula. To the extent that the approval of the U.S.G.A. would enhance the value of "instant handicaps," the U.S.G.A. has an opportunity, if it wishes to exercise it, of offering either Data-Max or other companies the use of the U.S.G.A. name in marketing its products and services.

Id. at 1040-1041. Can a similar argument be made for a computer program that provides the only means of communicating with a mainframe computer?

3. Under what circumstances should the owner of a trade secret be able to "contract around" the reverse engineering rule? Contracts that purport to do so are relatively common in the software industry, but their enforceability is open to some question. We discuss this issue in more detail in Chapter 6.

4. While reverse engineering clearly is not an infringement of civil trade secrets statutes, its status under the new Economic Espionage Act (EEA) is less clear. Some commentators have argued that, read literally, the EEA makes reverse engineering a crime.

> The most troubling thing about 18 U.S.C. §1831(a)(2) is that it arguably prohibits many forms of heretofore lawful reverse engineering activity. While reverse engineering is not expressly prohibited under this section, neither is it expressly permitted. Rather, its legality appears to be judged according to whether the reverse engineer engages in any of the prohibited acts.[103] To be sure, some types of reverse engineering, such as looking at or tasting a lawfully acquired product in order to determine what is in it, will not be illegal under the EEA. On the other hand, several of the restrictions in section (2) will if read literally encompass some forms of reverse engineering. For example, reverse engineering of computer software by "decompilation" almost always involves the making of a prohibited "copy" of the program. Reverse engineering of mechanical devices and computer hardware may well involve prohibited "sketching, drawing, or photographing" of the trade secret contained in the publicly sold device. And it is even possible that the prohibition against "altering" a trade secret will be interpreted to prevent chemical analysis of a trade secret product if such analysis involves the use of chemical reactants which bond to secret chemicals or which precipitate out certain elements from the formula.
>
> The legislative history of the EEA is not encouraging to reverse engineers. The Senate Report suggests that "the important thing is to focus on whether the accused has committed one of the prohibited acts of this statute rather than whether he or she has 'reverse engineered.' If someone has law-

---

103. See S. Rep., 142 Cong. Rec. S12212.

fully gained access to a trade secret and can replicate it without violating copyright, patent *or this law*, then that form of 'reverse engineering' should be fine."[106] The Report goes on to suggest that observing a lawfully purchased product, or drinking a Coca-Cola, are legitimate activities.[107] On the other hand, there appears to be no reverse engineering defense protecting any of the forms of analysis suggested above. A computer programmer has the right to decompile a software program in certain circumstances under the Uniform Act, copyright law, and the common law without fear of civil liability. Under the EEA, though, that programmer has apparently committed a felony.

James H.A. Pooley et al., Understanding the Economic Espionage Act of 1996, 5 Tex. Intell. Prop. L.J. 177 (1997). On the other hand, other commentators have pointed out that abolishing reverse engineering would work a radical change in the structure of trade secret law, and it is unlikely Congress intended to enact such a change sub rosa. And even Pooley et al. go on to argue that criminalizing reverse engineering would be unwise and that reverse engineering cases are not appropriate for prosecution. To date, no case has been brought that would test the proposition.

Note on Encryption

Of late, two very popular topics of discussion on the Internet have been encryption technology and the evil of patent and, to a lesser degree, copyright law. Recently some have even synthesized the two, suggesting that encryption, or "crypto-bottling," replace patent and copyright as the means for defining intellectual property rights in cyberspace.[108] While cryptography may be extremely useful in establishing high electronic security barriers to unauthorized access, it is hardly a new paradigm destined to supplant the entirety of intellectual property law. Instead, cryptography simply establishes more credible barriers to reverse engineering (in this case decryption) than does embedding a program in object code. Fundamentally, trade secret law is at work, but with more powerful tools. Even assuming that the technique provides perfect security, which it does not, the encryption merely shifts the problems of trade secret law to focus on the end user. Software must be decrypted to be valuable to purchasers and finally to end users of the integrated software system. While encryption may enhance the vendor's protection against unauthorized *access* to the software, it can do nothing about unauthorized use or disclosure of the component by those who have legitimately acquired and decrypted it.

106. 142 Cong. Rec. at S12212-13 (emphasis added).
107. *Id.* at S12213. Cf. Mason v. Jack Daniels Distillery, 518 So. 2d 130 (Ala. Civ. App. 1987).
108. See, e.g., John P. Barlow, *The Economy of Ideas*, Wired, Mar. 1994, at 84, 129 (suggesting encryption as a means to protect intellectual property in the digital age).

Thus, encryption may be a useful way of restricting reverse engineering by those who have access to the program only in encrypted form. It may also constitute a "reasonable precaution" that helps preserve the secrecy of the encrypted program. It is an imperfect barrier, however, that alone can do nothing about either reverse engineering or misappropriation by end users who know how to decrypt the program.

We return to the issue of encryption and circumvention in the next chapter, when we consider the Digital Millennium Copyright Act, a 1998 law that makes decryption illegal in many circumstances.

PROBLEM

Problem 1-3. Return to Problem 1-1, above. Assume for the moment that Microsoft has succeeded in maintaining the secrecy of its computer operating system, and has taken reasonable efforts to protect that secrecy. Are competing applications programmers entitled to decompile the operating system in order to prepare applications programs that will run on Microsoft's OS? Is there anything Microsoft can do that will prevent its competitors from legally reverse engineering its product?

2

Copyright Law

A. THE ORIGINS OF COPYRIGHT PROTECTION FOR COMPUTER SOFTWARE

Computer software, by its very nature as written work intended to serve utilitarian purposes, defies easy categorization within our intellectual property system. Copyright law has traditionally served as the principal source of legal protection for original literary work, while the patent system and trade secret law have been the primary means for protecting novel utilitarian works.

With time, it became evident to many that trade secret licensing alone would not be a viable way to protect software products, especially if a mass market in software were to develop. In the mid-1960s, when computer programmers first approached the U.S. Copyright Office about protecting programs by copyright law, the Office expressed some doubts about whether machine-executable forms of programs could be protected by copyright law because of their utilitarian nature. The Office viewed the difference between source and object code versions of programs to be akin to the difference between an engineering drawing (copyrightable as a drawing) and a bridge design depicted therein (not copyrightable because of its utilitarian character). Eventually the Office began issuing copyright registration certificates to computer programs under its "rule of doubt." (Such certificates indicated that the Copyright Office had doubts about the copyrightability of machine-readable versions of the claimed program, but would leave the legal question to the courts if litigation occurred.) While "rule of doubt" registrations might have discouraged some software developers from applying to the Office for a certificate of registration, a more powerful deterrent to registration was the Office's requirement that the full text of the source code be deposited with the Office. Like other deposit copies, this source code would be made available for public inspection. Such public availability of source code posed a threat to the trade secret status of the contents of software. Between 1966 and 1978, only about 1,200 copyright registration certificates had been issued.

Because a number of controversial new technology issues were holding up enactment of a major revision of the 1909 Copyright Act, Congress decided in 1974 to establish the Commission on New Technological Uses of Copyright (CONTU) to investigate and make recommendations on these issues. One such issue was whether computer programs could be copyrighted. In its final report in 1978, CONTU declared its view that programs already were copyrighted under the Copyright Act of 1976 but recommended some changes to this Act to make appropriate rules for programs.

In light of the computer software industry's relative youth and anticipated rapid growth, CONTU's rough empirical judgment that copyright would best promote the invention, development, and diffusion of new and better software products was, by necessity, highly speculative. See, e.g., Pamela Samuelson, CONTU Revisited: The Case Against Copyright Protection for Computer Programs in Machine-Readable Form, 1984 Duke L.J. 663 (criticizing some misleading statements in the CONTU Report about the way computer programs work and how copyright law could protect them). As CONTU recognized, it was impossible in 1978 to establish a precise line between copyrightable expression of computer programs and the uncopyrightable processes that they implement. Yet the location of this line—the idea/expression dichotomy—was critical to the rough cost-benefit analysis that guided CONTU's recommendation. Drawing the line too liberally in favor of copyright protection would bestow strong monopolies upon those who develop operating systems that would become industry standards and would thereby inhibit other creators from developing improved programs and computer systems. Drawing the line too conservatively would allow programmers' efforts to be copied easily, thus discouraging the creation of all but modest incremental advances. The wisdom of Congress's decision to bring computer programs within the scope of copyright law thus depends critically on where the courts draw this line. See generally Peter S. Menell, An Epitaph for Traditional Copyright Protection of Network Features of Computer Software, 43 Antitrust Bull. 651 (1998).

We begin with the first generation of copyright infringement suits under the 1980 amendments, which focus on whether and to what extent literal copying of computer software violates copyright law. Section B examines the second generation of copyright infringement suits, focusing on the extent to which nonliteral forms of copying constitute copyright infringement. We then turn to protection for program outputs and user interfaces. Finally, we discuss a number of issues related to infringement and fair use. A distinct set of issues related to the role of copyright on the Internet is reserved for Chapter 10.

B. THE SCOPE OF SOFTWARE COPYRIGHT

1. Protection for Literal Elements of Program Code

The first questions about copyright for computer programs involved the simplest form of copyright infringement—direct copying of the program code. Because the copying in these early cases was "literal"—that is, the accused infringer took the actual text of the work, not merely the structure, organization, or output of the programs—there is no question of scope of protection or "substantial similarity." Rather, the disputed issue in these early cases was whether computer programs could be protected by copyright at all.

Apple Computer, Inc. v. Franklin Computer Corp.
United States Court of Appeals for the Third Circuit
714 F.2d 1240 (3d Cir. 1983)

SLOVITER, Circuit Judge.

I. Introduction

Apple Computer, Inc. appeals from the district court's denial of a motion to preliminarily enjoin Franklin Computer Corp. from infringing the copyrights Apple holds on fourteen computer programs. . . .

In this case the district court denied the preliminary injunction, inter alia, because it had "some doubt as to the copyrightability of the programs." Apple Computer, Inc. v. Franklin Computer Corp., 545 F. Supp. 812, 812 (E.D. Pa. 1982). This legal ruling is fundamental to all future proceedings in this action and . . . has considerable significance to the computer services industry. Because we conclude that the district court proceeded under an erroneous view of the applicable law, we reverse the denial of the preliminary injunction and remand.

II. Facts and Procedural History

Apple, one of the computer industry leaders, manufactures and markets personal computers (microcomputers), related peripheral equipment such as disk drives (peripherals), and computer programs (software). It presently manufactures Apple II computers and distributes over 150 programs. Apple has sold over 400,000 Apple II computers, employs approximately 3,000 people, and had annual sales of $335,000,000 for fiscal year 1981. One of the by-products of Apple's success is the independent development by third parties of numerous computer programs which are designed to run on the Apple II computer.

Franklin, the defendant below, manufactures and sells the ACE 100 personal computer and at the time of the hearing employed about 75 people and had sold fewer than 1,000 computers. The ACE 100 was designed to be "Apple compatible," so that peripheral equipment and software developed for use with the Apple II computer could be used in conjunction with the ACE 100. Franklin's copying of Apple's operating system computer programs in an effort to achieve such compatibility precipitated this suit. . . .

. . . The district court held a three day evidentiary hearing limited to the copyright infringement claims. Apple produced evidence at the hearing in the form of affidavits and testimony that programs sold by Franklin in conjunction with its ACE 100 computer were virtually identical with those covered by the fourteen Apple copyrights. The variations that did exist were minor, consisting merely of such things as deletion of reference to Apple or its copyright notice. James Huston, an Apple systems programmer, concluded that the Franklin programs were "unquestionably copied from Apple and could not have been independently created." He reached this conclusion not only because it is "almost impossible for so many lines of code" to be identically written, but also because his name, which he had embedded in one program (Master Create), and the word "Applesoft", which was embedded in another (DOS 3.3), appeared on the Franklin master disk. Apple estimated the "works in suit" took 46 man-months to produce at a cost of over $740,000, not including the time or cost of creating or acquiring earlier versions of the programs or the expense of marketing the programs.

Franklin did not dispute that it copied the Apple programs. Its witness admitted copying each of the works in suit from the Apple programs. Its factual defense was directed to its contention that it was not feasible for Franklin to write its own operating system programs. David McWherter, now Franklin's vice-president of engineering, testified he spent 30-40 hours in November 1981 making a study to determine if it was feasible for Franklin to write its own Autostart ROM program and concluded it was not because "there were just too many entry points in relationship to the number of instructions in the program." Entry points at specific locations in the program can be used by programmers to mesh their application programs with the operating system program. McWherter concluded that use of the identical signals was necessary in order to ensure 100% compatibility with application programs created to run on the Apple computer. He admitted that he never attempted to rewrite Autostart ROM and conceded that some of the works in suit (i.e. Copy, Copy A, Master Create, and Hello) probably could have been rewritten by Franklin. Franklin made no attempt to rewrite any of the programs prior to the lawsuit except for Copy, although McWherter testified that Franklin was "in the process of redesigning" some of the Apple programs and that "[w]e had a fair degree of certainty that that would probably work." Apple introduced evidence that Franklin could have rewritten programs, including the Autostart ROM program, and that there are in existence operating programs written by third parties which are compatible with Apple II.

Franklin's principal defense at the preliminary injunction hearing and before us is primarily a legal one, directed to its contention that the Apple operating system programs are not capable of copyright protection. . . .

IV. Discussion

A.   *Copyrightability of a Computer Program Expressed in Object Code*

Certain statements by the district court suggest that programs expressed in object code, as distinguished from source code, may not be the proper subject of copyright. We find no basis in the statute for any such concern. Furthermore, our decision in Williams Electronics, Inc. v. Artic International, Inc., supra, laid to rest many of the doubts expressed by the district court. In 1976, after considerable study, Congress enacted a new copyright law to replace that which had governed since 1909. Act of October 19, 1976, Pub.L.No. 94-553, 90 Stat. 2541 (codified at 17 U.S.C. §§101 et seq.). Under the law, two primary requirements must be satisfied in order for a work to constitute copyrightable subject matter—it must be an "original wor[k] of authorship" and must be "fixed in [a] tangible medium of expression." 17 U.S.C. §102(a). . . .

Although section 102(a) does not expressly list computer programs as works of authorship, the legislative history suggests that programs were considered copyrightable as literary works. See H.R.Rep.No. 1476, 94th Cong., 2d Sess. 54, reprinted in 1976 U.S. Code Cong. & Ad. News 5659, 5667 ("'literary works' . . . includes . . . computer programs"). Because a Commission on New Technological Uses ("CONTU") had been created by Congress to study, inter alia, computer uses of copyrighted works, Pub.L.No. 93-573, §201, 88 Stat. 1873 (1974), Congress enacted a status quo provision, section 117, in the 1976 Act concerning such computer uses pending the CONTU report and recommendations.

The CONTU Final Report recommended that the copyright law be amended, inter alia, "to make it explicit that computer programs, to the extent that they embody an author's original creation, are proper subject matter of copyright." National Commission on New Technological Uses of Copyrighted Works, Final Report 1 (1979) [hereinafter CONTU Report].

CONTU recommended two changes relevant here: that section 117, the status quo provision, be repealed and replaced with a section limiting exclusive rights in computer programs so as "to ensure that rightful possessors of copies of computer programs may use or adapt these copies for their use," id.; and that a definition of computer program be added to section 101. Id. at 12. Congress adopted both changes. Act of Dec. 12, 1980, Pub.L.No. 96-517, §10, 94 Stat. 3015, 3028. The revisions embodied CONTU's recommendations to clarify the law of copyright of computer software. H.R.Rep.No. 1307, 96th Cong., 2d Sess. 23, reprinted in 1980 U.S. Code Cong. & Ad. News 6460, 6482.

The 1980 amendments added a definition of a computer program:

> A "computer program" is a set of statements or instructions to be used directly or indirectly in a computer in order to bring about a certain result.

17 U.S.C. §101. The amendments also substituted a new section 117 which provides that "it is not an infringement for the owner of a copy of a computer program to make or authorize the making of another copy or adaptation of that computer program" when necessary to "the utilization of the computer program" or "for archival purposes only." 17 U.S.C. §117. The parties agree that this section is not implicated in the instant lawsuit. The language of the provision, however, by carving out an exception to the normal proscriptions against copying, clearly indicates that programs are copyrightable and are otherwise afforded copyright protection.

We considered the issue of copyright protection for a computer program in Williams Electronics, Inc. v. Artic International, Inc., and concluded that "the copyrightability of computer programs is firmly established after the 1980 amendment to the Copyright Act." 685 F.2d at 875. At issue in *Williams* were not only two audiovisual copyrights to the "attract" and "play" modes of a video game, but also the computer program which was expressed in object code embodied in ROM and which controlled the sights and sounds of the game. Defendant there had argued "that when the issue is the copyright on a computer program, a distinction must be drawn between the "source code" version of a computer program, which . . . can be afforded copyright protection, and the "object code" stage, which . . . cannot be so protected," an argument we rejected. *Id.* at 876.

The district court here questioned whether copyright was to be limited to works "designed to be "read" by a human reader [as distinguished from] read by an expert with a microscope and patience", 545 F.Supp. at 821. The suggestion that copyrightability depends on a communicative function to individuals stems from the early decision of White-Smith Music Publishing Co. v. Apollo Co., 209 U.S. 1 (1908), which held a piano roll was not a copy of the musical composition because it was not in a form others, except perhaps for a very expert few, could perceive. See 1 Nimmer on Copyright §2.03[B][1] (1983). However, it is clear from the language of the 1976 Act and its legislative history that it was intended to obliterate distinctions engendered by White-Smith. H.R.Rep.No. 1476, supra, at 52, reprinted in 1976 U.S. Code Cong. & Ad. News at 5665.

Under the statute, copyright extends to works in any tangible means of expression "from which they can be perceived, reproduced, or otherwise communicated, either directly or with the aid of a machine or device." 17 U.S.C. §102(a). Further, the definition of "computer program" adopted by Congress in the 1980 amendments is "sets of statements or instructions to be used directly or indirectly in a computer in order to bring about a certain result." 17 U.S.C. §101. As source code instructions must be translated into object code before the computer can act upon them, only instructions expressed in object code can be used "directly" by the computer. See Midway Manufacturing Co. v. Strohon, No. 82 C 1305, slip op. at 25-26 (N.D.Ill. June 1, 1983). This definition was adopted following the CONTU Report in which the majority clearly took the position that object codes are proper subjects of copyright. See CONTU Report at 21. The majority's conclusion was reached although confronted by a dissent based upon the theory that the "machine-control phase" of a program is not directed at a human audience. See CONTU Report at 28-30 (dissent of Commissioner Hersey).

The defendant in *Williams* had also argued that a copyrightable work "must be intelligible to human beings and must be intended as a medium of communication to human beings," *id*. at 876-77. We reiterate the statement we made in *Williams* when we rejected that argument: "[t]he answer to defendant's contention is in the words of the statute itself." 685 F.2d at 877.

The district court also expressed uncertainty as to whether a computer program in object code could be classified as a "literary work."[7] However, the category of "literary works", one of the seven copyrightable categories, is not confined to literature in the nature of Hemingway's *For Whom the Bell Tolls*. The definition of "literary works" in section 101 includes expression not only in words but also "numbers, or other . . . numerical symbols or indicia", thereby expanding the common usage of "literary works." Cf. Harcourt, Brace & World, Inc. v. Graphic Controls Corp., 329 F.Supp. 517, 523-24 (S.D.N.Y. 1971) (the symbols designating questions or response spaces on exam answer sheets held to be copyrightable "writings" under 1909 Act); Reiss v. National Quotations Bureau, Inc., 276 F. 717 (S.D.N.Y. 1921) (code book of coined words designed for cable use copyrightable). Thus a computer program, whether in object

---

7. The district court stated that a programmer working directly in object code appears to think more as a mathematician or engineer, that the process of constructing a chip is less a work of authorship than the product of engineering knowledge, and that it may be more apt to describe an encoded ROM as a pictorial three-dimensional object than as a literary work. 545 F.Supp. at 821-22. The district court's remarks relied in part on a quotation about "microcode", see id. at 821 n.14; Apple introduced testimony that none of the works in suit contain "microcode." Moreover, Apple does not seek to protect the ROM's architecture but only the program encoded upon it.

code or source code, is a "literary work" and is protected from unauthorized copying, whether from its object or source code version. *Accord* Midway Mfg. Co. v. Strohon, slip op. at 25-27; see also GCA Corp. v. Chance, 217 U.S.P.A. at 719-20.

B. Copyrightability of a Computer Program Embedded on a ROM

Just as the district court's suggestion of a distinction between source code and object code was rejected by our opinion in *Williams* issued three days after the district court opinion, so also was its suggestion that embodiment of a computer program on a ROM, as distinguished from in a traditional writing, detracts from its copyrightability. In *Williams* we rejected the argument that "a computer program is not infringed when the program is loaded into electronic memory devices (ROMs) and used to control the activity of machines." 685 F.2d at 876. Defendant there had argued that there can be no copyright protection for the ROMs because they are utilitarian objects or machine parts. We held that the statutory requirement of "fixation", the manner in which the issue arises, is satisfied through the embodiment of the expression in the ROM devices. Id. at 874, 876; see also Midway Mfg. Co. v. Strohon, slip op. at 27-30; Tandy Corp. v. Personal Micro Computers, Inc., 524 F.Supp. at 173; cf. Stern Electronics, Inc. v. Kaufman, 669 F.2d 852, 855-56 (2d Cir. 1982) (audiovisual display of video game "fixed" in ROM). Therefore we reaffirm that a computer program in object code embedded in a ROM chip is an appropriate subject of copyright. See also Note, Copyright Protection of Computer Program Object Code, 96 Harv.L.Rev. 1723 (1983); Note, Copyright Protection for Computer Programs in Read Only Memory Chips, 11 Hofstra L.Rev. 329 (1982).

C. Copyrightability of Computer Operating System Programs

We turn to the heart of Franklin's position on appeal which is that computer operating system programs, as distinguished from application programs, are not the proper subject of copyright "regardless of the language or medium in which they are fixed." Apple suggests that this issue too is foreclosed by our *Williams* decision because some portion of the program at issue there was in effect an operating system program. Franklin is correct that this was not an issue raised by the parties in *Williams* and it was not considered by the court. Thus we consider it as a matter of first impression.

Franklin contends that operating system programs are per se excluded from copyright protection under the express terms of section 102(b) of the

Copyright Act, and under the precedent and underlying principles of Baker v. Selden, 101 U.S. 99 (1879). These separate grounds have substantial analytic overlap. . . .

1. "Process", "System" or "Method of Operation"

Franklin argues that an operating system program is either a "process", "system", or "method of operation" and hence uncopyrightable. Franklin correctly notes that underlying section 102(b) and many of the statements for which Baker v. Selden is cited is the distinction which must be made between property subject to the patent law, which protects discoveries, and that subject to copyright law, which protects the writings describing such discoveries. However, Franklin's argument misapplies that distinction in this case. Apple does not seek to copyright the method which instructs the computer to perform its operating functions but only the instructions themselves. The method would be protected, if at all, by the patent law, an issue as yet unresolved. See Diamond v. Diehr, 450 U.S. 175 (1981).

Franklin's attack on operating system programs as "methods" or "processes" seems inconsistent with its concession that application programs are an appropriate subject of copyright. Both types of programs instruct the computer to do something. Therefore, it should make no difference for purposes of section 102(b) whether these instructions tell the computer to help prepare an income tax return (the task of an application program) or to translate a high level language program from source code into its binary language object code form (the task of an operating system program such as "Applesoft", . . .). Since it is only the instructions which are protected, a "process" is no more involved because the instructions in an operating system program may be used to activate the operation of the computer than it would be if instructions were written in ordinary English in a manual which described the necessary steps to activate an intricate complicated machine. There is, therefore, no reason to afford any less copyright protection to the instructions in an operating system program than to the instructions in an application program.

Franklin's argument, receptively treated by the district court, that an operating system program is part of a machine mistakenly focuses on the physical characteristics of the instructions. But the medium is not the message. We have already considered and rejected aspects of this contention in the discussion of object code and ROM. The mere fact that the operating system program may be etched on a ROM does not make the program either a machine, part of a machine or its equivalent. Furthermore, as one of Franklin's witnesses testified, an operating system does not have to be permanently in the machine in ROM, but it may be on some other medium, such as a diskette or magnetic tape, where it could be readily transferred into the temporary memory space of the computer. In fact, some of the operating systems at issue were on diskette. As the CONTU majority stated,

> Programs should no more be considered machine parts than videotapes should be considered parts of projectors or phonorecords parts of sound re-production equipment. . . . That the words of a program are used ultimately in the implementation of a process should in no way affect their copy-rightability.

CONTU Report at 21.

Franklin also argues that the operating systems cannot be copyrighted because they are "purely utilitarian works" and that Apple is seeking to block the use of the art embodied in its operating systems. This argument stems from the following dictum in Baker v. Selden:

> The very object of publishing a book on science or the useful arts is to com-municate to the world the useful knowledge which it contains. But this object would be frustrated if the knowledge could not be used without incurring the guilt of piracy of the book. And where the art it teaches cannot be used with-out employing the methods and diagrams used to illustrate the book, or such as are similar to them, such methods and diagrams are to be considered as necessary incidents to the art, and given therewith to the public; not given for the purpose of publication in other works explanatory of the art, but for the purpose of practical application.

101 U.S. at 103. We cannot accept the expansive reading given to this language by some courts, see, e.g., Taylor Instrument Companies v. Fawley-Brost Co., 139 F.2d 98 (7th Cir. 1943), *cert. denied*, 321 U.S. 785 (1944). In this respect we agree with the views expressed by Professor Nimmer in his treatise. See 1 Nimmer on Copyright §2.18[C].

Although a literal construction of this language could support Frank-lin's reading that precludes copyrightability if the copyrighted work is put to a utilitarian use, that interpretation has been rejected by a later Supreme Court decision. In Mazer v. Stein, 347 U.S. 201, 218 (1954), the Court stated: "We find nothing in the copyright statute to support the argument that the intended use or use in industry of an article eligible for copyright bars or invalidates its registration. We do not read such a limitation into the copyright law." *Id*. at 218. The CONTU majority also rejected the expansive view some courts have given Baker v. Selden, and stated, "That the words of a program are used ultimately in the implementation of a process should in no way affect their copyrightability." *Id*. at 21. It referred to "copyright practice past and present, which recognizes copyright protection for a work of authorship regardless of the uses to which it may be put." *Id*. The Commission continued: "The copyright status of the written rules for a game or a system for the operation of a machine is unaffected by the fact that those rules direct the actions of those who play the game or carry out the process." *Id*. As we previously noted, we can consider the CONTU Report as accepted by Congress since Congress wrote into the law the majority's recommendations almost verbatim. See 18 Cong.Rec. H10767 (daily ed. Nov. 17, 1980) (Rep. Kastenmeier: Bill "eliminates confusion about the legal status of computer software by enacting the recommendations of [CONTU] clarifying the law of copyright of computer software"); 18 Cong.Rec. S14766 (daily ed. Nov. 20, 1980) (Sen. Bayh: "[t]his language reflects that proposed by [CONTU"]).

Perhaps the most convincing item leading us to reject Franklin's argument is that the statutory definition of a computer program as a set of instructions to be used in a computer in order to bring about a certain result, 17 U.S.C. §101, makes no distinction between application programs and operating programs. Franklin can point to no decision which adopts the distinction it seeks to make. In the one other reported case to have considered it, Apple Computer, Inc. v. Formula International, Inc., 562 F.Supp. 775 (C.D.Cal. 1983), the court reached the same conclusion which we do, i.e. that an operating system program is not per se precluded from copyright. It stated, "There is nothing in any of the statutory terms which suggest a different result for different types of computer programs based upon the function they serve within the machine." *Id.* at 780. Other courts have also upheld the copyrightability of operating programs without discussion of this issue. See Tandy Corp. v. Personal Micro Computers, Inc., 524 F.Supp. at 173 (input-output routine stored in ROM which translated input into machine language in a similar fashion as Applesoft and Apple Integer Basic proper subject of copyright); GCA Corp. v. Chance, 217 U.S.P.Q. at 719-20 (object code version of registered source code version of operating programs is the same work and protected).

2. Idea/Expression Dichotomy

Franklin's other challenge to copyright of operating system programs relies on the line which is drawn between ideas and their expression. Baker v. Selden remains a benchmark in the law of copyright for the reading given it in Mazer v. Stein, supra, where the Court stated, "Unlike a patent, a copyright gives no exclusive right to the art disclosed; protection is given only to the expression of the idea—not the idea itself." 347 U.S. at 217 (footnote omitted).

The expression/idea dichotomy is now expressly recognized in section 102(b) which precludes copyright for "any idea." This provision was not intended to enlarge or contract the scope of copyright protection but "to restate . . . that the basic dichotomy between expression and idea remains unchanged." H.R.Rep.No. 1476, supra, at 57, reprinted in 1976 U.S. Code Cong. & Ad. News at 5670. The legislative history indicates that section 102(b) was intended "to make clear that the expression adopted by the programmer is the copyrightable element in a computer program, and that the actual processes or methods embodied in the program are not within the scope of the copyright law." *Id.*

Many of the courts which have sought to draw the line between an idea and expression have found difficulty in articulating where it falls. See, e.g., Nichols v. Universal Pictures Corp., 45 F.2d 119, 121 (2d Cir. 1930) (L. Hand, J.); see discussion in 3 Nimmer on Copyright §13.03[A]. We believe that in the context before us, a program for an operating system, the line must be a pragmatic one, which also keeps in consideration "the preservation of the balance between competition and protection reflected in the patent and copyright laws". Herbert Rosenthal Jewelry Corp. v. Kalpakian, 446 F.2d 738, 742 (9th Cir. 1971). As we stated in Franklin Mint Corp. v. National Wildlife Art Exchange, Inc., 575 F.2d 62, 64 (3d Cir.), *cert. denied*, 439 U.S. 880 (1978), "Unlike a patent, a copyright protects originality rather than novelty or invention." In that opinion, we quoted approvingly the following passage from Dymow v. Bolton, 11 F.2d 690, 691 (2d Cir. 1926):

> Just as a patent affords protection only to the means of reducing an inventive idea to practice, so the copyright law protects the means of expressing an idea; and it is as near the whole truth as generalization can usually reach that, if the same idea can be expressed in a plurality of totally different manners, a plurality of copyrights may result, and no infringement will exist.

We adopt the suggestion in the above language and thus focus on whether the idea is capable of various modes of expression. If other programs can be written or created which perform the same function as an Apple's operating system program, then that program is an expression of the idea and hence copyrightable. In essence, this inquiry is no different than that made to determine whether the expression and idea have merged, which has been stated to occur where there are no or few other ways of expressing a particular idea. See, e.g., Morrissey v. Procter & Gamble Co., 379 F.2d 675, 678-79 (1st Cir. 1967); Freedman v. Grolier Enterprises, Inc., 179 U.S.P.Q. 476, 478 (S.D.N.Y. 1973) ("[c]opyright protection will not be given to a form of expression necessarily dictated by the underlying subject matter"); CONTU Report at 20.

The district court made no findings as to whether some or all of Apple's operating programs represent the only means of expression of the idea underlying them. Although there seems to be a concession by Franklin that at least some of the programs can be rewritten, we do not believe that the record on that issue is so clear that it can be decided at the appellate level. Therefore, if the issue is pressed on remand, the necessary finding can be made at that time.

Franklin claims that whether or not the programs can be rewritten, there are a limited "number of ways to arrange operating systems to enable a computer to run the vast body of Apple-compatible software". This claim has no pertinence to either the idea/expression dichotomy or merger. The idea which may merge with the expression, thus making the copyright unavailable, is the idea which is the subject of the expression. The idea of one of the operating system programs is, for example, how to translate source code into object code. If other methods of expressing that idea are not foreclosed as a practical matter, then there is no merger. Franklin may wish to achieve total compatibility with independently developed application programs written for the Apple II, but that is a commercial and competitive objective which does not enter into the somewhat metaphysical issue of whether particular ideas and expressions have merged.

In summary, Franklin's contentions that operating system programs are per se not copyrightable is unpersuasive. The other courts before whom this issue has been raised have rejected the distinction. Neither the CONTU majority nor Congress made a distinction between operating and application programs. We believe that the 1980 amendments reflect Congress' receptivity to new technology and its desire to encourage, through the copyright laws, continued imagination and creativity in computer programming. Since we believe that the district court's decision on the preliminary injunction was, to a large part, influenced by an erroneous view of the availability of copyright for operating system programs and unnecessary concerns about object code and ROMs, we must reverse the denial of the preliminary injunction and remand for reconsideration. . . .

V.

For the reasons set forth in this opinion, we will reverse the denial of the preliminary injunction and remand to the district court for further proceedings in accordance herewith.

COMMENTS AND QUESTIONS

1. Is there any legal basis for drawing a distinction between operating system code and application program code? What would be the policy basis for such a distinction? Are there any drawbacks to such an approach?

2. The court rejects the contention that object code (the actual implementation of the program in 1s and 0s in magnetic memory or on a circuit) cannot itself be copyrightable. The idea that object code is copyrightable is not terribly controversial today. In part, copyrightability of object code stems from what might be thought a slippery-slope argument: that since source code is copyrightable and since source code can readily be translated into object code, object code must also be copyrightable. See Dan L. Burk, Software as Speech, 8 Seton Hall Const. L.J. 683, 687-688 (1998) (discussing this rationale).

But this argument has some troubling implications. One of the fundamental rules of computing is that anything that can be implemented in software can in principle be implemented in hardware too. Indeed, "software" itself is nothing more than a temporary (rather than permanent) way of ordering circuit switches in hardware. So if object code is copyrightable, why not more permanent instantiations in hardware—the microcode instructions embedded in computer chips, for example, or the layout of a circuit board itself?

Copyright law does sometimes protect the design elements of utilitarian objects: the sculpture/lamp of Mazer v. Stein, cited in *Apple*, is a prominent example. But while courts have had difficulty at times separating the artistic from the utilitarian, they have steadfastly refused to extend copyright protection to the utilitarian aspects of three dimensional objects such as lamps, jewelry, and mannequins. Protecting object code and microcode raises many of the same troubling issues. How should courts separate the unprotectable utilitarian aspects of a computer program from the protectable expressive aspects? We see how the courts have dealt with this issue in the sections that follow.

3. The court also holds that operating system programs—as distinct from applications programs—are copyrightable. This conclusion has been universally followed by subsequent decisions. There is no question today that computer programs of any type can be copyrighted as long as they contain original expression. Of course, as the court's references to Baker v. Selden make clear, copyright in any computer program will not extend to ideas or methods embodied in that program.

But *should* we treat operating systems just like applications programs? There are arguably some important differences between the two. First, operating systems are designed to communicate with other computer elements, not with people. Some scholars have suggested that the absence of a "communicative function" should render an operating system uncopyrightable. See, e.g., David Luettgen, Functional Usefulness vs. Communicative Usefulness: Thin Copyright Protection for the Nonliteral Elements of Computer Programs, 4 Tex. Intell. Prop. L.J. 233 (1996). But the 1976 Copyright Act seems to reject this argument, offering protection to works even if they can be perceived or reproduced only with the aid of a computer or other device.

Still, one might reasonably suggest that there is a difference between a videotape or CD, which encodes information that can only be read by a machine but that the machine translates into words, pictures, or sounds that people can understand, and an operating system component that *never* communicates information to a human recipient. Does it make sense to extend copyright protection to the latter sorts of programs?

Commissioner Hersey, in his dissent to the CONTU Report, highlighted the fact that computer "[p]rograms are profoundly different from the various forms of 'works of authorship' secured under the Constitution by copyright. Works of authorship have always been intended to be circulated to human beings and to used by them—to be read, heard, or seen, for either pleasurable or practical ends. Computer programs, in their mature phase, are addressed to machines." Hersey argued that copyright protection should "not extend to a computer program in the form in which it is capable of being used to control computer operations." Do you agree with Hersey's critique of bringing computer software, in all of its forms, within the copyright law? Does the Constitution limit copyright protection for "works of authorship" solely to works intended to be directly "read, heard, or seen" by humans? Should protection for computer software be limited in this way? Would Hersey's proposed limitation on the scope of copyright protection for software better balance the social interests affected by legal protection for software? What might justify CONTU's decision to accord software full inclusion within the copyright law, irrespective of whether it is directed toward operating machines or communicating with humans?

For a detailed discussion of the problems raised by Commissioner Hersey in his dissent, see Pamela Samuelson, CONTU Revisited: The Case Against Copyright Protection for Computer Programs in Machine-Readable Form, 1984 Duke L.J. 663 (1984).

Second, the operating systems market is characterized by significant network effects. Operating systems markets tend towards standardization around a single product, because consumers benefit from using the same operating system that everyone else uses. Some scholars have suggested that strong copyright protection for operating systems is inappropriate because of these market characteristics. See Peter S. Menell, An Epitaph for Traditional Copyright Protection of Network Features of Computer Software, 43 Antitrust Bull. 651 (1998); Peter S. Menell, An Analysis of the Scope of Copyright Protection for Computer Programs, 41 Stan. L. Rev. 1045, 1101 (1989).

4. The *Apple* court concludes that the "idea" of Apple's operating system is to run the Apple computer, and that the particular way in which Apple runs its computer is protectable expression. Because it defines the idea of the program in very broad terms, the decision gives broad protection to Apple's operating system. In particular, the court rejects without serious consideration Franklin's claim that it has a right to produce "Apple-compatible" programs. This result is controversial for two different reasons. First, it gives a broad scope of protection to Apple's program. Second, it denies a right to reverse engineer in order to achieve compatibility. We return to both of these issues in greater detail in Sections B.3 and D.2. For a contrary result, see Control Data Systems, Inc. v. Infoware, Inc., 903 F. Supp. 1316 (D. Minn. 1995) (accepting defendant's argument that in making an emulation module, it necessarily had to copy elements of plaintiff's program).

5. Because object code consists only of a series of "on" and "off" switches in which data can be stored, the conclusion that object code falls within the subject matter of copyright means that not only computer

programs but *any* original expression stored as data in a computer is subject to copyright protection. Thus the discussion herein is important not only for those who program computers but for anyone who uses a computer to store any sort of data. We will discuss the implications of copyright protection for such "digital information" in more detail below.

PROBLEM

Problem 2-1. LETNI Corp. produces microprocessors, the central component of microcomputer systems. These "computers on a chip" are integrated circuits capable of performing arithmetic functions, manipulation of data, and other operations in response to object code instructions. At one time, LETNI's 684 microprocessor commanded a 70 percent market share of the microcomputer market. LETNI's 684 chip utilizes a single "bus" or path for transferring data. It features 512 lines of microcode, each of which is 21 bits long, that enable the microprocessor to interpret 133 assembly instructions.

CEN Corp., a competing microprocessor manufacturer, seeks to sell semiconductor chips capable of running the same software as LETNI's 684 microprocessor. A prior patent cross-licensing agreement entitles CEN to duplicate LETNI's 684 micro-architecture and hardware to the extent comprehended by the LETNI's patent. In order to increase processing speed and capability relative to LETNI's 684 chip, CEN designed its U2 microprocessor with a dual bus system and a larger micro instruction word size (29 bits). The 1,024 lines of microcode enable the microprocessor to interpret 156 assembly instructions. Five hundred fifty-two of these lines carry out the instruction set of the LETNI 684 microprocessor. The remaining lines perform other functions not carried out by the 684 chip. Because of the dual bus architecture and larger word size, CEN was able to write shorter and more efficient microcode.

Nonetheless, there were a number of similarities in the microcodes of the two microprocessors. LETNI brought suit, alleging: (1) microprograms are computer programs and hence protected by the Copyright Act; and (2) CEN's U2 microcode infringed the copyright of LETNI's 684 chip.

Applying the analysis of Apple v. Franklin, how should this case be resolved? Should microcode be copyrightable? If so, what should be the scope of protection?

Can a hardware manufacturer obtain copyright protection for the configuration of the hardwiring of its computer? If so, under what theory? If your answer is different from that for microcode, what explains the distinction?

2. Protection for Nonliteral Elements of Program Code

The Apple v. Franklin decision established an important baseline principle that exact copying of computer program code was copyright infringement. It was almost inevitable, however, that software developers would test whether copyright protection for computer programs would extend to other aspects of programs, such as their "look and feel" or their structure, sequence, and organization. This subsection explores how courts have assessed such claims for nonliteral copying of internal structural details of software design, user interface elements, or the interactive behavior of programs.

Whelan Associates, Inc. v. Jaslow Dental Laboratory, Inc.
United States Court of Appeals for the Third Circuit
797 F.2d 1222 (3d Cir. 1986)

BECKER, Circuit Judge.

This appeal involves a computer program for the operation of a dental laboratory, and calls upon us to apply the principles underlying our venerable copyright laws to the relatively new field of computer technology to determine the scope of copyright protection of a computer program. More particularly, in this case of first impression in the courts of appeals, we must determine whether the structure (or sequence and organization) of a computer program is protectible by copyright, or whether the protection of the copyright law extends only as far as the literal computer code. . . .

I. Factual Background

[Jaslow Dental Laboratory, Inc. (Jaslow Lab) hired Strohl Systems, Inc. (Strohl), a custom software firm, to develop a computer program that would organize the bookkeeping and administrative tasks of its business—manufacturing dental prosthetics and devices. The contract provided that Strohl could market the program to other dental laboratories after installation at Jaslow Lab, with Jaslow Lab receiving a 10% royalty. Strohl assigned the project to Elaine Whelan, an experienced programmer. After interviewing Jaslow Lab employees and studying the dental laboratory business, Whelan wrote a program called Dentalab in EDL (Event Driven Language), a computer language that ran on Jaslow Lab's IBM Series One computer.

Elaine Whelan subsequently left Strohl to form Whelan Associates, Inc. in order to pursue the market for Dentalab. Whelan Associates acquired Strohl's interest in Dentalab and entered into an agreement with

Jaslow Lab obliging Jaslow Lab to use its "best efforts and to act diligently in the marketing of the Dentalab package" and requiring Whelan Associates to "use its best efforts and to act diligently to improve and augment the previously successfully designed Dentalab package."

During the period of the agreement, Rand Jaslow, an officer and shareholder of Jaslow Lab, began development of the Dentcom PC program (Dentcom program), which performed the same functions as Dentalab but was written in the BASIC computer language, enabling it to run on a broader range of computers. Jaslow Lab subsequently ended the business relationship with Whelan Associates, formed Dentcom, Inc. to market dental laboratory software, and hired a professional computer programmer to complete the Dentcom program. Dentcom subsequently marketed the Dentalab and Dentcom programs, advertising the Dentcom program as "a new version of the Dentalab computer system."]

II. Procedural History

[On June 30, 1983, Jaslow Lab filed suit against Whelan Associates in state court alleging that Whelan Associates has misappropriated its trade secrets. Whelan Associates responded by filing this copyright action against Jaslow Lab, Dentcom, Inc., Rand Jaslow, and other officers of Dentcom in federal district court. The actions were consolidated in federal court.]

The principal witnesses were Elaine Whelan, Rand Jaslow, and two expert witnesses, Dr. Thomas Moore for Whelan Associates and Stephen Ness on behalf of the defendants. Whelan and Jaslow testified about the dealings and negotiations between the parties. Dr. Moore and Mr. Ness examined the programs and testified about the programs' similarities and differences. Dr. Moore testified that although the Dentcom program was not a translation of the Dentlab system, the programs were similar in three significant respects. He testified that most of the file structures, and the screen outputs, of the programs were virtually identical. He also testified that five particularly important "subroutines" within both programs— order entry, invoicing, accounts receivable, end of day procedure, and end of month procedure—performed almost identically in both programs. Mr. Ness compared the source and object codes of the Dentalab, Dentcom, and Datamaster programs, and testified at length about the many ways that the programs differed from one another. He concluded that "substantive differences in programming style, in programming structure, in algorithms and data structures, all indicate that the Dentcom system is not directly derived from either of the other systems." In his written report, however, which was entered into evidence, Mr. Ness conceded that the Dentalab and Dentcom programs had "overall structural similarities."

The district court ruled for Whelan Associates. . . .

III. Technological Background . . .

The creation of a program often takes place in several steps, moving from the general to the specific. Because programs are intended to accomplish particular tasks, the first step in creating the program is identifying the problem that the computer programmer is trying to solve. In this case, Rand Jaslow went to Strohl and stated that his problem was record-keeping for his business. Although this was an accurate statement of the problem, it was not specific enough to guide Elaine Whelan. Before she could write the Dentalab program, she needed to know more about Jaslow Lab's business—how orders were processed, what special billing problems might arise, how inventory might be correlated to orders, and other characteristics of the dental prosthetics trade.

As the programmer learns more about the problem, she or he may begin to outline a solution. The outline can take the form of a flowchart, which will break down the solution into a series of smaller units called "subroutines" or "modules," each of which deals with elements of the larger problem. See Note, Defining of Scope of Copyright Protection for Computer Software, 38 Stan. L. Rev. 497, 500-01 (1986). A program's efficiency depends in large part on the arrangements of its modules and subroutines. Although two programs could produce the same result, one might be more efficient because of different internal arrangements of modules and subroutines. Because efficiency is a prime concern in computer programs (an efficient program being obviously more valuable than a comparatively inefficient one), the arrangement of modules and subroutines is a critical factor for any programmer. In the present case, the Dentalab program had numerous modules pertaining to inventory, accounts receivable, various dentist-patient matters, and payroll, among others. Some of the modules were simple; others were quite complex and involved fairly elaborate logical development.

As the program structure is refined, the programmer must make decisions about what data is needed, where along the program's operations the data should be introduced, how the data should be inputted, and how it should be combined with other data. The arrangement of the data is accomplished by means of data files . . . and is affected by the details of the programs' subroutines and modules, for different arrangements of subroutines and modules may require data in different forms. Once again, there are numerous ways the programmer can solve the data-organization problems she or he faces. Each solution may have particular characteristics —efficiencies or inefficiencies, conveniences or quirks—that differentiate it from other solutions and make the overall program more or less desirable. Because the Dentalab program was intended to handle all of the business-related aspects of a dental laboratory, it had to accommodate and interrelate many different pieces and types of data including patients' names, dentists' names, inventory, accounts receivable, accounts payable, and payroll.

Once the detailed design of the program is complete, the coding begins. Each of the steps identified in the design must be turned into a language that the computer can understand. . . .

As this brief summary demonstrates, the coding process is a comparatively small part of programming. By far the larger portion of the expense and difficulty in creating computer programs is attributable to the development of the structure and logic of the program, and to debugging, documentation and maintenance, rather than to the coding. See Frank, Critical Issues in Software 22 (1983) (only 20% of the cost of program development goes into coding); Zelkowitz, Perspective on Software Engineering, 10 Computing Surveys 197-216 (June, 1978). See also InfoWorld, Nov. 11, 1985 at 13 ("the 'look and feel' of a computer software product often involves much more creativity and often is of greater commercial value than the program code which implements the product . . ."). The evidence in this case is that Ms. Whelan spent a tremendous amount of time studying Jaslow Labs, organizing the modules and subroutines for the Dentalab program, and working out the data arrangements, and a comparatively small amount of time actually coding the Dentalab program.

IV. Legal Background . . .

B. *The appropriate test for substantial similarity in computer program cases*—The leading case of Arnstein v. Porter, 154 F.2d 464, 468-69 (2d Cir. 1946), suggested a bifurcated substantial similarity test whereby a finder of fact makes two findings of substantial similarity to support a copyright violation. First, the fact-finder must decide whether there is sufficient similarity between the two works in question to conclude that the alleged infringer used the copyrighted work in making his own. On this issue, expert testimony may be received to aid the trier of fact. (This is called the "extrinsic" test of substantial similarity. Sid & Marty Krofft Television Prods, Inc. v. McDonald's Corp., 562 F.2d at 1164-65.) Second, if the answer to the first question is in the affirmative, the fact-finder must decide without the aid of expert testimony, but with the perspective of the "lay observer," whether the copying was "illicit," or "an unlawful appropriation" of the copyrighted work. (This is called an "intrinsic" test of substantial similarity. *Id.*) The *Arnstein* test has been adopted in this circuit. See *Universal Athletic Sales Co.*, 511 F.2d at 907.

The district court heard expert testimony. It did not bifurcate its analysis, however, but made only a single finding of substantial similarity. See Whelan Associates v. Jaslow Dental Laboratory, 609 F. Supp. at 1321-22. It would thus appear to have contravened the law of this circuit. Nevertheless, for the reasons that follow, we believe that the district court applied an appropriate standard.

The ordinary observer test, which was developed in cases involving novels, plays, and paintings, and which does not permit expert testimony, is of doubtful value in cases involving computer programs on account of the programs' complexity and unfamiliarity to most members of the public. See Note, Copyright Infringement of Computer Programs: A Modification of the Substantial Similarity Test, 68 Minn. L. Rev. 1264, 1285-88 (1984). Cf. Note, Copyright Infringement Actions: The Proper Role for Audience Reactions in Determining Substantial Similarity, 54 S. Cal. L. Rev. 385 (1981) (criticizing lay observer standard when objects in question are intended for particular, identifiable audiences). Moreover, the distinction between the two parts of the *Arnstein* test may be of doubtful value when the finder of fact is the same person for each step: that person has been exposed to expert evidence in the first step, yet she or he is supposed to ignore or "forget" that evidence in analyzing the problem under the second step. Especially in complex cases, we doubt that the "forgetting" can be effective when the expert testimony is essential to even the most fundamental understanding of the objects in question.

On account of these problems with the standard, we believe that the ordinary observer test is not useful and is potentially misleading when the subjects of the copyright are particularly complex, such as computer programs. We therefore join the growing number of courts which do not apply the ordinary observer test in copyright cases involving exceptionally difficult materials, like computer programs, but instead adopt a single substantial similarity inquiry according to which both lay and expert testimony would be admissible. See E.F. Johnson Co. v. Uniden Corp., 623 F. Supp. 1485, 1493 (D. Minn. 1985). . . . That was the test applied by the district court in this case. . . .

V. The Scope of Copyright Protection of Computer Programs

It is well, though recently, established that copyright protection extends to a program's source and object codes. Stern Elecs., Inc. v. Kaufman, 669 F.2d 852, 855 n.3 (2d Cir. 1982) (source code); Apple Computer, Inc. v. Franklin Computer Corp., 714 F.2d 1240, 1246-47 (3d Cir. 1983) (source and object code), cert. dismissed, 464 U.S. 1033, 104 S. Ct. 690, 79 L. Ed. 2d 158 (1984); Williams Elecs., Inc. v. Artic International, Inc. 685 F.2d 870 (3d Cir. 1982) (object code). In this case, however, the district court did not find any copying of the source or object codes, nor did the plaintiff allege such copying. Rather, the district court held that the Dentalab copyright was infringed because the overall structure of Dentcom was substantially similar to the overall structure of Dentalab. Whelan Associates v. Jaslow Dental Laboratory, 609 F. Supp. at 1321-22. The question therefore arises whether mere similarity in the overall structure of programs can be the basis for a copyright infringement, or, put differently, whether a program's copyright protection covers the structure of the program or only the program's literal elements, i.e., its source and object codes.

Title 17 U.S.C. §102(a)(1) extends copyright protection to "literary works," and computer programs are classified as literary works for the purposes of copyright. See H.R. Rep. No. 1476, 94th Cong., 2d Sess. 54, reprinted in 1976 U.S. Code Cong. & Ad. News 5659, 5667. The copyrights of other literary works can be infringed even when there is no substantial similarity between the works' literal elements. One can violate the copyright of a play or book by copying its plot or plot devices. See, e.g., Twentieth Century-Fox Film Corp. v. MCA, Inc., 715 F.2d 1327, 1329 (9th Cir. 1983) (13 alleged distinctive plot similarities between Battlestar Galactica and Star Wars may be basis for a finding of copyright violation): *Sid & Marty Krofft Television Productions, Inc.*, 562 F.2d at 1167 (similarities between McDonaldland characters and H.R. Pufnstuf characters can be established by "'total concept and feel'" of the two productions (quoting Roth Greeting Cards v. United Card Co., 429 F.2d 1106, 1110 (9th Cir. 1970)); Sheldon v. Metro-Goldwyn Pictures Corp., 81 F.2d 49, 54-55 (1936); Nichols v. Universal Pictures Corp., 45 F.2d 119, 121 (2d Cir. 1930) (copyright "cannot be limited literally to the text, else a plagiarist would escape by immaterial variations"). By analogy to other literary works, it would thus appear that the copyrights of computer programs can be infringed even absent copying of the literal elements of the program. Defendants contend, however, that what is true of other literary works is not true of computer programs. They assert two principal reasons, which we consider in turn.

A. Section 102(b) and the dichotomy between idea and expression—It is axiomatic that copyright does not protect ideas, but only expressions of ideas. . . .

Defendants argue that the structure of a computer program is, by definition, the idea and not the expression of the idea, and therefore that the structure cannot be protected by the program copyright. Under the defendants' approach, any other decision would be contrary to §102(b). We divide our consideration of this argument into two parts. First, we examine the caselaw concerning the distinction between idea and expression, and derive from it a rule for distinguishing idea from expression in the context of computer programs. We then apply that rule to the facts of this case.

1. A rule for distinguishing idea from expression in computer programs —It is frequently difficult to distinguish the idea from the expression thereof. No less an authority than Learned Hand, after a career that included writing some of the leading copyright opinions, concluded that the distinction will "inevitably be ad hoc." Peter Pan Fabrics, Inc. v. Martin Weiner Corp., 274 F.2d 487, 489 (2d Cir. 1960). See also

Knowles & Palmeri, Dissecting Krofft: An Expression of New Ideas in Copyright?, 8 San. Fern. Val. L. Rev. 109, 126 (1980) (arguing that there can be no meaningful distinction between idea and expression). Although we acknowledge the wisdom of Judge Hand's remark, we feel that a review of relevant copyright precedent will enable us to formulate a rule applicable in this case. In addition, precisely because the line between idea and expression is elusive, we must pay particular attention to the pragmatic considerations that underlie the distinction and copyright law generally. In this regard, we must remember that the purpose of the copyright law is to create the most efficient and productive balance between protection (incentive) and dissemination of information, to promote learning, culture and development. See U.S. Const. Art. I §8 cl. 8 (Copyright Clause) (giving Congress the power to "promote the Progress of Science and useful Arts").[27] . . .

The Court's test in Baker v. Selden suggests a way to distinguish idea from expression. Just as Baker v. Selden focused on the end sought to be achieved by Selden's book, the line between idea and expression may be drawn with reference to the end sought to be achieved by the work in question. In other words, *the purpose or function of a utilitarian work would be the work's idea, and everything that is not necessary to that purpose or function would be part of the expression of the idea.* Cf. Apple Computer, Inc. v. Formula Int'l, Inc., 562 F. Supp. 775, 783 (C.D. Cal. 1983) ("Apple seeks here not to protect ideas (i.e. making the machine perform particular functions) but rather to protect their particular *expressions . . .*"), *aff'd*, 725 F.2d 521 (9th Cir. 1984). Where there are various means of achieving the desired purpose, then the particular means chosen is not necessary to the purpose; hence, there is expression, not idea.[28]

Consideration of copyright doctrines related to *scenes a faire* and fact-intensive works supports our formulation, for they reflect the same underlying principle. *Scenes a faire* are "incidents, characters or settings

27. Achieving the proper incentive has been a longstanding task of courts. See, e.g., Sayre v. Moore, 102 Eng. Rep. 138, 140 n.6 (1785) (Lord Manfield):

> [W]e must take care to guard against two extremes equally prejudicial; the one, that men of ability, who have employed their time for the service of the community, may not be deprived of their just merits, and the reward for their ingenuity and labour; the other, that the world may not be deprived of improvements, nor the progress of the arts be retarded.

See also Twentieth Century Music Corp. v. Aiken, 422 U.S. 151, 156, 45 L. Ed. 2d 84, 95 S. Ct. 2040 (1975); Apple Computer, 714 F.2d at 1253 (Sloviter, J.) ("the line must be a pragmatic one, which also keeps in consideration 'the preservation of the balance between competition and protection reflected in the patent and copyright laws.'" (quoting Herbert Rosenthal Jewelry Corp. v. Kalpakian, 446 F.2d 738, 742 (9th Cir. 1971)).

28. This test is necessarily difficult to state, and it may be difficult to understand in the abstract. It will become more clear as we discuss and explain it in the textual discussion that follows this footnote. See also infra (discussion of the copyrightability of file structures that raise many of the issues considered here). As will be seen, see infra, the idea of the Dentalab program was the efficient management of a dental laboratory (which presumably has significantly different requirements from those of other businesses). Because that idea could be accomplished in a number of different ways with a number of different structures, the structure of the Dentalab program is part of the program's expression, not its idea.

which are as a practical matter indispensable . . . in the treatment of a given topic." Atari, Inc. v. North American Philips Consumer Elecs. Corp., 672 F.2d 607, 616 (7th Cir.), *cert. denied,* 459 U.S. 880, 74 L. Ed. 2d 145, 103 S. Ct. 176 (1982). See also See v. Durang, 711 F.2d 141, 143 (9th Cir. 1983). It is well-settled doctrine that *scenes a faire* are afforded no copyright protection.

Scenes a faire are afforded no protection because the subject matter represented can be expressed in no other way than through the particular scene a faire. Therefore, granting a copyright "would give the first author a monopoly on the commonplace ideas behind the scenes a faire." Landsberg v. Scrabble Crossword Game Players, Inc., 736 F.2d at 489. This is merely a restatement of the hypothesis advanced above, that the purpose or function of a work or literary device is part of that device's "idea" (unprotectible portion). It follows that anything necessary to effecting that function is also, necessarily, part of the idea, too.

Fact intensive works are given similarly limited copyright coverage. See, e.g., *Landsberg,* 736 F.2d at 488; Miller v. Universal City Studios, Inc., 650 F.2d 1365, 1372 (5th Cir. 1981). Once again, the reason appears to be that there are only a limited number of ways to express factual material, and therefore the purpose of the literary work—telling a truthful story—can be accomplished only by employing one of a limited number of devices. *Landsberg,* 736 F.2d at 488. Those devices therefore belong to the idea, not the expression, of the historical or factual work.

Although the economic implications of this rule are necessarily somewhat speculative, we nevertheless believe that the rule would advance the basic purpose underlying the idea/expression distinction, "the preservation of the balance between competition and protection reflected in the patent and copyright laws." Herbert Rosenthal Jewelry Corp. v. Kalpakian, 446 F.2d 738, 742 (9th Cir. 1971); see also *Apple Computer,* 714 F.2d at 1253 (quoting *Kalpakian*); supra n.27. As we stated above . . . , among the more significant costs in computer programming are those attributable to developing the structure and logic of the program. The rule proposed here, which allows copyright protection beyond the literal computer code, would provide the proper incentive for programmers by protecting their most valuable efforts, while not giving them a stranglehold over the development of new computer devices that accomplish the same end.

The principal economic argument used against this position—used, that is, in support of the position that programs' literal elements are the only parts of the programs protected by the copyright law—is that computer programs are so intricate, each step so dependent on all of the other steps, that they are almost impossible to copy except literally, and that anyone who attempts to copy the structure of a program without copying its literal elements must expend a tremendous amount of effort and creativity. In the works of one commentator: "One cannot simply 'approximate' the entire copyrighted computer program and create a similar operative program without the expenditure of almost the same amount of time as the original programmer expended." Note, 68 Minn. L. Rev. at 1290 (footnote omitted). According to this argument, such work should not be discouraged or penalized. A further argument against our position is not economic but jurisprudential; another commentator argues that the concept of structure in computer programs is too vague to be useful in copyright cases. Radcliffe, Recent Developments in Copyright Law Related to Computer Software, 4 Computer L. Rep. 189, 194-97 (1985). He too would therefore appear to advocate limiting copyright protection to programs' literal codes.

Neither of the two arguments just described is persuasive. The first argument fails for two reasons. In the first place, it is simply not true that "approximation" of a program short of perfect reproduction is valueless. To the contrary, one can approximate a program and thereby gain a significant advantage over competitors even though additional work is needed to complete the program. Second, the fact that it will take a great deal of effort to copy a copyrighted work does not mean that the copier is not a copyright infringer. The issue in a copyrighted case is simply whether the copyright holder's expression has been copied, not how difficult it was to do the copying. Whether an alleged infringer spent significant time and effort to copy an original work is therefore irrelevant to whether he has pirated the expression of an original work.

As to the second argument, it is surely true that limiting copyright protection to computers' literal codes would be simpler and would yield more definite answers than does our answer here. Ease of application is not, however, a sufficient counterweight to the considerations we have adduced on behalf of our position.

Finally, one commentator argues that the process of development and progress in the field of computer programming is significantly different from that in other fields, and therefore requires a particularly restricted application of the copyright law. According to this argument, progress in the area of computer technology is achieved by means of "stepping-stones," a process that "requires plagiarizing in some manner the underlying copyrighted work." Note, 68 Minn. L. Rev. at 1292 (footnote omitted). As a consequence, this commentator argues, giving computer programs too much copyright protection will retard progress in the field.

We are not convinced that progress in computer technology or technique is qualitatively different from progress in other areas of science or the arts. In balancing protection and dissemination, the copyright law has always recognized and tried to accommodate the fact that all intellectual pioneers build on the work of their predecessors.[33] Thus, copyright principles derived from other areas are applicable in the field of computer programs.

---

33. Long before the first computer, Sir Issac Newton humbly explained that "if [he] had seen farther than other men, it was because [he] had stood on the shoulders of giants."

2. Application of the general rule to this case—The rule proposed here is certainly not problem-free. The rule has its greatest force in the analysis of utilitarian or "functional" works, for the purpose of such works is easily stated and identified. By contrast, in cases involving works of literature or "non-functional" visual representations, defining the purpose of the work may be difficult. Since it may be impossible to discuss the purpose or function of a novel, poem, sculpture or painting, the rule may have little or no application to cases involving such works. The present case presents no such difficulties, for it is clear that the purpose of the utilitarian Dentalab program was to aid in the business operations of a dental laboratory.[34] It is equally clear that the structure of the program was not essential to that task; there are other programs on the market, competitors of Dentalab and Dentcom, that perform the same functions but have different structures and designs.

This fact seems to have been dispositive for the district court:

> The mere idea or concept of a computerized program for operating a dental laboratory would not in and of itself be subject to copyright. Copyright law protects the manner in which the author expresses an idea or concept, but not the idea itself. Albert E. Price v. Metzner, 574 F. Supp. 281 (E.D. Pa. 1983). Copyrights do not protect ideas—only expressions of ideas. Universal Athletic Sales Co. v. Salkeld, 511 F.2d 904, 908 (3d Cir. 1975). There are many ways that the same data may be organized, assembled, held, retrieved and utilized by a computer. *Different computer systems may functionally serve similar purposes without being copies of each other. There is evidence in the record that there are other software programs for the business management of dental laboratories in competition with plaintiff's program. There is no contention that any of them infringe although they may incorporate many of the same ideas and functions.* The "expression of the idea" in a software computer program is the manner in which the program operates, controls and regulates the computer in receiving, assembling, calculating, retaining, correlating, and producing useful information either on a screen, print-out or by audio communication.

Whelan Associates v. Jaslow Laboratory, 609 F. Supp. at 1320 (emphasis added). We agree. The conclusion is thus inescapable that the detailed structure of the Dentalab program is part of the expression, not the idea, of that program. . . .

Our solution may put us at odds with Judge Patrick Higginbotham's scholarly opinion in Synercom Technology, Inc. v. University Computing Co., 462 F. Supp. 1003 (N.D. Tex. 1978), which dealt with the question whether the "input formats" of a computer program—the configurations

---

34. We do not mean to imply that the idea or purpose behind every utilitarian or functional work will be precisely what it accomplishes, and that structure and organization will therefore always be part of the expression of such works. The idea or purpose behind a utilitarian work may be to accomplish a certain function in a certain way, see, e.g., Baker v. Selden, 101 U.S. at 100 (referring to Selden's book as explaining "a peculiar system of book-keeping"), and the structure or function of a program might be essential to that task. There is no suggestion in the record, however, that the purpose of the Dentalab program was anything so refined; it was simply to run a dental laboratory in an efficient way.

and collations of the information entered into the program—were idea or expression. The court held that the input formats were ideas, not expressions, and thus not protectible. Synercom did not deal with precisely the materials at issue here—input formats are structurally simple as compared to full programs—and it may therefore be distinguishable. However, insofar as the input formats are devices for the organization of data into forms useful for computers, they are similar to programs: thus, Synercom is relevant and we must come to grips with it.

Central to Judge Higginbotham's analysis was his conviction that the organization and structure of the input formats was inseparable from the idea underlying the formats. Although the court acknowledged that in some cases structure and sequence might be part of expression, not idea, see *id.* at 1014, it stated that in the case of input formats, structure and organization were inherently part of the idea. The court put its position in the form of a powerful rhetorical question: "if sequencing and ordering [are] expression, what separable idea is being expressed?" *Id.* at 1013.

To the extent that *Synercom* rested on the premise that there was a difference between the copyrightability of sequence and form in the computer context and in any other context, we think that it is incorrect. As just noted, the Copyright Act of 1976 demonstrates that Congress intended sequencing and ordering to be protectible in the appropriate circumstances, and the computer field is not an exception to this general rule. Although Congress was aware that computer programs posed a novel set of issues and problems for the copyright law, Congress did not then make, and has not since made, any special provision for ordering and sequencing in the context of computer programs. There is thus no statutory basis for treating computer programs differently from other literary works in this regard.

Despite the fact that copyright protection extends to sequence and form in the computer context, unless we are able to answer Judge Higginbotham's powerful rhetorical question—"if sequencing and ordering [are] expression, what separable idea is being expressed?"—in our own case, we would have to hold that the structure of the Dentalab program is part of its idea and is thus not protectible by copyright. Our answer has already been given, however: the idea is the efficient organization of a dental laboratory (presumably, this poses different problems from the efficient organization of some other kinds of laboratories or businesses). Because there are a variety of program structures through which that idea can be expressed, the structure is not a necessary incident to that idea. . . .

VI. Evidence of Substantial Similarity

Defendants' second argument is that even if copyright protection is not limited to computer programs' literal elements as a matter of law, there is insufficient evidence of substantial similarity presented in this case to support a finding of copyright infringement. The defendants claim that all three parts of Dr. Moore's expert testimony as to the similarity of the programs, see supra, were flawed, and also that the district court erred in evaluating the relative weight of Dr. Moore's and Mr. Ness' testimony. We consider these arguments in turn.

A. *File structures*—Defendants claim that Dr. Moore's examination and conclusions with respect to file structures are irrelevant to the question whether there was a copyright violation. Defendants analogize files to blank forms, which contain no information but merely collect and organize information that is entered from another source. They argue, relying on Baker v. Selden, that, as a matter of law, blank forms cannot be copyrighted. Thus, they conclude, neither can file structures be part of the copyright of a program.

Defendants' description of the file structures is indeed correct. Dr. Moore himself described a computer's file as "a storage place for data, and it's really no different in a computer than it is in a file drawer, it's like a manila folder that contains all the data on a particular subject category in a computer." (Another analogy, particularly accessible to lawyers, is to a very complex cataloguing structure like the structure of Lexis or Westlaw without any entries yet made.) Defendants' legal conclusion is not correct, however. Although some courts have stated that the meaning of Baker v. Selden is that blank forms cannot be copyrighted, this circuit, like the majority of courts that have considered the issue, has rejected this position and instead have held that blank forms may be copyrighted if they are sufficiently innovative that their arrangement of information is itself informative. *Apple Computer, Inc.*, 714 F.2d at 1250. See also Manpower, Inc. v. Temporary Help of Harrisburg, Inc., 246 F. Supp. 788 (E.D. Pa. 1965) (upholding copyrightability of form for vacation schedules).

This is not to say that *all* blank forms or computer files are copyrightable. Only those that by their arrangement and organization convey some information can be copyrighted. Cf. 1 Nimmer at 2-201: "Thus books intended to record the events of baby's first year, or a record of a European trip, or any one of a number of other subjects, may evince considerable originality in suggestions of specific items of information which are to be recorded, and in the arrangement of such items." (footnote omitted). Defendants do not contend, however, that the file structures convey no information, and it appears to us that the structures are sufficiently complex and detailed that such an argument would not succeed. As we have noted, supra, there are many ways in which the same goal—the organization of the business aspects of a dental laboratory—might be accomplished, and several of these approaches might use significantly different file structures.[43]

---

43. Defendants' expert, Mr. Ness, testified that, given the problem to be solved, there were in fact few possible, efficient, file structures, and that the similarity in the programs' file structures was therefore neither surprising nor probative. The district court apparently did not

The file structures in the Dentalab and Dentcom systems require certain information and order that information in particular fashion. Other programs might require different information or might use the same information differently. When we compare the comprehensiveness and complexity of the file structures at issue here with the "blank forms" at issue in the cases mentioned above, we have no doubt that these file structures are sufficiently informative to deserve copyright protection. . . .

C. The five subroutines—With respect to the final piece of evidence, Dr. Moore's testimony about the five subroutines found in Dentalab and Dentcom, defendants state that they "fail to understand how a substantial similarity in structure can be established by a comparison on only a small fraction of the two works." The premise underlying this declaration is that one cannot prove substantial similarity of two works without comparing the entirety, or at least the greater part, of the works. We take this premise to be the defendants' argument.

The premise does not apply in other areas of copyright infringement. There is no general requirement that most of each of two works be compared before a court can conclude that they are substantially similar. In the case of literary works—novels, movies, or plays, for example—it is often impossible to speak of "most" of the work. . . .

Computer programs are no different. Because all steps of a computer program are not of equal importance, the relevant inquiry cannot therefore be the purely mechanical one of whether most of the programs' steps are similar. Rather, because we are concerned with the overall similarities between the programs, we must ask whether the most significant steps of the programs are similar. See Midway Mfg. Co. v. Strohon, supra, 564 F. Supp. at 753. This is precisely what Dr. Moore did. . . .

VII. Conclusion

We hold that (1) copyright protection of computer programs may extend beyond the programs' literal code to their structure, sequence, and organization, and (2) the district court's finding of substantial similarity between the Dentalab and Dentcom programs was not clearly erroneous. The judgment of the district court will therefore be affirmed.

---

find Mr. Ness persuasive on this point, however, and we defer to the court's assessment. Had the defendants offered more evidence to support their position, our answer might have been different. It is true that for certain tasks there are only a very limited number of file structures available, and in such cases the structures might not be copyrightable and similarity of file structures might not be strongly probative of similarity of the program as a whole. We are simply not convinced that this is such a case.

COMMENTS AND QUESTIONS

1. The *Whelan* court is concerned with choosing a rule that promotes innovation in the development and diffusion of computer software.
In particular, the court is inclined to reward what it describes as the most
time- and cost-intensive parts of computer programming. Is the cost of
creation a valid factor to consider in affording copyright protection? In this
regard, consider Feist v. Rural Telephone Services, 499 U.S. 340 (1991),
in which the Supreme Court definitively rejected the "sweat of the brow"
theory of copyright law. There, the court held that factual works that took
a great deal of effort to compile are not protectable under copyright if the
work that went into them did not meet a threshold standard of originality.
If telephone books are not entitled to copyright protection, why should
computer programs get protection merely because they took a great deal of
effort to write?

Even if you agree that the court properly rewarded the hard work of
Whelan's programmers, it is possible to quibble with the court's factual
conclusions about programming. What does the court see as the most
time-intensive and costly stages in the development of application programs? How do these conclusions influence its interpretation of copyright
law? In particular, consider whether the court would have reached a
different conclusion if it had focused on the importance to programmers of
building on the works of others (the "On the Shoulders of Giants"
principle discussed above).

Jerry Reichman has cautioned against the expansion of copyright law
to protect "applied know-how." J.H. Reichman, Computer Programs as
Applied Scientific Know-How: Implications of Copyright Protection for
Commercialized University Research, 42 Vand. L. Rev. 639 (1989). His
concern is that a decision like *Whelan*, having concluded that most of the
value in a computer program lies in the development of its utilitarian,
functional aspects, will extend copyright protection to those aspects of the
program notwithstanding the traditional limits of the idea-expression
dichotomy. Is this a fair characterization of what *Whelan* did?

2. What "rule" does the *Whelan* court develop for distinguishing
idea from expression in the nonliteral elements of application program
code? Applying this rule, what did the court find to be the unprotectable
idea of the Dentalab program? What is the protectable expression? Does
this test comport with section 102(b) and Baker v. Selden?

In applying *Baker* to this case, two points deserve special mention.
First, Judge Learned Hand described copyright analysis as relying on a
series of "levels of abstraction" of increasing generality. See *Nichols*, cited
above. At what level of abstraction has *Whelan* defined the idea of the
computer program? Is it reasonable to conclude that "to run a dental
laboratory efficiently" is the idea of the program? Why not choose a less
abstract idea, along the lines of "collecting input on the following five
subjects, and directing courses of action to maximize the following three

constraints"? On the other hand, can you describe the "idea" of the program as "to make money," and everything else as merely one expression of that idea?

Although the *Whelan* court purports to derive its rule for distinguishing idea from expression from Baker v. Selden, it is interesting to apply the *Whelan* rule to the facts of Baker v. Selden. Applying the *Whelan* test, what is the idea expressed in Selden's work? What is the protectable expression? Does the result of the case change?

3. The second point about the idea-expression dichotomy is evident from the Second Circuit's decision in Hoehling v. Universal City Studios, 618 F.2d 972 (2d Cir. 1980) (holding that facts are not protectable under copyright and therefore granting only thin copyright protection to a history book). Ideas are not the only elements of a work not subject to copyright protection. *Scenes a faire* are mentioned by the court as another unprotectable element. In addition, facts, information or works in the public domain, and creations of insufficient originality to deserve protection are all unprotectable elements, according to copyright law. Does *Whelan*'s analysis take these unprotectable elements into account? If so, how?

Consider in this regard the evidence of copying the court actually relied on. Is it surprising that both programs "require certain information and order that information in a particular fashion"? That certain subroutines performing certain functions are similar between the two programs? Could this be a function of the necessities of the dental business? Of the operating systems used by the programs? Of the particular way Jaslow has historically run his business?

4. Section 102(b) provides that "In no case does copyright protection for an original work of authorship extend to any idea, procedure, process, system, method of operation, concept, principle, or discovery, regardless of the form in which it is described, explained, illustrated or embodied in such work." While this provision is clearly intended to codify the idea-expression dichotomy of Baker v. Selden, there is more to the statutory language. Consider whether *Whelan* provides protection for the process, method of operation, concept, procedure or principle of Whelan's computer program. While most courts have not given these statutory words independent meaning, we will discuss below one case that does so: the First Circuit's decision in Lotus v. Borland.

5. The *Whelan* court rejected the classic "ordinary observer" test as well as its bifurcated variant in Arnstein v. Porter in favor of "a single substantial similarity inquiry," according to which both lay and expert testimony would be admissible. Does the *Whelan* approach make sense here? In computer software generally? If you reject expert testimony, who is the appropriate "ordinary observer" in computer software cases? The reasonable programmer? The ordinary user of dental laboratory management programs? The person in the street?

PROBLEM

Problem 2-2. The Midwest Corn Cooperative Association (MCCA) is a nonprofit agricultural cooperative comprised of approximately 15,000 corn farmers in the midwestern states. MCCA's purpose is to assist its members in the growing and marketing of corn. During the mid-1970s, MCCA developed a computer software system called "CornMart," which provides users with information regarding corn prices and availability, accounting services, and a means for electronically completing actual sales. The Cornmart system is used by corn farmers and buyers through terminals connected to MCCA's large central computer by telephone lines.

CornMart was developed by a team of programmers that included George Cusher and Ben Fishman. In the early 1980s, after the program had been up and running for a number of years, Cusher and Fishman decided that the system would have much greater usefulness if the CornMart program could be operated on personal computers, which were by then increasingly used by members of MCCA. Cusher and Fishman took a complete source code version of CornMart and supporting program documentation when they departed MCCA.

In 1985, Cusher and Fishman formed Cornware, Inc., and began work on a personal computer version of CornMart. By early 1986, they succeeded in writing this version, which they marketed as Cornware. Soon after they began marketing their new software, MCCA sued, alleging copyright infringement.

Expert testimony at trial established that Cornware and CornMart were very similar in terms of functional specification, overall structure, and documentation. The main difference between the systems is that CornMart is designed to run on a mainframe computer and Cornware is designed to run on a personal computer. There was, however, no literal copying of code. Cusher and Fishman testified that they had not copied or modified the CornMart program but instead had "drawn on their knowledge of the corn industry and expertise in computer programming and design gained over many years." Expert testimony at trial indicated that it would take significant effort to modify a program as complex as CornMart to run on a personal computer—perhaps more effort than rewriting the program entirely. Nonetheless, there remained significant structural similarities between the programs, although two experts testified that residual similarity between the programs reflected features of the corn market and that different programmers knowledgeable about the corn industry could conceivably make similar judgments. For example, both programs were designed to present the same information as is contained on a corn recap sheet, a standard form used for corn transactions.

How would you argue the case for MCCA? For Cornware? How would this case be resolved under the *Whelan* test?

The *Whelan* court held that computer software can be protected from nonliteral infringement in at least some instances. On this point, *Whelan* has prevailed. Every circuit today holds that software copyright can be infringed by taking the "structure, sequence and organization" of the program. See, e.g., Kepner-Tregoe, Inc. v. Leadership Software, 12 F.3d 527 (5th Cir. 1994) (expressly overruling the *Synercom* case discussed in *Whelan*).

But determining that the structure and organization of computer programs is entitled to protection does not answer the question of *how much* protection is appropriate. In 1992, the Second Circuit addressed this issue in an influential case.

═══ *Computer Associates International v. Altai, Inc.*
United States Court of Appeals for the Second Circuit
982 F.2d 693 (2d Cir. 1992)

WALKER, Circuit Judge: . . .

This appeal comes to us from the United States District Court for the Eastern District of New York, the Honorable George C. Pratt, Circuit Judge, sitting by designation. By Memorandum and Order entered August 12, 1991, Judge Pratt found that defendant Altai, Inc.'s ("Altai"), OSCAR 3.4 computer program had infringed plaintiff Computer Associates' ("CA"), copyrighted computer program entitled CA-SCHEDULER. Accordingly, the district court awarded CA $364,444 in actual damages and apportioned profits. Altai has abandoned its appeal from this award. With respect to CA's second claim for copyright infringement, Judge Pratt found that Altai's OSCAR 3.5 program was not substantially similar to a portion of CA-SCHEDULER called ADAPTER, and thus denied relief. . . .

II. Facts . . .

The subject of this litigation originates with one of CA's marketed programs entitled CA-SCHEDULER. CA-SCHEDULER is a job scheduling program designed for IBM mainframe computers. Its primary functions are straightforward: to create a schedule specifying when the computer should run various tasks, and then to control the computer as it executes the schedule. CA-SCHEDULER contains a sub-program entitled ADAPTER, also developed by CA. ADAPTER is not an independently marketed product of CA; it is a wholly integrated component of CA-SCHEDULER and has no capacity for independent use.

Nevertheless, ADAPTER plays an extremely important role. It is an "operating system compatibility component," which means, roughly speaking, it serves as a translator. An "operating system" is itself a program that manages the resources of the computer allocating those resources to other programs as needed. The IBM System 370 family of computers, for which CA-SCHEDULER was created, is, depending upon the computer's size, designed to contain one of three operating systems: DOS/VSE, MVS, or CMS. As the district court noted, the general rule is that "a program written for one operating system, e.g., DOS/VSE, will not, without modification, run under another operating system such as MVS." Computer Assocs., 775 F.Supp. at 550. ADAPTER's function is to translate the language of a given program into the particular language that the computer's own operating system can understand.

The district, court succinctly outlined the manner in which ADAPTER works within the context of the larger program. In order to enable CA-SCHEDULER to function on different operating systems, CA divided the CA-SCHEDULER into two components:

- a first component that contains only the task-specific portions of the program, independent of all operating system issues, and
- a second component that contains all the interconnections between the first component and the operating system.

In a program constructed in this way, whenever the first, task-specific, component needs to ask the operating system for some resource through a "system call", it calls the second component instead of calling the operating system directly.

The second component serves as an "interface" or "compatibility component" between the task-specific portion of the program and the operating system. It receives the request from the first component and translates it into the appropriate system call that will be recognized by whatever operating system is installed on the computer, e.g., DOS/VSE, MVS, or CMS. Since the first, task-specific component calls the adapter component rather than the operating system, the first component need not be customized to use any specific operating system. The second, interface, component insures that all the system calls are performed properly for the particular operating system in use. Id. at 551. ADAPTER serves as the second, "common system interface" component referred to above.

A program like ADAPTER, which allows a computer user to change or use multiple operating systems while maintaining the same software, is highly desirable. It saves the user the costs, both in time and money, that otherwise would be expended in purchasing new programs, modifying existing systems to run them, and gaining familiarity with their operation. The benefits run both ways. The increased compatibility afforded by an ADAPTER-like component, and its resulting popularity among consumers, makes whatever software in which it is incorporated significantly more marketable.

Starting in 1982, Altai began marketing its own job scheduling program entitled ZEKE. The original version of ZEKE was designed for use in conjunction with a VSE operating system. By late 1983, in response to customer demand, Altai decided to rewrite ZEKE so that it could be run in conjunction with an MVS operating system.

[At that time, James P. Williams, then an employee of Altai and now its president, recruited Claude F. Arney, III, a long-standing friend and computer programmer who worked for CA, to assist Altai in designing an MVS version of ZEKE. Unknown to Williams, Arney was intimately familiar with CA's ADAPTER program and he took VSE and MVS source code versions of ADAPTER with him when he left CA to join Altai. Without disclosing his knowledge of ADAPTER, Arney persuaded Williams that the best way to modify ZEKE to run on an MVS operating system was to introduce a "common system interface" component, an approach that stemmed from Arney's familiarity with ADAPTER. Arney subsequently developed a component-program named OSCAR using the ADAPTER source code. Approximately 30 percent of the first generation of OSCAR was copied from CA's ADAPTER program. In mid-1988, CA discovered the copying from ADAPTER and brought this copyright infringement and trade secret action. Altai learned of its employees' copying from the complaint.]

Upon advice of counsel, Williams initiated OSCAR's rewrite. The project's goal was to save as much of OSCAR 3.4 as legitimately could be used, and to excise those portions which had been copied from ADAPTER. Arney was entirely excluded from the process, and his copy of the ADAPTER code was locked away. Williams put eight other programmers on the project, none of whom had been involved in any way in the development of OSCAR 3.4. Williams provided the programmers with a description of the ZEKE operating system services so that they could rewrite the appropriate code. The rewrite project took about six months to complete and was finished in mid-November 1989. The resulting program was entitled OSCAR 3.5.

From that point on, Altai shipped only OSCAR 3.5 to its new customers. . . .

Discussion

[The district court concluded that version 3.5 was not substantially similar to CA-ADAPTER.]

I. *Copyright Infringement . . .*

As a general matter, and to varying degrees, copyright protection extends beyond a literary work's strictly textual form to its non-literal components. As we have said, "[i]t is of course essential to any protection of literary property that the right cannot be limited literally to the text, else a plagiarist would escape by immaterial variations." Nichols v. Universal

Pictures Co., 45 F.2d 119, 121 (2d Cir.1930) (L. Hand, J.), *cert. denied,* 282 U.S. 902, 51 S.Ct. 216, 75 L.Ed. 795 (1931). Thus, where "the fundamental essence or structure of one work is duplicated in another," 3 Nimmer, §13.03(A)[1], at 13-24, courts have found copyright infringement. . . . This black letter proposition is the springboard for our discussion.

A. Copyright Protection for the Non-Literal Elements of Computer Programs

It is now well settled that the literal elements of computer programs, i.e., their source and object codes, are the subject of copyright protection. . . . Here, as noted earlier, Altai admits having copied approximately 30% of the OSCAR 3.4 program from CA's ADAPTER source code, and does not challenge the district court's related finding of infringement.

In this case, the hotly contested issues surround OSCAR 3.5. As recounted above, OSCAR 3.5 is the product of Altai's carefully orchestrated rewrite of OSCAR 3.4. After the purge, none of the ADAPTER source code remained in the 3.5 version; thus, Altai made sure that the literal elements of its revamped OSCAR program were no longer substantially similar to the literal elements of CA's ADAPTER.

According to CA, the district court erroneously concluded that Altai's OSCAR 3.5 was not substantially similar to its own ADAPTER program. CA argues that this occurred because the district court "committed legal error in analyzing [its] claims of copyright infringement by failing to find that copyright protects expression contained in the non-literal elements of computer software." We disagree.

CA argues that, despite Altai's rewrite of the OSCAR code, the resulting program remained substantially similar to the structure of its ADAPTER program. As discussed above, a program's structure includes its non-literal components such as general flow charts as well as the more specific organization of inter-modular relationships, parameter lists, and macros. In addition to these aspects, CA contends that OSCAR 3.5 is also substantially similar to ADAPTER with respect to the list of services that both ADAPTER and OSCAR obtain from their respective operating systems. We must decide whether and to what extent these elements of computer programs are protected by copyright law.

The statutory terrain in this area has been well explored. . . . While computer programs are not specifically listed as part of the statutory definition, the legislative history leaves no doubt that Congress intended them to be considered literary works. See H.R.Rep. No. 1476, 94th Cong., 2d Sess. 54, reprinted in 1976 U.S.C.C.A.N. 5659, 5667 (hereinafter "House Report"); Whelan, 797 F.2d at 1234; Apple Computer, 714 F.2d at 1247.

The syllogism that follows from the foregoing premises is a powerful one: if the non-literal structures of literary works are protected by copyright; and if computer programs are literary works, as we are told by the legislature; then the non-literal structures of computer programs are protected by copyright. See *Whelan*, 797 F.2d at 1234 ("By analogy to other literary works, it would thus appear that the copyrights of computer programs can be infringed even absent copying of the literal elements of the program."). We have no reservation in joining the company of those courts that have already ascribed to this logic. See, e.g., Johnson Controls, Inc. v. Phoenix Control Sys., Inc., 886 F.2d 1173; 1175 (9th Cir. 1989); Lotus Dev. Corp., 740 F.Supp. at 54; Digital Communications Assocs., Inc. v. Softhlone Distrib. Corp., 659 F.Supp. 449, 455-56 (N.D.Ga.1987); Q-Co Indus., Inc. v. Hoffman, 625 F.Supp. 608, 615 (S.D.N.Y.1985); SAS Inst., Inc. v. S & H Computer Sys., Inc., 605 F.Supp. 816, 829-30 (M.D.Tenn.1985). However, that conclusion does not end our analysis. We must determine the scope of copyright protection that extends to a computer program's non-literal structure.

As a caveat, we note that our decision here does not control infringement actions regarding categorically distinct works, such as certain types of screen displays. These items represent products of computer programs, rather than the programs themselves, and fall under the copyright rubric of audiovisual works. . . . In this case, . . . we are concerned not with a program's display, but the program itself, and then with only its non-literal components. In considering the copyrightability of these components, we must refer to venerable doctrines of copyright law.

1) Idea vs. Expression Dichotomy

It is a fundamental principle of copyright law that a copyright does not protect an idea, but only the expression of the idea. . . .

Drawing the line between idea and expression is a tricky business. Judge Learned Hand noted that "[n]obody has ever been able to fix that boundary, and nobody ever can," *Nichols*, 45 F.2d at 121. Thirty years later his convictions remained firm. "Obviously, no principle can be stated as to when an imitator has gone beyond copying the 'idea,' and has borrowed its 'expression,'" Judge Hand concluded. "Decisions must therefore inevitably be ad hoc." Peter Pan Fabrics, Inc. v. Martin Weiner Corp., 274 F.2d 487, 489 (2d Cir.1960).

The essentially utilitarian nature of a computer program further complicates the task of distilling its idea from its expression. See *SAS Inst.*, 605 F.Supp. at 829; cf. *Englund*, at 893. In order to describe both computational processes and abstract ideas, its content "combines creative and technical expression." See *Spivack*, at 755. The variations of expression found in purely creative compositions, as opposed to those contained in utilitarian works, are not directed towards practical application. For example, a narration of Humpty Dumpty's demise, which would clearly be a creative composition, does not serve the same ends as, say, a recipe for scrambled eggs—which is a more process-oriented text. Thus, compared to aesthetic works, computer programs hover even more closely to the elusive boundary line described in §102(b).

[The court reviewed the facts and holding of Baker v. Selden.]

To the extent that an accounting text and a computer program are both "a set of statements or instructions . . . to bring about a certain result," 17 U.S.C. §101, they are roughly analogous. In the former case, the processes are ultimately conducted by human agency; in the latter, by electronic means. In either case, as already stated, the processes themselves are not protectable. But the holding in *Baker* goes farther. The Court concluded that those aspects of a work, which "must necessarily be used as incident to" the idea, system or process that the work describes, are also not copyrightable. 101 U.S. at 104. Selden's ledger sheets, therefore, enjoyed no copyright protection because they were "necessary incidents to" the system of accounting that he described. *Id.* at 103. From this reasoning, we conclude that those elements of a computer program that are necessarily incidental to its function are similarly unprotectable.

While Baker v. Selden provides a sound analytical foundation, it offers scant guidance on how to separate idea or process from expression, and moreover, on how to further distinguish protectable expression from that expression which "must necessarily be used as incident to the work's underlying concept." In the context of computer programs, the Third Circuit's noted decision in Whelan has, thus far, been the most thoughtful attempt to accomplish these ends.

[The court quoted from the Whelan v. Jaslow decision reproduced above.]

So far, in the courts, the *Whelan* rule has received a mixed reception. While some decisions have adopted its reasoning, see, e.g., Bull HN Info. Sys., Inc. v. American Express Bank, Ltd., 1990 Copyright Law Dec. (CCH) P 26,555 at 23,278 (S.D.N.Y.1990); Dynamic Solutions, Inc. v. Planning & Control, Inc., 1987 Copyright Law Dec. (CCH) P 26,062 at 20,912 (S.D.N.Y.1987); Broderbund Software Inc. v. Unison World, Inc., 648 F.Supp. 1127, 1133 (N.D.Cal.1986), others have rejected it. See Plains Cotton Co-op v. Goodpasture Computer Serv. Inc., 807 F.2d 1256, 1262 (5th Cir.), cert. denied, 484 U.S. 821, 108 S.Ct. 80, 98 L.Ed.2d 42 (1987); cf. Synercom Technology, Inc. v. University Computing Co., 462 F.Supp. 1003, 1014 (N.D.Tex.1978) (concluding that order and sequence of data on computer input formats was idea not expression).

Whelan has fared even more poorly in the academic community, where its standard for distinguishing idea from expression has been widely criticized for being conceptually overbroad. See, e.g., Englund, at 881; Menell, at 1074, 1082; Kretschmer, at 837-39; Spivack, at 747-55; Thomas M. Gage, Note, Whelan Associates v. Jaslow Dental Laboratories: Copyright Protection for Computer Software Structure—What's the Purpose?, 1987 Wis.L.Rev. 859, 860-61 (1987). The leading commentator in the field has stated that, "[t]he crucial flaw in [*Whelan*'s] reasoning is that it assumes that only one 'idea,' in copyright law terms, underlies any computer program, and that once a separable idea can be identified, everything else must be expression." 3 Nimmer §13.03[F], at 13-62.34. This criticism focuses not upon the program's ultimate purpose but upon the reality of its structural design. As we have already noted, a computer program's ultimate function or purpose is the composite result of interacting subroutines. Since each subroutine is itself a program, and thus, may be said to have its own "idea," *Whelan*'s general formulation that a program's overall purpose equates with the program's idea is descriptively inadequate.

Accordingly, we think that Judge Pratt wisely declined to follow *Whelan*. See Computer Assocs., 775 F.Supp. at 558-60. In addition to noting the weakness in the *Whelan* definition of "program-idea," mentioned above, Judge Pratt found that *Whelan*'s synonymous use of the terms "structure, sequence, and organization," see *Whelan*, 797 F.2d at 1224 n. 1, demonstrated a flawed understanding of a computer program's method of operation. See Computer Assocs., 775 F.Supp. at 559-60 (discussing the distinction between a program's "static structure" and "dynamic structure"). Rightly, the district court found *Whelan*'s rationale suspect because it is so closely tied to what can now be seen—with the passage of time—as the opinion's somewhat outdated appreciation of computer science.

2) Substantial Similarity Test for Computer Program Structure: Abstraction-Filtration-Comparison

We think that *Whelan*'s approach to separating idea from expression in computer programs relies too heavily on metaphysical distinctions and does not place enough emphasis on practical considerations. Cf. *Apple Computer*, 714 F.2d at 1253 (rejecting certain commercial constraints on programming as a helpful means of distinguishing idea from expression because they did "not enter into the somehwat metaphysical issue of whether particular ideas and expressions have merged"). As the cases that we shall discuss demonstrate, a satisfactory answer to this problem cannot be reached by resorting, *a priori*, to philosophical first principles.

As discussed herein, we think that district courts would be well-advised to undertake a three-step procedure, based on the abstractions test utilized by the district court, in order to determine whether the non-literal elements of two or more computer programs are substantially similar. This approach breaks no new ground; rather, it draws on such familar copyright doctrines as merger, *scenes a faire*, and public domain. In taking this approach, however, we are cognizant that computer technology is a dynamic field which can quickly outpace judicial decisionmaking. Thus, in cases where the technology in question does not allow for a literal application of the procedure we outline below, our opinion should not be read to foreclose the district courts of our circuit from utilizing a modified version.

In ascertaining substantial similarity under this approach, a court would first break down the allegedly infringed program into its constituent structural parts. Then, by examining each of these parts for such things as incorporated ideas, expression that is necessarily incidental to those ideas, and elements that are taken from the public domain, a court would then be able to sift out all non-protectable material. Left with a kernel, or possibly kernels, of creative expression after following this process of elimination, the court's last step would be to compare this material with the structure of an allegedly infringing program. The result of this comparison will determine whether the protectable elements of the programs at issue are substantially similar so as to warrant a finding of infringement. It will be helpful to elaborate a bit further.

Step One: Abstraction

As the district court appreciated, see *Computer Assocs.*, 775 F.Supp. at 560, the theoretic framework for analyzing substantial similarity expounded by Learned Hand in the *Nichols* case is helpful in the present context. In *Nichols*, we enunciated what has now become known as the "abstractions" test for separating idea from expression:

> Upon any work . . . a great number of patterns of increasing generality will fit equally well, as more and more of the incident is left out. The last may perhaps be no more than the most general statement of what the [work] is about, and at times might consist only of its title; but there is a point in this series of abstractions where they are no longer protected, since otherwise the [author] could prevent the use of his "ideas," to which, apart from their expression, his property is never extended.

Nichols, 45 F.2d at 121.

While the abstractions test was originally applied in relation to literary works such as novels and plays, it is adaptable to computer programs. In contrast to the *Whelan* approach, the abstractions test "implicitly recognizes that any given work may consist of a mixture of numerous ideas and expressions." 3 Nimmer §13.03[F] at 13-62.34-63.

As applied to computer programs, the abstractions test will comprise the first step in the examination for substantial similarity. Initially, in a manner that resembles reverse engineering on a theoretical plane, a court should dissect the allegedly copied program's structure and isolate each level of abstraction contained within it. This process begins with the code and ends with an articulation of the program's ultimate function. Along the way, it is necessary essentially to retrace and map each of the designer's steps—in the opposite order in which they were taken during the program's creation.

As an anatomical guide to this procedure, the following description is helpful:

At the lowest level of abstraction, a computer program may be thought of in its entirety as a set of individual instructions organized into a hierarchy of modules. At a higher level of abstraction, the instructions in the lowest-level modules may be replaced conceptually by the functions of those modules. At progressively higher levels of abstraction, the functions of higher-level modules conceptually replace the implementations of those modules in terms of lower-level modules and instructions, until finally, one is left with nothing but the ultimate function of the program. . . . A program has structure at every level of abstraction at which it is viewed. At low levels of abstraction, a program's structure may be quite complex; at the highest level it is trivial.

Englund, at 897-98. Cf. Spivack, at 774.

Step Two: Filtration

Once the program's abstraction levels have been discovered, the substantial similarity inquiry moves from the conceptual to the concrete. Professor Nimmer suggests, and we endorse, a "successive filtering method" for separating protectable expression from non-protectable material. See generally 3 Nimmer §13.03[F]. This process entails examining the structural components at each level of abstraction to determine whether their particular inclusion at that level was "idea" or was dictated by considerations of efficiency, so as to be necessarily incidental to that idea; required by factors external to the program itself; or taken from the public domain and hence is non-protectable expression. See also Kretschmer, at 844-45 (arguing that program features dictated by market externalities or efficiency concerns are unprotectable). The structure of any given program may reflect some, all, or none of these considerations. Each case requires its own fact specific investigation.

Strictly speaking, this filtration serves "the purpose of defining the scope of plaintiff's copyright." Brown Bag Software v. Symantec Corp., 960 F.2d 1465, 1475 (9th Cir.) (endorsing "analytic dissection" of computer programs in order to isolate protectable expression), *cert. denied*, 113 S.Ct. 198 (1992). By applying well developed doctrines of copyright law, it may ultimately leave behind a "core of protectable material." 3 Nimmer §13.03[F][5], at 13-72. Further explication of this second step may be helpful.

(a) Elements Dictated by Efficiency

The portion of Baker v. Selden, discussed earlier, which denies copyright protection to expression necessarily incidental to the idea being expressed, appears to be the cornerstone for what has developed into the doctrine of merger. See Morrissey v. Procter & Gamble Co., 379 F.2d 675, 678-79 (1st Cir.1967) (relying on *Baker* for the proposition that expression embodying the rules of a sweepstakes contest was inseparable from the idea of the contest itself, and therefore were not protectable by copyright); see also *Digital Communications,* 659 F.Supp. at 457. The doctrine's underlying principle is that "[w]hen there is essentially only one way to express an idea, the idea and its expression are inseparable and copyright is no bar to copying that expression." Concrete Machinery Co. v. Classic Lawn Ornaments. Inc., 843 F.2d 600, 606 (1st Cir.1988). Under these circumstances, the expression is said to have "merged" with the idea itself. In order not to confer a monopoly of the idea upon the copyright owner, such expression should not be protected. See Herbert Rosenthal Jewelry Corp. v. Kalpakian, 446 F.2d 738, 742 (9th Cir.1971).

CONTU recognized the applicability of the merger doctrine to computer programs. In its report to Congress it stated that:

> [C]opyrighted language may be copied without infringing when there is but a limited number of ways to express a given idea. . . . In the computer context, this means that when specific instructions, even though previously copyrighted, are the only and essential means of accomplishing a given task, their later use by another will not amount to infringement.

CONTU Report at 20. While this statement directly concerns only the application of merger to program code, that is, the textual aspect of the program, it reasonably suggests that the doctrine fits comfortably within the general context of computer programs.

Furthermore, when one considers the fact that programmers generally strive to create programs "that meet the user's needs in the most efficient manner," Menell, at 1052, the applicability of the merger doctrine to computer programs becomes compelling. In the context of computer program design, the concept of efficiency is akin to deriving the most concise logical proof or formulating the most succinct mathematical computation. Thus, the more efficient a set of modules are, the more closely they approximate the idea or process embodied in that particular aspect of the program's structure.

While, hypothetically, there might be a myriad of ways in which a programmer may effectuate certain functions within a program—i.e., express the idea embodied in a given subroutine—efficiency concerns may so narrow the practical range of choice as to make only one or two forms of expression workable options. See 3 Nimmer §13.03[F][2], at 13-63; see also *Whelan,* 797 F.2d at 1243 n. 43 ("It is true that for certain tasks there are only a very limited number of file structures available, and in such cases the structures might not be copyrightable. . . ."). Of course, not all program structure is informed by efficiency concerns. See Menell, at 1052 (besides efficiency, simplicity related to user accommodation has become a programming priority). It follows that, in order to determine whether the merger doctrine precludes copyright protection to an aspect of a program's structure that is so oriented, a court must inquire "whether the use of *this particular set of modules* is necessary efficiently to implement that part of the program's process" being implemented. Englund, at 902. If the answer is yes, then the expression represented by the programmer's choice of a specific module or group of modules has merged with their underlying idea and is unprotected. *Id.* at 902-03.

Another justification for linking structural economy with the application of the merger doctrine stems from a program's essentially utilitarian nature and the competitive forces that exist in the software marketplace. See Kretschmer, at 842. Working in tandem, these factors give rise to a problem of proof which merger helps to eliminate. Efficiency is an industry-wide goal. Since, as we have already noted, there may be only a limited number of efficient implementations for any given program task, it is quite possible that multiple programmers, working independently, will design the identical method employed in the allegedly infringed work. Of course, if this is the case, there is no copyright infringement. See Roth Greeting Cards v. United Card Co., 429 F.2d 1106, 1110 (9th Cir.1970); *Sheldon*, 81 F.2d at 54.

Under these circumstances, the fact that two programs contain the same efficient structure may as likely lead to an inference of independent creation as it does to one of copying. See 3 Nimmer §13.03[F][2], at 13-65; cf. *Herbert Rosenthal Jewelry Corp.*, 446 F.2d at 741 (evidence of independent creation may stem from defendant's standing as a designer of previous similar works). Thus, since evidence of similarly efficient structure is not particularly probative of copying, it should be disregarded in the overall substantial similarity analysis. See 3 Nimmer §13.03[F][2], at 13-65. . . .

(b) Elements Dictated by External Factors

We have stated that where "it is virtually impossible to write about a particular historical era or fictional theme without employing certain 'stock' or standard literary devices," such expression is not copyrightable. Hoeh-ling v. Universal Studios, Inc., 618 F.2d 972, 979 (2d Cir.), *cert. denied*, 449 U.S.1 841, 101 S.Ct. 42, 66 L.Ed.2d 1 (1980). . . .

Professor Nimmer points out that "in many instances it is virtually impossible to write a program to perform particular functions in a specific computing environment without employing standard techniques." 3 Nimmer §13.03[F][3], at 13-65. This is a result of the fact that a programmer's freedom of design choice is often circumscribed by extrinsic considerations such as (1) the mechanical specifications of the computer on which a particular program is intended to run; (2) compatibility requirements of other programs with which a program is designed to operate in conjunction; (3) computer manufacturers' design standards; (4) demands of the industry being serviced; and (5) widely accepted programming practices within the computer industry. *Id.* at 13-65-71. . . .

(c) Elements Taken from the Public Domain

Closely related to the non-protectability of *scenes a faire*, is material found in the public domain. Such material is free for the taking and cannot be appropriated by a single author even though it is included in a copyrighted work. See E.F. Johnson Co. v. Uniden Corp. of America, 623 F.Supp. 1485, 1499 (D. Minn.1985); see also *Sheldon*, 81 F.2d at 54. We see no reason to make an exception to this rule for elements of a computer program that have entered the public domain by virtue of freely accessible program exchanges and the like. See 3 Nimmer §13.03[F][14]; see also *Brown Bag Software*, 960 F.2d at 1473 (affirming the district court's finding that "[p]laintiffs may not claim copyright protection of an . . . expression that is, if not standard, then commonplace in the computer software industry."). Thus, a court must also filter out this material from the allegedly infringed program before it makes the final inquiry in its substantial similarity analysis.

Step Three: Comparison

The third and final step of the test for substantial similarity that we believe appropriate for non-literal program components entails a comparison. Once a court has sifted out all elements of the allegedly infringed program which are "ideas" or are dictated by efficiency or external factors, or taken from the public domain, there may remain a core of protectable expression. In terms of a work's copyright value, this is the golden nugget. See *Brown Bag Software*, 960 F.2d at 1475. At this point, the court's substantial similarity inquiry focuses on whether the defendant copied any aspect of this protected expression, as well as an assessment of the copied portion's relative importance with respect to the plaintiff's overall program. See 3 Nimmer §13.03[F][5]; *Data East USA*, 862 F.2d at 208 ("To determine whether similarities result from unprotectable expression, analytic dissection of similarities may be performed. If . . . all similarities in expression arise from use of common ideas, then no substantial similarity can be found.").

3) Policy Considerations

We are satisfied that the three step approach we have just outlined not only comports with, but advances the constitutional policies underlying the Copyright Act. Since any method that tries to distinguish idea from expression ultimately impacts on the scope of copyright protection afforded to a particular type of work, "the line [it draws] must be a pragmatic one, which also keeps in consideration 'the preservation of the balance between competition and protection. . . .'" *Apple Computer*, 714 F.2d at 1253 (citation omitted).

CA and some amici argue against the type of approach that we have set forth on the grounds that it will be a disincentive for future computer program research and development. At bottom, they claim that if programmers are not guaranteed broad copyright protection for their work, they will not invest the extensive time, energy and funds required to design and improve program structures. While they have a point, their argument cannot carry the day. The interest of the copyright law is not in simply conferring a monopoly on industrious persons, but in advancing the public welfare through rewarding artistic creativity, in a manner that permits the free use and development of non-protectable ideas and processes.

In this respect, our conclusion is informed by Justice Stewart's concise discussion of the principles that correctly govern the adaptation of the copyright law to new circumstances. In Twentieth Century Music Corp. v. Aiken, he wrote:

> The limited scope of the copyright holder's statutory monopoly, like the limited copyright duration required by the Constitution, reflects a balance of competing claims upon the public interest: Creative work is to be encouraged and rewarded, but private motivation must ultimately serve the cause of promoting broad public availability of literature, music, and the other arts. The immediate effect of our copyright law is to secure a fair return for an "author's" creative labor. But the ultimate aim is, by this incentive, to stimulate artistic creativity for the general public good. . . . When technological change has rendered its literal terms ambiguous, the Copyright Act must be construed in light of this basic purpose.

422 U.S. 151, 156 (1975) (citations and footnotes omitted).

Recently, the Supreme Court has emphatically reiterated that "[t]he primary objective of copyright is not to reward the labor of authors. . . ." Feist Publications, Inc. v. Rural Tel. Serv. Co., —U.S.—, 111 S.Ct. 1282, 1290 (1991). While the *Feist* decision deals primarily with the copyrightability of purely factual compilations, its underlying tenets apply to much of the work involved in computer programming. *Feist* put to rest the "sweat of the brow" doctrine in copyright law. *Id*. 111 S.Ct. at 1295. The rationale of that doctrine "was that copyright was a reward for the hard work that went into compiling facts." *Id*. 111 S.Ct. at 1291. The Court flatly rejected this justification for extending copyright protection, noting that it "eschewed the most fundamental axiom of copyright law—that no one may copyright facts or ideas." *Id*.

Feist teaches that substantial effort alone cannot confer copyright status on an otherwise uncopyrightable work. As we have discussed, despite the fact that significant labor and expense often goes into computer program flow-charting and debugging, that process does not always result in inherently protectable expression. Thus, *Feist* implicitly undercuts the *Whelan* rationale, "which allow[ed] copyright protection beyond the literal computer code . . . [in order to] provide the proper incentive for programmers by protecting their most valuable efforts. . . ." *Whelan*, 797 F.2d at 1237 (footnote omitted). We note that *Whelan* was decided prior to *Feist* when the "sweat of the brow" doctrine still had vitality. In view of the Supreme Court's recent holding, however, we must reject the legal basis of CA's disincentive argument.

Furthermore, we are unpersuaded that the test we approve today will lead to the dire consequences for the computer program industry that plaintiff and some amici predict. To the contrary, serious students of the industry have been highly critical of the sweeping scope of copyright protection engendered by the *Whelan* rule, in that it "enables first comers to 'lock up' basic programming techniques as implemented in programs to perform particular tasks." Menell, at 1087; see also Spivack, at 765 (*Whelan* "results in an inhibition of creation by virtue of the copyright owner's quasi-monopoly power").

To be frank, the exact contours of copyright protection for non-literal program structure are not completely clear. We trust that as future cases are decided, those limits will become better defined. Indeed, it may well be that the Copyright Act serves as a relatively weak barrier against public access to the theoretical interstices behind a program's source and object codes. This results from the hybrid nature of a computer program, which, while it is literary expression, is also a highly functional, utilitarian component in the larger process of computing.

Generally, we think that copyright registration—with its indiscriminating availability—is not ideally suited to deal with the highly dynamic technology of computer science. Thus far, many of the decisions in this area reflect the courts' attempt to fit the proverbial square peg in a round hole. The district court, see *Computer Assocs.*, 775 F.Supp. at 560, and at least one commentator have suggested that patent registration, with its exacting up-front novelty and non-obviousness requirements, might be the more appropriate rubric of protection for intellectual property of this kind. See Randell M. Whitmeyer, Comment, A Plea for Due Processes: Defining the Proper Scope of Patent Protection for Computer Software, 85 Nw.U.L.Rev. 1103, 1123-25 (1991); see also Lotus Dev. Corp. v. Borland Int'l, Inc., 788 F.Supp. 78, 91 (D. Mass.1992) (discussing the potentially supplemental relationship between patent and copyright protection in the context of computer programs). In any event, now that more than 12 years have passed since CONTU issued its final report, the resolution of this specific issue could benefit from further legislative investigation—perhaps a CONTU II.

In the meantime, Congress has made clear that computer programs are literary works entitled to copyright protection. Of course, we shall abide by these instructions, but in so doing we must not impair the overall integrity of copyright law. While incentive based arguments in favor of broad copyright protection are perhaps attractive from a pure policy perspective, see *Lotus Dev. Corp.*, 740 F.Supp. at 58, ultimately, they have a corrosive effect on certain fundamental tenets of copyright doctrine. If the test we have outlined results in narrowing the scope of protection, as we expect it will, that result flows from applying, in accordance with Congressional intent, long-standing principles of copyright law to computer programs. Of course, our decision is also informed by our concern that these fundamental principles remain undistorted.

B. The District Court Decision . . .

2) Evidentiary Analysis

The district court had to determine whether Altai's OSCAR 3.5 program was substantially similar to CA's ADAPTER. . . .

The district court took the first step in the analysis set forth in this opinion when it separated the program by levels of abstraction. The district court stated:

> As applied to computer software programs, this abstractions test would progress in order of "increasing generality" from object code, to source code, to parameter lists, to services required, to general outline. In discussing the particular similarities, therefore, we shall focus on these levels.

Computer Assocs., 775 F.Supp. at 560. While the facts of a different case might require that a district court draw a more particularized blueprint of a program's overall structure, this description is a workable one for the case at hand.

Moving to the district court's evaluation of OSCAR 3.5's structural components, we agree with Judge Pratt's systematic exclusion of non-protectable expression. With respect to code, the district court observed that after the rewrite of OSCAR 3.4 to OSCAR 3.5, "there remained virtually no lines of code that were identical to ADAPTER." *Id*. at 561. Accordingly, the court found that the code "present[ed] no similarity at all." *Id*. at 562.

Next, Judge Pratt addressed the issue of similarity between the two programs' parameter lists and macros. He concluded that, viewing the conflicting evidence most favorably to CA, it demonstrated that "only a few of the lists and macros were similar to protected elements in ADAPTER; the others were either in the public domain or dictated by the functional demands of the program." *Id*. As discussed above, functional elements and elements taken from the public domain do not qualify for copyright protection. With respect to the few remaining parameter lists and macros, the district court could reasonably conclude that they did not warrant a finding of infringement given their relative contribution to the overall program. See Warner Bros., Inc. v. American Broadcasting Cos., Inc., 720 F.2d 231, 242 (2d Cir.1983) (discussing de minimis exception which allows for literal copying of a small and usually insignificant portion of the plaintiff's work); 3 Nimmer §13.03[F][5], at 13-74. In any event, the district court reasonably found that, for lack of persuasive evidence, CA failed to meet its burden of proof on whether the macros and parameter lists at issue were substantially similar. See *Computer Assocs.*, 775 F.Supp. at 562.

The district court also found that the overlap exhibited between the list of services required for both ADAPTER and OSCAR 3.5 was "determined by the demands of the operating system and of the applications program to which it [was] to be linked through ADAPTER or OSCAR. . . ." *Id.* In other words, this aspect of the program's structure was dictated by the nature of other programs with which it was designed to interact and, thus, is not protected by copyright.

Finally, in his infringement analysis, Judge Pratt accorded no weight to the similarities between the two programs' organizational charts, "because [the charts were] so simple and obvious to anyone exposed to the operation of the program[s]." *Id.* CA argues that the district court's action in this regard "is not consistent with copyright law"—that "obvious" expression is protected, and that the district court erroneously failed to realize this. However, to say that elements of a work are "obvious," in the manner in which the district court used the word, is to say that they "follow naturally from the work's theme rather than from the author's creativity." 3 Nimmer §13.03[F][3], at 1365. This is but one formulation of the *scenes a faire* doctrine, which we have already endorsed as a means of weeding out unprotectable expression. . . .

Since we accept Judge Pratt's factual conclusions and the results of his legal analysis, we affirm his dismissal of CA's copyright infringement claim based upon OSCAR 3.5. We emphasize that, like all copyright infringement cases, those that involve computer programs are highly fact specific. The amount of protection due structural elements, in any given case, will vary according to the protectable expression found to exist within the program at issue. . . .

COMMENTS AND QUESTIONS

1. How does the *Altai* court distinguish idea from expression? Compare this method to that proposed and applied in *Whelan*. How would the *Whelan* case have come out if the *Altai* test had been applied? How would Baker v. Selden be decided under the *Altai* approach?

2. *Computer Associates* seems to ask courts to analytically dissect a computer program to determine what is protectable and copied and compare this to the entire program, rather than to the protectable uncopied elements, to determine substantial similarity. Does this suggest that a program with relatively little protectable material can be freely copied?

One limitation on such copying may be the copyright protection afforded to *compilations* of uncopyrightable material. Even though all of the individual elements of a computer program may themselves be uncopyrightable, the expressive selection and arrangement of those uncopyrightable pieces may itself qualify for copyright protection. Indeed, the Second Circuit acknowledged this in Softel Inc. v. Dragon Medical and Scientific Communications Inc., 118 F.3d 955 (2d Cir. 1997), where it held that the "comparison" step was required even where all of the elements of a program had been filtered out. The court remanded the case "so that the district court may enter a finding as to whether the manner in which Softel combined the various design elements in its software was protectable expression, and, if it was, whether Dragon infringed that expression." *Id.*

If the elements of a computer program are all unprotectable—for example, because they are driven by functional considerations, how likely is it that the selection and arrangement of those elements will be expressive rather than functional? Won't the constraints of programming dictate not only which modules are chosen, but how they must interact with respect to each other?

3. Which approach—*Whelan* or *Altai*—comports better with section 102(b) and Baker v. Selden? Is there a more appropriate way of distinguishing idea from expression in the context of application program code?

4. The *Altai* case has been warmly praised by most commentators. See, e.g., David Bender, Computer Associates v. Altai: Rationality Prevails, Computer Law., Aug. 1992, at 1; Pamela Samuelson et al., The Nature of Copyright Analysis for Computer Program: Copyright Law Professors' Brief·Amicus Curiae in Lotus v. Borland, 16 Hastings Comm and Ent. L.J. 657 (1994) (brief of 24 copyright law professors endorsing *Altai*). However, the decision has also been bitterly attacked by lawyers and scholars representing large computer companies. See Jack Brown, Analytical Dissection of Copyrighted Computer Software—Complicating the Simple and Confounding the Complex, 25 Ariz. St. L.J. 801 (1993); Anthony L. Clapes & Jennifer M. Daniels, Revenge of the Luddites: A Closer Look at Computer Associates v. Altai, Computer Law., Nov. 1992, at 11. Professor Arthur Miller, a CONTU Commissioner, has expressed apprehension about the implications of the *Altai* approach:

> [A] court must employ considerable caution in excluding efficient or speedy program expression lest it undermine the effective protection of computer programs. For example, the mere fact that the expression is efficient should not, without more, bar protection for original authorship in the programming context any more than it does in prose work. An uncritical application of *Altai*'s language would penalize the most effective (and in some senses the most artistic) programmers.

Miller, Copyright Protection for Computer Programs, Databases, and Computer-Generated Works: Is Anything New Since CONTU?, 106 Harv. L. Rev. 977, 1004-1005 (1993) (footnotes omitted). Do you agree with Miller's view of the scope of copyright protection for the efficient elements of program structure? Is protection of decisions dictated by efficiency consistent with copyright cases outside the computer context? Or would it mean protecting function rather than expression?

5. The *Altai* test was rapidly adopted by most courts. Judicial convergence on the abstraction-filtration-comparison test has been so complete that every court to confront the issue since 1992 has chosen the *Altai* approach over the *Whelan* approach. See Bateman v. Mnemonics, Inc., 79 F.3d 1532, 1543-1545 (11th Cir. 1996); Apple Computer v. Microsoft Corp., 35 F.3d 1435 (9th Cir. 1994); Engineering Dynamics, Inc. v. Structural Software, Inc., 26 F.3d 1335 (5th Cir. 1994); Kepner-Tregoe, Inc. v. Leadership Software, 12 F.3d 527 (5th Cir. 1994); Gates Rubber Co. v. Bando Chemical Indus., 9 F.3d 823 (10th Cir. 1993); Atari Games Corp. v. Nintendo, 975 F.2d 832 (Fed. Cir. 1992); Control Data Systems, Inc. v. Infoware, Inc., 903 F. Supp. 1316 (D. Minn. 1995); CMAX/Cleveland, Inc. v. UCR, Inc., 804 F. Supp. 337 (M.D. Ga. 1992); Mark A. Lemley, Convergence in the Law of Software Copyright, 10 High Tech. L.J. 1 (1995). See also Brown Bag Software v. Symantec Corp., 960 F.2d 1465, 1475-1476 (9th Cir. 1992) (endorsing "analytic dissection" of the elements of a computer program prior to the *Altai* decision). Cf. MiTek Holdings Inc. v. Arce Engineering Co., 89 F.3d 1548 (11th Cir. 1996) (upholding *Altai* approach but allowing plaintiff to skip abstraction step by identifying in advance those elements it considers to be protectable and infringed). In addition, courts in Canada, the United Kingdom, and France have endorsed the *Altai* filtration analysis.

Not all of these courts have approached the abstraction-filtration-comparison analysis in precisely the same way, however. The Tenth Circuit decision in *Gates Rubber* is particularly notable for its elaboration of the test beyond the parameters of *Altai*. The *Gates Rubber* court acknowledged that "[a]pplication of the abstractions test will necessarily vary from case-to-case and program-to-program. Given the complexity and ever-changing nature of computer technology, we decline to set forth any strict methodology for the abstraction of computer programs." Nonetheless, the court identified six levels of "generally declining abstraction": (1) the main purpose of the computer program; (2) the structure or architecture of a program, generally as represented in a flowchart; (3) "modules" that comprise particular program operations or types of stored data; (4) individual algorithms or data structures employed in each of the modules; (5) the source code that instructs the computer to carry out each necessary operation on each data structure; and (6) the object code that is actually read by the computer. The court used these levels of abstraction to facilitate its analysis of the program at issue.

The *Gates Rubber* court also gave further content to the filtration part of the *Altai* analysis. The court filtered out six unprotectable elements: ideas, the processes or methods of the computer program,[2] facts, material

___

2. *Gates Rubber*, 9 F.3d at 836-837. The court cited the legislative history accompanying section 102(b) of the Copyright Act, which clearly indicates that the actual processes or methods used in a computer program are not entitled to copyright protection. *Id*. The court

in the public domain, expression that has "merged" with an idea or process, and expression that is so standard or common as to be a "necessary incident" to an idea or process.[3] Finally, the *Gates Rubber* court indicated that comparison of the protected elements of a program should be done on a case-by-case basis, with an eye toward determining whether a substantial portion of the protectable expression of the original work has been copied.

Is this analysis consistent with *Altai*? Is a court applying *Gates Rubber* likely to give more or less protection to a computer program than would the *Altai* court? Note that applying *Altai* does not mean that the nonliteral elements of computer programs get no protection at all. For example, in the Fifth Circuit, which has expressly adopted the *Gates Rubber* approach, one district court has concluded that a set of threshold values set by a computer manufacturer to indicate a failure threshold for replacement of a hard drive were copyrightable, because the business and engineering decisions that went into setting those values showed sufficient original expression to be protected. Compaq Computer v. Procom Technology, 908 F. Supp. 1409 (S.D. Tex. 1995). The court held that the merger and *scenes a faire* doctrines did not bar copyrightability, because the precise values Compaq chose were not necessary for competing manufacturers. See also Harbor Software Inc. v. Applied Systems Inc., 925 F. Supp. 1042 (S.D.N.Y. 1996) (finding nonliteral elements of a computer program protectable at a fairly low level of abstraction under the *Altai* test).

6. Note that while both *Whelan* and *Altai* are nominally about the scope of protection afforded computer programs under the copyright laws, both courts merge the analysis of infringement into the protectability analysis. This is particularly evident in *Altai*'s filtration analysis, where the comparison step involves identifying the similarities between the copyrighted program and the accused program.

PROBLEMS

Problem 2-3. Reassess the MCCA problem (Problem 2-2) based on the *Altai* methodology. Do you reach the same conclusion as before?

Problem 2-4. Demento Corporation (Demento) produces Demento II, the leading home video game system. The Demento II consists of a console, which runs game cartridges and attaches to a

---

noted that processes were most commonly found in the program architecture, module structure, and algorithms used. *Id.* at 837.

3. *Id.* This is the *scenes a faire* doctrine. The court held that such standard devices in computer programs include "those elements of a program that have been dictated by external factors," such as hardware and software standards, specifications, or compatibility requirements, customer design specifications, and basic industry practices. *Id.*

monitor or standard television, and a control device, which enables the user to manipulate characters or other images of particular games on the screen. Demento licenses a limited number of games per year.

In order to prevent unauthorized game producers from manufacturing games to run on the Demento II console, Demento developed a "lock-out" device that governs access to the console. The console contains a "master chip" or "lock" that will only run game cartridges that contain an appropriate "slave chip" or "key." When a user inserts an authorized game cartridge into the Demento II, the slave chip transmits an arbitrary data stream key, which is received by the master chip and unlocks the console, allowing the game to be played. The unlocking device is a sophisticated software program encoded in the master and slave chips. There is a multitude of different programs capable of generating the data stream that unlocks the console, although it would be almost impossible to decipher the "key" by trial and error. It would be like trying to find a needle in a haystack.

The rapid growth of the home video game market eroded the revenue base of Mutant Corporation (Mutant), a leading maker of arcade video games. Mutant sought to license the right to produce game cartridges for the Demento II system, but was put off by the limits on the number of new games that Demento would license per year and the high cost of each license. Mutant decided instead to develop its own slave chip that would unlock the Demento II game cartridge.

Mutant engineers first chemically peeled the layers of the Demento II chips to allow microsopic examination of the circuitry. Through this means, they were able to decipher the object code and construct the series of pulsating signals that unlock the master chip. Mutant discovered that only a relatively small portion of the coded message was necessary to unlock the Demento II console. From this information, Mutant software designers built a slave chip that successfully unlocked the Demento II console and enabled Mutant's game cartridges to run. It included the entire coded message for fear that Demento might later alter new versions of the Demento II system in such a way as to make Mutant's cartridges inoperable on newer units seeking the fuller coded message. In order to differentiate its product, the Mutant slave program was written in a different computer language and employed a microprocessor different from the Demento II system. Since the Mutant microprocessor operated at a faster speed than the Demento II chip, the Mutant program included numerous pauses.

Despite these differences, Demento promptly sued Mutant for copyright infringement after Mutant introduced its first game cartridge for the Demento II system. What is the unprotectable idea of the Demento II system? What is the protectable expression? Is the lockout code functional? How would this case be resolved in a jurisdiction adhering the *Whelan* test? The *Altai* test?

3. Protection for Functional Elements and Protocols

Many software copyright cases involve the taking of particular pieces of a plaintiff's program. Defendants in these cases may be those who attempt to clone the plaintiff's program, writing their own code to create a functionally equivalent program. See Lotus Dev. Corp. v. Paperback Software, 740 F. Supp. 37 (D. Mass. 1990). The defendants may also be those who simply attempt to reproduce the internal program interface necessary to make two programs compatible. Whether functional program elements could be protected under copyright law was tested in a series of cases involving the Lotus 1-2-3 spreadsheet.

≡
≡
≡
≡   *Lotus Development Corp. v. Borland International*
    United States Court of Appeals for the First Circuit
    49 F.3d 807 (1st Cir. 1995)

STAHL, Circuit Judge.

This appeal requires us to decide whether a computer menu command hierarchy is copyrightable subject matter. In particular, we must decide whether, as the district court held, plaintiff-appellee Lotus Development Corporation's copyright in Lotus 1-2-3, a computer spreadsheet program, was infringed by defendant-appellant Borland International, Inc., when Borland copied the Lotus 1-2-3 menu command hierarchy into its Quattro and Quattro Pro computer spreadsheet programs. See Lotus Dev. Corp. v. Borland Int'l, Inc., 788 F. Supp. 78 (D. Mass. 1992) (*"Borland I"*); Lotus Dev. Corp. v. Borland Int'l, Inc., 799 F. Supp. 203 (D. Mass. 1992) (*"Borland II"*); Lotus Dev. Corp. v. Borland Int'l, Inc., 831 F. Supp. 202 (D. Mass. 1993) (*"Borland III"*); Lotus Dev. Corp. v. Borland Int'l, Inc., 831 F. Supp. 223 (D. Mass. 1993) (*"Borland IV"*).

I. Background

Lotus 1-2-3 is a spreadsheet program that enables users to perform accounting functions electronically on a computer. Users manipulate and control the program via a series of menu commands, such as "Copy," "Print," and "Quit." Users choose commands either by highlighting them on the screen or by typing their first letter. In all, Lotus 1-2-3 has 469 commands arranged into more than 50 menus and submenus.

Lotus 1-2-3, like many computer programs, allows users to write what are called "macros." By writing a macro, a user can designate a series of command choices with a single macro keystroke. Then, to execute that series of commands in multiple parts of the spreadsheet, rather than typing the whole series each time, the user only needs to type the single pre-programmed macro keystroke, causing the program to recall and perform the designated series of commands automatically. Thus, Lotus 1-2-3 macros shorten the time needed to set up and operate the program.

Borland released its first Quattro program to the public in 1987, after Borland's engineers had labored over its development for nearly three years. Borland's objective was to develop a spreadsheet program far superior to existing programs, including Lotus 1-2-3. In Borland's words, "from the time of its initial release . . . Quattro included enormous innovations over competing spreadsheet products."

The district court found, and Borland does not now contest, that Borland included in its Quattro and Quattro Pro version 1.0 programs "a virtually identical copy of the entire 1-2-3 menu tree." *Borland III*, 831 F. Supp. at 212. In so doing, Borland did not copy any of Lotus's underlying computer code; it copied only the words and structure of Lotus's menu command hierarchy. Borland included the Lotus menu command hierarchy in its programs to make them compatible with Lotus 1-2-3 so that spreadsheet users who were already familiar with Lotus 1-2-3 would be able to switch to the Borland programs without having to learn new commands or rewrite their Lotus macros.

In its Quattro and Quattro Pro version 1.0 programs, Borland achieved compatibility with Lotus 1-2-3 by offering its users an alternate user interface, the "Lotus Emulation Interface." By activating the Emulation Interface, Borland users would see the Lotus menu commands on their screens and could interact with Quattro or Quattro Pro as if using Lotus 1-2-3, albeit with a slightly different looking screen and with many Borland options not available on Lotus 1-2-3. In effect, Borland allowed users to choose how they wanted to communicate with Borland's spreadsheet programs: either by using menu commands designed by Borland, or by using the commands and command structure used in Lotus 1-2-3 augmented by Borland-added commands.

Lotus filed this action against Borland in the District of Massachusetts on July 2, 1990, four days after a district court held that the Lotus 1-2-3 "menu structure, taken as a whole—including the choice of command terms [and] the structure and order of those terms," was protected expression covered by Lotus's copyrights. Lotus Dev. Corp. v. Paperback Software Int'l, 740 F. Supp. 37, 68, 70 (D. Mass. 1990) ("*Paperback*").[1] . . .

---

1. Judge Keeton presided over both the *Paperback* litigation and this case.

```
                                                           ┌───────┐
                                                           │MENU;│
┌──────────┐                                               └───────┘
│Worksheet│  Range  Copy  Move  File  Print  Graph  Data  Quit
└──────────┘
 Global,  Insert,  Delete,  Column-Width,  Erase,  Titles,  Window,  Status
          A         B         C         D         E         F         G         H
    1
    2
    3
    4
    5
    6
    7
    8
    9
   10
   11
   12
   13
   14
   15
   16
   17
   18
   19
   20
```

FIGURE 2-1
Facsimile of a Lotus 1-2-3 screen display.

On July 31, 1992, the district court denied Borland's motion [for summary judgment] and granted Lotus's motion in part. The district court ruled that the Lotus menu command hierarchy was copyrightable expression because

> [a] very satisfactory spreadsheet menu tree can be constructed using different commands and a different command structure from those of Lotus 1-2-3. In fact, Borland has constructed just such an alternate tree for use in Quattro Pro's native mode. Even if one holds the arrangement of menu commands constant, it is possible to generate literally millions of satisfactory menu trees by varying the menu commands employed.

Borland II, 799 F. Supp. at 217. The district court demonstrated this by offering alternate command words for the ten commands that appear in Lotus's main menu. Id. For example, the district court stated that "the 'Quit' command could be named 'Exit' without any other modifications," and that "the 'Copy' command could be called 'Clone,' 'Ditto,' 'Duplicate,' 'Imitate,' 'Mimic,' 'Replicate,' and 'Reproduce,' among others." Id. Because so many variations were possible, the district court concluded that the Lotus developers' choice and arrangement of command terms, reflected in the Lotus menu command hierarchy, constituted copyrightable expression.

In granting partial summary judgment to Lotus, the district court held that Borland had infringed Lotus's copyright in Lotus 1-2-3 . . . . *Borland II*, 799 F. Supp. at 223. The court nevertheless concluded that while the Quattro and Quattro Pro programs infringed Lotus's copyright, Borland had not copied the entire Lotus 1-2-3 user interface, as Lotus had contended. . . .

Immediately following the district court's summary judgment decision, Borland removed the Lotus Emulation Interface from its products. Thereafter, Borland's spreadsheet programs no longer displayed the Lotus 1-2-3 menus to Borland users, and as a result Borland users could no longer communicate with Borland's programs as if they were using a more sophisticated version of Lotus 1-2-3. Nonetheless, Borland's programs continued to be partially compatible with Lotus 1-2-3, for Borland retained what it called the "Key Reader" in its Quattro Pro programs. Once turned on, the Key Reader allowed Borland's programs to understand and perform some Lotus 1-2-3 macros. With the Key Reader on, the Borland programs used Quattro Pro menus for display, interaction, and macro execution, except when they encountered a slash ("/") key in a macro (the starting key for any Lotus 1-2-3 macro), in which case they interpreted the macro as having been written for Lotus 1-2-3. Accordingly, people who wrote or purchased macros to shorten the time needed to perform an operation in Lotus 1-2-3 could still use those macros in Borland's programs. The district court permitted Lotus to file a supplemental complaint alleging that the Key Reader infringed its copyright.

The parties agreed to try the remaining liability issues without a jury. The district court held two trials, the Phase I trial covering all remaining issues raised in the original complaint (relating to the Emulation Interface) and the Phase II trial covering all issues raised in the supplemental complaint (relating to the Key Reader). . . .

In its Phase I trial decision, the district court found that "each of the Borland emulation interfaces contains a virtually identical copy of the 1-2-3 menu tree and that the 1-2-3 menu tree is capable of a wide variety of expression." *Borland III*, 831 F. Supp. at 218. The district court also rejected Borland's affirmative defenses of laches and estoppel. Id. at 218-23.

In its Phase II trial decision, the district court found that Borland's Key Reader file included "a virtually identical copy of the Lotus menu tree structure, but represented in a different form and with first letters of menu command names in place of the full menu command names." *Borland IV*, 831 F. Supp. at 228. In other words, Borland's programs no longer included the Lotus command terms, but only their first letters. The district court held that "the Lotus menu structure, organization, and first letters of the command names . . . constitute part of the protectable expression found in [Lotus 1-2-3]." *Id.* at 233. Accordingly, the district court held that with its Key Reader, Borland had infringed Lotus's copyright. *Id.* at 245. The district court also rejected Borland's affirmative defenses of waiver, laches, estoppel, and fair use. *Id.* at 235-45. The district court then entered a permanent injunction against Borland, *id.* at 245, from which Borland appeals. . . .

II. Discussion

On appeal, Borland does not dispute that it factually copied the words and arrangement of the Lotus menu command hierarchy. Rather, Borland argues that it "lawfully copied the unprotectable menus of Lotus 1-2-3." Borland contends that the Lotus menu command hierarchy is not copyrightable because it is a system, method of operation, process, or procedure foreclosed from protection by 17 U.S.C. §102(b). Borland also raises a number of affirmative defenses.

A. Copyright Infringement Generally

. . . In this appeal, we are faced only with whether the Lotus menu command hierarchy is copyrightable subject matter in the first instance, for Borland concedes that Lotus has a valid copyright in Lotus 1-2-3 as a whole and admits to factually copying the Lotus menu command hierarchy. As a result, this appeal is in a very different posture from most copyright-infringement cases, for copyright infringement generally turns on whether the defendant has copied protected expression as a factual matter. Because of this different posture, most copyright-infringement cases provide only limited help to us in deciding this appeal. This is true even with respect to those copyright-infringement cases that deal with computers and computer software.

B. Matter of First Impression

Whether a computer menu command hierarchy constitutes copyrightable subject matter is a matter of first impression in this court. While some other courts appear to have touched on it briefly in dicta, see, e.g., Autoskill, Inc. v. National Educ. Support Sys., Inc., 994 F.2d 1476, 1495 n.23 (10th Cir.), cert. denied, 126 L. Ed. 2d 254, 114 S. Ct. 307 (1993), we know of no cases that deal with the copyrightability of a menu command hierarchy standing on its own (i.e., without other elements of the user interface, such as screen displays, in issue). Thus we are navigating in uncharted waters.

Borland vigorously argues, however, that the Supreme Court charted our course more than 100 years ago when it decided Baker v. Selden, 101 U.S. 99, 25 L. Ed. 841 (1879). In Baker v. Selden, the Court held that Selden's copyright over the textbook in which he explained his new way to do accounting did not grant him a monopoly on the use of his accounting system. Borland argues:

> The facts of Baker v. Selden, and even the arguments advanced by the parties in that case, are identical to those in this case. The only difference is that the "user interface" of Selden's system was implemented by pen and paper rather than by computer.

. . . We do not think that Baker v. Selden is nearly as analogous to this appeal as Borland claims. Of course, Lotus 1-2-3 is a computer spreadsheet, and as such its grid of horizontal rows and vertical columns certainly resembles an accounting ledger or any other paper spreadsheet. Those grids, however, are not at issue in this appeal for, unlike Selden, Lotus does not claim to have a monopoly over its accounting system. Rather, this appeal involves Lotus's monopoly over the commands it uses to operate the computer. Accordingly, this appeal is not, as Borland contends, "identical" to Baker v. Selden.

C. Altai

Before we analyze whether the Lotus menu command hierarchy is a system, method of operation, process, or procedure, we first consider the applicability of the test the Second Circuit set forth in Computer Assoc. Int'l, Inc. v. Altai, Inc., 982 F.2d 693 (2d Cir. 1992). The Second Circuit designed its *Altai* test to deal with the fact that computer programs, copyrighted as "literary works," can be infringed by what is known as "nonliteral" copying, which is copying that is paraphrased or loosely paraphrased rather than word for word. See *id.* at 701 (citing nonliteral-copying cases); see also 3 Melville B. Nimmer & David Nimmer, Nimmer on Copyright §13.03[A][1] (1993). When faced with nonliteral-copying cases, courts must determine whether similarities are due merely to the fact that the two works share the same underlying idea or whether they instead indicate that the second author copied the first author's expression. The Second Circuit designed its *Altai* test to deal with this situation in the computer context, specifically with whether one computer program copied nonliteral expression from another program's code. . . .

In the instant appeal, we are not confronted with alleged nonliteral copying of computer code. Rather, we are faced with Borland's deliberate, literal copying of the Lotus menu command hierarchy. Thus, we must determine not whether nonliteral copying occurred in some amorphous sense, but rather whether the literal copying of the Lotus menu command hierarchy constitutes copyright infringement.

While the *Altai* test may provide a useful framework for assessing the alleged nonliteral copying of computer code, we find it to be of little help in assessing whether the literal copying of a menu command hierarchy constitutes copyright infringement. In fact, we think that the *Altai* test in this context may actually be misleading because, in instructing courts to abstract the various levels, it seems to encourage them to find a base level that includes copyrightable subject matter that, if literally copied, would make the copier liable for copyright infringement.[8] While that base (or literal) level would not be at issue in a nonliteral-copying case like *Altai*, it is precisely what is at issue in this appeal. We think that abstracting menu command hierarchies down to their individual word and menu levels and then filtering idea from expression at that stage, as both the *Altai* and the district court tests require, obscures the more fundamental question of whether a menu command hierarchy can be copyrighted at all. The initial inquiry should not be whether individual components of a menu command hierarchy are expressive, but rather whether the menu command hierarchy as a whole can be copyrighted. But see Gates Rubber Co. v. Bando Chem. Indus., Ltd., 9 F.3d 823 (10th Cir. 1993) (endorsing *Altai*'s abstraction-filtration-comparison test as a way of determining whether "menus and sorting criteria" are copyrightable).

D. The Lotus Menu Command Hierarchy: A "Method of Operation"

Borland argues that the Lotus menu command hierarchy is uncopyrightable because it is a system, method of operation, process, or procedure foreclosed from copyright protection by 17 U.S.C. §102(b). Section 102(b) states: "In no case does copyright protection for an original work of authorship extend to any idea, procedure, process, system, method of operation, concept, principle, or discovery, regardless of the form in which it is described, explained, illustrated, or embodied in such work." Because we conclude that the Lotus menu command hierarchy is a method of operation, we do not consider whether it could also be a system, process, or procedure.

We think that "method of operation," as that term is used in §102(b), refers to the means by which a person operates something, whether it be a car, a food processor, or a computer. Thus a text describing how to operate something would not extend copyright protection to the method of operation itself; other people would be free to employ that

---

8. We recognize that *Altai* never states that every work contains a copyrightable "nugget" of protectable expression. Nonetheless, the implication is that for literal copying, "it is not necessary to determine the level of abstraction at which similarity ceases to consist of an 'expression of ideas,' because literal similarity by definition is always a similarity as to the expression of ideas." 3 Melville B. Nimmer & David Nimmer, Nimmer on Copyright §13.03[A][2] (1993).

method and to describe it in their own words. Similarly, if a new method of operation is used rather than described, other people would still be free to employ or describe that method.

We hold that the Lotus menu command hierarchy is an uncopyrightable "method of operation." The Lotus menu command hierarchy provides the means by which users control and operate Lotus 1-2-3. If users wish to copy material, for example, they use the "Copy" command. If users wish to print material, they use the "Print" command. Users must use the command terms to tell the computer what to do. Without the menu command hierarchy, users would not be able to access and control, or indeed make use of, Lotus 1-2-3's functional capabilities.

The Lotus menu command hierarchy does not merely explain and present Lotus 1-2-3's functional capabilities to the user; it also serves as the method by which the program is operated and controlled. The Lotus menu command hierarchy is different from the Lotus long prompts, for the long prompts are not necessary to the operation of the program; users could operate Lotus 1-2-3 even if there were no long prompts. The Lotus menu command hierarchy is also different from the Lotus screen displays, for users need not "use" any expressive aspects of the screen displays in order to operate Lotus 1-2-3; because the way the screens look has little bearing on how users control the program, the screen displays are not part of Lotus 1-2-3's "method of operation." The Lotus menu command hierarchy is also different from the underlying computer code, because while code is necessary for the program to work, its precise formulation is not. In other words, to offer the same capabilities as Lotus 1-2-3, Borland did not have to copy Lotus's underlying code (and indeed it did not); to allow users to operate its programs in substantially the same way, however, Borland had to copy the Lotus menu command hierarchy. Thus the Lotus 1-2-3 code is not an uncopyrightable "method of operation."

The district court held that the Lotus menu command hierarchy, with its specific choice and arrangement of command terms, constituted an "expression" of the "idea" of operating a computer program with commands arranged hierarchically into menus and submenus. *Borland II*, 799 F. Supp. at 216. Under the district court's reasoning, Lotus's decision to employ hierarchically arranged command terms to operate its program could not foreclose its competitors from also employing hierarchically arranged command terms to operate their programs, but it did foreclose them from employing the specific command terms and arrangement that Lotus had used. In effect, the district court limited Lotus 1-2-3's "method of operation" to an abstraction.

Accepting the district court's finding that the Lotus developers made some expressive choices in choosing and arranging the Lotus command terms, we nonetheless hold that that expression is not copyrightable because it is part of Lotus 1-2-3's "method of operation." We do not think that "methods of operation" are limited to abstractions; rather, they are the means by which a user operates something. If specific words are essential to operating something, then they are part of a "method of operation" and, as such, are unprotectable. This is so whether they must be highlighted, typed in, or even spoken, as computer programs no doubt will soon be controlled by spoken words.

The fact that Lotus developers could have designed the Lotus menu command hierarchy differently is immaterial to the question of whether it is a "method of operation." In other words, our initial inquiry is not whether the Lotus menu command hierarchy incorporates any expression. Rather, our initial inquiry is whether the Lotus menu command hierarchy is a "method of operation." Concluding, as we do, that users operate Lotus 1-2-3 by using the Lotus menu command hierarchy, and that the entire Lotus menu command hierarchy is essential to operating Lotus 1-2-3, we do not inquire further whether that method of operation could have been designed differently. The "expressive" choices of what to name the command terms and how to arrange them do not magically change the uncopyrightable menu command hierarchy into copyrightable subject matter.

Our holding that "methods of operation" are not limited to mere abstractions is bolstered by Baker v. Selden. In *Baker*, the Supreme Court explained that

> the teachings of science and the rules and methods of useful art have their final end in application and use; and this application and use are what the public derive from the publication of a book which teaches them. . . . The description of the art in a book, though entitled to the benefit of copyright, lays no foundation for an exclusive claim to the art itself. The object of the one is explanation; the object of the other is use. The former may be secured by copyright. The latter can only be secured, if it can be secured at all, by letters-patent.

Baker v. Selden, 101 U.S. at 104-05. Lotus wrote its menu command hierarchy so that people could learn it and use it. Accordingly, it falls squarely within the prohibition on copyright protection established in Baker v. Selden and codified by Congress in §102(b).

In many ways, the Lotus menu command hierarchy is like the buttons used to control, say, a video cassette recorder ("VCR"). A VCR is a machine that enables one to watch and record video tapes. Users operate VCRs by pressing a series of buttons that are typically labelled "Record, Play, Reverse, Fast Forward, Pause, Stop/Eject." That the buttons are arranged and labeled does not make them a "literary work," nor does it make them an "expression" of the abstract "method of operating" a VCR via a set of labeled buttons. Instead, the buttons are themselves the "method of operating" the VCR.

When a Lotus 1-2-3 user chooses a command, either by highlighting it on the screen or by typing its first letter, he or she effectively pushes a button. Highlighting the "Print" command on the screen, or typing the letter "P," is analogous to pressing a VCR button labeled "Play."

Just as one could not operate a buttonless VCR, it would be impossible to operate Lotus 1-2-3 without employing its menu command hierarchy. Thus the Lotus command terms are not equivalent to the labels on the VCR's buttons, but are instead equivalent to the buttons themselves. Unlike the labels on a VCR's buttons, which merely make operating a VCR easier by indicating the buttons' functions, the Lotus menu commands are essential to operating Lotus 1-2-3. Without the menu commands, there would be no way to "push" the Lotus buttons, as one could push unlabeled VCR buttons. While Lotus could probably have designed a user interface for which the command terms were mere labels, it did not do so here. Lotus 1-2-3 depends for its operation on use of the precise command terms that make up the Lotus menu command hierarchy. . . .

Computer programs, unlike VCRs, are copyrightable as "literary works." 17 U.S.C. §102(a). Accordingly, one might argue, the "buttons" used to operate a computer program are not like the buttons used to operate a VCR, for they are not subject to a useful-article exception. The response, of course, is that the arrangement of buttons on a VCR would not be copyrightable even without a useful-article exception, because the buttons are an uncopyrightable "method of operation." Similarly, the "buttons" of a computer program are also an uncopyrightable "method of operation."

That the Lotus menu command hierarchy is a "method of operation" becomes clearer when one considers program compatibility. Under Lotus's theory, if a user uses several different programs, he or she must learn how to perform the same operation in a different way for each program used. For example, if the user wanted the computer to print material, then the user would have to learn not just one method of operating the computer such that it prints, but many different methods. We find this absurd. The fact that there may be many different ways to operate a computer program, or even many different ways to operate a computer program using a set of hierarchically arranged command terms, does not make the actual method of operation chosen copyrightable; it still functions as a method for operating the computer and as such is uncopyrightable.

Consider also that users employ the Lotus menu command hierarchy in writing macros. Under the district court's holding, if the user wrote a macro to shorten the time needed to perform a certain operation in Lotus 1-2-3, the user would be unable to use that macro to shorten the time needed to perform that same operation in another program. Rather, the user would have to rewrite his or her macro using that other program's menu command hierarchy. This is despite the fact that the macro is clearly the user's own work product. We think that forcing the user to cause the computer to perform the same operation in a different way ignores Congress's direction in §102(b) that "methods of operation" are not copyrightable. That programs can offer users the ability to write macros in many different ways does not change the fact that, once written, the macro allows the user to perform an operation automatically. As the Lotus menu command hierarchy serves as the basis for Lotus 1-2-3 macros, the Lotus menu command hierarchy is a "method of operation." . . .

We also note that in most contexts, there is no need to "build" upon other people's expression, for the ideas conveyed by that expression can be conveyed by someone else without copying the first author's expression. In the context of methods of operation, however, "building" requires the use of the precise method of operation already employed; otherwise, "building" would require dismantling, too. Original developers are not the only people entitled to build on the methods of operation they create; anyone can. Thus, Borland may build on the method of operation that Lotus designed and may use the Lotus menu command hierarchy in doing so.

Our holding that methods of operation are not limited to abstractions goes against *Autoskill*, 994 F.2d at 1495 n.23, in which the Tenth Circuit rejected the defendant's argument that the keying procedure used in a computer program was an uncopyrightable "procedure" or "method of operation" under §102(b). The program at issue, which was designed to test and train students with reading deficiencies, *id.* at 1481, required students to select responses to the program's queries "by pressing the 1, 2, or 3 keys." *Id.* at 1495 n.23. The Tenth Circuit held that, "for purposes of the preliminary injunction, . . . the record showed that [this] keying procedure reflected at least a minimal degree of creativity," as required by *Feist* for copyright protection. *Id.* As an initial matter, we question whether a programmer's decision to have users select a response by pressing the 1, 2, or 3 keys is original. More importantly, however, we fail to see how "a student selecting a response by pressing the 1, 2, or 3 keys," *id.*, can be anything but an unprotectable method of operation.[14] . . .

Reversed.

BOUDIN, Circuit Judge, concurring.

The importance of this case, and a slightly different emphasis in my view of the underlying problem, prompt me to add a few words to the majority's tightly focused discussion.

I.

Most of the law of copyright and the "tools" of analysis have developed in the context of literary works such as novels, plays, and films. In this milieu, the principal problem—simply stated, if difficult to resolve—is to stimulate creative expression without unduly limiting access by others to the broader themes and concepts deployed by the author. The middle of

---

14. The Ninth Circuit has also indicated in dicta that "menus, and keystrokes" may be copyrightable. Brown Bag Software v. Symantec Corp., 960 F.2d 1465, 1477 (9th Cir.), *cert. denied*, BB Asset Management, Inc. v. Symantec Corp., 121 L. Ed. 2d 141, 113 S. Ct. 198 (1992). In that case, however, the plaintiff did not show that the defendant had copied the plaintiff's menus or keystrokes, so the court was not directly faced with whether the menus or keystrokes constituted an unprotectable method of operation. *Id.*

the spectrum presents close cases; but a "mistake" in providing too much protection involves a small cost: subsequent authors treating the same themes must take a few more steps away from the original expression.

The problem presented by computer programs is fundamentally different in one respect. The computer program is a means for causing something to happen; it has a mechanical utility, an instrumental role, in accomplishing the world's work. Granting protection, in other words, can have some of the consequences of patent protection in limiting other people's ability to perform a task in the most efficient manner. Utility does not bar copyright (dictionaries may be copyrighted), but it alters the calculus.

Of course, the argument for protection is undiminished, perhaps even enhanced, by utility: if we want more of an intellectual product, a temporary monopoly for the creator provides incentives for others to create other, different items in this class. But the "cost" side of the equation may be different where one places a very high value on public access to a useful innovation that may be the most efficient means of performing a given task. Thus, the argument for extending protection may be the same; but the stakes on the other side are much higher.

It is no accident that patent protection has preconditions that copyright protection does not—notably, the requirements of novelty and non-obviousness—and that patents are granted for a shorter period than copyrights. This problem of utility has sometimes manifested itself in copyright cases, such as Baker v. Selden, 101 U.S. 99, 25 L. Ed. 841 (1879), and been dealt with through various formulations that limit copyright or create limited rights to copy. But the case law and doctrine addressed to utility in copyright have been brief detours in the general march of copyright law.

Requests for the protection of computer menus present the concern with fencing off access to the commons in an acute form. A new menu may be a creative work, but over time its importance may come to reside more in the investment that has been made by users in learning the menu and in building their own mini-programs—macros—in reliance upon the menu. Better typewriter keyboard layouts may exist, but the familiar QWERTY keyboard dominates the market because that is what everyone has learned to use. See P. David, CLIO and the Economics of QWERTY, 75 Am. Econ. Rev. 332 (1985). The QWERTY keyboard is nothing other than a menu of letters.

Thus, to assume that computer programs are just one more new means of expression, like a filmed play, may be quite wrong. The "form"— the written source code or the menu structure depicted on the screen— look hauntingly like the familiar stuff of copyright; but the "substance" probably has more to do with problems presented in patent law or, as already noted, in those rare cases where copyright law has confronted industrially useful expressions. Applying copyright law to computer programs is like assembling a jigsaw puzzle whose pieces do not quite fit. . . .

II.

In this case, the raw facts are mostly, if not entirely, undisputed. Although the inferences to be drawn may be more debatable, it is very hard to see that Borland has shown any interest in the Lotus menu except as a fall-back option for those users already committed to it by prior experience or in order to run their own macros using 1-2-3 commands. At least for the amateur, accessing the Lotus menu in the Borland Quattro or Quattro Pro program takes some effort.

Put differently, it is unlikely that users who value the Lotus menu for its own sake—independent of any investment they have made themselves in learning Lotus' commands or creating macros dependent upon them—would choose the Borland program in order to secure access to the Lotus menu. Borland's success is due primarily to other features. Its rationale for deploying the Lotus menu bears the ring of truth.

Now, any use of the Lotus menu by Borland is a commercial use and deprives Lotus of a portion of its "reward," in the sense that an infringement claim if allowed would increase Lotus' profits. But this is circular reasoning: broadly speaking, every limitation on copyright or privileged use diminishes the reward of the original creator. Yet not every writing is copyrightable or every use an infringement. The provision of reward is one concern of copyright law, but it is not the only one. If it were, copyrights would be perpetual and there would be no exceptions.

The present case is an unattractive one for copyright protection of the menu. The menu commands (e.g., "print," "quit") are largely for standard procedures that Lotus did not invent and are common words that Lotus cannot monopolize. What is left is the particular combination and subgrouping of commands in a pattern devised by Lotus. This arrangement may have a more appealing logic and ease of use than some other configurations; but there is a certain arbitrariness to many of the choices.

If Lotus is granted a monopoly on this pattern, users who have learned the command structure of Lotus 1-2-3 or devised their own macros are locked into Lotus, just as a typist who has learned the QWERTY keyboard would be the captive of anyone who had a monopoly on the production of such a keyboard. Apparently, for a period Lotus 1-2-3 has had such sway in the market that it has represented the de facto standard for electronic spreadsheet commands. So long as Lotus is the superior spreadsheet—either in quality or in price—there may be nothing wrong with this advantage.

But if a better spreadsheet comes along, it is hard to see why customers who have learned the Lotus menu and devised macros for it should remain captives of Lotus because of an investment in learning made by the users and not by Lotus. Lotus has already reaped a substantial reward for being first; assuming that the Borland program is now better, good reasons exist for freeing it to attract old Lotus customers: to enable the old customers to take advantage of a new advance, and to reward Borland in turn for making a better product. If Borland has not made a better product, then customers will remain with Lotus anyway.

Thus, for me the question is not whether Borland should prevail but on what basis. Various avenues might be traveled, but the main choices are between holding that the menu is not protectable by copyright and devising a new doctrine that Borland's use is privileged. No solution is perfect and no intermediate appellate court can make the final choice.

To call the menu a "method of operation" is, in the common use of those words, a defensible position. After all, the purpose of the menu is not to be admired as a work of literary or pictorial art. It is to transmit directions from the user to the computer, i.e., to operate the computer. The menu is also a "method" in the dictionary sense because it is a "planned way of doing something," an "order or system," and (aptly here) an "orderly or systematic arrangement, sequence or the like." Random House Webster's College Dictionary 853 (1991).

A different approach would be to say that Borland's use is privileged because, in the context already described, it is not seeking to appropriate the advances made by Lotus' menu; rather, having provided an arguably more attractive menu of its own, Borland is merely trying to give former Lotus users an option to exploit their own prior investment in learning or in macros. The difference is that such a privileged use approach would not automatically protect Borland if it had simply copied the Lotus menu (using different codes), contributed nothing of its own, and resold Lotus under the Borland label.

The closest analogue in conventional copyright is the fair use doctrine. E.g., Harper & Row, Publishers, Inc. v. Nation Enters., 471 U.S. 539, 85 L. Ed. 2d 588, 105 S. Ct. 2218 (1985). Although invoked by Borland, it has largely been brushed aside in this case because the Supreme Court has said that it is "presumptively" unavailable where the use is a "commercial" one. See *id*. at 562. In my view, this is something less than a definitive answer; "presumptively" does not mean "always" and, in any event, the doctrine of fair use was created by the courts and can be adapted to new purposes.

But a privileged use doctrine would certainly involve problems of its own. It might more closely tailor the limits on copyright protection to the reasons for limiting that protection; but it would entail a host of administrative problems that would cause cost and delay, and would also reduce the ability of the industry to predict outcomes. Indeed, to the extent that Lotus' menu is an important standard in the industry, it might be argued that any use ought to be deemed privileged.

In sum, the majority's result persuades me and its formulation is as good, if not better, than any other that occurs to me now as within the reach of courts. Some solutions (e.g., a very short copyright period for menus) are not options at all for courts but might be for Congress. In all events, the choices are important ones of policy, not linguistics, and they should be made with the underlying considerations in view.

Digital Communications Associates v. Softklone Distributing Corp., 659 F. Supp. 449 (N.D. Ga. 1987):

> After review of the evidence, the court concludes that the status screen [of plaintiff's program], even if found to be a form, clearly expresses and conveys information and, therefore, is copyrightable. The arrangement of the commands under descriptive parameter headings aids the user in easier understanding of the availability, importance, and functioning of the various commands. Likewise, the highlighting and capitalizing of certain letters of the commands assist the user in knowing which symbols to enter to activate the various commands. While it is true that the status screen alone would be insufficient to completely explain to a novice user either the availability of commands, the meaning of the commands, or the symbols necessary to enter certain commands, this fact is not dispositive. Whether or not an explanatory work is complete for all users is not determinative of whether the work is explanatory in nature. The status screen clearly "undertakes to express." *Synercom*, 462 F. Supp. at 1011.
>
> The basic principle behind denying copyright protection to "blank forms" lies in the concern that providing such protection would give the copyright owner undue protection over the idea underlying the form, i.e., there are often very few methods to express the content of a form such as a calendar or time sheet and one individual could draw up these variations, copyright them, and thus obtain a virtual monopoly on such clearly useful ideas as a record of the days and of one's time and activities. Further, the majority of such forms are simple and require little ingenuity to design, so little incentive (protection) is required to motivate designers, while the use (communication) of the form is very important to society.
>
> Application of this principle to plaintiff's status screen, which undisputedly required substantial effort to author and which has innumerable possible variations so that its copyrighting would not permit the plaintiff to monopolize its underlying ideas, argues for granting it copyright protection. Despite defense counsel's arguments of the particular importance of standardization in the computer industry, an argument similar to the one rejected in *Whelan*, 797 F.2d at 1238 ("we are not convinced that progress in computer technology or technique is qualitatively different from progress in other areas of science or the arts"), this court concludes that the proper balance of protection and communication supports the copyrightability of the status screen arrangement and design. By granting the plaintiff a copyright on the arrangement and design of the status screen, the court is not granting plaintiff control over the ideas of a command driven program, a "status" screen depicting the status of the program's operations, or the use of particular command terms or symbols.

COMMENTS AND QUESTIONS

1. The issues raised by the *Lotus* decision remain unsettled. The Supreme Court granted certiorari in the case, but deadlocked 4-4, and therefore affirmed the First Circuit, but produced no precedential opinion. Lotus Dev. Corp. v. Borland Int'l, 516 U.S. 233 (1996). Note that the First Circuit concedes that its opinion is at odds with the Tenth Circuit's decision in Autoskill, Inc. v. National Educational Support Systems, 994 F.2d 1476, 1495 n.23 (10th Cir. 1993), and dictum from the Ninth Circuit's decision in Brown Bag Software v. Symantec Corp., 960 F.2d 1465, 1477 (9th Cir. 1992). It is also arguably inconsistent with the Fifth Circuit's decision in Engineering Dynamics, Inc. v. Structural Software Inc., 26 F.3d 1335 (5th Cir. 1994), which gave broad copyright protection to program interfaces and relied extensively on Judge Keeton's prior decision in Lotus Dev. Corp. v. Paperback Software, 740 F. Supp. 37 (D. Mass. 1990).

On the other hand, the *Lotus* approach seems consistent with the legislative history of 17 U.S.C. section 102(b). The House Report accompanying that section states:

> Section 102(b) is intended, among other things, to make clear that the expression adopted by the programmer is the copyrightable element in a computer program, and that the actual processes or methods embodied in the program are not within the scope of the copyright law.

H.R. Rep. No. 1476, 94th Cong., 2d Sess. 57 (1976), *reprinted in* 1976 U.S.C.C.A.N. 5659, 5670. Further, most commentators seem to agree with the ultimate result in *Lotus*, though many are troubled by the court's reasoning. See, e.g., Brief Amicus Curiae of Copyright Law Professors in Support of Respondent in Lotus v. Borland, No. 94-2003 (U.S. 1995) (brief submitted by 34 copyright professors urging affirmance for a variety of reasons); Mark A. Lemley, Convergence in the Law of Software Copyright, 10 High Tech. L.J. 1 (1995); Glynn S. Lunney Jr., Lotus v. Borland: Copyright and Computer Programs, 70 Tul. L. Rev. 2397 (1996); Peter S. Menell, The Challenges of Reforming Intellectual Property Protection for Computer Software, 94 Colum. L. Rev. 2644, 2653 (1994). Finally, at least one court has followed the First Circuit's ruling in *Lotus*. The court used section 102(b) to reject a copyright claim to a menu tree structure, noting that granting copyright on such a structure would infringe on the province of patent law. MiTek Holdings v. Arce Engineering Co., 89 F.3d 1548 (11th Cir. 1996). But see Mitel, Inc. v. Iqtel, Inc., 124 F.3d 1366 (10th Cir. 1997) ("We conclude that although an element of a work may be chararcterized as a method of operation, that element may nevertheless contain expression that is eligible for copyright protection. . . . Thus, we decline to adopt the *Lotus* court's approach to section 102(b), and continue to adhere to our abstraction-filtration-comparison approach.").

2. Contrast the analysis of section 102(b) and Baker v. Selden in the *Lotus* case with that in Apple v. Franklin. Applying the *Lotus* court's logic, isn't object code a "method of operation" for instructing a CPU how to process information? If so, how can the copyrightability of computer programs be reconciled with the exclusion from copyright of "methods of operation"?

3. Note that the *Lotus* court chose to reject the filtration test adopted by the Second Circuit in Computer Associates v. Altai and followed by most other circuits. Is the holding in *Lotus* really incompatible with *Altai*'s abstraction-filtration-comparison test? One possible way to reconcile *Lotus* and *Altai* is to treat *Lotus* not as a case involving "literal" copying of a menu structure but as a case involving nonliteral copying of the program itself. Lotus distributed object code that in certain combinations produces physical images on a screen that represent certain words and that have certain effects. Borland did not copy that code; rather, it wrote its own code, which produced similar images and had the same effects as the Lotus code. The court could then have applied *Altai*'s abstraction-filtration-comparison analysis. Perhaps this is in effect what the *Lotus* court did —although when it reached the "filtration" step, it determined that the entire program was unprotectable at the menu command hierarchy level. See Mark A. Lemley, Convergence in the Law of Software Copyright?, 10 High Tech. L.J. 1, 21-22 (1995).

Do the *Altai* and *Lotus* cases really present analogous issues? Is a "filtration" analysis that filters out the entire copyrighted work at one level of abstraction within the contemplation of the *Altai* court?

4. The *Lotus* court compares the 1-2-3 menu command hierarchy to the buttons on a VCR, which it says are uncopyrightable because they are methods of operation. But is this the right analogy? Lotus claimed that Borland had infringed its copyright by copying the structure, sequence, and organization of its menu hierarchy, not the words of the menus themselves. This "structure, sequence and organization" seems the equivalent of the location and arrangement of the VCR buttons rather than the buttons themselves. Would an original way of arranging the buttons on a VCR be copyrightable? Should it? Is the question one of originality and the idea-expression dichotomy, or is there some reason not to copyright the arrangement of buttons on a VCR even if it were original and expressive?

5. In the predecessor case to Lotus v. Borland, defendant Paperback Software argued that the command structure of the Lotus program is in essence a language. It can be used to create macros and to run the spreadsheet. Is this a fair characterization? The district court attacked this analogy (which it called "strained") on two basic grounds: that Lotus 1-2-3 was not in fact a language, and that languages could be copyrightable. The first conclusion is certainly debatable: one's definition of a language (or, alternatively, a "system") will go a long way toward answering this question. But consider the court's second premise—that languages might be

copyrightable. Is copyrighting "natural" (i.e., human) languages consistent with what you know of copyright law? Is a language functional, or does it express? Does it matter whether the plaintiff is claiming the creation of certain words or the entire system of grammar and interaction between words? Cf. Reiss v. National Quotation Bureau, 276 F. 717 (S.D.N.Y. 1921) (suggesting in dictum that Esperanto could be copyrighted). On this point, compare Ronald Johnson & Allen Grogan, Copyright Protection for Command Driven Interfaces, 8:6 Computer Law. 1 (June 1991) (advocating copyright protection for languages) with Pamela Samuelson, How to Interpret the Lotus Decision; And How Not To, 33:11 Communications of the ACM 27 (Nov. 1990), and Elizabeth G. Lowry, Comment, Copyright Protection for Computer Languages: Creative Incentive or Technological Threat, 39 Emory L.J. 1293 (1990) (both opposing such protection).

Does the First Circuit's decision in Lotus v. Borland shed any light on this issue? Are languages "systems" or "methods of operation" that are denied protection under section 102(b)? An Australian case, Data Access Corp. v. Powerflex Services Pty., No. VG473 (Fed. Ct. Aus., Melbourne 1996), may prove instructive. The Federal Court in that case (the trial court) held that even a single word serving a menu command function may be copyrightable, because it is a concatenation of letters. Copyright protection therefore clearly extended to the computer language at issue in that case, which consisted of 225 words. But the appellate panel reversed, concluding that the words in that case were not themselves sufficiently creative to be deserving of copyright protection.

6. Both the majority and Judge Boudin's concurrence express concern over the harm that would be done to users of Lotus 1-2-3 if they could not copy their macros for use on Quattro Pro. Certainly, users have invested time and effort in using Lotus 1-2-3, and this may make them reluctant to change spreadsheet programs, even if Borland's program really is superior. But is this the sort of problem with which the copyright law should be concerned? Why isn't a customer preference for a known and trusted product part of the reward that the copyright owner is entitled to reap?

Is the QWERTY keyboard protectable by copyright? Why or why not? Does the answer depend on timing—whether the QWERTY keyboard has just been introduced or whether it is well-established as the industry standard for typewriters? How would you apply section 102(b) in each case?

7. In his concurrence, Judge Boudin proposes (although he does not necessarily adopt) an alternative rationale for the Lotus decision: that Lotus's menu command hierarchy was copyrightable but that Borland's use of the menu hierarchy in this case was privileged because it was done for the purpose of making the two programs compatible. The "privileged use" rationale is narrower than the majority's "method of operation" rule. Because the majority holds the menu command hierarchy entirely uncopy-

rightable, Lotus has no power to prevent anyone from copying its menu structure, regardless of the circumstances in which the copying occurs.

Suppose that, without taking any protected source or object code, a small company managed to acquire an early copy of Lotus 1-2-3. It replicated the menu command hierarchy and began to sell "clone" programs that looked and worked just like Lotus 1-2-3. Cf. Lotus Dev. Corp. v. Paperback Software, 740 F. Supp. 37 (D. Mass. 1990), a prior decision by Judge Keeton that is apparently overruled by the First Circuit's decision. In such a case, the equities might seem to tilt towards *Lotus* more than they did in the *Borland* case. Nonetheless, under the majority's rule, the clone manufacturer has the right to make such copies. By contrast, the "privileged use" rationale might not protect the clone manufacturer from a copyright infringement suit. Does Judge Boudin's "privileged use" approach better address this circumstance? Some commentators have argued for the First Circuit's result in *Lotus* on these narrower grounds— that in the particular circumstances of this case Borland's improvement on the Lotus 1-2-3 program was sufficiently great that it should justify the taking. See Mark A. Lemley, The Economics of Improvement in Intellectual Property Law, 75 Tex. L. Rev. 989 (1997). For a more detailed discussion of a privilege to copy certain aspects of a computer program in order to achieve compatibility, see Section E below.

For an argument that the effort that goes into program design should be protected against misappropriation, though not by copyright law, see Pamela Samuelson et al., A Manifesto Concerning the Legal Protection of Computer Programs, 94 Colum. L. Rev. 2308 (1994).

8. In *Lotus*, the menu command hierarchy served both as a functional part of the program (structuring the way the program itself functioned) and as a user interface. Borland's emulation products (though not its Key Reader feature) copied this user interface and under certain conditions therefore presented the same appearance to the user as the Lotus 1-2-3 program. It might therefore be appropriate to think of *Lotus* as a user interface copyright case as well as a protocol copyright case. We discuss the protection of user interfaces in subsection B.5 below.

Note on the Protection of Computer Protocols After Lotus

The *Lotus* decision—and those rejecting it—are directly relevant to the copyright protection that will be afforded various software protocols governing data communication, applications program interfaces (APIs), and numerous other operational components of computer programs. The First Circuit's opinion in *Lotus* would seem to suggest that such APIs are, as a system of operation, themselves uncopyrightable in their entirety. As noted above, however, most courts do not take this absolute approach.

Even if an interface protocol is eligible for copyright protection, however, it may still lose protection against all but the most literal copying if a court concludes during its filtration analysis that virtually all of the elements of the interface are unprotectable. For example, in *Mitel*, the Tenth Circuit concluded that the arbitrary selection of code numbers in the operation of telephone call controllers was not sufficiently original to qualify for copyright protection. *Mitel* supra, 124 F.3d at 1366. But see Atari Games Corp. v. Nintendo of America, 975 F.2d 832, 840 (Fed. Cir. 1992) (arbitrary string of numbers in a lock-out device was not dictated by function and therefore could be copyrighted); American Dental Ass'n v. Delta Dental Plans, 44 U.S.P.Q.2d 1296 (7th Cir. 1997) (listing of code numbers assigned to each element was a copyrightable part of a taxonomy of information, because different numbers could have been chosen).

Program interface elements will also be uncopyrightable if they are dictated by external factors, such as the requirements of compatibility with a particular hardware or software platform. Thus, the Tenth Circuit concluded that the selection of values matched to codes in Mitel's call controllers, while sufficiently original to qualify for copyright protection, could not be protected because they were dictated by the needs of the industry. *Mitel*, supra, 124 F.3d at 1366. See also *Altai*, 982 F.2d at 707-709. On the other hand, other courts have found similar program elements to be copyrightable—e.g., *Atari*, 975 F.2d at 845; *Engineering Dynamics*, 26 F.3d at 1347; CMAX/Cleveland, Inc v. UCR, Inc., 804 F. Supp. 337, 355-356 (M.D. Ga. 1992).

Initially, it makes considerable difference which approach a court takes. The program implementing the protocols may well contain a significant amount of code. Even if facts and other unprotectable elements were to be filtered out of both the program and the documentation, it is evident that there is ample protectable expression remaining in both to allow the copyright owner to prevent literal copying of either the program itself or the documentation that accompanies it. Factual books, compilations of data, and computer programs that contain much less detailed expressive information than these programs have nonetheless been protected under copyright law—e.g., *Apple Computer*, 714 F.2d at 1240 (protecting early Apple operating system containing relatively few lines of code by modern standards); *American Dental*, supra, 126 F.3d at 977 (protecting individual words and numbers in a taxonomy containing short descriptions of dental treatments); Lipton v. Nature Co., 71 F.3d 464 (2d Cir. 1995) (protecting short list of "terms of venery"). The words chosen in the documentation to explain the program, and the actual code written to implement the program, necessarily contain myriad expressive choices, and those choices are protectable under the idea-expression dichotomy. Indeed, the program and the documentation are clearly protectable not only against literal copying, but even against the copying of a substantial part of the works. See Central Point Software v. Nugent, 903 F. Supp. 1057, 1060 (E.D. Tex. 1995) (copying of 50 percent of program code held infringement). By contrast, a court applying the *Lotus* approach might well circumvent this process, concluding that the entire protocol (including the supporting code) was unprotectable.

Nonetheless, *Mitel* suggests that even courts applying the abstraction-filtration-comparison approach may conclude that the protocol as a whole is uncopyrightable. However, not all courts follow *Mitel*'s approach. In particular, two decisions find that even the seemingly logical selection of a few number options can be copyrightable expression. In *Autoskill*, for example, the court protected a procedure under which reading test subjects keyed 1, 2, or 3 on the keyboard in response to material displayed on the screen. The court rejected the argument that this process was an uncopyrightable "method of operation." 994 F.2d at 1495 & n.23. While the program used in *Autoskill* contained many elements other than the three-key user input, the decision clearly indicates that the input system itself is protectable.

To similar effect is Compaq Computer Corp. v. ProCom Technology, 908 F. Supp. 1409 (S.D. Tex. 1995). In that case, Compaq successfully claimed copyright in a set of five numerical parameters that it used to warn of potential hard drive failure. The court distinguished *Feist* on the grounds that the selection of five parameters to monitor, and the choice of threshold values indicative of drive failure for each of those parameters, reflected expressive "selection and arrangement" entitling Compaq to copyright protection. This was true despite the fact that the selection of the parameters to be used was dictated by the function of the software and that "a third party seeking compatibility with [Compaq's system] has no choice but to use those five parameters as well." *Id.* at 1421. *Accord, Atari Games*, 975 F.2d at 843-844; *American Dental Ass'n*, 126 F.3d at 977. These cases provide some support for the copyrightability of protocol elements themselves.

Further, even if individual elements of the protocol are determined to be uncopyrightable because they are dictated by function, the entire protocol may be copyrightable as a compilation of uncopyrightable elements. *Compaq*, 908 F. Supp. at 1418 ("Compaq's compilation of the five threshold values meets the standard announced in *Feist*."). Cf. Apple Computer v. Microsoft Corp., 35 F.3d 1435, 1446 (9th Cir. 1994) (compilation of uncopyrightable elements protectable against virtually identical copying); *MiTek*, 89 F.3d at 1558-1559 (same). On the other hand, at least one court following *Lotus* has concluded that data structures are uncopyrightable as a whole. See Baystate Technologies v. Bentley Systems, Inc., 946 F. Supp. 1079 (D. Mass. 1996). That court concluded that the selection and arrangement of data file elements was "dictated mainly by external factors," notably the need for compatibility and programming efficiency, and was therefore not protectable.

Of course, even if the protocol is copyrighted, not all uses of copyrighted data will be infringing. In particular, a number of courts have held that in appropriate circumstances the copying of elements of a computer program for purposes of achieving interoperability may be a "fair use." For a more detailed discussion of this issue, see Section D below.

COMMENTS AND QUESTIONS

1. Should APIs be copyrightable? Why or why not? Do we need to provide protection to program interfaces in order to encourage the creation of new ones? Do network effects mean that protecting APIs is likely to give too much control to the copyright owner?

4. Protection for Program Outputs: Screen Displays

Stern Electronics, Inc. v. Kaufman
United States Court of Appeals for the Second Circuit
669 F.2d 852 (2d Cir. 1982)

NEWMAN, Circuit Judge:

This appeal from the grant of a preliminary injunction concerns primarily the availability of copyright protection for the visual images electronically displayed by a coin operated video game of the sort currently enjoying widespread popularity throughout the country. Omni Video Games, Inc., its distributor, and two of its officers appeal from an order . . . preliminarily enjoining them from infringing the copyright of Stern Electronics, Inc. in the audiovisual work entitled "Scramble". . . . Appellants contend that the visual images and accompanying sounds of the video game fail to satisfy the fixation and originality requirements of the Copyright Act, 17 U.S.C.A. §102(a) (1976). . . .

Video games like "Scramble" can roughly be described as computers programmed to create on a television screen cartoons in which some of the action is controlled by the player. In Stern's "Scramble," for example, the video screen displays a spaceship moving horizontally through six different scenes in which obstacles are encountered. With each scene the player faces increasing difficulty in traversing the course and scoring points. The first scene depicts mountainous terrain, missile bases, and fuel depots. The player controls the altitude and speed of the spaceship, decides when to release the ship's supply of bombs, and fires lasers that can destroy attacking missiles and aircraft. He attempts to bomb the missile bases (scoring points for success), bomb the fuel depots (increasing his own diminishing fuel supply with each hit), avoid the missiles being fired from the ground, and avoid crashing his ship into the mountains. And that is only scene one. In subsequent scenes the hazards include missile-firing enemy aircraft and tunnel-like airspaces. The scenes are in color, and the action is accompanied by battlefield sounds.

The game is built into a cabinet containing a cathode ray tube, a number of electronic circuit boards, a loudspeaker, and hand controls for the player. The electronic circuitry includes memory storage devices called PROMs, an acronym for "programmable read only memory." The PROM stores the instructions and data from a computer program in such a way that when electric current passes through the circuitry, the interaction of the program stored in the PROM with the other components of the game produces the sights and sounds of the audiovisual display that the player sees and hears. The memory devices determine not only the appearance and movement of the images but also the variations in movement in response to the player's operation of the hand controls.

Stern manufactures amusement equipment, including video games, for distribution worldwide. In January 1981 at a London trade exhibit Stern became aware of "Scramble," an electronic video game developed in late 1980 by a Japanese corporation, Konami Industry Co., Ltd. The audiovisual display constituting what Stern alleges is the copyrightable work was first published in Japan on January 8, 1981. Stern secured an exclusive sub-license to distribute the "Scramble" game in North and South America from Konami's exclusive licensee, and began selling the game in the United States on March 17, 1981. Even in the fast-paced world of video games, "Scramble" quickly became a big success. Approximately 10,000 units were sold at about $2,000 each in the first two months for an initial sales volume of about $20 million.

On April 14, 1981, a Certificate of Copyright Registration for the audiovisual work "Scramble" was issued to Konami by the United States Copyright Office, and shortly thereafter documents were filed with the Copyright Office reflecting the license and sub-license to Stern. To satisfy the statutory requirement for deposit of copies of a work to be copyrighted, 17 U.S.C.A. §408(b) (1976), Konami submitted video tape recordings of the "Scramble" game, both in its "attract mode" and in its "play mode."

Omni alleges that, concurrently with Stern's sales of the "Scramble" game and even earlier, it was endeavoring to sell a line of video game products so constructed that each unit could be equipped for playing different games by substituting a PROM containing the program for a particular game. . . . In April 1981 Omni began to sell a video game called "Scramble" that not only bears the same name as the "Scramble" game Stern was then marketing, but also is virtually identical in both sight and sound. It sold this copy of Stern's "Scramble" game, known in the trade as a "knock-off," for several hundred dollars less than Stern's game.

1. Copyright Issues

In challenging the preliminary injunction that bars distribution of its "Scramble" game, Omni does not dispute that Konami and its sub-licensee

Stern are entitled to secure some copyright protection for their "Scramble" game. Omni contends that Konami was entitled to copyright only the written computer program that determines the sights and sounds of the game's audiovisual display. While that approach would have afforded some degree of protection, it would not have prevented a determined competitor from manufacturing a "knock-off" of "Scramble" that replicates precisely the sights and sounds of the game's audiovisual display. This could be done by writing a new computer program that would interact with the hardware components of a video game to produce on the screen the same images seen in "Scramble," accompanied by the same sounds. Such replication is possible because many different computer programs can produce the same "results," whether those results are an analysis of financial records or a sequence of images and sounds. . . .

To secure protection against the risk of a "knock-off" of "Scramble" based upon an original program, Konami eschewed registration of its program as a literary work and chose instead to register the sights and sounds of "Scramble" as an audiovisual work. See 17 U.S.C.A. §102(a)(6) (1976). The Act defines "audiovisual works" as "works that consist of a series of related images which are intrinsically intended to be shown by the use of machines, or devices such as projectors, viewers, or electronic equipment, together with accompanying sounds, if any, regardless of the nature of the material objects, such as films or tapes, in which the works are embodied." 17 U.S.C.A. §101 (1976). Omni contends that Konami is not entitled to secure a copyright in the sights and sounds of its "Scramble" game because the audiovisual work is neither "fixed in any tangible medium of expression" nor "original" within the meaning of §102(a). Both contentions arise from the fact that the sequence of some of the images appearing on the screen during each play of the game will vary depending upon the actions taken by the player. For example, if he fails to avoid enemy fire, his spaceship will be destroyed; if he fails to destroy enough fuel depots, his own fuel supply will run out, and his spaceship will crash; if he succeeds in destroying missile sites and enemy planes, those images will disappear from the screen; and the precise course travelled by his spaceship will depend upon his adjustment of the craft's altitude and velocity.

If the content of the audiovisual display were not affected by the participation of the player, there would be no doubt that the display itself, and not merely the written computer program, would be eligible for copyright. The display satisfies the statutory definition of an original "audiovisual work," and the memory devices of the game satisfy the statutory requirement of a "copy" in which the work is "fixed."[4] The Act defines "copies"

---

4. In arguing that the permanent "imprinting" of the computer program in the game's memory devices satisfies the requirement of fixation in a tangible medium, appellees direct our attention to the PROM, which contains, in electronically usable form, the computer program for the game. While the PROM device contains the program specifically written for the "Scramble" game, there are undoubtedly some items of program stored in memory devices located in other components of the game. Whether located in the PROM prepared for this

as "material objects . . . in which a work is fixed by any method now known or later developed, and from which the work can be perceived, reproduced, or otherwise communicated, either directly or with the aid of a machine or device" and specifies that a work is "fixed" when "its embodiment in a copy . . . is sufficiently permanent or stable to permit it to be perceived, reproduced, or otherwise communicated for a period of more than transitory duration." 17 U.S.C.A. §101 (1976). The audiovisual work is permanently embodied in a material object, the memory devices, from which it can be perceived with the aid of the other components of the game.

We agree with the District Court that the player's participation does not withdraw the audiovisual work from copyright eligibility. No doubt the entire sequence of all the sights and sounds of the game are different each time the game is played, depending upon the route and speed the player selects for his spaceship and the timing and accuracy of his release of his craft's bombs and lasers. Nevertheless, many aspects of the sights and the sequence of their appearance remain constant during each play of the game. These include the appearance (shape, color, and size) of the player's spaceship, the enemy craft, the ground missile bases and fuel depots, and the terrain over which (and beneath which) the player's ship flies, as well as the sequence in which the missile bases, fuel depots, and terrain appears. Also constant are the sounds heard whenever the player successfully destroys an enemy craft or installation or fails to avoid an enemy missile or laser. It is true, as appellants contend, that some of these sights and sounds will not be seen and heard during each play of the game in the event that the player's spaceship is destroyed before the entire course is traversed. But the images remain fixed, capable of being seen and heard each time a player succeeds in keeping his spaceship aloft long enough to permit the appearances of all the images and sounds of a complete play of the game. The repetitive sequence of a substantial portion of the sights and sounds of the game qualifies for copyright protection as an audiovisual work.

Appellants' claim that the work lacks originality proceeds along two lines. Repeating their attack on fixation, they assert that each play of the game is an original work because of the player's participation. The videotape of a particular play of the game, they assert, secured protection only for that one "original" display. However, the repeated appearance of the same sequence of numerous sights and sounds in each play of the game defeats this branch of the argument. Attacking from the opposite flank, appellants contend that the audiovisual display contains no originality because all of its reappearing features are determined by the previously created computer program. This argument is also without merit. The visual and aural features of the audiovisual display are plainly original variations sufficient to render the display copyrightable even though the underlying

---

particular game or elsewhere in the total assembly, all portions of the program, once stored in memory devices anywhere in the game, are fixed in a tangible medium within the meaning of the Act.

written program has an independent existence and is itself eligible for copyright. Nor is copyright defeated because the audiovisual work and the computer program are both embodied in the same components of the game. The same thing occurs when an audio tape embodies both a musical composition and a sound recording. Moreover, the argument overlooks the sequence of the creative process. Someone first conceived what the audiovisual display would look like and sound like. Originality occurred at that point. Then the program was written. Finally, the program was imprinted into the memory devices so that, in operation with the components of the game, the sights and sounds could be seen and heard. The resulting display satisfies the requirement of an original work.

We need not decide at what point the repeating sequence of images would form too insubstantial a portion of an entire display to warrant a copyright, nor the somewhat related issue of whether a sequence of images (e.g., a spaceship shooting down an attacking plane) might contain so little in the way of particularized form of expression as to be only an abstract idea portrayed in noncopyrightable form, see Nichols v. Universal Pictures Corp., 45 F.2d 119, 121 (2d Cir. 1930), *cert. denied*, 282 U.S. 902 (1931). Assessing the entire effect of the game as it appears and sounds, we conclude that its repetitive sequence of images is copyrightable as an audiovisual display. . . .

COMMENTS AND QUESTIONS

1. Why are computer programs entitled to two different types of copyright protection—protection of the code (and nonliteral structural elements) as a literary work and protection of the output as a pictorial or audiovisual work? One possible answer lies in the unique nature of computer programs. The "literary work" protected by copyright is not actually readable by humans. When it is read by the computer, what the computer displays is not the code itself, but a screen display that is based on that code. Because what goes into the computer bears no physical resemblance to what comes out, limiting copyright protection to the code of a program would leave software vulnerable to being "copied" by other programmers, who would be free to write *their own* code to produce similar or even identical screen displays. Because the screen display is all that is visible to the user, allowing the display to be copied would significantly undermine the value of copyright protection.

Could we solve this problem by applying the rules of nonliteral code infringement to cases where what is alleged to have been copied is the screen display? How would the *Lotus* court resolve such a claim?

For an argument that infringement of screen displays (and the broader but overlapping category of "user interfaces," discussed below) should be treated as a subset of the more general question of whether the program itself has been infringed, see Pamela Samuelson, Computer Programs, User

Interfaces, and Section 102(b) of the Copyright Act of 1976: A Critique of Lotus v. Paperback, 6 High Tech. L.J. 209, 264-269 (1991).

2. How broad is the scope of protection for screen displays? Many computer audiovisual works—particularly video games—often display sequences of vivid and fanciful images accompanied by music and other sounds. Because of their highly expressive content, these video screen displays enjoy the broad scope of copyright protection that is accorded cartoon movies and similar works. On the other hand, copyright protection for video displays treated as an audiovisual work does not extend to the underlying game or program itself. See generally Last Frontier Report on Copyright Protection of Computer Software, 30 Jurimetrics J. 15, 32 (1989).

3. How should video game manufacturers register their works with the Copyright Office—as literary works or as audiovisual works? Are two separate copyright registrations required? The Copyright Office has ruled that

> all copyrightable expression owned by the same claimant and embodied in a computer program, or first published as a unit with a computer program, including computer screen displays, is considered a single work and should be registered on a single application form. . . . Ordinarily, where computer program authorship is part of the work, literary authorship will predominate, and one registration should be made on application Form TX. Where, however, audiovisual authorship predominates, the registration should be made on Form PA.

Registration and Deposit of Computer Screen Displays, 53 Fed. Reg. 21,817-18 (1988). What is the importance of the type of form on which a work is registered? Cf. Jefferson Airplane v. Berkeley Systems, 32 U.S.P.Q.2d 1632 (N.D. Cal. 1994) (registration of sound recordings did not extend to art contained on album cover).

Does it matter whether a computer program is treated as a literary work or an audiovisual work? On this point, see Manufacturers Technologies, Inc. v. CAMS, Inc., 706 F. Supp. 984, 992-993 (D. Conn. 1989), approaching the protectability of screen displays by treating "the single registration of a computer program as accomplishing two interrelated yet distinct registrations; one of the program itself and one of the screen displays or user interface of that program, to the extent that each contains copyrightable subject matter."

PROBLEM

Problem 2-5. Atari Games Corp. seeks to register BREAKOUT, a video game program. The game simulates a ball and paddle game. BREAKOUT's audiovisual display features a wall formed by red, amber, green, and blue layers of rectangles representing bricks. The screen shows the two players' scores at the top. The player manipulates a control knob that causes a rectangular "paddle" to hit a square "ball" against the brick wall. When the ball hits a brick, that brick disappears from its row, the player scores points, and a brick on a higher row becomes exposed. A "breakout" occurs when the ball penetrates through all rows of bricks to the empty space beyond, where it ricochets at greatly increased speed until it reemerges. The game produces four different tones as the ball touches different objects or places on the screen. The ball's movement depends on where it contacts the paddle. The size of the paddle diminishes and the motion of the ball accelerates as the game is played.

Should the Copyright Office register BREAKOUT as an audiovisual work?

Note on the Copyrightability of Computer-Generated Works

Who is the author of a computer-generated work? In *Stern Electronics*, Judge Newman comments that the player's participation does not nullify copyright protection for a video game. But in that case the court acknowledged that the exact video output being protected varied with each game, depending on the particular person playing the game and what actions she took. Who is the author of the images created on the video game? The creator of the program? The user? Both the creator of the program and the user as joint authors? The computer?

CONTU took a traditional copyright approach to the question of copyrightability of computer-generated works. "If a work created through application of computer technology meets th[e] minimal test of originality, it is copyrightable." CONTU Report at 45. With regard to authorship, CONTU reasoned as follows:

> Computers are enormously complex and powerful instruments which vastly extend human powers to calculate, select, arrange, display, design, and do other things involved in the creation of works. However, it is a human power they extend. The computer may be analogized or equated with, for example, a camera, and the computer affects the copyright status of a resultant work no more than the employment of a still or motion-picture camera, a tape recorder, or a typewriter. Hence, it seems clear that the copyright problems with respect to the authorship of new works produced with the assistance of a computer are not unlike those posed by the creation of more traditional works. . . .
>
> Finally, we confront the question of who is the author of a work produced through the use of a computer. The obvious answer is that the author is one who employs the computer. The simplicity of this response may ob-

scure some problems, though essentially they are the same sort of problems encountered in connection with works produced in other ways.

One such problem is that often a number of persons have a hand in the use of a computer to prepare, for example, a complex statistical table. They may have varying degrees and kinds of responsibility for the creation of the work. However, they are typically employees of a common employer, engaged in creating a work-for-hire, and the employer is the author. When the authors work together as a voluntary team and not as employees of a common employer, the copyright law with respect to works of joint authorship is as applicable here as to works created in more conventional ways, and the team itself may define by agreement the relative rights of the individuals involved.

To be used in the creation of a work, a computer must be controlled by a program and must ordinarily utilize data input from other sources. Both the program and the data may be copyrighted or parts of copyrighted works. The question has been raised whether authorship or proprietorship of the program or data base establishes or may establish a claim of authorship of the final work. It appears to the Commission that authorship of the program or of the input data is entirely separate from authorship of the final work, just as authorship of a translation of a book is distinct from authorship of the original work. It is, of course, incumbent on the creator of the final work to obtain appropriate permission from any other person who is the proprietor of a program or data base used in the creation of the ultimate work. The ultimate use of a program or data base might limit or negate the author's claim of copyright in the ultimate work, just as a failure of a translator to obtain a license from the proprietor of the translated work might prevent securing copyright in and making use of the translation. But this is not a question of authorship itself, and the author of the original work does not become the author of a translation merely because it is made from the original work without permission. Here, too, the situation with respect to works produced by the use of a computer does not appear to differ from that with respect to works otherwise created. . . .

However, the Commission recognizes that the dynamics of computer science promise changes in the creation and use of authors' writings that cannot be predicted with certainty. The effects of these changes should have the attention of Congress and its appropriate agencies to ensure that those who are the responsible policy makers maintain an awareness of the changing impact of computer technology on both the needs of authors and the role of authors in the information age. . . .

CONTU Report at 45-46.

COMMENTS AND QUESTIONS

1. On the copyright ownership implications of "artificial intelligence" programs, see generally Arthur Miller, Copyright Protection for Computer Programs, Databases, and Computer-Generated Works: Is Anything New Since CONTU? 106 Harv. L. Rev. 977, 1042-1072

(1993); Pamela Samuelson, Allocating Ownership Rights in Computer-Generated Works, 47 U. Pitt. L. Rev. 1185 (1986).

One case has addressed the issue of non-human creativity, albeit in a different context. In Urantia Foundation v. Maaherra, 114 F.3d 955 (9th Cir. 1997), the plaintiff was a church that claimed that its sacred text was written by a divine being, as channeled through a psychiatric patient. When it sued the defendant (a church splinter group) for copying the text, the defendant claimed that "there can be no valid copyright in the Book because it lacks the requisite ingredient of human creativity, and that therefore the Book is not a 'work of authorship' within the meaning of the Copyright Act." The court seemed to agree that human authorship was required: "it is not the creations of divine beings that the copyright laws were intended to protect, . . . in this case some element of human creativity must have occurred in order for the Book to be copyrightable. At the very least, for a worldly entity to be guilty of infringing a copyright, that entity must have copied something created by another worldly entity." *Id.* Nonetheless, the court found that the Book was copyrightable because humans had "compiled" the teachings of the divine being in question.

What does *Urantia* suggest for computer-generated works? Are they ineligible for copyright protection? Or could a computer program be a "worldly entity" within the language of the court?

2. Is the CONTU report on ownership consistent with the court's decision in *Stern*? In particular, CONTU emphasizes that "authorship of the program or of the input data is entirely separate from authorship of the final work." The Report goes on to suggest that it is the user of the computer, not the author of the program, who owns the final work. In some contexts, this makes perfect sense. It would be unreasonable to suggest, for example, that the creator of a word-processing program owned the documents written using that program. But what does this suggest about the ownership of video game screen displays? If the programmer merely set up some possible screen elements and the game player put them together into the actual screen displays shown, why should the programmer own those screen displays? Does it matter whether the actual displays shown are "fixed" in a tangible medium of expression other than the screen itself?

PROBLEM

Problem 2-6. Analyze the copyrightability and authorship of the output generated by the computer programs described below. Assume that there is no prior agreement between the program creator and the user.

(a) The user of a video game for home computers controls the movement of characters with a joy stick. The user decides to write a book about strategies for mastering the game. She prints out a number of visual displays that she arranged through placement of game characters for her book.

(b) SoftDesign, a computer program for architects, depicts floor plans in three-dimensional perspective. In addition, the program allows architects to see how sunlight will reflect through structures over the course of the day. Users enter the dimensions of a structure into the program either by tracing floor plans onto the screen or by entering dimensions directly.

(c) Instant Poet is a sophisticated computer program that enables users to develop poems for a variety of occasions. The basic program contains 120 vocabularies of 30 to over 5,000 words. Each vocabulary contains a particular type of word, such as articles, verbs in the imperative mode, or nouns. The program structures the relationship among categories in order to generate poems. Users select a number of variables—such as type of poem (romance, comedy, birthday), name of object, key attributes of object (e.g., age, interests). The program then generates a poem, prompting the user with a variety of choices along the way.

(d) Composer enables novice musicians to compose sophisticated musical compositions by combining digital samples of different instrument tracts.

(e) Car Repair is a diagnostic tool for evaluating car automotive problems. The computer asks the user a series of questions. Depending on how the user answers, the computer guides the user through a decision tree, eventually diagnosing the particular problem.

(f) Weatherware enables users to develop weather forecasts for a particular geographical area. The program is based on correlation analysis. The user first defines the geographical area by entering a set of six cities and their locations with respect to the location for which forecasts are sought. The user then enters daily information on temperature, wind speed, cloud cover, and precipitation for each of the cities. After the computer has a statistically significant body of data, it can generate up to four-day forecasts, along with margins for error.

(g) Translator is a sophisticated program for translating from English to French and French to English. The user merely enters the text to be translated. The program generates the translated text.

(h) PoMo is an automatic "postmodern literary theory paper generator." At the click of a button, PoMo generates prose similar in style to much postmodern literary criticism. The prose is "original" in the sense that it is not copied from anywhere else, although because PoMo is designed to mimic an existing genre, it uses words and phrases that commonly appear in that genre.

Note on the Fixation Requirement

Copyright law protects "works of authorship." But what is a work of authorship? The law has long required that a work be "fixed" in a tangible form before it is entitled to protection. This presumably distinguishes identifiable creative efforts (protectable) from an "author's" unrecorded thoughts (unprotectable).[4]

Technology continually pushes the frontiers of the fixation requirement. Where once it was possible to delineate rather clearly between things that were recorded on paper or canvas and things that weren't, the development of new recording media has led Congress to expand the notion of a fixed record. Magnetic tape, electrical circuits, and grooves and indentations on plastic are all common means today of recording information in machine-readable form. Congress drafted the fixation requirement in the 1976 Act to accommodate these technological developments. While the copyright law requires that a work be "fixed in a tangible medium of expression," fixation may be in any medium "now known or later developed" and is satisfied even if the work can be "perceived, reproduced, or otherwise communicated" only "with the aid of a machine or device." 17 U.S.C. §102(a).

There are two main fixation issues the courts have had to deal with in software copyright cases. One has to do with whether an infringing copy has been created. We discuss that issue in the next Section. The other application involves the "fixation" of interactive audiovisual works, such as video games and multimedia works. In both cases, the visual display of the program (as distinct from the program itself) is not predetermined. Instead, what is actually displayed depends on the actions of the user of the program. In Stern Electronics v. Kaufman, 669 F.2d 852 (2d Cir. 1982), the court analyzed the problem this way:

> We agree with the District Court that the player's participation does not withdraw the audiovisual work from copyright eligibility. No doubt the entire sequence of all the sights and sounds of the game are different each time the game is played, depending upon the route and speed the player selects for his spaceship and the timing and accuracy of his release of his craft's bombs and lasers. Nevertheless, many aspects of the sights and the sequence of their appearance remain constant during each play of the game. These include the appearance (shape, color, and size) of the player's spaceship, the enemy craft, the ground missile bases and fuel depots, and the terrain over which (and be-

---

4. Because "works of authorship" must be fixed in order to qualify for copyright, and works must be fixed to constitute "copies" under section 106, the fixation requirement arises both when determining the scope of copyright protection and when considering infringement. We return to the fixation question in the next Section, when we consider what constitutes a "copy" fixed in a tangible medium of expression for purposes of infringement.

neath which) the player's ship flies, as well as the sequence in which the missile bases, fuel depots, and terrain appears. Also constant are the sounds heard whenever the player successfully destroys an enemy craft or installation or fails to avoid an enemy missile or laser. It is true, as appellants contend, that some of these sights and sounds will not be seen and heard during each play of the game in the event that the player's spaceship is destroyed before the entire course is traversed. But the images remain fixed, capable of being seen and heard each time a player succeeds in keeping his spaceship aloft long enough to permit the appearances of all the images and sounds of a complete play of the game. The repetitive sequence of a substantial portion of the sights and sounds of the game qualifies for copyright protection as an audiovisual work.

Id. at 856. Is this argument persuasive? In particular, consider two possible problems with the *Stern* court's conclusion: (1) it links the supposedly independent copyright in the audiovisual work directly to the copyright in the underlying literary work (the program code), and may therefore mean that writing new code to achieve similar visual effects does not infringe the copyright; (2) it is dependent on the repetition of "a substantial portion of the sights and sounds" of the game during each occurrence, so that a truly interactive program would not be fixed under the court's analysis.

What is the purpose of the fixation requirement in the context of computer programs? Should it be enough that the audiovisual work is generated from a fixed source, whether or not it is repeatable?

PROBLEM

Problem 2-7. FractalArt is a computer graphics company that writes artistic software for the computer. In particular, FA's new program generates fractal patterns that partially replicate those found in nature at a microscopic level. The software includes a set of pseudo-random number generators which create new fractal patterns that are not stored anywhere in the program itself. The fractal patterns are displayed on a computer screen for approximately five minutes each as screen savers. After five minutes, the fractals are replaced by a new image. Because of the number of fractals that the program is capable of generating, it is extremely unlikely that a precise image will ever be repeated. FA has registered a copyright in its program.

A purchaser of the FA program likes the fractals displayed on his computer. Upset that he cannot "save" particularly attractive fractals, he photographs a number of the images, develops the photos, and publishes them in an art book without FA's permission. Is the purchaser liable for copyright infringement?

═══
═══ **Data East USA, Inc. v. Epyx, Inc.**
═══ *United States Court of Appeals for the Ninth Circuit*
═══ *862 F.2d 204 (9th Cir. 1988)*

TROTT, Circuit Judge:

[Data East, a video game manufacturer, received audio-visual copyright certificates for arcade and home computer versions of its video game "Karate Champ." Epyx subsequently commenced distribution of a video game designed to run on Commodore computers called "World Karate Championship."]

Each competing product . . . consists of the audio-visual depiction of a karate match or matches conducted by two combatants, one clad in a typical white outfit and the other in red. Successive phases of combat are conducted against varying stationary background images depicting localities or geographic scenes. The match is supervised by a referee who directs the beginning and end of each phase of combat and announces the winning combatant of each phase by means of a cartoon-style speech balloon. Each game has a bonus round where the karate combatant breaks bricks and dodges objects. Similarities also exist in the moves used by the combatants and the scoring method.

Data East alleged that the overall appearance, compilation, and sequence of the audio-visual display of the video game "World Karate Championship" infringed its copyright for "Karate Champ" as embodied in the arcade and home versions of the video game. Data East also charged Epyx with trademark and trade dress infringement.

The district court found that except for the graphic quality of Epyx's expressions, part of the scoreboard, the referee's physical appearance, and minor particulars in the "bonus phases," Data East's and Epyx's games are qualitatively identical. The district court then held that Epyx's game infringes the copyright Data East has in "Karate Champ." . . .

II. Discussion

A district court's determination of findings of fact is subject to the clearly erroneous standard of review. . . .

As in most infringement cases of this kind, no direct evidence was developed that [Epyx or the company from whom Epyx licensed its game] copied any version of Data East's product. There seldom is any direct evidence of copying in these matters. Therefore, copying may be established instead by circumstantial evidence of (1) the defendant's access to the copyrighted work prior to defendant's creation of its work, and (2) the substantial similarity of both the general ideas and expression between the copyrighted work and defendant's work. *Id.*; Baxter v. MCA, Inc., 812 F.2d 421, 423 (9th Cir. 1987), *cert. denied*, 108 S. Ct. 346 (1987). In essence, the question of copying becomes a matter of reasonable inferences. Because we find no substantial similarity, we decline to address the issue of access. . . .

B. *Substantial Similarity*

"To show that two works are substantially similar, plaintiff must demonstrate that the works are substantially similar in both ideas and expression." Frybarger v. International Business Machines Corp., 812 F.2d 525, 529 (9th Cir. 1987). Although plaintiff must first show that the ideas are substantially similar, the ideas themselves are not protected by copyright and therefore, cannot be infringed. It is an axiom of copyright law that copyright protects only an author's expression of an idea, not the idea itself. Mazer v. Stein, 347 U.S. 201, 217-18 (1954). There is a strong public policy corollary to this axiom permitting all to use freely ideas contained in a copyrightable work, so long as the protected expression itself is not appropriated. Landsberg v. Scrabble Crossword Game Players, Inc., 736 F.2d 485, 488 (9th Cir. 1984), *cert. denied,* 469 U.S. 1037 (1984). Thus, to the extent the similarities between plaintiff's and defendant's works are confined to ideas and general concepts, these similarities are noninfringing.

The Ninth Circuit has developed a two-step test for the purposes of determining substantial similarity. *McCulloch,* 823 F.2d at 319; *Krofft,* 562 F.2d at 1164. First, an "extrinsic" test is used to determine whether two ideas are substantially similar. This is an objective test which rests upon specific criteria that can be listed and analyzed. *Krofft, id.* Second, an "intrinsic" test is used to compare forms of expression. This is a subjective test which depends on the response of the ordinary reasonable person. *Id.*

In applying the extrinsic test, the district court found that the idea expressed in plaintiff's game and in defendant's game is identical. The idea of the games was described by the court as follows:

> . . . a martial arts karate combat game conducted between two combatants, and presided over by a referee, all of which are represented by visual images, and providing a method of scoring accomplished by full and half point scores for each player, and utilizing dots to depict full point scores and half point scores.

The district court further found that:

> In each of the games, the phases of martial arts combat are conducted against still background images purporting to depict geographic or locality situses and located at the top of the screen as the game is viewed. The action of the combatants in each of the games takes place in the lower portion of the screen as the game is viewed, and is against a one color background in that portion of the screen as the game is viewed.

Once an idea is found to be similar or identical, as in this case, the second or intrinsic step is applied to determine whether similarity of the expression of the idea occurs. This exists when the "total concept and feel of the works" is substantially similar. Aliotti v. R. Dakin & Co., 831 F.2d 901 (9th Cir. 1987). Analytic dissection of the dissimilarities as opposed to the similarities is not appropriate under this test because it distracts a reasonable observer from a comparison of the total concept and feel of the works. *Id.*

The rule in the Ninth Circuit, however, is that "[n]o substantial similarity of expression will be found when 'the idea and its expression are . . . inseparable,' given that 'protecting the expression in such circumstances would confer a monopoly of the idea upon the copyright owner.'" *Id.* (quoting Herbert Rosenthal Jewelry Corp. v. Kalpakian, 446 F.2d 738, 742 (9th Cir. 1971)); see also *Landsberg*, 736 F.2d at 489 (factual works); see v. Durang, 711 F.2d 141, 143 (9th Cir. 1983) (*scenes a faire* doctrine); *Krofft*, 562 F.2d at 1168.

Nor can copyright protection be afforded to elements of expression that necessarily follow from an idea, or to "*scenes a faire*," i.e., expressions that are "as a practical matter, indispensable or at least standard in the treatment of a given [idea]." *Aliotti*, 831 F.2d at 901 (quoting Atari, Inc. v. North American Phillips Consumer Elecs. Corp., 672 F.2d 607, 616 (7th Cir. 1982), *cert. denied*, 459 U.S. 880 (1982)).

To determine whether similarities result from unprotectable expression, analytic dissection of similarities may be performed. If this demonstrates that all similarities in expression arise from use of common ideas, then no substantial similarity can be found. *Id.*

The district court performed what can be described as an analytic dissection of similarities in its findings of fact and stated:

> Plaintiff's and defendant's games each encompass the idea of depicting the performance of karate martial arts combat in each of the following respects:
>
> A. Each game has fourteen moves.
> B. Each game has a two-player option.
> C. Each game has a one-player option.
> D. Each game has forward and backward somersault moves and about-face moves.
> E. Each game has a squatting reverse punch wherein the heel is not on the ground.
> F. Each game has an upper-lunge punch.
> G. Each game has a back-foot sweep.
> H. Each game has a jumping sidekick.
> I. Each game has low kick.
> J. Each game has a walk-backwards position.
> K. Each game has changing background scenes.
> L. Each game has 30-second countdown rounds.
> M. Each game uses one referee.

N. In each game the referee says "begin," "stop," "white," "red," which is depicted by a cartoon-style speech balloon.

O. Each game has a provision for 100 bonus points per remaining second.

The district court found that the visual depiction of karate matches is subject to the constraints inherent in the sport of karate itself. The number of combatants, the stance employed by the combatants, established and recognized moves and motions regularly employed in the sport of karate, the regulation of the match by at least one referee or judge, and the manner of scoring by points and half points are among the constraints inherent in the sport of karate. Because of these constraints, karate is not susceptible of a wholly fanciful presentation. Furthermore, the use of the Commodore computer for a karate game intended for home consumption is subject to various constraints inherent in the use of that computer. Among the constraints are the use of sprites,[5] and a somewhat limited access to color, together with limitations upon the use of multiple colors in one visual image.

The fifteen features listed by the court "encompass the idea of karate." These features, which consist of the game procedure, common karate moves, the idea of background computer graphics, and result from either constraints inherent in the sport of karate or computer restraints. After careful consideration and viewing of these features, we find that they necessarily follow from the *idea* of a martial arts karate combat game, or are inseparable from, indispensable to, or even standard treatment of the idea of the karate sport. As such, they are not protectable. "When idea and expression coincide, there will be protection against nothing other than identical copying." *Krofft*, 562 F.2d at 1168. A comparison of the works in this case demonstrates that identical copying is not an issue.

Accordingly, we hold that the court did not give the appropriate weight and import to its findings which support argument that the similarities result from unprotectable expression. Consequently, it was clear error for the district court to determine that protectable substantial similarity existed based upon these facts.

The lower court erred by not limiting the scope of Data East's copyright protection to the author's contribution—the scoreboard and background scenes. In actuality, however, the backgrounds are quite dissimilar and the method of scorekeeping, though similar, is inconsequential. Based upon these two features, a discerning 17.5 year-old boy[6]

---

5. A "sprite" involves the use of a special technique for creating mobile graphic images on a computer screen that is appropriate for animation. An increase in sophistication of sprite techniques used in the computer program will increase the graphic quality of the game's animation.

6. The district court found that the average age of individuals purchasing "Karate Champ" is 17.5 years, that the purchasers are predominantly male, and comprise a knowledgeable, critical, and discerning group.

could not regard the works as substantially similar. Accordingly, Data East's copyright was not infringed on this basis either. . . .

COMMENT AND QUESTION

Data East, like most software copyright cases (but unlike many more traditional copyright cases) seems to combine the copyrightability and substantial similarity inquiries, identifying similarities between the two works and then attempting to determine if the similarities were copyrightable. See also Interactive Network v. NTN Communications, 875 F. Supp. 1398 (N.D. Cal. 1995), *aff'd*, 57 F.3d 1083 (Fed. Cir. 1996) (NTN's interactive football game was not infringed by similar IN game, since most of the copying of the game was a result of the rules of football and the idea of an interactive prediction game). We have seen this combined approach before in *Altai's* abstraction-filtration-comparison test. Is this also the correct analytical approach to a screen display case?

5. Protection for Program Outputs: User Interfaces

Source and object code (as well as the nonliteral elements of program structure) are protectable as literary works. Screen displays (the output of the computer program) are protectable as audiovisual or pictorial works. Given these two rules, it might be considered evident that user interfaces— the screen displays that mediate the input to and output from a computer program—should also be protected by copyright.

Acknowledging this does not, however, tell us what *portions* of the user interface can be considered copyrightable expression. To a greater extent than other types of screen displays, user interfaces are dictated by market standards and functional considerations. As a result, assessing claims of copyright infringement is a challenging task.

Apple Computer, Inc. v. Microsoft Corp.
United States Court of Appeals for the Ninth Circuit
35 F.3d 1435 (9th Cir. 1994)

RYMER, Circuit Judge:

Lisa and Macintosh are Apple computers. Each has a graphical user interface ("GUI") which Apple Computer, Inc. registered for copyright as an audiovisual work. Both GUIs were developed as a user-friendly way for ordinary mortals to communicate with the Apple computer; the Lisa Desktop and the Macintosh Finder are based on a desktop metaphor with windows, icons and pull-down menus which can be manipulated on the screen with a hand-held device called a mouse. When Microsoft Corporation released Windows 1.0, having a similar GUI, Apple complained. As a result, the two agreed to a license giving Microsoft the right to use and sublicense derivative works generated by Windows 1.0 in present and future products. Microsoft released Windows 2.03 and later, Windows 3.0; its licensee, Hewlett-Packard Company (HP), introduced NewWave 1.0 and later, NewWave 3.0, which run in conjunction with Windows to make IBM-compatible computers easier to use. Apple believed that these versions exceed the license, make Windows more "Mac-like," and infringe its copyright. This action followed.

[The district court held that the only triable issue of fact was whether certain minor parts of the Windows interface were "virtually identical" to the Apple GUI. Apple appealed.]

Apple asks us to reverse because of two fundamental errors in the district court's reasoning. First, Apple argues that the court should not have allowed the license for Windows 1.0 to serve as a partial defense. Second, Apple contends that the court went astray by dissecting Apple's works so as to eliminate unprotectable and licensed elements from comparison with Windows 2.03, 3.0 and NewWave as a whole, incorrectly leading it to adopt a standard of virtual identity instead of substantial similarity. We disagree. . . .

III

Apple makes a number of related arguments challenging the district court's copyright analysis. It contends that the district court deprived its works of meaningful protection by dissecting them into individual elements and viewing each element in isolation. Because the Macintosh GUI is a dynamic audiovisual work, Apple argues that the "total concept and feel" of its works—that is, the selection and arrangement of related images and their animation—must be compared with that of the Windows and NewWave GUIs for substantial similarity. Apple further asserts that in this case, the court had no occasion to dissect its works into discrete elements because Microsoft and HP virtually mimicked the composition, organization, arrangement and dynamics of the Macintosh interface, as shown by striking similarities in the animation of overlapping windows and the design, layout and animation of icons. Apple also argues that even if dissection were appropriate, the district court should not have eliminated from jury consideration those elements that are either licensed or unprotected by copyright. Though stated somewhat differently, all of these contentions boil down to the same thing: Apple wants an overall comparison of its works to the accused works for substantial similarity rather than virtual identity.

The fact that Apple licensed the right to copy almost all of its visual displays fundamentally affects the outcome of its infringement claims. Authorized copying accounts for more than 90% of the allegedly infringing features in Windows 2.03 and 3.0, and two-thirds of the features in NewWave. More than that, the 1985 Agreement and negotiations leading up to Microsoft's license left Apple no right to complain that selection and arrangement of licensed elements make the interface as a whole look more "Mac-like" than Windows 1.0.

Thus, we do not start at ground zero in resolving Apple's claims of infringement. Rather, considering the license and the limited number of ways that the basic ideas of the Apple GUI can be expressed differently, we conclude that only "thin" protection, against virtually identical copying, is appropriate. Apple's appeal, which depends on comparing its interface as a whole for substantial similarity, must therefore fail. . . .

Although this litigation has raised difficult and interesting issues about the scope of copyright protection for a graphical user interface, resolving this appeal is a matter of applying well-settled principles. In this, as in other cases, the steps we find helpful to follow are these:

(1) The plaintiff must identify the source(s) of the alleged similarity between his work and the defendant's work.

(2) Using analytic dissection, and, if necessary, expert testimony, the court must determine whether any of the allegedly similar features are protected by copyright. Where, as in this case, a license agreement is involved, the court must also determine which features the defendant was authorized to copy. Once the scope of the license is determined, unprotectable ideas must be separated from potentially protectable expression; to that expression, the court must then apply the relevant limiting doctrines in the context of the particular medium involved, through the eyes of the ordinary consumer of that product.

(3) Having dissected the alleged similarities and considered the range of possible expression, the court must define the scope of the plaintiff's copyright—that is, decide whether the work is entitled to "broad" or "thin" protection. Depending on the degree of protection, the court must set the appropriate standard for a subjective comparison of the works to determine whether, as a whole, they are sufficiently similar to support a finding of illicit copying. . . .

B

It is not easy to distinguish expression from ideas, particularly in a new medium. However, it must be done, as the district court did in this case. Baker v. Selden, 101 U.S. 99, 25 L. Ed. 841 (1879). As we recognized long ago in the case of competing jeweled bee pins, similarities derived from the use of common ideas cannot be protected; otherwise, the first to come up with an idea will corner the market. Herbert Rosenthal

Jewelry Corp. v. Kalpakian, 446 F.2d 738, 742 (9th Cir. 1971). Apple cannot get patent-like protection for the idea of a graphical user interface, or the idea of a desktop metaphor which concededly came from Xerox. It can, and did, put those ideas together creatively with animation, overlapping windows, and well-designed icons; but it licensed the visual displays which resulted.

The district court found that there are five other basic ideas embodied in the desktop metaphor: use of windows to display multiple images on the computer screen and to facilitate user interaction with the information contained in the windows; iconic representation of familiar objects from the office environment; manipulation of icons to convey instructions and to control operation of the computer; use of menus to store information or computer functions in a place that is convenient to reach, but saves screen space for other images; and opening and closing of objects as a means of retrieving, transferring and storing information. *Apple V*, 799 F. Supp. at 1026. No copyright protection inheres in these ideas. Therefore, substantial similarity of expression in unlicensed elements cannot be based on the fact that the Lisa, the Finder, Windows 2.03, 3.0 and NewWave all have windows, icons representing familiar objects from the office environment that describe functions being performed and that can be moved around the screen to tell the computer what to do, menus which give easy access to information or functions without using space on the screen, or objects that open and close.

Well-recognized precepts guide the process of analytic dissection. First, when an idea and its expression are indistinguishable, or "merged," the expression will only be protected against nearly identical copying. *Krofft*, 562 F.2d at 1167-68; *Kalpakian*, 446 F.2d at 742. For example, in this case, the idea of an icon in a desktop metaphor representing a document stored in a computer program can only be expressed in so many ways. An iconic image shaped like a page is an obvious choice.

The doctrine of *scenes a faire* is closely related. As we explained in Frybarger v. International Business Machines Corp., 812 F.2d 525 (9th Cir. 1987), when similar features in a videogame are "'as a practical matter indispensable, or at least standard, in the treatment of a given [idea],'" they are treated like ideas and are therefore not protected by copyright. Id. at 530 (quoting Atari, Inc. v. North Am. Philips Consumer Elecs. Corp., 672 F.2d 607, 616 (7th Cir.), *cert. denied*, 459 U.S. 880, 74 L. Ed. 2d 145, 103 S. Ct. 176 (1982)). Furthermore, as Frybarger holds, "the mere indispensable expression of these ideas, based on the technical requirements of the videogame medium, may be protected only against virtually identical copying." *Id.*; see also *Data East*, 862 F.2d at 209 (visual displays of karate match conducted by two combatants, one of whom wears red shorts and the other white as in the sport, and who use the same moves, are supervised by a referee and are scored alike as in the sport, are inherent in the sport of karate itself and as such are unprotectable). In this case, for example, use of overlapping windows inheres in the idea of windows. A programmer has only two options for displaying more than one window at a time: either a tiled system, or an overlapping system. As demonstrated by Microsoft's *scenes a faire* video, overlapping windows have been the clear preference in graphic interfaces. Accordingly, protectable substantial similarity cannot be based on the mere use of overlapping windows, although, of course, Apple's particular expression may be protected.

Apple suggests that *scenes a faire* should not limit the scope of its audiovisual copyright, or at least that the interactive character of GUIs and their functional purpose should not outweigh their artistry. While user participation may not negate copyrightability of an audiovisual work, see, e.g., Midway Mfg. Co. v. Artic Int'l, Inc., 704 F.2d 1009, 1011-12 (7th Cir.), *cert. denied*, 464 U.S. 823, 78 L. Ed. 2d 98, 104 S. Ct. 90 (1983); Stern Elecs., Inc. v. Kaufman, 669 F.2d 852, 856 (2d Cir. 1982), the district court did not deny protection to any aspect of Apple's works on this basis. In any event, unlike purely artistic works such as novels and plays, graphical user interfaces generated by computer programs are partly artistic and partly functional. They are a tool to facilitate communication between the user and the computer; GUIs do graphically what a character-based interface, which requires a user to type in alphanumeric commands, does manually. Thus, the delete function is engaged by moving an icon on top of a trash can instead of hitting a "delete" key. In Apple's GUI, the ability to move icons to any part of the screen exemplifies an essentially functional process, indispensable to the idea of manipulating icons by a mouse.

To the extent that GUIs are artistic, there is no dispute that creativity in user interfaces is constrained by the power and speed of the computer. See Manufacturers Technologies, Inc. v. Cams, Inc., 706 F. Supp. 984, 994-95 (D. Conn. 1989) (denying protection to formatting style of plaintiff's screen displays because of constraints on viable options available to programmers). For example, hardware constraints limit the number of ways to depict visually the movement of a window on the screen; because many computers do not have enough power to show the entire contents of the window as it is being moved, the illusion of movement must be shown by using the outline of a window or some similar feature. Design alternatives are further limited by the GUI's purpose of making interaction between the user and the computer more "user-friendly." These, and similar environmental and ergonomic factors which limit the range of possible expression in GUIs, properly inform the scope of copyright protection.

Originality is another doctrine which limits the scope of protection. As the Supreme Court recently made clear, protection extends only to those components of a work that are original to the author, although original selection and arrangement of otherwise uncopyrightable components may be protectable. Feist Publications, Inc. v. Rural Tel. Serv. Co., 499 U.S. 340, 348-51, 113 L. Ed. 2d 358, 111 S. Ct. 1282 (1991). Apple's argument that components should not be tested for originality because its interface as a whole meets the test, see Roth Greeting Cards v. United Card Co., 429 F.2d 1106, 1109 (9th Cir. 1970) ("The originality necessary to support a copyright merely calls for independent creation, not novelty."), is therefore misplaced. Beyond that, Apple admits that it borrowed heavily from the iconic treatments in the Xerox Star and an IBM Pictureworld research report but disputes several of the district court's individual determinations. For instance, Apple claims that its file folder and page icon designs are original. Even if they are, these particular icons add so little to the mix of protectable material that the outcome could not reasonably be affected.

In sum, the district court's analytic dissection was appropriately conducted under the extrinsic portion of our test for whether sufficient copying to constitute infringement has taken place. We are not persuaded to the contrary by Apple's arguments that the district court shouldn't have dissected at all, or dissected too much; that it "filtered out" unprotectable and licensed elements instead of viewing the Macintosh interface as a whole; and that it should have recognized protectability of arrangements and the "total concept and feel" of the works under a substantial similarity standard.

First, graphical user interface audiovisual works are subject to the same process of analytical dissection as are other works. We have dissected videogames, which are audiovisual works and therefore closely analogous, see, e.g., *Data East*, 862 F.2d at 208-09 (performing analytic dissection of similarities to determine whether similarities resulted from unprotectable expression); *Frybarger*, 812 F.2d at 529-30 (district court correctly concluded that similar features in videogames were unprotectable ideas and that no reasonable jury could find expressive elements substantially similar), and we have dissected nonliteral elements of computer programs, which are somewhat analogous, see, e.g., *Brown Bag*, 960 F.2d at 1475-77 (rejecting argument similar to Apple's about propriety of analytic dissection of computer program components such as screens, menus and keystrokes); Johnson Controls, Inc. v. Phoenix Control Sys., Inc., 886 F.2d 1173, 1176 (9th Cir. 1989) (noting special master's detailed analysis of similarities). Other courts perform the same analysis, although articulated differently. See, e.g., Computer Assocs. Int'l, Inc. v. Altai, Inc., 982 F.2d 693, 706-11 (2d Cir. 1992) (adopting "abstraction-filtration-comparison" test for analyzing nonliteral structure of computer program, relying in part on our own approach); Gates Rubber Co. v. Bando Chem. Indus., 9 F.3d 823, 834, 841 (10th Cir. 1993) (adopting *Altai* test, but suggesting that comparison of works as a whole may be appropriate as preliminary step before filtering out unprotected elements); Engineering Dynamics, Inc. v. Structural Software, Inc., 26 F.3d 1335, 1342-43 (5th Cir. 1994) (adopting *Gates Rubber/Altai* test to analyze scope of copyright protection for user interface, input formats and output reports); Lotus Dev. Corp. v. Borland Int'l, Inc., 788 F. Supp. 78, 90, 93 (D. Mass. 1992) (describing similar three-part test); cf. Whelan Assocs. v. Jaslow Dental

Lab., Inc., 797 F.2d 1222, 1236 (3d Cir. 1986) (defining idea of utilitarian work as its purpose or function, and everything not necessary to that purpose as expression), *cert. denied*, 479 U.S. 1031, 93 L. Ed. 2d 831, 107 S. Ct. 877 (1987).

Nor did the district court's dissection run afoul of the enjoinder in such cases as *Johnson Controls*, 886 F.2d at 1176, *Krofft*, 562 F.2d at 1167, and *Roth*, 429 F.2d at 1110, to consider the "total concept and feel" of a work. Here, the court did not inappropriately dissect dissimilarities, and so did nothing to distract from subjectively comparing the works as a whole. See Aliotti v. R. Dakin & Co., 831 F.2d 898, 901 (9th Cir. 1987) (indicating that as the concern of *Krofft*).

As we made clear in *Aliotti*, the party claiming infringement may place "no reliance upon any similarity in expression resulting from" unprotectable elements. *Id.* (Similarities between competing stuffed dinosaur toys on account of posture and body design, and being cuddly, stem from the physiognomy of dinosaurs or from the nature of stuffed animals and are thus unprotectable.) Otherwise, there would be no point to the extrinsic test, or to distinguishing ideas from expression. In this case, it would also effectively rescind the 1985 Agreement. This does not mean that at the end of the day, when the works are considered under the intrinsic test, they should not be compared as a whole. See McCulloch v. Albert E. Price, Inc., 823 F.2d 316, 321 (9th Cir. 1987) (contrasting artistic work at issue, where decorative plates were substantially similar in more than the one unprotectable element (text), with factual works which have many unprotectable elements and very little protectable expression). Nor does it mean that infringement cannot be based on original selection and arrangement of unprotected elements. However, the unprotectable elements have to be identified, or filtered, before the works can be considered as a whole. See *Harper House*, 889 F.2d at 207-08 (reversing because "total impact and effect" test of jury instruction did not distinguish between protectable and unprotectable material, thereby improperly making it possible for jury to find copying based on unprotected material instead of selection and arrangement); see also *Pasillas*, 927 F.2d at 443 (copyright holder could not rely on unprotectable elements to show substantial similarity of expression); *Frybarger*, 812 F.2d at 529 (to extent that similarities between works were confined to ideas and general concepts, they were noninfringing).

C

The district court's conclusion that the works as a whole are entitled only to limited protection and should be compared for virtual identity follows from its analytic dissection. By virtue of the licensing agreement, Microsoft and HP were entitled to use the vast majority of features that Apple claims were copied. Of those that remain, the district court found no unauthorized, protectable similarities of expression in Windows 2.03 and 3.0, and only a handful in NewWave. Thus, any claim of infringement that Apple may have against Microsoft must rest on the copying of Apple's unique selection and arrangement of all of these features. Under *Harper House* and *Frybarger*, there can be no infringement unless the works are virtually identical.

Apple, however, contends that its audiovisual work with animation and icon design cannot be analogized to factual works such as game strategy books, see Landsberg v. Scrabble Crossword Game Players, Inc., 736 F.2d 485, 488 (9th Cir.) ("Similarity of expression may have to amount to verbatim reproduction or very close paraphrasing before a factual work will be deemed infringed."), *cert. denied*, 469 U.S. 1037, 83 L. Ed. 2d 403, 105 S. Ct. 513 (1984), accounting systems, see Selden, 101 U.S. at 104 (copyright in book describing new accounting system not infringed when defendant copied ledger sheets used in system), or organizers, see *Harper House*, 889 F.2d at 205 (as compilations consisting largely of uncopyrightable elements, plaintiff's organizers entitled only to protection against "bodily appropriation of expression"), which are afforded only "thin" protection because the range of possible expression is narrow. See *Feist*, 499 U.S. at 349. Rather, it submits that the broader protection accorded artistic works is more appropriate. See, e.g., *McCulloch*, 823 F.2d at 321 (artistic work like a decorative plate receives broader protection because of endless variations of expression available to artist).

Which end of the continuum a particular work falls on is a call that must be made case by case. We are satisfied that this case is closer to *Frybarger* than to *McCulloch*. See also Atari Games Corp. v. Oman, 298 U.S. App. D.C. 303, 979 F.2d 242, 245 (D.C. Cir. 1992) (analogizing audiovisual work like a videogame to compilation of facts). Accordingly, since Apple did not contest summary judgment under the virtual identity standard on the merits, judgment was properly entered. . . .

We therefore hold that the district court properly identified the sources of similarity in Windows and NewWave, determined which were licensed, distinguished ideas from expression, and decided the scope of Apple's copyright by dissecting the unauthorized expression and filtering out unprotectable elements. Having correctly found that almost all the similarities spring either from the license or from basic ideas and their obvious expression, it correctly concluded that illicit copying could occur only if the works as a whole are virtually identical.

COMMENTS AND QUESTIONS

1. What is the appropriate standard for testing infringement of the user interfaces of computer programs? The traditional test for evaluating copying has been the "substantial similarity" standard. *Apple*'s "virtual

identicality" test comes from a number of cases, including Hoehling v. Universal City Studios, Inc., 618 F.2d 972 (2d Cir. 1980), that deal with "thin" copyrights. It has been endorsed by at least one software case as well. See MiTek Holdings, Inc. v. ARCE Engineering Co., 89 F.3d 1548, 1558 (11th Cir. 1996) ("we join the Ninth Circuit in adopting the 'bodily appropriation of expression' or 'virtual identicality' standard" for claims of software infringement based on a compilation of uncopyrightable elements). See also Mark A. Lemley, Convergence in the Law of Software Copyright?, 10 High Tech. L.J. 1 (1995) (endorsing this test for "high-level" copying of program elements).

Is it appropriate to vary the standard for infringement with the scope of copyright protection, or does that "double count" the results of the filtration analysis?

2. To what extent is user interface design constrained by utilitarian considerations? As discussed in the introductory chapter, many programmers think of interface design as a "science" governed by fundamental principles of desirability. If certain goals are indeed inherently desirable— the "what you see is what you get" principle, say—what impact does that have on copyright protection for user interfaces?

3. In certain nonliteral software infringement cases, as well as in *Apple*, the vast majority of the copied work is determined to be uncopyrightable for one reason or another. If only a few "kernels" of copyrightable expression are mixed in with a large amount of public domain material, how should the courts test the "substantiality" of copying? Put another way, suppose that at trial Apple could prove only that a defendant had copied its "trash can" icon used for deleting files. Should copying of that one piece be sufficient to find infringement? If not, why not?

4. Consider the effect of dissection on copyright incentives. Does the fragmented protection that copyright affords to functional works such as computer programs really encourage creation of more programs? Does it encourage programmers to be more expressive when writing programs? If so, is that a desirable goal?

Before *Apple* and *Lotus*, a number of courts had given protection to relatively small individual elements of a user interface that they considered "artistic." See, e.g., Broderbund Software, Inc. v. Unison World, 648 F. Supp. 1127, 1134 (N.D. Cal. 1986) (choice of typeface on user interface screen and choice of words "Choose a Font" as title for a Print Shop screen were examples of audiovisual displays "dictated primarily by artistic and aesthetic consideration, and not by utilitarian or mechanical ones"); Lotus Dev. Corp. v. Paperback Software, 740 F. Supp. 37 (D. Mass. 1990) (choice of particular words to describe interface commands was expressive and therefore protectable). Is *Apple* inconsistent with protecting such microlevel design choices? Or is it simply harder to do so now?

5. Is Lotus Dev. Corp. v. Borland Int'l, reprinted above, really a case about command structures or about user interfaces? If the court approached it as a user interface case, should it reach the same result?

Would it? Cf. Mitel Inc. v. Iqtel, Inc., 896 F. Supp. 1050 (D. Colo. 1995), where the district court followed the First Circuit's decision in *Lotus* and in addition rejected the plaintiff's claim that its command codes were protectable as a user interface. On appeal, the Tenth Circuit affirmed, but it expressly refused to rely on *Lotus,* turning instead to *Altai*'s filtration approach. Mitel, Inc. v. Iqtel, Inc., 124 F.3d 1366 (10th Cir. 1997).

One court has held that user interfaces are really a species of nonliteral computer program elements and are not separately copyrightable. See O.P. Solutions Inc. v. Intellectual Property Network, 50 U.S.P.Q.2d 1399 (S.D.N.Y. 1999).

PROBLEM

Problem 2-8. Pueblo Graphics sells software that produces a variety of word processing fonts. (Fonts control the appearance of letters and numbers in typesetting.) The software allows the fonts to appear on the screen in exactly the same way they will appear on the printed page. Pueblo's software contains a number of "classic" print fonts, such as Geneva, Helvetica, and Times Roman Bold. In addition, however, Pueblo has designed several new fonts that look significantly different from any fonts previously produced.

Pueblo would like to assert a copyright infringement suit against a competitor who has copied its fonts. The competitor wrote its own program to implement those fonts, so Pueblo wants to know if it can get copyright protection in the fonts themselves. How would you advise Pueblo? Is their company's claim appropriately characterized as one for a "user interface"? Why or why not?

C. EXCLUSIVE RIGHTS IN COMPUTER PROGRAMS

1. The Right to Make "Copies"

Most of the cases we have considered in this chapter have involved the copying of all or part of a program by a company that sold a competing program. "Copying" has a potentially broader meaning in the computer context, however. The use of any modern computer program necessarily involves the creation of transitory copies in the RAM memory of a computer, and because running a computer program necessarily involves copying the program from long-term memory (ROM, CD-ROM, or disk) into the short-term memory of the computer, it is virtually impossible to use any computer program without making a "copy" of the entire program. However, that copy is not saved; it is erased whenever the application is exited or the computer is turned off. Whether such copies are fixed —and therefore potentially violate the copyright owner's rights under section 106(1)—has been a matter of some debate.

In 1993, the Ninth Circuit held that loading a computer program into RAM involved making a copy for purposes of section 106. MAI Systems Corp. v. Peak Computer, Inc., 991 F.2d 511, 518 (9th Cir. 1993). The court reasoned:

> The district court's grant of summary judgment on MAI's claims of copyright infringement reflects its conclusion that a "copying" for purposes of copyright law occurs when a computer program is transferred from a permanent storage device to a computer's RAM. This conclusion is consistent with its finding, in granting the preliminary injunction, that: "the loading of copyrighted computer software from a storage medium (hard disk, floppy disk, or read only memory) into the memory of a central processing unit ('CPU') causes a copy to be made. In the absence of ownership of the copyright or express permission by license, such acts constitute copyright infringement." We find that this conclusion is supported by the record and by the law.
>
> Peak concedes that in maintaining its customer's computers, it uses MAI operating software "to the extent that the repair and maintenance process necessarily involved turning on the computer to make sure it is functional and thereby running the operating system." It is also uncontroverted that when the computer is turned on the operating system is loaded into the computer's RAM. As part of diagnosing a computer problem at the customer site, the Peak technician runs the computer's operating system software, allowing the technician to view the systems error log, which is part of the operating system, thereby enabling the technician to diagnose the problem.
>
> Peak argues that this loading of copyrighted software does not constitute a copyright violation because the "copy" created in RAM is not "fixed." However, by showing that Peak loads the software into RAM and is then able to view the system error log and diagnose the problem with the computer, MAI has adequately shown that the representation created in the RAM is "sufficiently permanent or stable to permit it to be perceived, reproduced, or otherwise communicated for a period of more than transitory duration."
>
> After reviewing the record, we find no specific facts (and Peak points to none) which indicate that the copy created in the RAM is not fixed. . . .
>
> We have found no case which specifically holds that the copying of software into RAM creates a "copy" under the Copyright Act. However, it is generally accepted that the loading of software into a computer constitutes the creation of a copy under the Copyright Act. See, e.g., Vault Corp. v. Quaid Software, 847 F.2d 255, 260 (5th Cir. 1988) ("the act of loading a program from a medium of storage into a computer's memory creates a copy of the program"); 2 Nimmer on Copyright, §8.08 at 8-105 (1983) ("Inputting a computer program entails the preparation of a copy."); Final Report of the National Commission on the New Technological Uses of Copyrighted Works, at 13 (1978) ("the placement of a work into a computer is the preparation of a copy"). We recognize that these authorities are somewhat trou-

bling since they do not specify that a copy is created regardless of whether the software is loaded into the RAM, the hard disk or the read only memory ("ROM"). However, since we find that the copy created in the RAM can be "perceived, reproduced, or otherwise communicated," we hold that the loading of software into the RAM creates a copy under the Copyright Act.

COMMENTS AND QUESTIONS

1. If the Ninth Circuit is correct, every use of a computer or any computer program involves the making of at least one (and probably multiple) copies of the computer program. The fact that it is impossible to read or use a computer program without making such copies means that the application of the copyright laws to computer software is potentially far broader than to other types of works. While you can "use" a book without making a copy, under *MAI* any use of a computer program—even turning the computer on!—necessarily implicates the copyright laws. But cf. NFLC, Inc. v. Devcom Mid-America, Inc., 45 F.3d 231 (7th Cir. 1995) (suggesting that the use of dumb terminals to view a work located elsewhere might not make an infringing copy of that work).

Perhaps in recognition of this problem, Congress enacted section 117 of the Copyright Act in 1980. Section 117 makes it possible for users of computer programs to make certain copies without fear of liability. It was amended in 1998 to permit RAM copies specifically for the purpose of hardware maintenance (and therefore to overturn, at least in a narrow sense, the holding of *MAI*). We discuss section 117 in detail in the next Section; for now, keep in mind that making a copy is not always a violation of the copyright laws.

Does the specific enactment by Congress of a statutory provision permitting a user to make copies "necessary" to run a program suggest that Congress agreed that RAM copies were "fixed" for copyright purposes?

2. *MAI* is arguably inconsistent with both prior case law and the intent of Congress. In Apple Computer v. Formula Int'l, 594 F. Supp. 617, 621-622 (C.D. Cal. 1984), a case cited with apparent approval in *MAI*, the court indicated that copies stored in RAM, unlike those loaded in ROM, were only "temporary." And the House Report discussing the definition of "fixed" in section 101 of the Act had this to say on the subject of computer memory: "[T]he definition of 'fixation' would exclude from the concept purely evanescent or transient reproductions such as those projected briefly on a screen, shown electronically on a television or other cathode ray tube, or captured momentarily in the 'memory' of a computer." H.R. Rep. No. 94-1476, 94th Cong., 2d Sess. 52-53 (1976). More recently, the Fifth Circuit rejected the notion that remote viewing of a copyrighted computer program made a copy of that program. See Hogan Sys. v. Cybresource Int'l, 158 F.3d 319, 324 (5th Cir. 1998).

On the other hand, a number of courts have followed *MAI*'s lead in holding that copies loaded in RAM are fixed for purposes of copyright infringement. See Triad Systems v. Southeastern Express Co., 64 F.3d 1330 (9th Cir. 1995); Stenograph L.L.C. v. Bossard Assocs., 144 F.3d 96 (D.C. Cir. 1998); In re Independent Service Organizations Antitrust Litigation, 910 F. Supp. 1537, 1541 (D. Kan. 1995); MAI v. ACS, 845 F. Supp. 356 (E.D. Va. 1994).

Is RAM memory perceivable for "more than a transitory duration"? Is it more like movies projected on a screen or like movies stored on videotape?

3. Most commentators have been critical of the *MAI* decision. See, e.g., Niva Elkin-Koren, Copyright Law and Social Dialogue on the Information Superhighway: The Case Against Copyright Liability of Internet Providers, 13 Cardozo Arts & Ent. L.J. 345, 381-382 (1995); Michael E. Johnson, Note, The Uncertain Future of Computer Software Users' Rights in the Aftermath of MAI Systems, 44 Duke L.J. 327 (1994); Ronald Katz & Janet S. Arnold, An Unprecedented Opinion with Sparse Analysis, Computer Law., May 1993; Mark A. Lemley, Dealing with Overlapping Copyrights on the Internet, 22 U. Dayton L. Rev. 547, 550-552 (1997); Katrine Levin, Note, MAI v. Peak: Should Loading Operating System Software Into RAM Constitute Copyright Infringement?, 24 Golden Gate U.L. Rev. 649 (1994); Jessica Litman, The Exclusive Right to Read, 13 Cardozo Arts & Ent. L.J. 29, 41-43 (1994); David Nimmer, Brains and Other Paraphernalia of the Digital Age, 10 Harv. J.L. & Tech. 1 (1997); Carol G. Stovsky, Note, MAI Systems Corp. v. Peak Computer, Inc.: Using Copyright Law to Prevent Unauthorized Use of Computer Software, 56 Ohio St. L.J. 593 (1995). On the other hand, the Clinton administration has enthusiastically endorsed *MAI* in its White Paper on copyright and the Internet. See NII Working Group on Intellectual Property, Intellectual Property and the National Information Infrastructure (August 1995). The White Paper read *MAI* as authority for the proposition that reading a book online was an act of copyright infringement.

4. Two courts have held that copyright owners committed "copyright misuse" by attempting to extend their control over copyrights to RAM copies. DSC Communications Corp. v. DGI Technologies, Inc., 81 F.3d 597 (5th Cir. 1996); Tricom v. EDS, 902 F. Supp. 741 (E.D. Mich. 1995); see also Nimmer, supra (arguing that *MAI* should really have been a copyright misuse case). Presumably these cases implicitly reject the finding of MAI v. Peak, since it is hard to see how making a legitimate assertion of copyright infringement could be "misuse" of the copyright. Cf. 35 U.S.C. §271(d)(3) (not a misuse of patent rights to bring suit against infringers). On this point, see Mark A. Lemley, Beyond Preemption: The Law and Policy of Intellectual Property Licensing, 87 Cal. L. Rev. 111 (1999). The Fifth Circuit seemed to strengthen this inference in Hogan Systems Inc. v. Cybresource Int'l, 158 F.3d 319 (5th Cir. 1998), when it held that accessing a computer program from a remote location did not make a copy of the program. While the court did not discuss *MAI*, its conclusion was inconsistent with that case.

Note on the "Special" Problem of Multimedia

In the early 1990s, "multimedia" became an industry buzzword used to refer to the vast domain of products made possible through the integration of sound, graphics, film, and other works in modern interactive computer systems. Virtually everyone in the legal community and the popular press seemed to agree that the future of education and entertainment lies in multimedia. With this attention came a significant focus on the legal issues surrounding the creation of multimedia products. By and large, these are copyright issues.

The term "multimedia" itself refers to a rather amorphous group of actual or planned products that use computer technology to transcend the categories of traditional copyright law. For example, a multimedia CD-ROM might contain text, audio recordings, audiovisual works, and computer graphics and animation, along with hypertext search capabilities. Each of these elements has been digitized and placed onto a computer disk. Multimedia products are often (but not always) "interactive," which means that (like a video game) what occurs on the computer screen is a function of the choices made by the user of the software.

Despite the intense legal and industry interest in the law of multimedia, there are relatively few *legal* issues specific to multimedia, and most of those are well-settled principles of copyright law. Multimedia law might fairly be described as copyright law, only more so. The legal difficulties that plague producers of multimedia works result not from the novelty of the medium but from the aggregation of copyright issues already present in a number of old media.[5]

The typical multimedia program will incorporate dozens, if not hundreds, of "clips" or samples of preexisting works. The genius of the multimedia program lies in the collection and organization of these prior works—putting different pieces relating to a single subject in the same place, and designing a hypertext network that allows the user to "jump" from one piece to another in both predictable and spontaneous ways. Such programs present two types of copyright issues. First, program authors must get permission to use each of the copyrighted works in their program. Second, authors who have "compiled" these works into a unique format would like to copyright their compilation in order to prevent others from copying it.

Neither of these copyright issues is new. The process of obtaining copyright permissions for sound recordings, audiovisual works, photographs, text, and works of art is straightforward—copyright licensing has

---

5. One exception to this statement is the unification of different types of copyrighted works as digital content. Pictorial works, literary works, audiovisual works, and even architectural works can all be reduced to 1s and 0s in the digital medium. Arguably, therefore, they all become literary works. Since copyright law has historically given different rights to different types of works, this unification creates some potential problems. For a discussion of these issues, see Pamela Samuelson, Fair Use for Computer Programs and Other Copyrightable Works in Digital Form: The Implications of *Sony, Galoob,* and *Sega,* 1 J. Intell. Prop. L. 49 (1993).

been going on as long as copyright law has been in existence. While the fact that the multimedia product takes only a small "sample" from each preexisting work may distinguish multimedia from many copyright infringement cases, copyright has dealt with sampling before, notably in the context of rap music. See, e.g., Tin Pan Apple v. Miller Brewing Co., 30 U.S.P.Q.2d 1791 (S.D.N.Y. 1994); Jarvis v. A&M Records, 827 F. Supp. 282 (D.N.J. 1993); Grand Upright Music v. Warner Bros. Records, 780 F. Supp. 182 (S.D.N.Y. 1991). Whether a particular sample infringes the copyright on the original work depends on whether the taking from the original is substantial rather than de minimis.

Likewise, the protection of multimedia works can be treated according to well-established copyright principles. Program authors who write their own hypertext code or search engines can protect that code (and the nonliteral elements of the program) in the same way that they could protect any other computer program. And if the author has exercised creativity and originality in selecting preexisting materials for her multimedia program, she is entitled to a "compilation" copyright protecting that creativity against one who would copy her selection outright. 17 U.S.C. §103(a).

The problem copyright lawyers seem to have with multimedia is an eminently practical one—it is extraordinarily expensive and time-consuming to obtain hundreds of copyright permissions in order to put out a single product. Further, missing or intractable copyright owners can create "holdout" problems by leaving critical gaps in a multimedia work or charging exorbitant fees for the final pieces of a work. But these difficult problems inhere in the idea of copyright as a property right granted to authors and backed up by the force of injunctive relief.

The solution to these problems—if there is one—will take one of three forms. First, multimedia products may just be hard to produce or be incomplete and expensive. No novel interpretation of copyright law is required to achieve this result; it follows naturally from the economics of the copyright system.

Second, Congress could change the law to encourage the development of multimedia. The obvious candidate for legislative reform is the creation of some form of compulsory license that allows multimedia programmers to take works freely as long as they pay a set (or easily determinable) fee to the original copyright owner. This outcome seems unlikely, however. Not only has the United States been notoriously hostile to compulsory licensing, but multimedia by its nature would require a broad compulsory license governing most if not all types of copyrightable works. Unless the compulsory license were somehow limited to use in multimedia (a prospect that seems unworkable in practice), Congress could not accommodate the multimedia industry without revamping all of copyright law in a significant way.

Finally, it is possible that private organizations will develop that facilitate licensing of multiple works on a voluntary basis. Precursors of such groups already exist in some industries: American Society for Composers, Authors and Publishers (ASCAP) and Broadcast Music, Inc. (BMI) administer public performance rights to musical compositions, and the Copyright Clearance Center (CCC) grants the right to photocopy literary works, for example. See Robert P. Merges, Contracting Into Liability Rules: Institutions Supporting Transactions in Intellectual Property Rights, 84 Cal. L. Rev. 1293 (1996) (intellectual property rights support the development of private licensing organizations). But for multimedia to thrive, these voluntary organizations would have to expand into other areas (particularly with sound recordings and audiovisual works), and a significant percentage of copyright owners would have to sign on to the idea of automatically licensing their works to strangers. Unless and until that happens, the development of multimedia works will be hampered (though not prevented) by the problem of copyright licenses.

2. Copies and Section 117

As noted above, making copies is an essential part of using computer programs. Because of this important difference between computer software and other types of copyrightable material, Congress followed the recommendations of CONTU and passed section 117. That section provides in relevant part:

> Notwithstanding the provisions of section 106, it is not an infringement for the owner of a copy of a computer program to make or authorize the making of another copy or adaptation of that computer program provided:
>   (1) that such a new copy or adaptation is created as an essential step in the utilization of the computer program in conjunction with a machine and that it is used in no other manner, or
>   (2) that such new copy or adaptation is for archival purposes only and that all archival copies are destroyed in the event that continued possession of the computer program should cease to be rightful.

17 U.S.C. §117.

Section 117's right to make archival copies has not been controversial. It allows computer users to make backup copies of their programs as well as to load the programs onto hard drives from a floppy disk. See Vault Corp. v. Quaid Software Ltd., 847 F.2d 255 (5th Cir. 1988); ProCD, Inc. v. Zeidenberg, 908 F. Supp. 640 (W.D. Wis. 1996), *rev'd on other grounds*, 86 F.3d 1447 (7th Cir. 1996). The language of the statute also contemplates that multiple archival copies may be made of a single computer program. It clearly does *not* allow users of a program to make copies and distribute them to others for commercial purposes. See, e.g., Allen Myland Inc. v. IBM, 746 F. Supp. 520 (E.D. Pa. 1990); Apple Computer v. Formula Int'l, 594 F. Supp. 617 (C.D. Cal. 1984).

The right to make "essential" copies has proven more controversial. The basic intention of the section seems to be to allow copies like those made in *MAI v. Peak,* above. Further, the language of section 117(1) extends not only to identical copies, but to such "adaptation" of programs as is necessary to use them with a particular computer. In *Vault,* the Fifth Circuit held that such adaptations were not limited to those intended by the software vendor. In that case, Vault sold a computer program called PROLOK, which was used to "copy-protect" software.[6] Quaid reverse engineered Vault's program in order to create its own program, called RAMKEY, which disabled PROLOK's copy protection. In the course of writing RAMKEY, Quaid loaded the PROLOK program into its computer memory. The Court rejected Vault's claim of copyright infringement:

> In order to develop RAMKEY, Quaid analyzed Vault's program by copying it into its computer's memory. Vault contends that, by making this unauthorized copy, Quaid directly infringed upon Vault's copyright. The district court held that "Quaid's actions clearly fall within [the §117(1)] exemption. The loading of [Vault's] program into the [memory] of a computer is an 'essential step in the utilization' of [Vault's] program. Therefore, Quaid has not infringed Vault's copyright by loading [Vault's program] into [its computer's memory]." *Vault,* 655 F.Supp. at 758.
>
> Section 117(1) permits an owner of a program to make a copy of that program provided that the copy "is created as an essential step in the utilization of the computer program in conjunction with a machine and that it is used in no other manner." Congress recognized that a computer program cannot be used unless it is first copied into a computer's memory, and thus provided the §117(1) exception to permit copying for this essential purpose. See CONTU Report at 31. Vault contends that, due to the inclusion of the phrase "and that it is used in no other manner," this exception should be interpreted to permit only the copying of a computer program for the purpose of using it for *its intended purpose.* Because Quaid copied Vault's program into its computer's memory for the express purpose of devising a means of defeating its protective function, Vault contends that §117(1) is not applicable.
>
> We decline to construe §117(1) in this manner. Even though the copy of Vault's program made by Quaid was not used to prevent the copying of the program placed on the PROLOK diskette by one of Vault's customers (which is the purpose of Vault's program), and was, indeed, made for the express purpose of devising a means of defeating its protective function, the copy made by Quaid was "created as an essential step in the utilization" of Vault's program. Section 117(1) contains no language to suggest that the copy it permits must be employed for a use intended by the copyright owner, and, absent clear congressional guidance to the contrary, we refuse to read such limiting language into this exception. We therefore hold that Quaid did

---

6. Copy protection, which was common during the early 1980s, refers to programs that attempt to prevent unauthorized copies of software—for example, by disabling a copy from running at all or by requiring a user to enter a key word from the manual before each operation.

not infringe Vault's exclusive right to reproduce its program in copies under §106(1).

Vault Corp. v. Quaid Software Ltd., 847 F.2d 255 (5th Cir. 1988).

To whom does section 117 apply? By its terms, the statute authorizes copies or adaptations made by "the owner of a copy of a computer program" or persons she authorizes to make such copies. In its Final Report, the CONTU Commission indicated its intention "that *persons in rightful possession of copies of programs* be able to use them freely without fear of exposure to copyright liability." CONTU Final Report at 13 (emphasis added). The report seems to indicate that section 117 applies to anyone who has not obtained the program by improper means.

Without discussion or explanation, Congress changed "persons in rightful possession of copies" to "owners of copies." Does this mean that section 117 doesn't benefit licensees—a group that on some readings encompasses all users of a computer program? Or should the phrase "owner of a copy of a computer program" be interpreted to refer to the rightful possessor of the physical copy, regardless of who retains the copyright in the program itself? This issue was addressed at length by the Federal Circuit in DSC Communications Corp. v. Pulse Communications Inc., 170 F.3d 1354 (Fed. Cir. 1999):

> The district court concluded that making copies of the POTS-DI software (in the resident memory of POTS cards) was an "essential step in the utilization" of the POTS-DI software and that there was no evidence that the RBOCs used the software in any other manner that would constitute infringement. Accordingly, under the district court's theory of the case there was no direct infringement (and thus no contributory infringement) if the RBOCs were section 117 "owners" of copies of the POTS-DI software.
>
> The district court then held that the RBOCs were "owners" of copies of the POTS-DI software because they obtained the software by making a single payment and obtaining a right to possession of the software for an unlimited period. Those attributes of the transaction, the court concluded, made the transaction a "sale."
>
> DSC challenges the district court's conclusion that, based on the terms of the purchase transactions between DSC and the RBOCs, the RBOCs were "owners" of copies of the POTS-DI software. In order to resolve that issue, we must determine what attributes are necessary to constitute ownership of copies of software in this context.
>
> Unfortunately, ownership is an imprecise concept, and the Copyright Act does not define the term. Nor is there much useful guidance to be obtained from either the legislative history of the statute or the cases that have construed it. The National Commission on New Technological Uses of Copyrighted Works ("CONTU") was created by Congress to recommend changes in the Copyright Act to accommodate advances in computer technology. In its final report, CONTU proposed a version of section 117 that is identical to the one that was ultimately enacted, except for a single change.

The proposed CONTU version provided that "it is not an infringement for the rightful possessor of a copy of a computer program to make or authorize the making of another copy or adaptation of that program. . . ." Final Report of the National Commission on New Technological Uses of Copyrighted Works, U.S. Dept. of Commerce, PB-282141, at 30 (July 31, 1978). Congress, however, substituted the words "owner of a copy" in place of the words "rightful possessor of a copy." See Pub.L. No. 96-517, 96th Cong., 2d Sess. (1980). The legislative history does not explain the reason for the change, see H.R.Rep. No. 96-1307, 96th Cong., 2d Sess., pt. 1, at 23 (1980), but it is clear from the fact of the substitution of the term "owner" for "rightful possessor" that Congress must have meant to require more than "rightful possession" to trigger the section 117 defense.

In the leading case on section 117 ownership, the Ninth Circuit considered an agreement in which MAI, the owner of a software copyright, transferred copies of the copyrighted software to Peak under an agreement that imposed severe restrictions on Peak's rights with respect to those copies. See MAI Sys. Corp. v. Peak Computer, Inc., 991 F.2d 511, 26 USPQ2d 1458, 1462 (9th Cir.1995). The court held that Peak was not an "owner" of the copies of the software for purposes of section 117 and thus did not enjoy the right to copy conferred on owners by that statute. The Ninth Circuit stated that it reached the conclusion that Peak was not an owner because Peak had licensed the software from MAI. See *id*. at 518 n. 5. That explanation of the court's decision has been criticized for failing to recognize the distinction between ownership of a copyright, which can be licensed, and ownership of copies of the copyrighted software. See, e.g., 2 Melville B. Nimmer, Nimmer on Copyright ¶8.08[B][1], at 8-119 to 121 (3d ed.1997). Plainly, a party who purchases copies of software from the copyright owner can hold a license under a copyright while still being an "owner" of a copy of the copyrighted software for purposes of section 117. We therefore do not adopt the Ninth Circuit's characterization of all licensees as non-owners. Nonetheless, the MAI case is instructive, because the agreement between MAI and Peak, like the agreements at issue in this case, imposed more severe restrictions on Peak's rights with respect to the software than would be imposed on a party who owned copies of software subject only to the rights of the copyright holder under the Copyright Act. And for that reason, it was proper to hold that Peak was not an "owner" of copies of the copyrighted software for purposes of section 117. See also Advanced Computer Servs. of Mich. v. MAI Sys. Corp., 845 F. Supp. 356, 367, 30 USPQ2d 1443, 1452 (E.D.Va.1994) ("MAI customers are not 'owners' of the copyrighted software; they possess only the limited rights set forth in their licensing agreements"). We therefore turn to the agreements between DSC and the RBOCs to determine whether those agreements establish that the RBOCs are section 117 "owners" of copies of the copyrighted POTS-DI software. [The court concluded after a detailed analysis of the facts of the transaction that certain agreements in that case did not transfer ownership of the particular copies of the program at issue but that other transactions did involve a transfer of ownership.]

Id. at 1359-1362. It is worth noting that *DSC* involved a negotiated agreement between sophisticated parties—the buyers were the regional Bell operating companies. By contrast, in the mass-market context, most (though by no means all) cases that have considered the issue have concluded that mass-market, over-the-counter transfers of computer programs at retail stores constitute "sales of goods" subject to the Uniform Commercial Code rather than license agreements. See Chapter 6 (discussing these cases).

The Digital Millennium Copyright Act, passed by Congress in 1998, reversed the holding of MAI v. Peak but in a very narrow way. Rather than declare that section 117 applies to rightful possessors of a computer program, as CONTU intended, the DMCA altered section 117 to create a particular exemption from liability for the owner or lessee of a computer to make or authorize the making of a copy of a computer program for purposes of maintenance or repair of the computer hardware. However, the copy thus made must be made solely by turning the machine on and be used for no other purpose; and no other programs can be copied. Further, the new provision does not apply to maintenance or repair of software—just hardware.

Does this solve the problem created by the *MAI* case? Or does it give legislative sanction to the idea that RAM copies are not permitted except in the narrow circumstances covered by the new Act? One might read this new exemption as creating a negative implication that all other copies made by lessees or licensees were illegal, even if they fell within subsections 117(1) or (2). Thus, this change may benefit independent service organizations that service computer hardware, but it does nothing for computer users in general.

Is there a social interest in maintaining a competitive market for hardware and software maintenance? One way of thinking about the issue is to determine whether the copyright in a computer program should permit its owner to control the markets for hardware and software maintenance, or whether using the copyright to prevent competition in that market would expand copyright protection beyond its intended boundaries. For a discussion of the competitive interest in software maintenance, see Pamela Samuelson, Modifying Copyrighted Software: Adjusting Copyright Doctrine to Accommodate a Technology, 28 Jurim. J. 179 (1988).

3. Derivative Works

Copyright Act section 106(2) grants the copyright owner the exclusive right to prepare "derivative works" based on the original copyrighted work. (This right, like the right to make copies, is subject to section 117.) Because computer programs are inherently easy to modify, the "derivative works" right has taken on particular significance in the computer context.

Midway Manufacturing Co. v. Artic International, Inc.
United States Court of Appeals for the Seventh Circuit
704 F.2d 1009 (7th Cir. 1983), cert. denied, 464 U.S. 923 (1983)

CUMMINGS, Chief Judge. . . .

Plaintiff manufactures video game machines. Inside these machines are printed circuit boards capable of causing images to appear on a television picture screen and sounds to emanate from a speaker when an electric current is passed through them. On the outside of each machine are a picture screen, sound speaker, and a lever or button that allows a person using the machine to alter the images appearing on the machine's picture screen and the sounds emanating from its speaker. Each machine can produce a large number of related images and sounds. These sounds and images are stored on the machine's circuit boards—how the circuits are arranged and connected determines the set of sounds and images the machine is capable of making. When a person touches the control lever or button on the outside of the machine he sends a signal to the circuit boards inside the machine which causes them to retrieve and display one of the sounds and images stored in them. Playing a video game involves manipulating the controls on the machine so that some of the images stored in the machine's circuitry appear on its picture screen and some of its sounds emanate from its speaker.

Defendant sells printed circuit boards for use inside video game machines. One of the circuit boards defendant sells speeds up the rate of play —how fast the sounds and images change—of "Galaxian," one of plaintiff's video games, when inserted in place of one of the "Galaxian" machine's circuit boards. Another of defendant's circuit boards stores a set of images and sounds almost identical to that stored in the circuit boards of plaintiff's "Pac-Man" video game machine so that the video game people play on machines containing defendant's circuit board looks and sounds virtually the same as plaintiff's "Pac-Man" game.

Plaintiff sued defendant alleging that defendant's sale of these two circuit boards infringes its copyrights in its "Galaxian" and "Pac-Man" video games. . . .

The final argument of defendant's that we address is that selling plaintiff's licensees circuit boards that speed up the rate of play of plaintiff's video games is not an infringement of plaintiff's copyrights. Speeding up the rate of play of a video game is a little like playing at 45 or 78 revolutions per minute ("RPM's") a phonograph record recorded at 33 RPM's. If a discotheque licensee did that, it would probably not be an infringement of the record company's copyright in the record. One might argue by analogy that it is not a copyright infringement for video game licensees to speed up the rate of play of video games, and that it is not a contributory infringement for the defendant to sell licensees circuit boards that enable them to do that.

There is this critical difference between playing records at a faster than recorded speed and playing video games at a faster than manufactured rate: there is an enormous demand for speeded-up video games but there is little if any demand for speeded-up records. Not many people want to hear 33 RPM records played at 45 and 78 RPM's so that record licensors would not care if their licensees play them at that speed. But there is a big demand for speeded-up video games. Speeding up a video game's action makes the game more challenging and exciting and increases the licensee's revenue per game. Speeded-up games end sooner than normal games and consequently if players are willing to pay an additional price-per-minute in exchange for the challenge and excitement of a faster game, licensees will take in greater total revenues. Video game copyright owners would undoubtedly like to lay their hands on some of that extra revenue and therefore it cannot be assumed that licensees are implicitly authorized to use speeded-up circuit boards in the machines plaintiff supplies.

Among a copyright owner's exclusive rights is the right "to prepare derivative works based upon the copyrighted work." 17 U.S.C. §106(2). If, as we hold, the speeded-up "Galaxian" game that a licensee creates with a circuit board supplied by the defendant is a derivative work based upon "Galaxian," a licensee who lacks the plaintiff's authorization to create a derivative work is a direct infringer and the defendant is a contributory infringer through its sale of the speeded-up circuit board. See, e.g., Gershwin Publishing Corp. v. Columbia Artists Mgmt., Inc., 443 F.2d 1159, 1162 (2d Cir.1971); Universal City Studios, Inc. v. Sony Corp. of America, 659 F.2d 963, 975 (9th Cir.1981), *certiorari granted,* 457 U.S. 1116, 102 S.Ct. 2926, 73 L.Ed.2d 1326 (1982).

Section 101 of the 1976 Copyright Act defines a derivative work as "a work based upon one or more preexisting works, such as a translation, musical arrangement, dramatization, fictionalization, motion picture version, sound recording, art reproduction, abridgment, condensation, or any other form in which a work may be recast, transformed, or adapted." It is not obvious from this language whether a speeded-up video game is a derivative work. A speeded-up phonograph record probably is not. Cf. Shapiro, Bernstein & Co. v. Jerry Vogel Music Co., 73 F.Supp. 165, 167 (S.D.N.Y.1947) ("The change in time of the added chorus, and the slight variation in the base of the accompaniment, there being no change in the tune or lyrics, would not be 'new work'"); 1 Nimmer on Copyright §3.03 (1982). But that is because the additional value to the copyright owner of having the right to market separately the speeded-up version of the recorded performance is too trivial to warrant legal protection for that right. A speeded-up video game is a substantially different product from the original game. As noted, it is more exciting to play and it requires some creative effort to produce. For that reason, the owner of the copyright on the game should be entitled to monopolize it on the same theory that he is entitled to monopolize the derivative works specifically listed in Section 101. The current rage for video games was not anticipated in 1976, and like any new technology the video game does not fit with complete ease the definition of derivative work in Section 101 of the 1976 Act. But the amount by which the language of Section 101 must be stretched to accommodate speeded-up video games is, we believe, within the limits within which Congress wanted the new Act to operate. Cf. *WGN Continental Broadcasting Co.*, supra, 693 F.2d at 627; *Williams Electronics, Inc.*, supra, 685 F.2d at 873-874; *Atari*, supra, 672 F.2d at 614-620. . . .

Recall Vault Corp. v. Quaid Software Ltd., 847 F.2d 255 (5th Cir. 1988), discussed above. Early versions of RAMKEY had contained some characters from the original Vault program. The court found that this copying of characters was insufficient to make RAMKEY a derivative of the original PROLOK program:

> Section 106(2) of the Copyright Act provides the copyright owner exclusive rights "to prepare derivative works based on the copyrighted work." Section 101 defines a derivative work as:
>
>> a work based on one or more preexisting works, such as a translation, musical arrangement, dramatization, fictionalization, motion picture version, sound recording, art reproduction, abridgment, condensation, or any other form in which a work may be recast, transformed, or adapted. A work consisting of editorial revisions, annotations, elaborations or other modifications which, as a whole, represent an original work of authorship is a "derivative work."
>
> To constitute a derivative work, "the infringing work must incorporate in some form a portion of the copyrighted work." Litchfield v. Spielberg, 736 F.2d 1352, 1357 (9th Cir.1984), *cert. denied*, 470 U.S. 1052, 105 S.Ct. 1753, 84 L.Ed.2d 817 (1985). In addition, the infringing work must be substantially similar to the copyrighted work. *Id.*
>
> The 1984 version of RAMKEY contained approximately 30 characters of source code copied from Vault's program. Vault's program contained the equivalent of approximately 50 pages of source code, and the 1984 version of RAMKEY contained the equivalent of approximately 80 pages of source code. By all accounts, the 30 character sequence shared by RAMKEY and Vault's program constituted a quantitatively minor amount of source code. In response to Vault's contention that RAMKEY constitutes a derivative work, the district court found that "the copying in 1984 was not significant" and that "there has been no evidence . . . that there has been any further duplication." Holding that "RAMKEY is not a substantially similar copy of PROLOK," the court concluded that "RAMKEY is not a derivative work." *Vault*, 655 F.Supp. at 759.
>
> Vault now contends that the district court, in evaluating the 1984 version of RAMKEY, incorrectly emphasized the *quantity* of copying instead of the *qualitative* significance of the copied material, and cites Whelan Assoc's., Inc. v. Jaslow Dental Laboratory, Inc., 797 F.2d 1222 (3d Cir.1986), *cert. denied*, — U.S. —, 107 S.Ct. 877 (1987), for the proposition that a "court must make a qualitative, not quantitative, judgment about the character of

the work as a whole and the importance of the substantially similar portions of the work." *Id*. at 1245. See Midway Mfg. Co. v. Artic Int'l, Inc., 704 F.2d 1009, 1013-14 (7th Cir.), *cert. denied*, 464 U.S. 923 (1983). The sequence copied, Vault asserts, constituted the identifying portion of Vault's program which interacts with the "fingerprint" to confirm that the original PROLOK diskette is in the computer's disk drive. Vault contends that, because this sequence was crucial to the operation of Vault's program and RAMKEY's ability to defeat its protective function, the copying was qualitatively significant.

The cases upon which Vault relies, *Whelan* and *Midway*, both involved situations where the derivative work performed essentially the same function as the copyrighted work. In this case, Vault's program and RAMKEY serve opposing functions; while Vault's program is designed to prevent the duplication of its customers' programs, RAMKEY is designed to facilitate the creation of copies of Vault's customers' programs. Under these circumstances, we agree with the district court that the 1984 copying was not significant and that this version of RAMKEY was not a substantially similar copy of Vault's program.

While Vault acknowledges that the latest version of RAMKEY does not contain a sequence of characters from Vault's program, Vault contends that this version is also a derivative work because it "alters" Vault's program. Vault cites *Midway* for the proposition that a product can be a derivative work where it alters, rather than copies, the copyrighted work. The court in *Midway*, however, held that the sale of a product which speeded-up plaintiff's programs constituted contributory infringement because the speeded-up programs were derivative works. 704 F.2d at 1013-14. The court did not hold, as Vault asserts, that defendant's product itself was a derivative work. We therefore reject Vault's contention that the latest version of RAMKEY constitutes a derivative work.

COMMENTS AND QUESTIONS

1. What is the scope of the derivative works right under *Midway* decision? The court suggests that any nontrivial variation that would result in added revenues constitutes a derivative work. Is this consistent with the case law on derivative works outside the computer context? See Litchfield v. Spielberg, 736 F.2d 1352 (9th Cir. 1984) (works cannot be derivative unless they are substantially similar to the underlying work). In United States v. Manzer, 69 F.3d 222 (8th Cir. 1995), the court held that a 70 percent similarity between the code of two programs was sufficient to support a finding that one was an infringing derivative of the other. Would application of the *Litchfield* rule provide an easy way to resolve the "derivative works" issue in *Vault*?

It is also possible to criticize the *Midway* decision for reading the scope of derivative works too narrowly. After all, why should it matter whether there is a market for a particular derivative work? Shouldn't the property right of the program's owner include the right to prevent modifications whether or not they turn out to be commercially successful?

2.   To what extent does the first-sale doctrine (17 U.S.C. §109(a)) protect makers of "add-on" software and hardware? Should it matter whether the underlying computer program is sold or licensed? See H.R. Rep. No. 94-1476, 94th Cong., 2d Sess. (1976) (licensors can control or prevent exercise of first sale rights by users).[7]

Note on Derivative Works and Section 117

In many circumstances, computer system and software manufacturers encourage the development of "add-on" software so as to make their products more attractive to users and to build large networks of users. As the *Midway* and *Vault* cases highlight, however, the interests of add-on developers and original program manufacturers can conflict, making the scope of the derivative-works right critical to the innovative environment. Whose rights should prevail in such a conflict may depend on your evaluation of the economics of software development. Preventing independent derivative works will certainly give a greater reward to the originator of the initial program, but by giving a monopoly on subsequent development it may slow the creation of improvements or add-ons to the program.

In certain cases, such as *Vault*, the entire point of an add-on is to defeat or render useless the original program. In such cases, is there some policy goal that would be served by giving the copyright owner a veto right over such "improvements" to his program? Is the *Vault* case more like the mutilation or destruction of a work of art, which many countries prohibit under moral rights statutes, or like a parody that should be legal precisely *because* copyright owners will refuse to license it?

The Copyright Act provides that the owner of a copy of a computer program has the right to adapt that program "provided that such . . . adaptation is created as an essential step in the utilization of the computer program in conjunction with a machine." 17 U.S.C. §117. To what extent does section 117 give the owners of computer programs the right to make derivative works for their own use? In Aymes v. Bonnelli, 47 F.3d 23 (2d Cir. 1995), the Second Circuit held that the rightful owner of a copy of a computer program had the right under section 117 "to add features to the program that were not present at the time of rightful acquisition," and to modify it for internal use, but not to distribute the work to others. The court relied on CONTU's explanation of section 117: "Buyers should be able to adapt a purchased program for use on the buyer's computer

---

7. Note that a user's rights under the first-sale doctrine are limited in the computer context. Under the Software Rental Amendments Act of 1990, section 109 of the Act was amended to preclude those in possession of a copy of a computer program from "disposing of" it "by rental, lease, or lending, or by any other act or practice in the nature of rental, lease or lending." See Central Point Software Inc. v. Global Software & Accessories, 880 F. Supp. 957 (E.D.N.Y. 1995) ("Deferred Billing Plan" amounted to a de facto rental of software and was prohibited).

because without modifications, the program may work improperly, if at all."

Does *Aymes* justify the production of new versions of software? The translation of a program to run on a different operating system?

Some commentators have argued for a narrow scope for the derivative-works right in the context of computer program add-ons. See Richard Stern, Copyright Infringement by Add-On Software: Beyond Deconstruction of the Mona Lisa Moustache Paradigm and Not Taking Video Game Cases Too Seriously, 31 Jurimetrics J. 205 (1991); Christian H. Nadan, Comment, A Proposal to Recognize Component Works: How a Teddy Bears on the Competing Ends of Copyright Law, 78 Cal. L. Rev. 1633 (1990). Stern argues that allowing the creator of the original program to control add-ons not incorporated within that product would provide little additional incentive to develop the product, while inhibiting subsequent developers of add-on programs. Are there any other adverse effects of a narrow derivative-works right for add-on software? To what extent would Stern's argument apply to other fields of copyrightable works? On this issue, see Mark A. Lemley, The Economics of Improvement in Intellectual Property Law, 75 Tex. L. Rev. 989 (1997).

COMMENTS AND QUESTIONS

1. The Ninth Circuit took a much more limited view of add-on programs and enhancements in Micro Star v. Formgen, 154 F.3d 1107 (9th Cir. 1998). There, the copyright infringement plaintiff was Formgen, the owner of a popular computer game called "Duke Nukem 3D," in which characters adventured on multiple "levels." Players of the game had an established practice of writing and trading their own levels. Writing a level involved writing certain specifications that called on established graphics in the copyrighted game itself. However, the programs (MAP files) that created these add-on levels did not actually incorporate any of the code or graphics of the original computer game directly. Formgen permitted this practice so long as the levels were not sold. When Micro Star tried to compile and market add-on levels for the game, Formgen sued. The Ninth Circuit held that the levels were infringing derivative works, despite the fact that they did not themselves incorporate any aspect of the game in fixed form.[8]

---

8. When a user played the game, Formgen's graphics would be incorporated, but only for a brief and arguably unfixed period of time. The court concluded that some sort of quasi-fixation was indeed a requirement for derivative works, but that the audiovisual works produced during game play were sufficiently fixed to qualify as derivative works because the audiovisual displays were described in exact detail in the user-created level specifications (MAP files). Note, however, that the MAP files themselves did not copy any of Formgen's protected program code, but merely told the game which files to display from the 'Duke Nukem' graphics library.

Does this result make sense? Is it consistent with *Vault?* With *Aymes?* Note that the effect of this case is to give the copyright owner control over add-on works that merely interoperate with, rather than directly incorporate, the original copyrighted works. But see Lewis Galoob Toys v. Nintendo of America, 964 F.2d 965 (9th Cir. 1992) (concluding that a similar device that allowed users to alter the play of a video game was not a derivative work at all and in addition was fair use).

PROBLEM

Problem 2-9. Evaluate whether the following products would be deemed within the section 106(2) exclusive right to prepare derivative works.

(a) Demento Corporation (Demento) produces Demento II, the leading home video game system. The Demento II consists of a console, which runs game cartridges and attaches to a monitor or standard television, and a control device, which enables the user to manipulate characters or other images of particular games on the screen. Demento licenses a limited number of games per year.

Users of the Demento II, principally teenagers, quickly master the existing games. Without obtaining a license from Demento, MC Corporation developed a device to enable users to get more enjoyment out of the Demento games. Its product, Master Controller, allows users to alter the speed of play and the capabilities of characters within Demento games. Master Controller functions by altering the data sent from the game cartridge to the console. It does not alter the data within the game cartridge and cannot be used without both the Demento II console and game cartridges.

(b) ACME Software Inc. has developed a program called Speechwriter that works in conjuction with a number of leading word processing programs. By blocking keywords within a document and entering "Alt Q," Speechwriter displays a series of famous quotations related to the selected keywords. The program is geared to the visual presentation format of the particular word processing program. Once in the Speechwriter mode, the program offers users a variety of convenient ways to search among quotations. The program allows the user to download the quotation into the document. The actual program is stored on a separate floppy disk or can be loaded onto the computer's hard drive. It contains some program code from the word processing programs needed to interact with the word processing software and the graphical interface of the computer.

D.   FAIR USE

§107. Limitations on Exclusive Rights: Fair Use

Notwithstanding the provisions of section 106, the fair use of a copyrighted work, including such use by reproduction in copies or phonorecords or by any other means specified by that section, for purposes such as criticism, comment, news reporting, teaching (including multiple copies for classroom use), scholarship, or research, is not an infringement of copyright. In determining whether the use made of a work in any particular case is a fair use the factors to be considered shall include —

(1) the purpose and character of the use, including whether such use is of a commercial nature or is for nonprofit educational purposes;

(2) the nature of the copyrighted work;

(3) the amount and substantiality of the portion used in relation to the copyrighted work as a whole; and

(4) effect of the use upon the potential market for or value of the copyrighted work.

The fact that a work is unpublished shall not itself bar a finding of fair use if such finding is made upon consideration of all the above factors.

It is well established that both the list of potential fair uses and the factors to be considered in determining fair use are illustrative rather than exhaustive. The House Report accompanying section 107 describes the four factors—and the list of possible fair uses—as "the result of a process of accretion" during the judicial development of the fair use doctrine at common law. According to the report, section 107 is designed to "offer some guidance" in determining fair use, not to formulate "exact rules." H.R. No. 94-1476, at 66 (1976).

Section 107 represents the first attempt to codify what has been a common law doctrine for some time. The first reference to fair use (albeit by a different name) is thought to be in Folsom v. Marsh, 9 F. Cas. 342 (C.C. Mass. 1841). The court there focused on the loss in value to the plaintiff from copying to determine whether the defendant had engaged in what it called a "justifiable use" of plaintiff's copyrighted work. However, more recent cases have also looked to the purpose of the use and the "public benefit" conferred thereby. See Rosemont Enterprises v. Random House, Inc., 366 F.2d 303 (2d Cir. 1966). Indeed, *Folsom* itself involved the publication of George Washington's private letters, and therefore contained a strong public interest component as well.

The inability of the courts or Congress even to articulate a complete list of the factors to be applied in determining fair use is evidence of the difficulty courts have had in applying the doctrine. Judge Learned Hand described the fair use doctrine as "the most troublesome in the whole law of copyright." Dellar v. Samuel Goldwyn, Inc., 104 F.2d 661 (2d Cir. 1939).

≡
≡ *Lewis Galoob Toys, Inc. v. Nintendo of America, Inc.*
≡ *United States Court of Appeals for the Ninth Circuit*
≡ *964 F.2d 965 (9th Cir. 1992)*

FARRIS, Circuit Judge:

Nintendo of America appeals the district court's judgment following a bench trial (1) declaring that Lewis Galoob Toys' Game Genie does not violate any Nintendo copyrights and dissolving a temporary injunction and (2) denying Nintendo's request for a permanent injunction enjoining Galoob from marketing the Game Genie. Lewis Galoob Toys, Inc. v. Nintendo of America, Inc., 780 F. Supp. 1283, 20 U.S.P.Q.2D (BNA) 1662 (N.D. Cal. 1991). We have appellate jurisdiction pursuant to 15 U.S.C. §1121 and 28 U.S.C. §§1291 and 1292(a)(1). We affirm.

Facts

The Nintendo Entertainment System is a home video game system marketed by Nintendo. To use the system, the player inserts a cartridge containing a video game that Nintendo produces or licenses others to produce. By pressing buttons and manipulating a control pad, the player controls one of the game's characters and progresses through the game. The games are protected as audiovisual works under 17 U.S.C. §102(a)(6).

The Game Genie is a device manufactured by Galoob that allows the player to alter up to three features of a Nintendo game. For example, the Game Genie can increase the number of lives of the player's character, increase the speed at which the character moves, and allow the character to float above obstacles. The player controls the changes made by the Game Genie by entering codes provided by the Game Genie Programming Manual and Code Book. The player also can experiment with variations of these codes.

The Game Genie functions by blocking the value for a single data byte sent by the game cartridge to the central processing unit in the Nintendo Entertainment System and replacing it with a new value. If that value controls the character's strength, for example, then the character can be made invincible by increasing the value sufficiently. The Game Genie is inserted between a game cartridge and the Nintendo Entertainment System. The Game Genie does not alter the data that is stored in the game cartridge. Its effects are temporary.

Discussion

[The court concluded that the Game Genie was not a derivative work, because it did not itself incorporate the copyrighted work. The court also distinguished Midway v. Artic, reproduced above, and apparently concluded that the end user does not create a derivative work either. Nonetheless, the court went on to discuss fair use by the end user.]

2. *Fair Use*

"The doctrine of fair use allows a holder of the privilege to use copyrighted material in a reasonable manner without the consent of the copyright owner." Narell v. Freeman, 872 F.2d 907, 913, 10 U.S.P.Q.2D (BNA) 1596 (9th Cir. 1989) (citations omitted). The district court concluded that, even if the audiovisual displays created by the Game Genie are derivative works, Galoob is not liable under 17 U.S.C. §107 because the displays are a fair use of Nintendo's copyrighted displays. "Whether a use of copyrighted material is a 'fair use' is a mixed question of law and fact. If the district court found sufficient facts to evaluate each of the statutory factors, the appellate court may decide whether defendants may claim the fair use defense as a matter of law." Abend v. MCA, Inc., 863 F.2d 1465, 1468, 9 U.S.P.Q.2D (BNA) 1337 (9th Cir. 1988), *aff'd sub nom.* Stewart v. Abend, 495 U.S. 207, 109 L. Ed. 2d 184, 110 S. Ct. 1750, 14 U.S.P.Q.2D (BNA) 1614 (1990).

Section 107 codifies the fair use defense. . . .

Much of the parties' dispute regarding the fair use defense concerns the proper focus of the court's inquiry: (1) Galoob or (2) consumers who purchase and use the Game Genie. Nintendo's complaint does not allege direct infringement, nor did it try the case on that theory. The complaint, for example, alleges only that "Galoob's marketing advertising [sic], promoting and selling of Game Genie has and will contribute to the creation of infringing derivatives of Nintendo's copyrighted . . . games.". Contributory infringement is a form of third party liability. See Melville B. Nimmer & David Nimmer, 3 Nimmer on Copyright ¶12.04[A]2, at 12-68 (1991). The district court properly focused on whether consumers who purchase and use the Game Genie would be infringing Nintendo's copyrights by creating (what are now assumed to be) derivative works.

Nintendo emphasizes that the district court ultimately addressed its direct infringement by authorization argument. The court concluded that, "because the Game Genie does not create a derivative work when used in conjunction with a copyrighted video game, Galoob does not 'authorize the use of a copyrighted work without the actual authority from the copyright owner.'" *Galoob*, 780 F. Supp. at 1298 (quoting *Sony*, 464 U.S. at 435 n.17). Although infringement by authorization is a form of direct infringement, this does not change the proper focus of our inquiry; a party cannot authorize another party to infringe a copyright unless the authorized conduct would itself be unlawful.

The district court concluded that "a family's use of a Game Genie for private home enjoyment must be characterized as a non-commercial, nonprofit activity." *Galoob*, 780 F. Supp. at 1293. Nintendo argues that Game Genie users are supplanting its commercially valuable right to make and sell derivative works. Nintendo's reliance on Harper & Row Publishers, Inc. v. Nation Enters., 471 U.S. 539, 562, 85 L. Ed. 2d 588, 105 S. Ct. 2218, 225 U.S.P.Q. (BNA) 1073 (1985), is misplaced. The commercially valuable right at issue in Harper & Row was the right of first publication; Nation Enterprises intended to publish the copyrighted materials for profit. See id. at 562-63. See also *Sony*, 464 U.S. at 449 ("If the Betamax were used to make copies for a commercial or profit-making purpose, such use would presumptively be unfair."). Game Genie users are engaged in a non-profit activity. Their use of the Game Genie to create derivative works therefore is presumptively fair. See *Sony*, 464 U.S. at 449.

The district court also concluded that "the [Nintendo] works' published nature supports the fairness of the use." *Galoob*, 780 F. Supp. at 1293. Nintendo argues that it has not published the derivative works created by the Game Genie. This argument ignores the plain language of section 107: "the factors to be considered shall include . . . the nature of the copyrighted work." The argument also would make the fair use defense unavailable in all cases of derivative works, including "criticism, comment, news reporting, teaching . . . , scholarship, or research." 17 U.S.C. §107. A commentary that incorporated large portions of For Whom the Bell Tolls, for example, would be undeserving of fair use protection because the incorporated portions would constitute an unpublished derivative work. This cannot be the law.

The district court further concluded that the amount of the portion used in relation to the copyrighted work as a whole "cannot assist Nintendo in overcoming the presumption of fair use." *Galoob*, 780 F. Supp. at 1293. The video tape recorders at issue in *Sony* allowed consumers to tape copyrighted works in their entirety. The Supreme Court nevertheless held that, "when one considers . . . that [video tape recording] merely enables a viewer to see such a work which he had been invited to witness in its entirety free of charge, the fact that the entire work is reproduced does not have its ordinary effect of militating against a finding of fair use." 464 U.S. 449 at 449-50 (citations omitted). Consumers are not invited to witness Nintendo's audiovisual displays free of charge, but, once they have paid to do so, the fact that the derivative works created by the Game Genie are comprised almost entirely of Nintendo's copyrighted displays does not militate against a finding of fair use.

Nintendo would distinguish *Sony* because it involved copying copyrighted works rather than creating derivative works based on those works. In other words, the consumers in *Sony* could lawfully copy the copyrighted works because they were invited to view those works free of charge. Game

Genie users, in contrast, are not invited to view derivative works based on Nintendo's copyrighted works without first paying for that privilege. *Sony* cannot be read so narrowly. It is difficult to imagine that the Court would have reached a different conclusion if Betamax purchasers were skipping portions of copyrighted works or viewing denouements before climaxes. *Sony* recognizes that a party who distributes a copyrighted work cannot dictate how that work is to be enjoyed. Consumers may use a Betamax to view copyrighted works at a more convenient time. They similarly may use a Game Genie to enhance a Nintendo Game cartridge's audiovisual display in such a way as to make the experience more enjoyable.

"The fourth factor is the 'most important, and indeed, central fair use factor.'" *Stewart*, 495 U.S. at 238 (quoting 3 Nimmer on Copyright ¶13.05[A], at 13-81). The district court concluded that "Nintendo has failed to show any harm to the present market for its copyrighted games and has failed to establish the reasonable likelihood of a potential market for slightly altered versions of the games at suit." *Galoob*, 780 F. Supp. at 1295. Nintendo's main argument on appeal is that the test for market harm encompasses the potential market for derivative works. Because the Game Genie is used for a noncommercial purpose, the likelihood of future harm may not be presumed. See *Sony*, 464 U.S. at 451. Nintendo must show "by a preponderance of the evidence that some meaningful likelihood of future harm exists." *Id.*

Nintendo's argument is supported by case law. Although the Copyright Act requires a court to consider "the effect of the use upon the potential market for or value of the copyrighted work," 17 U.S.C. §107(4), we held in Abend that "although the motion picture will have no adverse effect on bookstore sales of the [underlying] novel—and may in fact have a beneficial effect—it is 'clear that [the film's producer] may not invoke the defense of fair use.'" 863 F.2d at 1482 (quoting 3 Nimmer on Copyright ¶13.05[B], at 13-84). We explained: " 'If the defendant's work adversely affects the value of any of the rights in the copyrighted work . . . the use is not fair even if the rights thus affected have not as yet been exercised by the plaintiff.'" *Id.* (quoting 3 Nimmer on Copyright ¶13.05[B], at 13-84 to 13-85 (footnotes omitted)). The Supreme Court specifically affirmed our finding that the motion picture adaptation "impinged on the ability to market new versions of the story." *Stewart*, 495 U.S. at 238.

Still, Nintendo's argument is undermined by the facts. The district court considered the potential market for derivative works based on Nintendo game cartridges and found that: (1) "Nintendo has not, to date, issued or considered issuing altered versions of existing games," *Galoob*, 780 F. Supp. at 1295, and (2) Nintendo "has failed to show the reasonable likelihood of such a market." *Id.* The record supports the court's findings. According to Stephen Beck, Galoob's expert witness, junior or expert versions of existing Nintendo games would enjoy very little market interest because the original version of each game already has been designed to appeal to the largest number of consumers. Mr. Beck also testified that a new game must include new material or "the game player is going to feel very cheated and robbed, and [the] product will have a bad reputation and word of mouth will probably kill its sales." Howard Lincoln, Senior Vice President of Nintendo of America, acknowledged that Nintendo has no present plans to market such games.

The district court also noted that Nintendo's assertion that it may wish to re-release altered versions of its game cartridges is contradicted by its position in various other lawsuits:

> In those actions, Nintendo opposes antitrust claims by using the vagaries of the video game industry to rebut the impact and permanence of its market control, if any. Having indoctrinated this Court as to the fast pace and instability of the video game industry, Nintendo may not now, without any data, redefine that market in its request for the extraordinary remedy sought herein. . . . While board games may never die, good video games are mortal.

Galoob, 780 F. Supp. at 1295. The existence of this potential market cannot be presumed. See *Sony*, 464 U.S. at 451. See also Wright v. Warner Books, Inc., 953 F.2d 731, 739, 20 U.S.P.Q.2D (BNA) 1892 (2d Cir. 1991) (affirming district court's finding of no reasonable likelihood of injury to alleged market because "plaintiff has offered no evidence that the project will go forward"). The fourth and most important fair use factor also favors *Galoob*.

Nintendo's most persuasive argument is that the creative nature of its audiovisual displays weighs against a finding of fair use. The Supreme Court has acknowledged that "fair use is more likely to be found in factual works than fictional works." *Stewart*, 495 U.S. at 237. This consideration weighs against a finding of fair use, but it is not dispositive. See *Sony*, 464 U.S. at 448 (fair use defense is an "equitable rule of reason"). The district court could properly conclude that Game Genie users are making a fair use of Nintendo's displays. . . .

AFFIRMED.

COMMENTS AND QUESTIONS

1. Suppose that Nintendo had announced its intention to sell add-on devices to its entertainment system that would perform the same function as the Game Genie. Should this fact change the fair use analysis? Certainly Nintendo could prove that it was losing money to Galoob in this example. Does this fact sway the fourth factor in Nintendo's favor? What if Nintendo could show the existence of a "market" for *licensing* devices like the Game Genie? Is Galoob depriving Nintendo of a royalty payment? On this issue, cf. American Geophysical Union v. Texaco, 37 F.3d 881 (2d Cir. 1994) (existence of "market" for royalty payments of copies undercuts fair use argument); Princeton University Press v. Michigan Document

Servs., 99 F.3d 1381 (6th Cir. 1996) (en banc) (same); *contra* Williams & Wilkins Co. v. United States, 487 F.2d 1345 (Ct. Cl. 1973) (en banc).

2.   One of the reasons people play video games is for the challenge of overcoming obstacles. Does a device that gives a game character "super powers" or an infinite number of lives defeat this purpose? It is certainly possible that owners of the Game Genie will more quickly grow bored with video games than those without it.[9] If Nintendo can prove that the Game Genie will cut into its sales of games by making the games less challenging, should that affect its copyright argument?

Alternatively, does Nintendo have some "moral right" in the integrity of its audiovisual work that is being violated by Galoob's device?

3.   Most of Nintendo's games are not written by Nintendo itself, but by independent authors who write and sell them for use on the Nintendo system. Isn't it the authors, rather than Nintendo itself, who should be bringing this action? On this point, see Vault v. Quaid:

> Vault contends that, because purchasers of programs placed on PROLOK diskettes use the RAMKEY feature of CopyWrite to make unauthorized copies, Quaid's advertisement and sale of CopyWrite diskettes with the RAMKEY feature violate the Copyright Act by contributing to the infringement of Vault's copyright and the copyrights owned by Vault's customers. Vault asserts that it lost customers and substantial revenue as a result of Quaid's contributory infringement because software companies which previously relied on PROLOK diskettes to protect their programs from unauthorized copying have discontinued their use. . . .
>
> . . . The district court held that Vault lacked standing to raise a contributory infringement claim because "it is not Vault, but the customers of Vault who place their programs on PROLOK disks, who may assert such claims. Clearly the copyright rights to these underlying programs belong to their publishers, not Vault." *Vault*, 655 F.Supp. at 759. [The Court of Appeals did not reach this issue because it found that RAMKEY was capable of a substantial noninfringing use, and therefore Quaid could not be liable for contributory infringement in any event].

847 F.2d 255 (5th Cir. 1988).

Micro Star v. Formgen Inc.
United States Court of Appeals for the Ninth Circuit
154 F.3d 1107 (9th Cir. 1998)

KOZINSKI, Circuit Judge.

Duke Nukem routinely vanquishes Octabrain and the Protozoid Slimer. But what about the dreaded Micro Star?

---

9. Of course, this might induce them to buy more Nintendo games, rather than fewer. If that is the case, it is hard to see how Nintendo has been injured.

I

FormGen Inc., GT Interactive Software Corp. and Apogee Software, Ltd. (collectively FormGen) made, distributed and own the rights to Duke Nukem 3D (D/N-3D), an immensely popular (and very cool) computer game. D/N-3D is played from the first-person perspective; the player assumes the personality and point of view of the title character, who is seen on the screen only as a pair of hands and an occasional boot, much as one might see oneself in real life without the aid of a mirror. Players explore a futuristic city infested with evil aliens and other hazards. The goal is to zap them before they zap you, while searching for the hidden passage to the next level. The basic game comes with twenty-nine levels, each with a different combination of scenery, aliens, and other challenges. The game also includes a "Build Editor," a utility that enables players to create their own levels. With FormGen's encouragement, players frequently post levels they have created on the Internet where others can download them. Micro Star, a computer software distributor, did just that: It downloaded 300 user-created levels and stamped them onto a CD, which it then sold commercially as Nuke It (N/I). N/I is packaged in a box decorated with numerous "screen shots," pictures of what the new levels look like when played.

Micro Star filed suit in district court, seeking a declaratory judgment that N/I did not infringe on any of FormGen's copyrights. FormGen counterclaimed, seeking a preliminary injunction barring further production and distribution of N/I. Relying on Lewis Galoob Toys, Inc. v. Nintendo of Am., Inc., 964 F.2d 965 (9th Cir.1992), the district court held that N/I was not a derivative work and therefore did not infringe FormGen's copyright. The district court did, however, grant a preliminary injunction as to the screen shots, finding that N/I's packaging violated FormGen's copyright by reproducing pictures of D/N-3D characters without a license. The court rejected Micro Star's fair use claims. Both sides appeal their losses. . . .

III

To succeed on the merits of its claim that N/I infringes FormGen's copyright, FormGen must show (1) ownership of the copyright to D/N-3D, and (2) copying of protected expression by Micro Star. See Triad Systems Corp. v. Southeastern Express Co., 64 F.3d 1330, 1335 (9th Cir.1995). FormGen's copyright registration creates a presumption of ownership, see *id.*, and we are satisfied that FormGen has established its ownership of the copyright. We therefore focus on the latter issue.

FormGen alleges that its copyright is infringed by Micro Star's unauthorized commercial exploitation of user-created game levels. In order to understand FormGen's claims, one must first understand the way D/N-3D works. The game consists of three separate components: the game engine, the source art library and the MAP files. The game engine is the heart of the computer program; in some sense, it is the program. It tells the computer when to read data, save and load games, play sounds and project images onto the screen. In order to create the audiovisual display for a particular level, the game engine invokes the MAP file that corresponds to that level. Each MAP file contains a series of instructions that tell the game engine (and, through it, the computer) what to put where. For instance, the MAP file might say scuba gear goes at the bottom of the screen. The game engine then goes to the source art library, finds the image of the scuba gear, and puts it in just the right place on the screen.[3] The MAP file describes the level in painstaking detail, but it does not actually contain any of the copyrighted art itself; everything that appears on the screen actually comes from the art library. Think of the game's audiovisual display as a paint-by-numbers kit. The MAP file might tell you to put blue paint in section number 565, but it doesn't contain any blue paint itself; the blue paint comes from your palette, which is the low-tech analog of the art library, while you play the role of the game engine. When the player selects one of the N/I levels, the game engine references the N/I MAP files, but still uses the D/N-3D art library to generate the images that make up that level.

FormGen points out that a copyright holder enjoys the exclusive right to prepare derivative works based on D/N-3D. See 17 U.S.C. §106(2) (1994). According to FormGen, the audiovisual displays generated when D/N-3D is run in conjunction with the N/I CD MAP files are derivative works that infringe this exclusivity. Is FormGen right? The answer is not obvious.

The Copyright Act defines a derivative work as

> a work based upon one or more preexisting works, such as a translation, musical arrangement, dramatization, fictionalization, motion picture version, sound recording, art reproduction, abridgment, condensation, or any other form in which a work may be recast, transformed, or adapted. A work consisting of editorial revisions, annotations, elaborations, or other modifications which, as a whole, represent an original work of authorship, is a "derivative work."

Id. §101. The statutory language is hopelessly overbroad, however, for "[e]very book in literature, science and art, borrows and must necessarily borrow, and use much which was well known and used before." Emerson v. Davies, 8 F. Cas. 615, 619 (C.C.D.Mass.1845) (No. 4436), quoted in

---

3. Actually, this is all a bit metaphorical. Computer programs don't actually go anywhere or fetch anything. Rather, the game engine receives the player's instruction as to which game level to select and instructs the processor to access the MAP file corresponding to that level. The MAP file, in turn, consists of a series of instructions indicating which art images go where. When the MAP file calls for a particular art image, the game engine tells the processor to access the art library for instructions on how each pixel on the screen must be colored in order to paint that image.

1 Nimmer on Copyright, §3.01, at 3-2 (1997). To narrow the statute to a manageable level, we have developed certain criteria a work must satisfy in order to qualify as a derivative work. One of these is that a derivative work must exist in a "concrete or permanent form," *Galoob*, 964 F.2d at 967 (internal quotation marks omitted), and must substantially incorporate protected material from the preexisting work, see Litchfield v. Spielberg, 736 F.2d 1352, 1357 (9th Cir.1984). Micro Star argues that N/I is not a derivative work because the audiovisual displays generated when D/N-3D is run with N/I's MAP files are not incorporated in any concrete or permanent form, and the MAP files do not copy any of D/N-3D's protected expression. It is mistaken on both counts.

The requirement that a derivative work must assume a concrete or permanent form was recognized without much discussion in Galoob. There, we noted that all the Copyright Act's examples of derivative works took some definite, physical form and concluded that this was a require-ment of the Act. See *Galoob*, 964 F.2d at 967-68; see also Edward G. Black & Michael H. Page, Add-On Infringements, 15 Hastings Comm/Ent. L.J. 615, 625 (1993) (noting that in *Galoob* the Ninth Circuit "re-examined the statutory definition of derivative works offered in section 101 and found an independent fixation requirement of sorts built into the statutory definition of derivative works"). Obviously, N/I's MAP files themselves exist in a concrete or permanent form; they are burned onto a CD-ROM. See ProCD, Inc. v. Zeidenberg, 86 F.3d 1447, 1453 (7th Cir.1996) (computer files on a CD are fixed in a tangible medium of expression). But what about the audiovisual displays generated when D/N-3D runs the N/I MAP files—i.e., the actual game level as displayed on the screen? Micro Star argues that, because the audiovisual displays in *Galoob* didn't meet the "concrete or permanent form" requirement, neither do N/I's.

In *Galoob*, we considered audiovisual displays created using a device called the Game Genie, which was sold for use with the Nintendo Enter-tainment System. The Game Genie allowed players to alter individual features of a game, such as a character's strength or speed, by selectively "blocking the value for a single data byte sent by the game cartridge to the [Nintendo console] and replacing it with a new value." *Galoob*, 964 F.2d at 967. Players chose which data value to replace by entering a code; over a billion different codes were possible. The Game Genie was dumb; it functioned only as a window into the computer program, allowing players to temporarily modify individual aspects of the game. See Lewis Galoob Toys, Inc. v. Nintendo of Am., Inc., 780 F.Supp. 1283, 1289 (N.D.Cal.1991).

Nintendo sued, claiming that when the Game Genie modified the game system's audiovisual display, it created an infringing derivative work. We rejected this claim because "[a] derivative work must incorporate a protected work in some concrete or permanent form." *Galoob*, 964 F.2d at 967 (internal quotation marks omitted). The audiovisual displays generated by combining the Nintendo System with the Game Genie were not incorporated in any permanent form; when the game was over, they were gone. Of course, they could be reconstructed, but only if the next player chose to reenter the same codes.[4]

Micro Star argues that the MAP files on N/I are a more advanced version of the Game Genie, replacing old values (the MAP files in the original game) with new values (N/I's MAP files). But, whereas the audiovisual displays created by Game Genie were never recorded in any permanent form, the audiovisual displays generated by D/N-3D from the N/I MAP files are in the MAP files themselves. In *Galoob*, the audiovisual display was defined by the original game cartridge, not by the Game Genie; no one could possibly say that the data values inserted by the Game Genie described the audiovisual display. In the present case the audiovisual display that appears on the computer monitor when a N/I level is played is described—in exact detail—by a N/I MAP file.

This raises the interesting question whether an exact, down to the last detail, description of an audiovisual display (and—by definition—we know that MAP files do describe audiovisual displays down to the last detail) counts as a permanent or concrete form for purposes of *Galoob*. We see no reason it shouldn't. What, after all, does sheet music do but describe in precise detail the way a copyrighted melody sounds? See 1 William F. Patry, Copyright Law and Practice 168 (1994) ("[A] musical composition may be embodied in sheet music. . . ."). To be copyrighted, pantomimes and dances may be "described in sufficient detail to enable the work to be performed from that description." *Id.* at 243 (citing Compendium II of Copyright Office Practices §463); see also Horgan v. Macmillan, Inc., 789 F.2d 157, 160 (2d Cir.1986). Similarly, the N/I MAP files describe the audiovisual display that is to be generated when the player chooses to play D/N-3D using the N/I levels. Because the audiovisual displays assume a concrete or permanent form in the MAP files, *Galoob* stands as no bar to finding that they are derivative works.

In addition, "[a] work will be considered a derivative work only if it would be considered an infringing work if the material which it has derived from a preexisting work had been taken without the consent of a copyright proprietor of such preexisting work." Mirage Editions v. Albuquerque A.R.T. Co., 856 F.2d 1341, 1343 (quoting 1 Nimmer on Copyright §3.01 (1986)) (internal quotation marks omitted). "To prove infringement, [FormGen] must show that [D/N-3D's and N/I's audiovisual displays] are substantially similar in both ideas and expression." Litchfield

---

4. A low-tech example might aid understanding. Imagine a product called the Pink Screener, which consists of a big piece of pink cellophane stretched over a frame. When put in front of a television, it makes everything on the screen look pinker. Someone who manages to record the programs with this pink cast (maybe by filming the screen) would have created an infringing derivative work. But the audiovisual display observed by a person watching television through the Pink Screener is not a derivative work because it does not incorporate the modified image in any permanent or concrete form. The Game Genie might be described as a fancy Pink Screener for video games, changing a value of the game as perceived by the current player, but never incorporating the new audiovisual display into a permanent or concrete form.

v. Spielberg, 736 F.2d 1352, 1356 (9th Cir.1984) (emphasis omitted). Similarity of ideas may be shown by comparing the objective details of the works: plot, theme, dialogue, mood, setting, characters, etc. See *id*. Similarity of expression focuses on the response of the ordinary reasonable person, and considers the total concept and feel of the works. See *id*. at 1356-57. FormGen will doubtless succeed in making these showings since the audiovisual displays generated when the player chooses the N/I levels come entirely out of D/N-3D's source art library. Cf. Atari, Inc. v. North Am. Philips Consumer Elec. Corp., 672 F.2d 607, 620 (7th Cir.1982) (finding two video games substantially similar because they shared the same "total concept and feel").

Micro Star further argues that the MAP files are not derivative works because they do not, in fact, incorporate any of D/N-3D's protected expression. In particular, Micro Star makes much of the fact that the N/I MAP files reference the source art library, but do not actually contain any art files themselves. Therefore, it claims, nothing of D/N-3D's is reproduced in the MAP files. In making this argument, Micro Star misconstrues the protected work. The work that Micro Star infringes is the D/N-3D story itself—a beefy commando type named Duke who wanders around post-Apocalypse Los Angeles, shooting Pig Cops with a gun, lobbing hand grenades, searching for medkits and steroids, using a jetpack to leap over obstacles, blowing up gas tanks, avoiding radioactive slime. A copyright owner holds the right to create sequels, see Trust Co. Bank v. MGM/UA Entertainment Co., 772 F.2d 740 (11th Cir.1985), and the stories told in the N/I MAP files are surely sequels, telling new (though somewhat repetitive) tales of Duke's fabulous adventures. A book about Duke Nukem would infringe for the same reason, even if it contained no pictures.[5]

Micro Star nonetheless claims that its use of D/N-3D's protected expression falls within the doctrine of fair use. . . .

As a preliminary matter, Micro Star asks us to focus on the player's use of the N/I CD in evaluating the fair use claim, because—according to Micro Star—the player actually creates the derivative work. In *Galoob*, after we assumed for purposes of argument that the Game Genie did create derivative works, we went on to consider the fair use defense from the player's point of view. See *Galoob*, 964 F.2d at 970. But the fair use analysis in *Galoob* was not necessary and therefore is clearly dicta. More significantly, Nintendo alleged only contributory infringement—that *Galoob* was helping consumers create derivative works; FormGen here alleges direct infringement by Micro Star, because the MAP files encompass new Duke stories, which are themselves derivative works.

---

5. We note that the N/I MAP files can only be used with D/N-3D. If another game could use the MAP files to tell the story of a mousy fellow who travels through a beige maze, killing vicious saltshakers with paper-clips, then the MAP files would not incorporate the protected expression of D/N-3D because they would not be telling a D/N-3D story.

Our examination of the section 107 factors yields straightforward results. Micro Star's use of FormGen's protected expression was made purely for financial gain. While that does not end our inquiry, see Campbell v. Acuff-Rose Music, Inc., 510 U.S. 569, 584, 114 S.Ct. 1164, 127 L.Ed.2d 500 (1994), "every commercial use of copyrighted material is presumptively an unfair exploitation of the monopoly privilege that belongs to the owner of the copyright." Sony Corp. of Am. v. Universal City Studios, Inc., 464 U.S. 417, 451, 104 S.Ct. 774, 78 L.Ed.2d 574 (1984).[6] The Supreme Court has explained that the second factor, the nature of the copyrighted work, is particularly significant because "some works are closer to the core of intended copyright protection than others, with the consequence that fair use is more difficult to establish when the former works are copied." *Campbell*, 510 U.S. at 586, 114 S.Ct. 1164. The fair use defense will be much less likely to succeed when it is applied to fiction or fantasy creations, as opposed to factual works such as telephone listings. See United Tel. Co. v. Johnson Publ'g Co., 855 F.2d 604, 609 (8th Cir.1988); see also Stewart v. Abend, 495 U.S. 207, 237, 110 S.Ct. 1750, 109 L.Ed.2d 184 (1990). Duke Nukem's world is made up of aliens, radioactive slime and freezer weapons—clearly fantasies, even by Los Angeles standards. N/I MAP files "expressly use[] the [D/N-3D] story's unique setting, characters, [and] plot," *Stewart*, 495 U.S. at 238, 110 S.Ct. 1750; both the quantity and importance of the material Micro Star used are substantial. Finally, by selling N/I, Micro Star "impinged on [FormGen's] ability to market new versions of the [D/N-3D] story." *Stewart*, 495 U.S. at 238, 110 S.Ct. 1750; see also Twin Peaks Productions, Inc. v. Publications Int'l, Ltd., 996 F.2d 1366, 1377 (2d Cir.1993). Only FormGen has the right to enter that market; whether it chooses to do so is entirely its business. "[N/I] neither falls into any of the categories enumerated in section 107 nor meets the four criteria set forth in section 107." *Stewart*, 495 U.S. at 237, 110 S.Ct. 1750. It is not protected by fair use.

Micro Star also argues that it is the beneficiary of the implicit license FormGen gave to its customers by authorizing them to create new levels. Section 204 of the Copyright Act requires the transfer of the exclusive rights granted to copyright owners (including the right to prepare derivative works) to be in writing. See 17 U.S.C. §204(a); Effects Assocs., Inc. v. Cohen, 908 F.2d 555, 556 (9th Cir.1990). A nonexclusive license may, however, be granted orally or implied by conduct. See Effects, 908 F.2d at 558. Nothing indicates that FormGen granted Micro Star any written license at all; nor is there evidence of a nonexclusive oral license. The only written license FormGen conceivably granted was to players who designed

---

6. Of course, transformative works have greater recourse to the fair use defense as they "lie at the heart of the fair use doctrine's guarantee of breathing space within the confines of copyright . . . and the more transformative the new work, the less will be the significance of other factors, like commercialism, that may weigh against a finding of fair use." *Campbell*, 510 U.S. at 579, 114 S.Ct. 1164 (citations omitted). N/I can hardly be described as transformative; anything but.

their own new levels, but that license contains a significant limitation: Any new levels the players create "must be offered [to others] solely for free." The parties dispute whether the license is binding, but it doesn't matter. If the license is valid, it clearly prohibits commercial distribution of levels; if it doesn't, FormGen hasn't granted any written licenses at all.

In case FormGen didn't license away its rights, Micro Star argues that, by providing the Build Editor and encouraging players to create their own levels, FormGen abandoned all rights to its protected expression. It is well settled that rights gained under the Copyright Act may be abandoned. But abandonment of a right must be manifested by some overt act indicating an intention to abandon that right. See Hampton v. Paramount Pictures Corp., 279 F.2d 100, 104 (9th Cir.1960). Given that it overtly encouraged players to make and freely distribute new levels, FormGen may indeed have abandoned its exclusive right to do the same. But abandoning some rights is not the same as abandoning all rights, and FormGen never overtly abandoned its rights to profit commercially from new levels. Indeed, FormGen warned players not to distribute the levels commercially and has actively enforced that limitation by bringing suits such as this one.

IV

Because FormGen will likely succeed at trial in proving that Micro Star has infringed its copyright, we reverse the district court's order denying a preliminary injunction and remand for entry of such an injunction.

COMMENTS AND QUESTIONS

1. Exactly what protected expression did Micro Star copy? The MAP files produced by game players themselves contain entirely new program code, and contain no code at all copied from Formgen. It is true that these files are designed to run with Formgen's game engine and art library and, indeed, would be useless without them. But does it follow from that that the MAP files themselves are "copies" of the original Duke Nukem game?

The real basis of the court's argument seems to be that the MAP files are guides to produce an infringing work. If a user buys the Micro Star CD and runs the game using the MAP files, he will generate on his screen a new Duke Nukem "level" that incorporates Micro Star's protected art. That might possibly be an infringing act that Micro Star has contributed to or induced. But if that is the complaint, the court was wrong to distinguish *Galoob*. Indeed, *Galoob* looks precisely analogous: the defendant makes a product that does not itself contain any copyrighted expression but that end users can employ to generate altered versions of the copyrighted work. The same analytic problem infects the court's analysis of the third fair use factor, in which the court concluded that the use copied substantially from Duke Nukem. While the game played by the end user does copy substantially from Formgen's original, it is hard to see how anyone could argue that the MAP files themselves did so.

2. Does the court's analogy to a movie sequel support its result? Why exactly are sequels considered derivative works? If it were possible to imagine a sequel that didn't itself include any copyrighted expression, would it be infringing? Should it be? How does the court square its result with Litchfield v. Spielberg, cited in the case, which held that a work could not be an infringing derivative work unless it was substantially similar in protected expression to the original?

3. The court's fair use analysis has a number of problems. First, the court disposes of the first factor entirely by reference to the *Sony* "presumption" that commercially motivated uses are unfair. This approach was specifically rejected by the Supreme Court in Campbell v. Acuff-Rose Music, Inc., 510 U.S. 569, 584 (1994), which flatly rejected the use of any such presumption.

Second, the court suggests in a footnote that there is nothing transformative about the MAP files Micro Star sold. Why not? Aren't these files creative additions to the Duke Nukem universe?

Third, the court disposes of the market-effect factor by asserting that Micro Star's use interferes with Formgen's right to sell additional Duke Nukem levels. Does it matter whether Formgen has made any effort to do so? Whether it plans to do so in the future? Neither fact is considered in the court's opinion. It is also worth considering how Formgen's license to users to distribute their own levels for free on the Internet would affect the market for additional levels.

4. Is this case really about the scope of the license Formgen admittedly granted to the individual users who wrote the MAP files at issue? It appears that Micro Star could have collated and distributed those MAP files for free without running afoul of Formgen's license restriction. If the only basis for the suit is that Micro Star charged money for doing what it had a right to do for free, isn't this case better resolved under contract law than under copyright law?

For a more detailed discussion of the uncertain issue whether exceeding the scope of a license agreement constitutes copyright infringement or merely breach of contract, see Chapter 6.

5. We discuss one specific type of fair use—reverse engineering—in the next Section. For a discussion of a variety of other activities that may qualify for fair use in the digital environment, see Pamela Samuelson, Fair Use for Computer Programs and Other Copyrightable Works in Digital Form: The Implications of *Sony, Galoob,* and *Sega,* 1 J. Intell. Prop. L. 49 (1993).

E. REVERSE ENGINEERING

In view of the network externalities flowing from many software products and the cumulative nature of innovation in software, two critical issues in the computer industry are the extent to which and manner by which competitors can develop compatible or interoperable programs, competitive programs, and enhancements of programs. Of particular relevance is the permissibility of reverse engineering. "Reverse engineering" is loosely defined as "starting with the known product and working backward to divine the process which aided in its development or manufacture." Kewanee Oil Co. v. Bicron Corp., 416 U.S. 470 (1974). It typically involves two phases: (1) disassembly or decompilation of the program in order to create human-readable source code that may be analyzed; and (2) using the results of this analysis to create a commercially viable program.

Most computer programs are distributed only in object code form, a fact that makes it difficult to discover the ideas and principles contained in a program without reverse engineering. In addition, some programs have special devices designed to prevent inspection. Nonetheless, reverse engineering of software, while difficult, is possible in some limited circumstances and may be growing easier with time. There are a variety of approaches to reverse engineering of computer programs. One is referred to as "black box" testing. By systematically inputting instructions, a computer programmer can learn how the program processes information and can construct a program that produces the same outputs for given instructions. Because of the complexity of most programs today, however, this approach is often infeasible. A second method is to study the technical specifications and user manuals. These materials, however, often do not contain the information necessary to achieve compatibility and interoperability. In order to feasibly achieve these objectives, it is often necessary to take a machine apart and directly observe its operation or, as is more common with regard to software, to decompile the program. After a program is understood, the competitor can use the results of the analysis to create a commercially viable program.

Patent and trade secrets laws treat reverse engineering very differently. Reverse engineering a patented product necessarily constitutes infringement if it involves making, using, or selling the patented invention. There is no statutory defense for reverse engineering. By contrast, the Uniform Trade Secrets Act expressly provides that reverse engineering a commercially available product is a legitimate means of discovering a trade secret. See Chapter 1. (Of course, many companies have tried to avoid this rule by contract, as discussed in Section I.B).

Copyright occupies an intermediate position on the legality of reverse engineering.

═══
═══
═══
═══

Sega Enterprises Ltd. v. Accolade, Inc.
United States Court of Appeals for the Ninth Circuit
977 F.2d 1510 (9th Cir. 1992)

REINHART, Circuit Judge:

I. Background

Plaintiff-appellee Sega Enterprises, Ltd. ("Sega"), a Japanese corporation, and its subsidiary, Sega of America, develop and market video entertainment systems, including the "Genesis" console (distributed in Asia under the name "Mega-Drive") and video game cartridges. Defendant-appellant Accolade, Inc., is an independent developer, manufacturer, and marketer of computer entertainment software, including game cartridges that are compatible with the Genesis console, as well as game cartridges that are compatible with other computer systems.

Sega licenses its copyrighted computer code and its "SEGA" trademark to a number of independent developers of computer game software. Those licensees develop and sell Genesis-compatible video games in competition with Sega. Accolade is not and never has been a licensee of Sega. Prior to rendering its own games compatible with the Genesis console, Accolade explored the possibility of entering into a licensing agreement with Sega, but abandoned the effort because the agreement would have required that Sega be the exclusive manufacturer of all games produced by Accolade.

Accolade used a two-step process to render its video games compatible with the Genesis console. First, it "reverse engineered" Sega's video game programs in order to discover the requirements for compatibility with the Genesis console. As part of the reverse engineering process, Accolade transformed the machine-readable object code contained in commercially available copies of Sega's game cartridges into human-readable source code using a process called "disassembly" or "decompilation".[2] Accolade purchased a Genesis console and three Sega game cartridges, wired a decompiler into the console circuitry, and generated printouts of the resulting source code. Accolade engineers studied and annotated the printouts in order to identify areas of commonality among

---

2. Computer programs are written in specialized alphanumeric languages, or "source code". In order to operate a computer, source code must be translated into computer readable form, or "object code". Object code uses only two symbols, 0 and 1, in combinations which represent the alphanumeric characters of the source code. A program written in source code is translated into object code using a computer program called an "assembler" or "compiler", and then imprinted onto a silicon chip for commercial distribution. Devices called "disassemblers" or "decompilers" can reverse this process by "reading" the electronic signals for "0" and "1" that are produced while the program is being run, storing the resulting object code in computer memory, and translating the object code into source code. Both assembly and disassembly devices are commercially available, and both types of devices are widely used within the software industry.

the three game programs. They then loaded the disassembled code back into a computer, and experimented to discover the interface specifications for the Genesis console by modifying the programs and studying the results. At the end of the reverse engineering process, Accolade created a development manual that incorporated the information it had discovered about the requirements for a Genesis-compatible game. According to the Accolade employees who created the manual, the manual contained only functional descriptions of the interface requirements and did not include any of Sega's code.

In the second stage, Accolade created its own games for the Genesis. According to Accolade, at this stage it did not copy Sega's programs, but relied only on the information concerning interface specifications for the Genesis that was contained in its development manual. Accolade maintains that with the exception of the interface specifications, none of the code in its own games is derived in any way from its examination of Sega's code. In 1990, Accolade released "Ishido", a game which it had originally developed and released for use with the Macintosh and IBM personal computer systems, for use with the Genesis console.

Even before Accolade began to reverse engineer Sega's games, Sega had grown concerned about the rise of software and hardware piracy in Taiwan and other Southeast Asian countries to which it exported its products. Taiwan is not a signatory to the Berne Convention and does not recognize foreign copyrights. Taiwan does allow prosecution of trademark counterfeiters. However, the counterfeiters had discovered how to modify Sega's game programs to blank out the screen display of Sega's trademark before repackaging and reselling the games as their own. Accordingly, Sega began to explore methods of protecting its trademark rights in the Genesis and Genesis-compatible games. While the development of its own trademark security system (TMSS) was pending, Sega licensed a patented TMSS for use with the Genesis home entertainment system.

The most recent version of the Genesis console, the "Genesis III", incorporates the licensed TMSS. When a game cartridge is inserted, the microprocessor contained in the Genesis III searches the game program for four bytes of data consisting of the letters "S-E-G-A" (the "TMSS initialization code"). If the Genesis III finds the TMSS initialization code in the right location, the game is rendered compatible and will operate on the console. In such case, the TMSS initialization code then prompts a visual display for approximately three seconds which reads "PRODUCED BY OR UNDER LICENSE FROM SEGA ENTERPRISES LTD" (the "Sega Message"). All of Sega's game cartridges, including those disassembled by Accolade, contain the TMSS initialization code.

Accolade learned of the impending release of the Genesis III in the United States in January, 1991, when the Genesis III was displayed at a consumer electronics show. When a demonstration at the consumer electronics show revealed that Accolade's "Ishido" game cartridges would not operate on the Genesis III, Accolade returned to the drawing board.

During the reverse engineering process, Accolade engineers had discovered a small segment of code—the TMSS initialization code—that was included in the "power-up" sequence of every Sega game, but that had no identifiable function. The games would operate on the original Genesis console even if the code segment was removed. Mike Lorenzen, the Accolade engineer with primary responsibility for reverse engineering the interface procedures for the Genesis console, sent a memo regarding the code segment to Alan Miller, his supervisor and the current president of Accolade, in which he noted that "it is possible that some future Sega peripheral device might require it for proper initialization."

In the second round of reverse engineering, Accolade engineers focused on the code segment identified by Lorenzen. After further study, Accolade added the code to its development manual in the form of a standard header file to be used in all games. The file contains approximately twenty to twenty-five bytes of data. Each of Accolade's games contains a total of 500,000 to 1,500,000 bytes. According to Accolade employees, the header file is the only portion of Sega's code that Accolade copied into its own game programs. In this appeal, Sega does not raise a separate claim of copyright infringement with respect to the header file.

In 1991, Accolade released five more games for use with the Genesis III, "Star Control", "Hardball!", "Onslaught", "Turrican", and "Mike Ditka Power Football." With the exception of "Mike Ditka Power Football", all of those games, like "Ishido", had originally been developed and marketed for use with other hardware systems. All contained the standard header file that included the TMSS initialization code. According to Accolade, it did not learn until after the Genesis III was released on the market in September, 1991, that in addition to enabling its software to operate on the Genesis III, the header file caused the display of the Sega Message. All of the games except "Onslaught" operate on the Genesis III console; apparently, the programmer who translated "Onslaught" for use with the Genesis system did not place the TMSS initialization code at the correct location in the program.

[Sega sued Accolade for copyright infringement].

III. Copyright Issues

Accolade raises four arguments in support of its position that disassembly of the object code in a copyrighted computer program does not constitute copyright infringement. First, it maintains that intermediate copying does not infringe the exclusive rights granted to copyright owners in section 106 of the Copyright Act unless the end product of the copying is substantially similar to the copyrighted work. Second, it argues that disassembly of object code in order to gain an understanding of the ideas and functional concepts embodied in the code is lawful under section 102(b) of the Act, which exempts ideas and functional concepts from copyright protection. Third, it suggests that disassembly is authorized by section 117 of the Act, which entitles the lawful owner of a copy of a computer program to load the program into a computer. Finally, Accolade contends that disassembly of object code in order to gain an understanding of the ideas and functional concepts embodied in the code is a fair use that is privileged by section 107 of the Act.

Neither the language of the Act nor the law of this circuit supports Accolade's first three arguments. Accolade's fourth argument, however, has merit. . . .

A. Intermediate Copying

We have previously held that the Copyright Act does not distinguish between unauthorized copies of a copyrighted work on the basis of what stage of the alleged infringer's work the unauthorized copies represent. Walker v. University Books, 602 F.2d 859, 864 (9th Cir. 1979) ("[T]he fact that an allegedly infringing copy of a protected work may itself be only an inchoate representation of some final product to be marketed commercially does not in itself negate the possibility of infringement."). Our holding in *Walker* was based on the plain language of the Act. Section 106 grants to the copyright owner the exclusive rights "to reproduce the work in copies", "to prepare derivative works based upon the copyrighted work", and to authorize the preparation of copies and derivative works. 17 U.S.C. §106 (1)-(2). Section 501 provides that "anyone who violates any of the exclusive rights of the copyright owner as provided by sections 106 through 118 . . . is an infringer of the copyright." Id. §501(a). On its face, that language unambiguously encompasses and proscribes "intermediate copying". *Walker*, 602 F.2d at 863-64.

In order to constitute a "copy" for purposes of the Act, the allegedly infringing work must be fixed in some tangible form, "from which the work can be perceived, reproduced, or otherwise communicated, either directly or with the aid of a machine or device." 17 U.S.C. §101. The computer file generated by the disassembly program, the printouts of the disassembled code, and the computer files containing Accolade's modifications of the code that were generated during the reverse engineering process all satisfy that requirement. The intermediate copying done by Accolade therefore falls squarely within the category of acts that are prohibited by the statute.

Accolade points to a number of cases that it argues establish the lawfulness of intermediate copying. Most of the cases involved the alleged copying of books, scripts, or literary characters. See v. Durang, 711 F.2d 141 (9th Cir. 1983); Warner Bros. v. ABC, 654 F.2d 204 (2d Cir. 1981); Miller v. Universal City Studios, Inc., 650 F.2d 1365 (5th Cir. 1981). In each case, however, the eventual lawsuit alleged infringement only as to the final work of the defendants. We conclude that this group of cases does not alter or limit the holding of *Walker*.

The remaining cases cited by Accolade, like the case before us, involved intermediate copying of computer code as an initial step in the development of a competing product. Computer Assoc. Int'l v. Altai, Inc., [supra] (2d Cir. 1992) ("CAI"); NEC Corp. v. Intel Corp., 10 U.S.P.Q.2D (BNA) 1177 (N.D. Cal. 1989); E.F. Johnson Co. v. Uniden Corp., 623 F. Supp. 1485 (D. Minn. 1985). In each case, the court based its determination regarding infringement solely on the degree of similarity between the allegedly infringed work and the defendant's final product. A close reading of those cases, however, reveals that in none of them was the legality of the intermediate copying at issue. Sega cites an equal number of cases involving intermediate copying of copyrighted computer code to support its assertion that such copying is prohibited. Atari Games Corp. v. Nintendo of America, Inc., 18 U.S.P.Q.2D (BNA) 1935 (N.D. Cal. 1991); SAS Institute, Inc. v. S&H Computer Systems, Inc., 605 F. Supp. 816 (M.D. Tenn. 1985); S&H Computer Systems, Inc. v. SAS Institute, Inc., 568 F. Supp. 416 (M.D. Tenn. 1983); Hubco Data Products v. Management Assistance, Inc., 219 U.S.P.Q. (BNA) 450 (D. Idaho 1983). Again, however, it appears that the question of the lawfulness of intermediate copying was not raised in any of those cases.

In summary, the question whether intermediate copying of computer object code infringes the exclusive rights granted to the copyright owner in section 106 of the Copyright Act is a question of first impression. In light of the unambiguous language of the Act, we decline to depart from the rule set forth in Walker for copyrighted works generally. Accordingly, we hold that intermediate copying of computer object code may infringe the exclusive rights granted to the copyright owner in section 106 of the Copyright Act regardless of whether the end product of the copying also infringes those rights. If intermediate copying is permissible under the Act, authority for such copying must be found in one of the statutory provisions to which the rights granted in section 106 are subject.

B. *The Idea/Expression Distinction*

Accolade next contends that disassembly of computer object code does not violate the Copyright Act because it is necessary in order to gain access to the ideas and functional concepts embodied in the code, which are not protected by copyright. 17 U.S.C. §102(b). Because humans cannot comprehend object code, it reasons, disassembly of a commercially available computer program into human-readable form should not be considered an infringement of the owner's copyright. Insofar as Accolade suggests that disassembly of object code is lawful *per se*, it seeks to overturn settled law.

Accolade's argument regarding access to ideas is, in essence, an argument that object code is not eligible for the full range of copyright protection. Although some scholarly authority supports that view, we have previously rejected it based on the language and legislative history of the Copyright Act. Johnson Controls, Inc. v. Phoenix Control Sys., Inc., 886 F.2d 1173, 1175 (9th Cir. 1989). . . .

Nor does a refusal to recognize a *per se* right to disassemble object code lead to an absurd result. The ideas and functional concepts underlying many types of computer programs, including word processing programs, spreadsheets, and video game displays, are readily discernible without the need for disassembly, because the operation of such programs is visible on the computer screen. The need to disassemble object code arises, if at all, only in connection with operations systems, system interface procedures, and other programs that are not visible to the user when operating—and then only when no alternative means of gaining an understanding of those ideas and functional concepts exists. In our view, consideration of the unique nature of computer object code thus is more appropriate as part of the case-by-case, equitable "fair use" analysis authorized by section 107 of the Act. See infra Part III(D). Accordingly, we reject Accolade's second argument.

C. Section 117

Section 117 of the Copyright Act allows the lawful owner of a copy of a computer program to copy or adapt the program if the new copy or adaptation "is created as an essential step in the utilization of the computer program in conjunction with a machine and . . . is used in no other manner." 17 U.S.C. §117(1). Accolade contends that section 117 authorizes disassembly of the object code in a copyrighted computer program.

Section 117 was enacted on the recommendation of CONTU, which noted that "because the placement of any copyrighted work into a computer is the preparation of a copy [since the program is loaded into the computer's memory], the law should provide that persons in rightful possession of copies of programs be able to use them freely without fear of exposure to copyright liability." CONTU Report at 13. We think it is clear that Accolade's use went far beyond that contemplated by CONTU and authorized by section 117. Section 117 does not purport to protect a user who disassembles object code, converts it from assembly into source code, and makes printouts and photocopies of the refined source code version.

D. Fair Use

Accolade contends, finally, that its disassembly of copyrighted object code as a necessary step in its examination of the unprotected ideas and functional concepts embodied in the code is a fair use that is privileged by section 107 of the Act. Because, in the case before us, disassembly is the only means of gaining access to those unprotected aspects of the program, and because Accolade has a legitimate interest in gaining such access (in order to determine how to make its cartridges compatible with the Genesis console), we agree with Accolade. Where there is good reason for studying or examining the unprotected aspects of a copyrighted computer program, disassembly for purposes of such study or examination constitutes a fair use.

1.

As a preliminary matter, we reject Sega's contention that the assertion of a fair use defense in connection with the disassembly of object code is precluded by statute. First, Sega argues that not only does section 117 of the Act *not* authorize disassembly of object code, but it also constitutes a legislative determination that any copying of a computer program *other* than that authorized by section 117 cannot be considered a fair use of that program under section 107. That argument verges on the frivolous. Each of the exclusive rights created by section 106 of the Copyright Act is expressly made subject to all of the limitations contained in sections 107 through 120. 17 U.S.C. §106. Nothing in the language or the legislative history of section 117, or in the CONTU Report, suggests that section 117 was intended to preclude the assertion of a fair use defense with respect to uses of computer programs that are not covered by section 117, nor has section 107 been amended to exclude computer programs from its ambit.

Moreover, sections 107 and 117 serve entirely different functions. Section 117 defines a narrow category of copying that is lawful *per se.* 17 U.S.C. §117. Section 107, by contrast, establishes a *defense* to an otherwise valid claim of copyright infringement. . . .

Second, Sega maintains that the language and legislative history of section 906 of the Semiconductor Chip Protection Act of 1984 (SCPA) establish that Congress did not intend that disassembly of object code be considered a fair use. Section 906 of the SCPA authorizes the copying of the "mask work" on a silicon chip in the course of reverse engineering the chip. 17 U.S.C. §906. The mask work in a standard ROM chip, such as those used in the Genesis console and in Genesis-compatible cartridges, is a physical representation of the computer program that is embedded in the chip. The zeros and ones of binary object code are represented in the circuitry of the mask work by open and closed switches. Sega contends that Congress's express authorization of copying in the particular circumstances set forth in section 906 constitutes a determination that other forms of copying of computer programs are prohibited.

The legislative history of the SCPA reveals, however, that Congress passed a separate statute to protect semiconductor chip products because it believed that semiconductor chips were intrinsically utilitarian articles that were not protected under the Copyright Act. H.R. Rep. No. 781, 98th

Cong., 2d Sess. 8-10, reprinted in 1984 U.S.C.C.A.N. 5750, 5757-59. Accordingly, rather than amend the Copyright Act to extend traditional copyright protection to chips, it enacted "a sui generis form of protection, apart from and independent of the copyright laws." Id. at 10, 1984 U.S.C.C.A.N. at 5759. Because Congress did not believe that semiconductor chips were eligible for copyright protection in the first instance, the fact that it included an exception for reverse engineering of mask work in the SCPA says nothing about its intent with respect to the lawfulness of disassembly of computer programs under the Copyright Act. Nor is the fact that Congress did not contemporaneously amend the Copyright Act to permit disassembly significant, since it was focusing on the protection to be afforded to semiconductor chips. Here we are dealing not with an alleged violation of the SCPA, but with the copying of a computer program, which is governed by the Copyright Act. Moreover, Congress expressly stated that it did not intend to "limit, enlarge or otherwise affect the scope, duration, ownership or subsistence of copyright protection . . . in computer programs, data bases, or any other copyrightable works embodied in semiconductor chip products." Id. at 28, 1984 U.S.C.C.A.N. at 5777. Accordingly, Sega's second statutory argument also fails. We proceed to consider Accolade's fair use defense.

2.

. . . In determining that Accolade's disassembly of Sega's object code did not constitute a fair use, the district court treated the first and fourth statutory factors [of 17 U.S.C. section 107, reprinted above] as dispositive, and ignored the second factor entirely. Given the nature and characteristics of Accolade's direct use of the copied works, the ultimate use to which Accolade put the functional information it obtained, and the nature of the market for home video entertainment systems, we conclude that neither the first nor the fourth factor weighs in Sega's favor. In fact, we conclude that both factors support Accolade's fair use defense, as does the second factor, a factor which is important to the resolution of cases such as the one before us.

(a)

With respect to the first statutory factor, we observe initially that the fact that copying is for a commercial purpose weighs against a finding of fair use. *Harper & Row*, 471 U.S. at 562. However, the presumption of unfairness that arises in such cases can be rebutted by the characteristics of a particular commercial use. Hustler Magazine, Inc. v. Moral Majority, Inc., 796 F.2d 1148, 1152 (9th Cir. 1986); see also Maxtone-Graham v. Burtchaell, 803 F.2d 1253, 1262 (2d Cir. 1986), *cert. denied*, 481 U.S. 1059, 95 L. Ed. 2d 856, 107 S. Ct. 2201 (1987). Further "the commercial nature of a use is a matter of degree, not an absolute. . . ." *Maxtone-Graham*, 803 F.2d at 1262.

Sega argues that because Accolade copied its object code in order to produce a competing product, the *Harper & Row* presumption applies and precludes a finding of fair use. That analysis is far too simple and ignores a number of important considerations. We must consider other aspects of "the purpose and character of the use" as well. As we have noted, the use at issue was an intermediate one only and thus any commercial "exploitation" was indirect or derivative.

The declarations of Accolade's employees indicate, and the district court found, that Accolade copied Sega's software solely in order to discover the functional requirements for compatibility with the Genesis console—aspects of Sega's programs that are not protected by copyright. 17 U.S.C. §102(b). With respect to the video game programs contained in Accolade's game cartridges, there is no evidence in the record that Accolade sought to avoid performing its own creative work. Indeed, most of the games that Accolade released for use with the Genesis console were originally developed for other hardware systems. Moreover, with respect to the interface procedures for the Genesis console, Accolade did not seek to avoid paying a customarily charged fee for use of those procedures, nor did it simply copy Sega's code; rather, it wrote its own procedures based on what it had learned through disassembly. Taken together, these facts indicate that although Accolade's ultimate purpose was the release of Genesis-compatible games for sale, its direct purpose in copying Sega's code, and thus its direct use of the copyrighted material, was simply to study the functional requirements for Genesis compatibility so that it could modify existing games and make them usable with the Genesis console. Moreover, as we discuss below, no other method of studying those requirements was available to Accolade. On these facts, we conclude that Accolade copied Sega's code for a legitimate, essentially non-exploitative purpose, and that the commercial aspect of its use can best be described as of minimal significance.

We further note that we are free to consider the public benefit resulting from a particular use notwithstanding the fact that the alleged infringer may gain commercially. See *Hustler*, 796 F.2d at 1153 (quoting MCA, Inc. v. Wilson, 677 F.2d 180, 182 (2d Cir. 1981)). Public benefit need not be direct or tangible, but may arise because the challenged use serves a public interest. *Id.* In the case before us, Accolade's identification of the functional requirements for Genesis compatibility has led to an increase in the number of independently designed video game programs offered for use with the Genesis console. It is precisely this growth in creative expression, based on the dissemination of other creative works and the unprotected ideas contained in those works, that the Copyright Act was intended to promote. See Feist Publications, Inc. v. Rural Tel. Serv. Co., — U.S. —, 111 S. Ct. 1282, 1290, 113 L. Ed. 2d 358 (1991) (citing *Harper & Row*, 471 U.S. at 556-57). The fact that Genesis-compatible video games are not scholarly works, but works offered for sale on the market, does not alter our judgment in this regard. We conclude that given the purpose and character of Accolade's use of Sega's video game programs, the presumption of unfairness has been overcome and the first statutory factor weighs in favor of Accolade.

(b)

As applied, the fourth statutory factor, effect on the potential market for the copyrighted work, bears a close relationship to the "purpose and character" inquiry in that it, too, accommodates the distinction between the copying of works in order to make independent creative expression possible and the simple exploitation of another's creative efforts. We must, of course, inquire whether, "if [the challenged use] should become widespread, it would adversely affect the potential market for the copyrighted work," Sony Corp. v. Universal City Studios, 464 U.S. 417, 451 (1984), by diminishing potential sales, interfering with marketability, or usurping the market, *Hustler*, 796 F.2d at 1155-56. If the copying resulted in the latter effect, all other considerations might be irrelevant. The *Harper & Row* Court found a use that effectively usurped the market for the copyrighted work by supplanting that work to be dispositive. 471 U.S. at 567-69. However, the same consequences do not and could not attach to a use which simply enables the copier to enter the market for works of the same type as the copied work.

Unlike the defendant in *Harper & Row*, which printed excerpts from President Ford's memoirs verbatim with the stated purpose of "scooping" a Time magazine review of the book, 471 U.S. at 562, Accolade did not attempt to "scoop" Sega's release of any particular game or games, but sought only to become a legitimate competitor in the field of Genesis-compatible video games. Within that market, it is the characteristics of the game program as experienced by the user that determine the program's commercial success. As we have noted, there is nothing in the record that suggests that Accolade copied any of those elements.

By facilitating the entry of a new competitor, the first lawful one that is not a Sega licensee, Accolade's disassembly of Sega's software undoubtedly "affected" the market for Genesis-compatible games in an indirect fashion. We note, however, that while no consumer except the most avid devotee of President Ford's regime might be expected to buy more than one version of the President's memoirs, video game users typically purchase more than one game. There is no basis for assuming that Accolade's "Ishido" has significantly affected the market for Sega's "Altered Beast", since a consumer might easily purchase both; nor does it seem unlikely that a consumer particularly interested in sports might purchase both Accolade's "Mike Ditka Power Football" and Sega's "Joe Montana Football", particularly if the games are, as Accolade contends, not substantially similar. In any event, an attempt to monopolize the market by making it impossible for others to compete runs counter to the statutory purpose of promoting creative expression and cannot constitute a strong equitable basis for resisting the invocation of the fair use doctrine. Thus, we conclude that the fourth statutory factor weighs in Accolade's, not Sega's, favor, notwithstanding the minor economic loss Sega may suffer.

(c)

The second statutory factor, the nature of the copyrighted work, reflects the fact that not all copyrighted works are entitled to the same level of protection. The protection established by the Copyright Act for original works of authorship does not extend to the ideas underlying a work or to the functional or factual aspects of the work. 17 U.S.C. §102(b). To the extent that a work is functional or factual, it may be copied, Baker v. Selden, 101 U.S. 99, 102-04, (1879), as may those expressive elements of the work that "must necessarily be used as incident to" expression of the underlying ideas, functional concepts, or facts, id. at 104. Works of fiction receive greater protection than works that have strong factual elements, such as historical or biographical works, *Maxtone-Graham*, 803 F.2d at 1263 (citing Rosemont Enterprises, Inc. v. Random House, Inc., 366 F.2d 303, 307 (2d Cir. 1966), *cert. denied*, 385 U.S. 1009 (1967)), or works that have strong functional elements, such as accounting textbooks, *Baker*, 101 U.S. at 104. Works that are merely compilations of fact are copyrightable, but the copyright in such a work is "thin." *Feist Publications*, 111 S. Ct. at 1289.

Computer programs pose unique problems for the application of the "idea/expression distinction" that determines the extent of copyright protection. To the extent that there are many possible ways of accomplishing a given task or fulfilling a particular market demand, the programmer's choice of program structure and design may be highly creative and idiosyncratic. However, computer programs are, in essence, utilitarian articles—articles that accomplish tasks. As such, they contain many logical, structural, and visual display elements that are dictated by the function to be performed, by considerations of efficiency, or by external factors such as compatibility requirements and industry demands. Computer Assoc. Int'l, Inc. v. Altai, Inc. In some circumstances, even the exact set of commands used by the programmer is deemed functional rather than creative for purposes of copyright. "When specific instructions, even though previously copyrighted, are the only and essential means of accomplishing a given task, their later use by another will not amount to infringement." CONTU Report at 20; see *CAI*, 23 U.S.P.Q. 2d at 1254.

Because of the hybrid nature of computer programs, there is no settled standard for identifying what is protected expression and what is unprotected idea in a case involving the alleged infringement of a copyright in computer software. We are in wholehearted agreement with the Second Circuit's recent observation that "thus far, many of the decisions in this area reflect the courts' attempt to fit the proverbial square peg in a round hole." *CAI*, 23 U.S.P.Q. 2d at 1257. In 1986, the Third Circuit attempted to resolve the dilemma by suggesting that the idea or function of a computer program is the idea of the program as a whole, and "everything that is not necessary to that purpose or function [is] part of the expression of that idea." Whelan Assoc., Inc. v. Jaslow Dental Laboratory, Inc., 797 F.2d 1222, 1236 (3d Cir. 1986) (emphasis omitted). The *Whelan* rule, however, has been widely—and soundly—criticized as simplistic and overbroad. See *CAI*, 23 U.S.P.Q. 2d at 1252 (citing cases, treatises, and articles). In reality, "a computer program's ultimate function or purpose is the composite result of interacting subroutines. Since each subroutine is itself a program, and thus, may be said to have its own 'idea,' Whelan's general formulation . . . is descriptively inadequate." *Id.* For example, the computer program at issue in the case before us, a video game program, contains at least two such subroutines—the subroutine that allows the user to interact with the video game and the subroutine that allows the game cartridge to interact with the console. Under a test that breaks down a computer program into its component subroutines and sub-subroutines and then identifies the idea or core functional element of each, such as the test recently adopted by the Second Circuit in *CAI*, 23 U.S.P.Q.2D (BNA) at 1252-53, many aspects of the program are not protected by copyright. In our view, in light of the essentially utilitarian nature of computer programs, the Second Circuit's approach is an appropriate one.

Sega argues that even if many elements of its video game programs are properly characterized as functional and therefore not protected by copyright, Accolade copied protected expression. Sega is correct. The record makes clear that disassembly is wholesale copying. Because computer programs are also unique among copyrighted works in the form in which they are distributed for public use, however, Sega's observation does not bring us much closer to a resolution of the dispute.

The unprotected aspects of most functional works are readily accessible to the human eye. The systems described in accounting textbooks or the basic structural concepts embodied in architectural plans, to give two examples, can be easily copied without also copying any of the protected, expressive aspects of the original works. Computer programs, however, are typically distributed for public use in object code form, embedded in a silicon chip or on a floppy disk. For that reason, humans often cannot gain access to the unprotected ideas and functional concepts contained in object code without disassembling that code—i.e., making copies.[8] Atari Games v. Nintendo of America, 975 F.2d 832 (Fed. Cir. 1992).

---

8. We do not intend to suggest that disassembly is always the only available means of access to those aspects of a computer program that are unprotected by copyright. As we noted in Part III(B), supra, in many cases the operation of a program is directly reflected on the screen display and therefore visible to the human eye. In those cases, it is likely that a reverse engineer would not need to examine the code in order to understand what the program does.

Sega argues that the record does not establish that disassembly of its object code is the only available method for gaining access to the interface specifications for the Genesis console, and the district court agreed. An independent examination of the record reveals that Sega misstates its contents, and demonstrates that the district court committed clear error in this respect.

First, the record clearly establishes that humans cannot *read* object code. Sega makes much of Mike Lorenzen's statement that a reverse engineer can work directly from the zeros and ones of object code but "it's not as fun." In full, Lorenzen's statements establish only that the use of an electronic decompiler is not absolutely necessary. Trained programmers can disassemble object code by hand. Because even a trained programmer cannot possibly remember the millions of zeros and ones that make up a program, however, he must make a written or computerized copy of the disassembled code in order to keep track of his work. See generally Johnson-Laird, Technical Demonstration of "Decompilation," *reprinted in* Reverse Engineering: Legal and Business Strategies for Competitive Design in the 1990's 102 (Prentice Hall Law & Business ed. 1992). The relevant fact for purposes of Sega's copyright infringement claim and Accolade's fair use defense is that *translation* of a program from object code into source code cannot be accomplished without making copies of the code.

Second, the record provides no support for a conclusion that a viable alternative to disassembly exists. The district court found that Accolade could have avoided a copyright infringement claim by "peeling" the chips contained in Sega's games or in the Genesis console, as authorized by section 906 of the SCPA, 17 U.S.C. §906. Even Sega's amici agree that this finding was clear error. The declaration of Dr. Harry Tredennick, an expert witness for Accolade, establishes that chip peeling yields only a physical diagram of the *object code* embedded in a ROM chip. It does not obviate the need to translate object code into source code. *Atari Games Corp.*, slip op. at 22.

The district court also suggested that Accolade could have avoided a copyright infringement suit by programming in a "clean room". That finding too is clearly erroneous. A "clean room" is a procedure used in the computer industry in order to prevent direct copying of a competitor's code during the development of a competing product. Programmers in clean rooms are provided only with the functional specifications for the desired program. As Dr. Tredennick explained, the use of a clean room would not have avoided the need for disassembly because disassembly was necessary in order to discover the functional specifications for a Genesis-compatible game.

In summary, the record clearly establishes that disassembly of the object code in Sega's video game cartridges was necessary in order to understand the functional requirements for Genesis compatibility. The interface procedures for the Genesis console are distributed for public use only in object code form, and are not visible to the user during operation of the video game program. Because object code cannot be read by humans, it must be disassembled, either by hand or by machine. Disassembly of object code necessarily entails copying. Those facts dictate our analysis of the second statutory fair use factor. If disassembly of copyrighted object code is *per se* an unfair use, the owner of the copyright gains a de facto monopoly over the functional aspects of his work—aspects that were expressly denied copyright protection by Congress. 17 U.S.C. §102(b). In order to enjoy a lawful monopoly over the idea or functional principle underlying a work, the creator of the work must satisfy the more stringent standards imposed by the patent laws. Bonito Boats, Inc. v. Thunder Craft Boats, Inc., 489 U.S. 141, 159-64, 103 L. Ed. 2d 118, 109 S. Ct. 971 (1989). Sega does not hold a patent on the Genesis console. Because Sega's video game programs contain unprotected aspects that cannot be examined without copying, we afford them a lower degree of protection than more traditional literary works. See *CAI*, 23 U.S.P.Q. 2d at 1257. In light of all the considerations discussed above, we conclude that the second statutory factor also weighs in favor of Accolade.

(d)

As to the third statutory factor, Accolade disassembled entire programs written by Sega. Accordingly, the third factor weighs against Accolade. The fact that an entire work was copied does not, however, preclude a finding a fair use. *Sony Corp.*, 464 U.S. at 449-50; *Hustler*, 795 F.2d at 1155 ("*Sony Corp.* teaches us that the copying of an entire work does not preclude fair use per se."). In fact, where the ultimate (as opposed to direct) use is as limited as it was here, the factor is of very little weight. Cf. Wright v. Warner Books, Inc., 953 F.2d 731, 738 (2d Cir. 1991).

(e)

In summary, careful analysis of the purpose and characteristics of Accolade's use of Sega's video game programs, the nature of the computer programs involved, and the nature of the market for video game cartridges yields the conclusion that the first, second, and fourth statutory fair use factors weigh in favor of Accolade, while only the third weighs in favor of Sega, and even then only slightly. Accordingly, Accolade clearly has by far the better case on the fair use issue.

We are not unaware of the fact that to those used to considering copyright issues in more traditional contexts, our result may seem incongruous at first blush. To oversimplify, the record establishes that Accolade, a commercial competitor of Sega, engaged in wholesale copying of Sega's copyrighted code as a preliminary step in the development of a competing product. However, the key to this case is that we are dealing with computer software, a relatively unexplored area in the world of copyright law.

We must avoid the temptation of trying to force "the proverbial square peg into a round hole." *CAI*, 23 U.S.P.Q. 2d at 1257.

In determining whether a challenged use of copyrighted material is fair, a court must keep in mind the public policy underlying the Copyright Act. "'The immediate effect of our copyright law is to secure a fair return for an "author's" creative labor. But the ultimate aim is, by this incentive, to stimulate artistic creativity for the general public good.'" *Sony Corp.*, 464 U.S. at 432 (quoting Twentieth Century Music Corp. v. Aiken, 422 U.S. 151, 156 (1975)). When technological change has rendered an aspect or application of the Copyright Act ambiguous, "'the Copyright Act must be construed in light of this basic purpose.'" *Id*. As discussed above, the fact that computer programs are distributed for public use in object code form often precludes public access to the ideas and functional concepts contained in those programs, and thus confers on the copyright owner a de facto monopoly over those ideas and functional concepts. That result defeats the fundamental purpose of the Copyright Act—to encourage the production of original works by protecting the expressive elements of those works while leaving the ideas, facts, and functional concepts in the public domain for others to build on. *Feist Publications*, 111 S. Ct. at 1290.

Sega argues that the considerable time, effort, and money that went into development of the Genesis and Genesis-compatible video games militate against a finding of fair use. Borrowing from antitrust principles, Sega attempts to label Accolade a "free rider" on its product development efforts. In *Feist Publications*, however, the Court unequivocally rejected the "sweat of the brow" rationale for copyright protection. 111 S. Ct. at 1290-95. Under the Copyright Act, if a work is largely functional, it receives only weak protection. "This result is neither unfair nor unfortunate. It is the means by which copyright advances the progress of science and art." *Id*. at 1290; see also *id*. at 1292 ("In truth, 'it is just such wasted effort that the proscription against the copyright of ideas and facts . . . [is] designed to prevent.'") (quoting Rosemont Enterprises, Inc. v. Random House, Inc., 366 F.2d 303, 310 (2d Cir. 1966), *cert. denied* 385 U.S. 1009, 87 S. Ct. 714, 17 L. Ed. 2d 546 (1967)); *CAI*, 23 U.S.P.Q. 2d at 1257. Here, while the work may not be largely functional, it incorporates functional elements which do not merit protection. The equitable considerations involved weigh on the side of public access. Accordingly, we reject Sega's argument.

(f)

We conclude that where disassembly is the only way to gain access to the ideas and functional elements embodied in a copyrighted computer program and where there is a legitimate reason for seeking such access, disassembly is a fair use of the copyrighted work, as a matter of law. Our conclusion does not, of course, insulate Accolade from a claim of copyright infringement with respect to its finished products. Sega has reserved the right to raise such a claim, and it may do so on remand.

COMMENTS AND QUESTIONS

1. Commentators are sharply divided on whether compatibility and/or standardization should justify reverse engineering or copying of parts of a plaintiff's computer program. Virtually all recent courts, as well as most commentators, have endorsed reverse engineering in some circumstances. In addition to *Sega*, see DSC Communications v. DGI Technologies, 81 F.3d 597, 601 (5th Cir. 1996); Bateman v. Mnemonics, Inc., 79 F.3d 1532, 1539 n.18 (11th Cir. 1995); Lotus Dev. Corp. v. Borland Int'l, 49 F.3d 807, 817-818 (1st Cir. 1995) (Boudin, J., concurring); Atari Games Corp. v. Nintendo of America, 975 F.2d 832, 843-844 (Fed. Cir. 1992); Sega, Inc. v. Accolade, 977 F.2d 1510, 1527-1528 (9th Cir. 1992); Vault v. Quaid, 847 F.2d 255, 270 (5th Cir. 1988); Mitel Inc. v. Iqtel Inc., 896 F. Supp. 1050 (D. Colo. 1995), *aff'd on other grounds*, 124 F.3d 1366 (10th Cir. 1997); Jonathan Band & Masanobu Katoh, Interfaces on Trial (1995); Julie Cohen, Reverse Engineering and the Rise of Electronic Vigilantism: Intellectual Property Implications of "Lock-Out" Technologies, 68 S. Cal. L. Rev. 1091 (1995); Lawrence D. Graham & Richard O. Zerbe Jr., Economically Efficient Treatment of Computer Software: Reverse Engineering, Protection, and Disclosure, 22 Rutgers Computer & Tech. L.J. 61 (1996); Dennis S. Karjala, Copyright Protection of Computer Documents, Reverse Engineering, and Professor Miller, 19 U. Dayton L. Rev. 975, 1016-1018 (1994); David A. Rice, Sega and Beyond: A Beacon for Fair Use Analysis . . . At Least as Far as It Goes, 19 U. Dayton L. Rev. 1131, 1168 (1994).

On the other hand, some early decisions rejected compatibility as a justification for copying. See Apple Computer v. Franklin Computer, 714 F.2d 1240 (3d Cir. 1983) (*reprinted in* Section B.1, supra); Digital Communications Assoc. v. Softklone Distributing Corp., 659 F. Supp. 449 (N.D. Ga. 1987). See also Anthony Clapes, Confessions of an Amicus Curiae: Technophobia, Law and Creativity in the Digital Arts, 19 U. Dayton L. Rev. 903 (1994) (no right to reverse engineer software should exist) and Arthur Miller, Copyright Protection for Computer Programs, Databases, and Computer-Generated Works: Is Anything New Since CONTU?, 106 Harv. L. Rev. 977 (1993) (same). Most of these decisions, unlike *Sega*, involve copied code that appears in the defendant's final product, rather than just intermediate copying. Should the courts treat intermediate copying differently from copying for compatibility in a final product?

In DSC Communications Corp. v. Pulse Communications Inc., 170 F.3d 1354 (Fed. Cir. 1999), the court seemed to acknowledge that reverse engineering could be a fair use but held that it was not always fair. It wrote:

> The district court dismissed DSC's direct copyright infringement claim on the ground that Pulsecom's conduct was excused by the affirmative defense of fair use for reverse engineering, as discussed in Sega Enterprises, Ltd. v. Accolade, Inc., 977 F.2d 1510, 1520, 24 USPQ2d 1561, 1569 (9th Cir.1992). The *Sega* case, however, does not stand for the proposition that any form of copyright infringement is privileged as long as it is done as part of an effort to explore the operation of a product that uses the copyrighted software. On the basis of DSC's evidence at trial, Pulsecom's activities in creating copies of the POTS-DI software on its POTS cards by using the RBOCs' Litespan systems does not qualify as "fair use" under the *Sega* analysis. DSC's evidence showed that Pulsecom representatives made copies of the POTS-DI software on Pulsecom POTS cards as part of the ordinary operation of those cards, not as part of an effort to determine how the Litespan system worked. Rather than being part of an attempt at reverse engineering, the copying appears to have been done after Pulsecom had determined how the system functioned and merely to demonstrate the interchangeability of the Pulsecom POTS cards with those made and sold by DSC.

Id. at 1363. Why isn't there a valid social purpose in testing one's system to make sure it is compatible with the plaintiff's system? Does Pulse's use have a market-destroying effect here? If so, what is it? For a result in some tension with *Pulse*, see Alcatel USA Inc. v. DGI Technologies Inc., 166 F.3d 772 (5th Cir. 1999) (holding that it was copyright misuse for DSC to attempt to prevent a competitor from testing the compatibility of its cards with DSC's).

2. Do you agree with the *Sega* court's analysis of the fourth fair use factor? Hasn't Sega been injured because it can no longer control who produces games for its machine? Won't it lose the ability to charge a fee to game writers?

3. *Sega* suggests that the very nature of computer programs entitles them to less protection than other literary works, since programs must be copied in order for the user to have access to the uncopyrightable ideas and facts they contain. Does this reasoning apply only to copying to achieve compatibility, or does it suggest that *any* copying is more likely to constitute fair use?

4. Is standardization a valid rationale for copying? Professor Menell suggests that even arbitrary elements of user interfaces that become de facto industry standards should lose copyright protection in order to foster network externalities. Peter Menell, An Analysis of the Scope of Copyright Protection for Computer Programs, 41 Stan. L. Rev. 1045, 1101 (1989). He argues that the high premium that consumers place on widely learned standards makes compatibility with such standards critical to entering the marketplace. In effect, what began as an arbitrary element has become functional due to widespread consumer learning. See also Frederick Warren-Boulton et al., The Economics of Intellectual Property for Soft-

ware: The Proper Role for Copyright, Computer Law. (Feb. 1995); Mark A. Lemley & David McGowan, Legal Implications of Network Economic Effects, 86 Cal. L. Rev. 479 (1998).

On the other hand, not every case requires standardization. The *Sega* court is careful to note that intermediate copying qualifies as fair use only if it is necessary to produce an interoperable program. At least one court has rejected a claim of fair use on the grounds that the copyrighted material taken was not needed for interoperability. Compaq Computer v. Procom Technology, 908 F. Supp. 1409 (S.D. Tex. 1995).

5. Is the fair use doctrine an appropriate means of encouraging compatibility or standardization? Does accommodating those policy goals require stretching the doctrine too far? A number of commentators have suggested that encouraging compatability is best accomplished by legislating a right to reverse engineer, analogous to the right provided in the Semiconductor Chip Protection Act of 1984.[10] See, e.g., Timothy S. Teter, Merger and the Machines: An Analysis of the Pro-Compatibility Trend in Computer Software Copyright Cases, 45 Stan. L. Rev. 1061, 1089-1097 (1993).

6. Is Sega entitled to control not only the sales of its copyrighted software-hardware package but also video games that will run on the Sega system? The court's decision obliquely suggests that there are antitrust (or possibly copyright misuse) problems with giving Sega such power: "an attempt to monopolize the market by making it impossible for others to compete runs counter to the statutory purpose of promoting creative expression and cannot constitute a strong equitable basis for resisting the invocation of the fair use doctrine." *Sega*, 977 F.2d at 1523-1524. Is this concern properly addressed in the fair use doctrine? Are there other limits on Sega's ability to control the creation of compatible programs? See infra (discussing the copyright misuse doctrine).

7. At the time *Sega* was decided, reverse engineering a computer program was a difficult and time-consuming task. If reverse engineering were simple and flawless, should it still be legal? For an argument that "easy" reverse engineering would be problematic, see Pamela Samuelson et al., A Manifesto Concerning the Legal Protection of Computer Programs, 94 Colum. L. Rev. 2308 (1994).

Note on Reverse Engineering and the Digital Millennium Copyright Act

Congress enacted the Digital Millennium Copyright Act in 1998. That Act, which creates an entirely new cause of action against people who circumvent "copy protection" schemes or make devices that enable others to do so, is discussed in detail in Chapter 10. One provision is particularly

---

10. This statute is discussed in detail in Chapter 5.

important for reverse engineering, however. While the statute generally outlaws any activity that involves bypassing or disabling a copy protection system, there is an exception for certain sorts of reverse engineering. 17 U.S.C. section 1201(f) provides in part:

> (1) Notwithstanding the provisions of subsection (a)(1)(A), a person who has lawfully obtained the right to use a copy of a computer program may circumvent a technological measure that effectively controls access to a particular portion of that program for the sole purpose of identifying and analyzing those elements of the program that are necessary to achieve interoperability of an independently created computer program with other programs, and that have not previously been readily available to the person engaging in the circumvention, to the extent any such acts of identification and analysis do not constitute infringement under this title.

Subsections (2) and (3) further provide that people can develop tools to permit such reverse engineering, and can share the information they learn with others, subject to the same conditions identified in paragraph (1).

Is this provision an endorsement of *Sega*? On the one hand, Congress clearly determined that reverse engineering could serve valuable social purposes and protected it from liability. But the last clause of the statute seems to contemplate the possibility that reverse engineering even for such a laudable social purpose might be infringing. Cf. DSC v. Pulse, discussed supra. The statute does not appear to change the law in that case.

PROBLEM

Problem 2-10. Return to the Demento v. Mutant problem (Problem 2-4). Suppose that Mutant deciphered Demento's "key" program by decompilation. How would a court rule on the issue of fair use?

F. COPYRIGHT MISUSE

≣
≣ ***Lasercomb America, Inc. v. Reynolds***
≣ *United States Court of Appeals for the Fourth Circuit*
≣ *911 F.2d 970 (4th Cir. 1990)*

SPROUSE, Circuit Judge:

Appellants Larry Holliday and Job Reynolds appeal from a district court judgment holding them liable to appellee Lasercomb America, Inc., for copyright infringement and for fraud, based on appellants' unauthorized copying and marketing of appellee's software. We affirm in part, reverse in part, and remand for recomputation of damages.

I. Facts and Proceedings Below

Appellants and defendants below are Larry Holliday, president and sole shareholder of Holiday Steel Rule Die Corporation (Holiday Steel), and Job Reynolds, a computer programmer for that company. Appellee is Lasercomb America, Inc. (Lasercomb), the plaintiff below. Holiday Steel and Lasercomb were competitors in the manufacture of steel rule dies that are used to cut and score paper and cardboard for folding into boxes and cartons. Lasercomb developed a software program, Interact, which is the object of the dispute between the parties. Using this program, a designer creates a template of a cardboard cutout on a computer screen and the software directs the mechanized creation of the conforming steel rule die.

In 1983, before Lasercomb was ready to market its Interact program generally, it licensed four prerelease copies to Holiday Steel which paid $35,000 for the first copy, $17,500 each for the next two copies, and $2,000 for the fourth copy. Lasercomb informed Holiday Steel that it would charge $2,000 for each additional copy Holiday Steel cared to purchase. Apparently ambitious to create for itself an even better deal, Holiday Steel circumvented the protective devices Lasercomb had provided with the software and made three unauthorized copies of Interact which it used on its computer systems. Perhaps buoyed by its success in copying, Holiday Steel then created a software program called "PDS-1000," which was almost entirely a direct copy of Interact, and marketed it as its own CAD/CAM die-making software. These infringing activities were accomplished by Job Reynolds at the direction of Larry Holliday.

There is no question that defendants engaged in unauthorized copying, and the purposefulness of their unlawful action is manifest from their deceptive practices. For example, Lasercomb had asked Holiday Steel to use devices called "chronoguards" to prevent unauthorized access to Interact. Although defendants had deduced how to circumvent the chronoguards and had removed them from their computers, they represented to Lasercomb that the chronoguards were in use. Another example of subterfuge is Reynolds' attempt to modify the PDS-1000 program output so it would present a different appearance than the output from Interact.

When Lasercomb discovered Holiday Steel's activities, it registered its copyright in Interact and filed this action against Holiday Steel, Holliday, and Reynolds on March 7, 1986. . . .

Holliday and Reynolds raise several issues on appeal. They do not dispute that they copied Interact, but they contend that Lasercomb is barred from recovery for infringement by its concomitant culpability. They assert that, assuming Lasercomb had a perfected copyright, it impermissibly abused it. This assertion of the "misuse of copyright" defense is based on language in Lasercomb's standard licensing agreement, restricting licensees from creating any of their own CAD/CAM die-making software. . . .

II. Misuse of Copyright Defense

A successful defense of misuse of copyright bars a culpable plaintiff from prevailing on an action for infringement of the misused copyright. Here, appellants claim Lasercomb has misused its copyright by including in its standard licensing agreement clauses which prevent the licensee from participating in any manner in the creation of computer-assisted die-making software. The offending paragraphs read:

> D. Licensee agrees during the term of this Agreement that it will not permit or suffer its directors, officers and employees, directly or indirectly, to write, develop, produce or sell computer assisted die making software.
>
> E. Licensee agrees during the term of this Agreement and for one (1) year after the termination of this Agreement, that it will not write, develop, produce or sell or assist others in the writing, developing, producing or selling computer assisted die making software, directly or indirectly without Lasercomb's prior written consent. Any such activity undertaken without Lasercomb's written consent shall nullify any warranties or agreements of Lasercomb set forth herein.

The "term of this Agreement" referred to in these clauses is ninety-nine years.

Defendants were not themselves bound by the standard licensing agreement. Lasercomb had sent the agreement to Holiday Steel with a request that it be signed and returned. Larry Holliday, however, decided not to sign the document, and Lasercomb apparently overlooked the fact that the document had not been returned. Although defendants were not party to the restrictions of which they complain, they proved at trial that at least one Interact licensee had entered into the standard agreement, including the anticompetitive language.

The district court rejected the copyright misuse defense for three reasons. First, it noted that defendants had not explicitly agreed to the contract clauses alleged to constitute copyright misuse. Second, it found "such a clause is reasonable in light of the delicate and sensitive area of computer software." And, third, it questioned whether such a defense exists. We consider the district court's reasoning in reverse order.

A. Does a "Misuse of Copyright" Defense Exist?

We agree with the district court that much uncertainty engulfs the "misuse of copyright" defense. We are persuaded, however, that a misuse of copyright defense is inherent in the law of copyright just as a misuse of patent defense is inherent in patent law.

The misuse of a patent is a potential defense to suit for its infringement, and both the existence and parameters of that body of law are well established. Although there is little case law on the subject, courts from time to time have intimated that the similarity of rationales underlying the law of patents and the law of copyrights argues for a defense to an infringement of copyright based on misuse of the copyright. The origins of patent and copyright law in England, the treatment of these two aspects of intellectual property by the framers of our Constitution, and the later statutory and judicial development of patent and copyright law in this country persuade us that parallel public policies underlie the protection of both types of intellectual property rights. We think these parallel policies call for application of the misuse defense to copyright as well as patent law. . . .

Although a patent misuse defense was recognized by the courts as early as 1917, most commentators point to Morton Salt Co. v. G.S. Suppiger, 314 U.S. 488, 62 S.Ct. 402, 86 L.Ed. 363 (1942), as the foundational patent misuse case. In that case, the plaintiff Morton Salt brought suit on the basis that the defendant had infringed Morton's patent in a salt-depositing machine. The salt tablets were not themselves a patented item, but Morton's patent license required that licensees use only salt tablets produced by Morton. Morton was thereby using its patent to restrain competition in the sale of an item which was not within the scope of the patent's privilege. The Supreme Court held that, as a court of equity, it would not aid Morton in protecting its patent when Morton was using that patent in a manner contrary to public policy. Id. at 490-92, 62 S.Ct. at 404-05. . . .

3. The "Misuse of Copyright" Defense

Although the patent misuse defense has been generally recognized since *Morton Salt*, it has been much less certain whether an analogous copyright misuse defense exists. This uncertainty persists because no United States Supreme Court decision has firmly established a copyright misuse defense in a manner analogous to the establishment of the patent misuse defense by Morton Salt. The few courts considering the issue have split on whether the defense should be recognized, see Holmes, Intellectual Property §4.09 (collecting cases), and we have discovered only one case which has actually applied copyright misuse to bar an action for infringement. M. Witmark & Sons v. Jensen, 80 F.Supp. 843 (D.Minn.1948), *appeal dismissed*, 177 F.2d 515 (8th Cir.1949).

We are of the view, however, that since copyright and patent law serve parallel public interests, a "misuse" defense should apply to infringement actions brought to vindicate either right. As discussed above, the similarity of the policies underlying patent and copyright is great and historically has been consistently recognized. Both patent law and copyright law seek to increase the store of human knowledge and arts by rewarding inventors and authors with the exclusive rights to their works for a limited time. At the same time, the granted monopoly power does not extend to property not covered by the patent or copyright. *Morton Salt,* 314 U.S. at 492, 62 S.Ct. at 405; *Paramount Pictures,* 334 U.S. at 156-58, 68 S.Ct. at 928-29; cf. Baker v. Selden, 101 U.S. 99, 101-04, 25 L.Ed. 841 (1880).

Thus, we are persuaded that the rationale of *Morton Salt* in establishing the misuse defense applies to copyrights. In the passage from Morton Salt quoted above, the phraseology adapts easily to a copyright context:

> The grant to the [author] of the special privilege of a [copyright] carries out a public policy adopted by the Constitution and laws of the United States, "to promote the Progress of Science and useful Arts, by securing for limited Times to [Authors] . . . the exclusive Right . . . " to their ["original" works]. United States Constitution, Art. I, §8, cl. 8, [17 U.S.C.A. §102]. But the public policy which includes [original works] within the granted monopoly excludes from it all that is not embraced in the [original expression]. It equally forbids the use of the [copyright] to secure an exclusive right or limited monopoly not granted by the [Copyright] Office and which it is contrary to public policy to grant.

Cf. *Morton Salt,* 314 U.S. at 492, 62 S.Ct. at 405.

Having determined that "misuse of copyright" is a valid defense, analogous to the misuse of patent defense, our next task is to determine whether the defense should have been applied by the district court to bar Lasercomb's infringement action against the defendants in this case.

B. *The District Court's Finding that the Anticompetitive Clauses Are Reasonable*

In declining to recognize a misuse of copyright defense, the district court found "reasonable" Lasercomb's attempt to protect its software copyright by using anticompetitive clauses in their licensing agreement. In briefly expressing its reasoning, the court referred to the "delicate and sensitive" nature of software. It also observed that Lasercomb's president had testified that the noncompete language was negotiable.

If, as it appears, the district court analogized from the "rule of reason" concept of antitrust law, we think its reliance on that principle was misplaced. Such reliance is, however, understandable. Both the presentation by appellants and the literature tend to intermingle antitrust and misuse defenses. E.g., Holmes, Intellectual Property, at §4.09. A patent or copyright is often regarded as a limited monopoly—an exception to the general public policy against restraints of trade. Since antitrust law is the statutory embodiment of that public policy, there is an understandable association of antitrust law with the misuse defense. Certainly, an entity which uses its patent as the means of violating antitrust law is subject to a misuse of patent defense. However, *Morton Salt* held that it is not necessary to prove an antitrust violation in order to successfully assert patent misuse. . . .

So while it is true that the attempted use of a copyright to violate antitrust law probably would give rise to a misuse of copyright defense, the converse is not necessarily true—a misuse need not be a violation of antitrust law in order to comprise an equitable defense to an infringement action. The question is not whether the copyright is being used in a manner violative of antitrust law (such as whether the licensing agreement is "reasonable"), but whether the copyright is being used in a manner violative of the public policy embodied in the grant of a copyright.

Lasercomb undoubtedly has the right to protect against copying of the Interact code. Its standard licensing agreement, however, goes much further and essentially attempts to suppress any attempt by the licensee to independently implement the idea which Interact expresses. The agreement forbids the licensee to develop or assist in developing any kind of computer-assisted die-making software. If the licensee is a business, it is to prevent all its directors, officers and employees from assisting in any manner to develop computer-assisted die-making software. Although one or another licensee might succeed in negotiating out the noncompete provisions, this does not negate the fact that Lasercomb is attempting to use its copyright in a manner adverse to the public policy embodied in copyright law, and that it has succeeded in doing so with at least one licensee. Cf. Berlenbach v. Anderson & Thompson Ski Co., 329 F.2d 782, 784-85 (9th Cir.), *cert. denied*, 379 U.S. 830, 85 S.Ct. 60, 13 L.Ed.2d 39 (1964).

The language employed in the Lasercomb agreement is extremely broad. Each time Lasercomb sells its Interact program to a company and obtains that company's agreement to the noncompete language, the company is required to forego utilization of the creative abilities of all its officers, directors and employees in the area of CAD/CAM die-making software. Of yet greater concern, these creative abilities are withdrawn from the public. The period for which this anticompetitive restraint exists is ninety-nine years, which could be longer than the life of the copyright itself.

. . . Again, the analysis necessary to a finding of misuse is similar to but separate from the analysis necessary to a finding of antitrust violation. The misuse arises from Lasercomb's attempt to use its copyright in a particular expression, the Interact software, to control competition in an area outside the copyright, i.e., the idea of computer-assisted die manufacture, regardless of whether such conduct amounts to an antitrust violation.

C. *The Effect of Appellants Not Being Party to the Anticompetitive Contract*

In its rejection of the copyright misuse defense, the district court emphasized that Holiday Steel was not explicitly party to a licensing agreement containing the offending language. However, again analogizing to patent misuse, the defense of copyright misuse is available even if the defendants themselves have not been injured by the misuse. In *Morton Salt,* the defendant was not a party to the license requirement that only Morton-produced salt tablets be used with Morton's salt-depositing machine. Nevertheless, suit against defendant for infringement of Morton's patent was barred on public policy grounds. Similarly, in *Compton,* even though the defendant Metal Products was not a party to the license agreement that restrained competition by Compton, suit against Metal Products was barred because of the public interest in free competition. See also *Hensley Equip. Co.,* 383 F.2d at 261; cf. *Berlenbach,* 329 F.2d at 784-85.

Therefore, the fact that appellants here were not parties to one of Lasercomb's standard license agreements is inapposite to their copyright misuse defense. The question is whether Lasercomb is using its copyright in a manner contrary to public policy, which question we have answered in the affirmative.

In sum, we find that misuse of copyright is a valid defense, that Lasercomb's anticompetitive clauses in its standard licensing agreement constitute misuse of copyright, and that the defense is available to appellants even though they were not parties to the standard licensing agreement. Holding that Lasercomb should have been barred by the defense of copyright misuse from suing for infringement of its copyright in the Interact program, we reverse the injunction and the award of damages for copyright infringement.[22] . . .

COMMENTS AND QUESTIONS

1. A number of cases have applied copyright misuse to bar enforcement of the copyright, though many others have refused to do so. For cases applying the misuse doctrine, see, e.g., in addition to Lasercomb America v. Reynolds, 911 F.2d 970 (4th Cir. 1990), and DSC Communi-

---

22. This holding, of course, is not an invalidation of Lasercomb's copyright. Lasercomb is free to bring a suit for infringement once it has purged itself of the misuse. Cf. *United States Gypsum Co. v. National Gypsum Co.,* 352 U.S. 457, 465 (1957); *Hensley Equipment Co.,* 383 F.2d at 261, 386 F.2d at 443.

cations v. DGI Technologies, 81 F.3d 597 (5th Cir. 1996), which is discussed below, see Alcatel USA Inc. v. DGI Technologies, 166 F.3d 772 (5th Cir. 1999); Practice Management Info. Corp. v. American Med. Ass'n, 121 F.3d 516, 520-521 (9th Cir. 1997), *as amended* Jan. 9, 1998 (finding that AMA license of its works to government agency on the condition that they did not use a competing work was copyright misuse, even though the clause was not enforced); PRC Realty Sys. v. National Ass'n of Realtors, 1992 U.S. App. LEXIS 18017 (4th Cir. 1992) (unpublished) (invalidating a license agreement for copyright misuse because it precluded competition by licensees); F.E.L. Publications, Ltd. v. Catholic Bishop, 214 U.S.P.Q. 409, 413 n.9 (7th Cir. 1982) (noting that "it is copyright misuse to exact a fee for the use of a musical work which is already in the public domain"; dictum); Tamburo v. Calvin, 1995 WL 121539 (N.D. Ill. Mar. 17, 1995) (holding that a software license agreement that prevents the development of competing products, whether or not based in software, constituted patent misuse); qad, Inc. v. ALN Assocs., 770 F. Supp. 1261, 1267-1269 (N.D. Ill. 1991) (holding that wrongly asserting copyright infringement on the basis of material that in fact plaintiff copied from another was copyright misuse, precluding plaintiff from asserting even the original portions of the copyrighted work), *aff'd*, 974 F.2d 834 (7th Cir. 1992); Broadcast Music, Inc. v. Moor-Law, Inc., 527 F. Supp. 758, 772 n.24 (D. Del. 1981) ("Copyright misuse and antitrust analysis in this area are not necessarily coextensive."); Vogue Ring Creations, Inc. v. Hardman, 410 F. Supp. 609, 615-616 (D.R.I. 1976) (finding that material misstatements in copyright registration form constituted copyright misuse); cf. Coleman v. ESPN, Inc., 764 F. Supp. 290, 295 (S.D.N.Y. 1991) (holding that defendant could proceed to trial on its copyright misuse defense).

Of course, in many other cases courts have refused to find copyright misuse in the circumstances before them. And a few older decisions took the position that there was no such thing as a copyright misuse defense at all, but no courts have done so recently.

2. The *Lasercomb* court relies heavily on the patent law analogy. Patent misuse is generally tested according to antitrust (or at least antitrust-related) principles. Should copyright misuse likewise be limited to cases in which the copyright owner engages in the sort of conduct that brings antitrust scrutiny? Courts that have found misuse are likely to do so on principles that go beyond antitrust law and arise instead from copyright policy. See Practice Management Info. Corp. v. American Med. Ass'n, 121 F.3d 516 (9th Cir. 1997), *as amended* Jan. 9, 1998 (suggesting that copyright misuse need not constitute an antitrust violation); Lasercomb Am., Inc. v. Reynolds, 911 F.2d 970, 978 (4th Cir. 1990) (describing misuse as "an equitable defense to an infringement action" that applies where "the copyright is being used in a manner violative of the public policy embodied in the grant of a copyright"); cf. Bateman v. Mnemonics, Inc., 79 F.3d 1532, 1547 (11th Cir. 1996) (suggesting that copyright

misuse might be appropriate to prevent a copyright owner from capturing protection for an idea in violation of 17 U.S.C. §102(b)). But see Reed-Union Corp. v. Turtle-Wax, Inc., 77 F.3d 909 (7th Cir. 1996) (suggesting that copyright misuse is limited to cases in which the antitrust laws are violated).

Commentators too are divided on whether copyright misuse is broader than antitrust law but lean heavily toward the view that it is. See Sean Michael Aylward, The Fourth Circuit's Extension of the Misuse Doctrine to the Area of Copyright: A Misuse of the Misuse Doctrine?, 17 U. Dayton L. Rev. 661 (1992) (copyright misuse doctrine is broader than antitrust law but shouldn't be); Julie E. Cohen, Reverse Engineering and the Rise of Electronic Vigilantism: Intellectual Property Implications of "Lock-Out" Technologies, 68 S. Cal. L. Rev. 1091 (1995) (arguing for application of misuse outside the antitrust context); Timothy H. Fine, Misuse and Antitrust Defenses to Copyright Infringement Actions, 17 Hastings L.J. 315 (1965) (arguing that misuse can occur without an antitrust violation); Marshall Leaffer, Engineering Competitive Policy and Copyright Misuse, 19 U. Dayton L. Rev. 1087, 1099 (1994) ("Most courts have declared that the misuse defense does not require proof of an antitrust violation."); John G. Mills, Possible Defenses to Complaints for Copyright Infringement and Reverse Engineering of Computer Software: Implications for Antitrust and I.P. Law, 80 J. Pat. & Trademark Off. Soc'y 101, 119 (1998) (arguing that copyright misuse does not require a showing of injury to competition); Maureen A. O'Rourke, Drawing the Boundary Between Copyright and Contract: Copyright Preemption of Software Licensing Terms, 45 Duke L.J. 479, 534 (1995) ("it seems that the quantum of proof is somewhat less" in a copyright misuse than in an antitrust case); Troy Paredes, Copyright Misuse and Tying: Will Courts Stop Misusing Misuse?, 9 High Tech. L.J. 271 (1994) (arguing that copyright misuse should be abolished, and only antitrust violations should be considered); David Scher, The Viability of the Copyright Misuse Defense, 20 Fordham Urb. L.J. 89 (1993) (arguing that misuse should cover all extensions of copyright); Richard Stitt, Copyright Self-Help Protection as Copyright Misuse: Finally, the Other Shoe Drops, 57 UMKC L. Rev. 899 (1989) (arguing that misuse is distinct from antitrust); Toshiko Takenaka, Extending the New Patent Misuse Limitation to Copyright, 5 Software L.J. 739, 746-748 (1992) (arguing for an antitrust-based approach to misuse); James A.D. White, Misuse or Fair Use? That Is the Software Copyright Question, 12 Berkeley Tech. L.J. 251, 302-305 (arguing that "misuse is independent of antitrust" and should be, at least for software); Philip Abromats, Comment, Copyright Misuse and Anticompetitive Software Licensing Restrictions, 52 U. Pitt. L. Rev. 629 (1991) (arguing for antitrust-based treatment of misuse); Ramsey Hanna, Note, Misusing Antitrust: The Search for Functional Copyright Misuse Standards, 46 Stan. L. Rev. 401 (1994) (arguing that misuse should be independent of but narrower than antitrust); Note, Clarifying the Copyright Misuse Defense: The Role of Antitrust Standards and First Amendment Values, 104 Harv. L. Rev. 1289 (1991) (arguing that copyright misuse should properly have both antitrust and pro-dissemination objectives).

For an interesting argument that network effects in the software industry support reliance on misuse principles independent of antitrust, see White, supra, at 277-280; cf. Mark A. Lemley & David McGowan, Could Java Change Everything? The Competitive Propriety of a Proprietary Standard, 43 Antitrust Bull. 715 (1998) (same).

Does it make sense to test copyright misuse by principles other than those derived from antitrust law? If so, what should those guiding principles be? Many of the cases finding copyright misuse are vulnerable to the criticism that the challenged practices were really alleged antitrust violations to which the court applied a more lenient standard (refusing to require a showing of market power in the *Lasercomb* case, for example).

3. To what extent can the copyright misuse doctrine do the work of doctrines like fair use? A recent application of the copyright misuse doctrine in a context analogous to Sega v. Accolade is DSC Comm. Corp. v. DGI Technologies, 81 F.3d 597, 601 (5th Cir. 1996). In that case, the Fifth Circuit held that a plaintiff was not likely to prevail on a claim of copyright infringement stemming from the creation of RAM copies of its operating system because the plaintiff's assertion of such a copyright claim was likely to constitute copyright misuse. The court reasoned:

> DSC seems to be attempting to use its copyright to obtain a patent-like monopoly over unpatented microprocessor cards. Any competing microprocessor card developed for use on DSC phone switches must be compatible with DSC's copyrighted operating system software. In order to ensure that its card is compatible, a competitor such as DGI must test the card on a DSC phone switch. Such a test necessarily involves making a copy of DSC's copyrighted operating system, which copy is downloaded into the card's memory when the card is booted up. If DSC is allowed to prevent such copying, then it can prevent anyone from developing a competing microprocessor card, even though it has not patented the card. The defense of copyright misuse "forbids the use of the copyright to secure an exclusive right or limited monopoly not granted by the Copyright Office, including a limited monopoly over microprocessor cards."

See also Tricom v. EDS, 902 F. Supp. 741 (E.D. Mich. 1995) (attempting to enforce copyright law against RAM copying constituted copyright misuse). In Sega v. Accolade is it reasonable to argue that Sega was misusing its copyright? Would application of the misuse doctrine provide a narrower rationale on which to decide the case? Is such a narrower rationale desirable? See Julie E. Cohen, Reverse Engineering and the Rise of

Electronic Vigilantism: Intellectual Property Implications of "Lock-Out" Technologies, 68 S. Cal. L. Rev. 1091 (1995) (suggesting that such a misuse-based approach may be warranted); David Nimmer, Brains and Other Paraphernalia of the Digital Age, 10 Harv. J. L. & Tech. 1 (1997) (arguing that the *MAI* decision should have been reversed on misuse grounds).

3

Patent Protection

A.   IS SOFTWARE PATENTABLE SUBJECT MATTER?

The computing industry has always relied on patents to a substantial degree. Patents on computer hardware have generally proved uncontroversial. Given the high level of innovation and the industry's prosperity, there is reason to think that the patent system has contributed to the success in this industry. Given the equivalence of hardware and software, it may be surprising to know that patents for software or software-related inventions have been controversial for about four decades. For most of this time, substantial questions existed about whether programs or program-related inventions were patentable subject matter. Indeed, an early Supreme Court case suggested that important categories of computer software were not patentable at all. More recently, courts have at first grudgingly, and then enthusiastically, accepted software patents, and the debate about software patents has focused on how sound are examiner judgments about the novelty and nonobviousness of claimed software inventions. Notwithstanding this debate, software developers have increasingly come to rely on patents (if for no other reason than to have something to trade).

Although the debates over patenting software have subsided to some degree, it is still useful to understand why software inventions have been regarded as troublesome for the patent system, because remnants of these arguments still surface from time to time in the United States and elsewhere. Further, the early unwillingness of the U.S. Patent Office (PTO) and courts to grant patents on software set the stage for the next two decades of legal protection for computer software, bringing trade secrets and copyright to the forefront. And finally, the history of software patents has influenced the nature of legal protection to this day. We therefore begin with some historical perspective on the patentability of software.

1. The Patentability of Mathematical Algorithms

On several notable occasions, early programmer/applicants brought their fight to patent software to the Supreme Court. These early cases—and, indeed, the vast majority of software patent cases to date—focused on the question of whether an "invention" consisting of the use of a mathematical algorithm could be patentable subject matter under 35 U.S.C. section 101. We begin with the first Supreme Court opinion on this issue.

Gottschalk v. Benson
Supreme Court of the United States
409 U.S. 63, 175 U.S.P.Q. (BNA) 673 (1972)

MR. JUSTICE DOUGLAS delivered the opinion of the Court.

Respondents filed in the Patent Office an application for an invention which was described as being related "to the processing of data by program and more particularly to the programmed conversion of numerical information" in general-purpose digital computers. They claimed a method for converting binary-coded decimal (BCD) numerals into pure binary numerals. The claims were not limited to any particular art or technology, to any particular apparatus or machinery, or to any particular end use. They purported to cover any use of the claimed method in a general-purpose digital computer of any type. Claims 8 and 13 were rejected by the Patent Office but sustained by the Court of Customs and Patent Appeals.

The question is whether the method described and claimed is a "process" within the meaning of the Patent Act.[2]

A digital computer, as distinguished from an analog computer, operates on data expressed in digits, solving a problem by doing arithmetic as a person would do it by head and hand. Some of the digits are stored as components of the computer. Others are introduced into the computer in a form which it is designed to recognize. The computer operates then upon both new and previously stored data. The general-purpose computer is designed to perform operations under many different programs.

---

2. Title 35 U.S.C. §100(b) provides:

The term "process" means process, art or method, and includes a new use of a known process, machine, manufacture, composition of matter, or material.

Title 35 U.S.C. §101 provides:

Whoever invents or discovers any new and useful process, machine, manufacture, or composition of matter, or any new and useful improvement thereof, may obtain a patent therefor, subject to the conditions and requirements of this title.

The representation of numbers may be in the form of a time series of electrical impulses, magnetized spots on the surface of tapes, drums, or discs, charged spots on cathode-ray tube screens, the presence or absence of punched holes on paper cards, or other devices. The method or program is a sequence of coded instructions for a digital computer.

The patent sought is on a method of programming a general-purpose digital computer to convert signals from binary-coded decimal form into pure binary form. A procedure for solving a given type of mathematical problem is known as an "algorithm." The procedures set forth in the present claims are of that kind; that is to say, they are a generalized formulation for programs to solve mathematical problems of converting one form of numerical representation to another. From the generic formulation, programs may be developed as specific applications.

The decimal system uses as digits the 10 symbols 0, 1, 2, 3, 4, 5, 6, 7, 8, and 9. The value represented by any digit depends, as it does in any positional system of notation, both on its individual value and on its relative position in the numeral. Decimal numerals are written by placing digits in the appropriate positions or columns of the numerical sequence, *i.e.*, "unit" (10^0), "tens" (10^1), "hundreds" (10^2), "thousands" (10^3), etc. Accordingly, the numeral 1492 signifies $(1\times10^3)+(4\times10^2)+(9\times10^1)+(2\times10^0)$.

The pure binary system of positional notation uses two symbols as digits—0 and 1, placed in a numerical sequence with values based on consecutively ascending powers of 2. In pure binary notation, what would be the tens position is the twos position; what would be hundreds position is the fours position; what would be the thousands position is the eights. Any decimal number from 0 to 10 can be represented in the binary system with four digits or positions as indicated in the following table.

Shown as the sum of powers of 2

		2^3		2^2		2^1		2^0		
Decimal		*(8)*		*(4)*		*(2)*		*(1)*		*Pure Binary*
0	=	0	+	0	+	0	+	0	=	0000
1	=	0	+	0	+	0	+	2^0	=	0001
2	=	0	+	0	+	2^1	+	0	=	0010
3	=	0	+	0	+	2^1	+	2^0	=	0011
4	=	0	+	2^2	+	0	+	0	=	0100
5	=	0	+	2^2	+	0	+	2^0	=	0101
6	=	0	+	2^2	+	2^1	+	0	=	0110
7	=	0	+	2^2	+	2^1	+	2^0	=	0111
8	=	2^3	+	0	+	0	+	0	=	1000
9	=	2^3	+	0	+	0	+	2^0	=	1001
10	=	2^3	+	0	+	2^1	+	0	=	1010

The BCD System using decimal numerals replaces the character for each component decimal digit in the decimal numeral with the corresponding four-digit binary numeral, shown in the righthand column of the table. Thus decimal 53 is represented as 0101 0011 in BCD, because decimal 5 is equal to binary 0101 and decimal 3 is equivalent to binary 0011. In pure binary notation, however, decimal 53 equals binary 110101. The conversion of BCD numerals to pure binary numerals can be done mentally through use of the foregoing table. The method sought to be patented varies the ordinary arithmetic steps a human would use by changing the order of the steps, changing the symbolism for writing the multiplier used in some steps, and by taking subtotals after each successive operation. The mathematical procedures can be carried out in existing computers long in use, no new machinery being necessary. And, as noted, they can also be performed without a computer.

The Court stated in Mackay Co. v. Radio Corp., 306 U.S. 86, 94 [1939], that "[w]hile a scientific truth, or the mathematical expression of it, is not a patentable invention, a novel and useful structure created with the aid of knowledge of scientific truth may be." That statement followed the longstanding rule that "[a]n idea of itself is not patentable." "A principle, in the abstract, is a fundamental truth; an original cause; a motive; these cannot be patented, as no one can claim in either of them an exclusive right." Le Roy v. Tatham, 14 How. [55 U.S.] 156, 175 [1853]. Phenomena of nature, though just discovered, mental processes, and abstract intellectual concepts are not patentable, as they are the basic tools of scientific and technological work. As we stated in Funk Bros. Seed Co. v. Kalo Co., 333 U.S. 127, 130 [1948], "He who discovers a hitherto unknown phenomenon of nature has no claim to a monopoly of it which the law recognizes. If there is to be invention from such a discovery, it must come from the application of the law of nature to a new and useful end." We dealt there with a "product" claim, while the present case deals with a "process" claim. But we think the same principle applies.

Here the "process" claim is so abstract and sweeping as to cover both known and unknown uses of the BCD to pure binary conversion. The end use may (1) vary from the operation of a train to verification of drivers' licenses to researching the law books for precedents and (2) be performed through any existing machinery or future-devised machinery or without any apparatus.

In O'Reilly v. Morse, 15 How. [56 U.S.] 62 [1853], Morse was allowed a patent for a process of using electromagnetism to produce distinguishable signs for telegraphy. *Id.*, at 111. But the Court denied the eighth claim in which Morse claimed the use of "electro magnetism, however developed for marking or printing intelligible characters, signs, or letters, at any distances." *Id.*, at 112. The Court in disallowing that claim said, "If this claim can be maintained, it matters not by what process or machinery the result is accomplished. For aught that we now know, some future inventor, in the onward march of science, may discover a mode of writing or printing at a distance by means of the electric or galvanic current, without using any part of the process or combination set forth in the plaintiff's specification. His invention may be less complicated—less liable to get out of order—less expensive in construction, and in its operation.

But yet, if it is covered by this patent, the inventor could not use it, nor the public have the benefit of it, without the permission of this patentee." *Id.*, at 113.

In *The Telephone Cases*, 126 U.S. 1, 534 [1887], the Court explained the *Morse* case as follows: "The effect of that decision was, therefore, that the use of magnetism as a motive power, without regard to the particular process with which it was connected in the patent, could not be claimed, but that its use in that connection could." Bell's invention was the use of electric current to transmit vocal or other sounds. The claim was not "for the use of a current of electricity in its natural state as it comes from the battery, but for putting a continuous current in a closed circuit into a certain specified condition suited to the transmission of vocal and other sounds, and using it in that condition for that purpose." *Ibid.* The claim, in other words, was not "one for the use of electricity distinct from the particular process with which it is connected in his patent." *Id.*, at 535. The patent was for that use of electricity "both for the magneto and variable resistance methods." *Id.*, at 538. Bell's claim, in other words, was not one for all telephonic use of electricity.

In Corning v. Burden, 15 How. [56 U.S.] 252, 267-268 [1853], the Court said, "One may discover a new and useful improvement in the process of tanning, dyeing, etc., irrespective of any particular form of machinery or mechanical device." The examples given were the "arts of tanning, dyeing, making waterproof cloth, vulcanizing India rubber, smelting ores." *Id.*, at 267. Those are instances, however, where the use of chemical substances or physical acts, such as temperature control, changes articles or materials. The chemical process or the physical acts which transform the raw material are, however, sufficiently definite to confine the patent monopoly within rather definite bounds.

Cochrane v. Deener, 94 U.S. 780 [1876], involved a process for manufacturing flour so as to improve its quality. The process first separated the superfine flour and then removed impurities from the middlings by blasts of air, reground the middlings, and then combined the product with the superfine. *Id.*, at 785. The claim was not limited to any special arrangement of machinery. *Ibid.* The Court said,

> That a process may be patentable, irrespective of the particular form of the instrumentalities used, cannot be disputed. If one of the steps of a process be that a certain substance is to be reduced to a powder, it may not be at all material what instrument or machinery is used to effect that object, whether a hammer, a pestle and mortar, or a mill. Either may be pointed out; but if the patent is not confined to that particular tool or machine, the use of the others would be an infringement, the general process being the same. A process is a mode of treatment of certain materials to produce a given result. It is an act, or a series of acts, performed upon the subject-matter to be transformed and reduced to a different state or thing.

Id., at 787-788.

It is argued that a process patent must either be tied to a particular machine or apparatus or must operate to change articles or materials to a "different state or thing." We do not hold that no process patent could ever qualify if it did not meet the requirements of our prior precedents. It is said that the decision precludes a patent for any program servicing a computer. We do not so hold. It is said that we have before us a program for a digital computer but extend our holding to programs for analog computers. We have, however, made clear from the start that we deal with a program only for digital computers. It is said we freeze process patents to old technologies, leaving no room for the revelations of the new, onrushing technology. Such is not our purpose. What we come down to in a nutshell is the following.

It is conceded that one may not patent an idea. But in practical effect that would be the result if the formula for converting BCD numerals to pure binary numerals were patented in this case. The mathematical formula involved here has no substantial practical application except in connection with a digital computer, which means that if the judgment below is affirmed, the patent would wholly pre-empt the mathematical formula and in practical effect would be a patent on the algorithm itself.

It may be that the patent laws should be extended to cover these programs, a policy matter to which we are not competent to speak. The President's Commission on the Patent System rejected the proposal that these programs be patentable:

> Uncertainty now exists as to whether the statute permits a valid patent to be granted on programs. Direct attempts to patent programs have been rejected on the ground of nonstatutory subject matter. Indirect attempts to obtain patents and avoid the rejection, by drafting claims as a process, or a machine or components thereof programmed in a given manner, rather than as a program itself, have confused the issue further and should not be permitted. The Patent Office now cannot examine applications for programs because of a lack of a classification technique and the requisite search files. Even if these were available, reliable searches would not be feasible or economic because of the tremendous volume of prior art being generated. Without this search, the patenting of programs would be tantamount to mere registration and the presumption of validity would be all but nonexistent.
>
> It is noted that the creation of programs has undergone substantial and satisfactory growth in the absence of patent protection and that copyright protection for programs is presently available.[1]

If these programs are to be patentable, considerable problems are raised which only committees of Congress can manage, for broad powers of investigation are needed, including hearings which canvass the wide variety of views which those operating in this field entertain. The techno-

---

1. "To Promote the Progress of . . . Useful Arts," Report of the President's Commission on the Patent System 13 (1966). [—EDS.]

logical problems tendered in the many briefs before us indicate to us that considered action by the Congress is needed. Reversed.

Appendix to Opinion of the Court

Claim 8 reads:

"The method of converting signals from binary coded decimal form into binary which comprises the steps of

"(1) storing the binary coded decimal signals in a re-entrant shift register,

"(2) shifting the signals to the right by at least three places, until there is a binary 1 in the second position of said register,

"(3) masking out said binary 1 in said second position of said register,

"(4) adding a binary 1 to the first position of said register,

"(5) shifting the signals to the left by two positions,

"(6) adding a 1 to said first position, and

"(7) shifting the signals to the right by at least three positions in preparation for a succeeding binary 1 in the second position of said register."

COMMENTS AND QUESTIONS

1. Recall the idea-expression merger doctrine in copyright law, which is invoked to refuse protection to otherwise copyrightable expression if it will allow the author to effectively appropriate the idea underlying the work. Does *Benson* create a similar merger doctrine in patent law? Is this approach consistent with other patent cases?

2. Prior to the *Benson* case, the Court of Customs and Patent Appeals (CCPA) had heard eight appeals from applicants claiming computer program-related inventions. According to an in-depth analysis of these cases and other matters pertaining to *Benson*,

[a] curious thing about these eight pre-*Benson* cases is that none of them, not even the CCPA's decision in the *Benson* case, makes any more than an incidental use of the word "algorithm" in discussing the patentability issue. Hence, none of the analysis contained in these lower court decisions focused on the patentability of "algorithms." It was the Supreme Court's decision in *Benson* that shifted the focus of attention to "algorithms."

Pamela Samuelson, Benson Revisited: The Case Against Patent Protection for Algorithms and Other Computer Program-Related Inventions, 39 Emory L.J. 1025, 1042-1043 (1990). After *Benson*, Samuelson states, the case law "is focused almost exclusively on algorithms." *Id.*, at 1059.

3. Donald Chisum, the author of the authoritative patent law treatise, has criticized the *Benson* decision and called for it to be overruled. The result in the case, he argues, "stemmed from an antipatent judicial bias that cannot be reconciled with the basic elements of the patent system established by Congress." Donald Chisum, The Future of Software Protection: The Patentability of Algorithms, 47 U. Pitt. L. Rev. 959, 961 (1986). Chisum states that the "awkward distinctions and seemingly irreconcilable results of the case law since *Benson* . . . are the product of the analytical and normative weakness of *Benson* itself." *Id.*, at 961-962. Professor Chisum believes there are strong policy reasons to favor the patentability of computer algorithms.

Consider the section 101 cases outside the computer context, such as Diamond v. Chakrabarty, 447 U.S. 303 (1980). Is this a fair criticism? Has the *Benson* Court treated software differently than it does other inventions?

Some commentators argue that Chisum's proposed remedy—overruling *Benson*—has in effect been carried out already. See Thomas P. Burke, Note, Software Patent Protection: Debugging the Current System, 69 Notre Dame L. Rev. 1115, 1164 (1994) ("*Benson* has been so limited that a decision explicitly overruling it would not work a great change in the substantive law."). For more discussion of *Benson*'s subsequent treatment in the courts, see the following cases in this Section.

4. Of what value would a patent be if the inventor were limited in her claims to *existing* technology? On the other hand, what about the objection stated in the *Morse* case—that allowing Morse to patent "*any method*" of communicating via electric signals at a distance would preempt much future inventive work? Would this claim have covered microwave communication, space satellites, or fiber optics?

5. Justice Douglas writes: "Transformation and reduction of an article 'to a different state or thing' is the clue to the patentability of a process claim that does not include particular machines." What argument would you make to show that Benson's invention did this? The quoted phrase comes from Cochrane v. Deener, 94 U.S. 780 (1876), a nineteenth century case. This attempt to tie software patentability to some tangible (rather than abstract) transformation presages the direction of the caselaw after Diamond v. Diehr, excerpted below.

6. Recall this statement from Justice Douglas' opinion:

> Here the "process" claim is so abstract and sweeping as to cover both known and unknown uses of the BCD to pure binary conversion. The end use may (1) vary from the operation of a train to verification of drivers' licenses to researching the law books for precedents and (2) be performed through any existing machinery or future-devised machinery or without any apparatus.

Is this truly a section 101 objection, or is it an objection to the *scope* of the claims sought by the patentee? How are the two related? Is section 101 designed to exclude from patentability discoveries and inventions so basic and fundamental to future advances that patenting them would unduly burden future inventors? Recall the statement by Justice Douglas in *Benson* that "mental processes" (which he holds includes algorithms) represent "the basic tools of scientific and technological work." 409 U.S. at 67. Again, the thought seems to be that these inventions are so basic—have so many applications—that they are not an appropriate subject for patents.

This objection has been made with respect to software patents in general; see the excerpt from the League for Programming Freedom below. And yet if this is true, then *any* invention that has a very wide range of applications might be thought to be unpatentable. Yet these are perhaps the most valuable types of inventions!

If section 101 is not the appropriate place to address this scope problem, what is? Or is it even a problem?

Note on the "Mental Steps" Doctrine

In *Benson*, Justice Douglas states: "Phenomena of nature, though just discovered, *mental processes*, and abstract intellectual concepts are not patentable, as they are the basic tools of scientific and technological work." 409 U.S. at 67 (emphasis added). The Court's invocation of what had been known as the "mental steps" doctrine followed the lead of several software-related cases that had been decided by the CCPA prior to the 1972 decision in *Benson*. See, e.g., In re Prater, 415 F.2d 1378 (C.C.P.A. 1968), *modified on reh'g*, 415 F.2d 1393 (C.C.P.A. 1969). Indeed, the pre-*Benson* cases were primarily concerned with the application of the "mental process" or "mental steps" doctrine, and only tangentially referred to the concept of an algorithm. The mental steps doctrine was eventually repudiated by the C.C.P.A. in In re Musgrave, 431 F.2d 882 (C.C.P.A. 1970), but the Supreme Court's reference to "mental processes" in the passage above makes it unclear whether the doctrine has been entirely eliminated from current law. In any event, the issues that were debated under the banner of "mental steps" are still very much with us, so a brief review of some of the cases and concepts connected with it is in order.

In its 1968 *Prater* decision the CCPA affirmed the Patent Office's rejection of process claims for identifying the optimal set of equations for determining the gaseous composition of materials subjected to spectrographic analysis—i.e., analysis based on radiation reflected off a sample. The CCPA noted that the applicant in *Prater I* had failed to limit his claims to machine implementations of his method. If the claims were allowed, said the court, then merely working through the claimed procedure by hand or in one's head would constitute infringement. This would run afoul of the "mental steps" doctrine developed in earlier cases. See, e.g., In re Shao Wen Yuan, 188 F.2d 377 (C.C.P.A. 1951) (finding mathematical means to determine optimal profile of airfoil exhibiting desired aerodynamic characteristics not patentable); In re Heritage, 150 F.2d 554 (C.C.P.A. 1945) (finding method of color-coating fiber board not patentable because the only novel feature of the method was in its process of selecting the amount of coating material to be used); Halliburton Oil Well Cementing Co. v. Walker, 146 F.2d 817 (9th Cir. 1944) (finding method of computing to determine depth of oil well not patentable), *rev'd on other grounds,* 329 U.S. 1 (1946); Don Lee, Inc. v. Walker, 61 F.2d 58 (9th Cir. 1932) (finding formula for computing the centrifugal force of engine shafts to determine the appropriate mass and positions of counterbalances not patentable). See also Diamond v. Diehr, 450 U.S. 175, 195-196 nn.6-9 (1981) (Stevens, J., dissenting) (citing other "mental step" or mental process" cases). See generally 1 Donald Chisum, Patents §1.06[6] (1978 & Supp. 1998).

The earlier "mental steps" cases are aptly summarized by Professor Samuelson in her article, *Benson* Revisited: The Case Against Patent Protection for Algorithms and Other Computer Program-Related Inventions, 39 Emory L.J. 1025, 1034-1035 (1990):

> These decisions involved claims for patenting processes in which human beings took measurements about something, and after making calculations with data derived from these measurements, learned useful information about how to solve a problem in a technological field. The measurements, calculations, and interpretations of data are the "mental processes" or "mental steps" to which the cases refer.
>
> One of these cases, In re Abrams, endorsed a set of "rules" by which to judge processes involving mental steps. [*Abrams,* 188 F.2d at 166.] The first rule is that if a process is "purely mental," it is not patentable. The second is that if a process contains both mental and physical steps, but the advance over the prior art is found in the mental steps, it too is not patentable. The third is that if both mental and physical steps have been claimed and there is some novelty in the physical as well as the mental steps, then the process is patentable. The courts deciding *Abrams* and the other "mental process" cases, although they spoke frequently about "mental processes" and "mental steps," largely seemed to be concerned not with the "mental" character of the invention (all inventions, after all, are mental conceptions). Instead, these courts concentrated on not granting patent protection to data collection and analysis, just as the courts deciding the "printed matter" cases concentrated on not granting patent protection to data representation or presentation.

Although, as mentioned, the "mental steps" doctrine has faded into obscurity since the *Benson* case, it contains the kernel of an objection to software patents that many observers feel is very important: the sacrosanct legal status of human thinking. To claim a thought process, the objection goes, is to assert ownership over something that should simply not be owned. (Note the similarity to the "gut-level" objection many people have to patenting living organisms.) Indeed, First Amendment objections were raised in some of the earliest software patent cases—the thought being that these patents might infringe a person's right to think certain thoughts. See Samuelson, supra, at 1044 n.60 (discussing Patent Office brief in the first *Prater* case, discussed above).

A prominent computer scientist and pioneer in the field of machine or "artificial" intelligence, Professor Alan Newell, voiced this objection in a response to the article by Professor Chisum cited earlier.

> Next consider algorithms and mental steps. The main line of progress in psychology for the last thirty years (called cognitive psychology) has been to describe human behavior as computational. We model what is going on inside the thinking human brain, as the carrying out of computational steps. Therefore, humans think by means of algorithms. Sequences of mental steps and algorithms are the same thing. Any attempt in the law to make distinctions that depend upon contrasting mental steps versus algorithms is doomed to eventual confusion. It is not important whether you accept this computational view of human thinking. There can be controversy about whether such an approach is the correct one for psychology. What is important is that such a view is a major one in the study of the human mind—that many psychologists see the mind this way and that thousands of technical papers are written from within this view, covering large expanses of psychological phenomena. Any attempt to erect a patent system for algorithms that tries to distinguish algorithms as one sort of thing and mental steps as another, will ultimately end up in a quagmire.
>
> Just avoiding the use of this distinction is only half the story. *An identity between algorithms and mental steps leads to such questions as whether you can keep people from thinking patented thoughts.* You might attempt to avoid such an untenable position by invoking a doctrine of fair use. Indeed, I found the comments by Professor Chisum on the problem of fair use interesting. But the implications of this identity go much further. We are talking about people who engage in those patented thoughts daily and hourly—even every few seconds—in the pursuit of their business and who make their money and their livelihood by so doing. I expect that any doctrine of fair use would experience substantial strain under such challenges.

Newell, The Models Are Broken, The Models Are Broken!, 47 U. Pitt L. Rev. 1023, 1025 (1986) (emphasis added).

Later in the same article, Professor Newell considers a series of problems with the legal status of software patents, and comments on the problems that would attend the use of a basic algorithm that had been patented:

> [C]ertainly one might contemplate patenting addition. . . . [I]f you want actually to do addition—that requires doing a sequence of things, not to the integers, which are abstract (so you cannot do things to them anyhow), but to some representation of the integers. Doing addition is accomplished by carrying out an algorithm. If algorithms are patentable, then I can keep you from doing addition with the algorithms invented for it. There would be ever so many things that the poor would not be able to do, such as add up their grocery bill.

Id., at 1027.

COMMENTS AND QUESTIONS

1. What exactly is wrong with patenting addition? It seems strange to us, but isn't that simply because addition is so well established in the prior art? Didn't the first person to come up with the idea of addition make a significant advance for the world, one that ought to be encouraged?

2. For examples of the "printed matter" rule referred to in the preceding excerpt, see In re Rice, 132 F.2d 140 (C.C.P.A. 1942) (holding pictorial method of writing sheet music not patentable); In re Russell, 48 F.2d 668 (C.C.P.A. 1931) (holding method of arranging directories in a phonetic order not patentable); Guthrie v. Curlett, 10 F.2d 725 (2d Cir. 1926) (holding consolidated tariff index not patentable). In Boggs v. Robertson, 13 U.S.P.Q. (BNA) 214 (D.C. Cir. 1931), which involved a patent for a map projection system, the court regarded printed matter as unpatentable when it merely reduces an abstract idea to written form. See Note, The Patentability of Printed Matter: Critique and Proposal, 18 Geo. Wash. L. Rev. 475 (1950).

3. Some scholars have argued that the "mental steps" rule should be rejected. See McClaskey, The Mental Process Doctrine: Its Origin, Legal Basis, and Scope, 55 Iowa L. Rev. 1148 (1970); Comment, The Mental Steps Doctrine, 48 Tenn. L. Rev. 903 (1981).

4. In footnote 15 of *Benson*, the Court states: "The underlying notion is that a scientific principle, such as that expressed in respondent's algorithm, reveals a relationship that has always existed." This idea is explored below.

Note on the Philosophy of Protecting Algorithms: Is Mathematics Discovered or Invented?

In comparing computer algorithms to natural products and laws of nature, Justice Douglas states in *Benson*:

> Phenomena of nature, though just discovered, mental processes, and abstract intellectual concepts are not patentable, as they are the basic tools of scientific and technological work.

What view of algorithms, and mathematics as a whole, is implicit in this statement?

The debate among mathematicians on the exact nature of what they do has taken many forms. However, it is possible to simplify the various positions by marshaling them into two main groups. First are the Platonists, who believe that mathematics is a real phenomenon that is discovered by mathematicians in the course of their research. In this view, mathematicians simply discover the ordered relationships that nature has laid down.

The alternative view is that mathematics is simply a formal game that mathematicians "make up" in accordance with strict rules. According to this "formalist" theory, mathematics does not describe any underlying reality. One must simply be careful to state mathematical assertions according to the accepted "rules of the game." This view comes closer to a theory that math is "invented" by mathematicians.

One overview of the field states:

> Most writers on the subject seem to agree that the typical working mathematician is a Platonist on weekdays and a formalist on Sundays. That is, when he is doing mathematics he is convinced that he is dealing with an objective reality whose properties he is attempting to determine. But then, when challenged to give a philosophical account of this reality, he finds it easiest to pretend that he does not believe in it after all.

P. Davis & R. Hersh, The Mathematical Experience (1981).

The view that math is invented is more starkly stated in the philosophy of Imre Lakatos. Lakatos, whose Proofs and Refutations was published in 1976, sets out a theory of mathematics that places it more properly within modern traditions of the history of science. That is, Lakatos believed that mathematics grows by the criticism and corrections of theories that are never entirely free of ambiguity or the possibility of error. According to Davis and Hersh,

> [s]tarting from a problem or a conjecture, there is a simultaneous search for proofs and counterexamples. New proofs explain old counterexamples, new counterexamples undermine old proofs. To Lakatos, "proof" in this context of informal mathematics does not mean a mechanical procedure which carries truth in an unbreakable chain from assumptions to conclusions. Rather, it means explanations, justifications, elaborations which make the conjecture more plausible, more convincing, while it is being made more detailed and accurate under the pressure of counterexamples.

Davis & Hersh, supra, at 347. Note that in this passage the authors are discussing Lakatos's view of that part of mathematics that is in the process of growth and discovery rather than "settled" mathematics. However, the authors point out that "informal" or unsettled mathematics "is of course mathematics as it is known to mathematicians and students of mathematics"—that is, the most significant part of the field.

These two authors conclude that neither the Platonist nor the formalist philosophy of mathematics is ultimately satisfying. They propose instead a view of mathematics that combines the objectivity of the Platonist view with the reliance on social consensus of the formalist view:

> Mathematics is not the study of an ideal, preexisting nontemporal reality. Neither is it a chess-like game with made-up symbols and formulas. Rather, it is the part of human studies which is capable of achieving a science-like consensus, capable of establishing *reproducible* results. The existence of the sub-

ject called mathematics is a fact, not a question. This fact means no more and no less than the existence of modes of reasoning and argument about ideas which are compelling and conclusive, noncontroversial when once understood.

Davis & Hersh, supra, at 410.

Mathematics, the authors conclude, has "conclusions [that] are compelling, like the conclusions of natural science. They are not simply products of opinion, and not subject to permanent disagreement like the ideas of literary criticism." That is, while admitting that at any given time certain propositions at the frontiers of mathematics may be fallible or correctable, they deny that this makes mathematics a meaningless battle of symbols.

What does all this mean for the patent system? First of all, it sheds some light on the somewhat naive Platonism of the early Supreme Court opinions on algorithms, especially *Benson*. As Davis and Hersh point out, there is no consensus among mathematicians that they are in fact discovering a preexisting reality. Thus, the Supreme Court's treatment of algorithms—as akin to other "found" natural objects, such as products of nature—conflicts with the views that many sophisticated mathematicians seem to have of their field. Of course, these views are normally expressed only when "frontier" or pioneer mathematics is at issue; much of the applied mathematics that is the subject matter of algorithm claims would probably be considered outside the discussion of mathematical philosophy anyway. Even these applied algorithms raise some of the same philosophical problems. It must be noted, however, that since applied mathematics strives to emulate underlying physical relationships, there is a much stronger pull toward the Platonist position when this branch of mathematics is under investigation.

Perhaps this explains some of the cases we will examine. For instance, the use of the Arrhenius equation in the rubber-curing process at issue in the *Diehr* case, discussed below, is well within the realm of applied mathematics. That is, this equation tries to capture a physical relationship and state it as a "law." For the variable stated in this equation, the relationship that it sets forth will always hold. On the other hand, consider the algorithm at issue in the *Benson* case. This was a "pure" mathematical algorithm that converts binary coded decimal numerals into their binary equivalents. Since numbers of a given base (e.g., base 2 or base 10, the decimal system) do not really correspond to any physical objects, this is an algorithm that states only an abstract relationship. (Compare this to the variables in the Arrhenius equation, which stand for physical properties— pressure, heat, and so on.) Perhaps the differences between the Arrhenius equation in the *Diehr* case and the "pure" number conversion algorithm in the *Benson* case go a long way toward explaining the different outcomes of the two cases. In any event, the statements made in *Benson* about the nature of mathematics surely conflict both with the offhanded treatment of the mathematical aspects of the *Diehr* process and with the way in which mathematicians themselves view their field—or at least that part of it that deals with purely abstract matters.

This debate over the nature of mathematical algorithms is very much a part of patent law. Consider the following statements by mathematicians, quoted in the popular press:

> Unlike an industrial technology, an algorithm, the step-by-step recipe for carrying out a mathematical calculation, might seem more like something that is discovered than invented. But in the last few years, corporations have been patenting these abstract procedures, leading many mathematicians to complain that the free flow of ideas is in danger of being interrupted.
>
> "The tradition in algorithms has been that they should be free," said Ronald Rivest, a mathematician at the Massachusetts Institute of Technology, who said he had mixed feelings on the subject. "Research generally has proceeded on that basis."
>
> Michael Ian Shamos, a mathematician and computer scientist at Carnegie-Mellon University in Pittsburgh and a lawyer in private practice, said that the patenting of important algorithms is contrary to the best interests of science.
>
> "Mathematical facts are the building blocks of research," he said. "I'm an intellectual property attorney. I like patents. But the patent law was never designed to apply to algorithms. The argument that you spent lots of money developing an algorithm and therefore you should be able to protect it is nonsense."

Gina Kolata, Mathematicians Are Troubled by Claims on Their Recipes, N.Y. Times, Mar. 12, 1989, sec. 4, at 26.

L. Thorne McCarty, professor of law and computer science at Rutgers University, said: "What if the court had gone the other way in 1964 or 1965, and we had freely granted patents on algorithms? All of the basic texts" in computer science "would be under patent, and that is perhaps worrisome."

E. Andrews, Patents on Equations: Some See a Danger, N.Y. Times, Feb. 15, 1989, at D1.

COMMENTS AND QUESTIONS

1. Is there a difference between the term "algorithm" as used by mathematicians and "algorithm" in the context of computer software? The Patent Office's official position on algorithms in the 1980s included the following statement:

> Scientific principles, such as the relationship between mass and energy [$E = mc^2$], and laws of nature, such as the acceleration of gravity, namely $a = 32$ ft/sec.^{2}, can be represented in mathematical format. However, some mathematical algorithms and formulae do not represent ideas or mental processes

and are simply logical vehicles for communicating possible solutions to complex problems. See also Safe Flight Instrument Corp. v. Sundstrand Data Control, Inc., 706 F.Supp. 1146, 10 USPQ2d 1733 (D.Del. 1989) (mathematical algorithm representing a natural phenomenon, windshear). No distinction is made between mathematical algorithms invented by man, and mathematical algorithms representing discoveries of scientific principles and laws of nature which reveal a relationship that has always existed.

F. McKelvey, PTO Report on Patentable Subject Matter: Mathematical Algorithms and Computer Programs, *reprinted in* 38 Pat., Copyright & Trademark J. 563 (Sept. 21, 1989). Cf. Steven M. Santisi, Note, In re Warmerdam: When Is a Software Process Too Abstract to Merit Patent Protection?, 13 J. Marshall J. Computer & Info. L. 667 (1995) (suggesting that patentability depends on the level of abstraction at which the algorithm is implemented in software).

2. The patent office has issued a number of "pure" algorithm patents. The most notable of these are the Karmarkar patent on improvements to the "simplex method" algorithm in the field of operations research, U.S. Patent No. 4,744,028; and the Bracewell patent on the Discrete Bracewell Transform, a replacement for the Fast Fourier Transform in signal processing that does not require the use of complex numbers, U.S. Patent No. 4,646,256. Other pure algorithm patents include those issued to Diffie-Hellman and RSA for the application of large-number factoring methods in public-key cryptography.

Do the policy justifications for protecting software algorithms extend to these "pure" algorithm patents?

3. While computer programming is obviously mathematical in nature, at least in some respects, it incorporates elements from other disciplines as well. Computer programming occurs using "syntax" and "programming languages," evoking language and linguistics at least as metaphors. How should one think about patenting a new programming language? Is a programming language a mathematical algorithm or something different?

Attempts to patent software did not end in the wake of *Benson*. Perhaps encouraged by the Court's insistence that it was not precluding computer program patents entirely, computer companies continued to file applications claiming computer software in various forms. In the 1970s, most of these applications were not for what we think of today as "pure software" but instead for the use of special-purpose computers or programs in a particular industrial environment.

The Supreme Court addressed the patentability of such programs in the case of Parker v. Flook, 437 U.S. 584 (1978). The Court held that a patent on a method of updating alarm limits using a computer to monitor temperature and pressure and trigger an alarm when a certain level was reached was not patentable subject matter. The Court noted that the only novel part of the patented invention was the mathematical formula used to calculate the alarm limit, and concluded that the invention was not patentable where the "point of novelty" did not constitute patentable subject matter. Yet the Court backed away from some of the more expansive interpretations of *Benson*:

> The notion that post-solution activity, no matter how conventional or obvious in itself, can transform an unpatentable principle into a patentable process exalts form over substance. A competent draftsman could attach some form of post-solution activity to almost any mathematical formula; the Pythagorean theorem would not have been patentable, or partially patentable, because a patent application contained a final step indicating that the formula, when solved, could be usefully applied to existing surveying techniques.
>
> Yet it is equally clear that a process is not unpatentable simply because it contains a law of nature or a mathematical algorithm. For instance, in Mackay Radio & Telegraph Co. v. Radio Corp. of America, 306 U.S. 86 [1939], the applicant sought a patent on a directional antenna system in which the wire arrangement was determined by the logical application of a mathematical formula. Putting the question of patentability to one side as a preface to his analysis of the infringement issue, Mr. Justice Stone, writing for the Court, explained:
>
>> While a scientific truth, or the mathematical expression of it, is not patentable invention, a novel and useful structure created with the aid of knowledge of scientific truth may be.
>
> [This and other cases indicate that the] process itself, not merely the mathematical algorithm, must be new and useful. Indeed, the novelty of the mathematical algorithm is not a determining factor at all. Whether the algorithm was in fact known or unknown at the time of the claimed invention, as one of the "basic tools of scientific and technological work," see Gottschalk v. Benson, it is treated as though it were a familiar part of the prior art.
>
> The rule that the discovery of a law of nature cannot be patented rests, not on the notion that natural phenomena are not processes, but rather on the more fundamental understanding that they are not the kind of "discoveries" that the statute was enacted to protect. The obligation to determine what type of discovery is sought to be patented must precede the determination of whether that discovery is, in fact, new or obvious.
>
> To a large extent our conclusion is based on reasoning derived from opinions written before the modern business of developing programs for computers was conceived. The youth of the industry may explain the complete absence of precedent supporting patentability. Neither the dearth of precedent, nor this decision, should therefore be interpreted as reflecting a judgment that patent protection of certain novel and useful computer programs will not promote the progress of science and the useful arts, or that such protection is undesirable as a matter of policy. Difficult questions of policy concerning the kinds of programs that may be appropriate for patent protection and the form and duration of such protection can be answered by Congress on the basis of current empirical data not equally available to this tribunal.

COMMENTS AND QUESTIONS

1. According to Professor Samuelson, after *Flook*, "[i]ncreasingly, the [CCPA] emphasized the 'industrial' or 'transformative' character of program-related process claims under review." She goes on to state:

> [Among the] CCPA decisions typical of this new emphasis [was] the *Bradley* case. [In In re Bradley, 600 F.2d 807 (C.C.P.A. 1979)], Bradley's microcode-related invention was characterized as a new combination of tangible hardware elements, even though Bradley's claims seemed to be for a new data structure for a microprogram function. Such characterizations, which gave the claims the flavor of traditional industrial processes and hardware, enhanced the likelihood of getting positive review from the Supreme Court. Even unsuccessful claimants tended to pick up on this theme in the third post-*Benson* period and made efforts to characterize their inventions as "transformative" or technological in nature. One claimant tried to make his claim appear more technological by drafting his claims in apparatus form. [Citing In re Maucorps, 609 F.2d 481, 203 U.S.P.Q. (BNA) 812 (C.C.P.A. 1979).]

Samuelson, *Benson* Revisited, at 1089-1090.

2. One attempt to seize on the industrial/nonindustrial distinction came quite early in the history of software patents, when applicants attempted to characterize their claims as hardware claims. The thought was that a program running on a computer makes that computer a different machine because the program is a series of instructions embodied in some physical form (e.g., magnetically recorded patterns) that causes physical events inside the computer—the movement of electrons in semiconductors, for example. See In re Bernhart, 417 F.2d 1395 (C.C.P.A. 1969) (upholding the patentability of apparatus and method claims for improved way to depict three-dimensional objects in two-dimensional form). In *Bernhart* the CCPA accepted the argument that "if a machine is programmed in a certain new and unobvious way, it is physically different from the machine without that program. . . . The fact that these physical changes are invisible to the eye should not tempt us to conclude that the machine has not been changed." *Id.* at 1400.

This idea was to gain much currency in the wake of the Supreme Court's next software patent case, Diamond v. Diehr.

≡≡≡ *Diamond v. Diehr*
≡≡≡ **Supreme Court of the United States**
≡≡≡ **450 U.S. 175, 209 U.S.P.Q. (BNA) 1 (1981)**

REHNQUIST, J.

We granted certiorari to determine whether a process for curing synthetic rubber which includes in several of its steps the use of a mathematical formula and a programmed digital computer is patentable subject matter under 35 U.S.C. §101.

I

The patent application at issue was filed by the respondents on August 6, 1975. The claimed invention is a process for molding raw, uncured synthetic rubber into cured precision products. The process uses a mold for precisely shaping the uncured material under heat and pressure and then curing the synthetic rubber in the mold so that the product will retain its shape and be functionally operative after the molding is completed.[1]

Respondents claim that their process ensures the production of molded articles which are properly cured. Achieving the perfect cure depends upon several factors including the thickness of the article to be molded, the temperature of the molding process, and the amount of time that the article is allowed to remain in the press. It is possible using well-known time, temperature, and cure relationships to calculate by means of the Arrhenius equation[2] when to open the press and remove the cured product. Nonetheless, according to the respondents, the industry has not been able to obtain uniformly accurate cures because the temperature of the molding press could not be precisely measured, thus making it difficult to do the necessary computations to determine cure time. Because the temperature inside the press has heretofore been viewed as an uncontrollable variable, the conventional industry practice has been to calculate the cure time as the shortest time in which all parts of the product will definitely be cured, assuming a reasonable amount of mold-opening time during loading and unloading. But the shortcoming of this practice is that operating with an uncontrollable variable inevitably led in some instances to overestimating the mold-opening time and overcuring the rubber, and in other instances to underestimating that time and undercuring the product.

Respondents characterize their contribution to the art to reside in the process of constantly measuring the actual temperature inside the mold. These temperature measurements are then automatically fed into a computer which repeatedly recalculates the cure time by use of the Arrhenius

1. A "cure" is obtained by mixing curing agents into the uncured polymer in advance of molding, and then applying heat over a period of time. If the synthetic rubber is cured for the right length of time at the right temperature, it becomes a usable product.

2. The equation is named after its discoverer Svante Arrhenius and has long been used to calculate the cure time in rubber-molding presses. The equation can be expressed as follows:

$$\ln v = CZ + x$$

wherein $\ln v$ is the natural logarithm of v, the total required cure time; C is the activation constant, a unique figure for each batch of each compound being molded, determined in accordance with rheometer measurements of each batch; Z is the temperature in the mold; and x is a constant dependent on the geometry of the particular mold in the press. A rheometer is an instrument to measure flow of viscous substances.

equation. When the recalculated time equals the actual time that has elapsed since the press was closed, the computer signals a device to open the press. According to the respondents, the continuous measuring of the temperature inside the mold cavity, the feeding of this information to a digital computer which constantly recalculates the cure time, and the signaling by the computer to open the press, are all new in the art.

The patent examiner rejected the respondents' claims on the sole ground that they were drawn to nonstatutory subject matter under 35 U.S.C. §101.[5] . . .

II

Last Term in Diamond v. Chakrabarty, 447 U.S. 303 (1980), this Court discussed the historical purposes of the patent laws and in particular 35 U.S.C. §101. As in *Chakrabarty*, we must here construe 35 U.S.C. §101.

In cases of statutory construction, we begin with the language of the statute. Unless otherwise defined, "words will be interpreted as taking their ordinary, contemporary, common meaning," and, in dealing with the patent laws, we have more than once cautioned that "courts 'should not read into the patent laws limitations and conditions which the legislature has not expressed.'" Diamond v. Chakrabarty, supra, at 308, quoting United States v. Dubilier Condenser Corp., 289 U.S. 178, 199 (1933).

---

5. Respondents' application contained 11 different claims. [Two] examples are claims 1 [and] 2, which provide:

"1. A method of operating a rubber-molding press for precision molded compounds with the aid of a digital computer, comprising:

"providing said computer with a data base for said press including at least,

"natural logarithm conversion data (ln),

"the activation energy constant (C) unique to each batch of said compound being molded, and

"a constant (x) dependent upon the geometry of the particular mold of the press,

"initiating an interval timer in said computer upon the closure of the press for monitoring the elapsed time of said closure,

"constantly determining the temperature (Z) of the mold at a location closely adjacent to the mold cavity in the press during molding,

"constantly providing the computer with the temperature (Z),

"repetitively calculating in the computer, at frequent intervals during each cure, the Arrhenius equation for reaction time during the cure, which is

"$\ln v = CZ + x$

"where v is the total required cure time,

"repetitively comparing in the computer at said frequent intervals during the cure each said calculation of the total required cure time calculated with the Arrhenius equation and said elapsed time, and

"opening the press automatically when a said comparison indicates equivalence."

"2. The method of claim 1 including measuring the activation energy constant for the compound being molded in the press with a rheometer and automatically updating said data base within the computer in the event of changes in the compound being molded in said press as measured by said rheometer."

The Patent Act of 1793 defined statutory subject matter as "any new and useful art, machine, manufacture or composition of matter, or any new or useful improvement [thereof]." Act of Feb. 21, 1793, ch. 11, §1, 1 Stat. 318. Not until the patent laws were recodified in 1952 did Congress replace the word "art" with the word "process." It is that latter word which we confront today, and in order to determine its meaning we may not be unmindful of the Committee Reports accompanying the 1952 Act which inform us that Congress intended statutory subject matter to "include anything under the sun that is made by man." S. Rep. No. 1979, 82d Cong., 2d Sess., 5 (1952); H.R. Rep. No. 1923, 82d Cong., 2d Sess., 6 (1952).

Although the term "process" was not added to 35 U.S.C. §101 until 1952, a process has historically enjoyed patent protection because it was considered a form of "art" as that term was used in the 1793 Act.

. . . [W]e think that a physical and chemical process for molding precision synthetic rubber products falls within the §101 categories of possibly patentable subject matter. That respondents' claims involve the transformation of an article, in this case raw, uncured synthetic rubber, into a different state or thing cannot be disputed. The respondents' claims describe in detail a step-by-step method for accomplishing such, beginning with the loading of a mold with raw, uncured rubber and ending with the eventual opening of the press at the conclusion of the cure. Industrial processes such as this are the types which have historically been eligible to receive the protection of our patent laws.

III

Our conclusion regarding respondents' claims is not altered by the fact that in several steps of the process a mathematical equation and a programmed digital computer are used. This Court has undoubtedly recognized limits to §101 and every discovery is not embraced within the statutory terms. Excluded from such patent protection are laws of nature, natural phenomena, and abstract ideas. Only last Term, we explained:

[A] new mineral discovered in the earth or a new plant found in the wild is not patentable subject matter. Likewise, Einstein could not patent his celebrated law that $E=mc^2$; nor could Newton have patented the law of gravity. Such discoveries are "manifestations of . . . nature, free to all men and reserved exclusively to none."

Diamond v. Chakrabarty, 447 U.S., at 309, quoting Funk Bros. Seed Co. v. Kalo Inoculant Co., supra, at 130.

Our recent holdings in Gottschalk v. Benson, supra, and Parker v. Flook, supra, both of which are computer-related, stand for no more than these long-established principles. In *Benson*, we held unpatentable claims for an algorithm used to convert binary code decimal numbers to equivalent pure binary numbers. The sole practical application of the algorithm was in connection with the programming of a general purpose digital computer. We defined "algorithm" as a "procedure for solving a given type of mathematical problem," and we concluded that such an algorithm, or mathematical formula, is like a law of nature, which cannot be the subject of a patent.

Parker v. Flook presented a similar situation. The claims were drawn to a method for computing an "alarm limit." An "alarm limit" is simply a number and the Court concluded that the application sought to protect a formula for computing this number. Using this formula, the updated alarm limit could be calculated if several other variables were known. The application, however, did not purport to explain how these other variables were to be determined, nor did it purport "to contain any disclosure relating to the chemical processes at work, the monitoring of process variables, or the means of setting off an alarm or adjusting an alarm system. All that it provides is a formula for computing an updated alarm limit." 437 U.S., at 586.

In contrast, the respondents here do not seek to patent a mathematical formula. Instead, they seek patent protection for a process of curing synthetic rubber. Their process admittedly employs a well-known mathematical equation, but they do not seek to pre-empt the use of that equation. Rather, they seek only to foreclose from others the use of that equation in conjunction with all of the other steps in their claimed process. These include installing rubber in a press, closing the mold, constantly determining the temperature of the mold, constantly recalculating the appropriate cure time through the use of the formula and a digital computer, and automatically opening the press at the proper time. Obviously, one does not need a "computer" to cure natural or synthetic rubber, but if the computer use incorporated in the process patent significantly lessens the possibility of "overcuring" or "undercuring," the process as a whole does not thereby become unpatentable subject matter.

Our earlier opinions lend support to our present conclusion that a claim drawn to subject matter otherwise statutory does not become non-statutory simply because it uses a mathematical formula, computer program, or digital computer. In Gottschalk v. Benson we noted: "It is said that the decision precludes a patent for any program servicing a computer. We do not so hold." 409 U.S., at 71. Similarly, in Parker v. Flook we stated that "a process is not unpatentable simply because it contains a law of nature or a mathematical algorithm." 437 U.S., at 590. It is now commonplace that an *application* of a law of nature or mathematical formula to a known structure or process may well be deserving of patent protection. As Justice Stone explained four decades ago:

> While a scientific truth, or the mathematical expression of it, is not a patentable invention, a novel and useful structure created with the aid of knowledge of scientific truth may be.

Mackay Radio & Telegraph Co. v. Radio Corp. of America, 306 U.S. 86, 94 (1939).

We think this statement in *Mackay* takes us a long way toward the correct answer in this case. Arrhenius' equation is not patentable in isolation, but when a process for curing rubber is devised which incorporates in it a more efficient solution of the equation, that process is at the very least not barred at the threshold by §101.

In determining the eligibility of respondents' claimed process for patent protection under §101, their claims must be considered as a whole. It is inappropriate to dissect the claims into old and new elements and then to ignore the presence of the old elements in the analysis. This is particularly true in a process claim because a new combination of steps in a process may be patentable even though all the constituents of the combination were well known and in common use before the combination was made. The "novelty" of any element or steps in a process, or even of the process itself, is of no relevance in determining whether the subject matter of a claim falls within the §101 categories of possibly patentable subject matter.

IV

We have before us today only the question of whether respondents' claims fall within the §101 categories of possibly patentable subject matter. We view respondents' claims as nothing more than a process for molding rubber products and not as an attempt to patent a mathematical formula. We recognize, of course, that when a claim recites a mathematical formula (or scientific principle or phenomenon of nature), an inquiry must be made into whether the claim is seeking patent protection for that formula in the abstract. A mathematical formula as such is not accorded the protection of our patent laws, Gottschalk v. Benson, and this principle cannot be circumvented by attempting to limit the use of the formula to a particular technological environment. Similarly, insignificant postsolution activity will not transform an unpatentable principle into a patentable process. To hold otherwise would allow a competent draftsman to evade the recognized limitations on the type of subject matter eligible for patent protection. On the other hand, when a claim containing a mathematical formula implements or applies that formula in a structure or process which, when considered as a whole, is performing a function which the patent laws were designed to protect (*e.g.*, transforming or reducing an article to a different state or thing), then the claim satisfies the requirements of §101. Because we do not view respondents' claims as an attempt to patent a mathematical formula, but rather to be drawn to an industrial process for the molding of rubber products, we affirm the judgment of the Court of Customs and Patent Appeals.

COMMENTS AND QUESTIONS

1. Does *Diehr* overrule *Flook?*

2. In applying *Diehr* (and, to a lesser extent, *Flook*), the Court of Customs and Patent Appeals and its successor, the United States Court of Appeals for the Federal Circuit, created a two-part test for the patentability of computer programs. Under the decisions in In re Freeman, 573 F.2d 1237 (C.C.P.A. 1978), In re Walter, 618 F.2d 758 (C.C.P.A. 1980), and In re Abele, 684 F.2d 902 (C.C.P.A. 1982), the proper way to evaluate patentability was, first, to determine whether a patent claim recites an algorithm "directly or indirectly." If it did, the second part of the test asked whether the claimed invention as a whole is no more than the algorithm itself. If so, the claim must be rejected under section 101; if not, it was patentable. Under the *Freeman-Walter-Abele* test, a program could be patentable even if the only *new* idea was the algorithm itself, as long as other process steps or physical structures were included in the patent claims.

Does the *Diehr* approach, as implemented by the CCPA, exalt artful drafting above the substance of the patented invention? Is there any software program that cannot be described and claimed in terms that will meet the *Freeman-Walter-Abele* test?

In re Iwahashi, 888 F.2d 1370; 12 U.S.P.Q.2d (BNA) 1908 (Fed. Cir. 1989), centered on an invention in the field of computer pattern recognition, with special application to the recognition of human speech. The invention involves a new technique for what amounts to indexing or cataloguing discrete parts of a pattern. As it applies to speech, for instance, the invention takes as its "input" some snippet of human speech. The speech is first converted into its electronic equivalent, a waveform, which can be represented on an oscilloscope (a television-like monitor for displaying visual representations of waves). The aim of the invention is to catalogue or classify the segments of speech. In the speech recognition art, the first step in doing this is to assess certain key features of the electronic version of the speech fragment. The invention at issue assigns some of these features by means of a mathematical operation known as "autocorrelation," which essentially involves comparing snippets of speech with other snippets from the same input. The output of this mathematical operation is a series of numerical "tags" called "autocorrelation coefficients"; these are numerical values that reflect key characteristics or features of the various speech segments. By taking the speech input, breaking it up into segments, and assigning coefficients to the segments, a computer can "understand" the meaning of the speech. The specific advance of the invention is its improved method for calculating autocorrelation coefficients. In the prior art, these coefficients were calculated using a lengthy and time-consuming digital electronic circuit, which involved bulky multiplication operations. The invention at issue in the case represented a new technique—one that is much faster—for calculating these coefficients. The new technique involves looking up the square of a number in a table rather than multiplying the number by itself to get the square. This saves a good deal of calculating time, which is important in pattern recognition applications that must respond quickly to actual human inquiries or commands—that is, ones that operate in real time.

The applicant in *Iwahashi* claimed the invention in a means-plus-function format. The key claim in the case recited

[a]n auto-correlation unit . . . comprising . . . means for extracting N pieces of sampled input values . . . means for calculating the sum of the sample values . . . a read only memory associated with said means for calculating . . . means for storing in said read only memory the squared value of each sum. . . .

The court held:

Though the claim starts out by saying . . . that it is a "unit", appellants prefer to characterize what they claim as apparatus with specific structural limitations. By the Solicitor's own analysis of the claim, we are constrained to agree. Appellants emphasize that they specify a ROM . . . to which is fed an input from an adder. . . . Next are means in the form of disclosed electronic circuitry which take from the ROM its output in the form of squares of numbers supplied as ROM input and feed them to a calculating circuit. . : . The claim as a whole certainly defines apparatus in the form of a combination of interrelated means and we cannot discern any logical reason why it should not be deemed statutory subject matter as either a machine or a manufacture as specified in §101. The fact that the apparatus operates according to an algorithm does not make it nonstatutory. We therefore hold that the claim is directed to statutory subject matter.

At least one commentator criticized the reasoning in *Iwahashi*. Richard Stern argued that the court's approval of means-plus-function claims would, despite its intentions, lead patent attorneys to draft all software-related claims in this form. Richard Stern, Patenting Algorithms in America: Part I—*Benson* to *Iwahashi*, It's Deja Vu All Over Again, 8 Eur. Intellectual Prop. Rev. 292 (1990), and Richard Stern, Patenting Algorithms in America: Part II—Back from *Iwahashi*, 9 Eur. Intellectual Prop. Rev. 321 (1990) (arguing against the sort of nominal hardware limitation present in *Iwahashi* and pointing out that "means plus function" language is capable of converting any process claim into a claim for a very broad class of "structures"). Indeed, means-plus-function claims were quite common in software patents in this era, though their popularity has declined since.

While Stern seems to object to means-plus-function claims because they are too broad, there is actually good evidence that such claims may, if anything, be too narrow. See infra, where a number of cases are discussed that find noninfringement of means-plus-function claims.

3. *Diehr* seems unequivocally to endorse the industrial/nonindustrial distinction raised in the post-*Flook* cases discussed above. For this

reason, it is not surprising that patent applicants after *Diehr* began to describe their software inventions as being part of a larger machine or process. This shift is well-documented in Samuelson, *Benson* Revisited, at 1089-1090. These patentees met with considerable success: by 1994, there were an estimated 14,000 software patents issued in the United States. Most, but not all, such patents were cloaked in other terms—describing themselves as patents on processes, machines, or systems that merely happened to be implemented in software. Nonetheless, the Federal Circuit was still debating the patentability of software per se.

In re Alappat
United States Court of Appeals for the Federal Circuit
31 U.S.P.Q.2d 1545, 33 F.3d 1526 (Fed. Cir. 1994) (en banc)

RICH, J., with whom . . . as to Part II (Merits): NEWMAN, LOURIE, MICHEL, PLAGER, and RADER, JJ., join; ARCHER, C.J., and NIES, J., dissent. . . .

Kuriappan P. Alappat, Edward E. Averill, and James G. Larsen (collectively Alappat) appeal the April 22, 1992, reconsideration decision of the Board of Patent Appeals and Interferences (Board) of the United States Patent and Trademark Office (PTO), Ex Parte Alappat, 23 USPQ2d 1340 (BPAI, 1992), which sustained the Examiner's rejection of claims 15-19 of application Serial No. 07/149,792 ('792 application) as being unpatentable under 35 U.S.C. Section 101 (1988). . . .

[In Part I, the Federal Circuit held that the "reconsideration decision" was rendered by a legally constituted panel of the Board of Appeals and Interferences, and therefore the Federal Circuit could properly move to a consideration of the merits.]

II. The Merits

Our conclusion is that the appealed decision should be reversed because the appealed claims are directed to a "machine" which is one of the categories named in 35 U.S.C. Section 101, as the first panel of the Board held.

A. Alappat's Invention

Alappat's invention relates generally to a means for creating a smooth waveform display in a digital oscilloscope. The screen of an oscillosope is the front of a cathode-ray tube (CRT), which is like a TV picture tube, whose screen, when in operation, presents an array (or raster) of pixels arranged at intersections of vertical columns and horizontal rows, a pixel being a spot on the screen which may be illuminated by directing an electron beam to that spot, as in TV. Each column in the array represents a different time period, and each row represents a different magnitude. An input signal to the oscilloscope is sampled and digitized to provide a waveform data sequence (vector list), wherein each successive element of the sequence represents the magnitude of the waveform at a successively later time. The waveform data sequence is then processed to provide a bit map, which is a stored data array indicating which pixels are to be illuminated. The waveform ultimately displayed is formed by a group of vectors, wherein each vector has a straight line trajectory between two points on the screen at elevations representing the magnitudes of two successive input signal samples and at horizontal positions representing the timing of the two samples.

Because a CRT screen contains a finite number of pixels, rapidly rising and falling portions of a waveform can appear discontinuous or jagged due to differences in the elevation of horizontally contiguous pixels included in the waveform. In addition, the presence of "noise" in an input signal can cause portions of the waveform to oscillate between contiguous pixel rows when the magnitude of the input signal lies between values represented by the elevations of the two rows. Moreover, the vertical resolution of the display may be limited by the number of rows of pixels on the screen. The noticeability and appearance of these effects is known as aliasing.

To overcome these effects, Alappat's invention employs an anti-aliasing system wherein each vector making up the waveform is represented by modulating the illumination intensity of pixels having center points bounding the trajectory of the vector. The intensity at which each of the pixels is illuminated depends upon the distance of the center point of each pixel from the trajectory of the vector. Pixels lying squarely on the waveform trace receive maximum illumination, whereas pixels lying along an edge of the trace receive illumination decreasing in intensity proportional to the increase in the distance of the center point of the pixel from the vector trajectory. Employing this anti-aliasing technique eliminates any apparent discontinuity, jaggedness, or oscillation in the waveform, thus giving the visual appearance of a smooth continuous waveform. In short, and in lay terms, the invention is an improvement in an oscilloscope comparable to a TV having a clearer picture.

Reference to Fig. 5A of the '792 application, reproduced below, better illustrates the manner in which a smooth appearing waveform is created.

Each square in this figure represents a pixel, and the intensity level at which each pixel is illuminated is indicated in hexadecimal notation by the number or letter found in each square. Hexadecimal notation has sixteen characters, the numbers 0-9 and the letters *A-F,* wherein *A* represents 10, *B* represents 11, *C* represents 12, *D* represents 13, *E* represents 14, and *F* represents 15. The intensity at which each pixel is illuminated increases from 0 to *F.* Accordingly, a square with a 0 (zero) in it represents a pixel having no illumination, and a square with an *F* in it represents a pixel

FIGURE 3-1
Facsimile diagram from the '792 application.

having maximum illumination. [The hexadecimal intensity level is stored in a "bit map" in Alappat's system as a binary number.]

Points 54 and 52 in Fig. 5A represent successive observation points on the screen of an oscilliscope. Without the benefit of Alappat's anti-aliasing system, points 54 and 52 would appear on the screen as separate, unconnected spots. [That is, without Alappat's algorithm to "interpolate" between points, only the pixels labelled 54 and 52 would be illuminated on the oscilloscope screen, and none of the points in between would be illuminated.] In Alappat's system, the different intensity level at which each of the pixels is illuminated produces the appearance of the line 48, a so-called vector.

The intensity at which each pixel is to be illuminated is determined as follows, using pixel 55 as an example. First, the vertical distance between the Y coordinates of observation points 54 and 52 (ΔY_i) is determined. In this example, this difference equals 7 units, with one unit representing the center-to-center distance of adjacent pixels. Then, the elevation of pixel 55 above pixel 54 (ΔY_{ij}) is determined, which in this case is 2 units. The Y_i and Y_{ij} values are then "normalized," which Alappat describes as converting these values to larger values which are easier to use in mathematical calculations. In Alappat's example, a barrel shifter is used to shift the binary input to the left by the number of bits required to set the most significant (left-most) bit of its output signal to "1." The ΔY_i and ΔY_{ij} values are then plugged into a mathematical equation for determining the intensity at which the particular pixel is to be illuminated. In this particular example, the equation $I'(i,j) = [1 - (\Delta Y_{ij}/\Delta Y_i)]\ F$, wherein F is 15 in hexadecimal notation, suffices. The intensity of pixel 55 in this example would thus be calculated as follows: $[1 - (2/7)]15 = (5/7)15 = 10.71 = 11$ (or B).

Accordingly, pixel 55 is illuminated at 11/15 of the intensity of the pixels in which observation points 54 and 52 lie. Alappat discloses that the particular formula used will vary depending on the shape of the waveform.

B. The Rejected Claims

Claim 15, the only independent claim in issue, reads:

> A rasterizer for converting vector list data representing sample magnitudes of an input waveform into anti-aliased pixel illumination intensity data to be displayed on a display means comprising:
> (a) means for determining the vertical distance between the endpoints of each of the vectors in the data list;
> (b) means for determining the elevation of a row of pixels that is spanned by the vector;
> (c) means for normalizing the vertical distance and elevation; and
> (d) means for outputting illumination intensity data as a predetermined function of the normalized vertical distance and elevation.

Each of claims 16-19 depends directly from claim 15 and more specifically defines an element of the rasterizer claimed therein. Claim 16 recites that means (a) for determining the vertical distance between the endpoints of each of the vectors in the data list, described above, comprises an arithmetic logic circuit configured to perform an absolute value function. Claim 17 recites that means (b) for determining the elevation of a row of pixels that is spanned by the vector, j described above, comprises an arithmetic logic circuit configured to perform an absolute value function. Claim 18 recites that means (c) for normalizing the vertical distance and elevation comprises a pair of barrel shifters. Finally, claim 19 recites that means (d) for outputting comprises a read only memory (ROM) containing illumination intensity data. As the first Board panel found, each of (a)-(d) was a device known in the electronics arts before Alappat made his invention.

C. The Examiner's Rejection and Board Reviews

The Examiner's final rejection of claims 15-19 was under 35 U.S.C. Section 101 "because the claimed invention is non statutory subject matter," and the original three-member Board panel reversed this rejection. That Board panel held that, although claim 15 recites a mathematical algorithm, the claim as a whole is directed to a machine and thus to statutory subject matter named in Section 101. In reaching this decision, the original panel construed the means clauses in claim 15 pursuant to 35 U.S.C. Section 112, paragraph six (Section 112 Para. 6), as corresponding to the respective structures disclosed in the specification of Alappat's application, and equivalents thereof.

In its reconsideration decision, the five member majority of the expanded, eight-member Board panel "modified" the decision of the original panel and affirmed the Examiner's Section 101 rejection. The majority held that the PTO need not apply Section 112 Para. 6 in rendering patentability determinations, characterizing this court's statements to the contrary in In re Iwahashi, 888 F.2d 1370, 1375, 12 USPQ2d 1908, 1912 (Fed. Cir. 1989), "as dicta," and dismissing this court's discussion of Section 112 Para. 6 in Arrhythmia Research Technology, Inc. v. Corazonix Corp., 958 F.2d 1053, 1060, 22 USPQ2d 1033, 1038 (Fed. Cir. 1992) on the basis that the rules of claim construction in infringement actions differ from the rules for claim interpretation during prosecution in the PTO. The majority stated that, during examination, the PTO gives means-plus-function clauses in claims their broadest interpretation and does not impute limitations from the specification into the claims. See Applicability of the Last Paragraph of 35 USC Section 112 to Patentability Determinations Before the Patent and Trademark Office, 1134 TMOG 633 (1992); Notice Interpreting In Re Iwahashi (Fed. Cir. 1989), 1112 OG 16 (1990). Accordingly, the majority held that each of the means recited in claim 15 reads on any and every means for performing the particular function recited.

The majority further held that, because claim 15 is written completely in "means for" language and because these means clauses are read broadly in the PTO to encompass each and every means for performing the recited functions, claim 15 amounts to nothing more than a process claim wherein each means clause represents only a step in that process. The majority stated that each of the steps in this postulated process claim recites a mathematical operation, which steps combine to form a "mathematical algorithm for computing pixel information," *Alappat*, 23 USPQ2d at 1345, and that, "when the claim is viewed without the steps of this mathematical algorithm, no other elements or steps are found." *Alappat*, 23 USPQ2d at 1346. The majority thus concluded that the claim was directed to nonstatutory subject matter.

In its analysis, the majority further stated:

> It is further significant that claim 15, as drafted, reads on a digital computer "means" to perform the various steps under program control. In such a case, it is proper to treat the claim as if drawn to a method. We will not presume that a stored program digital computer is not within the Section 112 Para. 6 range of equivalents of the structure disclosed in the specification.

The disclosed ALU, ROM and shift registers are all common elements of stored program digital computers. Even if appellants were willing to admit that a stored program digital computer were not within the range of equivalents, Section 112 Para. 2 requires that this be clearly apparent from the claims based upon limitations recited in the claims.

Alappat, 23 USPQ2d at 1345. The Board majority also stated that dependent claims 16-19 were not before them for consideration because they had not been argued by Alappat and thus not addressed by the Examiner or the original three-member Board panel. *Alappat*, 23 USPQ2d at 1341 n.1.

D. Analysis

(1) Section 112, Paragraph Six

As recently explained in In re Donaldson, 16 F.3d 1189, 1193, 29 USPQ2d 1845, 1050 (Fed. Cir. 1994), the PTO is not exempt from following the statutory mandate of Section 112 Para. 6, which reads:

> An element in a claim for a combination may be expressed as a means or step for performing a specified function without the recital of structure, material, or acts in support thereof, and such claim shall be construed to cover the corresponding structure, material, or acts described in the specification and equivalents thereof.

35 U.S.C. Section 112, paragraph 6 (1988). The Board majority therefore erred as a matter of law in refusing to apply Section 112 Para. 6 in rendering its Section 101 patentable subject matter determination.

Given Alappat's disclosure, it was error for the Board majority to interpret each of the means clauses in claim 15 so broadly as to "read on any and every means for performing the functions" recited, as it said it was doing, and then to conclude that claim 15 is nothing more than a process claim wherein each means clause represents a step in that process. Contrary to suggestions by the Commissioner, this court's precedents do not support the Board's view that the particular apparatus claims at issue in this case may be viewed as nothing more than process claims. . . .

When independent claim 15 is construed in accordance with Section 112 Para. 6, claim 15 reads as follows, the subject matter in brackets representing the structure which Alappat discloses in his specification as corresponding to the respective means language recited in the claims:

> A rasterizer [a "machine"] for converting vector list data representing sample magnitudes of an input waveform into anti-aliased pixel illumination intensity data to be displayed on a display means comprising:

(a) [an arithmetic logic circuit configured to perform an absolute value function, or an equivalent thereof] for determining the vertical distance between the endpoints of each of the vectors in the data list;

(b) [an arithmetic logic circuit configured to perform an absolute value function, or an equivalent thereof] for determining the elevation of a row of pixels that is spanned by the vector;

(c) [a pair of barrel shifters, or equivalents thereof] for normalizing the vertical distance and elevation; and

(d) [a read-only memory (ROM) containing illumination intensity data, or an equivalent thereof] for outputting illumination intensity data as a predetermined function of the normalized vertical distance and elevation.

As is evident, claim 15 unquestionably recites a machine, or apparatus, made up of a combination of known electronic circuitry elements.

Despite suggestions by the Commissioner to the contrary, each of dependent claims 16-19 serves to further limit claim 15. Section 112 Para. 6 requires that each of the means recited in independent claim 15 be construed to cover at least the structure disclosed in the specification corresponding to the "means." Each of dependent claims 16-19 is in fact limited to one of the structures disclosed in the specification.

(2) Section 101

The reconsideration Board majority affirmed the Examiner's rejection of claims 15-19 on the basis that these claims are not directed to statutory subject matter as defined in Section 101. . . . As discussed . . . supra, claim 15, properly construed, claims a machine, namely, a rasterizer "for converting vector list data representing sample magnitudes of an input waveform into anti-aliased pixel illumination intensity data to be displayed on a display means," which machine is made up of, at the very least, the specific structures disclosed in Alappat's specification corresponding to the means-plus-function elements (a)-(d) recited in the claim. According to Alappat, the claimed rasterizer performs the same overall function as prior art rasterizers, but does so in a different way, which is represented by the combination of four elements claimed in means-plus-function terminology. Because claim 15 is directed to a "machine," which is one of the four categories of patentable subject matter enumerated in Section 101, claim 15 appears on its face to be directed to Section 101 subject matter.

This does not quite end the analysis, however, because the Board majority argues that the claimed subject matter falls within a judicially created exception to Section 101 which the majority refers to as the "mathematical algorithm" exception. Although the PTO has failed to support the premise that the "mathematical algorithm" exception applies to true apparatus claims, we recognize that our own precedent suggests that this may be the case. . . . Even if the mathematical subject matter exception to Section 101 does apply to true apparatus claims, the claimed subject matter in this case does not fall within that exception.

(a)

The plain and unambiguous meaning of Section 101 is that any new and useful process, machine, manufacture, or composition of matter, or any new and useful improvement thereof, may be patented if it meets the requirements for patentability set forth in Title 35, such as those found in Sections 102, 103, and 112. The use of the expansive term "any" in Section 101 represents Congress's intent not to place any restrictions on the subject matter for which a patent may be obtained beyond those specifically recited in Section 101 and the other parts of Title 35. Indeed, the Supreme Court has acknowledged that Congress intended Section 101 to extend to "anything under the sun that is made by man." Diamond v. Chakrabarty, 447 U.S. 303, 309 (1980). . . . Thus, it is improper to read into Section 101 limitations as to the subject matter that may be patented where the legislative history does not indicate that Congress clearly intended such limitations. . . .

Despite the apparent sweep of Section 101, the Supreme Court has held that certain categories of subject matter are not entitled to patent protection. In *Diehr*, its most recent case addressing Section 101, the Supreme Court explained that there are three categories of subject matter for which one may not obtain patent protection, namely "laws of nature, natural phenomena, and abstract ideas." *Diehr*, 450 U.S. at 185. Of relevance to this case, the Supreme Court also has held that certain mathematical subject matter is not, standing alone, entitled to patent protection. . . . A close analysis of *Diehr*, *Flook*, and *Benson* reveals that the Supreme Court never intended to create an overly broad, fourth category of subject matter excluded from Section 101. Rather, at the core of the Court's analysis in each of these cases lies an attempt by the Court to explain a rather straightforward concept, namely, that certain types of mathematical subject matter, standing alone, represent nothing more than abstract ideas until reduced to some type of practical application, and thus that subject matter is not, in and of itself, entitled to patent protection. . . .

(b)

Given the foregoing, the proper inquiry in dealing with the so called mathematical subject matter exception to Section 101 alleged herein is to see whether the claimed subject matter as a whole is a disembodied mathematical concept, whether categorized as a mathematical formula, mathematical equation, mathematical algorithm, or the like, which in essence represents nothing more than a "law of nature," "natural phenomenon," or "abstract idea." If so, *Diehr* precludes the patenting of that subject matter. That is not the case here.

Although many, or arguably even all, of the means elements recited in claim 15 represent circuitry elements that perform mathematical calculations, which is essentially true of all digital electrical circuits, the claimed invention as a whole is directed to a combination of interrelated elements which combine to form a machine for converting discrete waveform data samples into anti-aliased pixel illumination intensity data to be displayed on a display means. This is not a disembodied mathematical concept which may be characterized as an "abstract idea," but rather a specific machine to produce a useful, concrete, and tangible result.

The fact that the four claimed means elements function to transform one set of data to another through what may be viewed as a series of mathematical calculations does not alone justify a holding that the claim as a whole is directed to nonstatutory subject matter. See In re Iwahashi, 888 F.2d at 1375, 12 USPQ2d at 1911. Indeed, claim 15 as written is not "so abstract and sweeping" that it would "wholly pre-empt" the use of any apparatus employing the combination of mathematical calculations recited therein. See *Benson*, 409 U.S. at 68-72 (1972). Rather, claim 15 is limited to the use of a particularly claimed combination of elements performing the particularly claimed combination of calculations to transform, i.e., rasterize, digitized waveforms (data) into anti-aliased, pixel illumination data to produce a smooth waveform.

Furthermore, the claim preamble's recitation that the subject matter for which Alappat seeks patent protection is a rasterizer for creating a smooth waveform is not a mere field-of-use label having no significance. Indeed, the preamble specifically recites that the claimed rasterizer converts waveform data into output illumination data for a display, and the means elements recited in the body of the claim make reference not only to the inputted waveform data recited in the preamble but also to the output illumination data also recited in the preamble. Claim 15 thus defines a combination of elements constituting a machine for producing an anti-aliased waveform.

The reconsideration Board majority also erred in its reasoning that claim 15 is unpatentable merely because it "reads on a general purpose digital computer 'means' to perform the various steps under program control." *Alappat*, 23 USPQ2d at 1345. The Board majority stated that it would "not presume that a stored program digital computer is not within the Section 112 Para. 6 range of equivalents of the structure disclosed in the specification." *Alappat*, 23 USPQ2d at 1345. Alappat admits that claim 15 would read on a general purpose computer programmed to carry out the claimed invention, but argues that this alone also does not justify holding claim 15 unpatentable as directed to nonstatutory subject matter. We agree. We have held that such programming creates a new machine, because a general purpose computer in effect becomes a special purpose computer once it is programmed to perform particular functions pursuant to instructions from program software. In re Freeman, 573 F.2d 1237, 1247 n.11, 197 USPQ 464, 472 n.11 (CCPA 1978); In re Noll, 545 F.2d 141, 148, 191 USPQ 721, 726 (CCPA 1976); In re Prater, 415 F.2d at 1403 n.29, 162 USPQ at 549-50 n.29.

Under the Board majority's reasoning, a programmed general purpose computer could never be viewed as patentable subject matter under Section 101. This reasoning is without basis in the law. The Supreme Court has never held that a programmed computer may never be entitled to patent protection. Indeed, the *Benson* court specifically stated that its decision therein did not preclude "a patent for any program servicing a computer." *Benson*, 409 U.S. at 71. Consequently, a computer operating pursuant to software may represent patentable subject matter, provided, of course, that the claimed subject matter meets all of the other requirements of Title 35. In any case, a computer, like a rasterizer, is apparatus not mathematics.

Conclusion

For the foregoing reasons, the appealed decision of the Board affirming the examiner's rejection is
REVERSED.

ARCHER, C.J., with whom NIES, J., joins, concurring in part and dissenting in part. . . .

I disagree with the majority's conclusion that Alappat's "rasterizer," which is all that is claimed in the claims at issue, constitutes an invention or discovery within 35 U.S.C. Section 101. I would affirm the board's decision sustaining the examiner's rejection of claims 15-19 to the rasterizer under 35 U.S.C. Section 101 because Alappat has not shown that he invented or discovered a machine within Section 101.

In 1873, George Curtis made certain general observations about patent law, the scope of patentable subject matter being at its heart. He stated them with such force and eloquence, and in my view they have such relevance to the issue we face today, that I repeat them as follows:

> It is necessary . . . to have clear and correct notions of the true scope of a patent right . . . which may be found to assist, in particular cases, the solution of the question, whether a particular invention or discovery is by law a patentable subject.
>
> In this inquiry it is necessary to commence with the process of exclusion; for although, in their widest acceptation, the terms "invention" and "discovery" include the whole vast variety of objects on which the human intellect may be exercised, so that in poetry, in painting, in music, in astronomy, in metaphysics, and in every department of human thought, men constantly invent or discover, in the highest and the strictest sense, their inventions and discoveries in these departments are not the subjects of the patent law. . . . The patent law relates to a great and comprehensive class of discoveries and inventions of some new and useful effect or result in matter, not referable to the department of the fine arts. The matter of which our globe is composed is the material upon which the creative and inventive faculties of man are exercised, in the production of whatever ministers to his

convenience or his wants. Over the existence of matter itself he has no control. . . .

The direct control of man over matter consists, therefore, in placing its particles in new relations. This is all that is actually done, or that can be done, namely, to cause the particles of matter existing in the universe to change their former places, by moving them, by muscular power or some other force. But as soon as they are brought into new relations, it is at once perceived that there are vast latent forces in nature, which come to the aid of man, and enable him to produce effects and results of a wholly new character, far beyond the mere fact of placing the particles in new positions. He moves certain particles of matter into a new juxtaposition, and the chemical agencies and affinities called into action by this new contact produce a substance possessed of new properties and powers, to which has been given the name of gunpowder. He takes a stalk of flax from the ground, splits it into a great number of filaments, twists them together, and laying numbers of the threads thus formed across each other, forms a cloth, which is held together by the tenacity or force of cohesion in the particles, which nature brings to his aid. He moves into new positions and relations certain particles of wood and iron, in various forms, and produces a complicated machine, by which he is able to accomplish a certain purpose, only because the properties of cohesion and the force of gravitation cause it to adhere together and enable the different parts to operate upon each other and to transmit the forces applied to them, according to the laws of motion. It is evident, therefore, that the whole of the act of invention, in the department of useful arts, embraces more than the new arrangement of particles of matter in new relations. The purpose of such new arrangements is to produce some new effect or result, by calling into activity some latent law, or force, or property, by means of which, in a new application, the new effect or result may be accomplished. In every form in which matter is used, in every production of the ingenuity of man, he relies upon the laws of nature and the properties of matter, and seeks for new effects and results through their agency and aid. Merely inert matter alone is not the sole material with which he works. Nature supplies powers, and forces, and active properties, as well as the particles of matter, and these powers, forces, and properties are constantly the subjects of study, inquiry, and experiment, with a view to the production of some new effect or result in matter.

Any definition or description, therefore, of the act of invention, which excludes the application of the natural law, or power, or property of matter, on which the inventor has relied for the production of a new effect, and the object of such application, and confines it to the precise arrangement of the particles of matter which he may have brought together, must be erroneous.

G. Curtis, A Treatise on the Law of Patents for Useful Inventions at xxiii-xxv (4th ed. 1873). . . .

Alappat has arranged known circuit elements to accomplish nothing other than the solving of a particular mathematical equation represented in the mind of the reader of his patent application. Losing sight of the forest for the structure of the trees, the majority today holds that any claim reciting a precise arrangement of structure satisfies 35 U.S.C. Section 101. As I shall demonstrate, the rationale that leads to this conclusion and the majority's holding that Alappat's rasterizer represents the invention of a machine are illogical, inconsistent with precedent and with sound principles of patent law, and will have untold consequences.

B.

. . . The terms used in Section 101 have been used for over two hundred years—since the beginnings of American patent law—to define the extent of the subject matter of patentable invention. . . . Coexistent with the usage of these terms has been the rule that a person cannot obtain a patent for the discovery of an abstract idea, principle or force, law of nature, or natural phenomenon, but rather must invent or discover a practical "application" to a useful end. Diamond v. Diehr. . . .

Thus patent law rewards persons for inventing technologically useful applications, instead of for philosophizing unapplied research and theory. . . .

Additionally, unapplied research, abstract ideas, and theory continue to be the "basic tools of scientific and technological work," which persons are free to trade in and to build upon in the pursuit of among other things useful inventions. *Flook*, 437 U.S. at 589, 198 USPQ at 197 (quotations omitted). Even after a patent has been awarded for a new, useful, and nonobvious practical application of an idea, others may learn from the underlying ideas, theories, and principles to legitimately "design around" the patentee's useful application. See Slimfold Mfg. Co. v. Kinkead Indus., Inc., 932 F.2d 1453, 1457, 18 USPQ2d 1842, 1845-46 (Fed. Cir. 1991). . . .

In addition to the basic principles embodied in the language of Section 101, the section has a pragmatic aspect. That subject matter must be new (Section 102) and nonobvious (Section 103) in order to be patentable is of course a separate requirement for patentability, and does not determine whether the applicant's purported invention or discovery is within Section 101. . . . Section 101 must be satisfied before any of the other provisions apply, and in this way Section 101 lays the predicate for the other provisions of the patent law. . . . When considering that the patent law does not allow patents merely for the discovery of ideas, principles, and laws of nature, ask whether, were it not so, the other provisions of the patent law could be applied at all. If Einstein could have obtained a patent for his discovery that the energy of an object at rest equals its mass times the speed of light squared, how would his discovery be meaningfully judged for nonobviousness, the sine qua non of patentable invention? 35 U.S.C. Section 103. When is the abstract idea "reduced to practice" as opposed to being "conceived"? See *id.* Section 102(g). What conduct amounts to the "infringement" of another's idea? See *id.* Section 271. . . .

Consider for example the discovery or creation of music, a new song. Music of course is not patentable subject matter; a composer cannot obtain exclusive patent rights for the original creation of a musical composition. But now suppose the new melody is recorded on a compact disc. In such case, the particular musical composition will define an arrangement of minute pits in the surface of the compact disc material, and therefore will define its specific structure. See D. Macaulay, The Way Things Work 248-49 (Houghton Mifflin 1988). Alternatively suppose the music is recorded on the rolls of a player piano or a music box.

Through the expedient of putting his music on known structure, can a composer now claim as his invention the structure of a compact disc or player piano roll containing the melody he discovered and obtain a patent therefor? The answer must be no. The composer admittedly has invented or discovered nothing but music. The discovery of music does not become patentable subject matter simply because there is an arbitrary claim to some structure.

And if a claim to a compact disc or piano roll containing a newly discovered song were regarded as a "manufacture" and within Section 101 simply because of the specific physical structure of the compact disc, the "practical effect" would be the granting of a patent for a discovery in music. Where the music is new, the precise structure of the disc or roll would be novel under Section 102. Because the patent law cannot examine music for "nonobviousness," the Patent and Trademark Office could not make a showing of obviousness under Section 103. The result would well be the award of a patent for the discovery of music. The majority's simplistic approach of looking only to whether the claim reads on structure and ignoring the claimed invention or discovery for which a patent is sought will result in the awarding of patents for discoveries well beyond the scope of the patent law. . . .

So what did Alappat invent or discover? Alappat's specification clearly distinguishes between an "oscilloscope" and a "rasterizer," and Alappat claims his invention in claims 15-19 to be only the "rasterizer."

The "rasterizer" as claimed is an arrangement of circuitry elements for converting data into other data according to a particular mathematical operation. The rasterizer begins with vector "data"—two numbers. [Appellants claim that] "it does not matter how they are ascertained." The two numbers, as they might to any algebra student, "represent" endpoints of a line.

The claimed "rasterizer" ends with other specific "data"—an array of numbers, as the original and reconsideration panels of the board both expressly agreed. . . .

Alappat admits that each of the circuitry elements of the claimed "rasterizer" is old. He says they are merely "form." Thus, they are only a convenient and basic way of electrically representing the mathematical operations to be performed, that is, converting vector data into matrix or raster data. In Alappat's view, it is the new mathematic operation that is the "substance" of the claimed invention or discovery. Claim 15 as a whole thus claims old circuitry elements in an arrangement defined by a mathematical operation, which only performs the very mathematical operation that defines it. Rather than claiming the mathematics itself, which of course Alappat cannot do, Alappat claims the mathematically defined structure. But as a whole, there is no "application" apart from the mathematical operation that is asserted to be the invention or discovery. What is going on here is a charade. . . .

COMMENTS AND QUESTIONS

1. Does Alappat's invention—essentially, interpolating between points to display a line on an oscilloscope's screen—seem straightforward? Does the Federal Circuit say that this invention deserves a patent? What is the precise legal holding of the opinion?

Certain language in *Alappat* suggests an extremely broad reading of section 101. The court acknowledges that Alappat's claims will read on "a general purpose computer programmed to carry out the claimed invention," but says that the claim is nonetheless patentable because "such programming creates a new machine, because a general purpose computer in effect becomes a special purpose computer once it is programmed to perform particular functions pursuant to instructions from programmed software." Is there any program for which this is not true? What remains of the section 101 limitation in light of this language?

2. In one portion of one of the many omitted opinions, Judge Pauline Newman, concurring on the merits, states: "Mathematics is not a monster to be struck down or out of the patent system, but simply another resource whereby technological advance is achieved." In re Alappat, 33 F.3d 1526, 31 U.S.P.Q.2d 1545, 1579 (Newman, J., concurring). Is this sentiment inconsistent with the view taken in *Benson*? How about in *Diehr*? What is the difference between (1) pure mathematics; (2) applied mathematics, as that term is used in mathematics department course catalogs; and (3) mathematics applied to solve a problem in the real world?

Note on Post-*Alappat* Developments

Alappat is by no means the last word on software patents from the Federal Circuit. Several cases decided shortly after the en banc decision in *Alappat* suggested that the Federal Circuit remained deeply divided on this issue. For example, late in 1994 a three-judge panel invalidated method (process) and means-plus-function claims to a technique in "graph theory" for determining the shortest (or cheapest) path between two points. In re Trovato, 42 F.3d 1376 (Fed. Cir. 1994). In the panel's view,

[u]nlike the invention claimed in *Diehr*, the specifications involved here provide no grasp of any underlying physical process. Although cursory references

to such diverse apparatus as robots, dynamic emergency exit routes and electronic maps are present, no computer architecture is provided, no circuit diagram is revealed, and no hardware at all receives more than a brief mention. Indeed, the specifications note the inventions' "general applicability to numerical methods" and seek to describe them "[f]rom a mathematical point of view." When questioned during oral argument before this Court, counsel for Trovato admitted that neither specification includes a hardware enablement of the claimed invention. Instead, the entire disclosure consists of flow charts and program code computing the least cost path from starting to goal states based upon the data in the configuration space. We therefore conclude that Trovato claims nothing more than the process of performing a numerical calculation. Simply stated, viewing the claims absent the algorithm, and as a whole, no statutory subject matter is present. . . .

Although some of Trovato's claims describe an electronic readout of the computed data, it is well established that mere post-solution display does not render patentable a mathematical algorithm. As our predecessor court noted in *Walter*, "[i]f Section 101 could be satisfied by the mere recordation of the results of a nonstatutory process on some record medium, even the most unskilled patent draftsman could provide for such a step." . . . Nor do Trovato's applications describe inventions which manipulate physical qualities, as with the inventions held to fall within statutory subject matter in cases such as *Arrhythmia* [Research Technology Inc. v. Corazonix Corp., 958 F.2d 1053, (Fed. Cir. 1992)]. . . . Indeed, the claimed invention does not even take the actual step of gathering the data from the "physical task space" that is arranged into the recited "configuration space data structure," a procedure which in itself cannot render an otherwise nonstatutory subject matter patentable. . . .

Trovato's applications fail even to explain how the claimed inventions actually employ the numbers derived to control movement. Although the inventions likely employ techniques known to the art to move an object along the lowest cost path it calculates, the absence of even a cursory description of how the computed values are implemented further indicates that the claimed methods comprise only numerical manipulation.

Does the *Trovato* panel succeed in distinguishing this case from *Alappat*? A majority of the Federal Circuit apparently thought not: in July 1995, the court sitting en banc vacated the panel opinion in *Trovato* and remanded the case to the PTO for further proceedings consistent with *Alappat*. In re Trovato, 60 F.3d 807 (Fed. Cir. 1995) (en banc).

While this rather unusual step might suggest an emerging consensus in support of *Alappat*'s broad reading of section 101, other cases leave the outcome in doubt. Two cases decided just after *Alappat* differed over the patentability of data structures, an issue not directly presented in *Alappat* but certainly related to it. Compare In re Lowry, 32 F.3d 1579 (Fed. Cir. 1994) (upholding as patentable abstract claims to a type of software data structure wherein data "objects" are arranged in complex relationships) with In re Warmerdam, 33 F.3d 1354 (Fed. Cir. 1994) (affirming rejection of process claims to data structure for representing proximity and shape of objects in the immediate environment—e.g., for use by a mobile machine with robot vision, and based on idea of representing objects in computer memory as increasingly fine-grained "bubbles"). See also In re Schraeder, 22 F.3d 290 (Fed. Cir. 1994) (holding unpatentable claims to method for competitively bidding on plurality of related items, such as contiguous tracts of land, since mathematical algorithm is implicit in claim, and since algorithm is not applied to or limited by physical elements or process steps: mere entering of bids in "record" is insufficient to impart patentability under the cases); Schlafly v. Public Key Partners, 155 F.3d 565 (Fed. Cir. 1998) (unpublished) (following *Alappat*, holding that a claim to an algorithm drafted in means-plus-function format does not preempt the use of that algorithm).

In 1995, IBM appealed the PTO's rejection of a claim to "software contained on a floppy disk" to the Federal Circuit. See In re Beauregard, 53 F.3d 1583 (Fed. Cir. 1995). While the appeal was pending, the PTO decided not to oppose the claim and promised the court that it would shortly issue new examining guidelines for software patents. After several false starts, the PTO did issue final Examination Guidelines for Computer-Implemented Inventions in January of 1996. These Guidelines direct examiners as follows:

> The subject matter courts have found to be outside the four statutory categories of invention is limited to abstract ideas, laws of nature and natural phenomena. While this is easily stated, determining whether an applicant is seeking to patent an abstract idea, a law of nature or a natural phenomenon has proven to be challenging. These three exclusions recognize that subject matter that is not a *practical application or use* of an idea, a law of nature or a natural phenomenon is not patentable. . . .
>
> Claims to computer-related inventions that are clearly non-statutory fall into the same general categories as non-statutory claims in other arts, namely natural phenomena such as magnetism, and abstract ideas or laws of nature which constitute "descriptive material." Descriptive material can be characterized as either "functional descriptive material" or "non-functional descriptive material." In this context, "functional descriptive material" consists of data structures and computer programs which impart functionality when encoded on a computer-readable medium. "Non-functional descriptive material" includes but is not limited to music, literary works and a compilation or mere arrangement of data.
>
> Both types of "descriptive material" are non-statutory when claimed as descriptive material *per se*. When functional descriptive material is recorded on some computer-readable medium it becomes structurally and functionally interrelated to the medium and will be statutory in most cases. When non-functional descriptive material is recorded on some computer-readable medium, it is not structurally and functionally interrelated to the medium but is merely carried by the medium. Merely claiming non-functional descriptive material stored in a computer-readable medium does not make it statutory. Such a result would exalt form over substance. Thus, non-statutory music does not become statutory by merely recording it on a compact disk. Protection for this type of work is provided under the copyright law. . . .

Data structures not claimed as embodied in computer-readable media are descriptive material *per se* and are not statutory because they are neither physical "things" nor statutory processes. Such claimed data structures do not define any structural and functional interrelationships between the data structure and other claimed aspects of the invention which permit the data structure's functionality to be realized. In contrast, a claimed computer-readable medium encoded with a data structure defines structural and functional interrelationships between the data structure and the medium which permit the data structure's functionality to be realized, and is thus statutory.

Similarly, computer programs claimed as computer listings *per se*, *i.e.*, the descriptions or expressions of the programs, are not physical "things," nor are they statutory processes, as they are not "acts" being performed. Such claimed computer programs do not define any structural and functional interrelationships between the computer program and other claimed aspects of the invention which permit the computer program's functionality to be realized. In contrast, a claimed computer-readable medium encoded with a computer program defines structural and functional interrelationships between the computer program and the medium which permit the computer program's functionality to be realized, and is thus statutory. Accordingly, it is important to distinguish claims that define descriptive material *per se* from claims that define statutory inventions. . . .

Since a computer program is merely a set of instructions capable of being executed by a computer, the computer program itself is not a process and Office personnel should treat a claim for a computer program, without the computer-readable medium needed to realize the computer program's functionality, as non-statutory functional descriptive material. When a computer program is claimed in a process where the computer is executing the computer program's instructions, Office personnel should treat the claim as a process claim. When a computer program is recited in conjunction with a physical structure, such as a computer memory, Office personnel should treat the claim as a product claim. . . .

Where certain types of descriptive material, such as music, literature, art, photographs and mere arrangements or compilations of facts or data, are merely stored so as to be read or outputted by a computer without creating any functional interrelationship, either as part of the stored data or as part of the computing processes performed by the computer, then such descriptive material alone does not impart functionality either to the data as so structured, or to the computer. Such "descriptive material" is not a process, machine, manufacture or composition of matter.

The policy that precludes the patenting of non-functional descriptive material would be easily frustrated if the same descriptive material could be patented when claimed as an article of manufacture. For example, music is commonly sold to consumers in the format of a compact disc. In such cases, the known compact disc acts as nothing more than a carrier for non-functional descriptive material. The purely non-functional descriptive material cannot alone provide the practical application for the manufacture.

Office personnel should be prudent in applying the foregoing guidance. Non-functional descriptive material may be claimed in combination with other functional descriptive material on a computer-readable medium to provide the necessary functional and structural interrelationship to satisfy the requirements of §101. The presence of the claimed non-functional descriptive material is not necessarily determinative of non-statutory subject matter. For example, a computer that recognizes a particular grouping of musical notes read from memory and upon recognizing that particular sequence, causes another defined series of notes to be played, defines a functional interrelationship among that data and the computing processes performed when utilizing that data, and as such is statutory because it implements a statutory process. . . .

Office personnel must treat each claim as a whole. The mere fact that a hardware element is recited in a claim does not necessarily limit the claim to a specific machine or manufacture. If a product claim encompasses *any and every* computer implementation of a process, when read in light of the specification, it should be examined on the basis of the underlying process. Such a claim can be recognized as it will:

- define the physical characteristics of a computer or computer component exclusively as functions or steps to be performed on or by a computer, and
- encompass *any and every* product in the stated class (*e.g.*, computer, computer-readable memory) *configured in any manner* to perform that process.

. . . If a claim is found to encompass any and every product embodiment of the underlying process, and if the underlying process is statutory, the product claim should be classified as a statutory product. By the same token, if the underlying process invention is found to be non-statutory, Office personnel should classify the "product" claim as a "non-statutory product." If the product claim is classified as being a non-statutory product on the basis of the underlying process, Office personnel should emphasize that they have considered all claim limitations and are basing their finding on the analysis of the underlying process. . . .

A claim that requires one or more acts to be performed defines a process. However, not all processes are statutory under §101. To be statutory, a claimed computer-related process must either: (1) result in a physical transformation outside the computer for which a practical application in the technological arts is either disclosed in the specification or would have been known to a skilled artisan (discussed in (i) below), or (2) be limited by the language in the claim to a practical application within the technological arts (discussed in (ii) below). The claimed practical application must be a further limitation upon the claimed subject matter if the process is confined to the internal operations of the computer. If a physical transformation occurs outside the computer, it is not necessary to claim the practical application. A disclosure that permits a skilled artisan to practice the claimed invention, *i.e.*, to put it to a practical use, is sufficient. On the other hand, it is necessary to claim the practical application if there is no physical transformation or if the process merely manipulates concepts or converts one set of numbers into another. . . .

There is always some form of physical transformation within a computer because a computer acts on signals and transforms them during its operation and changes the state of its components during the execution of a process.

Even though such a physical transformation occurs within a computer, such activity is not determinative of whether the process is statutory because such transformation alone does not distinguish a statutory computer process from a non-statutory computer process. What is determinative is not how the computer performs the process, but what the computer does to achieve a practical application.

A process that merely manipulates an abstract idea or performs a purely mathematical algorithm is non-statutory despite the fact that it might inherently have some usefulness. For such subject matter to be statutory, the claimed process must be limited to a practical application of the abstract idea or mathematical algorithm in the technological arts. For example, a computer process that simply calculates a mathematical algorithm that models noise is non-statutory. However, a claimed process for digitally filtering noise employing the mathematical algorithm is statutory. . . .

If the "acts" of a claimed process manipulate only numbers, abstract concepts or ideas, or signals representing any of the foregoing, the acts are not being applied to appropriate subject matter. Thus, a process consisting solely of mathematical operations, *i.e.*, converting one set of numbers into another set of numbers, does not manipulate appropriate subject matter and thus cannot constitute a statutory process.

COMMENTS AND QUESTIONS

1. The law of software patents in the last 15 years can be criticized as exalting form over substance, allowing patent attorneys to circumvent the limitations of section 101 through artful drafting. Do the Guidelines solve this problem? Or are they formalist as well? In particular, consider what distinguishes a patentable data structure from an unpatentable one under the Guidelines. Is it anything other than the language of the claims?

Take as an example claims to software on a floppy disk. Richard Stern argues that a *Beauregard*-style claim ought merely to affect who is a direct infringer, and not expand the sorts of subject matter covered by section 101. Thus, he claims, if an algorithm were unpatentable as a process or apparatus, it shouldn't become patentable simply by virtue of being placed on a floppy disk. Richard Stern, An Attempt to Rationalize Floppy Disk Claims, 17 J. Marshall J. Computer & Info. L. 183, 198 (1998). Are the Guidelines consistent with this approach?

2. Do the Guidelines' provisions on patentable subject matter affect the scope of the patents that result? One possible explanation for the formal distinctions drawn in the Guidelines is that they are designed to allow narrow patent claims while excluding broad ones. For example, a claim directed to a computer program itself is not statutory, but a claim for a program implemented on a particular medium is statutory. Does this imply that the claim is infringed only by the use of the same program *recorded on the same medium*? Is such a restriction consistent with *Alappat*, supra, where the court acknowledged that various possible computer

implementations of a program were functionally equivalent? For a discussion of this question, see the cases that follow.

3. Patent and copyright protection have coexisted uneasily for some time in the software arena. Do the Guidelines draw a line between material that is patentable and material that is copyrightable? In particular, is the fact that a particular program element receives copyright protection evidence that it is (or should be) unpatentable? Can you think of a way to patent copyrighted material in a computer-based medium that would pass muster under the Guidelines?

4. While the PTO Guidelines for examiners are obviously important to the continued development of the law in this area, they cannot substitute for the judgment of the courts. If the Federal Circuit decides, for example, that "software on a floppy disk" is not within the ambit of 35 U.S.C. section 101, the PTO does not have the power to issue such patents regardless of the Court decision. Similarly, the PTO cannot reject an application under section 101 if the courts have decided that it is patentable subject matter. Thus, while important, the Guidelines do not represent the final word on the section 101 issue. For an argument that the Guidelines accurately reflect the case law, see Ruben Bains, A Comparison of the PTO's Computer-Implemented Guidelines with the Current Case Law, 5 Tex. Intell. Prop. L.J. 27 (1996).

At the same time, the evidence is growing that the courts may not have the final say on section 101 either. With over 40,000 software or software-related patents in force in the United States and several thousand more being issued every year, the real world seems to have left the courts (and perhaps even the Guidelines) behind. Numerous issued patents cover pure data structures (see, e.g., U.S. Patent No. 5,488,717, U.S. Patent No. 5,414,701, methods for performing calculations in a data processor; U.S. Patent No. 5,386,375, data compression algorithms; U.S. Patent No. 5,051,745 and software-based encryption algorithms; U.S. Patent No. 5,530,752; and U.S. Patent No. 4,405,829), despite the apparent non-statutory nature of such claims. The "cognitive dissonance" that results between what the law is and what the actual practice has been suggests either that the law can be expected to change or that a large number of issued patents will have to be held invalid. Keith Witek offers an exhaustive guide to patenting computer programs and algorithms in a number of different forms, along with some analysis of the advantages and disadvantages of each. Keith E. Witek, Developing a Comprehensive Claim Drafting Strategy for U.S. Software Patents, 11 Berkeley Tech. L.J. 363 (1996).

For an argument that congressional action is necessary to clarify the section 101 issues surrounding software patents, see Lee Hollaar, Justice Douglas Was Right: The Need for Congressional Action on Software Patents, 24 AIPLA Q.J. 283 (1996); Maximilian R. Peterson, Note, Now You See It, Now You Don't: Was It a Patentable Machine or an Unpatentable "Algorithm"? On Principle and Expediency in Current Patent Law

Doctrines Relating to Computer-Implemented Inventions, 64 Geo. Wash. L. Rev. 90 (1995).

PROBLEMS

Problem 3-1. Yoshimoto, a company that makes software for video games, seeks a patent on a new and nonobvious computer program. Yoshimoto claims the program "implemented in a read-only memory (ROM) readable by a computer." Is this claim patentable subject matter? How would this question be answered under (1) *Benson*? (2) *Flook*? (3) *Diehr*? (4) *Alappat*? (5) The PTO's Proposed Guidelines? (6) *State Street* infra?

Problem 3-2. Lynn, a programmer who specializes in computer-assisted design tools, develops a new and more efficient way of cataloguing data in a computer representative of "virtual objects." The virtual objects are in turn computer graphics used to model real-world objects. She claims "a data structure resident in a computer-readable memory." The data structure is further described and defined in the claims, but the memory is not. Is Lynn's claim patentable under the PTO's Proposed Guidelines? Is there any form of software such a claim would not cover?

What other types of legal protection might Lynn be able to obtain?

≡ **State Street Bank & Trust v. Signature**
≡ **Financial Services**
≡ *United States Court of Appeals for the Federal Circuit*
≡ *149 F.3d 1368 (Fed. Cir. 1998)*

RICH, Circuit Judge.

Signature Financial Group, Inc. (Signature) appeals from the decision of the United States District Court for the District of Massachusetts granting a motion for summary judgment in favor of State Street Bank & Trust Co. (State Street), finding U.S. Patent No. 5,193,056 (the '056 patent) invalid on the ground that the claimed subject matter is not encompassed by 35 U.S.C. sec. 101 (1994). See State Street Bank & Trust Co. v. Signature Financial Group, Inc., 927 F.Supp. 502, 38 USPQ2d 1530 (D.Mass.1996). We reverse and remand because we conclude that the patent claims are directed to statutory subject matter.

Background

Signature is the assignee of the '056 patent which is entitled "Data Processing System for Hub and Spoke Financial Services Configuration." The '056 patent issued to Signature on March 9, 1993, naming R. Todd Boes as the inventor. The '056 patent is generally directed to a data processing system (the system) for implementing an investment structure which was developed for use in Signature's business as an administrator and accounting agent for mutual funds. In essence, the system, identified by the proprietary name Hub and Spoke®, facilitates a structure whereby mutual funds (Spokes) pool their assets in an investment portfolio (Hub) organized as a partnership. This investment configuration provides the administrator of a mutual fund with the advantageous combination of economies of scale in administering investments coupled with the tax advantages of a partnership.

State Street and Signature are both in the business of acting as custodians and accounting agents for multi-tiered partnership fund financial services. State Street negotiated with Signature for a license to use its patented data processing system described and claimed in the '056 patent. When negotiations broke down, State Street brought a declaratory judgment action asserting invalidity, unenforceability, and noninfringement in Massachusetts district court, and then filed a motion for partial summary judgment of patent invalidity for failure to claim statutory subject matter under sec. 101. The motion was granted and this appeal followed.

Discussion

. . . The patented invention relates generally to a system that allows an administrator to monitor and record the financial information flow and make all calculations necessary for maintaining a partner fund financial services configuration. As previously mentioned, a partner fund financial services configuration essentially allows several mutual funds, or "Spokes," to pool their investment funds into a single portfolio, or "Hub," allowing for consolidation of, inter alia, the costs of administering the fund combined with the tax advantages of a partnership. In particular, this system provides means for a daily allocation of assets for two or more Spokes that are invested in the same Hub. The system determines the percentage share that each Spoke maintains in the Hub, while taking into consideration daily changes both in the value of the Hub's investment securities and in the concomitant amount of each Spoke's assets.

In determining daily changes, the system also allows for the allocation among the Spokes of the Hub's daily income, expenses, and net realized and unrealized gain or loss, calculating each day's total investments based on the concept of a book capital account. This enables the determination of a true asset value of each Spoke and accurate calculation of allocation ratios between or among the Spokes. The system additionally tracks all the relevant data determined on a daily basis for the Hub and each Spoke, so that aggregate year end income, expenses, and capital gain or loss can be determined for accounting and for tax purposes for the Hub and, as a result, for each publicly traded Spoke.

It is essential that these calculations are quickly and accurately performed. In large part this is required because each Spoke sells shares to the public and the price of those shares is substantially based on the Spoke's percentage interest in the portfolio. In some instances, a mutual fund administrator is required to calculate the value of the shares to the nearest penny within as little as an hour and a half after the market closes. Given the complexity of the calculations, a computer or equivalent device is a virtual necessity to perform the task. . . .

The district court began its analysis by construing the claims to be directed to a process, with each "means" clause merely representing a step in that process. However, "machine" claims having "means" clauses may only be reasonably viewed as process claims if there is no supporting structure in the written description that corresponds to the claimed "means" elements. See In re Alappat, 33 F.3d 1526, 1540-41, 31 USPQ2d 1545, 1554 (Fed.Cir.1994) (in banc). This is not the case now before us.

When independent claim 1 is properly construed in accordance with section 112, para. 6, it is directed to a machine, as demonstrated below, where representative claim 1 is set forth, the subject matter in brackets stating the structure the written description discloses as corresponding to the respective "means" recited in the claims.

> 1. A data processing system for managing a financial services configuration of a portfolio established as a partnership, each partner being one of a plurality of funds, comprising:
>> (a) computer processor means [a personal computer including a CPU] for processing data;
>> (b) storage means [a data disk] for storing data on a storage medium;
>> (c) first means [an arithmetic logic circuit configured to prepare the data disk to magnetically store selected data] for initializing the storage medium;
>> (d) second means [an arithmetic logic circuit configured to retrieve information from a specific file, calculate incremental increases or decreases based on specific input, allocate the results on a percentage basis, and store the output in a separate file] for processing data regarding assets in the portfolio and each of the funds from a previous day and data regarding increases or decreases in each of the funds, [sic, funds'] assets and for allocating the percentage share that each fund holds in the portfolio;
>> (e) third means [an arithmetic logic circuit configured to retrieve information from a specific file, calculate incremental increases and decreases based on specific input, allocate the results on a percentage basis and store the output in a separate file] for processing data regarding

daily incremental income, expenses, and net realized gain or loss for the portfolio and for allocating such data among each fund;

(f) fourth means [an arithmetic logic circuit configured to retrieve information from a specific file, calculate incremental increases and decreases based on specific input, allocate the results on a percentage basis and store the output in a separate file] for processing data regarding daily net unrealized gain or loss for the portfolio and for allocating such data among each fund; and

(g) fifth means [an arithmetic logic circuit configured to retrieve information from specific files, calculate that information on an aggregate basis and store the output in a separate file] for processing data regarding aggregate year-end income, expenses, and capital gain or loss for the portfolio and each of the funds.

Each claim component, recited as a "means" plus its function, is to be read, of course, pursuant to sec. 112, para. 6, as inclusive of the "equivalents" of the structures disclosed in the written description portion of the specification. Thus, claim 1, properly construed, claims a machine, namely, a data processing system for managing a financial services configuration of a portfolio established as a partnership, which machine is made up of, at the very least, the specific structures disclosed in the written description and corresponding to the means-plus-function elements (a)-(g) recited in the claim. A "machine" is proper statutory subject matter under sec. 101. We note that, for the purposes of a sec. 101 analysis, it is of little relevance whether claim 1 is directed to a "machine" or a "process," as long as it falls within at least one of the four enumerated categories of patentable subject matter, "machine" and "process" being such categories.

This does not end our analysis, however, because the court concluded that the claimed subject matter fell into one of two alternative judicially-created exceptions to statutory subject matter. The court refers to the first exception as the "mathematical algorithm" exception and the second exception as the "business method" exception. . . .

The repetitive use of the expansive term "any" in sec. 101 shows Congress's intent not to place any restrictions on the subject matter for which a patent may be obtained beyond those specifically recited in sec. 101. Indeed, the Supreme Court has acknowledged that Congress intended sec. 101 to extend to "anything under the sun that is made by man." Diamond v. Chakrabarty, 447 U.S. 303, 309, 100 S.Ct. 2204, 65 L.Ed.2d 144 (1980); see also Diamond v. Diehr, 450 U.S. 175, 182, 101 S.Ct. 1048, 67 L.Ed.2d 155 (1981). Thus, it is improper to read limitations into sec. 101 on the subject matter that may be patented where the legislative history indicates that Congress clearly did not intend such limitations. See *Chakrabarty*, 447 U.S. at 308, 100 S.Ct. 2204 ("We have also cautioned that courts 'should not read into the patent laws limitations and conditions which the legislature has not expressed.'" (citations omitted)).

The "Mathematical Algorithm" Exception

The Supreme Court has identified three categories of subject matter that are unpatentable, namely "laws of nature, natural phenomena, and abstract ideas." *Diehr*, 450 U.S. at 185, 101 S.Ct. 1048. Of particular relevance to this case, the Court has held that mathematical algorithms are not patentable subject matter to the extent that they are merely abstract ideas. See *Diehr*, 450 U.S. 175, 101 S.Ct. 1048, passim; Parker v. Flook, 437 U.S. 584, 98 S.Ct. 2522, 57 L.Ed.2d 451 (1978); Gottschalk v. Benson, 409 U.S. 63, 93 S.Ct. 253, 34 L.Ed.2d 273 (1972). In *Diehr*, the Court explained that certain types of mathematical subject matter, standing alone, represent nothing more than abstract ideas until reduced to some type of practical application, i.e., "a useful, concrete and tangible result." *Alappat*, 33 F.3d at 1544, 31 USPQ2d at 1557.[4]

Unpatentable mathematical algorithms are identifiable by showing they are merely abstract ideas constituting disembodied concepts or truths that are not "useful." From a practical standpoint, this means that to be patentable an algorithm must be applied in a "useful" way. In *Alappat,* we held that data, transformed by a machine through a series of mathematical calculations to produce a smooth waveform display on a rasterizer monitor, constituted a practical application of an abstract idea (a mathematical algorithm, formula, or calculation), because it produced "a useful, concrete and tangible result"—the smooth waveform.

Similarly, in Arrhythmia Research Technology Inc. v. Corazonix Corp., 958 F.2d 1053, 22 USPQ2d 1033 (Fed.Cir.1992), we held that the transformation of electrocardiograph signals from a patient's heartbeat by a machine through a series of mathematical calculations constituted a practical application of an abstract idea (a mathematical algorithm, formula, or calculation), because it corresponded to a useful, concrete or tangible thing—the condition of a patient's heart.

Today, we hold that the transformation of data, representing discrete dollar amounts, by a machine through a series of mathematical calculations into a final share price, constitutes a practical application of a mathematical algorithm, formula, or calculation, because it produces "a useful, concrete and tangible result"—a final share price momentarily fixed for recording and reporting purposes and even accepted and relied upon by regulatory authorities and in subsequent trades.

The district court erred by applying the Freeman-Walter-Abele test to determine whether the claimed subject matter was an unpatentable abstract idea. . . .

After *Diehr* and *Chakrabarty*, the Freeman-Walter-Abele test has little, if any, applicability to determining the presence of statutory subject matter.

---

4. This has come to be known as the mathematical algorithm exception. This designation has led to some confusion, especially given the Freeman-Walter-Abele analysis. By keeping in mind that the mathematical algorithm is unpatentable only to the extent that it represents an abstract idea, this confusion may be ameliorated.

As we pointed out in *Alappat*, 33 F.3d at 1543, 31 USPQ2d at 1557, application of the test could be misleading, because a process, machine, manufacture, or composition of matter employing a law of nature, natural phenomenon, or abstract idea is patentable subject matter even though a law of nature, natural phenomenon, or abstract idea would not, by itself, be entitled to such protection. The test determines the presence of, for example, an algorithm. Under *Benson*, this may have been a sufficient indicium of nonstatutory subject matter. However, after *Diehr* and *Alappat*, the mere fact that a claimed invention involves inputting numbers, calculating numbers, outputting numbers, and storing numbers, in and of itself, would not render it nonstatutory subject matter, unless, of course, its operation does not produce a "useful, concrete and tangible result." *Alappat*, 33 F.3d at 1544, 31 USPQ2d at 1557. . . .

The question of whether a claim encompasses statutory subject matter should not focus on which of the four categories of subject matter a claim is directed to—process, machine, manufacture, or composition of matter— but rather on the essential characteristics of the subject matter, in particular, its practical utility. Section 101 specifies that statutory subject matter must also satisfy the other "conditions and requirements" of Title 35, including novelty, nonobviousness, and adequacy of disclosure and notice. See In re Warmerdam, 33 F.3d 1354, 1359, 31 USPQ2d 1754, 1757-58 (Fed.Cir.1994). For purpose of our analysis, as noted above, claim 1 is directed to a machine programmed with the Hub and Spoke software and admittedly produces a "useful, concrete, and tangible result." *Alappat*, 33 F.3d at 1544, 31 USPQ2d at 1557. This renders it statutory subject matter, even if the useful result is expressed in numbers, such as price, profit, percentage, cost, or loss.

COMMENTS AND QUESTIONS

1. Any thought that the new test announced in *State Street* was an aberration, or that it could easily be reconciled with prior precedent, was put to rest in AT&T v. Excel Communications, 172 F.3d 1352 (Fed. Cir. 1999). In that case, the court upheld as patentable subject matter method claims to a method for "generating a message record for an interexchange call" and recording who the call should be billed to. The court applied *State Street*'s "useful, concrete and tangible result" test, concluding that the generation of billing records was clearly useful. The court specifically rejected the argument that a patentable software claim must have physical structure associated with it, noting that physical transformation is only one of several possible ways to bring about a useful result. In sustaining the patent, the *AT&T* court laid to rest much of the history of the mathematical algorithm exception:

A mathematical formula alone, sometimes referred to as a mathematical algorithm, viewed in the abstract, is considered unpatentable subject matter. Courts have used the terms "mathematical algorithm," "mathematical formula," and "mathematical equation," to describe types of nonstatutory mathematical subject matter without explaining whether the terms are interchangeable or different. Even assuming the words connote the same concept, there is considerable question as to exactly what the concept encompasses. See, e.g., *Diehr*, 450 U.S. at 186 n. 9, 101 S.Ct. 1048 ("The term 'algorithm' is subject to a variety of definitions . . . [Petitioner's] definition is significantly broader than the definition this Court employed in Benson and Flook."); *accord* In re Schrader, 22 F.3d 290, 293 n. 5, 30 USPQ2d 1455, 1457 n. 5 (Fed.Cir.1994).

This court recently pointed out that any step-by-step process, be it electronic, chemical, or mechanical, involves an "algorithm" in the broad sense of the term. Because §101 includes processes as a category of patentable subject matter, the judicially-defined proscription against patenting of a "mathematical algorithm," to the extent such a proscription still exists, is narrowly limited to mathematical algorithms in the abstract. See also *Benson*, 409 U.S. at 65, 93 S.Ct. 253 (describing a mathematical algorithm as a "procedure for solving a given type of mathematical problem").

Since the process of manipulation of numbers is a fundamental part of computer technology, we have had to reexamine the rules that govern the patentability of such technology. The sea-changes in both law and technology stand as a testament to the ability of law to adapt to new and innovative concepts, while remaining true to basic principles. In an earlier era, the PTO published guidelines essentially rejecting the notion that computer programs were patentable. As the technology progressed, our predecessor court disagreed, and, overturning some of the earlier limiting principles regarding §101, announced more expansive principles formulated with computer technology in mind. In our recent decision in *State Street*, this court discarded the so-called "business method" exception and reassessed the "mathematical algorithm" exception, see 149 F.3d at 1373-77, 47 USPQ2d at 1600-04, both judicially-created "exceptions" to the statutory categories of §101. As this brief review suggests, this court (and its predecessor) has struggled to make our understanding of the scope of §101 responsive to the needs of the modern world. . . .

The State Street formulation, that a mathematical algorithm may be an integral part of patentable subject matter such as a machine or process if the claimed invention as a whole is applied in a "useful" manner, follows the approach taken by this court en banc in In re Alappat, 33 F.3d 1526, 31 USPQ2d 1545 (Fed.Cir.1994). . . . [T]he Alappat inquiry simply requires an examination of the contested claims to see if the claimed subject matter as a whole is a disembodied mathematical concept representing nothing more than a "law of nature" or an "abstract idea," or if the mathematical concept has been reduced to some practical application rendering it "useful." *Id.* at 1544, 31 USPQ2d at 1557. In *Alappat*, we held that more than an abstract idea was claimed because the claimed invention as a whole was directed toward forming a specific machine that produced the useful, concrete, and tangible result of a smooth waveform display. See *id*. at 1544, 31 USPQ2d at 1557.

In both *Alappat* and *State Street*, the claim was for a machine that achieved certain results. In the case before us, because Excel does not own or operate the facilities over which its calls are placed, AT&T did not charge Excel with infringement of its apparatus claims, but limited its infringement charge to the specified method or process claims. Whether stated implicitly or explicitly, we consider the scope of §101 to be the same regardless of the form—machine or process—in which a particular claim is drafted.

Id.

2. Related to the record generation claim in *AT&T*, but potentially even more far-reaching, is a new type of patent claim to "propagated signals." These claims are directed to "a manufactured transient phenomenon, such as an electrical, optical, or acoustical signal." Jeffrey R. Keuster et al., A New Frontier in Patents: Patent Claims to Propagated Signals, 17 J. Marshall J. Computer & Info. L. 75 (1998). The claim would be directly infringed by the sending of data covered by the claim over computer wires, telephone lines, or the airwaves.

After *State Street*, is there any reason such a claim would not be patentable? Does it produce a useful, concrete, and tangible result?

3. The PTO revised its Examination Guidelines in late 1998 in response to the decision in *State Street* by adding several "training examples" dealing with business, artificial intelligence, and mathematical processing claims. The examples show a reluctance on the part of the PTO to abandon the physical transformation approach that characterized the case law through *Alappat*.

PROBLEM

Problem 3-3. Safe Flight is an aircraft instrument company. It seeks to obtain a patent on avionic windshear equipment designed to give warnings to a plane's pilot on takeoff or landing when the plane encounters violent shifts in wind direction ("windshear"). This can result in disaster if the pilot cannot compensate quickly and properly for the changing conditions. Windshear is measured in Safe Flight's invention by means of an algorithm that compares the rate of change of the instantaneous airspeed (the speed of an aircraft measured against the surrounding air) with the change in groundspeed (the speed of an aircraft measured against the ground, which the patentee calls "horizontal inertial acceleration"). Safe Flight claims a "windshear measurement and control system" in an aircraft cockpit, which employs the algorithm to constantly recalculate windshear during landing and automatically generates a warning buzzer if windshear exceeds a certain threshold level.

Is Safe Flight's claim patentable subject matter under section 101? Should it be? Would it be patentable if it were not implemented in a computer?

2. Software as a "Method of Doing Business"

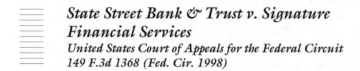

State Street Bank & Trust v. Signature Financial Services
United States Court of Appeals for the Federal Circuit
149 F.3d 1368 (Fed. Cir. 1998)

[The factual background of this case, and the court's decision on the mathematical algorithm exception, are reprinted above.]

The Business Method Exception

As an alternative ground for invalidating the '056 patent under sec. 101, the court relied on the judicially-created, so-called "business method" exception to statutory subject matter. We take this opportunity to lay this ill-conceived exception to rest. Since its inception, the "business method" exception has merely represented the application of some general, but no longer applicable legal principle, perhaps arising out of the "requirement for invention"—which was eliminated by sec. 103. Since the 1952 Patent Act, business methods have been, and should have been, subject to the same legal requirements for patentability as applied to any other process or method.[10]

The business method exception has never been invoked by this court, or the CCPA, to deem an invention unpatentable. Application of this particular exception has always been preceded by a ruling based on some clearer concept of Title 35 or, more commonly, application of the abstract idea exception based on finding a mathematical algorithm. Illustrative is the CCPA's analysis in In re Howard, 55 C.C.P.A. 1121, 394 F.2d 869,

---

10. As Judge Newman has previously stated,

[The business method exception] is . . . an unwarranted encumbrance to the definition of statutory subject matter in section 101, that [should] be discarded as error-prone, redundant, and obsolete. It merits retirement from the glossary of section 101. . . . All of the "doing business" cases could have been decided using the clearer concepts of Title 35. Patentability does not turn on whether the claimed method does "business" instead of something else, but on whether the method, viewed as a whole, meets the requirements of patentability as set forth in Sections 102, 103, and 112 of the Patent Act.

In re Schrader, 22 F.3d 290, 298, 30 USPQ2d 1455, 1462 (Fed.Cir.1994) (Newman, J., dissenting).

157 USPQ 615 (CCPA 1968), wherein the court affirmed the Board of Appeals' rejection of the claims for lack of novelty and found it unnecessary to reach the Board's section 101 ground that a method of doing business is "inherently unpatentable." Id. at 872, 55 C.C.P.A. 1121, 394 F.2d 869, 157 USPQ at 617.[12]

Similarly, In re Schrader, 22 F.3d 290, 30 USPQ2d 1455 (Fed. Cir. 1994), while making reference to the business method exception, turned on the fact that the claims implicitly recited an abstract idea in the form of a mathematical algorithm and there was no "transformation or conversion of subject matter representative of or constituting physical activity or objects." 22 F.3d at 294, 30 USPQ2d at 1459 (emphasis omitted).

State Street argues that we acknowledged the validity of the business method exception in *Alappat* when we discussed *Maucorps* and *Meyer*:

> *Maucorps* dealt with a business methodology for deciding how salesmen should best handle respective customers and *Meyer* involved a "system" for aiding a neurologist in diagnosing patients. Clearly, neither of the alleged "inventions" in those cases falls within any sec. 101 category.

Alappat, 33 F.3d at 1541, 31 USPQ2d at 1555. However, closer scrutiny of these cases reveals that the claimed inventions in both *Maucorps* and *Meyer* were rejected as abstract ideas under the mathematical algorithm exception, not the business method exception. See In re Maucorps, 609 F.2d 481, 484, 203 USPQ 812, 816 (CCPA 1979); In re Meyer, 688 F.2d 789, 796, 215 USPQ 193, 199 (CCPA 1982).

Even the case frequently cited as establishing the business method exception to statutory subject matter, Hotel Security Checking Co. v. Lorraine Co., 160 F. 467 (2d Cir.1908), did not rely on the exception to strike the patent. In that case, the patent was found invalid for lack of novelty and "invention," not because it was improper subject matter for a patent. The court stated "the fundamental principle of the system is as old as the art of bookkeeping, i.e., charging the goods of the employer to the agent who takes them." Id. at 469. "If at the time of [the patent] application, there had been no system of bookkeeping of any kind in restaurants, we would be confronted with the question whether a new and useful system of cash registering and account checking is such an art as is patentable under the statute." Id. at 472.

This case is no exception. The district court announced the precepts of the business method exception as set forth in several treatises, but noted

---

12. See also Dann v. Johnston, 425 U.S. 219, 96 S.Ct. 1393, 47 L.Ed.2d 692 (1976) (the Supreme Court declined to discuss the section 101 argument concerning the computerized financial record-keeping system, in view of the Court's holding of patent invalidity under section 103); In re Chatfield, 545 F.2d 152, 157, 191 USPQ 730, 735 (CCPA 1976); Ex parte Murray, 9 USPQ2d 1819, 1820 (Bd.Pat.App & Interf. 1988) ("[T]he claimed accounting method [requires] no more than the entering, sorting, debiting and totaling of expenditures as necessary preliminary steps to issuing an expense analysis statement. . . .") states grounds of obviousness or lack of novelty, not of nonstatutory subject matter.

as its primary reason for finding the patent invalid under the business method exception as follows:

> If Signature's invention were patentable, any financial institution desirous of implementing a multi-tiered funding complex modelled (sic) on a Hub and Spoke configuration would be required to seek Signature's permission before embarking on such a project. This is so because the '056 Patent is claimed [sic] sufficiently broadly to foreclose virtually any computer-implemented accounting method necessary to manage this type of financial structure.

927 F.Supp. 502, 516, 38 USPQ2d 1530, 1542. Whether the patent's claims are too broad to be patentable is not to be judged under §101, but rather under §§102, 103 and 112. Assuming the above statement to be correct, it has nothing to do with whether what is claimed is statutory subject matter.

. . . [T]he U.S. Patent and Trademark 1996 Examination Guidelines for Computer Related Inventions now read:

> Office personnel have had difficulty in properly treating claims directed to methods of doing business. Claims should not be categorized as methods of doing business. Instead such claims should be treated like any other process claims.

Examination Guidelines, 61 Fed.Reg. 7478, 7479 (1996). We agree that this is precisely the manner in which this type of claim should be treated. Whether the claims are directed to subject matter within sec. 101 should not turn on whether the claimed subject matter does "business" instead of something else.

Conclusion

The appealed decision is reversed and the case is remanded to the district court for further proceedings consistent with this opinion.

COMMENTS AND QUESTIONS

1. *State Street* is not the first case to permit a patent on a business method implemented in computer form. In Paine Webber Jackson & Curtis, Inc. v. Merrill Lynch, Pierce, Fenner & Smith, Inc., 564 F. Supp. 1358 (D. Del. 1983), the court permitted a similar program to be patented over the objection that it covered a business method. For criticism of the *Paine Webber* case, which the author says allowed the preemption of a broad program idea, see Comment, A Plea for Due Process: Defining the

Proper Scope of Patent Protection for Computer Software, 85 Nw. U.L. Rev. 1103 (1991).

2. A number of patents on basic business methods in electronic commerce issued during 1998. These included patents to PriceLine for its system of matching buyers and sellers online (U.S. Pat. No. 5,794,207), to Cybergold for the concept of paying customers to view online ads (U.S. Pat. No. 5,794,210), and to OpenMarket for its online auction system. Other recently issued electronic commerce patents include U.S. Patent No. 5,778,173 (for a method of performing secure purchases on the Web), U.S. Patent No. 5,778,067 (for Mondex's electronic cash system), and U.S. Patent No. 5,768,385 (for "untraceable electronic cash," patented by Microsoft). Each of these patent applications was filed long before *State Street* was decided, but they are clearly part of a trend towards patenting the new models of electronic commerce.

3. Is the process of playing a musical instrument any less "technological" than the process of implementing a business plan? Does *State Street* suggest that other "inventions" that don't fit easily within traditional technological categories may nonetheless be patentable? Does *State Street* prove that the dissent in *Alappat* was right? For an argument that the door has now been opened to the patenting of all sorts of ideas in the "liberal professions," see John R. Thomas, The Patenting of the Liberal Professions, — B.C. L. Rev. — (forthcoming 2000).

Should this expansion be troubling? Is there any reason to patent technological advances but not advances in the liberal arts or professions?

Note on *Musgrave* and the "Technological Arts"

Consider the following passage from Parker v. Flook:

> The rule that the discovery of a law of nature cannot be patented rests, not on the notion that natural phenomena are not processes, but rather on the more fundamental understanding that they are not the kind of "discoveries" that the statute was enacted to protect.

437 U.S. at 593.

This passage suggests that computer programs, or at least some aspects of them, were not within the class of human "inventions." An early version of this argument was made in the 1966 Presidential Commission Report on the patent system, entitled To Promote the Progress of Science and the Useful Arts . . . , and in the first set of Patent Office Guidelines on patenting computer programs, 33 Fed. Reg. 15,609 (1968). In one sense it is simply a restatement of the core of the "mental steps" doctrine as applied to software. But in In re Musgrave, 431 F.2d 882 (C.C.P.A. 1970), the CCPA had attempted to make it the cornerstone of patentability in this area. Near the end of the *Musgrave* opinion, which reversed the Patent Office Board of Appeals and upheld the patentability of a process for determining subsurface geological characteristics with computer assistance, the CCPA made the following statement:

> We cannot agree with the board that these claims (all the steps of which can be carried out by the disclosed apparatus) are directed to non-statutory processes merely because some or all the steps therein can also be carried out in or with the aid of the human mind or because it may be necessary for one performing the processes to think. All that is necessary, in our view, to make a sequence of operational steps a statutory "process" within 35 USC §101 is that it be in the technological arts so as to be in consonance with the Constitutional purpose to promote the progress of "useful arts." Const. Art. 1, sec. 8.

The effort to define software patentability according to whether a particular set of claims falls within the "technological arts" has its supporters, most notably Professor Donald Chisum, who wrote that *Musgrave* was "the highwater mark of rationality" in the software patent debate. Chisum, The Future of Software Protection: The Patentability of Algorithms, 47 U. Pitt. L. Rev. 959, 961 (1986). Even so, the technological arts argument was met with immediate skepticism in a concurring opinion by Judge Baldwin in *Musgrave*:

> It seems that whenever a court decides to go beyond what is necessary to decide the case before it, more problems are generated than are solved. I foresee quite a few with the majority's new holding.
>
> First and foremost will be the problem of interpreting the meaning of "technological arts". . . .
>
> Justifying the decision finding claims drawn entirely to purely mental processes to be statutory, the majority states that "[a] step requiring the exercise of subjective judgment without restriction might be objectionable as rendering a claim indefinite." It should not require much imagination to see the many problems sure to be involved in trying to decide whether a step requiring certain human judgment evaluations is definite or not.
>
> As one more example, suppose a claim happens to contain a sequence of operational steps which can reasonably be read to cover a process performable both within and without the technological arts? This is not too far fetched. Would such a claim be statutory? Would it comply with section 112 [on enablement]? We will have to face these problems some day.

415 F.2d at 893-894.

The problems identified by Judge Baldwin are largely the result of the ever-expanding applications of computer programs. One case that illustrates this well is In re Toma, 575 F.2d 872, 877 (C.C.P.A. 1978). Toma's claim was for an algorithm for a computerized natural language translation process. The Patent Office rejected the claim because it was for an algorithm under *Benson* and for a mental process, and because it made a contribution to the liberal, not the technological, arts. Toma's claim, however, was eventually ruled patentable by the CCPA.

Do recent developments suggest a need for some limitation on patentable subject matter based on a distinction between technological and liberal arts? If so, where should the court draw such a line? For a suggestion to demarcate patent and copyright along Cartesian lines of objective versus subjective problems, with implications for software patents, see Allen B. Wagner, Patenting Computer Science: Are Computer Instruction Writings Patentable?, 17 J. Marshall J. Computer & Info. L. 5 (1998).

Note on the Potential Impact of Patents on the Financial Services Industry

It is not surprising that the door to patenting business methods was first opened by computer programs. Patents for computer software are now being granted much more freely by the Patent Office than ever before. And because today new financial instruments and techniques are almost universally implemented in software on computer systems, these instruments and techniques have been characterized as essentially *computer*-related inventions, with a predictable result: the Patent Office has been issuing patents on them for several years.

Before *State Street*, it was the very computer-dependence of these financial "inventions" that made them patentable. This is clear from the way most business method patents are drafted. Their claims describe them as "systems" or "apparatus." Merrill Lynch's patent, for example, is for a "Securities Brokerage-Cash Management System." Other recent patents include U.S. Patent No. 4,642,767, a "Bookkeeping and Accounting System" patent granted to one M. Lerner; U.S. Patent No. 4,648,038, a "Method and Apparatus for Restructuring Debt Obligations," issued to P. Roberts et al. and assigned to Lazard Freres & Co.; U.S. Patent No. 4,839,804, a "Method and Apparatus for Insuring the Funding of a Future Liability of Uncertain Cost," issued to P. Roberts et al. and assigned to College Savings Bank of Princeton, N.J. U.S. Patent No. 4,736,294, entitled "Data Processing Methods and Apparatus For Managing Vehicle Financing" (April 5, 1988); and U.S. Patent No. 4,694,397, entitled "Banking/Brokerage Computer Interface System," (granted September 15, 1987) are also examples of business method/software patents. The computer interface patent "uses a computer and associated program as an interface between a conventional bank account and a securities brokerage account." This is very similar to the inter-account communication function of the patent at issue in the *Paine Weber* case. The patent on "Vehicle Financing" processes vehicle financing data and provides information to assist the lender in granting a loan.

In each case the patent describes the invention as relating to "data processing," while in fact the real contribution of the inventor involves a new financial instrument or technique. In the past, courts have declined to uphold patents on a new bookkeeping system employing novel checkbooks,[2] and on a system for conducting commodities trades at a distance without using brokers.[3] In these cases, the courts distinguished between the *method* of doing business, or the new business concept, and the *physical apparatus* or tools needed to carry out the new method. If the tools met all the tests of patentability, they were patentable, the courts said, but the business concept itself never is.

State Street changes all that, of course. Unless the decision is reversed —en banc or by the Supreme Court—it is reasonable to expect claims drafted to business methods more generally, without the cloak of computer programs. Had this decision come down 20 years ago, one can readily imagine Federal Express patenting a business model involving guaranteed overnight package delivery. The next Federal Express probably *will* patent its business innovation.

Why Not Patent Business Methods?

The computer tie-in may allow the financial services industry to overcome the traditional objection to patenting business methods, but the question still remains: why not allow patents for financial instruments and techniques, or business methods in general?

Although the older cases do not articulate their reasoning very clearly, they seem to center around one idea: that the patent system was meant to protect *technology*—actual machines, devices, and new chemical compositions—rather than pure concepts. Since business methods were not tied to particular machinery or devices, they were mere concepts and hence not patentable. As we saw in *Musgrave*, though, that distinction is a hard one to implement in practice.

Even if courts no longer rely on the distinction between concepts and machines, the rule against business methods might be justified on other— primarily economic—grounds.

Are These Patents Necessary?

First, one might argue that such patents are simply not necessary. After all, there seemed to be no shortage of new accounting methods, financial instruments, or financial services techniques throughout the history of

---

2. In re Sterling, 70 F.2d 910 (C.C.P.A. 1934). Although conceding that Sterling's checkbook, which included both regular checks and checks designed to transfer funds to a savings account, was "an ingenious and convenient arrangement," the court refused patent protection because the physical structure presented no novelty.

3. In re Wait, 73 F.2d 982 (C.C.P.A. 1934). The patent applicant claimed a process that involved three functions: transmitting offers to buy or sell to distant locations where interested parties could see the offers posted, transmitting acceptances, and recording each transaction. The court ruled it was not patentable subject matter.

the American economy when business methods were not patentable. Even into the mid-1980s, when these patents were just beginning to appear, the United States was considered the world leader in this service industry. Thus, on this view, the proper question is: why fix it if it ain't broke? Three possible responses suggest themselves.

First, one might point out the rising cost of creating an innovative financial service or instrument—that is, the old rules might no longer provide enough of an incentive to innovate in this field. This argument is frequently made with respect to computer program patents—which also suffer from the "if it ain't broke" critique. But this argument requires empirical support, which so far has been lacking. In addition, it may be that a field crowded with intellectual property rights will raise the cost of innovation in this market even further.

A second response to the opponents of business method patents might be that it is simply unfair to exclude these innovations from the umbrella of patent protection. After all, it is argued, entrepreneurs work just as hard in this field as in biotechnology, organic chemistry, diesel engine design, and all the other fields in which patents are routinely handed out. Why discriminate on the basis of subject matter; why not simply reward hard work and innovative results in whatever form they take?[4]

A third argument is perhaps more speculative. This would concede that the financial services sector has performed admirably in the United States but that it would have done—and will do, in light of new patent rules—*even better* in the brave new world of financial services patents. Investments that were not made because of a fear of piracy will be made, now that companies know their innovations will be protected.

Alternatives to Patents

In deciding whether financial instrument patents are really necessary, it is important to consider alternative means by which companies can reap returns on innovative financial instruments and services. Empirical research has revealed that in many industries, patents are not necessary for firms to secure an adequate return on research and development investment.[5] In many industries, trade secrets or a head start on the competition allow firms to capture enough of the value of their research to continue doing it. In other industries, according to recent studies, firms use strategies such as

---

4. For a proposal to create a system of patent-like rights to protect *all* innovations at the point of market introduction, whether technological, business method, or otherwise, see Direct Protection of Innovation (William Kingston ed., 1987). Kingston proposes a system of property rights to come into effect only when a new product is actually introduced on the market. See *id.*, at 1-34.

5. See Levin et al., Appropriating the Returns from Industrial Research and Development, 3 Brookings Papers Econ. Activity 783 (1987).

ownership of complementary assets intimately tied to an innovation—such as service networks—to capture the value of that innovation. See David J. Teece, Profiting from Technological Innovation: Implications for Integration, Collaboration, and Public Policy, 15 Research Pol'y 285 (1986).

Regardless of specific strategies, the point is the same: firms can capture the value of innovations in many ways. The question for policymakers is whether patents should be permitted in light of the other appropriability mechanisms that are available. Again, the relatively frequent innovations in the financial services industry prior to the era of patentability suggest that firms had adequate means to appropriate the value of their new financial innovations.

What alternative, non-patent means have companies traditionally used to capture the value of their financial innovations? Three come to mind (and there may be more): head start, trade secrets, and promotional value. The head start advantage is obvious: if a particular firm was recognized as the originator of a novel financial instrument—an interest rate swap, for example—they could expect to garner clients and make money before competitors figured out how to put the instrument together and market it. Even after competitors adopt a new business model, being first may have reputational advantages. Federal Express has kept a significant share of the overnight package delivery market, for example, due in part to their first-mover advantage. Trade secrets have traditionally been used to protect a host of financial techniques; even now, the internal financial dealings of large firms are only made public to the extent SEC and IRS oversight make necessary. On a more general level, many methods of doing business, such as using vertical integration and just-in-time inventory practices, can be kept secret or at least quiet; it is only *after* such practices have shown good results that they become widely known. And as to promotional value, it has surely been common to tout one's firm as "the originator of debt-for-equity swaps," or "the company that invented unbundled stock units." The prestige this brings helps firm recover the costs of creating these instruments.

What Is the Cost?

To say that patents are not necessary to call forth innovations implies a further point: that granting patents may cost society too much. There are so many ways a new business method or financial instrument might be adapted to particular business situations that it might be deemed inefficient to give one patentee exclusive rights to the method or technique. The losses—in the form of foregone applications and modifications—may simply outweigh the gain of a greater incentive to innovate.

In addition, both the patent application process and patent licensing involve administrative costs, which can be substantial. If the industry becomes one in which patent licensing—or even owning your own patent portfolio—is an effective prerequisite to market entry, it will be much harder for small companies to enter the marketplace. This may not be of much concern in certain financial services industries, where most of the players are large, but it may have a disproportionately greater impact on new industries like electronic commerce.

Finally, one might view patents on business methods as more troubling in a capitalist economy than patents on scientific inventions. Capitalism is based on competition, after all. If a new company can effectively lock up a market by patenting its business model, consumers will shoulder the burden by paying higher prices to the monopoly patent holder. Even if the patent owner chooses to license new entrants, the idea that potential competitors must begin by agreeing with their future competitor raises legitimate antitrust concerns.

COMMENTS AND QUESTIONS

1.   As with computer software patents, those who oppose patents for business methods must confront the very broad language of section 101 of the Patent Code; surely business methods can be "processes" and "improvements thereon." Is legislation the only way to deal with this problem or is it possible to interpret the section 101 categories in light of the potential impact of patents on the particular field in question?

2.   It is worth noting that each of the patents that have been issued for business methods have involved those implemented in a computer program. At one level, that is no surprise. After all, most of the truly new business models are ones that take advantage of computers and the Internet. But there is nothing in *State Street* that would prevent the developer of a plain old-fashioned business plan—say, Federal Express's guaranteed overnight package delivery system—from patenting it.

Are patents on "ordinary" business methods somehow more troubling than those on business methods implemented in software? If so, why?

3.   Patent Policy and Software Patents

With the possible exception of patenting living organisms, no issue of patent law has drawn greater attention or provoked more emotion than the debate over the wisdom of patenting computer software. This debate occurs at two different levels—public policy disputes over the effect of software patents and philosophical disputes over the nature of software itself. It proceeds apace even today, when it appears well settled that software patents (at least in some form) are here to stay.

League for Programming Freedom, Software Patents: Is This the Future of Programming?
Dr. Dobb's Journal, Nov. 1990, at 56

Software patents threaten to devastate America's computer industry. Newly granted software patents are being used to attack companies such as Lotus and Microsoft for selling programs that they have independently developed. Soon new companies will be barred from the software arena— most major programs will require licenses for dozens of patents, and this will make them infeasible. This problem has only one solution: Software patents must be eliminated.

[The article goes on to criticize the fact that the Patent Office has not hired professional programmers with computer science degrees to examine computer science-related patent applications.]

Licensing may be prohibitively expensive, as in the case when the patent is held by a competitor. Even "reasonable" license fees for several patents can add up to make a project infeasible. Alternatively, the developer may wish to avoid using the patent altogether; but there may be no way around it.

A programmer reading a patent may not believe that his program violates the patent, but a federal court may rule otherwise. It is thus now necessary to involve patent attorneys at every phase of program development. . . . However, for the inexpensive programming project, the same extra cost [for dealing with the patent system] is prohibitive. Individuals and small companies especially cannot afford these costs. Software patents will put an end to software entrepreneurs.

For example, the implementors of the widely used public domain data compression program *Compress* followed an algorithm obtained from *IEEE Computer* Magazine. They and the user community were surprised to learn later that [U.S.] Patent #4,558,302 had been issued to one of the authors of the article. Now [the] Unisys [Co.] is demanding royalties for using this algorithm. [U]sing [this program] means risking a law suit.

Most large software companies are trying to solve the problem of patents by getting patents of their own. Then they hope to cross-license with the other large companies that own most of the patents, so they will be free to go on as before.

While this approach will allow companies such as Microsoft, Apple, and IBM to continue in business, it will shut new companies out of the field. A future start-up, with no patents of its own, will be forced to pay whatever price the giants choose to impose. That price might be high: Established companies have an interest in excluding future competitors.

There will be little benefit to society from software patents because invention in software was already flourishing before software patents, and inventions were normally published in journals for everyone to use. Invention flourished so strongly, in fact, that the same inventions were often found again and again.

By reducing the number of people engage [sic] in software development, software patents will actually impede innovation. . . . [W]hen patents make development more difficult, and cut down on development projects, they will also cut down on the byproducts of development—new techniques.

We recommend the passage of a law to exclude software from the domain of patents.

Overturning patents in a court requires *prior art*, which may not be easy to find. The League for Programming Freedom will try to serve as a clearing house for this information, to assist the defendants in software patent suits. This depends on your help. If you know about *prior art* for any software patent, please send the information to the League. . . .

To picture the effects [of patents], imagine that each square of pavement on the sidewalk has an owner and that pedestrians must obtain individual licenses to step on particular squares. Think of the negotiations necessary to walk an entire block under this system. That is what writing a program will be like in the future if software patents continue.

COMMENTS AND QUESTIONS

1. Are these objections unique to the software industry? Or could one make the same arguments about almost every industry for which patents are available—that it will make future invention more difficult, that only large companies will be able to afford patents, or that patent litigation is expensive and the outcome uncertain? If these arguments are valid, why do we maintain a patent system at all?

2. One point mentioned in the excerpt deserves further mention: the idea that so many individual algorithms may be patented that it will be very difficult and expensive to obtain the necessary licenses to incorporate them all in a new software product. According to conventional economic theory, which pays little attention to the costs of engaging in such transactions, this should really be no problem. Since patentees and those writing programs that incorporate patentees' algorithms would both gain from a licensing transaction, it is thought that the appropriate licenses would be easily arranged. Implicit in the foregoing excerpt is doubt that this would be so. And there is some support for such doubt: some research shows that technology licensing transactions are expensive to arrange and administer, due to such factors as the difficulty of placing an "objective" value on technology. See, e.g., F. Contractor, International Technology Licensing: Compensation, Costs, and Negotiation 104-105 (1981) (transaction costs averaged over $100,000 for licensing deals studied); David J. Teece, The Multinational Corporation and the Resource Cost of International Technology Transfer 44 (1976) (transfer costs constituted over 19 percent of total project costs in international projects studied); E. von Hippel, The Sources of Innovation 48 (1988) (summarizing empirical studies finding

generally low net returns from licensing). More subtle transaction costs, such as possible opportunistic behavior, are described in F. Bidault, Technology Pricing: From Principles to Strategy 126-127 (B. Page & P. Sherwood trans. 1989), and David J. Teece, Profiting from Technological Innovation: Implications for Integration, Collaboration, Licensing and Public Policy, 15 Res. Pol'y 285, 294 (1986). It has been suggested that high transaction costs make a presumption that efficient licensing will occur unwise, see Mark A. Lemley, The Economics of Improvement in Intellectual Property Law, 75 Tex. L. Rev. 989 (1997), and even that such transactions costs are a good rationale for the exclusion of certain subject matter from intellectual property protection altogether. See Stanley Besen & Leo Raskind, An Introduction to the Law and Economics of Intellectual Property, 5 J. Econ. Perspectives 3, 10 (1991).

On the other hand, in certain cases businesses have been fairly creative in solving the problem of excessive patent licensing costs; one interpretation of industry-wide "patent pools" is that they lower the transaction costs of exchanging patented new technology. See, e.g., Bittlingmayer, Property Rights, Progress, and the Aircraft Patent Agreement, 31 J.L. & Econ. 227, 232 (1988) (describing operation and efficiency of long-lived and industry-wide patent pool in aircraft industry). But cf. Dykman, Patent Licensing Within the Manufacturer's Aircraft Association (MAA), 46 J. Pat. Off. Soc'y 646, 647 (1964) (describing formation of industry licensing pool at behest of government because "[n]o one would license the other under anything like a reasonable basis"). For a comprehensive analysis of group licensing efforts, see Robert P. Merges, Contracting Into Liability Rules: Institutions Supporting Transactions in Intellectual Property Rights, 84 Cal. L. Rev. 1293 (1996). In another context, artists' rights groups have been formed to issue "blanket licenses" of all members' works to media outlets. Formation of these groups is widely believed to be the only effective way for individual artists to have their works available for licensing. See, e.g., Stanley Besen et al., An Economic Analysis of Copyright Collectives, 78 Va. L. Rev. 383 (1992). To some extent, then, the debate over software patents may be viewed as a debate about how well the market for licenses of patented algorithms can be expected to work.

3. Given the record of success in the software industry, should we worry about permitting extensive patenting of software and algorithms? Is this a relevant concern when interpreting section 101 of the Patent Code?

Many of the issues that vex the software industry in relation to patents are *transitional* issues; they are problems that are occurring, or are feared, due to the fact that the industry was born in an era when software was generally viewed as unpatentable subject matter. Should Congress worry about who would win and who would lose during the transition from a pre-patent to a post-patent industry? Should we become alarmed over the cases where patents have erroneously issued on simple programming techniques long known to the field, or should we expect the normal court invalidation procedure to work if the patents are ever asserted? (Note that there have been industry efforts to set up a database to collect prior art to help in these cases.)

In countries in which a software industry was slow to develop, copyright protection has been credited with helping to create conditions that permitted a domestic industry to take root. See Intellectual Property Rights in Science, Technology and Economic Performance (F. Rushing & C. Brown eds., 1990), where the authors point to the case of India. On this general theme, see Robert P. Merges, A Comparative View of Property Rights in Software, *in* The International Computer Software Industry: A Comparative Study of Industry Evolution and Structure (David Mowery ed., 1994), where the author argues that strengthening property rights can not only encourage overall industry growth but also influence industry structure by making freestanding software firms more viable.

Should we expect similar transitional problems in responding to business method patents?

4. For an argument that implicitly criticizes patents for data structures and other high-level programming structures, see Randall M. Whitmeyer, Comment, A Plea for Due Process: Defining the Proper Scope of Patent Protection for Computer Software, 85 Nw. U. L. Rev. 1103, 1106 (1991):

> This Comment concludes that in the computer software context only narrow algorithms, as the term is understood by computer scientists, should be patentable. These types of algorithms best meet the patent law's policy goals of encouraging both innovation and the disclosure of technical information. At the same time, patent protection for software algorithms will not unduly hinder incremental improvements of computer software. Computer "program flows," which do little more than describe the underlying structure of a computer program, should not be considered patentable subject matter for two central reasons. First, substantial economic inefficiencies would result from these patents because of a relatively greater chance for monopoly and competitors' inability to make incremental improvements or to design around the patented method. In addition, the recent expansion of copyright protection for computer software provides protection for program flows that more appropriately balance the interests of society and software developers.

For a powerful argument that patents on software algorithms are necessary to encourage continued software development, see Donald Chisum, The Future of Software Protection: The Patentability of Algorithms, 47 U. Pitt. L. Rev. 959, 1014-1015 (1986). Professor Chisum's main argument is that producing new software is becoming more expensive and is inherently uncertain. Unless the design elements of software are protected, he argues, they will rapidly be copied, thus providing a substantial disincentive to investing in future software research and development. See also Mark A. Lemley & David W. O'Brien, Encouraging Software Reuse, 49 Stan. L. Rev. 255 (1997) (suggesting that the development of a market for reusable software components requires the stronger protection of patent law in some cases). Cf. Pamela Samuelson et al., A Manifesto Concerning the Legal Protection of Computer Programs, 94 Colum. L. Rev. 2308 (1994) (making a similar argument but suggesting a new category of software design protection in place of software patents).

B. EXAMINATION AND VALIDITY OF SOFTWARE PATENTS

Deciding whether (and under what circumstances) computer programs qualify as patentable subject matter is only the first hurdle in obtaining a software patent. A valid patent must pass four other tests in examination in the Patent Office: it must be useful (35 U.S.C. §101), novel (35 U.S.C. §102), nonobvious (35 U.S.C. §103), and clearly described in the patent application (35 U.S.C. §112 ¶1). Utility is not a particularly strict test; most computer programs that work will meet it easily. But each of the other steps in the patent examination process presents unique issues in the software context.

1. Novelty and Nonobviousness

Lockwood v. American Airlines, Inc.
United States Court of Appeals for the Federal Circuit
107 F.3d 1565 (Fed. Cir. 1997)

LOURIE, Circuit Judge.

Lawrence B. Lockwood appeals from the final judgment of the United States District Court for the Southern District of California, Lockwood v. American Airlines, Inc., No. 91-1640E (CM) (S.D.Cal. Dec. 19, 1995), granting summary judgment in favor of American Airlines, Inc. In that summary judgment, the court held that (1) U.S. Patent Re. 32,115, U.S. Patent 4,567,359, and U.S. Patent 5,309,355 were not infringed by American's SABREvision reservation system, and that (2) the '355 patent and the asserted claims of the '359 patent were invalid under 35 U.S.C. §102 and 35 U.S.C. §103, respectively. Lockwood v. American Airlines, Inc., 834 F.Supp. 1246, 28 USPQ2d 1114 (S.D.Cal.1993), *req. for reconsideration denied*, 847 F.Supp. 777 (S.D.Cal.1994) (holding the '115 and '359 patents not infringed); Lockwood v. American Airlines, Inc., 877 F.Supp. 500, 34 USPQ2d 1290 (S.D.Cal.1994) (holding the asserted claims of the '355 patent invalid and not infringed); Lockwood v. American Airlines, Inc., 37 USPQ2d 1534, 1995 WL 822659 (S.D.Cal.1995) (holding the '359 patent invalid). Because the district court correctly determined that there were no genuine issues of material fact in dispute and that American was entitled to judgment as a matter of law, we affirm.

Background

The pertinent facts are not in dispute. Lockwood owns the '115, '355, and '359 patents, all of which relate to automated interactive sales terminals that provide sales presentations to customers and allow the customers to order goods and services. Lockwood sued American asserting that American's SABREvision airline reservation system infringed all three patents. SABREvision is used by travel agents to access schedule and fare information, to book itineraries, and to retrieve photographs of places of interest, including hotels, restaurants, and cruises, for display to consumers. It improves upon American's SABRE reservation system, which originated in the 1960s and which cannot display photographs. . . .

The '359 patent discloses a system of multiple interactive self-service terminals that provide audio-visual sales presentations and dispense goods and services from multiple institutions. Claim 1, the only independent claim, reads in pertinent part:

> A system for automatically dispensing information, goods, and services for a plurality of institutions in a particular industry, comprising: . . .
> at least one customer sales and information terminal . . .
> . . . said sales and information terminal including:
> audio-visual means for interaction with a customer, comprising:
> means for storing a sequence of audio and video information to be selectively transmitted to a customer;
> means for transmitting a selected sequence of said stored information to the customer; customer operated input means for gathering information from a customer. . . .

The district court held that SABREvision did not infringe the '359 patent because it lacked the "audio-visual means" and "customer operated input means." The court also held the '359 patent invalid because it would have been obvious in light of the original SABRE system in combination with the self-service terminal disclosed in U.S. Patent 4,359,631, which issued in 1982 and was subsequently reissued as the '115 patent. . . .

Discussion . . .

A. *Validity*

The district court held that the asserted claims of the '359 patent would have been obvious in light of the prior art '631 patent and the original SABRE system. A determination of obviousness under 35 U.S.C.

§103 is a legal conclusion involving factual inquiries. Uniroyal, Inc. v. Rudkin-Wiley Corp., 837 F.2d 1044, 1050, 5 USPQ2d 1434, 1438 (Fed.Cir. 1988). Lockwood argues that the subject matter of the '359 claims would not have been obvious and that the district court impermissibly drew adverse factual inferences in concluding that the patent was invalid. Lockwood first argues that the district court erred in concluding that the SABRE system qualified as prior art.

American submitted an affidavit averring that the SABRE system was introduced to the public in 1962, had over one thousand connected sales desks by 1965, and was connected to the reservation systems for most of the other airlines by 1970. Lockwood does not dispute these facts, but argues that because "critical aspects" of the SABRE system were not accessible to the public, it could not have been prior art. American's expert conceded that the essential algorithms of the SABRE software were proprietary and confidential and that those aspects of the system that were readily apparent to the public would not have been sufficient to enable one skilled in the art to duplicate the system. However, American responds that the public need not have access to the "inner workings" of a device for it to be considered "in public use" or "used by others" within the meaning of the statute.

We agree with American that those aspects of the original SABRE system relied on by the district court are prior art to the '359 patent. The district court held that SABRE, which made and confirmed reservations with multiple institutions (e.g., airlines, hotels, and car rental agencies), combined with the terminal of the '631 patent rendered the asserted claims of the '359 patent obvious. The terminal of the '631 patent admittedly lacked this "multiple institution" feature. It is undisputed, however, that the public was aware that SABRE possessed this capability and that the public had been using SABRE to make travel reservations from independent travel agencies prior to Lockwood's date of invention.

If a device was "known or used by others" in this country before the date of invention or if it was "in public use" in this country more than one year before the date of application, it qualifies as prior art. See 35 U.S.C. §102(a) and (b) (1994). Lockwood attempts to preclude summary judgment by pointing to record testimony that one skilled in the art would not be able to build and practice the claimed invention without access to the secret aspects of SABRE. However, it is the claims that define a patented invention. See Constant v. Advanced Micro-Devices, Inc., 848 F.2d 1560, 1571, 7 USPQ2d 1057, 1064 (Fed.Cir.1988). As we have concluded earlier in this opinion, American's public use of the high-level aspects of the SABRE system was enough to place the claimed features of the '359 patent in the public's possession. See In re Epstein, 32 F.3d 1559, 1567-68, 31 USPQ2d 1817, 1823 (Fed.Cir.1994) ("Beyond this 'in public use or on sale' finding, there is no requirement for an enablement-type inquiry."). Lockwood cannot negate this by evidence showing that other, unclaimed aspects of the SABRE system were not publicly available. Moreover, the '359 patent itself does not disclose the level of detail that Lockwood would have us require of the prior art. For these reasons, Lockwood fails to show a genuine issue of material fact precluding summary judgment.

Lockwood further argues that even if the SABRE system is effective prior art, the combination of that system and the '631 patent would not have yielded the invention of the '359 patent. The terminal in the claims of the '359 patent includes a number of means-plus-function limitations, subject to 35 U.S.C. §112, ¶6, including "means for gathering information from a customer" and "means for storing a sequence of audio and video information to be selectively transmitted to a customer." Means-plus-function clauses are construed "as limited to the corresponding structure[s] disclosed in the specification and equivalents thereof." In re Donaldson Co., 16 F.3d 1189, 1195, 29 USPQ2d 1845, 1850 (Fed.Cir.1994) (in banc); see 35 U.S.C. §112, ¶6 (1994). Lockwood argues that the structures disclosed in the '359 patent differ substantially from the terminal disclosed in the '631 patent and that, at the very least, his expert's declaration raised genuine issues of material fact sufficient to preclude summary judgment.

We do not agree. We believe that American has met its burden, even in light of the presumption of patent validity, to show that the means limitations relating to the terminal in the claims of the '359 patent appear in the '631 specification. Lockwood has failed to respond by setting forth specific facts that would raise a genuine issue for trial. Specifically, Lockwood has not alleged that the '631 disclosure lacks the structures disclosed in the '359 patent specification or their equivalents. As the district court noted, Lockwood's expert, Dr. Tuthill, relied on structures that are not mentioned in either the '631 or the '359 patents. For example, Tuthill states that the claimed invention differs from the '631 patent because the terminal described in the '631 patent uses a "backward-chaining" system to solve problems while the '359 patent uses a "forward-chaining" system. Yet neither the '359 nor the '631 patents mentions backward- or forward-chaining. Nor does the '359 specification describe any hardware or software structure as being limited to any particular problem-solving technique. In addition, Lockwood argues that the hardware and software disclosed in the two patents are not equivalent to each other. However, the '359 patent claims the hardware and software in broad terms, and the patents both describe similar computer controlled self-service terminals employing video disk players that store and retrieve audio-visual information. For example, with regard to the "means for controlling said storage and transmitting means," Lockwood's expert avers that the "structure described in the '359 patent which corresponds to this means is the processor unit and the application program which the processor executes." Yet, the only software descriptions in the '359 patent consist of high level exemplary functional flowcharts. Lockwood's arguments and his expert's statements are thus conclusory. They fail to identify which structures in the

'359 patent are thought to be missing from the '631 patent disclosure. Accordingly, we agree with the district court that Lockwood's and his expert's declarations have not adequately responded to American's motion by raising genuine issues of material fact, and we therefore conclude that the district court properly held the asserted claims of the '359 patent to have been obvious as a matter of law. . . .

AFFIRMED.

COMMENTS AND QUESTIONS

1. The court holds that the SABRE system was "known or used by others" before the critical date of the '359 patent. But is affirmatively secret use sufficient to constitute prior art? Has the public really "known or used" the invention if they are prevented from seeing how it works or duplicating it? Does it matter whether American protected the SABRE system as a trade secret during the 1960s? In patent law, the answer appears to depend on whether the use was nominally open to the public, even if as a practical matter it was impossible for the public to find out about it. If it was open, it was in public use; if not, it does not constitute prior art. See, e.g., Rosaire v. National Lead Co., 218 F.2d 72 (5th Cir. 1955) (work done "openly" constituted prior art, even if it was done underground on private property); National Tractor Pullers Ass'n v. Watkins, 205 U.S.P.Q. 892 (N.D. Ill. 1980) (prior knowledge must be "reasonably accessible" to the public). For discussion of a related issue, "concealment" under 35 U.S.C. section 102(g), see infra.

2. The court notes that Lockwood has not disclosed much more structural detail in his patent specification than the prior art '631 patent, and therefore cannot claim to have differentiated his invention from that prior patent. Does this holding improperly conflate the enablement requirement and the test for obviousness?

3. Is a design alternative that accomplishes the same goal as a prior program, but does so in a different way, necessarily obvious? Or should programmers be entitled to patent their new designs that accomplish well-known goals? One practitioner provides this advice for those prosecuting software-related patents:

> [T]here are one or two rejections that seem to arise more often with software inventions than with other types of inventions. First, examiners in software cases are very quick to assert that differences between a claimed invention and a prior art reference represent "mere design alternatives" of no weight in determining patentability. Thus, the burden shifts to the applicant to argue (or reiterate, if the specification was properly written the first time) why the claimed distinctions are meritorious. The second observation of examiners in this area is that they tend to support their prior art rejections somewhat less fully than in other areas. For instance, the specifics of such a rejection might read:

> The Babbage reference does not teach a method involving Fourier Transforms. However, it would have been obvious to one skilled in the art at the time of the invention to combine the teaching of Babbage with the use a Fourier Transform in the manner claimed.

Oftentimes, such brief explanations without a description of how such teachings are likely to be combined proves unhelpful toward gaining an understanding of the examiner's reasoning. . . .

Although prior art rejections in software patent cases may tend toward the ordinary, that does not mean that responses to such rejections are necessarily conventional. In fact, because the field is still fairly undeveloped from a patent prosecution point of view, software invention prior art rejections are typically easier to handle than rejections in many other fields. Indeed, it is in litigation, rather than prosecution, that the prior art issue becomes more of a problem.

Stuart P. Meyer, Obtaining and Enforcing Patents for Software-related Inventions: Avoiding the Pitfalls, 5 Software L.J. 715 (1992).

A related question is the relevance of how competitors in the industry have addressed the same problem. For example, it is not uncommon in the software industry for many companies to come up with the same invention at roughly the same time. See, e.g., John Kasdan, Obviousness and New Technologies (working paper 1999) (noting that in one software spreadsheet case, Refac Int'l v. Lotus Dev. Corp., 15 U.S.P.Q.2d 1747 (S.D.N.Y. 1990), every company in the industry had independently come to the same conclusion that the plaintiff patented). Should such simultaneous invention be evidence of obviousness? On this point, compare In re Merck & Co., 800 F.2d 1091, 1098 (Fed. Cir. 1986) (independent invention can be evidence of obviousness), with Hybritech v. Monoclonal Antibodies, 802 F.2d 1367, n.2 (Fed. Cir. 1986) (independent invention is not evidence of obviousness).

4. A study by Greg Ahronian confirms that examiners cite less prior art in allowing software patents than in allowing any other form of patent. Why aren't patent examiners citing more prior art? Knowledgeable observers of the patent system offer at least three explanations. First, because software was not thought to be patentable until recently, the Patent Office has only recently taken steps to hire patent examiners qualified in computer software or related fields.[6] During the 1980s and the early part of the 1990s, the flood of software patent applications were handled largely by people operating outside their area of expertise. While the Meyer excerpt above suggests that this may be a problem for patent applicants, it is at least as big a problem for the public. Abundant evidence indicates that the Patent Office has issued software patents on a number of applications that did not meet the standard tests of novelty and nonobviousness. For anec-

---

6. See Scott Thurm, A Flood of Web Patents Stirs Dispute Over Tactics, Wall St. J., Oct. 9, 1998, at B1 (asserting that the PTO did not hire its first examiner with a degree in computer science until 1995).

dotes discussing some of the more extreme examples, see Simson L. Garfinkel, Patently Absurd, Wired, July 1994, at 104.

Second, for similar reasons, the PTO's classification system is not equipped to handle software patents. As a result, software patents tend to be classified according to the field in which the software will ultimately be used, rather than according to the nature of the software invention. This makes it much harder for examiners to find what prior art exists, a problem that could also be solved, either by reclassification or by an increased emphasis on computer search systems.

The final problem with prior art in the software field is more enduring: prior art in this particular industry may be difficult or, in some cases, impossible to find because of the nature of the software business. As Julie Cohen explains:

> [I]n the field of computers and computer programs, much that qualifies as prior art lies outside the areas in which the PTO has traditionally looked—previously issued patents and previous scholarly publications. Many new developments in computer programming are not documented in scholarly publications at all. Some are simply incorporated into products and placed on the market; others are discussed only in textbooks or user manuals that are not available to examiners on line. In an area that relies so heavily on published, "official" prior art, a rejection based on "common industry knowledge" that does not appear in the scholarly literature is unlikely. Particularly where the examiner lacks a computer science background, highly relevant prior art may simply be missed. In the case of the multimedia data retrieval patent granted to Compton's New Media,[7] industry criticism prompted the PTO to reexamine the patent and ultimately to reject it because it did not represent a novel and nonobvious advance over existing technology. However, it would be inefficient, and probably impracticable, to reexamine every computer program-related patent, and the PTO is unlikely to do so.

Julie E. Cohen, Reverse Engineering and the Rise of Electronic Vigilantism: Intellectual Property Implications of "Lock-Out" Technologies, 68 S. Cal. L. Rev. 1091, 1179 (1995). The current PTO Examination Guidelines for Computer-Related Inventions direct that examiners must "conduct a thorough search of the prior art," but they give no indication of how to accomplish that task.

One initiative that has received at least verbal support from a cross-section of the software industry is the work of the Software Patent Institute (SPI). Funded by a number of software publishers, the SPI seeks to create a "prior art" database of software techniques with an emphasis on those that have not been patented and are not otherwise available. They also

---

7. Compton's received a patent on an application filed in the late 1980s which purported to cover basic use of hypertext. When Compton's announced the existence of the patent at a computer trade show, and offered everyone in the multimedia industry a chance to license it, public outrage prompted the PTO to initiate a reexamination proceeding sua sponte. The PTO rejected the application after considering a number of prior art references submitted by third parties. [— EDS.]

hope to offer educational services directed to patent examiners, to address complaints about the quality of patent examinations in this field. Such online collections of software prior art may help to alleviate some of the problems Professor Cohen describes. But they are unlikely to address other problems, such as the large body of prior art published only in object code form in certain commercial or semicommercial programs. This "secret" prior art is discussed in more detail in the next Section.

Do the problems discovering software prior art suggest that the Patent Office should be more cautious about granting inventions in this industry than in other technologies? If not, what should be done about this problem?

5. For a collection of sources of prior art in the software industry, see Gregory A. Stobbs, Software Patents 109-147 (1995).

Note on Obviousness and Computer-Implemented Inventions

It is not enough that an applicant for a patent simply invent something new. To qualify for patent protection, the new invention must also show an "inventive leap" over the prior art—it must not be merely obvious to one skilled in the art. 35 U.S.C. §103. Application of the nonobviousness standard is never easy, because it requires examiners and courts to make a judgment call regarding what would have been considered obvious to scientists in the field at the time the invention was made. But as Professor Cohen points out, determining obviousness is particularly problematic in the case of inventions that use a computer to solve problems outside the field of programming itself:

> Intuitively, the most troubling aspect of many computer program-related patents is that they appear to reward the inventor for recognizing the obvious—that a given function may be performed more efficiently or more accurately if computerized—and using general purpose computer equipment and standard programming techniques to computerize it. Other computer program-related patents simply reward the programmer for developing otherwise unpatentable mathematical formulas. . . .
>
> In response to *Iwahashi*, Richard Stern, former chief of the Department of Justice's Intellectual Property Section, proposed reconceiving the standard for nonobviousness for computer program-related inventions. His solution, which may be termed the "innovative programmer" standard, adds a third step to the *Freeman-Walter-Abele* test. If a claimed invention recites a mathematical algorithm, but appears to be statutory subject matter when taken as a whole, the examiner must ask whether the claimed invention would have been obvious to "a person of ordinary skill . . . who: (a) knew the particular algorithm; (b) desired to accomplish the function or task to be performed; and (c) desired to do so with the aid of a computer. . . ." If not, it is nonobvious, and so patentable. By taking general purpose computer equipment and the mathematical algorithm as part of the prior art for purposes of

assessing nonobviousness, the innovative programmer standard is intended to avoid [granting patents to the first person to implement a known physical process on a computer, regardless of how straightforward that implementation might be].

Cohen, supra, at 1170. *Accord* Vincent Chiappetta, Patentability of Computer Software Instruction as an "Article of Manufacture": Software as Such as the Right Stuff, 17 J. Marshall J. Computer & Info. L. 89, 169-170 (1998). Does the Stern-Cohen proposal make sense? Is it consistent with patent law outside the computer context, or would it require the creation of a new, higher standard of examination specific to computer-implemented inventions? See Mark A. Lemley & David W. O'Brien, Encouraging Software Reuse, 49 Stan. L. Rev. 255 (1997) (suggesting that patent law is too lenient to inventions of the form "*A*, a known entity, plus *B*, a known entity," and that this explains many of the bad software patents currently in force).

The first case involving the obviousness of a software-implemented invention is, perhaps surprisingly, a Supreme Court case from the 1970s. In Dann v. Johnston, 425 U.S. 219 (1976), the Court held a patent on a "machine system for automatic record-keeping of bank checks and deposits" invalid for obviousness. The Court took a rather broad view of obviousness in the computer industry, focusing on whether systems analogous to the patentee's had been implemented in computer before, rather than analyzing the precise differences between the patentee's program and the prior art programs. The clear implication of the opinion is that if a reasonably skilled programmer could produce a program analogous to the patented one, and if there was motivation in the prior art to do so, the patented program is obvious.

On the other hand, the Federal Circuit in In re Zurko, 111 F.3d 887 (Fed. Cir. 1997), held that a patented invention was nonobvious even though each of the elements of the invention could be found in the prior art where the prior art did not identify the problem to be solved. This offers another outlet for patentees: they can focus their invention on solving a previously unknown problem rather than on the particular elements of their solution.

2. Trade Secrets, Section 102(g), and the Software Industry

Under 35 U.S.C. section 102(g), an inventor who keeps an invention secret may lose her right to a patent in a priority contest with an independent inventor who files a patent application. This section reads in part:

35 U.S.C. §102 Novelty and loss of right

An inventor shall be entitled to a patent unless —

(g) before the applicant's invention thereof the invention was made in this country *by another who had not abandoned, suppressed, or concealed it.*

(Emphasis added.)

Trade secret protection has been important in the software industry, particularly during its formative years. As a consequence of section 102(g) and the growing importance of patents in this industry, some commentators have expressed concern that software creators who keep their software as trade secrets could wind up having to license a later inventor of the same software, or even being forced to stop using their software altogether. See Albert C. Smith & Jared A. Slosberg, Beware! Trade Secret Software May Be Patented by a Later Inventor, 7 Computer Law. 15 (1990); Gates, Trade Secret Software: Is It Prior Art?, 6 Computer Law. 11 (1989). This results from the argument that exploiting an invention by treating it as a trade secret can amount to concealment under section 102(g) of the Patent Code. If so, the concealed invention cannot be offered as prior art to bar a different, later inventor from patenting the same invention!

In the era after *Benson*, this was not much of a threat because patents for software were generally not available. Now, however, software is clearly patentable, whether or not it is defined in physical terms. The result: later inventors may possibly leapfrog over earlier inventors of the same software. This follows from section 102(g), which not only makes it impossible for the first inventor to obtain a patent, but also directs the Patent Office and courts to disregard the first inventor's secret use when evaluating the validity of the second inventor's patent. In short, the combination of the section 102(g) rule and the growing role of patents creates the possibility of a serious threat to established software vendors who have been relying on trade secret protection for a long time. In some such cases, the second inventor will have in effect barred the first inventor from using her own invention. This is so even if—indeed, *especially* if—the first inventor invented long before the second.

On the other hand, in those cases where the first inventor's actions are not deemed intentional, or her delay in filing for a patent is not deemed excessive, her invention will defeat the novelty of the second inventor's patent application due to section 102(g).

Judge Learned Hand of the Second Circuit delivered an important opinion on the issue of prior invention in Gillman v. Stern, 114 F.2d 28 (2d Cir. 1940). The court held that a completed invention will be deemed abandoned, suppressed, or concealed if no steps are taken to make the invention publicly known within a reasonable time. The inventor in *Gillman* kept his invention completely secret from the outside world, which included his employees and his wife. The court held that such a secret invention could not be used as prior art against the patent of a subsequent inventor. An important point regarding *Gillman* is that the invention at issue was a pneumatic "puffing" machine used for quilting. Only the *output* of the machine—the products it produced—was offered for sale; the machine itself "was always kept as strictly secret as possible, consistently with its exploitation." 114 F.2d at 30. Thus, even though the quilting produced by the machine was publicly available, the machine itself was still deemed to have been concealed and hence could not be used as prior art to defeat the patentability of a later, independently developed version of the machine. See also Horwath v. Lee, 564 F.2d 948 (C.C.P.A. 1977) (the longer an inventor delays in filing application after reduction to practice, the greater are the equities that may be raised on behalf of one who made the same invention and promptly filed); Brokaw v. Vogel, 429 F.2d 476 (C.C.P.A. 1970) (five-year delay between reduction to practice and filing of patent application was too long).

If one were to analogize software object code to the quilting in *Gillman* and compare source code to the hidden-from-view quilting machine, this case could pose a serious threat to any seller of software who relies on source code trade secrecy for legal protection for an extended period of time.

Fortunately, the suggested rule in *Gilman* has not yet clearly prevailed. The Federal Circuit has held, for instance, that merely because research is secret does not mean it has necessarily been "abandoned, suppressed or concealed" under section 102(g). See E.I. du Pont de Nemours & Co. v. Phillips Petroleum Co., 849 F.2d 1430 (Fed. Cir.), *cert. denied*, 488 U.S. 986 (1988). Cf. Lockwood v. American Airlines, 107 F.3d 1565 (Fed. Cir. 1997) (secret computer program could be prior art under section 102(a) where it was "known or used by others," even though they could not see how it worked). Further, at least one court has concluded that an invention that was the subject of a secrecy order was not "concealed" within the meaning of section 102(g). Del Mar Engineering Labs v. United States, 524 F.2d 1178 (Ct. Cl. 1975). And an important recent case allows a patentee to avoid a charge of concealment despite a long delay as long as she resumes active pursuit of a patent before the second inventor's entry into the field. Paulik v. Rizkalla, 760 F.2d 1270, 226 U.S.P.Q. (BNA) 224 (Fed. Cir. 1985).

Despite the policy objective of encouraging early filing of patents, cases such as *Gillman* are troubling. To rule that secret use renders a prior invention "abandoned, suppressed or concealed" under section 102(g) is to punish those who elect to keep their inventions as trade secrets. Under *Gillman* and related cases, a later inventor who files a patent application can avoid the prior art effect of earlier secret uses by arguing that the earlier inventor abandoned, suppressed, or concealed the invention. This removes it from the definition of "prior art" under a section 102(g) and clears the way for the later inventor/patent applicant to obtain a patent. (Note that this assumes that the earlier use of the secret invention will not constitute section 102(a) "known or used by others" prior art; there is a strong possibility that section 102(a) would not defeat novelty, given the prevailing interpretation of knowledge or use as implying some degree of *public* knowledge or use.)

The rule proposed in *Gillman* is troubling because many industries rely heavily on trade secret protection to appropriate the value of their research and development. See, e.g., Levin et al., Appropriating the Returns from Industrial Research and Development, 1987 Brookings Papers Econ. Activity 783 (1987) (reporting results of extensive empirical survey of research and development personnel at U.S. corporations; many industries value trade secrets more highly than patents as appropriability mechanism, although non-legal techniques such as lead time advantages were valued most highly in most industries). Also, although several cases have held that state trade secret law may co-exist with federal patent law, see, e.g., Kewanee Oil Co. v. Bicron Corp., 416 U.S. 470 (1974), section 102(g)'s implicit "punishment" for those who elect trade secret protection raises the question how far the patent statute can or should go in disfavoring state law forms of protection.

Finally, note that the system of "prior user" rights in Europe protects the rights of first inventors/later filers in those countries. Prior inventors are allowed to continue their use of the invention after a patent issues to the second inventor. See William Neukom, A Prior User Right for The Community Patent Convention, 5 Eur. Intell. Prop. Rev. 165 (1990); Brownlee, Trade Secret Use of Patentable Inventions, Prior User Rights and Patent Law Harmonization, 72 J. Pat. & Trademark Off. Soc'y 523 (1990).

COMMENTS AND QUESTIONS

1. Because of the swiftness with which technology changes in the software industry, even relatively quick pendency times can catch the industry unawares. Late 1996 and 1997 saw the issuance of the first wave of patents directed to basic parts of the Internet, based on applications filed in the preceding years. See, e.g., U.S. Patent No. 5,572,643 ("Web browser with dynamic display of information objects during linking"). Does this rapid change suggest that software and the Internet should not be governed by patent law? Alternatively, can you think of a way to protect the prior inventor's rights over her technology while still giving voice to the patent system's policy of promoting disclosure of inventions? Note that the software industry is currently undergoing a transition from being a nonpatent industry to one where patents are important. Since many software firms have come to rely on trade secret protection, some may be hurt by the section 102(g) rule during the transitional period. Is there a way to afford these firms temporary relief, either through interpretation of the statute or by legislation?

Incidentally, one commentator has noted that patentees may be loath to risk having their patents invalidated by bringing infringement suits against prior inventors, a risk that is presumably large in light of the equities favoring the earlier trade secret user. Consequently, according to this commentator, we would expect to see a settlement of any such dispute, perhaps by cross-licenses. Karl Jorda, The Rights of the First Inventor-Trade Secret User As Against Those of the Second Inventor-Patentee (Part II), 61 J. Pat. Off. Soc'y 593, 601 (1979).

2. Would prior user rights that allowed the first inventor to continue her use of the invention make sense for the United States? See, e.g., Franklin Pierce Law Center: Third Patent System Major Problems Conference, 32 Idea 1, 41-64 (1991) (discussion of need for prior user rights system in United States). See also U.S. Congress, Committee on the Judiciary, Subcommittee on Intellectual Property and the Administration of Justice, Oversight Hearings on Prior User Rights, Tuesday, Sept. 13, 1994 (statement of Professor Robert P. Merges), at 8-9, 15, 17:

> Trade secret protection has been important in the software industry, for example. As a consequence of §102(g) and the growing importance of patents in this industry, some commentators have shown concern that software creators who keep their software as trade secrets could wind up having to license a later inventor of the same software, or even being forced to stop using their software altogether. As the Commissioner of Patents recently testified:

>> Several companies, particularly small software start-up firms from Silicon Valley, expressed concerns over potential liability for patent infringement based on their use of "old" or "well known" software techniques. These individuals believe that patents have been granted that cover such techniques, in part because the techniques were not documented in patents or printed publications. The proposed prior use defense could address one aspect of the problem these companies have described. It would enable a company that had made the requisite degree of commercial use of the "old" technique under the appropriate circumstances to avoid liability for patent infringement. It would provide this relief without requiring the company to prove that the patent being asserted against them is invalid. Importantly, the type of evidence that could be used to establish a successful prior use defense could encompass forms of evidence that do not fit cleanly within our current definitions of prior art. And while we are unsure as to how frequently this scenario may arise, we believe the legislation would address the concerns as they have described.

> Hearings on Patent Infringement, Subcommittee on Patents, Copyrights and Trademarks, U.S. Senate Committee on the Judiciary, August 9, 1994 (testimony of Bruce Lehman, U.S. Commissioner of Patents). . . . This is especially important because the software industry is currently undergoing a transition from being a non-patent industry to one where patents are important. Since many software firms have come to rely on trade secret protection, some may be hurt by the §102(g) rule. Prior user rights could afford them relief.

> . . . [T]he prior user right gives the prior inventor a "fallback" position in the event the patentee is able to prove that the prior inventor concealed the invention, and hence that the prior invention does not invalidate the pat-

entee's patent. The extra bargaining power conferred by a prior user right would encourage inventors to consider trade secret protection as a viable, although by no means equal, alternative to a patent.

A prior user right would affect the cost of negotiations as well, *if* the law provided objective, straightforward criteria for establishing the right. Under these circumstances, it would be much easier for negotiating parties to determine if a prior inventor qualified for a prior user right than it would be for them to determine the relevant §102(g) issues, including whether the prior inventor had concealed the invention. Aside from this purely evidentiary advantage, prior user rights would lower the stakes in a prior inventor/subsequent inventor-patentee dispute. Currently, the only defense available to a prior inventor who wants to continue using technology he or she developed is to invalidate the subsequent inventor's patent. Because the patent system is set up to safeguard patents from charges of invalidity, the procedural and evidentiary burdens required to establish a defense of invalidity are substantial.

. . . [T]ransfers from prior user right holders to patentees ought to be encouraged. Such a transfer would give the patentee absolutely exclusive rights, just as she receives now in the face of a holding that the prior user concealed the invention. Under a transferable prior user right regime, however, the prior user could ask for compensation for her R&D costs and the loss to her business stemming from non-practice of her invention. Of course, if she asked for too much, the subsequent patentee could decline the deal; the prior user would then be permitted to use her invention on a limited basis, as specified in the statute. The point is that by explicitly permitting transferability from prior users to subsequent patentees the law would allow absolute exclusivity, subject to some appropriate compensation (agreed to by the parties) for the loss to the prior user of her trade secret rights.

As an aside, the compensation under these deals would be a good measure of the value of the trade secret rights to the prior user. The anticipation of such compensation would then form part of the incentive to develop trade secret technologies. Again, note that this would generally be much less of an incentive than a patent, but that it would be something.

3. Under what circumstances can software that is publicly distributed only in object code form trigger the "on-sale" bar of 35 U.S.C. section 102(b)? Recall from Chapter 1 that software vendors can successfully maintain their programs as trade secrets under certain circumstances by distributing them only as object code, even though they are widely used. While one might argue that the patented invention was not disclosed to the public by such distribution, the Federal Circuit has recently foreclosed this defense. In In re Epstein, 32 F.3d 1559 (Fed. Cir. 1994), the court held that section 102(b) did not require that an invention be disclosed to trigger the bar—just that it be on sale. And as the Supreme Court made clear recently, an invention doesn't even have to be finished to be put on sale. See Pfaff v. Wells Electronics, 525 U.S. 55 (1998).

Even if the distribution of the product itself does not bar a patent more than one year afterwards, the dissemination of product marketing literature may do so if it discloses the advances claimed in the patent. See Constant v. Advanced Micro Devices, 848 F.2d 1560 (Fed. Cir. 1988).

3.   Enablement of Software Inventions

35 U.S.C.   Section 112, ¶1

The specification shall contain a written description of the invention, and of the manner and process of making and using it, in such full, clear, concise and exact terms as to enable any person skilled in the art to which it pertains, or with which it is most nearly connected, to make and use the same, and shall set forth the best mode contemplated by the inventor of carrying out his invention.

The primary issue for software patents under section 112, the disclosure provision of the patent code, has been whether a patent applicant must deposit source code to meet the enablement (i.e., "how to make and use") requirement of section 112, para. 1. Two cases in particular have defined the terms of this debate.

In White Consolidated Industries v. Vega Servo-Control, Inc., 713 F.2d 788 (Fed. Cir. 1983), the Federal Circuit invalidated a patent for a machine tool control system that was run by a computer program. Part of the invention was a programming language translator designed to convert an input program into machine language, which the system could then execute. The patent specification identified an example of a translator program, the so-called "SPLIT" program, which was a trade secret of Sundstrand, a company that later became the plaintiff White Consolidated. When the application was filed, the SPLIT program was available exclusively from Sundstrand.

The defendant, Vega, asserted patent invalidity as a defense to the infringement claim. Specifically, Vega argued that the SPLIT program was the only suitable translator program, and merely identifying it was not sufficient to meet the standards of section 112. White claimed that widely available equivalent translators could be also be used and that, in any event, the specification described the characteristics of the necessary translator program in terms that enabled a programmer of ordinary skill to create it from scratch.

The court held that the program translator was an integral part of the invention and that mere identification of it was not sufficient to discharge the applicant's duty under section 112. The court seemed concerned that maintaining the translator program as a trade secret would allow White to extend the patent beyond the 17-year term then specified in the patent code.

In Northern Telecom, Inc. v. Datapoint Corp., 908 F.2d 931 (Fed. Cir.), *cert. denied*, 498 U.S. 920 (1990), the Federal Circuit once again confronted the enablement requirement in the context of an invention containing a computer program. In *Northern Telecom*, the court reversed the district court's holding of invalidity on enablement grounds. Here the patent claimed an improved method of entering, verifying, and storing (or "batching") data with a special data entry terminal. The district court invalidated certain claims of the patent on the grounds that they were inadequately disclosed under section 112.

In a decision reversing this aspect of the district court's ruling, the Federal Circuit held that when claims pertain to a computer program that implements a claimed device or method, the enablement requirement varies according to the nature of the claimed invention as well as the role and complexity of the computer program needed to implement it. Under the facts in this case, the core of the claimed invention was the combination of components or steps, rather than the details of the program the applicant actually used. The court noted expert testimony that various programs could be used to implement the invention, and that it would be "relatively straightforward [in light of the specification] for a skilled computer programmer to design a program to carry out the claimed invention." *Id.* at 941-942. The court continued:

> The computer language is not a conjuration of some black art, it is simply a highly structured language. . . . [T]he conversion of a complete thought (as expressed in English and mathematics, i.e. the known input, the desired output, the mathematical expressions needed and the methods of using those expressions) into a language a machine understands is necessarily a mere clerical function to a skilled programmer.

Id.

The court refused to state categorically that a program listing would never have to be disclosed, however, especially in cases, such as *White*, where it was estimated that it would take two years for a skilled programmer to produce a working program of the type called for by the specification.

COMMENTS AND QUESTIONS

1. Failure to disclose the specifics of a program that would take two years to re-create renders a patent invalid under section 112. What if the program were to take one year to re-create? How about six months? One month?

2. For more on this issue, see Gregory A. Stobbs, Software Patents 170-223 (1995) (detailing means of describing software inventions in the specification and giving examples); David Bender, Anthony R. Barkume, Disclosure Requirements for Software-related Patents, 8 Computer Law. 1

(1991); Michael Bondi, Upholding the Disclosure Requirements of 35 U.S.C. §112 Through the Submission of Flow Charts with Computer Software Patent Applications, 5 Software L.J. 635 (1992); D.C. Toedt III, Patents for Inventions Utilizing Computer Software: Some Practical Pointers, 9 Computer Law. 12 (1992) (suggesting disclosure of "pseudocode" —i.e., cryptic, general-term code not in a particular programming language, to satisfy section 112 and discussing pros and cons of disclosing actual source code). See also Thomas P. Burke, Note, Software Patent Protection: Debugging the Current System, 69 Notre Dame L. Rev. 1115, 1158-1160 (1994):

> A software patent without source code is like a law review piece filled with case names but missing citations to case reporters. A person of ordinary skill in legal research might be able to track down the full text of all the opinions. Marbury v. Madison would be found quicker than a state trial court opinion. But, would anyone think that such a practice was enabling or the best mode? As it is now, the disclosure requirements can be met using such devices as specifications, flowcharts, and pseudo-code. Professor Randall Davis of MIT summed it up at the National Research Counsel in 1990:
>
> > There is almost no way to visualize software. Sure, we have flow charts, we have data-flow diagrams, we have control flow diagrams, and everybody knows how basically useless those are. Flow charts are documentation you write afterward —because management requires them, not because they are a useful tool.
>
> A patent is most similar to a real property deed specifying the metes and bounds for a parcel of land. Both documents are not easily understood but succeed if they secure the owners' interests in the specified claims. If the goal is to inform the world of an invention, software professionals have avenues more timely and less expensive than pursuing a patent application. In fostering the trade-off between the interests of inventors and the public, the source code is the best way to explain an algorithm.
>
> Under this proposal, a computer system's complete source code would not have to be appendixed to the patent. The applicant would only have to include the source code directly relevant to enabling the claim language. In cases where claims are broadly written (as in a means-plus-function apparatus claim that covers the automation of an entire industry), a nearly complete program listing would be required.

4. Best Mode and Software

Even where disclosure is adequate under the enablement standard, it can run into problems under the "best mode" aspect of section 112. An inventor runs afoul of the best mode requirement if she intentionally withholds from the patent specification information that discloses the best means of which she is aware for practicing her invention. Does the best mode requirement compel the disclosure of source code, on the theory that the actual way in which the programmer has implemented an invention must be the best way known to the inventor? Consider the following case.

═══ *Fonar Corp. v. General Electric Co.*
United States Court of Appeals for the Federal Circuit.
107 F.3d 1543 (Fed. Cir. 1997)

LOURIE, Circuit Judge. . . .

Background

The '966 patent concerns a technique for using a magnetic resonance imaging ("MRI") machine in order to obtain multiple image slices of a patient's body at different angles in a single scan, referred to as multi-angle oblique ("MAO") imaging. Prior art machines were able to obtain multiple parallel images along the same axis in a single scan, but they required multiple scans in order to obtain multiple images at varying angles. MAO resulted in shortened imaging times and hence allowed for the imaging of more patients per day. Claim 1 of the '966 patent recites this feature and reads in part:

> 1. A method for obtaining in the course of a single scan NMR [nuclear magnetic resonance] image data for a plurality of differently oriented selected planes in an object using nuclear magnetic resonance techniques, said method comprising the steps of:
>
> (a) positioning an object in a static homogeneous magnetic field;
>
> (b) determining first and second selected planes in said object for which NMR image data is to be obtained . . .
>
> (c) subjecting said object to a plurality of repetitions of a first repetition sequence composed of NMR excitation and magnetic gradient field pulses, each of said repetitions of said first repetition sequence including the steps of applying an excitation pulse and reading out of an NMR signal produced by said excitation pulse . . . said plurality of repetitions of said first repetition sequence being carried out in a manner to encode spatial information into a first collection of said NMR signals, said first collection of NMR signals being representative of NMR image data for said first selected plane; and
>
> (d) subjecting said object to a plurality of repetitions of a second repetition sequence composed of NMR excitation and magnetic field gradient pulses, each of said repetitions of said second repetition sequence including the steps of applying an excitation pulse and reading out of an NMR signal produced, by said excitation pulse . . . said plurality of repetitions of said second repetition sequence being carried out in a manner to encode spatial information into a second collection of NMR signals, said second collection of NMR signals being representative of NMR image data for said second selected plane;

said plurality of repetitions of said first and second repetition sequences each being carried out during the course of a single scan of said object and each being continued substantially throughout said single scan, the repetition time interval for repeating each of said first and second repetition sequences being substantially the same and said steps of applying an excitation pulse and reading out of an NMR signal for each repetition of said second repetition sequence being performed at a different time during said repetition time interval than each of said steps of applying an excitation pulse and reading out of an NMR signal for said first repetition sequence.

. . . Fonar sued GE for infringement of the two patents, asserting infringement of claims 1, 2, 4, 5, and 12 of the '966 patent and claims 1 and 2 of the '832 patent. A jury returned a verdict finding that the asserted claims were not invalid and were infringed. . . .

The court denied GE's motions for JMOL relating to its assertion of a violation of the best mode requirement and to damages for direct infringement of the '966 patent. The court concluded that the testimony of Fonar's witnesses provided substantial evidence to support the jury's finding that the patent satisfied the best mode requirement, and the court found that substantial evidence supported the jury's damages findings. The court summarily denied GE's motions for JMOL relating to the other issues now on appeal. The court awarded Fonar prejudgment interest and entered a final award against GE in the amount of $68,421,726.

GE now appeals to this court, arguing that the district court erred in its judgment concerning validity and infringement of the '966 patent. . . .

Discussion . . .

A. *Best Mode of the '966 Patent*

GE argues that the patent fails to disclose two software routines, the LGRAD and GETMAO programs, which the inventors testified were the best means they knew of to accomplish MAO imaging. GE also argues that a critical aspect of the invention, a gradient multiplier board ("GMB"), was not disclosed in sufficient detail to satisfy the best mode requirement. Furthermore, GE argues that the inventors failed to identify a new integrated circuit "chip" for implementing certain functions of the hardware.

Fonar responds that its disclosure was adequate to satisfy the best mode requirement, that the specification adequately describes the functions of the software, and that it is not necessary that the actual computer program be disclosed. According to Fonar, providing a description of the software's functions is what is important for a best mode disclosure, rather than actual source code, because the code was tailored to a specific hardware embodiment and it thus would not necessarily have worked with other hardware. Fonar also argues that the '966 specification adequately disclosed the GMB and the functions of the new "chip."

The patent statute requires that a patent specification "shall set forth the best mode contemplated by the inventor of carrying out his invention." 35 U.S.C. §112 (1994). Determining whether a patent satisfies the best mode requirement involves two factual inquiries. First, a fact-finder must determine whether at the time an applicant filed an application for a patent, he or she had a best mode of practicing the invention; this is a subjective determination. Second, if the inventor had a best mode of practicing the invention, the fact-finder must determine whether the best mode was disclosed in sufficient detail to allow one skilled in the art to practice it, which is an objective determination. United States Gypsum Co. v. National Gypsum Co., 74 F.3d 1209, 1212, 37 USPQ2d 1388, 1390 (Fed.Cir.1996); Chemcast Corp. v. Arco Indus. Corp., 913 F.2d 923, 927-28, 16 USPQ2d 1033, 1036 (Fed.Cir.1990).

We agree with Fonar that the jury's finding that the '966 patent satisfied the best mode requirement was supported by substantial evidence. There was evidence that the inventors had a best mode, and that the software, the GMB, and the "chip" were part of that best mode. However, with respect to the software routines, Fonar's witnesses testified that the '966 patent contained a sufficient description of the software's functions. Specifically, Robert Wolf, one of the inventors, testified as follows:

Q. From that written description, is there sufficient description to a software engineer, such as yourself, of what software needs to be written in order to perform the multi-angle oblique invention?

A. Yes. . . .

Q. In any event, the software, itself, as we see in the hundred pages of Exhibit 816, is not reproduced in its entirety in the patent. Is that right?

A. That's correct.

Q. Why is that?

A. For a few reasons. First of all, it's large as you can see. It's several hundred pages. It wouldn't help someone to have that software anyway because that software only works on a Fonar machine. What's much more important is to have a description of what the software has to do, and that is what you will find in the patent.

Fonar's witnesses further testified that providing the functions of the software was more important than providing the computer code. We agree.

As a general rule, where software constitutes part of a best mode of carrying out an invention, description of such a best mode is satisfied by a disclosure of the functions of the software. This is because, normally, writing code for such software is within the skill of the art, not requiring undue experimentation, once its functions have been disclosed. It is well established that what is within the skill of the art need not be disclosed to satisfy the best mode requirement as long as that mode is described. Stating the functions of the best mode software satisfies that description test.

We have so held previously and we so hold today. See In re Hayes Micro-computer Prods., Inc. Patent Litigation, 982 F.2d 1527, 1537-38, 25 USPQ2d 1241, 1248- 49 (Fed.Cir.1992); In re Sherwood, 613 F.2d 809, 816-17, 204 USPQ 537, 544 (CCPA 1980). Thus, flow charts or source code listings are not a requirement for adequately disclosing the functions of software. See *Sherwood*, 613 F.2d at 816-17, 204 USPQ at 544. Here, substantial evidence supports a finding that the software functions were disclosed sufficiently to satisfy the best mode requirement. See *Hayes*, 982 F.2d at 1537, 25 USPQ2d at 1248-49 (stating that there was no best mode violation where the specification failed to disclose a firmware listing or flow charts, but did disclose sufficient detail to allow one skilled in the art to develop a firmware listing for implementing the invention).

A finding that the GMB was sufficiently disclosed to satisfy the best mode requirement was also supported by substantial evidence. Fonar's witness testified that the '966 patent provided a description of the function of the GMB with reference to the components within the dotted line in Figure 7 of the '966 patent, reproduced on p. 347.

David Hertz, one of the inventors, testified in particular that the patent provides a description of the functions required for one skilled in the art to build a GMB that will work with a general MRI system and that the GMB disclosed in the patent is the one built by Fonar. More importantly, he testified that the GMB used in the Fonar machine was not the only means to accomplish MAO imaging and that it was not necessarily the best way to do it for every machine. GE argues nonetheless that the '966 patent failed to disclose the use of comparators as part of the GMB, which it alleged were an essential element of the best mode. However, Hertz testified that if an MRI machine performing MAO imaging according to the '966 patent were to require a comparator as part of the GMB, a skilled engineer would know that a comparator should be used. He further testified that each MRI machine has its own set of requirements for the functionality of the GMB, which is why the '966 patent described in general terms how to build the invention. Hertz's testimony provides substantial evidence to support a finding that there was no best mode violation with respect to the GMB.

Substantial evidence also supports the finding that the functions of the new "chip" were disclosed sufficiently to satisfy the best mode requirement. The '966 patent schematically disclosed the functions of that "chip" in Figure 7 and provided a textual description of its functions. See '966 patent, col. 13, lines 41-64. Because adequate disclosure of the functions of the "chip" was in the specification, failure to specifically identify a particular manufacturer's "chip" was not fatal to satisfaction of the best mode requirement. Accordingly, the jury's finding that the '966 patent satisfied the best mode requirement was supported by substantial evidence, and the district court did not err in denying GE's motion for JMOL concerning that issue. . . .

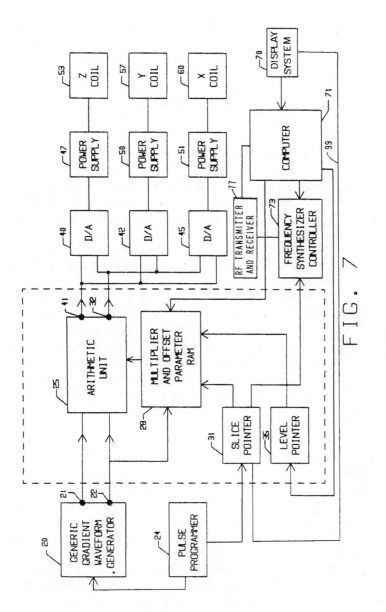

FIG. 7

FIGURE 3-2

Figure 7 of the '966 patent.

Conclusion

The district court did not err in its judgment denying GE's motions for JMOL and sustaining the jury's verdict that the '966 patent was not invalid for failure to satisfy the best mode requirement. . . .

AFFIRMED IN PART AND REVERSED IN PART.

COMMENTS AND QUESTIONS

1. Most software patent cases have taken a similar position. See In re Hayes Microcomputer Products, Inc. Patent Litigation, 982 F.2d 1527 (Fed. Cir. 1992) (maker of Hayes modems was not required to disclose secret settings used on those modems in patent application, because settings were arbitrarily chosen). Indeed, in two cases decided in 1997, the Federal Circuit concluded that the patentees satisfied the best-mode requirement for inventions implemented in software even though they did not use the terms "computer" or "software" anywhere in the specification! See Robotic Vision Systems, Inc. v. View Engineering, Inc., 42 U.S.P.Q.2d 1619 (Fed. Cir. 1997) (it would be "plainly apparent" to one of ordinary skill in the art that software would be required, and it was not necessary to further disclose the nature of the code actually used); In re Dossel, 42 U.S.P.Q.2d 1881 (Fed. Cir. 1997) (means-plus-function claim that includes a "means for reconstructing data" is obviously implemented in software, so disclosure of that fact is not required; software program itself did not have to be disclosed).

2. The PTO's Examination Guidelines for Computer-Implemented Inventions clearly assume that source code need not be disclosed in many cases. In the section discussing enablement, the Guidelines note that "[i]n many instances, an applicant will describe a programmed computer by outlining the significant elements of the programmed computer using a functional block diagram." Examiners facing such a disclosure are merely instructed to make sure that the block diagram adequately discloses the existence of each hardware element as well as the software elements.

3. Patent applicants presumably view the dramatic relaxation of the best-mode requirement in software cases with some relief. But should they? Note that the Federal Circuit considers the disclosure of software code and flow charts unnecessary because "normally, writing code for such software is within the skill of the art, not requiring undue experimentation, once its functions have been disclosed." If this is so, what does it suggest about the obviousness or nonobviousness of inventions whose improvement lies in more efficient code? Does the court's opinion presage a stricter standard of obviousness, at least for applications in which code improvements are claimed as the patentable invention? (For an example of this type of patent, see U.S. Patent No. 5,572,207 ("method and apparatus for numeric-to-string conversion").)

C. INFRINGEMENT

≡
≡
≡
≡
Pennwalt Corp. v. Durand-Wayland, Inc.
United States Court of Appeals for the Federal Circuit
833 F.2d 931 (Fed. Cir. 1987) (en banc)

BISSELL, Circuit Judge.

This appeal and cross-appeal are from a judgment of the United States District Court for the Northern District of Georgia, 225 U.S.P.Q. (BNA) 558 (N.D. Ga. 1984). The district court found that Durand-Wayland's accused devices do not infringe any claim, literally or under the doctrine of equivalents. Unable to view that finding as clearly erroneous under Fed. R. Civ. P. 52(a), we affirm the judgment of noninfringement. . . .

Background

Pennwalt sued Durand-Wayland for infringing claims 1, 2, 10 and 18 (claims-at-issue) of its U.S. Patent No. 4,106,628 (the '628 patent) on an invention of Aaron J. Warkentin and George A. Mills, entitled "Sorter for Fruit and the Like." Following a nonjury trial on the issues of patent infringement and validity, the district court, on March 22, 1984, issued an opinion concluding that (1) the claims-at-issue were not anticipated by the prior art, (2) the '628 patent had not run afoul of the "on sale" bar of 35 U.S.C. §102(b) (1982), and (3) the accused devices did not infringe any of the claims-at-issue, either literally or under the doctrine of equivalents. . . .

Opinion

The '628 patent claims a sorter. The principal object of the invention is to provide a rapid means for sorting items, such as fruit, by color, weight, or a combination of these two characteristics. The sorter recited in claims 1 and 2 conveys items along a track having an electronic-weighing device that produces an electrical signal proportional to the weight of the item, along with signal comparison means, clock means, position indicating means, and discharge means, each of which performs specified functions. The specification describes the details of a "hard-wired" network consisting of discrete electrical components which perform each step of the claims, e.g., by comparing the signals from the weighing device to reference signals and sending an appropriate signal at the proper time to discharge the item into the container corresponding to its weight. The combined sorter of claims 10 and 18 is a multifunctional apparatus whereby the item is conveyed across the weighing device and also carried past an optical scanner that produces an electrical signal proportional to the color of the item. The signals from the weighing device and color sensor are combined and an appropriate signal is sent at the proper time to discharge the item into the container corresponding to its color and weight.

Durand-Wayland manufactures and sells two different types of sorting machines. The first accused device, the "Microsizer," sorts by weight only and employs software labeled either Version 2 or Version 5. The second accused device employs software labeled Version 6 and sorts by both color and weight through the use of the "Microsizer" in conjunction with a color detection apparatus called a "Microsorter." . . .

I. Literal Infringement

Pennwalt asserts on appeal that all limitations set forth in claims 1 and 2 and some limitations set forth in claims 10 and 18 can be read literally on the accused devices. Pennwalt contends that the district court erred in interpreting the claims by going beyond the means-plus-function language of a claim limitation and comparing the structure in the accused devices with the structure disclosed in the specification. Such comparison allegedly resulted in the court's reading nonexistent structural limitations into the claims. Pennwalt relies on the statement in Graver Tank & Mfg. Co. v. Linde Air Prods. Co., 339 U.S. 605, 607, 94 L. Ed. 1097, 70 S. Ct. 854 (1950): "If accused matter falls clearly within the claim, infringement is made out and that is the end of it." In view of the literal breadth of means-plus-function language in the claims, that "test" for literal infringement would encompass any means that performed the function of a claim element. 35 U.S.C. §112 (1982). This is not the "test." . . .

. . . [S]ection 112, paragraph 6, rules out the possibility that any and every means which performs the function specified in the claim literally satisfies that limitation. While encompassing equivalents of those disclosed in the specification, the provision, nevertheless, acts as a restriction on the literal satisfaction of a claim limitation. Data Line Corp. v. Micro Technologies, Inc., 813 F.2d 1196, 1201, 1 U.S.P.Q.2d (BNA) 2052, 2055 (Fed. Cir. 1987). If the required function is not performed exactly in the accused device, it must be borne in mind that section 112, paragraph 6, equivalency is not involved. Section 112, paragraph 6, plays no role in determining whether an equivalent function is performed by the accused device under the doctrine of equivalents.

Thus, it was not legal error (as Pennwalt asserts) for the district court to have made a comparison between Durand-Wayland's structure and the structure disclosed in the specification for performing a particular function. The statute means exactly what it says: To determine whether a claim limitation is met literally, where expressed as a means for performing a stated function, the court must compare the accused structure with the disclosed structure, and must find equivalent structure as well as identity of claimed function for that structure. . . .

We need not, and do not, determine whether the district court correctly found no equivalency in structure because the district court also found that the accused devices, in any event, did not perform the same functions specified in the claim. For example, the district court found that the accused devices had no position indicating means which tracked the location of the item being sorted. That finding negates the possibility of finding literal infringement.

II. *Infringement under the Doctrine of Equivalents*

Under the doctrine of equivalents, infringement may be found (but not necessarily) if an accused device performs substantially the same overall function or work, in substantially the same way, to obtain substantially the same overall result as the claimed invention. Perkin-Elmer Corp. v. Computervision Corp., 732 F.2d 888, 901-02, 221 U.S.P.Q. (BNA) 669, 679 (Fed. Cir.), *cert. denied*, 469 U.S. 857, 83 L. Ed. 2d 120, 105 S. Ct. 187 (1984); *Graver Tank*, 339 U.S. at 608. That formulation, however, does not mean one can ignore claim limitations. As this court recently stated in Perkin-Elmer Corp. v. Westinghouse Elec. Corp., 822 F.2d 1528, 3 U.S.P.Q.2d (BNA) 1321 (Fed. Cir. 1987):

> One must start with the claim, and though a "non-pioneer" invention may be entitled to some range of equivalents, a court may not, under the guise of applying the doctrine of equivalents, erase a plethora of meaningful structural and functional limitations of the claim on which the public is entitled to rely in avoiding infringement. . . . Though the doctrine of equivalents is designed to do equity, and to relieve an inventor from a semantic strait jacket when equity requires, it is not designed to permit wholesale redrafting of a claim to cover non-equivalent devices, i.e., to permit a claim expansion that would encompass more than an insubstantial change. (Citations omitted.)
>
> . . . In applying the doctrine of equivalents, each limitation must be viewed in the context of the entire claim. . . . "It is . . . well settled that each element of a claim is material and essential, and that in order for a court to find infringement, the plaintiff must show the presence of every element or its substantial equivalent in the accused device." Lemelson v. United States, 752 F.2d 1538, 1551, 224 U.S.P.Q. (BNA) 526, 533 (Fed. Cir. 1985) (footnote omitted). To be a "substantial equivalent," the element substituted in the accused device for the element set forth in the claim must not be such as would substantially change the way in which the function of the claimed invention is performed.

Id. at 1532-33, 3 U.S.P.Q.2d at 1324-25.

Pennwalt argues that the "accused machines simply do in a computer what the patent illustrates doing with hard-wired circuitry," and asserts that "this alone is insufficient to escape infringement," citing Decca Ltd. v. United States, 210 Ct. Cl. 546, 544 F.2d 1070, 1080-81, 191 U.S.P.Q. (BNA) 439, 447 (1976). If Pennwalt was correct that the accused devices differ only in substituting a computer for hard-wired circuitry, it might have a stronger position for arguing that the accused devices infringe the claims. The claim limitations, however, require the performance of certain specified functions. Theoretically, a microprocessor could be programmed to perform those functions. However, the district court found that the microprocessor in the accused devices was not so programmed.

After a full trial, the district court made findings that certain functions of the claimed inventions were "missing" from the accused devices and those which were performed were "substantially different." *Pennwalt,* 225 U.S.P.Q. at 572. The district court observed that "because the 'Microsizer' uses different elements and different operations (on the elements it does use) than the elements and operations disclosed in the patent-in-suit to achieve the desired results, infringement can only be found if the different elements and operations are the legal equivalents of those disclosed in the patent-in-suit." *Id.* It is clear from this that the district court correctly relied on an element-by-element comparison to conclude that there was no infringement under the doctrine of equivalents, because the accused devices did not perform substantially the same functions as the Pennwalt invention. For example, the district court found in part:

> The machine described in the patent-in-suit uses shift registers that respond to "clock pulses" in order to indicate the various positions of the items to be sorted before each item is discharged. The "Microsizer" does not have any "indicating means" to determine positions of the items to be sorted since the microprocessor stores weight and color data, not the positions of the items to be sorted. After a piece of fruit has been analyzed by the "Microsorter" and while it is in transit from the optical detection means to the weight scale, the color value determined by the "Microsorter" is sorted in a color value queue. A color value queue pointer (which changes in value) points to the location of the data corresponding to the next piece of fruit to reach the weight scale. A weight value queue pointer (which also changes in value) is used to correspond to the number of cups between the weight scale and the drop location. The microprocessor software utilizes a random access memory that stores the digital numbers which resulted from the conversion of the analog signals generated by the "Microsorter" and the weight scale, and the queue pointers (under clock control) point to the memory location that has the data about a piece of fruit. The data is never "shifted" around, but rather is just stored in memory until the software routines call for data to be utilized in subsequent portions of the program(s). Thus, the "Microsizer" has neither a "first position indicating means" nor a "second position indicating means." The machine described in the patent-in-suit produces signals that indicate where the fruit is, i.e. track the progression of each cup. The "Microsizer" does not.

Id. at 569. . . .

The trial court found that the accused devices do not have any position indicating means to determine positions of the items to be sorted. Specifically with respect to claims 10 and 18, the court correctly held that "the microprocessor stores weight and color data, not the positions of the items to be sorted." *Pennwalt,* 225 U.S.P.Q. at 569. Since each of the claims-at-issue requires a position indicating means and the same analysis applies to each, we set forth only the relevant language of claim 10:

> first position indicating means responsive to a signal from said clock means and said signal from said second comparison means for continuously indicating the position of an item to be sorted while the item is in transit between said optical detection means and said electronic weighing means,
> second position indicating means responsive to the signal from said clock means, the signal from said first comparison means and said first position indicating means for generating a signal continuously indicative of the position of an item to be sorted after said item has been weighed.

. . . Second, the district court correctly rejected Pennwalt's assertion that the memory component of the Durand-Wayland sorter which stores information as to weight and color of an item performed substantially the same functions as claimed for the position indicating means. The district court found that a memory function is not the same or substantially the same as the function of "continuously indicating" where an item is physically located in a sorter. On this point the record is indisputable that before the words "continuously indicating" were added as an additional limitation, the claim was unpatentable in view of prior art which, like the accused machines, stores the information with respect to sorting criteria in memories, but did not "continuously" track the location. See, e.g., U.S. Patent No. 3,289,832 issued to Ramsey.

Thus, the facts here do not involve later-developed computer technology which should be deemed within the scope of the claims to avoid the pirating of an invention. On the contrary, the inventors could not obtain a patent with claims in which the functions were described more broadly. Having secured claims only by including very specific functional limitations, Pennwalt now seeks to avoid those very limitations under the doctrine of equivalents. This it cannot do. Graham v. John Deere Co., 383 U.S. 1, 33-34, 15 L. Ed. 2d 545, 86 S. Ct. 684 (1965); *Chemical Eng'g Corp.,* 795 F.2d at 1572 n. 8, 230 U.S.P.Q. at 391 n. 8; see also Exhibit Supply Co. v. Ace Patents Corp., 315 U.S. 126, 136, 86 L. Ed. 736, 62 S. Ct. 513 (1942); Coleco Indus., Inc. v. United States Int'l Trade Comm'n, 65 C.C.P.A. 105, 573 F.2d 1247, 1257-58, 197 U.S.P.Q. (BNA) 472, 479-80 (1978). Simply put, the memory components of the Durand-Wayland sorter were not programmed to perform the same or an equivalent function of physically tracking the items to be sorted from the scanner to the scale or from the scale to its appropriate discharge point as required by the claims.

[Affirmed. The dissent's discussion of the proper legal test for applying the doctrine of equivalents is omitted.]

Alpex Computer Corporation v. Nintendo Company Ltd.
United States Court of Appeals for the Federal Circuit
102 F.3d 1214 (Fed. Cir. 1996)

ARCHER, Chief Judge.

Nintendo Company, Ltd. and Nintendo of America, Inc. (collectively Nintendo) appeal the January 6, 1995, judgment of the United States District Court for the Southern District of New York, Alpex Computer Corp. v. Nintendo Co., 1994 U.S. Dist. LEXIS 17515, 34 U.S.P.Q.2D (BNA) 1167 (S.D.N.Y. 1994), holding U.S. Patent No. 4,026,555 (the '555 patent), owned by Alpex Computer Corporation (Alpex), not invalid, willfully infringed, and awarding $253,641,445 in damages and interest. We affirm the judgment as to validity and reverse the judgment of infringement.

I.

This case deals with an invention within the art of video games. The video game industry began in the early 1970s and includes two branches, arcade video games and home video games. Arcade video games are large, expensive, coin-operated machines that are placed in high traffic areas such as amusement arcades. These machines are generally referred to as "dedicated" because they can play only one game. Home video games, in contrast, are small, relatively inexpensive devices that are easily connected to the antennae terminals of a standard television.

The Magnavox Odyssey was the first home video game. It too was a dedicated system playing only one game which was referred to as the "ball and paddle" because a dot of light bounced between two player-controlled vertical lines. In early 1974, the inventors of the patent in suit conceived of a new microprocessor-based home video game system that used modular plug-in units—replaceable, read-only memory, or ROM, cartridges—to permit home video systems to play multiple games, including games with rotating images. The '555 patent on this invention issued to Alpex on May 31, 1977. The patented invention was commercialized in systems by Atari, Mattel, and Coleco. In the early 1980s, Nintendo entered the home video game market with the Nintendo Entertainment System (NES). After the NES was featured at the 1985 Consumer Electronics Show, Alpex notified Nintendo of possible infringement of the '555 patent. Soon thereafter, in February 1986, Alpex filed suit against Nintendo for patent infringement. . . . Following a four-week liability trial, the jury returned a verdict for Alpex. . . . Nintendo now appeals the judgment as to validity, infringement, and damages, and Alpex cross-appeals the amount of damages.

II.

The '555 patent claims a keyboard-controlled apparatus for producing video signals by means of random access memory (RAM) with storage positions corresponding to each discrete position of the raster for a standard television receiver. Figure 2 of the '555 patent depicts the structure of the invention, as follows: The television raster comprises numerous discrete dots or bars, approximately 32,000, which the cathode ray beam illuminates on a standard cycle, which in turn creates the image on the television screen. The patented invention requires sufficient RAM to accommodate each of the approximately 32,000 memory positions needed to represent the raster image. Thus, the RAM holds at least one "bit" of data for each position in the memory "map" of the raster. Accordingly, this video display system is called "bit-mapping." The advantage of this system, as disclosed in the patent, is that it provides for the representation of every image within the raster RAM, or display RAM, and thereby provides greater control of the display for the manipulation of complex images and symbols. To achieve this flexibility, however, bit-mapping requires the construction of each image within the display RAM before display, a process that requires the microprocessor to erase and rewrite each image. Because the microprocessor must refresh the display RAM for each frame to show the movement of images, the operation of the system is slowed down.

FIGURE 3-3
Figure 2 of the '555 patent.

The accused NES with its game cartridges is also an apparatus for producing video signals by means of storage positions corresponding to discrete positions of the raster for a standard television receiver. A trial exhibit illustrates the NES:

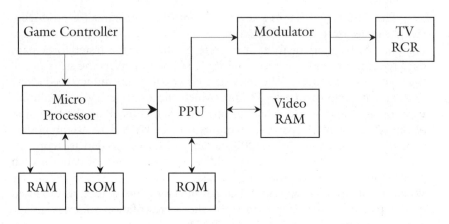

FIGURE 3-4
Illustration of structure of Nintendo device.

The video display system for the NES does not include RAM with storage positions corresponding to each discrete position of the raster. Instead, the NES utilizes a patented picture processing unit, or PPU, to perform the generation of images on the screen. The PPU receives preformed, horizontal slices of data and places each slice in one of eight shift registers, each of which can store a maximum of 8 pixels. These slices of data are then processed directly to the screen. The PPU repeats this process to assemble the initial image on the screen. Thereafter it repeats the process as necessary to form changes in images throughout the progression of the game. Nintendo refers to the PPU as an "on-the-fly" system. It is undisputed that the NES video display system, using shift registers to process slices of images (as opposed to entire screens), is a faster means of displaying movement of images on the video screen than the bit-mapping of the RAM-based system of the '555 patent. The claims at issue are 12 and 13 of the '555 patent:

> 12. Apparatus for playing games by displaying and manipulating player and ball image devices on the screen of a display tube, comprising
>> first means for generating a video signal representing a linear player image device aligned in a first direction,
>> second means for generating a video signal representing a ball image device,
>> manually operable game control means, and

means responsive to said manually operable game control means for causing said first means to generate a video signal representing the player image device rotated so that it is aligned in a second direction different from said first direction.

13. Apparatus according to claim 12, wherein said means for causing includes programmed microprocessor means and a replaceable memory having program game instructions stored therein for controlling said microprocessor means, whereby different games may be played with said apparatus by replacing said replaceable memory.

The parties dispute the proper claim construction of independent claim 12 (and thus dependent claim 13) and specifically the meaning and scope of "means for generating a video signal."

III.

. . . The following jury instruction with regard to the video display system claimed in the '555 patent was proposed by the special master:

> The structure corresponding to the elements of claims 12 and 13 for generating a video signal is the Figure 2 components without the television receiver and the keyboard. These components cooperate together to create a video signal as follows: The linear player image device and the ball image device to be displayed on the video unit 30 are stored as data within ROM 42A. The "intelligence" of the system is provided by micro-processor 40. The operation of the micro-processor 40 is under the control of a program stored in ROM 42A. Micro-processor 40 causes this information in ROM 42A to be written into RAM 32 by using the write control circuit 38. RAM 32 has discrete storage positions which correspond to each of the bars or pixels of the TV screen. TV interface 36 causes display RAM address 34 to scan each of these storage positions in display RAM 32 to provide the video signal to the TV receiver 30.

Alternatively, the special master recommended leaving the issue of claim construction to the jury. The district court chose only to adopt the first sentence of the special master's recommended jury instruction, relegating the remainder of the claim construction issues to the jury. After the jury returned a verdict of infringement, Nintendo challenged on motion for JMOL the interpretation that the jury appeared to give the claim in reaching its verdict, but the district court denied Nintendo's motion. The court seemed to adopt the entirety of the claim interpretation of the special master in ruling on the JMOL motion and held that there was sufficient evidence to support the jury's presumed claim construction. Nintendo argues that, by denying its JMOL, the district court approved an erroneous claim construction, allowing claims for a RAM-based, bit-map video display system to read on a device that used a shift register-based, on-the-fly video display system. Nintendo argues that the '555 patent requires the use of a RAM memory map for all of the 32,000 pixels in the raster, whereas the NES uses shift registers that only provide for a maximum of 64 pixels. Because of this difference in structure, Nintendo contends that there can be neither literal infringement nor infringement under the doctrine of equivalents. Nintendo further contends that Alpex is barred from claiming that the NES infringes the '555 patent because during prosecution Alpex distinguished the invention of the '555 patent from a relevant prior art patent using shift registers.

In prosecuting its patent application before the Patent and Trademark Office (PTO), Alpex specifically distinguished the RAM-based, bit-map video display structure of the '555 patent from a prior art patent, Okuda, which claimed a shift register-based video display structure. Alpex explained to the PTO that, unlike Alpex's bit-map system, the Okuda video display system comprised an entirely different structure than the Alpex system. Specifically, Alpex noted that Okuda was unable to modify selectively a single pixel on the screen. Alpex explained:

> Applicants' display system utilizes a random access memory (RAM) 32 which is under the control of a micro-processor 40. When the keyboard is operated, as explained in the specification, micro-processor 40 extracts an appropriate image device from the read-only memory (ROM) 42A and transfers this particular image device directly into the appropriate location within the RAM 32. The random access capability is important since this enables the selected image device to be located directly in any desired area of the RAM 32.
>
> Okuda, in contrast, does not use a random access memory but, instead, employs a series of shift registers as his refresh memory 17 which corresponds to applicants' RAM 32. Because random access to the shift registers is not possible, Okuda is unable to selectively modify a single bit in the memory 17 but, instead, must operate on a line at a time to modify the stored display data. . . .
>
> Okuda contemplates modification of one line of data at a time and there is no provision for modifying a single "dot." The random access techniques of applicants' invention enables any single point on the TV screen to be altered at will (under control of the micro-processor).

. . . Nintendo contends that the statements regarding the Okuda prior art patent were relevant and should have been considered for purposes of claim construction even though they may not give rise to prosecution history estoppel as to asserted claims 12 and 13. . . .

IV.

Prosecution history is relevant not only for purposes of prosecution history estoppel but also for construing the meaning and scope of the claims.

In this case, the Okuda patent is directly relevant to claim construction. The prosecution history of the '555 patent shows that the examiner rejected claim 1 of the application as being anticipated by Okuda. Claim 1 specified a series of limitations in means-plus-function format to a display control apparatus utilizing a RAM-based, bit-map system. Alpex distinguished Okuda before the PTO based on the structural difference of a RAM-based versus a shift register-based video display system: "Claim 1, as amended, now clearly distinguishes over Okuda. The claim requires a random access memory which, as indicated previously, is not disclosed in Okuda." . . .

The district court recognized that claims 12 and 13, and the specification of the '555 patent, call for the use of a RAM-based, bit-map video display system. Moreover, the statements made by Alpex during prosecution with regard to the Okuda prior art patent emphasize that Alpex claimed a video display system based on the use of RAM capable of modifying a single bit, or pixel, on the television receiver. These statements distinguish any video display system based on shift registers, as shift registers do not allow the selective modification of a single bit in memory, that is, a single pixel. It is undisputed that the NES utilized this type of video display system. Indeed, Alpex's own technical expert, Mr. Milner, testified that the NES utilized shift registers, not RAM. Further, Mr. Milner explained that the NES could not directly modify a single pixel. Thus, Mr. Milner's testimony confirms that random access capability is not possible by use of shift registers. In short, the structure and operation of the NES paralleled the structure and operation of the Okuda video display system.

Alpex attempts to distinguish Okuda from the NES because Okuda only allows the modification of horizontal lines on the raster, whereas the NES allows the modification of any 8-bit slice on the raster. This distinction, however, affects neither the structural similarities (both Okuda and the NES use shift registers) nor the pertinent functional similarities (both Okuda and the NES cannot modify a single pixel). Therefore, because Alpex admitted during prosecution that its claims do not cover a video display system based on shift registers as in Okuda, i.e., it argued that a system based on shift registers is not structurally or functionally equivalent to a RAM based system that can randomly access a single bit, Alpex's claims cannot now be construed to cover the NES, which possesses the same structural and functional traits as Okuda.

V.

On the jury verdict form, Interrogatory 1 asked the following: "Do you find that claims 12 and 13 require a structure that includes a display RAM which has discrete storage positions which correspond to each of the bars or pixels of the TV screen?" The jury answered this question in the affirmative. This response is consistent with and supported by the prosecution history of the '555 patent.

The jury then found that the accused products, the NES and most of its accompanying game cartridges, infringed claims 12 and 13 of the 555 patent, implicitly finding structural equivalence between a RAM-based, bit-map video display system and a shift register-based, NES system under §112, & 6. The district court determined that these findings were supported by substantial evidence and denied the motion for JMOL. See Kearns v. Chrysler Corp., 32 F.3d 1541, 1547-48, 31 U.S.P.Q.2D (BNA) 1746, 1751 (Fed. Cir. 1994) (deeming reversal proper "only if the jury's factual findings, presumed or express, are not supported by substantial evidence or, if they are, that the legal conclusions implied from the jury's verdict cannot in law be supported by those findings"); Perkin-Elmer Corp. v. Computervision Corp., 732 F.2d 888, 893, 221 U.S.P.Q. (BNA) 669, 673 (Fed. Cir. 1984) ("Only when the court is convinced upon the record before the jury that reasonable persons would not have reached a verdict for the non-mover, should it grant the motion for [JMOL]."). We review the district court's JMOL ruling applying the same standard. Read Corp. v. Portec, Inc., 970 F.2d 816, 821, 23 U.S.P.Q.2D (BNA) 1426, 1431 (Fed. Cir. 1992).

The district court held that Nintendo had literally infringed claims 12 and 13 of the '555 patent based primarily on the testimony of Alpex's expert Mr. Milner that the distinction between a bit-map system and the NES "is insignificant and insufficient to defeat a claim of equivalence under section 112(6)." Accordingly, the district court concluded that the NES is not only a functional equivalent but also a structural equivalent to the bit-map structure. For the reasons stated above, however, the NES cannot infringe claims 12 and 13 of the '555 patent as equivalents under §112, ¶6, under a proper claim construction. . . .

Moreover, while Mr. Milner's testimony purports to be an analysis of the structure of the specification and the accused device, it actually provides no more than an analysis of functional equivalency. Mr. Milner described the shift registers of the NES as storing "just one little slice of an object" to be imaged; whereas he said the bit-map system "stores the whole screen." He concluded that displaying a slice of an object is equivalent to displaying the "whole screen." Specifically, Mr. Milner testified that "the reason they are equivalent is by storing one line at a time and using it over and over and over again very quickly you can do the same thing." Thus, Mr. Milner concluded that by repeating the NES process the entire screen will eventually be imaged as is done with the bit map system. This is a conclusion, however, of equivalency of function—both systems store data and will eventually display an image on the whole screen. Mr. Milner did not compare the structure of the NES with the bit map structure disclosed in the specification. Moreover, the bit map structure was clearly distinguished over a shift register structure during the prosecution of the '555 patent.

Because Alpex defined its claims during the prosecution of the '555 patent as not covering a system using shift registers and because the testimony relied on by Alpex to establish infringement under §112, ¶6, was based only on a functional, not a structural, analysis, we conclude the court erred in sustaining the jury verdict of literal infringement.

VI.

The district court also denied Nintendo's motion for JMOL on the issue of infringement under the doctrine of equivalents primarily based on its conclusion that the jury could reasonably have found infringement under §112, ¶6. The court reasoned that equivalence under the doctrine of equivalents is a slightly broader concept than equivalence under §112, ¶6, and that, as a result, its discussion of equivalence for literal infringement applied equally to infringement under the doctrine of equivalents.

While equivalency under the doctrine of equivalents and equivalency under §112, ¶6, both relate to insubstantial changes, each has a separate origin, purpose and application. Valmont Indus., Inc. v. Reinke Mfg. Co., 983 F.2d 1039, 1043-44, 25 U.S.P.Q.2D (BNA) 1451, 1454 (Fed. Cir. 1993). Under §112, the concern is whether the accused device, which performs the claimed function, has the same or an equivalent structure as the structure described in the specification corresponding to the claim's means. D.M.I. Inc. v. Deere & Co., 755 F.2d 1570, 1575, 225 U.S.P.Q. (BNA) 236, 239 (Fed. Cir. 1985). Under the doctrine of equivalents, on the other hand, the question is whether the accused device is only insubstantially different than the claimed device. Hilton Davis Chem. Co. v. Warner-Jenkinson Co., 62 F.3d 1512, 1517, 35 U.S.P.Q.2D (BNA) 1641, 1644-45 (Fed. Cir. 1995) (in banc), *cert. granted*, 116 S. Ct. 1014 (1996). The latter question often turns on whether the accused device performs substantially the same function in substantially the same way to achieve substantially the same result. See *id.* at 1518, 35 U.S.P.Q.2D (BNA) at 1645.

In this case, the court concluded, based on the testimony of Alpex's expert, Mr. Milner, that the jury's finding of infringement under the doctrine of equivalents was supported by substantial evidence. However, Mr. Milner's testimony that the claimed and accused devices were substantially the same in terms of function/way/result was merely conclusory as acknowledged by the district court. However, the court said that Mr. Milner's conclusory statements on function/way/result, when considered with his testimony in relation to infringement under the §112, ¶6, were sufficient to establish infringement under the doctrine of equivalents.

As discussed earlier, however, Mr. Milner's testimony concerning §112, ¶6, only related to equivalence of the functional result. Neither he nor the court considered whether the accused device and the claimed device operated in substantially the same way. Indeed, in describing equivalency for §112, ¶6, purposes, Mr. Milner acknowledged that the accused and claimed devices do not operate in the same way. For example, Mr. Milner testified that the bit map system creates an image by copying the bit map (the entire stored image) into the display RAM and then reading out the entire image onto the full screen. On the other hand, he explained that the NES creates an image by taking a piece of the image, placing it in temporary storage, and then reading only that piece of the image onto the screen. According to Mr. Milner, by repeating this process "a little bit at a time" until the entire image is placed on the screen, the NES can achieve the same functional result as the bit-map system. This testimony does not support a conclusion that the claimed system and the NES operate in substantially the same way. . . .

AFFIRMED IN PART and REVERSED IN PART.

COMMENTS AND QUESTIONS

1. To similar effect as *Alpex* is Wiener v. NEC Electronics, Inc., 41 U.S.P.Q.2d 1023 (Fed. Cir. 1996). In that case, the Federal Circuit upheld the district court's finding of noninfringement under the doctrine of equivalents because there were substantial differences between the patent's requirement that a computer program "call on" columns of data one byte at a time and the defendant's product, where the columns alleged to be equivalent were not in the data matrix and therefore were not called upon to read data. The court rejected the "conclusory" declaration of plaintiff's expert that the two processes were identical. In General Electric v. Nintendo of America, 50 U.S.P.Q.2d 1910 (Fed. Cir. 1999), the court held that Nintendo's video game systems did not infringe GE's television switch patents because the patents, written in means-plus-function format, did not disclose a function for the switches identical to Nintendo's function. And in Digital Biometrics, Inc. v. Identix, Inc., 149 F.3d 1335 (Fed. Cir. 1998), the court construed narrowly a patent claim to "image arrays" storing a two-dimensional slice of video data and that were merged into a "composite array" storing a fingerprint image. The court held that the defendant's systems, which constructed the composite array directly rather than by using two-dimensional slices, did not create "image arrays" within the meaning of the claims.

The trend in software infringement cases seems to be toward interpreting the claims narrowly. Does this make sense, in light of what we know about the validity of software patents? Or does it render software patents ineffective, particularly in view of the fast-changing nature of the technology? One possible explanation for the narrow construction given software patents in infringement cases to date is that most of those patents have claim elements written in means-plus-function format.

2. A large number of early software patent claims were drafted in means-plus-function language, largely in order to meet the "structure"

requirements the courts have imposed on patentees under section 101. How should the "corresponding structure or equivalents thereof" in the specification be interpreted for infringement purposes? Does *Alpex* provide guidance on this issue? In particular, suppose that a patentee, to fall within the dictates of section 101, claims a "means for processing data" of a particular type. In the specification, the patentee discloses the use of an IBM-compatible personal computer with a Pentium microprocessor. Is this claim infringed by a defendant who runs the same software on a 486 microprocessor? An Apple computer using a Motorola microprocessor? A Sun Microsystems SPARC workstation? A Cray supercomputer? See IGT v. Global Gaming Technology Inc., 42 U.S.P.Q.2d 1144 (D. Nev. 1997) (microprocessors in a computer game were equivalent to hard-wired logic circuits disclosed in the patent, and therefore literally infringed under Section 112, para. 6).

3. Is a computer-implemented process "equivalent" to an older physical or analog process? The Federal Circuit has been struggling with this issue for some time. Compare Texas Instruments, Inc. v. International Trade Comm'n, 805 F.2d 1558 (Fed. Cir. 1986) (modern calculators did not infringe TI's original patent on the integrated circuit) with Hughes Aircraft Co. v. United States, 717 F.2d 1351 (Fed. Cir. 1983) (patent on means for controlling satellites from the ground via telemetry was infringed by use of on-board microprocessors to control satellites). For a case applying the doctrine of equivalents in a software context, see Safe Flight Instrument Corp. v. Sundstrand Data Control, Inc., 706 F. Supp. 1146 (D. Del. 1989).

In addition to the doctrine of equivalents, patent infringement analysis also requires application of the "reverse doctrine of equivalents." As the name suggests, the reverse doctrine of equivalents operates to protect patent defendants whose products fall within the literal scope of patent claims but that are in fact substantially different from the patented invention. This doctrine may be of particular importance in the software industry, because the application of computer technology has resulted in major changes in the way in which certain physical operations are performed.

4. In 1994, a jury ruled that Microsoft had infringed data compression software patents held by Stac Electronics and awarded damages of $120 million to Stac. J. Burgess, Microsoft Found Guilty of Patent Infringement: Software Giant Ordered to Pay $120 Million, Wash. Post, Feb. 24, 1994, at D11.[15] According to reports in the press, Microsoft tried to license the patents from Stac, but the parties failed to reach an agreement. After the verdict, Microsoft temporarily excised the infringing code

---

15. Although two software patents were asserted, the jury failed to specify whether one or both of them were infringed. Interestingly, the jury also found that Stac had misappropriated Microsoft's trade secrets relating to data compression and awarded Microsoft $13.6 million in damages.

from its MS-DOS operating system software but later settled the case by licensing the technology for a substantial sum. The case clearly shows the potential impact of software patents—Stac was able to force Microsoft to temporarily pull a multimillion dollar product from the market. To some, this case serves as an example of why patents for software are so problematic. See, e.g., L.M. Fisher, The Executive Computer: Will Users Be the Big Losers in Software Patent Battles?, N.Y. Times, May 6, 1994, at §3, p.7.

Judging from the volume of issued software patents, the flood of software patent litigation is just beginning. E-Data has sued a number of companies (and notified thousands of others of potential infringement) on its U.S. Patent 4,528,643, a "system for reproducing information in material objects at a point of sale location." See Interactive Gift Express v. Compuserve, 47 U.S.P.Q.2d 1797 (S.D.N.Y. 1998) (construing the E-Data patent narrowly). Eolas has sued Microsoft for infringing a patent that, if valid and broadly construed, would cover the use of "plug-ins" and "applets" on the Web. And recent litigation between Adobe and Quantel over Quantel's claim to own patents covering font software received a great deal of press attention in 1998.

D. DESIGN PATENTS ON SOFTWARE

While the most common form of patent is a "utility" patent, described in 35 U.S.C. §101, patents are also available for certain industrial designs. 35 U.S.C. §171 et seq. Relatively recently, some software designers have attempted to protect elements of their user interface as design patents.

Ex Parte Donaldson
Board of Patent Appeals and Interferences
26 U.S.P.Q.2d 1250 (Bd. Pat. App. & Int. 1992)

MANBECK, Commissioner.

This is an appeal from the examiner's decision finally rejecting the sole claim in the application.

The subject matter on appeal is a design for an icon. The sole claim on appeal states:

The ornamental design for a softkey display or the like, as shown and described.

The design as shown in the drawing figures is reproduced below:

Mode	Draw	Draw	Transform		Type	Active	Horiz	Vertical		Origin	Style
Select	∼	Text	Scale		None	All	4	4		Pin Point	None
Relation	∼•−	□	Stretch		Linear	Horiz	6	6			Dot
Grid	−	○	Rotate		Angular	Vert	12	12			
View	•		Flip				18	18			
Tools			Shear				36	36			

Fig. 4

Mode	Draw	Draw	Transform		Type	Active	Distance	Angle		Origin	Style
Select	∼	Text	Scale		None	All	4	30		Pin Point	None
Relation	∼•−	□	Stretch		Linear	Distance	6	45			Dot
Grid	−	○	Rotate		Angular	Angle	12	57.3			
View	•		Flip				18	60			
Tools			Shear				36	90			

Fig. 5

Mode	Draw	Draw	Transform		Scale %			
Select	∼	Text	Scale		50			
Relation	∼•−	□	Stretch		90			
Grid	−	○	Rotate		100			
View	•		Flip		400			
Tools			Shear		800			

Fig. 6

FIGURE 3-5
Ornamental design for a Softkey display.

. . . The sole claim stands rejected as unpatentable under 35 U.S.C. §171. After careful consideration of appellant's arguments presented in the briefs and at oral hearing, we affirm the examiner's rejection.

Section 171 of Title 35 provides:

> Whoever invents any new, original and ornamental design for an article of manufacture may obtain a patent therefor, subject to the conditions and requirements of this title.

The examiner concluded that the claimed design was nonstatutory, finding that the design was not an "ornamental design for an article of manufacture. . . ." While the examiner set forth her reasoning in great detail, the thrust of her position is that the design, as claimed, is merely a picture or surface ornamentation per se rather than a design applied to an article. The examiner notes that the specification does not describe, claim or show the claimed design applied to any article of manufacture. Appellant argues that the

> claimed invention is an ornamental design for the display screen of a programmed computer system. A programmed computer system, comprising a processor, a display device and a program executing on the processor is an article of manufacture. The claimed design is surface ornamentation for a particular region of the display screen, and thus qualifies as statutory subject matter.

The examiner responded stating:

> The fact that a programmed computer system running the necessary software may be an article of manufacture, does not help appellant here. No programmed computer system is either depicted or described. Section 1.152 [of 37 C.F.R.] is explicit in requiring that the article of manufacture be shown in the drawings.

The respective positions of the examiner and appellant require us to consider the meaning of "ornamental design for an article of manufacture" as used in §171.

The phrase "design for an article of manufacture" has long appeared in the design statutes. The language appears in Revised Statutes §4929, May 9, 1902, ch. 783, 32 Stat. 209; was reenacted in 35 U.S.C. §73 (1946) and again reenacted in 35 U.S.C. §171 (1952). The CCPA construed the phrase in In re Schnell, 46 F.2d 203, 8 USPQ 19 (CCPA 1931). The court noted that the language "new, original and ornamental design for an article of manufacture encompassed at least three kinds of designs: 1) a design for an ornament, impression, print or picture to be applied to an article of manufacture (surface ornamentation); 2) a design for the shape or configuration of an article of manufacture; and 3) a combination of the first two categories. 46 F.2d at 209, 8 USPQ at 26. With respect to the first category the court indicated the design statute required more than a mere picture.

> We think that Assistant Commissioner Clay was right in saying [in Ex parte Cady, 1916 Dec. Com'r. Pat. 57, 58] that the design must be shown not to be the mere invention of a picture, irrespective of its manner of use, but that the applicant should be required to show by an appropriate drawing the manner of its application.

46 F.2d at 209, 8 USPQ at 26. The Court went on to state:

> It is the application of the design to an article of manufacture that Congress wishes to promote, and an applicant has not reduced his invention to practice and has been of little help to the art if he does not teach the manner of applying his design.

46 F.2d at 209, 8 USPQ at 26.

The CCPA again interpreted the phrase in In re Zahn, 617 F.2d 261, 204 USPQ 988 (CCPA 1980). The issue in *Zahn* was whether or not §171 permitted claiming a design for a portion of an article of manufacture, a drill tool. The court noted that under §171 a design must be "embodied" in an article:

> Section 171 authorizes patents on ornamental designs *for* articles of manufacture. While the design must be *embodied* in some article, the statute is not limited to designs for complete articles, or "discrete" articles, and certainly not to articles separately sold. . . . Here the design is embodied in the shank portion of a drill and a drill is unquestionably an article of manufacture. It is applied design as distinguished from abstract design. (Emphasis original.)

617 F.2d at 268, 204 USPQ at 995.

These decisions indicate that a picture standing alone is not protect-able by a design patent. The factor which distinguishes statutory design subject matter from mere pictures or surface ornamentation per se (i.e., abstract designs) is the embodiment of the design in an article of manu-facture. In order to meet this threshold requirement of an applied design, we conclude that an applicant's specification must expressly disclose some article of manufacture ornamented by the design.

We find that appellant's claimed design, as disclosed in the application before us, is merely a picture. Appellant's specification does not show, describe or claim the design embodied in any article of manufacture. Only pictures of the icon are shown or described. The claimed subject matter, therefore, does not meet the requirements of 35 U.S.C. §171.

Appellant asserts that the design should be considered surface orna-mentation upon the display screen of a computer system. We have no doubt that the claimed design, like all surface ornamentation-type designs, could be used to ornament a wide variety of articles, including computers. However, the phrase "design for an article of manufacture" in §171 re-quires more than a depiction of the surface ornamentation alone. It re-quires disclosure of the ornamentation applied to or embodied in an article of manufacture. More than an applicant's generalized intent to ornament some article is required. It is the application of the design to an article which separates mere pictures from a design protectable by a patent. With-out express disclosure of an article, the design is not an applied design contemplated for protection under §171.

Consistent with §171, PTO regulations expressly require such disclo-sure. Thus, 37 CFR §1.153(a) states:

> (a) The title of the design must designate the particular article. No de-scription, other than a reference to the drawing, is ordinarily required. The claim shall be in formal terms to the ornamental design for the article (speci-fying name) as shown, or as shown and described. . . .

37 CFR §1.152 states:

> The design must be represented by a drawing made in conformity with the rules laid down for drawings of mechanical inventions and must contain a sufficient number of views to constitute a *complete disclosure of the appearance of the article.* Appropriate surface shading must be used to show the character or contour of the surfaces represented. Broken lines may be used to show visible environmental structure, but may not be used to show hidden planes and surfaces which cannot be seen through opaque materials. (Emphasis added [by court].)

Appellant has not described, shown or claimed the design as surface ornamentation for a computer system. The word "icon" does not limit the design to use with a display screen of a computer or any other article of manufacture. Icons are and have been used with a variety of articles. As we stated above, appellant's design, as shown and described, is merely a pic-ture which has not been disclosed applied to any article.

AFFIRMED 37 CFR §1.196(b).

COMMENTS AND QUESTIONS

1.   In a companion case to *Donaldson*, the Board of Patent Applications and Interferences (BPAI) held that an applicant was not entitled to claim an icon on a computer screen as a design patent, for essentially the same reasons. Ex parte Strijland, 26 U.S.P.Q.2d 1259 (Bd. Pat. App. & Int. 1992). However, the Board suggested that if the patentee had claimed an "information icon for display screen of a programmed computer system," and submitted a drawing *of the entire computer system* showing the icon on the screen, the Board would have held the claim to be patentable subject matter. Indeed, the Board even offered a proposed drawing as an appendix to the opinion.

FIGURE 3-6
Proposed drawing of acceptable computer system.

Why does it matter how the design is described in the drawings?

2.   On March 20, 1996, the PTO issued final guidelines governing the examination of design patent applications directed to computer icons. The guidelines follow the suggestion in *Strijland* that icons are patentable so long as they are shown on a computer screen, monitor, "or a portion thereof." The guidelines also suggest that computer-generated type fonts may be the subject of design patent protection. This is only the latest twist in a history of vacillations by the PTO over whether icons and other user interface elements should be entitled to design patents.

3.   Design patents are not available for designs that are "dictated by functional considerations." See Power Controls Corp. v. Hybrinetics, Inc., 806 F.2d 234, 238 (Fed. Cir. 1986). To what extent does this limit the availability of design patent protection for the screen displays in *Donaldson*? For the icon in *Strijland*?

4.   Design patents are in many respects more like trademarks than like utility patents. It is worth considering the extent to which design patent protection for computer icons overlaps with copyright and trademark protection. We consider trademark and trade dress protection in the next chapter.

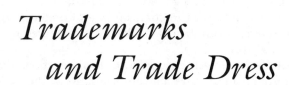

4

Trademarks
and Trade Dress

The computer industry relies not only on trade secrecy, copyrights, and patents, but also on trademark and trade dress protection. Some of the strongest brands in America are computer industry brands—IBM, Intel, and Microsoft—and many others are household names. Even where products are technically interchangeable, campaigns like "Intel inside" have given consumers a preference for specific brands.

In part, the reliance of this industry on trademarks is due to network effects. Consumers place significant value on obtaining application programs that are compatible with popular operating systems and peripheral equipment that connects with their base computer systems. Equipment and software manufacturers, therefore, use trademarks as an important part of their overall strategy to protect and market their products. Trademarks can signal or suggest compatibility and can serve as guarantors that a product meets a certain standard. In this way, trademark protection can significantly enhance the protection for new technology. On the other hand, trademark protection can also potentially inhibit competition if it limits the ability of new entrants to inform consumers of the compatible attributes of their products. Similar problems exist with respect to trademark law and Internet domain names.[1]

In the United States, protection for trademarks and trade dress is provided by the Lanham Act, 15 U.S.C. §1051 et seq., and by state common law. Trademark law generally applies to computers and computer companies in the same way that it does to other industries. For instance, Apple Computer is entitled to prevent competitors from selling computers with names confusingly similar to Apple (such as Pineapple). Apple Computer v.

---

1. Those problems are discussed in Chapter 10.

Formula Int'l, 562 F. Supp. 775 (C.D. Cal. 1983). Intel is not entitled to protect its "386" name for microprocessors because the x86 designation has been generic in the industry for some time, at least among the computer industry professionals who buy such chips and resell them in computers. Intel v. Advanced Micro Devices, 756 F. Supp. 1292 (N.D. Cal. 1991). In this chapter, though, we are not concerned with "ordinary" trademark issues that happen to come up in the computer context; rather, we focus on several circumstances in which the computer industry presents unique trademark issues.

We identify three such circumstances in the sections that follow. As you work through these cases and problems, assess the degree to which trademark law promotes (or retards) innovation in the computer industry, and consider whether that is even the goal of trademark law.

A. PROTECTING PROGRAMS THROUGH TRADEMARK

Note on Protection of Product Configurations

Trademarks are traditionally thought of as words or other written symbols or logos describing a product, service, or company. However, the Lanham Act also protects "trade dress"—a term that encompasses the total design of product packaging, including its shape and color. This protection has recently been expanded to protect the configuration of the product itself, on the same terms as other forms of trade dress. See Two Pesos, Inc. v. Taco Cabana, 505 U.S. 763 (1992) (total design of the interior of a fast-food Mexican restaurant was entitled to Lanham Act protection).

There remains some disagreement among the courts concerning precisely how to treat product configurations, however. In Duraco Products v. Joy Plastic Enterprises, 40 F.3d 1431 (3d Cir. 1994), the Third Circuit rejected the proposition (arguably mandated by *Two Pesos*) that traditional trade dress doctrine applies to product configurations. Instead, the Circuit developed a new, stricter test for protecting product configurations. Under the *Duraco* test, a product configuration qualifies as inherently distinctive (and therefore protectable without proof of secondary meaning) only if it is (1) unusual and memorable, (2) capable of being conceptually separated from the product itself, and (3) likely to serve primarily as a trademark rather than utilitarian function. See also Knitwaves, Inc. v. Lollytogs, Ltd., 71 F.3d 996 (2d Cir. 1995) (adopting a similarly restrictive test for protection of product configurations). By contrast, the Eighth Circuit has specifically rejected the *Duraco* test, holding that product configurations need not be "memorable" or "striking in appearance" to qualify as inherently distinctive. Stuart Hall Co. v. Ampad Corp., 51 F.3d 780 (8th Cir. 1995).

This dispute is relevant to the computer industry because some—and perhaps all—of the products capable of trademark protection in that industry qualify as product configurations. Certainly, the shape of a computer or monitor such as the iMac is a product configuration. Cf. Digital Computer Controls v. C. Itoh, 229 U.S.P.Q. 598 (D.N.J. 1985) (evaluating product configuration protection for the shape of a computer monitor). Arguably, so is the layout of icons and menus on a computer screen—though the "product" being shaped in the latter case is a bit more ephemeral. Cf. Ex parte Donaldson, discussed in the previous chapter, relating to design patents. If the Third Circuit standard prevails, trade dress protection may be harder to obtain for GUIs and other software configurations.

In previous chapters, we have discussed various means of protecting computer software and hardware against imitation by others. In a recent article, Lauren Fisher Kellner suggests that trademark could also be used to protect the "look and feel" of computer software against imitation. As you review her argument, consider whether graphical user interfaces should be thought of as trade dress or as product configuration and, indeed, whether it makes sense to protect them under trademark law at all.

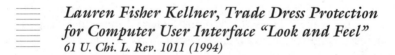

Lauren Fisher Kellner, Trade Dress Protection for Computer User Interface "Look and Feel"
61 U. Chi. L. Rev. 1011 (1994)

An employee on the way back to his office glances at the illuminated screen of a nearby computer. He sees the small trash can in the lower right corner; graphics of labeled folders, documents, and applications in the center; and a strip of words across the top of the screen. He immediately assumes that the computer is an Apple Macintosh. A spreadsheet programmer determines that an application program requires her to use a backslash to access multi-layered command menus and to strike the first letter of layered menu items in sequence in order to execute any series of commands. She knows the software must be Lotus 1-2-3.

Apple and Lotus realize that computer users rely on these elements to identify computer programs. Accordingly, both companies have invested time and money to build consumer recognition of their programs and have sought legal protection for their user interfaces. . . .

Both the academic literature and litigants' briefs have focused on copyright as a way to protect a developer's intellectual property rights in a software product's "look and feel." Trademark law, however, would be a better source of protection. Trademark law recognizes consumers' interests in identifying a product's source, and trade dress law, a subset of trademark law, protects a product's overall appearance to the purchasing public. While trade dress infringement claims have become more common in all product areas over the past few years, only a few attorneys have aggressively sought trade dress protection for the "look and feel" of user interfaces. . . .

The first requirement for trademark protection of any product feature or set of features is "distinctiveness"—the feature must be able to indicate the source of the product. . . .

Some user interfaces create an inherently distinctive visual impression. For example, Berkeley Systems's After Dark screen saver program features a stylized underwater scene: colorful fish, gurgling noises, and winged toasters. That visual display is unique and unusual enough to qualify as inherently distinctive. In general, then, program developers that create unique visual displays should be able to meet trademark law's distinctiveness requirement without showing secondary meaning. . . .

The trend toward standardization of user interfaces presents a potential obstacle to manufacturers' attempts to establish distinctiveness. Most user interfaces are unique when introduced. But microcomputer markets are moving toward "standard user interfaces" among programs in an attempt to reduce the time it takes to learn a new application. This "family look" promotes sales *within* product lines (among all programs designed to run on one type of computer) and *across* product lines (between programs designed for different computer systems) by increasing consumer confidence in and familiarity with standard techniques. Standardization may make it difficult, if not impossible, for a plaintiff to establish distinctiveness because "in markets with standard user interfaces, programs are *expected* to look and feel the same." [Gregory Wrenn, Federal Intellectual Property Protection for Computer Software Audiovisual Look and Feel: The Lanham, Copyright, and Patent Acts, 4 High Tech. L.J. 279, 284 (1989).]

. . . The likelihood of point-of-sale consumer confusion seems low because computers and software are typically sold in clearly marked packages. It is thus unlikely (though conceivable) that a purchaser intending to buy Lotus 1-2-3 would end up buying, say, VP-Planner instead.

In contrast, potential consumers of computer products may see a computer's user interface on co-workers' desks or in store windows and assume that they are viewing the Apple Macintosh or Lotus 1-2-3 interface. By the time they eventually discover that they were really viewing Microsoft Windows or VP-Planner, they may already have invested time and energy in researching and shopping for the wrong product. Microsoft Windows or VP-Planner retailers could then convince these potential consumers that the look-alike products are indistinguishable from the Macintosh or Lotus 1-2-3; they will have used Apple's or Lotus's reputation and customer recognition to lure customers into investigating and ultimately purchasing look-alike products. Trade dress law attempts to prevent precisely this kind of misappropriation of another product's good reputation.

COMMENTS AND QUESTIONS

1. "Distinctiveness" is a term of art that encompasses trademarks that are arbitrary, suggestive, or fanciful, or that are descriptive of the products they identify but have acquired "secondary meaning" in the minds of consumers as identifying a product from a particular source. Trademark protection does not extend to trademarks or trade dress that are merely descriptive of the things being identified. Further, in no case can a generic term or dress be protected. Kellner suggests that many user interfaces will be inherently distinctive because the way the interface works is unrelated to the nature of the functions performed. In practice, however, individual elements of the user interface may merely be descriptive of the functions performed. How would a court classify the "trash can" icon in the Macintosh graphical user interface (GUI), which serves to delete files? The Lotus 1-2-3 program's choice of the "D" key for delete, "F" for file, or "Q" for quit? See Lotus v. Borland, discussed in Chapter 2. Note that these problems are not necessarily specific to computer icons; arguably, any trade dress or product configuration is hard to classify using guidelines designed for word marks. See Knitwaves Inc. v. Lollytogs, Ltd., 71 F.3d 996 (2d Cir. 1995).

Must these individual elements be distinctive in order to be protected, or is it sufficient that the interface *as a whole* is not "descriptive" of a computer operating system? Note the parallels here to the copyright case of Apple v. Microsoft, reprinted in Chapter 2. There, Apple argued for a wholistic "look and feel" approach to copyright infringement—an approach rejected by the court. Is there any reason to prefer such an approach in trademark law? Would *Apple* have been decided differently if Apple had alleged trademark rather than copyright infringement?

2. User interfaces may also run afoul of the "genericide" doctrine. If a particular interface has become the de facto standard in the industry, so people naturally use that interface for a certain type of program, the interface is likely to be generic and therefore unprotectable. A good example is the QWERTY keyboard, an "interface" that may have been arbitrary as a means of organizing letters when it was introduced but that has since become a universal keyboard standard. Because consumers do not associate the QWERTY keyboard with a particular maker, but rather with the general idea of a typewriter, that keyboard is generic and therefore incapable of trademark protection. The same fate may befall certain elements of graphical user interfaces, such as pull-down menus. Even if the use of pull-down menus once identified the computer as an Apple, their prevalence in numerous programs today suggests that Apple may no longer be able to claim to own them.

Does it make sense that the very success of a GUI should be its undoing from the standpoint of trademark law? Quite possibly. One effect of the genericness rule is to prevent a particular company from using trademark law to corner the market on an industry standard and thereby foreclose competition in the underlying products. We discuss this issue in more detail in the next Section.

3. Kellner acknowledges that consumers are unlikely to be confused between different GUIs at the point of sale. There is no question that Apple and Microsoft, for example, package their products very differently. Neither is attempting to trade on the business goodwill of the other. But she suggests that post-sale confusion is still possible—that is, that consumers will see one operating system in action, think it is the other, and proceed to buy the wrong computer. (The last step in this chain is critical, because the Lanham Act is concerned with the likelihood of confusion among *consumers* of the products at issue.)

Whether you think such post-sale confusion is likely depends in part on your assessment of the sophistication of the purchasing public. Several courts have found confusion unlikely in the computer context because the buyers were relatively sophisticated and they were purchasing "big ticket" items. See, e.g., Engineering Dynamics, Inc. v. Structural Software, Inc., 26 F.3d 1335, 1350 (5th Cir. 1994) (competing software programs did not create a likelihood of confusion among sophisticated users in a limited market; consumers pay little attention to trade dress in determining which product to purchase); Intel v. Advanced Micro Devices, 756 F. Supp. 1292 (N.D. Cal. 1991) (purchasers of Intel microprocessors were computer hardware manufacturers, not end users; hardware manufacturers were sophisticated enough to distinguish between Intel 386 and AMD 386 chips).

4. Even if consumers are not confused, might programmers have a cause of action for trademark dilution, a theory that protects certain famous marks against any use in connection with other goods, even if consumers are not confused? See 15 U.S.C. §1125(c) (standards under new federal antidilution act). Can the Macintosh GUI be said to be "famous"? If so, does the use of pull-down menus by other companies reduce the identification value of the Apple mark?

5. How does protecting GUIs under trademark law comport with the purposes of the Lanham Act? Does it overreach—and thus destroy useful competition in an attempt to prevent some relatively minor instances of consumer confusion? In this regard, it is worth noting that the use of trade dress law to protect user interfaces has so far been rare. In 1996, one commentator reported that only two decisions had considered the question of interface trade dress protection, and both had rejected the trade dress claim. See Lisa T. Oratz, User Interfaces: Copyrights vs. Trade Dress Protection, 13 Computer Law. 1, 3 (1996).

6. The most significant limitation on trade dress protection for computer programs is functionality. Trademark protection does not extend to any part of the dress that is functional. Since computer icons normally serve a purpose, application of functionality should significantly limit their protection. Further, since the goal of interface design is to simplify a consumer's interaction with the machine, certain types of user interface

elements (say, those based on the principle "what you see is what you get") may inherently serve a useful function.

Recall that much of the debate over the appropriate scope of protection for GUIs in the copyright context had to do with whether elements of the interface were dictated by functional considerations. See Apple Computer v. Microsoft Corp., 35 F.3d 1435 (9th Cir. 1994). Isn't that debate likely to be replicated in the trademark context, with courts disagreeing over whether particular portions of the GUI are economically or aesthetically functional? If so, is there any advantage to seeking trademark rather than copyright protection?

One possible difference between trademark and copyright law may be the way in which functionality is tested. There is a debate in trademark law over whether the functionality of trade dress is to be tested by looking at the dress as a whole or by evaluating the purpose of individual elements. On this point, see Stormy Clime Ltd. v. Progroup, Inc., 809 F.2d 971 (2d Cir. 1987) (jacket contained a unique and protectable combination of functional elements). This debate, too, has its parallels in the copyright context, though it is all but resolved that copyright focuses on the individual elements rather than the program as a whole in determining functionality. Compare Computer Associates v. Altai, 982 F.2d 693 (2d Cir. 1992), and its progeny with Whelan Associates v. Jaslow Dental Laboratory, 797 F.2d 1222 (3d Cir. 1986).

An "element by element" approach to trademark functionality may be particularly appropriate in the software context, where alleged infringers take only a few key pieces of the plaintiff's trade dress (such as overlapping folders and pull-down menus from the Macintosh interface). If the elements taken are all functional, presumably no court would find trademark infringement even if the interface as a whole is protectable.

Is there reason for trademark owners to prefer one of these approaches over the other? It is reasonable to assume that testing functionality as a whole will allow greater leeway for protecting partially functional trade dress, but the *Digital* court suggests the reverse may be true: if any part of the interface is functional, none of it is protectable. Digital Computer Controls v. C. Itoh, 229 U.S.P.Q. 598 (D.N.J. 1985).

7. Protecting software product configurations obviously overlaps not only with copyright law but also with design patent law, which now protects computer icons in certain circumstances. See A. Hugo Word, The New Guidelines on Protection of Computer-Generated Icons and Typeface, 24 AIPLA Q.J. 415 (1996). Should such overlap be permissible? Note that some courts are unwilling to permit product configurations that are the subject of a utility patent to be protected under trade dress law as well, perhaps out of a concern that the owner of the design will be able to extend protection beyond the term of the patent. See Vornado Air Circulation Systems v. Duracraft Corp., 58 F.3d 1498 (10th Cir. 1995). For a detailed discussion of this issue, see Jay Dratler, Jr., Trade Dress Protection for Product Configurations: Is There a Conflict With Patent Policy?, 24

AIPLA Q.J. 427 (1996); Michael S. Perez, Reconciling the Patent Act and the Lanham Act: Should Product Configurations Be Entitled to Trade Dress Protection After the Expiration of a Utility or Design Patent?, 4 Tex. Intell. Prop. L.J. 383 (1996).

PROBLEMS

Problem 4-1. Apple's Macintosh graphical user interface has three main components that are copied by Kiwi Computer in its competing operating system. The three components are pull-down menus, in which the user commands are contained in a bar at the top of the screen that can be opened by clicking on the relevant command with a mouse and by dragging the mouse downward; a series of icons on the right-hand side of the screen to perform common commands or to open particular folders; and overlapping windows that show the most recently used document or program on top of other open applications.

Apple contends that none of these three components are functional and points to other ways in which Kiwi could have implemented a graphical user interface. For example, Apple argues that Kiwi could have used "pull-up" or "pull-across" menus, or an expandable list of commands controlled by the keyboard or by voice rather than by the mouse. Kiwi responds that it is easier and more logical for most computer users to drag the mouse downward than to push it up or across. Apple points to alternatives to its overlapping windows such as "tiled windows" that appear side by side; Kiwi responds that tiled windows are inefficient because they limit both the number of windows that can be open and the size of each open window.

Are Apple's design features functional? Does you answer depend on the legal standard you apply?

Problem 4-2. Intel manufactures generations of microprocessor chips with identifying number sequences. For reference, these number sequences are shortened to the last three digits and are commonly referred to by computer users in this way (e.g., the 286, 287, 386, 387, 486, etc.). Advanced Micro Devices, a competing microprocessor manufacturer, refers to its comparable chips by the same number sequences. Has AMD infringed an Intel trademark?

Intel refers to its latest generation of chip as the Pentium. From a trademark perspective, what are the advantages and disadvantages of this change-in-naming convention?

Problem 4-3. Sun Microsystems is a leading manufacturer of computer systems. A recent entrant in the computer workstation market is thinking about using the name SunRiver Systems. Would Sun Microsystems be likely to enjoin the use of this name? What information would you need to know in order to answer this question properly?

B.   COMPATIBILITY AND STANDARDIZATION

A second way in which trademark law may operate to influence the market for computer products directly is in the areas of standardization and compatibility.[2] Because computer hardware and software are sold in complex markets with high network externalities both among and between products, there is tremendous value to be gained not only in identifying one's own product, but in describing for consumers how it interacts with other products on the market. For example, the sellers of applications programs want to be able to tell their customers whether or not their program will run with a particular operating system. Because identifying the operating system often involves the use of a competitor's trademark, however, trademark law stands as a potential barrier to this form of compatibility identification.

═══ *Creative Labs, Inc. v. Cyrix Corporation*
═══ *United States District Court for the Northern District of California*
═══ *42 U.S.P.Q.2d 1872 (N.D. Cal. 1997)*

WILKEN, District Judge.

Plaintiffs Creative Labs and Creative Technology (collectively "Creative") move for a preliminary injunction against Defendants Cyrix Corporation and Tiger Direct, Inc. ("Tiger") for copyright infringement and false advertising. Defendants oppose the motion. The matter was heard on May 2, 1997. On May 2, 1997, Creative also filed an ex parte application for an order to show cause re contempt. Having considered all of the papers filed by the parties and oral argument on the motion, the Court GRANTS the motion for a preliminary injunction and DENIES the ex parte application for an order to show cause.

---

2. We have already encountered standardization in the previous Section in the context of genericness.

Background

Plaintiff Creative is the maker of the Sound Blaster line of sound cards, devices that interact with computer hardware and software to create sound effects. Sound Blaster is currently the dominant sound card on the market. Defendant Cyrix has recently introduced a microprocessor, the Media GX, which is capable of producing audio effects without the assistance of a sound card. The audio component of the Media GX is referred to as XpressAUDIO.

Cyrix has advertised XpressAUDIO as "compatible with Sound Blaster" and as "fully compatible with Sound Blaster." Tiger, a computer manufacturer which plans to introduce a line of computers that use the Media GX, claims that its products feature "integrated SoundBlaster 16/Pro compatible audio." Compaq uses the Media GX in one of its computers, the Presario 2100, but does not advertise that the Presario 2100 is Sound Blaster compatible.

Creative tested the Media GX on a Presario 2100 computer to determine whether Cyrix's claims concerning XpressAUDIO's compatibility with Sound Blaster were accurate. In a study testing 200 computer games, Creative discovered that sixteen games, or 8% of the total tested, did not run properly on the Presario 2100. Creative also found that the Presario 2100 did not support two functions supported by Sound Blaster: Adaptive Delta Pulse Code Modulation ("ADPCM") and Musical Instrument Digital Interface ("MIDI").

Creative also learned that Cyrix was making some Creative Labs software programs available for copying by the public on Cyrix's website.

Creative filed suit against Cyrix for copyright infringement, 17 U.S.C. §510 et seq.; against Cyrix and Tiger for false advertising and trademark dilution, 15 U.S.C. §1125(a), (c); and against Cyrix, Tiger, and Compaq for trademark infringement, 15 U.S.C. §§1114(a), 1125(a), and unfair competition, Cal.Bus. & Prof.Code §17200 et seq. The Court granted Creative's application for a temporary restraining order against Cyrix and Tiger. Creative now seeks a preliminary injunction enjoining all Defendants from trademark infringement, Cyrix and Tiger from false advertising, and Cyrix from copyright violations. In this order, the Court considers only the claims concerning false advertising and copyright infringement.

Discussion . . .

B. *False Advertising*

Creative alleges that Cyrix and Tiger advertisements which assert that the XpressAUDIO system is "compatible" with Sound Blaster constitute false advertising in violation of Lanham Act §43(a), 15 U.S.C. §1125(a). The elements of a Lanham Act false advertising claim are:

(1) a false statement of fact by the defendant in a commercial advertisement about its own or another's product; (2) the statement actually deceived or has the tendency to deceive a substantial segment of its audience; (3) the deception is material, in that it is likely to influence the purchasing decision; (4) the defendant caused its false statement to enter interstate commerce; and (5) the plaintiff has been or is likely to be injured as a result of the false statement, either by direct diversion of sales from itself to defendant or by a lessening of the goodwill associated with its products.

Southland Sod Farms v. Stover Seed Co., 108 F.3d 1134, 1139 (9th Cir.1997). Plaintiffs do not need to prove injury to be entitled to injunctive relief. *Id.* at 1145-46.

Plaintiffs seek to enjoin Cyrix and Tiger from advertising that their systems are Sound Blaster compatible. Cyrix and Tiger respond that XpressAUDIO is compatible with Sound Blaster. The dispute thus turns on the definition of the term "compatible." Creative maintains that competing computer products are compatible only if "the first product can be used in place of the second product without producing any difference in performance and that the first product has the same capabilities and functions as the second product." Creative supplied the declaration of an individual who works in the computer games industry asserting that the phrase "Sound Blaster compatible" indicates that the hardware "will properly play any software title that plays properly on a genuine Creative Labs Sound Blaster." Creative also refers to three dictionary definitions to support its interpretation. One provides that "[c]ompatibility means that the hardware ideally operates in all respects like the standard on which it is based." The second dictionary defines compatibility as, "[t]he capability of a peripheral [or] program . . . to function with or substitute for a given make and model of computer. . . . To be truly compatible, a program or device should operate on a given system without modification; all features should operate as intended, and a computer claiming to be compatible with another should run all the other computer's software without modification." By referring to a device for measuring how IBM-compatible personal computers are, however, the definition suggests that compatibility is not necessarily a matter of all or nothing. The third dictionary provides that compatibility is "[t]he extent to which a given piece of hardware or software conforms to an accepted standard. . . . This implies that the device will perform in every way just like the standard device." Cyrix cites a dictionary which defines the term "compatible" as describing a product which meets some, but not all, parts of a specification.

Princeton Graphics Operating, L.P. v. NEC Home Electronics (U.S.A.), Inc., 732 F.Supp. 1258 (S.D.N.Y.1990), supports Creative's definition of compatibility. In *Princeton Graphics*, the court chose the more restrictive definition because of the importance of precise definitions in the computer industry. *Id.* at 1261. It also believed that it is appropriate to apply a more precise definition of compatibility when a well-known industry standard is being used. *Id.* at 1262 n. 9. The Court therefore finds that a product advertising itself as Sound Blaster compatible must support the same functions as Sound Blaster.

Creative argues that XpressAUDIO is not compatible with Sound Blaster because it does not support all games that can function with Sound Blaster. Creative relies on a study in which sixteen computer games, 8% of all games tested, did not function properly on a Presario 2100 computer. The study, however, does not establish that those failures were due to incompatibilities between XpressAUDIO and Sound Blaster. Cyrix counters that it did not encounter problems when running six of these games on a properly configured computer. *Id.* Cyrix's own study indicates a failure rate of approximately 2%. Even if the failure rate of games played on computers with XpressAUDIO is closer to 2% than 8%, the evidence indicates that some games that function with Sound Blaster do not function with XpressAUDIO.

Creative also argues that XpressAUDIO is not Sound Blaster compatible because it does not support two specific functions supported by Sound Blaster: ADPCM and MIDI. Cyrix concedes that XpressAUDIO does not support ADPCM, but it maintains that few games employ ADPCM, that those games are not currently being sold, and that ADPCM does not meet consumer expectations of sound quality. The lack of ADPCM support, while perhaps insufficient to establish lack of compatibility alone, supports such a finding.

Creative also maintains that XpressAUDIO does not support Sound Blaster's MIDI function. XpressAUDIO, however, does support MIDI. The MIDI function can be turned off by the computer manufacturer. Compaq has turned off the MIDI feature on the XpressAUDIO systems used in Presario 2100 computers. Cyrix has not advertised that Presario 2100s are Sound Blaster compatible.

Because some computer games that function with Sound Blaster do not function with XpressAUDIO, the Court finds that XpressAUDIO is probably not compatible with Sound Blaster. Cyrix and Tiger's claims that systems using XpressAUDIO are Sound Blaster compatible will probably mislead consumers who would interpret the claim of Sound Blaster compatibility to mean that any product that functions with Sound Blaster would also function with XpressAUDIO.

Because Creative has established the likelihood of consumer confusion, it has also established the possibility of irreparable harm. The Court also finds that injunctive relief would further the public's interest in being protected from false trade descriptions. See U-Haul Int'l, Inc. v. Jartran, Inc., 681 F.2d 1159, 1162 (9th Cir.1982).

The Court therefore grants Creative's motion for a preliminary injunction enjoining Cyrix and Tiger from claiming that XpressAUDIO and computer systems using XpressAUDIO are Sound Blaster compatible. . . .

E. Temporary Restraining Order

The first part of the temporary restraining order signed March 28, 1997, was premised on the assumption that Cyrix motherboards or Media GX Architectural Systems caused computer systems to misidentify sound devices as Sound Blasters. The record no longer supports a finding that Cyrix hardware causes the misidentification. The portion of the temporary restraining order enjoining Cyrix and Tiger from selling hardware that causes computer systems to misidentify sound devices as Sound Blaster is therefore vacated.

Conclusion

For the foregoing reasons, Creative's motion for a preliminary injunction is GRANTED with regard to false advertising and copyright infringement.

1. Defendant Cyrix shall be and hereby is enjoined from distributing Creative's proprietary "applet" software; and

2. Defendants Cyrix Corporation and Tiger Direct, Inc. are hereby ordered to cease all advertising, promotional material, or packaging which claim that the Media GX chip or microprocessor system, or the Xpress-AUDIO feature provided by the Media GX chip or microprocessor system, or any personal computer based on the Media GX chip or microprocessor system, including the "Tiger Gx86", is Sound Blaster compatible. Defendants Cyrix and Tiger may resume advertising XpressAUDIO or computer systems using XpressAUDIO as Sound Blaster compatible only if they render XpressAUDIO Sound Blaster compatible.

IT IS SO ORDERED.

COMMENTS AND QUESTIONS

1. In *Princeton Graphics*, cited in *Creative Labs*, Princeton, the maker of a monitor for IBM computers, sued NEC, a competing maker of monitors, because NEC had claimed its monitor was "compatible" with the new IBM video standard (a claim Princeton could not make for its own monitors). The court determined that the term "compatible" had a precise meaning specific to the computer industry, and that it required a high degree of interoperability:

We find that within the "retail channel," the term "compatible" does not have the broad and flexible meaning as suggested by defendant when, as here, there is a possibility that a more precise definition may be applied.[8] Indeed, if

---

8. We make no finding as to the understanding of the term "compatible" in the broader consumer market.

there was one over-arching impression left on this court after the testimony given in this case it was that the computer industry is concerned with and depends upon accuracy. Thus, the testimony confirms our view that in an industry which depends upon accuracy, a lack of precision in the use of common terms, particularly in circumstances where those terms have the potential to be specific, would be an anomaly.

. . . We therefore find that in light of the evidence the definition of "compatible" as understood in the "retail channel" of sophisticated users has a clear and definite meaning—i.e., when a clearly defined standard, like IBM's VGA standard, exists and is widely accepted within the industry, a "compatible" product must meet that standard or at least perform in a manner equivalent to the standard's requirements.[11]

Princeton Graphics Operating v. NEC Home Electronics USA, 732 F. Supp. 1258 (S.D.N.Y. 1990). The court went on to conclude that falsely advertising compatibility could affect market purchasing decisions, and therefore cause actionable injury:

> We believe that plaintiff has presented a reasonable basis for its belief it was likely that defendant's advertising caused it damage. First, it is logical to conclude that had consumers been faced with two monitor products in the spring and summer of 1987, neither of which claimed PS/2 compatibility, some might have chosen plaintiff's. It is also reasonable to assume that had there been no compatibility claim on the part of defendant in the spring of 1987, some consumers would have waited until the summer of 1987 to buy plaintiff's PS/2 compatible UltraSync. Accordingly, we conclude that plaintiff has standing to bring this action.[16]

11. We find that the dictionary and glossary definitions offered by defendant were of little probative value. Either the exhibit indicated only what the understanding might be within the general population and not the "retail channel," or the definition was worded in such a way to lend support to either party's position. The definitions set forth in the exhibits did little to indicate the common construction and understanding of the term within the "retail channel" when applied to concrete products.

Further, defendant offered articles published in trade magazines as evidence that "compatible" had a broad and flexible meaning within the "retail channel." However, the context of the use of "compatibility" varied in those articles. In certain articles "compatibility" was used in relation to "Super VGA" capability or in relation to a monochrome gas plasma video display's VGA capability. Thus, in those articles "compatibility" was being discussed in a different context than the instant situation. For example, testimony at trial indicated that "Super VGA" (800 x 600 resolution) is not an IBM standard. Accordingly, defendant's articles are not of great persuasive weight since we believe that a broader understanding of compatible is favored by the "retail channel" in the absence of a clear industry standard.

Moreover, although the articles were not offered for the truth of their contents, we note only one short article offered by defendant explicitly stated that the MultiSync was "fully compatible" with VGA, and that explicit representation was only contained in a caption to the article's accompanying illustration.

16. Defendant asserts that since many customers in the "retail channel" research and test a monitor's capabilities before buying, even if defendant's claims were false it is unlikely that many in the "retail channel" were misled. Since the action has been bifurcated between liability and relief, during this liability phase plaintiff was not required to show proof of actual loss and to what extent any within the "retail channel" were actually influenced by defendant's claims to purchase MultiSync monitors. Thus, our conclusion that plaintiff has standing to bring this Lanham Act action does not imply that this court has reached any conclusion as to damages.

Does holding NEC to such a high threshold for compatibility help or hurt consumers? On the one hand, preventing NEC from falsely claiming that it is fully compatible with IBM's VGA standard prevents consumers from buying the monitor under false pretenses. In this sense, defining compatibility strictly ensures that consumers will know what they are getting. On the other hand, this strict definition means that at that time, no one except IBM could claim that they made a VGA-compatible monitor. If consumers are unwilling to buy products unless they are advertised as compatible, the effect is to give IBM a monopoly on monitor sales associated with IBM computers. From a consumer standpoint, this may actually be less desirable. If a consumer is willing to settle for a cheaper, 95 percent compatible monitor, shouldn't they be allowed to do so?

Should NEC or Cyrix be allowed to advertise their "near-compatibility"? Under these decisions, how could they do so?

2. Both of the *Creative Labs* and *Princeton Graphics* cases arose under the false advertising provisions of section 43(a) of the Lanham Act. The Lanham Act's prohibition on false advertising operates in parallel to its protection of trademarks. (Because Princeton Graphics did not own the IBM or VGA trademarks, it had no right to bring a claim for trademark infringement.) Presumably IBM could have brought a similar case for false advertising. See Intel Corp. v. Advanced Micro Devices, Computer Indus. Lit. Rptr. 11730 (N.D. Cal. Aug. 27, 1990) (enjoining AMD from claiming that its products were compatible with Intel's 287 microprocessor).

3. In *Princeton Graphics*, the issue was whether NEC's monitor was in fact compatible with the VGA standard. Presumably Princeton would not have had a cause of action against NEC if its statements regarding compatibility were accurate. But would IBM have a cause of action for trademark infringement? After all, NEC is in some sense trading on the value of the IBM standard by associating its product with IBM in the minds of consumers.

The answer to this question is complex. The doctrine of non-trademark use provides that it is acceptable to use a party's trademark *to refer to that party's product*. The Lanham Act is concerned only with the appropriation of that trademark to refer to another product. See New Kids on the Block v. News America Publishing, 971 F.2d 302 (9th Cir. 1992). Just as it is allowable to identify a competitor's product accurately in a comparative advertisement, shouldn't it be allowable to make an accurate statement that your product works well with another product?

In a case parallel to *Creative Labs*, Creative claimed that Cyrix's advertisements constituted trademark infringement because they referred to Creative too often and might therefore create confusion as to sponsorship or affiliation in the minds of consumers. How should this argument be evaluated? If a consumer sees an NEC advertisement and assumes either (1) that IBM is selling the NEC monitor or (2) that IBM has endorsed or somehow approved the NEC monitor, the consumer's purchasing decision may be influenced. Confusion as to source and sponsorship are actionable under the Lanham Act. Companies such as IBM and Microsoft may try to prevent the use of their trademarks as compatibility identifiers, either because they are afraid of being associated with an inferior product or because restricting the use of the marks for compatibility purposes will boost their own sales of competing products.

Should trademark law prevent true statements concerning compatibility? The answer depends on the relative weight you place on competing policies. If you believe that a trademark confers strong property rights and that trademark owners are right to be concerned about free riders selling inferior goods on the basis of their compatibility, you might favor trademark protection in this context. On the other hand, if you believe that compatibility ought to be encouraged, you are likely to think consumers benefit from access to more accurate information about product alternatives.

4. The setting of industry standards, particularly where it is done by a group of industry representatives, may be protected as a collective or certification mark.[3] A certification mark is a mark used to designate goods that meet certain quality or accuracy standards. Rather than belonging to a particular company, use of the certification mark is open to anyone who meets the standards set out by the owner of the mark. If VGA was protected by a certification mark, IBM could sue anyone who falsely claimed to meet the VGA compatibility standard but would have to permit use of its mark to identify goods that were in fact in compliance with the standard.

A number of companies have already established such certification standards. Examples include "SPARC" for computer equipment that meets standards set by Sun Microsystems, and "Windows—Ready to Run" for third-party programs that run on Microsoft's Windows operating system. See Mark F. Radcliffe, Trademarks in the Computer Industry: A New Role, 18:2 New Matter 1 (1993). Standards may also be set by third-party organizations, such as International Organization for Standardization (ISO) or American National Standards Institute (ANSI). Companies who submit their product specifications as a standard to such groups generally give up control over the trademark to the standard-setting organization, which will permit anyone who meets the specification to use the mark. (A notable exception is Sun's Java trademark. Sun has applied to ISO to have Java declared a standard but is seeking to reserve the rights to the term "Java-compatible" to itself. At this writing, Sun was locked in litigation with Microsoft over whether Microsoft could refer to its altered version of Java as "Java-compatible." See Sun Microsystems v. Microsoft Corp., 999 F. Supp. 1301 (N.D. Cal. 1998); David McGowan & Mark A. Lemley, Could Java Change Everything? The Competitive Propriety of a Proprietary Standard, 43 Antitrust Bull. 715 (1998).)

---

3. 15 U.S.C. §1054 provides that a certification mark may be registered under the same standards as a normal trademark.

Is the use of certification marks a reasonable compromise between the competing policies outlined above? Does it solve the problem of free-riding?

PROBLEM

Problem 4-4. Microsoft, one of the largest sellers of computer operating systems and applications software, seeks to trademark its term "Windows" for its operating system interface. Should Microsoft be entitled to a trademark? How would you classify the mark? Against whom could Microsoft enforce the mark? How could manufacturers of application programs that make use of the "Windows" interface advertise compatibility with that interface?

C. TRADEMARKS AS LOCKOUT DEVICES

The final way in which a trademark might be used to help control a computer product market is by incorporating the trademark into the product itself.

Sega Enterprises Ltd. v. Accolade, Inc.
United States Court of Appeals for the Ninth Circuit
977 F.2d 1510 (9th Cir. 1992)

REINHART, Circuit Judge.

[The factual background of this case is set out in Chapter 2, Section E. Briefly, Sega manufactures video games under the Genesis label and permits only authorized programmers to write Sega-compatible games. To prevent the use of unauthorized games, Sega incorporated a "lockout" program in its Genesis game box. Accolade reverse engineered the code of the box in order to find a way to defeat the lockout program and to make its games compatible.]

All of Accolade's Genesis-compatible games are packaged in a similar fashion. The front of the box displays Accolade's "Ballistic" trademark and states "for use with Sega Genesis and Mega Drive Systems." The back of the box contains the following statement: "Sega and Genesis are registered trademarks of Sega Enterprises, Ltd. Game 1991 Accolade, Inc. All rights reserved. Ballistic is a trademark of Accolade, Inc. Accolade, Inc. is not associated with Sega Enterprises, Ltd. All product and corporate names are trademarks and registered trademarks of their respective owners." . . .

IV. Trademark Issues

Ordinarily in a trademark case, a trademark holder contends that another party is misusing the holder's mark or is attempting to pass off goods or services as those of the trademark holder. The other party usually protests that the mark is not being misused, that there is no actual confusion, or that for some other reason no violation has occurred. This case is different. Here, both parties agree that there is a misuse of a trademark, both agree that there is unlawful mislabeling, and both agree that confusion may result. The issue, here, is—which party is primarily responsible? Which is the wrongdoer—the violator? Is it Sega, which has adopted a security system governing access to its Genesis III console that displays its trademark and message whenever the initialization code for the security system is utilized, even when the video game program was manufactured by a Sega competitor? Or is it Accolade, which, having discovered how to gain access to the Genesis III through the initialization code, uses that code even though doing so triggers the display of Sega's trademark and message in a manner that leads observers to believe that Sega manufactured the Accolade game cartridge? In other words, is Sega the injured party because its mark is wrongfully attached to an Accolade video game by Accolade? Or is Accolade wronged because its game is mislabeled as a Sega product by Sega? The facts are relatively straightforward and we have little difficulty answering the question.

Sega's trademark security system (TMSS) initialization code not only enables video game programs to operate on the Genesis III console, but also prompts a screen display of the SEGA trademark and message. As a result, Accolade's inclusion of the TMSS initialization code in its video game programs has an effect ultimately beneficial neither to Sega nor to Accolade. A Genesis III owner who purchases a video game made by Accolade sees Sega's trademark associated with Accolade's product each time he inserts the game cartridge into the console. Sega claims that Accolade's inclusion of the TMSS initialization code in its games constitutes trademark infringement and false designation of origin in violation of sections 32(1)(a) and 43(a) of the Lanham Trademark Act, 15 U.S.C. §§1114(1)(a), 1125(a), respectively. Accolade counterclaims that Sega's use of the TMSS to prompt a screen display of its trademark constitutes false designation of origin under Lanham Act section 43(a), 15 U.S.C. §1125(a).

Because the TMSS has the effect of regulating access to the Genesis III console, and because there is no indication in the record of any public or industry awareness of any feasible alternate method of gaining access to the Genesis III, we hold that Sega is primarily responsible for any resultant confusion. Thus, it has not demonstrated a likelihood of success on the merits of its Lanham Act claims. Accordingly, the preliminary injunction it obtained must be dissolved with respect to the trademark claim also. However, we decline to instruct the district court to grant Accolade's request for preliminary injunctive relief at this time. The decision whether to grant such relief requires the making of factual and equitable determinations in light of the legal conclusions we express here. Such determinations are best left in the first instance to the district court.

A. False Labeling

Section 32(1)(a) of the Lanham Act creates a cause of action for trademark infringement against any person who, without the consent of the trademark owner, "uses in commerce any reproduction . . . of a registered mark in connection with the sale, offering for sale, distribution, or advertising of any goods or services on or in connection with which such use is likely to cause confusion, or to cause mistake, or to deceive. . . ." 15 U.S.C. §1114(1)(a). Section 43(a) proscribes the use in commerce of a false designation of origin in connection with goods or services where such use is "likely to cause confusion, or . . . mistake." *Id.* §1125(a). Both Sega and Accolade agree that the screen display of the Sega trademark and message creates a likelihood of consumer confusion regarding the origin of Accolade's games. The question is: which party is legally responsible for that confusion? We disagree with the answer given by the district court.

The district court found that Accolade bore primary responsibility for any consumer confusion that resulted from the display of the false Sega Message. However, Accolade had no desire to cause the Sega Message to appear or otherwise to create any appearance of association between itself and Sega; in fact, it had precisely the opposite wish. It used the TMSS initialization code only because it wanted to gain access for its products to the Genesis III, and was aware of no other method for doing so. On the other hand, while it may not have been Sega's ultimate goal to mislabel Accolade's products, the record is clear that the false labeling was the result of a deliberate decision on the part of Sega to include in the Genesis III a device which would both limit general access and cause false labeling. The decision to use the SEGA trademark as an essential element of a functional device that regulates access and to cause the SEGA trademark and message to be displayed whenever that functional device was triggered compels us to place primary responsibility for consumer confusion squarely on Sega.

With respect to Accolade, we emphasize that the record clearly establishes that it had only one objective in this matter: to make its video game programs compatible with the Genesis III console. That objective was a legitimate and a lawful one. There is no evidence whatsoever that Accolade wished Sega's trademark to be displayed when Accolade's games were played on Sega's consoles. To the contrary, Accolade included disclaimers on its packaging materials which stated that "Accolade, Inc. is not associated with Sega Enterprises, Ltd." When questioned regarding the Sega Message and its potential effect on consumers, Alan Miller testified that Accolade does not welcome the association between its product and Sega and would gladly avoid that association if there were a way to do so. Miller testified that Accolade's engineers had not been able to discover any way to modify their game cartridges so that the games would operate on the Genesis III without prompting the screen display of the Sega Message.

In contrast, Sega officials testified that Sega incorporated the TMSS into the Genesis console, known in Asia as the Mega-Drive, in order to lay the groundwork for the trademark prosecution of software pirates who sell counterfeit cartridges in Taiwan and South Korea, as well as in the United States. Sega then marketed the redesigned console worldwide. Sega intended that when Sega game programs manufactured by a counterfeiter were played on its consoles, the Sega Message would be displayed, thereby establishing the legal basis for a claim of trademark infringement. However, as Sega certainly knew, the TMSS also had the potential to affect legitimate competitors adversely. First, Sega should have foreseen that a competitor might discover how to utilize the TMSS, and that when it did and included the initialization code in its cartridges, its video game programs would also end up being falsely labeled. Sega should also have known that the TMSS might discourage some competitors from manufacturing independently developed games for use with the Genesis III console, because they would not want to become the victims of such a labeling practice. Thus, in addition to laying the groundwork for lawsuits against pirates, Sega knowingly risked two significant consequences: the false labeling of some competitors' products and the discouraging of other competitors from manufacturing Genesis-compatible games. Under the Lanham Act, the former conduct, at least, is clearly unlawful.

"Trademark policies are designed '(1) to protect consumers from being misled . . . (2) to prevent an impairment of the value of the enterprise which owns the trademark; and (3) to achieve these ends in a manner consistent with the objectives of free competition.'" Anti-Monopoly, Inc. v. General Mills Fun Group, 611 F.2d 296, 300-01 (9th Cir. 1979) (quoting HMH Publishing Co. v. Brincat, 504 F.2d 713, 716 (9th Cir. 1974)). Sega violated the first and the third of these principles. "The trademark is misused if it serves to limit competition in the manufacture and sales of a product. That is the special province of the limited monopolies provided pursuant to the patent laws." Id. at 301 (citation omitted).

Sega makes much of the fact that it did not adopt the TMSS in order to wage war on Accolade in particular, but rather as a defensive measure against software counterfeiters. It is regrettable that Sega is troubled by software pirates who manufacture counterfeit products in other areas of the world where adequate copyright remedies are not available. However, under the Lanham Act, which governs the use of trademarks and other designations of origin in this country, it is the effect of the message display that matters. Whatever Sega's intent with respect to the TMSS, the device serves to limit competition in the market for Genesis-compatible games and to mislabel the products of competitors. Moreover, by seeking injunctive relief based on the mislabeling it has itself induced, Sega seeks once again to take advantage of its trademark to exclude its competitors from the market. The use of a mark for such purpose is inconsistent with the Lanham Act.

B. Functionality

Sega argues that even if the legal analysis we have enunciated is correct, the facts do not support its application to this case. Specifically, Sega contends that the TMSS does not prevent legitimate unlicensed competitors from developing and marketing Genesis III-compatible cartridges that do not trigger a display of the Sega trademark and message. In other words, Sega claims that Accolade could have "engineered around" the TMSS. Accolade strongly disagrees with Sega's factual assertions. It contends that the TMSS initialization sequence is a functional feature that must be included in a video game program by a manufacturer in order for the game to operate on the Genesis III. Sega's factual argument stands or falls on the Nagashima declaration and the accompanying modified game cartridges that Sega introduced at the hearing. Having carefully reviewed the declaration, we conclude that Sega has not met its burden of establishing nonfunctionality.

Based on the Nagashima declaration and on the modified cartridges, the district court concluded that the TMSS initialization sequence was not a necessary component of a Genesis-compatible game. The court found that Accolade could have created a game cartridge that lacked the TMSS initialization code but would still operate on the Genesis III, or could have programmed its games in such a way that the false Sega Message would not be displayed on the screen. The court further found that either modification could have been accomplished at minimal additional expense to Accolade. Accordingly, the court ruled that Accolade could not assert a functionality defense.

. . . Viewed in the correct light, the record before us supports only one conclusion: The TMSS initialization code is a functional feature of a Genesis-compatible game and Accolade may not be barred from using it.

"Functional features of a product are features 'which constitute the actual benefit that the consumer wishes to purchase, as distinguished from an assurance that a particular entity made, sponsored, or endorsed a product.'" Vuitton et Fils S.A. v. J. Young Enterprises, Inc., 644 F.2d 769, 774 (9th Cir. 1981) (quoting International Order of Job's Daughters v. Lindeburg & Co., 633 F.2d 912, 917 (9th Cir. 1980), *cert. denied,* 452 U.S. 941, 69 L. Ed. 2d 956, 101 S. Ct. 3086 (1981)). A product feature thus is functional "if it is essential to the use or purpose of the article or if it affects the cost or quality of the article." *Inwood Laboratories*, 456 U.S. at 850 n.10. The Lanham Act does not protect essentially functional or utilitarian product features because such protection would constitute a grant of a perpetual monopoly over features that could not be patented. Keene Corp. v. Paraflex Industries, Inc., 653 F.2d 822, 824 (3d Cir. 1981). Even when the allegedly functional product feature is a trademark, the trademark owner may not enjoy a monopoly over the functional use of the mark. *Job's Daughters*, 633 F.2d at 918-19.

In determining whether a product feature is functional, a court may consider a number of factors, including—but not limited to—"the availability of alternative designs; and whether a particular design results from a comparatively simple or cheap method of manufacture." Clamp Mfg. Co. v. Enco Mfg. Co., Inc., 870 F.2d 512, 516 (9th Cir.), *cert. denied*, 493 U.S. 872 (1989). The availability of alternative methods of manufacture must be more than merely theoretical or speculative, however. The court must find "that commercially feasible alternative configurations *exist.*" *Id.* (emphasis added). Moreover, some cases have even suggested that in order to establish nonfunctionality the party with the burden must demonstrate that the product feature "'serves no purpose other than identification.'" *Keene Corp.*, 653 F.2d at 826 (quoting SK&F Co. v. Premo Pharmaceutical Laboratories, Inc., 625 F.2d 1055, 1063 (3d Cir. 1980)). With these principles in mind, we turn to the question whether the TMSS initialization code is a functional feature of a Genesis-compatible game.

It is indisputable that, in the case before us, part of "the actual benefit that the consumer wishes to purchase" is compatibility with the Genesis III console. The TMSS initialization code provides that compatibility. Sega argues that the modified cartridges that were introduced in the district court establish the actual existence of technically and commercially feasible alternative methods of gaining access to the Genesis III. The cartridges were prepared by Nagashima, an employee in Sega's Hardware Research and Development Department who was "familiar with the TMSS system." At most, the Nagashima affidavit establishes that an individual familiar with the operation of the TMSS can discover a way to engineer around it. It does not establish that a competitor with no knowledge of the workings of the TMSS could do so. Nor is there any evidence that there was any public or industry awareness of any alternate method for gaining access to the Genesis III. Evidence that an individual, even an independent expert, produced one or more cartridges is not sufficient proof that an alternate method exists. What is needed for proof of that fact is proof of the method itself. Here, such proof is totally lacking. What is also needed is proof that knowledge of the alternate method exists or is readily available to knowledgeable persons in the industry. That proof also is totally lacking here. Accordingly, the district court erred as a matter of law in concluding that the Nagashima declaration and the modified cartridges were sufficient to establish nonfunctionality.

Because the TMSS serves the function of regulating access to the Genesis III, and because a means of access to the Genesis III console without using the TMSS initialization code is not known to manufacturers of competing video game cartridges, there is an insufficient basis for a finding of nonfunctionality. Moreover, we note that the only evidence in the record (other than the Nagashima declaration) relating to Accolade's ability to gain access to the Genesis III through the use of any process other than the TMSS is the affidavit of Alan Miller. Miller stated that Accolade's software engineers—who, absent any evidence to the contrary, we presume to be reasonably competent representatives of their profession—have not been able to discover such a method. This evidence supports our conclusion that Sega has not met its burden of establishing nonfunctionality. . . .

In summary, because Sega did not produce sufficient evidence regarding the existence of a feasible alternative to the use of the TMSS initialization code, it did not carry its burden and its claim of nonfunctionality fails. Possibly, Sega will be able to meet its burden of proof at trial. We cannot say. However, we conclude that in light of the record before the district court, Sega was not entitled to preliminary injunctive relief under the Lanham Act.[11]

COMMENTS AND QUESTIONS

1. In considering Sega's claim of copyright infringement, the Ninth Circuit held that Accolade had a right to make intermediate and final copies of Sega's code to the extent necessary to its purpose of achieving compatibility. Does the court's trademark holding depend on this conclusion? If the court had decided that Accolade could not copy any Sega code or that there was no right to create compatible programs, would Accolade be guilty of trademark as well as copyright infringement? If not, why not?

2. Is there any merit to *Accolade*'s claim for trademark infringement? Surely Sega did not intend to identify Accolade's products as its own, since

---

11. Sega contends that even if the TMSS code is functional, Accolade, as the copier, was obligated to take the most effective measures reasonably available to eliminate the consumer confusion that has arisen as a result of the association of Sega's trademark with Accolade's product. . . . When a product feature is both functional and source-identifying, the copier need only take reasonable measures to avoid consumer confusion. American Greetings Corp. v. Dan-Dee Imports, Inc., 807 F.2d 1136, 1141 (3d Cir. 1986); *Job's Daughters*, 633 F.2d at 919 (the degree of protection afforded a product feature that has both functional and source-identifying aspects depends on the characteristics of the use and on the copier's merchandising practices). Assuming arguendo that the rules applicable to copiers apply here, the measures adopted by Accolade satisfy a reasonableness standard. Accolade placed disclaimers on its packaging materials which stated that "Accolade, Inc. is not associated with Sega Enterprises, Ltd." While Accolade could have worded its disclaimer more strongly, the version that it chose would appear to be sufficient.

it did not intend Accolade to have access to its system at all. Can consumers really be said to be confused if they have bought their products from Accolade?

3. Has the Sega mark itself become functional? Has it done so in this particular context?

5

Sui Generis Protection
of Computer
Technology

Previous chapters have explored the ways in which courts have applied existing laws to computer technology, particularly to computer software. As we have seen, the "fit" between existing law (which largely evolved to deal with the challenges of a manufacturing-based economy) and some aspects of computer technology, particularly computer software (which is arguably at the heart of an emerging information-based economy), has sometimes been difficult to achieve. No wonder, then, that the past several decades have witnessed numerous proposals to protect some aspects of computer technology with new forms of intellectual property law specially devised for them. This has included not only computer software and semiconductor chip designs, but also computer databases, computer-generated works, and digital audio recording devices.

These proposals have generally been grounded on a theory that existing law did not provide sufficient protection to provide incentives for necessary levels of investment in their development and distribution, or on a theory that it would unduly distort existing laws to apply them to provide appropriate incentives for such innovations. Such "sui generis" (of its own kind) proposals have generally been an amalgam of existing legal concepts drawn or adapted from copyright law or patent, along with some specially tailored rules aimed at addressing particular concerns of the industry sector. J.H. Reichman speaks of these sui generis proposals as "legal hybrids between the patent and copyright paradigms" and offers a thesis (discussed below) to explain why these regimes have proliferated in the past several decades. See J.H. Reichman, Legal Hybrids Between the Patent and Copyright Paradigms, 94 Colum. L. Rev. 2432 (1994).

In view of the pervasive orthodoxy of using copyright law to protect computer programs, it may come as a surprise to learn that in the 1970s and through the 1980s, many thought that computer programs should be protected by a sui generis regime. The World Intellectual Property Organization, for example, proposed a sui generis form of legal protection for computer programs in the 1970s. The principal rationale for these proposals for software protection arose from concerns that it would distort copyright principles to apply this law to protect such a highly utilitarian subject matter. See, e.g., Pamela Samuelson, CONTU Revisited: The Case Against Copyright Protection for Computer Programs in Machine-Readable Form, 1984 Duke L.J. 663 (1984). The lack of experience in the copyright field in protecting utilitarian subject matters also meant that it might lack workable doctrines with which to analyze infringement claims.

In the early 1980s, the Japanese Ministry for International Trade (MITI) proposed a sui generis form of legal protection for computer programs built on modified copyright principles. Early on, MITI recognized that computer programs would pose compatibility and standardization issues that a legal regime protecting software would need to address. MITI expressed concern about the market power that computer firms might attain if the law conferred on them exclusive rights that enabled them to block the development of compatible systems. See Dennis S. Karjala, Lessons From the Computer Software Protection Debate in Japan, 1984 Ariz. St. L. Rev. 53 (1984) (discussing the MITI proposal). Owing in substantial part to strong U.S. opposition to the MITI proposal—especially to its compulsory license provisions—the government of Japan decided to follow the U.S. lead and use copyright law to protect computer programs. *Id.*

Even in the late 1980s and into the very early 1990s, the European Union (EU) was seriously considering a sui generis form of legal protection for computer programs. When in 1991 the EU issued its directive on such programs, which adopted the copyright model (see Chapter 8), the sui generis debate on an international level was largely settled as a political matter. However, the decompilation and interoperability provisions of the European directive are arguably sui generis rules within the body of copyright law that respond to the same concerns as were raised by MITI about undue market power if copyright protection could be used to stop the development of interoperable programs. One way to think about the U.S. experience with software protection is to say that the United States has, more or less, developed a sui generis form of legal protection for computer software within the body of copyright law through a common law litigation process. The courts have addressed unprecedented issues, such as the decompilation, interoperability, look and feel, and related issues in computer program cases and have devised new tests of infringement.

Although it did not emerge as the favored means for protecting computer software, sui generis legislation has been adopted for some other computer-related products. One example is the Semiconductor Chip Protection Act of 1984 in the United States (and its counterpart laws in other countries) that protect the topography of integrated circuits. A second example is the sui generis legal regime that the EU adopted in 1996 to protect the contents of databases (distinct from copyright protection for the creative selection and arrangement of data). Similar sui generis legislation has been pending for three legislative sessions in the U.S. Congress. Proponents assert that the U.S. Supreme Court's repudiation of the "sweat of the brow" theory of originality in Feist Publications v. Rural Telephone Serv., 499 U.S. 340 (1991) opened up a "gap" in legal protection available to database developers that makes them vulnerable to market-destructive appropriations. Some, however, question the existence of such a gap or its extent. Also debated is whether an unfair competition approach, rather than an exclusive property rights approach, to legal protection should be used to fill any gap that might exist. A third example of computer-related sui generis legislation is the form the United Kingdom adopted some years ago to protect computer-generated works (e.g., of music or pictorial images). All three of these legal regimes have been built primarily on modified copyright principles, although, as will become more evident below, the Semiconductor Chip Protection Act (SCPA) has some modified patent features as well.

But other legislation with a sui generis character has also been adopted in response to challenges arising from advances in computer-related technologies. This includes the Audio Home Recording Act of 1992 (requiring the installation of copy-control systems in digital audio recording devices) and the anti-circumvention provisions of the Digital Millennium Copyright Act of 1998 (see Chapter 10), which outlaws circumvention of technical measures used by copyright owners to protect access to their works and the manufacture or distribution of technologies primarily designed to bypass such technical measures. No underlying copyright infringement (e.g., illegal copying or public performance of a work) need occur to violate either of these laws.

Even though the political debate over sui generis protection for computer software has died down, questions continue to arise as to whether the law actually protects the "right" things about computer programs, just as questions continue to occur about whether the patent system can appropriately protect computer program inventions. This chapter includes some consideration of these issues and some proposals to protect software in part because they illustrate the difficulties that may arise when rules initially devised to create incentives for innovation in a manufacturing economy are applied to promote innovation in an information economy. As you review these materials, recall issues raised in previous chapters and consider whether patent and copyright laws can successfully be adapted to regulate the new information technology environment or whether new paradigms of intellectual property law need to be devised.

A. THE SEMICONDUCTOR CHIP PROTECTION ACT

United States firms were the initial world market leaders in the production of semiconductor chips. In the late 1970s, however, the U.S. semiconductor industry was in a serious slump, in part because of the rise of Asian competitors who were making substantial headway in the world market for semiconductor chips. One contributing cause of this slump, according to representatives of certain U.S. chip producers (Intel Corp. prominently among them), was that the law did not provide sufficient legal protection to the layout of integrated circuits on semiconductor chips. In one congressional hearing on this problem, Intel pointed out that it might need to invest tens of millions of dollars to develop a new family of chips. However, once these chips appeared in the open market, they could be quickly copied by a competitor with an investment of only about $50,000 of equipment. The disparity between the high cost of development and low cost of copying was, Intel officials reported, having a chilling effect on Intel's willingness to make such substantial investments. Moreover, Intel was not the only innovative U.S. chip producer being hurt by both offshore and domestic competitive copying.

Intel initially sought to deal with the gap-in-protection problem by claiming copyright protection in the layout of circuits on its semiconductors. It first registered copyright claims in drawings of its chip circuit layouts and then sought to register masks made from those drawings as derivative works of the drawings. The U.S. Copyright Office accepted registration of the drawings but refused the request to register the masks because of their utilitarian character (i.e., the masks were intended for use in the semiconductor chip manufacturing process). Intel then asked Congress to amend the copyright law to add semiconductor designs or mask works to the subject matter of copyright. In hearings on this legislation before Congress, Professor Arthur Miller, who had chaired the Commission on New Technological Uses of Copyright (CONTU) subcommittee responsible for recommending copyright protection for computer programs, argued that the same arguments that CONTU relied on to decide that copyright protection was appropriate for software applied to computer chips as well. Miller likened the design of semiconductor chips to Mondrian paintings. However, the Copyright Office and others raised objections to the use of copyright law as such to protect layout designs for circuits in semiconductors, saying that the "useful article" limitation on the scope of copyright protection for pictorial, sculptural, and graphic works was too fundamental to American copyright law. Representative Kastenmeier eventually introduced a sui generis bill for the legal protection of mask works (adapted from an industrial design bill that had nearly been made part of the Copyright Act of 1976). The legislative history and development of SCPA is described in Robert W. Kastenmeier & Michael J. Remington, The Semiconductor Chip Protection Act of 1984: A Swamp or Firm Ground?, 70 Minn. L. Rev. 417 (1985). The main provisions of SCPA are discussed in the case that follows.

≡ **Brooktree Corp. v. Advanced Micro Devices, Inc.**
≡ *United States Court of Appeals for the Federal Circuit*
≡ *977 F.2d 1555 (Fed. Cir. 1992)*

NEWMAN, Circuit Judge.

Brooktree Corporation brought suit against Advanced Micro Devices, Inc. (herein AMD) for patent infringement, 35 U.S.C. §271, and infringement of mask work registrations, 17 U.S.C. §910, in connection with certain semiconductor chips used in color video displays. The United States District Court for the Southern District of California entered judgment that the patents were valid and infringed and that the registered mask works were infringed, assessing damages.

. . . [F]or issues of fact and law under the Semiconductor Chip Protection Act we apply the discernible law of the Ninth Circuit, in accordance with the principles set forth in Atari, Inc. v. JS & A Group, Inc., 747 F.2d 1422, 1438-40, 223 USPQ 1074, 1086-87 (Fed. Cir. 1984) (en banc) (applying copyright law of the circuit in which the case was tried, thus avoiding creating new opportunities for forum shopping). Judicial consideration of the Semiconductor Chip Protection Act has thus far been sparse, and we have given particular attention to the statute and its history, for the parties dispute significant aspects of statutory interpretation. . . .

I. Mask Works

The Semiconductor Chip Protection Act

The Semiconductor Chip Protection Act of 1984, Pub.L. 98-620, Title III, 98 Stat. 3347, codified at 17 U.S.C. §§901-914, arose from concerns that existing intellectual property laws did not provide adequate protection of proprietary rights in semiconductor chips that had been designed to perform a particular function. The Act, enacted after extensive congressional consideration and hearings over several years, adopted relevant aspects of existing intellectual property law, but for the most part created a new law, specifically adapted to the protection of design layouts of semiconductor chips.

Chip design layouts embody the selection and configuration of electrical components and connections in order to achieve the desired electronic functions. The electrical elements are configured in three dimensions, and are built up in layers by means of a series of "masks" whereby, using photographic depositing and etching techniques, layers of metallic, insulating, and semiconductor material are deposited in the desired pattern on a wafer of silicon. This set of masks is called a "mask work", and is part of the semiconductor chip product. The statute defines a mask work as:

> a series of related images, however fixed or encoded
>
> (A) having or representing the predetermined, three dimensional pattern of metallic, insulating, or semiconductor material present or removed from the layers of a semiconductor chip product; and
>
> (B) in which series the relation of the images to one another is that each image has the pattern of the surface of one form of a semiconductor chip product.

17 U.S.C. §901(a)(2). The semiconductor chip product in turn is defined as:

> the final or intermediate form of any product—
>
> (A) having two or more layers of metallic, insulating, or semiconductor material, deposited or otherwise placed on, or etched away or otherwise removed from, a piece of semiconductor material in accordance with a predetermined pattern; and
>
> (B) intended to perform electronic circuitry functions.

17 U.S.C. §901(a)(1).

The design of a satisfactory chip layout may require extensive effort and be extremely time consuming, particularly as new and improved electronic capabilities are sought to be created. A new semiconductor chip may incur large research and development costs, yet after the layout is imprinted in the mask work and the chip is available in commerce, it can be copied at a fraction of the cost to the originator. Thus there was concern that widespread copying of new chip layouts would have adverse effects on innovative advances in semiconductor technology, as stated in the Senate Report:

> In the semiconductor industry, innovation is indispensable; research breakthroughs are essential to the life and health of the industry. But research and innovation in the design of semiconductor chips are threatened by the inadequacies of existing legal protection against piracy and unauthorized copying. This problem, which is so critical to this essential sector of the American economy, is addressed by the Semiconductor Chip Protection Act of 1984. . . .
>
> The Semiconductor Chip Protection Act of 1984, . . . would prohibit "chip piracy"—the unauthorized copying and distribution of semiconductor chip products copied from the original creators of such works.

S.Rep. No. 425, 98th Cong., 2d Sess., 1 (1984) (hereinafter Senate Report).

In the evolution of the Semiconductor Chip Protection Act it was first proposed simply to amend the Copyright Act, 17 U.S.C. §101 et seq., to include semiconductor chip products and mask works as subject of copyright. See H.R. 1028, 98th Cong., 1st Sess. (1983). However, although some courts had interpreted copyright law as applicable to computer software imbedded in a semiconductor chip, see Apple Computer, Inc. v. Franklin Computer Corp., 714 F.2d 1240, 1249, 219 USPQ 113, 121 (3d Cir. 1983), *cert. dismissed*, 464 U.S. 1033, 104 S. Ct. 690, 79 L.Ed.2d 158 (1984), it was uncertain whether the copyright law could protect against copying of the pattern on the chip itself, if the pattern was deemed inseparable from the utilitarian function of the chip. Indeed, the Copyright Office had refused to register patterns on printed circuit boards and semiconductor chips because no separate artistic aspects had been demonstrated. Copyright Protection for Semiconductor Chips: Hearings on H.R. 1028 Before the Subcomm. on Courts, Civil Liberties, and the Administration of Justice of the House Comm. on the Judiciary, 98th Cong., 1st Sess., 77 (1983) (hereinafter 1983 House Hearings) (statement of Dorothy Schrader, Associate Register of Copyrights for Legal Affairs). Concern was also expressed that extension of the copyright law to accommodate the problems of mask works would distort certain settled copyright doctrines, such as fair use. 1983 House Hearings at 16-17 (statement of Jon A. Baumgarten, Copyright Counsel, Association of American Publishers, Inc.).

The patent system alone was deemed not to provide the desired scope of protection of mask works. Although electronic circuitry and electronic components are within the statutory subject matter of patentable invention, see 35 U.S.C. §101, and some original circuitry may be patentable if it also meets the requirements of the Patent Act, as is illustrated in this case, Congress sought more expeditious protection against copying of original circuit layouts, whether or not they met the criteria of patentable invention. Senate Report at 8.

The Semiconductor Chip Protection Act of 1984 was an innovative solution to this new problem of technology-based industry. While some copyright principles underlie the law, as do some attributes of patent law, the Act was uniquely adapted to semiconductor mask works, in order to achieve appropriate protection for original designs while meeting the competitive needs of the industry and serving the public interest.

The Semiconductor Chip Protection Act provides for the grant of certain exclusive rights to owners of registered mask works, including the exclusive right "to reproduce the mask work by optical, electronic, or any other means", and the exclusive right "to import or distribute a semiconductor chip product in which the mask work is embodied". 17 U.S.C. §905. Mask works that are not "original", or that consist of "designs that are staple, commonplace, or familiar in the semiconductor industry, or variations of such designs, combined in a way that, considered as a whole, is not original", are excluded from protection. 17 U.S.C. §902(b). Protection is also not extended to any "idea, procedure, process, system, method of operation, concept, principle, or discovery, regardless of the form in which it is described, explained, illustrated or embodied" in the mask work. 17 U.S.C. §902(c). The sponsors and supporters of this legislation foresaw that there would be areas of uncertainty in application of this new law to particular situations, and referred to "gray areas" wherein factual situations could arise that would not have easy answers. Those areas are emphasized by both parties in the assignments of error on this appeal.

Brooktree's Mask Work Registrations

Brooktree was granted mask work registration MW 2873 on August 6, 1987, and registration MW 3838 on July 6, 1988, for its chips identified as Bt451 and Bt458. These Brooktree chips embody a circuit design that combines the functions of a static random access memory (SRAM) and a digital to analog converter (DAC). This circuitry, sometimes referred to as RAMDAC, acts as a "color palette", producing the colors in color video displays having high speed and enhanced picture resolution. A Brooktree witness described these chips as a technological breakthrough, exceeding limits in speed and performance that had been believed impossible to exceed. Brooktree stated that a single Bt458 chip replaced a previously used set of 36 chips (an AMD product) and offered many advantages. A Brooktree witness testified that these chips were extremely successful commercially, and were soon incorporated into new designs for video display systems made by several large manufacturers.

A critical component of the Brooktree chips is the core cell, a ten-transistor SRAM cell which is repeated over six thousand times in an array covering about eighty percent of the chip area. Each core cell consists of ten transistors and metal conductors electrically connecting the transistors throughout the three dimensions of the multilayered cell. Brooktree charged that this core cell was copied by AMD, thus infringing Brooktree's mask work registrations.

AMD does not challenge the validity of these mask work registrations, or dispute Brooktree's position that its chips are protected under the Semiconductor Chip Protection Act. AMD does, however, assert that its accused chips are not infringements, for reasons we shall discuss.

Infringement

The Semiconductor Chip Protection Act defines an "infringing semiconductor chip product" as one which is "made, imported, or distributed in violation of the exclusive rights" of the mask work owner. 17 U.S.C. §901(a)(9). The text of the Semiconductor Chip Protection Act sets forth the subject matter of protection in terms of certain exclusive rights, including, *inter alia*, the exclusive right to "reproduce the mask work", 17 U.S.C. §905. This usage mirrors the words of the Copyright Act, which states the exclusive rights of copyright owners "to reproduce the copyrighted work". 17 U.S.C. §106. Although the Semiconductor Chip Protection Act does not use the word "copy" to describe infringement, the parallel language reflects the incorporation of the well-explicated copyright principle of substantial similarity into the Semiconductor Chip Protection Act, as discussed infra.

The jury instruction on the criteria for establishing infringement included the instruction that infringement requires substantial similarity to a material portion of the registered mask work:

> To establish infringement, Brooktree must show that A.M.D.'s mask works are substantially similar to a material portion of the mask works in Brooktree's chips covered by Brooktree's mask work registration. No hard and fast rule or percentage governs what constitutes a "substantial similarity." Substantial similarity may exist where an important part of the mask work is copied, even though the percentage of the entire chip which is copied may be relatively small. It is not required that A.M.D. make a copy of the entire mask work embodied in the Brooktree chip.

AMD states that it does not on appeal challenge this jury instruction. Instead, AMD argues that because the non-SRAM portion of its accused chip was not copied, the chips are not "substantially similar", whatever the materiality of the SRAM cell to the total mask work. It was undisputed that there was not duplication of the entire chip. AMD states that the Semiconductor Chip Protection Act requires copying of the entire chip, and therefore that it was entitled to judgment in its favor as a matter of law, or at least to a new trial on the issue.

The principle of substantial similarity recognizes that the existence of differences between an accused and copyrighted work may not negate infringement if a material portion of the copyrighted work is appropriated. Shaw v. Lindheim, 919 F.2d 1353, 1362, 15 USPQ2d 1516, 1523 (9th Cir. 1990). If the copied portion is qualitatively important, the finder of fact may properly find substantial similarity under copyright law, Baxter v. MCA, Inc., 812 F.2d 421, 425, 2 USPQ2d 1059, 1063 (9th Cir.), *cert. denied*, 484 U.S. 954, 108 S. Ct. 346, 98 L.Ed.2d 372 (1987), and under the Semiconductor Chip Protection Act.

Brooktree agrees that the SRAM portion of the accused chips covers only eighty percent of the chip area, and that the remaining circuitry was not copied by AMD. Infringement under the statute does not require that all parts of the accused chip be copied. The district court's explanation to the jury was in full accord with the statutory grant of exclusive rights to reproduce the mask work. The statutory interpretation now pressed by AMD, *viz.*, that the entire chip must have been copied, is unsupported. Indeed, the House Report states that it was contemplated that the cell layout alone could be misappropriated:

> Mask works sometimes contain substantial areas (of so-called "cells") whose layouts involve creativity and are commercially valuable. In appropriate fact

settings, the misappropriation of such a cell—assuming it meets the original standards of this chapter—could be the basis for an infringement action under this chapter.

H.R.Rep. No. 781, 98th Cong., 2d Sess., 26, 27 (1984), reprinted in 1984 U.S. Code Cong. & Admin. News 5708, 5750, 5775, 5776 (hereinafter House Report) (footnote omitted). As explained in the Explanatory Memorandum—Mathias-Leahy Amendment to S. 1201, 130 Cong. Rec. S12,916 (daily ed. Oct. 3, 1984) (hereinafter Mathias-Leahy Memorandum), written to explain the House and Senate bills as they were enacted, *id.* at S12,923, the Congressional intention was to protect against "piecemeal copying" and "copying of a material portion" of a chip:

> . . . the amendment, like both bills, incorporates the familiar copyright principle of substantial similarity. Although as a practical matter, copying of an insubstantial portion of a chip and independent design of the remainder is not likely, copying of a material portion nevertheless constitutes infringement. This concept is particularly important in the semiconductor industry, where it may be economical, for example, to copy 75% of a mask work from one chip and combine that with 25% of another mask work, if the copies are transferable modules, such as units from a cell library.
>
> As the Senate report notes, no hard and fast percentages govern what constitutes a "substantial" copying because substantial similarity may exist where an important part of a mask work is copied even though the percentage copied may be relatively small. Nonetheless, mask work owners are protected not only from wholesale copying but also against piecemeal copying of substantial or material portions of one or more mask works.

Mathias-Leahy Memorandum at S12,917.

Whether an appropriation of a cell layout constitutes infringement in a particular case is for the trier of fact, and can not be decided as a matter of law. See Sid & Marty Krofft Television Productions, Inc. v. McDonald's Corp., 562 F.2d 1157, 1164, 196 USPQ 97, 102-03 (9th Cir. 1977) (question of substantial similarity under copyright law is for the trier of fact). We shall discuss this question post, for it was litigated in the context of AMD's defense of reverse engineering.

The Reverse Engineering Defense

AMD's position at trial, and on appeal, was that its core cell was the product of reverse engineering of the Brooktree chip, and therefore does not constitute infringement under the Semiconductor Chip Protection Act. Reverse engineering is a statutory defense, included in the Act upon extensive congressional attention to the workings of the semiconductor chip industry.

The statute provides that it is not an infringement of a registered mask work for

(1) a person to reproduce the mask work solely for the purpose of teaching, analyzing, or evaluating the concepts or techniques embodied in the mask work or the circuitry, logic flow, or organization of components used in the mask work; or

(2) a person who performs the analysis or evaluation described in paragraph (1) to incorporate the results of such conduct in an original mask work which is made to be distributed.

17 U.S.C. §906(a). The statute thus provides that one engaged in reverse engineering shall not be liable for infringement when the end product is itself original. In performing reverse engineering a person may disassemble, study, and analyze an existing chip in order to understand it. This knowledge may be used to create an original chip having a different design layout, but which performs the same or equivalent function as the existing chip, without penalty or prohibition. Congress was told by industry representatives that reverse engineering was an accepted and fair practice, and leads to improved chips having "form, fit, and function" compatibility with the existing chip, thereby serving competition while advancing the state of technology. Senate Report at 21.

Much attention was given by Congress and by witnesses to the question of how to determine whether a chip layout was born of legitimate reverse engineering or of copying. It was foreseen that there would be a "gray area" wherein the rights of the parties, on the facts of a particular chip design, would require resolution on a fact-dependent, case-by-case basis. The following colloquy illustrates concerns raised at the hearings:

Rep. Edwards: . . . Is the chief reservation here the idea that reverse engineering, which all the witnesses agree is appropriate, might be confused with pirating and that any kind of reverse engineering might be interpreted under this law as pirating?

Mr. MacPherson (of Fairchild Camera & Instrument Corp.): I think that's one of the very strong concerns that we have, yes. There is a very gray area here in the very nature of reverse engineering, which would leave an individual engaged in that practice uncertain what his ultimate rights would be should he use that particular result in another product.

Copyright Protection for Imprinted Design Patterns on Semiconductor Chips: Hearings Before the Subcomm. on Courts, Civil Liberties, and the Administration of Justice of the House Comm. on the Judiciary, 96th Cong., 1st Sess., 66 (1979).

This aspect was explored over the several years of legislative gestation. The reverse engineering procedure was described by witnesses, and distinguished in purpose and mechanism from the copying against which the Semiconductor Chip Protection Act was intended to guard. It was explained that a person engaged in reverse engineering seeks to understand the design of the original chip with the object of improving the circuitry, the chip layout, or both. The presence of innovation and improvement was stressed as the hallmark of an original layout. A witness explained the difference as determining "was anything innovative done in the process or was it simply a reproduction of what was already there?" The Semiconductor Chip Protection Act of 1983: Hearings on S. 1201 Before the Subcomm. on Patents, Copyrights, and Trademarks of the Senate Comm. on the Judiciary, 98th Cong., 1st Sess., 84 (1983) (testimony of Stanley C. Corwin). Another witness explained that reverse engineering generally produces a "paper trail" recording the engineer's efforts to understand the original chip and to design a different version after reverse engineering:

> Whenever there is a true case of reverse engineering, the second firm will have prepared a great deal of paper—logic and circuit diagrams, trial layouts, computer simulations of the chip, and the like; it will also have invested thousands of hours of work. All of these can be documented by reference to the firm's ordinary business records. A pirate has no such papers, for the pirate does none of this work. Therefore, whether there has been a true reverse engineering job or just a job of copying can be shown by looking at the defendant's records. The paper trail of a chip tells a discerning observer whether the chip is a copy or embodies the effort of reverse engineering.

Senate Report at 22 (quoting statement of Leslie L. Valdasz, Senior Vice President, Intel Corporation). The Committee reports and the statements of the Semiconductor Chip Protection Act's supporters show the belief that evidence of the presence or absence of such a paper trail would significantly reduce the gray area between legitimate and illegitimate behavior. See Mathias-Leahy Memorandum at S12,917; House Report at 21.

Senators Mathias and Leahy explained that §906(a) includes a provision

> to clarify the intent of both chambers that competitors are permitted not only to study the protected mask works, but also to use the results of that study to design, distribute and import semiconductor chip products embodying their own original mask works. . . .
> The end product of the reverse engineering process is not an infringement, and itself qualifies for protection under the Act, if it is an original mask work as contrasted with a substantial copy. If the resulting semiconductor chip product is not substantially identical to the original, and its design involved significant toil and investment, so that it is not mere plagiarism, it does not infringe the original chip, even if the layout of the two chips is, in substantial part, similar.

Mathias-Leahy Memorandum at S12,917.

In illuminating the meaning of "original" in the context of reverse engineering, Senators Mathias and Leahy distinguished between a substantial copy, on one hand, and the product of reverse engineering which might be similar to the original, but if not a substantial copy would not be an infringement. For the latter, the "paper trail" was expected to document efforts in "analyzing, or evaluating the concepts or techniques embodied in the mask work or the circuitry, logic flow, or organization of components used in the mask work", as the effort required would be reflected in the documents. *Id.*

AMD's defense was that its chips were independently designed after the Brooktree chips were subjected to reverse engineering to learn the Brooktree design. The question of whether AMD's activities were acceptable reverse engineering, or unacceptable copying, was explained to the jury as follows:

> Reverse engineering is permitted and is authorized by the Chip Protection Act. It is not infringement of an owner's exclusive right and protected mask work for another person, through reverse-engineering, to photograph and to study the mask work for the purpose of analyzing its circuitry—correction—the circuitry, logic flow and organization of the components used in the mask work and to incorporate such analysis into an original mask work.
>
> The end product of the reverse-engineering process may be an original mask work, and therefore not an infringing mask work, if the resulting semiconductor chip product is not substantially identical to the protected mask work and its design involved significant toil and investment so that it is not mere plagiarism.
>
> You should place great weight on the existence of reverse paperwork trail in determining whether the defendant's mask work is an original mask work from reverse-engineering.
>
> A.M.D. mask work constitutes an original mask work if A.M.D.'s mask work incorporates its own new design elements which offered improvements over or an alternative to Brooktree's mask work.

These instructions focus the jury on whether AMD produced an original mask work, as the statute requires. The instructions were not challenged by AMD on its motion for new trial or on appeal, and were adapted from AMD's proposed instructions. Brooktree calls the instructions "too lenient". Whether or not too lenient, they were not objected to by AMD at trial, and are not now criticized by AMD as incorrect. They are the law applied in this case. See Fed. R. Civ. P. 51; Herrington v. County of Sonoma, 834 F.2d 1488, 1500 n.12 (9th Cir. 1987), *cert. denied*, 489 U.S. 1090, 109 S. Ct. 1557, 103 L.Ed.2d 860 (1989) (failure to object to a jury instruction precludes appellate review).

The Trial

The factual premises of the issues of infringement and AMD's reverse engineering defense were extensively explored at trial, through examination and cross-examination of witnesses, exhibits, displays, and attorney argument. To summarize, AMD argued at trial, and repeats on this appeal, that it did not intend to copy Brooktree's layout, and did not do so. AMD pointed to its "paper trail" of its two and a half years of effort at a cost in excess of three million dollars. AMD stated that if its intent had been to copy the Brooktree layout, it would simply have directed duplication of the circuit layouts, requiring a matter of months, not years. AMD stressed differences between its chips and those of Brooktree, and pointed out its aversion to piracy. According to AMD, this case is not in the gray area where reasonable minds could differ over whether there was reverse engineering or copying. AMD argues that Congress could not have intended that mask work infringement be found in the circumstances of this case, and that this court should hold, as a matter of law, that AMD did not infringe Brooktree's mask work registrations.

Brooktree, on its part, argued that AMD's cell layout is not original, but was directly copied from Brooktree's SRAM core cell, and repeated 6,000 times. Brooktree stressed AMD's lengthy and expensive failures at designing a layout. Brooktree observed that AMD had incorrectly analyzed Brooktree's chip during its attempts at reverse engineering, and that throughout this entire period of attempted duplication of function, AMD was unable to come close to Brooktree's results. Brooktree pointed to the rapidity with which AMD changed to Brooktree's layout when the error in analysis was discovered, AMD immediately producing, without further experimentation, a substantially identical SRAM cell.

At trial there was extensive evidence of AMD's design efforts, including its full paper trail. Evidence included the following: William Plants, AMD's assigned designer of the SRAM core cell, testified that AMD initiated a project to design a color palette chip in January, 1986, based on Brooktree's announcement of such a chip the previous November and introduction of its Bt451 chip in February 1986. In April AMD obtained several Brooktree Bt451 chips.

Plants opened up one of the chips and had it photographed, including blow-ups of the SRAM portion, which he said was of particular interest to him. After studying the chip he prepared a "reverse engineering report" in June, 1986. Plants incorrectly concluded that the Brooktree chip had eight transistors in each SRAM cell rather than ten. Plants then abandoned his efforts to design an SRAM cell based on six transistors, and attempted, over the next six months, to create an SRAM core cell design based on eight transistors. These attempts were not successful.

There was evidence of increasing pressure to complete the design, including suggestions by AMD supervisors that Plants reexamine the Brooktree chip because the project had gotten "bogged down". Plants did so some time in late January or early February. Plants testified that it was toward the end of January 1987 when he changed to a ten-transistor design in the same arrangement as Brooktree's design. Plants admitted that he did "solve the problem in a week" by adopting the ten-transistor design. Plants denied, however, that he learned of the ten-transistor design from his reexamination of the Brooktree chip, but explained that the design had been suggested to him by a job candidate he interviewed during that period. That candidate did not testify, and an AMD witness said he was dead.

There was extensive exploration at trial of the events during this period, of Plants' design processes, and of the timing and other details of the successful AMD ten-transistor design. For instance, Plants testified that his reexamination of the Brooktree chip was prompted not by pressure from his supervisors, but by a memory flash, like a "bolt from the blue", of something he had seen previously in the Brooktree chip.

In addition, there was extensive testimony and demonstrative and documentary evidence that the similarities in the circuit designs led to the substantial identity between the layouts of the Brooktree and AMD core cells. For example, Plants testified that in laying out the ten-transistor SRAM cell for fabrication in silicon, he never changed the locations of the ten transistors in his design, and never considered alternatives to Brooktree's transistor arrangement. Michael Brunolli, the engineer responsible for the layout of the Brooktree SRAM cell, testified that, in contrast, he had gone through about six changes of transistor layout before he achieved the final design.

Brooktree's expert witness Richard Crisp testified that the layout of the Brooktree SRAM cell was unique and original, and was not a commonplace or staple design. Crisp stated that the most important factor in layout of the SRAM cell is the location of the transistors. Crisp showed the jury exhibits picturing alternative layouts of electrically identical ten-transistor SRAM core cells in other chips, illustrating different layouts of the same circuitry. Plants had agreed that "you could conceivably come up with an infinite number of layouts" for the ten-transistor cell.

Plants admitted that the metal lines connecting the transistors in one layer of his layout were in the same sequence or order as the corresponding lines in the Brooktree chip, although his design had an extra metal line in it. Crisp testified that the extra metal line in AMD's layout did not relate to any function of the SRAM core cell itself. Plants also admitted that he originally included 45-degree angled portions in the polysilicon layer of his initial layout, a feature found in the Brooktree layout. Plants said he later removed the angles at the request of AMD's production engineers because it was incompatible with AMD's process methodology. Brunolli testified that the 45-degree angled portions arose in his design as a result of design rules used at Brooktree, and that he chose the angles to make his cell layout more compact.

Crisp testified that the transistors, which "form the substance of the cell" were "grouped together in the same way" in the AMD and Brooktree layouts. Crisp showed a videotape of the Brooktree and AMD SRAM cells side-by-side and then overlaid. (This tape was shown four times, including once in the jury room.) He stopped the tape at various points to illustrate the similarities in the layout of the two chips, and explained that the differences were primarily the result of AMD's smaller technology and removal of the 45-degree angles.

Crisp testified that the differences between the cells were "very minor, trivial, insignificant", and "insignificant electrically", and that "the substance of the cells is the same." Plants had testified that minor differences in design layout would arise because the differing technologies of AMD and Brooktree resulted in each firm having different standard design rules for layout of semiconductor chips. . . .

A reasonable jury could have placed weight on the evidence that AMD did not use an alternative transistor configuration but used Brooktree's configuration. A reasonable jury could have inferred that AMD's paper trail, insofar as it related to the SRAM cell, related entirely to AMD's failures, and that as soon as the Brooktree chip was correctly deciphered by reverse engineering, AMD did not create its own design but copied the Brooktree design. A reasonable jury could have resolved credibility questions in favor of Brooktree. Issues of credibility of witnesses are for the jury, and are not amenable to appellate review. Nicholson v. Rushen, 767 F.2d 1426, 1427 (9th Cir. 1985).

AMD argues on appeal that the sheer volume of paper established the reverse engineering defense "as a matter of law". AMD appears to misperceive the process, whereby the jury is instructed on the law, and applies the law to the facts and inferences reasonably drawn therefrom, based on the evidence adduced at trial. When there was sufficient evidence to support the verdict in light of the entire record, and upon correct or unobjected instructions of law, the jury's verdict must stand. . . .

The jury was instructed on the law of the reverse engineering defense, and was told to place "great weight" on the paper trail. . . .

AMD's proposed interpretation of the reverse engineering defense is not supported in the statute. 17 U.S.C. §906(a) requires, as an element of the defense of reverse engineering, that the product be original. The Senate Report described reverse engineering as activity that "spurs innovation and technological progress, as competitors seek to develop ever faster or more efficient chips, to perform similar or related functions". Senate Report at 21. The statute does not reflect an intent to excuse copying, as a matter of law, if the copier had first tried and failed to do the job without copying. The paper trail is evidence of independent effort, but it is not conclusive or incontrovertible proof of either originality or the absence of copying.

The questions of originality and copying are heavily fact-dependent, not absolutes of law. Where the evidence is such that reasonable minds could draw different conclusions, such questions are the province of the jury, as illustrated in analogous copyright cases, e.g., Twentieth Century-Fox Film Corp. v. MCA, Inc., 715 F.2d 1327, 1329, 217 USPQ 611, 612 (9th Cir. 1983) (question of whether there was copying was a "close enough question" to require trial); Dezendorf v. Twentieth Century-Fox Film Corp., 99 F.2d 850, 851 (9th Cir. 1938) (issue of originality is for the jury, not for the court).

AMD points out that there was conflicting evidence as to whether the AMD chips were improved. For example, AMD points to evidence that its accused chips were smaller, and as a result faster, than those of Brooktree, while Brooktree points to evidence that this was because AMD used 1.6 micron technology as opposed to Brooktree's older 2 micron technology. (The micron size refers to the length across a transistor gate.)

There was also extensive evidence of differences in the circuit layouts, and their significance. For example, AMD's expert, Dominick Richiuso, testified to specific differences between the AMD and Brooktree chips in the layouts of the interconnections between the SRAM cells and other portions of the chips, and in the SRAM cells themselves. These differences were acknowledged by Brooktree's expert Crisp, who testified that the similarities in the chip layouts, including the locations and interconnections of the transistors, were of far greater significance than the differences.

These fact-dependent areas were thoroughly aired at trial. The grant of judgment as a matter of law, by the trial judge or by the appellate court, is appropriate only when the evidence, with inferences drawn favorably to the party with the verdict, could not reasonably support the verdict. Dean v. Trans World Airlines, Inc., 924 F.2d 805, 810 (9th Cir. 1991).

We conclude that there was a legally sufficient evidentiary basis whereby a reasonable jury could have found infringement of the mask work registrations.

The judgment is affirmed.

COMMENTS AND QUESTIONS

1. Review sections 905 and 906 of the SCPA. What exactly is illegal? Section 905 makes it illegal to reproduce a mask work, and *Brooktree* applies the copyright standard for reproduction: it is illegal to copy not only a whole work but even a significant part of the work. At the same time, section 906 provides that others may reverse engineer a mask work in order to "evaluate the concepts or techniques embodied in the mask work or the circuitry, logic flow or organization of components used in the mask work" *and* that they may "incorporate the results of" this reverse engineering in their own chips.

But isn't that exactly what AMD did here? The court seems to hinge liability on AMD's adoption of Brooktree's 10-transistor design. But AMD learned of that design through reverse engineering, and it certainly represents the "circuitry, logic flow, or organization of components used" in Brooktree's chip. See Richard H. Stern, Determining Liability for Infringement of Mask Works Under the Semiconductor Chip Protection Act, 70 Minn. L. Rev. 271, 295 n.81 (1985) ("aspects of mask works that are dictated by chip function are not protected."). So why isn't AMD safe unless they physically duplicated the Brooktree chip for production? Notice that there is no derivative work right in section 905.

The statute clearly analogizes mask works to copyright law, both in prohibiting copying and in allowing reverse engineering. Section 906 seems to be suggesting that there is an "idea-expression dichotomy" in the

SCPA, and that third parties are free to copy the unprotectable "idea" of a chip design. See Stern, supra, at 299-300. But how can we distinguish idea from expression in the context of semiconductor technology? Does *Brooktree* help draw a line? After *Brooktree*, what can AMD safely do with the chips it reverse engineers?

2. The court applies a "substantially identical" standard for determining infringement—tougher than the normal standard of "substantial similarity"—as long as the defendant can produce a paper trail establishing reverse engineering. Does this inappropriately burden the plaintiff in enforcing the SCPA? Alternatively, does it largely address the piracy concern that motivated the Act and ensure substantial lead-time advantages to registrants of mask works?

3. Some years ago Professor Raskind predicted that SCPA's reverse engineering provision would have "ramifications wider and deeper than than the Chip Act itself," perhaps reshaping the law's understanding about acts that should be considered fair use or unfair competition in the high technology field. See Leo J. Raskind, Reverse Engineering, Unfair Competition, and Fair Use, 70 Minn. L. Rev. 385 (1985). Think back to the Sega v. Accolade decision in Chapter 2 and consider what, if any, impact the SCPA provision might have had on the Ninth Circuit's ruling in that case. Would it affect your view to know that Sega argued in *Accolade* that the legislative history of SCPA supported its position that decompilation was not fair use? Some witnesses in congressional hearings on the chip protection legislation had expressed doubts about whether reverse engineering would be lawful under the fair use doctrine if semiconductor masks were added to the subject matter of copyright.

4. Although several aspects of SCPA are copyright-like (e.g., its originality requirement, its restatement of the idea/expression distinction, and the substantial similarity and substantial identity tests for infringement), other aspects of SCPA are more patent-like. The 10-year duration of protection, for example, is more patent- than copyright-like. SCPA also requires registration of mask works within two years of the first commercial exploitation of the mask work in order for SCPA rights to last up to 10 years. See 17 U.S.C. §908(a). The 10-year term of protection begins from the date of registration or first commercial use, whichever comes first. 17 U.S.C. §904(a). Registration is relatively straightforward and is modeled after copyright registration rather than the more detailed and time-consuming patent or trademark applications.

5. One of the most remarkable aspects of SCPA has been the dearth of litigation. Indeed, *Brooktree* is the only reported case litigated under the Act. Given that congressional testimony prior the SCPA's enactment indicated that there had been rampant piracy, the paucity of litigation has been surprising. A number of explanations have been offered for this discrepancy. First, it may be that most "piracy" prior to the Act was due to uncertainty about the scope of mask work protection under the copyright law. The SCPA clarified the law, according to this argument, thereby

leading firms to conform their behavior to the requirements of the Act. Is this explanation persuasive? Based on *Brooktree*, is it fair to say that the scope of the law is clear?

Ron Laurie, a leading computer law practitioner, has suggested an alternative explanation—that the outright piracy alluded to during the hearings either did not exist or has become technologically obsolete. Highly integrated modern mask works cannot be quickly and accurately duplicated without using a fabrication process virtually identical to the original manufacturer's. Because such processes are highly proprietary, it is unlikely that pirates could have duplicated complex, high density chip designs without reverse engineering. Ronald S. Laurie, The First Year's Experience Under the Chip Act or "Where Are the Pirates Now That We Need Them?" 3 Computer Law. 11, 21 (Feb. 1986). In addition, the technologies of chip production have moved beyond the use of "masks," thereby rendering the subject matter for protection under SCPA outmoded. Other nations have characterized the subject matter of their laws as covering the layout or topography of integrated circuits.

Commentators differ in their assessment of SCPA's success (or lack thereof). Compare John Barton, Adapting the Intellectual Property System to New Technologies (viewing SCPA as a success) and Morton David Goldberg, Semiconductor Chip Protection As a Case Study (viewing SCPA as a failure) *in* Global Dimensions of Intellectual Property Rights in Science and Technology (Mitchel B. Wallerstein et al., eds., 1993).

6. Congress decided to adopt a reciprocity rule for masks works produced by foreign nationals. For reasons that will be explained in Chapter 8, this decision was probably a strategic mistake. However, SCPA still provides that to have mask work rights under SCPA, an owner of a mask work first commercially exploited in a foreign country must be a "national, domiciliary, or sovereign authority of a foreign nation that is a party to a treaty affording protection to mask works to which the U.S. is a party," §902(a)(1)(A), or the President must issue a proclamation finding that the owner's country provides protection to owners of U.S. mask works "on substantially the same basis as that on which the country extends protection to its own mask work owners and to mask works first commercially exploited in that country" and "on substantially the same basis as provided by the SCPA," §902(a)(2). For further consideration of the international dimensions of chip protection, see Chapter 8.

7. Had CONTU been asked to consider whether semiconductor chip designs should be protected by copyright law, it might have said yes. See, e.g., Pamela Samuelson, Creating a New Kind of Intellectual Property Law: Applying the Lessons of the Chip Law to Computer Programs, 70 Minn. L. Rev. 471 (1985) (arguing that CONTU's rationale for advocating the use of copyright law to protect computer programs also applied to chip designs and, conversely, that the same rationale Congress had for choosing to protect semiconductor chips with a sui generis form of legal protection also applied to computer programs).

PROBLEM

Problem 5-1. Amazingly Large-Scale Integrated Circuits, Inc. (ALSI) obtains a commercially sold version of a competitor's new semiconductor chip, which cost millions of dollars to design. ALSI engages in the process of reverse engineering the chip, peeling away its various layers and developing cross-section photographs and materials analyses. Based on this investigation, ALSI produces a layout diagram of the chip for around $30,000. Using a commercially available computer program that designs mask works automatically given a logic-level layout diagram, ALSI produces a chip with a mask different from its competitor's but with identical functionality and circuit design. The total cost to ALSI is about $65,000.

Has ALSI violated the SCPA? Would your answer be any different if the computer program produced masks virtually identical to the competitor's?

B. SUI GENERIS PROTECTION FOR DATABASES

Advances in computer technology are largely responsible for the recent spate of sui generis proposals aimed at protecting the contents of databases. There are at least three reasons for this. One is that digital technologies make it so much easier and cheaper to appropriate information, regardless of whether it is in print form (e.g., by scanning) or in digital form (e.g., by stripping digitized information from a CD). Second, much of the value in databases lies not in the creativity of the compiler's selection and arrangement of the data, but rather in the data themselves. Especially when data are in electronic form, it is, moreover, very easy to reselect and rearrange the data in a manner so as to avert copyright liability, even though the appropriation may have competitively harmful consequences. Third, a large number of commercially valuable databases are products of automated data collection processes, are comprehensive in character and organized in a standard or functionally determined way, or require only modest and uncreative adjustments (e.g., correcting spelling or citations) to maintain. As a result, there may be insufficient originality in selection and arrangement of the data to support a claim of copyright. Although the legal protection of factual information has been a difficult area for copyright for many years, see, e.g., Jane C. Ginsburg, Creation and Commercial Value: Copyright Protection for Works of Information, 90 Colum. L. Rev. 1865 (1990), advances in computer technology have made the problem more acute.

The EU emphasized the vulnerability of databases to market-destructive appropriations when it proposed a new form of legal protection for databases. In fact, the first draft of the European Directive on the Legal Protection of Computer Databases would have provided a sui generis right to control the extraction and reuse of data from electronic databases. Partly because the drafters realized that digital technologies could be used to appropriate print as well as electronic information, subsequent drafts and the final directive confer this right on makers of "databases," which are defined as "a collection of independent works, data or other materials arranged in a systematic or methodical way and individually accessible by electronic or other means." Chapter 8 discusses the European sui generis right in greater detail. For purposes of this chapter, however, readers should know that the U.S. Congress has considered adopting a similar, if not equivalent, law. Chances are that a sui generis law to protect compilations of information from market-destructive appropriations is likely to be enacted, although it may differ from the European Directive in some significant details. For a detailed discussion of the database proposal, its shortcomings, and the need for database protection, see J.H. Reichman & Pamela Samuelson, Intellectual Property Rights in Data?, 50 Vand. L. Rev. 51 (1997).

The debate over database protection raises a number of philosophical issues central to intellectual property protection for software. Deciding whether and how to protect computer databases requires that a legislature consider what protection already exists and how well the industry would perform without sui generis protection. If it decides to adopt a system of database protection, it then needs to consider how to provide incentives for investment while at the same time minimizing the damage that would be done to competition. To date, much of this discussion has been missing from the debate over database protection. The *Warren* case, below, demonstrates the limitations on copyright protection for factual compilations in the post-*Feist* environment. Not surprisingly, Warren has been among the most ardent advocates of sui generis database protection legislation in the United States.

Warren Publishing, Inc. v. Microdos Data Corp.
United States Court of Appeals for the Eleventh Circuit
115 F.3d 1509 (11th Cir. 1997)

BIRCH, Circuit Judge: . . .

Warren Publishing, Inc. ("Warren") compiles and publishes annually a printed directory called the Television & Cable Factbook ("Factbook"), which provides information on cable television systems throughout the United States. The Factbook contains two volumes, the "Station" volume and the "Cable and Services" volume. The focus of this case is the "Cable

& Services" volume of the 1988 edition of the Factbook, and, in particular, the two sections of this volume entitled "Directory of Cable Systems" and "Group Ownership of Cable Systems in the United States." These sections are comprised of approximately 1,340 pages of factual data on 8,413 cable systems throughout the country and their owners.

The "Directory of Cable Systems" section contains extensive information on cable systems, including, inter alia, the name, address, and telephone number of the cable system operator, the number of subscribers, the channels offered, the price of service, and the types of equipment used. The entries in this section are arranged state by state in alphabetical order, and, within each state, all of the communities receiving cable television service are listed alphabetically. The "Group Ownership" section contains listings of selected information on "all persons or companies which have an interest in 2 or more systems or franchises." Factbook, Cable and Services Volume, at B-1301. The persons or entities listed in the group ownership section are known as multiple-system operators ("MSOs"), as contrasted with single-systems operators ("SSOs").

In the "Directory of Cable Systems" section, the factual data for each cable system is not printed under the name of each community that the cable system serves. The reason for this is that many communities are part of multiple-community cable systems, and it would be duplicative to list the same factual information under the individual community names for each community that comprises a multiple-community system. Therefore, a determination is made as to what community is the "principal" or "lead" (hereinafter "principal") community served by a particular cable system, and Warren prints the data only under the name of the principal community. Under the entries for the nonprincipal communities of a multiple-community cable system, there is a cross-reference to the principal community listing. Communities in north-central Georgia are cross-referenced to Atlanta in the 1988 Factbook: Alpharetta, Avondale Estates, Clarkston, College Park, Decatur, DeKalb County, East Point, Lithonia, Pine Lake, Sandy Springs, and Stone Mountain. In addition, Fulton County, although it has its own separate listing with factual data (since it is served by cable system different from that which serves Atlanta), also has a cross-reference that states "See also ATLANTA, GA." We infer from these listings that there are portions of Fulton County that are served by the cable system listed under the Fulton County heading, and that there are other portions of Fulton County served by the cable system listed under the Atlanta heading. The same holds true for DeKalb County, which is cross-referenced to both Atlanta and Chamblee, Georgia. We note that, in many cases, a cable system is a single-community system, and thus there is only one possible principal community.

Microdos Data Corp. and Robert Payne ("Microdos") also market a compilation of facts about cable systems. Robert Payne is the principal officer and shareholder of Microdos. Microdos's compilation comes in the form of a computer software package called "Cable Access." The Cable

Access program, like the Factbook, provides detailed information on both SSOs and MSOs. The district court described the format of Cable Access as follows:

> The Cable Access software package is broken into three databases. The first database provides information on the individual cable systems. This database is referred to as "the system database." The second database provides information on multiple system operators and is simply referred to as "the MSO database." The third database is a historical database which provides selected information on the cable industry from 1965 to the present. . . .
>
> Defendant's Cable Access software package comes pre-sorted by state and city. The customer may rearrange the data in a format of its choosing. The customer may construct searches of the database's information on cable systems as required to fit its particular needs, as well as output the data to a hard copy in various formats, again to fit the specific needs of the customer.

There is no dispute that Warren's Factbook predates the Cable Access program. Warren has been publishing cable television information since 1948, whereas Microdos began marketing Cable Access in 1989. Shortly after Warren became aware of the existence of the Cable Access software, it notified Microdos that it believed that the Cable Access program infringed its copyright in the Factbook. In 1989, Microdos ceased marketing the original version of Cable Access, and, after some delay, began marketing a second version of Cable Access. Subsequently, a third and fourth version of Cable Access were marketed.

In July of 1990, Warren filed suit against Microdos, alleging copyright infringement and unfair competition. Warren alleged that all four versions of Cable Access infringed upon its compilation copyright in the 1988 Factbook. . . . Warren contended that Microdos infringed its compilation copyright in the Factbook in three areas: (1) the communities covered/principal community system, (2) the data fields, and (3) the data field entries. Following discovery, Warren and Microdos each moved for partial summary judgment on these three copyright infringement issues. With respect to the data fields issue, the district court found that Microdos had not infringed Warren's data field format. With respect to the data field entries issue, the district court found that these entries were uncopyrightable facts, and therefore Warren's "sweat of the brow" argument on this issue could not prevail in light of the Supreme Court's *Feist* decision. Accordingly, the district court entered partial summary judgment for Microdos on these two issues.

The district court, however, reached a different conclusion on the communities covered issue. It found that the principal community system utilized by Warren in presenting the data on cable systems in its Factbook was "sufficiently creative and original to be copyrightable." (footnote omitted). The district court then analyzed the selection of communities employed by Microdos and found it to be "substantially similar" to that of Warren. Based on this finding, and its conclusion that Microdos failed to prove that it obtained its information from a source independent of the Factbook, the district court denied Microdos's motion for summary judgment on the principal community system and granted Warren's cross-motion on that issue. The district court subsequently denied Microdos's motion for reconsideration of the order and granted Warren's motion for a "permanent" injunction. The court "enjoined [Microdos] from violating [Warren's] copyright of the Factbook through the use, copying, distribution or selling of any version of [Microdos's] Cable Access products." Microdos appeals the interlocutory order granting the injunction.

II.   Discussion

Microdos argues that the district court improperly granted Warren's motion for an injunction based on an erroneous ruling of law. As a predicate for injunctive relief, the district court granted Warren's motion for partial summary judgment on the principal community system issue. Microdos contends that the district court erred, as a matter of law, in finding the principal community system protectable under copyright law.

A.   Review of Relevant Statutory Provisions and Case Law . . .

The Supreme Court, in its most recent decision focusing on compilation copyrights, noted that "[t]he sine qua non of copyright is originality." *Feist*, 499 U.S. at 345, 111 S. Ct. at 1287, 113 L. Ed. 2d 358. The Court emphasized that originality is a constitutional requirement, noting that the Constitution "authorizes Congress to 'secur[e] for limited times to Authors . . . the exclusive Right to their respective Writings.'" *Id*. at 346, 111 S. Ct. at 1288, 113 L. Ed. 2d 358 (quoting U.S. Const. art. I, §8, cl. 8). The Court also admonished that:

> Facts, whether alone or as part of a compilation, are not original and therefore may not be copyrighted. A factual compilation is eligible for copyright if it features an original selection or arrangement of facts, but the copyright is limited to the particular selection or arrangement. In no event may copyright extend to the facts themselves.

Id. at 350, 111 S. Ct. at 1290, 113 L. Ed. 2d 358.

Thus, the compiler's choices as to selection, coordination, or arrangement are the only portions of the compilation that arguably are even entitled to copyright protection. As the *Feist* Court noted, these choices must be made "independently by the compiler and entail a minimal degree of creativity" in order to be entitled to compilation copyright protection.

Id. at 348, 111 S. Ct. at 1289, 113 L. Ed. 2d 358. The *Feist* Court further explained:

> This protection is subject to an important limitation. The mere fact that a work is copyrighted does not mean that every element of the work may be protected. Originality remains the sine qua non of copyright; accordingly, copyright protection may extend only to those components of a work that are original to the author.

Id. Given these limitations on the scope of copyright protection in a factual compilation, it is abundantly clear that "copyright in a factual compilation is thin." *Id.* at 349, 111 S. Ct. at 1289, 113 L. Ed. 2d 358. Only when one copies the protected selection, coordination, or arrangement in a factual compilation has one infringed the compilation copyright; copying of the factual material contained in the compilation is not infringement.

B. The Principal Community System Employed by Warren

. . . The district court found that "Warren has developed a system for selecting communities which is original in the industry. This selection process represents a part of the format of the compilation which *is* copyrightable" (emphasis added). Since the district court concluded that Microdos had "substantially appropriated the copyrightable selection of communities portion of the format of Warren's Factbook," it held that "Microdos ha[d] infringed Warren's copyright in the Factbook." The district court was correct in employing "substantial similarity" analysis once it concluded that Warren's system for selecting communities was copyrightable. Where it erred, however, was in concluding that Warren's system of selection was copyrightable in the first place.

1. Warren's "System" of Selection

Section 102(b) of the Copyright Act specifically excludes "any idea, procedure, process, system, method of operation, concept, principle, or discovery" from copyright protection "regardless of the form in which it is described, explained, illustrated, or embodied in such work." 17 U.S.C. §102(b). Nonetheless, the district court concluded that Warren's "system" of selecting communities was original and entitled to copyright protection. This conclusion is contrary to the plain language of 17 U.S.C. §102(b), and is clearly incorrect. If Warren actually does employ a system to select the communities to be represented in the book, then section 102(b) of the Act bars the protection of such a system.

Even if we were to assume that the district court incorrectly denominated Warren's selection of communities as a "system," such an assumption would not validate the district court's finding of copyrightability. Warren contends that it has a unique method of choosing which communities to include in its directory, based on its "principal community" system. Warren defines a "cable system" as an entity offering subscribers in one or more communities the same cable services for the same price. As the district court found, "[t]he principal community, used to represent the entire cable system, is then selected by contacting the cable operator to determine which community is considered the lead community within the cable system. Other communities within the same cable system are then listed under the principal community, not independently." The Federal Communication Commission ("FCC"), unlike Warren, does not use a principal community system; rather, it lists individually every geographical community having cable service. As a result, if there are five communities served by one "cable system," Warren would list the system's data under the principal community name, and there would be cross-references under the listings of the names of the other four communities. The FCC, on the other hand, would list the data on all five communities separately.

At oral argument, Warren asserted, and the dissent agrees, that the district court was correct in finding that Warren is entitled to copyright protection in its "selection" of communities, which is based on its putatively unique definition of a cable system. The problem with this is that Warren does not undertake any "selection" in determining what communities to include in the Factbook. Warren claims that its system of listing communities does not include the entire universe of cable systems, and thus there is "selection" involved as to which communities they include in their Factbook. This assertion, however, is plainly wrong.

The district court found that the FCC, which attempts to list individually every community across the country with a cable system, had 724 communities listed for Illinois. Warren, it observed, listed 406 communities under its principal community concept. It did note that "[n]umerous additional communities were listed under the various principal communities," but stated that they were not separately listed. Given that Warren did not list all of the communities that the FCC did, the district court concluded that Warren did "select" which communities to include in the Factbook, and thus its selection was copyrightable. In an unintentionally prescient footnote, however, the district court noted that:

> This is not to say that the selection of cable systems would be copyrightable in all cases. Had Warren selected every cable system listed by the F.C.C., then there would not be sufficient originality in the "selection" to warrant copyrightability.

Yet, this is precisely what Warren did. The district court made the mistake of comparing the number of principal communities listed with the number of individual communities listed by the FCC. Given the way the principal community system works, however, that is like comparing apples to oranges. The proper method is to compare the 724 individual communities listed by the FCC for Illinois with the total number of communities listed by Warren for Illinois; in other words, include not only the principal communities listed, but also those that are listed and are cross-referenced to one of the 406 principal communities. Our count of the total number of communities listed for Illinois by Warren, both principal and nonprincipal, is approximately 1,000. Therefore, Warren seems to have included not only all that the FCC listed, but also some others that the FCC did not.

The Second Circuit has noted that "[s]election implies the exercise of judgment in choosing which facts from a given body of data to include in a compilation." Key Publications, Inc. v. Chinatown Today Publishing Enters., Inc., 945 F.2d 509, 513 (2d Cir. 1991). In *Key Publications*, the record indicated that the compilation copyright holder did not include the entire relevant universe in her directory; she testified that she chose to exclude certain businesses based on her belief that they would not remain open for very long. As the court noted, "[t]his testimony alone indicates thought and creativity in the selection of businesses included in the 1989-90 Key Directory." *Id.* Warren, to the contrary, has failed to make such a showing in this case. It did not exercise any creativity or judgment in "selecting" cable systems to include in its Factbook, but rather included the entire relevant universe known to it. The only decision that it made was that it would not list separately information for each community that was part of a multiple-community cable system; in other words, it decided to make the Factbook commercially useful. Therefore, it cannot prevail in its claim that it "selected" which communities to include in its Factbook. The district court erred in determining that Warren's system of selecting communities was copyrightable.

2. The Originality Requirement

Even were we to assume that the presentation of the selection of principal communities made by Warren was creative and original and therefore copyrightable, its claim that it is entitled to protection would nonetheless fail, because the selection is not its own, but rather that of the cable operators. The district court found that the principal community was "selected by contacting the cable operator to determine which community is considered the lead community within the cable system." As we observed in *BellSouth*, "these acts are not acts of authorship, but techniques for the discovery of facts." 999 F.2d at 1441.

In *BellSouth*, a case involving a "yellow pages" classified business directory, we held that Donnelley Information Publishing, Inc. ("Donnelley"), "[b]y copying the name, address, telephone number, business type, and unit of advertisement purchased for each listing in the BAPCO [Bell-South Advertising & Publishing Corporation] directory . . . copied no original element of selection, coordination or arrangement," and thus Donnelley was entitled to summary judgment on BAPCO's copyright infringement claim. *Id.* at 1446. The en banc court stated that "[w]hile BAPCO may select the headings that are offered to the subscriber, it is the subscriber who selects from those alternatives the headings under which the subscriber will appear in the directory. The headings that actually appear in the directory thus[] do not owe their origin to BAPCO. . . ." *Id.* at 1444. In this case, Warren employed a method similar to that of BAPCO in "selecting" the principal community heading under which to list the data for the multiple-community systems.

Lynn Levine, the Director of Market Research and Data Sales for Warren, stated in her deposition that Warren determines the names of the communities served by a cable system by contacting the operators of the cable systems and asking them which communities they serve. In addition, she stated that Warren, in gathering data for the Factbook, relied in "great part" on the questionnaire responses received from the various cable operators. *Id.* at 35. These acts are nothing more than techniques for the discovery of facts. Simply because Warren may have been the first to discover and report a certain fact on cable systems does not translate these acts of discovery into acts of creation entitled to copyright protection. See *Feist,* 499 U.S. at 347, 111 S. Ct. at 1288, 113 L. Ed. 2d 358 (distinguishing creation from discovery). "Just as the Copyright Act does not protect 'industrious collection,' it affords no shelter to the resourceful, efficient, or creative collector." *BellSouth,* 999 F.2d at 1441.

The record indicates that it is the cable operators, not Warren, that determine, in the case of a multiple-community system, the community name under which to list the factual data for the entire cable system. Therefore, Warren cannot prevail in its claim that it undertakes original selection in employing the principal community concept. Rather, it has created an effective system for determining where the cable operators prefer to have the data listed. While Warren may have found an efficient method of gathering this information, it lacks originality, which is the sine qua non of copyright. See *Feist,* 499 U.S. at 345, 111 S. Ct. at 1287, 113 L. Ed. 2d 358. Thus, the district court erred in finding that Warren's principal community "system" was sufficiently creative and original to be entitled to copyright protection. . . .

COMMENTS AND QUESTIONS

1. Three judges dissented in *Warren* and offered the following observations about Warren's selection of facts:

> At the initial stage of choosing the facts that it wanted, Warren moved from idea to intellectual expression through selection. The selection of facts it wanted were not the facts that previously the industry had compiled in terms of community. Rather Warren chose to select and present facts that reflected the way the industry is currently actually operating. Its choice was reflected in functional service/operations/management terms. The building block, the data-reporting unit, for selection and presentation of industry data was the

"cable system" as newly defined by Warren, "an entity composed as one or more communities that are offered the same service by the same cable system owner at the same price." Warren had . . . devised a framework for the data to be assembled and had formulated selective rules and categories. Reporting data by a functional unit was a new and original concept, and the implementing definition of "cable system" was new to the industry and crafted by Warren.

Next, it was necessary for Warren to define and identify the universe of raw data from which it would select and present information. It chose a universe composed of all geographic communities (in the state of Illinois, the representative state) having cable television service. This defined universe was itself new. It consisted of 1,000 plus geographic communities (1,017 by one count, 1,045 by another). It included cities, towns, and villages, and also included counties and townships, which historically were not usual franchise-granting units. The FCC maintained its own list of cable systems (as it defined them), composed of cities, towns and villages, that is, franchise-granting units. FCC's universe was 724 communities. Warren's functional/operational definition swept in non-franchising geographic areas receiving service. Its universe of raw data was thus new in concept and some 40% larger in number of communities than the FCC universe.

As its next step Warren identified and selected from its universe 406 data-reporting units in Illinois, each a "cable system" pursuant to its functional definition. Then, drawing from the 1,000 plus universe, Warren had to identify and properly locate within the proper unit of the 406 each geographic community enjoying cable service. More than half of the 406 Illinois cable operations turned out to be single-system operations (SSO's), that is, each served only a single community. A multiple community system (MSO) served more than one community. Each SSO, because of its singularity, fell within Warren's same operator/same service/same price definition of a cable system. The name under which its data was presented was necessarily that of the single community it served. Having located within the proper cable system (MSO or SSO) each community served, for MSO's Warren had to merge or combine the operating data for each community into one unitary body of operating data to be reported for the system. Data relating to each geographic community served was no longer independently listed community-by-community but instead was included in the unitary system data. The name of an individual (nonprincipal) geographic community whose service was operated and managed as part of a cable system appeared but without data and was cross-referenced to the system where its data was included in the unitary data. This referencing was necessary, of course, because data-reporting was unitary rather than individual.

As part of Warren's acts of selection it was necessary for it to choose a name by which each cable system would be listed and identified and under which the system data would be set out. For this purpose Warren elected to use a geographic name, and the type of geographic name it chose was that of the "lead" or "principal" geographic community within the system. Obviously, for an SSO the name of the single community served was selected. When these acts were concluded Warren's selection (406 units) consisted of 45% fewer data-reporting units than the FCC's listing of 724. . . .

Warren's selection entails more than the required degrees of originality and creativity. Warren saw the need, chose the facts it wanted to compile, chose how it wanted to arrange them in gathering points for data rather than by individualized presentations. It employed a new concept of gathering cable data into a smaller number of units and, for this purpose, it devised a new concept of a cable system as functionally defined and a new concept (and new title) of "principal community." It is sufficient if there is a "small spark of distinctiveness," but this is no small spark. It is a fundamental change in reporting data of a changing and developing industry. The fact that some of the data-reporting units were SSO's does not diminish the fact of Warren's acts of selection or of the originality and creativity of the selection, which required Warren to determine whether each of the 1,000 plus systems was a single community system (SSO) or part of a multiple community system (MSO) and to assemble and report system data accordingly.

Does this additional information about Warren's activities change your perception about whether the majority correctly ruled that there was insufficient originality in Warren's compilation?

2. Microdos would almost certainly be liable for a violation of the sui generis right created by the European Directive if that law applied to its actions. Article 7 provides: "[T]he maker of a database which shows that there has been a qualitatively and/or quantitatively substantial investment in either the obtaining, verification, or presentation of the contents [of the database shall have the right] to prevent the extraction and/or reutilization of the whole or a substantial part, evaluated qualitatively and/or quantitatively, of the contents of the database." The Directive provides for very limited exceptions to the norm for private study, for teaching or research, and for administrative proceedings.

Consider how Microdos would fare under the various bills that have recently been considered in the U.S. Congress.

The principal norm of H.R. 354, as first introduced in the 106th Congress, was:

> Any person who extracts, or uses in commerce, all or a substantial part, measured either quantitatively or qualitatively, of a collection of information gathered, organized, or maintained by another person through the investment of substantial monetary or other resources, so as to cause harm to the actual or potential market of that other person, or a successor in interest of that other person, for a product or service that incorporates that collection of information and is offered or intended to be offered for sale or otherwise in commerce by that other person, or a successor in interest of that person, shall be liable to that person or successor in interest for the remedies set forth in section 1406.

Some months later, this norm changed under a substitute H.R. 354. It would outlaw making available to others or extracting to make available to others all or a substantial part of another's collection of information so as to cause material harm to the primary market or a related market of that person. House Report 354 also provides for some exclusions from protection (principally for government information) and for some permitted acts (e.g., for news reporting, verification, and scientific or educational uses).

Consider also the principal norm of an alternative bill, H.R. 1858, that has been endorsed by a substantial number of high technology companies:

> It is unlawful for any person, by any means or instrumentality of interstate or foreign commerce or communications, to sell or distribute to the public a database that—
>> (1) is a duplicate of another database that was collected and organized by another person; and
>> (2) is sold or distributed in commerce in competition with that other database.

Why would high technology firms prefer H.R. 1858 to either version of H.R. 354? Is it accurate to characterize any of these approaches as unfair competition-based, as contrasted with the exclusive property rights approach of the European Directive? What are the relevant pros and cons of an unfair competition versus an exclusive property rights approach? Which, if any, of the approaches should Congress adopt and why?

3. In view of the Court's insistence in *Feist* on the constitutional nature of the originality requirement, questions have arisen about what power the U.S. Congress has to adopt sui generis protection to unoriginal databases. See, e.g., Jane C. Ginsburg, No "Sweat"? Copyright and Other Protection of Works of Information After Feist v. Rural Telephone, 92 Colum. L. Rev. 338, 348 (1992).

4. Advances in technology may provide new opportunities for appropriating information, and state law can sometimes be used to challenge such appropriations. However, copyright law may preempt some uses of state misappropriation law, as illustrated by National Basketball Ass'n v. Motorola, 105 F.3d 841 (2d Cir. 1997):

> Our conclusion, therefore, is that only a narrow "hot-news" misappropriation claim survives preemption for actions concerning material within the realm of copyright. . . .
> In our view, the elements central to an INS claim are: (i) the plaintiff generates or collects information at some cost or expense . . . ; (ii) the value of the information is highly time-sensitive . . . ; (iii) the defendant's use of the information constitutes free-riding on the plaintiff's costly efforts to generate or collect it . . . ; (iv) the defendant's use of the information is in direct competition with a product or service offered by the plaintiff . . . ; (v) the ability of other parties to free-ride on the efforts of the plaintiff would so reduce the incentive to produce the product or service that its existence or quality would be substantially threatened. . . . *INS*, 248 U.S. at 241. ("[INS's conduct] would render [AP's] publication profitless, or so little profitable as in effect to

cut off the service by rendering the cost prohibitive in comparison with the return.")

INS is not about ethics; it is about the protection of property rights in time-sensitive information so that the information will be made available to the public by profit-seeking entrepreneurs. If services like AP were not assured of property rights in the news they pay to collect, they would cease to collect it. The ability of their competitors to appropriate their product at only nominal cost and thereby to disseminate a competing product at a lower price would destroy the incentive to collect news in the first place. The newspaper-reading public would suffer because no one would have an incentive to collect "hot news."

We therefore find the extra elements—those in addition to the elements of copyright infringement—that allow a "hot-news" claim to survive preemption are: (i) the time-sensitive value of factual information, (ii) the free-riding by a defendant, and (iii) the threat to the very existence of the product or service provided by the plaintiff.

We conclude that Motorola and STATS have not engaged in unlawful misappropriation under the "hot-news" test set out above. To be sure, some of the elements of a "hot-news" *INS*-type claim are met. The information transmitted to SportsTrax is not precisely contemporaneous, but it is nevertheless time-sensitive. Also, the NBA does provide, or will shortly do so, information like that available through SportsTrax. It now offers a service called "Gamestats" that provides official play-by-play game sheets and half-time and final box scores within each arena. It also provides such information to the media in each arena. In the future, the NBA plans to enhance Gamestats so that it will be networked between the various arenas and will support a pager product analogous to SportsTrax. SportsTrax will of course directly compete with an enhanced Gamestats.

However, there are critical elements missing in the NBA's attempt to assert a "hot-news" *INS*-type claim. As framed by the NBA, their claim compresses and confuses three different informational products. The first product is generating the information by playing the games; the second product is transmitting live, full descriptions of those games; and the third product is collecting and retransmitting strictly factual information about the games. The first and second products are the NBA's primary business: producing basketball games for live attendance and licensing copyrighted broadcasts of those games. The collection and retransmission of strictly factual material about the games is a different product: e.g., box-scores in newspapers, summaries of statistics on television sports news, and real-time facts to be transmitted to pagers. In our view, the NBA has failed to show any competitive effect whatsoever from SportsTrax on the first and second products and a lack of any free-riding by SportsTrax on the third.

With regard to the NBA's primary products—producing basketball games with live attendance and licensing copyrighted broadcasts of those games—there is no evidence that anyone regards SportsTrax or the AOL site as a substitute for attending NBA games or watching them on television. In fact, Motorola markets SportsTrax as being designed "for those times when you cannot be at the arena, watch the game on TV, or listen to the radio. . . ."

The NBA argues that the pager market is also relevant to a "hot-news" *INS*-type claim and that SportsTrax's future competition with Gamestats satisfies any missing element. We agree that there is a separate market for the real-time transmission of factual information to pagers or similar devices, such as STATS's AOL site. However, we disagree that SportsTrax is in any sense free-riding off Gamestats.

An indispensable element of an INS "hot-news" claim is free-riding by a defendant on a plaintiff's product, enabling the defendant to produce a directly competitive product for less money because it has lower costs. SportsTrax is not such a product. The use of pagers to transmit real-time information about NBA games requires: (i) the collecting of facts about the games; (ii) the transmission of these facts on a network; (iii) the assembling of them by the particular service; and (iv) the transmission of them to pagers or an on-line computer site. Appellants are in no way free-riding on Gamestats. Motorola and STATS expend their own resources to collect purely factual information generated in NBA games to transmit to SportsTrax pagers. They have their own network and assemble and transmit data themselves.

To be sure, if appellants in the future were to collect facts from an enhanced Gamestats pager to retransmit them to SportsTrax pagers, that would constitute free-riding and might well cause Gamestats to be unprofitable because it had to bear costs to collect facts that SportsTrax did not. If the appropriation of facts from one pager to another pager service were allowed, transmission of current information on NBA games to pagers or similar devices would be substantially deterred because any potential transmitter would know that the first entrant would quickly encounter a lower cost competitor free-riding on the originator's transmissions.

However, that is not the case in the instant matter. SportsTrax and Gamestats are each bearing their own costs of collecting factual information on NBA games, and, if one produces a product that is cheaper or otherwise superior to the other, that producer will prevail in the marketplace. This is obviously not the situation against which INS was intended to prevent: the potential lack of any such product or service because of the anticipation of free-riding.

For the foregoing reasons, the NBA has not shown any damage to any of its products based on free-riding by Motorola and STATS, and the NBA's misappropriation claim based on New York law is preempted.

Would any of the sui generis proposals for database protection cover cases like *NBA*? Should they?

5. The ready appropriability of digital information may give rise to additional proposals for sui generis protection. Consider, for example, what courts will do if computer-generated works eventually become commercially valuable. In a pre-*Feist* era, it might have been possible to argue that copyright protection might extend to such works. See, e.g., Pamela Samuelson, Allocating Ownership Rights in Computer-Generated Works, 47 U. Pitt. L. Rev. 1185 (1986). Post-*Feist*, however, this seems unlikely.

Especially because of the vulnerability of personal information in digital networked environments, some economists have even proposed that legislatures create a sui generis property right in personal information as a way to protect privacy. See, e.g., Kenneth C. Laudon, Markets and Privacy, 39 Comm. ACM 92 (Sept. 1996). Would this be a good idea? Why or why not?

C. PROPOSALS FOR SUI GENERIS PROTECTION FOR SOFTWARE

A number of commentators have suggested that Congress should adopt for computer software a type of protection similar to the SCPA but tailored specifically to the needs of the computer software industry. These commentators normally call attention to three perceived problems with existing legal rules. First, they argue that the term of protection afforded the owners of copyrights (75 years for works for hire) and patents (20 years from the application date) is simply too long for the rapidly changing software industry. Some proposals are for patent-like protection but with a quicker application process and a term of five to seven years. Second, they argue that the overlapping protection now afforded computer software both confuses the market and distorts incentives to create and distribute software, because it is not always obvious what rights exist in a particular program. Sui generis protection is generally envisioned as a replacement for other forms of intellectual property protection. Finally, supporters of sui generis protection argue that none of the existing intellectual property regimes works particularly well in the software context. For instance, trade secrets law must stretch to protect mass-market software code, and cannot expect to protect screen displays at all. Copyright law protects only certain parts of computer programs—generally not the parts that the programmers generally consider most valuable. Patent protection is expensive and generally takes several years to get. Arguably, it provides too much protection once it has been acquired.

How to remedy these problems has been the subject of considerable academic debate. Consider the following views.

Peter S. Menell, Tailoring Legal Protection for Computer Software
39 Stan. L. Rev. 1329 (1987)

. . . B.   Tailoring Legal Protection for Operating Systems

Part of the reason for copyright's inability to promote economic efficiency in the provision of computer products is that the public goods and network externality problems suggest conflicting modes of legal protection. Public goods problems are alleviated by expanding legal protection for intellectual work. External benefits from networks are promoted by facilitating access to a standard. Thus, the difficult policy question is how to promote standardization while at the same time encouraging continuing innovation (along the entire spectrum from software to hardware). By closely tailoring legal protection to reward desired innovation while permitting reasonable access to industry standards, it is possible to reach a satisfactory accommodation of these apparently conflicting objectives.

In theory, patent law is more appropriate than copyright for protecting the intellectual work contained in computer operating systems. A patent protects new and useful processes and machines. Given the interchangeability of hardware and software, it seems logical to protect computer operating systems and dedicated computers that embody a particular operating system with the same form of legal protection. Because patent law protects ideas, those who create patentable operating systems could be better assured of appropriating a substantial portion of the benefits of their efforts.

. . . [I]t is difficult to obtain patent protection for computer programs.[1] It should be pointed out, however, that although the scope of patent protection for computer software is uncertain, some of the recent cases that have upheld the patentability of computer programs involved programs that manipulate the internal operations of a computer. Moreover, the importance of network externalities flowing from widespread access to a common mini- and microcomputer operating system suggests that legal protection should be hard to come by and relatively short in duration.

To encourage innovation in operating system technology, Congress should consider creating a hybrid form of patent protection specifically tailored to accommodate the market failures endemic to the provision of computer operating systems.[190] As with traditional patent law, the standard for protection should be novelty, nonobviousness, and usefulness; dominant firms (or anyone else) should not be able to "lock up" an industry standard simply by expressing it in a unique way.

To be feasible, the modified form of patent protection for computer operating systems should be based on a timely examination of patent applications. And given the rapid pace of technological change in the computer field and the interest in promoting access to industry standards,

---

1. [Keep in mind that this article was written in 1987. — EDS.]

190. Congress has recently followed a sui generis approach in designing legal protection for semiconductor chips. . . . Other commentators have also urged Congress to create a hybrid form of legal protection for computer software. See Davidson, [Protecting Computer Software: A Comprehensive Analysis, 1983 Ariz. St. L.J. 611, 673-674]; Galbi, Proposal for New Legislation to Protect Computer Programming, 17 J. Copyright Soc'y 280 (1970); Karjala, [Lessons from the Computer Software Protection Debate in Japan, 1984 Ariz. St. L.J. 53, 63]; Samuelson, Creating a New Kind of Intellectual Property: Applying the Lessons of the Chip Law to Computer Programs, 70 Minn. L. Rev. 471, 507, 529-31 (1985); Stern, The Case of the Purloined Object Code: Can It Be Solved? (Part 2), Byte, Oct. 1982, at 210, 222.

patent protection for operating systems should be shorter in duration than traditional patent protection.

In order to promote continued innovation in widely used operating systems, the operating system patent code should, like the Semiconductor Chip Protection Act, permit some limited form of reverse engineering. And like traditional patent law, the hybrid code should allow consumers to buy a ROM chip or other device containing a patented operating system and modify it for sale to a third person.

Because traditional patent law affords absolute protection, however, it would inhibit realization of network externalities from operating systems satisfying the above subject matter requirements. In order to facilitate realization of network externalities, therefore, the hybrid patent code should contain a flexible compulsory licensing provision. Such a provision would promote access to an industry standard while assuring rewards to the creator of an innovative and socially valuable operating system. It would also limit the ability of dominant firms in the industry to engage in anticompetitive practices.

The need for compulsory licensing as a means for promoting competition and rewarding innovation is brought into focus by the decision of the Ninth Circuit Court of Appeals in Digidyne Corp. v. Data General Corp. In *Data General*, the defendant (Data General), a manufacturer of computers, refused to license its RDOS operating system to firms using a central processing unit other than Data General's "NOVA" system. Recognizing the anticompetitive effects of this practice in a market with network externalities,[196] the Ninth Circuit held that Data General's licensing practices were an unlawful tying arrangement that violated federal antitrust law.

In light of the strong network externalities flowing from compatibility, computer operating systems serve as "essential facilities" in computer hardware markets. Unless a firm can get onto the network, its products will be at a great disadvantage relative to those that can run the vast stock of application programs designed for the industry standard. The operating system royalty rate per use should be set so as to compensate true innovators for the cost of building a useful "highway" for the market plus a fair profit (adjusted for the risk of failure). For high volume products, these rates would probably be low. In the microcomputer market, for example, the rate would probably be less than one dollar for access to the major operating systems (assuming that the Apple and IBM operating systems merited hybrid patent protection at all).

---

196. The court accepted the plaintiffs' proof of market power on the basis of software "lock-in." Software lock-in occurs when a computer user develops or purchases application software designed to run on a particular operating system. This installed base locks the consumer into the hardware products of the owner of that operating system if competitors cannot gain access to the operating system and the costs of converting software to run on different operating systems are high. But see Helein, Software Lock-in and Antitrust Tying Arrangements: The Lessons of Data General, 5 Computer/L.J. 329, 337, 342-43 (1985) (suggesting that conversion costs might not be so high as to justify a finding of market power).

A patent code for operating systems based on the above outline strikes a preferable balance of the conflicting policy concerns raised by computer operating systems. By providing solid protection for truly innovative and useful operating systems, the code would reward innovation in operating systems. The limits on this regime of protection—moderate duration, reverse engineering, adaptation—and the provision for compulsory licensing would promote access to operating systems that emerge as industry standards, wide diffusion of computer products, and innovation in hardware products. The code would also avoid wasteful expenditure of resources on efforts to emulate an industry standard.

The proposed operating system code would probably entail somewhat higher administrative costs than the current system. Patent examinations, though streamlined, would be significantly more expensive than the cost of copyright registration. Moreover, compulsory licensing proceedings, as well as the cost of monitoring use of protected operating systems, would add to the expense of the system. If the royalty rates were low (as the microcomputer example indicates), however, members of the industry could be expected to cooperate in ensuring that patent owners were properly compensated.

C. Tailoring Legal Protection for Application Programs

As with legal protection for operating systems, Congress should consider creating a special form of legal protection for application programs. Given the importance of improving existing programs as a primary mode of technological innovation and the presence of some network externalities, legal protection should be significantly shorter in duration than traditional copyright protection. The relatively short commercial life of most application programs indicates that legal protection should be correspondingly short.

The regime for protecting application programs should also allow for reverse engineering. In designing legal protection for semiconductor chips, Congress recognized the importance of reverse engineering in enabling researchers to advance a field in which innovations are cumulative. A limited reverse engineering provision in the application software code would similarly promote the advancement of application software technology.

Congress should also consider the desirability of a limited form of compulsory licensing of application packages. In order to realize the benefits of network externalities and to promote creativity in the integration of software programs, it would seem worthwhile to allow limited access to application programs, particularly those that emerge as industry standards. This could be achieved without dulling primary creative incentives by delaying the availability of compulsory licensing for a limited period to allow the creator of the program to reap the rewards of commercial success.

COMMENTS AND QUESTIONS

1. How does the Menell proposal compare with how copyright and patent protection have evolved to protect computer software? Think back to the cases in Chapter 2 and consider whether the software developers involved in those cases would have proceeded differently with their legal protection strategies had Menell's proposal been adopted.

2. How would Menell protect screen displays (if at all)? Mathematical algorithms embodied in computer software? Computer languages? Source code? Object code? Would all of these parts of a computer program require a different statute to protect them? Or should protection be subsumed within a broader "software" framework?

3. Presumably Menell's proposal would replace patent and copyright law. Should it also replace trademark and trade secret law insofar as they apply directly to computer software?

4. Does Menell's suggestion of treating applications programs differently from operating systems make sense? Are the differences between the two types of programs—something he discusses in detail in the balance of his piece—sufficient to warrant different statutory treatment? To the extent that there are differences, such as the standardization problem with operating systems, are they appropriately addressed in other ways? Recall that the Third Circuit in the Apple v. Franklin case rejected the idea of distinguishing between operating system and application programs.

≡≡≡ *Pamela Samuelson, Randall Davis, Mitchell D.*
≡≡≡ *Kapor, & J.H. Reichman, A Manifesto Concerning*
≡≡≡ *the Legal Protection of Computer Programs*
≡≡≡ 94 Colum. L. Rev. 2308 (1994)

1. Important Characteristics of Computer Programs

Computer programs have a number of important characteristics that have been difficult for legal commentators and decisionmakers to perceive. First, the primary source of value in a program is its behavior, not its text. Second, program text and behavior are independent in the sense that a functionally indistinguishable imitation can be written by a programmer who has never seen the text of the original program. Third, programs are, in fact, machines (entities that bring about useful behavior) that have been constructed in the medium of text (source and object code). The engineering designs embodied in programs could as easily be implemented in hardware as in software, and the user would be unable to distinguish between the two. Fourth, the industrial designs embodied in programs are typically incremental in character, the result of software engineering techniques and a large body of practical know-how. . . .

2.1.1 Programs Reveal a Substantial Amount of Their Know-How in Products Distributed in the Market

. . . Computer programs are an unusual kind of industrial product because the bulk of the know-how required to create them is accessible on or near the face of the product distributed in the marketplace. There are several reasons why this is so: (1) Software products need little specialized mass-production know-how; (2) they are particularly rich in design know-how; and (3) they are more susceptible in some respects to reverse engineering than traditional industrial products.

Software is easy to mass-produce because it is an information product. There is no steel to cut or bend, no wires to attach, and no parts to be cast in plastic or rubber. Mass production is as simple as loading copies onto floppy disks or tapes, a routine, inexpensive, and low-technology undertaking. Because there are no special processes required for mass production of the software products, there is no opportunity to accumulate specialized know-how about mass production. Lack of mass-production know-how matters because this is the kind of know-how that can most easily be kept out of the product, i.e., maintained as a trade secret. . . .

Software is, instead, rich in surface design know-how. This is particularly true for interactive software, i.e., programs that involve a great deal of hands-on usage. For such software, the metaphor or conception of the task is particularly important. . . .

Software is not only especially rich in design know-how; much of the value of software arises from it. . . .

The difficult task in creating interactive software, the innovations embodied in it, and the value of those innovations are typically found in conception and design: determining how to think about the task (e.g., the desktop metaphor), and then determining what capabilities the program should have (e.g., what can be done with documents, or folders). Determining the answers to these questions requires both informed insight and the time-consuming and expensive process of having real users test the software for extended periods. We can summarize by saying that interactive software is, by its nature, rich in design know-how.

Such know-how is, inescapably, present on the face of the product, and immediately evident on inspection. The hard-won insights and innovations embodied in surface design are prominently displayed by the program in operation; they are also explained in online help, and further detailed in the manual. Insights not readily explained by the tool or the manual will often become evident to a sophisticated user of the program who runs the program over a variety of examples. Since program innovation often lies in finding a way to make program behavior easier for people to use, the behavior and its insights must be evident to the user. . . .

We stress the triviality of some acquisitions of behavioral equivalence because this triviality can be the source of market-destructive effects. The particular means a firm uses to acquire behavioral equivalence is not important from a market-preservation standpoint. The crucial concern is whether it is trivially easy and quick to copy a software innovation that was very expensive to develop. If the disproportion in cost of copying and cost of innovation is substantial enough, it can destroy the innovator's opportunity to recoup its expenses, and consequently, can destroy incentives to invest in software innovation. . . .

2.2.3 Why Copyright Law Is Ill-Suited to Protecting Software Innovations

. . . Copyright law is mismatched to software, in part, because it does not focus on the principal source of value in a program (its useful behavior). As explained above, program text and behavior are largely independent, so that protecting program texts does not prevent second comers from copying valuable program behavior. The ability to copy valuable behavior legally would sharply reduce incentives for innovation, and thus thwart the policy behind legal protection. As we explain below, the right way out of this bind is not to conceive of behavior as a nonliteral element of the program's text, as some courts have done, but instead to regard it as the entity that an appropriate legal regime should protect.

Once one recognized that computer programs are machines whose medium of construction is text, it becomes obvious why copyright is an inappropriate vehicle for protecting most program behavior. Copyright law does not protect the behavior of physical machines (nor their internal constructions), no matter how much originality they may embody. Historically, innovations in the design of machine behavior have been left to the rigors of patent law. . . .

If the industrial designs of programs cannot generally be protected by patents because they do not meet the patent invention standard, but need some legal protection, one might ask whether copyright law could supply this protection. . . .

However, by enacting section 102(b), Congress intended to exclude industrial design elements of program—processes, procedures, systems and methods of operation—from the scope of copyright protection. . . .

This result does not change if one characterizes the abstract design of programs as an industrial compilation of applied know-how. Of course, copyright law has a long history of protecting compilations of information. It has, however, accorded either no or relatively thin protection to compilations of industrial or technological elements. Many industrial compilations (such as a combination of machine components) have been excluded from copyright protection because of their intrinsic utility. Others, such as those created when someone selects or arranges information in accordance with a method, system or other functionally determined design, are also unprotectable by copyright law. Even when copyright protection has been available for a work consisting largely of industrial information (such as a manual for operating a power plant), it has not protected the know-how, only the author's manner of describing the know-how. The commercially valuable aspects of industrial compilations of applied know-how have generally been protected by trade secret, not copyright.

[In the balance of the Manifesto, the authors propose a relatively brief period of anti-"cloning" protection in addition to the protection already provided by copyright law for program code and for expressive textual or pictorial material displayed on computer screens by the program code. While the authors regard patents as an inappropriate form of legal protection for software, they acknowledge that patent law is being used to protect software designs, and hope to provide an alternative protection mechanism that would permit firms to protect valuable functional designs without resort to the patent system.]

COMMENTS AND QUESTIONS

1. Mitchell D. Kapor, one of the co-authors of the Manifesto, was the founder and former CEO of Lotus Development Corp., as well as co-author of Lotus 1-2-3. The first of the Lotus "look and feel" lawsuits was initiated while Kapor was still with Lotus. Kapor's sponsorship of and participation in the Manifesto project was in part an attempt to grapple with how intellectual property law should deal with software innovations. The consensus among the co-authors of the Manifesto was that Paperback, Borland, Jaslow, and Microsoft had cloned industrial design and/or behavioral components of software products developed, respectively, by Lotus, Whelan, and Apple. Even though such cloning may have involved a competitively harmful trivial acquisition of equivalence, the Manifesto's authors would not have used copyright law to protect against such appropriations. They would, however, favor blocking clones for a period of years. See Manifesto, 94 Colum. L. Rev. at 2396-2399 (analyzing major cases).

2. A companion article to the Manifesto was J.H. Reichman, Legal Hybrids Between the Patent and Copyright Paradigms, 94 Colum. L. Rev. 2432, 2444 (1994). Richman suggested that the problems experienced by software developers were symptomatic of a larger problem confronting advanced technology innovators generally:

To avoid underinvestment in research and development of unpatentable innovation likely to ensure from a pervasive contraction of lead time in advanced technological sectors, the world's intellectual property system and the domestic competition laws with which it is allied have come under intense pressure to obtain artificial lead time through one legal device or another. . . . [G]overnments tend to respond by extending patent and copyright laws to protect subject matters for which these laws were not intended or by implementing legal hybrid [sui generis] regimes that grant exclusive property rights to new objects of protection that fall outside the classical legal framework. These ad hoc efforts to accommodate nontraditional forms of innovation have spawned a proliferation of restraints on trade that strain the international intellectual property system to the breaking point and weaken the competitive ethos from within.

Reichman explores at length the legal hybrid regimes built on modified copyright and modified copyright principles and suggests an alternative paradigm built on modified trade secrecy principles that would offer a short-term form of protection for industrial compilations of applied know-how.

In an earlier work, Reichman offered this explanation of the legal protection dilemma for high technology industries:

> The bulk of today's most valuable innovations flow from incremental improvements in applied scientific know-how. Traditionally, unpatentable industrial know-how remained exempt from free competition only so long as it was neither voluntarily disclosed nor reverse engineered. Because the task of reverse engineering took time and cost money, it endowed innovators with a period of natural lead time in which to secure a foothold in the market.
>
> In contrast, much of today's most advanced technology enjoys a less favorable competitive position than that of conventional machinery because of the unpatentable, intangible know-how responsible for its commercial value becomes embodied in products that are distributed on the open market. A product of the new technologies, such as a computer program, an integrated circuit design, or even a biogenetically altered organism may thus *bear its know-how on its face*, a condition that renders it as vulnerable to rapid appropriation by second-comers as any published literary or artistic work.
>
> From this perspective, a major problem with the kinds of innovative know-how underlying important new technologies is that they do not lend themselves to secrecy even when they represent the fruit of enormous investment in research and development. Because third parties can rapidly duplicate the embodied information and offer virtually the same products at lower prices than those of the originators, there is no secure interval of lead time in which to recuperate the originators' initial investment or their losses from unsuccessful essays, not to mention the goal of returning a profit.
>
> When innovators turn to the world's intellectual property system for relief, however, they find that its dominant paradigms are structured to protect "art" and "inventions." Present-day innovation fits imperfectly within either category. Viewed as industrial inventions, advances in the new technologies often appear too incremental and too small in scale to qualify as major breakthroughs under the "nonobviousness" or "inventive step" requirements

of patent law. At the same time, these technologies serve impersonal, functional goals that make them alien to the spirit of laws devised to protect literary and artistic works. Today's most economically significant technologies are thus likely to be *intermediate technologies* that fall between the patent and copyright paradigms. . . .

From a behavioral standpoint, investors in applied scientific know-how find the copyright paradigm attractive because of its inherent disposition to supply artificial lead time to all comers without regard to innovative merit and without requiring originators to preselect the products that are most worthy of protection.

J.H. Reichman, Design Protection and the New Technologies: The United States Experience in a Transnational Perspective, 1991 Indus. Prop. 220, 269, 271 (1991) (emphasis in original).

3. Some commentators on the Manifesto thought it might give too much reward to software developers. See Paul Goldstein, Comments on A Manifesto Concerning the Legal Protection of Computer Programs, 94 Colum. L. Rev. 2573, 2574-2575 (1994); Peter S. Menell, The Challenges of Reforming Intellectual Property Protection for Computer Software, 94 Colum. L. Rev. 2644, 2647 (1994). Other commentators questioned the timing of the Manifesto's call for new legislation. They pointed out that copyright law was providing a workable form of legal protection over the last few years and that drafting an entirely new statute would disturb this settling-in process. Further, the GATT agreement's Trade-Related Aspects of Intellectual Property (TRIPS) had just adopted copyright law as the dominant mode of legal protection for software throughout the world, and changing the rules of the game now would be a difficult and time-consuming process. See Jane C. Ginsburg, Four Reasons and a Paradox: The Manifest Superiority of Copyright Over Sui Generis Protection of Computer Software, 94 Colum. L. Rev. 2559 (1994); Menell, supra, at 2651-2654.

4. What is the appropriate level of protection for computer programs? Is it consistent with efforts to reward every inventive, creative, or time-consuming aspect of program development? Or should the goal be something less than that? Most economists would suggest that intellectual property rights ought to extend no further than necessary to encourage optimal investment in research and development. But how much protection is "just enough"?

5. Menell proposed that a sui generis statute for software should replace copyright and patent law. The Manifesto proposes that an additional form of legal protection should be available to software developers. Both papers evaluate software from an economic standpoint. What accounts for their different conclusions?

6. A larger issue pertains to the appropriate level of generality of a software protection statute. On the one hand, more specific statutes are easier to tailor to the particular needs of an industry, and they afford the legislature the opportunity to clarify the law. On the other hand, it is hard

to anticipate all possible circumstances in drafting legislation, and judicial flexibility may benefit litigants in the long run and guard against technological advances that render the statutes irrelevant. One commentator has argued against sui generis legislation on the following grounds:

> Now is the time to begin considering copyright law for the 21st century. Technology will change current concepts and policies faster than in the past. . . . [N]ew information processing technology like databases, personal computer workstations and optical disks will radically change the form of information and scholarship. We will soon see new computerized tools for creating music, industrial designs, entertainment and a myriad of other activities much more quickly. The distinctions copyright pundits now cherish will blur.
>
> We are at an intellectual property crossroads. One road is to man the bulwarks and preserve the traditional scope of copyright until new technology makes the contradictions in that approach all too apparent. Down that road lies repeated efforts to fine-tune the law with such sui generis experiments as the Semiconductor Chip Protection Act, until congressional delay and impatience pushes even the lawyers who benefit most from increased legislative complexity to yearn for a more comprehensive approach.
>
> The other road is to allow copyright to evolve, as it has when faced with new technology in the past. Recent software cases and practice are showing us where that road leads: to a misappropriation law where we are more concerned with the ethics and behavior of infringers than the technical details of infringement. The standards for proper and improper behavior (if trends continue) will reflect and reinforce a current consensus among engineers and users, and the new system will be largely self-enforcing. The fair use idea will expand to allow more flexibility in using new technology for private purposes. One can hope a common law license will develop allowing flexible, self-executing price and scope of use arrangements.
>
> Perhaps best of all, the method for analyzing infringement will be similar to the determination of misuse of information in a broad number of areas of law under the privacy rubric. This will reinforce the development of a lay understanding and appreciation of the boundaries of tortious activity in the information economy.
>
> We are at a seminal moment in history, equivalent to the beginnings of the industrial age. If our law can share the same vision as our engineering, we can promote the immense potential wealth in the information age.

Duncan M. Davidson, Common Law, Uncommon Software, 47 U. Pitt. L. Rev. 1037, 1116-1117 (1986).

Davidson advocated a common law evolution of copyright law that would allow it to serve as a misappropriation law applicable equally well to computer programs, appropriations of contents of databases, semiconductor chip designs, DNA sequences, and readily copied chemical compounds. The competitive norm embodied in Davidson's view of copyright was that persons could reverse engineer and copy externally visible aspects of these works but would be penalized for going inside the "black box" to reverse engineer internal details that he thought should be protected against unauthorized access, use, or disclosure. In what ways has copyright evolved as Davidson recommended, and in what ways has it diverged from his expectations? How would the computer software industry have been affected if Davidson's approach had been adopted? Would the result have been better or worse, or just different?

7. Consider this further proposal by Davidson:

> The common law development of copyright into a misappropriation law can create in effect a "common law license" that would work like self-executing licenses; it would delineate certain acceptable and unacceptable manners of reverse engineering, publishing or otherwise using products that contain information. Misappropriation law would be based on an underlying limited use doctrine that would apply if (1) the source of information was the plaintiff's products, and (2) the information was used beyond the reasonable expectations of the relationship. The "license" would result from the expectations of the parties; these expectations could vary depending upon the rights granted by the software company [or other information provider].

47 U. Pitt. L. Rev. at 1112. We will shortly be considering the enforceability of shrinkwrap, click-through, and other mass-market licenses. Although the legal status of these licenses has evolved by a common law process, it has not been in the context of copyright law. When reading in Chapter 6 about the proposed Uniform Computer Information Transactions Act, consider whether Davidson may have been more prescient than you might at first have thought.

8. Legal academics and technologists are not the only people to have suggested that advances in information technologies may bring about the need for new intellectual property laws. See, e.g., Lester Thurow, Needed: A New System of Intellectual Property Rights, Harv. Bus. Rev. 95, 95 (Sept.-Oct. 1995) (discussing software and biotechnology industries; expressing concern that inadequate legal protection will impede public disclosure of innovations in these knowledge-intensive industries; suggesting some characteristics of the new intellectual property rights he thinks are needed).

> Fundamental shifts in technology and in the economic landscape are rapidly making the current system of intellectual property rights unworkable and ineffective. Designed more than 100 years ago to meet the simpler needs of an industrial era, it is an undifferentiated, one-size-fits-all system. Although treating all advances in knowledge in the same way may have worked when most patents were granted for new mechanical devices, today's brainpower industries pose challenges that are far more complex.

In this essay, Thurow, like his MIT colleague, Nicholas Negroponte, expresses doubts about the viability of existing copyright law concepts as applied to digital information distributed via global networks. When reading Chapter 10's coverage on intellectual property issues in cyberspace, consider whether Thurow and Negroponte might be right.

6

Software Licensing

Typically, computer software vendors claim that their wares are licensed rather than sold. This arguably distinguishes software from most similar business or consumer goods, which are generally sold to customers, and even from much intellectual property (such as books, sound recordings, and patented devices), particular copies of which are sold to end users. Software licenses take a variety of forms—from complex agreements governing use and support obligations negotiated and signed by both parties to "shrinkwrap" licenses included with most mass-market software.

Licensing has been a fundamental paradigm of the distribution of computer software from the earliest days of the industry. Software developers have developed some innovative licensing schemes, often in response to customer demands: site licenses, network licenses, per-seat licenses, so-many-users-at-a-time licenses, and the like. Historically, most of these licenses were in effect leases of computer hardware, or "true" licenses of intellectual property rights (i.e., the right to make 500 copies of a program for use in a business). Negotiated licenses between software developers and their customers have generally presented many interesting *business* issues, but few novel legal challenges, except as regards warranty and performance issues.

As mass markets for software emerged, one might have expected licenses to wither away in favor of outright sales. Instead, software developers widely used shrinkwrap licenses in commercially distributing mass-market software products. The validity of these licenses, as a matter of both contract law and public policy (e.g., insofar as they purport to override rights otherwise available by intellectual property law) is the subject of ongoing controversy. Similar licenses are becoming common in the distribution of digital information more generally, and here too the

439

validity and scope of such licenses have been hotly contested. Legislation to validate mass-market licenses for computer information transactions is currently under consideration. Thus the licensing approach may become more important not just for software but for digital information more generally. Using licenses in place of sales may enable more flexibility and price discrimination but may also conflict with intellectual property law or policy.

This chapter addresses two issues critical to software licensing: (1) ownership rights in licensed software, and (2) the power of licenses to alter the legal rules that would otherwise apply to software. It is perhaps best to begin by noting that the entire concept of licensing software is a controversial one. Licensing is a paradigm that has traditionally been applied to intellectual property. By contrast, no one speaks of licensing tangible goods (such as books), even if those goods contain intellectual property within them. Similarly, David Nimmer has suggested that there is properly no licensing of tangible software merely because the computer program that is transferred contains intellectual property within it. David Nimmer et al., The Metamorphosis of Contract into Expand, 87 Cal. L. Rev. 17 (1999). By contrast, proponents of software licensing contend that software is not itself a product—that, like pure intellectual property licenses, "the license is the product." See Robert Gomulkiewicz, The License Is the Product: Comments on the Promise of Article 2B for Software and Information Licensing, 13 Berkeley Tech. L.J. 891 (1998). We discuss this debate in more detail below.

Information licensing takes many forms indeed. One useful typology is to break transactions down into basic types: negotiated and non-negotiated, otherwise called standard form contracts. The former are the norm when complex one-of-a-kind information is being transferred for a very specific purpose. The latter are becoming more and more common in conjunction with numerous off-the-shelf types of consumer information products—from online newspaper subscriptions entered into over the Internet to the purchase of prepackaged software in a retail store. Although we touch on an important example of negotiated agreements at the end of this chapter, for the most part we will be discussing mass-market information transactions. This means, in the main, that we will be considering standard form contracts.[1] Issues such as how these contracts are entered into and whether they are binding on the parties and the like are discussed throughout this chapter.

---

1. It is worth noting that mass-market transactions in software aren't necessarily sales to individual *consumers*, though many transactions do involve consumers. Small and even large businesses also buy mass-market software, and are therefore subject to the same license provisions. The draft Uniform Computer Information Transactions Act (UCITA) distinguishes in certain ways between the rules that apply to mass-market transactions and those that apply to consumer transactions. See infra.

A. LICENSE VERSUS SALE

Virtually all software vendors would like to license rather than sell their software, not only for the economic reasons we discuss below but because licensing may allow them to avoid the restraints and limitations intellectual property law imposes on them. This Section discusses the circumstances under which a software transaction constitutes a "license." In particular, it explores the extent to which the vendor can create a license by fiat—that is, by declaring that the transaction is in fact a license.

Communications Groups v. Warner Communications, Inc.
Civil Court of the City of New York, New York County
138 Misc. 2d 80; 527 N.Y.S.2d 341 (Civ. Ct. N.Y. 1988)

COHEN, J.

Plaintiff Communications Groups, Inc. (CGI) moves to dismiss defendant Warner Communications Inc.'s (Warner) first through third counterclaims which are identical to defendant's second through fourth affirmative defenses, respectively, pursuant to CPLR 3211 (a) (1), (7) and (b).

This action arises out of an alleged breach of a written agreement dated July 18, 1986 for the licensing, installation and servicing of a certain computer software package (the Agreement). Subsequently, the parties entered into two subcontracts for additional software and related hardware. As per the Agreement, defendant paid 50% of the amount due upon signing the Agreement. The remaining 50% was to be paid upon installation of the software. It is undisputed that defendant has not paid this remaining amount due under the Agreement.

The complaint, dated October 23, 1987, sets forth three causes of action for breach of contract to recover payment in the total amount of $16,650 still due and owing from defendant to plaintiff. Defendant does not dispute nonpayment, but defendant's answer asserts four affirmative defenses and three counterclaims: the second affirmative defense/first counterclaim (first counterclaim) claims breach of an implied warranty of fitness of the computer software for defendant's specified known purposes; the third affirmative defense/second counterclaim (second counterclaim) claims breach of an express and/or implied warranty of merchantability of the software system and the good working order of its system and repair services; and the fourth affirmative defense/third counterclaim (third counterclaim) claims breach of contract in failing to provide support services to keep the system operational and in good working order.

As to the first and second counterclaims alleging implied warranties of merchantability and fitness for a specified known business purpose, the movant, CGI, contends that the Agreement provided for a software system or package which was neither for a tangible and movable product or goods nor a transaction for a sale or lease of either services or goods. Rather, CGI claims the Agreement was a license for computer software as an intangible service for limited use by defendant of "copyrightable information" and for the acquisition of the "abstract right" only "to listen" as with music on a record or disk. As a consequence, CGI argues that since implied warranties of fitness for a particular purpose or merchantability are remedies exclusively for contracts of the sale of goods and because the Agreement herein is not such a transaction of goods, the implied warranty counterclaims lack merit and cannot be maintained either under common law or under the Uniform Commercial Code (UCC).

Moreover, movant contends that even if the contract was for a sale of goods or a lease of goods, the contract, by its terms, provides for an express disclaimer of any implied warranties of fitness and merchantability. Therefore, movant urges that the first two counterclaims should be dismissed on this ground.

As for the third counterclaim, movant characterizes this claim as a breach of express warranties of the good working order and adequate support services of the computer software. Movant contends that such express warranties are lacking under the terms of the Agreement. Movant argues that any prior or subsequent oral promises or warranties which may have been made by movant cannot be considered part of the Agreement based on the parol evidence rules under common law and the UCC. Therefore, movant contends that the third counterclaim also lacks merit and fails to state a cause of action and should be dismissed.

The threshold issue presented is whether the software computer package or system provided for under the Agreement involved a transaction of "goods" as defined under UCC 2-105 (1) to mean "all things (including specially manufactured goods) which are movable at the time of identification to the contract for sale".

A review of the Agreement, the sole documentary and evidentiary matter submitted on these motion papers, shows that the computer software referred to therein is not defined. Nor have either of the parties in their motion papers articulated the precise form of the instant software. Software, however, is a widely used term and has several meanings. (See, University Computing Co. v Lykes-Youngstown Corp., 504 F2d 518, 527 [5th Cir 1974] [software includes programs and computer language listings]; In re Law Research Servs. v General Automation, 494 F2d 202, 204, n 3 [2d Cir 1974] [software includes magnetic cards or paper cards programmed to instruct the computer]; Com-Share, Inc. v Computer Complex, 338 F Supp 1229 [US Dist Ct, ED Mich 1971] [software refers to programs used in the computer]; see generally, Note, Computer Programs As Goods Under The UCC, 77 Mich L Rev 1149 [1979].)

Regardless of the software's specific form or use, it seems clear that computer software, generally, is considered by the courts to be a tangible, and movable item, not merely an intangible idea or thought and therefore qualifies as a "good" under article 2 of the UCC. (RRX Indus. v Lab-Con, Inc., 772 F2d 543 [9th Cir 1985]; Chatlos Sys. v National Cash Register Corp., 479 F Supp 738 [US Dist Ct, NJ 1979], *affd* 670 F2d 1304 [3d Cir 1982]; Triangle Underwriters v Honeywell, Inc., 457 F Supp 765 [US Dist Ct, ED NY 1978], *affd in part, revd in part and remanded on other grounds* 604 F2d 737 [2d Cir 1979]; see also, Note, 77 Mich L Rev 1149.) Moreover, UCC 1-102 provides that the act shall be liberally construed and applied to promote its underlying purposes and policies.

Here, the Agreement clearly provides, in part, for the installation by CGI of its specially designed software equipment for defendant's particular telephone and computer system, needs and purposes. This equipment is expressly listed on schedules annexed and made a part of the Agreement. Said schedules clearly reflect installation by CGI of identifiable and movable equipment such as recording, accounting and traffic analysis and optimizations, modules, buffer, directories and an operational user guide and other items. A review of the counterclaim allegations shows that a software computer system and equipment were designed for defendant's special and unique known needs to store data relating to thousands of defendant's monthly telephone calls and to process and print this data on defendant's main computer frame so that defendant's operations would prove more time and labor efficient. Although the ideas and concepts of the CGI-designed software system remained its intellectual and copyrightable property under the Agreement, the court finds in the context of the case law and the UCC that the contract terms clearly provided for a transaction of computer software equipment involving movable, tangible and identifiable products or goods and not solely intangible ideas and services and, in fact, such goods were installed by CGI for defendant's special purposes. Therefore, the first and second counterclaims are not dismissible on the ground of an exclusive contractual intangible services transaction as urged by movant.

The next issue raised by movant is that the contractual transaction failed to constitute either a sale or lease but merely was a license to use and service the software, therefore precluding defendant from relying on the common law or the UCC implied warranties of merchantability (UCC 2-314) and fitness for a particular known purpose (UCC 2-315).

The court finds that the Agreement clearly constituted a lease for the use of CGI's goods despite the terms expressed therein of a "license to use" CGI "proprietary" software for the payment of a one-time perpetual license fee in accordance with attached pricing schedules. The Agreement, although labeled a license agreement, is clearly analogous to a lease for chattels or goods. The movant has not addressed nor presented a distinction, factually or legally, between a license to use goods from an ordinary lease to use goods. Plaintiff's argument is based on an alleged contractual license to provide intangible services which, as hereinabove, the court rejects. Therefore, the court finds the Agreement clearly is a lease for the use of plaintiff's goods, despite the contractual label of a "license".

The law is clear that common-law rights exist to state a cause of action or counterclaim for breach of implied warranties of merchantability and/or fitness for a particular known purpose involving the lease of chattels or goods without reliance on the UCC. (Industralease Automated & Scientific Equip. Corp. v R. M. E. Enters., 58 AD2d 482 [2d Dept 1977]; Atlantic Tug & Equip. Co. v S & L Paving Corp., 40 AD2d 589 [4th Dept 1972]; Vander Veer v Tyrrell, 29 AD2d 255 [3d Dept 1968]; Laudisio v Amoco Oil Co., 108 Misc 2d 245 [Sup Ct, NY County 1981].) The cases cited by movant suggesting the nonexistence of common-law rights of implied warranties are inapposite as they involve the provision of contractual services as distinguished from products and goods as found hereinabove.

Therefore, the defendant has sufficiently stated in its first and second counterclaims a common-law breach of implied warranties under a contractual lease of goods. However, these counterclaims allege a purchase and sale of the software products. In this regard the contract specifically provided that the CGI software was to be its sole and exclusive property and upon termination of the agreement the defendant would return the software to CGI. Thus, CGI contends the transaction was not a sale within the meaning of UCC 2-106 (UCC 2-401) as no title passed from seller to buyer for a price and therefore defendant is precluded from asserting UCC's implied warranties.

However, New York courts have liberally construed the meaning of "transaction" under UCC 2-102, choosing to analyze the underlying facts of the agreement at issue in determining whether it sufficiently resembles a sale. (In re O.P.M. Leasing Servs., 61 Bankr 596, 603 [US Dist Ct, SD NY 1986]; Uniflex, Inc. v Olivetti Corp., 86 AD2d 538, 539 [1st Dept 1982]; Barco Auto Leasing Corp. v PSI Cosmetics, 125 Misc 2d 68, 72-73 [Civ Ct 1984]; Aguiar v Harper & Row Publishers, 114 Misc 2d 828, 832 [Civ Ct 1982].)

Courts in this jurisdiction have consistently applied article 2 of the UCC to the leasing of chattels. (See, Industralease Automated & Scientific Equip. Corp. v R. M. E. Enters., supra; Laudisio v Amoco Oil Co., supra; United States Leasing Corp. v Franklin Plaza Apts., 65 Misc 2d 1082 [Civ Ct 1971]; Hertz Commercial Leasing Corp. v. Transportation Credit Clearing House, 59 Misc 2d 226 [Civ Ct 1969], *revd on other grounds* 64 Misc 2d 910.) Even if the lessor retains title to the goods, where the contract price of a lease is as large as the sales price of the same item, the transaction is analogous to a sale and will be covered by the UCC. (Barco Auto Leasing Corp., supra; Uniflex, Inc. v. Olivetti Corp., supra; United States Leasing Corp. v Franklin Plaza Apts., supra.)

Therefore, the analysis used by the courts in this jurisdiction to determine whether or not a lease sufficiently resembles a sale so as to bring it within the scope of the UCC may be applicable to the Agreement herein.

Although the Agreement specifically provides that plaintiff will retain title to the software, the Agreement appears to have no term and, in fact, is referred to as a "perpetual license." The economic effect of the Agreement is unclear from the sole submitted documentary evidence of the Agreement itself. Despite the Agreement spelling out the fee to be paid by defendant to plaintiff for use of the software, the court lacks information as to the actual value of the software. (But see, Note, op. cit., 77 Mich L Rev 1149, 1156 ["The economic result of a software loan is indistinguishable from a software sale. The price is apt to be the same in either case"], citing United States Leasing Corp. v Franklin Plaza Apts., supra.)

Neither party has submitted an affidavit by a person with knowledge of the transaction at issue nor is the intent of the parties and surrounding circumstances of the whole transaction between the parties clear from the Agreement alone as to whether this transaction was a sale or only a lease of computer software goods. In the context of the case law, as hereinabove, the contractual retention of title to the goods by CGI in and of itself is not determinative of whether this lease transaction resembled a sale for UCC applicability. There are factual triable issues raised in this regard and therefore dismissal of the implied warranty counterclaims for a sale for failure to sufficiently state a counterclaim or affirmative defense is not warranted. The court for purposes of this type of motion must accept the facts as alleged in the counterclaim as true. (219 Broadway Corp. v Alexander's, Inc., 46 NY2d 506 [1979].) Here there is a sufficient showing to support legally cognizable counterclaims for the breach of implied warranties of fitness and merchantability for a sale of goods within the scope of the UCC. . . .

Accordingly, the plaintiff's motion is denied in its entirety.

Microsoft Corp. v. Harmony Computers & Electronics, Inc.
United States District Court for the Eastern District of New York
846 F. Supp. 208 (E.D.N.Y. 1994)

DEARIE, District Judge.

This is an action for copyright infringement, trademark infringement, and related statutory and common law claims. Plaintiff Microsoft Corporation, a developer, manufacturer, and marketer of computer software programs, seeks declaratory and injunctive relief and treble damages against Harmony Computers & Electronics Inc. ("Harmony") and its president, Stanley Furst (together the "defendants"), for allegedly selling, without license or authorization, copyrighted Microsoft MS-DOS and Microsoft Windows software programs and accompanying materials ("Microsoft Products" or "Products").

Background . . .

Plaintiff argues that because defendants are not licensed by Microsoft, they are not legitimately in possession of, and are not entitled to sell, any Microsoft Products, whether counterfeit or not. To the extent that defendants bought their Microsoft Products from legitimate Microsoft licensees, plaintiff argues that defendants violated Microsoft's licensing restrictions by distributing the Products "stand-alone," that is, by themselves rather than bundled with one of the personal computer systems manufactured by Microsoft licensees. Furthermore, plaintiff alleges, and defendants acknowledge, that defendants persisted in their sales of Microsoft Products despite being notified of the alleged illegality of their activity by plaintiff's cease and desist letters of April 19, June 16, July 14, and September 14, 1993. Plaintiff has advised the Court, by the declarations of Robert Wanezek, Program Manager of Microsoft's Replication Group, and of Lee Gates, its Software Design Test Engineer, that twenty-one pieces of the Products seized from defendants' premises were counterfeit.

Defendants do not contest that they sold Microsoft Products, or that they sold such Products stand-alone as well as loaded onto the hard disks of computers. Defendants argue, however, that because the Products they sold were purchased from Microsoft licensees, they are immune from liability for copyright infringement under the first sale doctrine. In response, plaintiff argues that the first sale doctrine does not apply to the present case because Microsoft never sells but rather only licenses its Products. Defendants also deny that any of the Microsoft Products that they sold were counterfeit. Alternatively, defendants argue, even if any of the Products were counterfeit, they bought them from Microsoft licensees under the good faith belief that the Products were genuine. . . .

Discussion . . .

B. Unauthorized Distribution

Defendants are not Microsoft licensees and therefore are not authorized to sell Microsoft Products. Barbara Schmidt, an accounting supervisor for Microsoft's domestic Original Equipment Manufacturer ("OEM") licensing, declares that defendant Harmony was never at any time a Microsoft licensee. Defendants do not contest this fact. Furthermore, although defendant Stanley Furst was a signatory to a license agreement dated December 2, 1993, between Microsoft and another one of Furst's companies, Everything Computers, Inc., Mr. Furst was not himself a Microsoft licensee. The license held by Everything Computers does not authorize defendants Harmony or Furst to distribute Microsoft Products.

Defendants sold Microsoft Products, as evidenced by the fact that private investigators hired by Microsoft successfully bought various Microsoft

Products from defendants, that Harmony advertised the sale of MS-Dos 6.0, and that persons who had bought Microsoft Products from Harmony had called Microsoft's Piracy Hotline to question the legitimacy of their purchases. Defendants do not contest that they sold Microsoft Products, nor do they dispute that such activity would constitute copyright infringement absent the protection of the first sale doctrine. Because defendants are not authorized by Microsoft to distribute Microsoft Products, their distribution of those Products constitutes a prima facie case, that is, a likelihood of success on the merits of plaintiff's copyright infringement claim. Irreparable harm to plaintiff is therefore presumed.

Defendants argue that they in good faith believed that they were buying Products from authorized Microsoft licensees, and that their sales of the Products were therefore lawful. It is unlikely, in this case, that defendants were innocent infringers, as they were notified by Microsoft of the unlawfulness of their activities by letters dated April 19, June 16, July 14, and September 14, of 1993. Moreover, good faith is no defense against liability for copyright infringement. ISC-Bunker Ramo Corp. v. Altech, Inc., 765 F. Supp. 1310, 1331 (N.D.Ill. 1990) ("there is no such thing as a bona fide purchase for value in copyright law"). Accordingly, defendants' good faith defense must fail.

Finally, it is undisputed that any sale of counterfeit Microsoft Products by defendants would violate the federal copyright laws. Plaintiff has submitted the declarations of Robert L. Wanezek, Program Manager of Microsoft's Replication Group, and of Lee R. Gates, a Software Design Test Engineer for Microsoft, and samples of seized "counterfeit" Microsoft Products from defendants' premises, to support their claim that defendants sold counterfeit Products. Although defendants deny that any of the Products they sold were counterfeit, they provide no evidence to contradict plaintiff's sworn assertions. In the absence of an evidentiary hearing, and given that plaintiff is likely to succeed on the merits of its copyright infringement claim on the grounds that defendants were not licensees and therefore not authorized to distribute any Microsoft products, counterfeit or not, the Court declines at this juncture to make a finding as to the genuineness of the Microsoft Products sold by defendants.

III. First Sale Doctrine Does Not Apply

Defendants argue that even though they sold Microsoft Products without a license, they are immune under the first sale doctrine from liability for copyright infringement. Defendants fail to prove that the first sale doctrine applies because they do not trace their purchase of Microsoft Products to a "first sale" by Microsoft or any party authorized by Microsoft to sell the Products.

The first sale doctrine is codified at section 109(a) of title 17 of the United States Code, which provides that:

(a) Notwithstanding the provisions of section 106(3), the owner of a particular copy . . . lawfully made under this title, or any person authorized by such owner, is entitled, without the authority of the copyright owner, to sell or otherwise dispose of the possession of that copy . . .

17 U.S.C. §109(a) (1977). This statute "restates and confirms the principle that, where the copyright owner has transferred ownership of a particular copy . . . of a work, the person to whom the copy . . . is transferred is entitled to dispose of it by sale . . . or any other means." Historical Note to 17 U.S.C. §109. In civil actions for copyright infringement, the defendant has the burden of proving that the particular pieces of the copyrighted work that he sold were lawfully made or acquired. See Historical Note to 17 U.S.C. §109, cited in American Int'l Pictures, Inc. v. Foreman, 576 F.2d 661, 663 n.1 (5th Cir. 1978).

Defendants argue that a "first sale" occurred when they bought their Microsoft Products from entities whom they believed to be authorized Microsoft licensees. Although a sale of a copyrighted work by a party authorized by the copyright holder may constitute a "first sale" for purposes of the first sale doctrine, see Burke & Van Heusen Inc. v. Arrow Drug, Inc., 233 F. Supp. 881, 884 (E.D.Pa. 1964), defendants have the burden of tracing the chain of title to show that their authority to sell Microsoft Products flows from the copyright holder. American Int'l Pictures, Inc., 576 F.2d at 664-65; Microsoft Corp. v. ATS Computers, Inc. et al., CV 93-1273, at 14 (S.D.Cal. 1993).

Defendants' only evidence of a chain of title for any of their Products is an invoice of their purchase of several pieces of Microsoft Products from an entity called Innovative Datronics Corp. The fact that defendants bought their Microsoft Products from another party does not by itself establish a first sale. "Even an unwitting purchaser who buys a copy in the secondary market can be held liable for infringement if the copy was not the subject of a first sale by the copyright holder. . . . [U]nless title to the copy passes through a first sale by the copyright holder, subsequent sales do not confer good title." American Int'l Pictures, Inc., 576 F.2d at 664. See also Platt & Munk Co. v. Republic Graphics, Inc., 315 F.2d 847 (2d Cir. 1963) ("it has been held that sale of a book purchased from a merchant who bought it from an agent of the copyright proprietor, where the agent had been entrusted with possession of the book but not with actual authority to sell it, is infringement"). No evidence has been presented to show that Innovative Datronics or any party in the chain of title was a licensee of Microsoft and authorized to sell the product.

Defendants' failure to trace their Microsoft Products to a "first sale" by the copyright holder is aggravated by the fact that plaintiff has "established a course of conduct . . . consistent with an intention to retain all the rights associated with the grant of copyright" of the Microsoft Products. American Int'l Pictures, Inc., 576 F.2d at 665. Plaintiff's counsel declares that Microsoft only licenses and does not sell its Products. Entering a license agreement is not a "sale" for purposes of the first sale doctrine.

ISC-Bunker Ramo Corp., 756 F. Supp. at 1331. Moreover, the only chain of distribution that Microsoft authorizes is one in which all possessors of Microsoft Products have only a license to use, rather than actual ownership of the Products.

Defendants' failure to meet their burden of proving a chain of title distinguishes this case from *Burke* and precludes the applicability of the first sale doctrine to this case.

IV. Exceeding Scope of License Agreements

Plaintiff is likely to succeed on its claim that defendants are liable for copyright infringement for exceeding the scope of Microsoft's license agreements.

Plaintiff has traced a unit of MS-DOS 6.0 that Harmony had sold to plaintiff's undercover investigators, back to Amax Engineering, a Microsoft licensee that was authorized to distribute MS-DOS 6.0 exclusively with the sale of its personal computer systems. Plaintiff has also traced four of the MS-DOS 6.2 units seized from defendants' premises, back to Arche Technologies, a Microsoft licensee that was authorized to distribute MS-DOS and Windows only with its computer systems. The remainder of the Microsoft software seized from defendants' premises were not traceable to a specific licensee, but plaintiff's counsel affirms that none of the Products was authorized to be sold stand-alone.

To the extent that defendants bought their Microsoft Products from authorized Microsoft licensees, they were subject to the same licensing restrictions under which those licensees operated. See Major League Baseball Promotion v. Colour-Tex, 729 F. Supp. 1035, 1041, 1042 (D.N.J. 1990). Plaintiff's counsel have represented to the Court that every Microsoft license agreement contains the same licensing language, which provides in relevant part, that licensees:

> . . . shall distribute Product(s) only with [licensee's] Customer System(s) . . . for the particular Product(s) and only inside the Customer System package. [The licensee] shall provide a copy of the . . . Product with, and only with, each Customer System on which the corresponding Preinstalled Product Software is distributed.

(Microsoft License Agreement, P 5(a)(i)). This restriction requires that Microsoft Products only be sold together with a "Customer System," that is, a "single user computer system." (Microsoft License Agreement, P 1(c)), rather than on a stand-alone basis. Indeed, plaintiff's in-house counsel declares that "it is generally known in the computer software industry that except for upgrade products, Microsoft does not authorize anyone to distribute standalone MS-DOS product." Plaintiff explains that Products that are sold stand-alone or otherwise outside the scope of Microsoft's license agreements, though identical in exterior appearance to authorized Microsoft Products, do not come with the product support system, warranties, and assured compatibility with their personal computer systems that Microsoft provides for its legitimately distributed Products. Therefore, plaintiff argues, the sale of stand-alone Products irreparably harms Microsoft's goodwill and reputation as a reliable software producer. *Id.* . . .

COMMENTS AND QUESTIONS

1. Is it possible to reconcile *CGI* and *Harmony?* What did Microsoft do that the parties in *CGI* did not to characterize its transaction as a license?

Indeed, could one argue that the results in *both* cases where wrong? *CGI* involved a signed, presumably bargained agreement between two business parties. If two such parties wish for whatever reason to treat their transaction as a license, why shouldn't they be able to do so? By contrast, there is very little in the "license" at issue in *Harmony* to suggest any agreement whatsoever to depart from the traditional rules of commerce. Isn't *Harmony* actually a stronger case than *CGI* for treating the transaction as a sale?

2. Both *CGI* and *Harmony* point to significant legal reasons why a software vendor might prefer to characterize their transaction as a license rather than a sale. First, licensees may be able to avoid rules in the Uniform Commercial Code governing product warranties. Second, licensors retain certain rights under copyright law that sellers do not. (We discuss below whether software vendors may use license provisions to *alter* substantive copyright law.) Note that these legal consequences are in addition to the economic reasons for licensing discussed in the previous section.

On the other hand, a product licensed to a user with a "no resale" restriction would be expected to sell at a lower price than one sold without such a restriction. The obvious example here is a car lease versus an outright purchase. Do the transaction costs of such an arrangement make sense for a single copy of software? If it is impossible to enforce a "no resale" clause against the average individual, perhaps its only effective use would be against large-volume resellers. Does this affect your view about whether "no resale" clauses should be legally permitted?

3. The *Harmony* court certainly seems to be influenced by the fact that the defendants in that case were apparently counterfeiting Microsoft programs. But is the opinion limited to that circumstance, or does it extend further? In particular, what if Harmony had purchased copies of Microsoft programs only from legitimate end users, who had bought them along with computers they no longer wanted. Do the original end users have a right to dispose of their copies as they see fit? Does it depend on the terms of the license written by Microsoft? Who are the parties to that license agreement? Even without contractual "privity," a copyright owner

may sue a secondary purchaser or sublicensee for copyright infringement. But would contractual restrictions apply to such a party—i.e., would there be a breach of contract cause of action as well? *Cf.* Robert P. Merges, *The End of Friction? Property Rights and Contract in the 'Newtonian' World of On-line Commerce*, 12 Berkeley Tech. L.J. 115, 118-121 (1997).

In the context of mass-market transactions for software, virtually all courts have looked to the totality of the circumstances surrounding the transaction in concluding that it was in fact a sale rather than a license. An instructive example is DSC Communications Corp. v. Pulse Communications, Inc., 170 F.3d 1354 (Fed. Cir. 1999). In that case, the court came to two different conclusions regarding the status of different copies of the same computer program. One of those copies was governed by a complex bargained license agreement. The court concluded that this program was licensed rather than sold:

> Not only do the agreements characterize the RBOCs as non-owners of copies of the software, but the restrictions imposed on the RBOCs' rights with respect to the software are consistent with that characterization. In particular, the licensing agreements severely limit the rights of the RBOCs with respect to the POTS-DI software in ways that are inconsistent with the rights normally enjoyed by owners of copies of software. . . .
>
> The fact that the right of possession is perpetual, or that the possessor's rights were obtained through a single payment, is certainly relevant to whether the possessor is an owner, but those factors are not necessarily dispositive if the possessor's right to use the software is heavily encumbered by other restrictions that are inconsistent with the status of owner.

By contrast, different copies of the same software obtained by resale from a previous buyer were sold rather than licensed, because they were purchased "on the open market" and "without restriction on their use." *Id.*

In a typical mass-market software transaction, there is no bargaining over license terms. The purchaser (licensee?) commonly obtains a single copy of the software, along with documentation, in a box at a retail software store. The box contains a single price, which the purchaser pays up front and which constitutes the entire payment for the "license." The purchaser pays sales tax on the "license." The license does not run for a definite term and need not be renewed, but it is perpetual unless terminated by the vendor (something that almost never occurs).

In light of these indicia, and because most purchasers think they are *buying* a physical copy of a program, almost all courts and commentators that have considered the issue have concluded that a shrinkwrap license transaction involving software is a sale of goods rather than a license, and is therefore covered by Article 2 of the current UCC. See, e.g., Step-Saver Data Sys. v. Wyse Technology, 939 F.2d 91 (3d Cir. 1991); Advent Sys. v. Unisys Corp., 925 F.2d 670 (3d Cir. 1991); Arizona Retail Sys. v. Software Link, Inc., 831 F. Supp. 759 (D. Ariz. 1993); Hospital Computer Sys. v. Staten Island Hosp., 788 F. Supp. 1351 (D.N.J. 1992); In re

Amica, Inc., 135 B.R. 534 (Bankr. N.D. Ill. 1992); Neilson Bus. Equip. Center v. Italo Monteleone, 524 A.2d 1172 (Del. 1987); Photo Copy, Inc. v. Software, Inc., 510 So. 2d 1337 (La. Ct. App. 1987); USM Corp. v. Arthur Little Sys., 546 N.E.2d 888 (Mass. Ct. App. 1989); Drier Co. v. Unitronix Corp., 3 U.C.C. Rep. Serv. 2d 1728 (App. Div. N.J. 1987); Schroeders, Inc. v. Hogan Sys., 522 N.Y.S.2d 404 (Sup. Ct. 1987); Communications Groups, Inc. v. Warner Communications, 527 N.Y.S.2d 341 (Civ. Ct. 1988). Cf. ProCD, Inc. v. Zeidenberg, 86 F.3d 1447 (7th Cir. 1996) (concluding that a mass market transaction involving software was a "sale of goods" to which UCC Article 2 applied but nonetheless enforcing a "license agreement" under Article 2). The *ProCD* case is discussed in more detail below.

4. In an insightful article, David Nimmer has challenged the entire concept of a license of tangible goods, as opposed to a license of intellectual property. In Nimmer's view, there are two basic types of transactions involving software: (1) leases or other transactions in which title to the physical goods does not pass, and they are returned after a fixed term of periodic payments; and (2) sales of goods that happen to embody intellectual property. He faults *Harmony* for failing to establish what transfer mechanism was actually in use:

> Which circumstance actually obtained in Microsoft v. Harmony, the exemplar of the "licensing" paradigm? Sadly, the opinion fails to clarify the matter, and that inability to distinguish between differing paradigms is only too typical. Nonetheless, lack of clarity does not create a new "licensing" paradigm. Instead, if there were a bona fide *lease* of the physical goods, then one legal regime pertained; if Microsoft actually *sold* or otherwise permanently disposed of those physical goods, retaining full copyright ownership in itself, then another legal regime governed. Current copyright law does not recognize any regime of "licensing" that stands intermediate between those two possibilities.

David Nimmer et al., The Metamorphosis of Contract into Expand, 87 Cal. L. Rev. 17, 38 (1999). See also David A. Rice, Digital Information As Property and Product: U.C.C. Article 2B, 22 U. Dayton L. Rev. 621 (1997). It is worth noting that the "licensing" approach has been tried before, with sound recordings and with books, but courts always rejected the idea that a good was being licensed rather than sold merely because it embodied intellectual property.

Software industry lawyers dispute this characterization, of course. They have argued that licenses are indeed a valid, albeit new, method of distribution. The primary argument seems to be one of *fait accompli*: because virtually all software vendors provide shrinkwrap licenses or the equivalent along with their software, refusing to enforce them would upset settled commercial expectations. See Robert W. Gomulkiewicz, The License Is the Product: Comments on the Promise of Article 2B for Software and Information Licensing, 13 Berkeley Tech. L.J. 891 (1998);

Robert W. Gomulkiewicz & Mary Williamson, A Brief Defense of End-User Licensing Agreements, 19 Rutgers Computer & Tech. L.J. 335 (1996). It is certainly true that most software vendors expect their license agreements to be enforceable, despite case law to the contrary. See Michael Rustad & Lori E. Eisenschmidt, The Commercial Law of Internet Security, 10 High Tech. L.J. 213 (1995) (reporting results of a survey of software company lawyers in which two-thirds thought shrinkwrap licenses were enforceable). Should this fact be used by courts to enforce the licenses? For a contrary argument, see Mark A. Lemley, The Law and Economics of Internet Norms, 73 Chi.-Kent L. Rev. 1257, 1273-1274 (1999) (arguing that the assumptions of vendors regarding such licenses are at odds with the assumptions of consumers and that as a result there is no industry "norm" to which courts can reasonably defer).

Note on the Uniform Computer Information Transactions Act

The legal distinction between a license and sale, and more general questions regarding the applicability of the UCC to transfers of software and other information-intensive assets, were some of the forces behind a move to draft a new law governing software transactions, the Uniform Computer Information Transactions Act (UCITA).[2] One recent draft (August 1998) defines the mission of UCITA as follows:

Project History

Although it now involves far broader participation by motion picture, broadcast, publishing, database, banking, and other industries, Article 2B began with a focus on software and on-line contracting for information, covering the entire range of contracts in these industries. Over several years, committees of NCCUSL [National Conference of Commissioners of Uniform State Laws], the ABA and other groups examined the consequences of a mismatch in concept between a contract law aimed at defining relationships for the sale of goods (Article 2) and contract relationships in which information is the center of the transaction and the contractual format most often is a license, rather than a sale. The conclusion entails two basic observations:

1. **Distinct From Sales.** Information transactions and, especially, licenses of information, differ substantively from transactions involving the sale or lease of goods. The differences are manifested in both the conditional nature of the transaction and that the value lies not in the goods, but in information and rights that severable from the goods. A law tailored to transactions whose primary purpose is to transfer title to goods cannot be simply applied to transactions whose purpose is to convey rights in information. Separate treatment is needed.

---

2. UCITA was originally drafted as a new article of the UCC, Article 2B. It was not approved by the American Law Institute, however, and will not be included in the UCC.

2. Commercial Significance. The information industry has obvious commercial importance. Software and related information technologies account for in excess of 6% of the gross national product and the size of the industry continues to grow. Adding in other industries (publishing, motion pictures, on-line systems) swells the figure to a huge share of the economy. . .

Nature of a License.

The paradigmatic transaction is a *license* of information, rather than a sale of goods.[6] The transaction is characterized by 1) the *conditional* nature of the rights or privileges conveyed to use the information, and 2) the *focus* on information, rather than goods for the value conveyed. A license is unlike a sale or lease of goods in many ways, including what the transferee received by the contract. The Federal Circuit Court of Appeals, for example, has stated: "[A] patent license agreement is in essence nothing more than a promise by the licensor not to sue the licensee [even] if couched in terms of '[L]icensee is given the right to make, use, or sell X.'"[7]

Licenses are commercial transactions. Licensing is a primary means of commerce in digital information; it is important in all information industries. In licensing, contract terms play an important role in defining the product conveyed that transcends sale of goods terms dealing with warranties, time of delivery, and the like. The terms of a license also typically provide for express grants of rights (or permission) to use information and express limitations on use. The grant and restrictions are product and are often buttressed by the licensor's property right to control various uses of the information under patent, copyright or similar law. A license for computer software is a much different commercial value if it grants a right to commercially reproduce 100,000 copies than if it grants the right to personal use of a single copy. Yet, the information and perhaps the particular copy may be identical in both cases.

Typically, license use restrictions are enforceable unless a particular term in a particular context conflicts with general doctrines against intellectual property misuse or similar constraints. Courts have enforced license restrictions precluding commercial use of a digital database, limiting a right to access, barring the making of a copy of software, limiting use to a specific computer, limiting use to internal operations of the licensee, controlling redistribution to a particular package of software and hardware, precluding modifications, and various other contract limitations. Article 2B does not *create* contract law here—it merely provides a more coherent base for contracting.

Many commercial licenses deal with rights in intellectual property, but in many other cases the license is not based on intellectual property rights. For example, numerous licenses in Internet or for on-line services grant one party permission to enter the [sic] and obtain information from the computer

---

6. U.C.C. §2B-102.

7. Spindelfabrik Suessen-Schurr v. Schubert & Salzer, 829 F.2d 1075, 1081 (Fed.Cir.1987), *cert. denied*, 484 U.S. 1063 (1988). See also General Talking Pictures Corp. v. Western Electric Co., 304 U.S. 175, 181 (1938) (patent license "a mere waiver of the right to sue."); Cohen v. Paramount Pictures Corp., 845 F.2d 851 (9th Cir 1988).

of the other.[8] That form of licensing is increasingly important in the digital world. Article 2B describes this framework as an "access contract."[9] Where the relationship extends over time, it creates various ongoing obligations (e.g., the obligation to pay, the obligation to maintain accessibility) not present in other licenses.

Commercial Context.

As in commerce in goods, licensing spans a wide range of commercial practices and also occurs in the mass market. Article 2B focuses on many commercially important transactions, but does not apply to all information licensing. It excludes, for example, most forms of patent and trademark licenses.[10]

There are a wide range of companies. Many are large entities, but to an extent far greater than in the fields of selling goods or leasing them, the vast majority of information *providers* are small companies, reflecting the often small overhead of software and other information enterprise and the role of the software and other information industries as a focus for modern entrepreneurs. The average size of a software company in California, for example, is less than ten employees. The average in the state of Washington is twelve employees.

Similarly, while many people have their primary contact with licensing in reference to mass market transactions, in practice, the most significant forms of licensing and the center of major economic aspects of this field of commerce lie outside the mass market.

At every level of commerce, information providers that may be perceived as primarily licensors are in fact intimately and comprehensively both licensors and licensees with respect to most of their commercial practice. This is true because, for most information products, the product source involves combinations of information from numerous sources, obtained through licenses or similar transactions.

Transactional Context.

There are many different types of licensing, reflecting a diversity as great as that in fields of commerce associated with the production and sale of goods.[11]

One way of distinguishing among the various types of licenses in modern commerce differentiates between licenses that relate to information in copies physically transferred to a licensee, as contrasted to licenses that enable a licensee to access a computer in which information is located. Within transactions in which copies are made available on diskette or otherwise to a licen-

---

8. See Ticketron Ltd. Partnership v. Flip Side, Inc., No. 92 C 0911, 1993 WESTLAW 214164 (ND Ill. June 17, 1993).

9. Section 2B-102(a)(1). See Section 2B-615.

10. See Section 2B-104.

11. In addition, of course, especially in the mass market, many types of information are transferred in copies sold to customers. Except for computer software, Article 2B does not apply to sales of copies. It does not cover sales of books, magazines, records, or the like. These sales are not "licenses" because they do not involve express contractual restrictions on the transferee's use of the information. See Section 2B-102(28) (definition of license).

see subject to license conditions, a variety of transactional formats exist. In some, a licensor deals directly with the end user. In others, a chain of distribution intervenes; the publisher does not deal directly with the end user. In each case, the basis of the license resides in either the existence of intellectual property rights in the information or, more simply, the fact that the licensor has control over a source of the information that the licensee desires to utilize.

The distribution options are affected by the property rights involved. In areas covered by Article 2B, copyright law is a dominant (but not sole) source of intellectual property rights. Copyright law gives the copyright owner the exclusive right to *make copies* of its work, to *distribute* copies, to make *derivative* works, to *publicly display or perform* the work, and other rights. These rights are not relinquished by selling or transferring a copy of the information. Thus, a basic choice for a copyright owner is whether to license some or all of these rights or to sell copies of the work. A sale relinquishes some rights *with respect to the copy*. A license tailors what rights are granted. In text publishing, current practice in the non-electronic mass market involves a sale of copies, while transactions for distribution or acquisition of works use many different formats. In motion pictures, licensing is used to provide content to theaters, while in the consumer market, copies are either sold or rented under terms that preclude public performance. Computer programs are typically licensed, although computer game distribution frequently involves sales of copies.

Direct Licenses. Many licenses are face-to-face contracts between the copyright owner and the licensee. In most cases, direct licenses (often standard form agreements) transfer a copy to the licensee subject to express contractual use restrictions. Increasingly, copies are moved to the licensee's site electronically. An additional format involves no delivery of a copy, but licensed access to the information for brief periods as needed.

In direct licensing, common terms include limiting use to a designated system, for specific purposes (e.g., internal use only), subject to confidentiality conditions, transferability limits, and similar restrictions. In software licensing, a central factor of distribution recognizes that loading software into a computer and, even, moving it automatically from one part of memory to another part, constitutes making a copy that falls within the copyright owner's exclusive rights.

Direct licensing also occurs in the many contractual relationships in which information (software, text, movies) is developed for the licensee. Here, it is very common for small companies or individuals to be licensors. This illustrates an important point in the overall contract issues. While large providers are important factors, small company licensors are more numerous and are economically important.

Indirect Distribution Licensing. Commercial licensing also occurs in context of broader distribution chains. These are not analogous to distribution methods used in the sale of goods because of the intangible subject matter and the overlay of intellectual property rights which include the exclusive right to *distribute* copies. While it oversimplifies the matter, it is useful to discuss two distinct frameworks.

The first involves use of a master copy and is common in the movie industry and in software contracts. A "distributor" receives access to a single master copy of the work and a license to make and distribute additional copies or to make and publicly perform a copy. For example, Corel Software licenses a distributor to load its software into the distributor's computers. Corel limits the distributor to no more than 1,000 copies which can only be distributed in the computers and subject to an end user license. If the distributor does not perform within the limits of this license, since both making and distribution of copies are within the owner's copyright, the unauthorized acts would be infringements as well as contractual breaches.

An alternative uses tangible copies of the software. For example, Quicken may license a distributor to distribute its up to 1,000 copies of accounting software in packages provided by Quicken. While in some industries, the publisher will sell 1,000 copies to the distributor to achieve this result, a license is used in the software industry. In the license, the distributor is allowed to distribute copies to retailers, provided that conditions are met, such as terms of payment, use of the original packaging, and making the end user distribution subject to an end user license. The distribution right is an exclusive copyright right; distributions outside the license infringe the copyright.

In both formats, the information product eventually reaches an end user. If it does so in an ordinary chain complying with the distribution license, the end user is in rightful possession of a copy. If the authorized distribution involved sales of copies, no more is required to give the end user the very limited rights of the owner of a copy spelled out in copyright law (e.g., to transfer it, make a back-up if it is software, make some changes essential to use if it is software). If, however, the copyright owner elected a licensing framework, the end user's right to "use" (e.g., copy) the software depends on the end user license. Typically, this is in a license from the publisher to the end user. It creates a direct contractual relationship that would not otherwise exist. The contract leaps the chain of distribution and creates a direct link to the publisher by the end user. It is the only contract that enables the end user to make copies of the software.

COMMENTS AND QUESTIONS

1. Does the project history accurately describe the law existing before UCITA? Most commentators to consider the issue have argued that UCITA would in fact significantly change the rules governing transactions in software and digital information. Consider the following criticism, suggesting that UCITA "would remake the law of software and intellectual property licensing in a radical way":

UCC2B expands the scope and power of contracts in three ways. First, UCC2B reverses the well-settled rule of existing law that whether a transaction is a sale, a lease, or a license can only be determined by looking at the economic realities of an exchange. Under UCC2B, a transaction is automatically a license unless it constitutes an assignment of the intellectual property right itself. And if it is a license, UCC2B applies. UCC2B thus creates a new meaning of "licensing" intellectual property rights, one unknown to copyright or patent law and one that encompasses transactions that intellectual property has always dealt with as sales.

Second, UCC2B redefines what constitutes a contract, abandoning the focus on offer and acceptance, and therefore on the agreement at the time the parties conclude a deal, in favor of a rule that the intellectual property owner's standard form terms will be enforced, even if they are contained in a "shrinkwrap" or "clickwrap" license that the buyer cannot see until the transaction has already occurred. In so doing, UCC2B adopts a view that is decidedly in the minority among current courts, and that is dramatically to the benefit of the drafters of standard forms, who now do not even need a signature (or its electronic equivalent) in order to enforce their terms. Because of this shift, contracts under UCC2B are really more akin to property rights: the contracts can be viewed as equitable servitudes that "run with" the goods in much the way some property owners once tried to impose restrictions on chattel. This shift is extremely important. The existing relationship between intellectual property and contract law is based on a conception of what constitutes an enforceable contract. UCC2B changes that conception; as a result, it cannot help but change the relationship as well.

Finally, UCC2B makes virtually all of its default rules subject to change by "agreement of the parties". . . . And since UCC2B makes it so easy to write and enforce the terms of a contract, a software vendor with a good lawyer can quite easily enforce *virtually whatever terms it likes* simply by putting them "conspicuously" in a multi-page document the user cannot even see (much less agree to) until after buying, installing, and beginning to run the software. There are only a few limitations on a software vendor's power to create whatever terms it likes. . . . In short, UCC2B allows those who draft the contract terms to enforce almost any terms they desire.

Mark A. Lemley, Beyond Preemption: The Law and Policy of Intellectual Property Licensing, 87 Cal. L. Rev. 111 (1999) (footnotes omitted). See also Jessica Litman, The Tales That Article 2B Tells, 13 Berkeley Tech. L.J. 931 (1998) (criticizing UCITA as "disingenuous" with respect to its characterization of existing law); David McGowan, Free Contracting, Fair Competition, and Article 2B: Some Reflections on Federal Competition Policy, Information Transactions, and "Aggressive Neutrality," 13 Berkeley Tech. L.J. 1173 (1998) (disputing UCITA's characterization of itself as "neutral" in relation to existing law).

2. Recall David Nimmer's challenge to the concept of a "licensing" paradigm. If he is correct that there is no such paradigm, is there any need for UCITA? Certainly the main purpose of UCITA seems to be to set up uniform rules for licensing software and digital information.

UCITA does other things as well, of course. It updates the basic rules of contract law for the world of electronic commerce—for example, by setting up rules for digital signatures and authentication. But similar rules are being developed in the draft Uniform Electronic Transactions Act, which would apply not just to transactions in information products but to all transactions that occur online. And some commentators have questioned whether the rules UCITA would apply to electronic transactions are in fact the right ones. See A. Michael Froomkin, Article 2B as Legal Software for Electronic Contracting—Operating System or Trojan Horse?, 13 Berkeley Tech. L.J. 1023 (1998).

Novell, Inc. v. Network Trade Center
United States District Court for the District of Utah
25 F. Supp. 2d 1218 (D. Utah 1997)

GREENE, J.

Plaintiff Novell, Inc. ("Novell") is a developer, manufacturer, and distributor of computer software for use on microcomputers known as "personal computers." "NetWare" is one of Novell's computer software products. NetWare is a networking program designed to link separate computers together and allow the transfer of information between users. NetWare is marketed and sold in two forms: as an "original" product, and as an "upgrade" product which is substantially the same and equivalent to the "original" product. The "original" product is intended for the first time buyer of networking software. The "upgrade" product is restricted for use by either registered users of an older version of NetWare, or for the user of a competitor's qualifying networking software. The two forms of the program are identical in every respect except packaging and price. The "upgrade" is considerably less expensive.

Defendant Mark Bondiett ("Bondiett") is the sole shareholder, director, and officer of defendant Network Trade Center, Inc. ("NTC"). NTC operates as a software distributor which sells software programs, including NetWare, to purchasers who then use the software in business or otherwise.

NTC's original business practice was to purchase NetWare and older versions of other networking software in bulk, at low prices. Then, using the old software, NTC would order the "upgrade" version of the latest release of NetWare by filling out an upgrade form using qualifying information from the old software. Typically, the upgrade form was completed under Bondiett's name and purchased from an authorized distributor, or sometimes from Novell directly. Once received, the "upgrade" software would be sold to a purchaser at a profit, or placed in inventory to be sold later.

Beginning in 1995, NTC began advertising that it would sell older qualifying networking software to end-users and then help them order the latest "upgrade" release of Novell's NetWare. However, in June 1995, Novell announced that it would discontinue its competitive upgrade program for distributors, thus forcing end-users who wanted to purchase "upgrade" software to do so directly through Novell.

At all relevant times, plaintiff had valid federal trademark registrations for the terms "Novell" (No. 1,338,892) and "NetWare" (No. 1,328,271). Novell has continuously owned and used these trademarks without challenge for more than five years. Novell only authorizes use of its trademarks pursuant to written agreements. Authorized distributors, original equipment manufacturers, and certain resellers may receive written authorization from Novell to use its trademarks.

NTC and Bondiett have never applied for or received written authorization from Novell to use Novell's trademarks, nor is NTC authorized as a distributor of NetWare. Nevertheless, NTC has conducted and continues to conduct business throughout the United States and Mexico selling NetWare "upgrades" through direct mail and advertisements in national computer magazines. NTC's advertisements feature the "Novell" and "NetWare" trademarks and trade dress. NTC promotes the Novell software in its advertisements as being "New Retail" or as a "Special Novell Promotional Package." End-users who have made purchases of Novell software as a result of NTC advertising have complained to NTC as well as to Novell about the confusion concerning the nature and extent of rights obtained in the purchase. Some end-users were led to believe that the software they had purchased was an "original" rather than an "upgrade" product. Others thought they were entitled to register their NetWare product with Novell. Some end-users believed that Novell had sponsored and approved the sale of NetWare through NTC.

In July 1994, Novell notified NTC, in writing, that its advertisements, promotions, marketing, and sales of NetWare "upgrades" violated Novell's rights and policies, and demanded that NTC immediately discontinue all such forms of advertisement. Notwithstanding such notice, NTC has continued to advertise the NetWare product. Novell has also received complaints from some of its authorized distributors, reflecting perceived unfairness and dissatisfaction because of competition with NTC in sales of NetWare by NTC that consist of "upgrade" product represented to be "original" product and sold at prices below the authorized distributors' "original" product prices.

Novell asserts federal question claims against NTC and Bondiett for trademark infringement, unfair competition and false advertising, and copyright infringement. . . .

In order to establish a claim of trademark infringement under the Lanham Act, four elements must be established: (1) the mark is valid and legally protected; (2) the mark is owned by the plaintiff; (3) the defendant used the trademark in commerce without consent; and (4) defendant's use of the trademark will create the likelihood of confusion. [Validity and ownership were stipulated.]

Unauthorized use of another's registered trademarks in advertising constitutes trademark infringement. In this regard, the Fifth Circuit has declared that "[a]ffirmative misrepresentation, such as placing a plaintiff's trademark on the defendant's advertisements, is clearly a violation of section 1125(a)." Matrix Essentials, Inc. v. Emporium Drug Mart, Inc., 988 F.2d 587, 593 (5th Cir.1993).

In this case, it is clear that NTC used both the "Novell" and "NetWare" marks in advertisements placed in national computer magazines, and in direct mail sent to potential customers. The actions of NTC went well beyond any permissible build up of inventory of the NetWare product. . . . Otherwise unauthorized use of the marks of another can be justified when an implied license comes into being. An implied license can arise from conduct of the parties from which the existence of an agreement could reasonably be inferred. In *Birthright* [v. Birthright Inc., 827 F. Supp. 1114, 1133 (D.N.J. 1993)], an implied license authorizing the defendant to use plaintiff's mark and name was found to exist. 827 F. Supp. at 1134. Contrary to the facts in *Birthright*, however, there was no prior affiliation between the parties in this case, and there was never any conduct from which authorization to use the marks could be implied. Also, in July 1994, Novell notified NTC in writing that the advertisements, promotions, and marketing of Novell's marks by NTC was unauthorized and that Novell demanded NTC to cease using the marks immediately. It is apparent from the letter written by Novell, as well as other evidence in the record, that no implied agreement authorizing NTC to use the marks in advertising came into being.

In Sebastian Int'l, Inc. v. Longs Drug Stores Corp., 53 F.3d 1073, 1076 (9th Cir.1995), the Ninth Circuit reasoned that "[w]hen a purchaser resells a trademarked article under the producer's trademark, and nothing more, there is no actionable misrepresentation under the statute." Under the weight of authority, however, courts have held that trademark infringement does exist as in this case when a defendant goes beyond reselling the product. See, Stormor v. Johnson, 587 F. Supp. 275, 279 (W.D.Mich.1984). NTC argues that it has done nothing more than sell the "upgrade" software it acquired without altering the appearance of the box, and that there is nothing wrong with doing that. This Court finds, however, that in addition to reselling the software NTC used Novell's marks in its advertising, knowing that it was not authorized to do so. . . .

[The court then found likelihood of confusion, based on the mark's strength, a few instances of actual confusion, and other evidence.]

Based upon the foregoing, including consideration of all of the applicable factors and the totality of the record, this Court concludes that no genuine issue of material fact exists and that summary judgment in favor of plaintiff on the issue of trademark infringement under the Lanham Act should be granted.

COMMENTS AND QUESTIONS

1. Under the court's reasoning—that unauthorized use in advertising is an additional use beyond simple resale of a good—is an advertisement in the newspaper for sale of a used copy of software, or any product covered by a trademark, an infringement of the mark? Do ordinary consumers really violate trademark law every day by placing classified ads to resell their used cars, toasters, and blenders? Do supermarkets violate the

law by accurately advertising the brand products they have for sale unless implicitly authorized by license?

2. By the same token, assuming that commercial software is identified by its trademarked name in product reviews (e.g., comparing its performance to that of other products), would reviewers be liable for infringement if they failed to seek permission for that use? Can you see any problems or policy issues in such a rule? It is worth noting that at least some companies have included "no review" clauses in their software licenses.

In fact, the doctrine of "non-trademark use" (sometimes mistakenly called "fair use") provides that it does not infringe a trademark to use the mark, even in commerce or advertising, as an accurate description of the trademark owner's product. Thus, newspapers are entitled to use Microsoft trademarks in describing the company or its products, even if the descriptions are unflattering; competitors are entitled to use a company's trademarks in comparative advertising so long as the statements made are true; and people who own genuine Novell products are entitled to call those products what they are. See generally New Kids on the Block v. News America Publishing, 971 F.2d 302 (9th Cir. 1992) (discussing the doctrine of non-trademark use).

Novell may be part of a broader trend toward expanding trademark law beyond its natural boundaries without regard for the reasons we protect trademarks. See Mark A. Lemley, The Modern Lanham Act and the Death of Common Sense, 108 Yale L.J. 1687 (1999) (noting and criticizing this trend). In so doing, the court allows Novell to protect under trademark law what it could not get under copyright or contract law. (For the *Novell* court's conclusions on these issues, see Section C.1.a, infra.)

3. For recent Supreme Court treatment of first-sale issues, albeit in the copyright context, see Quality King Distributors, Inc. v. L'Anza Research Int'l, Inc., 118 S. Ct. 1125 (1998) (rejecting interpretation of distribution right under Copyright Act that would prevent importation and resale of authorized copies). For an interesting Federal Circuit case that raises as many questions as it answers regarding the first-sale right for patented items, see Mallinckrodt v. MediPart, 976 F.2d 700, 24 U.S.P.Q.2d 1173 (Fed. Cir. 1992) (excluding a patented product from the scope of the patent exhaustion doctrine because the product had a label affixed to it limiting the number of times it could be used).

B. WHAT IS AT STAKE IN THE LICENSE VERSUS SALE DEBATE

Having introduced the debate over whether software is transferred subject to a license agreement, we pause to ask a more profit-minded question: what does a seller of information want its customers to agree to, and why? In other words, why does it matter whether software is licensed or sold?

The particular answers depend on the nature of the industry, the distribution mode, and the costs of providing the information. This last factor in turn has two components, production cost and transaction cost.

1. Bundling

In some industries, sellers can make more money by selling bundles of information instead of individual, discrete components of it. The economics of this are well explained in an excellent recent book about the new information economy. Carl Shapiro & Hal R. Varian, Information Rules (Harvard Bus. School Press, 1998). The basic idea is that in many cases there is less variation in how consumers value bundles of information than in how they value individual components. This derives, paradoxically, from the fact that individual consumers value individual components differently.

Take as an example an online service that reports snow, weather, and crowd information for ski resorts across the United States. The service sells for $100 per year. One user, Anita, lives in Boston and usually skis in New England; for her, the regional reports for Vermont and New Hampshire are worth $75 per year, and the reports for the western United States are worth only $25. Another subscriber, Bill, lives in San Francisco and usually skis in the California Sierras. For him, the Western ski reports are the valuable ones: he would be willing to pay up to $75 for them. Because he occasionally skis in the East, the reports for New England are worth $25 to him.

If we make the simplifying (i.e., fantastical) assumption that Anita and Bill are the only consumers in the market, we can see that at $100 per year, the seller will sell subscriptions to both Anita and Bill and thereby earn revenues of $200. If the seller sold each regional service for $75, revenues would be only $150. (Neither Anita nor Bill would pay $75 for out-of-area information.) And if the seller sold regional service at a price Anita and Bill would be willing to pay—$25—it would still make only $100. It might also be more expensive to break the data down into regional reports, which would further eat into the seller's profit.

From an economic point of view, the ski report service is simply taking advantage of the variance or dispersion in individual buyers' valuation of the information. The revenue is higher in this case for a bundled product because consumers who value one component highly are likely to value another much less. If individuals who value one component very highly are more likely to value others highly, bundling would not work any better than selling individual components. One way to think about bundling is that different consumers may well have the same "average" valuation of each piece of information in the bundle but very different valuations of individual components. If high valuers of one component are likely to be low valuers of others, it behooves the seller to approximate this "average value" for a large number of consumers in pricing the bundle. See Yannis Bakos et al., Shared Information Goods, 42 J. Law & Econ. 199 (1999).

Bundling makes sense in the ski report example and, indeed, in many other examples. We can see this from the fact that bundling information is extremely common—everything from LEXIS law firm pricing to magazine subscriptions (which are really just bundles of individual stories, and meta-bundles of individual issues) bear this out. See Shapiro & Varian, Information Rules, supra.

From the point of view of legalities, the economic benefit of bundling explains a number of features of information licenses—for example (1) pay-up-front agreements; (2) subscription or multi-installment purchases; and, in some cases, (3) no ability to buy individual components. Unfortunately for producers, many forms of bundling violate the antitrust laws, an issue we shall return to in the next chapter.

2. Price Discrimination

In the ski report example above, the information seller was assumed not to know about the precise valuations of each user or—same thing—was presumed not to be able to do anything about it. Perhaps, for example, the cost of selling personally tailored information services is too high—it is too expensive to tell the high valuers for each region from the low valuers. (What the seller really worries about is selling information regarding Sierra ski conditions to Bill for $25 when Bill would have been willing to pay $75.)

But what if the seller could determine this? In our example, it would not add anything: charging Anita $75 for the Eastern ski report and charging her $25 for the Western one while charging Bill the opposite would yield the same revenue as with bundling. But if we change the numbers slightly, things change. Assume Anita is a more avid skier, or Bill values ski report information less overall (e.g., because California ski conditions are less variable). To be specific, let's say Anita is willing to pay $90 for Eastern information, but Bill will pay only $75 for Western information.

Now, if only the information seller can determine that this is so, it can capture the extra $15 in valuation from Anita. To be precise, if the seller can *find out* this information for less than it's worth—for less than $15—it will do so. Assuming the information is accurate, the seller can raise its price *to Anita* and reap the rewards. If the seller prices Anita's total bundle at $115, she will still buy; and by keeping Bill's the same as it was ($100), the seller will now earn revenues of $215.

The principle here is known as *price discrimination*—charge the higher valuer more and the lower valuer less, in layman's terms. In technical terms, take as much of the consumer surplus as you can. (If Anita is willing to pay $90 for Eastern ski reports but the seller has set a uniform price of $75 per region, Anita would have $15 in consumer surplus: the difference what she is willing to pay and what she in fact has to pay.)

If you want to price-discriminate, you need good information. If you raise the price of all regional reports to $90, Bill will no longer buy one— and you would lose money. (Anita's extra $15 will not offset the loss of Bill's $75.) In addition, you need something else: you need to be able to prevent one buyer from "buying low, selling high"—in a word, you need to prevent "arbitrage." The following excerpt describes this concept in more detail. (Note that the excerpt refers to a case called ProCD v. Zeidenberg, which the court viewed as an example of (attempted) arbitrage: the buyer of a set of CD-ROM directories made the public domain data in them available for free over the Internet in contravention of a licensing agreement contained on the product packaging. The case is excerpted and discussed in Section B of this chapter.)

≡
≡ *Michael J. Meurer, Price Discrimination,*
≡ *Personal Use and Piracy: Copyright Protection*
≡ *of Digital Works*
≡ *45 Buff. L. Rev. 845 (1997)*

Effective price discrimination requires: (1) measurement of consumer preferences; (2) a means to stop arbitrage by favored consumers; and (3) market power. Are the conditions for price discrimination met in ProCD? . . . Judge Easterbrook explains that commercial buyers have higher valuations. Elsewhere in the opinion he explains that a term in the software license precludes consumer buyers from making commercial use of the product. Such a term limits arbitrage. One can only speculate about whether ProCD has sufficient market power to successfully discriminate. Judge Easterbrook comments that ProCD has rivals. Market power declines as the number of rivals increases. But a firm does not have to be a monopolist to price discriminate. Some measure of market power is provided by the copyright which protects the search engine used in the software and the high fixed cost of selecting and maintaining the database. Time will tell. Persistent discriminatory pricing suggests sufficient market power. . . .

Economists use a three-way classification scheme for price discrimination depending on how preferences are measured. In third degree price discrimination, price differentials are tied to a characteristic of a buyer that is correlated with the buyer's valuation. An example is a senior citizen who gets a discounted movie ticket. The seller observes the characteristic and infers that on average this type of buyer has a lower valuation. In second degree price discrimination, price differentials are tied to actions chosen by the buyer. The seller believes that certain actions reflect the preferences of a low valuation buyer and other actions reflect the preferences of a high valuation buyer. In the movie example, a Tuesday night discount illustrates second degree price discrimination. In first degree price discrimination, the seller knows or learns the exact valuation of all buyers. This, of course, is an idealized benchmark.

The distinction between second and third degree discrimination is important because second degree discrimination is usually more costly to implement. The greater cost arises from the need to get buyers to sort themselves in a manner that makes discrimination possible. Economists call this a sorting condition. The price and characteristics of the good intended for the low end of the market must not attract the high end, and the price and characteristics of the good intended for the high end must not attract the low end. The sorting condition imposes an implicit cost on the seller because it restricts the freedom of the seller to set efficient prices. With third degree price discrimination the seller can choose prices for the two classes of consumers independently. With second degree price discrimination the prices are linked. Economic theory shows that a monopoly seller should set the efficient price for the high valuation consumers and an inefficient price for the low valuation consumers. This inefficiency yields the implicit cost of sorting.

Second degree price discrimination is common in the software market. A simple method is to grant a site license. A site license authorizes a customer to install a certain number of copies of software on stand alone machines at a site, or allow a certain number of networked users to access the software on a server. By making licensing fees sensitive to the number of users at a site, the seller can profitably discriminate as long as the number of users has a positive correlation to value.

Software publishers also use product design to facilitate second degree price discrimination. Educational versions of software may sell for a fraction of the price of standard versions. Sellers disable some of the features in the standard version so the quality is reduced. A similar strategy is to include documentation and customer support with the standard version and not with the educational version. Buyers who prize quality must pay more for the standard version, and students who are less sensitive to quality buy the cheaper version. Sorting will not occur unless the discount is large enough to justify the quality reduction to the low valuation buyers. But the discount cannot be too large or both types of buyers will purchase the cheap version.

If it is feasible to check student IDs before selling a cheap version then third degree price discrimination is possible. Comparing optimal second and third degree discrimination: both lead to the same price for the expensive version, while third degree price discrimination leads to a lower price on the cheap version and higher profits to the seller. The important intuition behind the economic theory is that the sorting condition reduces the seller's freedom and less freedom means lower profit. This discussion shows that sellers prefer third degree discrimination. But in many markets sellers are forced to rely on second degree discrimination because they cannot condition sales terms on directly relevant buyer characteristics.

A more sophisticated version of second degree price discrimination requires metering. In some cases metering can approximate first degree price discrimination. A classic example is provided in the antitrust case International Business Machines v. United States. IBM tied the sales of its tabulator machines to purchases of punch cards that were used in the machines. The likely purpose of this tied sale was to implement price discrimination. Discrimination was accomplished by charging a relatively low price for the tabulators, and a price above the competitive price for the punch cards. The purchase of punch cards meters (or measures) the frequency of use of the tabulator. The effect of the tied sale is to charge a high price to those who use the machine frequently and a low price to infrequent users. IBM reasonably believed that frequent use was positively correlated with high valuation.

Suppliers can sometimes directly meter the use of their product. Photocopy machines have counters that record the number of copies that have been made. Lease agreements often charge rates that depend directly on measured usage. Digital technology will expand the use of direct metering. For example, rather than selling hard copies of encyclopedias at a fixed price, a digital publisher could offer access to a digital encyclopedia and charge based on usage. Frequent users pay more for access and infrequent users pay less. As long as use is linked to value, metering can implement price discrimination. . . .

Arbitrage is limited by many factors; I concentrate on the role of transaction costs, technology, and law because they are especially relevant to digital works. Even though arbitrage is feasible sometimes it does not happen because the transaction costs are too high. In the movie example, even if the ticket taker is not very vigilant arbitrage would be limited by the hassle of setting up a secondary market in movie tickets. Further, theaters would resist arbitrage by limiting ticket sales to a small number per customer. In a digital world where it may be possible to buy individual songs or newspaper articles or photographs for pennies, small scale arbitrage might be too costly and large scale arbitrage too easily detected to be feasible.

When quality differentials are the source of price discrimination, arbitrage may be blocked by technology. As described above, educational discounts accompany software that has limited features compared to the higher priced version. Arbitrage is only possible if an educational user can alter the software to add or restore the missing features at a cost less than the discriminatory price differential.

New digital distribution technologies promise to limit arbitrage opportunities for digital works. Many transactions involving copyrighted works are being converted from sales of goods to sales of services. Text published in encyclopedias or legal digests can be resold, but a subscription to a database cannot. Videotapes can be resold but video that is delivered over the Internet by streaming technology cannot. On the other hand, the transaction costs that block arbitrage will fall as digital commerce appears.

The possibility of contract or copyright lawsuits raises the barrier to arbitrage of copyrighted works. The link between the first sale doctrine and arbitrage is obvious. If favored buyers can purchase a work and then sell or lease it to disfavored buyers then price discrimination may be defeated. Contract restrictions on resale or other transfers deter arbitrage.

Contract terms can impede arbitrage in other ways. In *ProCD* a field of use restriction in the software contract did the job. Customers were sorted into the commercial and consumer categories and charged different prices. The favored consumer buyers were discouraged from making commercial use of the database by the threat of contract litigation. The tying contract in *IBM* was designed to prevent high valuation customers from buying low cost punch cards in the open market. Contracts often limit the modification of software or the movement (migration) of software from one platform to another. One purpose of this limitation is to reduce arbitrage possibilities. For example, an application program like a statistics package can be designed to run on a DOS or UNIX operating system. The UNIX buyers tend to have more powerful machines and higher valuations for the software. If the price charged for UNIX versions is higher, then UNIX buyers may want to purchase a DOS version and modify it to run on UNIX. This arbitrage can be deterred if the price differential is less than the cost of modification. But the seller might want a larger price differential which makes the contract limitation valuable.

COMMENTS AND QUESTIONS

Sometimes licensors of information might want users to copy and disseminate an informational work, either because this will lead to indirect revenues (e.g., the later sale of related items), or because it will cause the copied work to become a standard of one sort or another, leading to enhanced revenues later. Consider the following from Lisa N. Takeyama, The Welfare Implications of Unauthorized Reproduction of Intellectual Property in the Presence of Demand Network Externalities, 42 J. Ind. Econ. 155 (1994):

> [U]nauthorized reproduction of intellectual property in the presence of demand network externalities can not only induce greater firm profits relative to the case where there is no copying, it can lead to a Pareto improvement in social welfare. Ceteris paribus, when network externalities are present, firms have a greater incentive to expand output because marginal revenue is higher and/or they may wish to create preemptive installed bases. [U]nauthorized copying can [also] be a relatively efficient means of achieving this by allowing the firm, in effect, to "price discriminate" among different classes of consumers.

This latter argument is dependent on the presence of strong network effects, so that expanding market share (even at a price of 0) brings its own rewards: existing and future customers value the product more highly than they would if it had a small market share. See also Mark A. Lemley & David McGowan, Legal Implications of Network Economic Effects, 86 Cal. L. Rev. 479, 523-541 (1998).

3. Control After Resale

Yet another economic motivation for vendors to license rather than sell their products is to enable them to retain control over those products after they have been delivered to customers. Both intellectual property and antitrust law draw a distinction between a vendor's control of its product before sale and attempts to control the product after it has been sold. Thus, copyright's "first sale" doctrine, 17 U.S.C. §109(a), provides that a copyright owner has no right to control the use or distribution of a particular copy of her work once it has been sold to another. The buyer can dispose of *that particular copy* as he wishes, at least so long as he does not violate another of the copyright owner's exclusive rights (e.g., by making additional copies or publicly performing the work). This means that a buyer is generally free to resell his copy of the work, to lend it to others, and in most cases even to rent it out for profit.[3] Similarly, patent law's "exhaustion" doctrine provides that the sale of a patented device to a customer carries with it an implied license to the customer allowing him to use or resell the device. Trademark law contains a similar exhaustion rule, which permits consumers, for example, to advertise and sell their used cars using the trademarked brand name. And antitrust law precludes certain efforts on the part of vendors to control the conditions under which a product may be resold—notably, efforts to set the resale price.

Why might a software vendor want to control the use or disposition of its product after it has been sold to a customer? A number of possible reasons come to mind. First, control over resale may be necessary to make a price discrimination scheme work. As noted above, price discrimination is possible only if the seller has some means to prevent arbitrage. If low-cost buyers could resell their products to high-cost buyers, they would swiftly undermine any such scheme for price discrimination. If the software vendor can control resale, either by precluding it entirely or by limiting the class of purchasers to whom a buyer can resell, the vendor may be able to prop up a price discrimination scheme.

Second, a software vendor may simply not be willing to sell to a particular class of purchasers at all, such as to its major competitor or to a company that it suspects might compete with it in a downstream market, or perhaps to a company that is suing it on an unrelated matter. Preventing

---

3. Section 109(c) of the Copyright Act creates an exception for computer software and music, which cannot be rented for profit. Other works in digital form, such as books, movies, and even video games, can be rented out by the owner of the copy without the permission of the copyright owner.

the resale of software by a buyer, or conditioning resale on prior approval from the vendor, is a way to achieve these goals. (Whether software vendors *should* be able to achieve these goals is another matter. Certainly some restrictions that vendors periodically impose, such as a contract provision prohibiting the buyer from competing against the seller, are potentially anticompetitive, especially when the software vendor has market power.)

For a discussion of restrictions on transferability, both under current law and under the draft UCITA, see David A. Rice, License with Contract and Precedent: Publisher-Licensor Protection Consequences and the Rationale Offered for the Nontransferability of Licenses Under Article 2B, 13 Berkeley Tech. L.J. 1239 (1998). Among other things, Rice argues that the idea of nontransferability is inconsistent with general principles of contract and commercial law.

COMMENTS AND QUESTIONS

It is worth noting that most of these rationales are not limited to the software industry. Sellers of books, cars, and copy machines would doubtless like to be able to bundle products, price-discriminate, and control the use of their products after a first sale. It is worth considering why all sorts of goods aren't licensed rather than sold. Is there something about the software industry that makes the license mechanism uniquely viable? Or should we expect to see a wide variety of manufacturers attempting to license their products in the future?

C. CONTRACT FORMATION, ENFORCEMENT, AND WARRANTIES

1. Contract Formation

a. *Contract Formation Under UCC Article 2*

Step-Saver Data Systems v. Wyse Technology
United States Court of Appeals for the Third Circuit
939 F.2d 91 (3d Cir. 1991)

WISDOM, Circuit Judge.

The "Limited Use License Agreement" printed on a package containing a copy of a computer program raises the central issue in this appeal. The trial judge held that the terms of the Limited Use License Agreement governed the purchase of the package, and, therefore, granted the software producer, The Software Link, Inc. ("TSL"), a directed verdict on claims of breach of warranty brought by a disgruntled purchaser, Step-Saver Data Systems, Inc. We disagree with the district court's determination of the legal effect of the license, and reverse and remand the warranty claims for further consideration. . . .

I.   Factual and Procedural Background

The growth in the variety of computer hardware and software has created a strong market for these products. It has also created a difficult choice for consumers, as they must somehow decide which of the many available products will best suit their needs. To assist consumers in this decision process, some companies will evaluate the needs of particular groups of potential computer users, compare those needs with the available technology, and develop a package of hardware and software to satisfy those needs. Beginning in 1981, Step-Saver performed this function as a value added retailer for International Business Machine (IBM) products. It would combine hardware and software to satisfy the word processing, data management, and communications needs for offices of physicians and lawyers. It originally marketed single computer systems, based primarily on the IBM personal computer. . . .

After evaluating the available technology, Step-Saver selected a program by TSL, entitled Multilink Advanced, as the operating system for the multi-user system. Step-Saver selected WY-60 terminals manufactured by Wyse, and used an IBM AT as the main computer. For applications software, Step-Saver included in the package several off-the-shelf programs, designed to run under Microsoft's Disk Operating System ("MS-DOS"), as well as several programs written by Step-Saver. Step-Saver began marketing the system in November of 1986, and sold one hundred forty-two systems mostly to law and medical offices before terminating sales of the system in March of 1987. Almost immediately upon installation of the system, Step-Saver began to receive complaints from some of its customers.

Step-Saver, in addition to conducting its own investigation of the problems, referred these complaints to Wyse and TSL, and requested technical assistance in resolving the problems. After several preliminary attempts to address the problems, the three companies were unable to reach a satisfactory solution, and disputes developed among the three concerning responsibility for the problems. As a result, the problems were never solved. At least twelve of Step-Saver's customers filed suit against Step-Saver because of the problems with the multi-user system.

Once it became apparent that the three companies would not be able to resolve their dispute amicably, . . . Step-Saver then filed a . . . complaint alleging breach of warranties by both TSL and Wyse and intentional misrepresentations by TSL. The district court's actions during the resolution of this second complaint provide the foundation for this appeal.

On the first day of trial, the district court specifically agreed with the basic contention of TSL that the form language printed on each package containing the Multilink Advanced program ("the box-top license") was the complete and exclusive agreement between Step-Saver and TSL under §2-202 of the Uniform Commercial Code (UCC).[6] Based on §2-316 of the UCC, the district court held that the box-top license disclaimed all express and implied warranties otherwise made by TSL. . . .

The trial proceeded on Step-Saver's breach of warranties claims against Wyse. At the conclusion of Wyse's evidence, the district judge denied Step-Saver's request for rebuttal testimony on the issue of the ordinary uses of the WY-60 terminal. The district court instructed the jury on the issues of express warranty and implied warranty of fitness for a particular purpose. Over Step-Saver's objection, the district court found insufficient evidence to support a finding that Wyse had breached its implied warranty of merchantability, and refused to instruct the jury on such warranty. The jury returned a verdict in favor of Wyse on the two warranty issues submitted.

Step-Saver appeals. . . .

II.   The Effect of the Box-Top License

The relationship between Step-Saver and TSL began in the fall of 1984 when Step-Saver asked TSL for information on an early version of the Multilink program. TSL provided Step-Saver with a copy of the early program, known simply as Multilink, without charge to permit Step-Saver to test the program to see what it could accomplish. Step-Saver performed some tests with the early program, but did not market a system based on it.

In the summer of 1985, Step-Saver noticed some advertisements in Byte magazine for a more powerful version of the Multilink program, known as Multilink Advanced. Step-Saver requested information from TSL concerning this new version of the program, and allegedly was assured by sales representatives that the new version was compatible with ninety percent of the programs available "off-the-shelf" for computers using MS-DOS. The sales representatives allegedly made a number of additional specific representations of fact concerning the capabilities of the Multilink Advanced program.

Based on these representations, Step-Saver obtained several copies of the Multilink Advanced program in the spring of 1986, and conducted tests with the program. After these tests, Step-Saver decided to market a multi-user system which used the Multilink Advanced program. From August of 1986 through March of 1987, Step-Saver purchased and resold 142 copies of the Multilink Advanced program. Step-Saver would typically

---

6. All three parties agree that the terminals and the program are "goods" within the meaning of UCC §§2-102 & 2-105. Cf. Advent Sys. Ltd. v. Unisys Corp., 925 F.2d 670, 674-76 (3d Cir. 1991). . . .

purchase copies of the program in the following manner. First, Step-Saver would telephone TSL and place an order. (Step-Saver would typically order twenty copies of the program at a time.) TSL would accept the order and promise, while on the telephone, to ship the goods promptly. After the telephone order, Step-Saver would send a purchase order, detailing the items to be purchased, their price, and shipping and payment terms. TSL would ship the order promptly, along with an invoice. The invoice would contain terms essentially identical with those on Step-Saver's purchase order: price, quantity, and shipping and payment terms. No reference was made during the telephone calls, or on either the purchase orders or the invoices with regard to a disclaimer of any warranties.

Printed on the package of each copy of the program, however, would be a copy of the box-top license. The box-top license contains five terms relevant to this action:

> (1) The box-top license provides that the customer has not purchased the software itself, but has merely obtained a personal, non-transferable license to use the program.
> (2) The box-top license, in detail and at some length, disclaims all express and implied warranties except for a warranty that the disks contained in the box are free from defects.
> (3) The box-top license provides that the sole remedy available to a purchaser of the program is to return a defective disk for replacement; the license excludes any liability for damages, direct or consequential, caused by the use of the program.
> (4) The box-top license contains an integration clause, which provides that the box-top license is the final and complete expression of the terms of the parties's agreement.
> (5) The box-top license states: "Opening this package indicates your acceptance of these terms and conditions. If you do not agree with them, you should promptly return the package unopened to the person from whom you purchased it within fifteen days from date of purchase and your money will be refunded to you by that person."

The district court, without much discussion, held, as a matter of law, that the box-top license was the final and complete expression of the terms of the parties's agreement. . . .

Step-Saver contends that the contract for each copy of the program was formed when TSL agreed, on the telephone, to ship the copy at the agreed price. The box-top license, argues Step-Saver, was a material alteration to the parties's contract which did not become a part of the contract under UCC §2-207.[10] Alternatively, Step-Saver argues that the undisputed

---

10. Section 2-207 provides:

Additional Terms in Acceptance or Confirmation.

(1) A definite and seasonable expression of acceptance or a written confirmation which is sent within a reasonable time operates as an acceptance even though it states

evidence establishes that the parties did not intend the box-top license as a final and complete expression of the terms of their agreement, and, therefore, the parol evidence rule of UCC §2-202 would not apply.[11]

TSL argues that the contract between TSL and Step-Saver did not come into existence until Step-Saver received the program, saw the terms of the license, and opened the program packaging. TSL contends that too many material terms were omitted from the telephone discussion for that discussion to establish a contract for the software. Second, TSL contends that its acceptance of Step-Saver's telephone offer was conditioned on Step-Saver's acceptance of the terms of the box-top license. Therefore, TSL argues, it did not accept Step-Saver's telephone offer, but made a counter-offer represented by the terms of the box-top license, which was accepted when Step-Saver opened each package. Third, TSL argues that, however the contract was formed, Step-Saver was aware of the warranty disclaimer, and that Step-Saver, by continuing to order and accept the product with knowledge of the disclaimer, assented to the disclaimer.

In analyzing these competing arguments, we first consider whether the license should be treated as an integrated writing under UCC §2-202, as a proposed modification under UCC §2-209, or as a written confirmation under UCC §2-207. Finding that UCC §2-207 best governs our resolution of the effect of the box-top license, we then consider whether, under UCC §2-207, the terms of the box-top license were incorporated into the parties's agreement.

A. Does UCC §2-207 Govern the Analysis?

As a basic principle, we agree with Step-Saver that UCC §2-207 governs our analysis. We see no need to parse the parties's various actions to

---

terms additional to or different from those offered or agreed upon, unless acceptance is expressly made conditional on assent to the additional or different terms.

(2) The additional terms are to be construed as proposals for addition to the contract. Between merchants such terms become part of the contract unless:

(a) the offer expressly limits acceptance to the terms of the offer;

(b) they materially alter it; or

(c) notification of objection to them has already been given or is given within a reasonable time after notice of them is received.

(3) Conduct by both parties which recognizes the existence of a contract is sufficient to establish a contract for sale although the writings of the parties do not otherwise establish a contract. In such case the terms of the particular contract consist of those terms on which the writings of the parties agree, together with any supplementary terms incorporated under any other provisions of the Act.

11. Two other issues were raised by Step-Saver. First, Step-Saver argued that the box-top disclaimer is either unconscionable or not in good faith. Second, Step-Saver argued that the warranty disclaimer was inconsistent with the express warranties made by TSL in the product specifications. Step-Saver argues that interpreting the form language of the license agreement to override the specific warranties contained in the product specification is unreasonable, citing Consolidated Data Terminals v. Applied Digital Data Sys., 708 F.2d 385 (9th Cir. 1983). See also Northern States Power Co. v. ITT Meyer Indus., 777 F.2d 405 (8th Cir. 1985). Because of our holding that the terms of the box-top license were not incorporated into the contract, we do not address these issues.

decide exactly when the parties formed a contract. TSL has shipped the product, and Step-Saver has accepted and paid for each copy of the program. The parties's performance demonstrates the existence of a contract. The dispute is, therefore, not over the existence of a contract, but the nature of its terms. When the parties's conduct establishes a contract, but the parties have failed to adopt expressly a particular writing as the terms of their agreement, and the writings exchanged by the parties do not agree, UCC §2-207 determines the terms of the contract.

As stated by the official comment to §2-207:

> 1. This section is intended to deal with two typical situations. The one is the written confirmation, where an agreement has been reached either orally or by informal correspondence between the parties and is followed by one or more of the parties sending formal memoranda embodying the terms so far as agreed upon and adding terms not discussed. . . .
>
> 2. Under this Article a proposed deal which in commercial understanding has in fact been closed is recognized as a contract. Therefore, any additional matter contained in the confirmation or in the acceptance falls within subsection (2) and must be regarded as a proposal for an added term unless the acceptance is made conditional on the acceptance of the additional or different terms.

Although UCC §2-202 permits the parties to reduce an oral agreement to writing, and UCC §2-209 permits the parties to modify an existing contract without additional consideration, a writing will be a final expression of, or a binding modification to, an earlier agreement only if the parties so intend. It is undisputed that Step-Saver never expressly agreed to the terms of the box-top license, either as a final expression of, or a modification to, the parties's agreement. In fact, Barry Greebel, the President of Step-Saver, testified without dispute that he objected to the terms of the box-top license as applied to Step-Saver. In the absence of evidence demonstrating an express intent to adopt a writing as a final expression of, or a modification to, an earlier agreement, we find UCC §2-207 to provide the appropriate legal rules for determining whether such an intent can be inferred from continuing with the contract after receiving a writing containing additional or different terms.

To understand why the terms of the license should be considered under §2-207 in this case, we review briefly the reasons behind §2-207. Under the common law of sales, and to some extent still for contracts outside the UCC, an acceptance that varied any term of the offer operated as a rejection of the offer, and simultaneously made a counteroffer. This common law formality was known as the mirror image rule, because the terms of the acceptance had to mirror the terms of the offer to be effective. If the offeror proceeded with the contract despite the differing terms of the supposed acceptance, he would, by his performance, constructively accept the terms of the "counteroffer", and be bound by its terms. As a result of these rules, the terms of the party who sent the last form, typically the seller, would become the terms of the parties's contract. This result was known as the "last shot rule".

The UCC, in §2-207, rejected this approach. Instead, it recognized that, while a party may desire the terms detailed in its form if a dispute, in fact, arises, most parties do not expect a dispute to arise when they first enter into a contract. As a result, most parties will proceed with the transaction even if they know that the terms of their form would not be enforced. The insight behind the rejection of the last shot rule is that it would be unfair to bind the buyer of goods to the standard terms of the seller, when neither party cared sufficiently to establish expressly the terms of their agreement, simply because the seller sent the last form. Thus, UCC §2-207 establishes a legal rule that proceeding with a contract after receiving a writing that purports to define the terms of the parties's contract is not sufficient to establish the party's consent to the terms of the writing to the extent that the terms of the writing either add to, or differ from, the terms detailed in the parties's earlier writings or discussions. In the absence of a party's express assent to the additional or different terms of the writing, section 2-207 provides a default rule that the parties intended, as the terms of their agreement, those terms to which both parties have agreed, along with any terms implied by the provisions of the UCC.

The reasons that led to the rejection of the last shot rule, and the adoption of section 2-207, apply fully in this case. TSL never mentioned during the parties's negotiations leading to the purchase of the programs, nor did it, at any time, obtain Step-Saver's express assent to, the terms of the box-top license. Instead, TSL contented itself with attaching the terms to the packaging of the software, even though those terms differed substantially from those previously discussed by the parties. Thus, the box-top license, in this case, is best seen as one more form in a battle of forms, and the question of whether Step-Saver has agreed to be bound by the terms of the box-top license is best resolved by applying the legal principles detailed in section 2-207.

B. Application of §2-207

TSL advances several reasons why the terms of the box-top license should be incorporated into the parties's agreement under a §2-207 analysis. First, TSL argues that the parties's contract was not formed until Step-Saver received the package, saw the terms of the box-top license, and opened the package, thereby consenting to the terms of the license. TSL argues that a contract defined without reference to the specific terms provided by the box-top license would necessarily fail for indefiniteness. Second, TSL argues that the box-top license was a conditional acceptance and counter-offer under §2-207(1). Third, TSL argues that Step-Saver, by continuing to order and use the product with notice of the terms of the box-top license, consented to the terms of the box-top license.

[The court held that the terms of the telephone agreement and purchase order were sufficiently definite to constitute a contract, and under UCC §2-204 the remaining terms (including warranly provisions) could be filled in with default rules provided in the UCC itself. Next, the court discusses TSL's argument that its acceptance of the order for goods was conditional upon the conditions of the box-top license:]

Using this test, it is apparent that the integration clause and the "consent by opening" language is not sufficient to render TSL's acceptance conditional. As other courts have recognized, this type of language provides no real indication that the party is willing to forego the transaction if the additional language is not included in the contract.

The second provision [providing for a refund if the buyer returns the software within 15 days] provides a more substantial indication that TSL was willing to forego the contract if the terms of the box-top license were not accepted by Step-Saver. On its face, the box-top license states that TSL will refund the purchase price if the purchaser does not agree to the terms of the license. Even with such a refund term, however, the offeree/counterofferor may be relying on the purchaser's investment in time and energy in reaching this point in the transaction to prevent the purchaser from returning the item. Because a purchaser has made a decision to buy a particular product and has actually obtained the product, the purchaser may use it despite the refund offer, regardless of the additional terms specified after the contract formed. But we need not decide whether such a refund offer could ever amount to a conditional acceptance; the undisputed evidence in this case demonstrates that the terms of the license were not sufficiently important that TSL would forego its sales to Step-Saver if TSL could not obtain Step-Saver's consent to those terms.

As discussed, Mr. Greebel testified that TSL assured him that the box-top license did not apply to Step-Saver, as Step-Saver was not the end user of the Multilink Advanced program. Supporting this testimony, TSL on two occasions asked Step-Saver to sign agreements that would put in formal terms the relationship between Step-Saver and TSL. Both proposed agreements contained warranty disclaimer and limitation of remedy terms similar to those contained in the box-top license. Step-Saver refused to sign the agreements; nevertheless, TSL continued to sell copies of Multilink Advanced to Step-Saver.

Additionally, TSL asks us to infer, based on the refund offer, that it was willing to forego its sales to Step-Saver unless Step-Saver agreed to the terms of the box-top license. Such an inference is inconsistent with the fact that both parties agree that the terms of the box-top license did not represent the parties's agreement with respect to Step-Saver's right to transfer the copies of the Multilink Advanced program. Although the box-top license prohibits the transfer, by Step-Saver, of its copies of the program, both parties agree that Step-Saver was entitled to transfer its copies to the purchasers of the Step-Saver multi-user system. Thus, TSL was willing to proceed with the transaction despite the fact that one of the terms of the box-top license was not included in the contract between TSL and Step-Saver. We see no basis in the terms of the box-top license for inferring that a reasonable offeror would understand from the refund offer that certain terms of the box-top license, such as the warranty disclaimers, were essential to TSL, while others such as the non-transferability provision were not.

Based on these facts, we conclude that TSL did not clearly express its unwillingness to proceed with the transactions unless its additional terms were incorporated into the parties's agreement. The box-top license did not, therefore, constitute a conditional acceptance under UCC §2-207(1).

3. Did the Parties's Course of Dealing Establish That the Parties Had Excluded Any Express or Implied Warranties Associated with the Software Program?

TSL argues that because Step-Saver placed its orders for copies of the Multilink Advanced program with notice of the terms of the box-top license, Step-Saver is bound by the terms of the box-top license. Essentially, TSL is arguing that, even if the terms of the box-top license would not become part of the contract if the case involved only a single transaction, the repeated expression of those terms by TSL eventually incorporates them within the contract. . . .

For two reasons, we hold that the repeated sending of a writing which contains certain standard terms, without any action with respect to the issues addressed by those terms, cannot constitute a course of dealing which would incorporate a term of the writing otherwise excluded under §2-207. First, the repeated exchange of forms by the parties only tells Step-Saver that TSL desires certain terms. Given TSL's failure to obtain Step-Saver's express assent to these terms before it will ship the program, Step-Saver can reasonably believe that, while TSL desires certain terms, it has agreed to do business on other terms—those terms expressly agreed upon by the parties. Thus, even though Step-Saver would not be surprised to learn that TSL desires the terms of the box-top license, Step-Saver might well be surprised to learn that the terms of the box-top license have been incorporated into the parties's agreement.

Second, the seller in these multiple transaction cases will typically have the opportunity to negotiate the precise terms of the parties's agreement, as TSL sought to do in this case. The seller's unwillingness or inability to obtain a negotiated agreement reflecting its terms strongly suggests that, while the seller would like a court to incorporate its terms if a dispute were to arise, those terms are not a part of the parties's commercial bargain. For these reasons, we are not convinced that TSL's unilateral act of repeatedly sending copies of the box-top license with its product can establish a course of dealing between TSL and Step-Saver that resulted in the adoption of the terms of the box-top license. . . .

4. Public Policy Concerns.

TSL has raised a number of public policy arguments focusing on the effect on the software industry of an adverse holding concerning the enforceability of the box-top license. We are not persuaded that requiring software companies to stand behind representations concerning their products will inevitably destroy the software industry. We emphasize, however, that we are following the well-established distinction between conspicuous disclaimers made available before the contract is formed and disclaimers made available only after the contract is formed.[45] When a disclaimer is not expressed until after the contract is formed, UCC §2-207 governs the interpretation of the contract, and, between merchants, such disclaimers, to the extent they materially alter the parties's agreement, are not incorporated into the parties's agreement.

If TSL wants relief for its business operations from this well-established rule, their arguments are better addressed to a legislature than a court.

C. *The Terms of the Contract*

Under section 2-207, an additional term detailed in the box-top license will not be incorporated into the parties's contract if the term's addition to the contract would materially alter the parties's agreement. Step-Saver alleges that several representations made by TSL constitute express warranties, and that valid implied warranties were also a part of the parties's agreement. Because the district court considered the box-top license to exclude all of these warranties, the district court did not consider whether other factors may act to exclude these warranties. The existence and nature of the warranties is primarily a factual question that we leave for the district court, but assuming that these warranties were included within the parties's original agreement, we must conclude that adding the disclaimer of warranty and limitation of remedies provisions from the box-top license would, as a matter of law, substantially alter the distribution of risk between Step-Saver and TSL. Therefore, under UCC §2-207(2)(b), the disclaimer of warranty and limitation of remedies terms of the box-top license did not become a part of the parties's agreement.

---

45. Compare Hill v. BASF Wyandotte Corp., 696 F.2d 287, 290-91 (4th Cir. 1982). In that case, a farmer purchased seventy-three five gallon cans of a herbicide from a retailer. Because the disclaimer was printed conspicuously on each can, the farmer had constructive knowledge of the terms of the disclaimer before the contract formed. As a result, when he selected each can of the herbicide from the shelf and purchased it, the law implies his assent to the terms of the disclaimer. See also Bowdoin v. Showell Growers, Inc., 817 F.2d 1543, 1545 (11th Cir. 1987) (disclaimers that were conspicuous before the contract for sale has formed are effective; post-sale disclaimers are ineffective); Monsanto Agricultural Prods. Co. v. Edenfield, 426 So. 2d at 575-76.

Based on these considerations, we reverse the trial court's holding that the parties intended the box-top license to be a final and complete expression of the terms of their agreement. Despite the presence of an integration clause in the box-top license, the box-top license should have been treated as a written confirmation containing additional terms. Because the warranty disclaimer and limitation of remedies terms would materially alter the parties's agreement, these terms did not become a part of the parties's agreement. We remand for further consideration the express and implied warranty claims against TSL. . . .

ProCD, Inc. v. Zeidenberg
United States Court of Appeals for the Seventh Circuit
86 F.3d 1447 (7th Cir. 1996)

EASTERBROOK, Circuit Judge.

Must buyers of computer software obey the terms of shrinkwrap licenses? The district court held not, for two reasons: first, they are not contracts because the licenses are inside the box rather than printed on the outside; second, federal law forbids enforcement even if the licenses are contracts. 908 F. Supp. 640 (W.D. Wis. 1996). The parties and numerous amici curiae have briefed many other issues, but these are the only two that matter—and we disagree with the district judge's conclusion on each. Shrinkwrap licenses are enforceable unless their terms are objectionable on grounds applicable to contracts in general (for example, if they violate a rule of positive law, or if they are unconscionable). Because no one argues that the terms of the license at issue here are troublesome, we remand with instructions to enter judgment for the plaintiff.

I

ProCD, the plaintiff, has compiled information from more than 3,000 telephone directories into a computer database. We may assume that this database cannot be copyrighted, although it is more complex, contains more information (nine-digit zip codes and census industrial codes), is organized differently, and therefore is more original than the single alphabetical directory at issue in Feist Publications, Inc. v. Rural Telephone Service Co., 499 U.S. 340, 113 L. Ed. 2d 358, 111 S. Ct. 1282 (1991). See Paul J. Heald, The Vices of Originality, 1991 Sup. Ct. Rev. 143, 160-68. ProCD sells a version of the database, called SelectPhone (trademark), on CD-ROM discs. (CD-ROM means "compact disc—read only memory." The "shrinkwrap license" gets its name from the fact that retail software packages are covered in plastic or cellophane "shrinkwrap," and some vendors, though not ProCD, have written licenses that become effective as soon as the customer tears the wrapping from the package.

Vendors prefer "end user license," but we use the more common term.) A proprietary method of compressing the data serves as effective encryption too. Customers decrypt and use the data with the aid of an application program that ProCD has written. This program, which is copyrighted, searches the database in response to users' criteria (such as "find all people named Tatum in Tennessee, plus all firms with 'Door Systems' in the corporate name"). The resulting lists (or, as ProCD prefers, "listings") can be read and manipulated by other software, such as word processing programs.

The database in SelectPhone™ cost more than $10 million to compile and is expensive to keep current. It is much more valuable to some users than to others. The combination of names, addresses, and SIC codes enables manufacturers to compile lists of potential customers. Manufacturers and retailers pay high prices to specialized information intermediaries for such mailing lists; ProCD offers a potentially cheaper alternative. People with nothing to sell could use the database as a substitute for calling long distance information, or as a way to look up old friends who have moved to unknown towns, or just as a electronic substitute for the local phone book. ProCD decided to engage in price discrimination, selling its database to the general public for personal use at a low price (approximately $150 for the set of five discs) while selling information to the trade for a higher price. It has adopted some intermediate strategies too: access to the SelectPhone (trademark) database is available via the America Online service for the price America Online charges to its clients (approximately $3 per hour), but this service has been tailored to be useful only to the general public.

If ProCD had to recover all of its costs and make a profit by charging a single price—that is, if it could not charge more to commercial users than to the general public—it would have to raise the price substantially over $150. The ensuing reduction in sales would harm consumers who value the information at, say, $200. They get consumer surplus of $50 under the current arrangement but would cease to buy if the price rose substantially. If because of high elasticity of demand in the consumer segment of the market the only way to make a profit turned out to be a price attractive to commercial users alone, then all consumers would lose out—and so would the commercial clients, who would have to pay more for the listings because ProCD could not obtain any contribution toward costs from the consumer market.

To make price discrimination work, however, the seller must be able to control arbitrage. An air carrier sells tickets for less to vacationers than to business travelers, using advance purchase and Saturday-night-stay requirements to distinguish the categories. A producer of movies segments the market by time, releasing first to theaters, then to pay-per-view services, next to the videotape and laserdisc market, and finally to cable and commercial tv. Vendors of computer software have a harder task. Anyone can walk into a retail store and buy a box. Customers do not wear tags saying "commercial user" or "consumer user." Anyway, even a commercial-user-detector at the door would not work, because a consumer could buy the software and resell to a commercial user. That arbitrage would break down the price discrimination and drive up the minimum price at which ProCD would sell to anyone.

Instead of tinkering with the product and letting users sort themselves —or example, furnishing current data at a high price that would be attractive only to commercial customers, and two-year-old data at a low price— ProCD turned to the institution of contract. Every box containing its consumer product declares that the software comes with restrictions stated in an enclosed license. This license, which is encoded on the CD-ROM disks as well as printed in the manual, and which appears on a user's screen every time the software runs, limits use of the application program and listings to non-commercial purposes.

Matthew Zeidenberg bought a consumer package of SelectPhone (trademark) in 1994 from a retail outlet in Madison, Wisconsin, but decided to ignore the license. He formed Silken Mountain Web Services, Inc., to resell the information in the SelectPhone (trademark) database. The corporation makes the database available on the Internet to anyone willing to pay its price—which, needless to say, is less than ProCD charges its commercial customers. Zeidenberg has purchased two additional Select-Phone (trademark) packages, each with an updated version of the database, and made the latest information available over the World Wide Web, for a price, through his corporation. ProCD filed this suit seeking an injunction against further dissemination that exceeds the rights specified in the licenses (identical in each of the three packages Zeidenberg purchased). The district court held the licenses ineffectual because their terms do not appear on the outside of the packages. The court added that the second and third licenses stand no different from the first, even though they are identical, because they might have been different, and a purchaser does not agree to —and cannot be bound by—terms that were secret at the time of purchase. 908 F. Supp. at 654.

II

Following the district court, we treat the licenses as ordinary contracts accompanying the sale of products, and therefore as governed by the common law of contracts and the Uniform Commercial Code. Whether there are legal differences between "contracts" and "licenses" (which may matter under the copyright doctrine of first sale) is a subject for another day. See Microsoft Corp. v. Harmony Computers & Electronics, Inc., 846 F. Supp. 208 (E.D. N.Y. 1994). Zeidenberg does not argue that Silken Mountain Web Services is free of any restrictions that apply to Zeidenberg himself, because any effort to treat the two parties as distinct would put Silken Mountain behind the eight ball on ProCD's argument that copying the application program onto its hard disk violates the copyright laws. Zeidenberg does argue, and the district court held, that placing the package of software on the shelf is an "offer," which the customer "accepts" by paying the asking price and leaving the store with the goods. Peters v. State, 154 Wis. 111, 142 N.W. 181 (1913). In Wisconsin, as elsewhere, a contract includes only the terms on which the parties have agreed. One cannot agree to hidden terms, the judge concluded. So far, so good—but one of the terms to which Zeidenberg agreed by purchasing the software is that the transaction was subject to a license. Zeidenberg's position therefore must be that the printed terms on the outside of a box are the parties' contract—except for printed terms that refer to or incorporate other terms. But why would Wisconsin fetter the parties' choice in this way? Vendors can put the entire terms of a contract on the outside of a box only by using microscopic type, removing other information that buyers might find more useful (such as what the software does, and on which computers it works), or both. The "Read Me" file included with most software, describing system requirements and potential incompatibilities, may be equivalent to ten pages of type; warranties and license restrictions take still more space. Notice on the outside, terms on the inside, and a right to return the software for a refund if the terms are unacceptable (a right that the license expressly extends), may be a means of doing business valuable to buyers and sellers alike. See E. Allan Farnsworth, 1 Farnsworth on Contracts §2.6 (1990); Restatement (2d) of Contracts §211 comment a (1981) ("Standardization of agreements serves many of the same functions as standardization of goods and services; both are essential to a system of mass production and distribution. Scarce and costly time and skill can be devoted to a class of transactions rather than the details of individual transactions."). Doubtless a state could forbid the use of standard contracts in the software business, but we do not think that Wisconsin has done so.

Transactions in which the exchange of money precedes the communication of detailed terms are common. Consider the purchase of insurance. The buyer goes to an agent, who explains the essentials (amount of coverage, number of years) and remits the premium to the home office, which sends back a policy. On the district judge's understanding, the terms of the policy are irrelevant because the insured paid before receiving them. Yet the device of payment, often with a "binder" (so that the insurance takes effect immediately even though the home office reserves the right to withdraw coverage later), in advance of the policy, serves buyers' interests by accelerating effectiveness and reducing transactions costs. Or consider the purchase of an airline ticket. The traveler calls the carrier or an agent, is quoted a price, reserves a seat, pays, and gets a ticket, in that order. The ticket contains elaborate terms, which the traveler can reject by canceling the reservation. To use the ticket is to accept the terms, even terms that in retrospect are disadvantageous. See Carnival Cruise Lines, Inc. v. Shute, 499 U.S. 585, 113 L. Ed. 2d 622, 111 S. Ct. 1522 (1991); see also Vimar Seguros y Reaseguros, S.A. v. M/V Sky Reefer, 132 L. Ed. 2d 462,

115 S. Ct. 2322 (1995) (bills of lading). Just so with a ticket to a concert. The back of the ticket states that the patron promises not to record the concert; to attend is to agree. A theater that detects a violation will confiscate the tape and escort the violator to the exit. One could arrange things so that every concertgoer signs this promise before forking over money, but that cumbersome way of doing things not only would lengthen queues and raise prices but also would scotch the sale of tickets by phone or electronic data service.

Consumer goods work the same way. Someone who wants to buy a radio set visits a store, pays, and walks out with a box. Inside the box is a leaflet containing some terms, the most important of which usually is the warranty, read for the first time in the comfort of home. By Zeidenberg's lights, the warranty in the box is irrelevant; every consumer gets the standard warranty implied by the UCC in the event the contract is silent; yet so far as we are aware no state disregards warranties furnished with consumer products. Drugs come with a list of ingredients on the outside and an elaborate package insert on the inside. The package insert describes drug interactions, contraindications, and other vital information—but, if Zeidenberg is right, the purchaser need not read the package insert, because it is not part of the contract.

Next consider the software industry itself. Only a minority of sales take place over the counter, where there are boxes to peruse. A customer may place an order by phone in response to a line item in a catalog or a review in a magazine. Much software is ordered over the Internet by purchasers who have never seen a box. Increasingly software arrives by wire. There is no box; there is only a stream of electrons, a collection of information that includes data, an application program, instructions, many limitations ("MegaPixel 3.14159 cannot be used with Byte-Pusher 2.718"), and the terms of sale. The user purchases a serial number, which activates the software's features. On Zeidenberg's arguments, these unboxed sales are unfettered by terms—so the seller has made a broad warranty and must pay consequential damages for any shortfalls in performance, two "promises" that if taken seriously would drive prices through the ceiling or return transactions to the horse-and-buggy age.

According to the district court, the UCC does not countenance the sequence of money now, terms later. (Wisconsin's version of the UCC does not differ from the Official Version in any material respect, so we use the regular numbering system. Wis. Stat. §402.201 corresponds to UCC §2-201, and other citations are easy to derive.) One of the court's reasons —that by proposing as part of the draft Article 2B a new UCC §2-2203 that would explicitly validate standard-form user licenses, the American Law Institute and the National Conference of Commissioners on Uniform Laws have conceded the invalidity of shrinkwrap licenses under current law, see 908 F. Supp. at 655-66—depends on a faulty inference. To propose a change in a law's text is not necessarily to propose a change in the law's effect. New words may be designed to fortify the current rule with a more precise text that curtails uncertainty. To judge by the flux of law review articles discussing shrinkwrap licenses, uncertainty is much in need of reduction—although businesses seem to feel less uncertainty than do scholars, for only three cases (other than ours) touch on the subject, and none directly addresses it. See Step-Saver Data Systems, Inc. v. Wyse Technology, 939 F.2d 91 (3d Cir. 1991); Vault Corp. v. Quaid Software Ltd., 847 F.2d 255, 268-70 (5th Cir. 1988); Arizona Retail Systems, Inc. v. Software Link, Inc., 831 F. Supp. 759 (D. Ariz. 1993). As their titles suggest, these are not consumer transactions. Step-Saver is a battle-of-the-forms case, in which the parties exchange incompatible forms and a court must decide which prevails. See Northrop Corp. v. Litronic Industries, 29 F.3d 1173 (7th Cir. 1994) (Illinois law); Douglas G. Baird & Robert Weisberg, Rules, Standards, and the Battle of the Forms: A Reassessment of §2-207, 68 Va. L. Rev. 1217, 1227-31 (1982). Our case has only one form; UCC §2-207 is irrelevant. *Vault* holds that Louisiana's special shrinkwrap-license statute is preempted by federal law, a question to which we return. And *Arizona Retail Systems* did not reach the question, because the court found that the buyer knew the terms of the license before purchasing the software.

What then does the current version of the UCC have to say? We think that the place to start is §2-204(1): "A contract for sale of goods may be made in any manner sufficient to show agreement, including conduct by both parties which recognizes the existence of such a contract." A vendor, as master of the offer, may invite acceptance by conduct, and may propose limitations on the kind of conduct that constitutes acceptance. A buyer may accept by performing the acts the vendor proposes to treat as acceptance. And that is what happened. ProCD proposed a contract that a buyer would accept by using the software after having an opportunity to read the license at leisure. This Zeidenberg did. He had no choice, because the software splashed the license on the screen and would not let him proceed without indicating acceptance. So although the district judge was right to say that a contract can be, and often is, formed simply by paying the price and walking out of the store, the UCC permits contracts to be formed in other ways. ProCD proposed such a different way, and without protest Zeidenberg agreed. Ours is not a case in which a consumer opens a package to find an insert saying "you owe us an extra $10,000" and the seller files suit to collect. Any buyer finding such a demand can prevent formation of the contract by returning the package, as can any consumer who concludes that the terms of the license make the software worth less than the purchase price. Nothing in the UCC requires a seller to maximize the buyer's net gains.

Section 2-606, which defines "acceptance of goods", reinforces this understanding. A buyer accepts goods under §2-606(1)(b) when, after an opportunity to inspect, he fails to make an effective rejection under §2-602(1). ProCD extended an opportunity to reject if a buyer should find the license terms unsatisfactory; Zeidenberg inspected the package, tried out the software, learned of the license, and did not reject the goods. We refer to §2-606 only to show that the opportunity to return goods can be important; acceptance of an offer differs from acceptance of goods after delivery, see Gillen v. Atalanta Systems, Inc., 997 F.2d 280, 284 n.1 (7th Cir. 1993); but the UCC consistently permits the parties to structure their relations so that the buyer has a chance to make a final decision after a detailed review.

Some portions of the UCC impose additional requirements on the way parties agree on terms. A disclaimer of the implied warranty of merchantability must be "conspicuous." UCC §2-316(2), incorporating UCC §1-201(10). Promises to make firm offers, or to negate oral modifications, must be "separately signed." UCC §§2-205, 2-209(2). These special provisos reinforce the impression that, so far as the UCC is concerned, other terms may be as inconspicuous as the forum-selection clause on the back of the cruise ship ticket in Carnival Lines. Zeidenberg has not located any Wisconsin case—for that matter, any case in any state—holding that under the UCC the ordinary terms found in shrinkwrap licenses require any special prominence, or otherwise are to be undercut rather than enforced. In the end, the terms of the license are conceptually identical to the contents of the package. Just as no court would dream of saying that SelectPhone (trademark) must contain 3,100 phone books rather than 3,000, or must have data no more than 30 days old, or must sell for $100 rather than $150—although any of these changes would be welcomed by the customer, if all other things were held constant—so, we believe, Wisconsin would not let the buyer pick and choose among terms. Terms of use are no less a part of "the product" than are the size of the database and the speed with which the software compiles listings. Competition among vendors, not judicial revision of a package's contents, is how consumers are protected in a market economy. Digital Equipment Corp. v. Uniq Digital Technologies, Inc., 73 F.3d 756 (7th Cir. 1996). ProCD has rivals, which may elect to compete by offering superior software, monthly updates, improved terms of use, lower price, or a better compromise among these elements. As we stressed above, adjusting terms in buyers' favor might help Matthew Zeidenberg today (he already has the software) but would lead to a response, such as a higher price, that might make consumers as a whole worse off.

III

The district court held that, even if Wisconsin treats shrinkwrap licenses as contracts, §301(a) of the Copyright Act, 17 U.S.C. §301(a), prevents their enforcement. 908 F. Supp. at 656-59. The relevant part of §301(a) preempts any "legal or equitable rights [under state law] that are equivalent to any of the exclusive rights within the general scope of copyright as specified by section 106 in works of authorship that are fixed in a tangible medium of expression and come within the subject matter of copyright as specified by sections 102 and 103". ProCD's software and data are "fixed in a tangible medium of expression", and the district judge held that they are "within the subject matter of copyright". The latter conclusion is plainly right for the copyrighted application program, and the judge thought that the data likewise are "within the subject matter of copyright" even if, after *Feist*, they are not sufficiently original to be copyrighted. 908 F. Supp. at 656-57. Baltimore Orioles, Inc. v. Major League Baseball Players Ass'n, 805 F.2d 663, 676 (7th Cir. 1986), supports that conclusion, with which commentators agree. E.g., Paul Goldstein, III Copyright §15.2.3 (2d ed. 1996); Melville B. Nimmer & David Nimmer, Nimmer on Copyright §101[B] (1995); William F. Patry, II Copyright Law and Practice 1108-09 (1994). One function of §301(a) is to prevent states from giving special protection to works of authorship that Congress has decided should be in the public domain, which it can accomplish only if "subject matter of copyright" includes all works of a type covered by sections 102 and 103, even if federal law does not afford protection to them. Cf. Bonito Boats, Inc. v. Thunder Craft Boats, Inc., 489 U.S. 141, 103 L. Ed. 2d 118, 109 S. Ct. 971 (1989) (same principle under patent laws).

But are rights created by contract "equivalent to any of the exclusive rights within the general scope of copyright"? Three courts of appeals have answered "no." National Car Rental Systems, Inc. v. Computer Associates International, Inc., 991 F.2d 426, 433 (8th Cir. 1993); Taquino v. Teledyne Monarch Rubber, 893 F.2d 1488, 1501 (5th Cir. 1990); Acorn Structures, Inc. v. Swantz, 846 F.2d 923, 926 (4th Cir. 1988). The district court disagreed with these decisions, 908 F. Supp. at 658, but we think them sound. Rights "equivalent to any of the exclusive rights within the general scope of copyright" are rights established by law—rights that restrict the options of persons who are strangers to the author. Copyright law forbids duplication, public performance, and so on, unless the person wishing to copy or perform the work gets permission; silence means a ban on copying. A copyright is a right against the world. Contracts, by contrast, generally affect only their parties; strangers may do as they please, so contracts do not create "exclusive rights." Someone who found a copy of SelectPhone (trademark) on the street would not be affected by the shrinkwrap license—though the federal copyright laws of their own force would limit the finder's ability to copy or transmit the application program.

Think for a moment about trade secrets. One common trade secret is a customer list. After *Feist*, a simple alphabetical list of a firm's customers, with address and telephone numbers, could not be protected by copyright. Yet Kewanee Oil Co. v. Bicron Corp., 416 U.S. 470, 40 L. Ed. 2d 315, 94 S. Ct. 1879 (1974), holds that contracts about trade secrets may be enforced—precisely because they do not affect strangers' ability to discover and use the information independently. If the amendment of §301(a) in 1976 overruled *Kewanee* and abolished consensual protection of those trade secrets that cannot be copyrighted, no one has noticed—though abolition is a logical consequence of the district court's approach. Think, too, about everyday transactions in intellectual property. A customer visits a video store and rents a copy of Night of the Lepus. The customer's contract with the store limits use of the tape to home viewing and requires its return in two days. May the customer keep the tape, on the ground that §301(a) makes the promise unenforceable?

A law student uses the LEXIS database, containing public-domain documents, under a contract limiting the results to educational endeavors; may the student resell his access to this database to a law firm from which LEXIS seeks to collect a much higher hourly rate? Suppose ProCD hires a firm to scour the nation for telephone directories, promising to pay $100 for each that ProCD does not already have. The firm locates 100 new directories, which it sends to ProCD with an invoice for $10,000. ProCD incorporates the directories into its database; does it have to pay the bill? Surely yes; Aronson v. Quick Point Pencil Co., 440 U.S. 257, 59 L. Ed. 2d 296, 99 S. Ct. 1096 (1979), holds that promises to pay for intellectual property may be enforced even though federal law (in *Aronson*, the patent law) offers no protection against third-party uses of that property. See also Kennedy v. Wright, 851 F.2d 963 (7th Cir. 1988). But these illustrations are what our case is about. ProCD offers software and data for two prices: one for personal use, a higher price for commercial use. Zeidenberg wants to use the data without paying the seller's price; if the law student and Quick Point Pencil Co. could not do that, neither can Zeidenberg.

Although Congress possesses power to preempt even the enforcement of contracts about intellectual property—or railroads, on which see Norfolk & Western Ry. v. Train Dispatchers, 499 U.S. 117, 111 S. Ct. 1156, 113 L. Ed. 2d 95 (1991)—courts usually read preemption clauses to leave private contracts unaffected. American Airlines, Inc. v. Wolens, 130 L. Ed. 2d 715, 115 S. Ct. 817 (1995), provides a nice illustration. A federal statute preempts any state "law, rule, regulation, standard, or other provision . . . relating to rates, routes, or services of any air carrier." 49 U.S.C. App. §1305(a)(1). Does such a law preempt the law of contracts—so that, for example, an air carrier need not honor a quoted price (or a contract to reduce the price by the value of frequent flyer miles)? The Court allowed that it is possible to read the statute that broadly but thought such an interpretation would make little sense. Terms and conditions offered by contract reflect private ordering, essential to the efficient functioning of markets. 115 S. Ct. at 824-25. Although some principles that carry the name of contract law are designed to defeat rather than implement consensual transactions, *id.* at 826 n.8, the rules that respect private choice are not preempted by a clause such as §1305(a)(1). Section 301(a) plays a role similar to §1301(a)(1): it prevents states from substituting their own regulatory systems for those of the national government. Just as §301(a) does not itself interfere with private transactions in intellectual property, so it does not prevent states from respecting those transactions. Like the

Supreme Court in *Wolens*, we think it prudent to refrain from adopting a rule that anything with the label "contract" is necessarily outside the preemption clause: the variations and possibilities are too numerous to foresee. *National Car Rental* likewise recognizes the possibility that some applications of the law of contract could interfere with the attainment of national objectives and therefore come within the domain of §301(a). But general enforcement of shrinkwrap licenses of the kind before us does not create such interference.

Aronson emphasized that enforcement of the contract between Aronson and Quick Point Pencil Company would not withdraw any information from the public domain. That is equally true of the contract between ProCD and Zeidenberg. Everyone remains free to copy and disseminate all 3,000 telephone books that have been incorporated into ProCD's database. Anyone can add sic codes and zip codes. ProCD's rivals have done so. Enforcement of the shrinkwrap license may even make information more readily available, by reducing the price ProCD charges to consumer buyers. To the extent licenses facilitate distribution of object code while concealing the source code (the point of a clause forbidding disassembly), they serve the same procompetitive functions as does the law of trade secrets. Rockwell Graphic Systems, Inc. v. DEV Industries, Inc., 925 F.2d 174, 180 (7th Cir. 1991). Licenses may have other benefits for consumers: many licenses permit users to make extra copies, to use the software on multiple computers, even to incorporate the software into the user's products. But whether a particular license is generous or restrictive, a simple two-party contract is not "equivalent to any of the exclusive rights within the general scope of copyright" and therefore may be enforced.

REVERSED AND REMANDED.

Novell, Inc. v. Network Trade Center, 25 F. Supp. 2d 1218 (D. Utah 1997). [NTC was a software reseller that purchased outdated copies of Novell's NetWare software and then requested upgrades under a Novell replacement policy. This allowed NTC to offer cut-rate copies of up-to-date Novell software to its customers. For a discussion of trademark infringement issues in the context of NTC's business model, see the excerpt at Section B, above.]

NTC argues that it was an owner because it purchased NetWare software from authorized distributors in compliance with Novell's "upgrade" policy, which required the purchaser to hold title to an older version of networking software. NTC then argues that because it bought and sold the software as a good, as defined by the U.C.C., its customers also became owners of the NetWare software they purchased from NTC. NTC maintains that when it sold the software to end-users, unopened and unaltered, it relinquished all rights to the software and therefore it was not and is not liable for copyright infringement.

Novell argues that it retains ownership and that the "shrinkwrap" license included with each copy of NetWare is binding, giving to authorized purchasers only a license to use the software. Novell submits that the license only allows end-users who have purchased the software in compliance with the "upgrade" policy to copy the software onto the hard drive.

Most courts that have addressed the validity of the shrinkwrap license have found them to be invalid, characterizing them as contracts of adhesion, unconscionable, and/or unacceptable pursuant to the U.C.C. *Step-Saver*, 939 F.2d 91; Vault Corp. v. Quaid Software Ltd., 847 F.2d 255 (5th Cir.1988); Rich, Mass Market Software and the Shrinkwrap License, 23 Colo. Law. 1321.[17] A minority of courts have determined that the shrinkwrap license is valid and enforceable. See, ProCD, Inc. v. Zeidenberg, 86 F.3d 1447, 1453 (7th Cir.1996); Microsoft v. Harmony Computers, 846 F.Supp. 208, 212 (E.D.N.Y.1994).

This Court holds that transactions making up the distribution chain from Novell through NTC to the end-user are "sales" governed by the U.C.C. Therefore, the first sale doctrine applies. It follows that the purchaser is an "owner" by way of sale and is entitled to the use and enjoyment of the software with the same rights as exist in the purchase of any other good. Said software transactions do not merely constitute the sale of a license to use the software. The shrinkwrap license included with the software is therefore invalid as against such a purchaser insofar as it purports to maintain title to the software in the copyright owner.

Based upon the foregoing, this Court rules that NTC's customers who obtained legally copyrighted materials from NTC did not violate the law and are therefore entitled to use the software in accordance with its intended use, including unrestricted copying of the software onto their hard drives.

COMMENTS AND QUESTIONS

1. As the district court in *Novell* indicates, *ProCD* is in the minority in enforcing a shrinkwrap license. Most courts that have considered the issue of shrinkwrap licenses have refused to enforce them. In addition to *Novell*, see Step-Saver v. Wyse Technology, 939 F.3d 91 (3d Cir. 1991); Vault Corp. v. Quaid, Inc., 847 F.2d 255 (5th Cir. 1988); Arizona Retail Sys. v. Software Link, Inc., 831 F. Supp. 759 (D. Ariz. 1993); cf. Morgan

---

17. The rationale in support of the majority position is that software users generally purchase the software through a retailer and consider the transaction as complete once the exchange of the software package is made at the register for the money. Later, as the new end-users attempt to use the software for the first time, they are presented an additional document setting forth conditions that in essence modify the original purchase agreement with the retailer. Courts are loathe to rule that such end-users should lose the benefits of ownership they had originally bargained for.

Labs, Inc. v. Micro Data Base Sys., 41 U.S.P.Q.2d 1850 (N.D. Cal. 1997) (refusing to allow a shrinkwrap license to modify a prior signed contract); Foresight Resource Corp. v. Pfortmiller, 719 F. Supp. 1006 (D. Kan. 1989) (dictum). The reasoning of these cases differs, however. Some courts (*Arizona Retail*, for instance) follow the rationale of *Step-Saver*, holding that the shrinkwrap license should be treated as a "battle of the forms" under U.C.C. section 2-207. Other courts (*Pfortmiller*, the district court in *Vault*) conclude that shrinkwrap licenses are unenforceable as contracts of adhesion. And the Fifth Circuit in *Vault* relied on the federal intellectual property laws to preempt contrary provisions in shrinkwrap licenses. (See infra.) For a contrary view that follows *ProCD* and enforces a shrinkwrap license, see M.A. Mortenson Co. v. Timberline Software Corp., 970 P.2d 803 (Wash. App. 1999).

The contract of adhesion rationale is suspect. Under traditional doctrines of contract law, a "contract of adhesion" is a standardized contract prepared entirely by one party and, due to the disparity in bargaining power between the parties, is effectively offered on a "take it or leave it" basis. Contrary to the holding of the district court in *Vault*, contracts of adhesion are generally enforceable unless certain other factors (such as unconscionability) are present. According to the Restatement (Second) of Contracts, §211(3), "[w]here the other party has reason to believe that the party manifesting such assent would not do so if he knew that the writing contained a particular term, the term is not part of the agreement." Comment f states that "[r]eason to believe [that the adherent would not knowingly have signed] may be inferred from the fact that the term is bizarre or oppressive, from the fact that it eviscerates the nonstandard terms explicitly agreed to, or form the fact that it eliminates the dominant purpose of the transaction."

On the other hand, a shrinkwrap license is not an ordinary contract of adhesion. Unlike most form contracts, in this case the party bound by the contract does not even sign or otherwise manifest consent to the terms that bind her. Indeed, in many cases she may not even be aware of them.

UCITA would enforce shrinkwrap licenses, provided that there was in fact an opportunity for consumers who disagree with the terms of the license to obtain a full and effective refund. UCITA §208. UCITA would enforce any terms in a shrinkwrap license that were not unconscionable. In so doing, the drafters of UCITA expressly reject Restatement (2d) of Contracts section 211.

2. Why did shrinkwrap licenses develop in the software context? They were certainly a fixture of the mass-market software industry by the early 1980s. One answer may be that shrinkwrap licenses serve (or once served) as a declaration of the vendor's rights. Generally, proprietary rights provisions of shrinkwrap licenses assert that the information contained in the accompanying computer software is confidential and proprietary to the vendor and may not be copied or disclosed without the vendor's permission. Software vendors who needed proof that they were not in fact dis-

closing their trade secrets by selling copies to whoever wanted them created the legal fiction that they were really licensing rather than selling their software. Because the "license" contained provisions that required customers to keep the software confidential, the trade secrets contained therein could be protected under decisions like *Data General.*

This rationale has much less force today, when it is clear that patent and copyright law are available to protect software sold on the mass market. Unlike trade secrets law, patent and copyright laws operate against the world and do not require proof of a confidential relationship (or, indeed, any relationship at all) between the parties.

3. Judge Easterbrook points out that certain contract terms have special contract formation procedures and requirements under the UCC. Finding none for shrinkwrap contracts, he reverts to the general formation procedure under Article 2. But is the Code section he relies on—section 2-204—the right one? Other courts have characterized shrinkwrap licenses under U.C.C. section 2-207 (dealing with the battle of the forms) or U.C.C. section 2-209 (dealing with modifications to an existing contract). The last provision seems particularly appropriate for a common class of shrinkwrap licenses that give no indication of the license terms until after the consumer has purchased the product and left the store.

Is *ProCD* such a case? The box containing the ProCD disks did not disclose the license terms but did at least indicate that there *were* additional terms contained in the box. Should this make a difference in deciding whether to enforce the terms?

4. For critiques of Judge Easterbrook's analysis of copyright preemption under 17 U.S.C. section 301, see Mark A. Lemley, Beyond Preemption: The Law and Policy of Intellectual Property Licensing, 87 Cal. L. Rev. 111 (1999) (footnotes omitted):

> There are a number of problems with the "contracts are different" idea. First, the reference to "equivalence" seems to direct the analysis only at copyright field preemption under section 301, and thus to ignore both copyright conflicts preemption and any form of patent preemption. Even if contract and copyright are not equivalent, it simply does not follow that federal law places no limits on the enforceability of contracts. Courts that take this position should also be troubled by the significant number of cases that *do* apply intellectual property rules to preempt contracts.
>
> Second, the viability of the distinction between private contracts and public legislation is diminishing day by day. One of the main changes Article 2B would make in current law would be to render enforceable contract "terms" to which the parties did not agree in the classic sense, and indeed of which one party may be entirely unaware. Article 2B would also enable the enforcement of such contract terms "downstream"—that is, against whomever later acquires the software—despite the fact that a first sale under both patent and copyright law would free the purchaser from upstream contractual restrictions. Technology facilitates this change by allowing a vendor to inter-

pose contract terms even in a downstream transaction that would not ordinarily be thought to demonstrate privity between the "contracting" parties.

. . . Third, even truly "private" contracts affect third parties who haven't agreed to the contract terms. Many contracts have significant negative externalities. . . .

On the distinction between "conflicts preemption" and copyright field preemption, see the amicus brief in the *ProCD* case on behalf of the American Committee for Interoperable Systems. See Brief of Amicus Curiae of American Committee for Interoperable Systems in support of Appellees (visited Oct. 26, 1998) <http://www.complaw.com/lawlibrary /brief.html>. See also David Nimmer et al., The Metamorphosis of Contract into Expand, 87 Cal. L. Rev. 17 (1999); Apik Minassian, Comment, The Death of Copyright: Enforceability of Shrinkwrap Licensing Agreements, 45 UCLA L. Rev. 569, 570 (1998) (arguing in favor of "a case-by-case, fact-specific approach to each shrinkwrap agreement to determine whether the license creates contractual rights that are equivalent to the exclusive rights of copyright law, and thus whether it implicates federal copyright preemption issues").

Is *ProCD* in fact a case of conflict between copyright and contract? The stage for such a conflict is set by the Supreme Court decision in *Feist*, which held that the telephone white pages at issue in *ProCD* were constitutionally ineligible for copyright protection. Does the fact that ProCD's shrinkwrap license gives, if anything, even greater protection than copyright would suggest there is a conflict here? If so, is there any way to prevent the sort of use Zeidenberg made of this data? Cf. Jessica Litman, The Tales That Article 2B Tells, 13 Berkeley Tech. L.J. 931 (1998) (arguing that UCITA wrongly presumes that there is some right to be licensed, even in circumstances like *ProCD*, where no intellectual property right exists in the data that was copied).

We discuss the enforceability of contract terms at odds with intellectual property law in more detail *below*.

5. In Judge Easterbrook's view, ProCD's business model relied heavily on the ability to price-discriminate between different classes of users.[4] Judge Easterbrook argues the benefits of this practice and of contracts to carry it out. Cf. Frank H. Easterbrook, Cyberspace and the Law of the Horse, 1996 U. Chi. Legal F. 205. Are there counterarguments or limits to the degree to which law ought to enable price discrimination? See the excerpt by Meurer in Section A, The Business Background, *supra*. And see generally, Wendy J. Gordon, Intellectual Property as Price Discrimination: Implications for Contract, 73 Chi.-Kent L. Rev. 1367 (1998).

---

4. In fact, there was no evidence introduced in the case that indicated ProCD would be willing to authorize a use such as Zeidenberg's at any price. The price discrimination rationale is a construct based on Judge Easterbrook's assumption about what a rational actor might do.

Note on "Clickwrap" Licenses and
Electronic Commerce

The shrinkwrap license cases discussed so far have all been based on a rather traditional model of software distribution in which software is sold off the shelf in a storefront or delivered in a box via the mail. Increasingly, however, software is not distributed by these means at all. Rather, software (and other forms of digital information) is likely to be distributed over the Internet directly. This new distribution mechanism has a number of implications for the contract rules that govern the transactions.

First, bits sent over a modem seem less like traditional, tangible goods to which Article 2 has traditionally applied. This doesn't necessarily mean that the information in question is licensed, of course. Software sold over the Internet is still distributed in the form of copies, at least in a copyright law sense; it's just that those copies are created at the buyer's site rather than being shipped there in physical form. Further, most of the indicia of sale in a mass-market transaction—the possession of one copy, with perpetual use rights in exchange for a single lump-sum payment—are still present in an online transaction. But even if the transaction looks more like a sale than a lease (or license), it is more and more difficult to apply Article 2 to such a deal, except perhaps by analogy.

Second, the nature of online sales gives vendors an opportunity to avoid the problems of shrinkwrap licenses entirely, by disclosing terms to buyers and obtaining an agreement to those terms before the purchase is completed. It is relatively common for Web sites to require agreement to certain terms and conditions by asking the user to click "OK" before proceeding. Such an agreement, entered into before the vendor sells the software or other information, is certainly a contract of adhesion. The buyer has no realistic choice other than to "take it or leave it." It is not a shrinkwrap license, however. The buyer has the opportunity to read and agree to the terms before she pays her money. It is not surprising, therefore, that such "clickwrap" licenses are easier to enforce than their shrinkwrap counterparts. See Hotmail Corp. v. Van Money Pie, 47 U.S.P.Q.2d 1020 (N.D. Cal. 1998) (assuming such an agreement was enforceable, without discussing the issue).

COMMENTS AND QUESTIONS

1.   Does the consumer really benefit from being able to see the terms in advance if they still have no choice regarding what those terms are? Is the real objection to shrinkwrap licenses their immutable monolithic character, and not how they are presented to the consumer? Cf. Robert P. Merges, Intellectual Property and the Costs of Commercial Exchange: A Review Essay, 93 Mich. L. Rev. 1570, 1612 (1995) (suggesting that shrinkwrap license terms should be preempted when there is sufficient

uniformity in the industry that the terms in effect amount to "private legislation" by software vendors); Maureen O'Rourke, Drawing the Boundary Between Copyright and Contract: Copyright Preemption of Software License Terms, 45 Duke L.J. 479 (1995); Maureen A. O'Rourke, Copyright Preemption After the *ProCD* Case: A Market-Based Approach, 12 Berkeley Tech. L.J. 53 (1997).

2. Despite the obvious legal advantages to giving consumers terms to review and approve before entering into a contract, many Web sites do not in fact require purchasers to read and agree to their terms. Can you think of any reason why they wouldn't do so? What does such a policy say about the importance of the terms to the vendor? To the transaction?

Hill v. Gateway 2000, Inc.
United States Court of Appeals for the Seventh Circuit
105 F.3d 1147 (7th Cir. 1997)

EASTERBROOK, Circuit Judge.

A customer picks up the phone, orders a computer, and gives a credit card number. Presently a box arrives, containing the computer and a list of terms, said to govern unless the customer returns the computer within 30 days. Are these terms effective as the parties' contract, or is the contract term-free because the order-taker did not read any terms over the phone and elicit the customer's assent?

One of the terms in the box containing a Gateway 2000 system was an arbitration clause. Rich and Enza Hill, the customers, kept the computer more than 30 days before complaining about its components and performance. They filed suit in federal court arguing, among other things, that the product's shortcomings make Gateway a racketeer (mail and wire fraud are said to be the predicate offenses), leading to treble damages under RICO for the Hills and a class of all other purchasers. Gateway asked the district court to enforce the arbitration clause; the judge refused, writing that "[t]he present record is insufficient to support a finding of a valid arbitration agreement between the parties or that the plaintiffs were given adequate notice of the arbitration clause." Gateway took an immediate appeal, as is its right.

The Hills say that the arbitration clause did not stand out: they concede noticing the statement of terms but deny reading it closely enough to discover the agreement to arbitrate, and they ask us to conclude that they therefore may go to court. Yet an agreement to arbitrate must be enforced "save upon such grounds as exist at law or in equity for the revocation of any contract." 9 U.S.C. §2. Doctor's Associates, Inc. v. Casarotto,— U.S.—, 116 S.Ct. 1652, 134 L.Ed.2d 902 (1996), holds that this provision of the Federal Arbitration Act is inconsistent with any requirement that an arbitration clause be prominent. A contract need not be read to be effective; people who accept take the risk that the unread terms may in retrospect prove unwelcome. Carr v. CIGNA Securities, Inc., 95 F.3d 544, 547 (7th Cir.1996); Chicago Pacific Corp. v. Canada Life Assurance Co., 850 F.2d 334 (7th Cir.1988). Terms inside Gateway's box stand or fall together. If they constitute the parties' contract because the Hills had an opportunity to return the computer after reading them, then all must be enforced.

ProCD, Inc. v. Zeidenberg, 86 F.3d 1447 (7th Cir.1996), holds that terms inside a box of software bind consumers who use the software after an opportunity to read the terms and to reject them by returning the product. Likewise, Carnival Cruise Lines, Inc. v. Shute, 499 U.S. 585, 111 S.Ct. 1522, 113 L.Ed.2d 622 (1991), enforces a forum-selection clause that was included among three pages of terms attached to a cruise ship ticket. *ProCD* and *Carnival Cruise Lines* exemplify the many commercial transactions in which people pay for products with terms to follow; *ProCD* discusses others. 86 F.3d at 1451-52. The district court concluded in *ProCD* that the contract is formed when the consumer pays for the software; as a result, the court held, only terms known to the consumer at that moment are part of the contract, and provisos inside the box do not count. Although this is one way a contract could be formed, it is not the only way: "A vendor, as master of the offer, may invite acceptance by conduct, and may propose limitations on the kind of conduct that constitutes acceptance. A buyer may accept by performing the acts the vendor proposes to treat as acceptance." *Id.* at 1452. Gateway shipped computers with the same sort of accept-or-return offer *ProCD* made to users of its software. *ProCD* relied on the Uniform Commercial Code rather than any peculiarities of Wisconsin law; both Illinois and South Dakota, the two states whose law might govern relations between Gateway and the Hills, have adopted the UCC; neither side has pointed us to any atypical doctrines in those states that might be pertinent; *ProCD* therefore applies to this dispute.

Plaintiffs ask us to limit *ProCD* to software, but where's the sense in that? *ProCD* is about the law of contract, not the law of software. Payment preceding the revelation of full terms is common for air transportation, insurance, and many other endeavors. Practical considerations support allowing vendors to enclose the full legal terms with their products. Cashiers cannot be expected to read legal documents to customers before ringing up sales. If the staff at the other end of the phone for direct-sales operations such as Gateway's had to read the four-page statement of terms before taking the buyer's credit card number, the droning voice would anesthetize rather than enlighten many potential buyers. Others would hang up in a rage over the waste of their time. And oral recitation would not avoid customers' assertions (whether true or feigned) that the clerk did not read term X to them, or that they did not remember or understand it. Writing provides benefits for both sides of commercial transactions. Customers as a group are better off when vendors skip costly and ineffectual steps such as telephonic recitation, and use instead a simple approve-or-return device. Competent adults are bound by such documents, read or unread. For what little it is worth, we add that the box from Gateway was crammed with software. The computer came with an operating system, without which it was useful only as a boat anchor. See Digital Equipment Corp. v. Uniq Digital Technologies, Inc., 73 F.3d 756, 761 (7th Cir.1996). Gateway also included many application programs. So the Hills' effort to limit *ProCD* to software would not avail them factually, even if it were sound legally—which it is not.

For their second sally, the Hills contend that *ProCD* should be limited to executory contracts (to licenses in particular), and therefore does not apply because both parties' performance of this contract was complete when the box arrived at their home. This is legally and factually wrong: legally because the question at hand concerns the formation of the contract rather than its performance, and factually because both contracts were incompletely performed. *ProCD* did not depend on the fact that the seller characterized the transaction as a license rather than as a contract; we treated it as a contract for the sale of goods and reserved the question whether for other purposes a "license" characterization might be preferable. 86 F.3d at 1450. All debates about characterization to one side, the transaction in *ProCD* was no more executory than the one here: Zeidenberg paid for the software and walked out of the store with a box under his arm, so if arrival of the box with the product ends the time for revelation of contractual terms, then the time ended in *ProCD* before Zeidenberg opened the box. But of course *ProCD* had not completed performance with delivery of the box, and neither had Gateway. One element of the transaction was the warranty, which obliges sellers to fix defects in their products. The Hills have invoked Gateway's warranty and are not satisfied with its response, so they are not well positioned to say that Gateway's obligations were fulfilled when the motor carrier unloaded the box. What is more, both *ProCD* and Gateway promised to help customers to use their products. Long-term service and information obligations are common in the computer business, on both hardware and software sides. Gateway offers "lifetime service" and has a round-the-clock telephone hotline to fulfil this promise. Some vendors spend more money helping customers use their products than on developing and manufacturing them. The document in Gateway's box includes promises of future performance that some consumers value highly; these promises bind Gateway just as the arbitration clause binds the Hills.

Next the Hills insist that *ProCD* is irrelevant because Zeidenberg was a "merchant" and they are not. Section 2-207(2) of the UCC, the infamous battle-of-the-forms section, states that "additional terms [following acceptance of an offer] are to be construed as proposals for addition to a contract. Between merchants such terms become part of the contract unless . . .". Plaintiffs tell us that *ProCD* came out as it did only because Zeidenberg was a "merchant" and the terms inside *ProCD*'s box were not excluded by the "unless" clause. This argument pays scant attention to the opinion in *ProCD*, which concluded that, when there is only one form,

"§2-207 is irrelevant." 86 F.3d at 1452. The question in *ProCD* was not whether terms were added to a contract after its formation, but how and when the contract was formed—in particular, whether a vendor may propose that a contract of sale be formed, not in the store (or over the phone) with the payment of money or a general "send me the product," but after the customer has had a chance to inspect both the item and the terms. *ProCD* answers "yes," for merchants and consumers alike. Yet again, for what little it is worth we observe that the Hills misunderstand the setting of *ProCD*. A "merchant" under the UCC "means a person who deals in goods of the kind or otherwise by his occupation holds himself out as having knowledge or skill peculiar to the practices or goods involved in the transaction", §2-104(1). Zeidenberg bought the product at a retail store, an uncommon place for merchants to acquire inventory. His corporation put *ProCD*'s database on the Internet for anyone to browse, which led to the litigation but did not make Zeidenberg a software merchant.

At oral argument the Hills propounded still another distinction: the box containing *ProCD*'s software displayed a notice that additional terms were within, while the box containing Gateway's computer did not. The difference is functional, not legal. Consumers browsing the aisles of a store can look at the box, and if they are unwilling to deal with the prospect of additional terms can leave the box alone, avoiding the transactions costs of returning the package after reviewing its contents. Gateway's box, by contrast, is just a shipping carton; it is not on display anywhere. Its function is to protect the product during transit, and the information on its sides is for the use of handlers rather than would-be purchasers.

Perhaps the Hills would have had a better argument if they were first alerted to the bundling of hardware and legal-ware after opening the box and wanted to return the computer in order to avoid disagreeable terms, but were dissuaded by the expense of shipping. What the remedy would be in such a case—could it exceed the shipping charges?—is an interesting question, but one that need not detain us because the Hills knew before they ordered the computer that the carton would include some important terms, and they did not seek to discover these in advance. Gateway's ads state that their products come with limited warranties and lifetime support. How limited was the warranty—30 days, with service contingent on shipping the computer back, or five years, with free onsite service? What sort of support was offered? Shoppers have three principal ways to discover these things. First, they can ask the vendor to send a copy before deciding whether to buy. The Magnuson-Moss Warranty Act requires firms to distribute their warranty terms on request, 15 U.S.C. §2302(b)(1)(A); the Hills do not contend that Gateway would have refused to enclose the remaining terms too. Concealment would be bad for business, scaring some customers away and leading to excess returns from others. Second, shoppers can consult public sources (computer magazines, the Web sites of vendors) that may contain this information. Third, they may inspect the documents after the product's delivery. Like Zeidenberg, the Hills took the third option. By keeping the computer beyond 30 days, the Hills accepted Gateway's offer, including the arbitration clause.

The Hills' remaining arguments, including a contention that the arbitration clause is unenforceable as part of a scheme to defraud, do not require more than a citation to Prima Paint Corp. v. Flood & Conklin Mfg. Co., 388 U.S. 395, 87 S.Ct. 1801, 18 L.Ed.2d 1270 (1967). Whatever may be said pro and con about the cost and efficacy of arbitration (which the Hills disparage) is for Congress and the contracting parties to consider. Claims based on RICO are no less arbitrable than those founded on the contract or the law of torts. Shearson/American Express, Inc. v. McMahon, 482 U.S. 220, 238-42, 107 S.Ct. 2332, 2343-46, 96 L.Ed.2d 185 (1987). The decision of the district court is vacated, and this case is remanded with instructions to compel the Hills to submit their dispute to arbitration.

COMMENTS AND QUESTIONS

1. Does it really comport with traditional principles of offer and acceptance to conclude that contract terms can always be added after the fact? Would *Hill* come out differently if the piece of paper included in the box was a demand for an additional $1,000? A contract term providing that the computer could not be used for more than 30 days? A provision that there were no warranties at all associated with the computer? If these terms were added after the fact, most courts (perhaps even *Hill*) would doubtless invalidate them. So why does it permit the term at issue here? Is it because it considers the term unimportant—at least in the sense that the deal wouldn't have foundered on it? Cf. Brower v. Gateway 2000, 676 N.Y.S.2d 579 (Sup. Ct. App. Div. 1998) (concluding in accordance with *Hill* that the arbitration term formed part of the contract, but going on to conclude that the term itself was substantively unconscionable). If the term isn't critical to the deal, why enforce it at all? Article 2 is full of default rules that the law will supply where the parties haven't bothered to agree about the issue. Realistically, isn't that exactly what happened here?

2. *Hill* seems to expand *ProCD* significantly. First, it is clear that the rule of *ProCD* is not limited to software—or even to "licenses." Any transaction can presumably be altered after the fact by the provision of additional terms. After *Hill*, one can readily imagine sales of standard goods and even services being made subject to these additional contract terms. Further, *Hill* dispenses with the *ProCD* requirement of at least some manifestation of assent to the terms—satisfied in the classic shrinkwrap case by tearing open the package after being offered an option to return it. Where is the "assent" here? Keeping the computer? Does silence really imply consent in this context, even when it might actually mean that the buyer never discovered the terms (or for that matter, didn't open the box in time)? Finally, the apparent requirement in *ProCD* that notice of addi-

tional terms be given before sale (in that case, on the outside of the box) disappears without discussion in *Hill.*

One way to approach this question is to ask whether the rule in *Hill* treats the parties neutrally. Suppose I mail additional terms to sellers after I buy a product and in that term sheet I announce that a failure to object (and to come to my house to refund my money and take back the software) implies assent. Would Judge Easterbrook enforce such a "contract"? After *Hill,* is there any legitimate reason not to?

b. Contract Formation Under UCITA

Several sections in the UCITA statute on information transactions would affect the outcome of cases such as *ProCD*: section 209, regarding mass-market licenses; and sections 203-205, on the electronic battle of the forms.

Section 209. Mass-Market Licenses

(a) A party adopts the terms of a mass-market license for purposes of Section 208 only if the party agrees to license, by manifesting assent, before or during the party's initial performance or use of or access to the information. A term is not part of the license if:

    (1) the term is unconscionable or is unenforceable under Section 105(a) or (b); or

    (2) subject to Section 301, the term conflicts with a term to which the parties to the license have expressly agreed.

    (b) If a mass-market license or a copy of the license is not available in a manner permitting an opportunity to review by the licensee before the licensee becomes obligated to pay and the licensee does not agree, such as by manifesting assent, to the license after having an opportunity to review, the licensee is entitled to a return under Section 112 and, in addition, to:

    (1) reimbursement of any reasonable expenses incurred in complying with the licensor's instructions for return or destruction of the computer information or, in the absence of instructions, expenses incurred for return postage or similar reasonable expense in returning the computer information; and

    (2) compensation for any reasonable and foreseeable costs of restoring the licensee's information processing system to reverse changes in the system caused by the installation, if:

        (A) the installation occurs because information must be installed to enable review of the license; and

        (B) the installation alters the system or information in it but does not restore the system or information after removal of the installed information because the licensee rejected the license.

(c) In a mass-market transaction, if the licensor does not have an opportunity to review a record containing proposed terms from the licensee before the licensor delivers or becomes obligated to deliver the information, and if the licensor does not agree, such as by manifesting assent, to those terms after having the opportunity, the licensor is entitled to a return.

Section 203.   Offer and Acceptance in General

Unless otherwise unambiguously indicated by the language or the circumstances:

(1) An offer to make a contract invites acceptance in any manner and by any medium reasonable under the circumstances.

(2) An order or other offer to acquire a copy for prompt or current delivery invites acceptance by either a prompt promise to ship or a prompt or current shipment of a conforming or nonconforming copy. However, a shipment of a nonconforming copy is not an acceptance if the licensor seasonably notifies the licensee that the shipment is offered only as an accommodation to the licensee.

(3) If the beginning of a requested performance is a reasonable mode of acceptance, an offeror that is not notified of acceptance or performance within a reasonable time may treat the offer as having lapsed before acceptance.

(4) If an offer in an electronic message evokes an electronic message accepting the offer, a contract is formed:

(A) when an electronic acceptance is received; or

(B) if the response consists of beginning performance, full performance, or giving access to information, when the performance is received or the access is enabled and necessary access materials are received.

Section 204.   Acceptance with Varying Terms

(a) In this section, an acceptance materially alters an offer if it contains a term that materially conflicts with or varies a term of the offer or that adds a material term not contained in the offer.

(b) Except as otherwise provided in Section 205, a definite and seasonable expression of acceptance operates as an acceptance even if the acceptance contains terms that vary from the terms of the offer, unless the acceptance materially alters the offer.

(c) If an acceptance materially alters the offer, the following rules apply:

(1) A contract is not formed unless:

(A) a party agrees, such as by manifesting assent, to the other party's offer or acceptance; or

(B) all the other circumstances, including the conduct of the parties, establish a contract.

(2) If a contract is formed by the conduct of both parties, the terms of the contract are determined under Section 210.

(d) If an acceptance varies from but does not materially alter the offer, a contract is formed based on the terms of the offer. In addition, the following rules apply:

(1) Terms in the acceptance which conflict with terms in the offer are not part of the contract.

(2) An additional non-material term in the acceptance is a proposal for an additional term. Between merchants, the proposed additional term becomes part of the contract unless the offeror gives notice of objection before, or within a reasonable time after it receives the proposed terms.

Section 205. Conditional Offer or Acceptance

(a) In this section, an offer or acceptance is conditional if it is conditioned on agreement by the other party to all the terms of the offer or acceptance.

(b) Except as otherwise provided in subsection (c), a conditional offer or acceptance precludes formation of a contract unless the other party agrees to its terms, such as by manifesting assent.

(c) If an offer and acceptance are in standard forms and at least one form is conditional, the following rules apply:

(1) Conditional language in a standard term precludes formation of a contract only if the actions of the party proposing the form are consistent with the conditional language, such as by refusing to perform, refusing to permit performance, or refusing to accept the benefits of the agreement, until its proposed terms are accepted.

(2) A party that agrees, such as by manifesting assent, to a conditional offer that is effective under paragraph (1) adopts the terms of the offer under Section 208 or 209, except a term that conflicts with an expressly agreed term regarding price or quantity.

COMMENTS AND QUESTIONS

1. Dissatisfaction with the draft of these sections, particularly section 208, was strong in the academic community, certain industries, and among those interested in consumer rights:

> Shrinkwrap licenses represent a significant further step away from the basic idea of contract law, stretching even the concept of blanket assent beyond its limits. Here, there is no signed writing at all. Indeed, the "contract" to be enforced is only discovered by the purchaser after the actual commercial transaction has already taken place.[216] The "fiction" of blanket assent has given way to fantasy in the case of shrinkwrap licenses.

---

216. Courts have been uniform in concluding that the commercially significant transaction that constitutes the basic "contract" is the exchange of money for software at the retail store, or (in the case of telephone orders) the telephonic agreement to exchange money for software.

Nor does the "notice assent" approach of most shrinkwrap licenses overcome this problem. In a typical mass-market software transaction, the consumer pays for software at the retail store and takes the box containing the software back to her home or office. Sometimes she will open the package relatively soon; in other circumstances, it could sit unopened for as long as a month.[217] When the box is opened, the user will encounter shrinkwrapped software. Assuming that she sees the license[218] and begins reading it before opening the package,[219] she will discover that she has in fact purchased only an option contract, and that she has (or once had) the "opportunity" to reject a new contract by returning the software to the store where she bought it (presumably at her own expense), and then relying on the timeliness of software vendors and the United States mail for her refund.

In these circumstances, it is simply unrealistic to believe that a failure to return the software for a refund constitutes any form of "agreement" to the terms of the form license. Even if we accept the notion of blanket assent uncritically, a significant portion of the consumers purchasing the software may be physically unable to return it for a refund. A second group may choose not to return the software because they believe the shrinkwrap license is unenforceable, a commonly held belief among software consumers and one with significant support in the current caselaw. A third group may choose not to return the software because it is simply too much effort, or because they need software right away and cannot afford to wait and select a different brand. A final group may object to particular terms in a license, but be unwilling to reject the software as a whole because of those objections.

The plight of this last group is particularly interesting. Shrinkwrap licenses purport to offer only a "yes or no" choice to consumers. The UCC draft ratifies this approach. This means that even where there is emphatically *not* a meeting of the minds on a particular term—for example, where a consumer expressly does not consent to that term—she may still be bound if she uses the software. At this point, we have come around 180 degrees from the doctrinal foundations of contract law. Contract law is based on agreement between the parties. Shrinkwrap licenses not only are not based on such agreement in any realistic sense, but may be enforceable even where it is utterly clear that they *do not* reflect agreement between the parties.

Mark A. Lemley, Intellectual Property and Shrinkwrap Licenses, 68 S. Cal. L. Rev. 1239 (1995) (footnotes omitted). See also Symposium: Intellec-

---

217. For example, programs that are purchased as gifts are unlikely to be opened immediately. Nor are software programs that must be installed on a network likely to be opened immediately by busy system administrators.

As an interesting aside, the nontransferability provisions of most shrinkwrap licenses, if enforceable, make it a breach of contract to give computer programs or games as birthday or Christmas presents. While this particular restriction seems unlikely to be tested in court in the near future, it is evidence of just how removed shrinkwrap licenses are from commercial reality.

218. If our customer picks up the package the wrong way, she is unlikely to notice the license until after the package has been opened, and she has already "consented" to the terms of the license.

219. While the idea of "notice assent" is premised on the user's opportunity to reject the "bargain" by returning the software unopened, the user can learn of that option only if she actually reads the license before opening the package. In spite of this fact, the UCC draft provides that the shrinkwrap license is enforceable whether or not the user ever even learns of its existence by reading it. [UCITA draft §208.]

tual Property and Contract Law in the Information Age: The impact of Article 2B of the Uniform Commercial Code on the Future of Transactions in Information and Electronic Commerce, 13 Berkeley Tech. L.J. 809 (1998).

2. UCITA undoubtedly endorses the result in *ProCD*, though the current version of section 208 provides a rather more robust refund right than current shrinkwrap licenses seem to envision. On the refund right, see Jeffrey C. Selman & Christopher S. Chen, Steering the Titanic Clear of the Iceberg: Saving the Sale of Software From the Perils of Warranties, 31 U.S.F. L. Rev. 531 (1997). It is worth noting that recent public efforts actually to collect a refund from Microsoft as provided in the shrinkwrap license have proven difficult if not impossible.

Section 111 governs the conduct necessary to "manifest assent." Earlier drafts of Article 2B explicitly rejected the *Hill* result, providing that "mere retention of a record without objection is not a manifestation of assent." But the current version of UCITA removes this restriction and appears to endorse the result in *Hill*.

PROBLEMS

Problem 6-1. Megaware, a major vendor of over-the-counter applications software, desires to characterize its transactions with consumers as sales rather than licenses. Megaware places its software in a box on store shelves. Conspicuous on the front of the box is a statement "THIS SOFTWARE IS FOR LICENSE, NOT FOR SALE." Megaware enforces a company policy that software stores refuse to release its software to a customer unless they sign a preprinted form "License Agreement" that Megaware has provided. Stores keep the forms behind their counter, and present them to customers at the point of sale. All other economic aspects of the transaction remain the same, however: the customer pays one price in exchange for perpetual rights to use one copy of the software, which they physically take with them.

Has Megaware sold, leased, or licensed its software? Does it matter whether the market for Megaware's software is composed of individual consumers or of businesses?

Problem 6-2. Terrell, an individual, buys a computer game from her local Brainiac Software outlet. The game is manufactured by Genesis Systems. Genesis has included inside the box a shrinkwrap license agreement. When Terrell returns home from the Brainiac store and opens her software, she discovers and reads the agreement, which contains terms that differ from those the UCC would otherwise imply. She nonetheless loads the game into her computer and plays it. The next day, she mails a postcard to Genesis that reads as follows:

"To whom it may concern: Thank you for your offer of additional terms to our recent contract. However, I must decline your offer. If you wish to cancel the contract, you may do so by appearing at my residence within the next 10 days to refund my money and collect your computer disk."

What terms govern the transaction under U.C.C. section 2-207? Under section 209?

2. Extra-Legal Enforcement: Self-Help and the Like

American Computer Trust Leasing v. Jack Farrell Implement Co.
United States District Court for the District of Minnesota
763 F. Supp. 1473 (D. Minn. 1991)

DOTY, J.

[This case arose out of the following facts: Plaintiff American Computer Trust Leasing (ACTL), a computer hardware leasing firm affiliated with a software firm called Automatic Data Processing, Inc. (ADP), brought suit against defendants Boerboom International, Inc. (Boerboom) and Jack Farrell Implement Co. (Farrell) to collect payments for computer hardware leased from ACTL. Defendants were agricultural equipment dealers who leased hardware and licensed software designed by ADP especially for farm equipment dealerships. Boerboom and Farrell each claimed that their obligation should be excused because the hardware did not work properly. The defendants also brought various counterclaims against plaintiffs ACTL and ADP, Navistar International Transportation Corporation (formerly International Harvester) (IH) and J.I. Case Company (Case), including a claim their computer software was wrongfully deactivated under the provisions of various state and federal statutes. The following excerpt is from the district court opinion granting plaintiffs' motion for summary judgment and dismissing the counterclaims. This opinion was in turn affirmed and remanded in part. See 967 F.2d 1208 (8th Cir. 1992).]

It is undisputed that ADP did deactivate Farrell's software. The deactivation occurred, however, as a result of Farrell's nonpayment under the terms of the software license agreement. Both Boerboom and Farrell signed agreements providing that the licenses granted by ADP for software could be canceled upon the client's default. Moreover, the software license agreements expressly provided that ADP retain full ownership of the software used by Boerboom and Farrell. Both Boerboom and Farrell stopped paying the software license fees due under the software license agreements. Steven Farrell testified that Farrell was aware of the fact that software services would be discontinued if payments were not made. After Farrell's account had fallen significantly past due, ADP notified Farrell on June 30, 1987 that it would terminate all processing and support services on July 8, 1987 if payment was not received by that date. On July 8, 1987, ADP deactivated Farrell's software as previously warned. After Farrell discovered that its software had been shut off for nonpayment, Farrell paid the amounts past due on its account and ADP promptly reactivated the software. At that point, ADP contends that Farrell disconnected its modem so that ADP could no longer access the system for service and support. Farrell made no further payments to ADP although ADP contends that Farrell continued to use ADP software and hardware.

The software deactivation claims do not support a RICO violation because the federal and state extortion statutes cited by the defendants do not apply to those claims based on the foregoing facts. The defendants assert that the software deactivation constitutes "extortion" in violation of Minn.Stat. §§609.27, 609.275 and 18 U.S.C. §§875, 1951. Violation of 18 U.S.C. §875 is not a racketeering activity listed under §1961(1) and thus cannot support the RICO claims. As discussed above, ADP suspended the defendants' use of its software because Boerboom requested deactivation when it changed to another type of computer system and because Farrell stopped paying ADP the license fees due under its software license agreement. ADP had a legal right to deactivate the defendants' software pursuant to the contracts and the extortion statutes do not apply. The federal statute defines extortion as the "obtaining of property from another, without his consent, induced by wrongful use of actual or threatened force, violence, or fear, or under color of official right." 18 U.S.C. §1951(b)(2). The Minnesota statute similarly requires "unlawful" activities. Minn.Stat. §609.27. Because ADP's deactivation was not unlawful or wrongful but merely an exercise of its rights under the software license agreement, its deactivation does not violate either extortion statute and thus is not a racketeering activity.

COMMENTS AND QUESTIONS

1. Software vendors whose customers default on lease payments or other obligations related to the software are in a difficult position. Unlike real property, it is not easy to repossess intellectual property. Even if the software vendor is entitled to the return of its computer disks, copies of its program may remain resident in off-site backup tapes, on floppy disks, on hard drives, or in a computer network. If the vendor's goal is to prevent the defaulting party from making any use of the software, it may be put to the time-consuming and ultimately impossible task of policing the computer systems of another company.

Some software vendors have tried to get around this problem by using "logic bombs" in their program. Logic bombs may take one of several different forms. The simplest method of attack is the brute-force method—the software vendor simply enters the company (physically or virtually) and disables the software. A more sophisticated vendor might plant "bombs" in their software before ever releasing it. The programmer may, for example, embed in the code a "refresher" lock that will shut down the program automatically if the programmer doesn't supply the proper key every so often (say, every six months). If the company stops payment, the vendor doesn't have to do anything—the software will simply stop working at some point.

2. The acceptability of self-help deactivation of a user's computer or program is hotly disputed. Notwithstanding the *Farrell* case above, courts have generally not been sympathetic to software vendors who apply such self-help remedies. In one case, a vendor who went to a customer site under the pretext of providing software maintenance and modified the program to shut down at a specific time was arrested and charged with computer tampering, a felony in New York! See Lance Rose, Next Time, Use a Collection Agency, Wired, May 1994, at 2. Virginia has a similar statute. Va. Code §18.2-152.7:1. Civil remedies are sometimes also available to the user whose software is affected. See Clayton X-Ray Co. v. Professional Systems Corp., 812 S.W.2d 565 (Mo. Ct. App. 1991) (finding software vendor liable for conversion and awarding punitive damages).

Even the pre-programmed logic bombs do not fare well in court, although their use may not be criminal. See Franks & Sons, Inc. v. Information Solutions, Inc., 1989 Computer Indus. Lit. Rptr. 8927 (N.D. Okla. Dec. 8, 1988) (enjoining the use of logic bomb); Werner, Zaroff, Slotnick, Stern & Askenazy v. Lewis, 588 N.Y.S.2d 960 (Civ. Ct. 1992) (awarding damages in the amount necessary to fix the software after the bomb "exploded," plus punitive damages).

3. Should the permissibility of self-help depend on whether the limitations are inherent in the device, or whether they are activated by the seller during a dispute? Whether the seller is in the right—that is, the seller turns out to have just cause to terminate the contract?

For a suggestion that lawfulness of logic bombs should depend on whether they were disclosed to the user at the time the original transaction occurred, see Esther C. Roditti, Is Self-Help a Lawful Contractual Remedy?, 21 Rutgers Computer & Tech. L.J. 431 (1995).

Note on Proposed Treatment Under UCITA

Three provisions of UCITA impact electronic self-help measures: sections 310, 815, and 816:

Section 2B-310. Electronic Regulation of Performance

(a) In this section, "restraint" means a program, code, device, or similar electronic or physical limitation that restricts use of information.

(b) A party entitled to enforce a limitation on use of information which does not depend on a breach of contract by the other party may include a restraint in the information or a copy of the information and use that restraint if:

(1) a term of the agreement authorizes use of the restraint;

(2) the restraint prevents uses of the information which are inconsistent with the agreement or with informational rights which were not granted to the licensee;

(3) the restraint prevents use of the information after expiration of the stated duration of the contract or a stated number of uses; or

(4) the restraint prevents use when the contract terminates, other than on expiration of a stated duration or number of uses, and the licensor gives reasonable notice to the licensee before further use is prevented.

(c) Unless authorized by a term of the agreement, this section does not permit a restraint that affirmatively prevents or makes impracticable a licensee's access to its own information in the licensee's possession by means other than by use of the licensor's information or informational rights.

(d) A party that includes or uses a restraint pursuant to subsection (b) or (c) is not liable for any loss caused by its authorized use of the restraint.

(e) This section does not preclude electronic replacement or disabling of an earlier copy of information by the licensor in connection with delivery of a new copy or version under an agreement to electronically replace or disable the earlier copy with an upgrade or other new information.

From the Reporter's Notes for this proposed section (December 1998 draft):

Subsection (b)(2) provides that for passive devices, notice is not required if the electronics merely restrict use without otherwise disabling the information. Thus, for example, assume that the contract restricts the licensee to making no more than one back-up copy and that applicable copyright law rules provide that same limitation. This subsection authorizes use of a devices [sic] to enforce that limitation, so long as the device does not destroy the licensed information. The permitted restraint enforces a contract, but does not impose a penalty for attempted breach. The limitations, for example, might entail a counter used to monitor the number of simultaneous uses or restrict use to a pre-agreed system. Although no notice is required, the agreement must support the electronic limitation. The licensee is protected by the fact that a limitation inconsistent with the licensor's rights is a breach of contract.

Illustration 1: The license provides that no more than five users may employ the word processing software at any one time. If a sixth user attempt [sic] to sign on for simultaneous use, that sixth user is electronically denied access until another user discontinues use. This limiting device is authorized without prior notice. If the limiting device disables the software if a sixth user attempts access, it is not authorized by subsection (b)(2).

c. Enforcing Property Rights. Subsection (b)(2) also allows use of passive devices that merely preclude infringing intellectual property rights. Merely preventing the act does not require contract or other notice. Thus, a contract that grants a right to make a back-up copy and to use a digital image, does not deal with the right of the licensee to transmit additional copies electronically. A device that precludes communication of the file electronically, but does not alter or erase the image in the event of an attempt to do so is authorized under (b)(2).

d. Enforcing Termination of the Contract. The restraints described in subsections (b)(3) and (b)(4) enforce termination of the license. Termination ends the license for reasons other than breach. Subsection (b)(3) corresponds to the right to terminate without notice either at the end of the fixed duration of the license, or on its termination on the happening of an agreed event. Both Article 2B and Article 2 recognize termination without notice in such cases and there is no principled reason to distinguish between termination enforced by automated means and any other form of termination. Subsection (b)(4), on the other hand, requires notice if termination is other than for the happening of an agreed event.

> **Illustration 2.** A license requires monthly payments of $1,000 due on the first of the month and a one year term. Licensee makes a payment five days late. Licensor uses an electronic device to turn off the software. That action is not authorized under this section since it enforces a breach of contract. Its enforceability under other law is not considered in this Article. If, however, there is no late payment, but the license reaches the end of the contractual time period and the restraint turns off the software, termination is valid under this section.

Section 815. Right to Possession and to Prevent Use

(a) On cancellation of a license, the licensor has the right to:

(1) possession of all copies of the licensed information in the possession or control of the licensee and any other materials pertaining to that information which by contract are to be returned or delivered by the licensee to the licensor; and

(2) prevent the continued exercise of contractual and informational rights in the licensed information under the license.

(b) Except as otherwise provided in Section 814, a licensor may exercise its rights under subsection (a) without judicial process only if this can be done:

(1) without a breach of the peace;

(2) without a foreseeable risk of personal injury or significant physical damage to information or property other than the licensed information; and

(3) in accordance with Section 816.

(c) In a judicial proceeding, the court may enjoin a licensee in breach of contract from continued use of the information and informational rights and may order the licensor or a judicial officer to take the steps described in Section 618.

(d) A party has a right to an expedited judicial hearing on a request for prejudgment relief to enforce or protect its rights under this section.

(e) The right to possession under this section is not available to the extent that the information, before breach of the license and in the ordinary course of performance under the license, was so altered or commingled that the information is no longer identifiable or separable.

(f) A licensee that provides information to a licensor subject to contractual use terms has the rights and is subject to the limitations of a licensor under this section with respect to the information it provides.

Section 816. Limitations on Electronic Self-Help

(a) In this section, "electronic self-help" means the use of electronic means to exercise a licensor's rights under Section 815(b).

(b) On cancellation of a license, electronic self-help is not permitted, except as provided in this section.

(c) A licensee shall separately manifest assent to a term authorizing use of electronic self-help. The term must:

(1) provide for notice of exercise as provided in subsection (d);

(2) state the name of the person designated by the licensee to which notice of exercise must be given and the manner in which notice must be given and place to which notice must be sent to that person; and

(3) provide a simple procedure for the licensee to change the designated person or place.

(d) Before resorting to electronic self-help authorized by a term of the license, the licensor shall give notice in a record to the person designated by the licensee stating:

(1) that the licensor intends to resort to electronic self-help as a remedy on or after 15 days following receipt by the licensee of the notice;

(2) the nature of the claimed breach that entitles the licensor to resort to self-help; and

(3) the name, title, and address including direct telephone number, facsimile number, or e-mail address to which the licensee may communicate concerning the claimed breach.

(e) A licensee may recover direct and incidental damages caused by wrongful use of electronic self-help. The licensee may also recover consequential damages for wrongful use of electronic self-help, whether or not such damages are excluded by the terms of the license, if:

(1) within the period specified in subsection (d)(1), the licensee gives notice to the licensor's designated person describing in good faith the general nature and magnitude of damages;

(2) the licensor has reason to know the damages of the type described in subsection (f) may result from the wrongful use of electronic self-help; or

(3) the licensor does not provide the notice required in subsection (d).

(f) Even if the licensor complies with subsections (c) and (d), electronic self-help may not be used if the licensor has reason to know that its use will result in substantial injury or harm to the public health or safety or grave harm to the public interest substantially affecting third persons not involved in the dispute.

(g) A court of competent jurisdiction of this State shall give prompt consideration to an application for injunctive relief and may enjoin, temporarily or permanently, the licensor from exercising electronic self-help even if authorized by a license term or enjoin the licensee from misappropriation or misuse of computer information, as may be appropriate, upon consideration of the following:

(1) grave harm of the kinds stated in subsection (f), or the threat thereof, whether or not the licensor has reason to know of those circumstances;

(2) irreparable harm or threat of irreparable harm to the licensee or licensor;

(3) whether the party seeking the relief is more likely than not to succeed under its claim when it is finally adjudicated;

(4) all the conditions to entitle a person to the relief under the laws of this State have been fulfilled; and

(5) the party that may be adversely affected is adequately protected against loss, including a loss because of misappropriation or misuse of computer information, that it may suffer because the relief is granted under this [Act].

(h) Before breach of contract, rights or obligations under this section may not be waived or varied by an agreement, but the parties, in the term referred to in subsection (c), may specify additional provisions more favorable to the licensee.

(i) This section does not apply if the licensor obtains possession of a copy without a breach of the peace and the electronic self-help is used solely with respect to that copy.

From the Reporter's Notes:

3. *Self-Help.* A license is a conditional transfer. Subsection (b) provides a right of self-help consistent with Article 2A and Article 9. The self-help right is constrained by 1) there being a breach sufficient to cancel the license and 2) the ability to exercise self-help without causing a "breach of the peace" or a foreseeable risk of personal injury or significant damage to information or property other than the licensed information. This places more restrictions on self-help than in Article 2A or Article 9. As in both of those

articles, this Section takes no position on whether self help can be pursued through electronic means.

4. *Expedited Hearing.* Subsection (d) provides for a right to an expedited hearing to enforce rights or possession and restriction of use. No effort has been made to define the contours of what that hearing timing may entail. This is left to state procedural law.

5. *Identifiability.* As indicated in subsection (e), there must be something identifiable with reference to which the rights can be applied. The right to posssession of copies cannot exist if the copies have been so commingled as to have lost their identifiability. This deals, for example, with cases where data are thoroughly intermingled with data of the other party *and* that intermingling occurs in the ordinary performance under the license. In such cases, repossession is impossible because of the expected performance of the parties under the contract.

This limitation does not necessarily apply to the right to prevent use. For example, if trade secret information was provided to the licensee under use restrictions, the ability to prevent further use hinges solely on whether a particular activity can be identified as involving use of the information. If an image, trademark, name or similar material is inseparable from other property of the party in breach, that does not preclude the injured party from preventing further use of the information by the party in breach. Thus, a license of the "Mickey Mouse" character which results in placing that image in a video game produced by the party in breach does not prevent the other party from barring continued use of the image on the hats in commerce.

Reporter's Note:

This section is a modified version of a proposal adopted in principle at the November meeting to provide a basis for a resolution of the electronic self-help issue based on concepts of prior notice. The prior Draft of the article provided that it took no position authorizing or prohibiting electronic self-help.

COMMENTS AND QUESTIONS

1. For criticism of UCITA's rules allowing electronic self-help measures, see Julie E. Cohen, Copyright and the Jurisprudence of Self-Help, 13 Berkeley Tech. L.J. 1089 (1998) (arguing that the provisions of proposed UCITA authorize an unprecedented degree of intrusion into private homes and offices, that they lack a sound theoretical basis, and that their adoption would threaten constitutionally mandated limits on copyright protection; and concluding that the law should afford *users* of digital works rights of electronic self-help where necessary to preserve the copyright balance). See also Gary J. Edwards, Comment, Self-Help Repossession of Software: Should Repossession Be Available in Article 2B of the UCC?, 58 U. Pitt. L. Rev. 763 (1997) (arguing that "the law of computer software transactions should not recognize any form of electronic repossession. Other remedies, such as injunctive relief, are easily obtainable and are

much more capable of protecting the interests of all parties to the dispute. The unilateral decision on the part of the software vendor to deprive the purchaser of access to the system should not be supported.").

2. For a broad-based defense of self-help and private ordering in general, see David Friedman, In Defense of Private Orderings: Comments on Julie Cohen's "Copyright and the Jurisprudence of Self-Help," 13 Berkeley Tech. L.J. 1151 (1998).

Is "private ordering" really what is at stake here? Or should the law place limits on what a software vendor can do even if the contract does provide for it? In this regard, note two things about the UCITA self-help rules: (1) the "contract" that authorizes them can be a shrinkwrap license or even the sort of "after the fact" terms permitted in *Hill*; and (2) section 716 clearly contemplates that self-help will be allowed even though it involves a "breach of the peace."

3. Section 715 permits some (but not all) forms of self-help to occur "without judicial process." Why? Would a rule that required some judicial process, akin to that required for repossession of physical items, impose an unfair burden on software vendors?

3. Warranties and Disclaimers

▬▬▬
▬▬▬
Neilson Business Equipment Center, Inc.
v. Monteleone
Supreme Court of Delaware
524 A.2d 1172 (Del. 1987)

MOORE, J.

Following a nonjury trial in the Superior Court, defendant Neilson Business Equipment Center, Inc. (Neilson), appeals a judgment awarding plaintiff, Dr. Italo V. Monteleone, P.A., damages of $34,983.42 for breaches of the warranties of merchantability and fitness arising from a lease contract for computer hardware, software and related services. The trial court found that the objects of the lease constituted "goods" under the Uniform Commercial Code and granted relief under the Code's implied warranties of merchantability and fitness. 6 Del.C. §§2-314(1) and 2-315.

Neilson's primary contentions are that the trial court erred (1) in classifying the computer software and related technical services as goods, and (2) in applying the Uniform Commercial Code's warranties to this transaction. Thus, we address for the first time the issue of computer software (programs) being treated as "goods" under the Code.

Both parties concede error in the computation of damages. We find that the classification of the contract as one involving "goods" is supported by substantial evidence. Accordingly, we affirm the judgment relating to breaches of the implied warranties of merchantability and fitness, but reverse and remand for a recomputation of damages.

I.

Dr. Monteleone is a neurologist. In March, 1982, his office began investigating various computer information systems, since record keeping was entirely manual. The doctor gave Toni Reed, his bookkeeper and office manager, complete authority to acquire a suitable computer system. However, Ms. Reed had no prior experience in buying computer technology.

She initially considered four possible computer dealers, including Neilson. An advertisement in the local telephone directory listed Neilson as a dealer in microcomputers. Ultimately, Ms. Reed chose Neilson, in part because she had previously purchased an office photocopier from the defendant with satisfactory results.

After an initial meeting at Neilson's office, the company sent two representatives to study Dr. Monteleone's manual billing system. The parties ultimately signed a lease/purchase option agreement covering hardware equipment and software. As part of the agreement, Neilson agreed to customize the computer system to meet Dr. Monteleone's needs. The purchase price was $18,995, but Dr. Monteleone chose to lease the equipment in order to obtain favorable cash flow and tax benefits. The total of all lease payments amounted to $32,800.80. Dr. Monteleone retained an option to purchase the system at the end of the lease at fair market value, not exceeding 10% of the original purchase price. In addition to the lease, the parties executed a separate maintenance agreement valued at $2,182.00. To facilitate the transaction, Neilson sold the equipment and software to Tri-Continental Leasing Corporation, who in turn leased the items to Dr. Monteleone.

Although Neilson did not design the software, it renamed the program it had acquired elsewhere the "Neilson Medical Office Management System." However, Neilson did alter the program at various times in an attempt to make it meet the doctor's needs.

The computer was delivered in July, 1982, and problems immediately developed. For example, the system printed a separate bill for each treatment rather than one bill encompassing the doctor's services to a patient for a specific period; the bills and medical insurance forms were not compatible with Dr. Monteleone's records; patient information was not as detailed as required; and incorrect balances appeared in the accounts receivable register. Attempts to modify the system failed, and in August, 1982, Neilson hired a program consultant to solve the problems.

In February, 1983, Dr. Monteleone notified Neilson that the lease was terminated for cause. Thereafter, plaintiff stopped using the computer, although in March, 1983, Neilson's program consultant successfully effected some modifications. In June, 1983, Neilson took possession of the system pursuant to an agreement which allowed Neilson to try and resell it. While in possession of the computer, Neilson modified the billing program and returned the system to Dr. Monteleone's office. The doctor never used the machine after its return, but continued timely lease payments under the contract.

The Superior Court ruled that the transaction involved goods and applied the warranty provisions of the Uniform Commercial Code. The trial court found that Neilson had breached the implied warranties of merchantability and fitness for a particular purpose, and awarded Dr. Monteleone damages totaling $34,983.42, with interest from March 11, 1983.

II.

[The court characterized the transaction as predominantly for the sale of goods, and so applied the UCC.]

Every contract of sale entered into by a merchant includes an implied warranty that the goods sold be "merchantable." The computer system, to be merchantable, must have been capable of passing without objection in the trade under the contract description, and be fit for the ordinary purposes for which it was intended. 6 Del.C. §2-314(1) and (2). There is no dispute that the computer system failed in that regard. In general, the computer system did not meet Dr. Monteleone's expressed record and bookkeeping needs, even though Neilson's sales representatives informed Ms. Reed that the system would do so. The trial court correctly found that plaintiff had established all the elements necessary to prove a breach of the warranty of merchantability, namely: (1) that a merchant sold the goods; (2) that such goods were not "merchantable" at the time of sale; (3) that plaintiff was damaged; (4) that the damage was caused by the breach of the warranty of merchantability; and (5) that the seller had notice of the damage. See F.E. Myers Co. v. Pipe Maintenance Servs., Inc., 599 F. Supp. 697, 703 (D. Del. 1984).

An implied warranty of fitness for a particular purpose arises when a seller, at the time of contracting, has reason to know a particular purpose of the buyer's for which the goods are required, and has reason to know that the buyer is relying on the seller's skill or judgment to select or furnish suitable goods. 6 Del.C. §2-315. The buyer need not provide the seller with actual knowledge of the particular purpose for which the goods are intended or of his reliance on the seller's skill and judgment, if the circumstances are such that the seller has reason to perceive the purpose intended or that reliance exists. See J. White and R. Summers, Uniform Commercial Code, Section 9-9 (2d ed. 1980).

Here, Neilson knew that Dr. Monteleone, through his assistant, Ms. Reed, sought a computer system to meet specific information processing needs. Neilson admits that it was responsible for selecting the proper equipment, and also agreed to customize the software so that the computer system would be compatible with Dr. Monteleone's manual records. There could hardly be a clearer case where a buyer relies on the professional expertise of the seller than that presented here. Dr. Monteleone needed a system that would perform specific functions, and relied on Neilson's professional expertise and experience in the computer and information processing field to develop and deliver a satisfactory computer system. Neilson clearly had reason to know of Monteleone's reliance on the company's expertise and breached the warranty of fitness for a particular purpose. Its liability is established under the Uniform Commercial Code.

COMMENTS AND QUESTIONS

1. Most provisions of the Uniform Commercial Code can be disclaimed or altered by contracting parties. Why should warranty terms be any different? What if two business parties agree that warranties are not appropriate in a particular situation (say, because the software is in an early stage of development and the customer wants to be able to use it before it is fully tested): should they be prevented from doing so?

2. What does a warranty on software cover? Is it limited to the price of the software, or is the vendor liable for lost data as a result of system crashes? For clients lost as a result of the failure to get a bid in on time, again traceable to software glitches? For consequential damages, including loss of life, in cases where the software runs a mission-critical system (a nuclear power plant, say, or an air traffic control center)?

3. Commentators regularly observe that software consumers are forced to put up with design defects and substandard performance that would be unthinkable in most other industries. See, e.g., Cem Kaner, Bad Software (1998). Why is this? For an argument that implied warranties have proven inadequate to assure performance in the software industry because they are universally disclaimed, see Peter A. Alces, W(h)ither Warranty: The B(l)oom of Products Liability Theory in Cases of Deficient Software Design, 87 Cal. L. Rev. 271 (1999). Alces criticizes draft UCITA for making it even easier to disclaim all warranties in software, and suggests that the appropriate solution may be to apply principles of products liability to computer programs.

Some software industry lawyers, by contrast, fear that warranties will destroy the software industry. See, e.g., Jeffrey C. Selman & Christopher S. Chen, Steering the Titanic Clear of the Iceberg: Saving the Sale of Software From the Perils of Warranties, 31 U.S.F. L. Rev. 531 (1997). Others have suggested compromises designed to create an implied warranty of merchantability that the software industry at least can live with. See Robert W. Gomulkiewicz, The Implied Warranty of Merchantability in Software Contracts: A Warranty No One Dares to Give and How to Change That, 16 J. Marshall J. Computer & Info. L. 393 (1998).

4. Should digital information be treated differently from software for warranty purposes? UCITA takes the position that it cannot impose any warranties regarding the accuracy of the information provided for fear of running afoul of the First Amendment. UCITA §404, Reporter's Note 3.b. ("Published informational content is the subject matter of general commerce in ideas, political, economic, entertainment or the like, whose distribution entails fundamental public policy interests in supporting distribution and not chilling this process through liability risks."). Some (but not all) cases have indeed taken that position, drawing from the libel cases a restrictive view of when speakers can be liable for making false statements of fact. See Daniel v. Dow Jones & Co., 520 N.Y.S.2d 334 (N.Y. City Ct. 1987).

On the other hand, courts regularly enforce contracts that restrict the free speech rights of parties to the contract. See Cohen v. Cowles Media, 501 U.S. 663 (1991). And courts in the trademark and false advertising contexts have no difficulty in imposing liability on those who make misleading statements, even if they do it unintentionally.

Should the law distinguish between liability for factual misstatements, which the First Amendment may protect, and liability for a database containing software flaws that crash someone's system?

D. THE CONTRACT-INTELLECTUAL PROPERTY BOUNDARY

In the case that follows, the software vendor attempted to circumvent copyright and trade secrets law by requiring the "licensee" to agree not to reverse engineer the computer program. Consider whether and under what circumstances vendors should be able to "contract around" intellectual property law.

≣
≣ *Vault Corp. v. Quaid Software Ltd.*
≣ *United States Court of Appeals for the Fifth Circuit*
≣ *847 F.2d 255 (5th Cir. 1988)*

REAVLEY, Circuit Judge: . . .

I

Vault produces computer diskettes under the registered trademark "PROLOK" which are designed to prevent the unauthorized duplication of programs placed on them by software computer companies, Vault's customers. Floppy diskettes serve as a medium upon which computer companies place their software programs. To use a program, a purchase loads the diskette into the disk drive of a computer, thereby allowing the computer to read the program into its memory. The purchaser can then remove the diskette from the disk drive and operate the program from the computer's memory. This process is repeated each time a program is used.

The protective device placed on a PROLOK diskette by Vault is comprised of two parts: a "fingerprint" and a software program ("Vault's program").[1] The "fingerprint" is a small mark physically placed on the magnetic surface of each PROLOK diskette which contains certain information that cannot be altered or erased. Vault's program is a set of instructions to the computer which interact with the "fingerprint" to prevent the computer from operating the program recorded on a PROLOK diskette (by one of Vault's customers) unless the computer verifies that the original PROLOK diskette, as identified by the "fingerprint", is in the computer's disk drive. While a purchaser can copy a PROLOK protected program onto another diskette, the computer will not read the program into its memory from the copy unless the original PROLOK diskette is also in one of the computer's disk drives. The fact that a fully functional copy of a program cannot be made from a PROLOK diskette prevents purchasers from buying a single program and making unauthorized copies for distribution to others.

Vault produced PROLOK in three stages. The original commercial versions, designated as versions 1.01, 1.02, 1.03, 1.04 and 1.06 ("version 1.0") were produced in 1983. Vault then incorporated improvements into the system and produced version 1.07 in 1984. The third major revision occurred in August and September of 1985 and was designated as versions 2.0 and 2.01 ("version 2.0"). Each version of PROLOK has been copyrighted and Vault includes a license agreement with every PROLOK package that specifically prohibits the copying, modification, translation, decompilation or disassembly of Vault's program.[2] Beginning with version

---

1. A PROLOK diskette contains two programs, the program placed on the diskette by a software company (e.g., word processing) and the program placed on the diskette by Vault which interacts with the "fingerprint" to prevent the unauthorized duplication of the software company's program. We use the term "software program" or "program" to refer to the program placed on the diskette by Vault's customers (a computer company) and "Vault's program" to refer to the program placed on the diskette by Vault as part of the protective device. We collectively refer to the "fingerprint" and Vault's program as the "protective device."

2. The license agreement refers to the program placed on the diskette by Vault, not the software program placed on the diskette by Vault's customers.... The companies that place their software programs on PROLOK diskettes, not Vault, own the copyright to their programs and may include a license agreement covering their programs in the package for sale to the public.

Vault's license agreement reads:

IMPORTANT! VAULT IS PROVIDING THE ENCLOSED MATERIALS TO YOU ON THE EXPRESS CONDITION THAT YOU ASSENT TO THE SOFTWARE LICENSE. BY USING ANY OF THE ENCLOSED DISKETTE(S), YOU AGREE TO THE FOLLOWING PROVISIONS. IF YOU DO NOT AGREE WITH THESE LICENSE PROVISIONS, RETURN THESE MATERIALS TO YOUR DEALER, IN ORIGINAL PACKAGING WITHIN 3 DAYS FROM RECEIPT, FOR A REFUND.

2.0 in September 1985, Vault's license agreement continued a choice of law clause adopting Louisiana law.[3]

Quaid's product, a diskette called "CopyWrite," contains a feature call "RAMKEY" which unlocks the PROLOK protective device and facilitates the creation of a fully functional copy of a program placed on a PROLOK diskette. The process is performed simply by copying the contents of the PROLOK diskette onto the CopyWrite diskette [which] can then be used to run the software program without the original PROLOK diskette in a computer disk drive. RAMKEY interacts with Vault's program to make it appear to the computer that the CopyWrite diskette contains the "finger-print," thereby making the computer function as if the original PROLOK diskette is in its disk drive. A copy of a program placed on a CopyWrite diskette can be used without the original, and an unlimited number of fully functional copies can be made in this manner from the program originally placed on the PROLOK diskette.

Quaid first developed RAMKEY in September 1983 in response to PROLOK version 1.0. In order to develop this version of RAMKEY, Quaid copied Vault's program into the memory of its computer and analyzed the manner in which the program operated. When Vault developed version 1.07, Quaid adapted RAMKEY in 1984 to defeat this new version. The adapted version of RAMKEY contained a sequence of approximately 30 characters found in Vault's program and was discontinued in July 1984. Quaid then developed the current version of RAMKEY which also operates to defeat PROLOK version 1.07, but does not contain the sequence of characters used in the discontinued version. Quaid has not yet modified RAMKEY to defeat PROLOK version 2.0, and has agreed not to modify RAMKEY pending the outcome of this suit. Robert McQuaid, the sole owner of Quaid, testified in his deposition that while a CopyWrite diskette can be used to duplicate programs placed on all disk-

1. This copy of the PROLOK Software Protection System and this PROLOK Software Protection Diskette (the "Licensed Software") are licensed to you, the end-user, for your own internal use. Title to the Licensed Software and all copyrights and proprietary rights in the Licensed Software shall remain with VAULT. You may not transfer, sublicense, rent, lease, convey, copy, modify, translate, convert to another programming language, decompile or disassemble the Licensed Software for any purpose without VAULT's prior written consent.

2. THE LICENSED SOFTWARE IS PROVIDED "AS-IS". VAULT DISCLAIMS ALL WARRANTIES AND REPRESENTATIONS OF ANY KIND WITH REGARD TO THE LICENSED SOFTWARE, INCLUDING THE IMPLIED WARRANTIES OF MERCHANTABILITY AND FITNESS FOR A PARTICULAR PURPOSE. UNDER NO CIRCUMSTANCES WILL VAULT BE LIABLE FOR ANY CONSEQUENTIAL, INCIDENTAL, SPECIAL OR EXEMPLARY DAMAGES EVEN IF VAULT IS APPRISED OF THE LIKELIHOOD OF SUCH DAMAGES OCCURRING. SOME STATES DO NOT ALLOW THE LIMITATION OR EXCLUSION OF LIABILITY FOR INCIDENTAL OR CONSEQUENTIAL DAMAGES, SO THE ABOVE LIMITATION OR EXCLUSION MAY NOT APPLY TO YOU.

3. The license agreement included the following language beginning with version 2.0:

To the extent the laws of the United States of America are not applicable, this license agreement shall be governed by the laws of the State of Louisiana.

ettes, whether copy-protected or not, the only purpose served by RAMKEY is to facilitate the duplication of programs placed on copy-protected diskettes. He also stated that without the RAMKEY feature, CopyWrite would have no commercial value.

II

Vault brought this action against Quaid seeking preliminary and permanent injunctions to prevent Quaid from advertising and selling RAMKEY, an order impounding all of Quaid's copies of CopyWrite which contain the RAMKEY feature, and monetary damages in the amount of $100,000,000. Vault asserted three copyright infringement claims. . . . Vault also asserted two claims based on Louisiana law, contending that Quaid breached its license agreement by decompiling or disassembling Vault's program in violation of the Louisiana Software License Enforcement Act, La.Rev.Stat.Ann. §51:1961 et seq. (West 1987), and that Quaid misappropriated Vault's program in violation of the Louisiana Uniform Trade Secrets Act, La.Rev.Stat.Ann. §51:1431 et seq. (West 1987).

[The court concluded that Quaid's reverse engineering did not violate the Copyright Act.]

IV. Vault's Louisiana Claims

Seeking preliminary and permanent injunctions and damages, Vault's original complaint alleged that Quaid breached its license agreement by decompiling or disassembling Vault's program in violation of the Louisiana Software License Enforcement Act (the "License Act"), La.Rev.Stat.Ann. §51:1961 et seq. (West 1987), and that Quaid misappropriated Vault's program in violation of the Louisiana Uniform Trade Secrets Act, La.Rev.Stat.Ann. §51:1431 et seq. (West 1987). On appeal, Vault abandons its misappropriation claim,[26] and, with respect to its breach of license claim, Vault only seeks an injunction to prevent Quaid from decompiling or disassembling PROLOK version 2.0.

Louisiana's License Act permits a software producer to impose a number of contractual terms upon software purchasers provided that the terms are set forth in a license agreement which comports with La.Rev.Stat.Ann. §§51:1963 & 1965, and that this license agreement accompanies the producer's software. Enforceable terms include the prohibition of: (1) any copying of the program for any purpose; and (2) modi-

---

26. While the district court held that the Louisiana Uniform Trade Secrets Act, La.Rev.Stat.Ann. §51:1431 et seq., was not preempted by the Copyright Act, the court held that the process of ascertaining information by "reverse engineering," used by Quaid to analyze the operation of Vault's program, did not constitute a violation of the Louisiana Trade Secrets Act. *Vault*, 655 F.Supp. at 761. This holding is not challenged on appeal.

fying and/or adapting the program in any way, including adaptation by reverse engineering, decompilation or disassembly. La.Rev.Stat.Ann. §51:1964.[28] The terms "reverse engineering, decompiling or disassembling" are defined as "any process by which computer software is converted from one form to another form which is more readily understandable to human beings, including without limitation any decoding or decrypting of any computer program which has been encoded or encrypted in any manner." La.Rev.Stat.Ann. §51:1962(3).

Vault's license agreement, which accompanies PROLOK version 2.0 and comports with the requirements of La.Rev.Stat.Ann. §§51:1963 & 1965, provides that "[y]ou may not . . . copy, modify, translate, convert to another programming language, decompile or disassembly" Vault's program. Vault asserts that these prohibitions are enforceable under Louisiana's License Act, and specifically seeks an injunction to prevent Quaid from decompiling or disassembling Vault's program.

The district court held that Vault's license agreement was "a contract of adhesion which could only be enforceable if the [Louisiana License Act] is a valid and enforceable statute." *Vault*, 655 F.Supp. at 761. The court noted numerous conflicts between Louisiana's License Act and the Copyright Act, including: (1) while the License Act authorizes a total prohibition on copying, the Copyright Act allows archival copies and copies made as an essential step tin the utilization of a computer program, 17 U.S.C. §117; (2) while the License Act authorizes a perpetual bar against copying, the Copyright Act grants protection against unauthorized copying only for the life of the author plus fifty years, 17 U.S.C. §302(a); and (3) while the

---

28. Section 51:1964 reads, in full:

Terms of which shall be deemed to have been accepted under R.S. 51:1963, if included in an accompanying license agreement which conforms to the provisions of R.S. 51:1965, may include any or all of the following:

(1) Provisions for the retention by the licensor of title to the copy of the computer software.

(2) If title to the copy of computer software has been retained by the licensor, provisions for the prohibition of any copying of the copy of computer software for any purpose and/or limitations on the purposes for which copies of the computer software can be made and/or limitations on the number of copies of the computer software which can be made.

(3) If title to the copy of computer software has been retained by the licensor, provisions for the prohibition or limitation of rights to modify and/or adapt the copy of the computer software in any way, including without limitation prohibitions on translating, reverse engineering, decompiling, disassembling, and/or creating derivative works based on the computer software.

(4) If title to the copy of computer software has been retained by the licensor, provisions for prohibitions on further transfer, assignment, rental, sale, or other disposition of that copy or any other copies made from that copy of the computer software, provided that terms which prohibit the transfer of a copy of computer software in connection with the sale or transfer by operation of law of all or substantially all of the operating assets of a licensee's business shall to that extent only not be deemed to have been accepted under R.S. 51:1963.

(5) Provisions for the automatic termination without notice of the license agreement if any provisions of the license agreement are breached by the licensee.

License Act places no restrictions on programs which may be protected, under the Copyright Act, only "original works of authorship" can be protected, 17 U.S.C. §102. *Vault*, 655 F.Supp. at 762-63. The court concluded that, because Louisiana's License Act "touched upon the area" of federal copyright law, its provisions were preempted and Vault's license agreement was unenforceable. *Id.* at 763.

In Sears, Roebuck & Co. v. Stiffel Co., 376 U.S. 225, 84 S.Ct. 784, 11 L.Ed.2d 661 (1964), the Supreme Court held that "[w]hen state law touches upon the area of [patent or copyright statutes], it is 'familiar doctrine' that the federal policy 'may not be set at naught, or its benefits denied' by the state law." *Id.* at 229, 84 S.Ct. at 787 (quoting Sola Elec. Co. v. Jefferson Elec. Co., 317 U.S. 173, 176, 63 S.Ct. 172, 173, 87 L.Ed. 165 (1942)). See Compco Corp. v. Day-Brite Lighting, Inc., 376 U.S. 234, 84 S.Ct. 779, 11 L.Ed.2d 669 (1964); see also Mitchell v. Penton/Indus. Publishing Co., 486 F.Supp. 22 (N.D. Ohio 1979) (holding that common law unfair competition claim preempted by the Copyright Act); Triangle Publications, Inc. v. Sports Eye, Inc., 415 F.Supp. 682, 686-87 (E.D.Penn. 1976) (holding that state regulation of unfair competition preempted as to matters falling within broad confines of the Copyright Act). Section 117 of the Copyright Act permits an owner of a computer program to make an adaptation of that program provided that the adaptation is either "created as an essential step in the utilization of the computer program in conjunction with a machine," §117(1), or "is for archival purpose only," §117(2). The provision in Louisiana's License Act, which permits a software producer to prohibit the adaptation of its licensed computer program by decompilation or disassembly, conflicts with the rights of computer program owners under §117 and clearly "touches upon an area" of federal copyright law. For this reason, and the reasons set forth by the district court, we hold that at least this provision of Louisiana's License Act is preempted by federal law, and thus that the restriction in Vault's license agreement against decompilation or disassembly is unenforceable. . . .

≡ *National Car Rental System, Inc. v. Computer*
≡ *Associates International, Inc.*
≡ **United States Court of Appeals for the Eighth Circuit**
≡ **991 F.2d 426, 26 U.S.P.Q.2d 1370 (8th Cir. 1993)**

MAGILL, Circuit Judge.

We here deal with the difficult question of the extent to which the Copyright Act preempts state breach of contract actions alleging that the licensee of computer software exceeded limitations on the use of computer software contained in the license agreements. Computer Associates International, Inc., appeals from the district court's order resolving a motion for judgment on the pleadings and dismissing its breach of contract claim against National Car Rental as preempted under the Copyright Act. We conclude that the district court failed to grant Computer Associates all reasonable inferences from its pleadings, and hold that as properly construed, the cause of action as pled is not preempted. We reverse.

I. Background

Computer Associates International, Inc. (CA), creates and licenses computer software. CA licensed its programs to the appellee, National Car Rental Systems, Inc. (National), to process National's data on National's hardware in Bloomington, Minnesota. The 1990 license agreement between CA and National provided, as did earlier licenses, that National may use the licensed programs "only for the internal operations of Licensee and for the processing of its own data." A separate order form, incorporated into the license agreement, similarly provided that "use of the Licensed Program[s] is restricted to the internal operations of Licensee and for the processing of its own data."

Sometime in 1990, National decided to cease its internal computer operations and contract with an independent computer services vendor for computer related information services. Ultimately, National retained Electronic Data Systems Corporation (EDS) to provide these services. In connection with this transaction, National, EDS, and CA entered into a supplement addendum, which provided that EDS could use the licensed programs to process National's data. The supplement addendum provided that EDS would use the programs for the benefit of National subject to the terms and conditions of the 1990 license agreement, and solely "to process data of Licensee and in no event for the processing of data . . . of any third party other than Licensee."

CA subsequently determined that National had been using the programs to process the data of third parties, including Lend Lease Trucks, Inc. (Lend Lease), and Tilden Car Rental, Inc. (Tilden), in violation of the license agreement, and that such use had continued through EDS under the supplement addendum. CA threatened to sue National if such use did not stop. National then brought a declaratory judgment action in the district court. National admitted in its complaint that it "has used the Licensed Software in its business activities . . . including the activities relating to Tilden and Trucks [Lend Lease]," but requested a declaration that its use of the programs neither breached the license agreement nor infringed CA's copyright. CA asserted two counterclaims. In the first, it claimed that National's use of the programs, either individually or through EDS, for the benefit of Lend Lease and Tilden, breached the license agreement. In the second, CA claimed that National infringed its copyright by making an unauthorized copy of the software.

National moved for judgment on the pleadings . . . , alleging that CA's first counterclaim was preempted under §301(a) of the Copyright Act. In resolving the motion, the district court concluded that CA alleged a lease agreement between National and the third parties: National permitted them to use the software in exchange for payment. The district court concluded that this cause of action, as pled, was "equivalent" to the exclusive copyright right of distribution of copies of the work, and held it was preempted.

The Copyright Act provides the exclusive source of protection for "all legal and equitable rights that are equivalent to any of the exclusive rights within the general scope of copyright as specified by section 106" of the Copyright Act. See 17 U.S.C. §301(a). Concomitantly, all non-equivalent rights are not preempted. A state cause of action is preempted if: (1) the work at issue is within the subject matter of copyright as defined in §§102 and 103 of the Copyright Act, and (2) the state law created right is equivalent to any of the exclusive rights within the general scope of copyright as specified in §106. Harper & Row, Publishers, Inc. v. Nation Enters., 723 F.2d 195, 200 (2d Cir.1983). . . .

In the first counterclaim, CA alleged, in pertinent part, that:

> The authorization for use granted National [pursuant to the 1990 License Agreement] was for the internal operations of National and for the processing of its own data. (First Counterclaim, P 31) Pursuant to the Supplement Addendum . . . it was agreed that the Licensed Programs would be used solely for the benefit of National and subject to the rights, obligations and benefits in all respects of the terms and conditions of the License Agreement. (First Counterclaim, P 32) Pursuant to the Supplement Addendum . . . National and EDS further agreed, among other things, to use the Licensed Programs . . . solely to process data of National and in no event for the processing of data of any third party other than National. (First Counterclaim, P 33) . . . In none of the License Agreements was [National] granted any authorization to use the licensed programs for the benefit of any company other than itself. (First Counterclaim, P 35) . . . National has used and permitted the use of the Licensed Programs for the processing of data for the benefit of third parties. This use of the Licensed Programs for the benefit of third parties includes the use for Lend Lease Trucks, Inc. and Tilden Car Rental, Inc. (First Counterclaim, P 36) . . . National has been unjustly enriched by any fees or other compensation received from those third-parties for use of the Licensed Programs for their benefit. (First Counterclaim, P 37)

The district court noted that the computer software in question was within the subject matter of copyright, and thus focused on whether CA's breach of contract action sought to protect rights equivalent to the exclusive copyright rights. The court noted that National had not alleged which copyright right was equivalent to CA's action, but concluded that the distribution right was the only right potentially equivalent.

In resolving the preemption issue, the court concluded that "[c]onstrued as true, CA's allegations reflect the existence of a lease arrangement between National and Lend Lease and Tilden: National has permitted Lend Lease and Tilden to use the licensed software in exchange for payment. The distribution right includes specifically the right to lease or lend." Mem. op. at 9-10. The court further concluded that the presence of a contract promise did not create a right qualitatively different from copyright, and stated: "In essence, CA alleges National breached the license agreement by infringing CA's copyrights in the licensed software." *Id.* at 10.

We believe that in reaching this conclusion, the district court either failed to give CA the benefit of all reasonable inferences from the pleadings or misinterpreted the law of copyright preemption. . . .

The only potential allegation of unauthorized distribution comes in CA's contention that National "permitted the use" of the programs. Because we must give CA the benefit of all reasonable inferences from the pleadings, we cannot conclude that an allegation that National "permitted the use" necessarily amounts to an allegation of the actual distribution of a copy of the program. Rather, we believe that such a pleading can be read, in context, to allege that National permitted EDS to use the programs for the benefit of Lend Lease and Tilden, with no copies ever going to Lend Lease and Tilden. . . .

We thus conclude that CA's pleadings cannot be read to allege that National breached its contract by actually distributing a copy of the licensed program to either Lend Lease or Tilden. . . .

C. Preemption of the Contractual Limitation on Use

The question then becomes whether CA's allegation that National breached their contract by using the program in a fashion not allowed under the contract protects a right equivalent to one of the exclusive copyright rights. We believe it does not.

We agree with the district court that the computer program in question is within the subject matter of copyright. Thus we focus on the second preemption issue: whether the right sought under state law is equivalent to the exclusive rights under copyright. We must consider whether a limitation on the uses to which a licensee may put a licensed work are preempted even though those uses do not involve the exclusive copyright rights. As noted above, courts and commentators have framed this inquiry as whether the right in question is "infringed by the mere act of reproduction, performance, distribution or display." 1 Nimmer on Copyright §1.01[B], at 1-13. Section 301 preempts only those state law rights that " 'may be abridged by an act which, in and of itself, would infringe one of the exclusive rights' provided by federal copyright law." Computer Assocs. Int'l, Inc. v. Altai, Inc., 982 F.2d 693, 716 (2d Cir.1992) (citing Harper & Row, Publishers, Inc. v. Nation Enters., 723 F.2d 195, 200 (2d Cir.1983), *rev'd on other grounds,* 471 U.S. 539, 105 S.Ct. 2218, 85

L.Ed.2d 588 (1985)). If an extra element is "required, instead of or in addition to the acts of reproduction, performance, distribution or display, in order to constitute a state-created cause of action, then the right does not lie 'within the general scope of copyright' and there is no preemption." 1 Nimmer on Copyright §1.01[B], at 1-14-15 (footnotes omitted). . . .

We conclude that the alleged contractual restriction on National's use of the licensed programs constitutes an extra element in addition to the copyright rights making this cause of action qualitatively different from an action for copyright.

National initially contends that any complaint alleging use of a copyrighted work that exceeds the uses allowable under the license must be brought as a copyright infringement claim; contract claims containing such allegations are preempted. In support of this proposition, National cites several cases finding copyright infringement when the licensee's "use" of a copyrighted and licensed work exceeded the uses allowed under the license. . . .

Because we find no general rule holding breach of contract actions such as this one preempted, we examine specifically whether this cause of action seeks to protect rights equivalent to the exclusive copyright rights. We conclude that the contractual restriction on use of the programs constitutes an additional element making this cause of action not equivalent to a copyright action.

National disagrees with this characterization and attempts to read the term "use" in the license agreement as synonymous with the rights given to the copyright holder. We believe it is not, as two recent cases make clear.

In a case very similar to this one, involving CA, the court held that a contractual restriction on use of a computer program was distinct from the exclusive copyright rights. In Computer Assocs. v. State St. Bank & Trust, 789 F.Supp. 470 (D.Mass.1992), the parties had executed a license that provided, inter alia: "Customer agrees to refrain from using the Equipment . . . for other customer-sites or customers on a service basis." *Id.* at 475. CA argued that State Street violated the provisions of the license agreement by allowing customers direct access to the programs to gain information. Because of that alleged breach, Computer Associates claimed that it could cancel their maintenance contract. State Street moved for a preliminary injunction prohibiting CA from cancelling the maintenance contract. CA then claimed that the violation of the agreements constituted copyright infringement, preventing State Street from claiming irreparable harm. In denying this claim, the court stated: infringement results only from the unauthorized copying of copyrighted material. A use of an authorized copy of copyrighted subject matter ordinarily is not infringing. . . . Therefore, applicable limitations on State Street's use of the programs, if any, must be derived initially from the license agreements, not copyright law. *Id.* at 472.

The Ninth Circuit reached a similar conclusion in G.S. Rasmussen & Assocs. v. Kalitta Flying Serv., 958 F.2d 896 (9th Cir.1992). In *Kalitta,* the plaintiff had received from the FAA a certificate (STC) allowing him to modify a plane design. The defendant took the certificate from an existing, modified plane and used it to modify another plane, without paying the plaintiff for doing so. Plaintiff sued for unfair competition, and the defendant raised the defense of copyright preemption. The court first noted that there was no allegation of copying. It went on to hold that:

> Federal copyright law governs only copying. . . . Enforcement of Rasmussen's property right in his STC leaves Kalitta free to make as many copies of the certificate as it wishes; to the extent the manual supplement is not protected by the copyright laws, the same is true of it. That Kalitta is prevented from then using these copies to obtain an airworthiness certificate from the FAA does not interfere in any way with the operation of the copyright laws.

Id. at 904.

In both of these cases, the courts distinguished restrictions on use of a copyrightable work that did not involve "copying" from the exclusive rights in copyright. CA's situation is the same. CA does not claim that National is doing something that the copyright laws reserve exclusively to the copyright holder, or that the use restriction is breached "by the mere act of reproduction, performance, distribution or display." Instead, on this posture, CA must be read to claim that National's or EDS's processing of data for third parties is the prohibited act. None of the exclusive copyright rights grant CA that right of their own force. Absent the parties' agreement, this restriction would not exist. Thus, CA is alleging that the contract creates a right not existing under the copyright law, a right based upon National's promise, and that it is suing to protect that contractual right. The contractual restriction on use of the programs constitutes an extra element that makes this cause of action qualitatively different from one for copyright.

We believe that the legislative history of the Copyright Act supports this conclusion. In elaborating the meaning of the term "equivalent rights" the House committee report to the Copyright Act suggests that breaches of contract were not generally preempted: "nothing in the bill derogates from the rights of parties to contract with each other and to sue for breaches of contract." See H.R.Rep. No. 94-1476, 94th Cong., 2d Sess. 132, *reprinted in* 1976 U.S.C.C.A.N. 5659, 5748. This is not the end of the inquiry, however.

National contends that while the bill as initially drafted might have excluded breaches of contract from preemption, the bill as passed did not. National notes that §301(b)(3) of the Copyright Act, as initially drafted and reported out of committee in the House, explicitly exempted breach of contract suits from preemption. This provision was then amended on the floor of the House to delete all the specific examples of non-preempted causes of action. National claims this action demonstrated congressional intent to remove the "safe harbor" from preemption for breach of contract actions. See, e.g., Wolff v. Institute of Elec. & Elecs. Eng'rs, Inc., 768 F.Supp. 66 (S.D.N.Y.1991) (deletion of safe harbor provision for breaches of contracts suggests that Congress did not intend generally to except them from preemption).

We disagree. Although the deletion of a provision from a final bill generally means that Congress intends to disavow what was formerly expressed, we believe in this case the facts surrounding the deletion of §301(b)(3) suggest Congress did not intend to reverse the presumption of non-preemption for the examples initially included in §301(b)(3). Instead, it appears that certain members of the House were concerned about the subsequent addition of the tort of misappropriation to the list of non-preempted causes of action, and suggested deletion of the specific examples in order to prevent confusion about the scope of preemption. . . . [W]e believe, the better view is that the legislative history suggests a congressional intent not to preempt breach of contract actions such as this one. . . .

We do not read CA to allege that National was unjustly enriched as a result of a wrongful exercise of one of the §106 rights. Rather, we read this allegation of damage as a further explanation of the damages CA intends to prove arising from the breach of contract. CA alleges generally that it has been damaged in an amount to be proved at trial, and it will have to prove those damages. In this context, we read its allegations of unjust enrichment as an attempt, albeit inartful, to allege that National received from Lend Lease and Tilden amounts that CA would have received had National not breached their contract. Second, National notes that CA requested return or destruction of any copies of its programs still in National's possession. It notes that the Copyright Act provides precisely that remedy, see 17 U.S.C. §504, and claims that the request for destruction shows the claim is equivalent to a copyright claim. We disagree. The parties' contract specifically provides for the return or destruction of the licensed programs upon any breach of the license agreement. This remedy would apply equally to this asserted breach (improper use) as to an action for breach of an agreement to pay royalties or license fees, which National admits would not be preempted. Furthermore, the copyright remedy of return or destruction applies even absent a preexisting relationship between the parties: it does not have to be stated in a contract or license agreement. We cannot conclude that this action is preempted simply because the parties' contract provides a remedy for breach identical to a remedy provided in copyright. . . .

III. Conclusion

For all the foregoing reasons, we conclude that CA's cause of action, as pled, is not preempted by the Copyright Act. Therefore, we reverse the order of the district court dismissing CA's first counterclaim with prejudice and remand for further proceedings consistent with this opinion.

COMMENTS AND QUESTIONS

1. It is worth noting that *Vault* is based on federal copyright preemption. Courts have generally not been concerned about contracts that avoid the provisions of state trade secrecy laws. See, e.g., Warner-Lambert Pharm. Co. v. Reynolds, Inc., 178 F. Supp. 655 (S.D.N.Y. 1959). But see Gary Van Zeeland Talent, Inc. v. Sandas, 267 N.W.2d 242 (Wis. 1978); Sarkes Tarzian, Inc. v. Audio Devices, Inc., 166 F. Supp. 250 (S.D. Cal. 1958), *aff'd*, 283 F.2d 696 (9th Cir. 1960) (refusing to enforce such agreements but not on preemption grounds).

Even if the Louisiana License Act is preempted by federal law, could state contract law (or the UCC) provide that agreements prohibiting reverse engineering will be enforced under state contract law? Would contract law as a whole be preempted in that case, on the grounds that it conflicts with the right to reverse engineer computer programs generally thought to exist in the Copyright Act? More likely, federal law would simply preclude the state from using its judicial power to enforce this contract term. On this point, compare Meehan v. PPG Indus., 802 F.2d 881, 886 (7th Cir. 1986), and Boggild v. Kenner Prods., 776 F.2d 1315 (6th Cir. 1985) (both finding illegal agreements to extend the term of patented or copyrighted products) with Aronson v. Quick Point Pencil Co., 440 U.S. 257 (1979) (contract could require the payment of royalties on an invention in the public domain).

2. Contract law is not as powerful a weapon for plaintiffs as is intellectual property law. For example, the House Committee Notes to section 109(a) of the Copyright Act provide that a contract limiting a user's first sale rights may be enforceable by an action for breach of contract but does not give rise to an action for copyright infringement. Thus the fact that an intellectual property owner may be entitled only to expectation damages, rather than unjust enrichment, statutory damages, attorney's fees, and an injunction, might be thought to weaken contract sufficiently that it is unlikely to supplant copyright law, just as a weak trade secrecy requirement was no threat to patent law. See generally Robert P. Merges, The End of Friction? Property Rights and Contract in the "Newtonian" World of On-line Commerce, 12 Berkeley Tech. L.J. 115 (1997) (making the familiar argument regarding the fundamental differences between contract and property).

Other scholars have challenged this argument, however. Mark Lemley offers this evaluation of proposals to allow copyright owners to opt out of copyright entirely and to rely *solely* on contractual protection:

Until recently, copyright owners would probably have found this an unattractive alternative, precisely because there were some types of conduct that copyright could reach but contract could not, and because the remedies for copyright infringement were so much stronger. The proposed expansion of contract in UCC2B to allow it to reach third parties not in privity with the vendor in any meaningful sense, coupled with the ability of vendors to write almost any remedy they wish into the contract, may make those differences disappear. Indeed, the possibility that intellectual property owners can get consequential and punitive damages, injunctive relief, extra-judicial self-help, and technological protection without having to meet any of the substantive requirements of intellectual property law, simply by contracting for it, might prove quite attractive to them.

The very fact that contract law will be augmented by UCC2B to give it the character and power of public legislation suggests that even in an "opt-out" scheme, contracts are not really "different" for preemption purposes. But in fact the problem with UCC2B is worse. It is *not* an opt-out statute. Rather, it permits intellectual property owners to pick and choose a combination of copyright and contractual rules and remedies. By adding its contract-enforcement regime to existing federal intellectual property rights, UCC2B distorts the balance that exists with contract alone.

Mark A. Lemley, Beyond Preemption: The Law and Policy of Intellectual Property Licensing, 87 Cal. L. Rev. 111 (1999).

Second, some courts have held that breach of a license agreement can itself violate the intellectual property laws. In Microsoft Corp. v. Harmony Computers, discussed supra, the court held:

> Third, if defendants purchased their Products from Microsoft licensees who were acting outside the scope of their licenses by selling the Products stand-alone, any distribution of the Products by defendants, whether within the scope of plaintiff's license agreement or not, would constitute copyright infringement. Microsoft Corp. v. ATS Computers, Inc. et al., CV 93-1273 (S.D.Cal. 1993); Major League Baseball Promotion v. Colour-Tex, 729 F. Supp. 1035, 1041 (D.N.J. 1990) ("A licensee who has failed to satisfy a condition of the license or has materially breached the licensing contract has no rights to give a sublicensee under which the sublicensee can take cover in a copyright infringement case, and therefore, both the licensee and the sublicensee can be held liable for acting without authorization and thereby infringing the licensor's copyright.").
>
> Finally, plaintiff's claim that defendants exceeded the scope of its license agreements states a claim for copyright infringement rather than breach of contract. Not being parties to any license agreement with Microsoft, defendants are "complete strangers" to Microsoft, and their violations of the licensing restrictions must of necessity be seen as claims arising under the copyright laws rather than the law of contracts. See Marshall v. New Kids on the Block Partnership, 780 F. Supp. 1005, 1008 (S.D.N.Y. 1991). Even if defendants were seen as parties to Microsoft's license agreements, their undisputed distribution of Products outside the scope of the license agreements

puts them in the same position as an infringer having no contractual relationship with the copyright holder and again makes them "strangers" to Microsoft. *Id.* at 1009; Kanakos v. MX Trading Corp., 1981 WL 1377, *2 (S.D.N.Y. Sept. 16, 1981). Accordingly, plaintiff's allegation that defendants exceeded the scope of the license agreement states a claim for copyright infringement.

Does this result make sense? Should the outcome turn on the nature of the breach—in particular, on whether the licensee was doing something that would have been illegal but for the license, or whether he was doing something (like reverse engineering) that he would otherwise have had a right to do?

3. The court states that since "National's or EDS's processing of data for third parties is the prohibited act," and since nothing in the Copyright Act limits the rights of certain parties to use a copyrighted work, the contract-based cause of action is not preempted. The court distinguishes this behavior—allowing an unauthorized third party to use a work—from the actual distribution of a copy of a work; since the behavior is not equivalent to a protected right under section 106, it is not preempted. What if National had made copies of the program and distributed them to third parties? Would not those third parties still have to use the work? Would this use—which occurs in this hypothetical *in addition to* the copyright-protected acts of copying and distribution rather than *instead of* them, as in the actual case—form the basis for a nonpreempted contract cause of action? If not, the case might make sense; it provides independent content to a state cause of action for breach of contract. But if use restrictions based on copying are not preempted, then allegations of "breach through improper use" will *always* be available to form the foundation for an alternative cause of action (breach of contractual use restriction) in what is otherwise a copyright infringement case.

4. The case for preempting contract terms that conflict with rights granted under intellectual property law is premised on two ideas. First, the entire right that the intellectual property owner is licensing was created by a federal statute that allocates only a limited set of rights to the licensor. Second, that allocation of rights reflects a "delicate balance" between many different interests, and not all of those interests are represented in licensing contracts. Allowing private parties to avoid the effects of intellectual property law would undermine that balance. For arguments in favor of preemption, see David A. Rice, Public Goods, Private Contract and Public Policy: Federal Preemption of Software License Prohibitions Against Reverse Engineering, 53 U. Pitt. L. Rev. 543 (1992); Mark A. Lemley, Intellectual Property and Shrinkwrap Licenses, 68 S. Cal. L. Rev. 1239 (1995); Julie E. Cohen, Reverse Engineering and the Rise of Electronic Vigilantism: Intellectual Property Implications of "Lock-Out" Programs, 68 S. Cal. L. Rev. 1091 (1995).

Does a pro-preemption stance suggest that government is in a better position than private parties to set the terms of licensing transactions? Is that view consistent with generally accepted economics principles? Or is there something about intellectual property licensing that suggests we cannot rely on the parties to the license to produce an efficient outcome?

5. *Vault* involved a shrinkwrap license. Would the court reach the same result if the provision at issue were a bargained contract between two commercial parties? Should it? Does *National* shed any light on this question?

Note on Anti-Propertization Agreements:
Copyleft and the Open Source Movement

Not all software is distributed on a traditional purchasing basis. Alternative distribution mechanisms such as "shareware" and "freeware" have played a significant role in the development of the software industry, particularly in the early days of both the software and Internet markets. Recently reconceived as the "open source code" movement, these alternative distribution schemes are gaining strength and mainstream credibility as commercial companies like IBM and Netscape have released their source code to the public to modify and redistribute.

How does copyright law apply to such transactions? Consider the case of "shareware"—software that is freely distributed either in full working versions or in sample versions. Shareware often requests that users pass on copies of the software to others. Payment is then due under the terms of the shareware "license" when a new user accepts the terms of transfer through continued use of the program or when the users request a full working version of the program. Shareware typically also restricts users from passing on copies for a price. Is this restriction enforceable? Is it enforceable after a re-transfer from one user to another? See Storm Impact, Inc. v. Software of the Month Club, Inc., 44 U.S.P.Q.2d 1441 (N.D. Ill. 1997) (suggesting the answer is yes to both).

Still other software is distributed free of any charge, frequently because the programmers believe in sharing information as widely and as freely as possible. Ironically, some distributors of such "freeware" have turned to contract law to protect their software—here, from incorporation into copyrighted commercial products:

> In the beginning, and still in many communities, the prevailing norm was free exchange. This freedom of exchange is a manifestation of the prevailing norm from the early days of software. One prominent organization, the Free Software Foundation, promotes this norm today through the institution of "copyleft," a copyright license that requires transferees of free software to promise not to incorporate it in a commercial product and to pass it on, even if embedded in a larger program, to others free of use restrictions.

By its own terms, the copyleft agreement is an unusual license; at the most basic level consider the problem of determining damages when the licensee frustrates the licensor's expectation of zero profits under the contract. But what is most significant about the agreement is that it purports to restrict subsequent transferees who receive software from a licensee, presumably even if the licensee fails to attach a copy of the agreement. As this new transferee is not in privity with the original copyleft licensor, the stipulation seems unenforceable.

Even so, copyleft no doubt carries some moral force in the on-line community. It therefore serves as an example of a non-binding, informal norm in cyberspace. The copyleft license in this community is the equivalent of a statement of good practices. Surely some programmers dutifully pass along the license and police cases where subsequent transferees receive code without such a license. In short, the notice is aimed at the perpetuation and enforcement of a norm that holds some force in this community, and it is therefore worth mentioning in a catalogue of rights in digital content.

Robert P. Merges, The End of Friction? Property Rights and Contract in the "Newtonian" World of On-Line Commerce, 12 Berkeley Tech. L.J. 115 (1997); see also Ira V. Heffan, Copyleft: Licensing Collaborative Works in the Digital Age, 49 Stan. L. Rev. 1487 (1997).

Note that while the author argues that the copyleft agreement is unenforceable against individuals not in privity with the original author, UCITA would create such privity by binding transferrees and successors to the terms of the contract. Ironically, therefore, a form of contract pushed by Microsoft may end up redounding to the benefit of the open source movement. See Robert Gomulkiewicz, How Copyleft Uses License Rights to Succeed in the Open Source Software Revolution and the Implications for Article 2B, 36 Hous. L. Rev. 179 (1999).

Open source software is not necessarily noncommercial, however. A number of companies have recently adopted an open source strategy because they believe they will make more money by giving their code away than by selling it. This seemingly counterintuitive notion builds on two facts about software: it is a network good, and it interrelates with a host of other goods. Companies who want to make money by giving software away are following one or both of two common strategies. The first strategy is to give the product away in order to build a market share in the hope that that market share will allow you to collect more money in later periods. Opening your source code allows you to benefit from the knowledge and expertise of thousands of users, and therefore to put the best product on the market. Once your product dominates the market, you can begin charging for upgrades and the like. An alternative strategy is to open a product for free use but to charge for some affiliated product or service that serious users are likely to want. Both Netscape (which gives away its Internet browser and has opened the browser source code but charges for server software) and Red Hat (which offers commercial support for the open-source Linux operating system) are following this second strategy.

COMMENTS AND QUESTIONS

1. For a copy of the "copyleft" agreement, consult *http://www. gnu.ai.mit.edu/copyleft/gpl.html.*

2. Should copyright law treat "prodissemination" contracts such as copyleft agreements as any differently from other agreements? If copyright is ultimately about getting works into the hands of consumers, perhaps so. On the other hand, why should courts foster contract law's goal of individual autonomy as manifested in private ordering in the case of copyleft agreements but not in the case of restrictive use agreements?

E. SOFTWARE CONSULTING AGREEMENTS

The emphasis on mass-market licensing and the issues it presents sometimes obscure an important fact: more than one-third of all software industry revenues in the United States come from custom, as opposed to off-the-shelf, software. The legal issues surrounding creation of custom software are very different from those involved in the prepackaged software market. Of paramount importance are:

- The status of the software engineer(s) who write the code—that is, employee or consultant;
- The understanding regarding reuse of the code; and
- Agreement regarding which party will maintain the software, and who is permitted to adapt and modify it.

1. Employee or Consultant?

Aymes v. Bonelli, 980 F.2d 857 (2d Cir. 1992) [In this typical case, a computer programmer named Aymes was paid to write software by Island, Inc., a company that installed swimming pools. After a dispute regarding payment and reuse of the programs Aymes had written—in particular a program called "CSALIB"—Aymes registered the copyright to the programs. This lawsuit followed. Island won below when the trial court determined that (a) there was no written agreement between the parties on which to base a determination of ownership; and (b) Aymes was an employee under the many-factored test laid down by the Supreme Court in CCNV v. Reid, 490 U.S. 730 (1989), thus rendering CSALIB a work for hire under the Copyright Act and making Island the owner of the work.]

A review of this analysis shows that the significant factors supporting Island's contention that Aymes was an employee include Island's right to control the means of CSALIB's creation and Island's right to assign other projects. The significant factors supporting Aymes's argument that he was an independent contractor include: the level of skill needed to create CSALIB; the decision of Island not to offer him benefits; and his payment of his own social security taxes. The other factors were either indeterminate, because they were evenly balanced between the parties, or of marginal significance, because they were inapplicable to these facts.

Examining the factors for each side in terms of their importance, we conclude that the only major factor strongly supporting Island is that it directed the creation of the program. Island did reserve the right to assign Aymes other projects, which is a major factor, but under these facts this was not necessarily inconsistent with an independent contractor relationship. Supporting Aymes's argument that he was an independent contractor, however, are several important factors—his skill, and the tax and benefit factors —that outweigh the elements supporting Island. The other factors outlined in *Reid* are either indeterminate or of negligible importance, and cannot outweigh the significance we attach to Island's choice to treat Aymes as an independent contractor when it was to Island's financial benefit. Now that this treatment is no longer to Island's benefit, the company must still adhere to the choice it made.

Note that the court's conclusion—that Aymes was an independent contractor—means that Aymes owns the copyright in the work. Absent an assignment agreement or even a written license, he, not the company, owns the right to make future copies and adaptations of the work regardless of how much the company paid him to write it.

COMMENTS AND QUESTIONS

1. The Copyright Act defines "work for hire" as follows:

A "work made for hire" is—
    (1) a work prepared by an employee within the scope of his or her employment; or
    (2) a work specially ordered or commissioned for use as a contribution to a collective work, as part of a motion picture or other audiovisual work, as a translation, as a supplementary work, as a compilation, as an instructional text, as a test, as answer material for a test, or as an atlas, if the parties expressly agree in a written instrument signed by them that the work shall be considered a work made for hire. . . .

17 U.S.C. §101 (1998).
2. In addition to *Aymes*, see Maclean Assocs. v. Wm. M. Merver-Meidinger-Hansen, Inc., 952 F.2d 769 (3d Cir. 1991), where a dispute erupted over personnel management software written for the defendant by ex-employee Barry MacLean:

We believe that consideration of the nine factors the Supreme Court listed in *Reid* could bring a rational jury to conclude that Mr. MacLean was not an actual servant of Mercer when JEMSystem was created. Mr. MacLean says he wrote the JEMSystem software after he left Mercer and continued in a consulting relationship with it on the NYSE project. His task of writing sophisticated computer software required skill and creativity. Mr. MacLean worked with his own software on his own computer at his own facility to complete Mercer's obligation under its contract with NYSE. Although Mr. MacLean was a principal of Mercer for almost five years, the duration of his relationship as a consultant for Mercer on the NYSE project was fairly short. Mercer did not have the right to assign additional projects to Mr. MacLean. Mr. MacLean had absolute discretion over when and how long to work. Mercer paid Mr. MacLean for the delivery of his services as a consultant, instead of paying him a regular periodic salary. It is obvious that Mercer's regular business is compensation consulting. It was not a part of Mercer's regular business at the relevant time to provide software for its clients' use on personal computers; instead, prior to Mr. MacLean's creation of the JEM-System software, Mercer took raw data its clients provided and produced for its clients computerized reports that evaluated and synthesized the data. Mercer did not pay any payroll or social security taxes on behalf of Mr. MacLean after he ceased to be one of Mercer's principals, nor did it thereafter provide him with workers' compensation coverage or contribute to unemployment insurance or workers' compensation funds. It is not known how Mercer treated its payments to Mr. MacLean for its own corporate tax purposes.

3. In the case of some types of copyrightable works, a written agreement prepared at the outset of the project can take care of all potential ownership claims, regardless of whether the work is prepared by an employee. See 17 U.S.C. §201(b) (1998). In other cases, employment status determines initial ownership: *Aymes* is an example. It is important to recognize that work-for-hire status only governs the initial ownership, however; technically, it defines who is the "author" of a work. Regardless of initial ownership, copyright in all works can be assigned. An agreement to assign a work before it is created is also fully enforceable. Hence work-for-hire issues are important as a practical matter only when the parties fail to specify ownership allocation in advance. This happens surprisingly often in the software world, however.

The impact of failing to obtain an assignment is fairly dramatic: a company that hires a consultant to write a program for the company's use and that pays the consultant for the program may end up not owning the program. Not only may the consultant resell the same program to a competitor, but the purchasing company's own ability to use the software may be put in jeopardy. It is critical, therefore, that the parties agree up front who will own what rights in the software to be created.

2. Rights to Re-Use Software

Even when it is clear that a consultant owns her work product, the parties can of course apportion use rights any number of ways by assignment or license. It is important to note that assignment is very different from even a very broad license. An assignment conveys title, which can be thought of as the right to decide what do with a work under all sorts of contingencies that the parties could not have even thought of when the agreement was signed. This can have very important practical ramifications, which by their nature are difficult to foresee.

Beyond that of ownership, the important threshold questions for the parties are (1) whether and to what extent each can re-use the work that is the subject of the contract; (2) whether and to what extent each or both can modify or adapt it; and (3) whether and to what extent the parties can resell the work, as originally created or in modified form.

Agreements on these terms take many forms, but some common ones include:

- The consultant owns the work outright, and the customer can only use it as originally delivered in its original form;
- The consultant owns the work, but the customer can reuse it and resell it in original or modified form, perhaps subject to limitations (no resale before a certain date; no resale to competitors of the consultant, etc.);
- The customer owns the work, but the consultant has the right to reuse it in meeting the needs of other customers, perhaps subject to a time limitation and/or a prohibition on reusing it in projects of the customer's direct competitors; or
- Both the customer and the consultant retain rights to use and license the work for their own purposes.

See generally Raymond Ocampo, Jr., Drafting and Negotiating Software Consulting Agreements (Glasser Legal Works, 1996 & Supp.).

7

Antitrust in the Computer Industry

Antitrust has recently taken on great prominence in the computer industry, to an extent not seen since the 1970s, when government and private cases against dominant computer manufacturer IBM captured the attention of the world. In the 1990s, it is a new market (software) and a new dominant player (Microsoft) that are the focus of antitrust scrutiny. Nonetheless, the multifarious cases against Microsoft are only a small part of the antitrust picture in the computer industry. There are a number of important issues relating to the interaction between antitrust and intellectual property law, for example. In addition, the confusing and fast-changing structure of the industry poses particular challenges for the sometimes-ponderous machinery of antitrust law. In this chapter, we approach all of these issues, paying particular attention to how antitrust rules interact with intellectual property and licensing in the computer context.

A. PRINCIPLES OF ANTITRUST LAW[1]

1. The Scope of Antitrust Law

Antitrust law protects competition and the competitive process by preventing certain types of conduct that threaten a free market. For example, antitrust prohibits competitors from agreeing on the price they will

---

1. This Section is provided for the benefit of those students who have not previously been exposed to antitrust law. Students with prior antitrust background are welcome to begin with Section B.

charge. It prohibits certain predatory practices designed to exclude competitors from the market, and it places certain limits on the behavior of firms with market power.

Competition is good for a variety of reasons. Basic economics tells us that competing firms produce more and price lower than monopolists. Monopolists not only take money away from consumers by raising prices, but they impose a "deadweight loss" on society by reducing their output below the level that consumers would be willing to purchase at a competitive price. A monopoly has other problems as well: it inherently reduces consumer choice, and provides fewer incentives to innovate than do competitive firms.

The first U.S. antitrust law was passed in 1890. The Sherman Act, as the statute is called, was a reaction to populist pressure on Congress to do something about the trusts that had come to dominate the American business landscape. The Sherman Act granted broad powers to government to break up trusts and other conspiracies in restraint of trade. The Sherman Act, which is still in force today, provides in part:

> Section 1 [15 U.S.C. §1]. Every contract, combination in the form of trust or otherwise, or conspiracy, in restraint of trade or commerce among the several States, or with a foreign nation, is declared to be illegal. . . .
>
> Section 2 [15 U.S.C. §2]. Every person who shall monopolize, or attempt to monopolize, or combine or conspire with any other person or persons, to monopolize any part of the trade or commerce among the several States, or with foreign nations, shall be deemed guilty of a felony. . . .

By their terms, these laws are broad indeed. In some sense, *every* contract necessarily restrains trade, because it forecloses options that were once open. Under the literal terms of section 1, employment contracts and sales contracts might be considered antitrust violations.

In practice, courts quickly gave the Sherman Act a more restrictive interpretation. The Supreme Court read section 1 as prohibiting only *unreasonable* restraints of trade. Much antitrust jurisprudence in the last century has attempted to distinguish reasonable from unreasonable restraints of trade.

The courts also limited the reach of section 2 to ensure that successful businesses would not be punished because of their success. Because the antitrust laws provide for felony criminal punishments, private treble damage actions and injunctions, and plaintiffs' attorneys' fees, the possibility of overdeterring legitimate business conduct is a real concern. To avoid this problem, the courts have distinguished between possessing a monopoly and actively acquiring or maintaining a monopoly through anticompetitive conduct. Section 2 prohibits only the latter.

Congress has never amended the core provisions of the Sherman Act. In 1914, however, in response to what it perceived as lax judicial enforcement of the antitrust laws, Congress passed the Clayton Act. The Clayton Act contains a number of specific provisions that serve to clarify the Sherman Act. For example, section 3 of the Clayton Act enumerates and prohibits certain types of agreements that are also included within the general scope of section 1.

The Clayton Act was amended in 1950 to prohibit certain types of mergers. Section 7 of the Act prohibits mergers and acquisitions (of a corporation, stock, or assets) where "the effect of such acquisition may be substantially to lessen competition or to tend to create a monopoly" in "any line of commerce . . . in any section of the country." Thus the antitrust laws prevent businesses from acting anticompetitively in three basic ways.

Monopolization. It is not illegal to have a monopoly. However, monopolists and firms gaining market power need to be very careful about their behavior. A monopolist violates section 2 if it has "market power" (defined as the power to raise prices or exclude competition in a relevant market) and engages in anticompetitive conduct designed to maintain or extend that power. Over time, the courts have identified a number of anticompetitive practices (and the circumstances in which they are actionable). We will discuss several in this chapter. A company may also be guilty of "attempted monopolization" if it intends to monopolize a market, engages in anticompetitive conduct, and has a "dangerous probability of successful monopolization." See, e.g., Spectrum Sports v. McQuillen, 506 U.S. 447 (1993).

To find that a defendant has monopolized a market, the court must first decide what the relevant market is. Specifically, the court must identify a product or set of products and a geographic region within which most consumers make their purchases. Controlling such a market will allow a monopolist to raise prices without losing customers to competitors from outside the market. The definition of a relevant market and the analysis of power in that market are both extremely complex questions, and a good deal of legal and economic work has gone into the attempt to define exactly what market power is. For a more detailed discussion of this issue, see U.S. Department of Justice and Federal Trade Commission, Revised Merger Guidelines §1 (April 2, 1992).

Agreements. Courts have identified two basic types of agreements that may be in restraint of trade—agreements among competitors (called "horizontal restraints") and agreements between buyers and sellers (called "vertical restraints").[2] Vertical restraints are generally less threatening to competition than horizontal restraints. With the exception of vertical price-fixing, they are generally judged under the rule of reason, under which the courts balance the anticompetitive harms of a restraint against its procom-

---

2. Actually, the term "vertical restraints" refers to a whole class of transactions between companies in a vertical relationship in the chain of distribution, including dealers, franchisors, distributors, resellers, etc.

petitive benefits. Only those restraints that produce harms significantly in excess of benefits to competition are deemed unreasonable.

Horizontal restraints are more troubling because they may allow the participants to create a cartel, which can then behave anticompetitively, much as a monopolist would. At first, most agreements between competitors were deemed illegal per se, without any necessity for a weighing of harms and benefits to competition. Today, the Supreme Court has retreated from that position, recognizing that certain agreements among competitors may be efficient and procompetitive. Many horizontal restraints are now judged under the rule of reason. Only certain forms of "naked" agreements to fix prices or divide territories remain illegal per se.

Mergers. Section 7 of the Clayton Act is intended to catch monopolies "in their incipiency." Because of this, the standard for proving the existence of market power is significantly lower in the case of a merger than in a section 2 monopolization claim. If a merger would substantially lessen competition in a relevant market, the courts may prohibit it. As with most other areas of antitrust law, however, courts are usually willing to consider a merger's potential benefits to competition in deciding whether it should be prevented.

Most merger enforcement takes place at the Antitrust Division of the U.S. Department of Justice and at the Federal Trade Commission (FTC). The Hart-Scott-Rodino Act of 1976 requires companies to file a statement with the Antitrust Division and the FTC and to seek approval for mergers over a certain size. If the Division or the FTC feels that a merger will restrain competition, it can challenge the merger in court before the merger takes place. 15 U.S.C. §7A.

Note on Antitrust Theory

The antitrust laws clearly reflect some congressional judgment that "big is bad." But *why* it is bad has been the subject of almost continuous debate since the enactment of the antitrust laws. At least three different rationales have been advanced to explain the antitrust laws. The first view may be called the "populist" view of antitrust. Populists take the position that big is *intrinsically* bad. It may be bad for a variety of reasons: it concentrates wealth; it reduces product diversity; or it concentrates political power, for example. But regardless of the reason, populists would use the antitrust laws as a weapon against all monopolies and against oligopolies as well. Populists can find substantial support for their position in the legislative history of the Sherman Act and in the political climate in the late nineteenth century. For an elaboration of the populist view, see Walter Adams, The Bigness Complex: Industry, Labor and Government in the American Economy (1986); Victor H. Kramer, The Supreme Court and Tying Arrangements: Antitrust as History, 69 Minn. L. Rev. 1013 (1985).

In the second view, antitrust is designed to protect small businesses from being driven out of the market. This view is related to the populist view, as both are likely to vigorously oppose monopolies and growing concentration in an industry, but these views differ in the perception of the instrumental value served by preventing monopoly. Advocates of this latter view tend to view antitrust as an unfair-competition statute, and to apply the antitrust laws to a number of practices that are bad for competitors but good for competition. For example, small-business advocates are likely to be skeptical of price cuts by large national companies, which they fear will "squeeze out" local independents. The legislative history of the Clayton Act and subsequent antitrust laws lends some support to this view.

The final view of the antitrust laws is the economic or "social welfare" model. This approach sees the purpose of the antitrust laws as promoting social welfare by ensuring that markets work freely and without interference. Antitrust law is aimed at practices that corrupt the market or usurp its function. In this view, antitrust is particularly concerned with preventing horizontal restraints of trade. While there is relatively little in the history of the antitrust laws that suggests Congress was concerned with economics,[3] this approach has gained great currency with courts and scholars in the last 25 years. See, e.g., Robert H. Bork, The Antitrust Paradox: A Policy at War with Itself (1978); Richard Posner, Antitrust Law: An Economic Perspective (1976). Most antitrust experts now use economic effects as the basis for their analysis of potentially anticompetitive practices, although they continue to disagree vigorously over *how* those effects are to be analyzed.

2. Intellectual Property and Antitrust Law

Intellectual property law grants certain exclusive rights to the creators, inventors, or discoverers of certain intangible but valuable assets. In previous chapters, we have discussed the nature of these rights at length. There is substantial disagreement as to whether intellectual property rights are "property" in the ordinary sense of the term. But whatever they are, intellectual property rights give their owners the right to exclude others from using or copying their inventions or creations.

Traditionally, the conventional wisdom has been that the antitrust laws and the intellectual property laws are in conflict. See, e.g., Stephen Calkins, Patent Law: The Impact of the 1988 Patent Misuse Reform Act and Noerr-Pennington Doctrine on Misuse Defenses and Antitrust Counterclaims, 38 Drake L. Rev. 175, 176 n.1 (1989) (noting this historic belief). Baldly stated, the conflict arises because the intellectual property

---

3. But cf. F.M. Scherer, Efficiency, Fairness, and the Early Contributions of Economists to the Antitrust Debate, 29 Washburn L.J. 243, 250-251 (1990) (arguing that the views of mainstream economists in 1890 were consistent with the goals of the Sherman Act).

laws grant "monopolies" to inventors, while the goal of the antitrust laws is to prevent or restrict monopoly.

However, scholars have increasingly taken the position that the two laws are not in conflict at all. Rather, they are complementary efforts to promote an efficient marketplace and long-run, dynamic competition through innovation. Professor Goldstein was an early proponent of the idea that the intellectual property laws were designed to promote competition. See Paul Goldstein, The Competitive Mandate: From Sears to Lear, 59 Cal. L. Rev. 971 (1971). He was soon joined by others.

≡
≡ *Ward Bowman, Jr., Patent and Antitrust*
≡ *Law: A Legal and Economic Appraisal*
≡ *(1973)*

. . . Antitrust law and patent law are frequently viewed as standing in diametric opposition. How can there be compatibility between antitrust law, which promotes competition, and patent law, which promotes monopoly? In terms of the economic goals sought, the supposed opposition between these laws is lacking. Both antitrust law and patent law have a common central economic goal: *to maximize wealth by producing what consumers want at the lowest cost.* In serving this common goal, reconciliation between patent and antitrust law involves serious problems of assessing effects, but not conflicting purposes. Antitrust law does not demand competition under all circumstances. Quite properly, it permits monopoly when monopoly makes for greater output than would the alternative of an artificially fragmented (inefficient) industry. The patent monopoly fits directly into this scheme insofar as its central aim is achieved. It is designed to provide something which consumers value and which they could not have at all or have as abundantly were no patent protection afforded.

Antitrust Law

Under the Sherman Act agreements in restraint of trade (section 1) and monopolization or an attempt to monopolize (section 2) are condemned as illegal. The economic rationale for this condemnation is that monopoly makes it possible to restrict output and raise prices so that consumers pay more for and get less of the things they want most. The output restriction made possible by monopoly idles, or transfers to less urgent uses, those resources, which but for the monopolistic restriction would be more efficiently employed. Conversely, a competitive market process allocate scarce resources to those uses the community values most highly. Insofar as the antitrust laws are successful, they promote a market-oriented, profit-incentive process unimpeded by artificial roadblocks to efficiency. Such is the rationale of market competition and the antitrust laws that support it.

Patent Law

Patent law, thought by some to be an exception to a general rule in favor of competition, shares with antitrust law its central purpose—efficiently providing those things consumers value. But the means are different. Patent law pursues this goal by encouraging the invention of new and better products. Invention, like other forms of productive activity, is not costless. Those who undertake it, therefore, must be rewarded. And so elusive a commodity as an idea which qualifies as invention is peculiarly susceptible to being freely appropriated by others. A patent is a legal device to insure that there can be a property right in certain ideas. Thus the temporary right of a patentee to exclude others is a means of preventing "free riding" so that the employment of useful private resources may be remunerated. Without a patent system, prevention of "free riding" would be severely limited. Ability to keep secrets and to enforce private "know-how" contracts would, without patent law, provide inventors very limited protection from rapid and widespread copying by others. Central to the economic justification of a patent system is the presumption that without the patent right, too few resources would be devoted to invention.

The "exclusive right to make, use and vend the invention or discovery," which Congress has long granted patentees, is thus a legal monopoly exempt from the more general proscription of trade restraints and monopolization under early common law and more recent antitrust statutes.

Goal Evaluation

The goal of both antitrust law and patent law is to maximize allocative efficiency (making what consumers want) and productive efficiency (making these goods with the fewest scarce resources). In achieving this goal under either antitrust or patent law the detriment to be avoided is output restriction. This may arise from monopolization which diverts production from more urgent to less urgent use or from legal rules requiring inefficient methods of production. The evil, then may be viewed as net output restriction after efficiency increases are accounted for. Both antitrust and patent law seek output expansion not output restriction. Competition deserves support insofar as it brings about this result. And so it is with patents. The temporary monopoly afforded by a patent, once a particular invention has come into being, will have all the output-restrictive disabilities of any monopoly. The argument for patents is that without this temporary monopoly there would be insufficient profit incentives to produce the invention, and that because an invention is profitable only if consumers are willing to pay what the patentee charges, the consumers are therefore better off than they would be without the invention, even if they are charged "monopoly" prices. If this is so, a trade-off (some monopoly restraint for greater output in the long run) is in the interest of socially desirable resource allocation. An appraisal of alleged conflicts between antitrust law and patent law depends upon understanding the role of profits in providing the incentive for undertaking efficient production of those things consumers value. . . .

As a public policy tool perfect competition does provide useful insights into the equilibrating forces of a competitive process unencumbered by either external or internal impediments to the flow of resources responding to price and profit signals. Monopoly and agreements in restraint of trade are such impediments, and, as has been stressed, they are condemned for this reason. This does not mean, however, and the antitrust laws have never interpreted to mean, that every departure from the perfect competitive model becomes illegal. Rather, these laws, when consistently and rationally applied, view competition as a process designed to work for the benefit of consumers. They take the world as it is and evaluate available alternatives. And the allocation of resources cannot be fully evaluated unless productive efficiencies (cost savings or better products) are assessed along with restraints. Stressing perfect competition as an ideal involves the danger of underplaying the importance of productive efficiencies: savings arising from large size and efficiencies arising from innovation in manufacturing and from company organization and management, as well as from dissemination of knowledge through sales effort and advertising. Employee relations and myriad other activities also are sources of productive efficiency. None of these commonplace examples would exist if competition were perfect. These examples, moreover, are not output restricting. Imperfect competition is not monopoly. Dealing with imperfections is what competition as a process rather than a static model is all about. . . .

Efficiency and Patents

If the temporary monopoly afforded to inventors is to be justified as on balance desirable, its existence and the uses to which it is put must face up to the kind of restraint/efficiency assessment applied under antitrust law. Analytically, the combination of two competing patents raises the same questions as the merger of two competing companies; both combine competing assets. That the productive efficiencies predictable from a patent pool may seem *de minimis* does not change the nature of the analysis. It may, however, seem more analogous to the antitrust cartel rule than to the rule on mergers. And, of course, jointly fixing the price to be charged for competing patents is an even more obvious analogy.

The problem of assessing permissible output restriction under patent law is, in one important sense, different from that under antitrust law. The legal propriety of a basic patent monopoly has to be recognized. Consequently, evaluating whether certain patent licensing practices should be sanctioned will involve the proper scope of the legal monopoly. Is more being monopolized than what the patent grants, or is the practice merely maximizing the reward attributable to the competitive advantage afforded by a patent? . . . [M]any cases of alleged patent misuse—many, indeed, which are said to violate antitrust law—involve vertical contract relationships between patentee and licensee in which no such extension of scope is explicable. Many such contracts between patentees and licensees, moreover, lead to productive efficiencies unattainable if the practices are prohibited. Given a legal patent monopoly, it is important not only to appraise whether the monopoly has been broadened—scope extension—but also to insure that prohibiting alleged misuses does not leave the holder of the patent a permissible alternative which, although less profitable, is more restrictive than the alleged misuse. The "misuse" may actually be the more efficient use of the patent from the social as well as the private point of view. It pays monopolists as well as competitors to be efficient, as has been stressed. . . .

Growth makes an economy richer in successive years. Achieving continuously more efficient resource allocation is not only compatible with growth but is an essential aspect of it. But economic growth is more often associated with a decision to produce more and newer products for tomorrow by foregoing consumption today. This may be done by voluntary savings and investment or by a centralized decision about what should be growing. In neither case, however, is there any compelling reason to believe that tomorrow is necessarily more important than today. And this is as true for that unique commodity information, the subject matter of patent law, as it is for other unpatentable commodities. Thus, even though the patent legislation looks to the promotion of the progress of science and useful arts, and the antitrust law prohibits artificial barriers to the entry of new products or new production methods, neither need favor or disfavor investment over current consumption, and neither need favor particular forms of investment. The allocative function which antitrust law should support and patent law should supplement is market motivation, making it profitable to produce the wide variety of things that people choose. Free exercise of choice is not limited to choices among goods, or choices between goods and services, or choices between either of these and leisure. Timing—the choice between having now and having later—is also involved.

The patent law is often described as a special inducement to growth. But, as has been indicated, the patent law, like antitrust law, does not foster growth for growth's sake. Rather, it is designed to make possible those new products and new production methods which customers deem worth paying for. Promoting science and the useful arts . . . is not to be viewed as a reasonably exact facsimile of a crop-support program for the over-production of invention. If the patent system works as it is designed to work, growth can be expected to be fostered. Scarce resources are diverted from current consumption to better products for tomorrow.

Growth under a patent system is thus not a separate goal competing with consumer choice. It is the result of it. . . .

Second, the patent system is sometimes described as a public contract with an inventor for the disclosure of his secrets. In exchange for temporary monopoly over a product, the argument goes, the public gets the benefit of information on how to make it. Thus one goal of patent policy seems to many to be the broad dissemination of knowledge. An alternative to the patent monopoly, therefore, is the private means of keeping the invention secret. Keeping secrets is not costless to inventors, however, and secrecy costs can be expected to differ with different kinds of invention. For some kinds of invention, private secrecy costs may be so high as to foreclose invention. On the other hand, the cost of secrecy may be so low that public disclosure of the invention at the price of a seventeen-year monopoly will be more costly than secrecy. Moreover, the costs of secrecy vary not only with the nature of the invention, but also with who does the inventing, the breadth and scale of participation through which the invention can be most efficiently exploited, and the amount of special know-how required for its practice. And of course, the longer the time span covered by the patent, the greater the reward available from disclosure. It also should be evident that inventions, especially processes, whose efficient exploitation requires production and therefore knowledge by a large number of firms, will have higher secrecy cost that those whose exploitation can be confined to a single form. And even within those single firms capable of exploiting an invention internally, the costs of secrecy will be lower the fewer the persons who must know the secret.

Public revelation of the secrets of invention, however, is not the primary function of patent law. Patent law insures that those who incur the costs of inventing will reap its reward if users find the result worth paying for. This cannot occur if others reap where the investor has sown. The patent system is thus designed to stop "free riding" so that the profit-incentive system may operate in the interest of the patentee and in the interest of consumers. Without patent protection, secrecy provides the principal means by which "free riding" may be avoided. In such circumstances, inventive resources would be directed toward invention having high secrecy potential. There are not obvious reasons to believe either that significant inventive results would occur or that those inventions which were brought forth would be valued more highly by consumers than those susceptible to easy copying. Avoidance of secrecy seems, therefore, clearly subordinate to that basic goal which antitrust and patent law share: the efficient allocation of scarce resources for those products and services consumers value. . . .

COMMENTS AND QUESTIONS

1. In the first half of this century, Joseph Schumpeter advanced the classic incentive theory that underlies much of intellectual property. In his

view, competition will lead to a focus on short-run marginal cost, to the exclusion of (long-run efficient) capital investments in research and development. In the absence of intellectual property protection, the result of competition is insufficient innovation. If that is true (and we have certainly assumed that it is for much of this book), what does it say about the wisdom of applying the antitrust laws to intellectual property? Is it a good idea to enforce competition in the computer industry? Or should the goal of antitrust law be modified somehow in this context?

2. Recent advances in economic thought have caused many economists to reconsider the arguments Professor Bowman makes in the last paragraph of the excerpt. In particular, a significant paper by Richard Levin and others forcefully demonstrates that different industries depend on different types of appropriability mechanisms. Richard Levin et al., Appropriating the Returns from Industrial Research and Development, 3 Brookings Papers on Economic Activity 783 (1987). The fact that appropriability varies from industry to industry significantly complicates the simple economic model of patents that Bowman sets forth. Further, recent work by David Teece and others suggests that firms within an industry will adapt strategically to the appropriability environment of that industry by taking advantage of what David Teece calls "co-specific assets." David J. Teece, Profiting from Technological Innovation: Implications for Integration, Collaboration, Licensing and Public Policy, 15 Res. Pol'y 285 (1986). The upshot of this recent work is that the economic model of patent incentives is substantially more complicated than it appeared to be a few years ago.

This new literature has particular application to the computer industry, where people frequently argue that innovation in software, for example, will be stifled if the innovators are not allowed to build on the work that went before them. We have discussed this argument before, calling it the "on the shoulders of giants" (OTSOG) principle. In copyright law, the argument is used to justify narrowing the scope of protection copyright affords to computer software. Does the same argument suggest a more active role for antitrust law in this industry?

3. Consider carefully what Professor Bowman is arguing. He asserts that both intellectual property and antitrust are not ends in themselves but ways toward a larger goal of wealth maximization. As a matter of policy, he is probably correct.

Professor Bowman's conclusion that the patent laws and the antitrust laws do not have conflicting purposes can be misleading, however. Bowman is best understood as saying that both patent law and antitrust law are tools to be used in promoting wealth maximization. They are designed to be used together to achieve a certain result. However, they strive toward that result in ways that are often in tension. Antitrust law seeks to maximize wealth by preventing monopoly, while patent law may in some cases encourage monopoly.

It is too facile to say that the patent laws give a monopoly to the patentee. Most patents cover a product or products that are only a small subset of a *product market*. It is therefore possible to have a perfectly competitive industry composed of patent holders if each holds a patent on one of several possible products in a market. Only where an innovation creates an entirely new market, or represents a quantum advance in an old one, is the patent likely to confer an economic monopoly directly.

There is room, therefore, for the patent and antitrust laws to coexist in the service of long-run, dymamic efficiencies. In this scheme, patents constitute an exception to the reach of the antitrust laws, and antitrust constrains what a patentee can do with its patent. Efficient wealth maximization requires that a line be drawn between conduct that is permissible and that which is impermissible. Drawing that line in the particular context of the computer industry is the subject of this chapter.

B.   MONOPOLIZATION

1.   Defining the Market

The first step in any antitrust inquiry is to define the relevant product and geographic markets. Monopolization does not occur in a vacuum. To be liable, an antitrust defendant must have monopolized *something, somewhere*. Market definition and market power analysis are well developed in antitrust law; thus we will not repeat the general issues here.

There are, however, some market definition issues that are specific to the computer industry. The first of these results from the importance of intellectual property to computer law. Antitrust courts have entertained a long-standing presumption that intellectual property rights confer market power. The Supreme Court has reasoned that, because a patent confers the right to exclude competitors *from practicing the patented invention*, it must confer monopoly power over that invention. Thus the Supreme Court has on several occasions presumed market power from the existence of patents or copyrights. E.g., Jefferson Parish Hospital District v. Hyde, 466 U.S. 2 (1984); United States v. Loew's, Inc., 371 U.S. 38 (1962). In the computer industry, the key case embodying this presumption is Digidyne Corp. v. Data General Corp., 734 F.2d 1336 (9th Cir. 1984). There, the court held that because Data General's operating system was copyrighted and therefore could not be copied without permission, it was a unique good that must be evaluated in a market by itself.

This presumption that intellectual property rights confer market power has little basis in fact. Patents grant the right to exclude in a tightly defined technological domain. In most cases, this does not translate into what an economist would call a "monopoly," because the technological domain is rarely co-extensive with an economic product market. For example, consider a typical mechanical patent—say, on a new type of muffler for lawn mowers. This typical patent does not confer the right to exclude others from making lawn mowers, of course; nor even from making most types of mufflers for lawn mowers. Only the new muffler is covered. Whether one considers the market for lawn mowers, for lawn mower components, or even for lawn mower mufflers, this patent does not confer a monopoly. *Only* in the very limited market defined by this new type of muffler and its close technological substitutes does the patent holder have exclusionary power—that is, a "monopoly."[4] Most patents are like that. Occasionally, however, a patent (and, even more rarely, a copyright) is granted on a "pioneering" or "basic" invention—for example, the lightbulb, or the laser, or the communication satellite, or recombinant DNA techniques. In these rare instances, the patent may confer exlusionary power over an entire market, and hence qualify as a true economic monopoly.

Commentators have been virtually unanimous in their criticism of the market power presumption. See, e.g., Philip Areeda & Louis Kaplow, Antitrust Analysis 441 (1987); Herbert Hovenkamp, Economics and Federal Antitrust Law §8.3, at 219 (1985); William Montgomery, Note, The Presumption of Economic Power for Patented and Copyrighted Products in Tying Arrangements, 85 Colum. L. Rev. 1140, 1156 (1985). Perhaps in response to this criticism, some courts have rejected the market power presumption in recent years. See Abbott Labs. v. Brennan, 952 F.2d 1346, 1354-1355 (Fed. Cir. 1991); A.I. Root Co. v. Computer/Dynamics, Inc., 806 F.2d 673 (6th Cir. 1986); 3 P.M., Inc. v. Basic Four Corp., 591 F. Supp. 1350 (E.D. Mich. 1984). Moreover, the new U.S. Department of Justice Antitrust Guidelines for the Licensing and Acquisition of Intellectual Property (Intellectual Property Guidelines) specifically reject the market power presumption:

> Market power is the ability profitably to maintain prices above, or output below, competitive levels for a significant period of time. The Agencies will not presume that a patent, copyright or trade secret necessarily confers market power upon its owner. Although the intellectual property right confers the power to exclude with respect to the *specific* product, process, or work in question, there will often be sufficient actual or potential close substitutes for such product, process or work to prevent the exercise of market power.

Intellectual Property Guidelines §2.2 (1995). Legislation has periodically been introduced in Congress to abolish the market power presumption. See H.R. 401, 105th Cong., 1st Sess. (1997).

---

4. It is sometimes asserted that a patent is merely a property right, as opposed to a monopoly, and that the exclusionary power of a patent should not be deemed any more forceful than property rights in one's house. This is misleading, however, because unlike a house or any piece of tangible (real or personal) property, a patent grants its owner the right to exclude others from doing certain things with their own physical property.

The economic literature on the market power issue is complex. See, e.g., David J. Teece et al., Assessing Market Power in Regimes of Rapid Technological Change, 2 Indus. & Corp. Change 3, 7 (1993) ("The more innovative the new product or process, the greater the conventional market power will appear, because price changes will have little or no influence on demand for a truly innovative product."); *id.* at 29 (proposing to measure market power by performance attributes, not price changes). See also Kenneth Burchfiel, Patent Misuse and Antitrust Reform: "Blessed Be the Tie," 4 Harv J.L. & Tech. 1 (1991) (suggesting simpler tests for determining market power, including: (1) whether a royalty was paid by licensees; (2) whether accused infringers chose to keep infringing during litigation; (3) the profit derived from the patented product); Jesse Markham, Concentration: A Stimulus or Retardant to Innovation?, in Industrial Concentration: The New Learning 247 (Harvey Goldschmid et al. eds., 1974) (summarizing empirical tests of the Schumpeterian hypothesis).

The Antitrust Division takes the position that markets may need to be defined differently in the intellectual property context. In addition to evaluating the effect of intellectual property rights on markets for goods, the Division has defined two additional types of markets:

3.2.2 Technology Markets

Technology markets consist of intellectual property that is licensed (the "licensed technology") and its close substitutes—that is, the technologies or goods that are close enough substitutes significantly to constrain the exercise of market power with respect to the intellectual property that is licensed.[19] When rights to intellectual property are marketed separately from the products in which they are used, the Agencies may rely on technology markets to analyze the competitive effects of a licensing arrangement.

To identify a technology's close substitutes and thus to delineate the relevant technology market, the Agencies will, if the data permit, identify the smallest group of technologies and goods over which a hypothetical monopolist of those technologies and goods likely would exercise market power —for example, by imposing a small but significant and nontransitory price increase. The Agencies recognize that technology often is licensed in ways that are not readily quantifiable in monetary terms. In such circumstances, the Agencies will delineate the relevant market by identifying other technologies and goods which buyers would substitute at a cost comparable to that of using the licensed technology.

In assessing the competitive significance of current and likely potential participants in a technology market, the Agencies will take into account all relevant evidence. When market share data are available and accurately reflect the competitive significance of market participants, the Agencies will include

---

19. For example, the owner of a process for producing a particular good may be constrained in its conduct with respect to that process not only by other processes for making that good, but also by other goods that compete with the downstream good and by the processes used to produce those other goods.

market share data in this assessment. The Agencies also will seek evidence of buyers' and market participants' assessments of the competitive significance of technology market participants. . . . When market share data or other indicia of market power are not available, and it appears that competing technologies are comparably efficient, the Agencies will assign each technology the same market share. For new technologies, the Agencies generally will use the best available information to estimate market acceptance over a two-year period, beginning with commercial introduction.

3.2.3 Research and Development: Innovation Markets

. . . A licensing arrangement may have competitive effects on innovation that cannot be adequately addressed through the analysis of goods or technology markets. For example, the arrangement may affect the development of goods that do not yet exist. Alternatively, the arrangement may affect the development of new or improved goods or processes in geographic markets where there is not actual or likely potential competition in the relevant goods.

An innovation market consists of the research and development directed to particular new or improved goods or processes, and the close substitutes for that research and development. The close substitutes are research and development efforts, technologies, and goods that significantly constrain the exercise of market power with respect to the relevant research and development, for example by limiting the ability and incentive of a hypothetical monopolist to retard the pace of research and development. The Agencies will delineate an innovation market only when the capabilities to engage in the relevant research and development can be associated with specialized assets or characteristics of specific firms.

In assessing the competitive significance of current and likely potential participants in an innovation market, the Agencies will take into account all relevant evidence. When market share data are available and accurately reflect the competitive significance of market participants, the Agencies will include market share data in this assessment. The Agencies also will seek evidence of buyers' and market participants' assessments of the competitive significance of innovation market participants. . . . The Agencies may base the market shares of participants in an innovation market on their shares of identifiable assets or characteristics upon which innovation depends, on shares of research and development expenditures, or on shares of a related product. When entities have comparable capabilities and incentives to pursue research and development that is a close substitute for the research and development activities of the parties to a licensing arrangement, the Agencies may assign equal market shares to such entities.

Intellectual Property Guidelines §§3.2.2, 3.2.3.

COMMENTS AND QUESTIONS

1. Does defining separate technology and innovation markets make sense? Another way of approaching this question is to ask whether these market definitions capture any anticompetitive conduct that could not be

challenged under a traditional product market definition. One possible answer is that alleging a market for innovation allows the Division to challenge mergers or anticompetitive conduct earlier than they could in product markets, as the Division need not wait until an actual product market is affected. Whether this is good or bad depends on your confidence in the ability of the courts to define innovation markets and assess anticompetitive effects accurately.

But it is also possible that technology and innovation markets allow the antitrust laws to reach conduct that could not be attacked under traditional product market definitions. For example, a dominant company in a product market may be able to merge with or drive out a competitor whose current market share is insignificant but who has the best technology and is therefore well placed to challenge the dominant firm. If nothing else, technology markets may make market power analysis more forward-looking by requiring the parties to focus on likely future market power rather than just current market shares. At the same time, technology and innovation markets may be used by the government to attack mergers that do not present product market overlaps at all.

Finally, technology markets may sometimes have the opposite effect: they could require the courts to consider as potential future competitors firms that do not now compete with the antitrust defendant. For an argument in favor of such "dynamic" market power analysis, see David Teece et al., Assessing Market Power in Regimes of Rapid Technological Change, 2 Indus. & Corp. Change 439 (1993).

2. How can we define a market for "research and development" (R&D)? The Guidelines suggest several possible ways of determining market shares, including arbitrarily assigning each participant an equal share. Is this reasonable? Is R&D expenditure a fair measure? One problem with the Guidelines' suggestion that innovation monopolists can "profitably retard or restrict innovation" is that it assumes a fairly static model of monopoly. Monopolists who cut back on R&D may reap the rewards in the short term but are likely to be left behind as new companies enter the market for R&D. Can an argument be made the other way—that the real danger is that a dominant firm will extend its product monopoly by spending excessively on research and development?

Market definition issues in the computer industry are complicated not only by the existence of intellectual property rights and the dynamic nature of market power, but also by the rather heavy interdependence of products in the industry. Defining a market may require consideration of upstream and downstream as well as horizontally competitive products. Further, the market may be constrained to some extent by compatibility requirements. Consider the following case.

Allen-Myland, Inc. v. International Business Machines Corp.
United States Court of Appeals for the Third Circuit
33 F.3d 194 (3d Cir. 1994)

NYGAARD, Circuit Judge.

Allen-Myland, Inc. ("AMI") appeals from the district court's judgment in favor of IBM in this intricate antitrust tying case. We conclude that the district court erred and will vacate its judgment and remand the cause for further proceedings.

I. Facts and Procedure

A. *Mainframes and Upgrades . . .*

IBM is the world's largest manufacturer of large-scale mainframe computers. These machines have the capacity to process millions of records at a time and manage a tremendous volume of information, making modern operations possible for large corporations, public utilities and government agencies. Without them, business would soon slow or halt. Mainframes are physically large machines, generally occupying significant floor space and requiring a full-time staff to keep them in operation. Needless to say, they are quite expensive, with prices commonly in excess of $1 million.

Mainframes are available in a wide range of computing capacities, to fit the needs of each individual customer. One common measure of capacity is computing speed, measured in millions of instructions per second ("MIPS"). IBM mainframes may also be upgraded, as its customers' computing needs change over time, in what is known as a MIPS upgrade.

Many IBM mainframes are not purchased outright from IBM by their end users, but are instead leased through third-party leasing companies such as CMI and Comdisco. A mainframe will typically be leased to several end users during its life cycle, and then when obsolete will be scrapped. Often, when the lease term expires and the mainframe returns to the lessor, the computer will need to be reconfigured to meet the needs of the next lessee.

Companies like AMI found a profitable market reconfiguring mainframe computers such as the IBM 303X series. Lessors could not afford to have their machines idle and generating no revenue while waiting for a reconfiguration, yet IBM often took months to install an upgrade. AMI, on the other hand, would turn the job around in a matter of only a few days. Either AMI or the leasing company would buy the required parts outright from IBM for inventory on what were known as SWRPQ terms, meaning that IBM installation was not included. It would then install the parts in the user's computer, set up the appropriate software and test the system. Old parts could often then be used on another computer. Because the 303X series of computers was based on "MST" circuit board technology, which required significant technical skill and time to reconfigure, AMI was in a position to add considerable value in terms of its labor. As a result, AMI grew into a company with $50 million in annual revenue.

In 1980, however, IBM introduced its next generation of mainframe computers, the 308X series, which caused a major erosion in AMI's reconfiguration business. . . .

In marketing its 308X series, IBM used a policy known as net pricing. Under this policy, IBM installation labor was bundled in with the price of the parts for TCM-based MIPS upgrades; SWRPQ pricing was either eliminated or was priced prohibitively high. In addition, any old TCMs recovered from a mainframe during reconfiguration became IBM's property. As a result, customers desiring non-IBM installation of upgrades were required to pay IBM's labor charge anyway. And because the net pricing policy limited the supply of the TCMs on the open market, acquiring parts from sources other than IBM became impractical. . . .

The district court found that IBM's net pricing structure did not constitute a per se section 1 violation, for two reasons: first, that IBM's share of the relevant market was not high enough to impose per se liability; and second, that net pricing did not foreclose AMI from a "viable business opportunity." The court also found that net pricing did not violate section 1 under a rule of reason analysis because sufficient procompetitive reasons existed for it. . . .

III. Scope of the Relevant Market

A. *Introduction*

AMI asserts that the tying product is the "large-scale mainframe computer," defined as computers that are "among the largest in memory capacity, the fastest in computing speed, and the most expensive of computers available." *Allen-Myland*, 693 F. Supp. at 270-71. Alternatively, it sets forth two submarkets consisting of the parts and services required for the conversion and upgrade of either IBM mainframes or all manufacturers' mainframes. AMI defines the tied product as the labor required to install upgrades.

The district court found AMI's proposed market definition and submarkets to be too narrow. When the court broadened the market to include various substitutes that it believed shared cross-elasticity of demand with large-scale mainframes, IBM's market share dropped from as high as 79% to under 34.4%, too low to impose per se liability. See *Jefferson Parish*, 466 U.S. at 26-27, 104 S. Ct. at 1566 (30% market share insufficient); Times-Picayune Publishing Co. v. United States, 345 U.S. 594, 611-12,

73 S. Ct. 872, 882, 97 L. Ed. 1277 (1953) (33-40% market share insufficient). The court stated:

> Standing alone, AMI's market share evidence tends to show that IBM enjoys substantial economic power. However, AMI's definitions of large scale mainframes and the relevant market are flawed in several respects and tend to overstate IBM's market share and power.

Allen-Myland, 693 F. Supp. at 271. The district court defined the relevant market to include not only large-scale mainframes, but also added upgrades to large-scale mainframes, leased and smaller capacity computers, peripheral products and software, "box swaps," and upgrades using customer-provided parts to the relevant market. . . .

B. Leasing Companies

The district court first added leasing companies into AMI's proposed market definition. It reasoned as follows: Leasing companies, such as Comdisco and CMI, purchase computer equipment from manufacturers and lease it to users. From a consumer's standpoint, they are an alternative source of computer equipment. They compete with IBM. Leasing companies own approximately 40 percent of all large scale mainframe computers, as defined by AMI. Prof. Levin testified that IBM's share of the market would be reduced by an amount he was unable to determine if leasing companies were taken into account in AMI's market definition. If leasing company transactions involving computers comparable and in many cases identical to the large scale mainframes marketed by IBM are included in the relevant market, and the market is measured on a "transaction basis," IBM's share of the market, according to Prof. Almarin Phillips, who testified for IBM as an expert economist, drops to 34.4 percent. Prof. Phillips testified that such a share would not reflect "overwhelming" activity in the market on IBM's part. *Allen-Myland*, 693 F. Supp. at 273-74 (footnote and record citations omitted). We cannot affirm the district court's finding that leasing companies form a part of the relevant market.

. . . [W]e think that the opinion reveals an analytical flaw. Leasing companies lease both new and used computers. They purchase new mainframes from IBM and lease them to end users; when the lease term is up, if the mainframe is not obsolete and can be leased again, the leasing company will place it with another end user. In addition, leasing companies deal in both IBM and non-IBM computers. There are important legal and competitive distinctions between the various types of equipment in which the leasing companies deal, so they cannot be lumped together.

New computers are, of course, already in the relevant market as defined by AMI. It was therefore incorrect to add them in again when end users lease new computers rather than purchase them outright. In this situation, leasing companies provide nothing more than an alternate way of financing a new computer, but do nothing to increase the supply of new machines. See Transamerica Computer Co. v. IBM Corp. (In re IBM Peripheral EDP Devices Antitrust Litig.), 481 F. Supp. 965, 979 (N.D. Cal. 1979), *aff'd*, 698 F.2d 1377 (9th Cir.), *cert. denied*, 464 U.S. 955, 104 S. Ct. 370, 78 L. Ed. 2d 329 (1983). They do not increase the number of new mainframes, as leasing companies still must purchase them from their manufacturers. Thus, to the extent that IBM had the power to set prices, that power would not be diminished, or at most would only be slightly diminished, by its sales to leasing companies rather than end users. Since these purchases are already in the relevant market, it was double counting to also include them as part of the leasing market. Cf. *id*.

With respect to leases of used computers, there is a significant difference whether those machines were made by IBM or by some other manufacturer. Where used IBM computers are leased, we think that United States v. Aluminum Co. of America ("Alcoa"), 148 F.2d 416 (2d Cir. 1945) is apposite. There, Alcoa controlled 90 percent of the market for virgin aluminum ingot. It sought to reduce its market share for antitrust purposes by arguing that secondary ingot derived from scrap competed with virgin ingot for sales. The court held that because all secondary ingot was ultimately derived from virgin ingot, Alcoa, by properly exercising its power over the supply of virgin, could indirectly control the supply of secondary as well. *Id*. at 425.

Alcoa's analysis is persuasive. Indeed, we think the case is even stronger here for excluding the secondary market. Refined aluminum can be melted down and reused repeatedly, and in any event, products made with it may last for decades before they are scrapped and the aluminum is recycled. It therefore may have been quite difficult for Alcoa to estimate future supply and demand for aluminum ingot over a long period of time with sufficient accuracy to maximize its profits by manipulating the supply of virgin ingot it produced. See 2 Phillip Areeda & Donald F. Turner, Antitrust Law ¶530c (1978).

Computers, however, have considerably more limited lives than aluminum ingot. Technology and price/performance ratios have been advancing so rapidly in the computer industry that used machines cannot be re-leased indefinitely. Accordingly, a powerful manufacturer like IBM was in a position to maximize its profits by carefully controlling the number of mainframes that would later appear on the used leasing market. This is particularly true when, as here, that control was enhanced by IBM's policy of recapturing old parts that could otherwise have been used to extend the useful service lives of existing used mainframes by allowing them to be upgraded and placed with new customers. We therefore conclude that the district court erred when it added leases of used IBM mainframes into the relevant market.

On the other hand, to the extent that leasing companies deal in used, non-IBM mainframes that have not already been counted in the sales market, these machines belong in the relevant market for large-scale mainframe computers. Unlike IBM, there is no allegation that the manufacturers of these computers possess the market power to control prices, much less that they would do so in concert with IBM. When these computers are placed in service by leasing companies, they provide an alternative that limits IBM's power in the market.

Accordingly, we conclude that the district court erred when it included all leasing company transactions in the relevant market. On remand, them court should include only leases of used, non-IBM mainframes and determine the extent to which those leases reduce IBM's market share.

C. Box Swaps

The district court also added "box swaps"—replacing an existing computer with a more powerful, new or used computer—into the relevant market, although it did not calculate the degree to which these box swaps eroded IBM's market share.

The analytical problem with this finding is similar to the error with respect to leasing companies. To the extent that a box swap involves purchasing a new IBM or a new or used non-IBM mainframe computer, it constitutes double counting to add box swaps to the market because those sales are already included in the market definition. On the other hand, if a used IBM computer is used in the swap, then to include that machine in the market is incorrect under *Alcoa* for the same reason it was error to include them in the leasing market.

D. Used Parts Upgrades

Including "used parts upgrades" in the relevant market was also error. A used parts upgrade is an upgrade performed with parts obtained from another computer, either one belonging to the organization needing the upgrade or one belonging to a leasing company. See *Allen-Myland*, 693 F. Supp. at 277.

The district court correctly recognized that the viability of used parts upgrades could be limited by the scarcity of the necessary parts. It then relied on the many memory and channel upgrades and downgrades that had been performed with used parts not acquired from IBM. The record indicates, however, that most memory and channel upgrade parts are not based on TCM technology and were thus not subject to IBM's net pricing and parts recapture policies. The parts required for MIPS upgrades, however, were mostly TCM-based and subject to net pricing and recapture. Thus, that other non-net priced parts were readily available does not support the implicit conclusion that there was no scarcity of MIPS upgrade parts.

Even if used parts were available to perform MIPS upgrades, the record does not suggest any manufacturer of those parts other than IBM. Hence, the reasoning of Alcoa is as controlling here as it was for used IBM computers. . . .

E. Smaller Capacity Computers

The district court considered AMI's proposed market definition to be too narrow because it failed to include "smaller capacity computers"—computers below the size and sophistication of a large-scale mainframe that nevertheless would be reasonable substitutes, either singly or in combination. See *Allen-Myland*, 693 F. Supp. at 274-75. AMI argues that it was error for the district court to include these smaller machines because there was not sufficient evidence of substitutability between these two types of computers. The district court rejected AMI's argument, citing evidence that smaller computers had effectively displaced mainframes in certain applications and noting a trend toward the replacement of large, centralized systems with "distributed" systems consisting of greater numbers of smaller capacity computers. *Id.*

AMI argues on appeal that this reasoning was flawed because it failed to consider the rapid development of technology over the life cycle of a typical computer. It agrees that some installations that initially required older generation mainframes might be satisfied with "smaller" machines when it came time to replace their mainframes, because the smaller machines would by then have all the power of the earlier mainframes. Nevertheless, AMI contends, the fact that some users of older mainframe computers might switch to smaller capacity machines proves nothing about whether those smaller machines effectively compete against IBM's current, more powerful mainframes, which are the focus of this litigation. AMI's argument is sound, but unavailing. There was testimony admitted at trial indicating that at least one smaller capacity computer, the Hewlett-Packard HP 3000 series, competed against the IBM 308X series "in many applications." The district court was entitled to, and did, credit this evidence. *Allen-Myland*, 693 F. Supp. at 275.

The amici argue that the district court failed to consider the problem of "lock-in." Although mainframes and smaller capacity computers may be substitutable when a new computer application is being developed or when an existing application is no longer useful and must be rewritten anyway, they argue that there are significant switching costs that prevent this from happening in the short run. For example, to "port" an existing application from a mainframe to a smaller computer, the applications software may have to be rewritten, the data files may have to be converted to new formats, and personnel may have to be extensively trained on the new system. The costs of doing so and the delay involved could well cause the computer user to remain with a mainframe-based system rather than convert to a smaller computer; indeed, one court has noted that, for compatibility reasons, over 80 percent of users remain loyal to the manufacturer of their original systems. See *Transamerica*, 481 F. Supp. at 980 & n.32.

. . . [T]his remains an issue of fact for the district court to resolve in the first instance. . . .

F. Peripheral Devices and Software

AMI also argues that the district court erred when it added peripheral devices and software into the relevant market. The court found that these items, which provide data input, storage and output capabilities and direct the computer in its processing of information, "provided significant and reasonable alternatives to a wide variety of upgrades and modifications of large scale mainframes." *Allen-Myland*, 693 F. Supp. at 276.

Similar or substitute products are those that "have the ability—actual or potential—to take significant amounts of business away from each other." SmithKline Corp. v. Eli Lilly & Co., 575 F.2d 1056, 1063 (3d Cir.), *cert. denied*, 439 U.S. 838, 99 S. Ct. 123, 58 L. Ed. 2d 134 (1978). Thus, the relevant product market "is composed of products that have reasonable interchangeability for the purposes for which they are produced —price, use and qualities considered." *Id.* at 1062-63 (quoting United States v. E.I. du Pont de Nemours & Co., 351 U.S. 377, 404, 76 S. Ct. 994, 1012, 100 L. Ed. 1264 (1956) (The Cellophane Case)); Tunis Bros. Co. v. Ford Motor Co., 952 F.2d 715, 722 (3d Cir. 1991), *cert. denied*, 120 L. Ed. 2d 903, 112 S. Ct. 3034 (1992).

"Interchangeability" implies that one product is roughly equivalent to another for the use to which it is put; while there might be some degree of preference for the one over the other, either would work effectively. A person needing transportation to work could accordingly buy a Ford or a Chevrolet automobile, or could elect to ride a horse or bicycle, assuming those options were feasible. The key test for determining whether one product is a substitute for another is whether there is a cross-elasticity of demand between them: in other words, whether the demand for the second good would respond to changes in the price of the first. *Tunis Bros.*, 952 F.2d at 722.

In the six years since the district court issued its opinion, the personal computer has consolidated its position in modern life, and what once seemed mired in impenetrable technical jargon is now within the vocabulary of the general public. Moreover, technology changes rapidly and if one has an older computer and wishes to use the latest software applications, one often must either upgrade the central processor—the equivalent of a MIPS upgrade—or buy a new computer. Increasing the size of the disk drive, buying more memory or installing the latest version of the operating system may help in some cases but in many others will be ineffective. It thus may be argued that the same situation obtains in the case of larger computers; that is, peripherals and software are complementary goods but are not substitutes for mainframe computers.

The issue, nevertheless, remains a factual one for the district court to resolve. Here, if peripherals and software are reasonable substitutes for mainframes, we should expect to see an increased demand for them as the price of mainframes rises, but the district court cited no evidence of this type. Instead, it relied on the fact that IBM considers peripheral products and software when pricing its computer systems. *Allen-Myland*, 693 F. Supp. at 276. Pricing a large mainframe system on the basis of peripherals included with it against competitive offerings by other manufacturers, however, is simply not evidence that peripherals and mainframes are substitutes for one another.

The district court relied even more heavily on several anecdotes in which large mainframe users had upgraded memory, disks, software or other peripherals rather than perform a MIPS upgrade. *Id.* at 276-77. This testimony fell into two categories. First, some users testified that it was possible to delay a MIPS upgrade for a while by upgrading peripherals or software: akin perhaps to saying that installing new brakes may delay the necessity of purchasing a new car, but it is not sufficient evidence on which to conclude that the products are reasonably interchangeable in use. See Kaiser Aluminum & Chemical Corp. v. Federal Trade Comm'n, 652 F.2d 1324, 1331-32 (7th Cir. 1981) ("specialties," which delayed the necessity of replacing refractory bricks in furnaces, did not belong in the same relevant market).

Second, there was testimony to the effect that there are many ways to enhance the performance of a computer system, including MIPS upgrades and peripheral/software upgrades. Although it is doubtless true that improvements to peripherals or software will improve a computer's performance somewhat under certain circumstances, we find no evidence on how much or under what conditions improvement could be expected. There was thus no evidence from which to conclude whether peripheral and software upgrades were reasonably interchangeable with either a MIPS upgrade or a different mainframe computer in enough cases that those alternate upgrades could properly be termed substitutes. Nor was there evidence that, because of a price change in mainframes, there was a greater or lesser demand for peripheral/software upgrades. In sum, the evidence was insufficient to support the wholesale inclusion of peripherals and software into the relevant market for large-scale mainframes.

We emphasize, however, that we are not holding that peripheral and software must be excluded from the relevant market, only that, upon review, the evidence cited in the district court's opinion is insufficient to warrant including them. On remand, the district court will of course determine whether there is some degree of interchangeability or other evidence of cross-elasticity of demand. If there is, then the court is free to adjust IBM's share of the market by its best estimate of the true competition from peripherals and software. . . .

VI. Conclusion

We will accordingly vacate the district court's judgment in favor of IBM and remand for further proceedings consistent with this opinion.

Telex Corp. v. IBM Corp., 510 F.2d 894 (10th Cir. 1975): In 1975, IBM was a major manufacturer of computer hardware. IBM sold both computers themselves and "peripheral devices" which could be plugged into IBM computers. Telex, which also made peripheral devices designed to be plugged into IBM computers, charged that IBM had monopolized the market for "IBM plug-compatible peripheral products." IBM contended that the market was "electronic data processing systems," and that it had no power in that market. The definition of the relevant market in which Telex and IBM competed was central to the case. The district court agreed with Telex, but the court of appeals reversed. It reasoned that peripheral devices which were not "IBM-compatible" were nonetheless "reasonably interchangeable" with IBM products because these devices could easily be modified for use with an IBM computer "by the use of interfaces designed for this purpose." Further, the court held that these competing products were part of a larger relevant market for computer *systems*, in which IBM competed with numerous other companies. This competition constrained any power IBM might have in the separate market for compatible peripherals.

COMMENTS AND QUESTIONS

Doesn't the relevant market in these cases depend on which consumers you consider, and when you consider them? It is surely true, as *Telex* suggests, that new computer purchasers look for entire systems of compatible products, and perhaps the competition of DEC, Wang, and others for computer systems prevented IBM from exercising market power over those consumers. However, once a consumer has purchased a computer, he may be significantly more limited in the peripheral devices he can buy to work with that computer. Should antitrust protect consumers from companies who would monopolize these "aftermarkets"? We will return to this issue in detail when we consider tying arrangements below.

PROBLEM

Problem 7-1. Two companies (*A* and *B*) agree to cross-license future patents relating to the development of a new system for modeling data structures in 3-D terms, in combination with a virtual reality device. Innovation in the development of the model requires the capability to interoperate with an advanced virtual reality helmet patented by a third party (*C*), which so far has been freely licensed to interested software developers. Aspects of the licensing arrangement between *A* and *B* raise the possibility that competition in research and development of this and related modeling programs will be lessened. Both *A* and *B* estimate that they are approximately two years away from marketing any software. The Antitrust Division is considering whether to define an innovation market in which to evaluate the competitive effects of the arrangement. What factors should it take into account in making this decision?

---

2. Anticompetitive Conduct

It is not enough to define a market and determine that an intellectual property owner is a monopolist, for monopoly alone is not illegal. Rather, it must be combined with some form of anticompetitive conduct. Assuming that the intellectual property owner has market power in a particular case, what conduct will suffice? It is in this context that the conflict between intellectual property and the antitrust laws arises most starkly.

Certainly, antitrust law must make some accommodation for monopolies that result from intellectual property if those intellectual property rights are to have any meaning. In particular, it is evident that merely possessing and enforcing a patent, copyright, trademark, or trade secret against competitors ought not violate the antitrust laws. See, e.g., Corsearch v. Thomson & Thomson, 3 CCH Computer Cases ¶46,645 (owner of copyright in a computer database did not violate the antitrust laws by denying a competitor access to that database; a copyright owner has the right to limit or terminate the use of its intellectual property as it deems appropriate).

If we start from the proposition that it cannot be illegal to possess a patent (or other intellectual property right), what role remains for antitrust law? Several types of factual situations may still present antitrust problems. First, the patentee may have acquired his patent illegally (for example, through fraud). Second, a patentee may use his patent to acquire or maintain power beyond that granted by the intellectual property right itself. In both situations, antitrust courts are properly concerned with the effects that anticompetitive use of the intellectual property right may have.

a.   *Enforcing Intellectual Property Rights*

Walker Process Equipment, Inc. v. Food Machinery & Chemical Corp.
Supreme Court of the United States
382 U.S. 172 (1965)

MR. JUSTICE CLARK delivered the opinion of the Court.

The question before us is whether the maintenance and enforcement of a patent obtained by fraud on the Patent Office may be the basis of an action under §2 of the Sherman Act . . . [Food Machinery sued Walker for patent infringement, and Walker counterclaimed for violations of the antitrust laws.] Walker then amended its counterclaim to charge that Food Machinery had "illegally monopolized interstate and foreign commerce by fraudulently and in bad faith obtaining and maintaining . . . its patent . . . well knowing that it had no basis for . . . a patent." It alleged fraud on the basis that Food Machinery had sworn before the Patent Office that it neither knew nor believed that its invention had been in public use in the United States for more than one year prior to filing its patent application when, in fact, Food Machinery was a party to prior use within such time.

[The District Court dismissed Walker's counterclaim, and the Court of Appeals affirmed.] . . .

. . . The gist of Walker's claim is that since Food Machinery obtained its patent by fraud it cannot enjoy the limited exception to the prohibitions of §2 of the Sherman Act, but must answer under that section and §4 of the Clayton Act in treble damages to those injured by any monopolistic action taken under the fraudulent patent claim. Nor can the interest in protecting patentees from "innumerable vexatious suits" be used to frustrate the assertion of rights conferred by the antitrust laws. It must be remembered that we deal only with a special class of patents, i.e. those procured by intentional fraud.

Under the decisions of this Court a person sued for infringement may challenge the validity of the patent on various grounds, including fraudulent procurement. In fact, one need not await the filing of a threatened suit by the patentee; the validity of the patent may be tested under the Declaratory Judgment Act. . . . At the same time, we have recognized that an injured party may attack the misuse of patent rights. To permit recovery of treble damages for the fraudulent procurement of the patent coupled with violations of §2 accords with these long-recognized procedures. It would also promote the purposes so well expressed in Precision Instrument [Mfg. Co. v. Automotive Maintenance Machinery, 324 U.S. 806 (1945)] at 816:

> A patent by its very nature is affected with a public interest. . . . [It] is an exception to the general rule against monopolies and to the right to access to a free and open market. The far-reaching social and economic consequences of

a patent, therefore, give the public a paramount interest in seeing that patent monopolies spring from backgrounds free from fraud or other inequitable conduct and that such monopolies are kept within their legitimate scope.

III.

Walker's counterclaim alleged that Food Machinery obtained the patent by knowingly and willfully misrepresenting facts to the Patent Office. Proof of this assertion would be sufficient to strip Food Machinery of its exemption from the antitrust laws. By the same token, Food Machinery's good faith would furnish a complete defense. This includes an honest mistake as to the effect of prior installation upon patentability—so-called "technical fraud."

To establish monopolization or attempt to monopolize a part of trade or commerce under §2 of the Sherman Act, it would then be necessary to appraise the exclusionary power of the illegal patent claim in terms of the relevant market for the product involved. Without a definition of that market there is no way to measure Food Machinery's ability to lessen or destroy competition. It may be that the device—knee-action swing diffusers—used in sewage treatment systems does not comprise a relevant market. There may be effective substitutes for the device which do not infringe the patent. This is a matter of proof, as is the amount of damages suffered by Walker.

[The Court remanded the case with instructions to consider the antitrust claim on its merits.]

COMMENTS AND QUESTIONS

1. The Supreme Court's decision in *Walker Process* has given rise to a whole series of antitrust claims (such as Brunswick Corp. v. Riegel Textile Corp., 752 F.2d 261 (7th Cir. 1984)) that are based on fraudulent procurement of a patent. Indeed, these antitrust suits have come to be referred to as "*Walker Process* claims."

However, the idea that fraudulent procurement of a patent itself violates the antitrust laws is highly misleading. As the last section of the Court's opinion makes clear, the only effect of the defendant's fraud was that it lost the protection of the patent laws. The Court still required that Walker prove all the substantive elements of a section 2 violation (market power, anticompetitive conduct, and—for attempt claims—intent to monopolize). Indeed, Justice Harlan concurred precisely in order to emphasize that point:

> We hold today that a treble-damage action for monopolization . . . may be maintained under §4 of the Clayton Act if two conditions are satisfied: (1) the relevant patent is shown to have been produced by knowing and willful

fraud . . . ; and (2) all the elements otherwise necesary to establish a §2 monopolization charge are proved. Conversely, such a private cause of action would *not* be made out if the plaintiff . . . failed to prove the elements of a §2 charge even though he has established actual fraud in the procurement of the patent and the defendant's knowledge of that fraud.

382 U.S. at 179. Thus, *Walker Process* is limited to removing the cloak of protection afforded by patent law to patents themselves where the patent in question was obtained by fraud.

2. Even if a patent is lawfully acquired, using it as an anticompetitive weapon might violate the antitrust laws. After all, baseless infringement suits on a valid patent are just as troubling as infringement suits on a baseless patent. Several courts have held that "anticompetitive litigation," standing alone, can suffice to violate the antitrust laws. See, e.g., Handgards, Inc. v. Ethicon, Inc., 601 F.2d 986, 996 (9th Cir. 1979); CVD, Inc. v. Raytheon Co., 769 F.2d 842, 851 (1st Cir. 1985). Still other courts have held that baseless litigation may constitute anticompetitive conduct sufficient to satisfy one element of the monopolization test. See Daralyn Durie & Mark A. Lemley, The Antitrust Liability of Labor Unions for Anticompetitive Litigation, 80 Cal. L. Rev. 757, 778 n.128 (1992) (collecting cases).

3. There is a significant limitation on antitrust claims or counterclaims that are based on the filing of an infringement suit. That limitation is the antitrust petitioning immunity doctrine. Before considering the merits of an antitrust counterclaim, courts must first decide whether the patentee is immune from antitrust liability under the *Noerr-Pennington* doctrine, a doctrine that protects antitrust defendants from liability for petitioning the government. The Supreme Court has consistently held that filing a lawsuit or an action before an administrative agency is "petitioning" and therefore is presumptively entitled to immunity from antitrust suit.

There is an exception to antitrust immunity for sham litigation, however. If a patent or copyright infringement lawsuit is a sham, rather than a "genuine effort . . . to influence" the court, it is not entitled to antitrust immunity, and the counterclaim will be evaluated on the merits. Allied Tube & Conduit Corp. v. Indian Head, Inc., 486 U.S. 492 (1988). Not surprisingly, there has been heated debate over the precise scope of the "sham" exception. The Supreme Court visited this issue in the 1993 case of Professional Real Estate Investors v. Columbia Pictures, Inc., 508 U.S. 49 (1993), in which Columbia Pictures had brought a copyright infringement suit against PREI based on PREI's performance of copyrighted movies in guests' hotel rooms. PREI counterclaimed on the grounds that Columbia had conspired to monopolize the market and restrain trade. Columbia lost its copyright case on summary judgment, but the district court held that PREI was not entitled to pursue its antitrust claim because Columbia's copyright suit, though unsuccessful, was not a sham.

The Supreme Court affirmed the application of antitrust immunity to PREI's counterclaim. In doing so, it set out a new two-part test to determine whether a lawsuit is a sham. "First, the lawsuit must be objectively baseless in the sense that no reasonable litigant could realistically expect success on the merits." *Id.* at 60. Second, "the court should focus on whether the baseless lawsuit conceals an attempt to interfere directly with the business relationships of a competitor through the use of governmental *process*—as opposed to the *outcome* of that process—as an anticompetitive weapon." *Id.* at 60-61 (emphasis in original). These are commonly referred to as the "objectively baseless" and "subjectively baseless" tests, respectively. Only if the suit is a sham under this definition will the court proceed to consider the substantive elements of an antitrust violation. *Id.* The effect of this new test is to make it extremely difficult to prevail in an antitrust counterclaim based on wrongful enforcement of an intellectual property right.

b. Other Anticompetitive Conduct

United States v. Microsoft Corporation
United States District Court for the District of Columbia
159 F.R.D. 318 (D.D.C. 1995), rev'd, 56 F.3d 1448 (D.C. Cir. 1995)

SPORKIN, District Judge:

The issue before this Court is whether the entry of a proposed antitrust consent decree between Microsoft Corporation and the United States is in "the public interest." Microsoft is the world's largest developer of computer software. On July 15, 1994, the Government filed a complaint charging Microsoft with violating Sections 1 and 2 of the Sherman Anti-Trust Act. 15 U.S.C. §§1-7 (1973). On the same day the parties filed a proposed consent judgment.

I. Background

The Government filed the complaint and proposed judgment after a four-year investigation of Microsoft. The Federal Trade Commission ("FTC") initiated the investigation in 1990. According to Microsoft, but not confirmed by the Government, the FTC considered a wide range of practices including: (1) that Microsoft gave its developers of applications software information about its operating systems software before providing it to other applications developers; (2) that Microsoft announced that it was developing a non-existent version of operating software to dissuade Original Equipment Manufacturers ("OEMs") from leasing a competitor's operating system; (3) that Microsoft required OEMs that licensed its operating system software also to license Microsoft applications; and (4) that Microsoft licensed its operating systems to OEMs on a per processor basis. Microsoft asserts that before the FTC investigation was completed, it was expanded to include every aspect of Microsoft's business.

There was never a majority vote among the FTC commissioners to file an administrative complaint against Microsoft. In late 1993, after a 2-2 deadlock by the commissioners, no administrative action was filed, and the FTC suspended its investigation of Microsoft.

Following the suspension of the FTC investigation, Assistant Attorney General Bingaman, the head of the Antitrust Division of the Department of Justice, decided to revive the investigation. In June, 1994 Microsoft and the Department of Justice initiated settlement negotiations. Approximately a month later the parties came to agreement and filed a proposed judgment with the Court.

II. The Complaint

The complaint charges that Microsoft violated Sections 1 and 2 of the Sherman Anti-Trust Act. 15 U.S.C. §§1-7. The primary allegations in the complaint concern licensing agreements between Microsoft and OEMs of personal computers ("PCs"). The complaint also addresses provisions of non-disclosure agreements ("NDAs") between Microsoft and other developers of applications software, known as independent software developers ("ISVs"). The complaint narrowly tailors the relevant product market to the market for certain operating systems software for x86 microprocessors. The geographic market is not limited. . . .

Microsoft has a monopoly on the market for PC operating systems. Microsoft's share of the operating systems market identified in the complaint is consistently well above 70%. According to Microsoft's 1993 Annual Report, as of June 30, 1993, 120 million PCs ran on Microsoft's MS-DOS. Microsoft also developed and sells Windows, a sophisticated operating system that runs on top of MS-DOS or a similar operating system. Windows allows a PC user to run more than one application at a time and shift between them. Windows is known as a "graphical user interface." Approximately 50 million PCs now use Windows. Microsoft generally does not sell its operating systems directly to consumers. Instead, it licenses its operating systems to OEMs for inclusion in the PCs they make.

Microsoft, the Justice Department, and a number of competitors who oppose the entry of the decree all agree that it is very difficult to enter the operating systems market. There are two main reasons for this, each of which reinforces the other. First, consumers do not want to buy PCs with an operating system that does not already have a large installed base because of their concern that there will not be a wide range of applications software available for that operating system. The second, complementary reason why there are large barriers to entry into the operating systems market is that ISVs do not want to spend time and money developing applications for operating systems that do not have a large installed base. They perceive that demand for that software will be low. As a result, OEMs have little incentive to license an operating system that does not have a large installed base and include it in their PCs.

In addition to these "natural" barriers to entry the complaint identifies Microsoft's use of per processor licenses and long term commitments as "exclusionary and anti-competitive contract terms to maintain its monopoly." A per processor license means that Microsoft licenses an operating system to an OEM which pays a royalty to Microsoft for each PC sold regardless of whether a Microsoft operating system is included in that PC. In other words, under a per processor license, if an OEM sells some PCs with a competitor's operating system installed (e.g., IBM'S OS/2), and others with MS-DOS installed, the OEM would pay Microsoft royalties for all PCs sold. In effect, the OEM pays twice every time it sells a PC with a non-Microsoft operating system—once to the company that licensed the operating system to the OEM and once to Microsoft. The complaint charges that per processor licenses discourage OEMs from licensing competing operating systems and/or cause OEMs to raise the price for PCs with a competing operating system to recoup the fee paid to Microsoft.

The complaint further alleges that Microsoft's use of long-term licensing agreements with or without minimum commitments, and the rolling over of unused commitments unreasonably extended some licensing agreements with Microsoft. These practices allegedly foreclosed OEMs from licensing operating systems from Microsoft's competitors.

The other anticompetitive practice cited in the complaint is the structure of Microsoft's non-disclosure agreements ("NDAs") with ISVs during the development of its new Windows operating system. ISVs work with Microsoft during the development and testing of new operating systems so they can produce applications that run with that operating system and release them around the time the operating system is released. This collaboration benefits Microsoft in two ways. First, Microsoft receives input from the ISVs on how to improve the operating system. Second, a new operating system is more attractive to consumers if there are compatible applications programs immediately available. In order to protect confidential information about its new software, Microsoft requires ISVs to sign NDAs in order to obtain product information.

The complaint alleges that the recent NDAs Microsoft has executed with ISVs are overly restrictive and anti-competitive. The Government alleges that the NDAs not only legitimately protect against the disclosure of confidential information to competing developers of operating systems but also discourage ISVs from developing their own competing operating systems and/or from developing applications for competing operating systems.

In sum, the Government alleges that the practices outlined above deprive competitors of substantial opportunities to license their operating systems to OEMs, preventing them from developing a large installed base.

This discourages both ISVs from designing software for competing operating systems and consumers from buying PCs with these competing operating systems. These practices also harm consumers by limiting the variety of available operating systems and raising the prices for non-Microsoft operating systems. . . .

III. The Proposed Decree

The proposed decree negotiated and entered into by the parties is significantly and substantially narrower than the requests contained in the prayer for relief in the complaint. The consent decree limits certain of Microsoft's contract and NDA practices. The prohibitions concern licensing agreements and NDAs for certain operating systems software; operating systems software for workstations are not covered. The decree does not address any of Microsoft's applications software.

The decree enjoins Microsoft from entering into any licensing agreement longer than one year, though OEMs may at their discretion include in the licensing agreement a one year option to renew. Microsoft can impose no penalty or charge on an OEM for its choice not to renew the licensing agreement, nor can it require an OEM to commit not to license a competitor's operating system.

Microsoft may only license the operating systems covered by the decree on a per copy basis, with one exception.[11] Microsoft cannot include minimum commitments in its covered licensing agreements. The agreements cannot be structured so that the OEM pays royalties for including MS-DOS in a fixed number of PCs, whether or not the OEM actually sells that number of PCs with a Microsoft operating system included.

The decree restricts the scope of the NDAs that Microsoft may negotiate with ISVs. Microsoft cannot enter into an NDA whose duration extends beyond, (i) commercial release of the operating system, (ii) an earlier public disclosure by Microsoft, or (iii) one year from the date of the disclosure of information covered by the NDA to a person subject to the NDA, whichever comes first. The decree also prohibits the use of NDAs that would prevent persons covered by that NDA from developing applications for competing operating systems unless the application entailed use of proprietary Microsoft information.

The decree explicitly states that it does not constitute "any evidence or admission by any party with respect to any issue of fact or law." Indeed, Microsoft has denied in its submissions to the Court that any of the allega-

---

11. This exception allows for certain Per System Licenses. A per system license means a license for a particular system or model. The decree allows OEMs to designate identical machines containing different operating systems as distinct systems. This is intended to prevent OEMs from paying royalties to Microsoft for all the computers of a certain system even if some do not include a Microsoft operating system.

tions set forth in the complaint constitute violations of the antitrust laws. . . .

V.

B. Public Interest Determination

The Court cannot find the proposed decree to be in the public interest for four reasons. First, the Government has declined to provide the Court with the information it needs to make a proper public interest determination. Second, the scope of the decree is too narrow. Third, the parties have been unable and unwilling adequately to address certain anticompetitive practices, which Microsoft states it will continue to employ in the future and with respect to which the decree is silent. Thus, the decree does not constitute an effective antitrust remedy. Fourth, the Court is not satisfied that the enforcement and compliance mechanisms in the decree are satisfactory. . . .

V.B.2. Scope of the Decree

The Court finds the decree on its face to be too narrow. Its coverage is restricted to PCs with x86 or Intel x86 compatible microprocessors. The decree covers only MS-DOS and Windows and its predecessor and successor products. Neither party has even addressed the Court's concern that the decree be expanded to cover all of Microsoft's commercially marketed operating systems. Given the pace of technological change, the decree must anticipate covering operating systems developed for new microprocessors.[25] In addition, taking into account Microsoft's penchant for narrowly defining the antitrust laws, the Court fears there may be endless debate as to whether a new operating system is covered by the decree.

V.B.3. Ineffective Remedy

The Court cannot find the proposed decree to be in the public interest because it does not find that the decree will "effectively pry open to competition a market that has been closed by defendant['s] illegal restraints." *AT&T*, 552 F. Supp. at 150. During the period in which this matter was before the Court the Government did little to show that the decree would meet this test beyond telling the Court that it had labored hard, that the decree was good, and that it should be approved. At the eleventh hour, only after the Court again requested information to allay its

---

25. It is difficult to imagine in this dynamic area that by the end of the period (7 years) the decree will be in effect, there will not be wholesale change with respect to microprocessors and operating systems.

concerns, did the Government finally produce an affidavit from Nobel Laureate economist, Professor Kenneth Arrow.

The affidavit made three main points: 1) that the market is an increasing returns market with large barriers to entry; 2) that the violations set forth in the complaint contributed in some part to Microsoft's monopoly position; and 3) that the decree will eliminate "artificial barriers that Microsoft had erected to prevent or slow the entry of competing suppliers of operating system software products."

The Court does not doubt the Government's position that the practices alleged in the complaint are artificial barriers. Nor does it doubt that the decree does address those practices. But what the Government fails to show is that the proposed decree will open the market and remedy the unfair advantage Microsoft gained in the market through its anticompetitive practices.

Professor Arrow's affidavit states that the operating systems market is an increasing returns market. In layman's terms that means that once a company has a monopoly position, it is extremely hard to dislodge it. Professor Arrow and the Government also concur that part of Microsoft's monopoly position is attributable to the artificial barriers it erected. Professor Arrow only argues that the decree prospectively removes these artificial barriers. He does not explain how the decree remedies the monopolist position Microsoft has achieved through alleged illegal means in an increasing returns market. If it is concededly difficult to open up an increasing returns market to competition once a company has obtained a monopoly position, the Government has not shown how prospectively prohibiting violative conduct that contributed to defendant's achieving its monopoly position will serve to return the market to where it should have been absent its anticompetitive practices. Simply telling a defendant to go forth and sin no more does little or nothing to address the unfair advantage it has already gained. In short, given the Government's expert's own analysis of this market, the decree is "too little, too late."

The proposed decree without going further, is not in the public interest because it does not meet the test of an effective antitrust remedy. The decree deals with licensing and nondisclosure practices that the Government found to be anticompetitive and detrimental to a free and open market. What the decree does not address are a number of other anticompetitive practices that from time to time Microsoft has been accused of engaging in by others in the industry. Since a Court cannot shut its eyes to the obvious, it has asked the parties to discuss these widespread public allegations. The Government has refused, and Microsoft has claimed that the accusations are false.

The accusations range from charges that Microsoft engages in the practice of vaporware i.e., the public announcement of a computer product before it is ready for market for the sole purpose of causing consumers not to purchase a competitor's product that has been developed and is either currently available for sale or momentarily about to enter the market. Other allegations include charges that Microsoft uses its dominant position in operating systems to give it an undue advantage in developing applications software and that it manipulates its operating systems so competitors' applications software are inoperable or more difficult for the consumers to utilize effectively.

Throughout these proceedings, this Court has expressed repeated concern about these allegations, in part, because it is concerned that if they are true and defendant continues to engage in them, it will continue to hold and possibly expand its monopoly position, even if it ceases the practices alleged in the complaint.

The Court has been particularly concerned about the accusations of "vaporware." Microsoft has a dominant position in the operating systems market, from which the Government's expert concedes it would be very hard to dislodge it. Given this fact, Microsoft could unfairly hold onto this position with aggressive preannouncements of new products in the face of the introduction of possibly superior competitive products. In other words, all participants concede that consumers and OEMs will be reluctant to shift to a new operating system, even a superior one, because it will mean not only giving up on both its old operating systems and applications, but also risking the possibility that there will not be adequate applications to run on the superior product. If this is true, Microsoft can hold onto its market share gained allegedly illegally, even with the introduction of a competitor's operating system superior to its own. By telling the public, "we have developed a product that we are about to introduce into the market (when such is not the case) that is just as good and is compatible with all your old applications," Microsoft can discourage consumers and OEMs from considering switching to the new product. It is for this reason that courts may consider practices outside the complaint. See *AT&T*, 552 F. Supp. at 150.

. . . [The court admitted two Microsoft documents submitted by an amicus curiae.] Both of these documents are internal Microsoft records. They are part of two Microsoft employee evaluation forms. In the first, the Microsoft employee writes that during the past six months he engaged in the following beneficial activities for Microsoft, "QB3 preannounce to hold off Turbo buyers."

The second document is even more specific. In a self-evaluation, a Microsoft employee wrote, "I developed a rollout plan for QuickC and CS that focused on minimizing Borland's first mover advantage by preannouncing with an aggressive communications campaign." These documents indicate that the highest officials of the company knew of the practices that were utilized to impact adversely on the market plans of a competitor. Whether the documents are actionable or not, certainly at a minimum they require explanation from the parties. No satisfactory explanation has been given.

Although Microsoft acknowledges the authenticity of the documents, it denies they describe the practice of vaporware and indeed, states that the practice that is described is a perfectly legitimate competitive practice. When pressed as to why the practices described in the documents were not vaporware, counsel for Microsoft stated he would limit "vaporware" to those instances where no product at all exists at the time of the so-called "preannouncement." According to counsel, it does not even matter that the date for introduction of the preannounced product is not met. Counsel further advised the Court that he would advise his client to continue to engage in the described practices. . . .

This Court cannot ignore the obvious. Here is the dominant firm in the software industry admitting it "preannounces" products to freeze the current software market and thereby defeat the marketing plans of competitors that have products ready for market. Microsoft admits that the preannouncement is solely for the purpose of having an adverse impact on a competitor's product. Its counsel states it has advised its client that the practice is perfectly legal and it may continue the practice. This practice of an alleged monopolist would seem to contribute to the acquisition, maintenance, or exercise of market share.

The Government has pressed for the adoption of its decree on the grounds that it will open up competition. Given the Government's desire to open up competition why does it not want to take on the vaporware issue?

When the Court gave Microsoft the opportunity to disavow this practice by an undertaking it declined to do so. What is more, the Government told the Court that if it conditioned its approval on Microsoft's undertaking no longer to engage in the practice, the Government would withdraw its approval of the decree even if Microsoft agreed to the undertaking.

The Court cannot sign off on a decree knowing that the defendant intends to continue to engage in an anticompetitive practice without the Government providing a full explanation as to its "no action" stance. It would almost be the equivalent of a Court accepting a probationary plea from a defendant who has told the Court he will go out and again engage in inappropriate conduct.

V.B.4. Compliance

The only change in the decree that the Government stated it would accept is the Court's suggestion that Microsoft establish an internal mechanism to monitor the decree. This too Microsoft has declined even to consider. Microsoft's position is that its 50 or so in-house lawyers, along with its outside retained counsel, are sufficient to monitor the decree. This is the same group that has advised its client that "product preannouncements" to impede competition is proper behavior.

This Court finds itself in a position similar to that of Judge Greene in *AT&T*, who refused to approve the decree without modification because of his concern as to its compliance and enforcement. *AT&T*, 552 F. Supp. at 214-17.

Based on Microsoft's counsel's representations to this Court, the Court is concerned about the question of compliance. This concern is heightened because even though the Company on prior occasions has publicly stated it does not and will not abuse its dominant position in the operating systems market vis-a-vis its development of application products, it has refused to give the Court the same assurance. Without a compliance mechanism, the Court cannot make the public interest finding. This is particularly so because Microsoft denies that the conduct charged in the Government's complaint to which it has consented, violates the antitrust laws.

This is clearly the kind of case that Congress had in mind when it passed the Tunney Act. Microsoft is a company that has a monopolist position in a field that is central to this country's well being, not only for the balance of this century, but also for the 21st Century. The Court is certainly mindful of the heroic efforts of the Antitrust Division to negotiate the decree. There is no doubt its task was formidable. Here is a company that is so feared by its competitors that they believe they will be retaliated against if they disclose their identity even in an open proceeding before a U.S. District Court Judge.

The picture that emerges from these proceedings is that the U.S. Government is either incapable or unwilling to deal effectively with a potential threat to this nation's economic well being. How else can the four year deadlocked investigation conducted by the FTC be explained. What is more, the Justice Department, although it labored hard in its follow up investigation, likewise was unable to come up with a meaningful result.

It is clear to this Court that if it signs the decree presented to it, the message will be that Microsoft is so powerful that neither the market nor the Government is capable of dealing with all of its monopolistic practices. The attitude of Microsoft confirms these observations. While it has denied publicly that it engages in anticompetitive practices, it refuses to give the Court in any respect the same assurance.[36] It has refused to take even a small step to meet any of the reasonable concerns that have been raised by the Court. . . .

Microsoft has done extremely well in its business in a relatively short period of time, which is a tribute both to its talented personnel and to this nation's great ethic that affords every citizen the ability to rise to the top. Microsoft, a rather new corporation, may not have matured to the position where it understands how it should act with respect to the public interest and the ethics of the market place. In this technological age, this nation's cutting edge companies must guard against being captured by their own technology and becoming robotized. . . .

---

36. Microsoft has stated to the Press over the years that there is a "Chinese Wall" between its operating systems and applications divisions. In Microsoft's submission to the Court, it maintains that there is no such separation and that one is not necessary.

[Judge Sporkin refused to accept the proposed consent decree between the Antitrust Division and Microsoft.]

Transamerica Computer Co. v. IBM Corp., 481 F. Supp. 965 (N.D. Cal. 1979), *aff'd*, 698 F.2d 1377 (9th Cir. 1983): IBM, which at that time held a dominant position in the mainframe and minicomputer markets, was accused of "predatory design changes." In particular, Transamerica (a maker of IBM-compatible peripheral devices) claimed that IBM frequently changed the design specifications of its peripheral interfaces, solely in order to make competing products obsolete and extend its own power into the market for peripherals. The court held that IBM was not liable for monopolizing the market, even though it acknowledged that IBM's "predominant intent . . . was undoubtedly to preclude or delay PCM competition and gain a competitive advantage." The court reasoned:

> It is not difficult to imagine situations where a monopolist could utilize the design of its own product to maintain market control or to gain a competitive advantage. For instance, the PCMs were only able to offer IBM's customers an alternative because they had duplicated the interface, the electrical connection between the IBM System/360 CPU and the IBM peripheral (or peripheral subsystem). Had IBM responded to the PCMs' inroads on its assumed monopoly by changing the System/360 interfaces with such frequency that PCMs would have been unable to attach and unable to economically adapt their peripherals to the ever-changing interface designs, and, if those interface changes had no purpose and effect other than the preclusion of PCM competition, this Court would not hesitate to find that such conduct was predatory. Or, if a monopolist frequently changed the teleprocessing interface by which its computers communicate with remote terminals in such a way that its terminals would continue to function while others would fail, and, if the only purpose and effect of the change was to gain a competitive advantage in the terminal market (where the monopolist lacked monopoly power), that use of monopoly power would be condemned.
>
> It is more difficult to formulate a legal standard for design conduct than it is to imagine clearly illegal situations. Any such standard must properly balance a concern for the preservation of desirable incentives with the need to prevent monopolization by technology. Like pricing, equipment design can have procompetitive as well as anticompetitive aspects. Truly new and innovative products are to be encouraged, and are an important part of the competitive process. For this reason, the acquisition or maintenance of monopoly power as a result of a superior product does not violate the Sherman Act. One court has even suggested that where there is a valid engineering dispute over a product's superiority the inquiry should end; the product is innovative and the design is legal. That view, probably the result of a concern for the creativity that has characterized the history of computers, is overprotective. It ignores the possibility that a superior product might be used as a vehicle for tying sales of other products, and would pronounce products superior even where the predominant evidence indicated they were not.

Another approach would be to examine the designers' intent. If a technological design were chosen for an illegal purpose (such as to effectuate a tie) and if that purpose was fulfilled, it would be illegal. If that standard were to apply only where the intent was solely an illegal one, creativity would not be stifled. But usually many results are intended, and if only one, even the predominating, intent is illegal, and thus punished, legitimate incentives will be imperiled. Discerning corporate intent is seldom easy, and, in any event, the law against monopolization is much more concerned with the effect of conduct rather than with its purpose. . . .

Large firms attempting to conform their conduct to Transamerica's proposed rule would have a difficult time indeed. Any successful action they might take to win sales necessarily tends to improve or preserve their market position. Disappointed competitors, if they can conceive of some alternative price, product, modification or practice they would have preferred, would be encouraged to bring suit. Even if the large firm recognizes and tries to resolve the problem, it cannot assure its safety. One alternative might exclude or restrict one set of potential plaintiffs, while another set would be affected by the other alternative. Management's safest course might be to do nothing, but that, of course, would violate their duty to shareholders, and would do nothing to benefit a healthy, innovative and competitive market.

It is an unwise policy for the law to coddle competitors, especially if the protection comes at the expense of destroying a larger firm's incentive to compete. Even companies that choose to enter dominated markets must be prepared to face competition on the merits. Where a monopolist chooses an alternative that does not unreasonably restrict competition, the law is not offended. It is the choice of an unreasonable alternative, not the failure to choose the least restrictive alternative, that leads to liability.

IBM did not lie dead in the water when faced with competition. It took action. And the action it took may have caused some competitors to suffer more than other actions would have. But the action IBM took, under the circumstances in which it acted, did not unreasonably restrict competition, and thus, did not violate the law.

COMMENTS AND QUESTIONS

1. Judge Sporkin's decision in United States v. Microsoft Corp. was reversed by the D.C. Circuit on appeal. United States v. Microsoft Corp., 56 F.3d 1448 (D.C. Cir. 1995). The Court of Appeals held that Judge Sporkin simply lacked the power under the Tunney Act, 15 U.S.C. §16(e), to expand his inquiry beyond the bounds of the complaint filed by the government. Thus, the Court of Appeals did not address the "vaporware" issue on the merits; it simply reversed on the grounds that the agreement between the United States and Microsoft *on the issues alleged in the complaint* was consonant with the public interest. The Court of Appeals also took the unusual step of ordering that the case be reassigned to another judge on remand.

2. Judge Sporkin in *Microsoft* expressed concern that the Antitrust Division has not taken sufficient steps to ensure compliance with the con-

sent decree. What additional steps would appropriately protect the public? In particular, consider Judge Sporkin's proposed prohibition on "vaporware," which he notes includes preannouncements as well as announcements concerning nonexistent products. How can the Justice Department ensure that Microsoft does not engage in vaporware announcements? Would government scrutiny of all Microsoft product announcements be too invasive a remedy?

For a discussion of the vaporware issue, see Stephan M. Levy, Should "Vaporware" Be an Antitrust Concern?, 42 Antitrust Bull. 33 (1997); Robert Prentice, Vaporware: Imaginary High-Tech Products and Real Antitrust Liability in a Post-Chicago World, 57 Ohio St. L.J. 1163 (1996).

3. Between 1991 and 1993, the FTC conducted an exhaustive investigation into the business practices of Intel Corp. Intel has been the dominant producer of microprocessors for IBM-compatible personal computers for some time, accounting for roughly 85 percent of the market in 1993. The FTC investigated allegations by Intel competitors, notably Advanced Micro Devices and Cyrix Corp., that Intel had threatened its distributors that if they carried Cyrix or AMD products, they would no longer be able to buy products from Intel. This practice is referred to in antitrust parlance as an "exclusive dealing arrangement." Recall that a similar sort of arrangement was used by Microsoft to guarantee its share of the operating systems market but that Microsoft agreed to stop this practice in settlement of the Justice Department's antitrust suit against it.

What is wrong with exclusive dealing arrangements? Companies agree all the time to buy from (or, more rarely, to sell to) only one source. Such agreements are arguably efficient because they reduce the transactions costs of both parties and assure a steady supply of a commodity. Do such efficiencies justify Intel's or Microsoft's actions? If not, how can we punish Intel and Microsoft without preventing a whole host of efficient supply agreements?

In 1993, the FTC dropped its investigation of Intel but cautioned that it had not found the company innocent of wrongdoing, and it reserved the right to reopen the investigation at a later date. See Ilene Knable Gotts & Howard W. Fogt, Jr., Clinton Administration Expresses More than Intellectual Curiosity in Antitrust Issues Raised by Intellectual Property Licensing, 22 AIPLA Q.J. 1, 21 (1994). Indeed, as we discuss below, the FTC has since investigated other practices by Intel.

4. Not all courts have agreed with *Transamerica* that product design changes cannot be predatory. An interesting development in the patent context is C.R. Bard v. M3 Systems, 157 F.3d 1340 (Fed. Cir. 1998), where the Federal Circuit (over a vigorous dissent by Judge Newman) held that deliberate acts to create incompatibility between a patented system and a competitor's product could be the sort of predatory conduct that was actionable under the antitrust laws.

c.   **Unilateral Refusals to Deal**

Data General Corp. v. Grumman Systems Support Corp.
United States Court of Appeals for the First Circuit
36 F.3d 1147 (1st Cir. 1994)

STAHL, Circuit Judge.

While this case raises numerous issues touching on copyright law, Grumman's most intriguing argument—presented below as both a defense and a counterclaim—is that DG illegally maintained its monopoly in the market for service of DG computers by unilaterally refusing to license ADEX to Grumman and other competitors. The antitrust claims are intriguing because they present a curious conflict, namely, whether (and to what extent) the antitrust laws, in the absence of any statutory exemption, must tolerate short-term harm to the competitive process when such harm is caused by the otherwise lawful exercise of an economically potent "monopoly" in a copyrighted work.

After a careful analysis, we affirm [a jury verdict for Data General on the question of copyright infringement] on all but one relatively minor issue concerning the calculation of damages.

I.   Background

DG and Grumman are competitors in the market for service of computers manufactured by DG, and the present litigation stems from the evolving nature of their competitive relationship. DG not only designs and manufactures computers, but also offers a line of products and services for the maintenance and repair of DG computers. Although DG has no more than a 5% share of the highly competitive "primary market" for minicomputers, DG occupies approximately 90% of the "aftermarket" for service of DG computers. As a group, various "third party maintainers" ("TPMs") earn roughly 7% of the service revenues; Grumman is the leading TPM with approximately 3% of the available service business. The remaining equipment owners (typically large companies in the high technology industry) generally maintain their own computers and peripherals, although they occasionally need outside service on a "time and materials" basis. . . .

From 1976 until some point in the mid-1980s, DG affirmatively encouraged the growth of TPMs with relatively liberal policies concerning TPM access to service tools. DG sold or licensed diagnostics directly to TPMs, and allowed TPMs to use diagnostics sold or licensed to DG equipment owners. DG did not restrict access by TPMs to spare parts manufactured by DG or other manufacturers. DG allowed (or at least tolerated) requests by TPMs for DG's repair depot to fix malfunctioning circuit boards, the heart of a computer's central processing unit ("CPU"). DG sold at least some schematics and other documentation to TPMs. DG also sold TPMs engineering change order kits. And finally, DG training classes were open to TPM field engineers. Grumman suggests that DG's liberal policies were beneficial to DG because increased capacity (and perhaps competition) in the service aftermarket would be a selling point for DG equipment.

3. Increased Restrictions

In the mid-1980s, DG altered its strategy. With the goal of maximizing revenues from its service business, DG began to refuse to provide many service tools directly to TPMs. DG would not allow TPMs to use the DG repair depot, nor would it permit TPMs to purchase schematics, documentation, "change order" kits, or certain spare parts. DG no longer allowed TPM technicians to attend DG training classes. Finally, DG developed and severely restricted the licensing of ADEX, a new software diagnostic for its MV computers. The MV series was at once DG's most advanced computer hardware and an increasingly important source of sales and service revenue for DG.

A number of items unavailable to TPMs directly from DG were either available to all equipment owners (even customers of TPMs) from DG, or were available to TPMs from sources other than DG. For example, DG depot service, change order kits, and at least some documentation were available to all equipment owners. There is also evidence that Grumman had its own repair depot and that Grumman could make use of repair depots run by other service organizations (sometimes called "fourth party maintainers"). Likewise, there is evidence that TPMs could purchase at least some spare parts from sources other than DG.

The situation was different with respect to ADEX. DG service technicians would use ADEX [a computer diagnostic program developed by Data General] in performing service for DG equipment owners. DG would also license ADEX for the exclusive use of the in-house technicians of equipment owners who perform most of their own service. However, DG would not license ADEX to its own service customers or to the customers of TPMs. Nor was ADEX available to TPMs from sources other than DG. At least two other diagnostics designed to service DG's MV computers may have become available as early as 1989, but no fully functional substitute was available when this case was tried in 1992.

Grumman found various ways to skirt DG's ADEX restrictions. Some former DG employees, in violation of their employment agreements, brought copies of ADEX when they joined Grumman. In addition, DG field engineers often stored copies of ADEX at the work sites of their service customers, who were bound to preserve the confidentiality of any DG proprietary information in their possession. Although DG service customers had an obligation to return copies of ADEX to DG should they cancel their service agreement and switch to a TPM, few customers did so. It is essentially undisputed that Grumman technicians used and duplicated copies of ADEX left behind by DG field engineers. There is also uncontroverted evidence that Grumman actually acquired copies of ADEX in this manner in order to maintain libraries of diagnostics so that Grumman technicians could freely duplicate and use any copy of ADEX to service any of Grumman's customers with DG's MV computers.

C. *The Present Litigation*

In 1988, DG filed suit against Grumman in the United States District Court for the District of Massachusetts. . . . In one count, DG alleged that Grumman's use and duplication of ADEX infringed DG's ADEX copyrights, and requested njunctive relief, 17 U.S.C. §502 (1988), as well as actual damages and profits, 17 U.S.C. §504(b) (1988). In another count, DG alleged that Grumman had violated Massachusetts trade secrets law by misappropriating copies of ADEX in violation of confidentiality agreements binding on former DG employees and DG service customers. . . .

b.   Antitrust Defenses

Grumman claimed that DG could not maintain its infringement action because DG had used its ADEX copyrights to violate Sections 1 and 2 of the Sherman Antitrust Act, 15 U.S.C. §§1 and 2 (1988 & Supp. IV 1992). Specifically, Grumman charged that DG misused its copyrights by (1) tying the availability of ADEX to a consumer's agreement either to purchase DG support services (a "positive tie") or not to purchase support services from TPMs (a "negative tie"), and (2) willfully maintaining its monopoly in the support services aftermarket by imposing the alleged tie-in and refusing to deal with TPMs. . . .

In rejecting Grumman's motion for reconsideration of the grant of summary judgment on the monopolization claim, the district court also directly addressed Grumman's contention that DG's refusal to license ADEX to TPMs constitutes exclusionary conduct. The court stated that DG's refusal to license ADEX to TPMs was not exclusionary because "DG offers to the public a license to use MV/ADEX on any computer owned by the customer," and therefore DG "'did not withhold from one member of the public a service offered to the rest[.]'" *Grumman III*, slip op. at 5 (citing Olympia Equip. Leasing Co. v. Western Union Tel. Co., 797 F.2d 370, 377 (7th Cir. 1986), *cert. denied*, 480 U.S. 934, 94 L. Ed. 2d 765, 107 S. Ct. 1574 (1987)). . . .

B.   Grumman's Antitrust Counterclaims . . .

2.   Monopolization . . .

a.   Unilateral Refusals to Deal

Because a monopolization claim does not require proof of concerted activity, even the unilateral actions of a monopolist can constitute exclusionary conduct. See 15 U.S.C. §2 (referring to "every person who shall monopolize . . . or combine or conspire with any other person . . . to monopolize") (emphasis added); Moore v. Jas. H. Matthews & Co., 473 F.2d 328, 332 (9th Cir. 1973) (observing that "section 2 is not limited to concerted activity"). Thus, a monopolist's unilateral refusal to deal with its competitors (as long as the refusal harms the competitive process) may constitute prima facie evidence of exclusionary conduct in the context of a Section 2 claim. See *Kodak*, 112 S. Ct. at 2091 n.32 (citing Aspen Skiing Co. v. Aspen Highlands Skiing Corp., 472 U.S. 585, 602-05, 86 L. Ed. 2d 467, 105 S. Ct. 2847 (1985)). A monopolist may nevertheless rebut such evidence by establishing a valid business justification for its conduct. See *Kodak*, 112 S. Ct. at 2091 n. 32 (suggesting that monopolist may rebut an inference of exclusionary conduct by establishing "legitimate competitive reasons for the refusal"); *Aspen Skiing*, 472 U.S. at 608 (suggesting that sufficient evidence of harm to consumers and competitors triggers further inquiry as to whether the monopolist has "persuaded the jury that its [harmful] conduct was justified by [a] normal business purpose"). In general, a business justification is valid if it relates directly or indirectly to the enhancement of consumer welfare. Thus, pursuit of efficiency and quality control might be legitimate competitive reasons for an otherwise exclusionary refusal to deal, while the desire to maintain a monopoly market share or thwart the entry of competitors would not. See *Kodak*, 112 S. Ct. at 2091 (discussing the validity and sufficiency of various business justifications); *Aspen Skiing*, 472 U.S. at 608-11 (same); see generally 7 Areeda & Turner ¶1504, at 377-83; 9 Areeda & Turner ¶¶1713, 1716-17, at 148-61, 185-239. In essence, a unilateral refusal to deal is prima facie exclusionary if there is evidence of harm to the competitive process; a valid business justification requires proof of countervailing benefits to the competitive process.

Despite the theoretical possibility, there have been relatively few cases in which a unilateral refusal to deal has formed the basis of a successful Section 2 claim. Several of the cases commonly cited for a supposed duty to deal were actually cases of joint conduct in which some competitors joined to frustrate others. See Associated Press v. United States, 326 U.S. 1, 89 L. Ed. 2013, 65 S. Ct. 1416 (1945); United States v. Terminal R.R. Ass'n, 224 U.S. 383, 56 L. Ed. 810, 32 S. Ct. 507 (1912). Prior to *Aspen*

Skiing, the case that probably came closest to condemning a true unilateral refusal to deal was Otter Tail Power Co. v. United States, 410 U.S. 366, 35 L. Ed. 2d 359, 93 S. Ct. 1022 (1973), which condemned the refusal of a wholesale power supplier either to sell wholesale power to municipal systems or to "wheel power" when Otter Tail's retail franchises expired and local municipalities sought to supplant Otter Tail's local distributors. The case not only involved a capital-intensive public utility facility—which could not effectively be duplicated and occupied a distinct separate market —but the Supreme Court laid considerable emphasis on "supported" findings in the district court "that Otter Tail's refusals to sell at wholesale or to wheel were solely to prevent municipal power systems from eroding its monopolistic position." 410 U.S. at 378.

In *Aspen Skiing*, the Court criticized a monopolist's unilateral refusal to deal in a very different situation, casting serious doubt on the proposition that the Court has adopted any single rule or formula for determining when a unilateral refusal to deal is unlawful. In that case, an "all-Aspen" ski ticket—valid at any mountain in Aspen—had been developed and jointly marketed when the three (later four) ski areas in Aspen were owned by independent entities. 472 U.S. at 589. Some time after Aspen Skiing Company ("Ski Co.") came into control of three of the four ski areas, Ski Co. refused to continue a joint agreement with Aspen Highlands Skiing Corp. ("Highlands"), the owner of the fourth area. *Id.* at 592-93. Although there was no "essential facility" involved, the Court found that it was exclusionary for Ski Co., as a monopolist, to refuse to continue a presumably efficient "pattern of distribution that had originated in a competitive market and had persisted for several years." *Id.* at 603.

It is not entirely clear whether the Court in *Aspen Skiing* merely intended to create a category of refusal-to-deal cases different from the essential facilities category or whether the Court was inviting the application of more general principles of antitrust analysis to unilateral refusals to deal. We follow the parties' lead in assuming that Grumman need not tailor its argument to a preexisting "category" of unilateral refusals to deal.

b. Unilateral Refusals to License

DG attempts to undermine Grumman's monopolization claim by proposing a powerful irrebuttable presumption: a unilateral refusal to license a copyright can never constitute exclusionary conduct. We agree that some type of presumption is in order, but reach that conclusion only after an exhaustive inquiry touching on the general character of presumptions, the role of market analysis in the copyright context, existing responses to the tension between the antitrust and patent laws, the nature of the rights extended by the copyright laws, and our duty to harmonize two conflicting statutes.

(1) The Propriety of a Presumption

We begin our analysis with two observations. First, DG's rule of law could be characterized as either an empirical assumption or a policy preference. For example, if we were convinced that refusals to license a copyright always have a net positive effect on the competitive process, we might adopt a presumption to this effect in order to preclude wasteful litigation about a known fact. On the other hand, if we were convinced that the rights enumerated in the Copyright Act should take precedence over the responsibilities set forth in the Sherman Act, regardless of the realities of the market, we might adopt a blanket rule of preference. DG's argument contains elements of both archetypal categories of presumptions.

Second, we note that the phrase "competitive process" may need some refinement in order to evaluate either an empirical assumption or a policy presumption concerning the desirability of unilateral refusals to license a copyright. Antitrust law generally seeks to punish and prevent harm to consumers in particular markets, with a focus on relatively specific time periods. See, e.g., *Jefferson Parish*, 466 U.S. at 18 (holding that "any inquiry into the validity of a tying arrangement must focus on the market or markets in which the two products are sold, for that is where the anti-competitive forcing has its impact"). Thus, in determining whether conduct is exclusionary in the context of a monopolization claim, we ordinarily focus on harm to the competitive process in the relevant market and time period. See generally 3 Areeda & Turner ¶¶517-28, at 346-88, ¶¶533-36, at 406-431. Confining the competitive process in this way assists courts in deciding particular disputes based primarily on case-specific adjudicative facts rather than generally-applicable "legislative" facts or assumptions. The use and protection of copyrights also affects the "competitive process," but it may not be appropriate to judge the effect of the use of a copyright by looking only at one market or one time period.

We now consider what appears to be an empirical proclamation from DG: "The refusal to make one's innovation available to rivals . . . is pro-competitive conduct." As support, DG cites *Grinnell*, 384 U.S. at 570-71, in which the Court held that willful maintenance of monopoly does not include "growth or development as a consequence of a superior product." It is not the superiority of a work that allows the author to exclude others, however, but rather the limited monopoly granted by copyright law. Moreover, one reason why the Copyright Act fosters investment and innovation is that it may allow the author to earn monopoly profits by licensing the copyright to others or reserving the copyright for the author's exclusive use. See Sony Corp. of Am. v. Universal City Studios, Inc., 464 U.S. 417, 429, 78 L. Ed. 2d 574, 104 S. Ct. 774 (1984) (explaining that the limited copyright monopoly "is intended to motivate the creative activity of authors and inventors by the provision of a special reward"). Thus, at least in a particular market and for a particular period of time, the Copyright Act tolerates behavior that may harm both consumers and competitors. Cf. SCM Corp. v. Xerox Corp., 645 F.2d 1195, 1203 (2d Cir. 1981) ("The primary purpose of the antitrust laws—to preserve competition—can be frustrated, albeit temporarily, by a holder's exercise of the patent's inherent exclusionary power during its term."), *cert. denied,* 455 U.S. 1016, 72 L. Ed. 2d 132, 102 S. Ct. 1708 (1982).

DG does not in fact argue that consumers are better off in the short term because of the inability of TPMs to license ADEX. Instead, DG suggests that allowing copyright owners to exclude others from the use of their works creates incentives which ultimately work to the benefit of consumers in the DG service aftermarket as well as to the benefit of consumers generally. In other words, DG seeks to justify any immediate harm to consumers by pointing to countervailing long-term benefits. Certainly, a monopolist's refusal to license others to use a commercially successful patented idea is likely to have more profound anti-competitive consequences than a refusal to allow others to duplicate the copyrighted expression of an unpatented idea (although such differences may become less pronounced if copyright law becomes increasingly protective of intellectual property such as computer software). But by no means is a monopolist's refusal to license a copyright entirely "pro-competitive" within the ordinary economic framework of the Sherman Act. Accordingly, it may be inappropriate to adopt an empirical assumption that simply ignores harm to the competitive process caused by a monopolist's unilateral refusal to license a copyright. Even if it is clear that exclusive use of a copyright can have anti-competitive consequences, some type of presumption may nevertheless be appropriate as a matter of either antitrust law or copyright law.

(2) Antitrust Law and the Accommodation of Patent Rights

Antitrust law is somewhat instructive. Although creation and protection of original works of authorship may be a national pastime, the Sherman Act does not explicitly exempt such activity from antitrust scrutiny and courts should be wary of creating implied exemptions. See Square D Co. v. Niagara Frontier Tariff Bureau, Inc., 476 U.S. 409, 421, 90 L. Ed. 2d 413, 106 S. Ct. 1922 (1986) ("Exemptions from the antitrust laws are strictly construed and strongly disfavored."); cf. Flood v. Kuhn, 407 U.S. 258, 32 L. Ed. 2d 728, 92 S. Ct. 2099 (1972) (holding that the long-standing judicially created exemption of professional baseball from the Sherman Act is an established "aberration" in which Congress has acquiesced). The Supreme Court has suggested that an otherwise reasonable yet anti-competitive use of a copyright should not "be deemed a per se violation of the Sherman Act," Broadcast Music, Inc. v. CBS, Inc., 441 U.S. 1, 19, 60 L. Ed. 2d 1, 99 S. Ct. 1551 (1979), but a monopolistic refusal to license might still violate the rule of reason, see Rural Tel. Serv. Co. v. Feist Publications, Inc., 957 F.2d 765, 767-69 (10th Cir.) (analyzing reasonableness of monopolist's unilateral refusal to license copyrighted telephone listings to a competing distributor of telephone directories), *cert. denied,*

121 L. Ed. 2d 429, 113 S. Ct. 490 (1992).[63] Should an antitrust plaintiff be allowed to demonstrate the anti-competitive effects of a monopolist's unilateral refusal to grant a copyright license? Would the monopolist then have to justify its refusal to license by introducing evidence that the protection of the copyright laws enabled the author to create a work which advances consumer welfare?

The courts appear to have partly settled an analogous conflict between the patent laws and the antitrust laws, treating the former as creating an implied limited exception to the latter. In Simpson v. Union Oil Co., 377 U.S. 13, 24, 12 L. Ed. 2d 98, 84 S. Ct. 1051 (1964), the Supreme Court stated that "the patent laws which give a 17-year monopoly on 'making, using, or selling the invention' are in pari materia with the antitrust laws and modify them pro tanto." Similarly, we have suggested that the exercise of patent rights is a "legitimate means" by which a firm may maintain its monopoly power. *Barry Wright*, 724 F.2d at 230. Other courts have specifically held that a monopolist's unilateral refusal to license a patent is ordinarily not properly viewed as exclusionary conduct. See *Miller Insituform*, 830 F.2d at 609 ("A patent holder who lawfully acquires a patent cannot be held liable under Section 2 of the Sherman Act for maintaining the monopoly power he lawfully acquired by refusing to license the patent to others."); *Westinghouse*, 648 F.2d at 647 (finding no antitrust violation because "*Westinghouse* has done no more than to license some of its patents and refuse to license others"); *SCM Corp.*, 645 F.2d at 1206 (holding that "where a patent has been lawfully acquired, subsequent conduct permissible under the patent laws cannot trigger any liability under the antitrust laws"); see also 3 Areeda & Turner ¶704, at 114 ("The patent is itself a government grant of monopoly and is therefore an exception to usual antitrust rules."). This exception is inoperable if the patent was unlawfully "acquired." *SCM Corp.*, 645 F.2d at 1208-09 (analyzing legality of Xerox's acquisition of plain-paper copier patent); see generally 3

---

63. It is in any event well settled that concerted and contractual behavior that threatens competition is not immune from antitrust inquiry simply because it involves the exercise of copyright privileges. See, e.g., *Kodak*, 112 S. Ct. at 2089 n.29 ("The Court has held many times that power gained through some natural and legal advantage such as a patent, copyright, or business acumen can give rise to liability if 'a seller exploits his dominant position in one market to expand his empire into the next.'") (quoting Times-Picayune Publishing Co. v. United States, 345 U.S. 594, 611, 97 L. Ed. 1277, 73 S. Ct. 872 (1953) (tying case)); United States v. Paramount Pictures, Inc., 334 U.S. 131, 143, 92 L. Ed. 1260, 68 S. Ct. 915 (1948) (holding that horizontal conspiracy to engage in price-fixing in copyright licenses is illegal per se); *id.* at 159 (holding that block-booking of motion pictures—"a refusal to license one or more copyrights unless another copyright is accepted"—is an illegal tying arrangement); Straus v. American Publishers' Ass'n, 231 U.S. 222, 234, 58 L. Ed. 192, 34 S. Ct. 84 (1913) ("No more than the patent statute was the copyright act intended to authorize agreements in unlawful restraint of trade. . . ."); Digidyne Corp. v. Data General Corp., 734 F.2d 1336 (9th Cir. 1984) (affirming finding of illegal tie between copyrighted software and computer hardware), *cert. denied*, 473 U.S. 908, 87 L. Ed. 2d 657, 105 S. Ct. 3534 (1985); cf. Miller Insituform, Inc. v. Insituform of N. Am., Inc., 830 F.2d 606, 608-09 & n.4 (6th Cir. 1987) (describing ways in which patent holder may violate the antitrust laws), *cert. denied*, 484 U.S. 1064, 98 L. Ed. 2d 988, 108 S. Ct. 1023 (1988); United States v. Westinghouse Elec. Corp., 648 F.2d 642, 646-47 (9th Cir. 1981) (same).

Areeda & Turner ¶¶705-707, at 117-45 (discussing effect of patent acquisition, internal development of patents, and improprieties in patent procurement on applicability of antitrust laws).

The "patent exception" is largely a means of resolving conflicting rights and responsibilities, i.e., a policy presumption. See, e.g., *Miller Insituform*, 830 F.2d at 609 (declaring summarily that "there is no adverse effect on competition since, as a patent monopolist, [the patent holder] had [the] exclusive right to manufacture, use, and sell his invention"). At the same time, the exception is grounded in an empirical assumption that exposing patent activity to wider antitrust scrutiny would weaken the incentives underlying the patent system, thereby depriving consumers of beneficial products. See, e.g., *SCM Corp.*, 645 F.2d at 1209 (holding that imposition of antitrust liability for an arguably unreasonable refusal to license a lawfully acquired patent "would severely trample upon the incentives provided by our patent laws and thus undermine the entire patent system").

(3) Copyright Law

Copyright law provides further guidance. The Copyright Act expressly grants to a copyright owner the exclusive right to distribute the protected work by "transfer of ownership, or by rental, lease, or lending." 17 U.S.C. §106. Consequently, "the owner of the copyright, if [it] pleases, may refrain from vending or licensing and content [itself] with simply exercising the right to exclude others from using [its] property." Fox Film Corp. v. Doyal, 286 U.S. 123, 127, 76 L. Ed. 1010, 52 S. Ct. 546 (1932). See also Stewart v. Abend, 495 U.S. 207, 229, 109 L. Ed. 2d 184, 110 S. Ct. 1750 (1990). We may also venture to infer that, in passing the Copyright Act, Congress itself made an empirical assumption that allowing copyright holders to collect license fees and exclude others from using their works creates a system of incentives that promotes consumer welfare in the long term by encouraging investment in the creation of desirable artistic and functional works of expression. See Feist Publications, Inc. v. Rural Tel. Serv. Co., 499 U.S. 340, 111 S. Ct. 1282, 1290, 113 L. Ed. 2d 358 (1991) ("The primary objective of a copyright is not to reward the labor of authors, but 'to promote the Progress of Science and useful Arts.'") (quoting U.S. Const. art. I. §8, cl. 8); Sony Corp., 464 U.S. at 429 (discussing goals and incentives of copyright protection); Twentieth Century Music Corp. v. Aiken, 422 U.S. 151, 156, 45 L. Ed. 2d 84, 95 S. Ct. 2040 (1975) ("The immediate effect of our copyright law is to secure a fair return for an 'author's' creative labor. But the ultimate aim is, by this incentive, to stimulate artistic creativity for the general public good."). We cannot require antitrust defendants to prove and reprove the merits of this legislative assumption in every case where a refusal to license a copyrighted work comes under attack. Nevertheless, although "nothing in the copyright statutes would prevent an author from hoarding all of his works during the term of the copyright," *Stewart*, 495 U.S. at 228-29, the Copyright Act does not explicitly purport to limit the scope of the Sherman Act. And, if the Copyright Act is silent on the subject generally, the silence is particularly acute in cases where a monopolist harms consumers in the monopolized market by refusing to license a copyrighted work to competitors.

We acknowledge that Congress has not been entirely silent on the relationship between antitrust and intellectual property laws. Congress amended the patent laws in 1988 to provide that "no patent owner otherwise entitled to relief for infringement . . . of a patent shall be denied relief or deemed guilty of misuse or illegal extension of the patent right by reason of [the patent owner's] refusal to license or use any rights to the patent." 35 U.S.C. §271(d) (1988). Section 271(d) clearly prevents an infringer from using a patent misuse defense when the patent owner has unilaterally refused a license, and may even herald the prohibition of all antitrust claims and counterclaims premised on a refusal to license a patent. See Stephen Calkins, Patent Law: The Impact of the 1988 Patent Misuse Reform Act and Noerr-Pennington Doctrine on Misuse Defenses and Antitrust Counterclaims, 38 Drake L. Rev. 192-97 (1988-89). Nevertheless, while Section 271(d) is indicative of congressional "policy" on the need for antitrust law to accommodate intellectual property law, Congress did not similarly amend the Copyright Act.

(4) Harmonizing the Sherman Act and the Copyright Act

Since neither the Sherman Act nor the Copyright Act works a partial repeal of the other, and since implied repeals are disfavored, e.g., Watt v. Alaska, 451 U.S. 259, 267, 68 L. Ed. 2d 80, 101 S. Ct. 1673 (1981), we must harmonize the two as best we can, *id.*, mindful of the legislative and judicial approaches to similar conflicts created by the patent laws. We must not lose sight of the need to preserve the economic incentives fueled by the Copyright Act, but neither may we ignore the tension between the two very different policies embodied in the Copyright Act and the Sherman Act, both designed ultimately to improve the welfare of consumers in our free market system. Drawing on our discussion above, we hold that while exclusionary conduct can include a monopolist's unilateral refusal to license a copyright, an author's desire to exclude others from use of its copyrighted work is a presumptively valid business justification for any immediate harm to consumers.[64]

---

64. Wary of undermining the Sherman Act, however, we do not hold that an antitrust plaintiff can never rebut this presumption, for there may be rare cases in which imposing antitrust liability is unlikely to frustrate the objectives of the Copyright Act.

c. DG's Refusal to License ADEX to non-CMOs

Having arrived at the applicable legal standards, we may resolve Grumman's principal allegation of exclusionary conduct. Although there may be a genuine factual dispute about the effect on DG equipment owners of DG's refusal to license ADEX to TPMs, DG's desire to exercise its rights under the Copyright Act is a presumptively valid business justification. . . .

Grumman attempts to analogize this case to *Aspen Skiing* by focusing on the fact that DG once encouraged firms to enter the DG service aftermarket by allowing liberal access to service tools, but no longer does so. The analytical framework of *Aspen Skiing* cannot function in these circumstances, however, because we are unable to view DG's market practices in both competitive and noncompetitive conditions. While TPMs have made inroads in the market for service of DG computers, DG has always been a monopolist in that market, and competitive conditions have never prevailed. Therefore, it would not be "appropriate to infer" from DG's change of heart that its former policies "satisfy consumer demand in free competitive markets." *Aspen Skiing*, 472 U.S. at 603.

Nor does it appear that Grumman would be able at trial to overcome the presumption on any other theory. There is no evidence that DG acquired its ADEX copyrights in any unlawful manner; indeed, the record suggests that DG developed all its software internally. Cf. 3 Areeda & Turner ¶706, at 127-28 (arguing that although an internally developed patent may be as exclusionary as one acquired from outside a firm, labelling the former as exclusionary would "discourage progressiveness by monopolists"). And, while there is evidence that DG knew that developing a "proprietary position" in the area of diagnostic software would help to maintain its monopoly in the aftermarket for service of DG computers, there is also evidence that DG set out to create a state-of-the-art diagnostic that would help to improve the quality of DG service. Cf. *id.* ¶706, at 128-29 (suggesting that "nearly all commercial research rests on a mixture of motivations" and that a search for an overriding "antisocial" motivation would be unilluminating). In fact, there is clearly some evidence that ADEX is a significant benefit to owners of DG's MV computers. ADEX is a better product than any other diagnostic for MV computers. The use of ADEX appears to have increased the efficiency and reduced the cost of service because technicians can locate problems more quickly and, through the use of the software's "remote assistance" capability, can arrive at customer sites having determined ahead of time what replacement parts are necessary. In addition to the possibility of lower prices occasioned by such gains in efficiency, ADEX also promises to lower prices through gains in effectiveness. For example, customers may save the cost of replacing expensive hardware components because the use of advanced diagnostics increases the possibility that technicians can locate a problem and repair the component.

COMMENTS AND QUESTIONS

Consider the court's conclusion that a refusal to license a copyrighted work is a presumptively valid business justification. How does this square with the rationales behind the copyright law? Is it inconsistent with the ultimate goal of copyright—to promote the *dissemination* of works of authorship to the general public?

Note on a Monopolist's Duty to Disclose

Antitrust law sometimes imposes burdens on monopolists that it does not impose on ordinary competitors. One of the most contentious issues in antitrust law is the duty of monopolists to give competitors access to their facilities. In limited circumstances, courts have been willing to require monopolists to provide such access on nondiscriminatory terms. For example, the Supreme Court has held that a group of railroads that together owned the central railroad switching yard in St. Louis, Missouri, could not deny access to that yard to nonmembers. United States v. Terminal Ry., 212 U.S. 1 (1912). *Terminal Railway* reasoned that because it was the only rail yard serving St. Louis and because of the importance of the city as a hub, the rail yard was an "essential facility" from which its owners could not exclude others to the detriment of competition. A more recent case held that the owner of ski resorts with local market power could not discontinue a multi-area ski lift ticket it had shared with a smaller competitor in the absence of a legitimate business justification, even though the Court was unwilling to describe the lift ticket as an "essential facility." Aspen Skiing Co. v. Aspen Highlands Skiing Corp., 472 U.S. 585 (1985).

With these limited exceptions, however, the general rule is that businesses—even monopolists—do not have to give their competitors access to their facilities. In Berkey Photo, Inc. v. Eastman Kodak Co., 603 F.2d 263 (2d Cir. 1979), the court rejected Berkey's argument that Kodak owed it a duty to predisclose its forthcoming products so Berkey could prepare compatible products. The court recognized that Kodak's size and advance knowledge of its own plans gave it an advantage over Berkey. But, the court said,

> a large firm does not violate section 2 simply by reaping the competitive rewards attributable to its efficient size, nor does an integrated business offend the Sherman Act whenever one of its departments benefits from association with a division possessing a monopoly in its own market. So long as we allow a firm to compete in several fields, we must expect it to seek the competitive advantages of its broad-based activity. . . .
>
> Berkey postulates that Kodak had a duty to disclose limited types of information to certain competitors under specific circumstances. But it is difficult to comprehend how a major corporation, accustomed though it is to making business decisions with antitrust considerations in mind, could pos-

sess the omniscience to anticipate all the instances in which a jury might one day in the future retrospectively conclude that predisclosure was warranted. And it is equally difficult to discern workable guidelines that a court might set forth to aid the firm's decision. For example, how detailed must the information conveyed be? And how far must research have progressed before it is "ripe" for disclosure? These inherent uncertainties would have an inevitable chilling effect on innovation. They go far, we believe, towards explaining why no court has ever imposed the duty Berkey seeks to create here.

Id.

The already difficult line between these two strands of cases is further complicated when the subject matter at issue is intellectual property. An intellectual property right is an exclusive right. It would be stripped of much of its value if antitrust law were to compel intellectual property owners to share it with their competitors. But there may be circumstances in which access to a patent or copyright has become an "essential facility" for competitors in the same or in a downstream market. In those circumstances, courts must face a direct conflict between the rights granted by intellectual property law and the prohibitions of antitrust law. Cf. David Scheffman, The Application of Raising Rivals' Costs Theory to Antitrust, 37 Antitrust Bull. 187 (1992) (suggesting that raising the cost of a key input to a rival creates a problem similar to the problem of denying access to an essential facility).

This problem has arisen on several different occasions in the computer industry. In each case, the issue is one of standardization. One company's system (protected by intellectual property rights) has become the de facto standard for an entire industry. Is the company entitled therefore to control the entire industry? To date, courts have not answered this question. Instead, they have dealt with these problems as problems of copyright law, and have not considered antitrust issues at all. See, e.g., Apple Computer v. Franklin Computer, 714 F.2d 1240 (3d Cir. 1983) (Franklin had no right to create programs compatible with the Apple II operating system that would justify access to Apple's operating system code); Sega v. Accolade, 977 F.2d 1510 (9th Cir. 1992) (Accolade had right under copyright fair use doctrine to reverse engineer Sega's copyrighted code in order to create games that would work on Sega's video game system). Cf. DSC Communications v. DGI Technologies, 81 F.3d 597 (5th Cir. 1996) (attempt to use copyright to prevent a competitor's access to microcode was copyright misuse). Issues of standardization and the role of monopolists with intellectual property will recur—in the computer industry and elsewhere.

COMMENTS AND QUESTIONS

1. As we shall see in the next section, antitrust law normally is intensely skeptical of agreements and exchanges of information between competitors. The plaintiff in *Berkey Photo* seems to be asking that the court

require that competitors share information about their new product specifications. Shouldn't the court be concerned about helping facilitate a cartel between the parties in an "essential facilities" case?

2. Some recent cases have cast doubt on the strength of the presumption that an intellectual property owner is always justified in unilaterally refusing to license its patents. In Kodak v. Image Technical Services, Inc., 125 F.3d 1195 (9th Cir. 1997), the court faced an appeal from a jury verdict that Kodak had tied the purchase of replacement parts for its copiers to the purchase of service from Kodak in an effort to drive independent service organizations out of business. (A prior Supreme Court ruling on the legal theory of this case is discussed in the section on tying, infra). One of Kodak's arguments on appeal was that because some of its spare parts were patented, it was free to refuse to license those patents to anyone it chose. The Ninth Circuit rejected that argument, reasoning that the "refusal to license" asserted in that case was really a part of an unlawful tying arrangement and that Kodak asserted its patents as a pretext. This result is perfectly consistent with the existing case law on patents and tying arrangements. Indeed, the court applied the *Data General* presumption: it simply concluded that the presumption was rebutted in this case. Strong language in the opinion suggests, however, that the Ninth Circuit is skeptical about the ability of patent owners to refuse to license under all conditions.

At least one court has expressly rejected the Ninth Circuit's holding, concluding that a refusal to license can *never* violate the antitrust laws. In re Independent Service Organizations Antitrust Litigation, 989 F. Supp. 1131 (D. Kan. 1997).

An even stronger challenge to the ability of patent owners to control licensing is presented by Intergraph Corp. v. Intel Corp., 3 F. Supp. 2d 1255 (N.D. Ala. 1998). In that case, Intergraph obtained an order from the district court requiring Intel to continue a long-standing business relationship with Intergraph by providing Intergraph with chips, technical information, and assistance regarding its new Pentium II chip architecture in advance of the chip's release. The court acknowledged that Intel owned patents, copyrights, and mask work registrations governing its chip architecture but concluded that Intel's intellectual property rights did not protect it from having to continue dealing with Intergraph.

In *Intergraph*, the district court also concluded that Intel's as-yet-unreleased Pentium II chip architecture was an "essential facility" because hardware and peripheral manufacturer's had to be able to make products compatible with the architecture sold by Intel, the dominant firm in the microprocessor industry. It therefore ordered Intel to provide advanced product information and technical support—as well as a guaranteed supply of chips—to Intergraph. The Federal Circuit reversed on appeal, however, concluding that because Intel did not compete with Intergraph its conduct could not form the basis for a monopolization claim.

This is precisely the sort of relief Berkey Photo sought. What, if anything, distinguishes the cases? If Intel's chip architecture is really an "essential facility," does Intel have a similar obligation to provide this information to its competitors in the microprocessor business? What does this case suggest about Microsoft's power to deny competitors access to the APIs of its Windows operating system? Cf. Aldridge v. Microsoft Corp., 995 F. Supp. 728 (S.D. Tex. 1998) (holding that Microsoft's Windows 95 operating system was potentially subject to an "essential facilities" claim but that the portions at issue in this case were not in fact essential facilities).

3. For an argument that intellectual property owners should not be compelled to license their rights to competitors even in a network market, see David McGowan, Networks and Intention in Antitrust and Intellectual Property, 24 J. Corp. L. 485 (1999); David McGowan, Regulating Competition in the Information Age: Computer Software as an Essential Facility Under the Sherman Act, 18 Hastings Comm. & Ent. L.J. 771 (1996).

C. AGREEMENTS TO RESTRAIN TRADE

1. Vertical Restraints

a. *Tying Arrangements*

In a tying arrangement, the seller forces the buyer to buy a product he does not want (the tied product) in order to get a product he does want (the tying product). According to traditional tying theory, sellers with market power in the tying product can leverage that monopoly into the tied product by forcing captive buyers to buy the tied product exclusively from them. Whether this strategy is economically viable has been the subject of heated debate, as we discuss below. Tying arrangements, like joint ventures, have proven difficult to pigeonhole for antitrust purposes. They have been attacked under section 1 of the Sherman Act as involving a conspiracy,[5] under section 2 of the Sherman Act as involving monopolization of the tied product market, and under section 3 of the Clayton Act as requiring an exclusive dealing arrangement.[6]

Tying is one of the theories most commonly asserted against intellectual property owners. A common antitrust complaint is that a patentee, who has some power in the (patented) tying product by virtue of her

---

5. The presumed "conspiracy" here is between the coercing seller and the coerced buyer. This is hardly the sort of collusion one normally thinks of as subject to section 1. But see Perma-Life Mufflers v. International Parts Corp., 392 U.S. 134 (1968) (defendant may be guilty of conspiracy with plaintiff he coerces under section 1).

6. Only some tying arrangements fall within the scope of this last provision. A tying arrangement can be either exclusive or nonexclusive, depending on whether it requires buyers to buy *all* of their supply of the tied product from the seller or only a specified amount of it. Further, section 3 by its terms applies only to transactions in goods, not services.

intellectual property right, is requiring buyers to purchase unpatented tied products as well. In the computer industry, in which components that interoperate (work together) play a fundamental role, the claim is often somewhat more subtle—that an intellectual property owner has tied some desirable part of the system to the purchase of the entire system.

An important 1992 Supreme Court case (not directly involving intellectual property) held that such a tying claim could be evaluated in the relevant antitrust "aftermarket" for parts or service for a single brand of photocopier, because consumers were "locked in" to that copier once they had purchased it. Eastman Kodak Co. v. Image Technical Servs., Inc., 504 U.S. 451 (1992). That case has obvious importance for the computer industry, in which consumer lock-in plays a major role.

≡ *Virtual Maintenance, Inc. v. Prime Computer, Inc.*
≡ *United States Court of Appeals for the Sixth Circuit*
≡ *11 F.3d 660 (6th Cir. 1993)*

Suhrheinrich, Circuit Judge. . . .

I.

. . . Defendant Prime Computer, Inc. ("Prime") manufactures and markets computer systems, and provides maintenance services for those systems. Of significance to this lawsuit is one of its hardware lines, the "50 Series" minicomputer, and one of its applications software products, the so-called Computer-Aided Design/Computer-Aided Manufacturing system ("CAD/CAM"), which can be used with the 50 Series minicomputers.

Ford Motor Company ("Ford") created and owns a CAD/CAM software design program for use in designing automobiles. Ford's CAD/CAM program is called Product Design Graphic System ("PDGS"). Ford frequently revises the software program, and requires the automotive design companies with which it does business to use the most recent version of Ford's PDGS in order to facilitate the transmission of design specifications through CAD/CAM software.

Ford licenses defendant Prime as the exclusive distributor of Ford's version of PDGS under a year-to-year contract. Ford's version of PDGS runs only in Prime's 50 Series minicomputers, but can be translated to other systems at a higher cost.

Prime also distributes software support (i.e., revisions, modifications, updates, and support services) for PDGS software. Prime offers this software support to Ford's design companies as part of a package that includes hardware maintenance on the Prime 50 Series minicomputers. PDGS revisions may be purchased separately from the hardware maintenance, but only at a prohibitive expense. In contrast, the general contract to purchase PDGS does not contain a hardware maintenance requirement.

Plaintiff Virtual Maintenance, Inc. ("Virtual") brought this antitrust action after unsuccessfully attempting to enter into hardware maintenance contracts with owners of Prime 50 Series computers. Virtual contended that Prime's package constituted an illegal tying arrangement in violation of §1 of the Sherman Act, 15 U.S.C. §1, by conditioning the purchase of software support required by Ford to hardware maintenance from Prime (the tying product). . . .

II. . . .

B. . . .

2.

Under Virtual's first per se claim, the district court defined the relevant market as "the sale of software revisions and support for the CAD/CAM industry in general." We found no error in the legal adequacy of the district court's definition, but concluded that Prime possessed at most an 11% share of the market, which is insufficient as a matter of law to confer market power. *Virtual I*, 957 at 1325 (citing *Jefferson Parish Hosp. Dist. No. 2* in *Hyde*, 466 U.S. 2, 26, 80 L. Ed. 2d 2, 104 S. Ct. 1551 (1984) (30% market share does not confer market power); A.I. Root v. Computer/Dynamics, Inc., 806 F.2d 673, 675 (6th Cir. 1986) (2-4% market share is insufficient); Grappone, Inc. v. Subaru of New England, Inc., 858 F.2d 792, 796 (1st Cir. 1985) (5% market share insufficient)). We find nothing in *Eastman Kodak* which requires us to alter this analysis. We therefore hold that a per se tying violation could not be established under Virtual's first per se theory because Prime lacks market power in the general CAD/CAM product market, for the reasons stated here and in section II.B.1. of our decision in *Virtual I*.

3.

Our ruling regarding Virtual's second per se claim requires much closer scrutiny. The other market that Virtual urged was defined as "the sale of software revisions and support of software necessary to do business with Ford Motor Company." *Virtual I*, 957 F.2d at 1325. Prime argued that this instruction defined the tying product market too narrowly as a matter of law, and we agreed. We found that market definition defective as a matter of law because it was "based solely on one customer's requirements," which "this court has held . . . does not create a separate product market." *Id.* at 1327 (citing International Logistics Group, Ltd. v. Chrysler Corp., 884 F.2d 904, 908 (6th Cir. 1989), *cert. denied*, 494 U.S. 1066, 108 L. Ed. 2d 784, 110 S. Ct. 1783 (1990); Dunn & Mavis, Inc. v. Nu-Car Driveaway, Inc., 691 F.2d 241 (6th Cir. 1982)).

In response to Virtual's contention that Ford is not the only customer of Prime's products, but that all of Ford's design suppliers made up the customer market for "Ford-required CAD/CAM," we stated:

> Virtual seeks to distinguish these cases by pointing out that Ford is not the only customer of Prime's products; rather, all of Ford's design suppliers make up the customer market for "Ford-required CAD/CAM." This ignores the fact that Ford requires its suppliers to purchase the software updates for Ford's benefit. Ford is ultimately the single consumer of its specialized design software because Ford's requirements define the demand for the software and the updates. But defining the market by Ford's requirements creates the appearance of market power based only upon the demand side of the market. Defining a market, or "submarket," on the basis of demand considerations alone is erroneous because such an approach fails to consider the supply side of the market. Philip E. Areeda & Herbert Hovenkamp, Antitrust Law, ¶518.1g at 471 & n.26 (Supp. 1990) (citing United States v. Central State Bank, 817 F.2d 22 (6th Cir. 1987)). The relevant product market cannot be determined without considering the cross-elasticity of supply.

957 F.2d at 1327.

Virtual countered that Prime has no supply side competition because of its exclusive license for PDGS. We rejected this argument as "confusing the tying product (software support for PDGS) with the interbrand market relevant for antitrust analysis," *id.*, and ruled that "the relevant tying market is comprised of all CAD/CAM software reasonably interchangeable with PDGS." *Id.* Critical to this analysis was the view that PDGS software support is an intrabrand "submarket":

> Prime has market power in the trivial sense that no one else makes PDGS. But true market power—power sufficient to change and sustain anti-competitive prices—cannot be inferred from this because were Prime to charge exorbitant prices for its software support, its customers would simply switch to some other manufacturer of PDGS-type software. Prime's lack of market power over the general market for CAD/CAM software thus prevents Prime from controlling the "submarket" for PDGS software.

957 F.2d at 1327-28. Upon refusing to view Ford-required PDGS software support as a separate tying product market, we rejected Virtual's lock-in and switching costs arguments as a matter of law:

> Virtual responds that Ford and its design suppliers cannot switch to a new supplier of software support because they are "locked-in" to Prime as the sole supplier due to their substantial investments in Prime 50 Series computers and other hardware. While Ford might believe it is "locked-in," this is due in large part to its own decision to purchase Prime's software and invest in Prime's computer systems. But a customer's initial purchase of a particular manufacturer's product does not justify a limited market definition. Defining the market by customer demand after the customer has chosen a single sup-

plier fails to take into account that the supplier (here Prime) must compete with other similar suppliers to be designated the sole source in the first place.

Id. at 1328 (citation omitted).

Under *Eastman Kodak*, our rejection of Virtual's second per se claim based on a tying product of Ford-required software support was misguided. That Ford had many competitors to choose from when it made its initial decision to grant the exclusive license to Prime cannot, after *Eastman Kodak*, preclude as a matter of law Virtual's proposed theory of market power because it ignores information costs. It follows that our rejection of Virtual's "lock-in" argument, on the basis of an interbrand competitive market in the initial purchase of Prime's software package and Prime 50 Series minicomputers, was also in error.

Eastman Kodak also requires us to rethink our characterization of the tying product market here as merely the preference of one customer. Unlike *Eastman Kodak*, the initial decision to purchase Prime equipment and software was made by a single consumer, Ford. However, by shifting the focus to the derivative aftermarket of software support, there is not a single consumer, but numerous automotive design companies doing business with Ford. In contrast with *International Logistics*, 894 F.2d at 904, which involved vertical nonprice restraints unilaterally imposed by defendant Chrysler upon its distributors, the automotive design companies in the present case are independent companies, not a part of Ford. Unlike *Dunn & Mavis*, 691 F.2d 241, where it was held that an agreement between a single seller of transportation services and a single automobile manufacturer was not an illegal "group boycott," the present case does not involve merely an arrangement between a single consumer and a single supplier. Thus, the market in this case is not defined by Ford, as a customer of Prime, but by Ford's requirements that affect the choice of Prime's other customers, Ford suppliers.

The similarities between this case and *Eastman Kodak* are apparent. As in *Eastman Kodak*, the alleged tie is not between equipment and parts, where interbrand competition would defeat market power and a per se tying claim. Rather, the alleged tie is in the derivative aftermarkets. Like Kodak, Prime is able to exercise control over the sale of software support because of its exclusive distribution license from Ford, and Ford's requirement that its automotive design suppliers use the most current version of Prime's software support. Thus, it can be argued that Prime enjoys a significant advantage in the Ford-required software support market by virtue of Ford's license and the requirement Ford places on the automotive design companies to use the most current version of PDGS. In other words, there is evidence to make the argument that Prime's tying arrangement bears that "essential characteristic" of an illegal tying arrangement, the ability to exploit control over the tying product to force the buyer to purchase an unwanted tied product. *Jefferson Parish*, 466 U.S. at 12. . . .

Virtual offered expert testimony concerning lock-in and switching costs. Virtual's industry experts testified that customers were "locked-in" to the hardware maintenance by the substantial cost incurred for hardware, maintenance, and training, most of which would be substantially worthless if the customer switched to another manufacturer's system. A Ford employee, called by Prime, testified that Ford itself felt "locked-in" to Prime, stating that Ford could not change from Prime's computer system and remain economically viable in the automotive industry. Virtual's expert also opined that Prime could substantially raise its maintenance prices before customers would abandon their investment.

Finally, Virtual made a showing that a "not insubstantial" amount of commerce was affected in that it stood to lose significant profits over a five-year period. Thus, under *Eastman Kodak*, we conclude that Virtual's second definition of tying product market was not improper.

COMMENTS AND QUESTIONS

1. Is market power required for an antitrust plaintiff to prevail on a tying claim? Historically, the answer has been no—tying two products together was illegal per se. In 1984, the Supreme Court addressed this issue in Jefferson Parish Hospital v. Hyde, 466 U.S. 2 (1984). In that case, the majority voted to maintain the per se rule in tying cases, but they did require some showing of a market effect. Four concurring justices would have required proof that the antitrust defendant had market power in the tying product, as well as there being a dangerous possibility of obtaining market power in the tied product.

2. Does *Virtual Maintenance* interpret *Kodak* correctly? Is an after-market for a single product *always* the correct market for antitrust purposes? If not, how can courts distinguish between single-firm monopolists and intrabrand competitors?

3. In the wake of *Kodak*, a number of similar cases were reopened in the computer industry. See Virtual Maintenance, Inc. v. Prime Computer, Inc., 957 F.2d 1318 (6th Cir. 1992), *vacated and remanded*, 113 S. Ct. 314 (1992), *on remand*, 995 F.2d 1324 (6th Cir. 1993) (the latter opinion was reproduced above); Datagate, Inc. v. Hewlett-Packard Co., 941 F.2d 864 (9th Cir. 1991), *cert. denied*, 503 U.S. 984 (1992). It also spurred a host of new cases. A large number of these post-*Kodak* cases turn on whether the plaintiff can characterize the tied product as having a genuinely separate product market. See, e.g., Tricom Inc. v. Electronic Data Systems, 902 F. Supp. 741 (E.D. Mich. 1995) (conditioning of a software lease agreement on the purchase of CPU time from the software dealer was actionable tying arrangement).

Many of these recent cases have limited the applicability of *Kodak* in the computer industry. For example, in Digital Equipment Corp. v. Uniq Digital Technologies, 73 F.3d 756 (7th Cir. 1996), the Seventh Circuit held that DEC was not liable for tying sales of its mid-range computers to its operating system because it lacked power in the market for mid-range computers. The court distinguished *Kodak*, calling the Supreme Court's conclusions an "assumption" rather than a holding and noting that in any event *Kodak* applied only to ties between two different aftermarkets. Two other cases have found sufficient market power but failed to find evidence that consumers were actually coerced to purchase the tied product. See Amerinet, Inc. v. Xerox Corp., 972 F.2d 1483 (8th Cir. 1992); Service & Training, Inc. v. Data General Corp., 963 F.2d 680 (4th Cir. 1992).

An example of such a limiting approach is Advanced Computer Services v. MAI Systems, 845 F. Supp. 356 (E.D. Va. 1994). MAI Systems has attempted for several years to prevent independent computer repair services from servicing its computers. In 1993, MAI convinced the Ninth Circuit that independent repairers were engaged in copyright infringement, as they necessarily made a copy of the operating system when they started the computer in an attempt to repair it. MAI v. Peak Computing, 991 F.2d 511 (9th Cir. 1993). After this decision, a number of computer repairers filed an antitrust claim against MAI, alleging that MAI was tying the sale of its operating system to the sale of repair service. The District Court granted summary judgment for MAI on the antitrust claim, reasoning that there was no separate market for MAI's operating system and that MAI lacked market power in the broader market for minicomputer operating systems.

What exactly would it mean to tie service to the initial product? What would be wrong with such an agreement? In SMS Systems Maintenance Services, Inc. v. Digital Equipment Corp., 188 F.3d 11 (1st Cir. 1999), the plaintiff claimed that DEC had entered into an unlawful tying arrangement by offering a three-year warranty with its computers. SMS reasoned that with a long-term warranty, buyers would have no incentive to use independent service organizations. The court rejected this claim because DEC did not have market power in the market for computers, and (unlike in *Kodak*) consumers could find out up front that their computer purchase came with a warranty. Further, the court argued that the warranty was generally of benefit to consumers: "a warranty has obvious virtue as a tool of competition. . . . [P]eople ordinarily associate warranties with consumer welfare and highly competitive markets."

4. Both *Kodak* and *Virtual Maintenance* are part of a raging debate on the role of tying claims in antitrust law. On the one hand, the *Kodak* court's analysis of the combined problems of imperfect information and consumer lock-in suggests serious imperfections in the market, which Kodak apparently was able to exploit. As one commentator has noted, this is the key to the *Kodak* decision. Richard Stern, Anti-trust Enforcement in the United States: Eastman Kodak Revives Tie-in Claims, 14 Eur. Intell. Prop. Rev. 369 (1992). The dissent attempts to refute these arguments but ultimately falls back on its assumption that "rational" consumers (that is, those with perfect information and who are not already locked in) will make the right choice. On the other hand, the dissent is surely correct in

stating that allowing antitrust to correct this market imperfection will dramatically expand the scope of antitrust law.

Is there a real danger that power in a computer equipment market could profitably be leveraged into aftermarkets—or, alternatively, markets for complementary goods, such as operating system programs? Economists have debated the validity of "leveraging" theory for some time. Both Judge Bork and Judge Posner have advanced the idea that leveraging is economically irrational. See Robert Bork, The Antitrust Paradox: A Policy with Itself (1978):

> The fallacy of the cases on tying arrangements may be shown through a hypothetical example based on the facts of *International Salt*. Suppose that a food canner is just willing to pay $100 for a one-year lease of a salt-dispensing machine. How is it possible for the lessor of the machine to make him pay $100 and, in addition, require him to take all his salt from the lessor? If the requirement is necessary, the lessee is giving up something he values. If the lessor has charged the full value of the machine, he cannot then charge still more in the form of coercion to take what amounts to a requirements contract for salt. That is double counting of monopoly power. The tying arrangement, whatever else it may accomplish, is obviously not a means of gaining two monopoly profits from a single monopoly.
>
> The argument is identical with respect to reciprocity. In *Consolidated Foods* the Supreme court struck down Consolidated's acquisition of Gentry, a small manufacturer of dehydrated onion and garlic, on the theory that Consolidated, a large food processor, might condition its purchases from food suppliers upon their willingness to purchase from Gentry. There is, however, no way in which that practice could be anti-competitive. Suppose that both Consolidated and Gentry buy and sell in fully competitive markets. Consolidated will then have no market power with which to force its suppliers to purchase from Gentry. The suppliers can turn to other customers. Suppose, however, that all markets involved display large elements of market power. Consolidated, before its acquisition of Gentry, may be presumed to have negotiated the best price if could from its suppliers. The acquisition of Gentry does not alter Consolidated's purchasing power, but the attempt after the acquisition to force Gentry's onions and garlic on suppliers as a condition of continued purchases by Consolidated is merely a way of demanding a still lower price from the suppliers. If the tactic works, Consolidated merely learns that it was paying too high a price to begin with: it would be better off renegotiating prices than cramming unwanted onions and garlic down its suppliers' throats. Nor is the theory improved by assuming that Consolidated understands all this and agrees to pay suppliers more in return for purchases from Gentry as a tactic of monopolizing the onion market. Rival sellers in Gentry's market can respond in a variety of ways, the most obvious being a price cut that just matches the price increase laid out by Consolidated. In that kind of price war, Consolidated has no advantages.
>
> But perhaps the most concise devastation of the law's tie-in theory was provoked by the Supreme Court's 1962 *Loew's* decision. Distributors of pre-1948 copyrighted motion-picture feature films for television exhibition engaged in the practice of block booking their films to television stations. The

stations had to take entire groups of films and could not pick and choose particular films from the proffered packages. The Court majority held, of course, that the practice violated Section I of the Sherman Act. The opinion's economic analysis of block booking was confined to a recitation of Justice Frankfurter's by then clearly indefensible dictum on the purpose of tying arrangements.

The inadequacy of the Supreme Court's theory of tying was well stated by George Stigler in a critique of the *Loew's* opinion:

> Consider the following simple example. One film, Justice Goldberg cited "Gone with the Wind," is worth $10,000 to the buyer, while a second film, the Justice cited "Getting Gertie's Garter," is worthless to him. The seller could sell the one for $10,000 and throw away the second, for no matter what its cost, bygones are forever bygones. Instead the seller compels the buyer to take both. But surely he can obtain no more than $10,000, since by hypothesis this is the value of both films to the buyer. Why not, in short, use his monopoly power directly on the desirable film? It seems no more sensible, on this logic, to blockbook the two films than it would be to compel the exhibitor to buy "Gone with the Wind" and seven Ouija boards, again for $10,000.

To these queries the law has no answers. Indeed, it has so far successfully managed to ignore the existence of the queries.

Id. at 372-374; *accord* Richard Posner, Antitrust Law (1976); cf. Melissa Hamilton, Software Tying Arrangements Under the Antitrust Laws: A More Flexible Approach, 71 Denv. U. L. Rev. 607 (1994) (making the rather different argument that tying is efficient in the software context because it allows programmers to continue to upgrade their products). The logic of Judge Bork's argument is appealing. But is it correct? Louis Kaplow has offered a powerful critique of the Bork-Posner theory. Louis Kaplow, Extension of Monopoly Power Through Leverage, 85 Colum. L. Rev. 515 (1985). There, he argues that

> There are a number of deficiencies in the analysis of recent commentators who have attempted to proclaim the death of leverage theory. The basic mistake in their central thesis is that antitrust law should be indifferent to the exploitation of monopoly power because extant power is a fixed sum and thus will result in the same damage regardless of how it is deployed. Although of some superficial appeal, it can readily be demonstrated that their analysis is strongly counterintuitive. Consider the case of a terrorist on the loose with one stick of dynamite. The fixed sum thesis posits that since the power is fixed—that is, the terrorist has one and only one dynamite stick—we should be indifferent to where the dynamite is placed. It is all too obvious, however, that the potential damage resulting from power in this context, as well as in virtually any other we can imagine, is overwhelmingly dependent upon how it may be used. . . .
>
> The position of these commentators [Bork, Posner, others] can be given more meaning only by developing it more extensively. The most rea-

sonable interpretation, I believe, is that their two categories represent an implicit attempt to distinguish between short-run and long-run phenomena— or, to use more technical language, between static and dynamic models. Profit-maximizing practices are meant to refer roughly to those actions that can have fairly direct and immediate effects, while monopoly extension refers to behavior designed to have implications on the magnitude of profits and welfare loss in the future. The prototypical example of a profit maximization device is a pricing decision by a firm with market power, a decision which can be implemented rather quickly. By contrast, practices designed to affect the market share and elasticity of market demand might be labelled monopoly extension devices. These practices do not increase short-run profits, and might even decrease them. The firm's motivation is to change the structural conditions it faces in the future in order that it may receive greater profits in the future.

Id. at 516, 523-524. Professor Kaplow goes on to point out a number of reasons why leveraging may be possible in the real world. His reasons include the dynamic nature of markets in which firms may give up short-run profits in order to maximize long-run gains and inherent imperfections in markets that may allow monopolists to gain limited power in new markets through leveraging. See also George Stigler, United States v. Loew's, Inc.: A Note on Block Booking, 1963 Sup. Ct. Rev. 152 (explaining price discrimination potential inherent in tying).

PROBLEMS

Problem 7-2. Intelligent Co. is the world's largest manufacturer of computer microprocessors, the semiconductor chips that power computers. Intelligent sells 78 percent of the 25 million personal computer microprocessors sold every year and 42 percent of the 4 million workstation and mid-range computer microprocessors. Intelligent carefully protects the design of its microprocessors, going to extreme measures to prevent employees from removing any data about its designs or manufacturing processes from the company's high-security facilities. Intelligent also has a number of patents related to its semiconductor manufacturing. Many of these patents govern the process by which its chips are made, but one Intelligent patent (as well as a number of mask work registrations) govern the layout of the current chip itself (called the 586 chip). Intelligent is in the process of designing a new and faster chip called the 686 but has not yet received any patent or SCPA protection for that chip.

Charybdis is a competing maker of computer microprocessors that sells a much smaller share (8 percent) of personal computer microprocessors each year. Charybdis does not sell microprocessors for other types of computers. Charybdis has filed an antitrust suit against Intelligent. In discovery, the following facts have come out:

- Intelligent comes out with new generations of microprocessors approximately every two years. For several months after it releases a new generation of chips, its competitors are unable to produce an equivalent chip. During this period, Intelligent faces competition only from the older generation of chips.
- The length of time it takes Charybdis to produce an equivalent chip is a function of Intelligent's intellectual property rights in its chips. If Charybdis were permitted to copy the design directly without risk of patent infringement, it could produce an equivalent chip in a much shorter period of time.
- Virtually all software vendors design their operating systems and applications programs to work with the Intelligent chip architecture. Thus, if another company wants to sell chips that will run these programs, it must design its chips to be compatible with Intelligent's. Only one company (Starfruit) uses a different architecture for PC microprocessors. It has only a 4 percent share of the PC microprocessors sold, and it writes its own software.
- The prices of Intelligent's chips drop by approximately 30 percent the day that Charybdis or another competitor first comes out with a similar chip.
- When Intelligent releases a new generation of chip, the chips are in great demand. Because Intelligent cannot produce them fast enough during the initial month of release, it has developed a system to "ration" demand for its new chips. Under its "preferred customer" policy, Intelligent will sell its new chips first to its good customers—defined as those who bought its last generation of chips and did not buy a competitor's chips.
- Intelligent has on occasion licensed its proprietary microprocessor design know-how to other competitors, though never to Charybdis. These licensing agreements require the competitors to give Intelligent the exclusive rights to any changes or improvements they make to the licensed technology, and require the competitors to sell only to a specified set of customers at a specified price.

Based on this evidence, Charybdis seeks a court order requiring Intelligent to make its microprocessor design technology available on "reasonable, nondiscriminatory terms" without the restrictions in Intelligent's current licenses. It also seeks an order ending Intelligent's "Preferred Customer" program. How should the court rule?

Problem 7-3. Nintendo of America sells the Nintendo Entertainment System (NES), one of the most popular videogame "boxes" on the market. Nintendo's box was particularly successful in the late 1980s, when its market share was over 80 percent. (The development by competitors of new, more technologically sophisticated games has reduced Nintendo's share of the market to around 45 percent today.)

Nintendo's box allows its owner to play a variety of video games by purchasing game cartridges that are plugged into the box. Nintendo does not directly require that its consumers buy games made or licensed by Nintendo. However, Nintendo has included in its box a lockout device that prevents non-Nintendo games from working on the NES box. As a result, owners of Nintendo boxes know that they must buy only Nintendo or Nintendo-licensed games.

Atari Games Corp., which makes games for a box that competes with Nintendo's, sued Nintendo, alleging that Nintendo was tying the sale of NES boxes to the sale of its game cartridges. How should this suit be resolved?

Note on Tying and Product Integration

In a much-reported decision, United States v. Microsoft Corp., 147 F.3d 935 (D.C. Cir. 1998), the D.C. Circuit considered the legality of Microsoft's bundling its Internet Explorer browser into its Windows 95 operating system.[7] The fundamental facts of the case were that Microsoft had originally sold Windows 95 and Internet Explorer separately but proceeded through various upgrades to link the two more closely together and to sell Windows 95 only in conjunction with Internet Explorer (though not vice versa). The Justice Department charged that this violated a 1994 consent decree. For purposes of interpreting that consent decree, the key question was whether the two bundled programs constituted a permissible "integrated product." The district court issued an injunction precluding Microsoft from offering Windows 95 only on the condition that the user also take Internet Explorer.

The D.C. Circuit reversed. The majority held that Microsoft's actions did not violate the consent decree. Two of the judges went beyond that

---

7. The inclusion of the browser in the later Windows 98 operating system is being litigated in a separately filed case, still pending at this writing. The district court issued a partial opinion in that case in November 1999. United States v. Microsoft Corp., —F. Supp. 2d— (D.D.C. Nov. 5, 1999).

question, however, and, in far-reaching dicta, addressed the propriety of a tying theory:

> The point of the test is twofold and may be illustrated by its application to the paradigm case of the Novell complaint and the subsequent release of Windows 95. First, "integration" suggests a degree of unity, something beyond merely placing disks in the same box. If an OEM or end user (referred to generally as "the purchaser") could buy separate products and combine them himself to produce the "integrated product," then the integration looks like a sham. If Microsoft had simply placed the disks for Windows 3.11 and MS-DOS in one package and covered it with a single license agreement, it would have offered purchasers nothing they could not get by buying the separate products and combining them on their own.[11]
>
> Windows 95, by contrast, unites the two functionalities in a way that purchasers could not; it is not simply a graphical user interface running on top of MS-DOS. Windows 95 is integrated in the sense that the two functionalities—DOS and graphical interface—do not exist separately: the code that is required to produce one also produces the other. Of course one can imagine that code being sold on two different disks, one containing all the code necessary for an operating system, the other with all the code necessary for a graphical interface. But as the code in the two would largely overlap, it would be odd to speak of either containing a discrete functionality. Rather, each would represent a disabled version of Windows 95. The customer could then "repair" each by installing them both on a single computer, but in such a case it would not be meaningful to speak of the customer "combining" two products. Windows 95 is an example of what Professor Areeda calls "physical or technological interlinkage that the customer cannot perform." X Areeda, Antitrust Law §1746b at 227, 228 (1996).
>
> So the combination offered by the manufacturer must be different from what the purchaser could create from the separate products on his own. The second point is that it must also be better in some respect; there should be some technological value to integration. Manufacturers can stick products together in ways that purchasers cannot without the link serving any purpose but an anticompetitive one. The concept of integration should exclude a case where the manufacturer has done nothing more than to metaphorically "bolt" two products together, as would be true if Windows 95 were artificially rigged to crash if IEXPLORE.EXE were deleted. Cf. ILC Peripherals Leasing Corp. v. International Business Machines Corp., 448 F.Supp. 228, 233 (N.D.Cal.1978) ("If IBM had simply bolted a disk pack or data module

---

11. The same analysis would apply to peripherals. If, for example, Microsoft tried to bundle its mouse with the operating system, it would have to show that the mouse/operating system package worked better if combined by Microsoft than it would if combined by OEMs. This is quite different from showing that the mouse works better with the operating system than other mice do. See X Areeda, Elhauge & Hovenkamp, Antitrust Law ¶1746b. Problems seem unlikely to arise with peripherals, because their physical existence makes it easier to identify the act of combination. It seems unlikely that a plausible claim could be made that a mouse and an operating system were integrated in the sense that neither could be said to exist separately. An operating system used with a different mouse does not seem like a different product. But Windows 95 without IE's code will not boot, and adding a rival browser will not fix this. If the add/remove utility is run to hide the IE 4 technologies, Windows 95 reverts to an earlier version, OEM service release ("OSR") 2.0.

into a drive and sold the two items as a unit for a single price, the 'aggregation' would clearly have been an illegal tying arrangement.") *aff'd per curiam sub nom.* Memorex Corp. v. International Business Machines Corp., 636 F.2d 1188 (9th Cir.1980); X Areeda, Elhauge & Hovenkamp, Antitrust Law ¶1746 at 227 (discussing literal bolting). Thus if there is no suggestion that the product is superior to the purchaser's combination in some respect, it cannot be deemed integrated.[12]

It might seem difficult to put the two elements discussed above together. If purchasers cannot combine the two functionalities to make Windows 95, it might seem that there is nothing to test Windows 95 against in search of the required superiority. But purchasers can combine the functionalities in their stand-alone incarnations. They can install MS-DOS and Windows 3.11. The test for the integration of Windows 95 then comes down to the question of whether its integrated design offers benefits when compared to a purchaser's combination of corresponding stand-alone functionalities. The decree's evident embrace of Windows 95 as a permissible single product can be taken as manifesting the parties' agreement that it met this test.

The short answer is thus that integration may be considered genuine if it is beneficial when compared to a purchaser combination. But we do not propose that in making this inquiry the court should embark on product design assessment. In antitrust law, from which this whole proceeding springs, the courts have recognized the limits of their institutional competence and have on that ground rejected theories of "technological tying." A court's evaluation of a claim of integration must be narrow and deferential. As the Fifth Circuit put it, "[S]uch a violation must be limited to those instances where the technological factor tying the hardware to the software has been designed for the purpose of tying the products, rather than to achieve some technologically beneficial result. Any other conclusion would enmesh the courts in a technical inquiry into the justifiability of product innovations." Response of Carolina, Inc. v. Leasco Response, Inc., 537 F.2d 1307, 1330 (5th Cir.1976). . . .

We emphasize that this analysis does not require a court to find that an integrated product is superior to its stand-alone rivals. See ILC Peripherals Leasing Corp. v. International Business Machines Corp., 458 F.Supp. 423, 439 (N.D.Cal.1978) ("Where there is a difference of opinion as to the advantages of two alternatives which can both be defended from an engineering standpoint, the court will not allow itself to be enmeshed 'in a technical inquiry into the justifiability of product innovations.'") (quoting *Leasco,* 537 F.2d at 1330), *aff'd per curiam sub nom.* Memorex Corp. v. IBM Corp., 636 F.2d 1188 (9th Cir.1980). We do not read §IV(E)(i) to "put[] judges and juries in the unwelcome position of designing computers." IX Areeda, Antitrust Law ¶1700j at 15 (1991). The question is not whether the integration is a net plus but merely whether there is a plausible claim that it brings some advantage. Whether or not this is the appropriate test for antitrust law generally, we believe it is the only sensible reading of §IV(E)(i).

---

12. Thus of course we agree with the separate opinion that "commingling of code . . . alone is not sufficient evidence of true integration." Commingling for an anticompetitive purpose (or for no purpose at all) is what we refer to as "bolting."

Judge Wald dissented from this opinion. She suggested a somewhat less deferential interpretation of the consent decree—and of tying law generally:

> I think the prohibition [in the consent decree on tying] and the proviso [allowing integrated products] could reasonably be construed to state that Microsoft may offer an "integrated" product to OEMs under one license only if the integrated product achieves synergies great enough to justify Microsoft's extension of its monopoly to an otherwise distinct market.

Id. at 957-958. Judge Wald would balance the productive efficiencies against the harm to competition in determining whether an antitrust violation had occurred.

COMMENTS AND QUESTIONS

1. Is the deference shown by the majority in *Microsoft* appropriate? Under Judge Williams's opinion, how likely is it that any "integrated" product will ever be held to be a tie? Does the *Microsoft* opinion have implications beyond the integration of software products—to cover the synergistic combination of any kind of products?

On the other hand, surely there is some value to embedding Internet Explorer in Windows 95 to make it easier for novice computer users to access the Internet without having to obtain separate software to do so. Is this valuable enough to outweigh the elimination of competition in the browser market that will almost certainly result from Microsoft's bundling?

2. The pros and cons of browser bundling are discussed in Mark A. Lemley & David McGowan, Could Java Change Everything? The Competitive Propriety of a Proprietary Standard, 43 Antitrust Bull. 715 (1998); Dan Gifford, Java and Microsoft: How Will the Antitrust Story Unfold?, 44 Vill. L. Rev. 501 (1999).

For an argument that Microsoft's conduct should not be evaluated under tying law at all, but rather as an instance of monopolization, see Thomas A. Piraino Jr., An Antitrust Remedy for Monopoly Leveraging by Electronic Networks, 93 Nw. U. L. Rev. 1 (1998) (arguing that Microsoft is improperly using an essential facility to leverage its monopoly power). Piraino points out that Microsoft cannot evade his approach simply by integrating the two products.

3. Yet another Microsoft case offers some interesting thoughts on the role of intellectual property law in justifying licensing restrictions. In United States v. Microsoft Corp., 1998-2 Trade Cas. ¶72,621 (D.D.C. 1998), the case brought against Windows 98, Microsoft defended its allegedly anticompetitive licensing restrictions in part on the ground that its license terms "merely highlight and expressly state the rights that Microsoft already enjoys under federal copyright law" and therefore could not violate the antitrust laws. The court rejected this argument, noting that the

copyright laws did not give Microsoft "unlimited" power over its software. The court wrote:

> [C]opyright law does not give Microsoft blanket authority to license (or refuse to license) its intellectual property as it sees fit. A copyright does not give its holder immunity from laws of general applicability, including the antitrust laws. Copyright holders are restricted in their ability to extend their control to other markets. They may not prevent the development and use of interoperable programs by competitors. Antitrust liability may also attach to other anticompetitive licensing restrictions involving copyrighted works.

Id. (citations omitted). That case was still pending at this writing. The district court issued a partial opinion in that case in November 1999. United States v. Microsoft Corp., — F. Supp. 2d — (D.D.C. Nov. 5, 1999).

b. Licensing Restrictions

One of the most difficult antitrust issues surrounding intellectual property rights concerns the limitations placed on the licensing of intellectual property. Intellectual property owners may wish to license their rights to others for a number of reasons: they may be ill-equipped to make the protected product; they may want a revenue stream without having to invest in producing and selling the product; they may wish to reserve one geographic or product market to themselves while allowing others to exploit the intellectual property right elsewhere; or they may simply feel that broad dissemination of their product will redound to their benefit— for example, because there is value in having their product become an industry standard. Economic theory encourages licensing because it allows the market to transfer the intellectual property right to the most productive user of that right.

There is no antitrust problem with licensing per se. Indeed, the Antitrust Division's Intellectual Property Guidelines take the position that licensing is essentially procompetitive:

> Intellectual property typically is one component among many in a production process and derives value from its combination with complementary factors. Complementary factors of production include manufacturing and distribution facilities, workforces, and other items of intellectual property. The owner of intellectual property has to arrange for its combination with other necessary factors to realize its commercial value. Often, the owner finds it most efficient to contract with others for these factors, to sell rights to the intellectual property, or to enter into a joint venture arrangement for its development, rather than supplying these complementary factors itself.
>
> Licensing, cross-licensing, or otherwise transferring intellectual property (hereinafter "licensing") can facilitate integration of the licensed property with complementary factors of production. This integration can lead to more

efficient exploitation of the intellectual property, benefiting consumers through the reduction of costs and the introduction of new products. Such arrangements increase the value of intellectual property to consumers and to the developers of the technology. By potentially increasing the expected returns from intellectual property, licensing also can increase the incentive for its creation and thus promote greater investment in research and development. . . .

Field-of-use, territorial and other limitations on intellectual property licenses may serve procompetitive ends by allowing the licensor to exploit its property as efficiently and effectively as possible. These various forms of exclusivity can be used to give a licensee an incentive to invest in the commercialization and distribution of products embodying the licensed intellectual property and to develop additional applications for the licensed property. The restrictions may do so, for example, by protecting the licensee against free-riding on the licensee's investments by other licensees or by the licensor. They may also promote the licensor's incentive to license, for example, by protecting the licensor from competition in the licensor's own technology in a market niche that it prefers to keep to itself. These benefits of licensing restrictions apply to patent, copyright, and trade secret licenses, and to know-how agreements.

Intellectual Property Guidelines §2.3. For many of these reasons, the Division's prior set of Guidelines governing intellectual property licensing (promulgated by the Reagan Administration in 1988 and contained in the International Guidelines) took a very "hands off" approach to intellectual property licensing transactions. That has changed with the current Guidelines, however. While the new Guidelines recognize the procompetitive benefits of licensing, they also identify some licensing arrangements that are cause for antitrust concerns:

> [A]ntitrust concerns may arise when [a] licensing arrangement harms competition among entities that would have been actual or likely potential competitors in a relevant market in the absence of a license (entities in a "horizontal relationship"). A restraint in a licensing arrangement may harm such competition, for example, if it facilitates market division or price fixing. In addition, license restrictions with respect to one market may harm such competition in another market by anticompetitively foreclosing access to, or significantly raising the price of, an important input, or by facilitating coordination to increase price or reduce output.

Id., §3.1.

COMMENTS AND QUESTIONS

1. Consider the Division's new policy statement—that they are concerned about agreements that reduce competition that would have existed but for the license. On the one hand, this policy can be (and has been) criticized as being too aggressive. By declaring that intellectual property is

like any other form of property, the Guidelines narrowly circumscribe the terms of licensing agreements. The effect may be to prevent some efficient licensing agreements from being signed, even though the procompetitive effects of the agreement would outweigh its negative effects on preexisting competition.

On the other hand, perhaps the policy can be criticized from the other side for not being aggressive enough. Why should the antitrust laws be concerned only with protecting competition that would have existed absent the license? If licensing is favored because it is procompetitive, doesn't antitrust law have some obligation to see that those procompetitive benefits that result from the license itself are not lost because of restrictive license provisions?

One way of resolving this debate is to distinguish between the effects inherent to the license, and the effects that result from restrictive provisions ancillary to the license. For example, an agreement to license a patent may promote competition in the market for the patented product, but the agreement may also contain a term dividing geographic territories or setting resale prices. To the extent that these restrictive terms can be severed from the balance of the license, antitrust law may be able to challenge them without threatening the license itself.

2. The Guidelines also establish that most licensing agreements will be treated under the rule of reason, rather than under the per se rule. Does this help to alleviate any concern that the Guidelines are too restrictive in their treatment of intellectual property licensing?

Note on Intellectual Property and Exclusive Dealing

Section 3 of the Clayton Act prohibits some "exclusive dealing arrangements" under the rule of reason. "Exclusive dealing" refers to agreements that prevent the agreeing party from buying or selling the goods of a competitor. For example, a company with a significant share of the market may attempt to drive its competitors out of business by requiring that all its customers buy exclusively from the company. If the customers consider the exclusive dealer to be their most important source of supply, they will likely agree to purchase all their goods from that dealer. The result may be that the dealer expands its market power into an actual monopoly.

On the other hand, exclusive dealing arrangements may have procompetitive justifications. Agreements to buy everything you need from (or sell everything you produce to) one source may significantly reduce transaction costs and may allow smaller companies to take advantage of discounts resulting from economies-of-scale purchasing. The problem for antitrust law is to distinguish exclusive dealing arrangements that restrict competition from those that merely serve to make business transactions easier. To draw this line, antitrust requires some showing of market power to make out a Clayton Act section 3 violation.

Intellectual property licenses often contain exclusivity provisions. Such provisions can bind either the licensor or the licensee (or conceivably both). The licensor might agree to grant an exclusive license for his patent that gives only the licensee the right to work the patent. The licensor cannot license anyone else to work the patent and in some circumstances gives up the right to work it himself. On the other end, a patent license may bind the licensee not to use or sell products other than the patentee's product. In either case, the contract expressly requires that one party deal exclusively with the other. The Antitrust Division's Intellectual Property Guidelines take the position that exclusive licenses do not raise antitrust concerns unless the parties to the agreement (or other potential licensees) would have been actual or potential competitors absent the exclusivity provision. See Intellectual Property Guidelines §4.3.2.

Exclusive dealing practices need not be express. Certain types of licensing provisions have the practical effect of coercing the licensee into using only the licensor's product. One example is a type of nonmetered royalty. In a recent complaint, the Antitrust Division charged that Microsoft had dominated the market for installed computer operating systems by requiring that computer manufacturers pay royalties to Microsoft on each computer they shipped, regardless of whether the computer had a Microsoft operating system installed. Because the manufacturers had to pay for Microsoft's operating system anyway, they were extremely unlikely to install a competitor's operating system, because if they did they would have had to pay twice for an operating system. United States v. Microsoft Corp., No. 94-1564 (D.D.C., filed July 15, 1994). When Microsoft settled the Division's complaint, it agreed to stop the use of nonmetered royalties.

COMMENTS AND QUESTIONS

1. Several companies have alleged that after they asserted their intellectual property rights against Intel—either by filing suit or by entering into license negotiations—Intel threatened to cut them off from the supply of its crucial technology unless they dropped their suits. In effect, the allegation is that Intel is using its power in the market for microprocessors to obtain royalty-free licenses to everyone else's intellectual property. Is this a reciprocal tying arrangement of a sort between Intel's technology and the intellectual property asserted against it? Is it an exclusive dealing arrangement? If so, does it violate the antitrust laws? See Intergraph Corp. v. Intel Corp., 3 F. Supp. 2d 1255 (N.D. Ala. 1998); In re Intel Corp., FTC No. 9288 (complaint filed June 8, 1998).

Intel and the FTC entered into a consent decree in 1999. Under that decree, Intel agreed not to terminate its supply of chips or information to a buyer merely because that buyer sued it for intellectual property infringement. Intel retained the right to terminate supply for a number of legitimate business reasons, however. Further, the consent decree provided that Intel could cut off any purchaser who sued it for infringement if that purchaser sought to enjoin the sale of Intel's core products. In essence, therefore, Intel has retained the power to demand a compulsory license of intellectual property rights from the companies with which it does business.

Is the consent decree an appropriate compromise between the positions of the parties? Is it likely to have procompetitive effects?

PROBLEM

Problem 7-4. Assume that Microsoft owns a registered trademark for Windows to identify its graphical user interface on a computer operating system. Microsoft agrees to license the Windows trademark to certain companies that wish to indicate that their applications programs are "Windows-compatible." However, assume that Microsoft requires as a condition of the license that the companies sell only applications programs that run exclusively on Microsoft Windows operating systems. Has Microsoft violated the antitrust laws? What role should market power play in the analysis? Does the Windows trademark itself confer market power?

Note on Other Common Licensing Restrictions

Besides exclusivity, a number of other common features of intellectual property licenses raise potential antitrust issues. We consider several here.

Grantback Clauses. Intellectual property owners sometimes require as a condition of the license that the licensee "grant back" to the licensor the rights to use any improvements the licensee makes in the technology. Some grantback clauses simply require that the licensee agree not to sue the licensor for infringing on any improvement patents that result from the licensee's work. Others are more strict, however; they require the assignment or exclusive license of the rights to any improvement.

One reason licensors use grantback clauses is obvious: they don't want to lose the right to practice their invention or be held "hostage" by their licensees. By retaining the right to use any improvements the licensee makes, the original intellectual property owner can ensure that she stays current in her technology. Grantback clauses may also help to avoid the "blocking patents" problem by ensuring that the senior intellectual property owner always has the dominant right.

The precise nature of the grantback clause may differ from case to case. Some patentees require that their licensee *assign* any improvement patents back to the licensee. In this instance, the grantback clause avoids the blocking-patents problem entirely, because the original patentee ends up owning both the original and the improvement patents. By contrast, if the original patentee requires only that the improver license back the right to use the improvement, the grantback clause looks more like an ex ante cross-licensing solution to a prospective blocking-patents problem.

On the other hand, grantback clauses may be used to stifle competition. Grantbacks allow a dominant industry player to license her intellectual property freely, without worrying that her licensees may develop an improved process for manufacturing her product and therefore compete with her. Indeed, such licenses may be an effective way of *preventing* serious competition, because they allow the dominant player to "capture" potential competitors and take advantage of their ideas. Further, because licensees no longer have the exclusive (or perhaps any) right to their improvements, they may be less willing to invest in research and development of such improvements.

Most grantback clauses have survived antitrust scrutiny. (A notable exception is United Shoe Machinery Co. v. United States, 258 U.S. 451 (1922).) The Antitrust Division's current Intellectual Property Guidelines, however, provide that "[i]n deciding whether to challenge a grantback, the Department will consider the extend to which, as compared with no license at all, the license with the grantback provision may diminish total research and development investment or lessen competition in innovation or technology markets." Intellectual Property Guidelines, §5.6. See John Barton, Patents and Antitrust: A Rethinking in Light of Patent Breadth and Sequential Innovation, 65 Antitrust L.J. 449, 461-462 (1997) (endorsing the Division's case-by-case approach).

Is this the right comparison to make? Does it suggest that the Division will treat patent grantbacks differently from copyright grantbacks (because of the difference between the blocking-patents rule and the rule in copyright)?[8]

Field-of-Use Restrictions. Alluded to earlier, field-of-use restrictions in intellectual property licenses grant licensees the right to work a patent in only a limited area. The area may be limited either geographically or by product market. Such restrictions may enable a patentee to exploit his technology efficiently in several markets while maintaining the exclusivity granted him by the patent laws. But field-of-use restrictions may also be an efficient means of enforcing a territorial market division agreement between horizontal competitors. Horizontal market division can have the effect of creating mini-monopolies in what would otherwise be a competitive mar-

---

8. On this difference, see Mark A. Lemley, The Economics of Improvement in Intellectual Property Law, 75 Tex. L. Rev. 989 (1997).

ket. If the patent licensed is a sham or is only a minor part of the business of the licensor and licensee, it is possible that the patent license is really a "front" for a market division scheme. Territorial market division is normally illegal per se under the rule of United States v. Topco Associates, 405 U.S. 596 (1972). However, the scope of that rule is limited in the patent area by 35 U.S.C. §261, which explicitly permits geographic field-of-use restrictions in patent licenses.

Are there legitimate reasons for some field-of-use restrictions that inhere in the nature of the intellectual property laws? Consider, for example, an geographic market division scheme that granted each licensee an exclusive territory in a different country. Because of the national nature of patents, this means that each licensee received the exclusive right to work the patent (although not the exclusive worldwide right to sell the technology). Is there anything wrong with such a scheme? See United States v. Westinghouse, 471 F. Supp. 532, *aff'd*, 648 F.2d 642 (9th Cir. 1991) (approving such an arrangement).

Extension of Patent or Copyright Term. This is primarily an issue in patent law, because patents have shorter terms than copyrights. A license may seek to extend the exclusive rights of the patent laws beyond the 20-year patent term, either by compelling the continued payment of royalties or by imposing collateral obligations (such as exclusive dealing arrangements or grantback clauses) that do not terminate when the patent expires.

Whether extensions of the patent term by contract should be of concern to anyone but the contracting parties themselves has been a matter of some debate. Compare Robert Merges, Reflections on Current Legislation Affecting Patent Misuse, 70 J. Pat. & Trademark Off. Soc'y 793, 801-802 (1988) (patent term extensions are anticompetitive) with Mark Lemley, Comment, The Economic Irrationality of the Patent Misuse Doctrine, 78 Cal. L. Rev. 1599, 1630 (1990) (agreements to extend patent term are not anticompetitive). In some sense, the issue here is the same as we have been considering repeatedly throughout this book—the right of private parties to change the scope of the intellectual property laws by contract.

In another sense, however, these issues have a different spin on them in the antitrust context. To the extent that patent term extensions reduce competition by removing the incentive for licensees to compete directly with the patentee after the patent expires, it is consumers and society who suffer the consequences. Cf. Lasercomb America v. Reynolds, 911 F.2d 970 (4th Cir. 1990) (invalidating 99-year software license under copyright misuse doctrine).

2. Horizontal Restraints

Cartels—loosely defined as agreements among competitors to restrict output and raise prices—are illegal under section 1 of the Sherman Act, 15

U.S.C. §1. When competitors have agreed to set prices or output levels or divide markets, the Sherman Act may be violated without regard to proof of market power or effect. This is the "per se" rule. However, the courts have been backing away from the per se rule in a number of situations involving horizontal agreements between competitors, particularly where the agreement arguably serves some procompetitive purpose, such as in the cases discussed below.

One example of such an arguably procompetitive arrangement is the "patent pool" under which competitors cross-license their patents. An argument can be made that patent pooling is more desirable than controls on the licensing of a single patent. The argument focuses on the problem of blocking patents. Where one company patents an original invention and a second company (presumably but not necessarily a licensee) patents an improvement on that invention, the law leaves the two companies in a rather peculiar situation. In order to make the most efficient use of the invention, each company wants to use both the original invention and its improvement. Alone, however, neither company can do so without infringing the other's patent. One obvious solution to the blocking-patents problem is for the companies to cross-license their patents, which allows both companies to use the invention efficiently and thereby benefit society and preserve some measure of competition.

The problem of blocking patents is common in the patent-antitrust literature. In addition to the examples cited by the courts, see E. Fox & L. Sullivan, Antitrust 353-54 (1989); Robert P. Merges, Intellectual Property Rights and Bargaining Breakdown: The Case of Blocking Patents, 62 Tenn. L. Rev. 75 (1994). Blocking patents can take one of two forms. First, two or more companies may have valid patents on different steps of a process in which each step is necessary to make the end product. This can be thought of as "pure" technical necessity. Without cross-licensing, neither company would be able to produce the product at all. The case against applying antitrust law is fairly clear: preventing patent-pooling will reduce rather than increase market participation. In this circumstance, at least some courts have been willing to permit pools of blocking patents. For example, in Carpet Seaming Tape Licensing Corp. v. Best Seam, Inc., 616 F.2d 1133 (9th Cir. 1980), cert. denied, 464 U.S. 818 (1983), the court held:

> A well-recognized legitimate purpose for a pooling agreement is exchange of blocking patents. The trial court . . . demonstrates a misunderstanding as to the nature of the relationship which can give rise to a blocking situation. The trial judge found that the Winkler and Clymin patents did not block the Burgess patents, but ignored the possibility that the Burgess patents may well have blocked the Winkler and Clymin patents despite well-established law that patents on basic processes and products may block patents on improvements to those products and processes. As the Supreme Court stated in Standard Oil Co. v. United States, 283 U.S. at 172, n.5:

> This is often the case where patents covering improvements of a basic process, owned by one manufacturer, are granted to another. A patent may be rendered quite useless, or 'blocked,' by another unexpired patent which covers a vitally related feature of the manufacturing process. Unless some agreementa can be reached, the parties are hampered and exposed to litigation. And, frequently, the cost of litigation to a patentee is greater than the value of a patent for a minor improvement. . . .

The economics underlying this attitude toward the accumulation of improvement patents is ably and succinctly stated by Professor Ward S. Bowman:

> "If . . . one patent was subservient to the other, and improvement patent unusable without infringing the basic patent, then combining or pooling them eliminates no user alternative. In terms of possible trade restraint, this case is indistinguishable from a vertical merger. The two patents combined . . . could not restrict output or raise price any more than if the two were exploited separately."
> W. Bowman, Patent and Antitrust Law at 201 (1973).

Id. at 1142. See also Clorox Co. v. Sterling Winthrop, 932 F. Supp. 469 (E.D.N.Y. 1996) (agreement settling trademark dispute over the terms "Lysol" and "Pine-Sol" by limiting the product markets in which each could sell was not anticompetitive because owner of Pine-Sol can compete with Lysol using other marks).

A more common problem involves a number of patents whose validity is open to question. This may be thought of as practical technical necessity. Rather than entering into prohibitively expensive and protracted litigation over the validity of their respective patents, can firms in this situation settle their differences by pooling their patents (at least one of which is presumably valid)? Standard Oil Co. v. United States, 283 U.S. 163 (1931), seems to suggest that such an agreement would be treated under the rule of reason. Of course, that does not mean that the agreement will always be upheld. If the companies with blocking patents together comprise only a small part of the industry, their agreement would presumably survive rule-of-reason scrutiny. But if the new technology encompassed by the patents dominates a market, even the *Standard Oil* rule presents an antitrust problem. Is this a desirable outcome?

On the one hand, allowing the agreement would get the product to market more quickly and inexpensively. Further, because each firm in our hypothetical holds an arguably valid patent, one firm (the firm whose patent is upheld) is likely to end up with a monopoly in the product anyway. On the other hand, allowing competitors to resolve their differences by cross-licensing their patents could foreclose any incentive for those firms to compete in the future. Instead of a monopoly patent holder being faced with several competitors trying to unseat it, the patent cartel would face no foreseeable competition. See John Barton, Patents and Antitrust: A Rethinking in Light of Patent Breadth and Sequential Innovation, 65 Antitrust L.J. 449, 462-465 (1997). Whether you believe the rule of reason or outright legality should govern this situation depends on your assessment of the relative costs of each approach.

Does it matter for antitrust analysis whether the parties to the pool are in the same market? Is the existence of the pool presumptive evidence that they are? Market definition problems have plagued patent-pooling cases. See Roger B. Andewelt, Analysis of Patent Pools Under the Antitrust Laws, 53 Antitrust L.J. 611 (1984).

Can a similar argument be made for copyright "pools"? Consider the following case.

a. Industry Standardization

Broadcast Music, Inc. v. Columbia Broadcasting System, Inc.
Supreme Court of the United States
441 U.S. 1 (1978)

MR. JUSTICE WHITE delivered the opinion of the Court.

This case involves an action under the antitrust and copyright laws brought by respondent Columbia Broadcasting System, Inc. (CBS), against petitioners, American Society of Composers, Authors and Publishers (ASCAP) and Broadcast Music, Inc. (BMI), and their members and affiliates. The basic question presented is whether the issuance by ASCAP and BMI to CBS of blanket licenses to copyrighted musical compositions at fees negotiated by them is price fixing *per se* unlawful under the antitrust laws. . . .

BMI, a nonprofit corporation owned by members of the broadcasting industry, was organized in 1939, is affiliated with or represents some 10,000 publishing companies and 20,000 authors and composers, and operates in much the same manner as ASCAP. Almost every domestic copyrighted composition is in the repertory either of ASCAP, with a total of three million compositions, or of BMI, with one million.

Both organizations operate primarily through blanket licenses, which give the licensees the right to perform any and all of the compositions owned by the members or affiliates as often as the licensees desire for a stated term. Fees for blanket licenses are ordinarily a percentage of total revenues or a flat dollar amount, and do not directly depend on the amount or type of music used. Radio and television broadcasters are the largest users of music, and almost all of them hold blanket licenses from both ASCAP and BMI. Until this litigation, CBS held blanket licenses from both organizations for its television network on a continuous basis since the late 1940's and had never attempted to secure any other form of license from either ASCAP or any of its members. *Id.*, at 752-754.

The complaint filed by CBS charged various violations of the Sherman Act and the copyright laws. CBS argued that ASCAP and BMI are unlawful monopolies and that the blanket license is illegal price fixing, an unlawful tying arrangement, a concerted refusal to deal, and a misuse of copyrights. The District Court, though denying summary judgment to certain defendants, ruled that the practice did not fall within the *per se* rule. 337 F.Supp. 394, 398 (SDNY 1972). After an 8-week trial, limited to the issue of liability, the court dismissed the complaint, rejecting again the claim that the blanket license was price fixing and a *per se* violation of §1 of the Sherman Act, and holding that since direct negotiation with individual copyright owners is available and feasible there is no undue restraint of trade, illegal tying, misuse of copyrights, or monopolization. 400 F.Supp., at 781-783.

[The Court of Appeals reversed, holding that the agreement was *per se* illegal.]

A

As a preliminary matter, we are mindful that the Court of Appeals' holding would appear to be quite difficult to contain. If, as the court held, there is a *per se* antitrust violation whenever ASCAP issues a blanket license to a television network for a single fee, why would it not also be automatically illegal for ASCAP to negotiate and issue blanket licenses to individual radio or television stations or to other users who perform copyrighted music for profit? Likewise, if the present network licenses issued through ASCAP on behalf of its members are *per se* violations, why would it not be equally illegal for the members to authorize ASCAP to issue licenses establishing various categories of uses that a network might have for copyrighted music and setting a standard fee for each described use?

Although the Court of Appeals apparently thought the blanket license could be saved in some or even many applications, it seems to us that the *per se* rule does not accommodate itself to such flexibility and that the observations of the Court of Appeals with respect to remedy tend to impeach the *per se* basis for the holding of liability.

CBS would prefer that ASCAP be authorized, indeed directed, to make all its compositions available at standard per-use rates within negotiated categories of use. 400 F.Supp., at 747 n. 7.[28] But if this in itself or in conjunction with blanket licensing constitutes illegal price fixing by copyright owners, CBS urges that an injunction issue forbidding ASCAP to issue any blanket license or to negotiate any fee except on behalf of an individual member for the use of his own copyrighted work or works.[29]

---

28. Surely, if ASCAP abandoned the issuance of all licenses and confined its activities to policing the market and suing infringers, it could hardly be said that member copyright owners would be in violation of the antitrust laws by not having a common agent issue per-use licenses. Under the copyright laws, those who publicly perform copyrighted music have the burden of obtaining prior consent. Cf. Zenith Radio Corp. v. Hazeltine Research, Inc., 395 U.S., at 139-140.

29. In its complaint, CBS alleged that it would be "wholly impracticable" for it to obtain individual licenses directly from the composers and publishing houses, but it now says that it would be willing to do exactly that if ASCAP were enjoined from granting blanket licenses to CBS or its competitors in the network television business.

Thus, we are called upon to determine that blanket licensing is unlawful across the board. We are quite sure, however, that the *per se* rule does not require any such holding.

B

In the first place, the line of commerce allegedly being restrained, the performing rights to copyrighted music, exists at all only because of the copyright laws. Those who would use copyrighted music in public performances must secure consent from the copyright owner or be liable at least for the statutory damages for each infringement and, if the conduct is willful and for the purpose of financial gain, to criminal penalties. Furthermore, nothing in the Copyright Act of 1976 indicates in the slightest that Congress intended to weaken the rights of copyright owners to control the public performance of musical compositions. Quite the contrary is true. Although the copyright laws confer no rights on copyright owners to fix prices among themselves or otherwise to violate the antitrust laws, we would not expect that any market arrangements reasonably necessary to effectuate the rights that are granted would be deemed a *per se* violation of the Sherman Act. Otherwise, the commerce anticipated by the Copyright Act and protected against restraint by the Sherman Act would not exist at all or would exist only as a pale reminder of what Congress envisioned.[32]

C

More generally, in characterizing this conduct under the *per se* rule, our inquiry must focus on whether the effect and, here because it tends to show effect, see United States v. United States Gypsum Co., 438 U.S. 422, 436 n. 13 (1978), the purpose of the practice are to threaten the proper operation of our predominantly free-market economy—that is, whether the practice facially appears to be one that would always or almost always tend to restrict competition and decrease output, and in what portion of the market, or instead one designed to "increase economic efficiency and render markets more, rather than less, competitive." *Id.*, at 441 n. 16; see National Society of Professional Engineers v. United States, 435 U.S., at 688; Continental T.V., Inc. v. GTE Sylvania Inc., 433 U.S., at 50 n. 16; Northern Pac. R. Co. v. United States, 356 U.S., at 4.

---

32. Cf. Silver v. New York Stock Exchange, 373 U.S. 341 (1963).

Because a musical composition can be "consumed" by many different people at the same time and without the creator's knowledge, the "owner" has no real way to demand reimbursement for the use of his property except through the copyright laws and an effective way to enforce those legal rights. See Twentieth Century Music Corp. v. Aiken, 422 U.S. 151, 162 (1975). It takes an organization of rather large size to monitor most or all uses and to deal with users on behalf of the composers. Moreover, it is inefficient to have too many such organizations duplicating each other's monitoring of use.

The blanket license, as we see it, is not a "naked restrain[t] of trade with no purpose except stifling of competition," White Motor Co. v. United States, 372 U.S. 253, 263 (1963), but rather accompanies the integration of sales, monitoring, and enforcement against unauthorized copyright use. See L. Sullivan, Handbook of the Law of Antitrust §59, p. 154 (1977). As we have already indicated, ASCAP and the blanket license developed together out of the practical situation in the marketplace: thousands of users, thousands of copyright owners, and millions of compositions. Most users want unplanned, rapid, and indemnified access to any and all of the repertory of compositions, and the owners want a reliable method of collecting for the use of their copyrights. Individual sales transactions in this industry are quite expensive, as would be individual monitoring and enforcement, especially in light of the resources of single composers. Indeed, as both the Court of Appeals and CBS recognize, the costs are prohibitive for licenses with individual radio stations, nightclubs, and restaurants, 562 F.2d, at 140 n. 26, and it was in that milieu that the blanket license arose.

A middleman with a blanket license was an obvious necessity if the thousands of individual negotiations, a virtual impossibility, were to be avoided. Also, individual fees for the use of individual compositions would presuppose an intricate schedule of fees and uses, as well as a difficult and expensive reporting problem for the user and policing task for the copyright owner. Historically, the market for public-performance rights organized itself largely around the single-fee blanket license, which gave unlimited access to the repertory and reliable protection against infringement. When ASCAP's major and user-created competitor, BMI, came on the scene, it also turned to the blanket license.

With the advent of radio and television networks, market conditions changed, and the necessity for and advantages of a blanket license for those users may be far less obvious than is the case when the potential users are individual television or radio stations, or the thousands of other individuals and organizations performing copyrighted compositions in public. But even for television network licenses, ASCAP reduces costs absolutely by creating a blanket license that is sold only a few, instead of thousands, of times, and that obviates the need for closely monitoring the networks to see that they do not use more than they pay for. ASCAP also provides the necessary resources for blanket sales and enforcement, resources unavailable to the vast majority of composers and publishing houses. Moreover, a bulk license of some type is a necessary consequence of the integration necessary to achieve these efficiencies, and a necessary consequence of an aggregate license is that its price must be established.

MR. JUSTICE STEVENS, dissenting.

The Court holds that ASCAP's blanket license is not a species of price fixing categorically forbidden by the Sherman Act. I agree with that holding. The Court remands the cases to the Court of Appeals, leaving open the question whether the blanket license as employed by ASCAP and BMI is unlawful under a rule-of-reason inquiry. I think that question is properly before us now and should be answered affirmatively. . . .

COMMENTS AND QUESTIONS

1. There is no "technical necessity" for the copyright collective in *Broadcast Music*. It is certainly possible in theory to require each copyright holder to offer licenses independently and to punish cooperation in the market for copyright licenses in the same way section 1 punishes other cooperation among competitors. But the result would be that most licenses currently offered would not be available because of prohibitive transaction costs. Economic necessity therefore requires that we exempt such sales from the per se rule. The Court concludes that the rule of reason applies, and remands the case.

The transactions-cost rationale seems to require that copyright collectives have a certain degree of market power. After all, if the industry were composed of thousands of small "collectives," transactions costs would still be a significant barrier to copyright licenses. In fact, the "efficient scale" of a copyright collective would seem to be the entire industry. Given this fact, should antitrust courts be less or more concerned about the market power of copyright collectives?

2. The Court reasons that since the market in question was created by the copyright laws in the first place, it ought to be protected from per se antitrust scrutiny. But is it fair to say that ASCAP and BMI created the market? Certainly, they facilitate the granting of copyright permissions, although they do so at the expense of competition among copyright owners in the sale of permissions. It may be that, absent large organizations such as BMI that have significant bargaining power, most musicians would trade away any performance right royalty in exchange for the public exposure that comes from having their songs played on the radio. If this is true, BMI skews the ordinary market distribution in favor of copyright owners, with the result that radio stations pay a higher price. Indeed, the Supreme Court has previously condemned similar copyright "aggregation" arrangements under the per se rule. See United States v. Loew's, Inc., 371 U.S. 38 (1962) ("block-booking" of movies in theatres illegal).

There are two possible responses to this argument. First, the transactions-cost problem discussed above may be so great that absent a copyright collective, artists and broadcasters might never connect at all. As a result, broadcasters would be unable to play songs by artists who would like to have their songs played. Second, BMI may actually restore equity to the bargaining situation by providing countervailing power to match the power of the broadcasters, and individual copyright owners might feel they have no choice but to give up their royalties. They are likely to be in a much better bargaining position as part of a large collective organization.

3. Can an analogous argument be made in favor of patent-pooling on the grounds that it reduces transactions costs? Consider the following excerpt:

> Patent pools arise because it makes sense for firms in industries characterized by crossing and conflicting IPRs [intellectual property rights] to "institutionalize" technology exchange. In many cases, pools are creatures of necessity. For example, where different firms hold patents on the basic building blocks of the industry's products, they will have to cross-license to produce at all. This was the case, for example, with the aircraft industry in the early days of the twentieth century, and with sewing machines. Even where no single patent or set of patents is essential, however, firms in an industry often find that they engage in such frequent negotiations that a regularized institution with formal rules, or even general guidelines, is helpful in reducing transaction costs. An example of a pool such as this is the one formed by the early shoe machinery industry. The economic literature on institutions explains this quite well; to use one popular metaphor, the "repeat-play" nature of an institution makes it easier to reach agreement on any particular issue, because disparities tend to balance out over many transactions. . . .
>
> All patent pools share one fundamental characteristic: they provide a regularized transactional mechanism in place of the statutory property rule baseline which requires an individual bargain for each transaction. But my review of particular pools shows that this general structure has encompassed a diversity of organizational forms. . . .
>
> Many patent pools are in essence contracts. Firms agree to consolidate patents and license them collectively. The royalties from licensing the patents, and sometimes from sales of products made by one or more parties to the pooling agreement, are divided according to a contractual formula. . . . In this simple example, the contract integrated numerous transactions that would otherwise have been negotiated separately. And, most importantly for present purposes, it translated the contribution of each major patent holder into a precise percentage of the royalty stream.

Robert P. Merges, Contracting into Liability Rules: Intellectual Property Rights and Collective Rights Organizations, 84 Cal. L. Rev. 1293, 1341-1342 (1996).

The music industry is not the only one to have developed collectives of copyright owners. In the publishing industry, an organization called the Copyright Clearance Center (CCC) has taken a leading role in granting permissions and collecting fees from people who photocopy pages out of books or periodicals. The CCC's standard fee for photocopying permissions is fairly high—a standard fee is 25 cents per page. (The royalty for copying a 200-page book at this rate would be $50. This price does not include any reproduction cost.) While the CCC is in much the same situation as BMI or ASCAP, the people with whom it is bargaining (individuals, corporations, and universities) are generally smaller than broadcasters and have less bargaining power. Does this fact make CCC's existence as the dominant publishing collective troublesome from an antitrust perspective? See Merges, supra; Stanley M. Besen et al., An Economic Analysis of

Copyright Collectives, 78 Va. L. Rev. 383 (1992) (copyright collectives lower transactions costs and are therefore generally procompetitive).

Note on Standards, Interoperability, and Standard-Setting Organizations

A significant portion of the intellectual property debate in the computer industry centers around the idea of interoperability or compatibility. A strong argument can be made that the efficient use of computers requires that they be able to "talk to" each other, so that work on one machine can be shared with other users. This argument is even stronger in the case of computer networks and the Internet, where the very existence of the network requires that computers be able to communicate in a standardized format.

How is this to be accomplished? If consumers are to be able to translate their word processing documents from one word processing program to another, someone who knows the nature of one system must write a compatibility component into the other system. Compatibility (particularly one-way compatibility—my system will run your documents, whether or not your system runs mine) does not require that the two programs be developed together or that two competitors work together. It does require that the party making the compatible product have the opportunity to reverse engineer the other product or otherwise have access to the applications programming interfaces (APIs). We have seen significant debate in the case law concerning the propriety of reverse engineering copyrighted software.

But reverse engineering has its problems. As we noted in the introductory chapter, it is an imperfect and time-consuming process. It also requires access to the competitor's product, something that may not be available until after the product is sold commercially. If reverse engineers must wait until a product reaches the shelves and then spend six months taking it apart in order to produce a compatible product, their new product may have only a short shelf life before a new revision of the original product renders the compatible software obsolete.

There is a better way. If the procompatibility programmers have advanced access to the new program—or, better yet, if the necessary compatibility components have been published—it is cheaper and easier to make compatible products, and society benefits. But such standardization requires cooperation among competitors, and such cooperation makes antitrust lawyers very nervous. There is a fine line between wanting to encourage the efficient production of software—which may mean the use of compatibility and interface standards—and wanting to deter cartels that limit innovation. For this reason, the antitrust status of standard-setting groups in the computer industry remains uncertain today.

At the same time, there is reason to be concerned about *not* allowing such groups to function. There is a natural tendency for the computer industry to coalesce around certain devices as industry standards. If those standards are not set by industry agreement, one company's product may become the de facto standard. If that product is difficult to reverse engineer, or if strong intellectual property protection prevents the development of compatible products, the standard-setter will become a monopolist. De facto standards controlled by a single company can be very hard to change, and they may continue to dominate an industry due to inertia long after they are technically obsolete.

In industries characterized by large standardization externalities—that is, where the market naturally tends toward a single product or type of product—group standard-setting organizations can serve valuable procompetitive purposes. They may allow a number of companies to make and sell competing products that are compatible with each other, thus allowing for more flexible use of the products by consumers and preventing one firm from dominating the market with a de facto standard. See Mark A. Lemley, Antitrust and the Internet Standardization Problem, 28 Conn. L. Rev. 1041 (1996).

Unfortunately, standard-setting organizations are sometimes subject to "capture" by a particular participant. In the context of high-technology markets, the most likely means of capturing a standard is by the strategic use of intellectual property rights.[9] For example, in 1992, the Video Electronics Standards Association (VESA) adopted a computer hardware standard called the VL-Bus standard, which governs the transmission of information between a computer's CPU and its peripheral devices. Each of the members voting to adopt the standard, including Dell Computer Corporation, was required by VESA rules to affirm that they did not own any patent rights that covered the VL-Bus standard.[10] Dell's representative did in fact make such a statement. Nonetheless, Dell asserted a patent against other VESA members for using the VL-Bus standard eight months later, after the standard had been widely adopted. By working to adopt as a group standard a technology Dell allegedly knew was proprietary,[11] Dell could obtain the help of its competitors in establishing a standard that it would ultimately be able to control.

---

9. In more traditional products markets, capture of standard-setting organizations sometimes takes the form of controlling the organization and using it to vote down a competitor's standard. This is what apparently happened in Allied Tube & Conduit Corp. v. Indian Head, Inc., 486 U.S. 492 (1988). That approach will not have the same effect in industries such as the software market unless the capturing party has intellectual property rights in the dominant standard. Absent such rights, competitors will alter their products to comply with the winning standard. This may require some time and expense, but the expense will be well worth it to competitors if the lock-in effects of the standard are significant.

10. Many standard-setting organizations, including the American National Standards Institute (ANSI) and Semiconductor Equipment and Materials International (SEMI) have similar rules.

11. Whether Dell in fact knew this is a matter of some dispute. In her dissent to the Commission's proposed consent decree, FTC Commissioner Mary L. Azcuenaga claimed that there was "no evidence to support such a finding of intentional conduct."

The competitive harms of this form of capture are relatively clear. Not only does the capturing party end up with exclusive control over the market standard, converting a group standard-setting process into a de facto one, but the capturing party can use the group standard to achieve a dominant position it could not have attained in an open standards competition. Had Dell announced up front that the standards it was backing were proprietary, it is unlikely that the affected industry would have chosen those standards. At the very least, those standards would have faced stiffer competition than they did.

The most likely avenue of antitrust attack against such capture does not involve Sherman Act section 1 at all but rather is an attempted monopolization claim under section 2. Attempted monopolization has three elements—intent to monopolize, anticompetitive conduct in furtherance of that intent, and a dangerous probability of success. Spectrum Sports v. McQuillen, 506 U.S. 447 (1993). Assuming the failure to disclose relevant intellectual property rights was intentional and not an oversight, the first element should be easy to satisfy. Efforts to capture an industry standard in any given case would constitute anticompetitive conduct precisely in the situation where those efforts are likely to threaten monopolization—that is, where the standard being set is one that will likely dominate the industry. Market power may be the necessary result of patent enforcement in some cases, while in others the patent owner's control over the market stems from a failure of information in the market, a failure that the patent owner herself has induced. While the fact that the antitrust defendant does own intellectual property rights governing the technology suggests some caution in applying the antitrust laws, the mere possession of an intellectual property right will not protect its owner from a charge of dominating a market by extending the scope of that right.[12] In the *Dell* case, the FTC entered into a consent decree in which Dell agreed not to assert its intellectual property rights in the VL-Bus. See In re Dell Computer Corp., No. 931-0097 (F.T.C. 1995).

---

12. In light of this, it is somewhat surprising that the Antitrust Division has taken a position in favor of allowing intellectual property ownership of group standards by a member of the group. In a series of negotiations regarding rules promulgated by the European Telecommunications Standards Institute (ETSI), the United States put substantial pressure on ETSI to back down from its original rule requiring disclosure and nondiscriminatory licensing of member intellectual property rights embodied in ETSI standards.

To be sure, this approach has precedent in some earlier U.S. cases condemning patent pools and cross-licenses. See United States v. New Wrinkle, 342 U.S. 371 (1951). Further, there were apparently some legitimate complaints about the reciprocity of the ETSI licensing provisions. See Allen N. Dixon, The ETSI Complaint and the European Commission's Communication on Standardization (working paper 1995); Prins & Schiessl, The New Telecommunications Standards Institute Policy: Conflicts Between Standardisation and Intellectual Property Rights, 8 Eur. Intell. Prop. Rev. 263 (1993). Nonetheless, the Division's approach seems at least to be in some tension with the FTC's arguments in the *Dell* case, in which the government opposed efforts by one party to use intellectual property rights to capture group standards with market power. For discussions of the evolving ETSI rule on intellectual property rights, see Raymond T. Nimmer, Standards, Antitrust and Intellectual Property, in Intellectual Property Antitrust (P.L.I. 1995).

Of course, not all patents-covering standards will necessarily be anti-competitive. While one approach to standards is to require them to be intellectual property-free (the Internet Engineering Task Force's approach, at least until recently), intellectual property can coexist with procompetitive standard-setting. For example, ANSI and other groups do not require that an intellectual property owner give up any claim to a standard but merely that they license their intellectual property rights on a reasonable basis. Other examples of reasonable and even procompetitive uses of intellectual property in the standard-setting context are possible. It is only in that subset of cases where the patent is used as a competitive weapon that concerns about market control are implicated.[13]

PROBLEM

Problem 7-5. The Graphics Interchange Format, or GIF, is a tool used to exchange images between computers on the Internet. While it is not the only format by which pictures can be exchanged, it is the most popular. The GIF format has been publicly available without restriction since the mid-1980s, and has been incorporated into many of the most popular Net-surfing programs (such as the Mosaic Web-browsing program).

In late 1994, Unisys Corp. asserted for the first time that it had a patent that covered GIF technology. It immediately began to approach commercial Internet providers, seeking to obtain royalties for their continuing use of its patented technology. The Unisys announcement (and its subsequent license with CompuServe Inc.) created a firestorm of controversy, with many Internet users accusing Unisys of deliberately waiting until GIF was adopted as an industry standard before asserting its patent rights.

Has Unisys violated the antitrust laws? If so, how? Does it matter whether Unisys deliberately waited to enforce its patent until GIF had achieved a dominant position in the industry?

---

13. In rare cases, a rule *precluding* patents on standards might be found to be anti-competitive. In In re American Soc'y of Sanitary Engg., 106 F.T.C. 324, 328-329 (1985), the FTC alleged that a standard-setting organization could not refuse to consider revising its standards to include a new product solely on the grounds that that product was patented. The case was settled by consent decree. It is significant that the standard in question was inclusive rather than exclusive, so allowing the complainant's product to be included would not have restricted the rights of other members to make use of other technology covered by the standard. Nonetheless, the case should serve as a caution for rules such as Internet Engineering Task Force's (IETF's) requiring participants to relinquish their intellectual property rights.

b. *Joint Ventures*

A form of cooperative behavior among competitors that has grown especially popular in high-technology industries is the joint venture or strategic alliance. A joint venture occupies a position somewhere between a cartel and a merger. While cartels research, develop, produce, and market goods independently, merely coordinating their output and pricing strategies, joint venturers are competitors who actively cooperate in the research and development of new products, their production, or their marketing. At the same time, they may compete vigorously with respect to sales, output, and pricing decisions.

Because of this unusual structure, joint ventures have long been a problem for traditional antitrust analysis. See Joseph Brodley, Joint Ventures and Antitrust Policy, 95 Harv. L. Rev. 1521 (1982); Thomas M. Jorde & David Teece, Innovation, Cooperation, and Antitrust: Balancing Cooperation and Competition, 4 High Tech. L.J. 1 (1989). Courts have treated them under either section 1 of the Sherman Act or under section 7 of the Clayton Act, depending on whether the court analogized the joint venture to a cartel or to a merger. At the same time, a growing number of scholars have argued that joint ventures deserve to be treated differently— and generally more favorably—than other horizontal agreements under Sherman Act section 1. These economists point to the competitive efficiencies that can result from the integration of joint venture assets and to the fact that joint ventures are better for competition than the alternative of merger between the same companies. Research and development joint ventures are particularly important in innovative industries, according to this argument, because of the high research costs in those industries and the speculative nature of new research projects. See Gene Grossman & Carl Shapiro, Research Joint Ventures: An Antitrust Analysis, 2 J.L. Econ. & Org. 315 (1986).

Because of the unique nature of joint ventures, courts have generally subjected them only to rule-of-reason treatment, even under section 1. See Northrop Corp. v. McDonnell Douglas Corp., 705 F.2d 1030 (9th Cir. 1983). In addition, courts have treated joint ventures under section 7 of the Clayton Act. United States v. Penn-Olin Corp., 378 U.S. 158 (1964), involved a joint venture between Pennsalt Chemicals and Olin Mathieson Chemical to produce and sell sodium chlorate. The Court held that section 7 applied to third companies created under joint ownership of two parents. In applying section 7, it wrote:

> The District Court found that "Pennsalt and Olin each possessed the resources and general capability needed to build its own plant in the southeast and to compete with Hooker and [American Potash] in that market. Each could have done so if it had wished." 217 F. Supp. 110, 129.[5] In addi-

---

5. The court explained further: "At the time when the joint venture was agreed upon Pennsalt and Olin each had an extensive background in sodium chlorate. Pennsalt had years of

tion, the District Court found that, contrary to the position of the management of Olin and Pennsalt, "the forecasts of each company indicated that a plant could be operated with profit." *Ibid*.

The District Court held, however, that these considerations had no controlling significance, except "as a factor in determining whether as a matter of probability *both* companies would have entered the market as individual competitors if Penn-Olin had not been formed. Only in this event would potential competition between the two companies have been foreclosed by the joint venture." *Id.*, at 130. In this regard the court found it "impossible to conclude that as a matter of reasonable probability *both* Pennsalt and Olin would have built plants in the southeast if Penn-Olin had not been created." *Ibid*. The court made no decision concerning the probability that one would have built "while the other continued to ponder." It found that this "hypothesized situation affords no basis for concluding that Penn-Olin had the effect of substantially lessening competition." *Ibid*. That would depend, the court said, "upon the competitive impact which Penn-Olin will have as against that which might have resulted if Pennsalt or Olin had been an individual market entrant." *Ibid*. The court found that this impact could not be determined from the record in this case. "Solely as a matter of theory," it said, ". . . no reason exists to suppose that Penn-Olin will be a less effective competitor than Pennsalt or Olin would have been. The contrary conclusion is the more reasonable." *Id.*, at 131.

We believe that the court erred in this regard. Certainly the sole test would not be the probability that *both* companies would have entered the market. Nor would the consideration be limited to the probability that one entered alone. There still remained for consideration the fact that Penn-Olin eliminated the potential competition of the corporation that might have remained at the edge of the market, continually threatening to enter. Just as a merger eliminates actual competition, this joint venture may well foreclose any prospect of competition between Olin and Pennsalt in the relevant sodium chlorate market. The difference, of course, is that the merger's foreclosure is present while the joint venture's is prospective. Nevertheless, "[potential] competition . . . as a substitute for . . . [actual competition] may restrain producers from overcharging those to whom they sell or underpaying those from whom they buy. . . . Potential competition, insofar as the threat survives [as it would have here in the absence of Penn-Olin], may compensate in part for the imperfection characteristic of actual competition in the great majority of competitive markets." Wilcox, Competition and Monopoly in American Industry, TNEC Monograph No. 21 (1940) 7-8. Potential competition cannot be put to a subjective test. It is not "susceptible of a ready and precise answer." As we found in United States v. El Paso Natural Gas Co., supra, at 660, the "effect on competition . . . is determined by the na-

---

experience in manufacturing and selling it. Although Olin had never been a commercial manufacturer, it possessed a substantially developed manufacturing technique of its own, and also had available to it a process developed by Vickers-Krebs with whom it had been negotiating to construct a plant. Olin had contacts among the southeastern pulp and paper mills which Pennsalt lacked, but Pennsalt's own estimates indicate that in a reasonable time it would develop adequate business to support a plant if it decided to build. A suitable location for a plant was available to each company—Calvert City, Kentucky for Pennsalt, and the TVA area around Chattanooga, Tennessee for Olin. The financing required would not have been a problem for either company." *Ibid*.

ture or extent of that market and by the nearness of the absorbed company to it, that company's eagerness to enter that market, its resourcefulness, and so on." The position of a company "as a competitive factor . . . was not disproved by the fact that it had never sold . . . there. . . . [I]t is irrelevant in a market . . . where incremental needs are booming." The existence of an aggressive, well equipped and well financed corporation engaged in the same or related lines of commerce waiting anxiously to enter an oligopolistic market would be a substantial incentive to competition which cannot be underestimated. . . .

Does it make sense to treat a new joint venture as a merger between the two parents? The Court says elsewhere that "[r]ealistically, the parents would not compete with their progeny." *Id.* at 168. Is that a fair assessment of all joint ventures? Or does it apply only where the joint venture itself will be the exclusive outlet for the products designed?

Joint venture agreements often contain some means of dividing the product or territorial markets. In *Northrop*, this agreement was that McDonnell would build only carrier-based aircraft and Northrop would build only land-based aircraft. What sort of scrutiny should these agreements receive? The *Northrop* court was quite deferential to the agreement in that case for two reasons. First, the court read the agreement as not foreclosing head-to-head competition between the companies, citing some evidence that such competition had in fact occurred. Second, the court reasoned that the joint venture was on balance procompetitive, because without the joint venture neither company would have entered the market. Since the joint venture produced one additional competitor (the joint venture), it promoted competition.

The *Penn-Olin* court's first reason for allowing market-splitting agreements is suspect. In *Northrop*, there was head-to-head competition only because McDonnell began to sell in Northrop's product territory (land-based fighters). Had the parties enforced their agreement to divide products, they would not have competed with each other. Territorial market-division agreements are common in joint ventures, but they may not be a necessary part of the joint venture. In the absence of market power, the contractual restraints in the joint venture agreement should be of little concern. If there is market power among the joint venture participants, it is important to know whether the joint venture would have succeeded absent the market-division mechanism. If so, the existence of that mechanism reduces competition with no offsetting benefit to society because the choice is between a competitive joint venture and a collusive one. It seems reasonable to evaluate such agreements separately from the rest of the joint venture and to strike down such agreements without holding the entire joint venture unlawful.

The court's second reason, that the joint venture was on balance procompetitive, has much economic force in principle. The force it has in practice, though, is highly dependent on the facts of individual cases. It is important to know whether either or both of the joint venturers would have entered the market absent the joint venture. Certainly, if both had entered and had done so successfully,[14] the effect of the joint venture would be to reduce competition.

Penn-Olin goes further than this, of course. The Court concludes that foreclosing "potential competition" by the joint venturers may still make the joint venture anticompetitive. While this may be true in certain limited circumstances, the Court almost certainly overstates its case. The doctrine of "contestable markets," or potential competition, ironically advanced in the 1980s as a reason to *weaken* antitrust scrutiny, see William Baumol et al., Contestable Markets and the Theory of Industry Structure (1982), has come under serious empirical attack. See, e.g., Randall L. Reed & Don E. Waldman, Mergers and Air Fares: 'Contestable Markets' in the Airline Industry, 20:3 Antitrust L. & Econ. Rev. 15 (1988); Steven A. Morrison & Clifford Winston, Empirical Implications and Tests of the Contestability Hypothesis, 30 J.L. & Econ. 53 (1987). It is unquestionably true that actual competition has far more effect than potential entry in restraining price increases.

The existence of these difficult factual issues in antitrust scrutiny of joint ventures counsels against the application of a per se rule to joint ventures. But joint venturers should be careful not to mistake the absence of a per se rule for the absence of any antitrust scrutiny at all. Because joint ventures receive special treatment, courts must also be careful not to let ordinary cartels be characterized as joint ventures. See Timken Roller Bearing Co. v. United States, 341 U.S. 592 (1951).

Is it reasonable to give greater leeway to joint ventures in the computer industry if they are directed toward creating or integrating standardized products? Consider the discussion in the previous section regarding the importance of industry standardization. Can an industry standard-setting group avoid or reduce antitrust scrutiny by recharacterizing itself as a joint venture? Should it be able to do so?

Note on the National Cooperative Research Act

Responding to many of the criticisms described above and in order to encourage the formation of research and development joint ventures, Congress in 1984 passed the National Cooperative Research Act (NCRA),

---

14. As Jorde and Teece note below, the mere fact that the joint venturers would have entered the market does not alone compel the conclusion that the joint venture reduced competition. For example, if each firm could have entered only at the fringes of a market dominated by an existing firm, a single joint venture that can compete on an equal basis with that dominant firm may be more desirable than two fringe competitors.

15 U.S.C. §§4301 et seq. NCRA provides that all joint ventures[15] must be judged under the rule of reason, and that prevailing defendants in an antitrust suit against a joint venture are entitled to collect attorneys' fees. In addition, it allowed joint venturers to register the venture with the Department of Justice. Registered joint ventures were subject only to single, rather than treble, damages.

A number of joint ventures were registered with the Department of Justice after passage of the 1984 Act. Most of these were efforts by small companies, however, and NCRA has received very little in the way of judicial elaboration. In an influential article, Professors Thomas Jorde and David Teece argued that the problem was twofold: NCRA didn't extend to development, production, and marketing joint ventures; and it didn't offer

---

[15] NCRA defines "joint venture" as follows:

§4301. Definitions . . .

(6) The terms "joint research and development venture" means any group of activities, including attempting to make, making or performing a contract, by two or more persons for the purpose of —

(A) theoretical analysis, experimentation, or systematic study of phenomena or observable facts,

(B) the development or testing of basic engineering techniques,

(C) the extension of investigative findings or theory of a scientific or technical nature into practical application for experimental and demonstration purposes, including the experimental production and testing of models, prototypes, equipment, materials, and processes,

(D) the collection, exchange, and analysis of research information, or

(E) any combination of the purposes specified in subparagraphs (A), (B), (C), and (D),

and may include the establishment and operation of facilities for the conducting of research, the conducting of such venture on a protected and proprietary basis, and the prosecuting of applications for patents and the granting of licenses for the results of such venture, but does not included any activity specified in subsection (b) of this section.

(b) The term "joint research and development venture" excludes the following activities involving two or more persons:

(1) exchanging information among competitors relating to costs, sales, profitability, prices, marketing or distribution of any product, process, or service, that is not reasonably required to conduct the research and development that is the purpose of such venture,

(2) entering into any agreement or engaging in any other conduct restricting, requiring, or otherwise involving the production or marketing by any person who is a party to such venture of any product, process, or service, other than the production or marketing of proprietary information developed through such venture, such as patents and trade secrets, and

(3) entering into any agreement or engaging in any other conduct —

(A) to restrict or require the sale, licensing, or sharing of inventions or developments not developed through such venture, or

(B) to restrict or require participation by such party in other research and development activities,

that is not reasonably required to prevent misappropriation of proprietary information contributed by any person who is a party to such venture or of the results of such venture.

enough protection to joint venturers. Thomas M. Jorde & David Teece, Innovation, Cooperation, and Antitrust: Balancing Competition and Cooperation, 4 High Tech. L.J. 1 (1989). They argued:

> While Congress should be applauded for its initial effort in this area, it is now clear that the Act fails to address fully the needs of innovation, and hence has not generated the hoped for response from private business. . . .
>
> Perhaps because it was Congress' first major effort in this area, it is not surprising that the NCRA failed to take important additional steps that we believe would provide greater incentives for cooperative innovation and commercialization arrangements without threatening competition.

a. The Importance of Commercialization to Successful Innovation Is Not Recognized

The substantive protections provided by the NCRA—guaranteed rule of reason treatment and reduction of damages—extend only to research and downstream commercial activity "reasonably required" for research and narrowly confined to marketing intellectual property developed through a joint R&D program. Treatment of commercialization agreements is thus left uncertain, to be determined only by interpretation of the "reasonably required" standard.

In our view, the NCRA is not sufficiently generous toward cooperative commercialization efforts in the context of cooperative innovation. By limiting protection to joint marketing of intellectual property only, for example,the NCRA unwisely precludes joint manufacturing and production of innovative products and processes,which in turn might provide the cooperating ventures with significant feedback information to aid in further innovation and product development. To be sure, it is possible that one might interpret the language "reasonably required" to include all commercialization efforts that aid continued and next generation research of the kind that we have described as critical to cooperative innovation. Whatever the proper reading, we think it would be better to recognize forthrightly that commercialization may be integral to successful, ongoing innovation efforts. To examine commercialization only in terms of whether it is "ancillary" to or "reasonably required" for joint research is likely only to perpetuate analytical confusion and unpredictability when the rule of reason is applied to cooperative innovation arrangements.

b. Rule of Reason Analysis Is Not Adequately Defined

The NCRA gives little guidance concerning the substantive content of its rule of reason approach. To its credit, it does, in requiring that markets be defined in the context of research, implicitly acknowledge the need to define market power in terms of identifiable markets that are tailored to the special characteristics of research and innovation. However, the NCRA fails either to create a market-power-based safe harbor or to specify factors to be considered within rule of reason analysis. It simply requires consideration of "all relevant factors affecting competition," paying no special attention to the special characteristics of the innovation process in a quickly changing industry. In this sense, it does not adequately reflect Congress' appreciation of the importance of innovation to American competitiveness.

c. The Registration Procedure Fails to Provide Effective Protection from Antitrust Exposure

While the NCRA's elimination of treble damages for registered ventures is an important step forward, cooperating firms are still not protected from antitrust litigation. The cost of defending antitrust suits is not materially reduced by the exceedingly narrow circumstances in which the Act permits an award of attorneys' fees to prevailing defendants. Moreover, single damages are still available. We believe that if an approval procedure existed under which procompetitive arrangements could obtain exemptions from further antitrust exposure to private damage actions, then many more competitively beneficial ventures would utilized the NCRA.

Id. To solve this problem, Jorde and Teece proposed that Congress do two things. First, they suggested that the definition of a "joint venture" be expanded to include the production, testing, and marketing of joint ventures. Second, they suggested creating a "safe harbor" protecting joint ventures with less than a 20-25 percent market share from any private antitrust litigation. Jorde and Teece drafted proposed legislation to this end. Congress enacted a similar bill, 15 U.S.C. §§4301 et seq., in 1993 to revise NCRA. The new Act includes production and testing (but not marketing) within the definition of a joint venture. It still does not contain a safe harbor provision, however, and it is limited to domestic companies.

COMMENTS AND QUESTIONS

1. Is there any reason not to enact the Jorde-Teece safe harbor proposal? A safe harbor will not prevent all antitrust litigation against small joint ventures—courts will still be called upon to define the market in order to determine market share, for example. But it would offer some protection to the small joint venture that does not seem to be an immediate threat to the competitive landscape. In this regard, it is worth noting that the Antitrust Division's Intellectual Property Guidelines do adopt a "safety zone" in licensing cases along the lines that Jorde and Teece suggested. Under this safety zone, the Division will not challenge restraints that are not illegal per se unless the licensor and licensees collectively account for more than 20 percent of the market. Intellectual Property Guidelines §4.1. The Division's policy should prevent Justice Department prosecution of small joint ventures, but it does not bar private suits.

For a potential argument against the proposal, see Joseph Brodley, Joint Ventures and Antitrust Policy, 95 Harv. L. Rev. 1521 (1982). Professor Brodley suggests that the result of applying the rule of reason to joint ventures "leads to unfocused, protracted litigation that places the party with the burden of proof at a severe disadvantage. Because the burden of proof normally falls on the government, the result is likely to be significant underenforcement of the antitrust laws." He suggests that courts allocate the burden of proof to the defendant joint venturers in cases where certain factors allow the court to presume a threshold risk of anticompetitive harm.

PROBLEM

Problem 7-6. In the summer of 1991, personal computer giants Apple and IBM announced plans to enter into a joint venture to produce a new type of operating system to run on "Power PC" computers. The "pink" operating system was intended to be used in connection with a new generation of high-speed microprocessors developed by Motorola that use reduced-instruction-set computing, or RISC. It had the added virtue of being able to run on several different types of microprocessors. Apple and IBM would each produce (compatible) computers using the new operating system and microprocessors.

At the time the joint venture was developed, both the operating system market and the microprocessor market were "slaves" to the personal computer market because all three ingredients must be integrated into one compatible set. Today, the IBM-compatible computer dominates the personal computer market, with Apple its most significant challenger. Microsoft (which makes the Windows operating system for use with IBM-compatible computers) dominates the operating system market, and Intel dominates the microprocessor market. Apple also participates in the operating system market, making an Apple-compatible operating system, and Motorola does the same in the microprocessor market. Finally, IBM has entered the operating system market in the past with its OS/2 operating system.

However, because the computer "sets" must be integrated, there was little or no direct competition between Apple and Microsoft in the operating system market, or between Intel and Motorola in the microprocessor market, until the introduction of the PowerPC. The Power PC was designed to be run either the Microsoft or Apple operating systems.

How should such a scheme be evaluated under the antitrust laws? Should it survive antitrust scrutiny? Do subsequent developments (i.e., the abandonment of both "pink" and the PowerPC) suggest a reason for caution about antitrust enforcement in general?

D. MERGERS AND ACQUISITIONS

Closely related to the problem of joint ventures is the problem of mergers and acquisitions of competing companies. Mergers between competitors have similar effects to horizontal agreements—in both cases, the result is to eliminate competition that existed before the mergers. Mergers may also be efficient, however, because they may prevent the duplication of unnecessary administrative costs or research and development activity.

Antitrust law also scrutinizes nonmerger transactions that involve the acquisition of the assets of one company by another. While the acquisition of intellectual property rights or licenses falls within the scope of this review, Automatic Radio Mfg. v. Hazeltine Research, Inc., 339 U.S. 827, 834 (1950), established the proposition that "[t]he mere accumulation of patents, no matter how many, is not in and of itself illegal." However, the strength of that case was diluted by the passage of the Clayton Act the same year. Section 7 of the Clayton Act prohibits the acquisition of any company, stock, *or asset* where such acquisition is likely to restrain competition. Courts have viewed patents and copyrights as "assets" subject to the provisions of that section. SCM Corp. v. Xerox Corp., 645 F.2d 1195 (2d Cir. 1981); see also United States v. Lever Bros., 216 F. Supp. 887, 889 (S.D.N.Y. 1963); United States v. Columbia Pictures Corp., 189 F. Supp. 153, 182-183 (S.D.N.Y. 1960). *SCM* recognizes that in some circumstances section 7 would prohibit patent acquisitions (or mergers between companies holding patents in the same market), even though in-house development of the same intellectual property would be perfectly legal.

Most intellectual property rights are not commercialized by the original inventor.[16] Companies that purchase a patent outright are subject to the Clayton Act; companies that develop a number of patents in-house are not. Is there more reason to be concerned about acquisitions than about internal growth? If not, why the differential treatment? One reason may have to do with the nature of the antitrust remedy. It is much easier to enjoin a proposed purchase or merger, or to order divestiture of a recently acquired asset, than it is to fashion a remedy against a company that has developed and patented its own research.

More common than outright purchase of patent rights is the long-term licensing of those rights by inventors to companies that will commercialize the invention. Do such licenses constitute the "acquisition" of an asset within the meaning of section 7? Should licenses fall within the scope of the Act? Does it matter whether the license is exclusive or non-exclusive?

---

16. In some fields, such as biotechnology, however, "bundled" patenting of groups of similar inventions are becoming increasingly common. For example, the designer of a synthetic analogue to a naturally occurring chemical may patent a whole series of similar analogues in order to prevent imitation by competitors. Large companies and universities that have major research departments are more likely to engage in bundled patenting than are small inventors. To the extent these patents are commercialized (and they often are not), they will normally be commercialized by the same firm.

The Antitrust Division's Intellectual Property Guidelines provide that exclusive licenses will be treated like acquisitions under section 7 but that nonexclusive licenses will not.

PROBLEM

Problem 7-7. In the summer of 1991, Borland International announced its plan to buy Ashton-Tate Corp. At the time, both companies were major players in the database software market for personal computers. Together, they were expected to become the dominant player in that market, beating out competitors that included Microsoft. However, the merged company also planned to enter the database software market for minicomputers, a market currently dominated by Oracle Corp. Should antitrust law permit the expected increase in competition in that market to offset the damage to competition in the PC market?

The Antitrust Division expressed concern that the combined intellectual property libraries of Borland and Ashton-Tate will allow it to prevent further entry into the database market. In particular, the Division was concerned that large potential entrants like Lotus Corp. will be deterred by the threat of intellectual property litigation by Borland. How would you evaluate a proposal by the Division, as a condition of permitting the merger, to require the new company to give up its right to sue new entrants for copyright infringement?

Note on Government Merger Enforcement

The U.S. Justice Department has recently recognized the role of intellectual property rights in determining industry structure. When emerging software giant Borland International sought to acquire Ashton-Tate, its chief rival in the prepackaged database software market, the Justice Department imposed a novel condition on the merger. The text of the consent decree in this case indicates the competitive importance the Department attached to copyrights. The decree, to which Borland and Ashton-Tate stipulated, enjoined Borland from asserting any claim or counterclaim for copyright infringement of "the command names, menu items, menu command hierarchies, command languages, programming languages and file structures used in and recognized by Ashton-Tate's dBASE family of products, standing alone and apart from other aspects of those computer programs." At the same time, the final judgment states that it does not preclude Borland from asserting its right to use these items, or "from asserting copyright protection in and copyright infringement of the computer program code (including its structure, sequence and organization) and other aspects of the user interface of Ashton-Tate's dBASE family of products." The decree prompted Borland to drop a lawsuit brought by Ashton-Tate (which it inherited in the merger) against a smaller database producer, Fox Software. Microsoft subsequently acquired Fox and thus immediately entered the market for Ashton-Tate-compatible database software.

Clearly the consent decree reflected the Justice Department's awareness of the impact of intellectual property rights on industry structure, especially entry. The dBASE family of software has acquired a huge and loyal following; the investments of time and money by these users mean that they face very significant "switching costs" if they were required to learn a dBASE-competitive database program. By injecting the dBASE command structure into the public domain, the Department sought to lower these switching costs and thereby make entry into the industry more likely. The desired effect is a reduction in the market power of the Borland/Ashton-Tate combine.

This episode illustrates the importance of intellectual property as a competitive weapon and a determinant of industry structure. The Department recognized that, as we saw earlier in the case of Japan, the availability and extent of intellectual property protection can have an impact on software industry structure. Unlike Japan, however, the problem in the United States was not that rights were too weak to induce the prepackaged segment of the industry to take off, but rather that rights might be *too strong* to permit a healthy, competitive rate of entry. In this industry and others, policymakers are beginning to see that intellectual property influences much more than R&D spending. It is a key asset with very important ramifications for industry strategy and evolution. In terms of the " 'perennial gale' of competition," intellectual property determines the degree of legal shelter an incumbent can count on. Strong protection, like a brick wall, protects such an incumbent from the winds stirred up by potential entrants, while weak protection is more like a tent—it helps, but cannot be relied on when the winds get too strong. The Justice Department in effect made Borland give up its brick structure for a tent, in exchange for more of a market share. The idea was not so much to encourage entry for its own sake but to permit the kind of cumulative advance (*across* firms) that can take place only in the presence of competition. In so doing, the U.S. government recognized the emergence of intellectual property in this industry as a key variable that is at least as important as productive capacity or labor force advantages in a more traditional industry.

The interest of the Justice Department has not been limited to the enforcement of intellectual property, however. The Antitrust Division also intervened in two cases involving ChipSoft, which at that time was the leading publisher of income tax preparation software for use by consumers. When ChipSoft announced its intention in 1993 to acquire MECA Software, which made the second most popular software package, the

Justice Department announced its intention to oppose the merger. The Justice Department defined the market narrowly, limiting it to consumer-oriented tax software and excluding both programs written for accountants and noncomputerized tax assistance. The government also imposed conditions on ChipSoft's 1993 merger with Intuit, a producer of general business software. Finally, the government blocked Microsoft's proposed acquisition of Intuit in 1995. See Ilene Knable Gotts & Howard W. Fogt, Jr., Clinton Administration Expresses More than Intellectual Curiosity in Antitrust Issues Raised by Intellectual Property Licensing, 22 AIPLA Q.J. 1, 22-23 (1994).

E. REMEDIES

The practical significance of the antitrust laws and other doctrines aimed at preventing the anticompetitive use of intellectual property are in large part determined by the sanctions imposed against violators.[17] There are a number of issues that arise specifically in the context of the patent-antitrust intersection that merit consideration here.[18]

Section 15 of Title 15 of the U.S. Code provides that a private anti-trust plaintiff may recover treble damages plus costs, attorney's fees, and, in some cases, interest from a defendant found to have violated the antitrust laws. In addition, prevailing plaintiffs are entitled to an injunction against further antitrust violations and, in some cases, to affirmative structural relief against the defendant (such as the 1982 decree breaking up AT&T).

COMMENTS AND QUESTIONS

1. The efficiency issues the treble damages provision raises are not specific to patent cases. However, in recent years commentators have suggested that treble damages are particularly inappropriate in innovation cases because they tend to deter legitimate and socially useful activity. The leading advocates of single antitrust damages have been Professors Thomas Jorde and David Teece:

> The Clayton Act permits private parties to sue for treble damages for alleged antitrust injuries, and allows state attorney generals to recover treble damages on behalf of persons residing in the state. Successful plaintiffs can also recover attorneys' fees. The availability of these remedies provides a pow-

17. See, e.g., Landes, Optimal Sanctions for Antitrust Violations, 50 U. Chi. L. Rev. 652 (1983); Block & Sidak, The Cost of Antitrust Deterrence: Why Not Hang a Price Fixer Now and Then?, 68 Geo. L.J. 1131 (1980).

18. For a general discussion of the problems of antitrust enforcement in the patent context, see Ward Bowman, Patent and Antitrust Law 239-256 (1973).

erful incentive for plaintiffs to litigate—and a powerful disincentive for businesses to form cooperative innovation arrangements and strategic alliances.

Treble damages and attorneys' fees are designed to deter anticompetitive conduct by giving private plaintiffs an incentive to ferret out anticompetitive conduct, particularly when such conduct (e.g. secret price fixing or territory divisions) might be difficult to detect. In our view, these incentives are unwarranted in the context of cooperative innovation, which promises such high returns to society. The effects of most cooperative innovation arrangements, which rarely involve price or territory agreements, are not ordinarily difficult to detect. While it is difficult to measure the underinvestment in cooperative innovation caused by the threat of treble damage litigation, out judgment is that it is substantial, largely due to ingrained habits caused by a hostile antitrust tradition.

Thomas M. Jorde & David Teece, Innovation, Cooperation and Antitrust: Balancing Cooperation and Competition, 4 High Tech. L.J. 1 (1989). Jorde and Teece advance two reasons for treating cooperative innovation differently from antitrust violations in other industries. First, they cite the high social returns to such cooperative activities. It is true that innovation provides a social benefit, while cooperation in most other industries does not. This consideration is tempered by two factors, however. First, it is important to differentiate social benefits that are achievable without risking antitrust liability from those that require questionable conduct; only the latter can properly be considered a benefit to *cooperative* innovation. Second, if those high social benefits are matched by high private returns to the cooperating firms, those firms will have an incentive to cooperate in spite of potential antitrust liability. Both of these are empirical matters that may affect the force of Jorde and Teece's argument.

The second argument the authors advance is that treble damages are not needed to encourage the detection of secret agreements, particularly in the context of joint ventures. There is no reason to believe, however, that this is true solely in the innovation context. Jorde and Teece's point here may support the conclusion that certain types of antitrust violations—such as joint ventures—should not be subject to treble damages in *any* industry. The validity of this argument is also contingent on the assumption that treble damages are designed to compensate for difficulty of detection, not other factors, such as lack of incentive for plaintiffs to sue or standing problems.

Others have argued, however, that treble damages may play a beneficial role. For example, William Breit & Kenneth Elzinga, Antitrust Penalty Reform: An Economic Analysis (1986), argue that like other punitive or criminal sanctions, treble damages provide a deterrent to illegal behavior even when punishing that behavior is uncertain. See also Robert Cooter & Daniel Rubinfeld, Economic Analysis of Legal Disputes and Their Resolution, 27 J. Econ. Lit. 1067 (1989) (In antitrust cases, "where reputational effects are important, and where the parties tend to be pessimistic, . . . treble damages lead to a decrease in the proportion of cases resolved by trial and an increase in the number of settlements."). Cooter and Rubin-feld cite other studies demonstrating a contrary result, however. See *id.* at 1081-1082.

2. Judicial decisions in the last 15 years have put substantial obstacles in the way of private antitrust plaintiffs (for example, by strictly limiting "standing to sue"). How does the increasing difficulty plaintiffs have in recovering on their antitrust claims affect Jorde and Teece's argument?

3. An alternative remedy available in intellectual property antitrust cases is the compulsory license, discussed in more detail in Chapter 2. Essentially, a compulsory license takes away the "exclusive" nature of an intellectual property right, leaving the intellectual property owner with only the right to collect "damages" (in the form of a court-imposed reasonable royalty). Courts have periodically ordered compulsory licensing of intellectual property as an antitrust remedy, reasoning that it will restore competition to the industry. See, e.g., Hartford-Empire Co. v. United States, 323 U.S. 386, 417 (1945); *ReaLemon,* 92 F.T.C. 669 (1978) (compulsory license of the ReaLemon trademark for lemon juice); American Cyanamid Co., 63 F.T.C. 1747 (1963) (compulsory license of patent for tetracycline). Note that the ReaLemon compulsory license was reversed by the full F.T.C., which held that remedies short of compulsory licensing were sufficient to dissipate monopoly power. See also Carl Kaysen, United States v. United Shoe Machinery Corp. 283 (1956) (discussing licensing restrictions as an antitrust remedy in the title case).

4. A final "antitrust remedy" is not directly connected with antitrust law at all. The patent, copyright, and trademark misuse doctrines provide remedies for infringers against intellectual property owners who have abused their intellectual property rights. Because misuse overlaps significantly with antitrust law, patentees who use their intellectual property to violate the antitrust laws may lose the ability to enforce their patent or copyright, in addition to whatever sanctions are imposed by the antitrust laws. On the overlap in remedies between the antitrust laws and the misuse doctrine, see Mark A. Lemley, Comment, The Economic Irrationality of the Patent Misuse Doctrine, 78 Cal. L. Rev. 1599 (1990).

Misuse doctrine has some currency in the computer industry. The first case acknowledging the validity of a copyright misuse defense involved improper practices in the licensing of computer software. Lasercomb America v. Reynolds, 911 F.2d 970 (4th Cir. 1990). Since that time, other cases have applied the misuse doctrine in a variety of contexts that would also constitute antitrust violations. For example, in Electronic Data Systems v. Computer Associates Int'l, 802 F. Supp. 1463 (N.D. Tex. 1992), the court refused to dismiss EDS's misuse defense based on Computer Associates' alleged tying together of multiple software products.

8

International Protection for Computer Technology

Because the market for computer technology is worldwide, the need for legal protection on an international scale is evident. Protecting computer technology in the international marketplace is complicated in part because of differences among national legal rules, traditions, procedures, and institutional frameworks. However, countries generally have the same basic types of legal protection for computer technology as those types discussed in earlier chapters. International treaties provide significant procedural and substantive protections to distributors of computer technology who do business in other lands.[1] In general, these treaties obligate member states to protect the innovations of foreign nationals on a "national treatment" basis—that is, they oblige countries not to discriminate against innovations originating in fellow treaty member states. This principle is fulfilled by a commitment to provide at least as much protection to the innovations of foreign nationals as local laws provide to the country's own nationals.

An especially significant development in international protection of computer technology occurred in 1994 when the Agreement on Trade-Related Aspects of Intellectual Property Rights (TRIPS) became an annex to

---

1. The Berne Convention for the Protection of Literary and Artistic Works, Sept. 9, 1886, as last revised at Paris on July 24, 1971, 828 U.N.T.S. 221, and the Paris Convention for the Protection of Industrial Property, Mar. 20, 1883, as revised at Stockholm on July 14, 1967, 21 U.S.T. 1583, have historically been the two principal international intellectual property treaties. Other multilateral treaties include the International Convention for the Protection of Performers, Producers of Phonograms, and Broadcasting Organizations (often referred to as the Rome Convention); the Universal Copyright Convention; the Patent Cooperation Treaty; and the Treaty on Intellectual Property in Respect of Integrated Circuits. There are, in addition, numerous bilateral or regional treaties with provisions on intellectual property rights. See, e.g., the North American Free Trade Agreement and the European Patent Convention.

643

the agreement establishing the World Trade Organization (WTO). TRIPS, like other international treaties, relies on national treatment and nondiscrimination principles to ensure that innovations, including computer technology, receive adequate protection in member state nations.[2] However, TRIPS also establishes detailed minimum standards for seven intellectual property regimes, five of which may be relied upon by U.S. software developers (i.e., copyright, patent, trade secrecy, trademark, and semiconductor chip design).[3] TRIPS not only requires WTO members to have substantive laws that meet the minimum standards of protection that TRIPS sets forth; it also requires that a generous array of remedies be available for infringement of intellectual property rights.[4] Furthermore, TRIPS commits WTO member states to adequate enforcement of intellectual property rights and remedies.[5] TRIPS thus offers international distributors of computer technology reason to be confident that their legal rights will be respected in WTO countries.

The TRIPS Agreement establishes a dispute resolution system by which one WTO member state may make a formal complaint against another member state about the inadequacy of intellectual property protection available to the complainant's nationals in that other state. These complaints, it should be noted, can only be made by one WTO member state against another, not by private parties. In general, it will take more than one erroneous ruling in a jurisdiction before a viable complaint can be made that a country is in violation of its TRIPS obligations. Moreover, a formal complaint will not lead to immediate litigation. The Dispute Settlement Body first attempts to help resolve disputes between countries informally, via mediation and consultations. However, if a dispute cannot be resolved informally, the Dispute Settlement Body will, at the request of one of the parties, empanel a tribunal of experts to consider a formal complaint and to make a determination that, for example, state X violated this or that provision of the TRIPS Agreement and that state Y's nationals suffered this or that harm. If a WTO panel determines that a complaint has merit, it can authorize the imposition of trade sanctions against products of the offending nation until that nation adapts its practices to conform to TRIPS requirements. An appeal process exists for WTO panel determinations, but once a determination has been affirmed on appeal, it is a final ruling with which the member state must comply. Compliance is ensured by sanctions,

---

2. Articles 3-4, TRIPS Agreement.

3. The principal way TRIPS establishes these minimum standards is by requiring members to comply with specified provisions of the Berne Convention, the Paris Convention, the Rome Convention, and the Treaty on Intellectual Property in Respect of Integrated Circuits. See arts. 2 and 9(1) of the TRIPS Agreement. Other substantive minima are set forth in arts. 9(2)-40.

4. See arts. 42-46.

5. See arts. 41 (generally), 61 (criminal measures). See also arts. 42-43, 47, 49-50 (procedural requirements). TRIPS also contains provisions aimed at establishing effective border measures to control trafficking in pirated goods. Arts. 51-60.

which may gradually extend to products not involved in the original dispute —products whose export is sufficiently im-portant to the offending nation that it will want to comply with the ruling to have the sanctions lifted. In all cases, the goal of the dispute resolution process is to bring states into compliance with TRIPS norms, not to punish them for past transgressions. See Rochelle C. Dreyfuss & Andreas F. Lowenfeld, Two Achievements of the Uruguay Round: Putting TRIPS and Dispute Settlement Together, 37 Va. Int'l L. Rev. 275 (1997).

This chapter, for the most part, parallels the structure of earlier chapters and provides representative cases, laws, regulations, and guidelines that indicate the nature and degree of protection available under various national laws for computer technology. It also describes major intellectual property treaties affecting international transactions in computer technology. Finally, it provides guidance on extraterritoriality issues of concern to computer hardware and software developers and their lawyers.

A. TRADE SECRECY

Given the well-established nature of trade secrecy law in the United States, it may come as a surprise to learn that the legal concept of trade secrecy is far from universally accepted in the international community. Some countries have U.S.-style trade secrecy laws, but some do not.[6] In countries that do not have U.S.-style trade secrecy laws, it will generally be possible to get a similar degree of protection by other means. It is common in other countries, for example, to protect commercially valuable secrets through license restrictions on use or disclosure of the information. Even where a licensing agreement is not explicit about the need to keep certain secret information confidential, courts in many jurisdictions may use implied contract theory to find that the parties to a contract intended that certain information not be disclosed. Many countries also have rules against disclosure of confidential information, including information of the sort that in the U.S. would be protected as a trade secret. Breaches of fiduciary duty may be, in an appropriate case, yet another way to protect what U.S. firms will consider to be trade secrets. Hence, the substance of U.S.-style trade secrecy protection can generally be achieved outside the U.S. by reliance on other legal theories.

---

6. Prior to the 1990 amendments to the Japanese Unfair Competition Act, Japan, for example, had no trade secrecy law as such and provided little protection by other means. See, e.g., Jay Dratler, Jr., Trade Secrets in the United States and Japan: A Comparison and Prognosis, 14 Yale J. Int'l L. 68 (1989). However, Japan now has a formal trade secrecy law. See Trade Secret Act, An Amendment of the Unfair Competition Prevention Act (118th Diet, 66th Act, 1990).

Northern Office Micro Computers (Pty)
Ltd. v. Rosenstein
Cape Provincial Division, South Africa
1981 (4) S.A. 123(C)

MARAIS, A.J.

[A former employee had developed a suite of programs during the course of employment. Under South African copyright law, he was the owner of the copyright in these programs. After determining that computer programs could be protected by South African copyright law and that the respondent, a former part-time employee of one of the applicants, was the owner of a valid copyright in the program at issue, the court turned to the main issue raised by the applicants.] . . .

May the Employer Prevent the Employee from Exploiting the Copyright?

At the outset, it is necessary to emphasize two things. Firstly, applicants' case is not based upon any claim to copyright in the programmes. Their case is based solely upon the threatened exploitation by respondent of their trade secrets. Secondly, the mere fact that a particular computer programme may qualify for copyright protection, does not mean that the programme is also a trade secret. Whether it is a trade secret, depends upon different considerations and is another enquiry altogether. If the result of such an enquiry is that the programme is found to be a trade secret, I fail to see how the fact that copyright in it vests in an employee, gives him the right to disregard the obligation which the common law imposes upon him to respect his employer's trade secrets. Section 41 (3) of the Copyright Act provides that nothing in the Act shall affect the operation of any rule of equity relating to breaches of trust or confidence. While it is so that this provision cannot be read as introducing in South African law principles of the English common law which do not exist here (Dun and Bradstreet (Pty) Ltd v SA Merchants Combined Credit Bureau Cape (Pty) Ltd 1968 (1) SA 209 (C) at 215), it is plainly intended to have some effect in South Africa. If it does not save the express or implied rights of employers to have their employees respect their trade secrets, it is difficult to conceive of any field of application which it might have.

But, even if sec. 41(3) had not existed, I would have been of the same opinion. It would be contrary to well-known principles of statutory construction to read the Copyright Act as abolishing, or derogating from, the common law rights of an employer unless express language, or the clearest of necessary implications, compelled such a reading. In my view, the mere fact that copyright is vested in an employee in certain circumstances does not mean that, even if the subject of the copyright is confidential and a trade secret, the employee may divulge it to whom he pleases. I do not think that the adoption of this view emasculates or nullifies the employee's copyright. He will still have *locus standi* to *protect* his copyright against infringement by third parties. Indeed, he will even be able to protect it against infringement by his employer, to the extent that the employer's use of it goes beyond what was expressly, or impliedly, authorised by the contract of employment. It is true that he will be hampered in his *exploitation* of the copyright if he has to respect his employer's trade secret, but I do not think the Legislature intended otherwise. To make copyright protection available to an employee is one thing. To strip an employer of his common law right to have his trade secrets respected is another. And, of course, if the subject of the copyright is not a trade secret, the employee is free to exploit it.

If I am right in so thinking, it follows that, if the suite of programmes in issue is a trade secret, it is no answer to the claim for an interdict for respondent to say that he is vested with the copyright. The critical question then is whether the applicants have established that the suite of programmes is indeed a trade secret and, if so, to what extent respondent should be restricted in dealing with it. That computer programmes may qualify for the protection which the common law accords to confidential matter and trade secrets seems to me to be plain. In his work Computer Law (1978) Tapper says this of computer programmes in the context of trade secrets and confidentiality:

> So far no reported cases on this topic in the United Kingdom have concerned computer programmes, but here too there can be no reasonable doubt that in principle such programmes are eligible for this sort of protection as soon as they have progressed beyond being merely a general idea and have been transmitted into a set of instructions.

(At 30.) I agree with this view of the matter, provided, of course, that the programme is not commonplace.

The dividing line between the use by an employee of his own skill, knowledge and experience, and the use by him of his employer's trade secrets is notoriously difficult to draw. An employer's trade secret may be no more than the result of the application by an employee of his own skill, knowledge and experience. But, if the employee was engaged to evolve the secret, it remains the employer's trade secret for all that. The employee may not simply copy it if, by copy, one means that literally. For example, if he has conducted a confidential market survey for his erstwhile employer to establish what demand, if any, exists in a particular area for a particular type of product, he cannot simply copy the survey and hand it to his new employer. But *non constat* that the employee may never again set out to establish the market demand for that particular type of product in the same area. Generally speaking, he cannot be prevented from using his own skill and experience to attain a particular result, merely because it is a result which he has achieved before for a previous employer. I say, generally speaking, because one can conceive of cases where the result sought to be achieved is so elusive that only a solution of the kind which legend has it prompted Archimedes to say "Eureka" will do, and the employee has been engaged specifically to find it. In such a case, it may well be that the employee who has evolved the solution may have to refrain from solving it in the same way for a future employer.

What have we here? The respondent is qualified in a particular technology, namely computer programming. He has learnt a computer language which is the *lingua franca* of the Datapac computers. It is not suggested by the applicants that the language of the Datapac computer is a trade secret. While in applicants' employ, respondent worked upon a particular project, namely the development of a suite of programmes which provide an accounting and administrative system for doctors and dentists. The object of the computer programme was to provide them with "a speedy, accurate and comprehensive source of information . . . relating to all aspects of their financial affairs".

The use of computer technology to achieve this purpose can hardly be described as inspired. This is the kind of thing which computers are vaunted to be able to do. Their field of application is virtually limitless. Programmes can be devised to cater for the needs of almost anybody, from banks, building societies and insurance companies to engineers, astronomers, and mariners. All this is common knowledge. That being so, I am unable to see that the *concept* of a computer programme of this kind for doctors and dentists is confidential to the applicants and so, a trade secret. Particularly when it is not disputed that some of applicants' competitors are already marketing, or have advertised their intention of marketing, computer programmes for doctors and dentists. (Applicants stress that the other systems are different, but the remarks which I have made are confined to the broad *concept* of a computer programme attuned to the needs of doctors and dentists.)

To pass from the general to the particular. What is there in this particular suite of programmes which gives it a quality of such confidentiality that respondent should be restrained

> from communicating all computer language instructions relating exclusively to the accounting and administrative requirements of doctors and dentists, whether in writing or otherwise, embodied in the suite of programmes designed by respondent for the purposes of producing an accounting system for doctors and dentists irrespective of the nature or type of computer in conjunction with which such instruction may be used?

In my view, the evidence before me does not enable me to conclude that what has gone into the development of this suite of programmes is of so confidential a character that respondent should be restrained in either of these ways. I emphasize that I am not here referring to the copying of the suite of programmes. That respondent plainly cannot do. It is common cause that much work, skill and time is needed to produce a suite of programmes of this kind. If respondent were permitted simply to copy it, he would be unfairly nullifying the advantage of the "long start" over anyone else to which applicants are entitled. To that limited extent, the suite of programmes is, in my opinion, a trade secret.

But it does not follow from this that respondent may not again apply his mind to the development of a suite of programmes to cater for the accounting and financial needs of doctors and dentists, or that, if he does, he must wipe clean from the slate of his memory (as if that were possible) any recollection he may have of the things which it seemed to him were appropriate for inclusion in such a suite of programmes, or of appropriate formulae, or the like. To accept the contrary view would halter respondent's use of his own training, skill and experience to an unacceptable degree. This remains so whether he is restrained permanently, or for a limited period of two years such as Mr. Dison suggested. As CROSS J said in Printers and Finishers Ltd v Holloway (1964) 3 All ER 731 at 736F:

> The law will defeat its own object if it seeks to enforce in this field standards which would be rejected by the ordinary man.

. . . But, as I have said, I think that applicants are entitled to have respondent restrained from copying, or permitting to be copied, the suite of programmes, or any part of it. They are entitled to have respondent restrained from making use of, or permitting anyone to make use of, any existing copy of the whole, or any part, of the suite of programmes. In saying this, I include, within the concept of copying, translating the programmes into any other computer language.

COMMENTS AND QUESTIONS

1. Why does the employee own the copyright in the program? He was hired to write it, and paid to write it. Contrast the U.S. rule, under which employees acting within the scope of their employment in creating copyrighted works do not own the works. Perhaps the South African rule reflects a more continental treatment of copyrighted works (including computer programs) as extensions of the "author's" personality.

On the other hand, it is worth noting that an independent contractor under U.S. law would still retain the copyright in a computer program written under contract for a company. Perhaps it is U.S. law that is inconsistent on this ownership issue.

2. If the court is correct in concluding that Rosenstein owns the copyright in his program, why should it come to a different result regarding ownership of the trade secret? What is the practical outcome of this case? Who—if anyone—is entitled to use the program? To make additional copies? To sell the program to another company?

3. How would the rule in *Northern Office* apply across international borders? Rosenstein's copyright is presumably protected under the Berne Convention in most countries in the world. Is Northern Office entitled to a worldwide injunction against his use of trade secrets abroad? Does it matter whether there is a similar international treaty guaranteeing trade secret rights? (There was no such agreement until 1994, when the TRIPS Agreement was adopted by most countries in the world. TRIPS includes sections establishing minimum substantive requirements for legal protection of confidential information in member states. See infra.)

4. The *Northern Office* court suggests that while Rosenstein can't copy his own program without misappropriating a trade secret, there is nothing to prevent him from using his own knowledge and skill to write another program. Compare this case with the U.S. decision in *Rivendell*, discussed in Chapter 1. Would U.S. courts be so lenient to a trade secret defendant?

Computer Workshops Ltd. v. Banner Capital Market Brokers Ltd.
Ontario High Court of Justice
64 O.R.(2d) 266, 21 C.P.R.3d 116 [1988]

CRAIG J.:

This an action for damages resulting from an alleged breach of contract by the defendants. The plaintiff company, having its office located in Toronto, is engaged in the sale of microcomputers and related accessories. The defendants Banner Capital Market Brokers Ltd. (Banner) and Shorcan International Brokers Limited (Shorcan) are bond brokers also having their offices located in Toronto. They are related corporations sharing common offices and having interlocking officers and directors.

Pursuant to the terms of an agreement between the plaintiff and the defendants, the plaintiff was to provide to the defendant 100 Toshiba T-300 microcomputers and accessories; also the plaintiff was to provide assistance in the adaptation of the appropriate software programs and in the installation of the hardware system. The defendants terminated the contract with the plaintiff at a time when 75 of the microcomputers had not yet been delivered.

The defendants allege breach of an implied term of the contract that the plaintiff:

(a) would keep confidential the knowledge it obtained of the defendants' business and of the system and would not reveal such knowledge to third parties or potential competitors, and

(b) would not attempt to sell the system or a comparable system to any competitor or potential competitor of the defendants.

Apart from the contractual relationship, the defendants further allege breach of:

(c) a relationship of confidentiality between the parties;
(d) infringement of copyright held by the defendants in the relevant software programs, and
(e) breach of a fiduciary relationship between the plaintiff and the defendants.

The ultimate issue in this case is whether the plaintiff is entitled to damages for breach of contract (wrongful termination of contract by the defendants).

The defendants submit that they were entitled to terminate the contract based upon allegations (a), (b), (c), (d) and (e) above; alternatively that they were entitled to terminate for breach of implied term alone because it was a breach of serious and major importance which was coupled with a breach of confidence, infringement of copyright and breach of fiduciary relationship or some of them.

. . . The plaintiff and the defendants entered into an agreement for the purchase and installation of 20 Toshiba T-100 microcomputers and accessories. In addition, the plaintiff was to provide assistance in adapting and developing the software programs. Morrison converted his software program for use on the Toshiba T-100. Upon testing the Toshiba T-100 did not meet Banner's requirements. It did not have the necessary communication ability; it was too slow; the "flashing" did not perform properly and there were other difficulties. One Wilfred Steimle, an independent consultant, was retained by the plaintiff to assist Morrison in making the required adjustments of the software programs to conform with the Toshiba T-100s and to arrange for the necessary configuration of the hardware. In this capacity Steimle acquired an intimate and detailed knowledge of the Shorcan system and proposed Banner system. On March 6, 1984, because the T-100s did not meet the defendant's requirements the plaintiff and the defendants agreed to the cancellation of the purchase of the T-100s and accessories; also that the defendants would purchase from the plaintiff 100 T-300 microcomputers and accessories. It was understood that the plaintiff would continue to provide assistance in the adaptation of Morrison's software programs and configuration of the hardware system. The plaintiff agreed to and did provide to the defendants a full credit on the return of the Toshiba T-100 microcomputers and accessories.

The configuration consisted of a host computer—with input terminals at the Banner office connected by wires to a modem. The modem was connected to a "bridge" which splits the signal into a certain number of identical amplified signals for transmission over dedicated data or phase lines to the exchange and then from the exchange to the customers' sites where it is connected to another modem which converts the analog signal back to a digital signal that is fed into the computers.

All of the above-mentioned equipment could be purchased "off the shelf", but I accept the evidence of Steimle that a "bridge" was designed for use in electrical alarm systems. Morrison and Steimle testified that they were not aware that a "bridge" had ever been used before in this particular application, and this evidence was not denied. This configuration was therefore unique in that sense. Also it resulted in a very substantial saving in costs because up until that time a separate modem for each customer would have been required at the Banner offices.

I find that the Banner system was unique in that the hardware configuration with the bridge had not been in place up to that time; the software had been written specifically and adapted for that application; it employed the use of colour (flashing) display screens at customer sites. I accept Steimle's evidence that to create a similar system "from scratch" would require six to nine months and the assistance from a person such as Morrison who was knowledgeable in the bond brokerage industry, at a cost of [Canadian] $50 per hour.

This was a commercial transaction between the plaintiff and the defendants, but upon my findings of fact and reasons to follow it is my view that the plaintiff stood in a fiduciary relationship to the defendants; the defendants through Morrison sought out the plaintiff and gave it confidential information. Because the defendants reposed trust and confidence in the plaintiff, the latter was not entitled to derive any profit or advantage, other than that which arose out of the contract, except with the knowledge and consent of the defendants.

In argument counsel for the plaintiff admitted (for the first time) that in order to give business efficacy to the contract between the plaintiff and the defendants it may be necessary to imply a term that the plaintiff would not sell a system similar to Banner to someone else. He submitted that the evidence did not go beyond an attempt to sell on the part of the plaintiff, and that an *attempt* to sell a similar system would not constitute breach of the implied term.

The information given to the plaintiff by the defendants (including Steimle) had the necessary quality of confidence (the uniqueness or novelty of the configuration and the copyright in the software). Steimle was an independent contractor, but for the purpose of performing the plaintiff's contract with the defendants he was the plaintiff's agent up until he "abandoned ship" on or about March 30, 1984. This is not to say that some aspects of the Banner system were not public property or publicly known. Applying the language of *Saltman* the defendants used their available brain power "to produce a result which can only be produced by someone who goes through the same process." The configuration of the hardware was simple but it was entitled to protection along with the software. If Crook wanted to devise his own system there could be no objection. What he was not entitled to was a copy of the Banner system. At least six months were required to develop the software and these programs had been carefully protected by Morrison. In my opinion, the Banner system as a unit was clearly confidential information. The plaintiff and/or Crook were entitled to compete but what happened was a classic case of wrongfully using the defendants' confidential information as a spring-board for activities detrimental or potentially detrimental to the defendants.

I find as fact that on March 28, 1984, the plaintiff formed an intention to duplicate and agreed to duplicate the Banner system for another customer (the defendants' competitor). The fact that there might be cosmetic changes is irrelevant. Having done that the plaintiff was in breach of the implied term of its contract with the defendants, and in breach of confidence and fiduciary duty. Whether there was only an attempted rather than an actual infringement of copyright is not material to the result in the circumstances of the case.

The plaintiff submits that Steimle acted without authority and unethically herein in making various disclosures to the defendants. If there is any substance to that allegation it is not relevant to the result in this action. Also any rights the plaintiff may have in relation to Steimle are not impaired by the judgment in this action.

Was the Breach of Implied Term of Such Major Importance That the Defendants Are Discharged from Liability?

As of March 28, 1984, the plaintiff and Denda intended to sell the Banner system to a competitor through Crook as a middleman. Cosmetic changes only were contemplated. On March 30th, Banner gave notice to the plaintiff that his proposed conduct was "unethical" and a "breach of Banner's copyright and proprietary rights, as well as breach of your obligation to Banner". On April 5th, and without notifying the defendants, Denda in his personal capacity entered into a contract with TEO to collect a commission for business generated through the Investment Dealers Association and/or Crook. On April 6th, the defendants again wrote to the plaintiff and Denda requiring the support of the plaintiff and Denda for the protection of the Banner system, and advising them of the importance of keeping the system confidential. On April 11, 1984 (and again without disclosing that he personally had contracted with TEO on April 5th), Denda made a counter-proposal on behalf of the plaintiff only. The defendants had become aware of the contract between Denda and TEO. On April 12th they wrote to both Denda and the plaintiff terminating their contract because of "misconduct and breaches of contract".

I find that there was a repudiation or breach of contract by the plaintiff of the implied term of the contract in circumstances where, on the part of the plaintiff, there was a breach of confidence, a breach of fiduciary duty and an infringement or attempted infringement of copyright. The implied term of the contract was of the utmost importance to the defendants. As stated by Morrison, it could be a matter of "life and death" for the defendants. It can also be said that it was a breach going to the root of the contract. The time for final performance by the plaintiff had not yet arrived (delivery of the 75 T-300 Toshiba computers). As indicated earlier, repudiation may occur before the time for final performance has arrived (anticipatory breach). For the reasons stated above the defendants were entitled to terminate the contract with the plaintiff on and after March 28, 1984. Nothing happened between that date and April 12, 1984 (the date of termination), that would preclude the defendants from exercising the right to terminate. In my opinion the defendants acted very reasonably in writing the above-mentioned letters of April 3rd and April 6th, expressing their urgent concerns and imposing certain requirements for the continuation of the contract and relationship. Denda himself was not a party to the contract but he was the sole directing mind of the plaintiff company and in the circumstance he himself stood in the same position to the defendants as the plaintiff.

COMMENTS AND QUESTIONS

What exactly did the defendants take in this case? The court suggests that the defendants may not use the plaintiff's proprietary program as a "springboard" to develop their own. Does this comport with the South African rule discussed above? With the U.S. case law?

Note on TRIPS and Trade Secret Protection

The prospects for improved legal protection for trade secrets in the international arena have increased considerably since adoption of the TRIPS Agreement. It includes a provision requiring WTO member states to provide adequate protection for undisclosed information. Article 39(2) of TRIPS sets forth the following obligations regarding undisclosed information protection:

1. In the course of ensuring effective protection against unfair competition as provided in Article 10bis of the Paris Convention (1967), Members shall protect undisclosed information in accordance with paragraph 2 and data submitted to governments or governmental agencies in accordance with paragraph 3.
2. Natural and legal persons shall have the possibility of preventing information lawfully within their control from being disclosed to, acquired by, or used by others without their consent in a manner contrary to honest commercial practices[10] so long as such informa-

---

10. For the purposes of this provision, 'a manner contrary to honest commercial practices' shall mean at least practices such as breach of contract, breach of confidence and inducement to breach, and includes the acquisition of undisclosed information by third parties

tion: (a) is secret in the sense that it is not, as a body or in the precise configuration and assembly of its components, generally known among or readily accessible to persons within the circles that normally deal with the kind of information in question; (b) has commercial value because it is secret; and (c) has been subject to reasonable steps under the circumstances, by the person lawfully in control of the information, to keep it secret.

3. Members, when requiring, as a condition of approving the marketing of pharmaceutical or of agricultural chemical products which utilize new chemical entities, the submission of undisclosed test or other data, the origination of which involves a considerable effort, shall protect such data against unfair commercial use. In addition, Members shall protect such data against disclosure, except where necessary to protect the public, or unless steps are taken to ensure that the data are protected against unfair commercial use.

The North American Free Trade Agreement (NAFTA) to which the United States, Canada, and Mexico are signatories, has a more explicit and detailed set of provisions binding its members to protect trade secrets. Article 1711(1) resembles Article 39(2) of the TRIPS Agreement, except that the NAFTA provision refers to protection of trade secrets as such, not just to protection of undisclosed information. It also regards trade secrecy protection to be available to information with potential, as well as actual, commercial value because it is unknown. Unlike the TRIPS provision, the NAFTA trade secrecy provision does not define "honest commercial practices." Neither agreement makes any explicit reference to reverse engineering as a legitimate way to obtain secret information.

Another noteworthy provision for computer technology is Article 1711(2), which permits NAFTA members to require in their national laws that "a trade secret must be evidenced in documents, electronic or magnetic means, optical discs, microfilms, films or other similar instruments." NAFTA members may not, however, under Article 1711(3) and (4), limit the duration of trade secrecy protection or discourage the voluntary licensing of trade secrets by the imposition of "excessive or discriminatory conditions on such licenses or conditions that dilute the value of the trade secrets."

COMMENTS AND QUESTIONS

1. What does the silence of NAFTA and TRIPS on the question of reverse engineering suggest for the legality of the U.S. reverse engineering exception? Is the exception permissible? Mandatory? Perhaps it could be

---

who knew, or were grossly negligent in failing to know, that such practices were involved in the acquisition.

inferred from language in TRIPS Article 39(2), which would punish only conduct that is "contrary to honest commercial practices." It is, however, worth noting that the new U.S. Economic Espionage Act, 18 U.S.C. §§1831 et seq., does not appear to permit reverse engineering either.

2. Does a trade secret exist in intangible form? Consider DSC v. Brown, a recent U.S. case in which an employer sued an employee who came up with a potentially valuable new idea and refused to disclose it to the company. United States trade secret law has no great difficulty in concluding that Brown had violated his obligation to the company in this situation, assuming the information really is the sort of thing DSC would have a claim to own. But because Brown never wrote the secret down, it is not clear that the case would produce the same result under TRIPS.

B. COPYRIGHT

Today copyright protection for computer programs is universally accepted in the international community, especially after incorporation of this rule in Article 10 of the TRIPS Agreement. This is noteworthy in part because some early legal decisions in the United States and elsewhere questioned the availability of copyright protection for computer programs. See, for example, the Australian case, Apple Computer Inc. v. Computer Edge Pty Ltd., 50 A.L.R. 581 (1983) (no breach of copyright because computer programs were not, under then existing copyright law, protectable "literary works"). During the late 1980s and into the early 1990s, largely at the urging of the U.S. Trade Representative, a trend emerged internationally toward using copyright as the principal form of legal protection for source and object code forms of computer programs. In the early 1980s, however, no clear consensus existed on this subject.

Some countries, notably Brazil, adopted a sui generis form of protection for computer programs. Others, including Japan and the European Economic Community (now the European Union), were considering a sui generis form of protection for programs. Indeed, the World Intellectual Property Organization (WIPO) was among the organizations to propose sui generis legislation for computer programs. By the late 1980s, however, WIPO had backed away from its own proposal and came to favor the copyright approach. Even within nations that did protect programs by means of copyright law, there were variations. France, for example, initially decided to place computer programs (a form, perhaps, of industrial literature) in the same legal category as works of industrial art. Among the implications of this designation was a more limited duration of copyright protection for programs. One notable German case seemed to require almost a patent-like level of creativity before a programmer's work product could qualify for copyright protection.

The decision of the European Commission in 1989 to adopt copyright protection for computer programs turned the international tide in favor of copyright. However, it was not until the 1994 TRIPS Agreement that there was an international treaty explicitly requiring countries to use copyright protection for computer programs. Article 10(1) of the TRIPS Agreement states simply that "[c]omputer programs, whether in source or object code, shall be protected as literary works under the Berne Convention (1971)." A very similar provision appears in Article 4 of the WIPO Copyright Treaty concluded in December 1996: "Computer programs are protected as literary works within the meaning of Article 2 of the Berne Convention [which defines the term 'literary work']. Such protection applies to computer programs, whatever may be the mode or form of their expression."

Even with this harmonization, variations in national laws continue to exist on basic issues regarding computer programs. Some writings may be "computer programs" under European Union (EU) law that would not be classified as such under U.S. law. In the EU, the term "computer program" includes "preparatory design materials," such as flowcharts. Flowcharts do not qualify as "computer programs" under U.S. law, although they may be protectable as pictorial, sculptural, or graphic works. Because of concerns that any specific definition might become technologically outmoded, the EU Directive does not define the term "computer program"; it protects computer programs regardless of their form. United States law, by contrast, defines this term as "a set of statements or instructions to be used, directly or indirectly, to bring about a certain result." 17 U.S.C. §101. Although Japanese copyright law defines "computer program" in a manner similar to U.S. law, Japanese authorities have expressed doubt that microcode programs fall within their statutory definition of "computer program."

While the TRIPS and WIPO Treaty provisions unquestionably require countries to protect the source and object code forms of programs from exact duplication, it is less clear whether these provisions require member or signatory countries to protect the nonliteral elements of programs, such as their structure, sequence, and organization or user interfaces. See, e.g., Charles R. McManis, Taking Trips on the Information Superhighway: International Intellectual Property Protection and Emerging Computer Protection, 41 Vill. L. Rev. 207, 232-251 (1996) (asserting TRIPS does not require copyright to protect structure); Eric Smith, Worldwide Copyright Protection Under the TRIPS Agreement, 29 Vand. J. Trans'l L. 559, 576-577 (1996) (anticipating a successful challenge before the WTO to jurisdictions not protecting structural elements of programs). Both TRIPS and the WIPO Copyright Treaty provide some guidance on scope of protection issues as regards computer programs. Article 9(2) of the TRIPS Agreement states: "Copyright protection shall extend to expressions and not to ideas, procedures, methods of operation, or mathematical concepts as such." The WIPO Copyright Treaty adopted two years later contains a virtually identical rule. Interestingly, this was the first explicit manifestation of the idea-expression distinction in a Berne Convention-related agreement.

Many national laws also contain provisions providing some guidance on scope of protection issues. Article 1(2) of the European Directive on the Legal Protection of Computer Programs states: "Protection in accordance with this Directive shall apply to the expression in any form of a computer program. Ideas and principles which underlie any element of a program, including those that underlie its interfaces, are not protected by copyright under this Directive." The Recitals of the Directive also indicate that "in accordance with this principle of copyright, to the extent that logic, algorithms, and programming languages comprise ideas and principles, those ideas and principles are not protected under this Directive." Recitals do not have the same authority as the black-letter provision of a Directive, but they provide some guidance about the intended interpretation to be given to any provision to which the Recital pertains.

Perhaps the most elaborate statutory statement on scope of protection issues can be found in Article 7 of China's regulations for the protection of computer software. It states that "[t]he protection provided to software under these regulations cannot be expanded to encompass the ideas, concepts, discoveries, principles, algorithms, processing methods and operations used in the development of software." In addition, Article 31 states that "[r]esulting similarities between software developed and software already in existence does not constitute a violation of the copyright of existing software in the following situations: (1) Because it is necessary for the execution of national policies, laws, and rules and regulations; (2) Because it is necessary for the setting of technical standards; (3) Because of the limited categories of forms of expression."

In keeping with their obligations under the Berne Convention (which establishes minimum standards for national copyright laws), most countries provide the owners of copyrights in computer programs with exclusive rights to reproduce the software, to make derivative works or adaptations of the software, and to control distribution of copies. Article 9(1) of the TRIPS Agreement incorporates the pertinent exclusive rights provisions of the Berne Convention and establishes them as minimum standards for the national laws of WTO members.

COMMENTS AND QUESTIONS

1. How similar or different would you expect interpretations to be of the exclusion from protection provisions found in both the TRIPS agreement and the WIPO Copyright Treaty? What significance should be attached to the "as such" language in the exclusion (i.e., that copyright shall not extend to ideas, etc. "as such")? Does this imply that ideas, processes, and the like *may* be protected by copyright under some circumstances?

How do these provisions compare with those in the European Directive and the Chinese software regulations?

2. How would you predict U.S. courts would treat program elements "necessary for the setting of technical standards," which are excluded from protection under Chinese law?

Further detail about copyright protection for computer programs under national laws outside the United States is presented in the subsections that follow. The first concerns copyright protection in Japan, the second considers the same legal protection in Europe, and the third provides a look at Australian software copyright law.

1. Copyright Protection for Computer Programs in Japan

Japan is one of the principal markets for computer software. Although there has sometimes been tension between the United States and Japan over the adequacy of legal protection of computer programs under Japanese law, these tensions are in abeyance. While Japanese copyright law clearly protects the source and object code forms of programs, it is somewhat unclear to what extent copyright protection is available for nonliteral elements of computer programs. This is mainly because Japanese law limits the scope of copyright protection in programs to a considerable degree. Article 10(3) of Japan's copyright law states that copyright protection for computer programs "shall not extend to any programming language, rule or algorithm used for making such work." This provision defines these terms as follows: "(i) 'programming language' means letters and other symbols as well as their systems for use as a means of expressing a program; (ii) 'rule' means a special rule on how to use in a particular program a programming language mentioned in the preceding item; (iii) 'algorithm' means methods of combining, in a program, instructions given to a computer." For further discussion of this provision of Japanese law and its implications for the scope of copyright protection in Japan, see Dennis S. Karjala, The Protection of Operating Software Under Japanese Law, 12 E.I.P.R. 359 (1988).

There has been relatively little litigation in Japan interpreting copyright law as applied to computer programs. ICM Corp. v. Met's, Inc.[7] is one of the few reported cases with an appellate ruling. This decision is discussed at length in the excerpt that appears below.

---

7. Toyko Dist. Ct. (Civ. Div. No. 29) Decision of 27 Feb. 1991, Heisei 1 (yo) no. 2577, *aff'd,* Tokyo High Court Decision of 31 March 1992. Karjala's article relies on an unpublished English translation of the ICM decision by Edward G. Durney.

Dennis S. Karjala, Programs and Data Files Under Japanese Law
[1993] Eur. Intell. Prop. Rev.

Facts of the Case and the Lower Court Decision

The petitioners in *ICM* held the copyright in a utility program called 'EO System', written in assembly language, that worked in conjunction with the MS-DOS operating system to help users in the hard disk installation and file management of some 81 selected application programs. EO System comprised a number of programs, including a main driver program written in assembly language called 'MENU.EXE' as well as the software at issue in the case, called 'IBF Files'.

IBF Files was a collection of 81 distinguishable pieces (files), one for each of the application programs that EO System was designed to install and manage. Each of the files included in IBF Files had the same overall format or structure and carried information or commands enabling MENU.EXE to carry out the function of installing the particular application program represented by that file. For example, there was an ID Line permitting MENU.EXE to recognise the file as one belonging to EO System, a Title Line identifying the application program covered by the file, a Command Line containing the command used to start the application program and allowing MENU.EXE to create an automatically executable batch file for that purpose with the correct parameters, a Message Line that would appear verbatim on the screen instructing the user to insert the application program floppy disk, and an Installation Sequence Line telling MENU.EXE the order in which to install application program files.

The respondents in the action offered a similar utility system covering, among others, some 42 of the 81 application programs handled by the petitioners' EO System. The respondents' main driver program was called 'MFD.EXE', written in the 'C' language, and the functional equivalent of IBF Files in the respondents' system was called 'HCA Files'. Although the petitioners argued that the respondents' overall system had the same functional objectives and similar operating characteristics as EO System, with almost identical program file composition and structure, their formal claim was only that HCA Files was copied from IBF Files, based on an asserted near one-to-one correspondence between the two works.

The issue of whether the IBF Files constituted programs was argued in the district court, but the judge elected not to decide it. Rather, based on the assumption that they did constitute programs, the Court denied relief on the ground that they nevertheless failed to qualify for copyright protection under the JCL because they lacked the statutorily required creativity.

The district court first determined that the overall structure of the individual IBF Files was unprotected because (1) it comprised a format or grammar excluded from protection by the 'programming languages' limitation of the JCL, and because (2) the format of the IBF Files was constrained by MENU.EXE. The Court next found that the content of the individual IBF Files also lacked creativity because such content was largely constrained either by MENU.EXE (such as the ID Line) or the application program (such as the Title Line) for each file, so there was no room for choice. The Court found some slight degree of freedom available in choosing the installation sequence of files from the application program being installed and in the message on the Installation Message Line, but concluded that the range of selection was too small to permit a finding of statutory creativity. Moreover, while admitting that there was some freedom of choice in determining which and how many application programs EO System should cover, the Court concluded that such a choice amounted to no more than an idea, and ideas cannot supply the expressive creativity required by the statute.

The Tokyo High Court Decision

The High Court opinion addresses the threshold issue whether IBF Files was [sic], in fact, a program within statutory definition. (Given its negative resolution of that question, the Court did not address any further issues.) Quite properly, the Court began with the statutory definition itself:

"Program" means a combination of instructions causing a computer to function so as to achieve a certain result.

The decision focuses strongly on the word 'instructions' in this definition in formulating its test for what constitutes a computer program:

[A] program under the Copyright Law must be a set of instructions for a computer that cause the computer to effect a specific process. . . .

Therefore, even where something is recorded electromagnetically in a storage medium as an electronic file that can be read by a computer, it is not a program if it does not carry out the above function.

In processing a program on a computer, one effects a specific process through calls on given programs in the system, and for this purpose, in addition to the program, data giving processing information are necessary, but for reasons of efficiency data are often kept in files separate from the main program. In these circumstances, the data file is read by the program and processed by the computer, but it cannot be said to include sets of instructions for the computer, and therefore it is not a program under the Copyright Law. Of course, when different files are used, the processing result will be different, but that follows from the differences in the data content stored in the files. Clearly we cannot say that the data give instructions to the computer. *Similarly, where data are described by specific symbols or letters ('symbols, etc.') that are defined by the program itself, we might concede that the program will read those symbols, etc., and effect the process contained in their meaning. But even so, this amounts to nothing more than the program's effecting a specific process upon reading the symbols, etc., as data, and we cannot say that the symbols, etc., are instructions for the computer. Therefore, the data contained in the symbols, etc., cannot be said to constitute a program under the Copyright Law* (emphasis added).

In applying its distinction between data files and program files to the IBF Files at issue in the case, the Court first rejected the appellants' (petitioners') argument that the individual IBF Files were batch files, apparently on the superficial ground that they did not employ the '.BAT' extension used by MS-DOS for batch files.

The Court next looked to the content of the individual IBF Files and concluded that they contained nothing more than installation information (name of the application software to be installed, device drivers, and so on) that was simply read by MENU.EXE as data. As a factual matter, it accepted the lower court determination that the role of IBF Files was over once it was read by MENU.EXE. It rejected, as 'clear', that the IBF Files were not ultimately converted into machine language effecting instructions to the computer.

The Court even applies this to the 'COPY', '!' and '?' symbols mutually employed by IBF Files and MENU.EXE:

> The 'COPY' used by IBF Files employs identical characters as the MS-DOS command 'COPY', but those characters are simply defined by the MENU. EXE program. They are character information read by the MENU.EXE program not a command causing a computer to operate. The symbols '!', '?', etc., are similar. They are simply defined by the MENU.EXE program and are nothing more than symbols that can be understood solely by that program.
>
> . . . [E]ven if we concede that, when a program processes data, the program processing will vary depending on the content of the symbols, etc., that is something that is determined by the program itself. The symbols, etc., and combinations do not function as commands; it is simply a question of the method of entering data defined by the program. The commands that appellants assert are uniquely valid for functioning with EO System, too, are simply entered according to the demands of the MENU.EXE program and are nothing more than symbols, etc., to be read as data by it. In other words, program means the descriptive expression based on combinations of instructions to cause a computer to function so as to achieve a particular result. The descriptive content of IBF Files is similar to the descriptive format of the MS-DOS start command, or 'DEVICE=' setting, or 'COPY' command, but in EO System they are no more than data. They do not cause a computer to function, so they do not have the characteristics of a program.

. . . Conclusion

The Tokyo High Court in the *ICM* case appears to have arrived at the correct result on the facts but on erroneous reasoning. Its conclusion that data files are not protected as computer programs, while technically finding justification in the specific language of the JCL, leaves such files vulnerable to slavish electronic copying as databases that show no creativity in selection or arrangement. A better approach may be to treat data files as potentially protected elements of programs but to ensure that protection is limited to unfair extraction of their content and does not extend to functional, efficient, standard or obvious aspects of their formats or to aspects in which industry or user standardisation is desirable.

COMMENTS AND QUESTIONS

1. How would the *ICM* case have been decided under U.S. copyright law? How would the analysis in an American court decision have differed from that of the Tokyo High Court?

2. How similar or different is the Japanese scope of protection provision from section 102(b) of U.S. copyright law, from the European Directive's provision, and from the Chinese scope of protection rule? Is it consistent with Article 9(2) of the TRIPS Agreement?

3. One of the stress points between the United States and Japan has concerned the decompilation of computer programs. When Japan proposed adoption of an explicit decompilation privilege in its copyright law (akin to that adopted in Europe, on which more below), some U.S. officials objected strenuously. Japanese officials eventually decided not to move forward with this initiative, but some commentators nevertheless believe that decompilation for purposes of interoperability is lawful in Japan. For a historical overview of divergent viewpoints on this issue, see Jonathan Band and Masanobu Katoh, Interfaces on Trial: Intellectual Property and Interoperability in the Global Software Industry (1995).

2. The European Union and Its Member States

The market for computer technology in Europe is strong, and, as one might expect, the legal protection environment is also strong. The most important development in European copyright law as applied to computer programs has undoubtedly been the adoption of the Council Directive on the Legal Protection of Computer Programs, 91/250, 1991 O.J. (L122) 42. Several provisions of this Directive appear below. However, even before the Directive took effect, courts in Europe found little difficulty in applying copyright protection to computer programs. It is difficult, in view of the paucity of European case law, to state with a great deal of confidence how broad or narrow copyright protection for computer programs is likely to be in Europe. There, as here, commentators disagree on some important scope of protection issues. However, the *Ibcos* case, which arose under U.K. copyright law prior to the U.K.'s implementation of the European Directive, provides a glimpse of a different approach to applying copyright law to computer programs than that which currently prevails in the United States.

IBCOS Computers Ltd. v. Barclay's Mercantile Highland Finance Ltd.
Chancery Division, United Kingdom
[1994] F.S.R. 275

[A programmer named Poole developed a suite of programs for license to an agricultural business owned by Clayton. Poole and Clayton formed a company, PK Ltd., to further develop and market this suite of programs under the name ADS. When Poole left this firm, Clayton insisted on Poole's agreement that the firm owned the copyright in ADS and further insisted on a restrictive covenant limiting Poole's ability to sell a similar comprehensive set of programs or be employed by another company intending to develop such software for two years. Poole developed a competing program, Unicorn, in his spare time and, after the expiration of the two-year restriction, undertook to distribute Unicorn through Highland. Ibcos, the successor to PK Ltd.'s interest in the software, sued Poole and Highland for copyright infringement.]

Was There Copying?

For infringement there must be copying. Whether there was or not is a question of fact. To prove copying the plaintiff can normally do no more than point to bits of his work and the defendant's work which are the same and prove an opportunity of access to his work. If the resemblance is sufficiently great then the court will draw an inference of copying. It may then be possible for the defendant to rebut the inference—to explain the similarities in some other way. For instance, he may be able to show both parties derived the similar bits from some third party or material in the public domain. Or he may be able to show that the similarity arises out of a functional necessity—that anyone doing this particular job would be likely to come up with similar bits. So much is common ground between the parties. The concept of sufficient similarities shifting the onus onto the defendant to prove non-copying is well recognised in copyright law. . . .

It should be noted that at this stage (namely "Was there copying?") both the important and the unimportant bits of the works being compared count. Indeed it is often identity of trivial matter which traps a copyist. As Hoffmann J observed in Billhofer Maschinenfabrik GmbH v Dixon & Co Ltd ([1990] FSR 105 at 123.):

It is the resemblances in inessentials, the small, redundant, even mistaken elements of the copyright work which carry the greatest weight. This is because they are least likely to have been the result of independent design.

What then is the position here? Is there an inference of copying? I have no doubt that there is. It is overwhelming. There are bits of ADS in Unicorn which cannot really be explained in any other way. It would be burdensome in this judgment to set out all the similarities which raise the inference. They were all well identified in Mr Turner's report for the plaintiffs before the trial began. I find it surprising that the defendant's experts did not seem to have addressed or faced up to these resemblances. Only at moments in the witness box did Mr Kenny (the better of the defendants' experts) seem to recognise that there were real difficulties in the way of a case of independent design.

I must set out some of the key items.

(a) *Common Spelling Mistakes*

Computer programs are inherently less tolerant of spelling mistakes than ordinary literary works. Normally only in comments can they appear without affecting the working of the program. And comments are apt to be short and limited in number, so there is limited material in which misspellings can occur. However in both ADS and Unicorn there are significant spelling mistakes in the comments. The words of particular interest are, "Alpfa," "PIONT," "Didgit," "NUMREIC," "detached," "Channal" and "Shedule." I have set out the words as they are used, namely where capitals are used and where lower case are used. These words appear in identical comments in both programs. To be more precise they appear in different programs within each suite of programs. Moreover each of those words is correctly spelt in a number of different places in other parts of each program, as Mr Howe's search program was able to reveal with ease.

I am quite incapable of believing that this is all due to coincidence or due to the fact that Mr Poole has difficulty in spelling (which seems to be the case). If the latter was the explanation then why are the words spelt correctly many times in other places? And why are the errors always in the same place? It will be recalled that if there is disk-to-disk copying then this kind of thing will be copied accurately. Only disk-to-disk copying from ADS can explain the identity of these misspelled words.

(b) *Headings*

Then there are the identical comment headings. A document called X11 conveniently shows a series of headings in comments which are the same in an important program of ADS (SKPER, for manufacturers' prices of spare parts) and the corresponding program in Unicorn (PAMUPP). For instance the word FORD is presented in a comment in both programs with 23 hyphens to the left and 30 to the right. Likewise the words INTERNA-TIONAL HARVESTER are presented with 21 hyphens to the left and 13 to the right. An explanation for this was suggested by counsel for Mr Poole in his re-examination. The idea was that a line of 60 hyphens was copied into a fresh line and then the name of the part manufacturer was typed over some of the hyphens. Mr Poole seemed keen to accept this explanation. It will not wash. First that does not explain the identical positioning of the manufacturers' names (no less than six in identical not quite alphabetical order). Secondly, the last two manufacturers have a missing hyphen at the end in both sets of programs which cannot be explained by sticking down 60 hyphens and overtyping. Thirdly, Mr Poole's evidence was that he added the manufacturers to Unicorn as and when he needed. However at the time when the plaintiffs obtained a copy of Unicorn pursuant to the 1989 delivery-up order he had not got customers who were dealers with some of the manufacturers to be found in PAMUPP.

I was also unhappy about his explanation of how he got any of the information as to manufacturers' price tape formats. It seemed to me that after the event a story was being concocted.

It is not only in this pair of programs where there are headings that are the same. For example in one place in another ADS program there is a heading, "**DEFFERED ENTRY**" which occurs also in the Unicorn program. Here it is not so much the misspelling which matters (for it seems Mr Poole regularly misspells "defer") as the surrounding **'s. This is atypical of the headings in either program. . . .

(e) Redundant and Unexplained Code in Both Programs

It is not only comments, labels and names which are involved in identity. There are bits of ADS and Unicorn in the program code which were also identical. These too would be copied by disk-to-disk copying. It would technically not matter if they were redundant codes or if they had a purpose in ADS and were redundant in Unicorn. But their presence would betray copying. The difficulty from Mr Poole's point of view is that those portions of code are in Unicorn at all. For if he was genuinely writing it from scratch one would not expect redundant code at all. That is the sort of thing that arises when a program is first written and then modified as time goes on. One would certainly not at all expect identical pieces of redundant code in Unicorn and ADS or bits of redundant code in Unicorn which had a function in ADS. Yet that is what we find here.

(f) Other Matter

One could go on with this list of detailed similarities. . . .

The upshot of all this is that the similarities between the two programs can only have resulted from disk to disk copying. The statistical chance of these resemblances occurring twice in the two programs must be infinitesimal. I say this bearing well in mind that many many lines in the two suites of programs are not the same. I am not prepared to accept that there was a fluke upon a fluke upon a fluke to the nth power. Nor can I understand why the defendants' experts did not see these details as overwhelming indicia of copying. They seem not to have focused on this aspect of the case at all. . . .

There is a danger in jumping from a conclusion that there was copying to a conclusion that a substantial part of a work has been taken. It is all too easy to say that a defendant who has lied about copying must have taken a lot. Of course it is likely in most cases that this is so. But the court must always go on to look at the further question of whether a substantial part was copied. In relation to conventional kinds of work this it can do reasonably readily. Even in the case of technical drawings it is possible to examine the parties' drawings to see whether a substantial part of the plaintiff's work is to be found in the defendant's. A good example of the right way to go about the problem is the *Billhofer* case. Even though there was copying (betrayed by the inessential details) there was no taking of sufficient visual features of the copyright drawing. In a computer program case, however, the court cannot so readily assess the question of substantial part unaided by expert evidence. I believe I should therefore be largely guided by such evidence. . . .

It is of course possible for two programs to be similar as a result of mere style. Such was the case of a minor program within Unicorn written not by Mr Poole but by one Joy Masters who had learned programming with Mr Poole at Supaflo many years earlier. In the case of Mr Poole's programs however the question is not whether the similarities could have arisen by reason of style and programming habits, but did they? Mr Poole was capable of producing something like Unicorn independently (though probably not in the time-frame within which it was done). He is manifestly good at programming. His skill in producing both ADS and Unicorn shows this. Unicorn is undoubtedly to the user a much friendlier program than ADS was at the time (it has now been much enhanced I understand). It has got convenient cursor movements, colour, error correction and so on, all absent from ADS as I was shown. Users doubtless think of the programs as very different because they present differently. Indeed Mr Dance, a customer, told me that was so in his case. But I think Mr Poole was taking short-cuts by starting with ADS and making considerable additions and modifications. Unicorn is a major enhancement of ADS, not a wholly independent creation. Given his failure to be "frank and candid" I think the proper inference is that the similarities identified by Mr Turner and not explained by independent evidence are due to copying. That is the guide by which I think it right to judge the question of whether a substantial part was taken. I turn to Mr Turner's similarities.

"Substantial Part": Program Structure

Under the head "program structure" Mr Turner has identified individual programs in each package which correspond. The correspondence is very close, though there are some cases where an individual Unicorn program corresponds to two or three ADS programs. Now is the compilation of ADS programs a copyright work in itself? True it is that most if not all of the functions achieved by these programs would have to be implemented by an independent programmer. But it by no means follows that he would achieve those functions by the same set of programs. As Mr Turner observes:

> The architect and designer of a software package has considerable freedom to decide how such functionality [ie of the program at system module level] is to be implemented.

I think that the putting together of the various programs in ADS, by a kind of organic growth over the years, did result in a copyright work. I of course bear in mind that within the set are some self evident programs (eg open printer) but the putting together of the whole package involved considerable skill and labour.

Was that copyright infringed? I think it was. It is true that in some cases several ADS programs have been combined into one (explicable by the improvements in hardware which make this possible) and that Unicorn has added to it many further programs which have no ADS equivalent as is shown by a list made by Mr Poole's solicitor. But I think Mr Poole took as his starting point the ADS set and that set remains substantially in Unicorn.

I should mention another level at which Mr Turner considered similarities, namely that of "design feature." He pointed out that both programs had the following identities:

— nine levels of security;
— a unique ability to create different invoice types (Mr Kenny suggested this was not unique but I was not convinced he understood what was being talked about);
— an internal sales system within the ordinary sales ledger package;
— month end sales audit combined with VAT;
— 22 character parts description;
— use of 3 separate programs for the stock ordering facility;
— 12 labour rates;
— 5 levels of sub-totalling;
— audit report by posting in identical form;
— automatic check on depreciation;
— holiday stamp facility (wholly inappropriate for an agricultural dealer. It was only in ADS as a historical accident).

Now these matters may well have arisen as a result of copying. I rather think they were. I found, for instance, Mr Poole's explanation of why there was a holiday stamp feature in Unicorn unconvincing. He said that he felt he had to have the facility as a sales point against ADS. But since no customer could conceivably want this it is a rotten sales point. One might as well put in a cube root facility. But I do not regard these matters as themselves constituting a copyright compilation. They are features of the package of interest to the customers and no more. We are here at a level of generality where there is little of the programmer's skill, labour and judgment. Even if the set were copyright, the mere taking of those functions would not be an infringement—it would be the taking of a mere general idea or scheme. . . .

Unicorn 2

This is a further revision of Unicorn issued in 1993. Many of the literal similarities which were present in Unicorn have disappeared. There has been a considerable cleaning up of comments. Mr Turner in an un-crossexamined further report concluded:

> In this brief examination into whether the literal similarities between the ADS and Unicorn software packages identified in [his earlier report] also exist in [Unicorn 2] no clear pattern has emerged. At one extreme many similarities no longer exist and original work has obviously been done to create an alternative solution. At the other, some similarities still exist intact, and no attempt has been made to create an alternative, original solution. Between the two extremes I have found a complete spectrum of cases including many instances of minimal cosmetic changes.

Plainly Unicorn 2 was made starting from Unicorn.

Mr Turner has considered whether the literal similarities in his 49 examples are present still in Unicorn 2 and has concluded that many are not. I do not have much detail on the evidence and in the circumstances I find myself in considerable difficulty in deciding one way or the other whether what remains in Unicorn is or is not a substantial part of an ADS copyright work. I do not propose to find infringement of matter I have been unable to consider in detail. However where Mr Turner has given unchallenged evidence that there has been virtually no change, or that changes were merely cosmetic, I accept that evidence. On that basis I hold that the following programs of Unicorn 2 infringe: TAX, MESS, NOMCBS, DATST, PRINT, PAMUPP, ASSAPM, PAYDIN, CUSCSH, PAYNAL, NAREC.

The overall structure remains virtually unchanged. Mr Turner says so. The copyright in ADS as a whole is likewise infringed.

COMMENTS AND QUESTIONS

1. The facts of *Ibcos* overwhelmingly suggest copyright infringement. In dictum, however, the court went on to sketch a vision of U.K. copyright law that is fundamentally different from the U.S. approach. In the excerpt that follows, the court suggests some truly radical differences between U.S. and U.K. law:

It was sometimes suggested in a general sort of way that because a particular program had a function, and especially if that function could only be achieved in one or a limited number of ways, there could be no copyright in it. The extreme form of this idea is expressed by Judge Baker in the *Total* case. He said:

> Secondly, stemming from the principle that copyright does not exist in ideas but in the expression of them is the line of authorities commencing with Kenrick v Lawrence that if there is only one way of expressing an idea that way is not the subject of copyright.

That statement is in error in two ways. First, *Kenrick* (the case about a drawing of a hand showing voters which way to vote on a voting slip) did not decide that if there is only one way of expressing an idea no copyright can subsist in it. What was held was that there was no copyright infringement in taking the idea of using a picture of a hand showing how to vote. Accordingly a different picture embodying the same idea was not a taking of a substantial part of the copyright work. In that sense only the principle that there is no copyright in an idea applied.

Secondly there is, I think, danger in the proposition that, "If there is only one way of expressing an idea that way is not the subject of copyright." As Lord Hailsham observed in LB Plastics v Swish ([1979] RPC 551):

> But of course as the late Professor Joad used to observe it all depends on what you mean by "ideas." What the respondents in fact copied from the appellants was no mere general idea.

It is of course true that copyright cannot protect any sort of general principle, such as the principle of drawing a hand to show how to vote, but it can protect a detailed literary or artistic expression. Thus in the case of an exhaust pipe it was said that the copyright was protecting the engineering principles which went into its design. Nevertheless there was copyright in the drawing and the copying of the drawing (via the medium of an exhaust pipe made from it) amounted to an infringement. This was so even though there was also a copying of the engineering principles that went into the original design. Thus Oliver LJ said in British Leyland v Armstrong ([1986] RPC 279 at 296):

> What the plaintiffs seek to protect is not the idea of an exhaust system, but their monopoly in the drawings of this particular exhaust system, the salient feature of which is the flow-line into which months of research have gone, and for the embodiment of which the drawings, taken together, form a complete set of working instructions.

The question in every case is no doubt, whether a given three-dimensional object "reproduces" the substance of the two-dimensional drawing or drawings, but I can see nothing in the Act which justifies a distinction being drawn, so far as the ambit of "reproduction" is concerned, between drawings which are purely functional, and drawings which have some aesthetic appeal. I can find no context at all for giving the word some different and more extended or restricted meaning according to the intention of the author, or the emotional response of the beholder.

To my mind that passage is inconsistent with Judge Baker's statement, which was not supported by any counsel before me. The true position is that where an "idea" is sufficiently general, then even if an original work embodies it, the mere taking of that idea will not infringe. But if the "idea" is detailed, then there may be infringement. It is a question of degree. The same applies whether the work is functional or not, and whether visual or literary.

It should be noted that the aphorism "there is no copyright in an idea" is likely to lead to confusion of thought. Sometimes it is applied to the question of subsistence of copyright (is there a "work" and if there is, is it "original"?). Sometimes it is applied to the different question of infringement (has a substantial part been taken?). That is not to say that the expression has no use: for instance if all a defendant has done is to copy a general idea then it does not matter whether there is copyright in the plaintiff's work, or whether the plaintiff owns that copyright.

In this context there was some appeal to United States cases on copyright. The fact is that United States copyright law is not the same as ours, particularly in the area of copyright works concerned with functionality and of compilations. The Americans (many would say sensibly) never developed copyright so that functional things like exhaust pipes could not be copied. This is partly due to their statute, which is different from our Act.

Moreover United States case law has, ever since Baker v Selden, been extremely careful to keep copyright out of the functional field, either by saying there is no copyright in, or that copyright cannot be infringed by taking, the functional. In *Baker* a design of ledger sheets which had a particular function was refused copyright. I doubt that would have happened here.

2.   Does the court's distinction between U.S. and U.K. law make sense? Does it explain the radically different vision of copyright law that the court articulates in *Ibcos*? Or has the *Ibcos* court arguably fallen into the same trap as the Third Circuit in Whelan v. Jaslow, in defining copyrightable expression in computer programs in an overbroad and simplistic way simply because the defendant in that case was so obviously guilty?

3.   Consider the implications of a copyright regime like the one the court describes. Copyright could presumably protect all sorts of machines and devices, whether functional or not, by the simple expedient of preventing the copying or use of plans or diagrams of the devices. Wouldn't the result be tremendous overlap between copyright and patent law? Is there anything wrong with such overlap? Have the devices set up in U.S. law to channel protection between copyright and patent worked very well? It should be noted that the U.K. eventually amended its copyright law to overturn the *British Leyland* decision to which Judge Jacob referred in *Ibcos*. However, as with U.S. copyright law, the new English copyright law limits the scope of copyright in drawings of functional designs; that is, copy-

righted drawings cannot be infringed by manufacturing the functional design depicted in the drawing. What implications might this change in English law have for computer programs that, after all, are classified as "literary works"?

4. In contrast to *Ibcos* is Judge Ferris's decision in John Richardson Computers Ltd. v. Flanders, [1993] F.S.R. 497, another pre-Directive U.K. decision. Although finding infringement based on the copying of some details of a computer program in that case, Judge Ferris took note of the Second Circuit decision in Computer Associates, Inc. v. Altai, Inc. and announced that he found nothing in English law that conflicted with the analytic approach of *Altai*. Further, he stated:

> But at the stage at which the substantiality of any copying falls to be assessed in an English case the question which has to be answered, in relation to the originality of the plaintiff's program and the separation of an idea from its expression, is essentially the same question as the United States court was addressing in *Computer Associates*. In my judgment it would be right to adopt a similar approach in England.

In *Ibcos*, Judge Jacobs took issue with Judge Ferris's conclusion, saying:

> For myself I do not find the route of going via United States case law particularly helpful. As I have said, United Kingdom copyright cannot prevent the copying of a mere general idea but can protect the copying of a detailed "idea." It is a question of degree where a good guide is the notion of overborrowing of the skill, labour and judgment which went into the copyright work. Going via the complication of the concept of a "core of protectable expression" merely complicates the matter so far as our law is concerned. It is likely to lead to overcitation of United States authority based on a statute different from ours. In the end the matter must be left to the value judgment of the court.

5. The defendant's explanation for many of the similarities between the two programs was that they resulted from his particular programming style. In light of the details in this case, the argument doesn't seem all that convincing. But it raises a more general issue: to what extent should programmers be able to take their skills, experience, and style to another company? A programmer who writes a program for one company and is then hired to write a similar program for a different company arguably couldn't start from scratch even if she wanted to. Her new program will necessarily look a bit like the old—presumably not at the level of shared typographical errors, but perhaps in sharing structure and even the odd line of code. Is this "copying"? If so, does the law effectively preclude programmers from pursuing their livelihood once they leave their employer?

6. Consider whether the European Directive on the Legal Protection of Computer Programs, which follows, would change the analysis in *Ibcos*.

See generally Pamela Samuelson, Comparing U.S. and E.C. Copyright Protection for Computer Programs: Are They More Different Than They Seem?, 13 J. Law & Comm. 279 (1994).

EC Council Directive on the Legal Protection of Computer Programs
E.C. 91/250, 1991 O.J. (L 122) 42

The Council of the European Communities, having regard to the treaty establishing the European Economic Community and in particular article 100a thereof, having regard to the proposal from the Commission, in cooperation with the European Parliament, having regard to the opinion of the economic and social committee,

whereas computer programs are at present not clearly protected in all member states by existing legislation and such protection, where it exists, has different attributes;

whereas the development of computer programs requires the investment of considerable human, technical and financial resources while computer programs can be copied at a fraction of the cost needed to develop them independently;

whereas computer programs are playing an increasingly important role in a broad range of industries and computer program technology can accordingly be considered as being of fundamental importance for the community's industrial development;

whereas certain differences in the legal protection of computer programs offered by the laws of the member states have direct and negative effects on the functioning of the common market as regards computer programs and such differences could well become greater as member states introduce new legislation on this subject;

whereas existing differences having such effects need to be removed and new ones prevented from arising, while differences not adversely affecting the functioning of the common market to a substantial degree need not be removed or prevented from arising;

whereas the community's legal framework on the protection of computer programs can accordingly in the first instance be limited to establishing that member states should accord protection to computer programs under copyright law as literary works and, further, to establishing who and what should be protected, the exclusive rights on which protected persons should be able to rely in order to authorize or prohibit certain acts and for how long the protection should apply;

whereas, for the purpose of this directive, the term 'computer program' shall include programs in any form, including those which are incorporated into hardware;

whereas this term also includes preparatory design work leading to the development of a computer program provided that the nature of the preparatory work is such that a computer program can result from it at a later stage;

whereas, in respect of the criteria to be applied in determining whether or not a computer program is an original work, no tests as to the qualitative or aesthetic merits of the program should be applied;

whereas the community is fully committed to the promotion of international standardization;

whereas the function of a computer program is to communicate and work together with other components of a computer system and with users and, for this purpose, a logical and, where appropriate, physical interconnection and interaction is required to permit all elements of software and hardware to work with other software and hardware and with users in all the ways in which they are intended to function;

whereas the parts of the program which provide for such interconnection and interaction between elements of software and hardware are generally known as 'interfaces';

whereas this functional interconnection and interaction is generally known as 'interoperability';

whereas such interoperability can be defined as the ability to exchange information and mutually to use the information which has been exchanged;

whereas, for the avoidance of doubt, it has to be made clear that only the expression of a computer program is protected and that ideas and principles which underlie any element of a program, including those which underlie its interfaces, are not protected by copyright under this directive;

whereas, in accordance with this principle of copyright, to the extent that logic, algorithms and programming languages comprise ideas and principles, those ideas and principles are not protected under this directive;

whereas, in accordance with the legislation and jurisprudence of the member states and the international copyright conventions, the expression of those ideas and principles is to be protected by copyright; . . .

whereas the provisions of this directive are without prejudice to the application of the competition rules under articles 85 and 86 of the treaty if a dominant supplier refuses to make information available which is necessary for interoperability as defined in this directive; whereas the provisions of this directive should be without prejudice to specific requirements of community law already enacted in respect of the publication of interfaces in the telecommunications sector or Council decisions relating to standardization in the field of information technology and telecommunication;

whereas this directive does not affect derogations provided for under national legislation in accordance with the Berne Convention on points not covered by this directive,

has adopted this directive:

Article 1   Object of Protection

1. In accordance with the provisions of this directive, member states shall protect computer programs, by copyright, as literary works within the meaning of the Berne Convention for the Protection of Literary and Artistic Works. For the purposes of this directive, the term 'computer programs' shall include their preparatory design material.

2. Protection in accordance with this directive shall apply to the expression in any form of a computer program. Ideas and principles which underlie any element of a computer program, including those which underlie its interfaces, are not protected by copyright under this directive.

3. A computer program shall be protected if it is original in the sense that it is the author's own intellectual creation. No other criteria shall be applied to determine its eligibility for protection.

Article 2   Authorship of Computer Programs

1. The author of a computer program shall be the natural person or group of natural persons who has created the program or, where the legislation of the member state permits, the legal person designated as the rightholder by that legislation. Where collective works are recognized by the legislation of a member state, the person considered by the legislation of the member state to have created the work shall be deemed to be its author.

2. In respect of a computer program created by a group of natural persons jointly, the exclusive rights shall be owned jointly.

3. Where a computer program is created by an employee in the execution of his duties or following the instructions given by his employer, the employer exclusively shall be entitled to exercise all economic rights in the program so created, unless otherwise provided by contract.

Article 3   Beneficiaries of Protection

1. Protection shall be granted to all natural or legal persons eligible under national copyright legislation as applied to literary works.

Article 4   Restricted Acts

1. Subject to the provisions of articles 5 and 6, the exclusive rights of the rightholder within the meaning of article 2, shall include the right to do or to authorize:

(a) the permanent or temporary reproduction of a computer program by any means and in any form, in part or in whole. Insofar as loading, displaying, running, transmission or storage of the computer program necessitate such reproduction, such acts shall be subject to authorization by the rightholder;

(b) the translation, adaptation, arrangement and any other alteration of a computer program and the reproduction of the results thereof, without prejudice to the rights of the person who alters the program;

(c) any form of distribution to the public, including the rental, of the original computer program or of copies thereof.

2. The first sale in the community of a copy of a program by the rightholder or with his consent shall exhaust the distribution right within the community of that copy, with the exception of the right to control further rental of the program or a copy thereof.

Article 5   Exceptions to the Restricted Acts

1. In the absence of specific contractual provisions, the acts referred to in article 4 (a) and (b) shall not require authorization by the rightholder where they are necessary for the use of the computer program by the lawful acquirer in accordance with its intended purpose, including for error correction.

2. The making of a back-up copy by a person having a right to use the computer program may not be prevented by contract insofar as it is necessary for that use.

3. The person having a right to use a copy of a computer program shall be entitled, without the authorization of the rightholder, to observe, study or test the functioning of the program in order to determine the ideas and principles which underlie any element of the program if he does so while performing any of the acts of loading, displaying, running, transmitting or storing the program which he is entitled to do.

Article 6   Decompilation

1. The authorization of the rightholder shall not be required where reproduction of the code and translation of its form within the meaning of article 4 (a) and (b) are indispensable to obtain the information necessary to achieve the interoperability of an independently created computer program with other programs, provided that the following conditions are met:

(a) these acts are performed by the licensee or by another person having a right to use a copy of a program, or on their behalf by a person authorized to do so;

(b) the information necessary to achieve interoperability has not previously been readily available to the persons referred to in subparagraph (a); and

(c) these acts are confined to the parts of the original program which are necessary to achieve interoperability.

2. The provisions of paragraph 1 shall not permit the information obtained through its application:

(a) to be used for goals other than to achieve the interoperability of the independently created computer program;

(b) to be given to others, except when necessary for the interoperability of the independently created computer program; or

(c) to be used for the development, production or marketing of a computer program substantially similar in its expression, or for any other act which infringes copyright.

Article 7 Special Measures of Protection

1. Without prejudice to the provisions of articles 4, 5 and 6, member states shall provide, in accordance with their national legislation, appropriate remedies against a person committing any of the acts listed in subparagraphs (a), (b) and (c) below:

(a) any act of putting into circulation a copy of a computer program knowing, or having reason to believe, that it is an infringing copy;

(b) the possession, for commercial purposes, of a copy of a computer program knowing, or having reason to believe, that it is an infringing copy;

(c) any act of putting into circulation, or the possession for commercial purposes of, any means the sole intended purpose of which is to facilitate the unauthorized removal or circumvention of any technical device which may have been applied to protect a computer program.

2. Any infringing copy of a computer program shall be liable to seizure in accordance with the legislation of the member state concerned.

3. Member states may provide for the seizure of any means referred to in paragraph 1 (c).

Article 8 Term of Protection

1. Protection shall be granted for the life of the author and for fifty years after his death or after the death of the last surviving author; where the computer program is an anonymous or pseudonymous work, or where a legal person is designated as the author by national legislation in accordance with article 2 (1), the term of protection shall be fifty years from the time that the computer program is first lawfully made available to the public. The term of protection shall be deemed to begin on the first of January of the year following the abovementioned events.

2. Member states which already have a term of protection longer than that provided for in paragraph 1 are allowed to maintain their pre-

sent term until such time as the term of protection for copyright works is harmonized by community law in a more general way.

Article 9   Continued Application of Other Legal Provisions

1. The provisions of this directive shall be without prejudice to any other legal provisions such as those concerning patent rights, trademarks, unfair competition, trade secrets, protection of semi-conductor products or the law of contract. Any contractual provisions contrary to article 6 or to the exceptions provided for in article 5 (2) and (3) shall be null and void.

2. The provisions of this directive shall apply also to programs created before 1 January 1993 without prejudice to any acts concluded and rights acquired before that date.

COMMENTS AND QUESTIONS

1.   The European Directive is far more explicit about some copyright issues in relation to computer programs than is U.S. copyright law. Do these more explicit provisions favor software developers?

2.   What implications should one draw about whether the structure, sequence, and organization of a computer program is protected by copyright from the Directive's characterization of computer programs as "literary works"? What implications might there be for user interface similarities or for "look and feel"?

3.   How would you predict ICM v. Met's would be decided under the Directive or under *Ibcos?*

4.   Some European countries do not have "work made for hire" rules in their copyright laws; they require instead a transfer-of-rights agreement with employees. How does the Directive deal with this matter?

5.   Notice the difference between the European Directive and U.S. law in terms of the exclusive rights conferred on authors. Does the absence of a public performance or display right have any significance?

6.   Compare Article 5's "Exceptions to the Restricted Acts" provision with 17 U.S.C. section 117. How are they similar or different?

7.   How does the decompilation privilege under Article 6 compare with the U.S. ruling in Sega Enterprises v. Altai? It may be worth knowing that the European Council adopted the Directive and its decompilation privilege before there had been a definitive ruling in the United States on the decompilation issue.

8.   The Directive's decompilation privilege under Article 6 is non-waivable by contract. How does this compare to U.S. law?

9.   Continental European law provides protection for the moral rights of authors as well as their economic interests. Notice that the Directive is totally silent on the issue of moral rights. Given the utilitarian nature of

computer programs and given that the texts of computer programs are generally not widely distributed, one might wonder whether authors of computer programs do or should have moral rights to stop customers from modifying their programs. At least one European case has applied moral rights law to programs. See Bodin v. AGOSAP (D. Ct. Paris, France, Jan. 20, 1993) (author of computer program retained moral right of integrity in program; modifying the source code to allow the program to run on a different operating system violated the author's moral rights). Japan, by contrast, has limited moral rights in computer programs in recognition that situations may arise in which users may need to modify computer programs to fix coding errors, make adjustments in its functioning, and the like.

3. Copyright in Computer Programs in Australia

Data Access Corporation v. Powerflex Services Pty Ltd.
High Court of Australia
[1999] H.C.A. 49

. . . Data Access owns the copyright in a system of computer programs which is known as "Dataflex".

. . . It is a system which allows a programmer or developer to develop customised database applications or databases.

The Dataflex system incorporates:

- a program development system, which provides the means to write, edit, compile and run programs under development;
- a computer programming language known as the "Dataflex language", which is an application development language in which the source code for all Dataflex programs is written or generated;
- a compiler program which translates the Dataflex source code programs written in the Dataflex language by using the program development system, into an internal format which is then able to be run by the runtime program; and
- a runtime program, which is the executable program required to run the compiled application programs developed using the program development system.

Mr Cory Casanave, Executive Vice-President of Data Access, gave evidence as to the nature of the language used in computer programs. He said:

A computer language defines the names of each word in the language and the rules governing the use of each word (syntax). Each word in a computer language is an instruction to the computer to invoke lower level proccesses, the word chosen to invoke those processes is generally chosen to suggest the nature of the process that will be invoked.

A computer language is comprised of a set of reserved words which are used in accordance with the rules of syntax governing their use. A computer language syntax, like the syntax of a human language, comprises the rules by which the words can be combined to form statements which are correct for the language. For each command or function there is a specific syntax which describes how arguments may be applied to the command. Arguments can be likened to a noun phrase, they describe what the command will act on. Various documents also refer to 'functions' as well as commands. Functions are a type of command which perform a computation and return a result.

Two hundred and fifty-four words of the Dataflex language are listed in the Dataflex encyclopedia. However, 29 of those words, which express commands for developing graphics, are not used at all in the PFXplus language. Of the other 225, 192 are used in the PFXplus language in a way which eventually causes the computer to perform the same function as those words perform in the Dataflex language.

At first instance, the reasons of Jenkinson J suggest that he considered that copyright subsisted in each of these 192 common words and that the use of them in PFXplus infringed Data Access' copyright in them. However, the orders made by his Honour restrain the use of only 169 of the common words, three of which are "Macros". It may be that, after judgment but before the orders were made, Data Access conceded that the remaining 23 words (which include words such as "SHOW" and "ENTRY") were not protected by copyright. Perhaps a concession was made during argument and, in a complex case, overlooked when the reasons for judgment were being prepared. But whatever the reason for not dealing with these 23 words, the issue of copyright in this Court is confined to the 169 words the subject of the order made by his Honour.

We will deal with the three "Macros" separately from the remaining 166 common words which can conveniently be called the "Reserved Words". Of these Reserved Words, at least 55 are unique to the Dataflex program. But many are ordinary English words—such as "BOX", "CHART", and "RETAIN". Others are a combination of two English words such as "PAGEBREAK". Some are not only common English words but are used in most, if not all, computer programs. Examples are "DIRECTORY" and "SAVE".

The PFXplus System

Some years ago, the third respondent, Dr David Bennett ("Dr Bennett"), became familiar with the Dataflex system. He decided to create and market an application development system which would be compatible with the Dataflex language and the Dataflex database file structure so that persons who were familiar with the Dataflex system would be able to use his new product.

The Full Court of the Federal Court found the following facts to be common ground between the parties to the appeal:

- by a process of reverse engineering and study of both the documentation and operation of the Dataflex system, Dr Bennett created a system of computer programs, which was originally known as "Powerflex", but is now known as "PFXplus", intending that the system would be compatible with the Dataflex system, i.e. that certain commands and "reserved words" (including the Macros) used as commands in the Dataflex system would operate in like manner in the PFXplus system;
- the source code in which the Dataflex system is written is quite different from the source code in which the PFXplus system is written; and
- there is not necessarily any similarity between the object code used in the Dataflex system and that used in the PFXplus system.

PFXplus achieved Dr Bennett's aim of being highly compatible with Dataflex. Dr Bennett and his wife subsequently incorporated a company, the second respondent, to sell PFXplus.

The Issues

The only allegations of copyright infringement that are now in issue are the claims that by publishing PFXplus the respondents have infringed the copyright which Data Access has in:

A. The Reserved Words.
B. The Macros.
C. The Dataflex Huffman compression table, to which reference will later be made.

A. *The Reserved Words*

The appellant contends:

1. Copyright subsists in each of the Reserved Words because each is a "computer program" within the definition in §10(1) of the Act.

2. Copyright subsists in the collocation of the Reserved Words comprising the Dataflex language because this collocation is a "computer program".

3. Alternatively to 2, even if the collocation of Reserved Words is not itself a literary work, it nevertheless forms a substantial part of a literary work (the Dataflex system) so that copying of it is an infringement of the appellant's copyright in the Dataflex system.

4. Copyright subsists in the table or compilation of Reserved Words in the Dataflex User's Guide on the footing that it is a literary work within par (a) of the definition in §10(1) of the Act.

We turn to consider each of these contentions.

1. Is Each of the Reserved Words a "Computer Program" within the Meaning of §10(1) of the Act?

The appellant contends that each of the Reserved Words is itself a "computer program" within the meaning of the definition in §10(1) of the Act. In order to determine the validity of the appellant's submissions, it is convenient to divide the definition of "computer program" into its component parts.

The definition of "computer program" requires that each Reserved Word be:

> (i) "an expression,"
> (ii) "in any language, code or notation,"
> (iii) "of a set of instructions (whether with or without related information)"
> (iv) "intended, either directly or after either or both of the following:
>> (a) conversion to another language, code or notation;
>> (b) reproduction in a different material form; to cause"
> (v) "a device having digital information processing capabilities to perform a particular function."

Each of the first four of these elements qualifies what follows and the scope of the definition is marked out by the requirement of an intention that the device be caused "to perform a particular function". In form, the definition of a computer program seems to have more in common with the subject matter of a patent than a copyright. Inventions when formulated as a manner of new manufacture traditionally fell within the province of patent law, with the scope of the monopoly protection being fixed by the terms of a public document, the patent specification. In Australia claims to computer programs which are novel, not obvious and otherwise satisfy the Patents Act 1990 (Cth) and which have the effect of controlling computers to operate in a particular way, have been held to be proper subject matter for letters patent, as "achieving an end result which is an artificially created state of affairs of utility in the field of economic endeavour", within the meaning of National Research Development Corporation v Commissioner of Patents.

The amendment of the definition of "literary work" in §10(1) of the Act to include as item (b) "a computer program or compilation of computer programs" obviously marked a significant departure from what previously had been the understanding of what was required for subsistence of copyright in an original literary work. It is true that copyright may subsist in a literary work which is related to the exercise of mechanical functions. A set of written instructions for the assembly and operation of a domestic appliance is an example. However, it is not to the point in copyright law that, if followed, the instructions do not cause the appliance to function. The protection of the function performed by the appliance will be for the patent law, including the law as to inutility. This is what was indicated by Bradley J in a passage in Baker v Selden which was repeated by Brennan J in *Computer Edge*. Bradley J said that no one would contend that the exclusive right to the manner of manufacture described in a treatise would be given by the subsistence of copyright in that work, and continued:

> The copyright of the book, if not pirated from other works, would be valid without regard to the novelty, or want of novelty, of its subject-matter. . . . To give to the author of the book an exclusive property in the art described therein, when no examination of its novelty has ever been officially made, would be a surprise and a fraud upon the public. That is the province of letters-patent, not of copyright.

Further, the requirement in copyright law that a work be "original" is to be distinguished from the requirements that an alleged invention be novel and that it not be obvious. The question for copyright law is whether "the work emanates from the person claiming to be its author, in the sense that he has originated it or brought it into existence and has not copied it from another". If so, the work does not lack originality because of the anterior independent work of another, although, in such circumstances, an invention might lack novelty.

Finally, to say that the copyright law does not protect function and extends only to the expression of systems or methods does not deny that a work may serve utilitarian rather than aesthetic ends. A map and a recipe book are obvious examples.

There is, with respect, some oversimplification of these principles in the following statement by Dawson J in Autodesk Inc v Dyason ("*Autodesk No 1*"):

> [W]hen the expression of an idea is inseparable from its function, it forms part of the idea and is not entitled to the protection of copyright.

The 1984 amendment departed from traditional principles by identifying for copyright purposes a species of literary work, the very subsistence of which requires an expression of a set of instructions intended to cause a device to perform a particular function. The difficulties which arise from accommodating computer technology protection to principles of copyright law have been remarked upon but the Act now expressly requires such an accommodation.

In the present case, no question arises with respect to the relationship between the Act and the protection given to the designers of computer chips by the Circuit Layouts Act 1989 (Cth). The first issue in the appeal turns solely on the application of the definition of "computer program" in §10(1) of the Act.

The appellant submits that each Reserved Word meets each component of the definition of "computer program". The appellant contends:

> (i) A Reserved Word itself is identified as being the relevant "expression" for the purposes of the definition. The term "expression" is used in the definition to preserve the distinction between the set of instructions and the manner in which the set is expressed in a particular programming language. The choice of expressions for words and commands in a language is determined by the author of the language.
>
> (ii) Each Reserved Word is in a code or notation, the relevant code or notation being the Dataflex language.
>
> (iii) Each Reserved Word expresses a set of instructions, that set being either the underlying set of instructions in source code, or the meaning and syntax of the word or command in question.
>
> (iv) and (v) Each Reserved Word is in a high level language, and each is intended, after conversion into a lower level language by a compiler and run-time program, to cause a computer (which is a device having digital information processing capabilities) to perform a particular function.

In our opinion, none of the Reserved Words satisfies the statutory definition. Each Reserved Word is undoubtedly in "code or notation"—the Dataflex language. It follows that whether a Reserved Word is a "computer program" within the meaning of the definition depends on whether it is an "expression . . . of a set of instructions . . . intended . . . to cause a device having digital information processing capabilities to perform a particular function". However, each of the Reserved Words is a single word; none is a set of instructions in the Dataflex language. Further, none of the Reserved Words intends to express, directly or indirectly, an algorithmic or logical relationship between the function desired to be performed and the physical capabilities of the "device having digital information processing capabilities".

We turn to explain these conclusions.

The Findings in the Courts Below

The trial judge held that each Reserved Word was itself a computer program. Jenkinson J said:

> Each of the words of the DataFlex language found also in the PFXplus language is in my opinion an expression of a set of instructions intended to cause

a device having digital information processing capabilities to perform a particular function. The circumstance that the expression of those instructions in source code is different is in my opinion immaterial. At the level of abstraction under consideration the objective similarity is complete: the set of instructions intended to cause the performance of the particular function is expressed, at that level where the "language, code or notation" is based upon concatenations of letters of the alphabet, by the same concatenation of letters in each language. If at that level some of the concatenations constitute or resemble words of the English language descriptive or suggestive of the functions to be performed, that may facilitate the use of the computer program by those who understand English. But each concatenation of letters is nonetheless an expression of a set of instructions intended to cause the device to perform a particular function, in my opinion, and therefore a "computer program" within the meaning of that expression in the Copyright Act.

The Full Court came to the opposite conclusion. It said:

Each of the words in the so-called Dataflex language is but a cipher. The underlying program is the set of instructions which directs the computer what to do when that cipher is in fact used, for example by being typed on to the screen. It is not to the point that the cipher bears some resemblance to an ordinary English word. The cipher or command is not an expression of the set of instructions, although it appears in that set of instructions. It is the trigger for the set of instructions to be given effect to by the computer.

It may not be inaccurate to describe each of the commands as itself an instruction. It is likewise not necessarily inaccurate to talk of each of those words as representing the set of instructions in the sense that the use of one of them triggers the instructions contained in the computer program to be acted upon. But it is in our view not accurate to refer to each of the words as being an expression of the set of instructions. The set of instructions is expressed in the source code which is the computer program and, at least at a higher level, includes the particular word which is a command. The computer program will also in other forms exist in lower level language, ultimately through to an object code in nonvisible form. Each of these representations will fall within the definition of "computer program". In each of them, in some language, code or notation, the word said to be part of the computer language will be able to be found.

The passage earlier quoted from the judgment of Gaudron J in *Autodesk*, placing as it does emphasis upon the requirement that it is the set of instructions in their entirety which is the computer program, also points to the conclusion that the individual words of command are not, themselves, computer programs within the definition. . . .

The Relevant "Set of Instructions" Executed by a Computer . . .

It is impossible to overemphasise the importance of the fact that a computer has no "intelligence" to execute instructions over and beyond the simple logical functions which are hard wired into its circuits. In order for the simple logical functions of a computer to translate into a useful result, it is necessary to express complex problems in terms of a sequence of a large number of these simple operations. A "set of instructions" will not cause a computer to execute a particular function unless that set of instructions can be ultimately expressed in terms of a sequence of the logical operations which are hard wired into the computer. No doubt it is very rare to express a complex computer program in terms of the simple logical operations which are hard wired into a computer. That is because the process of writing programs becomes practically unmanageable unless the "set of instructions" is perceived at a high level of abstraction. Such a level of abstraction is required in order to express what are millions of simple logical operations in terms of a manageable number of more complex instructions which themselves are reducible to these simple logical operations. . . .

No doubt, at the highest level of abstraction, the word "PRINT" is an expression of an instruction which is intended to cause a device having digital information processing capabilities to perform a particular function. Thus, at the highest level of abstraction, each of the Reserved Words in Dataflex may likewise be regarded as an expression of an instruction which is intended to cause a device having digital information processing capabilities to perform a particular function.

However, the appellant must show that each Reserved Word is an "expression, in any language, code or notation, of a set of instructions . . . intended, either directly or after . . . conversion to another language, code or notation . . . to cause a device having digital information processing capabilities to perform a particular function".

In order to overcome the difficulty that a Reserved Word is only one instruction in the Dataflex language, the appellant made two related arguments:

- first, that after "conversion to another language, code or notation" (i.e. source code), each Reserved Word is a "set of instructions" in source code and each Reserved Word is therefore the expression, in the Dataflex language, of this underlying set of instructions; and
- second, that each Reserved Word is an expression, in the Dataflex language, of, as the appellant put it, "the meaning and syntax of the word or command in question".

In relation to the first argument, it is true that after a Reserved Word is converted to source code, there is a "set of instructions" in source code.

The question then arises as to the level of abstraction (or in other words, the level of language) at which the appellant must show that the Reserved Word meets the definition of a computer program.

Two Competing Interpretations of "Computer Program"

In our view, there are two competing interpretations of the definition of "computer program" in §10(1) of the Act. The two competing interpretations arise from the effect of the words "in any language, code or notation" and the words "either directly or after . . . conversion to another language, code or notation" in the definition.

On one view, the effect of these words is that, if an item written in language *A* is not an "expression . . . of a set of instructions . . . intended . . . to cause a device having digital information processing capabilities to perform a particular function" in language *A*, but after conversion to language *B* is such an expression of a set of instructions in language *B*, the statutory requirements are met in respect of the expression in both language *A* and language *B*. Thus, the item would be regarded as a "computer program" in both language *A* and language *B*, even though it is only an "expression . . . of a set of instructions . . . intended . . . to cause a device having digital information processing capabilities to perform a particular function" in language *B*.

The second, opposing view is that the requirement that there be an "expression . . . of a set of instructions . . . intended . . . to cause a device having digital information processing capabilities to perform a particular function" is a requirement that must be applied to each new language in which the item may be expressed in order for the item to be a "computer program" in that language. On this view, if an item is not an "expression . . . of a set of instructions . . . intended . . . to cause a device having digital information processing capabilities to perform a particular function" in language *A*, its expression in language *A* is not a computer program, even if, after conversion to language *B*, the item meets the criteria of an "expression . . . of a set of instructions . . . intended . . . to cause a device having digital information processing capabilities to perform a particular function" in language *B*.

On the second view, the question whether an item is an "expression . . . of a set of instructions . . . intended . . . to cause a device having digital information processing capabilities to perform a particular function" must be determined separately for each language in which that item is expressed. The fact that an item meets the criteria of an "expression . . . of a set of instructions . . . intended . . . to cause a device having digital information processing capabilities to perform a particular function" in one language does not automatically mean that the item will meet that criteria in any other language in which that item may be expressed.

In our opinion, the second view is the preferable one. The definition of "computer program" begins with the words "an expression, in any language, code or notation". The phrase relates to a singular expression (the word "an" is used) and the words "any language" envisage that the expression will be in a particular language, whatever that language might be. However, the "expression" must be of a "set of instructions" which has a particular intention.

The meaning of the phrase "expression . . . of a set of instructions" was referred to in the Explanatory Memorandum to the Copyright Amendment Bill 1984:

The phrase "expression . . . of a set of instructions" is intended to make clear that it is not an abstract idea, algorithm or mathematical principle which is protected but rather a particular expression of that abstraction. The word "set" indicates that the instructions are related to one another rather than being a mere collection.

It is the particular selection, ordering, combination and arrangement of instructions within a computer program which provide its expression. A computer program in a particular language may be relatively inefficient because it uses many instructions to achieve the function that a single instruction could achieve. A computer program in a particular language may also operate relatively inefficiently because of the way it is structured, in terms of the ordering of the instructions and the sequence in which they are executed. Considerations of efficiency are largely a function of the particular language which is used. It is the skill of the programmer in a particular language which determines the expression of the program in that language.

The Explanatory Memorandum states that it is a "particular expression" of an abstract idea which is protected. As a particular expression is a function of the language of the expression, whether a word or words is or are a relevant expression of a set of instructions needs to be asked separately for each language in which there is purportedly a set of instructions.

For an item to be a computer program, it must not only be an "expression . . . of a set of instructions", but the expression of that set of instructions must also be designed to achieve a particular purpose. That is to say, it must be "intended . . . to cause a device having digital information processing capabilities to perform a particular function". The emphasis on a singular function in the phrase "a particular function" indicates that it is necessary to identify precisely the relevant function.

As we have already indicated, the only operations which a computer is physically capable of performing are those logic operations which are hard wired into its circuits. This physical limitation manifests itself at every level of computer programming, at different levels of abstraction. At the lowest level, when programming in object code, the limitation is perhaps most evident. That is because the computer program is written in terms which are closely related to physical events within the processor and memory of the computer. In higher level languages, the physical limitations of the computer manifest themselves to a programmer in a more subtle way. In the particular language in which a programmer is working, there is a limited set of commands which can be used. Each of these commands has its own syntactical and grammatical rules which must be followed in order for the command to be successfully recognised by the compiler program which converts the commands into object code. This is because each command in the high level language is nothing more than a "pre-packaged set" of sequences of the logic operations which the computer is capable of performing. The compiler program, upon reading a command, merely opens the pre-packaged set and launches the corresponding logic operations which the computer is capable of performing. If a set of instructions in a high level language is intended to cause a computer to perform a particular function, it is an expression which intends to express an algorithmic or logical relationship between the desired function and the physical capabilities of the computer, albeit indirectly. Owing to programming errors, or what are commonly called "bugs", it may not actually do so. The presence of "bugs" in a computer program, however, does not disentitle it to copyright protection, because as the Explanatory Memorandum stated:

> The phrase "intended . . . to cause" is used in preference to words such as "capable . . . of causing" to cover the situation where the program, as written, may not operate for technical reasons such as the presence of a programming error.

It is the ability to express in a computer language an algorithmic or logical relationship between an identifiable function which is desired to be performed and the physical capabilities of the computer, which is the true skill of the programmer. This remains true even if the programmer is working via the medium of a high level language and is unaware of the physical capabilities of the computer. It is the expression of this skill which is intended to be protected by the Act.

In our opinion, the foregoing conclusion also explains the reference in the definition of "computer program" to "a set of instructions (whether with or without any related information)". The Explanatory Memorandum stated:

> The phrase "whether with or without related information" is intended to make clear that the protected program may include material other than instructions for the computer (such as information for programmers or users of the program, or data to be used in connection with the execution of the program).

The distinction between "data" or "related information" on the one hand and "instructions for the computer" on the other indicates that Parliament has conceived of a "set of instructions" that are truly "instructions for the computer" in the sense that they are referable to the computer's physical capabilities. The inclusion in the definition of "computer program" of the words "(whether with or without related information)", in parenthesis, effected the legislative intent that the inclusion of "related information" within the "expression . . . of a set of instructions" would not take that expression outside the definition. "Data" or "related information" is that part of the computer program which is not in any sense referable to the computer's physical capabilities. The examples given in the Explanatory Memorandum indicate that it may be a wide category. It is unnecessary to consider what may constitute "information" which is not "related information", a matter removed from the task of construing the phrase "set of instructions".

In our opinion, whether what is claimed to be a "computer program" is an "expression . . . of a set of instructions . . . intended . . . to cause a device having digital information processing capabilities to perform a particular function" must be answered separately for each language in which the item in question is said to be a computer program.

Moreover, something is not a "computer program" within the meaning of the definition in §10(1) unless it intends to express, either directly or indirectly, an algorithmic or logical relationship between the function desired to be performed and the physical capabilities of the "device having digital information processing capabilities". Thus, in the sense employed by the definition, a program in object code causes a device to perform a particular function "directly" when executed. A program in source code does so "after . . . conversion to another language, code or notation".

Some support, by way of analogy, may be derived from considering the position in the United States. In Baystate Technologies Inc v Bentley Systems Inc, it was held that whilst the computer program comprising "CADKEY" was protected, the particular "data structures" with which the case was concerned "[did] not bring about any result on their own", so that they were protected, if at all, only as part of the whole computer program. This was because, as was later expressed in the judgment: "a computer cannot read data structures and perform any function".

Once these principles are applied to each Reserved Word in the Dataflex language, it is clear that they are not "computer programs". Each Reserved Word comprises but a single instruction in that language. Each Reserved Word, considered alone, is not a "set of instructions" in that language. It is not a "computer program" expressed in the Dataflex language.

Meaning and Syntax

There remains to be addressed the further argument of the appellant that the relevant set of instructions at the level of the Dataflex language is the "meaning and syntax of the word or command in question". In response to questions from members of this Court during the argument of the appeal, counsel for the appellant was asked on a number of occasions to identify the relevant "set of instructions". His answer was that it was the "meaning and syntax of the word or command in question".

However, the function which will be executed by a particular Reserved Word depends entirely on the source code underlying the Reserved Word. Thus, its "meaning" depends on the source code underlying it. This is also the case with the "syntax". There are, of course, grammatical and syntactical rules for the use of the Reserved Words. These rules would be written in the source code underlying the Dataflex commands. Equivalent rules would be written in the source code underlying the PFXplus commands. The meaning of the Reserved Words, and the grammatical and syntactical rules for their use, are not an "expression" until they are reduced to the underlying source code. However, the appellant does not, and could not, contend that Dr Bennett's source code expression of the meaning of commands or of the grammatical and syntactical rules in PFXplus is a reproduction of the source code expression of those meanings or rules in the Dataflex language. There was a finding that the source code of PFXplus was dissimilar to the source code of Dataflex.

Furthermore, as the Full Court of the Federal Court pointed out:

> It goes without saying that, but for ease of usage, the precise words used in a particular computer language are irrelevant. A particular program could use the letters "XZB", or any other combination of letters or symbols, so that when the computer was confronted with those letters it would perform a particular set of instructions, for example, displaying a particular item in a particular database. The use of a string of letters forming an English word such as "display" will, however, more easily be recalled and reproduced by the user than will a meaningless combination to that user.

Thus, from the computer's perspective, any of the Reserved Words in the Dataflex language could have been replaced with any other word or string of characters. If it had, the same function would have been performed provided the necessary modifications were made to the compiler and run-time programs. In our opinion, this shows that the particular characters of a Reserved Word in the Dataflex language, considered alone, do not intend to express a logical or algorithmic relationship between the function it intends to cause the computer to perform and the physical capabilities of the computer.

It is true that, from the user's perspective, the particular words chosen allow for ease of use. No doubt this explains the focus in the appellant's submissions on the "meaning" of a Reserved Word. However, ease of use is an intended function which the author of the Reserved Words had in relation to the user. It is not an intended function which the author of the Reserved Words had in relation to the computer. The definition of a computer program requires that the intention be in relation to the performance of a particular function by the computer.

It is true that in any high level language, the particular commands might be replaced with any other string of characters and necessary modifications made to the compiler program. But that does not mean that nothing expressed in a high level language could ever be a computer program. Once more than one instruction is expressed in a high level language with the intention that the expression will, after conversion to object code, cause a computer to perform a particular function, there will ordinarily be a computer program for the purposes of the Act. The choice and interrelationship of the particular instructions used and their sequence and structure will ordinarily constitute the expression of a logical or algorithmic relationship between the function intended to be performed and the physical capabilities of the computer.

The conclusion that the Reserved Words themselves are not a computer program in Dataflex does not mean that their expression in source code and object code is not a computer program. As the Full Court stated, correctly in our view:

[I]t is in our view not accurate to refer to each of the words as being an expression of the set of instructions. The set of instructions is expressed in the source code which is the computer program and, at least at a higher level, includes the particular word which is a command. The computer program will also in other forms exist in lower level language, ultimately through to an object code in non-visible form. Each of these representations will fall within the definition of a "computer program". In each of them, in some language, code or notation, the word said to be part of the computer language will be able to be found.

However, the appellant does not contend that the source code in PFXplus underlying any of the 166 commands in question is an infringement of the source code underlying the corresponding commands in Dataflex. That being so, the claim that each Reserved Word is a computer program fails.

2. Is the Collocation of the Reserved Words a Computer Program?

Furthermore, the collocation of the Reserved Words is not a "computer program". Although the Reserved Words together form "an expression . . . of a set of instructions", their simple listing together, without more, does not cause a computer to perform any identifiable function. There is no interrelationship of the instructions with one another which is an expression of a logical or algorithmic relationship between an identifiable function and the physical capabilities of the computer via the medium of the Dataflex language.

It is no answer that there is a set of instructions with a single identifiable function in that it provides a programmer with the vocabulary to enable him or her to program in the Dataflex language. As in the case of each individual Reserved Word, this is a function which the author of the Reserved Words intended them to perform in relation to the user, not in relation to the computer. As we have indicated, the definition of a "computer program" requires that the set of instructions be intended to cause the computer to perform a particular function.

3. Does the Collocation of the Reserved Words Form a Substantial Part of a Literary Work (the Dataflex System)?

The Dataflex system is a computer program. Hence it is a literary work for the purpose of the Act. The appellant contends that the collocation of Reserved Words, even if it is not itself a literary work, constitutes a substantial part of the Dataflex system. Section 14(1)(b) of the Act provides that in the Act "a reference to a reproduction . . . of a work shall be read as including a reference to a reproduction . . . of a substantial part of the work".

A copyright owner's exclusive right to reproduce a work is therefore infringed if another person reproduces a "substantial part" of the work.

In *Autodesk No 1*, this Court held that it was not necessary that the reproduction of a substantial part of a computer program should itself be a computer program. Relying on that reasoning, the appellant contends that its copyright is infringed because the collocation of Reserved Words is a substantial part of the Dataflex system.

Substantiality

The question whether something is a substantial part of a computer program created difficulty in *Autodesk No 1* and *Autodesk No 2*. In *Autodesk No 1*, in the course of determining whether the 127-bit series embedded in the EPROM in Dyason's Auto Key lock infringed the copyright in Autodesk's Widget C, Dawson J, with whom the other members of the Court agreed, said:

> For Widget *C* is a computer program and a substantial, indeed essential, part of that program is the look-up table by reference to which Widget *C* processes the information which it receives from the AutoCAD lock. . . . In effect, both Widget *C* and the Auto Key lock contain the same look-up table.
>
> . . . Whilst the 127-bit look-up table does not of itself constitute a computer program within the meaning of the definition—it does not by itself amount to a set of instructions—it is a substantial part of Widget *C* and its reproduction in the Auto Key lock is a reproduction of a substantial part of that program.

In *Autodesk No 2*, when discussing whether the 127-bit series embedded in the EPROM constituted a reproduction of a substantial part of Widget *C*, Brennan J said:

> A further submission is that the look-up table is not a substantial part of the relevant computer program. The bytes contained in the look-up table are but a minute fraction of the bytes in the whole of the Widget *C* program. Nevertheless, the series of digits in the look-up table is both original and critical to the set of instructions designed to cause the computer to run the AutoCAD application. When the running of the AutoCAD application is the purpose of the set of instructions expressed in that program, it would be difficult, if not impossible, to contend that the look-up table is not a substantial part of that program.

Gaudron J said:

> The only other matter on which the respondents rely is the question whether the look-up table can be said to be a substantial part of Widget *C*. In truth, the table was the linchpin of the program, to borrow an expression from a different technology. It was the critical part of the instructions in that the other parts depended on and were made by reference to it. Whatever may be the

situation in cases in which information plays a less significant role, given that the look-up table was crucial to Widget *C* and given that copyright protection extends to information as well as the commands involved in a set of instructions of the kind constituting a computer program as defined in §10 of the Act, there is, in my view, simply no basis for an argument that the look-up table was not a substantial part of Widget *C*.

The above passages in the various judgments in the two *Autodesk* cases relied on the "essentiality" or "criticality" of the look-up table to determine its substantiality. The reasoning appears to come close to a "but for" analysis, i.e. but for the look-up table, the AutoCAD program would not execute and therefore the look-up table was a "substantial part" of the program. To some degree the course taken in the above passages may reflect the statement by Dawson J that, although the 127-bit look-up table did not itself constitute a computer program within the meaning of the definition because it did not by itself amount to a set of instructions, so that no reliance was placed upon it as a literary work in itself, "there can be no doubt about the originality of authorship of the look-up table expressed as it is in Widget *C*". This may have suggested that what was "original" ought itself to be protected.

However, as Mr Prescott QC has said:

> In general, a computer program—any computer program—will not work if even one digit therein is altered or corrupted. It is therefore "essential". But it would be a startling conclusion to hold that not even a single number from a computer program may be copied. If one digit will not infringe, why should 127? Only if it takes substantially more skill and labour to create the 127. But it does not.

In Cantor Fitzgerald International v Tradition (UK) Ltd, Pumfrey J, sitting in the English Patents Court, observed of the reasoning in Autodesk No 1 that it "would result in any part of any computer program being substantial since without any part the program would not work, or at best not work as desired".

In *Autodesk No 2*, Mason CJ, who dissented, took a different view of the substantiality issue. His Honour thought that the judgment in *Autodesk No 1* should be re-opened in order to hear the respondent's argument as to whether the look-up table was a substantial part of Widget *C*. Mason CJ said:

> It is clear that the phrase "substantial part" refers to the quality of what is taken rather than the quantity. In Ladbroke (Football) Ltd v William Hill (Football) Ltd, Lord Pearce stated:
>
> > Whether a part is substantial must be decided by its quality rather than its quantity. The reproduction of a part which by itself has no originality will not normally be a substantial part of the copyright and therefore will not be protected. For that which would not attract copyright except by reason of its collocation will,

> when robbed of that collocation, not be a substantial part of the copyright and therefore the courts will not hold its reproduction to be an infringement. It is this, I think, which is meant by one or two judicial observations that "there is no copyright" in some unoriginal part of a whole that is copyright.

As this statement makes clear, in determining whether the quality of what is taken makes it a "substantial part" of the copyright work, it is important to inquire into the importance which the taken portion bears in relation to the work as a whole: is it an "essential" or "material" part of the work?

In this case, it is argued by the appellants that such an inquiry compels an affirmative answer as the look-up table is essential to the operation of the AutoCAD locking mechanism. Such an argument, however, misconceives the true nature of the inquiry and seeks to re-introduce by another avenue an emphasis upon the copyright work's function. True it is that the look-up table is essential to the functioning of the AutoCAD lock. However, in the context of copyright law, where emphasis is to be placed upon the "originality" of the work's expression, the essential or material features of a work should be ascertained by considering the originality of the part allegedly taken. This is particularly important in the case of functional works, such as a computer program, or any works which do not attract protection as ends in themselves (e.g., novels, films, dramatic works) but as means to an end (e.g., compilations, tables, logos and devices).

There is great force in the criticism that the "but for" essentiality test which is effectively invoked by the majority in *Autodesk No 2* is not practicable as a test for determining whether something which appears in a computer program is a substantial part of it. For that reason, we prefer Mason CJ's opinion that, in determining whether something is a reproduction of a substantial part of a computer program, the "essential or material features of [the computer program] should be ascertained by considering the originality of the part allegedly taken".

In order for an item in a particular language to be a computer program, it must intend to express, either directly or indirectly, an algorithmic or logical relationship between the function desired to be performed and the physical capabilities of the "device having digital information processing capabilities". It follows that the originality of what was allegedly taken from a computer program must be assessed with respect to the originality with which it expresses that algorithmic or logical relationship or part thereof. The structure of what was allegedly taken, its choice of commands, and its combination and sequencing of commands, when compared, at the same level of abstraction, with the original, would all be relevant to this inquiry.

That being so, a person who does no more than reproduce those parts of a program which are "data" or "related information" and which are irrelevant to its structure, choice of commands and combination and sequencing of commands will be unlikely to have reproduced a substantial part of the computer program. We say "unlikely" and not "impossible" because it is conceivable that the data, considered alone, could be sufficiently original to be a substantial part of the computer program.

It follows that we are unable to agree with the approach to determining "substantiality" which the majority took in *Autodesk No 1* and *Autodesk No 2*. Because of the importance of the question, we think that the Court should re-open the question of what constitutes a substantial part of a computer program. To depart from the reasoning in the *Autodesk* cases does not necessarily mean that the outcomes in those cases were wrong. In our view, the look-up table in Widget *C* was merely data and was not capable of being a substantial part of the AutoCAD program unless the data itself had its own inherent originality. However, re-opening the reasoning in the *Autodesk* cases does not require the Court to express a view on whether the look-up table in that case had its own inherent originality.

Substantiality and the Collocation of the Reserved Words

As they appear in the source code of the Dataflex system, the Reserved Words are irrelevant to the structure, choice of commands and combination and sequencing of the commands in source code. They are merely literal strings which, from the computer's perspective, could be replaced by any other literal string. Accordingly, they are not a substantial part of the Dataflex program as it appears in source code unless they have their own inherent originality.

The evidence is that at least 55 of the Reserved Words are unique to the Dataflex program. When looking at the list of the Reserved Words in respect of which the respondent was held at first instance to be infringing copyright, it can be seen that many of the words are ordinary English words which are suggestive of the function they perform, such as "BOX"; "CHART"; "CHECK"; "CLEAR"; "INDICATOR"; "INSERT"; "LOOP"; "NAME"; "PAD"; "PALETTE"; "PLOT"; "POINTS"; "REQUIRED"; "RETAIN"; "SELECTION"; "STATUS"; "TOTAL" and "UNLOCK".

Others are concatenations of two or more English words which together suggest the function performed, such as "AUTOFIND"; "AUTOPAGE"; "AUTORETURN"; "BACKFIELD"; "PAGEBREAK"; "PAGECHECK"; "PAGECOUNT"; "SAVE_GRAPHIC"; "SET_LINE_STYLE"; "SKIPFOUND" and "WINDOWINDEX".

Still other Reserved Words are single words which are in common use in other computer languages such as "DIRECTORY" and "SAVE", or concatenations of other words which are common computer terms such as "FILELIST", "MAKE_FILE", "RUNPROGRAM", and "SAVERECORD". As the Full Court pointed out, even those Reserved Words which are more removed from English usage than the examples above, such as "ENTAGAIN", "KEYPROC", and "MOVEINT", have a function which can be guessed from the English association.

In our opinion, even when the Reserved Words are considered as a collocation, they do not possess sufficient originality as data to constitute a substantial part of the computer program which is the Dataflex system.

4. Does Copyright Subsist in the Table or Compilation of the Reserved Words in the Dataflex User's Guide?

The Reserved Words are contained in the Dataflex User's Guide. The appellant did not submit that any of the Reserved Words themselves were traditional literary works protected by copyright, no doubt because they would face significant hurdles in the form of originality and substantiality. Given that the Reserved Words are arranged in alphabetical order in the Dataflex User's Guide, very little skill or labour was involved in compiling the Reserved Words in the form in which they appear in the User's Guide over and above the sum of the skill and labour involved in devising each individual Reserved Word. As the Full Court said:

> This is not a case where disconnected words are used in a particular order so that the order becomes the linchpin for copyright.

Furthermore, as we have already said, each of the Reserved Words is suggestive of the function it performs. In many cases, it is an ordinary English word, or a concatenation of two or more ordinary English words.

Even if the skill and labour involved in devising each individual Reserved Word is combined and consideration given to the total skill and labour, there may still be a real question as to whether there is sufficient originality for copyright to subsist in the combination. This is so even allowing for the inclusion in the definition of par (b) of "literary work" of a "compilation of computer programs".

The totality of the Reserved Words cannot be protected as a "compilation" within the definition because it requires a "compilation of computer programs" and the Reserved Words are not themselves programs. This does not necessarily preclude them together from protection as constituting a single program, but the set of instructions said to constitute such a program would still require identification. For the reasons leading to the conclusion that each of the Reserved Words does not constitute programs, a collection thereof does not constitute a program. The English letters which make them up are never at any stage executed by the computer. They are not instructions. They never cause a computer to perform a function. Their totality might be considered a "set", but of labels or data, rather than of instructions as required by the definition.

In any event, even if copyright does subsist in the table or compilation of the Reserved Words, we do not think that the respondents have infringed this copyright. The Reserved Words appear in the PFXplus source code program not as an alphabetical list, but as literal strings to which certain commands are assigned.

B. *The Macros*

The appellant also contends that copyright subsists in what are referred to as "Macros". It contends that each of these commands is a "computer program" within the statutory definition and that Dr Bennett made an adaptation of the Dataflex Macro commands. Consequently, it submits that Dr Bennett infringed the appellant's copyright in them.

Three particular commands in the Dataflex language, "REPORT", "ENTERGROUP" and "ENTER", are described as "Macros" because they cause the performance of a more complex function than any of the other Reserved Words. Executing a Macro command causes a sequence of other functions to be executed, so that the overall effect of performing a more complex function is achieved.

Are the Macros Computer Programs in Dataflex?

It follows from the nature of a "computer program" as defined in §10(1) of the Act that the words assigned to the Macros, comprising as they do one instruction in the Dataflex language, cannot qualify as a "computer program". However, the underlying source code of each Macro may qualify as a "computer program". In practice, the source code underlying each Macro is a small fragment of the source code of the overall Dataflex computer program (the relevant portion was said by the Full Court of the Federal Court to be some 229 lines).

The Full Court said that the question of whether a component part of a computer program is itself a computer program for the purposes of the Act is a question of fact. However, the Full Court went on to say that "[i]f a particular set of instructions is functionally separate from the entirety of the program, then . . . there is no difficulty in treating that set of instructions as being a literary work separate from the balance of the program". Although it did not expressly say so, the Full Court must have considered that the particular set of instructions comprising each Macro was not functionally separate from the remainder of the Dataflex compiler program. This is because it said that "the relevant program to be considered here would not be that small fragment of program which causes the macro command to perform its function (some 229 lines), but the Dataflex compiler program itself".

The Full Court stated no statutory basis for taking a "functionally separate" approach. If there is a statutory basis it must be found in the words of the definition "intended . . . to cause a device having digital information processing capabilities to perform a particular function". If the segment of the larger program in question can be said to have a function which is not merely one of the functions in the set of functions performed by the larger program, but is a separate and distinct particular function, it may be that this segment can be properly viewed as a computer program in and of itself. The *Autodesk* example given by the Full Court would illustrate that kind of distinction. The lock program in Widget *C* had a function (to prevent use of the software unless the correct key was inserted) which was not merely one of the functions in the set of functions performed by the computer aided design program which was AutoCAD.

The Full Court appears to have concluded in this case that as a matter of fact the function performed by the segment of the Dataflex source code which underlies each Macro is merely one of the functions performed by the larger program, and therefore that segment is not a computer program in and of itself. We need not consider that conclusion because even if it is not right and the segment of source code which underlies each Macro is a computer program, there was no reproduction and no adaptation of those works.

Reproduction or Adaptation of the Macros?

The learned trial judge found strong objective similarity between the underlying source code of the PFXplus Macros and the underlying source code of the Dataflex Macros. Jenkinson J did not find that Dr Bennett had reproduced the Dataflex Macros, but instead found that Dr Bennett had "made an adaptation of the expression in I-Code of each of the three sets of instructions". The finding of no reproduction was not challenged; the appellant contended that there was an adaptation.

The meaning of "adaptation" in relation to computer programs, as set out in §10(1) of the Act, is "a version of the work (whether or not in the language, code or notation in which the work was originally expressed) not being a reproduction of the work". In examining the meaning of the word "version", the Full Court referred to the meanings of the word "version" given by the Macquarie Dictionary "2. a translation. 3. a particular form or variant of anything".

The Full Court also quoted the following passages from the Explanatory Memorandum:

> 11. Copyright in literary works includes exclusive rights to reproduce or adapt such works and computer programs will be treated as literary works. However, the present definition of adaptation in relation to literary works only includes translation, conversion between dramatic and non-dramatic forms, and conversion to a pictorial form.
> 12. Of these, only translation is likely to be relevant to adaptation of programs and there are legal doubts as to whether this refers only to translations between human languages.
> 13. The new definition is intended to cover translation either way between the various so-called "high-level programming languages" in which the

programs may be written by humans (often called "source code") and languages, codes or notations which actually control computer operations (often called "machine code" or "object code"). Thus "adaptation" is intended, for example, to cover the compilation of a FORTRAN program to produce machine code which will directly control the operation of a computer. Languages, etc of intermediate level would also be covered.

14. It is also possible for a program to be converted from object code into source code, or between different languages of similar level. In some circumstances this process will result largely in a substantial reproduction of the original program. In other cases, however, such as compilation followed by decompilation, the differences may be so substantial that one cannot speak of a reproduction although the final product is clearly derived from the original. The new definition of adaptation is intended to cover such situations.

The Full Court said:

The evidence is clear that while Dr D Bennett carefully studied the Dataflex program so as to ensure that the PFXplus commands in question performed the same functions as the Dataflex commands, the expression of the source program as written by him was an original expression, albeit having much which was objectively similar to the expression of the source code in the Dataflex program. But it is clear that the process involved no translation from one form or language to another, nor did it involve the kind of process referred to in par 14 of the Explanatory Memorandum involving compilation followed by decompilation, or vice versa. In our view, a process of devising a source code to perform the same function as is performed in some other source code expressed in original language does not involve creating a version of the original source code.

Thus, the Full Court was of the opinion that there needed to be "translation from one form or language to another", or, alternatively, "the kind of process referred to in par 14 of the Explanatory Memorandum involving compilation followed by decompilation, or vice versa" in order for there to be a "version" within the meaning of the statute.

In response to this reasoning, the appellant contends that while the word "version" includes these two processes, it is not limited to these two processes. Furthermore, the appellant argues that the statutory context does not support the approach of the Full Court. It points out that where, in the course of the amendments to the Act that included the definition of "adaptation", Parliament wished to refer to conversion of a program from one language, code or notation to another, it used the word "conversion". The definition of "computer program" contains one example. Furthermore, so the appellant submits, the word "version" is ordinarily used in a much looser sense than that adopted by the Full Court. Ordinarily, it refers to the substance of the work but not the form. Examples are rendering a novel into a play or vice versa or turning a story into a series of pictures.

Paragraph 12 of the Explanatory Memorandum states that "only translation is likely to be relevant to adaptation of programs". This indicates that Parliament did not intend the word "version" to cover situations where, although the functionality of a computer program was copied, original code has been written to perform that function. The focus on translation indicates that Parliament was concerned to ensure that the different languages in which a computer program may be expressed did not provide a means by which copying could occur and infringement be avoided on the ground that the expression in the new language was not a "reproduction".

The use of the words "derived from the original" in par 14 of the Explanatory Memorandum also indicates that the focus is on copying. In accordance with the fundamental principle that copyright protects expression and not ideas, this must relate to the copying of the code (the "expression . . . of a set of instructions"), rather than a copying of the idea or function underlying the code.

There was no adaptation of the Macros.

C. The Dataflex Huffman Compression Table

The respondents seek special leave to cross-appeal against the Full Court's finding that they infringed the copyright which the appellant held in the Huffman compression table embedded in the Dataflex program.

Usually, in storing data, all of the 256 characters which a computer recognises are stored in memory as bit strings which are eight bits in length. Huffman compression is a method of reducing the amount of memory space consumed by data files. It stores characters in a data file as bit strings which have a length which relates to the character's frequency of occurrence in the data file. If a character occurs frequently in the data file, it is stored as a bit string of shorter length than a character which occurs infrequently in a data file. . . .

The Huffman algorithm, when expressed in source code, analyses a data file to determine the relative frequency of the occurrence of characters, and then assigns a bit string of appropriate length to each character, depending on its frequency of occurrence. There is no allegation in this case that Dr Bennett copied the source code of the Huffman algorithm from the Dataflex program. Dr Bennett states that he obtained "freely distributable" source code for this purpose.

In about 1992, Mr Cory Casanave created the "standard" or "default" Dataflex Huffman compression table by writing a program which applied the Huffman algorithm to a database file known as SERIAL.DAT. There is also provision in the Dataflex program for users to create their own custom Huffman compression tables. This enables the user to compress the data in his or her files with reference to the frequency of occurrence of characters in the actual file to be compressed, rather than with reference to the frequency of occurrence of characters in the file SERIAL.DAT. It appears that SERIAL.DAT simply served the purpose of being a representative sample of data which would suffice for standard compressions. If the user wanted the greater efficiency which would flow from the compression table actually being derived from the data in the file to be compressed, custom compression could be used.

Dr Bennett wished PFXplus to be able to compress and decompress Dataflex files, and vice versa, when standard compression was used. Consequently, he needed to be able to replicate precisely the default Huffman compression table used in Dataflex. Dr Bennett did not have access to the file SERIAL.DAT. For that reason, he could not replicate the Huffman table simply by applying the Huffman algorithm to that file. His evidence is that he refrained from "decompiling or looking inside the Dataflex runtime", and instead carried out the following process:

> The process I eventually devised was as follows. First I obtained a program which would dump out the contents of a file in bits, rather than the more usual hex dump.
>
> I then wrote a small Dataflex program which would create an empty database file using Standard compression, and would then add 256 records to the file. The records had the following appearance:
>
> AEAEAEAEAEAEAEA!AEAEAEAEAEAEAEAAEA
> AEAEAEAEAEAEAEA@AEAEAEAEAEAEAEAAEA
> AEAEAEAEAEAEAEA#AEAEAEAEAEAEAEAAEA
> AEAEAEAEAEAEAEA$AEAEAEAEAEAEAEAAEA
> AEAEAEAEAEAEAEA%AEAEAEAEAEAEAEAAEA
> and so on, for a total of 256 records.
>
> The position in the middle could be occupied by one of 256 possible characters, and the program cycled through all 256 possibilities. I knew that the pattern of AE repeated would create a distinctive and reproducible bit pattern in the Huffman encoding, to act as a background. It would then be possible to make out the single changed character, standing out in relief against the background.
>
> I ran the program, dumped the output to a file using the bit dump program, and printed out the result. I then marked out the 256 bit strings by pencil. . . . I found that they did indeed stand out well against the background. This process took just a few hours.

By this process, Dr Bennett deduced the bit string for each of the 256 characters as it appeared in the standard Dataflex compression table. This enabled him to create an identical table for use in PFXplus. . . .

In our opinion, the Dataflex Huffman table is a table expressed in figures and symbols, and falls squarely within the statutory definition of a "literary work". The reference in the Explanatory Memorandum to "data . . . stored in a computer as a table" clearly describes the Dataflex Huffman table. The Dataflex Huffman table is similar to the look-up table in Widget *C* which, in *Autodesk No 1*, Dawson J considered was a "literary work" within the meaning of the above definition. His Honour thought this was so even though no reliance was placed on that point by *Autodesk*.

For copyright to subsist in the standard Dataflex Huffman table, it must be an "original literary . . . work". As we have indicated, the requirement that a work be "original" in copyright law is a requirement that "the work emanates from the person claiming to be its author, in the sense that he has originated it or brought it into existence and has not copied it from another". At first instance, Jenkinson J found that "[t]he use of the Huffman system to produce a compression table requires the employment of substantial skill and judgment and a very great deal of hard work". The Full Court agreed with this finding.

The skill and judgment employed by Dataflex was perhaps more directed to writing the program setting out the Huffman algorithm and applying this program to a representative sample of data than to composing the bit strings in the Huffman table. Nevertheless, the standard Dataflex Huffman table emanates from Dataflex as a result of substantial skill and judgment. That being so, the Full Court was correct in holding that the standard Dataflex Huffman table constituted an original literary work.

In addition, in our opinion the Full Court was correct in holding that the process undertaken by Dr Bennett constituted a "reproduction" of the standard Dataflex Huffman table. The fact that Dr Bennett used an ingenious method of determining the bit string assigned to each character does not make the output of such a process any less a "reproduction" than if Dr Bennett had sat down with a print-out of the table and copy-typed it into the PFXplus program.

The finding that the respondents infringed the appellant's copyright in the Huffman table embedded in the Dataflex program may well have considerable practical consequences. Not only may the finding affect the relations between the parties to these proceedings, it may also have wider ramifications for anyone who seeks to produce a computer program that is compatible with a program produced by others. These are, however, matters that can be resolved only by the legislature reconsidering and, if it thinks it necessary or desirable, rewriting the whole of the provisions that deal with copyright in computer programs.

COMMENTS AND QUESTIONS

1. Consider how differently the court in *Powerflex* deals with the command language and macro issues than did the First Circuit in the Lotus v. Borland case in Chapter 2. Which decision is more persuasive?

2. The High Court's *Powerflex* decision calls into question the reasoning of Autodesk Inc. v. Dyason (1992), 173 C.L.R. 330, 176 C.L.R. 300, an earlier Australian software copyright case that had a substantial influence on the lower court's decision in *Powerflex*. The *Autodesk* court had determined that a "look-up table," though not itself a computer program, was a "substantial part" of a computer program such that reproduction of this table was an infringement of the copyright of the computer program of

which it was a part. How significant is this critique of *Autodesk* for other software copyright issues arising in Australia or elsewhere?

C. PATENTS

Patents are widely used to protect computer hardware throughout the world and are increasingly being used to protect software-related inventions. According to the Fenwick & West 1999 Update on International Intellectual Property Protection for Software, "[m]ore than 70 of the 176 countries in the world that grant patents permit the patenting of software related inventions, at least to some degree."[8] This report suggests that there has been a worldwide trend toward greater protection of software by patents. This trend has accelerated since the TRIPS Agreement,[9] even though there is no express mention of computer software in the patent provisions of TRIPS.

The TRIPS Agreement incorporates many provisions of the Paris Convention by reference and transforms them into minimum standards of patent protection for member states of the WTO. In addition, the TRIPS Agreement contains a number of other patent substantive minima. For example, Article 27(1) of TRIPS states that "patents shall be available for any inventions, whether products or processes, in all fields of technology, provided that they are new, involve an inventive step, and are capable of industrial application." Those who favor patent protection for program-related inventions may perceive in this provision a requirement that WTO member nations must grant patent protection to program inventions. After all, computer programs would seem to be part of a "field of technology." However, only a minority of patent-granting states presently provide patent protection to program-related inventions, and those that do have varying standards for what program-related inventions are patentable. Because of this, it is far from clear that TRIPS mandates patent protection for such inventions. Two prominent academic commentators, one a specialist in international trade and the other a specialist in intellectual property, have expressed doubts that a WTO panel would find a violation of TRIPS in a member state's denial of patent protection to software-related inventions. See Rochelle C. Dreyfuss & Andreas Lowenfeld, Two Achievements of the Uruguay Round: Putting TRIPS and Dispute Settlement Together, 37 Va. J. Int'l L. 275 (1997). Over time, if patents for program-related inventions become more widely accepted and international consensus arises, TRIPS may eventually encom-

---

8. Fenwick & West LLP, 1998 Update: International Legal Protection for Software (1999) at 18. The Fenwick & West annual update, which includes a chart identifying the countries that offer patent protection to program-related inventions, can be found on the Web at <http://www.softwareprotection.com>.
    9. *Id.*

pass an obligation to make patent protection for program-related inventions available. However, this may not occur soon.

Among those countries and regions that do protect computer program-related inventions, there are varying standards and tests for patentability. The Taiwanese Patent Office, for example, has adopted an approach consistent with the rule in the United States in the 1980s: hardware inventions that utilize software may be patented, but pure software inventions may not be. In Japan, mathematical algorithms, such as the Karmarkar linear programming algorithm that received patent protection in the United States, have been denied patent protection, even when the claims have been limited to certain industrial applications. Relatively common in the international community has been a requirement that a software-related invention represent a "technical solution" to an industrial problem or achieve "a technical effect"—for example, by enabling faster operations in a computer or more efficient execution of a chemical process. The Japanese Patent Office (JPO) has issued new guidelines concerning computer-related inventions, however, and its attitude may be changing.

Typical of the intermediate approach is the policy and practice of the European Patent Office (EPO). The EPO, it should be noted, is constrained to a significant degree by the European Patent Convention (EPC), which established the Office and under which the Office operates. The EPC mirrors the national laws of a number of European nations in its exclusion of computer programs from patent protection. Because several of the EPC exclusions may affect program-related inventions, it is worth reviewing both what is and is not patentable under the EPC. Article 52 of that treaty provides as follows:

(1) European patents shall be granted for any inventions which are susceptible of industrial application, which are new and which involve an inventive step.

(2) The following in particular shall not be regarded as inventions within the meaning of paragraph 1:

(a) discoveries, scientific theories, and mathematical methods;

(b) aesthetic creations;

(c) schemes, rules and methods for performing mental acts, playing games or doing business, and programs for computers;

(d) presentations of information.

This does not, however, mean that computer program-related inventions can never be patented in Europe. If patent applications are drawn with some care, program inventors can often obtain significant protection from the EPO.

The EPO Guidelines on the patentability of computer program-related inventions set forth the following criteria:

(1) A computer-related "invention" is a patentable invention if the real contribution which the alleged invention, when considered as a whole, adds to the known art is of a technical character;

(2) The "invention" issue is separate and distinct from the issues of novelty, inventiveness, and industrial applicability;

(3) A computer program (i.e., a list of instructions for a computer per se) is excluded from patentability. This ban must be seen as extending to computer instructions recorded on an ordinary computer disk, loaded on to an ordinary computer, or implemented through physical alteration of the circuitry of a computer;

(4) Nonetheless, an alleged invention featuring a program and which represents a technical process (e.g., a program-controlled manufacturing process) or which has a technical effect (e.g., a program which increases the working memory of a computer) must be seen as making a technical contribution and patentable.

Although the legal force of the Guidelines has been eroded by some recent decisions of the EPO, and the EPO's more recent interpretation of the EPC rules has brought the EPO closer to the U.S. and Japanese standards for software-related patents, a review of some of the older cases provides a better understanding of the evolution of the law on these matters in the EU. Application of the EPC rules was at issue in the case that follows.

IBM/Text Processing
European Patent Office, Technical Board of Appeal 3.5.1
T65/86 (1989)

Claim 1 is worded as follows:

1. A method for automatically detecting and correcting contextual homophone errors in a text document, in a text processing system comprising a processor (11) with a memory (23) and a process execution unit (24), a keyboard (10) with graphic symbol keys and control keys including a display cursor control key and a data enter key, said keyboard being connected to the input (21) of said processor (11) for entering data into a keystroke queue portion (26) of said memory (23), a text buffer portion (27) of said memory (23) being connected to said keystroke queue portion (26) for receiving data therefrom, and a display refresh buffer (12) connected to the output (23) of said processor (11) for controlling the generation of characters on a screen (40) of a display device (14) said method being *characterised in that* it includes the steps of:
a) defining sets of homophones and storing, under control of said execution unit (24), said sets of homophones in a portion (31) of said memory (23);

b) defining contextual characteristics for each said homophones and storing, under control of said execution unit (24), said characteristics in a portion (32) of said memory (23);

c) storing in a portion (34) of said memory (23) a set of data segments related to each homophone;

d) entering from said keyboard (10) a text document into said text buffer portion (27) and said display refresh buffer (12) for displaying by said display device (14);

e) controlling said execution unit (24) of said processor (11) to scan word-by-word the contents of said display refresh buffer (12) and to compare each scanned word to the said sets of homophones stored in said memory portion (31), in order to determine whether homophones are present in said display refresh buffer (12);

f) controlling said execution unit (24) to compare the data segments surrounding each homophone found in step (e) to the defined contextual characteristics stored in portion (32) for the homophone;

g) highlighting on said display device (14) each homophone whose surrounding data segments do not compare with said defined contextual characteristics;

h) controlling said executive unit (24) to access those sets of data segments stored in said memory portion (34), and related to said highlighted homophones, and to cause said display device (14) to display said sets of data segments;

i) moving said display cursor, through actuation of said cursor control key, underneath a data segment selected among the displayed set of data segments related to an highlighted homophone;

j) actuating said data enter key on the keyboard (10) to cause said cursored data segment to be substituted for the highlighted homophone in the said text document.

Claims 2 to 5 are dependent on Claim 1.

Reasons for the Decision

2. As can be seen from the opening words of Claim 1, the claim is directed to a method for automatically detecting and correcting contextual homophone errors in a text document. A 'contextual homophone error' occurs when one of a number of confusable words, such as 'affect' and 'effect' for example, has been used in an inappropriate context. In the opinion of the Board, a contextual homophone error is a purely linguistic error and has no technical significance at all.

3. Claim 1 goes on to specify that the method is carried out in a text processing system comprising a processor with a memory and a process execution unit, a keyboard with graphic symbol keys and control keys including

a display cursor control key and a data enter key, said keyboard being connected to the input of said processor for entering data into a keystroke queue portion of said memory, a text buffer portion of said memory being connected to said keystroke queue portion for receiving portion data therefrom, and display refresh buffer connected to the output of said processor for controlling the generation of characters on a screen of a display device. The appellant does not dispute the fact that the above mentioned hardware is conventional.

4.   In step (a) of Claim 1, namely 'defining sets of homophones and storing, under control or said execution unit (24), said sets of homophones in a portion (31) of said memory (23);' information required solely for linguistic purposes is entered and stored in a manner which is conventional from a technical point of view.

5.   In step (b) of Claim 1, namely 'defining contextual characteristics for each said homophone and storing, under control of said execution unit (24), said characteristics in a portion (32) of said memory (23);' information required solely for linguistic purposes is entered and stored in a manner which is conventional from a technical point of view.

6.   In step (c) of Claim 1, namely 'storing a portion (34) of said memory (23) a set of data segments related to each homophone,' information required solely for linguistic purposes is entered and stored in a manner which is conventional from a technical point of view.

7.   In step (d) of Claim 1, namely 'entering, from said keyboard (10) a text document into said text buffer portion (27) and said display refresh buffer (12) for displaying by said display device (14);' information required solely for linguistic purposes is entered and stored in a manner which is conventional from a technical point of view.

8.   In step (e) of Claim 1, namely 'controlling said execution unit (24) of said processor (11) to scan word-by-word the contents of said display refresh buffer (12) and to compare each scanned word to the sets of homophones stored in said memory portion (31), in order to determine whether homophones are present in said display refresh buffer (12);' data are compared in a manner which is conventional from a technical point of view for the sole purpose of determining whether the data in the display refresh buffer meet certain purely linguistic criteria.

9.   In step (f) of Claim 1, namely 'controlling the execution unit (24) to compare the data segments surrounding each homophone found in step (c) to defined contextual characteristics stored in portion (32) for the homophone;' data are compared in a manner which is conventional from a technical point of view for the sole purpose of determining whether the data in the display refresh buffer meet certain purely linguistic criteria.

10.   In step (g) of Claim 1, namely 'highlighting on said display device (14) each homophone whose surrounding data segments do not compare with said define contextual characteristics;' the outcome of the comparisons performed in step (f) is displayed to the operator in manner which is conventional from a technical point of view. The information displayed is

required solely for linguistic purposes, namely to indicate to the operator those of the detected homophones which are suspected of being incorrectly used.

11. In step (h) of Claim 1, namely 'controlling said execution unit (24) to access those sets of data segments stored in said memory portion (34), and related to said highlighted homophones, and to cause the display device (14) to display said sets of data segments;' information which is required solely for linguistic purposes, namely to assist the operator in selecting a homophonic for inclusion in the text, is retrieved and displayed in a manner which is conventional from a technical point of view.

12. In step (i) of Claim 1, namely 'moving said display cursor through actuation of said cursor control key, underneath a data segment selected among the displayed set of data segments related to a highlighted homophone;' the actual selection is made by the operator using only his skill and judgment. The selection of one of several displayed options by positioning the cursor under it is conventional from a technical point of view.

13. In step (j) of Claim 1, namely 'actuating said data entry key on the keyboard (10) to cause said cursored data segment to be substituted for the highlighted homophone in the said text document,' one item of data having only linguistic significance is replaced by another item of data having only linguistic significance. This is done in a manner which is conventional from a technical point of view.

14. It seems to the Board that a person who wishes to detect and correct homophone errors in a text document, doing everything by himself with pencil and paper, would have to proceed in a similar way and follow the same sequence of steps (a) to (j) as described in Claim 1, but without using the technical facilities described there he would:

(A) define sets of homophones and either hold them in his head or write them down;

(B) define contextual characteristics for each of said homophones and either hold them in his head or write them down;

(C) ascertain possible replacement words and their correct meanings and usage for each of said homophones and either hold them in his head or write them down;

(D) take up a text document to be checked and

(E) scan it word by word, comparing each scanned word with the sets of homophones defined in step (A) to determine whether any homophones are present in the text document;

(F) compare the words surrounding each homophone found in step (E) with the contextual characteristics defined in step (B) for that homophone;

(G) mark on the text document each homophone whose surrounding words do not satisfy said defined contextual characteristics;

(H) consider the possible word(s) and their correct meanings and usage for each of said marked homophones;

(I)   choose a replacement word and

(J)   substitute the chosen word for the marked word in the text document.

15.   Processing in this way, the said person would only use his skill and judgment and would consequently perform purely mental acts within the meaning of Article 52(2)(c) EPC. The schemes, rules and methods, that is, the steps as enumerated under the foregoing items (A) and (J), for performing these mental acts are not inventions within the meaning of Article 52 (1) EPC.

16.   The Board recognises that the use of technical means for carrying out a method, partly or entirely without human intervention, which method, if performed by a human being, would require him to perform mental acts, *may*, having regard to Article 52(3) EPC, render such a method a technical process or method and therefore an invention within the meaning of Article 52(1) EPC, that is, one which is not excluded from patentability under Article 52(2) (c) EPC. This is because paragraph 3 of Article 52 EPC makes it clear that patentability is excluded only to the extent to which the patent application relates to excluded subject-matter or activities as such. In the opinion of the Board, while it follows that the EPC does not prohibit the patenting of inventions consisting of a mix of excluded and non-excluded features (in conformity with T26/86 (J) EPO, 1988, 19) it does not necessarily follow that all such mixes are patentable. Since patentability is excluded only to the extent to which the patent application relates to excluded subject-matter or activities as such, it appears to be the intention of the EPC to permit patenting in those cases in which the invention involves some contribution to the art in a field not excluded from patentability. In other words, inventions involving such a contribution must be considered to constitute inventions within the meaning of paragraph 1 of Article 52 EPC.

17.   In the opinion of the Board, paragraph 1 of Article 52 EPC, as qualified by paragraphs 2 and 3 of that Article, states in effect that European patents shall be granted for any inventions (except those excluded by virtue of paragraphs 2 and 3 of Article 52 EPC) which are susceptible of industrial application, which are new and which involve an inventive step.

18.   The method claimed in Claim 1 of the present application does not appear to involve an inventive step. Once the step of the method for performing the mental acts in question (enumerated under the foregoing item 14) have been defined, the implementation of the technical means to be used in those steps, at least at the level of generality specified in Claim 1, involves no more than the straightforward application of conventional techniques of entering, storing, retrieving and comparing data, displaying, highlighting and selecting options from a menu, and must therefore be considered to be obvious to a person skilled in the technical art.

19.   Although a computer program is not expressly recited in Claim 1, it is clear to a reader skilled in the art that the claim covers the case in

which a computer program is used and, indeed, in the only embodiment disclosed in the application the text processing system is controlled by a set of programs and data stored in the memory.

20.   The overall effect of the method claimed in Claim 1 is that signals representing one linguistic expression in the text document are replaced with signals representing another linguistic expression. These signals are not different from a technical point of view. They differ only in that they represent different linguistic expressions, which are purely abstract expressions without any technical significance. The overall effect of the method is thus not technical.

21.   The present case is therefore distinguishable from the previous Decisions T208/84* (VICOM, OJ EPO, 1987, 14) and T26/86[†] (X-ray apparatus, OJ EPO, 1988, 19). In T208/84* the claimed method is patentable, even though it could be carried out by known hardware suitably programmed, because it makes a contribution in a field not excluded namely a more efficient restoration or enhancement of the technical quality of an image. Similarly, in T26/86[†] the claimed apparatus is patentable, even though the X-ray apparatus without the computer program known, because it makes a contribution in a field not excluded from patentability, namely controlling the X-ray tubes so that optimum exposure is obtained with adequate protection against overloading of the X-ray tubes.

22.   In the opinion of the Board, the method according to Claim 1 of the present application does not contribute to the art anything involving an inventive step within the meaning of Article 56 EPC in a field not excluded from patentability by Article 52(2)(c) EPC.

23.   It follows that Claim 1 cannot be accepted. The same applies to the dependent Claims 2 to 5, which concern further details of steps (b), (c) and (h), according to which only conventional operations are performed on non-technical data. These claims do not include anything which could involve an inventive step in a field not excluded from patentability by Article 52(2)(c) EPC.

24.   As far as the disclosed embodiment is concerned, some of its hardware is explicitly acknowledged to be conventional. Near the bottom of page 4, it says: 'The microprocessor may be an IBM Series 1, INTEL model 8086, or any of the functionally equivalent, currently available microprocessors.' On page 5, line 14, it says: 'The printer may be any suitable printer known in the art.' The description of the remaining hardware is not very detailed and does not mention any feature which is not conventional, it being assumed in the application that a person skilled in the art would know of suitable devices which may be used. The manner in which the hardware devices are interconnected is indicated only in a very general way. The required functions and interactions are achieved by means of programs and data stored in the memory.

25.   While it cannot be denied that there is an interaction between the programs and the hardware, since the programs without the hardware or the hardware without the programs could do nothing, but together they

make it possible to perform the method claimed in Claim 1, this fact alone cannot confer patentability on either the method or the apparatus. Since the only conceivable use for a computer program is the running of it on a computer, the exclusion from patentability of programs for computers would be effectively undermined if it could be circumvented by including in the claim a reference to conventional hardware features, such as a processor, memory, keyboard and display, which, in practice, are indispensable if the program is to be used at all. In the opinion of the Board, in such cases patentability must depend on whether the operations performed involve an inventive step in a field not excluded from patentability by Article 52(2) EPC.

26. In the present case, all the operations performed are conventional from a technical point of view and amount to no more than the processing of abstract data, for a non-technical purpose, by means of computer programs running on conventional hardware. The Board has found nothing in the claims, description and drawings of the present application which could be regarded as making a contribution to the art in a field which is not excluded from patentability by Article 52(2)(c) EPC.

In the opinion of the Board, therefore, the present application must be refused.

COMMENTS AND QUESTIONS

1. How plausible is it that someone using pen and paper—or her memory—would solve the problem in the same way? Is it really logical to talk about the algorithms at issue here as "mental steps"? If the goal is to prevent a patent that could be infringed by thinking "patented thoughts," this invention seems fairly low-risk.

2. Suppose IBM had built a machine to do the same thing. Is there any question that such a machine *would* be patentable subject matter? Is the EPC simply adopting metaphysical distinctions that once burdened U.S. law?

3. Is IBM entitled to *any* form of intellectual property protection for its invention? Would a broad interpretation of copyright law allow it to recoup its investment? If so, is copyright a better vehicle than patent for protecting this sort of creativity? Cf. Pamela Samuelson et al., A Legal Manifesto Concerning the Protection of Computer Programs, 94 Colum. L. Rev. 2308 (1994) (suggesting "gap-filling" protection between patent and copyright).

As you read the case that follows and compare it to the previous case, keep in mind the evolution of software-related patents in the United States, discussed in Chapter 3.

I. The respondent is proprietor of European patent No. 0 086 199. Claim 1 as granted reads as follows:

1. System for determining the queue sequence for serving customers at a plurality of service points comprising a turn-number allocating unit (4) for allocating a turn-number to every customer desiring to be served, a plurality of terminals (31, 32, 33, 34), one for each service point, and an information unit (2) receiving signals identifying the particular turn-number to be served and the particular free service point for indicating them to the customers, *characterised in that* the system comprises a selection unit (5) associated with the turn-number allocating unit (4) in a turn-number device (1), enabling customers to select a desired service point among said plurality of service points, computing means (6) for memorising the sequence of allocated turn-numbers with the selected desired service points, for receiving from the plurality of terminals (31, 32, 33, 34) signals identifying a particular service point which is free for serving a customer, for deciding which particular turn-number is to be served at the particular free service point and for feeding-out signals identifying this particular turn-number and the particular free service point to the information unit (2), the particular turn-number to be served being the next in turn in the memorised sequence of allocated turn-numbers for which no desired service point is selected or for which the selected desired service point is the particular free service point.

. . . The appellant (opponent) requested that the decision under appeal be set aside and that the European patent No. 0 086 199 be revoked. The respondent (patentee) requested that the appeal be dismissed and that the patent be maintained as granted.

Reasons for the Decision

1. Relationship between Article 52 EPC and Article 56 EPC

. . . [T]he appellant submitted in the Grounds of Appeal that the subject-matter of Claim 1 is a scheme, rule or method of doing business within the meaning of Article 52(2)(c) EPC, because the apparatus features of the claim are in very general terms corresponding to the steps of a method, which would be unpatentable, and such apparatus does not contribute anything more to the art than the method.

The submission was further developed during the oral hearing, when it was emphasised that the only feature in Claim 1 which was not disclosed in the Malmö [reference] prior to use was that set out in the last lines of the claim (column 7, lines 41 to 46), and that the feature was not a technical feature, so that the claimed subject-matter did not involve 'some contribution to the art in a field not excluded from patentability'.

In the Board's view, these submissions result from a misinterpretation of the relationship between Articles 52 and 56 EPC. In a case such as the present, a first question to be considered is whether the appellant is correct in his contention that the subject-matter of Claim 1 does not constitute an 'invention' within the meaning of Article 52(1) EPC. If, contrary to the appellant's contention, such subject-matter is not excluded from being patentable under Article 52 EPC, a further and separate question, also raised by the appellant, is whether the claimed subject-matter involves an inventive step.

2. Articles 52(2)(c) and (3) EPC

Article 52(2) EPC excludes patentability under the EPC for certain categories of 'subject-matter or activities as such', which are set out in subparagraphs (a) to (d) of Article 52(2) EPC. A common characteristic of such excluded categories is that their subject-matter is abstract in nature. In the present case the appellant has submitted that the apparatus system claimed in Claim 1 constitutes in effect a scheme, rule or method for doing business, which is one of the excluded categories. The Board does not accept this submission. The claimed apparatus is clearly technical in nature, and has practical application to the service of 'customers'. The fact that one such practical application of such apparatus concerns the service of customers of 'a business equipment' does not mean that the claimed subject-matter must be equated with a method of doing business, as such.

Thus in the Board's judgment the claimed subject matter is not excluded from patentability under Article 52(2) and (3) EPC. This conclusion is also supported by the following detailed considerations.

2.2 The wording of Claim 1 leaves no doubt that protection is sought for a 'system which is capable to determine the queue sequence of customers', and thus for a three-dimensional object with the aforementioned capacities. Claim 1 explicitly indicates that this system comprises: 'a turn-number allocation unit, a selection unit, terminals, an information unit and computing means'. Hence, the wording employed in the claim defines a technical item with at least five constructional components, which item clearly belongs to the category of an apparatus. Each of the five components is characterised in terms of its functions. In the present case, such a broad claiming is justified on the basis of the disclosed embodiments and examples. As generally recognised, a characterisation of an apparatus component by its function does not *per se* transform the corresponding claim feature into a measure which a user will exercise onto this apparatus component.

2.3 Among the functions indicated in Claim 1, there is a first group which can be exclusively interpreted as apparatus properties inherent to the corresponding system component. This first group consists of the following functions: 'Allocating a turn-number to every customer desiring to be served' is a property of the 'turn-number allocating unit'. 'Receiving signals identifying the particular turn-number to be served and the free service point for indicating them to the customers' is an attribute of the 'information unit'. Enabling customers to select a desired service point among said plurality of service points' is a function of the 'selection unit'. Memorising the sequence of allocated turn-numbers with the selected desired service point' is a hardware property of the 'computing means'. 'Receiving from the plurality of terminals signals identifying a particular service point which is free for serving a customer' specifies the circuit interconnection between terminal outputs and the input of the computing means. 'Feeding out signals identifying the particular turn-number and the particular free service point to the information unit' characterises the circuit interconnection between the output of the computing means and the input of the information unit. The above-mentioned functions do not correspond technically to the steps of a method, and therefore the true nature of the subject-matter of Claim 1 when considered as a whole cannot be interpreted as a method for doing business as such.

2.4 There remains only one more function in Claim 1. It describes the basic working principle of the claimed computing means: 'deciding which particular turn-number is to be served at the particular free service point' according to the rule: 'the particular turn-number to be served being the next in turn in the memorised sequence of allocated turn-numbers for which no desired service point is selected or (next in turn) for which the selected desired service point is the particular free service point'. In the Board's view only this functional term in Claim 1 is of an ambiguous nature in that it is a step of a method for doing business which may be performed by a mental act as well as a hardware capacity of the computing means, which allows the achievement of the intended technical result by the claimed subject-matter without human intervention. The activation of the selection unit by a customer and that of a terminal by a person attending the terminal are not to be considered as human interventions in a method of doing business, but as manual inputs of control data and trigger signals into a technical system. Taking Claim 1 as a whole, it is clear to the skilled reader that the above functional term is not an independent constituent underlying the entire claim, which can be examined on its own merits as an intellectual concept. The wording of Claim 1 links this functional term logically with the remaining technical features of the claim in an inseparable way, in that it is indispensable for achieving the intended technical result disclosed in the description column 1, lines 37 to 45. Hence, within the overall teaching of Claim 1, the nature of the above functional term is limited to a hardware property. Claim 1 excludes, in the Board's opinion, any interpretation of the above functional term as a step of an unpatentable method for doing business, and only allows the understanding of this functional term as a computer program according to which the claimed hardware operates.

2.5   Any interpretation of the above functional term as a step of an unpatentable method contradicts the integral technical information which the skilled reader derives from the total claim wording and would be the result of an interpretation of claim features in isolation from the remaining wording of the claim. In the Board's view, such an interpretation out of its context disregards the explicitly claimed technical co-operation between the claimed features, changes the disclosed nature of a particular feature and is therefore not justified.

2.6   As results from the above analysis, Claim 1 is directed to an apparatus which comprises, *inter alia*, computer hardware operating according to a particular computer program. The program-determined output signal of the hardware is used for an automatic control of the operation of another system component (information unit) and thus solves a problem which is completely of a technical nature. In such a case—according to the case law established by the Boards of Appeal—a mix of technical and non-technical elements shall not be excluded from patentability under Article 52(2) and (3) EPC. For this reason Claim 1 is allowed.

2.7   During the proceedings before the Opposition Division, the opponent relied on the fact that, in response to an opposition against the Swedish priority application in Sweden on the ground that the subject-matter was not patentable, the Swedish Patent Office rejected the application. In appeal proceedings, the Swedish Court of Patent Appeals also rejected the application. In a further appeal, the Swedish Supreme Administrative Court also rejected the application. The claims of the Swedish application were essentially in respect of the same subject-matter as the claims of the patent in suit. The ground of rejection of the Swedish application essentially corresponded to the ground of objection under Article 52(2) and (3) EPC against the patent in suit.

Although this history of the corresponding Swedish application was not specifically relied on by the opponent during the proceedings before the Board of Appeal, nevertheless in deference to the views expressed in support of the rejection of the Swedish application by the Swedish Patent Office, the Court of Patent Appeals and the Supreme Administrative Court, and in view of the object of harmonising patent protection within the Contracting States which underlies the EPC, the Board makes the following observations.

2.8   The Board notes that both the Swedish Patent Office and the Court of Patent Appeal regarded the subject-matter of the Swedish application as constituting a solution to a problem which was not of a technical nature, and therefore unpatentable. Although the supreme Administrative Court confirmed the rejection of the application, its judgment included a dissenting opinion.

Since the issue of these decisions in Sweden between 1983 and 1987, the case law of the Boards of Appeal concerning the interpretation of Article 52 EPC has been developed, and has been matched by corresponding development of the law in Sweden, as shown in the judgment of the Supreme

Administrative Court issued on 13 June 1990 in a case concerning an application by N.V. Philips Glocilampenfabricken. This judgment indicates that earlier Swedish case law, at the time of the above-identified decisions on the corresponding Swedish application, had deviated from the EPO case law.

Having regard to what is now established case law within the Boards of Appeal, and for the reasons set out in detail above, the Board does not agree with the reasoning which led to the rejection of the corresponding Swedish application.

COMMENTS AND QUESTIONS

1. Can this decision be reconciled with the previous one? What explains why this application receives a patent, but the IBM application didn't?

2. Why does it matter under the EPC whether an object is "three-dimensional"? Is it less likely to involve mathematics or mental steps if it is built in three dimensions? The formalism of this distinction is reminiscent of the U.S. rules for design patents, which grant protection to computer icons only if the entire computer is drawn, rather than merely the icon itself.

3. Are the EPC rules any less subject to evasion by artful drafting of patent claims than were the U.S. rules set out in Diamond v. Diehr?

Recent decisions of the EPO have continued the evolution of European computer patents toward greater harmony with the current U.S. model. Two of the most important of these decisions are discussed in the following excerpt.

Thomas C. Vinje, Computer Program Product Claims Allowed by the European Patent Office — Impact on Software Patent Claiming
Morrison & Foerster LLP

The Board of Appeal of the European Patent Office (EPO) recently rendered two important decisions relating to the patentability of software inventions in Europe. Both cases relate to patent applications filed by IBM Corporation. In these cases, the Board of Appeal decided in favor of computer program product claims (similar to those allowed in In re Beauregard, 53 F. 3d 1583 (Fed. Cir. 1995)). These decisions nullify, and reverse, a passage in the Guidelines for Examination in the European Patent Office, where it is stated that a computer program claimed by itself or as a record on a carrier is not patentable irrespective of its contents.

Under the reasoning of the Board, a computer program claimed by itself is not excluded from patentability if the program, when running on a computer or loaded into a computer, brings about, or is capable of bringing about, a technical effect which goes beyond the "normal" physical interactions between the program (software) and the computer (hardware) on which it is run. In addition, the Board said that it does not make any difference whether a computer program is claimed by itself or as a record on a carrier.

These decisions offer significant new patent protection for software, especially for a software-implemented invention which is supplied or downloaded over the Internet.

Background of the EPO Statutes on Computer Software

A threshold condition for patentability in the EPO is that the claimed invention must make a *technical* contribution to the prior art. Rules 27 and 29 EPC. In addition, Article 52 on "patentable Inventions" states in part that (1) "European patents shall be granted for any inventions which are susceptible of *industrial* application . . ."; (2) "The following in particular shall not be regarded as inventions within the meaning of paragraph (1): . . . (c) schemes, rules and methods for performing mental acts, playing games or doing business, and *programs for computers*;" (3) "The provisions of paragraph 2 shall exclude patentability . . . *only* to the extent to which . . . [a] European patent relates to such subject matter or activities *as such.*" In the past these restrictions on "*computer programs as such*" have been the basis for the EPO refusal to grant claims to a computer program product on a computer-readable medium or on a carrier wave. Guidelines for examination in the European Patent Office C-IV, 2.3 indicate that "[a] computer program claimed by itself or as a record on a carrier, is not patentable irrespective of its content." These two IBM case decisions, however, allowed such claims.

Subject Matter in the IBM Cases

In one case, T 0935/97-3.5.1, the invention relates to detecting where a second window in a computer display overlies part of a first window, obscuring information in a portion of the first window. The invention in this circumstance detects the overlay and causes the information obscured by the second window to be displayed in another portion of the first window not obscured by the second window by moving the obscured data to a portion of the first window not covered by the second window.

In the other case, T 1173/97-3.5.1, the invention relates to resource recovery in a computer system, including implementing a commit procedure for a work request; in the event that the commit procedure fails, notifying an application that it may continue; and, while the application continues to run, resynchronizing the incomplete commit procedure.

The Decisions in the Examination Division

In both cases, the Examination Division accepted system and method claims directed to the invention but rejected computer program product and element claims.

In T 0935/97, the Examiners allowed claims 1-6 directed to method and apparatus claims, indicating that the requirements of the European Patent Convention, and in particular those of novelty and inventive step, were fulfilled. Claims 7-10 were rejected as computer program code stored on a computer-readable medium. The Examiners concluded that "the subject matter claimed was distinguished from the prior art only by the information pattern represented by the stored program code. Therefore," the Examiners reasoned, "the problem solved would merely be how to store the particular computer program on a data carrier; this problem was well known in the prior art, so was its solution. Neither would this problem be a technical problem nor would any technical effects be achieved by its solution, since a computer program stored on a data carrier in the form of bits and bytes would still be nothing more than a computer program as such which was explicitly excluded from patentability by Article 52 (2) and (3) EPC."

Under similar reasoning, in case T 1173/97, the Examination Division allowed method and apparatus claims 1-19 and rejected claims 20 and 21 related to computer program products stored in computer-readable memory.

The Board of Appeal Decisions

In these decisions, the Board noted that, in the context of the interpretation of the EPC, the *technical character* of an invention is an essential requirement for patentability, referring to Rules 27 and 29 EPC.

Construing the phrase "as such" in 52(3), the Board considered that the exclusions from patentability of programs for computers *as such* in Article 52(2) and (3) EPC mean that programs are considered to be mere abstract creations, lacking in technical character, which necessarily follows if they are "not to be regarded as inventions." The Board concluded that it follows from this logic that *programs for computers must be considered as patentable inventions when they do have technical character.*

The Board spent some time discussing the *technical character* of programs for computers and indicated that the normal physical modifications of the hardware (e.g., the generation of electric currents) deriving from the execution of the instructions given by programs for computers *cannot per se* constitute the technical character required for avoiding the exclusion of those programs. However, technical character can be found in *further technical effects* deriving from the execution (by the hardware) of the instructions given by a computer program. Apparently, such a *further technical effect* could have the necessary technical character where, for example, it causes the software to solve a technical problem (see, for example, the VICOM decision T 208/84, OJ 1987, 14), or where technical considerations are involved to arrive at the invention (see, for example, the SOHEI decision T 769/92, OJ 1995, 525).

As to computer program product claims, the Board said the central question is what "*further technical effect*" can lead to this subject matter not being excluded under Article 52(2) and (3) EPC. Where a computer program product produces such a further technical effect when run on a computer, the Board described such a computer program product as having the potential to produce such a further technical effect. Accordingly, in a case where a specific computer program product, when run on a computer, brings about such a further technical effect, the Board could see no good reason to distinguish between a direct technical effect and an indirect technical effect.

Using a line of reasoning similar to the VICOM decision, the Board found that it would be illogical to grant a patent for a method, and an apparatus adapted for carrying out the same method, but not for the computer program, which comprises all the features enabling the implementation of the method and which, when loaded in a computer, is indeed able to carry out that method.

Accordingly, the Board stated that "a computer program claimed by itself is not excluded from patentability if the program, when running on a computer or loaded into a computer, brings about, or is capable of bringing about, a technical effect which goes beyond the 'normal' physical interactions between the program (software) and the computer (hardware) on which it is run." Also, referring to the findings in the BBC decision T 163/85, OJ 1990, 379, where it was held that a television signal was patentable, the Board concluded that it did not make any difference whether a computer program product is claimed by itself or as a record on a carrier.

As an interesting side note, IBM argued to the Board that a narrower interpretation of the "computer program as such" language would "accord with the TRIPS Agreement, especially Article 27," which says, "Patents shall be available for any inventions, whether products or processes, in all fields of technology." The Board noted pointedly that TRIPS is not directly applicable to the EPC, and that although TRIPS is binding on many of the EPC member states, not all of its members are so bound. Nevertheless, the Board recognized that cognizance of TRIPS and an interpretation of the EPC which is compatible with it is not inappropriate.

Conclusion

The Board of Appeal in these rulings has taken a giant step in bringing the treatment of computer program product claims in the European Patent Office in harmony with the treatment provided in the United States and Japan. Practitioners in the United States filing computer software applications must continue to be aware of the "technical effect" requirements of the EPO but should consider including computer program product claims in EPO filings, including, where appropriate, claims to a computer program product on a carrier wave, for example for a software-implemented invention supplied via the Internet.

COMMENTS AND QUESTIONS

1. In response to IBM's argument in the IBM/Data Processing case that Article 52(2) and (3) of the EPC violated Article 27(1) the TRIPS Agreement (which requires patents to be available "for any inventions, whether products or processes, in all fields of technology"), the Board stated: "[A]lthough TRIPS may not be applied directly to the EPC, the Board thinks it appropriate to take it into consideration, since it is aimed at setting common standards and principles concerning the availability, scope, and use of trade-related intellectual property rights, and therefore of patent rights." Do you expect other legal decision-makers will be as responsive to arguments about the interpretation of their laws in light of TRIPS? Why or why not?

2. The European Commission has recently suggested that it will prepare a draft directive to harmonize national laws on the patentability of computer programs. In addition, the Commission has proposed a modification to Article 52 of the European Patent Convention to omit computer programs from the list of nonpatentable inventions.

Note on the Japanese Patent Office Guidelines

Those seeking patent protection in Japan should refer to two sets of guidelines to judge whether computer-related inventions will be ruled patentable there and how best to claim such inventions. The Implementing Guidelines for Examination of Industrially Applicable Inventions defines what is and is not statutory subject matter under Japanese patent law. The Implementing Guidelines for Inventions in Specific Fields, Chapter 1 of which concerns computer software-related inventions, explains best practices for those drafting claims for software-related inventions. These guidelines may be found on the Web at <http://www.jpo-miti.go.jp>. Also on this Web site is the classification system that the JPO has devised for searching software technologies, in cooperation with the EPO and the U.S. PTO.

The Industrially Applicable Invention Guidelines begin by observing that section 29(1) of the Patent Law of Japan provides that "[a]ny person who has made an industrially applicable invention may obtain a patent therefor." This provision is understood in Japan to require both that the subject matter of the patent be a "statutory invention" and that it be "industrially applicable." The Guidelines set forth interpretations of both concepts. Its definition of "statutory invention," drawn from section 2(1) of the Patent Law of Japan, is "a highly advanced creation of technical ideas utilizing natural laws." To clarify the meaning of this definition, section 1 of the Guidelines identifies eight categories of "nonstatutory inventions." In addition to excluding natural laws as such and mere discoveries, the Guidelines exclude "laws or the like other than natural laws, and an invention in which solely such laws are utilized." The Guidelines explain: "If a claimed invention is any laws [sic] other than natural laws (economic laws, for example), arbitrary arrangements, mathematical methods or mental activities, or utilizes only these laws, the invention is not considered statutory." Nor are mere "presentations of information," a category that expressly includes computer program listings—that is, "representations of program codes by means of printing them on paper, displaying them on a screen, etc." When a technical feature resides in a presentation of information, however, that technical feature can be a statutory invention. The JPO Guidelines give as an example "[a] plastic card on which information is recorded with characters, letters, and figures embossed on it . . . [where] this card enables one to copy the information by affixing the card on a paper, and in this sense [a] technical feature resides in the presentation of information." Section 2 of the Industrial Application Guidelines articulates the standard for "industrial applicability." In general, an invention that doesn't fall within one of the specific exclusions in the Guidelines will be considered an industrially applicable invention. Methods of calculating numbers, of drawing geometric shapes, and of playing games are among the examples given in the Guidelines of inventions that are not industrially applicable.

The JPO Guidelines on Software-Related Inventions offer many helpful examples of successful and unsuccessful ways to claim such inventions, as well as information about the criteria that Japanese patent examiners will use to determine whether the application has complied with the "inventive step" requirement. In addition to permitting program-related inventions to be claimed as processes, the JPO Guidelines, as of April 1997, contemplate that claims can be made in the form "A computer-readable storage medium having a program recorded thereon, where the program is to make the computer execute procedure A, procedure B, procedure C, etc. . . . or where the program is to make the computer operate as (the combination of) means A, means B, means C." It also advises against claims for a program, data signals, or a data structure, none of which adequately identifies the category of invention for which the patent is sought. Even if a computer program solution utilizes natural laws, "when it is no more than the 'mere processing of information by using a computer,' 'mere recording of a program or data on a storage medium,' or 'mere processing of information by using a computer and mere recording of a program or data on a storage medium,' the claimed invention is deemed as nonstatutory." Very important under the JPO Guidelines is how the claims "suggest, directly or indirectly, how the hardware resources of the computer is [sic] utilized in the processing." Unless this is done, the claim will be considered nonstatutory. The Guidelines give an example of two claims which have in common the calculation of the sum of natural numbers from 'n' to 'n+k' with the use of a computer. The claim that made specific references to the role played by specific hardware resources in carrying out this function is considered statutory. By contrast, the claim for an apparatus to calculate such a sum without reference to these resources is deemed nonstatutory because it is a "mere processing of information by using a computer."

In the past, the United States and Japan have been at odds about procedural issues, and have had as well substantively different conceptions of the patentability of software-related inventions. The main concerns of U.S. officials about the Japanese patent system, according to a Letter of Agreement between the United States and Japan, dated August 16, 1994, was "the inability to make English-language filings in Japan that are followed up with Japanese translations; the long delays in the examination of patent application in the JPO; the pre-grant opposition system and the practice of addressing oppositions seriatim rather than at the same time; the narrow grant of patent claims; the availability of dependent patent compulsory licenses; and the lack of a full 12-month grace period. The U.S. representatives also raised concerns about delays in court cases in Japan and the absence of a mechanism to protect confidential information in court proceedings." The JPO responded to these concerns by committing itself to introduce legislation by April 1995 that would end pre-grant opposition and promote consolidation of oppositions. It established a target date of January 1996 to establish a procedure whereby applicants can request that their applications be fully processed within 36 months. And by July 1995, it undertook to restrict considerably the grant of compulsory licenses for dependent inventions.[10]

Note on International Patent Treaties and Substantive Harmonization

When seeking patent protection for computer-related inventions outside the United States, it is important to understand that other nations have significantly different rules, some of which are substantive, and some of which are procedural, for their patent systems. The U.S. patent system is, in fact, the exception rather than the rule in its adherence, for example, to a "first inventor" rather than a "first to file" rule to qualify for patent protection. In addition, outside the United States it is common for national patent laws to have absolute novelty rules (that is, the claimed invention must absolutely be new to the art, not merely new in the sense that it has not been described in a printed publication or other patent) and to require

---

10. By contrast, the United States still has not complied with *its* obligations under the executive agreement, because Congress has been unwilling to join the rest of the world in permitting patent applications to be published 18 months after filing.

publication of the patent application within 18 months of filing in that country. This obviously affects the ability of patent applicants to claim trade secrecy protection for an innovation for which a patent might be sought.

Over time, it is likely that there will be additional harmonization in the patent area and more cooperation among patent-granting countries so that an inventor need not file individual patent applications in all countries of the world at the same time. A significant regional development that enables inventors to use one application to get patent protection in many countries is the EPC that established the EPO. Under the EPC, inventors can choose to file one application and designate in which of the 20 participating countries it wishes to have patent protection. EPO patents are valid in those countries designated in the EPO application as long as there has been a subsequent perfection of the patent in each such country. There is, however, no pan-European enforcement mechanism. Enforcement of the patent must be done in national courts under the national law of that state. Alternatively, an inventor may file applications in individual European countries. This may be advantageous, for example, where the national law of an EPO member state has a broader view of the patentability of program-related inventions than the EPO itself has. Apart from regional treaties, such as EPC, there are several treaties affecting patent protection on an international scale. These treaties are critical to the effective international exploitation of a patented invention, as will be discussed below.

Coordinating International Prosecution

Patent lawyers face two problems in coordinating the prosecution of a series of national patents. First, a common priority date must be obtained to ensure that protection will be uniform and unaffected by prior art published (or otherwise having an effective date) before one or more of the national patent applications. Also, a common date will ensure that prosecution of a patent in country *A* does not somehow compromise the patentability of the invention in country *B*. Second, the patent lawyer has to deal with the logistics of international protection; she must oversee multiple filings in diverse languages in numerous countries. The wide variations in national practices and the high cost of conducting a large-scale application barrage make this one of the more challenging professional tasks in patent law.

Fortunately, two international agreements make these tasks a bit more tolerable. The first is the Paris Convention, whose primary function is to guarantee a uniform worldwide priority date across all member countries. An applicant may file in any member country of the Convention up to one year after an initial (typically home-country) filing without losing the priority date of the initial filing. (This treatment is provided under U.S. law in 35 U.S.C. section 119.) The second is the Patent Cooperation Treaty (PCT), which streamlines the filing of multiple national patent applications. Each agreement in its own way is an indispensable tool of the patent trade. Although detailed discussions of the agreements would take up too much room to fit in this volume, a few words about the essential features of each is in order.

a) The Paris Convention

The Paris Convention was signed in 1883, a product of the first true internationalization wave in the field of patent law. Paris Convention for the Protection of Industrial Property, as last revised, July 14, 1967, 21 U.S.T. 1583, T.I.A.S. No. 6295, 828 U.N.T.S. 305 (last revision, sometimes referred to as the Stockholm revision, entered into force April 26, 1970). Its primary function is to define a common priority date so that one may file an application in one member state and have the benefit of that same filing date when filing later in another member state. One purpose of this is to prevent interlopers from copying patents applied for or issued in one state and claiming them as their own in another before the legitimate owner has time to file in the other country.

The key provision in the Convention as regards priority is Article 4. The relevant portions read as follows:

Article 4

A(1)   Any person who has duly filed an application for a patent, or for the registration of a utility model, or of an industrial design, or of a trademark, in one of the countries of the Union, or his successor in title, shall enjoy, for the purpose of filing in the other countries, a right of priority in the periods hereinafter fixed.

A(2)   Any filing that is equivalent to a regular national filing under the domestic legislation of any country of the Union or under bilateral or multilateral treaties concluded between countries of the Union shall be recognized as giving rise to the right of priority.

A(3)   By a regular national filing is meant any filing that is adequate to establish the date on which the application was filed in the country concerned, whatever may be the subsequent fate of the application.

B.   Consequently, any subsequent filing in any of the other countries of the Union before the expiration of the periods referred to above shall not be invalidated by reason of any acts accomplished in the interval, in particular, another filing, the publication or exploitation of the invention, the putting on sale of copies of the design, or the use of the mark, and such acts cannot give rise to any third-party right or any right of personal possession. Rights acquired by third parties before the date of the first application that serves as the basis for the right of priority are reserved in accordance with the domestic legislation of each country of the Union.

C(1)   The periods of priority referred to above shall be twelve months for patents and utility models, and six months for industrial designs and trademarks.

Thus, filing in one country that is a signatory to the Paris Convention gives an applicant some breathing room—12 months in which to prepare to file in other signatory nations. The filing of an application for a patent in Canada on May 15, 1997, for example, will enable the inventor to have until May 15, 1998, to file patent applications for the same invention in other Paris Union states, such as Japan and Australia. If the inventor filed an application for a patent on this invention in Japan on April 10, 1998, Japan would consider the date of filing to be May 15, 1997, because of the earlier filing in a Paris Union jurisdiction (namely, Canada). This is especially important for those firms operating in the international environment, given the first-to-file and absolute novelty rules of most patent systems.

b) The Patent Cooperation Treaty

The Patent Cooperation Treaty (PCT) was signed in 1970 and opened for signature June 19, 1970, 28 U.S.T. 7645, T.I.A.S. No. 8733 (entered into force Jan. 24, 1978). Its major purpose is to streamline the early prosecution stages of patent applications filed in numerous countries. It is often described as a clearinghouse for international patent applications. As a practical matter, its major advantage is that it gives an inventor (and her patent lawyer) more time, a precious commodity in the prosecution of an application destined for many countries. The signatories to the PCT have agreed to permit an applicant to wait for up to 30 months after the initial filing of a patent application in one country to begin the in-depth prosecution of the application in other countries. This allows the inventor more time, compared to non-PCT prosecution, in which to test the product, decide which countries' protection is worthwhile, and pay the patent office filing fees in the various countries.

There are two main parts of the PCT. Chapter 1 provides that an applicant who files in a national patent office may elect within 12 months to add a PCT filing. The PCT filing is simply an additional filing in any national patent office designated in the PCT. In this case, the applicant has up to 20 months from the initial filing to request that the PCT preliminary prosecution procedure be initiated. At that time, the applicant must also select the PCT member nations that the applicant wishes to be covered under the PCT filing. Note that Chapter 1 preserves the applicant's priority date (in PCT member countries), without having to begin active prosecution, for eight months longer than the simple Paris Convention priority period.

Chapter 2 of the PCT extends the election period to 30 months. To qualify under Chapter 2, the applicant must make her PCT filing at most five months after the first national filing. Chapter 2 gives an inventor 18 extra months, compared to the Paris Convention, to select countries for coverage and to initiate multiple national prosecutions. In other words, so-called Chapter 2 PCT filings give the inventor up to 30 months to make his or her national elections.

The extra time is a substantial advantage. Besides simply delaying the expenditure of filing and examination fees, the PCT allows an inventor a significant extra period to assess the technical merits and commercial potential of the invention. This extra time helps the inventor save wasted filing fees for inventions that fail to blossom; for those that show great promise, the various patent applications that grow out of the PCT filing can be tailored to reflect the commercially significant embodiments that have emerged from the extensive testing.

D. SEMICONDUCTOR CHIP DESIGN PROTECTION

The market in semiconductors is, of course, as global as the market for computer technology generally. Outside the United States, makers of semiconductors can rely on patent, trade secrecy (or confidential information), and licensing laws for some of the legal protection they need, just as in the United States. Many countries also have industrial design laws that can be used to protect semiconductor chip designs or sui generis laws akin to the U.S. Semiconductor Chip Protection Act of 1984. There is, in addition, an international treaty specifically relating to semiconductor chip designs. A diplomatic conference hosted by the World Intellectual Property Organization produced the Treaty on Intellectual Property in Respect of Integrated Circuits (widely known as the Washington Convention).[11] Because some provisions of this Convention were unacceptable to the United States, it did not join this Convention. However, the United States successfully pushed for stronger international protection of semiconductor chip designs in the negotiations leading up to the successful conclusion of the TRIPS Agreement. As a result, minimum standards for international protection of semiconductor chip designs—or in the parlance of TRIPS, the layout-designs of integrated circuits—is now assured by Articles 35-38 of TRIPS.[12]

The main obligation is found in Article 35, which obliges WTO member states to provide protection to the layout designs of integrated circuits and incorporates by reference several provisions of the Washington Convention. Article 3 establishes important scope of protection rules that go beyond the protections of the Washington Convention. Article 36 makes it illegal to perform any of the following acts without authority of the rights

---

11. For a discussion of other national semiconductor chip laws, the Washington Convention, and the reasons it has been perceived to be deficient, see Carl A. Kukkonen III, The Need to Abolish Registration for Integrated Circuit Topographies Under TRIPS, 38 IDEA: J. L. & Tech. 105 (1997).

12. Very similar provisions may be found in Article 1710 of NAFTA.

holder: "importing, selling, or otherwise distributing for commercial purposes a protected layout-design, an integrated circuit in which a protected layout-design is incorporated, or an article incorporating such an integrated circuit only in so far as it continues to contain an unlawfully reproduced layout-design." Article 37 limits liability for violations of Article 36 when the person in violation neither knew nor had reason to know of the infringing acts of its supplier. Article 38 provides for a 10-year minimum term of protection for layout-designs of integrated circuits. The tangibility of semiconductors and devices in which they may be embedded will allow U.S. firms to look to border control measures to control trafficking in illegal chips. The TRIPS Agreement obligates WTO member states to institute border control measures to stop the flow of counterfeit products, including semiconductors.[13]

In view of these TRIPS obligations, computer lawyers are today unlikely to encounter significant difficulties in asserting legal protection of U.S. semiconductor designs distributed in the international market. Nevertheless, it is worth knowing something about the checkered history of international protection of semiconductor chip designs. When the U.S. Congress adopted a sui generis form of legal protection in the Semiconductor Chip Protection Act of 1984, 17 U.S.C. §901, et seq., it chose to accord protection to semiconductor chips manufactured by non-U.S. firms only if the countries of origin of these firms had been certified by the U.S. Secretary of Commerce as having a form of protection "equivalent" to the U.S. chip law. That is, the United States adopted a reciprocity-based, rather than a national treatment-based, approach to protecting the mask works of foreign nationals.[14]

The reciprocity provision of the U.S. semiconductor law may have been a tactical success, in that many nations thereafter adopted similar laws to protect mask works (that is, stencils used in the manufacturing process) or layout designs for integrated circuits,[15] but in retrospect it was a strategic mistake. The reciprocity provision of the U.S. chip law created considerable resentment in the international community as a kind of power play by the United States. This contributed to a lack of consensus and cooperation that in turn caused the Washington Convention, eventually negotiated in 1989, to be so unsatisfactory that none of the major semiconductor producing nations are even signatories of this treaty.[16]

---

13. See TRIPS, arts. 51-60. It should be noted that use of unilateral sanctions against another country for violation of TRIPS norms is itself a violation of TRIPS. One consequence of this is that the United States is not as free in the post-TRIPS environment to use special 301 sanctions as it was in the pre-TRIPS environment. See Charles R. McManis, Taking TRIPS on the Information Superhighway: International Intellectual Property Protection and Emerging Computer Technology, 41 Vill. L. Rev. 207 (1996).

14. See 17 U.S.C. §914 (setting forth procedures).

15. See Andrew Christie, Integrated Circuits and Their Contents: International Protection (1995).

16. See, e.g., Morton David Goldberg, Semiconductor Chip Protection as a Case Study, in Global Dimensions of Intellectual Property Rights in Science and Technology 329, 335 (Mitchel B. Wallerstein, et al., eds., 1993) (observing that the WIPO-negotiated treaty on semiconductor chips was so weak that leading chip-producing nations would not sign it).

The United States would likely have been better off in the long run had it worked more closely and cooperatively with the international community to build support for universal recognition of the need for legal protection for chip layouts. It might, for example, have promoted the idea that the unfair competition provisions of the Paris Convention (e.g., Article 10bis) already provided a basis for international legal protection for semiconductor designs. Or it might have worked with countries having industrial design laws to persuade them to protect chip layouts under these laws. This would have avoided establishing a precedent in the international community for using reciprocity rules in new legislation affecting high technology industries. The U.S. expenditure of political capital to adopt an international mask work protection system is particularly remarkable given that these laws, including the U.S. statute, are virtually never used.

The United States found itself on the unwelcome receiving end of a reciprocity rule when a 1996 European Directive established a new form of legal protection for the contents of databases on a reciprocity basis. This Directive essentially requires member states of the EU to deny protection to the contents of U.S. databases in Europe unless the United States has adopted a law that the Europeans deem equivalent to their law. We discuss this Directive in further detail in the next subsection.

E. DATABASE PROTECTION

The principal form of legal protection available to databases in the international arena is found in the law of copyright. Article 10(2) the TRIPS Agreement binds member states of the WTO to protect databases by copyright law. It provides that "[c]ompilations of data or other material, whether in machine readable or other form, which by reason of the selection or arrangement of their contents constitute intellectual creations shall be protected as such. Such protection, which shall not extend to the data or material itself, shall be without prejudice to any copyright subsisting in the data or material itself." The 1996 WIPO Copyright Treaty contains a very similar provision.[17]

A noteworthy feature of these treaty provisions is that they adopt an "intellectual creation" standard for copyright protection of databases. There has been a longstanding divide between two alternative conceptions of the basis for copyright protection: a creativity-based standard of originality, and a reward-based standard that protects the "sweat of the brow." The U.S. Supreme Court's decision in Feist Publications v. Rural Telephone Service came down strongly in favor of requiring creativity, not simply labor, as a condition for protection. *Feist* contributed to an erosion in the international

---

17. See art. 5.

community of "sweat of the brow" copyrights. In 1997, for example, the Canadian Federal Court of Appeals in Tele-Direct (Publications), Inc. v. American Business Information, Inc., interpreted its copyright law as imposing a *Feist*-like creativity standard of originality for data compilations. The U.K., the jurisdiction that originated "sweat of the brow" copyrights for data collections, has seemingly capitulated to the creativity-based originality standard, at least for data collections developed after the effective date of the European Directive on the legal protection of databases that harmonizes EU member states' copyright laws to an intellectual creation standard for databases.[18] Indeed, after TRIPS it is not entirely clear that a member state would even be *permitted* to protect unoriginal data compilations under copyright on a "sweat of the brow" or "industrious compilation" basis. On the one hand, Article 1(1) allows member states to adopt more extensive protection than the minima established by TRIPS. On the other hand, Article 10(2) indicates that the copyright protection it contemplates for databases cannot extend to the data in the database.

Several other aspects of the European Database Directive merit attention. The Directive defines the term "database" in Article 1 as "a collection of independent works, data or other materials arranged in a systematic or methodical way and individually accessible by electronic or other means." This provision may allow a wider array of databases to be protected under European copyright law than under U.S. copyright law. Systematic and methodical arrangements of data might be excluded from copyright protection under U.S. law by virtue of section 102(b)'s exclusion of systems, procedures, methods of operation, and the like, and the Baker v. Selden tradition of denying copyright protection to systematically arranged data.

Article 5 of the European Database Directive grants to authors of original databases a set of five exclusive rights to carry out or authorize:

(a) temporary or permanent reproduction by any means and in any form, in whole or in part;

(b) translation, adaptation, arrangement, and any other alteration; any form of distribution to the public of the database or copies thereof . . . ;

(c) any communication, display, or performance to the public;

(d) any reproduction, distribution, communication, display or performance to the public of the results of the acts referred to in (b).

While the database Directive is independent of copyright protection, the list of rights given to database owners is remarkably similar to the rights granted by the U.S. Copyright Act.

---

18. See European Parliament and Council Directive 96/9/EC of 11 March 1996 on the Legal Protection of Databases, 1996 O.J. (L 77) 20.

Article 5 also indicates that "[t]he first sale in the Community of a copy of the database by the rightsholder or with his consent shall exhaust the right to control resale of that copy within the Community."[19]

In addition to its provisions harmonizing the law of copyright as applied to databases, the European Database Directive also establishes a sui generis form of legal protection for the contents of databases in the EU. Prior to the Directive, some Nordic countries had adopted laws that protected the makers of certain uncreative data compilations, such as catalogs, against directly competitive appropriations. Other countries have used unfair competition law to protect data collections from market-destructive appropriations. Both to harmonize national laws within the EU and to promote a higher level of investment within the EU in database development, the European Commission and Council decided that this new sui generis law was necessary and desirable.

The key provision of the sui generis part of the European Database Directive is Article 7(1):

> Member states shall provide for a right for the maker of a database which shows that there has been a qualitatively or quantitatively substantial investment in either the obtaining, verification or presentation of the contents to prevent extraction and/or reutilization of the whole or a substantial part, evaluated qualitatively and/or quantitatively, of the contents of that database.

The Directive establishes a 15-year duration of protection for database contents. A substantial change in the contents of the database, whether by reason of deletions, additions, or alterations, can give rise to a new term of rights if a qualitatively or quantitatively substantial new investment was made to bring them about. The principal public policy limitation on the scope of the sui generis right is the nonwaivable right of lawful users of a database to take "insubstantial" parts of that database. Unfortunately, there is little guidance from the Commission about how to measure the substantiality or insubstantiality of a taking. Also, the Directive is so new, and the right it creates is so untested, that it is difficult to predict just how broad a right it grants to database makers.

There has been little litigation so far to clarify the scope of the new EU sui generis right in databases. However, the following Dutch case suggests that the Directive may have a profound effect on the outcome of future cases involving the appropriation of data in Europe.

---

19. Article 6 enables, but does not require, EU member states to adopt the following exceptions to or limitations on the exclusive rights granted under Article 5:

 (a) in the case of reproduction for private purposes of a non-electronic database;

 (b) where there is use of the sole purpose of illustration for teaching or scientific research, as long as the source is indicated and to the extent justified by the non-commercial purpose to be achieved;

 (c) where there is use for the purpose of public security or for the purpose of an administrative or judicial procedure;

 (d) where other exceptions to copyright which are traditionally authorized under national law are involved, without prejudice to points (a), (b), and (c).

Koninklijke Vermande B.V. v. Pavle Bojkovski
The District Court of the Hague
98/147 (1998)

Judge E.J. NUMANN
1. The facts of this case are as follows:

a. Since 1985 Vermande publishes the Verzameling Nederlandse Wetgeving (Collected Dutch Legislation) ("VNW"). This is a five-volume edition containing the full texts of a large number of laws and treaties. Vermande has derived the original legal texts and amendments from the Staatsblad (Official Journal), the Staatscourant (Official Gazette), the Official Journal of the European Communities, the Tractatenblad (official journal of treaties) and other sources.

Vermande has adapted these texts by adding marginal notes, summaries, intitulates, references, footnotes and other editorial information. Having been in the business of publishing legal texts for decades, Vermande invests substantial time and money in compiling—Vermande speaks of "consolidating"—the text of a single act from, sometimes many, Official Journals, Official Gazettes and other official publications. The same is true for the constant updating of the texts.

b. Since a number of years Vermande also publishes a digital version of the Collected Dutch Legislation (the "VNW-CD"), containing approximately 200 laws and other regulations. In the late summer of 1996 Vermande has distributed the VNW-CD (version 1996) gratis with the sale of the VNW book edition. The VNW-CD was included in the book edition in plastic shrink wrap.

c. Bojkovski, a student of international law, has copied from Vermande's CD-Rom approximately 60 laws and regulations, which he makes available—since the middle of December 1997—on a website under the name of "Legislatio". After being summoned by Vermande, Bojkovski has deleted, in January 1998, the headwords and marginal notes which Vermande had added to the legal texts on the CD-Rom. The address of the Legislatio website is: http//www.wetten.nu. . . .

2. Vermande demands, in sum:

a. an injunction against Bojkovski to cease and desist any further reproduction and/or a communication to the public of the contents of the VNW-CD and/or the Collected Dutch Legislation in book form and/or substantial parts thereof via the Internet or in any other way, subject to a penalty;

b. to order Bojkovski to provide Vermande with a specified, written and complete account, duly agreed by a register accountant, stating how many times Legislatio has been consulted on the Internet by third parties, subject to a penalty.

3. Vermande bases its claims on the facts mentioned under §1. According to Vermande Bojkovski infringes its copyrights and rights in "unpersonal writings" by copying the contents of the VNW-CD and making

them available on the Internet, as well as slavishly reproducing on the Internet the marginal texts, summaries (of legal articles not included), intitulates, references and footnotes of legal provisions and further editorial information.

According to Vermande the reproduction of the VNW files (even without editorial changes) must also be considered a wrongful act, in the light of Directive 96/9/EEC of 11 March 1996 (the Database Directive).

Moreover, according to Vermande, Bojkovski has infringed the general conditions of sale and delivery, and the general conditions of use of Vermande's databases, and thereby committed default against Vermande.. . .

Application of the Database Directive

9. On 11 March 1996 the European Directive 96/9/EC on the legal protection of databases (O.J. L77/20; hereinafter: the Directive) was adopted. Member States were to implement the Directive by 1 January 1998. However, the Dutch legislature has not met this deadline. Supposedly, one of the two draft bills produced by the parties at the oral hearing of the case has been adopted by the Dutch Council of Ministers and submitted to the Council of State. However, since these two versions differ in an aspect which is crucial to this case, and it is not clear which draft bill has passed the Council of Ministers, the text of the draft bill can play no further role in this proceeding.

10. Since the Directive should have been implemented into Dutch legislation, the national court has a duty to interpret existing national law in conformity with the Directive as much as possible. However, such interpretation will find its limits in requirements of legal security of the citizens to which the Directive, by its very nature, does not address itself. This implies that, in the first place, the question must be answered whether Vermande would have enjoyed protection under the Directive if it were timely transposed into Dutch law.

11. Bojkovski does not deny that the VNW-CD is a database within the meaning of article 1 of the Directive. However, Bojkovski maintains that a database of legislative texts—texts that are not protected by copyright pursuant to article 11 of the Dutch Copyright Act—falls outside the scope of the sui generis right of the Directive by virtue of article 13 of the Directive, which reads as follows:

This Directive shall be without prejudice to provisions concerning in particular [. . .] access to public documents [. . .].

Bojkovski also invokes Recital 52 of the Directive:

Whereas those Member States which have specific rules providing for a right comparable to the sui generis right provide for in this Directive should be permitted to retain, as far as the new right is concerned, the exceptions traditionally specified by such rules.

Since this is only one of the considerations which have led to the adoption of the Directive, and which are not part of the provisions of the Directive, it does not empower the national legislature to create exceptions to the Directive's regime, leaving aside that in the Court's opinion Bojkovski's argument that the protection of "non-original writings" is to be considered a right related to the database right provided by the Directive, and that therefore the existing traditional exception of article 11 of the Dutch Copyright Act may be maintained under the Directive's regime, does not appear to be correct.

12.   Should article 11 of the Dutch Copyright be considered a legal provision concerning the "access to public documents"? Parliamentary history of (the precursor of) article 11 teaches us that exempting (inter alia) laws from copyright protection is founded on the desire to prevent the State from exercising copyrights in respect of such texts, and to promote everyone's freedom to disseminate these texts. However, we must realise that the legislative activity in those days (1877, 1912) was not yet such that most laws could not be found in a single edition of the Official Journal, and that reproduction, storage and retrieval techniques were by no means comparable to the possibilities that are available to us today. Moreover, parties (correctly) agree that article 11 of the Dutch Copyright Act does not prevent a collection of laws from enjoying protection as a copyright work, if it is the result of a selection manifesting the author's personal vision (which, admittedly, is not the case).

13.   Against this background the Court provisionally opines that article 11 of the Dutch Copyright Act is not a provision concerning the *access* to public documents within the meaning of article 13 of the Directive.

Admittedly, the explanatory memorandum to one of the versions of the draft bill produced at the oral hearing, which contains a provision (article 8 §1) exempting databases of laws e.a. from the database right, refers to article 13 of the Directive, but no further arguments are given. . . .

However, it is unclear why a private producer of a database of laws should not enjoy ordinary database protection, whereas the production of such a database requires substantial investments that have become necessary because Government restricts itself to publishing official journals and similar publications containing legislative amendments without (except in special cases) making available consolidated texts of the laws in force. Whether or not the texts collected in those databases are exempted from copyright (pursuant to article 11 of the Dutch Copyright Act), is irrelevant for the application of the Directive.

The decision of the Dutch Supreme Court (Hoge Raad) in the case of the State v. Den Ouden (Hoge Raad 20 November 1987, Nederlandse Jurisprudentie 1988, 311) does not provide an argument for maintaining that article 11 of the Dutch Copyright Act (or its analogy) guarantees free access to (inter alia) legal texts. In the first place, that case concerned the reproduction of a recent legal text that had appeared in a single issue of the Official Journal (therefore the need to compile or to consolidate played no role). In the second place, it was the State itself (in its capacity of the former State Printing and Publishing company) that protested against the reproduction of its product, an action which the legislature had precisely attempted to prevent by way of article 11 of the Dutch Copyright Act.

14. The Court, therefore, provisionally opines that the Directive does not leave the legislature any freedom to categorically exempt databases of laws from the sui generis right, and thereby declare free for the taking the fruits of the labour which, in its place, has been invested over the years by private enterpreneurs. The circumstance that none of the (draft) implementation bills of other Member States which were produced by Vermande at the oral hearing provides for an exemption for databases of laws, reinforces the Court's doubts as to the possibility of the exemption argued by Bojkovski.

Interpretation in Conformity with the Directive? Wrongful Act?

15. This still leaves undecided the question raised in this procedure by Vermande. The Directive has not yet been implemented in the Netherlands and imposes only obligations on the State, without binding the citizens directly. However, Vermande has argued that the deadline for implementation of the Directive has been surpassed and that the Court, therefore, must interpret national law, at the very least since 1 January 1998, as much as possible in conformity with the Directive. In the pending case this implies that in Vermande's opinion the acts of Bojkovski must be considered wrongful under unwritten law. . . .

17. . . . Vermande's argument must be rejected. Until today, pursuant to article 11 of the Dutch Copyright Act, a right as provided by the Directive never existed in respect of collections of laws without a personal character; therefore, the Directive's regime is a breach with the past. Application of the law as proposed by Vermande would result in the Directive, indirectly, imposing obligations on a private citizen such as Bojkovski, which would contravene the principle of legal security.

18. The Court fails to see why article 10 §2 of the TRIPs Agreement would support the argument presented by Vermande. Judging from its wording, this provision relates only to databases which by the selection or arrangement of its contents constitute an intellectual creation, in other words: to databases which are copyright protected. In respect of Vermande's collection this is, admittedly, not the case.

Default?

19. Finally, Vermande has argued that Bojkovski, by copying the VNW-CD, has acted contrary to the term, which was visible to Bojkovski when the sale of the CD-Rom took place,

Unauthorised downloading or other kinds of copying prohibited,

which as a general condition of sale was part of the license to use the VNW-CD; thereby, in doing so, Bojkovski committed default.

20. Even if one were to accept that by the sale of the VNW book series to Bojkovski, including the gratis VNW-CD, a contractual relationship was established between Vermande and Bojkovski of which the quoted term is an element, this does not, in the provisional opinion of the Court, imply that Bojkovski has infringed that term.

It may be considered a fact of general knowledge that producers of data carriers or sound recordings regularly include statements of this nature on their products (as producers of phonograms have done in the past), and that the restrictions contained therein are usually broader, sometimes much broader, than the law provides. Therefore, there is no need for a consumer to interpret these statements as anything else than mere warnings of the existence of statutory restrictions of use. Bojkovski was free to interpret the statement in such a way that "unauthorised" meant nothing else than: unauthorised by law. Leaving aside the non-implemented Directive, Bojkovski has not infringed any statutory provisions.

Conclusion

21. All this leads to the conclusion that the provisional measures requested will be denied.

COMMENTS AND QUESTIONS

1. The European Database Directive, which creates a new intellectual property right, should not be confused with the roughly contemporaneous European Data Protection Directive. The latter provides individuals with substantial protections against the gathering and use of personal data by governments and corporations. For a general discussion of the European Data Protection Directive, see Paul M. Schwartz & Joel R. Reidenberg, Data Privacy Law (1997); Peter P. Swire & Robert E. Litan, None of Your Business: World Data Flows, Electronic Commerce, and the European Privacy Directive (1998).

2. The European Database Directive seems to adopt a copyright-like model for protection. Are the rights it grants equivalent to copyright? If so, why not protect databases under copyright law? Does the answer lie in the

limitations imposed by the Berne Convention and the TRIPS Agreement, which seem to contemplate some minimum creativity standard for copyright protection? Is the European Database Directive nothing more than an end run around the limitations of international copyright law? How is it different from an unfair competition-based model for database protection? Which approach is better and why?

3. The European Directive on the Legal Protection of Databases is not self-executing. It must be implemented in national laws, and member nations of the EU have significant leeway in adopting implementation legislation, especially as to remedies for violation of the sui generis extraction right.

4. By including a reciprocity provision in the database Directive, the European Commission very clearly intended to encourage the international community to adopt an equivalent form of legal protection for the contents of databases. United States database companies have understandably been nervous about the vulnerability of their data to depredations in Europe since the database Directive became effective in January 1998. However, a variety of legal protection mechanisms, including copyright, contract, and unfair competition law, should generally suffice to provide meaningful protection to U.S. database firms operating in Europe. Some commentators, notably Professor Charles McManis, have argued that the EU would be vulnerable to a challenge that the reciprocity provision of its database Directive violates the national treatment norm of the TRIPS Agreement. See Charles R. McManis, Taking TRIPS on the Information Superhighway: International Intellectual Property Protection and Emerging Computer Technology, 41 Vill. L. Rev. 207, 258-262 (1996). The United States is among the nations that have considered adopting some new form of legal protection for the contents of databases. However, this legislation has been controversial in the United States, and, to date, Congress has not enacted such a law.

5. United States and European officials pushed for a new multilateral treaty requiring member states to enact database protection laws as part of the 1996 WIPO treaty negotiations. The proposal was abandoned, however, because of myriad doubts expressed by numerous delegations just prior to commencement of the diplomatic conference. Their concerns echoed those expressed by scientific, library, academic, and user organizations present at the WIPO conference as nongovernment organizations. See, e.g., Pamela Samuelson, The U.S. Digital Agenda at WIPO, 37 Va. J. Int'l L. 369, 418-426 (1997).

F. TRADEMARK PROTECTION

Trademark law provides additional protection to computer technology firms operating in the global market. As with other laws discussed earlier in this chapter, there are some differences between U.S. and other national laws concerning trademark protection. Some of those differences are in substantive rules (for example, the extent to which trade dress protection is available at all or available through trademark law), but many are of a procedural nature. Managing trademark rights in an international marketplace can be challenging. Although counterfeiting of products and of trademarks has been a substantial problem in some parts the world market, the TRIPS Agreement's trademark provisions and border measures offer new measures to combat this kind of activity. However, attaining and maintaining trademark protection in the international arena is challenging because this law is less harmonized in some key respects than would be optimal, and because the United States has yet to join one of the international treaties that would ease the need for multiple registrations for trademark protection.

1. United States Trademarks Abroad: The Failure (So Far) of Internationalization

Despite the obvious desirability of international trademark registration, the United States has not joined an international convention that goes beyond the rather minimal protections afforded by the Paris Convention. Trademark owners still have to prosecute trademark applications in each country where they want their rights protected.[20] This is expensive: the various national filing fees, translations, and local counsel fees add up.[21] But trademark law in the United States is outside the structure of the Madrid Trademark Agreement (MTA), the main international trademark convention.[22] (In 1980, the United States refused to join an organization called the Trademark Registration Treaty, a minor international agreement;[23] and although the United States in 1994 did sign the Trademark Law Treaty (TLT), this is a limited agreement among many countries relating mostly to

---

20. A U.S. corporation may obtain the benefits of international registrations under the Madrid Trademark Agreement in the name of a subsidiary corporation domiciled in one of the Madrid Agreement member states, however. See MTA, *infra*, arts. 1(2), (3), 828 U.N.T.S. at 393.

21. Daniel C. Schulte, The Madrid Trademark Agreement's Basis in Registration-based Systems: Does the Protocol Overcome Past Biases? (Part I), 77 J. Pat. & Trademark Off. Soc'y 595, 597 (1995).

22. Madrid Agreement Concerning the International Registration of Marks, Apr. 14, 1891, 175 Consol.T.S. 57. This is an agreement under the Paris Convention for the Protection of Industrial Property, Stockholm Revision, done July 14, 1967, art. 2(1), 21 U.S.T. 1629, 1631, 828 U.N.T.S. 305, 313. There are approximately 40 members, including China and most of the European nations. See WIPO, World Intellectual Property Organization General Information 30 (1993). Various other international agreements exist, but for the most part they only cover relations between pairs of countries. See, e.g., 3 J. Thomas McCarthy, Trademarks and Unfair Competition §29.10[2] (describing bilateral treaties signed by the United States).

23. See Trademark Registration Treaty, Done at Vienna, June 12, 1973, and amended on Sept. 26, 1980, *reprinted in* World Intellectual Property Organization, Trademark Registration Treaty (1989).

subject matter and prosecution procedures.[24]) Now, with the advent of a new variant on the MTA—called the Madrid Protocol (MP)—there is renewed interest in trademark internationalization in the United States.[25]

The MTA does not of itself protect any trademark rights; it simply facilitates trademark prosecution in member states. It is effective in this regard, however: over 290,000 international Madrid registrations are now in force. On average, each international registration is extended to 10 countries.

Under the MTA, a trademark owner files a single registration with its domestic trademark office.[26] The owner may then extend this "basic registration" by filing, within six months of the original filing, an international application with the domestic trademark office designating other MTA member countries in which protection is sought.[27] The international application is then forwarded to the international trademark bureau of WIPO, which issues an international registration for the mark and publishes it in Les Marques Internationales, the gazette of the international trademark community. WIPO then forwards the application to the designated countries for prosecution under each country's national law.[28] Unless the trademark office or an opponent takes action to deny protection, the mark is registered in each of the designated countries.[29]

Several objections have prevented the United States from joining the MTA over the years. First, the MTA follows the international norm in its priority rule, which turns on registration rather than use.[30] Second, because of this, and under the MTA's reciprocity clause, foreign trademark registrants might well flood the U.S. trademark register with unused marks. Thus, by staying out of the MTA, the U.S. trademark community is preventing clutter on the trademark register—clutter that has a real cost in the form of higher search, clearance, and litigation costs. Third, the Madrid Agreement includes a provision known as the "central attack" provision, which provides that if the home country registration is successfully opposed or cancelled during the first five years after international registration, all related registrations fall with it. This would harm U.S. trademark owners disproportionately because of the many bases on which U.S. registrations

24. See Trademark Law Treaty, Oct. 28, 1994.

25. Protocol Relating to the Madrid Agreement Concerning the International Registration of Marks, June 28, 1989, *reprinted in* World Intellectual Property Organization, Protocol, Relating to the Madrid Agreement Concerning the International Registration of Marks [hereinafter Madrid Protocol]; S. 977, 103d Cong., 1st Sess. (1993); H.R. 2129, 103d Cong., 2d Sess. (1994). In early 1996, The Madrid Protocol had about 30 signatories but was not yet in force. Monique L. Cordray, GATT v. WIPO, 76 J. Pat. & Trademark Off. Soc'y 121, 124 (1994).

26. Madrid Agreement, art. 1(2), 828 U.N.T.S. at 393.

27. See arts. 3(1), 3^ter(1), 828 U.N.T.S. at 395, 397; Art. 4(2), 828 U.N.T.S. at 399; Paris Convention, supra, art. 4(C), 21 U.S.T. at 1632, 828 U.N.T.S. at 315 (six-month priority grace period for trademark registration filings).

28. Arts. 3(4), 5, 828 U.N.T.S. at 395-397, 399.

29. Art. 5(1), (2), (5), 828 U.N.T.S. at 399-401.

30. See Gerald D. O'Brien, The Madrid Agreement Adherence Question, 56 Trademark Rep. 326 (1966). See generally Jeffrey M. Samuels & Linda B. Samuels, The Changing Landscape of International Trademark Law, 27 Geo. Wash. J. Int'l L. & Econ. 433 (1994).

may be challenged under the Lanham Act relative to other countries. Finally, the MTA has only one official language: French.

Some knowledgeable observers believe that many of the traditional objections to U.S. adherence to the MTA no longer apply in light of the new MP.[31] Indeed, the MP was drafted with an eye to overcoming these very objections. The MP thus considerably softens some of the harsher impacts of the MTA, especially on the United States.[32] Specifically, recent legislation to implement the MP under U.S. law (1) allows for filing in English or French in the U.S. PTO or any other member country trademark office; (2) allows the filing of an international application based not only on a "basic" (home-country) registration, but also on a basic *application*—a substantial advantage given the relatively stringent prosecution standards in the United States, which can lead to long gaps between applications and registrations, especially now in light of intent-to-use registrations under the Lanham Act; and (3) substantially lessens the impact of the "central attack" provision by allowing an international registrant to convert a successfully attacked registration into a bundle of individual national registrations if the attack occurs during the first five years of the international registration.[33]

Although some problems remain,[34] and it had not yet passed in the United States when this book went to press, the MP faces better prospects

---

31. See U.S. House of Representatives, Committee on the Judiciary, Subcommittee on Courts and Intellectual Property, Hearings on Trademarks Legislation, July 19, 1995 (Statement of Nils Victor Montan, Trademark Counsel, Warner Bros., Inc.) (supporting passage of bill proposing U.S. version of MP).

32. Technically, members of the MP join the Madrid Union without signing the MTA. See MTA art. 1, 828 U.N.T.S. at 391 (states adhering to the Madrid Agreement "constitute a Special Union for the international registration of marks," known as the "Madrid Union."); Madrid Agreement Protocol, art. 1, at 9 (states adhering to the Madrid Agreement Protocol are also members of the Madrid Union).

33. MP art. 9, at 43-45.

34. See, e.g., Allan Zelnick, The Madrid Protocol—Some Reflections, 82 Trademark Rep. 651 (1992). Zelnick argues that U.S. companies might still prefer to pursue foreign trademark rights by filing individual foreign applications, because of the liberality of most foreign trademark systems regarding the classes of goods that can be identified with the mark in the application. (In many countries, a trademark application can specify *all* classes of goods —giving applicants substantially broader rights than under U.S. law.) According to Zelnick,

> [I]t seems likely that on the whole, most American trademark owners who file abroad today are unlikely to make use of the Madrid Protocol. The reason for this conclusion is that under our practice the specification of goods or services that will appear in the domestic application, on which the international application will be based, must be narrowly drawn to the specific goods or services in respect of which the mark shall have been used in interstate or foreign commerce of the United States (in the case of applications based on use) or restricted to the particular items or services identified by their common trade names in respect of which the applicant shall have a bona fide intention to use the mark. Since the international application under the Madrid Protocol will have the same specification of goods or services as the United States application upon which it is based, we will have, in effect, transferred our domestic practice in this regard to United States trademark owners' international filings.

Id. at 652.

than any trademark harmonization initiative in the recent past. Indeed, some degree of harmonization would seem to be incumbent, if only to keep up with trading partners. In Europe, for example, 1995 saw the advent of the Community Trademark Convention (CTC), a treaty providing for a single community trade mark (CTM) based on a single European trademark registration.[35] If further proof were needed, the CTC shows convincingly that the logic of trademark harmonization is compelling in this era of global trade and instantaneous communication.

2. Foreign Trademarks in the United States: Limited Internationalization

Because the United States does not yet adhere to any international trademark treaty, foreign trademark owners cannot avail themselves of a centralized prosecution system such as under the Trademark Registration Treaty or the Madrid Protocol. Even so, certain provisions of U.S. law do make some concessions to the need for foreign trademark owners to register their marks in the United States. Primarily, section 44 of the Lanham Act allows foreign trademark owners to register their marks in the United States. In particular, section 44 reads:

> (b) Rights of foreign owner of trademark. Any person whose country of origin is a party to any convention or treaty relating to trademarks, trade or commercial names, or the repression of unfair competition, to which the United States is also a party, or extends reciprocal rights to nationals of the United States by law, shall be entitled to the benefits of this section under the conditions expressed herein to the extent necessary to give effect to any provision of such convention, treaty,

---

35. Council Regulation (EC) no. 40/94 of 20 December 1993 on the Community Trademark, O.J. L 11/1. The CTM regulation built on a 1980 Directive that substantially harmonized the national trademark laws of the EC member states. Primary features of the recently added CTM are:

- Trademarks with renewable 10-year term, to be registered in the new European Trademark Office in Alicante, Spain;
- Marks valid in all member states but invalid everywhere if revoked;
- Substantive requirements for registration and grounds for opposition that would largely be familiar to American trademark practitioners—e.g., registration of non-distinctive marks upon proof of secondary meaning for limited class of goods or services, etc.
- The working languages are German, English, Spanish, French, and Italian. Applications can be filed in any Community language and are translated (for free); opposition proceedings are only conducted in one of the official languages, however, which must be selected at the time of filing.

See Eric P. Raciti, The Harmonization of Trademarks in the European Community: The Harmonization Directive and the Community Trademark, 78 J. Pat. & Trademark Off. Soc'y 51 (1996).

or reciprocal law, in addition to the rights to which any owner of a mark is otherwise entitled by this Act.

(c) Registration of mark in country of origin. No registration of a mark in the United States by a person described in subsection (b) of this section shall be granted until such mark has been registered in the country of origin of the applicant, unless the applicant alleges use in commerce. For the purposes of this section, the country of origin of the applicant is the country in which he has a bona fide and effective industrial or commercial establishment, or if he has not such an establishment the country in which he is domiciled, or if he has not a domicile in any of the countries described in subsection (b) of this section, the country of which he is a national.

(d) Effect of foreign application. An application for registration of a mark under sections 1051, 1053, 1054, 1091 or 1126(e) of this Act filed by a person described in subsection (b) shall be accorded the same force and efect as would be accorded to the same application if filed in the United States on the same date on which the application was first filed in such foreign country: *Provided*, that—

(1) the application in the United States is filed within 6 months from the date on which the application was first filed in the foreign country;

(2) the application conforms as nearly as practicable to the requirements of this Act, including a statement that the applicant has a bona fide intention to use the mark in commerce.

(3) the rights acquired by third parties before the date of the filing of the first application in the foreign country shall in no way be affected by a registration obtained on an application filed under this subsection (d);

(4) nothing in this subsection (d) shall entitle the owner of a registration granted under this section to sue for acts committed prior to the date on which his mark was registered in this country unless the registration is based on use in commerce.

Lanham Act §44, 15 U.S.C. §1126.

While section 44(d)(2) requires a statement of bona fide intent to use,[36] no subsequent proof of actual use in commerce in the United States is required. This allows foreign trademark owners to register their marks in the United States on terms slightly more favorable than those extended to domestic applicants under the Lanham Act.

---

36. This provision was added in 1988 (effective 1989) in response to the decision of the Trademark Trial and Appeal Board's decision in Crocker National Bank v. Canadian Imperial Bank of Commerce, 223 U.S.P.Q. (BNA) 909 (T.T.A.B. 1984), which held valid a trademark registration application filed by a Canadian bank despite the absence of an allegation of use anywhere in the world.

3. "Gray-Market" Goods

United States law prohibits the importation of any goods bearing a registered U.S. trademark without the consent of the domestic trademark owner, even if the goods are genuine and even if they are imported by a licensed manufacturer (or the original trademark owner itself). 19 U.S.C. §1526. The so-called "gray-market" or "parallel imports" problem is a troubling one for courts and commentators alike. The Supreme Court has described the problem as follows:

> The gray market arises in any of three general contexts. The prototypical gray-market victim (case 1) is a domestic firm that purchases from an independent foreign firm the rights to register and use the latter's trademark as a United States trademark and to sell its foreign-manufactured products here. Especially where the foreign firm has already registered the trademark in the United States or where the product has already earned a reputation for quality, the right to use that trademark can be very valuable. If the foreign manufacturer could import the trademarked goods and distribute them here, despite having sold the trademark to a domestic firm, the domestic firm would be forced into sharp intrabrand competition involving the very trademark it purchased. Similar intrabrand competition could arise if the foreign manufacturer markets its wares outside the United States, as is often the case, and a third party who purchases them abroad could legally import them. In either event, the parallel importation, if permitted to proceed, would create a gray market that could jeopardize the trademark holder's investment.
>
> The second context (case 2) is a situation in which a domestic firm registers the United States trademark for goods that are manufactured abroad by an affiliated manufacturer. In its most common variation (case 2a), a foreign firm wishes to control distribution of its wares in this country by incorporating a subsidiary here. The subsidiary then registers under its own name (or the manufacturer assigns to the subsidiary's name) a United States trademark that is identical to its parent's foreign trademark. The parallel importation by a third party who buys the goods abroad (or conceivably even by the affiliated foreign manufacturer itself) creates a gray market. Two other variations on this theme occur when an American-based firm establishes abroad a manufacturing subsidiary corporation (case 2b) or its own unincorporated manufacturing division (case 2c) to produce its United States trademarked goods, and then imports them for domestic distribution. If the trademark holder or its foreign subsidiary sells the trademarked goods abroad, the parallel importation of the goods competes on the gray market with the holder's domestic sales.
>
> In the third context (case 3), the domestic holder of a United States trademark authorizes an independent foreign manufacturer to use it. Usually the holder sells to the foreign manufacturer an exclusive right to use the trademark in a particular foreign location, but conditions the right on the foreign manufacturer's promise not to import its trademarked goods into the United States. Once again, if the foreign manufacturer or a third party imports into the United States, the foreign-manufactured goods will compete on the gray market with the holder's domestic goods.

K-Mart Corp. v. Cartier, Inc., 486 U.S. 281, 286-87 (1988).

What is wrong with importing gray-market goods? In this case, unlike the typical trademark dispute, there is no question that the goods are genuine and are being sold as precisely what they are. Further, there is no question that they originated with the trademark owner (at least at some point). If a gray-market transaction occurred entirely within the United States, would it constitute trademark infringement? If not, is there any reason to treat importation differently?

One obvious rationale for prohibiting gray-market imports is that the U.S. trademark owner is losing the benefit of what she thought was an exclusive right to sell the trademarked goods in the United States. But does she really have such an exclusive right? Certainly, the right to use the "Ford" trademark on cars in the United States does not prevent bona fide purchasers of Ford cars from identifying them as such upon resale. And even if the U.S. trademark owner did obtain the exclusive rights to the first sale of goods in the United States, isn't the problem here really one of breach of contract?

Section 1526, which regulates gray-market goods, may violate Article 2 of the Paris Convention because it treats U.S. trademark holders differently from foreign trademark holders, and U.S. infringers differently from foreign infringers. See Raimund Steiner & Robert Sabath, Intellectual Property and Trade Law Approaches to Gray Market Importation, and the Restructuring of Transnational Entities to Permit Blockage of Gray Goods in the United States, 15 Wm. Mitchell L. Rev. 433, 441 (1989) (after K-Mart, to obtain benefits of section 526 of Tariff Act of 1930 and Lanham Act, companies must separate ownership of foreign and domestic trademarks); see generally Note, The Use of Copyright Law to Block the Importation of Gray-Market Goods: The Black and White of It All, 23 Loy. L.A. L. Rev. 645 (1990).

There is a debate in the economics literature about the wisdom of permitting gray-market imports. The argument generally runs along these lines: those favoring restrictions on the gray market cite the importance of encouraging investments in brand quality by retailers, coupled with differing international product quality standards. In essence, the argument is that retailers will not engage in optimal expenditures to promote the product (advertising, clean showrooms, knowledgeable sales staff, etc.) if gray-market imports will undercut the retailers' prices. On the opposite side, those who support the gray market say it undercuts blatant price discrimination. See Robert J. Staaf, International Price Discrimination and the Gray Market, 4 Intellectual Prop. J. 301 (1989) (gray market presents an opportunity for arbitrage, allowing competitors to circumvent attempted price discrimination and therefore benefiting consumers).

The following case from the U.K. illustrates gray-market goods issues that sometimes arise in the context of computer software products.

Microsoft Corp. v. Computer Future Distribution Ltd.
United Kingdom Chancery Division
[1998] E.T.M.R. 597

RIMER J:

[Computer Future Distribution (CFD) lawfully acquired copies of Academic Edition (AE)-packaged Microsoft (MS) software from unnamed North American distributors. It then removed the outer packaging, which contained notices of restrictions on resale of the software outside North America and certificates of authentication (COA). CFD repackaged this software (correctly identifying Microsoft as its source) and then commercially distributed the software to various customers in the U.K. without inclusion of the end user license agreement (EULA) that Microsoft routinely includes in its packaged software. MS sued CFD for trademark infringement, passing off, and copyright infringement. When MS moved for summary judgment on all three counts, CFD argued that MS's sale of the software in North America exhausted its rights to control redistribution of the software in the U.K.]

Mr Baldwin submits that CFD's activities . . . constitute an infringement of Microsoft's registered trade marks. The action is governed by the Trade Marks Act 1994, which was passed to implement Council Directive 89/104/EEC, and which must be construed so as to give effect to the Directive. It is an infringement to use in the course of trade, without the consent of the proprietor, a sign identical to the registered trade mark in relation to goods identical to those for which it is registered: see ss.9 and 10 of the Act. In this case, CFD has used a sign identical to Microsoft's registered trade marks in relation to identical goods. Mr Baldwin submits that there has been no consent to CFD's acts.

An exhaustion defence is provided by s.12 of the Act, implementing Art.7 of the Directive. Mr Baldwin's position is that that cannot avail CFD since the relevant goods have not been marketed in the EEA by Microsoft or with its consent, but only in North America whence they have been imported. He claims that Microsoft's rights in respect of trade mark infringement are preserved in relation to goods marketed by or with its consent outside the EEA and he says that that is the position in relation to the supply of goods which are the subject of this action. He does not, however, ask the court to determine that particular point on this application. That is because the Austrian Supreme Court has recently referred the effect of Art. 7 to the ECJ: Silhouette v Hartlauer [1997] ETMR 219. Mr Baldwin concedes that, until that reference has been decided, the possibility of an international exhaustion defence based on the marketing of the goods in North America cannot be excluded.

He submits further, however, that even if an international exhaustion defence is available under s.12, it can anyway be of no assistance to CFD.

That is because Art. 7(2) of the Directive and s.12(2) of the 1994 Act recognise that, even if the goods were put on the market by or with the consent of the trade mark owner, such owner's rights will not be exhausted if there are legitimate reasons for him to oppose further dealing in the goods. Section 12(2) provides that:

> Subsection (1) does not apply where there exist legitimate reasons for the proprietor to oppose further dealings in the goods (in particular, where the condition of the goods has been changed or impaired after they have been put on the market).

Mr Baldwin submits that in this case Microsoft has legitimate reasons for opposing the manner in which CFD has been dealing with the brown box software, the licence packs and the family bundles.

As to the brown box software, it appears plain that the whole, or at least the main, point of removing Microsoft's original outer packaging, and in supplying the software in brown boxes, was to conceal from purchasers the fact that the product was originally destined exclusively for the North American market or intended solely for North American academic users. All this was made clear on the removed packaging, but is not apparent from the plain brown box.

The effect of the removal of the outer packaging was to enable the software to be sold to non-North American users who would or might buy in ignorance that the product was designed and intended exclusively for the North American market and who would or might find that they had no money back guarantee or guarantee of support. In addition, it would enable software products intended by Microsoft exclusively for North American academic users, and originally sold by it at the generous concessionary AE price, instead to find their way into the hands of ordinary users and at an increased price. Further, the removal of Microsoft's outer packaging results in an inferior looking product, with resultant damage to Microsoft's goodwill. Microsoft asserts that purchasers cannot be sure who has packaged the product which is being sold, they cannot be sure that the contents of the brown box have not been altered or tampered with since it left Microsoft's control, and the removal of the COA contained on the outer packaging removes part of the evidence of the authenticity of the product. The removal of the outer packaging also opens up the scope for splitting up the products in a way which Microsoft does not permit, for example by extracting the EULAs and providing them to users of other software as a purported licence.

Mr Baldwin makes like points in relation to CFD's practice of stripping out EULAs so as to create a market in bogus licences. The particular examples complained of and proved are CFD's supply of the licence pack to Option Technology and the 40 EULAs to Sussex Training. The product sold to Option Technology suffers from being an incomplete package presented as emanating from Microsoft; and that supplied to Sussex Training looks shoddy, containing nothing to attribute the re-packaging to CFD. The sale of such separate EULAs, unattached to particular software items, is without Microsoft's licence and its availability facilitates and encourages the use of unlicensed copies of Microsoft's software.

As for the family bundles, they are supplied in a form which falls short of including an EULA and a COA for each item of software supplied, whereas authentic family bundles do or should include an EULA and a COA for each item. This results in surplus EULAs and COAs being available for use in conferring spurious authenticity on other items of software. The purchaser is deprived of an indication that the goods are genuine Microsoft products and Microsoft is deprived of the opportunity of discovering whether the product is counterfeit. The packaging gives no indication of who is responsible for it and no notice of the re-packaging is given to Microsoft.

Mr Baldwin submits that all this means that, in relation to each of the items within the three classes of goods in question, Microsoft's trade marks are diminished as an indication of authenticity and quality. He submits that it follows that 'there exist legitimate reasons' within the meaning of s.12(2) for Microsoft's opposition to such dealings. If so, then, whatever the result of the reference in the Silhouette case, there will be no exhaustion defence available to CFD under s.12.

In considering the application of s.12(2) to this case, Mr Baldwin referred me in particular to the decision of the ECJ in Bristol-Myers Squibb v Paranova (1996) 34 BMLR 59, [1997] FSR 102. That case was concerned, inter alia, with the extent to which the trade mark owner could object to the repackaging and sale of imported pharmaceutical products to which the trade mark had been affixed. The case depended on Art. 7(2) of the Directive, to which s.12(2) gives effect. The court said that:

> 39. Article 7(2) of the Directive provides that the owner of a trade mark may oppose the further commercialisation of products where there is a legitimate reason for doing so, especially where the condition of the products has been changed or impaired since they were put on the market. The use of the word "especially" shows that the case envisaged is given only as an example.
>
> 40. Article 7 of the Directive, like Article 36 of the Treaty, is intended to reconcile the fundamental interest in protecting trade mark rights with the fundamental interest in the free movement of goods within the common market, so that those two provisions, which pursue the same result, must be interpreted in the same way. . . .
>
> 47. In answering the question whether a trade mark owner's exclusive rights include the power to oppose the use of the trade mark by a third party after the product has been repackaged, account must be taken of the essential function of the trade mark, which is to guarantee to the consumer or end user the identity of the trade-marked product's origin by enabling him to distinguish it without any risk of confusion from products of different origin. That guarantee of origin means that the consumer or end user can be certain that a trade-marked product offered to him has not been subject at a previous stage of marketing to interference by a third person, without the authorisation of

the trade mark owner, in such a way as to affect the original condition of the product (*Hoffmann-La Roche*, paragraph 7; *Pfizer*, paragraph 8).

48.   Therefore the right conferred upon the trade mark owner to oppose any use of the trade mark which is liable to impair the guarantee of origin so understood forms part of the specific subject-matter of the trade mark right, the protection of which may justify derogation from the fundamental principle of free movement of goods (*Hoffmann-La Roche*, paragraph 7; *Pfizer*, paragraph 9). . . .

58.   In the light of the arguments of the plaintiffs in the main actions, it should be clarified at the outset that the concept of adverse effects on the original condition of the product refers to the condition of the product inside the packaging.

59.   The trade mark owner may therefore oppose any repackaging involving a risk of the product inside the package being exposed to tampering or to influences affecting its original condition. To determine whether that applies account must be taken, as the Court held in paragraph 10 of the *Hoffmann-La Roche* judgment, of the nature of the product and the method of repackaging.

60.   As regards pharmaceutical products, it follows from the same paragraph in *Hoffmann-La Roche* that repackaging must be regarded as having been carried out in circumstances not capable of affecting the original condition of the product where, for example, the trade mark owner has placed the product on the market in double packaging and the repackaging affects only the external layer, leaving the inner packaging intact, or where the repackaging is carried out under the supervision of a public authority in order to ensure that the product remains intact. . . .

67.   If the repackaging is carried out in conditions which cannot affect the original condition of the product inside the packaging, the essential function of the trade mark as a guarantee of origin is safeguarded. Thus, the consumer or end user is not misled as to the origin of the products, and does, in fact, receive products manufactured under the sole supervision of the trade mark owner.

68.   Whilst, in these circumstances, the conclusion that the trade mark owner may not rely on his rights as owner in order to oppose the marketing under his trade mark of products repackaged by an importer is essential in order to ensure the free movement of goods, it does, nevertheless, confer on the importer certain rights which, in normal circumstances, are reserved for the trade mark owner himself.

69.   In the interests of the owner as proprietor of the trade mark, and to protect him against any misuse, those rights must therefore, as the Court held in *Hoffmann-La Roche*, be recognised only in so far as the importer complies with a number of other requirements.

70.   Since it is in the trade mark owner's interest that the consumer or end user should not be led to believe that the owner is responsible for the repackaging, an indication must be given on the packaging of who repackaged the product. . . .

75.   Even if the person who carried out the repackaging is indicated on the packaging of the product, there remains the possibility that the reputation of the trade mark, and thus of its owner, may nevertheless suffer from an inappropriate presentation of the repackaged product. In such a case, the trade

mark owner has a legitimate interest, related to the specific subject-matter of the trade mark right, in being able to oppose the marketing of the product. In assessing whether the presentation of the repackaged product is liable to damage the reputation of the trade mark, account must be taken of the nature of the product and the market for which it is intended. . . .

78. Finally, as the Court pointed out in *Hoffmann-La Roche*, the trade mark owner must be given advance notice of the repackaged product being put on sale. The owner may also require the importer to supply him with a specimen of the repackaged product before it goes on sale, to enable him to check that the repackaging is not carried out in such a way as directly or indirectly to affect the original condition of the product and that the presentation after repackaging is not likely to damage the reputation of the trade mark. Similarly, such a requirement affords the trade mark owner a better possibility of protecting himself against counterfeiting.

The essence of Mr Wilson's argument for CFD was that all that had been done to Microsoft's original packaging was that, in creating the brown box format, the goods had been de-labelled, not re-labelled or repackaged, which he submitted was not, or was arguably not, an activity involving any relevant alteration to the condition of the goods after they had been put onto the market by Microsoft. The customer would still be getting genuine, unaltered, Microsoft software in sealed jewel cases bearing Microsoft's trade marks, and he submitted that the reference to 'goods' in s.12(2) was to the contents of Microsoft's packaging, not to the packaging itself, a proposition supported by para 58 of the judgment in the Bristol-Myers case. Moreover, he said that CFD dealt only with OEMs, so that the appearance of the packages they were supplying was of less importance than if they were dealing with end users direct. He did not submit that these points were necessarily a complete answer to the case based on trade mark infringement, but he did submit that the question of whether Microsoft had 'legitimate reasons' to oppose CFD's dealings in the goods was a matter giving rise to a triable issue deserving full investigation and in respect of which CFD was entitled to leave to defend.

I feel unable to accept Mr Wilson's argument. I do not find the decision in the *Bristol-Myers* case of direct assistance in this case, since the circumstances there were rather different. I am inclined to agree with Mr Wilson that this case is not strictly about the repackaging of Microsoft's product. It is rather about the deliberate destruction of a material part of the packaging which Microsoft has applied to its products, the object of such exercise being to conceal from the purchaser features about the product which Microsoft had intentionally spelt out on the destroyed packaging, namely that the enclosed product was either designed and intended solely for the North American market or for North American academic users at the concessionary price. Products supplied by Microsoft for retail distribution in North America are only licensed for use by an end user if the first end user purchases in North America. Likewise, products supplied by Microsoft for retail distribution to academic users in North America are only licensed for use if the first end user is an academic who purchases in North America. The purpose of the destruction of Microsoft's outer packaging was to facilitate sales of the software which Microsoft had not authorised. CFD's dealings in supplying the licence packs and family bundles were similarly unauthorised by Microsoft.

I agree with Mr Wilson that marketing the products in plain brown boxes was not an exercise which was likely to have any adverse effects on the condition of the software itself. On the other hand, Microsoft does not sell its software separately, since it is a feature of its operations that a particular item of software must be accompanied by a related EULA. One possible effect of the marketing of the products in the brown boxes was the increased risk that there would be an intermediate splitting up of software and EULAs. Microsoft claims that this is what CFD did when selling MLP12 to Technology plc. CFD denies that, and I do not consider that I can resolve that factual dispute on this application. However, the point is that the brown box trade facilitated the tampering with the contents of the original product in this way. Further, I do not accept that CFD dealt only with OEMs. Mr Stuart's evidence is to the effect that his supply of EULAs to Option Technologies derived from software packages returned to CFD by dissatisfied purchasers, by which I interpret him to mean end users.

I have come to the conclusion that CFD's contention that Microsoft can have no legitimate reasons for opposing CFD's manner of trading is one that does not give rise to a triable issue. I accept Mr Baldwin's submission that Microsoft has established trade mark infringement by CFD with regard to all six heads of complaint. . . .

[Microsoft also prevailed on the passing off and copyright infringement counts. The latter was based on the theory that CFD did not have authority to license use of the software because Microsoft had not consented to this.]

G.   CONTRACTS AND LICENSING

Computer software is often distributed in the world market in packages containing shrinkwrap licenses, such as those discussed in Chapter 6. Although individually negotiated license agreements are generally enforceable in the international arena, national laws differ considerably as to whether or under what circumstances mass-market shrinkwrap licenses are enforceable, as the excerpts below explain:

Andrea Migdal,[37] *Shrinkwrap Licenses Abroad*
2 J. Internet L. 24 (June 1999)

Questions Regarding Enforceability

The problem of finding an "offer and acceptance" of shrinkwrap licenses has resulted in judicial uncertainty as to their enforceability, both at home and abroad. Until recently, courts in the United States refused to enforce shrinkwraps. However, in 1996, the Seventh Circuit upheld the provisions of a shrinkwrap license in the case of ProCD, Inc. v. Zeidenberg, departing from previous court decisions and creating a split in judicial precedent. Since *ProCD*, most US courts have upheld shrinkwrap licenses. Shrinkwraps are more likely to be upheld if the consumer has the opportunity to read the license requirements and, if the consumer disagrees with the terms of the license, is afforded the opportunity to return the software for a refund.

Similarly, the laws of foreign countries have swung back and forth and are unclear and incomplete in many instances as to the enforceability of shrinkwraps. Some nations expressly forbid the use of shrinkwraps; others allow them without limitation. Many other countries tread the middle ground by allowing the use of shrinkwraps subject to limitations.

This article provides a brief overview of the positions of selected foreign countries on the enforceability of shrinkwrap licenses. As will be noted in the information provided below, in many countries there has been neither a definitive court ruling on the enforceability of shrinkwraps nor legislation in favor of prohibiting shrinkwraps. Accordingly, conclusions reached regarding the enforceability of shrinkwraps in many countries is based on (1) analogy to the treatment of other consumer terms or (2) consumer acceptance.

Fairness to Consumers Governs
Shrinkwrap Enforcement

The countries noted below are divided roughly into two groups. The first consists of countries that appear to have either an extremely general policy or no articulated policy at all toward shrinkwraps. The second includes countries that appear to have developed at least a modest set of enforcement standards to govern shrinkwraps.

A number of countries generally enforce shrinkwrap licenses. These countries include Argentina (preliminary measures granted in favor of shrinkwraps), Belgium (shrinkwraps upheld when general conditions of validity are met), Egypt (shrinkwraps enforced without specific requirements),

37. Andrea Migdal is a partner in the Intellectual Property and Technology Group of Gray Cary Ware & Freidenrich in San Diego, CA.

Hong Kong (shrinkwraps upheld when they are reasonable and for which reasonable consideration has been given), and Malaysia (shrinkwraps upheld, though courts would defer to US or UK judicial decisions).

In contrast, there is a view among foreign counsel in a number of countries that shrinkwraps would not be enforced if the terms were actually tested by a consumer. These countries include Finland (shrinkwraps are commonly used, but are probably not enforceable), Italy (enforcement would probably not be possible unless shrinkwraps became an industry standard), Norway, Poland, Singapore, South Africa, Taiwan, and Venezuela.

In general, the extent of shrinkwrap enforcement is limited by a concern for fairness to consumers. Nations that have developed enforcement standards for shrinkwraps often restrict enforcement to prevent the same abuses sought to be prevented by the contracts doctrine of "unconscionability." Thus, not surprisingly, limitations on shrinkwraps are usually imposed in two ways. The first is by prohibiting "surprise" to the consumer by making sure shrinkwrap terms are visible and understandable to purchasers prior to purchase (procedural unconscionability). The second is by invalidating shrinkwrap terms that are grossly unfair or illegal (substantive unconscionability).

Other Countries Enforce Shrinkwraps
Subject to Limitations

A handful of countries enforce shrinkwrap licenses subject to articulated limitations. Various limitations are aimed at preventing surprise to the consumer. For example, many countries require the shrinkwrap to be in the purchaser's native language (e.g., Colombia, Denmark, France, Germany, Japan, and Italy). Other countries require clear and visible presentation of the license terms on the exterior of the packaging (e.g., Australia, Denmark, the Dominican Republic, France, Germany, Italy, Japan, and the United Kingdom).

Other limitations aim less at preventing surprise than at preventing substantive unfairness. For example, many countries prohibit shrinkwrap terms that are unduly burdensome or illegal. These countries include Austria (shrinkwraps are subject to certain restrictions under the Austrian Consumer Protection Law), Brazil (shrinkwraps must not violate "mandatory legal provisions"), Colombia (limits enforcement of shrinkwrap terms, requiring the payment of royalties), France (declares invalid severe limitations on reverse engineering and consumer remedies against the manufacturer), Germany (declares invalid severe limitations on consumer remedies and the purchaser's right to use the product), Italy (declares invalid severe limitations on consumer remedies and transferability), Israel (shrinkwraps are subject to the Standard Contracts Act of 1982, which invalidates depriving or restricting conditions), Japan (courts protect consumer remedies), and the United Kingdom (encroachment on European Community law is suspect; some limitations on consumer remedies and reverse engineering are invalid).

Conclusion

The use of shrinkwraps, though widespread as a business practice, is not universally and definitively recognized as a valid contract. Further, the wide variety of loosely articulated enforcement standards has created a potential maze for software manufacturers attempting to maximize the use of shrinkwraps internationally. However, even where no precedent or laws governing enforceability exist, shrinkwrap licenses can be useful to the licensor, at least as a potential deterrent to widespread copying, reverse engineering, and related licensing concerns. A licensor can also create the conditions for more likely enforcement of its shrinkwrap license by:

- providing a clear opportunity for the consumer to accept the license (e.g., "click here to accept and install");
- avoiding overly onerous terms, which might be voided as an adhesion contract or against public policy; and
- "localizing" licenses through translation and attention to other consumer law provisions.

≡ *Imprimatur, Report on Formation and Validity of*
≡ *On-Line Contracts in the European Union*
≡ *Institute for Information Law, U. Amsterdam, June 1998*

. . . Under British law the legal qualification of a shrinkwrap license is complex. First there is the doctrine of "privity of contract". This prescribes a direct contractual connection between parties. In the software business there is no such direct connection between producer and user. Software is sold through retailers. Secondly, according to the doctrine of "consideration" in order to achieve a binding license between producer and user, consideration has to be given for such a contract. It is doubtful whether merely breaking a cellophane seal can be said to amount to consideration. Judges confronted with a shrinkwrap case, will have to apply these doctrines, but may also want to give effect to a shrinkwrap license. To reconcile these interests is a dilemma under British law.

In December 1995 the first British judgment on the enforceability of shrinkwrap licences was passed: Beta v. Adobe. The facts of this case brought before a Scottish court are the following. Adobe placed an order with retailer Beta for the supply of software produced by Informix. Beta delivered the software package to user Adobe. Adobe ultimately did not want the software, and relying on the producer's shrinkwrap provisions including the right to return the software, tried to return the package. But Beta refused it and later sued Adobe for payment of the invoiced price. Beta contended that the purchaser had made an unconditional order. The supply had been made and so the price was due. Adobe's position was that the shrinkwrap terms were incorporated into the contract at point of sale. The court gave judgement to Adobe. It did give effect to the shrinkwrap license by applying the Scottish doctrine of *ius quaesitum tertio.* This doctrine allows a party to a bilateral contract (i.e. Beta) to create contractual rights for the benefit of a third party (i.e. the producer). This implies the third party is able to enforce these rights directly against the end user. . . .

Netherlands

Only one decision dealing with the enforceability of a shrinkwrap license has been reported. It is a judgment by the Amsterdam court of first instance of May 24, 1995 in the case of Coss Holland B.V. v. TM Data Nederland B.V. The facts of this case are the following. Distributor TM Data supplied software, produced by Raima, to user Coss. According to TM Data, the text of Raima's shrinkwrap license terms were enclosed in the packing of the software. Coss denied the terms were present in the packing. When the computer program turned out not to function properly and attempts to repair it failed, Coss claimed damages from TM Data. TM Data refused to pay damages contending that TM Data was not a party to the shrinkwrap license, the license being concluded between Raima and Coss. The court rejected this defence. It held a licence agreement cannot be formed by simply opening the packing of software. A license agreement can only be concluded validly if a user is aware that by opening a packing he becomes party to a license agreement. Moreover the contents of the license terms will have to be clear to the user beforehand.

From this judgement one can conclude that under Dutch law shrinkwrap licenses may be enforceable provided that users are aware of the use of such licenses and know the contents of the license terms before the agreement is formed. Dutch commentators opine that a user has to be familiar with the contents of the license terms before or at the moment the license agreement is formed.

Conclusion

. . . From case law it becomes clear that the enforceability of shrinkwrap licenses will be determined by the following factors:

- the awareness of the user of the existence of a shrinkwrap license: is a user aware that the product he ordered is subject to a shrinkwrap license? If so is he aware that by opening the product's packing he agrees to the license terms?

- the user's familiarity with the contents of the license terms. The license terms have to be available.
- the moment upon which the user was informed about the terms.

COMMENTS AND QUESTIONS

1.   The Scottish case cited by the Imprimatur Report involved an attempt by the recipient of a shrinkwrap license to enforce terms that were favorable to the purchaser. This reverses the normal model. Should this matter in determining the enforceability of the shrinkwrap license? Can a user turn the document drafted by the licensor into a binding contract by adopting it? If so, what, if any, support does this provide for efforts by licensors to enforce shrinkwrap licenses?

2.   Most shrinkwrap licenses contain provisions purporting to determine both the forum in which disputes may be litigated and the law that will apply to those disputes. If these provisions are enforceable in most countries, they will significantly skew the resolution of software disputes, probably toward certain states in the United States.

3.   Software vendors in the United States have been pushing for the adoption of the Uniform Computer Information Transactions Act, which would govern transactions involving computer software and digital information. This model law is discussed in detail in Chapter 6. There is no similar statute in the works in the rest of the world that would validate shrinkwrap licenses or enact many of the other provisions that benefit software vendors.

4.   For a discussion of the status of contract law in Japan, see, e.g., Tsuneo Matsumoto, Article 2B and Mass Market License Contracts: A Japanese Perspective, 13 Berkeley Tech. L.J. 1283 (1998).

H.   ANTITRUST AND COMPETITION POLICY

Approximately 60 countries in the world have antitrust-like laws. These countries typically use the term "competition law" to describe their body of law that performs the functions that antitrust law serves in the United States. Many of these competition laws are relatively new (i.e., less than 10 years old) and less fully developed than U.S. antitrust law. In general, computer technology firms are free to exercise their intellectual property rights in the international marketplace in a manner that will best serve the firm's interests. There are, however, several areas where competition policy issues tend to arise in regulation of the computer technology market-place.

One prominent example was an action that the Competition Director-ate of the European Commission took against IBM Corporation in the 1980s because IBM's alterations to program interfaces were perceived to have harmed competition in the market for peripheral devices. This case was settled with IBM's agreement to disclose changes in its interfaces. The Commission's experience in the IBM case contributed to the Commission's subsequent insistence that the European Council's Directive on the Legal Protection of Computer Programs include three competition-enhancing rules: (1) a rule that interfaces necessary for achieving interoperability of computer programs should not be protected by copyright law; (2) a rule that decompilation of computer program code should be permissible when necessary to achieve interoperability; and (3) a rule that contract terms aiming to override the decompilation privilege would be null and void.

Similar considerations led the European Commission to make the right of lawful users of a database to extract and reuse under the new sui generis right in the contents of databases nonwaivable by contract. Concerns about potential abuses of dominant firms in the database industry nearly led the Commission to adopt a compulsory license scheme for sole source and gov-ernment databases in the sui generis database law. However, the *Magill* de-cision (below) apparently persuaded the Commission that competition pol-icy could adequately address abuses of dominant positions in the database market. The Commission is sufficiently concerned about the potential for abuse by database providers that it intends to review and periodically report on licensing practices in this field. However, the *Magill* decision will apply more generally to the licensing of intellectual property rights in the EU.

Radio Telefis Eireann (RTE) and Independent Television Publications Ltd. (ITP) v. Commission of the European Communities
Court of Justice of the European Communities
1995 E.C.J. CELEX LEXIS 3670, [1995] E.C.R. I-743,
[1995] 4 C.M.L.R. 718

... 6 According to the judgments of the Court of First Instance, most households in Ireland and 30% to 40% of households in Northern Ireland can receive television programmes broadcast by RTE, ITV and BBC.

7 At the material time, no comprehensive weekly television guide was available on the market in Ireland or in Northern Ireland. Each television station published a television guide covering exclusively its own pro-grammes and claimed, under Irish and United Kingdom legislation, copy-right protection for its own weekly programme listings in order to prevent their reproduction by third parties. . . .

9   ITP, RTE and BBC practised the following policy with regard to the dissemination of programme listings. They provided their programme schedules free of charge, on request, to daily and periodical newspapers, accompanied by a licence for which no charge was made, setting out the conditions under which that information could be reproduced. Daily listings and, if the following day was a public holiday, the listings for two days, could thus be published in the press, subject to certain conditions relating to the format of publication. Publication of "highlights" of the week was also authorized. ITP, RTE and the BBC ensured strict compliance with the licence conditions by instituting legal proceedings, where necessary, against publications which failed to comply with them.

10   Magill TV Guide Ltd ("Magill") attempted to publish a comprehensive weekly television guide but was prevented from doing so by the appellants and the BBC, which obtained injunctions prohibiting publication of weekly television listings.

11   Magill lodged a complaint with the Commission on 4 April 1986 under Article 3 of Regulation No 17 of the Council of 6 February 1962, the First Regulation implementing Articles 85 and 86 of the Treaty (OJ, English Special Edition 1959-1962, p. 87) ("Regulation No 17") seeking a declaration that the appellants and the BBC were abusing their dominant position by refusing to grant licences for the publication of their respective weekly listings. The Commission decided to initiate a proceeding, at the end of which it adopted Decision 89/205/EEC of 21 December 1988 relating to a proceeding under Article 86 of the EEC Treaty (IV/31.851. Magill TV Guide/ITP, BBC and RTE) (OJ 1989 L 78, p. 43) (" the decision"), which was the subject-matter of the proceedings before the Court of First Instance.

12   In that decision the Commission found that there had been a breach of Article 86 of the EEC Treaty and ordered the three organizations to put an end to that breach, in particular "by supplying . . . third parties on request and on a non-discriminatory basis with their individual advance weekly programme listings and by permitting reproduction of those listings by such parties". It was also provided that, if the three organizations chose to grant reproduction licences, any royalties requested should be reasonable. . . .

24   So far as the existence of a dominant position is concerned, the Court of First Instance held that "ITP enjoyed, as a consequence of its copyright in ITV and Channel 4 programme listings, which had been transferred to it by the television companies broadcasting on those channels, the exclusive right to reproduce and market those listings. It was thus able, at the material time, to secure a monopoly over the publication of its weekly listings in the TV Times, a magazine specializing in the programmes of ITV and Channel 4". Consequently, in the opinion of the Court of First Instance, "the applicant clearly held at that time a dominant position both on the market represented by its weekly listings and on the market for the magazines in which they were published in Ireland and Northern Ireland.

Third parties such as Magill who wished to publish a general television magazine were in a situation of economic dependence on the applicant, which was thus in a position to hinder the emergence of any effective competition on the market for information on its weekly programmes" (*ITP* judgment, paragraph 49). With regard to RTE, the Court of First Instance reached the same conclusion in nearly identical terms (*RTE* judgment, paragraph 63).

25   So far as the existence of an abuse of that dominant position was concerned, the Court of First Instance considered that it was necessary to interpret Article 86 in the light of copyright in programme listings. It pointed out that, in the absence of harmonization of national rules or Community standardization, determination of the conditions and procedures under which copyright was protected was a matter for national rules (*ITP* judgment, paragraphs 50 and 51). The relationship between national intellectual property rights and the general rules of Community law was governed expressly by Article 36 of the EEC Treaty, which provided for the possibility of derogating from the rules relating to the free movement of goods on grounds of the protection of industrial or commercial property, subject to the conditions set out in the second sentence of Article 36. Article 36 thus emphasized that the reconciliation between the requirements of the free movement of goods and the respect to which intellectual property rights were entitled had to be achieved in such a way as to protect the legitimate exercise of such rights, which alone was justified within the meaning of that article, and to preclude any improper exercise thereof likely to create artificial partitions within the market or pervert the rules governing competition within the Community. The Court of First Instance took the view that the exercise of intellectual property rights conferred by national legislation had consequently to be restricted as far as was necessary for that reconciliation (*ITP* judgment, paragraph 52).

26   The Court of First Instance found, in the light of the case-law of the Court of Justice, that it followed from Article 36 of the Treaty that only those restrictions on freedom of competition, free movement of goods or freedom to provide services which were inherent in the protection of the actual substance of the intellectual property right were permitted in Community law. It based its view in particular on the judgment of the Court of Justice in Case 78/70 Deutsche Grammophon v Metro 1971 ECR 487, paragraph 11, in which the Court of Justice held that, although it permitted prohibitions or restrictions on the free movement of products which were justified for the purpose of protecting industrial and commercial property, Article 36 only admitted derogations from that freedom to the extent to which they were justified for the purpose of safeguarding rights which constituted the specific subject-matter of such property (*ITP* judgment, paragraph 54).

27   The Court of First Instance then observed that in principle the protection of the specific subject-matter of a copyright entitled the copy-

right-holder to reserve the exclusive right to reproduce the protected work (*ITP* judgment, paragraph 55).

28   However, the Court of First Instance took the view that, while it was plain that the exercise of the exclusive right to reproduce a protected work was not in itself an abuse, that did not apply when, in the light of the details of each individual case, it was apparent that that right was being exercised in such ways and circumstances as in fact to pursue an aim manifestly contrary to the objectives of Article 86. In that event, the Court of First Instance continued, the copyright was no longer being exercised in a manner which corresponded to its essential function, within the meaning of Article 36 of the Treaty, which was to protect the moral rights in the work and ensure a reward for the creative effort, while respecting the aims of, in particular, Article 86. From this the Court of First Instance concluded that the primacy of Community law, particularly as regards principles as fundamental as those of the free movement of goods and freedom of competition, prevailed over any use of a rule of national intellectual property law in a manner contrary to those principles (*ITP* judgment, paragraph 56).

29   In the present case, the Court of First Instance noted that the applicants, by reserving the exclusive right to publish their weekly television programme listings, were preventing the emergence on the market of a new product, namely a general television magazine likely to compete with their own magazines. The applicants were thus using their copyright in the programme listings produced as part of the activity of broadcasting in order to secure a monopoly in the derivative market of weekly television guides in Ireland and Northern Ireland. The Court of First Instance also regarded it as significant in that regard that the applicants had authorized, free of charge, the publication of their daily listings and highlights of their weekly programmes in the press in both Ireland and the United Kingdom.

30   The Court of First Instance accordingly took the view that conduct of that type . . . characterized by preventing the production and marketing of a new product, for which there was potential consumer demand, on the ancillary market of weekly television guides and thereby excluding all competition from that market solely in order to secure the applicants' respective monopolies clearly went beyond what was necessary to fulfil the essential function of the copyright as permitted in Community law. The applicants' refusal to authorize third parties to publish their weekly listings was, in this case, the Court of First Instance ruled, arbitrary in so far as it was not justified by the requirements peculiar to the activity of publishing television magazines. It was thus possible for the applicants to adapt to the conditions of a television magazine market which was open to competition in order to ensure the commercial viability of their weekly publications. The applicants' conduct could not, in those circumstances, be covered in Community law by the protection conferred by their copyright in the programme listings (*ITP* judgment, paragraph 58). . . .

32   The Court of First Instance accordingly dismissed the plea in law based on breach of Article 86.

33   RTE, supported by IPO, relies on the judgment in Case 238/87 Volvo v Veng 1988 ECR 6211 in arguing that the exercise by an owner of intellectual property rights of his exclusive rights, in particular his refusal to grant a licence, cannot in itself be regarded as an abuse of a dominant position.

34   According to RTE, ITP and IPO, one of the essential rights of the owner of a copyright, without which that right would be deprived of its substance, is the exclusive right of reproduction. That right, which has not been placed in question by the Treaty rules, entitles its holder to be rewarded by the exclusive sale of the products incorporating the protected work and to prevent competition by a third party in respect of those products.

35   ITP denies that the exercise of the exclusive right of reproduction is itself an abuse where it is in pursuit of an aim manifestly contrary to the objectives of Article 86 (*ITP* judgment, paragraph 56) since copyright owners ordinarily and naturally exercise their copyright in order to restrict competition with their own product by other products made using their copyright material, even on a derived market. That, it continues, is the essence of copyright.

36   IPO considers that copyright is by nature beneficial for competition, pointing out that it attributes exclusive proprietorial rights only to a particular expression of an idea or concept, not to the concept or idea itself.

37   RTE and IPO point out that, in the absence of Community harmonization, the scope of national copyright laws can be defined only by the legislature of each Member State. The definition of that scope cannot be altered by a measure adopted in implementation of Article 86, but only by specific Community legislation.

38   Moreover, according to RTE, the right of first marketing has been considered in the case-law of the Court of Justice as the specific subject-matter of all industrial property rights.

39   RTE contends that the owner of an intellectual property right is under no obligation to offer justification for his refusal to grant a licence, contrary to the view taken by the Court of First Instance. ITP adds that this view of the Court of First Instance is not supported by the case-law of the Court of Justice and that, due to the imprecision of the criteria used, it undermines legal certainty for copyright owners.

40   According to RTE and IPO, a refusal, by the owner of a right, to grant a licence forms part of the specific subject-matter of his exclusive right. RTE considers that this would constitute an abuse only in very particular circumstances and IPO adds that the use of an intellectual property right is justified if it is within the scope of the specific subject- matter of the right in question.

41   IPO and RTE criticize the approach, adopted by the Court of First Instance and the Commission in this case, of seeing copyright as a mere combination of the right of attribution of authorship and the right to compensation for exploitation. IPO claims that this is in marked contrast

not only to the laws of the various Member States but also to the Berne Convention and would represent a significant diminution of the protection afforded by copyright. ITP adds that this view overlooks the right of exclusive reproduction and distinguishes between the protection of moral rights and the protection of commercial rights with the result that assignees of the creator, such as ITP, cannot avail themselves of moral rights, which are inalienable, and will therefore be unable to exercise the right of exclusive reproduction.

42   RTE submits that consumer demand cannot justify application of Article 86 to the present cases and that it is for the national legislature alone to remedy such a situation, as has been done in the United Kingdom. ITP adds that it is ordinarily the case that a copyright owner who sells his own product made from his copyright material deprives consumers of the opportunity of obtaining it elsewhere.

43   Next, according to IPO, there is no presumption that the holder of an intellectual property right is in a dominant position within the meaning of Article 86 (judgments in Case 40/70 Sirena v EDA and Others 1971 ECR 69 and Case 78/70 *Deutsche Grammophon*, cited above). Relying in particular on the judgment in Case 322/81 Michelin v Commission 1983 ECR 3461, IPO takes the view that a dominant position presupposes a position of economic strength and for that reason it calls in question the analysis of the Court of First Instance that the appellants were dominant merely because they held copyrights without reference to any analysis whatever of economic power in the marketplace.

44   IPO also criticizes the Commission for having failed to apply the criterion of dominant position based on economic power and having taken the view that the appellants and the BBC held a factual monopoly. In doing so, the Commission takes the view that a factual monopoly is likely to arise wherever there exists a primary market and a secondary market and a third party wishes to avail itself of the products or services on the primary market in order to carry on business on the secondary market. According to IPO, the Commission considers that such a situation will result in a position of economic dependence which is characteristic of the existence of a dominant position.

45   IPO criticizes this conception in so far as it artificially links economic dependence with the intention of a third party, who would always have the possibility of undertaking some other economic venture. For IPO, the concept of "factual monopoly" appears to be an artificial construct whereby the Commission seeks to justify the use of competition law in order to change the specific subject-matter of copyright.

(a)   Existence of a Dominant Position

46   So far as dominant position is concerned, it is to be remembered at the outset that mere ownership of an intellectual property right cannot confer such a position.

47   However, the basic information as to the channel, day, time and title of programmes is the necessary result of programming by television stations, which are thus the only source of such information for an undertaking, like Magill, which wishes to publish it together with commentaries or pictures. By force of circumstance, RTE and ITP, as the agent of ITV, enjoy, along with the BBC, a de facto monopoly over the information used to compile listings for the television programmes received in most households in Ireland and 30% to 40% of households in Northern Ireland. The appellants are thus in a position to prevent effective competition on the market in weekly television magazines. The Court of First Instance was therefore right in confirming the Commission's assessment that the appellants occupied a dominant position (see the judgment in Case 322/81 *Michelin*, cited above, paragraph 30).

(b)   Existence of Abuse

48   With regard to the issue of abuse, the arguments of the appellants and IPO wrongly presuppose that where the conduct of an undertaking in a dominant position consists of the exercise of a right classified by national law as "copyright", such conduct can never be reviewed in relation to Article 86 of the Treaty.

49   Admittedly, in the absence of Community standardization or harmonization of laws, determination of the conditions and procedures for granting protection of an intellectual property right is a matter for national rules. Further, the exclusive right of reproduction forms part of the author's rights, so that refusal to grant a licence, even if it is the act of an undertaking holding a dominant position, cannot in itself constitute abuse of a dominant position (judgment in Case 238/87 *Volvo*, cited above, paragraphs 7 and 8).

50   However, it is also clear from that judgment (paragraph 9) that the exercise of an exclusive right by the proprietor may, in exceptional circumstances, involve abusive conduct.

51   In the present case, the conduct objected to is the appellants' reliance on copyright conferred by national legislation so as to prevent Magill or any other undertaking having the same intention from publishing on a weekly basis information (channel, day, time and title of programmes) together with commentaries and pictures obtained independently of the appellants.

52   Among the circumstances taken into account by the Court of First Instance in concluding that such conduct was abusive was, first, the fact that there was, according to the findings of the Court of First Instance, no actual or potential substitute for a weekly television guide offering information on the programmes for the week ahead. On this point, the Court of First Instance confirmed the Commission's finding that the complete lists of programmes for a 24-hour period and for a 48-hour period at week-

ends and before public holidays published in certain daily and Sunday newspapers, and the television sections of certain magazines covering, in addition, "highlights" of the week's programmes, were only to a limited extent substitutable for advance information to viewers on all the week's programmes. Only weekly television guides containing comprehensive listings for the week ahead would enable users to decide in advance which programmes they wished to follow and arrange their leisure activities for the week accordingly. The Court of First Instance also established that there was a specific, constant and regular potential demand on the part of consumers (see the *RTE* judgment, paragraph 62, and the *ITP* judgment, paragraph 48).

53 Thus the appellants, who were, by force of circumstance, the only sources of the basic information on programme scheduling which is the indispensable raw material for compiling a weekly television guide, gave viewers wishing to obtain information on the choice of programmes for the week ahead no choice but to buy the weekly guides for each station and draw from each of them the information they needed to make comparisons.

54 The appellants' refusal to provide basic information by relying on national copyright provisions thus prevented the appearance of a new product, a comprehensive weekly guide to television programmes, which the appellants did not offer and for which there was a potential consumer demand. Such refusal constitutes an abuse under heading (b) of the second paragraph of Article 86 of the Treaty.

55 Second, there was no justification for such refusal either in the activity of television broadcasting or in that of publishing television magazines (*RTE* judgment, paragraph 73, and *ITP* judgment, paragraph 58).

56 Third, and finally, as the Court of First Instance also held, the appellants, by their conduct, reserved to themselves the secondary market of weekly television guides by excluding all competition on that market (see the judgment in *Joined Cases* 6/73 and 7/73 Commercial Solvents v Commission 1974 ECR 223, paragraph 25) since they denied access to the basic information which is the raw material indispensable for the compilation of such a guide.

57 In the light of all those circumstances, the Court of First Instance did not err in law in holding that the appellants' conduct was an abuse of a dominant position within the meaning of Article 86 of the Treaty. . . .

91 In the present case, after finding that the refusal to provide undertakings such as Magill with the basic information contained in television programme listings was an abuse of a dominant position, the Commission was entitled under Article 3, in order to ensure that its decision was effective, to require the appellants to provide that information. As the Court of First Instance rightly found, the imposition of that obligation with the possibility of making authorization of publication dependent on certain conditions, including payment of royalties was the only way of bringing the infringement to an end.

COMMENTS AND QUESTIONS

1. Prior to adoption of the European Directive on the Legal Protection of Databases, U.K. copyright law allowed compilers of factual data to obtain copyright protection for their compilations on a "sweat of the brow" theory. Although the EU Directive now harmonizes European copyright law on an "intellectual creation" standard of originality, it "grandfathered" in copyright protection for compilations protected by national law prior to the effective date of the directive.

2. How would U.S. courts deal with the same issue as in *Magill*? In particular, it is interesting to contrast *Magill* with the Microsoft cases and the cases regarding mandatory disclosure of interfaces. Does *Magill* suggest that Microsoft might be forced to publish its APIs in a European court?

3. The *Magill* decision has been criticized in Europe for applying competition law too broadly. See, e.g., Per Jebsen & Robert Stevens, Assumptions, Goals, and Dominant Undertakings: The Regulation of Competition Under Article 86 of the European Union, 64 Antitrust L.J. 443, 461 (1996).

> "In that case, the primacy of Community Law, particularly as regards principles as fundamental as those of the free movement of goods and freedom of competition, prevails over any use of a rule of national intellectual property in a manner contrary to these principles." . . . With these words the CFI in *Radio Telefís Eireann* struck fear into the hearts of all businesses operating in sectors where intellectual property is of great significance. . . . The decision in *Radio Telefís Eireann*—undermining much of the assumed strength of intellectual property—is an appropriate place to begin our analysis of Article 86.

Seemingly consistent with *Magill*, however, is Article 8(2) of the TRIPS Agreement, which states that "[a]ppropriate measures . . . may be needed to prevent the abuse of intellectual property rights by rightsholders or the resort to practices which unreasonably restrain trade or adversely affect the international transfer of technology."

4. Both U.S. and EU law regulate competition matters by announcing broad principles against anticompetitive activity and leaving the specific application of these principles to the courts (and in the EU, the Commission) on a case-by-case basis. Article 81(1) (formerly 85(1)) of the Treaty Establishing the European Community, for example, outlaws all agreements that "have as their object or effect the prevention, restriction or distortion of competition within the common market," in particular those that:

(a) directly or indirectly fix purchase or selling prices or any other trading conditions;

(b) limit or control production, markets, technical development, or investment;

(c) share markets or sources of supply;

(d)   apply dissimilar conditions to equivalent transactions with other trading parties, thereby placing them at a competitive disadvantage;

(e)   make the conclusion of contracts subject to acceptance by the other parties of supplementary obligations which, by their nature or according to commercial usage, have no connection with the subject of such contracts.

Article 82 (formerly 86) defines "an abuse of a dominant position" as those acts done by a monopolist, which Article 81(1) (formerly 85(1)) (a), (b), (d), and (e) make illegal when done by combination among firms.

It is noteworthy that the EU, like the United States, recognizes the need for a flexible approach to certain practices that would be considered anticompetitive in an industrial economy but that may be necessary to the efficient exploitation of intellectual property rights. In Europe, this recognition comes in the form of block exemptions for many intellectual property licensing practices. See, e.g., Jiamming Shen, Block Exemption for Technology Licensing Agreements Under Commission Regulation (EC) No. 240/96, 20 B.C. Int'l & Comp. L. Rev. 251 (1997). European block exemptions are not found in the Treaty Establishing the European Community; they are implemented separately in the form of EC regulations.

5.   United States antitrust authorities have recognized that the global nature of the computer industry is a challenge for antitrust enforcers. Joel Klein of the U.S. Antitrust Division explained the U.S. strategy for applying antitrust to the global computer industry in this way:

> To seek effective antitrust enforcement in global industries, we in the Department of Justice have developed three approaches. First, we rely on coordinated enforcement actions, in which we pursue parallel investigations of particular practices with other national competition authorities through shared information and cooperation. Second, we invoke positive comity, a doctrine in which one enforcement agency requests enforcement action by another country where the latter may be better able to challenge or curb the anticompetitive activities in question. Finally, we directly apply our laws to conduct occurring in whole or in part in other jurisdictions where the effects of such conduct may be felt in the United States.

Joel Klein & Preeta Bansal, International Antitrust Enforcement in the Computer Industry, 41 Vill. L. Rev. 173 (1996) (giving examples of each strategy). See also U.S. Dep't of Justice & Fed. Trade Comm'n, Antitrust Enforcement Guidelines for International Operations (Apr. 1995).

6.   The lack of uniformity in competition policies around the world has alarmed some commentators, who suggest that, in a global market, companies should have to adhere to a single standard of conduct worldwide. For a discussion of the lack of uniformity among national antitrust laws, reasons for this diversity, and an explanation about why it may be difficult to get a WTO agreement on competition policy, see Eleanor M. Fox,

Trade, Competition, and Intellectual Property—TRIPS and Its Antitrust Counterparts, 29 Vand. J. Transnat'l L. 481, 494 (1996). On the problems with achieving international cooperation in applying antitrust principles, see Andrew T. Guzman, Is International Antitrust Possible?, 73 N.Y.U. L. Rev. 1501 (1998).

The problems with lack of antitrust uniformity are exacerbated by the growing tendency of the United States and some other countries to apply their laws extraterritorially. The United States, for example, has applied its criminal statute to a price-fixing agreement that occurred entirely within Japan because the consequences of the agreement could be felt in the United States. See, e.g., United States v. Nippon Paper, 109 F.3d 1 (1st Cir. 1997), *cert. denied*, 118 S. Ct. 685 (1998).

This extraterritoriality problem is a single instance of a much larger problem in international law, one that affects intellectual property rules as well. We discuss the question of extraterritorial effect in more detail in the next section.

I. EXTRATERRITORIALITY

Given the complexity of dealing with the many substantive, procedural, and remedial differences in the laws and legal systems of other nations, some companies may heartily wish to bring an action in U.S. courts to get remedies for infringements, even though some or all of the acts have occurred outside the United States. United States courts have generally been reluctant to accept cases involving extraterritorial infringement. However, a predicate act in the United States that relates to activities outside the United States may provide a basis for U.S. courts to exercise jurisdiction.

> *Expediters International of Washington, Inc. v. Direct Line Cargo Management Services, Inc.*
> United States District Court for the District of New Jersey
> *995 F. Supp. 468 (D.N.J. 1998)*

This matter involves the alleged wrongful use of a computer software program. Plaintiff Expediters International ("EI") claims that a Taiwan company, Direct Line Cargo Management Services, Inc. ("CMS-Taiwan"), became affiliated with it and assigned to it the rights of an allegedly copyrighted software program. Prior to EI's affiliation with CMS-Taiwan, CMS-Taiwan was associated with the New Jersey defendant, Direct Line Cargo Management Services, Inc., ("DLCMS-USA"), and a group of affiliated Asian companies. During its association with the defendant, CMS-Taiwan issued a license to the defendant and its affiliates which permitted the companies to make limited use of the software. When CMS-Taiwan became associated with the plaintiff, however, this license expired. This lawsuit arises from the defendant's and its affiliates' alleged wrongful use of the software subsequent to the expiration of the license.

a. Extraterritoriality

The defendant urges the Court to grant its motion because the Asian companies allegedly copied the Software overseas, beyond the jurisdiction of the United States Copyright Act. DLCMS-USA argues that the mere authorization of these infringing acts abroad is not sufficient to establish primary liability so as to bring the plaintiff's action within the jurisdiction of this Court. It also argues that, even if the Court were to attach primary liability to the mere act of authorizing infringement, there is no evidence that the defendant, in fact, authorized the Asian affiliates to copy the Software.

Section 501 of the Copyright Act states that "[a]nyone who violates any of the exclusive rights of the copyright owner as provided by sections 106 through 118 . . . is an infringer of the copyright. . . ." 17 U.S.C. §501(a). According to Section 106 of this act:

> [T]he owner of a copyright . . . has the exclusive rights to do and to authorize any of the following:
> (1) to reproduce the copyrighted work in copies or phonorecords;
> (2) to prepare derivative works based upon the copyrighted work;
> (3) to distribute copies . . . of the copyrighted work to the public by sale or other transfer of ownership, or by rental, lease or lending. . . .

17 U.S.C. §106 (1996).

There is a division among courts as to whether a claim for infringement can be brought under the Copyright Act when the alleged infringing conduct consists solely of the authorization within the United States of acts that occur entirely abroad. For example, the Ninth Circuit has held that such authorization, by itself, cannot support a United States infringement claim. See Subafilms, Ltd. v. MGM-Pathe Communications Co., 24 F.3d 1088 (9th Cir.1994). In contrast, a district court in the Sixth Circuit has held that, by authorizing the release of copyrighted music recordings overseas, a United States entity commits primary infringement that is actionable under Section 106. See Curb v. MCA Records, Inc., 898 F.Supp. 586 (M.D.Tenn.1995).

In *Subafilms*, the plaintiffs alleged that Warner Brothers violated its copyright in the Beatles's movie, "Yellow Submarine," by authorizing distributors to release video versions of the movie abroad. 24 F.3d 1088. The Court tied the authorization right in Section 106 solely to a claim of contributory infringement; it reasoned that a defendant in the United States could not be liable based on its authorization of infringing acts, where the overseas entity who actually copied the materials was not subject to United States Copyright Law. See *id.* at 1094. The Court noted that "to hold otherwise would produce the untenable anomaly, inconsistent with the general principles of third party liability, that a party could be held liable as an infringer for violating the 'authorization' right when the party that it authorized could not be considered an infringer under the Copyright Act." *Id.*

While the defendant urges the Court to apply Subafilms' interpretation of Section 106, the Court departs from the Ninth Circuit's interpretation and adopts the holding set forth in Curb v. MCA Records, Inc., 898 F.Supp. 586. In *Curb,* the defendant counterclaimed that a music company violated its licensing agreement by authorizing infringing acts abroad. See *id.* The Court denied the plaintiff's summary judgment motion, finding that there was a genuine issue of material fact as to whether the plaintiff engaged in primary infringement by merely authorizing the release of copyrighted sound recordings overseas. See *id.* The court held that authorizing infringing acts may constitute primary infringement in light of both the language and legislative history[13] of the Statute. See *id.* at 595-96. Furthermore, it reasoned that imposing direct liability for authorizing infringement more closely serves the underlying policies of the Copyright Act in this modern era. See *id.* at 595. Specifically, the Court noted:

> [P]iracy has changed since the Barbary days. Today, the raider need not grab the bounty with his own hands; he need only transmit his go-ahead by wire or telefax to start the presses in a distant land. Subafilms ignores this economic reality, and the economic incentives underpinning the Copyright clause designed to encourage creation of new works, and transforms infringement of the authorization right into a requirement of domestic presence by a primary infringer. Under this view, a phone call to Nebraska results in liability; the same phone call to France results in riches. In a global marketplace, it is literally a distinction without a difference.

Id.

This Court agrees with *Curb*'s literal interpretation of Section 106, which clearly lends "the owner of a copyright . . . the exclusive rights to do and to authorize" the reproduction and distribution of copyrighted materials. 17 U.S.C. §106. Furthermore, the Court appreciates the policy observations set forth in *Curb,* which appear more closely adapted to our modern age of telefaxes, Internet communication, and electronic mail systems. The purpose behind the Copyright Act is to protect a copyright owner's right to be free from infringement in the United States. To allow an entity to curtail this right by merely directing its foreign agent to do its "dirty work" would

---

13. The legislative history of Section 106 reveals: "Use of the phrase 'to authorize' is intended to avoid any questions as to the liability of contributory infringers. For example, a person who lawfully acquires an authorized copy of a motion picture would be an infringer if he or she engages in the business of renting it to others for purposes of unauthorized public performance." H.R.Rep. No. 1476, 94th Cong., 2d Sess. 61, *reprinted in* 1976 U.S.C.C.A.N. 5659, 5674, cited in *Curb,* 898 F.Supp. at 595.

be to hinder the deterrent effect of the statute and to thwart its underlying purpose. Because it is more closely aligned with the language, legislative history, and purpose of the statute, the Court adopts the *Curb* interpretation of Section 106 and finds that the mere authorization of infringing acts abroad constitutes direct infringement and is actionable under United States Copyright Law.

Having made this determination, the Court considers whether a reasonable jury could conclude that DLCMS-USA, in fact, authorized the Asian companies' actions. In light of DLCMS-USA's arguable motive and ability to control its affiliates, the Court cannot foreclose this possibility. A jury might reasonably infer that the defendant had a motive for authorizing the infringing acts, since the affiliates' use of the Software enabled the defendant to receive manifests and billing information to facilitate its consolidation ventures. McKenzie himself indicated that the Software was extremely valuable to the companies' business.[14] In its Answer to the Complaint, DLCMS-USA asserts as an affirmative defense that it signed the License Agreement limiting its use of the Software because it was under duress. Furthermore, during oral argument, defense counsel admitted that DLCMS-USA continued to use the Software after November 15, 1993 at the insistence of its customers. Finally, the fact that the defendant negotiated to use the Software during a transition period suggests that the defendant continued to need the Software, even after the license had expired.

In addition to motive, a jury might reasonably infer that the defendant had the ability to authorize the alleged infringing acts, owing to its close interaction with the affiliates. To prove this point, EI calls attention to the joint business dealings, the mutual agency agreements, and the shared profits, leadership, and ownership among the Asian companies and the defendant. Furthermore, it points to the defendant's own characterization of itself and its Asian affiliates as a "family of companies."

In light of the defendant's possible motive and power to authorize its affiliates to use the Software, the Court cannot, as a matter of law, find that the defendant did not direct its affiliates' actions. For this reason, the Court rejects the defendant's extraterritoriality argument.

COMMENTS AND QUESTIONS

1. Even when predicate acts in the United States permit the exercise of federal jurisdiction, U.S. courts will sometimes decide to dismiss infringement cases on forum non conveniens grounds. Two factors are relevant to this determination: (1) whether an adequate alternative forum exists, and (2) whether the balance of public and private interests warrants

---

14. McKenzie declared that he signed the June 1993 Agreement to permit DLCMS-USA's continued use of the Software; "if I refused to sign this document, DLCMS-Taiwan . . . would immediately withdraw from the DLCMS family and withhold further support of the computer systems. Such action would completely disrupt, if not completely destroy, the company."

dismissal. See, e.g., Creative Technology, Ltd. v. Aztech System Pte, Ltd., 61 F.3d 696 (9th Cir. 1995) (dismissing an infringement claim brought by one Singapore company against another Singapore company, even though much of the allegedly infringing activity had taken place in the United States). Although Judge Ferguson's vigorous dissent in *Creative Technology* criticized the majority's conclusion on the adequacy of the Singaporean courts as an alternative forum, a Singaporean court later ruled in favor of Creative Technology in a decision that granted it stronger copyright protection than would have applied in the United States. See, e.g., Jonathan Band & Taro Isshiki, Interoperability in the Pacific Rim: Reversal of Fortunes in Singapore and Australia, 9 J. Proprietary Rts. 2 (July 1997) (disassembly held not to be fair dealing under Singapore's copyright law).

2. For a detailed discussion of extraterritoriality issues of U.S. intellectual property laws, see Curtis A. Bradley, Territorial Intellectual Property Rights in an Age of Globalism, 37 Va. J. Int'l L. 505 (1997) (arguing for a more unified and narrower approach to judging extraterritoriality issues in patent, copyright, and trademark cases); Jane C. Ginsburg, Extraterritoriality and Multiterratoriality in Copyright Infringement, 37 Va. J. Int'l L. 587 (1997) (distinguishing between multiterritorial claims and extraterritorial claims; arguing that U.S. courts ought to be more willing to adjudicate multiterritorial cases and apply the laws of other jurisdictions to acts occurring outside the territorial bounds of the United States).

3. Different intellectual property statutes have different extraterritoriality rules. By and large, intellectual property statutes are supposed to be territorial in nature. Thus it is clear that the patent laws do not have extraterritorial effect. If you want a patent to cover competitor conduct in England, for example, you must get a U.K. patent. While there are certain rules designed to stop the *importation* of infringing products (and products made abroad by infringing processes), the law itself does not reach conduct that occurs outside the United States.

By contrast, courts are much more willing to apply the trademark laws extraterritorially. See, e.g., Playboy Enterprises, Inc. v. Chuckleberry Pub'g, Inc., 939 F. Supp. 1032 (S.D.N.Y. 1996) (enjoining Italian-based "Playmen" Web site from offering products and services in English on an Italian server upon contempt motion deriving from earlier ruling that "Playmen" magazine was a trademark infringement under U.S. law, even though not under Italian law). Copyright occupies a middle position, and as the *Expediters* case indicates, the precedent on this issue is conflicting. Certain language from the Supreme Court's recent decision in Quality King v. L'Anza, 118 S. Ct. 1125 (1998), suggests that the copyright laws do not have extraterritorial effect, at least based on the "authorization" theory adopted in *Expediters.*

4. The broad historical trend of international intellectual property law has been toward substantive harmonization. International treaties such as the Berne and Paris Conventions have established substantive rules for protection. They have also endorsed the principle of national treatment,

discussed supra, under which an author's copyright is protected in a foreign country by application of foreign laws. Further, GATT TRIPS created the WTO, a new multilateral enforcement mechanism for resolving trade disputes, including disputes over intellectual property protection.

Does the existence of these substantive and procedural rules for resolving international intellectual property disputes militate against the extraterritorial effect of any one country's laws?

5. How does the remedy for intellectual property infringement affect the extraterritoriality question? In an important software copyright case, Computer Associates v. Altai, discussed supra, the Second Circuit held that Altai's program did not infringe CA's copyright. As the trial was commencing in the United States, CA filed essentially the same suit against Altai in Bobigny, France. The trial court in France decided that, as a matter of French law, Altai did not violate CA's copyrights, and CA decided to appeal this ruling. The U.S. Second Circuit's copyright decision was handed down before the French case went to appeal, and Altai sought to enjoin the French appeal by alleging that the issue had already been finally adjudicated in a U.S. court. The Second Circuit, however, refused to bar the French suit, 126 F.3d 365 (2d Cir. 1997). In theory, at least, CA is now free to sue Altai in every country in which it sells its software. No matter how many times it loses, CA can always sue again elsewhere and relitigate the same case.

Suppose that CA wins one of these suits. To what remedies is it entitled? If the Second Circuit was right to conclude that a French copyright action is different from a U.S. copyright action, does it follow that the remedies in *either* action cannot extend beyond the national borders? Surely simple fairness requires such an outcome, else defendants could never win a case. But do copyright plaintiffs really benefit from a rule that requires them to go to court in every country in the world to get effective worldwide relief?

II | *INTERNET LAW*

Computer software was the first digital information product to challenge traditional legal categories and to require an adaptation of the law so that appropriate results could be achieved. Chapters 1 through 4 provide the results of this adaptation. It should be noted, however, that it took several decades before the contentious issues of software protection became relatively settled in the United States and the rest of the world. Later arising but nonetheless significant challenges to protection regimes have occurred as to semiconductor chip designs and computer databases. As Chapter 5 has shown, new legislation has been devised to meet the needs of these industries.

It should have been apparent that the ease with which digital information could be copied and redistributed, especially when made available in networked environments, would pose other challenges as well. As more information has become available in digital form, new copyright issues have arisen, and the law of copyright had to be adapted once again to answer new questions that the Internet posed. The challenges posed by digital information do not, however, pertain only to intellectual property law. Privacy is a big problem on the Internet in part because of the ease with which digital technologies can be used to collect and process personal data. Cryptography has become a major area for policy because digital implementations of this technology can protect digital information against abusive uses (such as copyright infringement or privacy invasions), overcoming in part some of the vulnerabilities that digital information would otherwise be subject to owing to the ease of duplication and dissemination. Yet cryptography can also be used to hide abusive activities, and this complicates the policy landscape, which might otherwise place great importance on enabling widespread adoption of strong encryption tools.

Part II will explore how the law is responding to the wider challenges posed by digital information in the global digital network environment (known today as the Internet). Given the state of flux in Internet law and the constant stream of developments that are yielding new Internet law questions, it may seem premature to include in this book a separate part on Internet law. However, the law on some key issues is relatively settled; where it is not yet settled, disputes over activities occurring in cyberspace present questions that the law will have to address. Students may benefit from exposure to the constantly evolving nature of the law of cyberspace. Some examples of how judges are grappling with these contentious issues may be useful even if the appellate courts or legislatures ultimately adopt different answers. There are, of course, some questions and legal developments in Internet law that are not dealt with in this book. New developments are especially likely in the law governing electronic commerce. Nonetheless, Part II provides a foundation concerning the law of the Internet at the end of the millennium.

9

Jurisdiction and Choice of Law

One of the first questions raised about law on the Internet had to do with jurisdiction. One of the advantages of the Internet is the way it compresses or obscures distance and makes things appear to be close even though they are far away. What is an advantage in technology can be a problem for the law, however. If people act "on the Internet," where are they? What law applies to their conduct, and where can they be sued? Many courts have struggled with these questions.

Cybersell, Inc. v. Cybersell, Inc.
United States Court of Appeals for the Ninth Circuit
130 F.3d 414 (9th Cir. 1997)

RYMER, Circuit Judge.

We are asked to hold that the allegedly infringing use of a service mark in a home page on the World Wide Web suffices for personal jurisdiction in the state where the holder of the mark has its principal place of business. Cybersell, Inc., an Arizona corporation that advertises for commercial services over the Internet, claims that Cybersell, Inc., a Florida corporation that offers web page construction services over the Internet, infringed its federally registered mark and should be amenable to suit in Arizona because cyberspace is without borders and a web site which advertises a product or service is necessarily intended for use on a world wide basis. The district court disagreed, and so do we. Instead, applying our normal "minimum contacts" analysis, we conclude that it would not comport with "traditional notions of fair play and substantial justice," Core-Vent Corp. v. Nobel Indus. AB, 11 F.3d 1482, 1485 (9th Cir.1993) (quoting International

775

Shoe Co. v. Washington, 326 U.S. 310, 316, 66 S.Ct. 154, 158, 90 L.Ed. 95 (1945)), for Arizona to exercise personal jurisdiction over an allegedly infringing Florida web site advertiser who has no contacts with Arizona other than maintaining a home page that is accessible to Arizonans, and everyone else, over the Internet. We therefore affirm.

I

Cybersell, Inc. is an Arizona corporation, which we will refer to as Cybersell AZ. It was incorporated in May 1994 to provide Internet and web advertising and marketing services, including consulting. The principals of Cybersell AZ are Laurence Canter and Martha Siegel, known among web users for first "spamming" the Internet. Mainstream print media carried the story of Canter and Siegel and their various efforts to commercialize the web.

On August 8, 1994, Cybersell AZ filed an application to register the name "Cybersell" as a service mark. The application was approved and the grant was published on October 30, 1995. Cybersell AZ operated a web site using the mark from August 1994 through February 1995. The site was then taken down for reconstruction.

Meanwhile, in the summer of 1995, Matt Certo and his father, Dr. Samuel C. Certo, both Florida residents, formed Cybersell, Inc., a Florida corporation (Cybersell FL), with its principal place of business in Orlando. Matt was a business school student at Rollins College, where his father was a professor; Matt was particularly interested in the Internet, and their company was to provide business consulting services for strategic management and marketing on the web. At the time the Certos chose the name "Cybersell" for their venture, Cybersell AZ had no home page on the web nor had the PTO granted their application for the service mark.

As part of their marketing effort, the Certos created a web page at *http://www.cybsell.com/cybsell/index.htm*. The home page has a logo at the top with "CyberSell" over a depiction of the planet earth, with the caption underneath "Professional Services for the World Wide Web" and a local (area code 407) phone number. It proclaims in large letters "Welcome to CyberSell!" A hypertext link allows the browser to introduce himself, and invites a company not on the web — but interested in getting on the web — to "Email us to find out how!"

Canter found the Cybersell FL web page and sent an e-mail on November 27, 1995 notifying Dr. Certo that "Cybersell" is a service mark of Cybersell AZ. Trying to disassociate themselves from the Canters, the Certos changed the name of Cybersell FL to WebHorizons, Inc. on December 27 (later it was changed again to WebSolvers, Inc.) and by January 4, 1996, they had replaced the CyberSell logo at the top of their web page with WebHorizons, Inc. The WebHorizons page still said "Welcome to CyberSell!"

II

The general principles that apply to the exercise of personal jurisdiction are well known. As there is no federal statute governing personal jurisdiction in this case, the law of Arizona applies. Under Rule 4.2(a) of the Arizona Rules of Civil Procedure, an Arizona court

> may exercise personal jurisdiction over parties, whether found within or outside the state, to the maximum extent permitted by the Constitution of this state and the Constitution of the United States.

The Arizona Supreme Court has stated that under Rule 4.2(a), "Arizona will exert personal jurisdiction over a nonresident litigant to the maximum extent allowed by the federal constitution." Uberti v. Leonardo, 181 Ariz. 565, 569, 892 P.2d 1354, 1358, *cert. denied*, —U.S. —, 116 S.Ct. 273, 133 L.Ed.2d 194 (1995). Thus, Cybersell FL may be subject to personal jurisdiction in Arizona so long as doing so comports with due process.

A court may assert either specific or general jurisdiction over a defendant. See Helicopteros Nacionales de Colombia, S.A. v. Hall, 466 U.S. 408, 414, 104 S.Ct. 1868, 1872, 80 L.Ed.2d 404 (1984). Cybersell AZ concedes that general jurisdiction over Cybersell FL doesn't exist in Arizona, so the only issue in this case is whether specific jurisdiction is available.

We use a three-part test to determine whether a district court may exercise specific jurisdiction over a nonresident defendant:

> (1) The nonresident defendant must do some act or consummate some transaction with the forum or perform some act by which he purposefully avails himself of the privilege of conducting activities in the forum, thereby invoking the benefits and protections[;] (2)[t]he claim must be one which arises out of or results from the defendant's forum-related activities[; and] (3)[e]xercise of jurisdiction must be reasonable.

Ballard v. Savage, 65 F.3d 1495, 1498 (9th Cir.1995) (citations omitted).

Cybersell AZ argues that the test is met because trademark infringement occurs when the passing off of the mark occurs, which in this case, it submits, happened when the name "Cybersell" was used on the Internet in connection with advertising. Cybersell FL, on the other hand, contends that a party should not be subject to nationwide, or perhaps worldwide, jurisdiction simply for using the Internet.

A

Since the jurisdictional facts are not in dispute, we turn to the first requirement, which is the most critical. As the Supreme Court emphasized in

Hanson v. Denckla, "it is essential in each case that there be some act by which the defendant purposefully avails itself of the privilege of conducting activities within the forum State, thus invoking the benefits and protections of its laws." 357 U.S. 235, 253, 78 S.Ct. 1228, 1239, 2 L.Ed.2d 1283 (1958). We recently explained in *Ballard* that

> the "purposeful availment" requirement is satisfied if the defendant has taken deliberate action within the forum state or if he has created continuing obligations to forum residents. "It is not required that a defendant be physically present within, or have physical contacts with, the forum, provided that his efforts 'are purposefully directed' toward forum residents."

Ballard, 65 F.3d at 1498 (citations omitted).

We have not yet considered when personal jurisdiction may be exercised in the context of cyberspace, but the Second and Sixth Circuits have had occasion to decide whether personal jurisdiction was properly exercised over defendants involved in transmissions over the Internet, see CompuServe, Inc. v. Patterson, 89 F.3d 1257 (6th Cir.1996); Bensusan Restaurant Corp. v. King, 937 F.Supp. 295 (S.D.N.Y.1996), *aff'd*, 126 F.3d 25 (2d Cir.1997), as have a number of district courts. Because this is a matter of first impression for us, we have looked to all of these cases for guidance. Not surprisingly, they reflect a broad spectrum of Internet use on the one hand, and contacts with the forum on the other. As *CompuServe* and *Bensusan* seem to represent opposite ends of the spectrum, we start with them.[4]

CompuServe is a computer information service headquartered in Columbus, Ohio, that contracts with individual subscribers to provide access to computing and information services via the Internet. It also operates as an electronic conduit to provide computer software products to its subscribers. Computer software generated and distributed in this way is often referred to as "shareware." Patterson is a Texas resident who subscribed to CompuServe and placed items of "shareware" on the Compu-Serve system pursuant to a "Shareware Registration Agreement" with CompuServe which provided, among other things, that it was "to be governed by and construed in accordance with" Ohio law. During the course of this relationship, Patterson electronically transmitted thirty-two master software files to CompuServe, which CompuServe stored and displayed to its subscribers. Sales were made in Ohio and elsewhere, and funds were transmitted through CompuServe in Ohio to Patterson in Texas. In effect, Patterson used CompuServe as a distribution center to market his software. When Patterson threatened litigation over allegedly infringing CompuServe software, CompuServe filed suit in Ohio seeking a declaratory judgment of noninfringement. The court found that Patterson's relation-

---

4. Since *Bensusan* was decided on the basis of New York's long-arm statute (which requires presence in the forum and is therefore more stringent than due process), its holding is not instructive, but the district court's analysis is. The district court dismissed for lack of personal jurisdiction under the long-arm statute as well as on due process grounds, while the Second Circuit affirmed on the statute and did not discuss the constitutional issue.

ship with CompuServe as a software provider and marketer was a crucial indicator that Patterson had knowingly reached out to CompuServe's Ohio home and benefitted from CompuServe's handling of his software and fees. Because Patterson had chosen to transmit his product from Texas to CompuServe's system in Ohio, and that system provided access to his software to others to whom he advertised and sold his product, the court concluded that Patterson purposefully availed himself of the privilege of doing business in Ohio.

By contrast, the defendant in *Bensusan* owned a small jazz club known as "The Blue Note" in Columbia, Missouri. He created a general access web page that contained information about the club in Missouri as well as a calendar of events and ticketing information. Tickets were not available through the web site, however. To order tickets, web browsers had to use the names and addresses of ticket outlets in Columbia or a telephone number for charge-by-phone ticket orders, which were available for pick-up on the night of the show at the Blue Note box office in Columbia. Bensusan was a New York corporation that owned "The Blue Note," a popular jazz club in the heart of Greenwich Village. Bensusan owned the rights to the "The Blue Note" mark. Bensusan sued King for trademark infringement in New York. The district court distinguished King's passive web page, which just posted information, from the defendant's use of the Internet in CompuServe by observing that whereas the Texas Internet user specifically targeted Ohio by subscribing to the service, entering into an agreement to sell his software over the Internet, advertising through the service, and sending his software to the service in Ohio,

> King has done nothing to purposefully avail himself of the benefits of New York. King, like numerous others, simply created a Web site and permitted anyone who could find it to access it. Creating a site, like placing a product into the stream of commerce, may be felt nationwide—or even worldwide—but, without more, it is not an act purposefully directed toward the forum state.

Bensusan, 937 F.Supp. at 301 (citing the plurality opinion in Asahi Metal Indus. Co. v. Superior Court, 480 U.S. 102, 112, 107 S.Ct. 1026, 1032, 94 L.Ed.2d 92 (1992)). Given these facts, the court reasoned that the argument that the defendant "should have foreseen that users could access the site in New York and be confused as to the relationship of the two Blue Note clubs is insufficient to satisfy due process." *Id*. at 301.

"Interactive" web sites present somewhat different issues. Unlike passive sites such as the defendant's in *Bensusan*, users can exchange information with the host computer when the site is interactive. Courts that have addressed interactive sites have looked to the "level of interactivity and commercial nature of the exchange of information that occurs on the Web site" to determine if sufficient contacts exist to warrant the exercise of jurisdiction. See, e.g., Zippo Mfg. Co. v. Zippo Dot Com, Inc., 952 F.Supp. 1119, 1124 (W.D.Pa.1997) (finding purposeful availment based on Dot Com's interactive web site and contracts with 3000 individuals and seven Internet access providers in Pennsylvania allowing them to download the electronic messages that form the basis of the suit); Maritz, Inc. v. Cybergold, Inc., 947 F.Supp. 1328, 1332-33 (E.D.Mo.) (browsers were encouraged to add their address to a mailing list that basically subscribed the user to the service), *reconsideration denied*, 947 F.Supp. 1338 (1996).

Cybersell AZ points to several district court decisions which it contends have held that the mere advertisement or solicitation for sale of goods and services on the Internet gives rise to specific jurisdiction in the plaintiff's forum. However, so far as we are aware, no court has ever held that an Internet advertisement alone is sufficient to subject the advertiser to jurisdiction in the plaintiff's home state. See, e.g., Smith v. Hobby Lobby Stores, 968 F.Supp. 1356 (W.D.Ark.1997) (no jurisdiction over Hong Kong defendant who advertised in trade journal posted on the Internet without sale of goods or services in Arkansas). Rather, in each, there has been "something more" to indicate that the defendant purposefully (albeit electronically) directed his activity in a substantial way to the forum state.

Inset Systems, Inc. v. Instruction Set, Inc., 937 F.Supp. 161 (D.Conn.1996), is the case most favorable to Cybersell AZ's position. Inset developed and marketed computer software throughout the world; Instruction Set, Inc. (ISI) provided computer technology and support. Inset owned the federal trademark "INSET"; but ISI obtained "INSET.COM" as its Internet domain address for advertising its goods and services. ISI also used the telephone number "1-800-US-INSET." Inset learned of ISI's domain address when it tried to get the same address, and filed suit for trademark infringement in Connecticut. The court reasoned that ISI had purposefully availed itself of doing business in Connecticut because it directed its advertising activities via the Internet and its toll-free number toward the state of Connecticut (and all states); Internet sites and toll-free numbers are designed to communicate with people and their businesses in every state; an Internet advertisement could reach as many as 10,000 Internet users within Connecticut alone; and once posted on the Internet, an advertisement is continuously available to any Internet user.

Cybersell AZ further points to the court's statement in EDIAS Software International, L.L.C. v. BASIS International Ltd., 947 F.Supp. 413 (D.Ariz.1996), that a defendant "should not be permitted to take advantage of modern technology through an Internet Web page and forum and simultaneously escape traditional notions of jurisdiction." *Id.* at 420. In that case, EDIAS (an Arizona company) alleged that BASIS (a New Mexico company) sent advertising and defamatory statements over the Internet through e-mail, its web page, and forums. However, the court did not rest its minimum contacts analysis on use of the Internet alone; in addition to the Internet, BASIS had a contract with EDIAS, it made sales to EDIAS and other Arizona customers, and its employees had visited Arizona during the course of the business relationship with EDIAS.

Some courts have also given weight to the number of "hits" received by a web page from residents in the forum state, and to other evidence that Internet activity was directed at, or bore fruit in, the forum state. See, e.g., Heroes, Inc. v. Heroes Found., 958 F.Supp. 1 (D.D.C.1996) (web page that solicited contributions and provided toll-free telephone number along with the defendant's use on the web page of the allegedly infringing trademark and logo, along with other contacts, provided sustained contact with the District), amended by No. Civ.A. 96-1260(TAF) (1997); Pres-Kap, Inc. v. System One, Direct Access, Inc., 636 So.2d 1351 (Fla. Dist. Ct. App. 1994) (declining jurisdiction where defendant consumer subscribed to plaintiff's travel reservation system but was solicited and serviced instate by the supplier's local representative).

In sum, the common thread, well stated by the district court in *Zippo*, is that "the likelihood that personal jurisdiction can be constitutionally exercised is directly proportionate to the nature and quality of commercial activity that an entity conducts over the Internet." *Zippo*, 952 F.Supp. at 1124.

B

Here, Cybersell FL has conducted no commercial activity over the Internet in Arizona. All that it did was post an essentially passive home page on the web, using the name "CyberSell," which Cybersell AZ was in the process of registering as a federal service mark. While there is no question that anyone, anywhere could access that home page and thereby learn about the services offered, we cannot see how from that fact alone it can be inferred that Cybersell FL deliberately directed its merchandising efforts toward Arizona residents.

Cybersell FL did nothing to encourage people in Arizona to access its site, and there is no evidence that any part of its business (let alone a continuous part of its business) was sought or achieved in Arizona. To the contrary, it appears to be an operation where business was primarily generated by the personal contacts of one of its founders. While those contacts are not entirely local, they aren't in Arizona either. No Arizonan except for Cybersell AZ "hit" Cybersell FL's web site. There is no evidence that any Arizona resident signed up for Cybersell FL's web construction services. It entered into no contracts in Arizona, made no sales in Arizona, received no telephone calls from Arizona, earned no income from Arizona, and sent no messages over the Internet to Arizona. The only message it received over the Internet from Arizona was from Cybersell AZ. Cybersell FL did not have an "800" number, let alone a toll-free number that also used the "Cybersell" name. The interactivity of its web page is limited to receiving the browser's name and address and an indication of interest—signing up for the service is not an option, nor did anyone from Arizona do so. No money changed hands on the Internet from (or through) Arizona. In short,

Cybersell FL has done no act and has consummated no transaction, nor has it performed any act by which it purposefully availed itself of the privilege of conducting activities, in Arizona, thereby invoking the benefits and protections of Arizona law.

We therefore hold that Cybersell FL's contacts are insufficient to establish "purposeful availment." Cybersell AZ has thus failed to satisfy the first prong of our three-part test for specific jurisdiction. We decline to go further solely on the footing that Cybersell AZ has alleged trademark infringement over the Internet by Cybersell FL's use of the registered name "Cybersell" on an essentially passive web page advertisement. Otherwise, every complaint arising out of alleged trademark infringement on the Internet would automatically result in personal jurisdiction wherever the plaintiff's principal place of business is located. That would not comport with traditional notions of what qualifies as purposeful activity invoking the benefits and protections of the forum state. See Peterson v. Kennedy, 771 F.2d 1244, 1262 (9th Cir.1985) (series of phone calls and letters to California physician regarding plaintiff's injuries insufficient to satisfy first prong of test).

III

Cybersell AZ also invokes the "effects" test employed in Calder v. Jones, 465 U.S. 783, 104 S.Ct. 1482, 79 L.Ed.2d 804 (1984), and Core-Vent Corp. v. Nobel Industries, 11 F.3d 1482 (9th Cir.1993), with respect to intentional torts directed to the plaintiff, causing injury where the plaintiff lives. However, we don't see this as a *Calder* case. Because Shirley Jones was who she was (a famous entertainer who lived and worked in California) and was libeled by a story in the National Enquirer, which was published in Florida but had a nationwide circulation with a large audience in California, the Court could easily hold that California was the "focal point both of the story and of the harm suffered" and so jurisdiction in California based on the "effects" of the defendants' Florida conduct was proper. *Calder*, 465 U.S. at 789, 104 S.Ct. at 1486. There is nothing comparable about Cybersell FL's web page. Nor does the "effects" test apply with the same force to Cybersell AZ as it would to an individual, because a corporation "does not suffer harm in a particular geographic location in the same sense that an individual does." *Core-Vent*, 11 F.3d at 1486. Cybersell FL's web page simply was not aimed intentionally at Arizona knowing that harm was likely to be caused there to Cybersell AZ.[6]

---

6. Likewise unpersuasive is Cybersell AZ's reliance on Panavision International v. Toeppen, 938 F.Supp. 616 (C.D.Cal.1996), where the court found the "purposeful availment" prong satisfied by the effects felt in California, the home state of Panavision, from Toeppen's alleged out-of-state scheme to register domain names using the trademarks of California companies, including Panavision, for the purpose of extorting fees from them. Again, there is nothing analogous about Cybersell FL's conduct.

IV

We conclude that the essentially passive nature of Cybersell FL's activity in posting a home page on the World Wide Web that allegedly used the service mark of Cybersell AZ does not qualify as purposeful activity invoking the benefits and protections of Arizona. As it engaged in no commercial activity and had no other contacts via the Internet or otherwise in Arizona, Cybersell FL lacks sufficient minimum contacts with Arizona for personal jurisdiction to be asserted over it there. Accordingly, its motion to dismiss for lack of personal jurisdiction was properly granted.

AFFIRMED.

COMMENTS AND QUESTIONS

1. Suppose there were many hits on the Florida site. Would that change the court's result? Should it?

2. Some scholars have questioned whether existing jurisdictional law can solve the problems of jurisdiction in cyberspace. In particular, two scholars, David Johnson and David Post, have argued in a number of articles that cyberspace should be its own jurisdiction, with its own courts (or "virtual magistrates") to resolve disputes that occur entirely online. For their arguments, see David R. Johnson & David Post, Law and Borders— The Rise of Law in Cyberspace, 48 Stan. L. Rev. 1367 (1996); David R. Johnson & David G. Post, And How Shall the Net Be Governed?: A Meditation on the Relative Virtues of Decentralized, Emergent Law, in Coordinating the Internet (Brian Kahin & James Keller eds., MIT Press, 1997). But see Lawrence Lessig, The Zones of Cyberspace, 48 Stan. L. Rev. 1403 (1996) (challenging the Johnson-Post model). For more discussion of the Johnson-Post model, see the section on Internet governance, infra.

3. There are numerous cases involving the Internet and personal jurisdiction, many involving trademark disputes. Since 1996, there have been literally hundreds of articles written about the problem of jurisdiction on the Internet. Among the better treatments of the problem are Dan L. Burk, Jurisdiction in a World Without Borders, 1 Va. J.L. & Tech. (1996), http://www.student.virginia.edu/~vjolt/vol1/BURK.htm; Katherine Sheehan, Predicting the Future: Personal Jurisdiction for the 21st Century, 66 U. Cin. L. Rev. 385 (1998); Dan Burk, Federalism in Cyberspace, 28 Conn. L. Rev. 1095 (1996); Ira S. Nathenson, Showdown at the Domain Name Corral: Property Rights and Personal Jurisdiction Over Squatters, Poachers and Other Parasites, 58 U. Pitt. L. Rev. 911 (1997); Allan R. Stein, The Unexceptional Problem of Jurisidiction in Cyberspace, 32 International Lawyer 1167 (1998); Jack Goldsmith, Against Cyberanarchy, 65 U. Chi. L. Rev. 1199 (1998); Jane C. Ginsburg, Copyright Without

Borders? Choice of Forum and Choice of Law for Copyright Infringement in Cyberspace, 15 Cardozo Arts & Ent. L.J. 153 (1997).

Generally, global "solutions" to the jurisdictional problem tend to resolve themselves in one of three ways:

(1) First, the defendant might be amenable to suit everywhere the Web page can be seen (essentially, this is everywhere in the world). *Inset Systems* took this approach to some extent. See also Maritz v. Cybergold, 947 F. Supp. 1328 (E.D. Mo. 1996) (a desire to transmit information everywhere in the world confers jurisdiction everywhere in the world). This assures the plaintiff a reasonable choice of forum but places an enormous burden on potential defendants, and may reduce online speech to the "least common denominator" acceptable to all jurisdictions worldwide.

(2) Second, the defendant might be amenable to suit only in its home forum (whether that "forum" is a physical state or an Internet locale, as Johnson and Post suggest). This relieves the burden on the defendant but imposes a corresponding burden on remote plaintiffs. It may also encourage the development of "data havens" that promise virtual immunity from trademark, copyright, or defamation laws to their residents.

(3) Finally, courts might attempt a rough compromise by applying traditional jurisdictional principles to determine on a case-by-case basis how fair the exercise of jurisdiction would be. *Cybersell* takes this approach. This last approach may produce the most reasonable results across a wide range of cases, though it is worth noting that it sacrifices a great deal of certainty and may produce a lot of litigation over jurisdictional issues.

4. Efforts to take this middle road require courts to distinguish between cases in which a Web site should confer jurisdiction and cases where it shouldn't. On what basis should courts make this distinction? One possible factor (used in *Cybersell*) is how often people visit the Web site. A second possible factor, raised in many other cases, is the existence of other contacts with the forum, such as sales into the jurisdiction or telephone orders. Finally, some decisions (including the one below) have suggested that the extent of the interactive or passive nature of the Web page should be relevant to the jurisdictional question.

≡ *Zippo Manufacturing Co. v. Zippo Dot Com, Inc.*
≡ *United States District Court for the Western District of Pennsylvania*
≡ *952 F. Supp. 1119 (W.D. Pa. 1997)*

McLAUGHLIN, District Judge.

This is an Internet domain name dispute. At this stage of the controversy, we must decide the Constitutionally permissible reach of Pennsylvania's Long Arm Statute, 42 Pa.C.S.A. §5322, through cyberspace. Plaintiff Zippo Manufacturing Corporation ("Manufacturing") has filed a five count complaint against Zippo Dot Com, Inc. ("Dot Com") alleging trademark dilution, infringement, and false designation under the Federal Trademark Act, 15 U.S.C. §§1051-1127. In addition, the Complaint alleges causes of action based on state law trademark dilution under 54 Pa.C.S.A. §1124, and seeks equitable accounting and imposition of a constructive trust. Dot Com has moved to dismiss for lack of personal jurisdiction and improper venue pursuant to Fed.R.Civ.P. 12(b)(2) and (3) or, in the alternative, to transfer the case pursuant to 28 U.S.C. §1406(a). For the reasons set forth below, Defendant's motion is denied.

I. Background

The facts relevant to this motion are as follows. Manufacturing is a Pennsylvania corporation with its principal place of business in Bradford, Pennsylvania. Manufacturing makes, among other things, well known "Zippo" tobacco lighters. Dot Com is a California corporation with its principal place of business in Sunnyvale, California. Dot Com operates an Internet Web site and an Internet news service and has obtained the exclusive right to use the domain names "zippo.com", "zippo.net" and "zipponews.com" on the Internet.

Dot Com's Web site contains information about the company, advertisements and an application for its Internet news service. The news service itself consists of three levels of membership—public/free, "Original" and "Super." Each successive level offers access to a greater number of Internet newsgroups. A customer who wants to subscribe to either the "Original" or "Super" level of service, fills out an on-line application that asks for a variety of information including the person's name and address. Payment is made by credit card over the Internet or the telephone. The application is then processed and the subscriber is assigned a password which permits the subscriber to view and/or download Internet newsgroup messages that are stored on the Defendant's server in California.

Dot Com's contacts with Pennsylvania have occurred almost exclusively over the Internet. Dot Com's offices, employees and Internet servers are located in California. Dot Com maintains no offices, employees or agents in Pennsylvania. Dot Com's advertising for its service to Pennsylvania residents involves posting information about its service on its Web page, which is accessible to Pennsylvania residents via the Internet. Defendant has approximately 140,000 paying subscribers worldwide. Approximately two percent (3,000) of those subscribers are Pennsylvania residents. These subscribers have contracted to receive Dot Com's service by visiting its Web site and filling out the application. Additionally, Dot Com has entered into agreements with seven Internet access providers in Pennsylvania to permit their subscribers to access Dot Com's news service. Two of these providers are located in the Western District of Pennsylvania.

The basis of the trademark claims is Dot Com's use of the word "Zippo" in the domain names it holds, in numerous locations in its Web site and in the heading of Internet newsgroup messages that have been posted by Dot Com subscribers. When an Internet user views or downloads a newsgroup message posted by a Dot Com subscriber, the word "Zippo" appears in the "Message-Id" and "Organization" sections of the heading. The news message itself, containing text and/or pictures, follows. Manufacturing points out that some of the messages contain adult oriented, sexually explicit subject matter. . . .

III. Discussion

A. Personal Jurisdiction

1. The Traditional Framework

Our authority to exercise personal jurisdiction in this case is conferred by state law. Fed.R.Civ.P. 4(e); *Mellon*, 960 F.2d at 1221. The extent to which we may exercise that authority is governed by the Due Process Clause of the Fourteenth Amendment to the Federal Constitution. Kulko v. Superior Court of California, 436 U.S. 84, 91, 98 S.Ct. 1690, 1696, 56 L.Ed.2d 132 (1978).

Pennsylvania's long arm jurisdiction statute is codified at 42 Pa.C.S.A. §5322(a). The portion of the statute authorizing us to exercise jurisdiction here permits the exercise of jurisdiction over non-resident defendants upon:

(2) Contracting to supply services or things in this Commonwealth.

42 Pa.C.S.A. §5322(a). It is undisputed that Dot Com contracted to supply Internet news services to approximately 3,000 Pennsylvania residents and also entered into agreements with seven Internet access providers in Pennsylvania. Moreover, even if Dot Com's conduct did not satisfy a specific provision of the statute, we would nevertheless be authorized to exercise jurisdiction to the "fullest extent allowed under the Constitution of the United States." 42 Pa.C.S.A. §5322(b).

The Constitutional limitations on the exercise of personal jurisdiction differ depending upon whether a court seeks to exercise general or specific jurisdiction over a non-resident defendant. *Mellon*, 960 F.2d at 1221. General jurisdiction permits a court to exercise personal jurisdiction over a non-resident defendant for non-forum related activities when the defendant has engaged in "systematic and continuous" activities in the forum state. Helicopteros Nacionales de Colombia, S.A. v. Hall, 466 U.S. 408, 414-16, 104 S.Ct. 1868, 1872-73, 80 L.Ed.2d 404 (1984). In the absence of general jurisdiction, specific jurisdiction permits a court to exercise personal jurisdiction over a non-resident defendant for forum-related activities where the "relationship between the defendant and the forum falls within the 'minimum contacts' framework" of International Shoe Co. v. Washington, 326 U.S. 310, 66 S.Ct. 154, 90 L.Ed. 95 (1945) and its progeny. *Mellon*, 960 F.2d at 1221. Manufacturing does not contend that we should exercise general personal jurisdiction over Dot Com. Manufacturing concedes that if personal jurisdiction exists in this case, it must be specific.

A three-pronged test has emerged for determining whether the exercise of specific personal jurisdiction over a non-resident defendant is appropriate: (1) the defendant must have sufficient "minimum contacts" with the forum state, (2) the claim asserted against the defendant must arise out of those contacts, and (3) the exercise of jurisdiction must be reasonable. *Id.* The "Constitutional touchstone" of the minimum contacts analysis is embodied in the first prong, "whether the defendant purposefully established" contacts with the forum state. Burger King Corp. v. Rudzewicz, 471 U.S. 462, 475, 105 S.Ct. 2174, 2183-84, 85 L.Ed.2d 528 (1985) (citing International Shoe Co. v. Washington, 326 U.S. 310, 319, 66 S.Ct. 154, 159-60, 90 L.Ed. 95 (1945)). Defendants who " 'reach out beyond one state' and create continuing relationships and obligations with the citizens of another state are subject to regulation and sanctions in the other State for consequences of their actions." *Id.* (citing Travelers Health Assn. v. Virginia, 339 U.S. 643, 647, 70 S.Ct. 927, 929, 94 L.Ed. 1154 (1950)). "[T]he foreseeability that is critical to the due process analysis is . . . that the defendant's conduct and connection with the forum State are such that he should reasonably expect to be haled into court there." World-Wide Volkswagen Corp. v. Woodson, 444 U.S. 286, 297, 100 S.Ct. 559, 567, 62 L.Ed.2d 490 (1980). This protects defendants from being forced to answer for their actions in a foreign jurisdiction based on "random, fortuitous or attenuated" contacts. Keeton v. Hustler Magazine, Inc., 465 U.S. 770, 774, 104 S.Ct. 1473, 1478, 79 L.Ed.2d 790 (1984). "Jurisdiction is proper, however, where contacts proximately result from actions by the defendant himself that create a 'substantial connection' with the forum State." *Burger King*, 471 U.S. at 475, 105 S.Ct. at 2183-84 (citing McGee v. International Life Insurance Co., 355 U.S. 220, 223, 78 S.Ct. 199, 201, 2 L.Ed.2d 223 (1957)).

The "reasonableness" prong exists to protect defendants against unfairly inconvenient litigation. *World-Wide Volkswagen*, 444 U.S. at 292, 100 S.Ct. at 564-65. Under this prong, the exercise of jurisdiction will be reasonable if it does not offend "traditional notions of fair play and substantial justice." *International Shoe*, 326 U.S. at 316, 66 S.Ct. at 158. When determining the reasonableness of a particular forum, the court must consider the burden on the defendant in light of other factors including: "the forum state's interest in adjudicating the dispute; the plaintiff's interest in obtaining convenient and effective relief, at least when that interest is not adequately protected by the plaintiff's right to choose the forum; the interstate judicial system's interest in obtaining the most efficient resolution of controversies; and the shared interest of the several states in furthering fundamental substantive social policies." *World-Wide Volkswagen*, 444 U.S. at 292, 100 S.Ct. at 564 (internal citations omitted).

2. The Internet and Jurisdiction

In Hanson v. Denckla, the Supreme Court noted that "[a]s technological progress has increased the flow of commerce between States, the need for jurisdiction has undergone a similar increase." Hanson v. Denckla, 357 U.S. 235, 250-51, 78 S.Ct. 1228, 1237-39, 2 L.Ed.2d 1283 (1958). Twenty seven years later, the Court observed that jurisdiction could not be avoided "merely because the defendant did not physically enter the forum state." *Burger King*, 471 U.S. at 476, 105 S.Ct. at 2184. The Court observed that:

> [I]t is an inescapable fact of modern commercial life that a substantial amount of commercial business is transacted solely by mail and wire communications across state lines, thus obviating the need for physical presence within a State in which business is conducted.

Id.

Enter the Internet, a global " 'super-network' of over 15,000 computer networks used by over 30 million individuals, corporations, organizations, and educational institutions worldwide." Panavision Intern., L.P. v. Toeppen, 938 F.Supp. 616 (C.D.Cal.1996) (citing American Civil Liberties Union v. Reno, 929 F.Supp. 824, 830-48 (E.D.Pa.1996)). "In recent years, businesses have begun to use the Internet to provide information and products to consumers and other businesses." *Id.* The Internet makes it possible to conduct business throughout the world entirely from a desktop. With this global revolution looming on the horizon, the development of the law concerning the permissible scope of personal jurisdiction based on Internet use is in its infant stages. The cases are scant. Nevertheless, our review of the available cases and materials reveals that the likelihood that personal jurisdiction can be constitutionally exercised is directly proportionate to the nature and quality of commercial activity that an entity conducts over the Internet. This sliding scale is consistent with well developed personal jurisdiction principles. At one end of the spectrum are situations where a defendant clearly does business over the Internet. If the defendant enters into contracts with residents of a foreign jurisdiction that involve the knowing and repeated transmission of computer files over the Internet, personal jurisdiction is proper. E.g. CompuServe, Inc. v. Patterson, 89 F.3d 1257 (6th Cir.1996). At the opposite end are situations where a defendant has simply posted information on an Internet Web site which is accessible to users in foreign jurisdictions. A passive Web site that does little more than make information available to those who are interested in it is not grounds for the exercise personal jurisdiction. E.g. Bensusan Restaurant Corp. v. King, 937 F.Supp. 295 (S.D.N.Y.1996). The middle ground is occupied by interactive Web sites where a user can exchange information with the host computer. In these cases, the exercise of jurisdiction is determined by examining the level of interactivity and commercial nature of the exchange of information that occurs on the Web site. E.g. Maritz, Inc. v. Cybergold, Inc., 947 F.Supp. 1328 (E.D.Mo.1996).

Traditionally, when an entity intentionally reaches beyond its boundaries to conduct business with foreign residents, the exercise of specific jurisdiction is proper. *Burger King*, 471 U.S. at 475, 105 S.Ct. at 2183-84. Different results should not be reached simply because business is conducted over the Internet. In CompuServe, Inc. v. Patterson, 89 F.3d 1257 (6th Cir.1996), the Sixth Circuit addressed the significance of doing business over the Internet. In that case, Patterson, a Texas resident, entered into a contract to distribute shareware through CompuServe's Internet server located in Ohio. *CompuServe*, 89 F.3d at 1260. From Texas, Patterson electronically uploaded thirty-two master software files to CompuServe's server in Ohio via the Internet. *Id.* at 1261. One of Patterson's software products was designed to help people navigate the Internet. *Id.* When CompuServe later began to market a product that Patterson believed to be similar to his own, he threatened to sue. *Id.* CompuServe brought an action in the Southern District of Ohio, seeking a declaratory judgment. *Id.* The District Court granted Patterson's motion to dismiss for lack of personal jurisdiction and CompuServe appealed. *Id.* The Sixth Circuit reversed, reasoning that Patterson had purposefully directed his business activities toward Ohio by knowingly entering into a contract with an Ohio resident and then "deliberately and repeatedly" transmitted files to Ohio. *Id.* at 1264-66.

In Maritz, Inc. v. Cybergold, Inc., 947 F.Supp. 1328 (E.D.Mo.1996), the defendant had put up a Web site as a promotion for its upcoming Internet service. The service consisted of assigning users an electronic mailbox and then forwarding advertisements for products and services that matched the users' interests to those electronic mailboxes. *Maritz*, 947 F.Supp. at 1330. The defendant planned to charge advertisers and provide users with incentives to view the advertisements. *Id.* Although the service was not yet operational, users were encouraged to add their address to a mailing list to receive updates about the service. *Id.* The court rejected the defendant's contention that it operated a "passive Web site." *Id.* at 1333-34. The court reasoned that the defendant's conduct amounted to "active solicitations" and "promotional activities" designed to "develop a mailing list of Internet users" and that the defendant "indiscriminately responded to every user" who accessed the site. *Id.* at 1333-34.

Inset Systems, Inc. v. Instruction Set, 937 F.Supp. 161 (D.Conn.1996) represents the outer limits of the exercise of personal jurisdiction based on the Internet. In *Inset Systems*, a Connecticut corporation sued a Massachusetts corporation in the District of Connecticut for trademark infringement based on the use of an Internet domain name. *Inset Systems*, 937 F.Supp. at 162. The defendant's contacts with Connecticut consisted of posting a Web site that was accessible to approximately 10,000 Connecticut residents and maintaining a toll free number. *Id.* at 165. The court exercised personal jurisdiction, reasoning that advertising on the Internet constituted the purposeful doing of business in Connecticut because "unlike television and radio advertising, the advertisement is available continuously to any Internet user." *Id.* at 165.

Bensusan Restaurant Corp. v. King, 937 F.Supp. 295 (S.D.N.Y.1996) reached a different conclusion based on a similar Web site. In *Bensusan*, the operator of a New York jazz club sued the operator of a Missouri jazz club for trademark infringement. *Bensusan*, 937 F.Supp. at 297. The Internet Web site at issue contained general information about the defendant's club, a calendar of events and ticket information. *Id.* However, the site was not interactive. *Id.* If a user wanted to go to the club, she would have to call or visit a ticket outlet and then pick up tickets at the club on the night of the show. *Id.* The court refused to exercise jurisdiction based on the Web site alone, reasoning that it did not rise to the level of purposeful availment of that jurisdiction's laws. The court distinguished the case from *CompuServe*, supra, where the user had " 'reached out' from Texas to Ohio and 'originated and maintained' contacts with Ohio." *Id.* at 301.

Pres-Kap, Inc. v. System One, Direct Access, Inc., 636 So.2d 1351 (Fla.App.1994), *review denied*, 645 So.2d 455 (Fla.1994) is not inconsistent with the above cases. In *Pres-Kap*, a majority of a three-judge intermediate state appeals court refused to exercise jurisdiction over a consumer of an on-line airline ticketing service. *Pres-Kap* involved a suit on a contract dispute in a Florida court by a Delaware corporation against its New York customer. *Pres-Kap*, 636 So.2d at 1351-52. The defendant had leased computer equipment which it used to access an airline ticketing computer located in Florida. *Id.* The contract was solicited, negotiated, executed and serviced in New York. *Id.* at 1352. The defendant's only contact with Florida consisted of logging onto the computer located in Florida and mailing payments for the leased equipment to Florida. *Id.* at 1353. *Pres-Kap* is distinguishable from the above cases and the case at bar because it addressed the exercise of jurisdiction over a consumer of on-line services as opposed to a seller. When a consumer logs onto a server in a foreign jurisdiction he is engaging in a fundamentally different type of contact than an entity that is using the Internet to sell or market products or services to residents of foreign jurisdictions. The *Pres-Kap* court specifically expressed concern over the implications of subjecting users of "on-line" services with contracts with out-of-state networks to suit in foreign jurisdictions. *Id.* at 1353.

3. Application to this Case

First, we note that this is not an Internet advertising case in the line of *Inset Systems* and *Bensusan*, supra. Dot Com has not just posted information on a Web site that is accessible to Pennsylvania residents who are connected to the Internet. This is not even an interactivity case in the line of *Maritz*, supra. Dot Com has done more than create an interactive Web site through which it exchanges information with Pennsylvania residents in hopes of using that information for commercial gain later. We are not being asked to determine whether Dot Com's Web site alone constitutes the purposeful availment of doing business in Pennsylvania. This is a "doing business over the Internet" case in the line of *CompuServe*, supra. We are being asked to determine whether Dot Com's conducting of electronic commerce with Pennsylvania residents constitutes the purposeful availment of doing business in Pennsylvania. We conclude that it does. Dot Com has contracted with approximately 3,000 individuals and seven Internet access providers in Pennsylvania. The intended object of these transactions has been the downloading of the electronic messages that form the basis of this suit in Pennsylvania.

We find Dot Com's efforts to characterize its conduct as falling short of purposeful availment of doing business in Pennsylvania wholly unpersuasive. At oral argument, Defendant repeatedly characterized its actions as merely "operating a Web site" or "advertising." Dot Com also cites to a number of cases from this Circuit which, it claims, stand for the proposition that merely advertising in a forum, without more, is not a sufficient minimal contact. This argument is misplaced. Dot Com has done more than advertise on the Internet in Pennsylvania. Defendant has sold passwords to approximately 3,000 subscribers in Pennsylvania and entered into seven contracts with Internet access providers to furnish its services to their customers in Pennsylvania.

Dot Com also contends that its contacts with Pennsylvania residents are "fortuitous" within the meaning of *World-Wide Volkswagen*, 444 U.S. 286, 100 S.Ct. 559 (1980). Defendant argues that it has not "actively" solicited business in Pennsylvania and that any business it conducts with Pennsylvania residents has resulted from contacts that were initiated by Pennsylvanians who visited the Defendant's Web site. The fact that Dot Com's services have been consumed in Pennsylvania is not "fortuitous" within the meaning of *World-Wide Volkswagen*. In *World-Wide Volkswagen*, a couple that had purchased a vehicle in New York, while they were New York residents, were injured while driving that vehicle through Oklahoma and brought suit in an Oklahoma state court. *World-Wide Volkswagen*, 444 U.S. at 288, 100 S.Ct. at 562-63. The manufacturer did not sell its vehicles in Oklahoma and had not made an effort to establish business relationships in Oklahoma. *Id.* at 295, 100 S.Ct. at 566. The Supreme Court characterized the manufacturer's ties with Oklahoma as fortuitous because they resulted entirely out of the fact that the plaintiffs had driven their car into that state. *Id.*

Here, Dot Com argues that its contacts with Pennsylvania residents are fortuitous because Pennsylvanians happened to find its Web site or heard about its news service elsewhere and decided to subscribe. This argument misconstrues the concept of fortuitous contacts embodied in *World-Wide*

Volkswagen. Dot Com's contacts with Pennsylvania would be fortuitous within the meaning of *World-Wide Volkswagen* if it had no Pennsylvania subscribers and an Ohio subscriber forwarded a copy of a file he obtained from Dot Com to a friend in Pennsylvania or an Ohio subscriber brought his computer along on a trip to Pennsylvania and used it to access Dot Com's service. That is not the situation here. Dot Com repeatedly and consciously chose to process Pennsylvania residents' applications and to assign them passwords. Dot Com knew that the result of these contracts would be the transmission of electronic messages into Pennsylvania. The transmission of these files was entirely within its control. Dot Com cannot maintain that these contracts are "fortuitous" or "coincidental" within the meaning of *World-Wide Volkswagen*. When a defendant makes a conscious choice to conduct business with the residents of a forum state, "it has clear notice that it is subject to suit there." *World-Wide Volkswagen*, 444 U.S. at 297, 100 S.Ct. at 567. Dot Com was under no obligation to sell its services to Pennsylvania residents. It freely chose to do so, presumably in order to profit from those transactions. If a corporation determines that the risk of being subject to personal jurisdiction in a particular forum is too great, it can choose to sever its connection to the state. *Id.* If Dot Com had not wanted to be amenable to jurisdiction in Pennsylvania, the solution would have been simple—it could have chosen not to sell its services to Pennsylvania residents.

Next, Dot Com argues that its forum-related activities are not numerous or significant enough to create a "substantial connection" with Pennsylvania. Defendant points to the fact that only two percent of its subscribers are Pennsylvania residents. However, the Supreme Court has made clear that even a single contact can be sufficient. *McGee*, 355 U.S. at 223, 78 S.Ct. at 201. The test has always focused on the "nature and quality" of the contacts with the forum and not the quantity of those contacts. *International Shoe*, 326 U.S. at 320, 66 S.Ct. at 160. The Sixth Circuit also rejected a similar argument in *CompuServe* when it wrote that the contacts were "deliberate and repeated even if they yielded little revenue." *CompuServe*, 89 F.3d at 1265.

We also conclude that the cause of action arises out of Dot Com's forum-related conduct in this case. The Third Circuit has stated that "a cause of action for trademark infringement occurs where the passing off occurs." Cottman Transmission Systems Inc. v. Martino, 36 F.3d 291, 294 (citing Tefal, S.A. v. Products Int'l Co., 529 F.2d 495, 496 n. 1 (3d Cir.1976); Indianapolis Colts v. Metro. Baltimore Football, 34 F.3d 410 (7th Cir.1994). In *Tefal*, the maker and distributor of T-Fal cookware sued a partnership of California corporations in the District of New Jersey for trademark infringement. *Tefal*, 529 F.2d at 496. The defendants objected to venue in New Jersey, arguing that the contested trademark accounted for only about five percent of national sales. *Id.* On appeal, the Third Circuit concluded that since substantial sales of the product bearing the allegedly infringing mark took place in New Jersey, the cause of action arose in New Jersey and venue was proper. *Tefal*, 529 F.2d at 496-97.

In *Indianapolis Colts*, also case cited by the Third Circuit in *Cottman*, an Indiana National Football League franchise sued a Maryland Canadian Football League franchise in the Southern District of Indiana, alleging trademark infringement. *Indianapolis Colts*, 34 F.3d at 411. On appeal, the Seventh Circuit held that personal jurisdiction was appropriate in Indiana because trademark infringement is a tort-like injury and a substantial amount of the injury from the alleged infringement was likely to occur in Indiana. *Id.* at 412.

In the instant case, both a significant amount of the alleged infringement and dilution, and resulting injury have occurred in Pennsylvania. The object of Dot Com's contracts with Pennsylvania residents is the transmission of the messages that Plaintiff claims dilute and infringe upon its trademark. When these messages are transmitted into Pennsylvania and viewed by Pennsylvania residents on their computers, there can be no question that the alleged infringement and dilution occur in Pennsylvania. Moreover, since Manufacturing is a Pennsylvania corporation, a substantial amount of the injury from the alleged wrongdoing is likely to occur in Pennsylvania. Thus, we conclude that the cause of action arises out of Dot Com's forum-related activities under the authority of both *Tefal* and *Indianapolis Colts*, supra.

Finally, Dot Com argues that the exercise of jurisdiction would be unreasonable in this case. We disagree. There can be no question that Pennsylvania has a strong interest in adjudicating disputes involving the alleged infringement of trademarks owned by resident corporations. We must also give due regard to the Plaintiff's choice to seek relief in Pennsylvania. *Kulko*, 436 U.S. at 92, 98 S.Ct. at 1696-97. These concerns outweigh the burden created by forcing the Defendant to defend the suit in Pennsylvania, especially when Dot Com consciously chose to conduct business in Pennsylvania, pursuing profits from the actions that are now in question. The Due Process Clause is not a "territorial shield to interstate obligations that have been voluntarily assumed." *Burger King*, 471 U.S. at 474, 105 S.Ct. at 2183. . . .

COMMENTS AND QUESTIONS

1.   Does it make sense to treat electronic commerce sites differently from "passive" Web pages? Is it the act of sale into a jurisdiction or the offer for sale that makes an electronic commerce site liable for suit in that jurisdiction?

One implication of the "offer for sale" approach would seem to be that if you offer products for sale over the Internet, you are subject to suit *everywhere in the world*. Does this result make sense? Is there a way to limit jurisdiction while still holding ecommerce sites liable for suit in jurisdictions in which their products or conduct actually cause injury?

Of course, as with virtually all discussions of Internet jurisdiction, we are talking about specific rather than general jurisdiction here. That is, each of these disputes is about amenability to suits arising out of the plaintiff's interaction with the Web site. A court recently confirmed that *general* jurisdiction—jurisdiction over all types of claims, whether or not related to the forum contacts—cannot be conferred by the mere accessibility of a Web site, regardless of how interactive it is. See Coastal Video Comm. Corp. v. The Staywell Corp., 59 F. Supp. 2d 562 (E.D. Va. 1999).

2. If a site does not itself sell products, should it automatically be considered passive? Many business models on the Internet today involve giving away useful information or services and funding the site with some other revenue source (such as advertising). Is a search engine interactive or passive within the meaning of the jurisdiction cases?

3. The case-by-case approach has drawn the adherence of a number of courts. Most courts to consider the question have concluded that passive Web pages alone are not enough for jurisdiction. In addition to *Cybersell*, see Bensusan Restaurant Corp. v. King, 937 F. Supp. 295 (S.D.N.Y. 1996); CD Solutions v. Tooker, 965 F. Supp. 17 (N.D. Tex. 1997); Rannoch Inc. v. Rannoch Corp., 52 F. Supp. 2d 681 (E.D. Va. 1999); Millennium Ents. v. Millennium Music, 33 F. Supp. 2d 907 (D. Or. 1999) (defining "passive" to include a Web page that was itself interactive but that could not be used to conduct commerce). By contrast, courts that found the presence of other "plus factors"—non-Internet advertising activities in the jurisdiction, for example, or sales or business relationships within the jurisdiction—are more likely to find personal jurisdiction. In addition to *Zippo*, see Heroes, Inc. v. Heroes Found., 958 F. Supp. 1 (D.D.C. 1996); Digital Equip. Corp. v. Altavista Tech., 960 F. Supp. 456 (D. Mass. 1997). The definition of "interactivity" is open to some dispute, however. By contrast to Millennium, see Bochan v. LaFontaine, 22 Media L. Rep. 2057 (E.D. Va. 1999) (Web site interactive despite inability to purchase products through it). For an expansive reading of what constitutes an "interactive" Web site, concluding that the ability to send email to the site owner qualifies, see Blumenthal v. Drudge, 992 F. Supp. 44 (D.D.C. 1998).

An interesting twist on this question occurs when the Web sites or servers used by the defendant are themselves located out of state. What happens when the defendant is sued not in the jurisdiction in which he resides, but the jurisdiction in which his ISP is located? Two cases have suggested that jurisdiction is proper there as well, because the Web sites are "located" there. See *Bochan*, supra; Krantz v. Air Line Pilots Assoc., 427 S.E.2d 326 (Va. 1993). Does this result make sense? Does it matter whether the defendant knows where the servers are physically located?

4. Should it matter what the defendant is accused of doing? Some courts have said yes. For example, in Panavision Int'l v. Toeppen, 141 F.3d 1316 (9th Cir. 1998), discussed in Chapter 10 in the Section on trade-

marks, defendant Toeppen was an Illinois resident who had registered the trademark "panavision" as an Internet domain name. Despite the fact that the registration did not take place in California, the court held that jurisdiction there was proper. It relied in part on the fact that Toeppen had knowingly registered a California corporation's mark as a domain name *in order to sell it to a California corporation* and therefore had purposefully "directed" his injurious activities into the forum in a way that had effects there.[1] A similar line of cases exists in the defamation context, where an intentional act of defamation against a person is held to be directed against that person, thereby conferring jurisdiction in that person's state of residence. See Calder v. Jones, 465 U.S. 783 (1984).

How far does this logic extend? Is trademark infringement always "directed" toward whatever jurisdiction the plaintiff resides in? How about copyright infringement? Does it matter whether the plaintiff alleges that the defendant's conduct was intentional? Whether they can prove it? Suppose that the defendant did not even *know* what state the plaintiff lived in. How can defamation be "directed toward" the state in that case? For a particularly expansive application of this principle, see Minnesota v. Granite Gate Resorts, 568 N.W.2d 715 (Minn. Ct. App. 1997).

5. In a novel approach to the jurisdiction question, Porsche recently brought an in rem action in Virginia (the home of Network Solutions (NSI), which registers most U.S. domain names) against a variety of domain names that it felt infringed its trademarks. Porsche argued that it need not prove personal jurisdiction over the variety of cybersquatters that had registered the domain names because the action was against the "property" itself, and the property was located in NSI's computers in Virginia. The Virginia trial court rejected this argument. Porsche AG v. porsch.com, et al., No. 99-0006-A (E.D. Va. Jan. 6, 1999). The Virginia Supreme Court accepted the case for review. If the court permits the in rem action, it will be a powerful new tool in a significant subset of jurisdictional disputes.

Note on International Jurisdiction

The problem of Internet jurisdiction is not just confined to the United States. A number of cases have considered the related problem of international jurisdiction. In one trademark case, Playboy Enterprises v. Chuckleberry Publishing, 939 F. Supp. 1032 (S.D.N.Y. 1996), the court held that an Italian Web site allegedly infringing Playboy's trademark was subject to jurisdiction in New York (though in that case jurisdiction was largely based on a prior case between the parties). This case raises the spectre not only of being haled into court anywhere in the world to answer for the contents of your Web page, but also the even more troubling problem of conforming your conduct to different substantive laws in different jurisdictions.

---

1. By contrast, had Toeppen merely registered the mark without offering to sell it, jurisdiction apparently would not have been proper.

Chuckleberry's site was legal under Italian trademark laws, because the Italian courts had ruled that its "Playmen" mark did not infringe "Playboy." But U.S. courts had held the opposite, and the court concluded that Chuckleberry was bound by the prior U.S. rulings. Cases like *Inset Systems,* cited in *Cybersell,* are even more troubling because they suggest that anyone who puts up a Web page can be sued anywhere in the world.

Solving the problem of international jurisdiction and conflicting legal rules may require, at a minimum, harmonizing the substantive laws governing the Internet on a worldwide basis. See David W. Maher, Trademark Law on the Internet—Will It Scale? The Challenge to Develop International Trademark Law, 16 J. Marshall J. Computer & Info. L. 3 (1997).

Harmonization has proven difficult enough even in relatively uncontroversial areas like trademark law, however. It may well be impossible to harmonize laws where there is less agreement on principles among nations —laws relating to free speech, for example. And even if that problem is solved, courts will have to do something about an individual's risk of being sued in remote jurisdictions if they are to avoid chilling speech on the Internet. The prospect of being subject to litigation in a number of different countries is likely to be extremely daunting to individuals and even small and medium-sized businesses. While the law has faced this problem before, in the past companies subject to worldwide jurisdiction were almost all large, sophisticated entities with offices and lawyers in many parts of the world. What is different about the Internet is precisely its ability to make anyone who can afford a computer an international publisher. Unfortunately, the responsibilities that traditionally come with that international status—like amenability to suit—carry a large price tag.

Note on Choice of Law

Choice of law is a neglected cousin to personal jurisdiction in Internet cases. Strictly speaking, determining where a defendant can be sued only settles where the case will take place—it does not settle the separate question of what jurisdiction's *legal rules* apply to the transaction. (As a practical matter, it may be that courts are inclined to favor applying the law of their own jurisdiction in close cases, since that is the law with which they are most familiar.)

Jurisprudence regarding choice of law has a long history, and we will not recapitulate it here. While courts historically inquired into the location of the contract (in contract cases) or the wrong (in tort cases), in modern times the choice of law inquiry in most jurisdictions has devolved into a multifactor test of general applicability. This test seeks to determine the jurisdiction with the most significant relationship to the transaction or injury in question, and to apply the law of that jurisdiction. See Restatement (Second) of Conflict of Laws §§148(2), 188(2). These factors may include the location of the plaintiff and defendant, the place where each of the acts relevant to the claim took place (i.e., where the contract was negotiated, where it was to be performed, where fraudulent representations were made, where a defamation was published, and so on).

On the Internet, it is likely that many of these locations will diverge between plaintiff and defendant. For example, where is an electronic contract formed—at the promisor's computer, or the promisee's? The logical answer would seem to be "both," but that is not terribly helpful in selecting one particular body of law to apply. One commentator has suggested that choice of law, like jurisdiction, will answer these questions differently for different causes of action. Thus,

> [plaintiff's] domicile will likely govern defamation actions arising in the [Internet]. Invasion of privacy claims, like defamation claims, are centered where the plaintiff lives and conducts his or her affairs, because that is where the privacy interest exists. The same result is appropriate for intellectual property actions unless the party arguing for the choice of different law can show that adversely affected markets are located elsewhere.

Henry H. Perritt Jr., Jurisdiction in Cyberspace, 41 Vill. L. Rev. 1 (1996). It is reasonable to predict that courts will generally apply well-worn rules of choice of law in Internet cases but will face new challenges in deciding *how* those rules apply to the Internet.

While courts have necessarily addressed choice of law questions in Internet cases, they have frequently done so *sub rosa*, assuming or concluding without much analysis that a particular law applied. For discussion and criticism of these cases, see Christopher P. Beall, The Scientological Defenestration of Choice-of-Law Doctrines for Publication Torts on the Internet, 15 J. Marshall J. Computer & Info. L. 361 (1997).

For further discussion of choice of law issues, particularly in the international context, see Kai Burmeister, Jurisdiction, Choice of Law, Copyright, and the Internet: Protection Against Framing in an International Setting, 9 Fordham Intell. Prop., Media & Ent. L.J. 625 (1999); John Rothchild, Protecting the Digital Consumer: The Limits of Cyberspace Utopianism, 74 Ind. L.J. 893, 918 (1999); Peter P. Swire, Of Elephants, Mice and Privacy: International Choice of Law and the Internet, 32 Int'l Law. 991 (1998); Matthew R. Burnstein, Conflicts on the Net: Choice of Law in Transnational Cyberspace, 29 Vand. J. Transnat'l L. 75 (1996).

10

Intellectual Property in Cyberspace

A. TRADEMARK LAW

In this section, we consider a number of issues of trademark law that have been litigated in the context of the Internet. We begin with a problem specific to the structure of the Internet itself, and that has generated abundant litigation: how domain names are treated under trademark law. We then consider a number of other trademark-related issues raised by the Internet.

1. Domain Names as Trademarks

> **Panavision International, L.P. v. Toeppen**
> *United States Court of Appeals for the Ninth Circuit*
> *141 F.3d 1316 (9th Cir. 1998)*

DAVID R. THOMPSON, Circuit Judge:

This case presents two novel issues. We are asked to apply existing rules of personal jurisdiction to conduct that occurred, in part, in "cyberspace." In addition, we are asked to interpret the Federal Trademark Dilution Act as it applies to the Internet. [The discussion of personal jurisdiction is omitted.]

Panavision accuses Dennis Toeppen of being a "cyber pirate" who steals valuable trademarks and establishes domain names on the Internet using these trademarks to sell the domain names to the rightful trademark owners. . . .

799

We conclude Panavision was entitled to summary judgment under the federal and state dilution statutes. Toeppen made commercial use of Panavision's trademarks and his conduct diluted those marks.

I Background

The Internet is a worldwide network of computers that enables various individuals and organizations to share information. The Internet allows computer users to access millions of web sites and web pages. A web page is a computer data file that can include names, words, messages, pictures, sounds, and links to other information.

Every web page has its own web site, which is its address, similar to a telephone number or street address. Every web site on the Internet has an identifier called a "domain name." The domain name often consists of a person's name or a company's name or trademark. For example, Pepsi has a web page with a web site domain name consisting of the company name, Pepsi, and .com, the "top level" domain designation: Pepsi.com.

The Internet is divided into several "top level" domains: .edu for education; .org for organizations; .gov for government entities; .net for networks; and .com for "commercial" which functions as the catchall domain for Internet users.

Domain names with the .com designation must be registered on the Internet with Network Solutions, Inc. ("NSI"). NSI registers names on a first-come, first-served basis for a $100 registration fee. NSI does not make a determination about a registrant's right to use a domain name. However, NSI does require an applicant to represent and warrant as an express condition of registering a domain name that (1) the applicant's statements are true and the applicant has the right to use the requested domain name; (2) the "use or registration of the domain name . . . does not interfere with or infringe the rights of any third party in any jurisdiction with respect to trademark, service mark, trade name, company name or any other intellectual property right"; and (3) the applicant is not seeking to use the domain name for any unlawful purpose, including unfair competition.

A domain name is the simplest way of locating a web site. If a computer user does not know a domain name, she can use an Internet "search engine." To do this, the user types in a key word search, and the search will locate all of the web sites containing the key word. Such key word searches can yield hundreds of web sites. To make it easier to find their web sites, individuals and companies prefer to have a recognizable domain name.

Panavision holds registered trademarks to the names "Panavision" and "Panaflex" in connection with motion picture camera equipment. Panavision promotes its trademarks through motion picture and television credits and other media advertising.

In December 1995, Panavision attempted to register a web site on the Internet with the domain name Panavision.com. It could not do that, however, because Toeppen had already established a web site using Panavision's trademark as his domain name. Toeppen's web page for this site displayed photographs of the City of Pana, Illinois.

On December 20, 1995, Panavision's counsel sent a letter from California to Toeppen in Illinois informing him that Panavision held a trademark in the name Panavision and telling him to stop using that trademark and the domain name Panavision.com. Toeppen responded by mail to Panavision in California, stating he had the right to use the name Panavision.com on the Internet as his domain name. Toeppen stated:

> If your attorney has advised you otherwise, he is trying to screw you. He wants to blaze new trails in the legal frontier at your expense. Why do you want to fund your attorney's purchase of a new boat (or whatever) when you can facilitate the acquisition of 'PanaVision.com' cheaply and simply instead?

Toeppen then offered to "settle the matter" if Panavision would pay him $13,000 in exchange for the domain name. Additionally, Toeppen stated that if Panavision agreed to his offer, he would not "acquire any other Internet addresses which are alleged by Panavision Corporation to be its property."

After Panavision refused Toeppen's demand, he registered Panavision's other trademark with NSI as the domain name Panaflex.com. Toeppen's web page for Panaflex.com simply displays the word "Hello."

Toeppen has registered domain names for various other companies including Delta Airlines, Neiman Marcus, Eddie Bauer, Lufthansa, and over 100 other marks. Toeppen has attempted to "sell" domain names for other trademarks such as intermatic.com to Intermatic, Inc. for $10,000 and americanstandard.com to American Standard, Inc. for $15,000.

Panavision filed this action against Toeppen in the District Court for the Central District of California. Panavision alleged claims for dilution of its trademark under the Federal Trademark Dilution Act of 1995, 15 U.S.C. §1125(c), and under the California Anti-dilution statute, California Business and Professions Code §14330. Panavision alleged that Toeppen was in the business of stealing trademarks, registering them as domain names on the Internet and then selling the domain names to the rightful trademark owners. The district court determined it had personal jurisdiction over Toeppen, and granted summary judgment in favor of Panavision on both its federal and state dilution claims. This appeal followed.

II Discussion . . .

B. *Trademark Dilution Claims*

The Federal Trademark Dilution Act provides:

> The owner of a famous mark shall be entitled . . . to an injunction against another person's commercial use in commerce of a mark or trade

name, if such use begins after the mark has become famous and causes dilution
of the distinctive quality of the mark. . . .

15 U.S.C. §1125(c).

The California Anti-dilution statute is similar. See Cal. Bus. & Prof.
Code §14330. It prohibits dilution of "the distinctive quality" of a mark
regardless of competition or the likelihood of confusion. The protection
extends only to strong and well recognized marks. Panavision's state law
dilution claim is subject to the same analysis as its federal claim.

In order to prove a violation of the Federal Trademark Dilution Act, a
plaintiff must show that (1) the mark is famous; (2) the defendant is making
a commercial use of the mark in commerce; (3) the defendant's use began
after the mark became famous; and (4) the defendant's use of the mark
dilutes the quality of the mark by diminishing the capacity of the mark to
identify and distinguish goods and services. 15 U.S.C. §1125(c).

Toeppen does not challenge the district court's determination that
Panavision's trademark is famous, that his alleged use began after the mark
became famous, or that the use was in commerce. Toeppen challenges the
district court's determination that he made "commercial use" of the mark
and that this use caused "dilution" in the quality of the mark.

1. Commercial Use

Toeppen argues that his use of Panavision's trademarks simply as his
domain names cannot constitute a commercial use under the Act. Case law
supports this argument. See Panavision International, L.P. v. Toeppen, 945
F.Supp. 1296, 1303 (C.D.Cal.1996) ("Registration of a trade[mark] as a
domain name, without more, is not a commercial use of the trademark and
therefore is not within the prohibitions of the Act."); Academy of Motion
Picture Arts & Sciences v. Network Solutions, Inc., 989 F.Supp. 1276,
1997 WL 810472 (C.D.Cal. Dec.22, 1997) (the mere registration of a
domain name does not constitute a commercial use); Lockheed Martin
Corp. v. Network Solutions, Inc., 985 F.Supp. 949 (C.D.Cal.1997) (NSI's
acceptance of a domain name for registration is not a commercial use within
the meaning of the Trademark Dilution Act).

Developing this argument, Toeppen contends that a domain name is
simply an address used to locate a web page. He asserts that entering a
domain name on a computer allows a user to access a web page, but a
domain name is not associated with information on a web page. If a user
were to type Panavision.com as a domain name, the computer screen would
display Toeppen's web page with aerial views of Pana, Illinois. The screen
would not provide any information about "Panavision," other than a
"location window" which displays the domain name. Toeppen argues that a
user who types in Panavision.com, but who sees no reference to the plaintiff
Panavision on Toeppen's web page, is not likely to conclude the web page
is related in any way to the plaintiff, Panavision.

Toeppen's argument misstates his use of the Panavision mark. His use is not as benign as he suggests. Toeppen's "business" is to register trademarks as domain names and then sell them to the rightful trademark owners. He "act[s] as a 'spoiler,' preventing Panavision and others from doing business on the Internet under their trademarked names unless they pay his fee." *Panavision*, 938 F.Supp. at 621. This is a commercial use. See Intermatic Inc. v. Toeppen, 947 F.Supp. 1227, 1230 (N.D.Ill.1996) (stating that "[o]ne of Toeppen's business objectives is to profit by the resale or licensing of these domain names, presumably to the entities who conduct business under these names.").

As the district court found, Toeppen traded on the value of Panavision's marks. So long as he held the Internet registrations, he curtailed Panavision's exploitation of the value of its trademarks on the Internet, a value which Toeppen then used when he attempted to sell the Panavision.com domain name to Panavision.

In a nearly identical case involving Toeppen and Intermatic Inc., a federal district court in Illinois held that Toeppen's conduct violated the Federal Trademark Dilution Act. Intermatic, 947 F.Supp. at 1241. There, Intermatic sued Toeppen for registering its trademark on the Internet as Toeppen's domain name, intermatic.com. It was "conceded that one of Toeppen's intended uses for registering the Intermatic mark was to eventually sell it back to Intermatic or to some other party." *Id.* at 1239. The court found that "Toeppen's intention to arbitrage the 'intermatic.com' domain name constitute[d] a commercial use." *Id*. See also Teletech Customer Care Management, Inc. v. Tele-Tech Co., 977 F.Supp. 1407 (C.D.Cal.1997) (granting a preliminary injunction under the Trademark Dilution Act for use of a trademark as a domain name).

Toeppen's reliance on Holiday Inns, Inc. v. 800 Reservation, Inc., 86 F.3d 619 (6th Cir.1996), *cert. denied*, —U.S.—, 117 S.Ct. 770, 136 L.Ed.2d 715 (1997) is misplaced. In *Holiday Inns*, the Sixth Circuit held that a company's use of the most commonly misdialed number for Holiday Inns' 1-800 reservation number was not trademark infringement.

Holiday Inns is distinguishable. There, the defendant did not use Holiday Inns' trademark. Rather, the defendant selected the most commonly misdialed telephone number for Holiday Inns and attempted to capitalize on consumer confusion.

A telephone number, moreover, is distinguishable from a domain name because a domain name is associated with a word or phrase. A domain name is similar to a "vanity number" that identifies its source. Using Holiday Inns as an example, when a customer dials the vanity number "1-800-Holiday," she expects to contact Holiday Inns because the number is associated with that company's trademark. A user would have the same expectation typing the domain name HolidayInns.com. The user would expect to retrieve Holiday Inns' web page.

Toeppen made a commercial use of Panavision's trademarks. It does not matter that he did not attach the marks to a product. Toeppen's commercial use was his attempt to sell the trademarks themselves.[5] Under the Federal Trademark Dilution Act and the California Anti-dilution statute, this was sufficient commercial use.

2. Dilution

"Dilution" is defined as "the lessening of the capacity of a famous mark to identify and distinguish goods or services, regardless of the presence or absence of (1) competition between the owner of the famous mark and other parties, or (2) likelihood of confusion, mistake or deception." 15 U.S.C. §1127.

Trademark dilution on the Internet was a matter of Congressional concern. Senator Patrick Leahy (D-Vt.) stated:

> [I]t is my hope that this anti-dilution statute can help stem the use of deceptive Internet addresses taken by those who are choosing marks that are associated with the products and reputations of others.

141 Cong. Rec. §19312-01 (daily ed. Dec. 29, 1995) (statement of Sen. Leahy). See also Teletech Customer Care Management, Inc. v. Tele-Tech Co., Inc., 977 F.Supp. 1407, 1413 (C.D.Cal.1997).

To find dilution, a court need not rely on the traditional definitions such as "blurring" and "tarnishment." Indeed, in concluding that Toeppen's use of Panavision's trademarks diluted the marks, the district court noted that Toeppen's conduct varied from the two standard dilution theories of blurring and tarnishment. *Panavision*, 945 F.Supp. at 1304. The court found that Toeppen's conduct diminished "the capacity of the Panavision marks to identify and distinguish Panavision's goods and services on the Internet." *Id.* See also *Intermatic*, 947 F.Supp. at 1240 (Toeppen's registration of the domain name, "lessens the capacity of Intermatic to identify and distinguish its goods and services by means of the Internet.").

This view is also supported by *Teletech*. There, TeleTech Customer Care Management Inc. ("TCCM"), sought a preliminary injunction against Tele-Tech Company for use of TCCM's registered service mark, "TeleTech," as an Internet domain name. *Teletech*, 977 F.Supp. at 1410. The district court issued an injunction, finding that TCCM had demonstrated a likelihood of success on the merits on its trademark dilution claim.

---

5. See Boston Pro. Hockey Assoc., Inc. v. Dallas Cap & Emblem Mfg., Inc., 510 F.2d 1004 (1975), which involved the sale of National Hockey League logos. The defendant was selling the logos themselves, unattached to a product (such as a hat or sweatshirt). The court stated: "The difficulty with this case stems from the fact that a reproduction of the trademark itself is being sold, unattached to any other goods or services." *Id.* at 1010. The court concluded that trademark law should protect the trademark itself. "Although our decision here may slightly tilt the trademark laws from the purpose of protecting the public to the protection of the business interests of plaintiffs, we think that the two become ... intermeshed. ..." *Id.* at 1011. "Whereas traditional trademark law sought primarily to protect consumers, dilution laws place more emphasis on protecting the investment of the trademark owners." *Panavision*, 945 F.Supp. at 1301.

Id. at 1412. The court found that TCCM had invested great resources in promoting its servicemark and Teletech's registration of the domain name teletech.com on the Internet would most likely dilute TCCM's mark. *Id.* at 1413.

Toeppen argues he is not diluting the capacity of the Panavision marks to identify goods or services. He contends that even though Panavision cannot use Panavision.com and Panaflex.com as its domain name addresses, it can still promote its goods and services on the Internet simply by using some other "address" and then creating its own web page using its trademarks.

We reject Toeppen's premise that a domain name is nothing more than an address. A significant purpose of a domain name is to identify the entity that owns the web site. "A customer who is unsure about a company's domain name will often guess that the domain name is also the company's name." Cardservice Int'l v. McGee, 950 F.Supp. 737, 741 (E.D.Va.1997). "[A] domain name mirroring a corporate name may be a valuable corporate asset, as it facilitates communication with a customer base." MTV Networks, Inc. v. Curry, 867 F.Supp. 202, 203-204 n. 2 (S.D.N.Y.1994).

Using a company's name or trademark as a domain name is also the easiest way to locate that company's web site. Use of a "search engine" can turn up hundreds of web sites, and there is nothing equivalent to a phone book or directory assistance for the Internet. See *Cardservice*, 950 F.Supp. at 741.

Moreover, potential customers of Panavision will be discouraged if they cannot find its web page by typing in "Panavision.com," but instead are forced to wade through hundreds of web sites. This dilutes the value of Panavision's trademark. We echo the words of Judge Lechner, quoting Judge Wood: "Prospective users of plaintiff's services who mistakenly access defendant's web site may fail to continue to search for plaintiff's own home page, due to anger, frustration or the belief that plaintiff's home page does not exist." Jews for Jesus v. Brodsky, 993 F.Supp. 282, 306-07 (D.N.J. 1998) (Lechner, J., quoting Wood, J. in Planned Parenthood v. Bucci, 1997 WL 133313 at *4); see also *Teletech*, 977 F.Supp. at 1410 (finding that use of a search engine can generate as many as 800 to 1000 matches and it is "likely to deter web browsers from searching for Plaintiff's particular web site").

Toeppen's use of Panavision.com also puts Panavision's name and reputation at his mercy. See *Intermatic*, 947 F.Supp. at 1240 ("If Toeppen were allowed to use 'intermatic.com,' Intermatic's name and reputation would be at Toeppen's mercy and could be associated with an unimaginable amount of messages on Toeppen's web page.").

We conclude that Toeppen's registration of Panavision's trademarks as his domain names on the Internet diluted those marks within the meaning of the Federal Trademark Dilution Act, 15 U.S.C. §1125(c), and the California Anti-dilution statute, Cal.Bus. & Prof.Code §14330.

III Conclusion

Toeppen engaged in a scheme to register Panavision's trademarks as his domain names on the Internet and then to extort money from Panavision by trading on the value of those names. Toeppen's actions were aimed at Panavision in California and the brunt of the harm was felt in California. The district court properly exercised personal jurisdiction over Toeppen.

We also affirm the district court's summary judgment in favor of Panavision under the Federal Trademark Dilution Act, 15 U.S.C. §1125(c), and the California Anti-dilution statute, Cal.Bus. & Prof.Code §14330. Toeppen made commercial use of Panavision's trademarks and his conduct diluted those marks.

AFFIRMED.

COMMENTS AND QUESTIONS

1. The interaction between NSI's "first-come, first-serve" rule for allocating Internet domain names and trademark law has been explored in great detail elsewhere. The following is only a sample of the many treatments of the subject. See, e.g., Dan L. Burk, Trademarks Along the Info-bahn: A First Look at the Emerging Law of Cybermarks, 1 Rich. J.L. & Tech. 1 (1995); David J. Loundy, A Primer on Trademark Law and Internet Addresses, 15 John Marshall J. Computer & Info. L. 465 (1997); James West Marcovitz, ronald@mcdonalds.com—"Owning a Bitchin'" Corporate Trademark as an Internet Address—Infringement?, 17 Cardozo L. Rev. 85 (1995); Carl Oppedahl, Remedies in Domain Name Lawsuits: How Is a Domain Name Like a Cow?, 15 John Marshall J. Computer & Info. L. 437 (1997). See also http://www.ll.georgetown.edu/lc/internic/domain1.html (cataloguing information about domain name trademark disputes).

2. As the courts have decided dozens of domain name cases, a basic consensus has emerged on some issues. Essentially, as to "cybersquatters" (those who obtain a domain name from NSI in order to deprive the trademark owner of it, or in order to sell it or confuse consumers), the rule in the cases is straightforward: the trademark owner wins. Numerous cases have established liability for using another's trademark as a domain name. See, e.g., Comp Examiner Agency v. Juris, Inc., 1996 U.S. Dist. LEXIS 20259 (C.D. Cal. Apr. 25, 1996) (injunction against direct competitor); Actmedia, Inc. v. Active Media Int'l, 1996 US Dist. LEXIS 20814 (N.D. Ill. July 17, 1996) (same); Lozano Enters. v. La Opinion Pub. Co., 44 U.S.P.Q.2d 1764 (C.D. Cal. 1997) (same); Cardservice Int'l v. McGee, 950 F. Supp. 737 (E.D. Va. 1997) (same); Planned Parenthood Federation v. Bucci, 42 U.S.P.Q.2d 1430 (S.D.N.Y. 1997) (anti-abortion activist can't use Planned Parenthood name); Intermatic, Inc. v. Toeppen, 947 F. Supp. 1227 (N.D. Ill. 1996) (same dilution analysis); Hasbro, Inc. v. Internet Entertainment

Group, 40 U.S.P.Q.2d 1479 (W.D. Wash 1996) (adult site dilutes famous name for children's game); Toys 'R' Us v. Akkaoui, 40 U.S.P.Q.2d 1836 (N.D. Cal. 1996) (dilution of "R Us" family of marks by defendant's "adultsrus" domain name); Inset Systems v. Instruction Set, Inc., 937 F. Supp. 161 (D. Conn. 1996) (dictum).

Not all domain name trademark cases involve cybersquatting, however. Sometimes two legitimate trademark owners with the same name dispute who should own a domain name. These problems often arise because trademarks that are widely separated in geographic or product space are thrown together on the Internet, which is worldwide and cuts across product lines. For example, "roadrunner" is the name of a bird, a computer company, a moving and storage company, and a Warner Brothers cartoon character. In the real world, all of these uses can coexist, because the products are so different that no one would be likely to confuse them. But on the Internet, only one company can register roadrunner.com.

Courts faced with disputes of this sort have a number of choices, but none seem especially satisfactory. First, they could uphold NSI's traditional "first-come, first-served" approach to registration. Whoever wins the race to the registrar gets the name, and everyone else loses. This result is certainly easy to administer; indeed, the courts need not get involved at all. It may end up increasing consumer confusion, however, especially where the larger of two coexisting companies loses the race.

Second, courts (or NSI) might try to decide which claimant to a name was the "best," or most famous. This may produce the fairest result in the final analysis, but only if there is some way to make that determination. NSI's policy of placing domain names on hold if a registered trademark owner complains has led to some problems here, particularly when both the registrant and the complainant had legitimate claims to the name. See Giacalone v. Network Solutions, 1996 U.S. Dist. LEXIS 20807 (N.D. Cal. June 14, 1996) (preliminary injunction against NSI placing a registered domain name on hold at the request of a trademark owner). One lawyer refers to the use of NSI's on-hold policy against a legitimate trademark owner as "reverse domain name hijacking." See Carl Oppedahl, Pursuing Domain Name Registrants Can Backfire, Nat'l L.J., Apr. 26, 1999, at B6 (discussing a number of cases rejecting NSI's policy in disputes between legitimate trademark owners).

Finally, courts might force the competing applicants to coexist—either by choosing similar names ("road-runner.com" and "roadrunner.com"), or by sharing a welcome page. The parties in Mattel v. Hasbro (C.D. Cal. 1997) chose the latter option. Hasbro owned the trademark rights to the game "Scrabble" in North America, and Mattel owned the rights elsewhere. The parties settled a trademark dispute by agreeing to create a joint page at scrabble.com that linked to both of their respective sites.

Whichever of these choices is most logical, it seems unlikely that trademark law or dilution will provide a cause of action against a legitimate user of a domain name. In Hasbro Inc. v. Clue Computing Inc., 66 F.

Supp. 2d 117 (D. Mass. 1999), the court refused to find trademark infringement or dilution by Clue Computing, which had registered the name clue.com, in a suit by the maker of the board game Clue. Even if the game Clue is famous, the court reasoned, it may be forced to coexist with other trademarks, and a legitimate trademark owner has not diluted the mark by using its own mark as a domain name.

3. A third set of cases involve suits by both sides against NSI for their role in domain name registration. Irate trademark owners sued NSI for allowing cybersquatters to register their marks, and demanding that the domain name be handed over to them. When NSI started putting domain names on hold, domain name owners not only sued the trademark owner who requested the hold, but in many cases also sued NSI for interfering with their rights. (The *Giacalone* case cited above is an example of the latter.) While either or both sides may have a claim based in property rights or tort, the courts have generally ruled that NSI's domain name registration policies do not themselves implicate the trademark laws. Lockheed Martin Corp. v. Network Solutions Inc., 985 F. Supp. 949 (C.D. Cal. 1997); Academy of Motion Picture Arts & Sciences v. Network Solutions, Inc., 989 F. Supp. 1276 (C.D. Cal. 1997). In both cases, the court concluded that the mere act by NSI of registering a domain name by placing the entry on the domain name server (DNS) database was not "use" necessary for a violation of the Lanham Act. The court opined in *Lockheed* that "the solution to the current difficulties faced by trademark owners on the Internet lies in . . . technical innovation, not in attempts to assert trademark rights over legitimate non-trademark uses of this important new means of communication." *Id.*

Is the court correct that accepting a domain name registration that infringes a trademark is a "legitimate non-trademark use"? Is *Lockheed* distinguishable from the result in *Panavision*?

4. There are numerous trademark disputes on the Internet that do not involve domain names but rather the content of Web sites themselves. For a discussion of many of these cases and some of the interesting issues they present, see Dan L. Burk, Trademark Doctrines for Global Electronic Commerce, 49 S.C. L. Rev. 695 (1998).

5. Despite a wave of decisions holding that cybersquatting is illegal, the trend has not abated. Many large companies face hundreds and even thousands of cybersquatters who have seized misspellings of their marks, variants or combinations using their marks, and domain names registered in other countries or in top-level domains (TLDs) other than .com. These cybersquatters know they will lose if they are sued, but they count on the cost and delay associated with the legal system to allow them to extort money out of legitimate trademark owners.

Trademark owners have sought to respond to this threat in a number of ways. One is the in rem action against the domain names themselves, discussed above in the Section on jurisdiction. An example of another innovative maneuver is a Texas class action suit brought by hundreds of mark owners against a major cybersquatter. Omega Protein Corp. v. Flom, No. H-98-3114 (S.D. Tex., filed Sept. 18, 1998). The defendant had hoped to settle individually with each mark owner for something less than the cost of litigation, but, if successful, this class action tactic may make litigation rather than settlement cost-effective. Still another response is to encourage or require alternative dispute resolution of cybersquatting disputes. We discuss this approach in more detail below.

A final approach is legislative. Congress recently passed a bill to punish cybersquatting as an independent civil wrong, whether or not it also constitutes trademark infringement. S. 1255 (105th Cong., 1st Sess.). (An earlier provision in the bill, since deleted, would have made cybersquatting a crime.) One problem with legislation of this sort is that it requires Congress to define "cybersquatting" and to distinguish it from the other sorts of cases discussed above. What exactly is cybersquatting? How would you define it in a statute?

6. From a policy perspective, punishing cybersquatters like Toeppen seems unobjectionable. But consider how well it really comports with trademark doctrine. Were consumers confused by Toeppen's use of the panavision.com domain? Perhaps initially—they might have gone to www.panavision.com expecting to find the Web site for the corporation, but any such confusion surely would have been quickly dispelled, because Toeppen's site had nothing to do with Panavision's business.[1] The obvious alternative is to apply dilution theory, but dilution requires the "commercial use in commerce" of a diluting mark by the defendant. 15 U.S.C. §1125(c). Has Toeppen really engaged in commercial use of the Panavision mark? What if he did not wish to sell it to Panavision at all, but instead simply wanted it for his own private use or to deprive Panavision of the ability to use the mark? Cf. Juno Online Servs. v. Juno Lighting, 979 F. Supp. 684 (N.D. Ill. 1997) (suggesting that mere registration of a domain name without using it could not be trademark infringement; defendant in that case had a legitimate claim to the mark, however). Alternatively, suppose Toeppen devoted the site to a political diatribe against Panavision's employment practices. It is hard to see how this would constitute dilution in the traditional sense. See also 15 U.S.C. §1125(c), which exempts from dilution any noncommercial use of a mark.

The *Panavision* court, like in many cybersquatting cases, grounded its rationale on dilution. Does this mean that only famous marks are entitled to protection against cybersquatters? Is there a way Toeppen could be said to cause consumer confusion? If so, how? Consider the following case.

---

1. A different (and much easier) issue is presented by cases in which one firm registers a competitor's domain name and uses it to put out information about the two products. This was the case, for example, when Princeton Review registered kaplan.com and devoted the site to comparing the two companies.

Avery Dennison Corporation v. Sumpton
United States Court of Appeals for the Ninth Circuit
51 U.S.P.Q.2d 1801 (9th Cir. 1999)

TROTT, Circuit Judge:

Jerry Sumpton and Freeview Listings Ltd. (together, "Appellants") appeal an injunction in favor of Avery Dennison Corp., entered after summary judgment for Avery Dennison on its claims of trademark dilution under the Federal Trademark Dilution Act of 1995 and the California dilution statute, Cal. Bus. & Prof. Code §14330 (West 1987). The district court published an opinion, 999 F.Supp. 1337 (C.D.Cal.1998), holding that Appellants' maintenance of domain name registrations for avery.net and dennison.net diluted two of Avery Dennison's separate trademarks, "Avery" and "Dennison." . . . The district court then entered an injunction ordering Appellants to transfer the domain-name registrations to Avery Dennison in exchange for $300 each.

We have jurisdiction under 28 U.S.C. §1291 (1994). Because Avery Dennison failed to create a genuine issue of fact on required elements of the dilution cause of action, we reverse and remand with instructions to enter summary judgment for Appellants and to consider Appellants' request for attorneys' fees in light of this decision. . . .

II Facts

Sumpton is the president of Freeview, an Internet e-mail provider doing business as "Mailbank." Mailbank offers "vanity" e-mail addresses to users for an initial fee of $19.95 and $4.95 per year thereafter, and has registered thousands of domain-name combinations for this purpose. Most SLDs that Mailbank has registered are common surnames, although some represent hobbies, careers, pets, sports interests, favorite music, and the like. One category of SLDs is titled "Rude" and includes lewd SLDs, and another category, titled "Business," includes some common trademark SLDs. Mailbank's TLDs consist mainly of .net and .org, but some registered domain name combinations, including most in the "Business" and "Rude" categories, use the TLD .com. Mailbank's surname archives include the domain-name combinations avery.net and dennison.net.

Avery Dennison sells office products and industrial fasteners under the registered trademarks "Avery" and "Dennison," respectively. "Avery" has been in continuous use since the 1930s and registered since 1963, and "Dennison" has been in continuous use since the late 1800s and registered since 1908. Avery Dennison spends more than $5 million per year advertising its products, including those marketed under the separate "Avery" and "Dennison" trademarks, and the company boasts in the neighborhood of $3 billion in sales of all of its trademarks annually. No evidence indicates what percentage of these dollar figures apply to the "Avery" or "Dennison" trademarks. Avery Dennison maintains a commercial presence on the Internet, marketing its products at avery.com and averydennison.com, and maintaining registrations for several other domain-name combinations, all using the TLD .com.

Avery Dennison sued Appellants, alleging trademark dilution under the Federal Trademark Dilution Act and California Business and Professional Code §14330. Avery Dennison also sued NSI, alleging contributory dilution and contributory infringement. The district court granted summary judgment to NSI on Avery Dennison's claims. The district court then concluded as a matter of law that the disputed trademarks were famous and denied summary judgment to Appellants and granted summary judgment to Avery Dennison on its dilution claims, entering an injunction requiring Appellants to transfer the registrations to Avery Dennison. 983 F.Supp. at 1342. . . .

V Dilution Protection

We now turn to the dilution causes of action at issue in this case, brought under the Federal Trademark Dilution Act and California Business and Professional Code §14330.

In *Panavision*, we held that both the Federal Trademark Dilution Act and §14330 were implicated when the defendant registered domain-name combinations using famous trademarks and sought to sell the registrations to the trademark owners. 141 F.3d at 1318, 1327. Three differences made *Panavision* easier than the instant case. First, the defendant did not mount a challenge on the famousness prong of the dilution tests. *Panavision*, 141 F.3d at 1324. Second, the *Panavision* defendant did not challenge the factual assertion that he sought to profit by arbitrage with famous trademarks. *Id.* at 1324-25. Third, the diluting registrations in *Panavision* both involved the TLD .com. In the instant case, by contrast, Appellants contest Avery Dennison's claim of famousness, Appellants contend that the nature of their business makes the trademark status of "Avery" and "Dennison" irrelevant, and the complained-of registrations involve the TLD .net.

A Famousness

The district court considered evidence submitted by Avery Dennison regarding marketing efforts and consumer association with its marks and concluded as a matter of law that "Avery" and "Dennison" were famous marks entitled to dilution protection. 999 F.Supp. at 1339. We hold that Avery Dennison failed to create a genuine issue of fact on the famousness element of both dilution statutes.

Dilution is a cause of action invented and reserved for a select class of marks—those marks with such powerful consumer associations that even non-competing uses can impinge on their value. See generally Frank L.

Schechter, The Rational Basis for Trademark Protection, 40 Harv. L. Rev. 813 (1927) (proposing a cause of action for dilution); Krafte-Jacobs, supra, at 689-91. Dilution causes of action, much more so than infringement and unfair competition laws, tread very close to granting "rights in gross" in a trademark. See 3 McCarthy, supra, §24:108. In the infringement and unfair competition scenario, where the less famous a trademark, the less the chance that consumers will be confused as to origin, see AMF Inc. v. Sleek-craft Boats, 599 F.2d 341, 349 (9th Cir.1979), a carefully-crafted balance exists between protecting a trademark and permitting non-infringing uses. In the dilution context, likelihood of confusion is irrelevant. See 15 U.S.C. §1127; Cal. Bus. & Prof.Code §14330; *Panavision*, 141 F.3d at 1326. If dilution protection were accorded to trademarks based only on a showing of inherent or acquired distinctiveness, we would upset the balance in favor of over-protecting trademarks, at the expense of potential non-infringing uses. See *Fruit of the Loom*, 994 F.2d at 1363 ("[The plaintiff] would sweep clean the many business uses of this quotidian word.").

We view the famousness prong of both dilution analyses as reinstating the balance—by carefully limiting the class of trademarks eligible for dilution protection, Congress and state legislatures granted the most potent form of trademark protection in a manner designed to minimize undue impact on other uses. See San Francisco Arts & Athletics, Inc. v. United States Olympic Comm., 483 U.S. 522, 564 n.25 (1987) (Brennan, J., dissenting) (citing 2 J. McCarthy, Trademarks & Unfair Competition §24:16, at 229 (2d ed.1984)) (discussing limits on the dilution doctrine that help prevent overprotection of trademarks).

Therefore, to meet the "famousness" element of protection under the dilution statutes, " 'a mark [must] be truly prominent and renowned.'" I.P. Lund Trading ApS v. Kohler Co., 163 F.3d 27, 46 (1st Cir.1998) (quoting 3 McCarthy, supra, §24.91). In a 1987 report, which recommended an amendment to the Lanham Act to provide a federal dilution cause of action, the Trademark Review Commission of the United States Trademark Association emphasized the narrow reach of a dilution cause of action: "We believe that a limited category of trademarks, those which are truly famous and registered, are deserving of national protection from dilution." Trademark Review Commission, Report & Recommendations, 77 Trademark Rep. 375, 455 (Sept.-Oct.1987).

The Federal Trademark Dilution Act lists eight non-exclusive considerations for the famousness inquiry, 15 U.S.C. §1125(c)(1)(A)-(H), which are equally relevant to a famousness determination under Business and Professional Code §14330, see *Panavision*, 141 F.3d at 1324 ("Panavision's state law dilution claim is subject to the same analysis as its federal claim."). These are:

(A)   the degree of inherent or acquired distinctiveness of the mark;
(B)   the duration and extent of use of the mark in connection with the goods or services with which the mark is used;

(C) the duration and extent of advertising and publicity of the mark;

(D) the geographical extent of the trading area in which the mark is used;

(E) the channels of trade for the goods or services with which the mark is used;

(F) the degree of recognition of the mark in the trading areas and channels of trade used by the mark's owner and the person against whom the injunction is sought;

(G) the nature and extent of use of the same or similar marks by third parties; and

(H) whether the mark was registered . . . on the principal register.

15 U.S.C. §1125(c)(1).

We note the overlap between the statutory famousness considerations and the factors relevant to establishing acquired distinctiveness, which is attained "when the purchasing public associates the [mark] with a single producer or source rather than just the product itself." First Brands Corp. v. Fred Meyer, Inc., 809 F.2d 1378, 1383 (9th Cir.1987). Proof of acquired distinctiveness is a difficult empirical inquiry which a factfinder must undertake, Taco Cabana Int'l, Inc. v. Two Pesos, Inc., 932 F.2d 1113, 1119-20 & n.7 (5th Cir.1991), *aff'd*, 505 U.S. 763 (1992), considering factors including:

> [1] whether actual purchasers . . . associate the [mark] with [the plaintiff]; [2] the degree and manner of [the plaintiff's] advertising; [3] the length and manner of [the plaintiff's] use of the [mark]; and [4] whether [the plaintiff's] use of the [mark] has been exclusive.

Clamp Mfg. Co. v. Enco Mfg. Co., 870 F.2d 512, 517 (9th Cir.1989). Furthermore, registration on the principal register creates a presumption of distinctiveness—in the case of a surname trademark, acquired distinctiveness. 15 U.S.C. §1057(b) (1994); Americana Trading Inc. v. Russ Berrie & Co., 966 F.2d 1284, 1287 (9th Cir.1992) ("[R]egistration carries a presumption of secondary meaning.").

However, the Federal Trademark Dilution Act and Business and Professional Code §14330 apply "only to those marks which are both truly distinctive and famous, and therefore most likely to be adversely affected by dilution." S.Rep. No. 100-515, at 42. The Trademark Review Commission stated that "a higher standard must be employed to gauge the fame of a trademark eligible for this extraordinary remedy." 77 Trademark Rep. at 461. Thus, "[t]o be capable of being diluted, a mark must have a degree of distinctiveness and 'strength' beyond that needed to serve as a trademark." 3 McCarthy, supra, §24:109; see also Krafte-Jacobs, supra, at 690 ("If all marks are distinctive, and a showing of distinctiveness meets the element of fame, what marks would be outside the protection of the FTDA? [T]he FTDA does not indicate that any particular degree of distinctiveness should end the inquiry." (interpreting the Federal Trademark Dilution Act)). We have previously held likewise under California Business and Professional Code §14330. Accuride Int'l, Inc. v. Accuride Corp., 871 F.2d 1531, 1539 (9th Cir.1989) (requiring more than mere distinctiveness).

Applying the famousness factors from the Federal Trademark Dilution Act to the facts of the case at bench, we conclude that Avery Dennison likely establishes acquired distinctiveness in the "Avery" and "Dennison" trademarks, but goes no further. Because the Federal Trademark Dilution Act requires a showing greater than distinctiveness to meet the threshold element of fame, as a matter of law Avery Dennison has failed to fulfill this burden.

1 Distinctiveness

We begin with the first factor in the statutory list: "inherent or acquired distinctiveness." §1125(c)(1)(A). No dispute exists that "Avery" and "Dennison" are common surnames—according to evidence presented by Appellants, respectively the 775th and 1768th most common in the United States. A long-standing principle of trademark law is the right of a person to use his or her own name in connection with a business. See Howe Scale Co. v. Wyckoff, Seamans & Benedict, 198 U.S. 118, 140 (1905). This principle was incorporated into the Lanham Act, which states that a mark that is "primarily merely a surname" is not protectable unless it acquires secondary meaning. 15 U.S.C. §1052(e)(4), (f) (1994); Abraham Zion Corp. v. Lebow, 761 F.2d 93, 104 (2d Cir.1985); see L.E. Waterman Co. v. Modern Pen Co., 235 U.S. 88, 94 (1914) (pre-Lanham Act case stating that protection from confusion is available to the holder of a surname trademark that has acquired public recognition); Horlick's Malted Milk Corp. v. Horluck's, Inc., 59 F.2d 13, 15 (9th Cir.1932) (pre-Lanham Act case limiting the defendant's right to use his surname as a trademark where the name had acquired public recognition from the efforts of a competitor). Avery Dennison cannot claim that "Avery" and "Dennison" are inherently distinctive, but must demonstrate acquired distinctiveness through secondary meaning.

The drafters of the Federal Trademark Dilution Act continued the concern for surnames when adding protection against trademark dilution to the federal scheme. On early consideration of the Act, the report from the Senate Judiciary Committee emphasized: "[T]he committee intended to give special protection to an individual's ability to use his or her own name in good faith." S.Rep. No. 100-515, at 43 (1988). The Federal Trademark Dilution Act imports, at a minimum, the threshold secondary-meaning requirement for registration of a surname trademark.

Avery Dennison maintains registrations of both "Avery" and "Dennison" on the principal register, prima facie evidence that these marks have achieved the secondary meaning required for protection from infringement and unfair competition. See Americana Trading, 966 F.2d at 1287. We reject Appellants' argument that the distinctiveness required for famousness under the Federal Trademark Dilution Act is inherent, not merely acquired distinctiveness. See 15 U.S.C. §1125(c)(1)(A) (referring to "inherent or acquired distinctiveness"). However, because famousness requires a showing greater than mere distinctiveness, the presumptive secondary meaning associated with "Avery" and "Dennison" fails to persuade us that the famousness prong is met in this case.

2   Overlapping Channels of Trade

We next consider the fifth and sixth factors of the statutory inquiry: the channels of trade for the plaintiff's goods and the degree of recognition of the mark in the trading areas and channels of trade used by plaintiff and defendant. §1125(c)(1)(E), (F). The drafters of the Federal Trademark Dilution Act broke from the Trademark Review Commission's recommendation that only marks "which have become famous throughout a substantial part of the United States" could qualify for protection. Report & Recommendation, 77 Trademark Rep. at 456. Instead, fame in a localized trading area may meet the threshold element under the Act if plaintiff's trading area includes the trading area of the defendant. S.Rep. No. 100-515, at 43; Washington Speakers Bureau, Inc. v. Leading Auths., Inc., 33 F.Supp.2d 488, 503-04 (E.D.Va.1999) (citing *I.P. Lund*, 163 F.3d at 46; Teletech Customer Care Mgt., Inc. v. TeleTech Co., 977 F.Supp. 1407, 1413 (C.D.Cal.1997)). The rule is likewise for specialized market segments: specialized fame can be adequate only if the "diluting uses are directed narrowly at the same market segment." *Washington Speakers*, 33 F.Supp.2d at 503. No evidence on the record supports Avery Dennison's position on these two prongs of the famousness inquiry.

In *Teletech*, fame in a narrow market segment was present when the plaintiff showed "that the Teletech Companies may be the largest provider of primarily inbound integrated telephone and Internet customer care nationwide." 977 F.Supp. at 1409. The defendant was "a contractor providing engineering and installation services to the telecommunications industry," and maintained the domain-name combination, teletech.com. *Id.* at 1409-10. The court held that the showing on the threshold element under the Federal Trademark Dilution Act was adequate to qualify for a preliminary injunction. *Id.* at 1413. In *Washington Speakers*, both the plaintiff and defendant were in the business of scheduling speaking engagements for well-known lecturers. 33 F.Supp.2d at 490, 503 & n.31 (citing cases). In the instant case, by contrast, Appellants' sought-after customer base is Internet users who desire vanity e-mail addresses, and Avery Dennison's customer base includes purchasers of office products and industrial fasteners. No evidence demonstrates that Avery Dennison possesses any degree of recognition among Internet users or that Appellants direct their e-mail services at Avery Dennison's customer base.

3 Use of the Marks by Third Parties

The seventh factor, "the nature and extent of use of the same . . . marks by third parties," §1125(c)(1)(G), undercuts the district court's conclusion as well. All relevant evidence on the record tends to establish that both "Avery" and "Dennison" are commonly used as trademarks, both on and off of the Internet, by parties other than Avery Dennison. This evidence is relevant because, when "a mark is in widespread use, it may not be famous for the goods or services of one business." Report & Recommendation, 77 Trademark Rep. at 461; see *Accuride*, 871 F.2d at 1539 (affirming the district court's holding that widespread use of elements of a trademark helped to defeat a dilution claim).

The record includes copies of five trademark registrations for "Avery" and "Averys," a computer printout of a list of several businesses with "Avery" in their names who market products on the Internet, and a list of business names including "Avery," which, according to a declaration submitted by NSI, is a representative sample of over 800 such businesses. The record also contains a computer printout of a list of several businesses with "Dennison" in their names which market products on the Internet and a list of business names including "Dennison," a representative sample of over 200 such businesses. Such widespread use of "Avery" and "Dennison" makes it unlikely that either can be considered a famous mark eligible for the dilution cause of action.

4 Other Famousness Factors

Avery Dennison argues that evidence of extensive advertising and sales, international operations, and consumer awareness suffices to establish fame. We agree that the remaining four statutory factors in the famousness inquiry likely support Avery Dennison's position. Both "Avery" and "Dennison" have been used as trademarks for large fractions of a century and registered for decades. Avery Dennison expends substantial sums annually advertising each mark, with some presumable degree of success due to Avery Dennison's significant annual volume of sales. In addition, Avery Dennison markets its goods internationally. See 15 U.S.C. §1125(c)(1)(B)-(D), (G). However, we disagree that Avery Dennison's showing establishes fame.

Avery Dennison submitted three market research studies regarding perceptions of the "Avery" and "Avery Dennison" brands. Discussion groups through which one study was conducted were formed "using Avery client lists," and produced the conclusion that the "Avery" name has "positive associations . . . among current customers." Surveyed persons in the other two studies were mostly "users and purchasers of office products" and "[o]ffice supply consumers." The one consumer group that did not necessarily include office supply purchasers for businesses was still required to be "somewhat" or "very" familiar with Avery products in order to be counted.

Avery Dennison's marketing reports are comparable to a survey we discussed in Anti-Monopoly, Inc. v. General Mills Fun Group, Inc., 684 F.2d 1316 (9th Cir.1981), proving only the near tautology that consumers already acquainted with Avery and Avery Dennison products are familiar with Avery Dennison. See *id.* at 1323-24. The marketing reports add nothing to the discussion of whether consumers in general have any brand association with "Avery" and "Avery Dennison," and no evidence of product awareness relates specifically to the "Dennison" trademark. Although proper consumer surveys might be highly relevant to a showing of fame, we reject any reliance on the flawed reports submitted by Avery Dennison.

Finally, Avery Dennison—like any company marketing on the Internet —markets its products worldwide. See 15 U.S.C. §1125(c)(1)(D). By itself, this factor carries no weight; worldwide use of a non-famous mark does not establish fame. Because famousness requires more than mere distinctiveness, and Avery Dennison's showing goes no further than establishing secondary meaning, we hold that Avery Dennison has not met its burden to create a genuine issue of fact that its marks are famous. Avery Dennison's failure to fulfill its burden on this required element of both dilution causes of action mandates summary judgment for Appellants.

5   Likelihood of Confusion Remains Irrelevant

We recognize that our discussion of the breadth of fame and overlapping market segments begins to sound like a likelihood of confusion analysis, and we agree with Avery Dennison that likelihood of confusion should not be considered under either the Federal Trademark Dilution Act or Business and Professional Code §14330. However, as we discuss above, the famousness element of the dilution causes of action serves the same general purpose as the likelihood of confusion element of an infringement or unfair competition analysis—preventing the trademark scheme from granting excessively broad protection at the expense of legitimate uses. See *Fruit of the Loom*, 994 F.2d at 1363 ("Whittling away will not occur unless there is at least some subliminal connection in a buyer's mind between the two parties' uses of their marks."). The close parallels between the two analyses are therefore not surprising; nor do they cause us concern.

B   *Commercial Use*

Addressing the second element of a cause of action under the Federal Trademark Dilution Act, the district court held that Appellants' registration of avery.net and dennison.net constituted commercial use. 999 F.Supp. at 1339-40. We disagree.

Commercial use under the Federal Trademark Dilution Act requires the defendant to be using the trademark as a trademark, capitalizing on its trademark status. See *Panavision*, 141 F.3d at 1325. Courts have phrased this requirement in various ways. In a classic "cybersquatter" case, one court referenced the defendants "intention to arbitrage" the registration which included the plaintiff's trademark. *Intermatic*, 947 F.Supp. at 1239. Another court, whose decision we affirmed, noted that the defendant "traded on the value of marks as marks." Panavision Int'l, L.P. v. Toeppen, 945 F.Supp. 1296, 1303 (C.D.Cal.1996), *aff'd*, 141 F.3d 1316 (9th Cir.1998). In our *Panavision* decision, we considered the defendant's "attempt to sell the trademarks themselves." 141 F.3d at 1325.

All evidence in the record indicates that Appellants register common surnames in domain-name combinations and license e-mail addresses using those surnames, with the consequent intent to capitalize on the surname status of "Avery" and "Dennison." Appellants do not use trademarks qua trademarks as required by the caselaw to establish commercial use. Rather, Appellants use words that happen to be trademarks for their non-trademark value. The district court erred in holding that Appellants' use of avery.net and dennison.net constituted commercial use under the Federal Trademark Dilution Act, and this essential element of the dilution causes of action likewise mandates summary judgment for Appellants.

C   Dilution

The district court then considered the dilution requirement under both statutes, holding that Appellants' use of avery.net and dennison.net caused dilution, or a likelihood of dilution, of "Avery" and "Dennison." 999 F.Supp. at 1340-41. We hold that genuine issues of fact on this element of the causes of action should have precluded summary judgment for Avery Dennison.

Two theories of dilution are implicated in this case. First, Avery Dennison argues that Appellants' conduct is the cybersquatting dilution that we recognized in *Panavision*. See 141 F.3d at 1326-27. Second, Avery Dennison argues that Appellants' conduct in housing the avery.net and dennison.net domain names in the same database as various lewd SLDs causes tarnishment of the "Avery" and "Dennison" marks.

1   Cybersquatting

Cybersquatting dilution is the diminishment of "'the capacity of the [plaintiff's] marks to identify and distinguish the [plaintiff's] goods and services on the Internet.'" *Panavision*, 141 F.3d at 1326 (quoting the *Panavision* district court, 945 F.Supp. at 1304). We recognized that this can occur if potential customers cannot find a web page at trademark.com. *Id.* at 1327; see also *Brookfield*, 174 F.3d at 1045 ("The Web surfer who assumes that "'*X*'.com" will always correspond to the web site of company *X* or trademark *X* will, however, sometimes be misled."). Dilution occurs because " '[p]rospective users of plaintiff's services . . . may fail to continue to search for plaintiff's own home page, due to anger, frustration or the belief that plaintiff's home page does not exist.'" *Panavision*, 141 F.3d at 1327 (quoting Jews for Jesus v. Brodsky, 993 F.Supp. 282, 306-07 (D.N.J.1998)).

In the instant case, Appellants registered the TLD .net, rather than .com, with the SLDs avery and dennison. As we recognized in *Panavision*, .net applies to networks and .com applies to commercial entities. 141 F.3d at 1318. Evidence on the record supports this distinction, and courts applying the dilution cause of action to domain-name registrations have universally considered trademark.com registrations. See Brown, Note, supra, at 251-54 (discussing cases); *id.* at 262-63 (addressing the .com versus .net distinction). Although evidence on the record also demonstrates that the .com and .net distinction is illusory, a factfinder could infer that dilution does not occur with a trademark.net registration. This genuine issue of fact on the question of cybersquatting dilution should have prevented summary judgment for Avery Dennison.

2 Tarnishment

Tarnishment occurs when a defendant's use of a mark similar to a plaintiff's presents a danger that consumers will form unfavorable associations with the mark. See Hasbro, Inc. v. Internet Ent. Group, Ltd., 40 U.S.P.Q.2d 1479, 1480 (W.D.Wash.1996) (candyland.com as a domain-name combination for a sexually explicit web site diluted plaintiff's trademark, "Candyland," for a children's game); 3 McCarthy, supra, §24:104. The district court did not reach Avery Dennison's claims regarding tarnishment.

Avery Dennison offers, as an alternative ground for affirming the district court, the fact that Appellants house avery.net and dennison.net at the same web site as lewd domain-name registrations. However, the evidence likewise indicates that to move from avery.net or dennison.net to a lewd SLD requires "linking" through the Mailbank home page, which might remove any association with the "Avery" and "Dennison" trademarks that the Internet user might have had. See *Fruit of the Loom*, 994 F.2d at 1363 (requiring some connection between the two parties' uses of their marks). Whether Appellants' use of the registrations presents a danger of tarnishment is an issue of fact that could not be decided on summary judgment. . . .

VII Conclusion

We reverse the district court's summary judgment in favor of Avery Dennison and remand with instructions to enter summary judgment for Sumpton and Freeview. We also remand Appellants' request for attorneys' fees for a determination by the district court. Finally, we deny Avery Dennison's motion to strike portions of Appellants' brief, and we deny Appellants' request for judicial notice.

REVERSED and REMANDED.

COMMENTS AND QUESTIONS

1. Is the court's distinction between cybersquatting and what Sumpton is doing persuasive? Is the difference simply the intent of the parties?

2. Suppose that Sumpton had registered "averydennison.com" and offered to sell it to the company. Clearly, in that case he would be a cybersquatter, just as Toeppen was. But under the rationale of the Ninth Circuit's decision, would Avery-Dennison have a cause of action against him? If so, for what?

A case presenting just such a problem is Archdiocese of St. Louis v. Internet Entertainment Group, 34 F. Supp. 2d 1145 (E.D. Mo. 1999). There, a well-known Internet pornographer registered "papalvisit.com" and "papalvisit1999.com" in advance of the Pope's visit to the United States. The site contained information about the Pope's visit, but also contained links to the defendant's porn sites. The district court held that the use of these names diluted the trademarks of the Catholic church. It seems quite implausible, however, that the church's unregistered mark "Papal Visit 1999," of recent and only casual usage, was really famous. Rather, the court seemed to be reacting to the defendant's intent to mislead those coming to the site.

3. One possible point of distinction between Toeppen and Sumpton is that Sumpton is not using the term in question *as a trademark. Avery-Dennison* is a difficult case, because Sumpton *is* selling the domain names for profit. But there is a distinction in trademark law between using a mark to identify goods or services and merely using the mark (for example, on T-shirts, or in a newspaper article). The domain name cases blur that line, in part because use of domain names is exclusive—that is, if I register a mark, you can't register the same mark. Still, it is important to distinguish different uses of the mark in question.

Some uses may not be commercial at all, rendering trademark law inapplicable. For example, in one widely reported dispute, a 12-year-old boy with the nickname "Pokey" registered pokey.org for his personal Web site. The company that owned the "Gumby" and "Pokey" trademarks threatened to sue but backed down in the face of adverse publicity. But if they had sued, they could not have proven trademark infringement or dilution. Do you see why?

Should the noncommercial nature of a defendant's use of a domain name always mean that trademark law does not apply? Consider the following case.

Planned Parenthood Federation of America, Inc. v. Bucci

United States District Court for the Southern District of New York
42 U.S.P.Q.2d 1430 (S.D.N.Y. 1997)

KIMBA M. WOOD, District Judge.

Plaintiff Planned Parenthood Federation of America, Inc. ("Planned Parenthood") has moved to preliminarily enjoin defendant Richard Bucci ("Bucci"), doing business as Catholic Radio, from using the domain name "plannedparenthood.com," and from identifying his web site on the Internet under the name "www.plannedparenthood.com." The Court held a hearing on February 20, 1997 and February 21, 1997, and now issues the preliminary injunction sought by Planned Parenthood.

I. Undisputed Facts

The parties do not dispute the following facts. Plaintiff Planned Parenthood, founded in 1922, is a non-profit, reproductive health care organization that has used its present name since 1942. Plaintiff registered the stylized service mark "Planned Parenthood" on the Principal Register of the United States Patent and Trademark Office on June 28, 1955, and registered the block service mark "Planned Parenthood" on the Principal Register of the United States Patent and Trademark Office on September 9, 1975. Plaintiff's 146 separately incorporated affiliates, in 48 states and the District of Columbia, are licensed to use the mark "Planned Parenthood." Plaintiff expends a considerable sum of money in promoting and advertising its services. The mark "Planned Parenthood" is strong and incontestable.

Plaintiff operates a web site at "www.ppfa.org," using the domain name "ppfa.org." Plaintiff's home page offers Internet users resources regarding sexual and reproductive health, contraception and family planning, pregnancy, sexually transmitted diseases, and abortion, as well as providing links to other relevant web sites. In addition, plaintiff's home page offers Internet users suggestions on how to get involved with plaintiff's mission and solicits contributions.[2]

Defendant Bucci is the host of "Catholic Radio," a daily radio program broadcast on the WVOA radio station in Syracuse, New York. Bucci is an active participant in the anti-abortion movement. Bucci operates web sites at "www.catholicradio.com" and at "lambsofchrist.com." On August 28, 1996, Bucci registered the domain name "plannedparenthood.com" with Network Solutions, Inc. ("NSI"), a corporation that administers the assignment of domain names on the Internet. After registering the domain name, Bucci set up a web site and home page on the Internet at the address "www.plannedparenthood.com."

---

2. Plaintiff's Houston affiliate owns the domain name "plannedparenthood.org," and is in the process of transferring that domain name to plaintiff.

Internet users who type in the address "www.plannedparenthood. com," or who use a search engine such as Yahoo or Lycos to find web sites containing the term "planned parenthood," can reach Bucci's web site and home page. Once a user accesses Bucci's home page, she sees on the computer screen the words "Welcome to the PLANNED PARENTHOOD HOME PAGE!" These words appear on the screen first, because the text of a home page downloads from top to bottom. Once the whole home page has loaded, the user sees a scanned image of the cover of a book entitled The Cost of Abortion, by Lawrence Roberge ("Roberge"), under which appear several links: "Foreword," "Afterword," "About the Author," "Book Review," and "Biography."

After clicking on a link, the user accesses text related to that link. By clicking on "Foreword" or "Afterword," the Internet user simply accesses the foreword or afterword of the book The Cost of Abortion. That text eventually reveals that The Cost of Abortion is an anti-abortion book. The text entitled "About the Author" contains the curriculum vitae of author Roberge. It also notes that "Mr. Roberge is available for interview and speaking engagements," and provides his telephone number. The "Book Review" link brings the Internet user to a selection of quotations by various people endorsing The Cost of Abortion. Those quotations include exhortations to read the book and obtain the book. "Biography" offers more information about Roberge's background.

II. Disputed Facts

The parties dispute defendant's motive in choosing plaintiff's mark as his domain name. Plaintiff alleges that defendant used plaintiff's mark with the "specific intent to damage Planned Parenthood's reputation and to confuse unwitting users of the Internet." Discussing the difference between the domain name at issue here and defendant's other web sites, defendant's counsel states that "[t]he WWWPLANNNEDPARENTHOOD.COM [sic] website . . . enables Defendant's message to reach a broader audience." Defendant's counsel made the following statement to the Court regarding defendant's use of plaintiff's mark to designate his web site:

> My belief is that it was intended to reach people who would be sympathetic to the proabortion position. . . . [I]t is an effort to get the . . . political and social message to people we might not have been otherwise able to reach. I think it's analogous to putting an advertisement in the New York Times rather than The National Review. You are more likely to get people who are sympathetic to the proabortion position, and that's who you want to reach. I believe that is exactly what Mr. Bucci did when he selected Planned Parenthood.

. . . Defendant's counsel also admitted that Bucci was trying to reach Internet users who thought, in accessing his web site, that they would be getting information from plaintiff.

Defendant stated that his motive in using plaintiff's mark as his domain name was "to reach, primarily, Catholics that are disobedient to the natural law." *Id.* at 21. In an affidavit submitted to the Court, defendant stated that he wanted his "anti-abortion message to reach as many people as possible, and particularly the people who do not think that abortion has an inimical effect on society." Defendant conceded that he was aware that by using plaintiff's mark to identify his web site, he was likely to draw in Internet users who are "pro-abortion." Defendant demonstrated full knowledge of plaintiff's name and activities, and admitted to an understanding that using plaintiff's mark as his domain name would attract "pro-abortion" Internet users to his web site because of their misapprehension as to the site's origin. I therefore now make the factual finding that defendant's motive in choosing plaintiff's mark as his domain name was, at least in part, to attract to his home page Internet users who sought plaintiff's home page.

III. Analysis . . .

B. *Whether the Lanham Act Is Applicable*

Defendant argues that his use of plaintiff's mark cannot be reached under the Lanham Act because it is non-commercial speech. Planned Parenthood has brought suit under §§1114, 1125(a), and 1125(c) of the Lanham Act, Title 15, United States Code. Section 1114 of the Lanham Act forbids a party to "use in commerce any reproduction, counterfeit, copy, or colorable imitation of a registered mark in connection with the sale, offering for sale, distribution, or advertising of any goods or services on or in connection with which such use is likely to cause confusion, or to cause mistake, or to deceive." An injunction under §1125(c) is proper to stop "commercial use in commerce of a mark or trade name" if that use causes dilution of a famous mark. Finally, with respect to §1125(a), defendant may be liable if he has used the plaintiff's mark "in commerce" in a way that either "is likely to cause confusion, or to cause mistake, or to deceive as to the affiliation, connection, or association of such person with another person, or as to the origin, sponsorship, or approval of his or her goods, services, or commercial activities by another person," §1125(a)(1)(A), or "in commercial advertising or promotion, misrepresents the nature, characteristics, qualities, or geographic origin of his or her or another person's goods, services, or commercial activities," §1125(a)(1)(B). Section 1125(c)(4)(B) specifically exempts from the scope of all provisions of §1125 the "noncommercial use of a mark."

As a preliminary matter, I note that although the parties agreed at a hearing before me on February 21, 1997 that defendant's use of plaintiff's mark is "in commerce" within the meaning of the Lanham Act, defendant now argues that his activities are not subject to the Lanham Act because they are not "in commerce." I find this argument meritless. The "use in commerce" requirement of the Lanham Act is a jurisdictional predicate to any law passed by Congress. It is well settled that the scope of "in commerce" as a jurisdictional predicate of the Lanham Act is broad and has a sweeping reach. Steele v. Bulova Watch Co., 344 U.S. 280, 283, 73 S.Ct. 252, 97 L.Ed. 319 (1952). The activity involved in this action meets the "in commerce" standard for two reasons. First, defendant's actions affect plaintiff's ability to offer plaintiff's services, which, as health and information services offered in forty-eight states and over the Internet, are surely "in commerce." Thus, even assuming, arguendo, that defendant's activities are not in interstate commerce for Lanham Act purposes, the effect of those activities on plaintiff's interstate commerce activities would place defendant within the reach of the Lanham Act. See Franchised Stores of New York. Inc. v. Winter, 394 F.2d 664, 669 (2d Cir.1968). Second, Internet users constitute a national, even international, audience, who must use interstate telephone lines to access defendant's web site on the Internet. The nature of the Internet indicates that establishing a typical home page on the Internet, for access to all users, would satisfy the Lanham Act's "in commerce" requirement. See Intermatic v. Toeppen, 947 F.Supp. 1227, 1239 (N.D.Ill.1996), quoting 1 Gilson, Trademark Protection and Practice, §5.11(2), p. 5-234 ("there is little question that the 'in commerce' requirement would be met in a typical Internet message"). Therefore, I conclude that defendant's actions are "in commerce" within the meaning of that term for jurisdictional purposes. I now turn to the specific language of each provision of the Lanham Act under which plaintiff has brought suit.

1. Section 1114

Notwithstanding its jurisdictional "in commerce" requirement, Section 1114 contains no commercial activity requirement; rather, it prohibits any person from, without consent of the registrant of a mark, using the mark "in connection with the sale, offering for sale, distribution, or advertising of any good or services on or in connection with which such use is likely to cause confusion, or to cause mistake, or to deceive." The question the Court must decide, then, is whether defendant's use of plaintiff's mark is properly viewed as in connection with the distribution or advertising of goods or services.

Defendant's use of plaintiff's mark satisfies the requirement of §1114 in a variety of ways. First, defendant has stated that he chose to place materials about The Cost of Abortion on the "www.plannedparenthood.com" web site because he wanted to help Roberge "plug" his book. In addition, defendant agreed that he, by this activity, was helping the author sell his book. Although defendant receives no money from any sales of the book that result from its exposure on his home page, there is no personal profit requirement in §1114. The materials on the home page, which are similar to a publisher's publicity kit, certainly relate to the advertisement and distribution of The Cost of Abortion.

Second, defendant's home page is merely one portion of his, and Catholic Radio's, broader effort to educate Catholics about the anti-abortion movement. With respect to that effort, defendant solicits funds and encourages supporters to join him in his protest activities. Much like plaintiff, defendant has a practical as well as a political motive. While plaintiff seeks to make available what it terms "reproductive services," including, inter alia, birth control and abortion services, defendant offers informational services for use in convincing people that certain activities, including the use of plaintiff's services, are morally wrong. In this way, defendant offers his own set of services, and his use of plaintiff's mark is in connection with the distribution of those services over the Internet. See MGM-Pathe Communications v. Pink Panther Patrol, 774 F.Supp. 869 (S.D.N.Y.1991) (holding that a group formed to offer the free service of protecting gay individuals from assault was subject to §1114).

In addition, defendant's use of plaintiff's mark is "in connection with the distribution of services" because it is likely to prevent some Internet users from reaching plaintiff's own Internet web site. Prospective users of plaintiff's services who mistakenly access defendant's web site may fail to continue to search for plaintiff's own home page, due to anger, frustration, or the belief that plaintiff's home page does not exist. One witness explained, "We didn't resume the search [for plaintiff's web site] after [finding defendant's web site] because . . . we were pretty much thrown off track." Therefore, defendant's action in appropriating plaintiff's mark has a connection to plaintiff's distribution of its services. For these reasons, §1114 is applicable to defendant's use of plaintiff's mark.

2. Section 1125(c)

Section 1125(c), the Lanham Act's anti-dilution provision, provides that the owner of a famous mark is entitled to an injunction against another person's "commercial use in commerce of a mark or trade name, if such use begins after the mark has become famous and causes dilution of the distinctive quality of the mark." The provision has no requirement that there be advertising or a sale of goods or services. Defendant argues that his use is not "commercial" within the meaning of §1125(c). I hold, however, that defendant's use of plaintiff's mark is "commercial" for three reasons: (1) defendant is engaged in the promotion of a book, (2) defendant is, in essence, a non-profit political activist who solicits funds for his activities, and (3) defendant's actions are designed to, and do, harm plaintiff commercially.

First, as discussed above, defendant's home page is a showcase for The Cost of Abortion, offering excerpts of the book, information about the author (specifically including how to contact the author for speaking engagements), and endorsements of the book (including statements such as "I want to see this book in the hands of EVERY Catholic priest and Protestant minister in the country"). This showcase is surely commercial in nature, despite the fact that defendant derives no monetary gain from these activities. Although defendant does not seek a profit from his actions, §1125(c) carries no "for-profit" requirement. Therefore, defendant's use of plaintiff's mark to further his self-styled effort to "plug" The Cost of Abortion falls within the purview of the commercial use requirement of §1125(c).

Second, defendant's use of plaintiff's mark to identify his web site is one part of defendant's sustained effort, through his radio show and other means, to achieve his end of persuading the public to eschew birth control and abortion. Defendant is a vocal supporter of the anti-abortion movement. Defendant also opposes the use of contraceptives. Through his radio program, he seeks to educate his listeners about the teachings of the Catholic church, specifically trying to discourage his audience from using birth control and obtaining abortions. In this connection, defendant is a vocal critic of plaintiff and plaintiff's activities.

In *MGM-Pathe*, 774 F.Supp. 869, Judge Leval considered whether a non-profit group that uses another's trademark in support of its own non-profit aims is subject to the Lanham Act. Specifically, he examined whether a group whose aim was to provide protection to the gay community and to educate the general public about violence against that community could appropriate a part of the name of a movie produced by plaintiff ("Pink Panther"). After finding that there was a likelihood of confusion, Judge Leval concluded that defendant's goal of political activism did not confer immunity from the Lanham Act, noting that "[t]he seriousness and virtue of a cause do not confer any right to the use of the trademark of another." Defendant attempts to distinguish *MGM-Pathe* from the case now before the Court on the ground that defendant in this action has used plaintiff's mark in an effort to criticize plaintiff, while the *MGM-Pathe* defendants had no intent to criticize the Pink Panther movies. The Court finds this distinction unhelpful. The mere fact that defendant seeks to criticize plaintiff cannot automatically immunize a use that is otherwise prohibited by the Lanham Act.

Additionally, defendant has testified that he solicits contributions on his "Catholic Radio" radio show and has solicited contributions on the air in connection with the instant lawsuit. Defendant's ownership of the domain name "plannedparenthood.com" is part and parcel of Catholic Radio's broader efforts in the anti-abortion movement. Specifically, defendant has told his radio listeners that "Catholic Radio owns the name 'Planned Parenthood.'" Courts have found that fund-raising activities may bring a defendant's actions within the scope of the Lanham Act. See Cancer Research Institute. Inc. v. Cancer Research Society, Inc., 694 F.Supp. 1051 (S.D.N.Y.1988) (enjoining defendant from using plaintiff's name for soliciting funds for cancer research), Girls Club of Am., Inc. v. Boys Clubs of Am., Inc., 683 F.Supp. 50, 53 (S.D.N.Y.), *aff'd*, 859 F.2d 148 (2d Cir.1988) (enjoining defendant from adding plaintiff's name to its own for broad range of non-profit activities including fundraising); Brach van Houten Holding v. Save Brach's Coalition, 856 F.Supp. 472 (N.D.Ill.1994) (enjoining defendant from use of plaintiff's name in soliciting funds); American Diabetic Assoc. v. National Diabetic Assoc., 533 F.Supp. 16, 20 (E.D.Pa.1981) (enjoining defendant from use of similar name in relation to its non-profit fund-raising). I find that defendant's use of plaintiff's mark is sufficiently tied to defendant's fund-raising efforts for the use to be deemed "commercial" within the meaning of §1125(c).

Finally, defendant's use is commercial because of its effect on plaintiff's activities. First, defendant has appropriated plaintiff's mark in order to reach an audience of Internet users who want to reach plaintiff's services and viewpoint, intercepting them and misleading them in an attempt to offer his own political message. Second, defendant's appropriation not only provides Internet users with competing and directly opposing information, but also prevents those users from reaching plaintiff and its services and message. In that way, defendant's use is classically competitive: he has taken plaintiff's mark as his own in order to purvey his Internet services—his web site—to an audience intending to access plaintiff's services. . . .

3. Section 1125(a)(1)(A)

In relevant part, §1125(a)(1)(A) prohibits a person from using in commerce any term or false designation of origin which "is likely to cause confusion . . . as to the affiliation, connection, or association of such person with another person, or as to the origin, sponsorship, or approval of his or her goods, services, or commercial activities by another person." Section 1125(a)(1) is also limited by §1125(c)(4)(B), which states that "noncommercial use of a mark" is not actionable under the Lanham Act.

Here, as discussed above, defendant offers informational services relating to the anti-abortion and anti-birth control movement, specifically providing his audience with relevant literature and the means to contact Roberge. In addition, defendant's solicitation of funds in relation to his anti-abortion efforts are commercial in nature. Therefore, because defendant's labelling of his web site with plaintiff's mark relates to the "origin, sponsorship, or approval" by plaintiff of defendant's web site, I find that §1125(a)(1)(A) may govern defendant's actions in this case. . . .

I therefore determine that §1114, §1125(c), and §1125(a)(1)(a) of the Lanham Act are applicable here. I turn now to whether defendant's use of plaintiff's mark results in a likelihood of confusion.

C. The Likelihood of Confusion

1. The Polaroid Factors

The Second Circuit set out the factors a court must consider in determining the likelihood of consumer confusion in Polaroid Corp. v. Polarad

Elecs. Corp., 287 F.2d 492, 495 (2d Cir.1961). Those factors include: the strength of plaintiff's mark, the degree of similarity between the two marks, the competitive proximity of the products or services, the likelihood that the plaintiff will bridge the gap between the two markets, the existence of actual confusion, the defendant's good faith in adopting the mark, the quality of the defendant's product, and the sophistication of the purchasers.

a. The Strength of the Mark

The strength of plaintiffs' mark is conceded by defendant, which is reasonable in light of plaintiffs' trademark registration of the mark and plaintiffs' continued use of the mark for over 50 years. The strength of plaintiffs' mark weighs in favor of likelihood of confusion.

b. The Degree of Similarity Between the Marks

The two marks, "Planned Parenthood" and "plannedparenthood. com" are nearly identical; the only distinctions are the latter's lack of initial capitalization, the lack of a space between words, and the ".com" that is necessary to designate a domain name. The degree of similarity between defendant's domain name and the domain name owned by plaintiff's affiliate, Planned Parenthood of Houston, "plannedparenthood.org," is even stronger. Plaintiff was originally under the impression that according to Internet usage, it could operate using only a ".org" designation. Currently, however, NSI allows non-profit corporations, as well as for-profit businesses and individuals, to use the ".com" designation. The ".com" designation is commonly used by businesses. The degree of similarity between the marks thus increases the likelihood of confusion among Internet users.

c. The Competitive Proximity of the Products or Services

The web sites of plaintiff and defendant are both located on the World Wide Web. Therefore, defendant's web site at "www.plannedparenthood. com" is close in proximity to plaintiff's own web site, "www.ppfa.org." Both sites compete for the same audience—namely, Internet users who are searching for a web site that uses plaintiff's mark as its address. The degree of competitive proximity, therefore, increases the likelihood of confusion among Internet users.

d. The Likelihood that Plaintiff Will Bridge the Gap Between the Markets

Because plaintiff's web site and defendant's web site are both on the Internet, the parties are vying for users in the same "market." Where the market for competing goods or services is the same, there is no need to consider whether plaintiff will bridge the gap between the markets. Paddington Corp. v. Attiki Importers & Distributors, Inc., 996 F.2d 577, 586 (2d Cir.1993). I therefore do not consider this factor in determining the likelihood of confusion.

e.   The Existence of Actual Confusion

Plaintiff has produced testimony demonstrating that actual confusion has occurred among Internet users. The confusion has occurred both in a user who attempted to go directly to "www.plannedparenthood.com," thinking that it was likely to be plaintiff's web address, and in a user who used a search engine to find web sites containing, or designated by, plaintiff's mark.

This specific testimony exemplifies the likelihood of confusion due to the nature of domain names and home page addresses. First, because ".com" is a popular designation for Internet domain names, an Internet user is likely to assume that ".com" after a corporation's name will bring her to that corporation's home page, if one exists. Second, an Internet user cannot immediately determine the content of a home page maintained by the owner of a particular domain name or located at a specific address. Only after a user has seen or entered "plannedparenthood.com" can she access the web site; such access occurs after at least a temporary delay. In addition, there is a delay while the home page "loads" into the computer. Because the words on the top of the page load first, the user is first greeted solely with the "Welcome to the Planned Parenthood Home Page!" It is highly likely that an Internet user will still believe that she has found plaintiff's web site at that point.

Even when the picture of The Cost of Abortion finally does appear on the screen, the user is unlikely to know that she is not at plaintiff's home page. The book's ambiguous title "The Cost of Abortion," alone, cannot disabuse every Internet user of the notion that she has found plaintiff's home page. The Internet user must actually click on a link to read excerpts from the book, biographical information about the author, or book endorsements. only in the course of reading those items can the user determine that she has not reached plaintiff's home page. Depending on which link the user has chosen to access, there may be an additional delay before the user can grasp that plaintiff is not the true provider of the home page. This lengthy delay between attempting to access plaintiff's home page and learning that one has failed to do so increases the likelihood of consumer confusion.

f.   The Defendant's Good Faith in Adopting the Mark

Defendant's testimony, and his counsel's admission at the hearing before this Court on the temporary restraining order, show that defendant chose his domain name and home page name with full knowledge and intent that some Internet users seeking to find plaintiff's home page would instead encounter his. However, defendant may have acted under the good faith assumption that his actions were protected by the First Amendment. I need not conclude that defendant acted in bad faith to conclude that there is a likelihood of confusion, and I therefore make no such finding at this time.

g. The Quality of Defendant's Product

A comparison of the quality of plaintiff's and defendant's products—their web sites—is irrelevant; the Court cannot compare the two web sites in terms of superior or inferior quality. However, I note that the two products are vastly different and convey quite divergent messages. Plaintiff's web site offers educational resources, suggests ways to get involved in plaintiff's activities, to join plaintiff in its advocacy mission, and to contribute to plaintiff, and offers links to plaintiff's local affiliates, related organizations, and job listings. In sum, plaintiff's web site provides Internet users with an array of information and services related to Planned Parenthood's mission of providing reproductive choice for women. Defendant's home page bearing plaintiff's mark offers users information, including an advertisement for a book, and ways to contact a vocal anti-abortion advocate. Any ensuing confusion resulting from defendant's use of plaintiff's mark as his domain name and home page address is likely to be destructive to the image that plaintiff, the senior user of the mark, has established. See *MGM-Pathe*, 774 F.Supp. at 876.

h. The Sophistication of the Purchasers

Plaintiff argues that its primary purchasers are low income, relatively unsophisticated women. I note that those with access to the Internet may not be coextensive with the segment of the population to whom plaintiff normally offers its services; those with Internet access may be more sophisticated. However, testimony has shown that even sophisticated Internet users were confused by defendant's web site. Although the sophisticated Internet user may discover, after reading the text of one of the links on defendant's home page, that she has not reached plaintiff's web site, some users may not be so immediately perspicacious. Because the sophistication of the user is no guarantee, here, that the consumer will not be confused, I find that this factor is of limited value in determining whether the consumer is likely to be confused.

In sum, I find that the bulk of the Polaroid factors demonstrate that there is a significant likelihood of confusion that warrants the granting of a preliminary injunction.

D. *Defendant's Additional Defenses*

Defendant also argues that his use of plaintiff's mark is protected from injunction because (1) it is a parody, and (2) it is protected speech under the First Amendment. I consider these arguments in turn.

1. The Parody Exception

Defendant argues that his use of the "planned parenthood" mark is not likely to confuse because it is similar to a parody. A parody "depends on a lack of confusion to make its point," and "'must convey two simultaneous—and contradictory—messages: that it is the original, but also that it is not the original and is instead a parody.'" Hormel Food Corp. v. Jim Henson Productions, Inc., 73 F.3d 497, 503 (2d Cir.1996) (internal citations omitted). Here, an Internet user may either find the defendant's web site through a search engine or may simply enter the words "planned parenthood" in the expectation that she will find the plaintiff's web site. Seeing or typing the "planned parenthood" mark and accessing the web site are two separate and nonsimultaneous activities. Furthermore, the greeting "Welcome to the Planned Parenthood Home Page!" does not immediately contradict an Internet user's assumption that she has accessed the plaintiff's home page. Only when an Internet user actually "clicks" on one of the topics and accesses commentary on The Cost of Abortion does she encounter defendant's message.

I am not persuaded by defendant's argument that the message of the home page provides an ironic and contrasting allusion to plaintiff, nor do I find convincing his argument that the banner heading of the home page is sarcastic. Similarly, I do not conclude that defendant's use of the term "planned parenthood" in the context described above is intended not to confuse the user into an association with plaintiff, but rather "to reference Plaintiff as the 'enemy.'" Because defendant's use of "planned parenthood" does not convey the simultaneous message that the home page and web site are those of plaintiff and those of defendant, defendant's argument that his use of the mark is a parody fails. Thus, the Polaroid factors must govern the issue of whether there is a likelihood of confusion. Here, I have found that the Polaroid factors demonstrate that there is a likelihood of confusion that arises from defendant's use of the domain name "plannedparenthood.com," the home page address "www.plannedparenthood.com," and the banner at the top of the home page stating, "Welcome to the Planned Parenthood Home Page!"

2. The First Amendment Exception

Defendant also argues that his use of the "planned parenthood" mark is protected by the First Amendment. As defendant argues, trademark infringement law does not curtail or prohibit the exercise of the First Amendment right to free speech. I note that plaintiff has not sought, in any way, to restrain defendant from speech that criticizes Planned Parenthood or its mission, or that discusses defendant's beliefs regarding reproduction, family, and religion. The sole purpose of the Court's inquiry has been to determine whether the use of the "planned parenthood" mark as defendant's domain name and home page address constitutes an infringement of plaintiff's trademark. Defendant's use of another entity's mark is entitled to First Amendment protection when his use of that mark is part of a communicative message, not when it is used to identify the source of a product. Yankee Publishing. Inc. v. News America Publishing, Inc., 809 F.Supp. 267, 275 (S.D.N.Y.1992). By using the mark as a domain name and home page address and by welcoming Internet users to the home page with the message "Welcome to the Planned Parenthood Home Page!" defendant identifies the web site and home page as being the product, or forum, of plaintiff. I therefore determine that, because defendant's use of the term "planned parenthood" is not part of a communicative message, his infringement on plaintiff's mark is not protected by the First Amendment.

Defendant argues that his use of the "Planned Parenthood" name for his web site is entitled to First Amendment protection, relying primarily on the holding of *Yankee Publishing*, 809 F.Supp. at 275. In that case, Judge Leval noted that the First Amendment can protect unauthorized use of a trademark when such use is part of an expression of a communicative message: "the Second Circuit has construed the Lanham Act narrowly when the unauthorized use of the trademark is for the purpose of a communicative message, rather than identification of product origin." *Id*. Defendant argues that his use of the "Planned Parenthood" name for his web site is a communicative message.

However, *Yankee Publishing* carefully draws a distinction between communicative messages and product labels or identifications:

> When another's trademark . . . is used without permission for the purpose of source identification, the trademark law generally prevails over the First Amendment. Free speech rights do not extend to labelling or advertising products in a manner that conflicts with the trademark rights of others.

Id. at 276. Defendant offers no argument in his papers as to why the Court should determine that defendant's use of "plannedparenthood.com" is a communicative message rather than a source identifier. His use of "plannedparenthood.com" as a domain name to identify his web site is on its face more analogous to source identification than to a communicative message; in essence, the name identifies the web site, which contains defendant's home page. The statement that greets Internet users who access defendant's web site, "Welcome to the Planned Parenthood Home Page," is also more analogous to an identifier than to a communication. For those reasons, defendant's use of the trademarked term "planned parenthood" is not part of a communicative message, but rather, serves to identify a product or item, defendant's web site and home page, as originating from Planned Parenthood.

Defendant's use of plaintiff's mark is not protected as a title under Rogers v. Grimaldi, 875 F.2d 994, 998 (2d Cir.1989). There, the Court of Appeals determined that the title of the film "Ginger and Fred" was not a misleading infringement, despite the fact that the film was not about Ginger Rogers and Fred Astaire, because of the artistic implications of a title. The Court of Appeals noted that "[f]ilmmakers and authors frequently rely on word-play, ambiguity, irony, and allusion in titling their works." *Id*. The Court of Appeals found that the use of a title such as the one at issue in *Rogers* was acceptable "unless the title has no artistic relevance to the underlying work"; even when the title has artistic relevance, it may not be used to "explicitly mislead[ ] [the consumer] as to the source or content of the work." *Id*. Here, even treating defendant's domain name and home page address as titles, rather than as source identifiers, I find that the title "plannedparenthood.com" has no artistic implications, and that the title is being used to attract some consumers by misleading them as to the web site's source or content. Given defendant's testimony indicating that he knew, and intended, that his use of the domain name "plannedparenthood.com" would cause some "pro-abortion" Internet users to access his web site, he cannot demonstrate that his use of "planned parenthood" is entitled to First Amendment protection.

Because defendant's use of plaintiff's mark is subject to the Lanham Act, because the Polaroid factors demonstrate that there is a likelihood of confusion arising from defendant's use of plaintiff's mark, and because defendant has not raised a defense that protects his use of the mark, plaintiff has met its burden of demonstrating that a preliminary injunction against defendant's use of plaintiff's mark is warranted. *Hasbro*, 858 F.2d at 73.

E. Whether a Disclaimer Will Cure the Confusion

Defendant argues that a disclaimer, rather than an injunction, is the appropriate remedy here. I disagree. Due to the nature of Internet use, defendant's appropriation of plaintiff's mark as a domain name and home page address cannot adequately be remedied by a disclaimer. Defendant's domain name and home page address are external labels that, on their face, cause confusion among Internet users and may cause Internet users who seek plaintiff's web site to expend time and energy accessing defendant's web site. Therefore, I determine that a disclaimer on defendant's home page would not be sufficient to dispel the confusion induced by his home page address and domain name. . . .

COMMENTS AND QUESTIONS

1. The district court's opinion was affirmed without opinion by the Second Circuit. 152 F.3d 920 (2d Cir. 1998). For a similar result, see Jews

for Jesus v. Brodsky, 46 U.S.P.Q.2d 1652 (D.N.J. 1998) (enjoining the use of the jewsforjesus.com domain name by a Jewish group opposed to Jews for Jesus), *aff'd without opinion,* 159 F.3d 1351 (3d Cir. 1998). But cf. Playboy Enter. Inc. v. Universal Tel-A-Talk, 48 U.S.P.Q.2d 1779 (E.D. Pa. 1998) (use of the Playboy term as a link to Playboy's Web site was not trademark infringement or counterfeiting).

2. Does it make sense to use the traditional analysis of likelihood of confusion here? What exactly is Bucci selling? In what way are the goods or services similar to those of Planned Parenthood?

3. Why was Bucci's use "commercial use in commerce," as the federal dilution statute requires? Was it because he promoted someone else's book on the site? What if he hadn't done so? Isn't it rather more plausible that this Web page was using the Planned Parenthood name for political purposes, not as a trademark to sell goods or services? If so, should this affect the court's analysis? For an argument that courts are distorting trademark principles in this and related cases in order to reach what appears to be a just result, see Mark A. Lemley, The Modern Lanham Act and the Death of Common Sense, 108 Yale L.J. 1687 (1999).

If the court determined that the speech in question was political, not commercial, presumably the trademark laws would not apply. But does that mean that Bucci would avoid liability altogether? Arguably, his use of plannedparenthood.com and his title "Welcome to the Planned Parenthood Home Page" are false statements of fact, and therefore unprotectable under First Amendment principles.

For a political speech dispute that seems more like a parody, compare www.gwbush.com (a parody site not authorized by the George Bush presidential campaign) with the real site (www.georgewbush.com).

4. A clearer case for speech protected by the First Amendment (because it is not misleading) is presented by the "sucks" cases. A number of individuals have registered "[companynamehere]sucks.com" in order to post "gripe sites" complaining about a company. Companies are understandably upset about being criticized. A number of them have attempted to use trademark law to prevent the registration of such domain names. While trademark owners have sometimes prevailed in these suits, this seems a misuse of trademark law to trample on free expression. For an opinion reaffirming the right of individuals to use such sites, see Bally Total Fitness Holding Corp. v. Faber, 29 F. Supp. 2d 1161 (C.D. Cal. 1998) (use of a "ballysucks" Web page (though not domain name) was permissible free speech). Of course, there is nothing to prevent a company from registering "[itsname]sucks.com" itself to prevent anyone else from doing it.

Note on the Domain Name
Dispute Resolution Process

Trademark owners faced with multiple cybersquatters have expressed concern about the amount of money it would cost to sue them all. Some innovative solutions to this problem are discussed above. But by far the most popular solution has been to turn to some form of alternative dispute resolution (ADR). Because the parties cannot always agree to mediation or arbitration after the dispute has arisen, a more common (and more controversial) approach is to mandate ADR beforehand. NSI has had a wide variety of dispute resolution policies during the years it has been registering domain names. Its policies have generally provided that domain name registrants agree to arbitrate disputes with NSI. They have not, however, mandated arbitration between trademark owners and domain name registrants.

A recent policy adopted by Internet Corporation for Assigned Names and Numbers (ICANN),[2] the not-for-profit corporation that has recently been given authority over the domain name system, would require arbitration of disputes between trademark owners and alleged cybersquatters. ICANN would achieve this by requiring all domain name registrars to in turn require registrants to agree to arbitrate disputes arising out of their registration of the domain names. A number of commentators have been critical of this mandatory ADR policy, arguing that it could deprive domain name registrants of their right to go to court. ICANN has attempted to limit its mandatory dispute resolution procedures to claims of bad faith registration of domain names identical to registered trademarks. In so doing, it has in effect tried to define "cybersquatting" and exclude disputes between legitimate trademark owners from the ADR process.

2. Other Uses of Trademarks

While domain names have captured much of the public and judicial attention in Internet trademark law, there are a number of other Internet practices that present interesting trademark questions. In this section, we explore several such issues.

a. Metatagging

≡ *Brookfield Communications, Inc. v. West Coast*
≡ *Entertainment Corporation*
≡ **United States Court of Appeals for the Ninth Circuit**
≡ **174 F.3d 1036 (9th Cir. 1999)**

O'SCANNLAIN, Circuit Judge:
We must venture into cyberspace to determine whether federal trademark and unfair competition laws prohibit a video rental store chain from

2. For more on ICANN, see Chapter 15.

using an entertainment-industry information provider's trademark in the domain name of its web site and in its web site's metatags.

I

Brookfield Communications, Inc. ("Brookfield") appeals the district court's denial of its motion for a preliminary injunction prohibiting West Coast Entertainment Corporation ("West Coast") from using in commerce terms confusingly similar to Brookfield's trademark, "MovieBuff." Brookfield gathers and sells information about the entertainment industry. Founded in 1987 for the purpose of creating and marketing software and services for professionals in the entertainment industry, Brookfield initially offered software applications featuring information such as recent film submissions, industry credits, professional contacts, and future projects. These offerings targeted major Hollywood film studios, independent production companies, agents, actors, directors, and producers.

Brookfield expanded into the broader consumer market with computer software featuring a searchable database containing entertainment-industry related information marketed under the "MovieBuff" mark around December 1993. Brookfield's "MovieBuff" software now targets smaller companies and individual consumers who are not interested in purchasing Brookfield's professional level alternative, The Studio System, and includes comprehensive, searchable, entertainment-industry databases and related software applications containing information such as movie credits, box office receipts, films in development, film release schedules, entertainment news, and listings of executives, agents, actors, and directors. This "Movie-Buff" software comes in three versions—(1) the MovieBuff Pro Bundle, (2) the MovieBuff Pro, and (3) MovieBuff—and is sold through various retail stores, such as Borders, Virgin Megastores, Nobody Beats the Wiz, The Writer's Computer Store, Book City, and Samuel French Bookstores.

Sometime in 1996, Brookfield attempted to register the World Wide Web ("the Web") domain name "moviebuff.com" with Network Solutions, Inc. ("Network Solutions"), but was informed that the requested domain name had already been registered by West Coast. Brookfield subsequently registered "brookfieldcomm.com" in May 1996 and "moviebuffonline .com" in September 1996. Sometime in 1996 or 1997, Brookfield began using its web sites to sell its "MovieBuff" computer software and to offer an Internet-based searchable database marketed under the "MovieBuff" mark. Brookfield sells its "MovieBuff" computer software through its "brookfieldcomm.com" and "moviebuffonline.com" web sites and offers subscribers online access to the MovieBuff database itself at its "inhollywood.com" web site.

On August 19, 1997, Brookfield applied to the Patent and Trademark Office (PTO) for federal registration of "MovieBuff" as a mark to designate both goods and services. Its trademark application describes its product as "computer software providing data and information in the field of the motion picture and television industries." Its service mark application describes its service as "providing multiple-user access to an on-line network database offering data and information in the field of the motion picture and television industries." Both federal trademark registrations issued on September 29, 1998. Brookfield had previously obtained a California state trademark registration for the mark "MovieBuff" covering "computer software" in 1994.

In October 1998, Brookfield learned that West Coast—one of the nation's largest video rental store chains with over 500 stores—intended to launch a web site at "moviebuff.com" containing, inter alia, a searchable entertainment database similar to "MovieBuff." West Coast had registered "moviebuff.com" with Network Solutions on February 6, 1996 and claims that it chose the domain name because the term "Movie Buff" is part of its service mark, "The Movie Buff's Movie Store," on which a federal registration issued in 1991 covering "retail store services featuring video cassettes and video game cartridges" and "rental of video cassettes and video game cartridges." West Coast notes further that, since at least 1988, it has also used various phrases including the term "Movie Buff" to promote goods and services available at its video stores in Massachusetts, including "The Movie Buff's Gift Guide"; "The Movie Buff's Gift Store"; "Calling All Movie Buffs!"; "Good News Movie Buffs!"; "Movie Buffs, Show Your Stuff!"; "the Perfect Stocking Stuffer for the Movie Buff!"; "A Movie Buff's Top Ten"; "The Movie Buff Discovery Program"; "Movie Buff Picks"; "Movie Buff Series"; "Movie Buff Selection Program"; and "Movie Buff Film Series." . . .

In its first amended complaint filed on November 18, 1998, Brookfield alleged principally that West Coast's proposed offering of online services at "moviebuff.com" would constitute trademark infringement and unfair competition in violation of sections 32 and 43(a) of the Lanham Act, 15 U.S.C. §§1114, 1125(a). Soon thereafter, Brookfield applied ex parte for a temporary restraining order ("TRO") enjoining West Coast "[f]rom using . . . in any manner . . . the mark MOVIEBUFF, or any other term or terms likely to cause confusion therewith, including moviebuff.com, as West Coast's domain name, . . . as the name of West Coast's website service, in buried code or metatags on their home page or web pages, or in connection with the retrieval of data or information on other goods or services."

On November 27, West Coast filed an opposition brief in which it argued first that Brookfield could not prevent West Coast from using "moviebuff.com" in commerce because West Coast was the senior user. West Coast claimed that it was the first user of "MovieBuff" because it had used its federally registered trademark, "The Movie Buff's Movie Store," since 1986 in advertisements, promotions, and letterhead in connection with retail services featuring videocassettes and video game cartridges. Alternatively, West Coast claimed seniority on the basis that it had garnered common-law rights in the domain name by using "moviebuff.com" before

Brookfield began offering its "MovieBuff" Internet-based searchable database on the Web. In addition to asserting seniority, West Coast contended that its planned use of "moviebuff.com" would not cause a likelihood of confusion with Brookfield's trademark "MovieBuff" and thus would not violate the Lanham Act. . . .

II . . .

Using a Web browser, such as Netscape's Navigator or Microsoft's Internet Explorer, a cyber "surfer" may navigate the Web—searching for, communicating with, and retrieving information from various web sites. See *Microsoft*, 147 F.3d at 939-40, 950. A specific web site is most easily located by using its domain name. See *Panavision*, 141 F.3d at 1327. Upon entering a domain name into the web browser, the corresponding web site will quickly appear on the computer screen. Sometimes, however, a Web surfer will not know the domain name of the site he is looking for, whereupon he has two principal options: trying to guess the domain name or seeking the assistance of an Internet "search engine."

Oftentimes, an Internet user will begin by hazarding a guess at the domain name, especially if there is an obvious domain name to try. Web users often assume, as a rule of thumb, that the domain name of a particular company will be the company name followed by ".com." See *id.;* Playboy Enterprises v. Universal Tel-A-Talk, Inc., No. 96-6961, 1998 WL 767440, at *2 (E.D.Pa. Nov.3, 1998); Cardservice Int'l, Inc. v. McGee, 950 F.Supp. 737, 741 (E.D.Va.1997), *aff'd* by, 129 F.3d 1258 (4th Cir.1997). For example, one looking for Kraft Foods, Inc. might try "kraftfoods.com," and indeed this web site contains information on Kraft's many food products. Sometimes, a trademark is better known than the company itself, in which case a Web surfer may assume that the domain address will be "'trademark'.com." See *Panavision,* 141 F.3d at 1327; Beverly v. Network Solutions, Inc., No. 98-0337, 1998 WL 320829, at *1 (N.D.Cal. June 12, 1998) ("Companies attempt to make the search for their web site as easy as possible. They do so by using a corporate name, trademark or service mark as their web site address."). One interested in today's news would do well visiting "usatoday.com," which features, as one would expect, breaking stories from Gannett's USA Today. Guessing domain names, however, is not a risk-free activity. The Web surfer who assumes that "'X'.com" will always correspond to the web site of company X or trademark X will, however, sometimes be misled. One looking for the latest information on Panavision, International, L.P., would sensibly try "panavision.com." Until recently, that Web surfer would have instead found a web site owned by Dennis Toeppen featuring photographs of the City of Pana, Illinois. . . .

A Web surfer's second option when he does not know the domain name is to utilize an Internet search engine, such as Yahoo, Altavista, or Lycos. See ACLU v. Reno, 31 F.Supp.2d 473, 484 (E.D.Pa.1999); Washington Speakers Bureau, Inc. v. Leading Authorities, Inc., 33 F.Supp.2d 488, 499 (E.D.Va.1999). When a keyword is entered, the search engine processes it through a self-created index of web sites to generate a (sometimes long) list relating to the entered keyword. Each search engine uses its own algorithm to arrange indexed materials in sequence, so the list of web sites that any particular set of keywords will bring up may differ depending on the search engine used. See Niton Corp. v. Radiation Monitoring Devices, Inc., 27 F.Supp.2d 102, 104 (D.Mass.1998); Intermatic Inc. v. Toeppen, 947 F.Supp. 1227, 1231-32 (N.D.Ill.1996); Shea v. Reno, 930 F.Supp. 916, 929 (S.D.N.Y.1996), *aff'd*, 521 U.S. 1113, 117 S.Ct. 2501, 138 L.Ed.2d 1006 (1997). Search engines look for keywords in places such as domain names, actual text on the web page, and metatags. Metatags are HTML code intended to describe the contents of the web site. There are different types of metatags, but those of principal concern to us are the "description" and "keyword" metatags. The description metatags are intended to describe the web site; the keyword metatags, at least in theory, contain keywords relating to the contents of the web site. The more often a term appears in the metatags and in the text of the web page, the more likely it is that the web page will be "hit" in a search for that keyword and the higher on the list of "hits" the web page will appear. See *Niton*, 27 F.Supp.2d at 104.

With this basic understanding of the Internet and the Web, we may now analyze the legal issues before us. . . .

[The court concluded that Brookfield was the senior user of the mark, because West Coast's prior use of "The Movie Buff's Movie Store" was too dissimilar to "moviebuff.com" to allow it to trace priority to the use of that phrase.]

V

Establishing seniority, however, is only half the battle. Brookfield must also show that the public is likely to be somehow confused about the source or sponsorship of West Coast's "moviebuff.com" web site—and somehow to associate that site with Brookfield. [The court went on to enjoin West Coast's use of moviebuff.com after concluding that it was likely to cause confusion with Brookfield's "Movie Buff" mark.]

B

So far we have considered only West Coast's use of the domain name "moviebuff.com." Because Brookfield requested that we also preliminarily enjoin West Coast from using marks confusingly similar to "MovieBuff" in metatags and buried code, we must also decide whether West Coast can, consistently with the trademark and unfair competition laws, use "Movie-Buff" or "moviebuff.com" in its HTML code.[23]

At first glance, our resolution of the infringement issues in the domain name context would appear to dictate a similar conclusion of likelihood of confusion with respect to West Coast's use of "moviebuff.com" in its metatags. Indeed, all eight likelihood of confusion factors outlined in Part V-A—with the possible exception of purchaser care, which we discuss below—apply here as they did in our analysis of domain names; we are, after all, dealing with the same marks, the same products and services, the same consumers, etc. Disposing of the issue so readily, however, would ignore the fact that the likelihood of confusion in the domain name context resulted largely from the associational confusion between West Coast's domain name "moviebuff.com" and Brookfield's trademark "MovieBuff." The question in the metatags context is quite different. Here, we must determine whether West Coast can use "MovieBuff" or "moviebuff.com" in the metatags of its web site at "westcoastvideo.com" or at any other domain address other than "moviebuff.com" (which we have determined that West Coast may not use).

Although entering "MovieBuff" into a search engine is likely to bring up a list including "westcoastvideo.com" if West Coast has included that term in its metatags, the resulting confusion is not as great as where West Coast uses the "moviebuff.com" domain name. First, when the user inputs "MovieBuff" into an Internet search engine, the list produced by the search engine is likely to include both West Coast's and Brookfield's web sites. Thus, in scanning such list, the Web user will often be able to find the particular web site he is seeking. Moreover, even if the Web user chooses the web site belonging to West Coast, he will see that the domain name of the web site he selected is "westcoastvideo.com." Since there is no confusion resulting from the domain address, and since West Coast's initial web page prominently displays its own name, it is difficult to say that a consumer is likely to be confused about whose site he has reached or to think that Brookfield somehow sponsors West Coast's web site.

Nevertheless, West Coast's use of "moviebuff.com" in metatags will still result in what is known as initial interest confusion. Web surfers looking for Brookfield's "MovieBuff" products who are taken by a search engine to "westcoastvideo.com" will find a database similar enough to "MovieBuff" such that a sizeable number of consumers who were originally looking for Brookfield's product will simply decide to utilize West Coast's offerings instead. Although there is no source confusion in the sense that consumers know they are patronizing West Coast rather than Brookfield, there is nevertheless initial interest confusion in the sense that, by using "movie-

---

23. As we explained in Part II, metatags are HTML code not visible to Web users but used by search engines in determining which sites correspond to the keywords entered by a Web user. Although Brookfield never explained what it meant by "buried code," the leading trademark treatise explains that "buried code" is another term for the HTML code that is used by search engines but that is not visible to users. See 3 McCarthy, supra, at §25:69 n. 1. We will use the term metatags as encompassing HTML code generally.

buff.com" or "MovieBuff" to divert people looking for "MovieBuff" to its web site, West Coast improperly benefits from the goodwill that Brookfield developed in its mark. Recently in *Dr. Seuss*, we explicitly recognized that the use of another's trademark in a manner calculated "to capture initial consumer attention, even though no actual sale is finally completed as a result of the confusion, may be still an infringement." *Dr. Seuss*, 109 F.3d at 1405 (citing Mobil Oil Corp. v. Pegasus Petroleum Corp., 818 F.2d 254, 257-58 (2d Cir.1987)).[24]

The *Dr. Seuss* court, in recognizing that the diversion of consumers' initial interest is a form of confusion against which the Lanham Act protects, relied upon *Mobil Oil*. In that case, Mobil Oil Corporation ("Mobil") asserted a federal trademark infringement claim against Pegasus Petroleum, alleging that Pegasus Petroleum's use of "Pegasus" was likely to cause confusion with Mobil's trademark, a flying horse symbol in the form of the Greek mythological Pegasus. Mobil established that "potential purchasers would be misled into an initial interest in Pegasus Petroleum" because they thought that Pegasus Petroleum was associated with Mobil. *Id.* at 260. But these potential customers would generally learn that Pegasus Petroleum was unrelated to Mobil well before any actual sale was consummated. See *id*. Nevertheless, the Second Circuit held that "[s]uch initial confusion works a sufficient trademark injury." *Id.*

Mobil Oil relied upon its earlier opinion in Grotrian, Helfferich, Schulz, Th. Steinweg Nachf. v. Steinway & Sons, 523 F.2d 1331, 1341-42 (2d Cir.1975). Analyzing the plaintiff's claim that the defendant, through its use of the "Grotrian-Steinweg" mark, attracted people really interested in plaintiff's "Steinway" pianos, the Second Circuit explained:

> We decline to hold, however, that actual or potential confusion at the time of purchase necessarily must be demonstrated to establish trademark infringement under the circumstances of this case.
>
> The issue here is not the possibility that a purchaser would buy a Grotrian-Steinweg thinking it was actually a Steinway or that Grotrian had some connection with Steinway and Sons. The harm to Steinway, rather, is the likelihood that a consumer, hearing the "Grotrian-Steinweg" name and thinking it had some connection with "Steinway," would consider it on that basis. The "Grotrian-Steinweg" name therefore would attract potential customers based on the reputation built up by Steinway in this country for many years.

Grotrian, 523 F.2d at 1342.

Both *Dr. Seuss* and the Second Circuit hold that initial interest confusion is actionable under the Lanham Act, which holdings are bolstered by

---

24. The *Dr. Seuss* court discussed initial interest confusion within its purchaser care analysis. As a district court within our circuit recognized in a recent case involving a claim of trademark infringement via metatags usage, "[t]his case . . . is not a standard trademark case and does not lend itself to the systematic application of the eight factors." Playboy Enters. v. Welles, 7 F.Supp.2d 1098 (S.D.Cal.1998). Because we agree that the traditional eight-factor test is not well-suited for analyzing the metatags issue, we do not attempt to fit our discussion into one of the *Sleekcraft* factors.

the decisions of many other courts which have similarly recognized that the federal trademark and unfair competition laws do protect against this form of consumer confusion. See *Green Prods.*, 992 F.Supp. 1070, 1076 (N.D.Iowa 1997) ("In essence, ICBP is capitalizing on the strong similarity between Green Products' trademark and ICBP's domain name to lure customers onto its web page."); Securacomm Consulting, Inc. v. Securacom Inc., 984 F.Supp. 286, 298 (D.N.J.1997) ("'Infringement can be based upon confusion that creates initial customer interest, even though no actual sale is finally completed as a result of the confusion.'") (citing 3 McCarthy §23:6), *rev'd on other grounds*, 166 F.3d 182, 186 (3d Cir.1999) ("In this appeal, [appellant] does not challenge the district court's finding of infringement or order of injunctive relief."); Kompan A.S. v. Park Structures, Inc., 890 F.Supp. 1167, 1180 (N.D.N.Y.1995) ("Kompan argues correctly that it can prevail by showing that confusion between the Kompan and Karavan lines and names will mistakenly lead the consumer to believe there is some connection between the two and therefore develop an interest in the Karavan line that it would not otherwise have had."); Blockbuster Entertainment Group v. Laylco, Inc., 869 F.Supp. 505, 513 (E.D.Mich.1994) ("Because the names are so similar and the products sold are identical, some unwitting customers might enter a Video Busters store thinking it is somehow connected to Blockbuster. Those customers probably will realize shortly that Video Busters is not related to Blockbuster, but under [Ferrari S.P.A. Esercizio v. Roberts, 944 F.2d 1235 (6th Cir.1991)] and *Grotrian* that is irrelevant."); Jordache Enters., Inc. v. Levi Strauss & Co., 841 F.Supp. 506, 514-15 (S.D.N.Y.1993) ("Types of confusion that constitute trademark infringement include where . . . potential consumers initially are attracted to the junior user's mark by virtue of its similarity to the senior user's mark, even though these consumers are not actually confused at the time of purchase."); Sara Lee Corp. v. Kayser-Roth Corp., No. 92-00460, 1992 WL 436279, at *24 (W.D.N.C. Dec. 1, 1992) ("That situation offers an opportunity for sale not otherwise available by enabling defendant to interest prospective customers by confusion with the plaintiff's product."); Television Enter. Network, Inc. v. Entertainment Network, Inc., 630 F.Supp. 244, 247 (D.N.J.1986) ("Even if the confusion is cured at some intermediate point before the deal is completed, the initial confusion may be damaging and wrongful."); Koppers Co. v. Krupp-Koppers GmbH, 517 F.Supp. 836, 844 (W.D.Pa.1981) ("[S]ecuring the initial business contact by the defendant because of an assumed association between the parties is wrongful even though the mistake is later rectified."). See also Forum Corp. of North America v. Forum, Ltd., 903 F.2d 434, 442 n. 2 (7th Cir.1990) ("We point out that the fact that confusion as to the source of a product or service is eventually dispelled does not eliminate the trademark infringement which has already occurred."). But see Astra Pharm. Prods., Inc. v. Beckman Instruments, Inc., 718 F.2d 1201, 1206-08 (1st Cir.1983) (suggesting that only confusion that affects "the ultimate decision of a purchaser whether to buy a particular product" is actionable);

Teletech Customer Care Mgmt. (Cal.), Inc. v. Tele-Tech Co., 977 F.Supp. 1407, 1410, 1414 (C.D.Cal.1997) (finding likelihood of initial interest confusion but concluding that such "brief confusion is not cognizable under the trademark laws").

Using another's trademark in one's metatags is much like posting a sign with another's trademark in front of one's store. Suppose West Coast's competitor (let's call it "Blockbuster") puts up a billboard on a highway reading—"West Coast Video: 2 miles ahead at Exit 7"—where West Coast is really located at Exit 8 but Blockbuster is located at Exit 7. Customers looking for West Coast's store will pull off at Exit 7 and drive around looking for it. Unable to locate West Coast, but seeing the Blockbuster store right by the highway entrance, they may simply rent there. Even consumers who prefer West Coast may find it not worth the trouble to continue searching for West Coast since there is a Blockbuster right there. Customers are not confused in the narrow sense: they are fully aware that they are purchasing from Blockbuster and they have no reason to believe that Blockbuster is related to, or in any way sponsored by, West Coast. Nevertheless, the fact that there is only initial consumer confusion does not alter the fact that Blockbuster would be misappropriating West Coast's acquired goodwill. See *Blockbuster*, 869 F.Supp. at 513 (finding trademark infringement where the defendant, a video rental store, attracted customers' initial interest by using a sign confusingly [similar] to its competitor's even though confusion would end long before the point of sale or rental); see also *Dr. Seuss*, 109 F.3d at 1405; *Mobil Oil*, 818 F.2d at 260; *Green Prods.*, 992 F.Supp. at 1076.

The few courts to consider whether the use of another's trademark in one's metatags constitutes trademark infringement have ruled in the affirmative. For example, in a case in which Playboy Enterprises, Inc. ("Playboy") sued AsiaFocus International, Inc. ("AsiaFocus") for trademark infringement resulting from AsiaFocus's use of the federally registered trademarks "Playboy" and "Playmate" in its HTML code, a district court granted judgment in Playboy's favor, reasoning that AsiaFocus intentionally misled viewers into believing that its Web site was connected with, or sponsored by, Playboy. See Playboy Enters. v. Asiafocus Int'l, Inc., No. CIV.A. 97-734-A, 1998 WL 724000, at *3, *6-*7 (E.D.Va. Apr.10, 1998).

In a similar case also involving Playboy, a district court in California concluded that Playboy had established a likelihood of success on the merits of its claim that defendants' repeated use of "Playboy" within "machine readable code in Defendants' Internet Web pages, so that the PLAYBOY trademark [was] accessible to individuals or Internet search engines which attempt[ed] to access Plaintiff under Plaintiff's PLAYBOY registered trademark" constituted trademark infringement. See Playboy Enters. v. Calvin Designer Label, 985 F.Supp. 1220, 1221 (N.D.Cal.1997). The court accordingly enjoined the defendants from using Playboy's marks in buried code or metatags. See *id*. at 1221-22.

In a metatags case with an interesting twist, a district court in Massachusetts also enjoined the use of metatags in a manner that resulted in initial interest confusion. See *Niton*, 27 F.Supp.2d at 102-05. In that case, the defendant Radiation Monitoring Devices ("RMD") did not simply use Niton Corporation's ("Niton") trademark in its metatags. Instead, RMD's web site directly copied Niton's web site's metatags and HTML code. As a result, whenever a search performed on an Internet search engine listed Niton's web site, it also listed RMD's site. Although the opinion did not speak in terms of initial consumer confusion, the court made clear that its issuance of preliminary injunctive relief was based on the fact that RMD was purposefully diverting people looking for Niton to its web site. See *id.* at 104-05.

Consistently with *Dr. Seuss*, the Second Circuit, and the cases which have addressed trademark infringement through metatags use, we conclude that the Lanham Act bars West Coast from including in its metatags any term confusingly similar with Brookfield's mark. West Coast argues that our holding conflicts with *Holiday Inns*, in which the Sixth Circuit held that there was no trademark infringement where an alleged infringer merely took advantage of a situation in which confusion was likely to exist and did not affirmatively act to create consumer confusion. See *Holiday Inns*, 86 F.3d at 622 (holding that the use of "1-800-405-4329"—which is equivalent to "1-800-H[zero]LIDAY"—did not infringe Holiday Inn's trademark, "1-800-HOLIDAY"). Unlike the defendant in *Holiday Inns*, however, West Coast was not a passive figure; instead, it acted affirmatively in placing Brookfield's trademark in the metatags of its web site, thereby creating the initial interest confusion. Accordingly, our conclusion comports with *Holiday Inns*.

C

Contrary to West Coast's contentions, we are not in any way restricting West Coast's right to use terms in a manner which would constitute fair use under the Lanham Act. See New Kids on the Block v. News America Pub., Inc., 971 F.2d 302, 306-09 (9th Cir.1992); see also August Storck K.G. v. Nabisco, Inc., 59 F.3d 616, 617-18 (7th Cir.1995). It is well established that the Lanham Act does not prevent one from using a competitor's mark truthfully to identify the competitor's goods, see, e.g., Smith v. Chanel, Inc., 402 F.2d 562, 563 (9th Cir.1968) (stating that a copyist may use the originator's mark to identify the product that it has copied), or in comparative advertisements, see *New Kids on the Block*, 971 F.2d at 306-09. This fair use doctrine applies in cyberspace as it does in the real world. See Radio Channel Networks, Inc. v. Broadcast.Com, Inc., No. 98 Civ. 4799, 1999 WL 124455, at *5-*6 (S.D.N.Y. Mar.8, 1999); Bally Total Fitness Holding Corp. v. Faber, 29 F.Supp.2d 1161 (C.D.Cal.1998); *Welles*, 7 F.Supp.2d at 1103-04; Patmont Motor Werks, Inc. v. Gateway

Marine, Inc., No. 96-2703, 1997 WL 811770, at *3-*4 & n. 6 (N.D.Cal. Dec.18, 1997); see also *Universal Tel-A-Talk*, 1998 WL 767440, at *9.

In *Welles*, the case most on point, Playboy sought to enjoin former Playmate of the Year Terri Welles ("Welles") from using "Playmate" or "Playboy" on her web site featuring photographs of herself. See 7 F.Supp.2d at 1100. Welles's web site advertised the fact that she was a former Playmate of the Year, but minimized the use of Playboy's marks; it also contained numerous disclaimers stating that her site was neither endorsed by nor affiliated with Playboy. The district court found that Welles was using "Playboy" and "Playmate" not as trademarks, but rather as descriptive terms fairly and accurately describing her web page, and that her use of "Playboy" and "Playmate" in her web site's metatags was a permissible, good faith attempt to index the content of her web site. It accordingly concluded that her use was permissible under the trademark laws. See *id.* at 1103-04.

We agree that West Coast can legitimately use an appropriate descriptive term in its metatags. But "MovieBuff" is not such a descriptive term. Even though it differs from "Movie Buff" by only a single space, that difference is pivotal. The term "Movie Buff" is a descriptive term, which is routinely used in the English language to describe a movie devotee. "MovieBuff" is not. The term "MovieBuff" is not in the dictionary. See Merriam-Webster's Collegiate Dictionary 762 (10th ed.1998); American Heritage College Dictionary 893 (3d ed.1997); Webster's New World College Dictionary 889 (3d ed.1997); Webster's Third New Int'l Dictionary 1480 (unabridged 1993). Nor has that term been used in any published federal or state court opinion. In light of the fact that it is not a word in the English language, when the term "MovieBuff" is employed, it is used to refer to Brookfield's products and services, rather than to mean "motion picture enthusiast." The proper term for the "motion picture enthusiast" is "Movie Buff," which West Coast certainly can use. It cannot, however, omit the space.

Moreover, West Coast is not absolutely barred from using the term "MovieBuff." As we explained above, that term can be legitimately used to describe Brookfield's product. For example, its web page might well include an advertisement banner such as "Why pay for MovieBuff when you can get the same thing here for FREE?" which clearly employs "MovieBuff" to refer to Brookfield's products. West Coast, however, presently uses Brookfield's trademark not to reference Brookfield's products, but instead to describe its own product (in the case of the domain name) and to attract people to its web site in the case of the metatags. That is not fair use. . . .

VII

As we have seen, registration of a domain name for a Web site does not trump long-established principles of trademark law. When a firm uses a competitor's trademark in the domain name of its web site, users are likely to be confused as to its source or sponsorship. Similarly, using a competitor's trademark in the metatags of such web site is likely to cause what we have described as initial interest confusion. These forms of confusion are exactly what the trademark laws are designed to prevent.

Accordingly, we reverse and remand this case to the district court with instructions to enter a preliminary injunction in favor of Brookfield in accordance with this opinion.

≡
≡ *Playboy Enterprises, Inc. v. Welles*
≡ United States District Court for the Southern District of California
≡ *7 F. Supp. 2d 1098 (S.D. Cal. 1998)*

KEEP, District Judge.

On February 27, 1998, plaintiff Playboy Enterprises, Inc. (PEI) filed a Complaint against defendant Terri Welles. The Complaint consists of five causes of action: 1) trademark infringement pursuant to 15 U.S.C. §1114(1); 2) false designation of origin and unfair competition under 15 U.S.C. §1125(a); 3) dilution of trademarks pursuant to 15 U.S.C. 1125(c); 4) trademark infringement and unfair competition under California common law; 5) unfair competition in violation of Cal.Bus. & Prof.Code §17200, et seq. . . .

I. Background

The following background facts are taken from the parties' contentions in their papers, but the court does not make any ultimate findings of fact with respect to this case. Plaintiff Playboy Enterprises, Inc. (PEI) is an international publishing and entertainment company. Since 1953, PEI has published Playboy magazine, a widely popular magazine with approximately ten (10) million readers each month. PEI also publishes numerous specialty magazines such as Playboy's Playmate Review, Playboy's Playmates of the Year, and Playboy's Calendar Playmates among other publications. In addition to its publishing ventures, PEI produces television programming for cable and direct-to-home satellite transmission and sells and licenses various goods and services including videos.

PEI has established two websites. According to plaintiff, its free website, http://www.playboy.com, has become one of the most popular sites on the Web and is used to promote its magazine, goods, and services. Its other website, called the "Playboy Cyber Club," http://www.cyber.playboy.com, is devoted to promoting current and former PEI models.

PEI owns federally registered trademarks for the terms Playboy, Playmate, Playmate of the Month, and Playmate of the Year. The term Playmate of the Year is sometimes abbreviated "PMOY." PEI does not have a federally registered trademark in the abbreviation "PMOY," although PEI argues that "PMOY" is worthy of trademark protection because it is a well-known abbreviation for the trademark Playmate of the Year.

Defendant Terri Welles is a self-employed model and spokesperson, who began her modeling career with Playboy magazine in 1980. In May of 1980, Ms. Welles appeared on the cover of Playboy magazine and was subsequently featured as the "Playmate of the Month" in the December 1980 issue. Ms. Welles received the "Playmate of the Year" award in June of 1981. Since 1980, Ms. Welles has appeared in no less than thirteen (13) issues of Playboy magazine and eighteen (18) newsstand specials published by PEI. Defendant claims that she has always referred to herself since 1980 as a "Playmate" or "Playmate of the Year" with the knowledge of PEI.

On June 29, 1997, Ms. Welles opened a website, http://www.terriwelles.com, which includes photographs of herself and others (both nude and clothed), a fan club posting board, an autobiography section, and a listing of current events and personal appearances. The domain name for defendant's site is "terriwelles," the heading for the website is "Terri Welles—Playmate of the Year 1981," and title of the link page is "Terri Welles—Playboy Playmate of the Year 1981." Each of the pages uses "PMOY '81" as a repeating watermark in the background. According to defendant, eleven (11) of the fifteen (15) free web pages include a disclaimer at the bottom of the pages, in varying font sizes depending on the page, which indicates that the website is not endorsed by PEI; the disclaimer reads as follows: "This site is neither endorsed, nor sponsored by, nor affiliated with Playboy Enterprises, Inc. PLAYBOY, PLAYMATE OF THE YEAR and PLAYMATE OF THE MONTH are registered trademarks of Playboy Enterprises, Inc." Defendant uses the terms Playboy and Playmate along with other terms within the keywords section of the meta tags, which constitutes the internal index of the website used by some search engines.

The site contains link pages to other erotic, adult-oriented websites. It also contains advertising "banners" for some of those websites.

Since May of 1997, defendant has been in contact with plaintiff about the design and creation of her website. Defendant claims that plaintiff, through Marcia Terrones, the director of the "Rights and Permission" department at PEI, informed her that she could identify herself as the "Playmate of the Year 1981" but that she could not reproduce the rabbit head logo on her proposed website. Various communications between defendant and plaintiff ensued. According to defendant, PEI, through Hugh Hefner, initially complimented her website and encouraged her use of the title "Playmate of the Year 1981." However, Mr. Hefner later informed defendant that use of PEI's trademarks were restricted; instead, he invited defendant to join PEI's new Cyber Club. Defendant refused this invitation, and PEI continued to demand that defendant remove the "Playmate of the Year" title from the home page as well as remove the PMOY watermark from the background.

Plaintiff has moved for a preliminary injunction which would enjoin defendant from 1) using the trademarked term Playmate of the Year in the title of the home page and the link page; 2) from using the watermark "PMOY '81" in the background; and 3) from using the trademarked terms Playboy and Playmate in the meta-tagging of defendant's site. Therefore, the task before the court is to determine whether a preliminary injunction against defendant is warranted in this instance. . . .

III. Discussion

In general, plaintiff argues that defendant's use of the Playboy and Playmate trademarks in conjunction with her website is likely to cause confusion, mistake or deception. Specifically, PEI avers that these alleged infringements are harming it and its trademarks since websurfing consumers are likely to believe that defendant's website is authorized, sponsored or otherwise approved by PEI when it is not. *Id.* Defendant, on the other hand, contends that her use of the title Playmate of the Year and the abbreviation PMOY is merely a descriptive use of those terms so as to identify herself to her customers. She argues that any other use of PEI's trademarked terms is merely used in an editorial fashion.

In this motion, plaintiff concentrates on defendant's use of the Playmate of the Year title in Ms. Welles' web page heading and link page, her use of the PMOY '81 term as a watermark in the web page background, and her use of the Playboy and Playmate marks as meta tags. These appear to be the only infringements alleged by PEI; accordingly, the court will focus on these three particular issues in this order. . . .

B. *Likelihood of Success in Trademark Causes of Action*

Plaintiff asserts that defendant is infringing on its registered trademarks in violation of Section 32(1) of the Lanham Act, 15 U.S.C. §1114(1), and that said infringement is causing confusion, mistake, or deception which constitutes false designation of origin and unfair competition in violation of Section 43(a) of the Lanham Act, 15 U.S.C. §1125(a). The purpose of a trademark is to allow for customer identification of the manufacturer or sponsor of a good or the provider of a service. See New Kids on the Block v. New Am. Pub., Inc., 971 F.2d 302, 305 (9th Cir.1992).

It is undisputed that PEI owns federally-registered trademarks for the words Playboy, Playmate, Playmate of the Month, and Playmate of the Year. The term Playboy has gained widespread public recognition and is distinctive due in large part to the long-standing success and popularity of Playboy magazine and related publications from PEI. See Playboy Enters., Inc. v. Chuckleberry Publishing, Inc., 687 F.2d 563, 566-67 (2d Cir.1982) (holding that the Playboy mark is distinctive, widely recognized, and of great value). However, the other trademarks such as Playmate are not only trademarks related to Playboy magazine, but they are titles bestowed upon particular models who appear in that magazine. From the papers submitted and the oral arguments, it appears that the terms Playmate, Playmate of the Month, and Playmate of the Year are titles which Playboy magazine awards to certain Playboy models, who then use the title to describe themselves. Much like Academy Award winners, crowned Miss Americas, and Heisman Trophy winners, Playboy Playmates are given a title which becomes part of their identity and adds value to their name. Indisputably, these winners represent the awarding organization or sponsor, but the title becomes part of who they are to the public.

In the case of Playboy Playmates, PEI encourages these select models to use their titles for their self-promotion and the promotion of its magazines and assorted goods and services. In the case of Ms. Welles, it appears that PEI had no objection to her use of the terms Playmate of the Year or Playboy Playmate until she launched her competing website. In oral argument, PEI conceded that these models may use their title for their own benefit, as in the title of an autobiography. PEI also admitted that Ms. Welles is not contractually restricted from using the terms Playmate of the Month or Playmate of the Year based on her previous contracts with PEI. However, it contends that Ms. Welles may not trade on PEI's marks so as to compete with PEI; specifically, PEI argues that the prominent use of its marks to attract the attention of potential customers is a trademark infringement as well as a dilution of its marks.

In the papers submitted, the parties engage in an extensive analysis of whether defendant's use of PEI's trademarks creates confusion among websurfers. Indeed, the dispositive legal issue in the standard trademark case concerns "customer confusion." See WCVB-TV v. Boston Athletic Ass'n, 926 F.2d 42, 44 (1st Cir.1991). The Ninth Circuit has articulated an eight-factor test which the court may consider in determining the likelihood of confusion: 1) the strength of the mark; 2) proximity or relatedness of the goods; 3) similarity in appearance, sound, and meaning of the marks; 4) evidence of actual confusion; 5) degree to which the marketing channels converge; 6) type of good and degree of care customers are likely to exercise in purchasing them; 7) evidence of the intention of defendant in selecting and using the alleged infringing name; and 8) likelihood that the parties will expand their product lines. See Metro Pub. Ltd. v. San Jose Mercury News, 987 F.2d 637, 640 (9th Cir.1993); see also Century 21 Real Estate Corp. v. Sandlin, 846 F.2d 1175, 1178-79 (9th Cir.1988) (applying a similar six-factor test). These factors are simply helpful guidelines for the determination of potential customer confusion. See *Metro Pub.*, 987 F.2d at 640.

This case, however, is not a standard trademark case and does not lend itself to the systematic application of the eight factors. In the case at bar, defendant has used the terms Playmate of the Year and its abbreviation

PMOY on her website. She has also used the terms Playboy and Playmate as meta tags for her site so that those using search engines on the Web can find her website if they were looking for a Playboy Playmate. The problem in this case is that the trademarks that defendant uses, and the manner in which she uses them, describe her and identify her. This raises a question of whether there is a "fair use" of these marks pursuant to 15 U.S.C. §§1115(b)(4) and 1125(c)(4). See *New Kids*, 971 F.2d at 306 (noting that the "fair use" defense arises when the trademark also describes a person, a place or an attribute of a product). Terri Welles was and is the "Playmate of the Year for 1981." Plaintiff has conceded this fact and has not submitted any evidence for the court to conclude that PEI may prevent defendant from using that term to identify herself and her award; as noted above, PEI conceded that there are no contractual agreements between it and defendant which restrict her use of any of the marks. Thus, defendant has raised a "fair use" defense which must be overcome by the plaintiff before a potential infringement under Section 43(a) of the Lanham Act or trademark dilution under Section 43(c) of the Lanham Act may be found.

In a case where the "mark is used only to 'describe the goods or services of [a] party, or their geographic origin,' trademark law recognizes a 'fair use' defense." *Id.* (quoting 15 U.S.C. §1115(b)(4)). Title 15 U.S.C. §1115(b)(4) states the following:

> That the use of the name, term, or device charged to be an infringement is a use, otherwise than as a mark, of the party's individual name in his own business, or of the individual name of anyone in privity with such party, or of a term or device which is descriptive of and used fairly and in good faith only to describe the goods or services of such party, or their geographic origin. . . .

Id. "'The "fair use" defense, in essence, forbids a trademark registrant to appropriate a descriptive term for his exclusive use and so prevent others from accurately describing a characteristic of their goods.'" *New Kids*, 971 F.2d at 306 (quoting Soweco, Inc. v. Shell Oil Co., 617 F.2d 1178, 1185 (5th Cir.1980)). In the case at bar, Ms. Welles has used the trademark term Playmate of the Year to identify and describe herself. As the court noted above, Ms. Welles earned the title of "Playboy Playmate of the Year" in 1981 and has used that title ever since, without objection from PEI.

From the exhibits submitted with the parties' papers and presented at oral argument, it is evident that Ms. Welles has minimized her references to Playboy on her website and has not attempted to trick consumers into believing that they are viewing a Playboy-endorsed website. In Volkswagenwerk Aktiengesellschaft v. Church, 411 F.2d 350, 352 (9th Cir.1969), the Ninth Circuit held that the defendant was able to advertise that he repaired Volkswagen vehicles as long as he did not do so in a manner "which is likely to suggest to his prospective customers that he is part of Volkswagen's organization of franchised dealers and repairmen." *Id.* In the case at bar, Ms. Welles has not created a Playboy-related website. She does not use Playboy or Playmate in her domain name, she does not use the classic Playboy bunny logo, she inserted disclaimers which clearly state that the website is not endorsed by PEI, and the font of the Playmate of the Year 1981 title is not recognizable as a Playboy magazine font.

It is clear that defendant is selling Terri Welles and only Terri Welles on the website. There is no overt attempt to confuse the websurfer into believing that her site is a Playboy-related website. In this case, then, defendant's use of the term Playmate of the Year 1981 "is descriptive of and used fairly and in good faith only to describe [herself]." 15 U.S.C. §1115(b)(4). As such, the use of the abbreviation PMOY '81 is also permissible since it makes reference to her title as "Playmate of the Year 1981." Since the court finds that "PMOY '81" is a fair description of Ms. Terri Welles, it is not necessary to rule on whether the abbreviation PMOY is a protected trademark.

With respect to the meta tags, the court finds there to be no trademark infringement where defendant has used plaintiff's trademarks in good faith to index the content of her website. The meta tags are not visible to the websurfer although some search engines rely on these tags to help websurfers find certain websites. Much like the subject index of a card catalog, the meta tags give the websurfer using a search engine a clearer indication of the content of a website. The use of the term Playboy is not an infringement because it references not only her identity as a "Playboy Playmate of the Year 1981," but it may also reference the legitimate editorial uses of the term Playboy contained in the text of defendant's website. Plaintiff conceded, both in its papers and in oral argument, that defendant may properly use the term Playboy in an editorial fashion (i.e. in reference to the Playboy Mansion). Therefore, the court finds that defendant has not infringed on defendant's trademarks by using them in her website meta tags.

Since defendant is entitled to the "fair use" defense pursuant to 15 U.S.C. §1115(b)(4), it is not necessary to determine the likelihood of confusion in this case. However, even if the court were to determine the likelihood of confusion in this case, it does not appear that there is a likelihood that websurfers would think that Ms. Welles' website is endorsed or sanctioned in any way by PEI. Even if Ms. Welles were not entitled to the fair use defense, plaintiff has failed to demonstrate that there is a likelihood of confusion for websurfers. Certainly, the PEI trademarks are strong and are used by PEI to sell adult entertainment on the Internet. Defendant claims she is selling a different class of goods since she is offering her promotional services and related goods like her line of cigars. However, it appears that PEI and Terri Welles are in competition for websurfers who pay money for on-line erotica, regardless of the underlying promotion.

Other factors weigh in defendant's favor. Though she is using the trademarks, she has done nothing else to make her use identical to the Playboy trademark. There is no bunny logo, the font for the terms is different, and there is no other indication that PEI is sponsoring the website. Plaintiff has presented no empirical evidence to show that there is actual confusion among consumers. Though not necessary, the lack of any such demonstration weighs in defendant's favor. Finally, it appears that defendant has used the trademarks in good faith. She has removed some of the references per PEI's request, has not used the bunny logo, and has added a disclaimer to the vast majority of her free web pages. See Consumers Union of U.S. v. General Signal Corp., 724 F.2d 1044, 1053 (2d Cir.1983) ("Disclaimers are a favored way of alleviating consumer confusion as to source or sponsorship."). This indicates good faith in the use of the trademarks and weighs in favor of defendant. Hence, even if the court were to apply the Ninth Circuit's eight-factor test, plaintiff has failed to demonstrate that it would likely succeed in proving that defendant's use of the trademarks causes a likelihood of confusion for the consumer. As the court has already noted, the Terri Welles web page appears to promote Terri Welles only and makes no attempt to connect itself with Playboy or PEI.

C. Dilution Claim

Given that the court has found that defendant is entitled to the "fair use" defense pursuant to 15 U.S.C. §1115(b)(4), plaintiff cannot make a sufficient dilution claim under 15 U.S.C. §1125(c) to warrant the granting of a preliminary injunction. Dilution is defined as "the lessening of the capacity of a famous mark to identify and distinguish goods or services, regardless of the presence or absence of . . . (2) likelihood of confusion, mistake, or deception." 15 U.S.C. §1127. . . . The section provides factors the court may consider in determining whether a mark is distinctive and famous. See 15 U.S.C. §1125(c)(1)(A-H). Though PEI's marks are arguably famous, their distinctiveness does not preclude defendant from the fair use of those items.

Under the Federal Trademark Dilution Act, a dilution claim is not actionable if there is a "[f]air use of a famous mark by another person in comparative commercial advertising or promotion to identify the competing goods or services of the owner of the famous mark." 15 U.S.C. §1125(c)(4)(A). As the court has indicated, Ms. Welles' use of the terms Playmate and Playmate of the Year constitute identification of herself. The use of those terms, in the website and in the meta tags, allows websurfers and potential customers to identify her services, whether it be her line of cigars, her promotional services, or her nude photographs. Given that Ms. Welles is the "Playmate of the Year 1981," there is no other way that Ms. Welles can identify or describe herself and her services without venturing into absurd descriptive phrases. In cases where the trademarked term must be used to identify the individual or a good, infringement and dilution laws do not apply. See *New Kids*, 971 F.2d at 306 ("In such cases, use of the trademark does not imply sponsorship or endorsement of the product because the mark is used only to describe the thing, rather than to identify its source."). Accordingly, plaintiff has failed to show that there is a likelihood of success on the merits of its dilution claim.

IV. Conclusion

In Prestonettes v. Coty, 264 U.S. 359, 368, 44 S.Ct. 350, 68 L.Ed. 731 (1924), Justice Holmes explained the purpose of trademark protection and noted that "[w]hen the mark is used in a way that does not deceive the public we see no such sanctity in the word as to prevent its being used to tell the truth. It is not taboo." In this case, Ms. Welles has used PEI's trademarks to identify herself truthfully as the "Playmate of the Year 1981." Such use is not "taboo" under the law. Based on the foregoing analysis, the court finds that plaintiff has failed to demonstrate that a preliminary injunction is warranted since there is not a strong likelihood of success on the merits. Consequently, the court cannot find that the balance of harm tips strongly enough in plaintiff's favor to overcome the lack of meritoriousness the court has found. See Stokely-Van Camp Inc. v. Coca-Cola. Co., 2 U.S.P.Q.2d 1225, 1227 (N.D.Ill.1987). In addition, it is unclear that irreparable harm would ensue from the continued operation of Ms. Welles' website since plaintiff has not demonstrated that there is a likelihood of confusion. As such, the court, hereby, DENIES plaintiff's Motion for a Preliminary Injunction.

COMMENTS AND QUESTIONS

1. The denial of a preliminary injunction in *Welles* was affirmed by the Ninth Circuit in an unpublished opinion. See 162 F.3d 1169 (9th Cir. 1998). However, the case is still pending at this writing.

2. Is initial interest confusion really the sort of thing trademark law should be concerned with? All the metatag cases seem to assume that consumers will not be confused at the time they make any purchase decisions—that is, that any confusion will be dispelled once they actually reach the site using the metatags. If that is true, what harm has been done? Does it matter what the Web site does or sells—that is, whether it is selling products in the real world, or whether its real "product" is consumer attention?

One possible harm, cited in *Brookfield*, is the "diversion" of consumer interest to the metatagging site. But this assumes that consumers will believe that all of the search engine results they get are necessarily relevant. If consumers understand the misuse of metatags and know to ignore irrelevant-looking sites in their search engine results, they may not be drawn in by the misuse of metatags.

A trademark owner might still be harmed in this instance, however, because the search will have gotten more complex. For example, a search for "Playboy" on a major search engine is likely to pull up thousands of hits, most of which are not official pages of Playboy Magazine. Does a trademark owner have a right to a "clean" search result—that is, one in which only relevant sites appear?

3.   A number of district court cases have held that the use of a competitor's trademark in your metatags is illegal. See, e.g., Playboy Ents. v. AsiaFocus Int'l, 1998 WL 724000 (1998); Playboy Ents. v. Calvin Designer Label, 985 F. Supp. 1218 (N.D. Cal. 1997). But a more difficult issue is posed when the site using the trademark in a metatag is not in fact a competitor. For example, in Oppedahl & Larson v. Advanced Concepts, No. 97CV1592 (D. Colo., filed July 24, 1997), the law firm of Oppedahl & Larson challenged the use of its name in a metatag by a site that provided totally different products. Is there consumer confusion here? Alternatively, can a trademark owner maintain a cause of action for dilution via metatagging?

4.   The *Welles* decision points up an important limit on the theory of initial interest confusion. While most metatagging cases involve Web sites with no legitimate right to use the mark in question, there are a number of circumstances in which a Web page might legitimately use another company's trademark. It might appear in a resumé, for example (essentially what was at issue in *Welles*), in an article about the trademark owner on a news site, or in comparative advertising by a competitor ("four out of five doctors prefer Brand X to Brand Y"). If a Web site is making legitimate use of a trademark, should it also be able to put that mark in its metatags?

5.   For a good discussion of metatag trademark issues, see Maureen A. O'Rourke, Defining the Limits of Free-Riding in Cyberspace: Trademark Liability for Metatagging, 33 Gonzaga L. Rev. 277 (1998); Katherine E. Gasparek, Comment, Applying the Fair Use Defense in Traditional Trademark Infringement and Dilution Cases to Internet Meta Tagging or Linking Cases, 7 Geo. Mason L. Rev. 787 (1999); Ira S. Nathenson, Internet Infoglut and Invisible Ink: Spamdexing Search Engines with Meta Tags, 12 Harv. J. L. & Tech. 43 (1998).

b.   Keyword Buys

Playboy Enterprises, Inc. v. Excite, Inc.
United States District Court for the Central District of California
55 F. Supp. 2d 1070 (C.D. Cal. 1999)

STOTLER, District J. . . .

II.   Factual Background

Defendants operate search engines on the Internet. When a person searches for a particular topic in either search engine, the search engine compiles a list of sites matching or related to the user's search terms, and then posts the list of sites, known as "search results."

Defendants sell advertising space on the search result pages. Known as "banner ads," the advertisements are commonly found at the top of the screen. The ads themselves are often animated and whimsical, and designed to entice the Internet user to "click here." If the user does click on the ad, she is transported to the web site of the advertiser.

As with other media, advertisers seek to maximize the efficacy of their ads by targeting consumers matching a certain demographic profile. Savvy web site operators accommodate the advertisers by "keying" ads to search terms entered by users. That is, instead of posting ads in a random rotation, defendants program their servers to link a pre-selected set of banner ads to certain "key" search terms. Defendants market this context-sensitive advertising ability as a value-added service and charge a premium.

Defendants key various adult entertainment ads to a group of over 450 terms related to adult entertainment, including the terms "playboy" and "playmate." Plaintiff contends that inclusion of those terms violates plaintiff's trademarks rights in those words.

III. Parties' Contentions

Plaintiff has a trademark on "Playboy®" and "Playmate®." Plaintiff contends that defendants are infringing and diluting its trademarks (1) by marketing and selling the group of over 450 words, including "playboy" and "playmate," to advertisers, (2) by programming the banner ads to run in response to the search terms "playboy" and "playmate" (i.e., "keying"), and (3) by actually displaying the banner ad on the search results page. As a result, plaintiff contends, Internet users are diverted from plaintiff's official web site and web sites sponsored or approved by plaintiff, which generally will be listed as search results, to other adult entertainment web sites. Plaintiff further argues that defendants intend to divert the users to the non-PEI sites. Plaintiff does not contend, however, that defendants infringe or dilute the marks when defendants' search engines generate a list of Web sites related to "playboy" or "playmate."

Defendants respond that while plaintiff may have a trademark on "Playboy®" and "Playmate®," defendants do not actually "use" the trademarks qua trademarks. Moreover, even if defendants do use the trademarks, defendants argue that a trademark does not confer an absolute property right on all uses of the protected terms, and that defendants' use of the terms is permitted. Finally, defendants dispute that they have any intent to divert users from clicking on search results (such as PEI's sites) to clicking on banner ads.

IV. Discussion . . .

C. *Trademark Use*

Integral to plaintiff's success on the merits of its case, on either the infringement or dilution theory, is a showing that defendants use plaintiff's trademarks in commerce. Plaintiff does not so show. Rather, plaintiff can only contend that the use of the words "playboy" and "playmate," as keywords or search terms, is equivalent to the use of the trademarks "Playboy®" and "Playmate®." However, it is undisputed that an Internet user cannot conduct a search using the trademark form of the words, i.e., Playboy® and Playmate®. Rather, the user enters the generic word "playboy" or "playmate." It is also undisputed that the words "playboy" and "playmate" are English words in their own right, and that there exist other trademarks on the words wholly unrelated to PEI. Thus, whether the user is looking for goods and services covered by PEI's trademarks or something altogether unrelated to PEI is anybody's guess. Plaintiff guesses that most users searching the Web for "playboy" and "playmate" are indeed looking for PEI sites, goods and services. Based on that theory, plaintiff argues that since defendants also speculate that users searching for "playboy" and "playmate" are looking for things related to Playboy® and Playmate®, defendants use the trademarks when they key competing adult entertainment goods and services to the generic "playboy" and "playmate."

Plaintiff has not shown that defendants use the terms in their trademark form, i.e., Playboy® and Playmate®, when marketing to advertisers or in the algorithm that effectuates the keying of the ads to the keywords. Thus, plaintiff's argument that defendants "use" plaintiff's trademarks falls short.

D. Trademark Infringement and Dilution

Even if use of the generic "playboy" and "playmate" were construed to be use of the trademark terms Playboy® and Playmate®, plaintiff still must show that the use violates trademark law. Plaintiff has asserted two theories, trademark infringement and trademark dilution.

1. Infringement

"The core element of trademark infringement is the likelihood of confusion, i.e., whether the similarity of the marks is likely to confuse customers about the source of the products." Official Airline Guides, Inc. v. Goss, 6 F.3d 1385, 1391 (9th Cir.1993). Assuming arguendo that defendants' use of "playboy" and "playmate" is use of plaintiff's marks, plaintiff must still show that confusion is likely to result from that use. Plaintiff has not so shown.

Rather, plaintiff relies on the recent case from the Court of Appeals for the Ninth Circuit, Brookfield Communications, Inc. v. West Coast Entertainment Corp., —F.3d—, 1999 WL 232014, *22-*24 (9th Cir.1999), for the proposition that defendants cause "initial interest confusion" by the use of the words "playboy" and "playmate." Initial interest confusion, as coined by the Ninth Circuit, is a brand of confusion particularly applicable to the Internet. Generally speaking, initial interest confusion may result when a user conducts a search using a trademark term and the results of the search include web sites not sponsored by the holder of the trademark search term, but rather of competitors. *Id.* The Ninth Circuit reasoned that the user may be diverted to an unsponsored site, and only realize that she has been diverted upon arriving at the competitor's site. Once there, however, even though the user knows she is not in the site initially sought, she may stay. In that way, the competitor has captured the trademark holder's potential visitors or customers. *Id.*

Brookfield is distinguishable from this case, and where applicable, supportive of defendants' position.

First, the trademark at issue in *Brookfield* was not an English word in its own right. In *Brookfield*, the Court compared Brookfield's trademark "MovieBuff" with competitor West Coast's use of the domain name "moviebuff.com," and found them to be "essentially identical" despite the differences in capitalization, which the Court considered "inconsequential in light of the fact that Web addresses are not caps-sensitive. . . ." *Id.* at *14. However, the Court held that West Coast could use the term "Movie Buff" (or, presumably, "movie buff") with the space, as such is the "proper term for the 'motion picture enthusiast'. . . . It cannot, however, omit the space." *Id.* at 26. On the other hand, "[i]n light of the fact that it is not a word' in the English language, when the term 'MovieBuff' is employed, it is used to refer to Brookfield's products and services, rather than to mean 'motion picture enthusiast.'" *Id.* at *26.

As English words, "playboy" and "playmate" cannot be said to suggest sponsorship or endorsement of either the web sites that appear as search results (as in *Brookfield*) or the banner ads that adorn the search results page. Although the trademark terms and the English language words are undisputedly identical, which, presumably, leads plaintiff to believe that the use of the English words is akin to use of the trademarks, the holder of a trademark may not remove a word from the English language merely by acquiring trademark rights in it. *Id.*

Second, the use by defendant of plaintiff's trademark in *Brookfield* was more suspect because the parties compete in the same market—as online providers of film industry information. See *id.*, at *16-*17 ("[n]ot only are they not non-competitors, the competitive proximity of their products is actually quite high"). The Ninth Circuit analogized the capture of unsuspecting Internet users by a competitor to highways and billboards. . . .

Here, the analogy is quite unlike that of a devious placement of a road sign bearing false information. This case presents a scenario more akin to a driver pulling off the freeway in response to a sign that reads "Fast Food Burgers" to find a well-known fast food burger restaurant, next to which stands a billboard that reads: "Better Burgers: 1 Block Further." The driver, previously enticed by the prospect of a burger from the well-known restaurant, now decides she wants to explore other burger options. Assuming that the same entity owns the land on which both the burger restaurant and the competitor's billboard stand, should that entity be liable to the burger restaurant for diverting the driver? That is the rule PEI contends the Court should adopt.

2. Dilution

Trademark dilution is defined as "the lessening of the capacity of a famous mark to identify and distinguish goods or services." 15 U.S.C. §1127. However, dilution is "not intended to serve as a mere fallback protection for trademark owners unable to prove trademark infringement." I.P. Lund Trading ApS v. Kohler Co., 163 F.3d 27, 48 (1st Cir.1998).

To establish dilution, plaintiff must show that "(1) [defendants have] made use of a junior mark sufficiently similar to the famous mark to evoke in a relevant universe of consumers a mental association of the two that (2) has caused (3) actual economic harm to the famous mark's economic value by lessening its former selling power as an advertising agent for its goods and services." Ringling Bros.-Barnum & Bailey Combined Shows, Inc. v. Utah Div'n of Travel Dept., 170 F.3d 449, 459 (4th Cir.1999). Dilution generally occurs through the blurring of a famous mark or tarnishment of the mark, but is not limited to these categories. See Panavision Int'l, L.P. v. Toeppen, 141 F.3d 1316, 1326 (9th Cir.1998). Plaintiff has not shown blurring of its marks, which would occur if defendants used the marks to identify defendants' goods or services. *Id.* at 1326 n. 7. First, as discussed supra, plaintiff has not shown that defendant uses its marks Playboy® and Playmate®. Further, plaintiff has not presented any evidence that defendants' use of the words "playboy" and "playmate" causes any severance of the association between plaintiff and its marks Playboy® and Playmate®, much less in the minds of Internet users.

Plaintiff has also failed to show tarnishment, which occurs when a famous mark is associated improperly with an inferior or offensive product or service. *Id.* at 1326 n. 7. Plaintiff contends that because the content of the banner ads is more sexually explicit that PEI's content, PEI's marks are being tarnished. Again, plaintiff's argument is based on the incorrect assumption that defendants use plaintiff's marks, rather than the generic words "playboy" and "playmate." But even if the defendants could be said to use plaintiff's marks, plaintiff would still be required to show that associating marks admittedly famous for adult entertainment with other purveyors of adult entertainment somehow harms plaintiff's marks. Whether PEI is a cut above the rest, as it contends, is undercut by the fact that PEI's marks are associated with other purveyors of adult entertainment in other marketing channels, as defendants' exhibits graphically establish. Adoption of plaintiff's tarnishment would secure near-monopoly control of the placement of plaintiff's marks and the associated goods and services on the

Internet, where, arguably, "placement" is a nebulous concept. A greater showing of harm is required.

V. Conclusion

Accordingly, and for the foregoing reasons, the plaintiff's motion is denied. . . .

COMMENTS AND QUESTIONS

1. Are you persuaded that Web users searching for "playboy" are often searching not for sites related to plaintiff's trademark but for sites using the term in its generic sense?

2. Keyword buys affect the advertising that appears alongside search results in a search engine. Are consumers likely to confuse ads with search results? When you see ads on a search result page, do you assume that they are somehow related to or sponsored by the owner of the trademark you have searched for? If not, how exactly has Playboy been injured by the keyword buy?

3. A variety of other conduct may be alleged to suggest a connection or affiliation between one Web site and another. Trademark cases have been litigated over links from one page to another, "frames" that display two pages in proximity to each other, and the use of logos to identify a link. Because these cases generally also involve copyright questions, we defer discussion of them until the next Section.

B. COPYRIGHT LAW

1. Direct Infringement

≡ *Playboy Enterprises v. Webbworld*
≡ *United States District Court for the Northern District of Texas*
≡ *991 F. Supp. 543 (N.D. Tex. 1997)*

SANDERS, Senior District Judge. . . .

On December 2, 1996, Plaintiff Playboy Enterprises, Inc. ("PEI"), filed this action for copyright infringement, trademark infringement, and unfair competition. After a hearing on December 9, 1996, the Court granted a temporary restraining order, and on January 6, 1997, the Court entered an agreed preliminary injunction. Both orders forbad Defendants, owners and operators of an adult-oriented Internet website, from directly or indirectly infringing PEI's copyright and trademark registrations.

On June 27, 1997, Judge Dale E. Saffels, a visiting judge to whom the case was referred, granted summary judgment against Defendant Webbworld, Inc., for direct copyright infringement of sixty-two PEI images. See Playboy Enterprises, Inc. v. Webbworld, Inc., 968 F.Supp. 1171 (N.D.Tex.1997) ("Webbworld"). Moreover, Judge Saffels found two of the individual Defendants, Bentley Ives and Benjamin Brian Ellis, jointly and severally liable for vicarious infringement. . . .

In the present opinion, the Court disturbs neither the conclusion nor the reasoning of Judge Saffels's summary judgment. The issues remaining for decision after non-jury trial are PEI's claims for the following: (1) copyright infringement of twenty-nine PEI registrations—the sixteen on which Judge Saffels reserved opinion, plus thirteen not included in PEI's motion for summary judgment; (2) vicarious liability of Defendants Ellis and Ives for the remaining twenty-nine alleged infringements, and of Defendant Gurkin for all of the alleged infringements; (3) willfulness; (4) trademark infringement and unfair competition under the Lanham Act; (5) Texas common-law unfair competition; (6) dilution of PEI's trademarks; and (7) contempt against Ellis for alleged violation of the preliminary injunction. PEI requests statutory, actual, and punitive damages, a permanent injunction, and attorney's fees.

II. Factual Background

Since approximately 1953, Playboy Enterprises, Inc. ("PEI"), has published the monthly Playboy magazine and other publications. It is undisputed here that PEI owns valid trademark or service mark registrations for the famous "Rabbit Head" design, for the name "Playboy," for the name "Playboy's Playmate Review," and for the name "Playmate." It is also undisputed that PEI holds valid copyrights for the images in its magazine issues and other publications.

Defendant Webbworld, Inc. ("Webbworld"), is a Texas corporation that operated "Netpics," an adult-oriented site on the Internet's World Wide Web, from about May 1996 until February 1997. Webbworld ceased operating at that time upon seizure of their equipment in a raid by the Fort Worth police on charges of child pornography. The gravamen of PEI's Complaint here is that the Defendants infringed certain copyrighted nude and semi-nude female images ("the images"), some of which bore PEI trademarks. Webbworld made those images available on the Netpics site to Internet users for a monthly subscription fee.

Webbworld had three principals, individual Defendants Bentley Ives ("Ives"), James Gurkin ("Gurkin"), and Benjamin Brian Ellis ("Ellis"). Ellis had the original idea for the Netpics site and wrote the software that allowed it to function. Gurkin and Ives contributed the start-up capital. Ives was, until the final month of the company's existence, sole shareholder and president of Webbworld. Gurkin worked as Webbworld's customer service representative. The net profits of the business were distributed 50% to Ellis, and 25% each to Gurkin and Ives.

The equipment for Webbworld's Netpics website consisted of fifteen personal computers, a modem, and three telephone lines, all of which were located in an office building in Dallas, Texas. One of the computers functioned as a news server; one handled accounting and administrative data; and the remaining twelve were used as web servers. The web servers were where the Netpics site "existed" on the World Wide Web. They were used to store, reproduce, display, and distribute adult images to Webbworld subscribers.

Webbworld obtained the images that it sold from selected adult-oriented Internet "newsgroups." A newsgroup is an Internet forum for the exchange of ideas by people of similar interests. Newsgroups exist on the Usenet, which like the World Wide Web is an aspect of the Internet. A newsgroup typically specializes in a certain subject area, such as sports, for example, or Cajun cooking. A substantial number of newsgroups are devoted to sexually explicit material. Newsgroups feature discrete collections of information called "articles." Newsgroup participants may "post" (upload) articles, which consist of text and/or images. Images may be posted by using hardware called a scanner to convert, for example, a photograph to a digital file, which may then be uploaded onto the newsgroup in the same way that text is transferred. Once online and within a newsgroup, a participant may post an article, may view one of many articles on the computer screen, and may download an article to his or her computer for later retrieval or printing. None of the Defendants here themselves posted any of the PEI images at issue to any of the newsgroups.

Webbworld obtained its images from selected newsgroups according to the following general method. Defendant Ellis selected the particular adult-oriented newsgroups to be downloaded. Periodically, Webbworld received a "news feed," which consisted of digital files from the selected adult newsgroups. The information was downloaded onto the news server computer. The feed consisted of both text and images, representing all of the new material that had been posted onto the newsgroup since the last feed.

The heart of the Webbworld operation was "ScanNews," software that Ellis had developed. ScanNews took the news feed, discarded most of the text, and retained the sexually-oriented images. A small amount of identifying text was sometimes retained. After the news feed was edited, the news server would announce to the twelve web servers, via the ScanNews software, that its images were ready to be transferred. Each of the web servers would contact the news server computer and copy into memory the new adult images stored there. The news server then discarded that data to make room for the next news feed.

Besides discarding text, the ScanNews software altered the news feed in a second way. It created two "thumbnail" copies, one large and one small, for each of the adult images downloaded from the Usenet. The thumbnail images enabled Webbworld to display many images on a single screen. Moreover, the thumbnails could be downloaded more quickly than full-sized images. The thumbnails were not part of the news feed; they were created by the ScanNews software to facilitate Webbworld's sale of the images they represented.

After being loaded onto the web servers, the thumbnail and full-sized adult images were available to any Internet user willing to pay Webbworld a subscription fee of $11.95 per month. The subscription process could be completed online in about 30 seconds with a major credit card. Before gaining access to the Webbworld Netpics site on the World Wide Web, a potential user would first have had to gain access to the Internet via his or her Internet service provider ("ISP"), sometimes called an access provider ("IAP"). Then, the person would employ browser software to access various sites on the World Wide Web. Webbworld's Internet address was "http://www.netpics.com." That address would be typed into a user's browser software for immediate access to Webbworld's site.

Upon entering Netpics, a subscriber was given the choice whether to view images in large or small thumbnail format. After making that choice, the user could view a full-sized image by clicking on the corresponding thumbnail. Webbworld provided instructions to its subscribers about viewing images and about downloading them into the memories of their own computers for later retrieval.

Every day, Webbworld obtained between 5,000 and 10,000 new images. An approximately equal number were deleted to make room for the new arrivals. On average, an image was stored on Webbworld's computers and thus made available to subscribers for about six days before being deleted. Webbworld normally stored and displayed about 40,000 to 70,000 images at any given time.

During the time Webbworld was in operation, many hundreds of copyrighted PEI images appeared on the website. Some of those images appeared in close association with one or more of PEI's trademarks. PEI never authorized Webbworld to reproduce, display, or distribute any of those images or marks.

III. Direct Copyright Infringement

Based on the facts related above, PEI alleges that Defendant Webbworld is directly liable for copyright infringement. For the reasons that follow, the Court agrees.

To prevail on a claim for direct copyright infringement, PEI must prove (1) ownership of the asserted copyrights, and (2) "copying" by Webbworld. See Lakedreams v. Taylor, 932 F.2d 1103 (5th Cir.1991); Central Point Software, Inc. v. Nugent, 903 F.Supp. 1057, 1059 (E.D.Tex.1995). Direct infringement does not require intent or any particular state of mind. Religious Tech. Center v. Netcom On-Line Comm.

Servs., 907 F.Supp. 1361, 1367 (N.D.Cal.1995); see Playboy Enterprises, Inc. v. Frena, 839 F.Supp. 1552, 1559 (M.D.Fla.1993) ("Intent or knowledge is not an element of infringement, and thus even an innocent infringer is liable. . . ."); Key Maps, Inc. v. Pruitt, 470 F.Supp. 33, 38 (S.D.Tex.1978) (explaining that intent to infringe need not be proved).

In this case, PEI has submitted to the Court twenty-nine copyright certificates of registration. The parties have stipulated that the registrations are valid and enforceable. Accordingly, the sole element of infringement remaining for PEI to prove is whether Webbworld "copied" the registered images.

"Copying" is a judicial shorthand for the infringement of any of a copyright owner's exclusive rights. Worlds of Wonder, Inc. v. Veritel Learning Systems, Inc., 658 F.Supp. 351, 354 (N.D.Tex.1986); see 17 U.S.C. §106 (setting forth a copyright owner's rights). Because direct proof of copying is rarely available to a copyright owner, copying is normally shown by proving (a) that a defendant had access to the copyrighted work; and (b) substantial similarity between the copyrighted work and the accused work. *Lakedreams*, 932 F.2d at 1107. Alternatively, where proof of access is absent, copying may be proved by showing a "striking similarity" between the copyrighted work and the accused work. Ferguson v. National Broadcasting Co., 584 F.2d 111, 113 (5th Cir.1978) (holding that if two works are so strikingly similar as to preclude the possibility of independent creation, copying may be proved without a showing of access).

In this case, Webbworld cannot claim to have lacked access to PEI's famous publications. The uncontroverted testimony at trial is that PEI's periodicals are widely distributed throughout the United States.

Even if proof of access were lacking, however, the Court would still find "copying" to exist. The electronic images downloaded from Webbworld's computers and offered as evidence at trial are not merely "strikingly similar" to PEI's photographs, but are virtually identical. See Exh. 5 (consisting of twenty-nine tabs with the relevant copyright registration, a photocopy of the copyrighted images, and copies of identical images downloaded from the Netpics site). Furthermore, a few of Netpics' electronic copies self-proclaim their origin by bearing a PEI title or emblem.

Having established that the accused electronic files are copies of PEI's photographs, PEI must establish that Webbworld has violated one or more of the five exclusive rights granted to a copyright holder. See Playboy Enterprises, Inc. v. Starware Pub. Corp., 900 F.Supp. 433, 437-38 (S.D.Fla.1995); *Frena*, 839 F.Supp. at 1555-56; Meadowgreen Music Co. v. Voice in the Wilderness Broadcasting, Inc., 789 F.Supp. 823, 825 (E.D.Tex.1992). Under The Copyright Act, the bundle of rights enjoyed by a copyright owner includes, among other things, the exclusive right to do, or to authorize, any of the following:

(1) Reproduce the copyrighted work;

(2) Distribute copies of the copyrighted work to the public by sale or other transfer of ownership; and/or

(3) Display the copyrighted work publicly.

17 U.S.C. §106. Using, or authorizing the use of, a copyrighted work in any one of these three ways, without permission of the copyright owner, constitutes actionable copyright infringement. *Starware Publishing Corp.*, 900 F.Supp. at 438-39; *Frena*, 839 F.Supp. at 1555-56; *Worlds of Wonder*, 658 F.Supp. at 354; 17 U.S.C. §501(a). In this case, PEI has established by a preponderance of the evidence that Webbworld violated all three of these rights.

First, Webbworld "reproduced" unauthorized copies of copyrighted PEI images. On each of the twelve Webbworld web server computers and for each of the images at issue, Webbworld created two thumbnail copies and also reproduced a full-sized image downloaded from the newsgroup. See MAI Systems Corp. v. Peak Computer, Inc., 991 F.2d 511, 519 (9th Cir.1993), *cert. dism'd*, 510 U.S. 1033, 114 S.Ct. 671, 126 L.Ed.2d 640 (1994) (holding that copying occurs when a computer program is transferred from a permanent storage device to a computer's random access memory).

Second, Webbworld "distributed" PEI's copyrighted works by allowing its users to download and print copies of electronic image files. Those files, stored on the web servers, contained virtually exact reproductions of copyrighted PEI images. Thus, Webbworld violated PEI's exclusive right to distribute its copyrighted works. See *Central Point Software, Inc.*, 903 F.Supp. at 1061 (ordering forfeiture of all computer hardware used to distribute plaintiff's copyrighted software on an electronic bulletin board); *Frena*, 839 F.Supp. at 1556 (finding a similar violation).

Finally, Webbworld violated PEI's exclusive right to "display" its copyrighted works. To display a work means "to show a copy of it, either directly or by means of a film, slide, television image, or any other device or process." 17 U.S.C. §101. Webbworld allowed its paying subscribers to view PEI's copyrighted works on their computer monitors while online. Such action constitutes a display, as the *Frena* court explains:

> The concept of display is broad. It covers "the projection of an image on a screen or other surface by any method, the transmission of an image by electronic or other means, and the showing of an image on a cathode ray tube, or similar viewing apparatus connected with any sort of information storage and retrieval system." H.R.Rep. No. 1476, 94th Cong., 2d Sess. 64 (Sept. 3, 1976), *reprinted in* 1976 U.S.Code Cong. & Admin.News 5659, 5677. The display right precludes unauthorized transmission of the display from one place to another, for example, by a computer system. See H.R.Rep. No. 1476, 94th Cong., 2d Sess. 80 (Sept. 3, 1976), *reprinted in* 1976 U.S.Code Cong. & Admin.News 5659, 5694.

839 F.Supp. at 1556-57.

Defendant Ives testified that no image existed until the Netpics subscriber downloaded it. That assertion is disingenuous. The image existed in digital form on Webbworld's servers, which made it available for decoding as an image file by the subscriber's browser software. The subscriber could view the images merely by visiting the Webbworld site. The evidence unequivocally shows that Webbworld electronically reproduced, distributed, and displayed PEI's protected images.

Webbworld's primary defense to the claim of copyright infringement is that, as a provider of access to Usenet images, it served as a mere conduit between its subscribers and adult-oriented newsgroups. See Religious Technology Center v. Netcom On-Line Communication Services, Inc., 907 F.Supp. 1361, 1372-73 (N.D.Cal.1995) ("RTC"). In *RTC*, the district court held that an Internet access provider and Internet bulletin board service operator were not directly liable for copyright infringement. *Id.* at 1366-72, 1381-82. The court reasoned, in part, that they were mere conduits for unaltered information, even though infringing files were temporarily stored on their computers. *Id.* Here, Webbworld principals testified similarly that the infringing images would have existed on the Usenet whether or not Webbworld provided access to them or not. They argue that to hold them liable would be to hold the entire Internet liable for activities that cannot reasonably be monitored or deterred.

Webbworld's argument was rejected at summary judgment and is similarly unavailing after the additional evidence presented at trial. See *Webbworld*, 968 F.Supp. at 1177. Unlike the defendant service provider in *RTC*, Webbworld did not function as a mere provider of access. To visit the Netpics site, a subscriber first was required to gain access to the Internet itself by using an Internet service provider such as the defendant in *RTC*. Webbworld did not sell access; it sold adult images.

Also unlike the Defendant in *RTC*, Webbworld did not function as a passive conduit of unaltered information. Instead, Webbworld functioned primarily as a store, a commercial destination within the Internet. Just as a merchant might re-package and sell merchandise from a wholesaler, so did Webbworld re-package (by deleting text and creating thumbnails) and sell images it obtained from the various newsgroups. In contrast to the defendants in *RTC*, Webbworld took "affirmative steps to cause the copies to be made." *RTC*, 907 F.Supp. at 1381. Such steps included using the ScanNews software to troll the Usenet for Webbworld's product.

Webbworld contends that it had no control over the information its software retrieved from the Usenet and no control over the images posted therein. See *RTC*, 907 F.Supp. at 1372 (finding no liability because the defendant access provider "does not create or control the content of the information available to its subscribers"). On the contrary, Webbworld exercised total dominion over the content of its site and the product it offered its clientele. As a shop owner may choose from what sources he or she contracts to buy merchandise, so, too, did Webbworld have the ability to choose its newsgroup sources. Clearly, a newsgroup named, for example, "alt.sex.playboy" or "alt.mag.playboy" might instantly be perceived as problematic from the standpoint of federal copyright law. Alternatively, Webbworld might simply have refrained from conducting business until it had developed software or a manual system of oversight to prevent, or at least to minimize the possibility of, copyright infringement. In any event, having developed and launched the ScanNews software for commercial use, Webbworld cannot now evade liability by claiming helplessness in the face of its "automatic" operation.

For those reasons, the Court rejects Webbworld's defenses and holds it directly liable for infringing PEI's twenty-nine copyright registrations at issue in trial of this case.

IV. Willfulness

PEI claims that Webbworld's infringement was willful. A defendant acts willfully if he knows his actions constitute an infringement; the actions need not have been malicious. Broadcast Music, Inc. v. Xanthas, Inc., 855 F.2d 233, 236 (5th Cir.1988). The practical significance of the issue of wilfulness is to increase the amount of statutory damages available to a plaintiff up to $100,000 per infringement. 17 U.S.C. §504(c)(2).

At trial, PEI offered evidence of certain images downloaded from the Webbworld site that infringed five of its copyright registrations. These images appeared on Netpics and were downloaded by PEI after Webbworld was on notice, by way of a temporary restraining order issued by this Court, that its site contained infringing material. Many of the images are instantly recognizable as belonging to PEI because of the trademark phrases or emblems printed on them. Furthermore, the images originated from a newsgroup called "alt.binaries.erotica.centerfolds." The title of that particular newsgroup, though not a PEI trademark, is sufficiently closely associated with PEI magazines to have put Webbworld on notice that the newsgroup potentially contained PEI images. Webbworld continued to carry that newsgroup until the business closed in February 1997.

Defendant Ives, president of Webbworld, testified at trial that anyone would have known that most of the images at issue belonged to PEI. Ives further testified that he knew that the "centerfolds" newsgroup contained infringing images and that he did not take any steps to prevent its use.

Defendants Ives and Ellis also testified, however, that the infringements were innocent. They maintained that identification and elimination of all PEI images was impossible and therefore that no infringement might be termed "willful."

The Court disagrees. Elimination by manual monitoring would have been difficult and expensive, but not impossible, particularly for images as obviously infringing as the ones at issue here. The evidence shows that Webbworld implemented substantial effort to combat the infringement. Notwithstanding its "compliance program," Webbworld chose to continue to copy from a newsgroup that essentially advertised by its "centerfolds" name that it carried PEI images. After it was on notice of infringement, Webbworld chose to stay in business without implementing a system that would reliably delete even such obvious transgressions. Such an action constitutes willful infringement. See *Broadcast Music, Inc.*, 855 F.2d at 236 (holding that a music vendor's choice to stay in business and thereby to continue to infringe copyrighted music was patently willful). For the five copyright registrations infringed by the many images Webbworld copied from the "centerfolds" newsgroup after the TRO was entered in this case, the Court makes a finding of willfulness. . . .

XI. Conclusion

For the reasons set out above, the Court rules as follows. Plaintiff has proved its claim for infringement of twenty-nine copyrights in addition to the sixty-two infringements found on summary judgment. Of those infringements, five were willful. The Court awards statutory damages of $129,000, in addition to the $310,000 awarded at summary judgment. Individual Defendants Ellis and Ives are vicariously liable for all infringements and are therefore jointly and severally liable for the damages awarded. . . .

PEI's request for a permanent injunction prohibiting future copyright infringement is GRANTED. . . .

COMMENTS AND QUESTIONS

1. The district court's opinion was affirmed by the Fifth Circuit without opinion. 168 F.3d 486 (5th Cir. 1999).

2. The defendants in *Webbworld* wrote software that automatically searched millions of Usenet postings to pull out the ones containing nude pictures. How likely is it that they actually checked—or feasibly could check—the origin of each picture? Has the court set an impossible burden on anyone who wants to filter messages from the Internet? Suppose that the same computer program was used by a group of concerned parents who wanted to protect their children from pornography. Would they be liable for copyright infringement on a similar theory if some of the messages they allowed through were copyrighted? If not, what distinguishes these cases?

A somewhat easier case was presented by Playboy Ents. v. Hardenburgh, 982 F. Supp. 503 (N.D. Ohio 1997). There, the court wrote:

> As a legal matter, the court would agree with Judge Whyte that a finding of direct copyright infringement requires some element of direct action or participation, for two primary reasons. First, the statute is cast in terms of activities which are reserved to copyright owners. 17 U.S.C. §106. It follows that an infringer must actually engage in one of those activities in order to di-

rectly violate the statute. Setting up a computer bulletin board is not one of those activities. Merely encouraging or facilitating those activities is not proscribed by the statute. Second, it is the area of contributory liability which allows "the imposition of liability on certain parties who have not themselves engaged in the infringing activity." Sony Corp. v. Universal Studios, Inc., 464 U.S. 417, 435, 104 S.Ct. 774, 785, 78 L.Ed.2d 574 (1984) (footnote omitted). There would be no reason to bifurcate copyright liability into the separate categories of direct and contributory if any remote causal connection to copyright infringement could be analyzed under theories of direct infringement.

That being said, the facts in this case, unlike *Frena, Sega,* and *Netcom,* are sufficient to establish that Defendants themselves engaged in two of the activities reserved to copyright owners under 17 U.S.C. §106. The court finds that Defendants distributed and displayed copies of PEI photographs in derogation of PEI's copyrights. This finding hinges on two crucial facts: (1) Defendants' policy of encouraging subscribers to upload files, including adult photographs, onto the system, and (2) Defendants' policy of using a screening procedure in which RNE employees viewed all files in the upload file and moved them into the generally available files for subscribers.

These two facts transform Defendants from passive providers of a space in which infringing activities happened to occur to active participants in the process of copyright infringement. Defendants admit that they were operating a service where the quantity of adult files available to customers increased the attractiveness of the service. Defendants actively encouraged their subscribers to upload such files. Defendants had control over which files were discarded and which files were moved into the general system. Defendants knew that there was a possibility that PEI photographs were being uploaded onto the system, but failed to adopt procedures which ensured that any and all PEI photographs would be discarded. It is inconsistent to argue that one may actively encourage and control the uploading and dissemination of adult files, but cannot held liable for copyright violations because it is too difficult to determine which files infringe upon someone else's copyrights.

For a different approach to the filtering issue, see the Section that follows concerning defamation.

3. The court concludes that the act of taking a picture from Usenet and loading it onto your own server involves the making of a copy. It cites *MAI,* discussed in Chapter 2, which holds that loading material into computer memory even temporarily is copying that violates section 106. Given this, is everyone who ever uses the Internet guilty of copyright infringement? After all, under *MAI*'s definition it is impossible to download information from the Web without making a copy. Mark Lemley has explained the problem as follows:

> Resolution of these debates will affect the number of copies made in routine Net transactions, and may also affect who is liable for making those copies. But it should be clear that under any definition, most activities on the Net involve the making of one or more permanent copies that unquestionably implicate §106(1). Sending electronic mail to someone makes at least one copy of the message sent—the copy that resides in semipermanent memory in

the recipient computer. Because many computer users regularly back up their systems, another semipermanent copy of the e-mail may be created on tape or floppy disk. Still other copies may be made if the recipient forwards the message to another, stores it in a computer file, or prints a hard copy. Similarly, posting material on a Web page involves making a long-term copy of it on the Web server, and transmitting still other copies to whomever accesses the page. Those who access the page may in turn make permanent or semipermanent copies of the Web page, either by storing or printing the material, forwarding it to another, or by "caching" the page automatically for a certain period of time.

If one accepts the argument that RAM copies are actionable under §106(1), the number of copies made in even the most routine Net transactions increases dramatically. Obviously, each act of uploading or downloading makes a RAM copy in the recipient's computer, but that is only the beginning. When a picture is downloaded from a Web site, the modem at each end will buffer each byte, as will the router, the receiving computer, the Web browser, the video decompression chip, and the video display board. Those seven copies will be made on each such transaction. Further, since most Internet transmissions do not travel directly between sender and receiver, more copies will be made of the individual packets at each node they pass through on their way to the end point.

Finally, consider who is responsible for making these copies. Some are generated by the computer where the message originates, and might therefore be within the control of the individual sending the message (or creating the Web site). But others are made automatically by the recipient's computer, meaning that under the rationale of *MAI* coupled with *Playboy* even innocently receiving an e-mail message may well infringe the copyright in that message. For similar reasons, anyone who browses the Net and unintentionally runs across infringing material is making infringing copies under this rationale. This includes not only the millions of casual Web browsers, but all the major search engine companies, which use "spiders" to crawl the Internet cataloguing Web sites and making RAM copies in the process. Further, intermediaries are also generating RAM copies and therefore infringing copyright under *MAI*. Intermediaries potentially held liable include not only the Internet service providers playing host to the message originator (for example, Netcom in the *RTC* case) but also every node on every intermediate network that routes one or more of the packets toward its destination, since those routers also buffer the packets they forward. It may be impossible to tell who made copies of which e-mails without conducting a packet routing analysis for each message. And for certain Net functions (notably Usenet and IRC), even the host of the network is a concept that cannot be clearly defined. As Judge Whyte warned in *RTC*, taking the RAM copying and direct infringement theories seriously

> would also result in liability for every single Usenet server in the worldwide link of computers transmitting [each] message to every other computer. These parties, who are liable under plaintiff's theory, do no more than operate or implement a system that is essential if Usenet messages are to be widely distributed.

There is nothing in the nature of the Net that suggests the copyright laws will not apply to conduct occurring there. Rather, the problem seems to be how to cabin the definition of copying within reasonable bounds.

Mark A. Lemley, Dealing With Overlapping Copyrights on the Internet, 22 U. Dayton L. Rev. 547 (1997). Lemley goes on to point out that transmission or downloading of material over the Internet not only makes a copy, but is potentially also a public distribution, a public performance, and a public display. Indeed, the *Webbworld* court found the defendants to have violated several of the plaintiff's section 106 rights.

The fact that everything is a copy on the Internet has two important implications. First, it can expand the set of activities that copyright owners get to control. Jessica Litman has argued that copyright owners may obtain what she terms "the exclusive right to read" in cyberspace. See Jessica Litman, The Exclusive Right to Read, 13 Cardozo Arts & Ent. L.J. 29 (1994). She points out that in real space, a customer who buys a book can read the book as many times as he wants, can lend or sell it to others, and can dispose of it as he chooses. By contrast, each new visit to a Web site to read a book—or for that matter, each time the consumer opens a computer file to read the book—is a separate copy over which the copyright owner has control. Litman worries that copyright owners may use that control to price-discriminate or at least to monitor what users are doing in the online environment. See also Julie E. Cohen, A Right to Read Anonymously: A Closer Look at "Copyright Management" in Cyberspace, 28 Conn. L. Rev. 981 (1996).

Second, if everything a user can do on the Internet involves making a copy, every user is a potential infringer. If a user has made a copy of a copyrighted work, he is presumptively liable for infringement. Unless users generally have some sort of defense to copyright infringement, the entire operation of the Internet would seem to be illegal.

One possible defense is to claim an "implied license," an argument which has some plausibility. Companies presumably put information on their Web sites because they want people to be able to access that information. In so doing, they might be said to have granted an implied license to download that information. Cf. Effects, Inc. v. Cohen, 908 F.2d 555 (9th Cir. 1990) (discussing implied copyright licenses). But an implied license relies on the desire of the copyright owner to have the information downloaded. Implied licenses can be expressly disclaimed, which would leave copying illegal. Even if an implied license does exist, its scope may be unclear. Finally, and most significantly, implied license will protect only those who download information from the copyright owner itself or a legitimate licensee. A user who unwittingly stumbles across an infringing page and downloads it will be unable to rely on an implied license defense.

An alternative defense is fair use. Some people place strong reliance on the defense of fair use in the context of computer networks. They argue or assume that even if multiple copies, distributions, and performances occur in the everyday course of running a network, those uses will likely be deemed fair, exempting from liability those who make the copies. It is undoubtedly true that some of the copies at issue here, such as the copies made by routers passing through Internet message packets, ought to be deemed fair use. Nonetheless, exclusive reliance on fair use to justify the very existence of the Net seems unwise. First, it is a defense, and the Supreme Court has made quite clear that defendants face a strong evidentiary burden in demonstrating entitlement. Second, the fair use analysis is extremely fact-specific, which means both that it is hard to predict in advance and that it will be expensive to prove. Finally, courts periodically hold or suggest that exact copying of entire works for commercial purposes is unfair regardless of the circumstances. This is an approach that should worry commercial Internet service providers—and perhaps others as well. See Lemley, Overlapping Copyrights, at 566-567.

Finally, it may be that, as a practical matter, even if what individual users are doing is illegal, no one will bother to sue. The harm caused by an individual browsing the Internet may not be great enough—or the potential damages large enough—to justify an infringement suit. This arguably explains the paucity of Internet copyright decisions to date.

While individuals may take some solace in that fact, it will not always protect them. Statutory damages can mount up quickly in some cases of infringement. See Playboy v. Sanfilipo, —F. Supp.— (1998) (awarding minimum statutory damages of over $3 million for the copying of numerous Playboy photographs). Further, as the lead case in the next Section indicates, copyright plaintiffs do not always sue for monetary reasons.

4. Another copyright issue that comes up with regularity on the Net, at least in theory, is the problem of caching. Trotter Hardy describes the issue as follows:

> Computerized information traveling over a network like the Internet sometimes arrives at its destination quickly and sometimes slowly—often painfully slowly, as any frequent "surfer" on the World Wide Web can attest. Speed of communications depends on many things: the speed of the computer that is providing the information initially; the speed of the slowest "link" in the network chain; the number of other users using the same computer or the same network at the same time; and so on. Other things being equal, if a unit of information can originate at a point closer to the ultimate consumer rather than farther, or from a computer that is faster or less congested than another, the consumer will be able to obtain it more quickly.
>
> Mechanisms to do that—to store information temporarily "closer" to the consumer or on a more powerful or less congested computer, in order to speed up access—are generally referred to as "caching."
>
> The concept of a "temporary" storage location or "cache" for computer-handled information has a wide variety of interpretations. Do we mean "temporary" in human time? Then perhaps a cache would last a few days. Or do we mean "temporary" in computer time, which might mean a few milliseconds. Or do we mean something in between: seconds, minutes, or hours. All of these differing times can be and often are thought of as "caching," which perhaps means like beauty, "temporariness" is in the eye of the beholder.
>
> Whenever a temporary—however defined—copy of information is created, it will likely be a copy not just for computer purposes, but also for copyright purposes.

I. Trotter Hardy, Computer RAM "Copies": A Hit or a Myth? Historical Perspectives on Caching as a Microcosm of Current Copyright Concerns, 22 U. Dayton L. Rev. 423 (1997). Hardy suggests that this is not a problem, because caching can in fact do harm to the copyright owner (by skewing hit counts on a Web site, for example), and because in any event we should expect efficient caching to be licensed.

Do you agree? Is there anything wrong with caching? Or is this just another example of conduct that is made illegal automatically by the rule in *MAI*, without much thought to whether it ought to be considered infringement? See David Hayes, Advanced Copyright Issues on the Internet, 7 Tex. Intell. Prop. L.J. 1 (1998).

The Digital Millennium Copyright Act, passed by Congress in 1998, creates a limited safe harbor for one type of caching—automatic and temporary caching done by an Internet service provider. See 17 U.S.C. §512(b). More detail on the ISP safe harbors is given in the next Section.

5. Not all Internet copyright issues originate online. One recent set of disputes has pitted authors against publishers who make their back issues available online, either over the Web or in proprietary databases. The Second Circuit held in Tasini v. New York Times, 192 F.3d 356 (2d Cir. 1999) that a license to publish a copyrighted work that was silent on the issue of electronic rights did not give the publisher a right to move the print work online. If widely adopted, this decision may make it difficult to put archives of previously published material online. (Presumably, contracts signed in the future will treat the issue of electronic rights expressly.)

2. Indirect and Contributory Infringement

Most of the early Internet copyright disputes came up in the context of the liability not of those who posted or downloaded infringing material, but of the ISPs or other intermediaries who passed it on. The reason for this is simple: ISPs had deeper pockets than most individual defendants.

The law of ISP liability was significantly changed in 1998, when Congress passed the Digital Millennium Copyright Act, discussed in detail below. The case that follows is still important, however, not only because it sets out the rules that apply to non-ISPs, but because it frames the debate over liability for serving as an intermediary.

≡ *Religious Technology Center v. Netcom On-Line*
≡ *Communication Services, Inc.*
≡ **United States District Court for the Northern District of California**
≡ **907 F. Supp. 1361 (N.D. Cal. 1995)**

RONALD M. WHYTE, United States District Judge.

This case concerns an issue of first impression regarding intellectual property rights in cyberspace. Specifically, this order addresses whether the operator of a computer bulletin board service ("BBS"), and the large Internet access provider that allows that BBS to reach the Internet, should be liable for copyright infringement committed by a subscriber of the BBS.

Plaintiffs Religious Technology Center ("RTC") and Bridge Publications, Inc. ("BPI") hold copyrights in the unpublished and published works of L. Ron Hubbard, the late founder of the Church of Scientology ("the Church"). Defendant Dennis Erlich ("Erlich") is a former minister of Scientology turned vocal critic of the Church, whose pulpit is now the Usenet newsgroup alt.religion.scientology ("a.r.s."), an on-line forum for discussion and criticism of Scientology. Plaintiffs maintain that Erlich infringed their copyrights when he posted portions of their works on a.r.s. Erlich gained his access to the Internet through defendant Thomas Klemesrud's ("Klemesrud's") BBS "support.com." Klemesrud is the operator of the BBS, which is run out of his home and has approximately 500 paying users. Klemesrud's BBS is not directly linked to the Internet, but gains its connection through the facilities of defendant Netcom On-Line Communications, Inc. ("Netcom"), one of the largest providers of Internet access in the United States.

After failing to convince Erlich to stop his postings, plaintiffs contacted defendants Klemesrud and Netcom. Klemesrud responded to plaintiffs' demands that Erlich be kept off his system by asking plaintiffs to prove that they owned the copyrights to the works posted by Erlich. However, plaintiffs refused Klemesrud's request as unreasonable. Netcom similarly refused plaintiffs' request that Erlich not be allowed to gain access to the Internet through its system. Netcom contended that it would be impossible to prescreen Erlich's postings and that to kick Erlich off the Internet meant kicking off the hundreds of users of Klemesrud's BBS. Consequently, plaintiffs named Klemesrud and Netcom in their suit against Erlich, although only on the copyright infringement claims.

On June 23, 1995, this court heard the parties' arguments on eight motions, three of which relate to Netcom and Klemesrud and are discussed in this order: (1) Netcom's motion for summary judgment; (2) Klemesrud's motion for judgment on the pleadings; and (3) plaintiffs' motion for a preliminary injunction against Netcom and Klemesrud. For the reasons set forth below, the court grants in part and denies in part Netcom's motion for summary judgment and Klemesrud's motion for judgment on the pleadings and denies plaintiffs' motion for a preliminary injunction.

I. Netcom's Motion for Summary Judgment of Noninfringement . . .

B. *Copyright Infringement* . . .

1. Direct Infringement

Infringement consists of the unauthorized exercise of one of the exclusive rights of the copyright holder delineated in section 106. 17 U.S.C.

§501. Direct infringement does not require intent or any particular state of mind, although willfulness is relevant to the award of statutory damages. 17 U.S.C. §504(c). . . .

a. Undisputed Facts

The parties do not dispute the basic processes that occur when Erlich posts his allegedly infringing messages to a.r.s. Erlich connects to Klemesrud's BBS using a telephone and a modem. Erlich then transmits his messages to Klemesrud's computer, where they are automatically briefly stored. According to a prearranged pattern established by Netcom's software, Erlich's initial act of posting a message to the Usenet results in the automatic copying of Erlich's message from Klemesrud's computer onto Netcom's computer and onto other computers on the Usenet. In order to ease transmission and for the convenience of Usenet users, Usenet servers maintain postings from newsgroups for a short period of time—eleven days for Netcom's system and three days for Klemesrud's system. Once on Netcom's computers, messages are available to Netcom's customers and Usenet neighbors, who may then download the messages to their own computers. Netcom's local server makes available its postings to a group of Usenet servers, which do the same for other servers until all Usenet sites worldwide have obtained access to the postings, which takes a matter of hours.

Unlike some other large on-line service providers, such as CompuServe, America Online, and Prodigy, Netcom does not create or control the content of the information available to its subscribers. It also does not monitor messages as they are posted. It has, however, suspended the accounts of subscribers who violated its terms and conditions, such as where they had commercial software in their posted files. Netcom admits that, although not currently configured to do this, it may be possible to reprogram its system to screen postings containing particular words or coming from particular individuals. Netcom, however, took no action after it was told by plaintiffs that Erlich had posted messages through Netcom's system that violated plaintiffs' copyrights, instead claiming that it could not shut out Erlich without shutting out all of the users of Klemesrud's BBS.

b. Creation of Fixed Copies

The Ninth Circuit addressed the question of what constitutes infringement in the context of storage of digital information in a computer's random access memory ("RAM"). MAI Systems Corp. v. Peak Computer, Inc., 991 F.2d 511, 518 (9th Cir. 1993). In *MAI*, the Ninth Circuit upheld a finding of copyright infringement where a repair person, who was not authorized to use the computer owner's licensed operating system software, turned on the computer, thus loading the operating system into RAM for long enough to check an "error log." *Id.* at 518-19. Copyright protection subsists in original works of authorship "fixed in any tangible medium of expression, now known or later developed, from which they can be perceived, reproduced, or otherwise communicated, either directly or with the aid of a machine or device." 17 U.S.C. §102. A work is "fixed" when its "embodiment in a copy . . . is sufficiently permanent or stable to permit it to be perceived, reproduced, or otherwise communicated for a period of more than transitory duration." *Id.* §101. *MAI* established that the loading of data from a storage device into RAM constitutes copying because that data stays in RAM long enough for it to be perceived. *MAI Systems*, 991 F.2d at 518.

In the present case, there is no question after *MAI* that "copies" were created, as Erlich's act of sending a message to a.r.s. caused reproductions of portions of plaintiffs' works on both Klemesrud's and Netcom's storage devices. Even though the messages remained on their systems for at most eleven days, they were sufficiently "fixed" to constitute recognizable copies under the Copyright Act. See Information Infrastructure Task Force, Intellectual Property and the National Information Infrastructure: The Report of the Working Group on Intellectual Property Rights 66 (1995) ("IITF Report").

c. Is Netcom Directly Liable for Making the Copies?

Accepting that copies were made, Netcom argues that Erlich, and not Netcom, is directly liable for the copying. *MAI* did not address the question raised in this case: whether possessors of computers are liable for incidental copies automatically made on their computers using their software as part of a process initiated by a third party. Netcom correctly distinguishes *MAI* on the ground that Netcom did not take any affirmative action that directly resulted in copying plaintiffs' works other than by installing and maintaining a system whereby software automatically forwards messages received from subscribers onto the Usenet, and temporarily stores copies on its system. Netcom's actions, to the extent that they created a copy of plaintiffs' works, are necessary to having a working system for transmitting Usenet postings to and from the Internet. Unlike the defendants in *MAI*, neither Netcom nor Klemesrud initiated the copying. The defendants in *MAI* turned on their customers' computers thereby creating temporary copies of the operating system, whereas Netcom's and Klemesrud's systems can operate without any human intervention. Thus, unlike *MAI*, the mere fact that Netcom's system incidentally makes temporary copies of plaintiffs' works does not mean Netcom has caused the copying. The court believes that Netcom's act of designing or implementing a system that automatically and uniformly creates temporary copies of all data sent through it is not unlike that of the owner of a copying machine who lets the public make copies with it.[12] Although some of the people using the machine may directly infringe copyrights, courts analyze the machine owner's liability under the rubric of contributory infringement, not direct infringement. See, e.g., RCA Records v. All-Fast Systems, Inc., 594 F. Supp. 335 (S.D.N.Y. 1984); 3 Melville B. Nimmer & David Nimmer, Nimmer on Copyright §12.04[A][2][b], at 12-78 to -79 (1995) ("Nimmer on Copyright"); *Elkin-Koren*, supra, at 363 (arguing that "contributory infringement is more appropriate for dealing with BBS liability, first, because it focuses attention on the BBS-users relationship and the way imposing liability on BBS operators may shape this relationship, and second because it better addresses the complexity of the relationship between BBS operators and subscribers"). Plaintiffs' theory would create many separate acts of infringement and, carried to its natural extreme, would lead to unreasonable liability. It is not difficult to conclude that Erlich infringes by copying a protected work onto his computer and by posting a message to a newsgroup. However, plaintiffs' theory further implicates a Usenet server that carries Erlich's message to other servers regardless of whether that server acts without any human intervention beyond the initial setting up of the system. It would also result in liability for every single Usenet server in the worldwide link of computers transmitting Erlich's message to every other computer. These parties, who are liable under plaintiffs' theory, do no

---

12. Netcom compares itself to a common carrier that merely acts as a passive conduit for information. In a sense, a Usenet server that forwards all messages acts like a common carrier, passively retransmitting every message that gets sent through it. Netcom would seem no more liable than the phone company for carrying an infringing facsimile transmission or storing an infringing audio recording on its voice mail. As Netcom's counsel argued, holding such a server liable would be like holding the owner of the highway, or at least the operator of a toll booth, liable for the criminal activities that occur on its roads. Since other similar carriers of information are not liable for infringement, there is some basis for exempting Internet access providers from liability for infringement by their users. The IITF Report concluded that "if an entity provided only the wires and conduit—such as the telephone company, it would have a good argument for an exemption if it was truly in the same position as a common carrier and could not control who or what was on its system." IITF Report at 122. Here, perhaps, the analogy is not completely appropriate as Netcom does more than just "provide the wire and conduits." Further, Internet providers are not natural monopolies that are bound to carry all the traffic that one wishes to pass through them, as with the usual common carrier. See *id.* at 122 n.392 (citing Federal Communications Commission v. Midwest Video Corp., 440 U.S. 689, 701, 59 L. Ed. 2d 692, 99 S. Ct. 1435 (1979)). Section 111 of the Copyright Act codifies the exemption for passive carriers who are otherwise liable for a secondary transmission. 3 Melville B. Nimmer & David Nimmer, Nimmer on Copyright §12.04[B][3], at 12-99 (1995). However, the carrier must not have any direct or indirect control over the content or selection of the primary transmission. *Id.*; 17 U.S.C. §111(a)(3). Cf. infra part I.B.3.a. In any event, common carriers are granted statutory exemptions for liability that might otherwise exist. Here, Netcom does not fall under this statutory exemption, and thus faces the usual strict liability scheme that exists for copyright. Whether a new exemption should be carved out for online service providers is to be resolved by Congress, not the courts. Compare Comment, "Online Service Providers and Copyright Law: The Need for Change," 1 Syracuse J. Legis. & Pol'y 197, 202 (1995) (citing recommendations of online service providers for amending the Copyright Act to create liability only where a "provider has actual knowledge that a work is being or has been transmitted onto, or stored on, its system is infringing, and has the 'ability and authority' to stop the transmission, and has, after a reasonable amount of time, allowed the infringing activity to continue") with IITF Report at 122 (recommending that Congress not exempt service providers from strict liability for direct infringements).

more than operate or implement a system that is essential if Usenet messages are to be widely distributed. There is no need to construe the Act to make all of these parties infringers. Although copyright is a strict liability statute, there should still be some element of volition or causation which is lacking where a defendant's system is merely used to create a copy by a third party.

Plaintiffs point out that the infringing copies resided for eleven days on Netcom's computer and were sent out from it onto the "Information Superhighway." However, under plaintiffs' theory, any storage of a copy that occurs in the process of sending a message to the Usenet is an infringement. While it is possible that less "damage" would have been done if Netcom had heeded plaintiffs' warnings and acted to prevent Erlich's message from being forwarded, this is not relevant to its direct liability for copying. The same argument is true of Klemesrud and any Usenet server. Whether a defendant makes a direct copy that constitutes infringement cannot depend on whether it received a warning to delete the message. See D.C. Comics, Inc. v. Mini Gift, 912 F.2d 29, 35 (2d Cir. 1990). This distinction may be relevant to contributory infringement, however, where knowledge is an element. See infra part I.B.2.a.

The court will now consider two district court opinions that have addressed the liability of BBS operators for infringing files uploaded by subscribers.

d.   Playboy Case

Playboy Enterprises, Inc. v. Frena involved a suit against the operator of a small BBS whose system contained files of erotic pictures. 839 F. Supp. 1552, 1554 (M.D. Fla. 1993). A subscriber of the defendant's BBS had uploaded files containing digitized pictures copied from the plaintiff's copyrighted magazine, which files remained on the BBS for other subscribers to download. *Id.* The court did not conclude, as plaintiffs suggest in this case, that the BBS is itself liable for the unauthorized reproduction of plaintiffs' work; instead, the court concluded that the BBS operator was liable for violating the plaintiff's right to publicly distribute and display copies of its work. *Id.* at 1556-57.

In support of their argument that Netcom is directly liable for copying plaintiffs' works, plaintiffs cite to the court's conclusion that "there is no dispute that [the BBS operator] supplied a product containing unauthorized copies of a copyrighted work. It does not matter that [the BBS operator] claims he did not make the copies himself." *Id.* at 1556. It is clear from the context of this discussion that the Playboy court was looking only at the exclusive right to distribute copies to the public, where liability exists regardless of whether the defendant makes copies. Here, however, plaintiffs do not argue that Netcom is liable for its public distribution of copies. Instead, they claim that Netcom is liable because its computers in fact made copies. Therefore, the above-quoted language has no bearing on the issue of direct liability for unauthorized reproductions. Notwithstanding *Playboy*'s holding that a BBS operator may be directly liable for distributing or displaying to the public copies of protected works, this court holds that the storage on a defendant's system of infringing copies and retransmission to other servers is not a direct infringement by the BBS operator of the exclusive right to reproduce the work where such copies are uploaded by an infringing user. *Playboy* does not hold otherwise.

e. *Sega* Case

A court in this district addressed the issue of whether a BBS operator is liable for copyright infringement where it solicited subscribers to upload files containing copyrighted materials to the BBS that were available for others to download. Sega Enterprises Ltd. v. MAPHIA, 857 F. Supp. 679, 683 (N.D. Cal. 1994). The defendant's "MAPHIA" BBS contained copies of plaintiff Sega's video game programs that were uploaded by users. *Id.* at 683. The defendant solicited the uploading of such programs and received consideration for the right to download files. *Id.* Access was given for a fee or to those purchasing the defendant's hardware device that allowed Sega video game cartridges to be copied. *Id.* at 683-84. The court granted a preliminary injunction against the defendant, finding that plaintiffs had shown a prima facie case of direct and contributory infringement. *Id.* at 687. The court found that copies were made by unknown users of the BBS when files were uploaded and downloaded. *Id.* Further, the court found that the defendant's knowledge of the infringing activities, encouragement, direction and provision of the facilities through his operation of the BBS constituted contributory infringement, even though the defendant did not know exactly when files were uploaded or downloaded. *Id.* at 686-87.

This court is not convinced that *Sega* provides support for a finding of direct infringement where copies are made on a defendant's BBS by users who upload files. Although there is some language in *Sega* regarding direct infringement, it is entirely conclusory:

> Sega has established a prima facie case of direct copyright infringement under 17 U.S.C. §501. Sega has established that unauthorized copies of its games are made when such games are uploaded to the MAPHIA bulletin board, here with the knowledge of Defendant Scherman. These games are thereby placed on the storage media of the electronic bulletin board by unknown users.

Id. at 686. The court's reference to the "knowledge of Defendant" indicates that the court was focusing on contributory infringement, as knowledge is not an element of direct infringement. Perhaps, *Sega*'s references to direct infringement and that "copies . . . are made" are to the direct liability of the "unknown users," as there can be no contributory infringement by a defendant without direct infringement by another. See 3 Nimmer on

Copyright §12.04[A][3][a], at 12-89. Thus, the court finds that neither *Playboy* nor *Sega* requires finding Netcom liable for direct infringement of plaintiffs' exclusive right to reproduce their works.[17]

f. Public Distribution and Display?

Plaintiffs allege that Netcom is directly liable for making copies of their works. They also allege that Netcom violated their exclusive rights to publicly display copies of their works. There are no allegations that Netcom violated plaintiffs' exclusive right to publicly distribute their works. However, in their discussion of direct infringement, plaintiffs insist that Netcom is liable for "maintaining copies of [Erlich's] messages on its server for eleven days for access by its subscribers and 'USENET neighbors'" and they compare this case to the *Playboy* case, which discussed the right of public distribution. Plaintiffs also argued this theory of infringement at oral argument. Because this could be an attempt to argue that Netcom has infringed plaintiffs' rights of public distribution and display, the court will address these arguments.

Playboy concluded that the defendant infringed the plaintiff's exclusive rights to publicly distribute and display copies of its works. 839 F. Supp. at 1556-57. The court is not entirely convinced that the mere possession of a digital copy on a BBS that is accessible to some members of the public constitutes direct infringement by the BBS operator. Such a holding suffers from the same problem of causation as the reproduction argument. Only the subscriber should be liable for causing the distribution of plaintiffs' work, as the contributing actions of the BBS provider are automatic and indiscriminate. Erlich could have posted his messages through countless access providers and the outcome would be the same: anyone with access to Usenet newsgroups would be able to read his messages. There is no logical reason to draw a line around Netcom and Klemesrud and say that they are uniquely responsible for distributing Erlich's messages. Netcom is not even the first link in the chain of distribution—Erlich had no direct relationship with Netcom but dealt solely with Klemesrud's BBS, which used Netcom to gain its Internet access. Every Usenet server has a role in the distribution, so plaintiffs' argument would create unreasonable liability. Where the BBS merely stores and passes along all messages sent by its subscribers and others, the BBS should not be seen as causing these works to be publicly distributed or displayed.

Even accepting the *Playboy* court's holding, the case is factually distinguishable. Unlike the BBS in that case, Netcom does not maintain an

---

17. To the extent that *Sega* holds that BBS operators are directly liable for copyright infringement when users upload infringing works to their systems, this court respectfully disagrees with the court's holding for the reasons discussed above. Further, such a holding was dicta, as there was evidence that the defendant knew of the infringing uploads by users and, in fact, actively encouraged such activity, thus supporting the contributory infringement theory. *Id*. at 683.

archive of files for its users. Thus, it cannot be said to be "supplying a product." In contrast to some of its larger competitors, Netcom does not create or control the content of the information available to its subscribers; it merely provides access to the Internet, whose content is controlled by no single entity. Although the Internet consists of many different computers networked together, some of which may contain infringing files, it does not make sense to hold the operator of each computer liable as an infringer merely because his or her computer is linked to a computer with an infringing file. It would be especially inappropriate to hold liable a service that acts more like a conduit, in other words, one that does not itself keep an archive of files for more than a short duration. Finding such a service liable would involve an unreasonably broad construction of public distribution and display rights. No purpose would be served by holding liable those who have no ability to control the information to which their subscribers have access, even though they might be in some sense helping to achieve the Internet's automatic "public distribution" and the users' "public" display of files.

g. Conclusion

The court is not persuaded by plaintiffs' argument that Netcom is directly liable for the copies that are made and stored on its computer. Where the infringing subscriber is clearly directly liable for the same act, it does not make sense to adopt a rule that could lead to the liability of countless parties whose role in the infringement is nothing more than setting up and operating a system that is necessary for the functioning of the Internet. Such a result is unnecessary as there is already a party directly liable for causing the copies to be made. Plaintiffs occasionally claim that they only seek to hold liable a party that refuses to delete infringing files after they have been warned. However, such liability cannot be based on a theory of direct infringement, where knowledge is irrelevant. The court does not find workable a theory of infringement that would hold the entire Internet liable for activities that cannot reasonably be deterred. Billions of bits of data flow through the Internet and are necessarily stored on servers throughout the network and it is thus practically impossible to screen out infringing bits from noninfringing bits. Because the court cannot see any meaningful distinction (without regard to knowledge) between what Netcom did and what every other Usenet server does, the court finds that Netcom cannot be held liable for direct infringement. Cf. IITF Report at 69 (noting uncertainty regarding whether BBS operator should be directly liable for reproduction or distribution of files uploaded by a subscriber).

2. Contributory Infringement

Netcom is not free from liability just because it did not directly infringe plaintiffs' works; it may still be liable as a contributory infringer.

Although there is no statutory rule of liability for infringement committed by others,

> the absence of such express language in the copyright statute does not preclude the imposition of liability for copyright infringement on certain parties who have not themselves engaged in the infringing activity. For vicarious liability is imposed in virtually all areas of the law, and the concept of contributory infringement is merely a species of the broader problem of identifying the circumstances in which it is just to hold one individual accountable for the actions of another.

Sony Corp. v. Universal City Studios, Inc., 464 U.S. 417, 435, 78 L. Ed. 2d 574, 104 S. Ct. 774 (1984) (footnote omitted). Liability for participation in the infringement will be established where the defendant, "with knowledge of the infringing activity, induces, causes or materially contributes to the infringing conduct of another." Gershwin Publishing Corp. v. Columbia Artists Management, Inc., 443 F.2d 1159, 1162 (2d Cir. 1971).

a. Knowledge of Infringing Activity

Plaintiffs insist that Netcom knew that Erlich was infringing their copyrights at least after receiving notice from plaintiffs' counsel indicating that Erlich had posted copies of their works onto a.r.s. through Netcom's system. Despite this knowledge, Netcom continued to allow Erlich to post messages to a.r.s. and left the allegedly infringing messages on its system so that Netcom's subscribers and other Usenet servers could access them. Netcom argues that it did not possess the necessary type of knowledge because (1) it did not know of Erlich's planned infringing activities when it agreed to lease its facilities to Klemesrud, (2) it did not know that Erlich would infringe prior to any of his postings, (3) it is unable to screen out infringing postings before they are made, and (4) its knowledge of the infringing nature of Erlich's postings was too equivocal given the difficulty in assessing whether the registrations were valid and whether Erlich's use was fair. The court will address these arguments in turn.

Netcom cites cases holding that there is no contributory infringement by the lessors of premises that are later used for infringement unless the lessor had knowledge of the intended use at the time of the signing of the lease. See, e.g., Deutsch v. Arnold, 98 F.2d 686, 688 (2d Cir. 1938). The contribution to the infringement by the defendant in *Deutsch* was merely to lease use of the premises to the infringer. Here, Netcom not only leases space but also serves as an access provider, which includes the storage and transmission of information necessary to facilitate Erlich's postings to a.r.s. Unlike a landlord, Netcom retains some control over the use of its system. See infra part I.B.3.a. Thus, the relevant time frame for knowledge is not when Netcom entered into an agreement with Klemesrud. It should be when Netcom provided its services to allow Erlich to infringe plaintiffs' copyrights. Cf. Screen Gems-Columbia Music, Inc. v. Mark-Fi Records, Inc., 256 F. Supp. 399, 403 (S.D.N.Y. 1966) (analyzing knowledge at time that defendant rendered its particular service). It is undisputed that Netcom did not know that Erlich was infringing before it received notice from plaintiffs. Netcom points out that the alleged instances of infringement occurring on Netcom's system all happened prior to December 29, 1994, the date on which Netcom first received notice of plaintiffs' infringement claim against Erlich. Thus, there is no question of fact as to whether Netcom knew or should have known of Erlich's infringing activities that occurred more than 11 days before receipt of the December 28, 1994 letter.

However, the evidence reveals a question of fact as to whether Netcom knew or should have known that Erlich had infringed plaintiffs' copyrights following receipt of plaintiffs' letter. Because Netcom was arguably participating in Erlich's public distribution of plaintiffs' works, there is a genuine issue as to whether Netcom knew of any infringement by Erlich before it was too late to do anything about it. If plaintiffs can prove the knowledge element, Netcom will be liable for contributory infringement since its failure to simply cancel Erlich's infringing message and thereby stop an infringing copy from being distributed worldwide constitutes substantial participation in Erlich's public distribution of the message. Cf. R.T. Nimmer, The Law of Computer Technology ¶15.11B, at S15-42 (2d ed. 1994) (opining that "where information service is less directly involved in the enterprise of creating unauthorized copies a finding of contributory infringement is not likely").

Netcom argues that its knowledge after receiving notice of Erlich's alleged infringing activities was too equivocal given the difficulty in assessing whether registrations are valid and whether use is fair. Although a mere unsupported allegation of infringement by a copyright owner may not automatically put a defendant on notice of infringing activity, Netcom's position that liability must be unequivocal is unsupportable. While perhaps the typical infringing activities of BBSs will involve copying software, where BBS operators are better equipped to judge infringement, the fact that this involves written works should not distinguish it. Where works contain copyright notices within them, as here, it is difficult to argue that a defendant did not know that the works were copyrighted. To require proof of valid registrations would be impractical and would perhaps take too long to verify, making it impossible for a copyright holder to protect his or her works in some cases, as works are automatically deleted less than two weeks after they are posted. The court is more persuaded by the argument that it is beyond the ability of a BBS operator to quickly and fairly determine when a use is not infringement where there is at least a colorable claim of fair use. Where a BBS operator cannot reasonably verify a claim of infringement, either because of a possible fair use defense, the lack of copyright notices on the copies, or the copyright holder's failure to provide the necessary documentation to show that there is a likely infringement, the operator's lack of knowledge will be found reasonable and there will be no liability for contributory infringement for allowing the continued distribution of the works on its system.

Since Netcom was given notice of an infringement claim before Erlich had completed his infringing activity, there may be a question of fact as to whether Netcom knew or should have known that such activities were infringing. Given the context of a dispute between a former minister and a church he is criticizing, Netcom may be able to show that its lack of knowledge that Erlich was infringing was reasonable. However, Netcom admits that it did not even look at the postings once given notice and that had it looked at the copyright notice and statements regarding authorship it would have triggered an investigation into whether there was infringement. These facts are sufficient to raise a question as to Netcom's knowledge once it received a letter from plaintiffs on December 29, 1994.

b. Substantial Participation

Where a defendant has knowledge of the primary infringer's infringing activities, it will be liable if it "induces, causes or materially contributes to the infringing conduct of" the primary infringer. *Gershwin Publishing*, 443 F.2d at 1162. Such participation must be substantial. Apple Computer, Inc. v. Microsoft Corp., 821 F. Supp. 616, 625 (N.D. Cal. 1993), *aff'd*, 35 F.3d 1435 (9th Cir. 1994); Demetriades v. Kaufmann, 690 F. Supp. 289, 294 (S.D.N.Y. 1988).

Providing a service that allows for the automatic distribution of all Usenet postings, infringing and noninfringing, goes well beyond renting a premises to an infringer. See Fonovisa, Inc. v. Cherry Auction, Inc., 847 F. Supp. 1492, 1496 (E.D. Cal. 1994) (finding that renting space at swap meet to known bootleggers not "substantial participation" in the infringers' activities). It is more akin to the radio stations that were found liable for rebroadcasting an infringing broadcast. See, e.g., Select Theatres Corp. v. Ronzoni Macaroni Corp., 59 U.S.P.Q. 288, 291 (S.D.N.Y. 1943). Netcom allows Erlich's infringing messages to remain on its system and be further distributed to other Usenet servers worldwide. It does not completely relinquish control over how its system is used, unlike a landlord. Thus, it is fair, assuming Netcom is able to take simple measures to prevent further damage to plaintiffs' copyrighted works, to hold Netcom liable for contributory infringement where Netcom has knowledge of Erlich's infringing postings yet continues to aid in the accomplishment of Erlich's purpose of publicly distributing the postings. Accordingly, plaintiffs do raise a genuine issue of material fact as to their theory of contributory infringement as to the postings made after Netcom was on notice of plaintiffs' infringement claim.

3. Vicarious Liability

Even if plaintiffs cannot prove that Netcom is contributorily liable for its participation in the infringing activity, it may still seek to prove vicarious infringement based on Netcom's relationship to Erlich. A defendant is liable for vicarious liability for the actions of a primary infringer where the defendant (1) has the right and ability to control the infringer's acts and (2) receives a direct financial benefit from the infringement. See Shapiro, Bernstein & Co. v. H.L. Green Co., 316 F.2d 304, 306 (2d Cir. 1963). Unlike contributory infringement, knowledge is not an element of vicarious liability. 3 Nimmer on Copyright §12.04[A][1], at 12-70.

a. Right and Ability to Control

The first element of vicarious liability will be met if plaintiffs can show that Netcom has the right and ability to supervise the conduct of its subscribers. Netcom argues that it does not have the right to control its users' postings before they occur. Plaintiffs dispute this and argue that Netcom's terms and conditions, to which its subscribers[22] must agree, specify that Netcom reserves the right to take remedial action against subscribers. Plaintiffs argue that under "netiquette," the informal rules and customs that have developed on the Internet, violation of copyrights by a user is unacceptable and the access provider has a duty take measures to prevent this; where the immediate service provider fails, the next service provider up the transmission stream must act. Further evidence of Netcom's right to restrict infringing activity is its prohibition of copyright infringement and its requirement that its subscribers indemnify it for any damage to third parties. Plaintiffs have thus raised a question of fact as to Netcom's right to control Erlich's use of its services.

Netcom argues that it could not possibly screen messages before they are posted given the speed and volume of the data that goes through its system. Netcom further argues that it has never exercised control over the content of its users' postings. Plaintiffs' expert opines otherwise, stating that with an easy software modification Netcom could identify postings that contain particular words or come from particular individuals. Plaintiffs further dispute Netcom's claim that it could not limit Erlich's access to Usenet without kicking off all 500 subscribers of Klemesrud's BBS. As evidence that Netcom has in fact exercised its ability to police its users' conduct, plaintiffs cite evidence that Netcom has acted to suspend subscribers' accounts on over one thousand occasions. See Ex. J (listing suspensions of subscribers by Netcom for commercial advertising, posting obscene

---

22. In this case, Netcom is even further removed from Erlich's activities. Erlich was in a contractual relationship only with Klemesrud. Netcom thus dealt directly only with Klemesrud. However, it is not crucial that Erlich does not obtain access directly through Netcom. The issue is Netcom's right and ability to control the use of its system, which it can do indirectly by controlling Klemesrud's use.

materials, and off-topic postings). Further evidence shows that Netcom can delete specific postings. Whether such sanctions occurred before or after the abusive conduct is not material to whether Netcom can exercise control. The court thus finds that plaintiffs have raised a genuine issue of fact as to whether Netcom has the right and ability to exercise control over the activities of its subscribers, and of Erlich in particular.

b. Direct Financial Benefit

Plaintiffs must further prove that Netcom receives a direct financial benefit from the infringing activities of its users. For example, a landlord who has the right and ability to supervise the tenant's activities is vicariously liable for the infringements of the tenant where the rental amount is proportional to the proceeds of the tenant's sales. *Shapiro, Bernstein*, 316 F.2d at 306. However, where a defendant rents space or services on a fixed rental fee that does not depend on the nature of the activity of the lessee, courts usually find no vicarious liability because there is no direct financial benefit from the infringement. See, e.g., Roy Export Co. v. Trustees of Columbia University, 344 F. Supp. 1350, 1353 (S.D.N.Y. 1972) (finding no vicarious liability of university because no financial benefit from allowing screening of bootlegged films); *Fonovisa*, 847 F. Supp. at 1496 (finding swap meet operators did not financially benefit from fixed fee); see also Kelly Tickle, Comment, The Vicarious Liability of Electronic Bulletin Board Operators for the Copyright Infringement Occurring on Their Bulletin Boards, 80 Iowa L. Rev. 391, 415 (1995) (arguing that BBS operators "lease cyberspace" and should thus be treated like landlords, who are not liable for infringement that occurs on their premises).

Plaintiffs argue that courts will find a financial benefit despite fixed fees. In Polygram International Publishing, Inc. v. Nevada/TIG, Inc., 855 F. Supp. 1314, 1330-33 (D. Mass. 1994), the court found a trade show organizer vicariously liable for the infringing performance of an exhibitor because, although the infringement did not affect the fixed rental fee received by the organizers, the organizers benefitted from the performances, which helped make the show a financial success. But see Artists Music, Inc. v. Reed Publishing, Inc., 1994 U.S. Dist. LEXIS 6395, 31 U.S.P.Q.2D (BNA) 1623, 1994 WL 191643, at *6 (S.D.N.Y. 1994) (finding no vicarious liability for trade show organizers where revenues not increased because of infringing music performed by exhibitors). Plaintiffs cite two other cases where, despite fixed fees, defendants received financial benefits from allowing groups to perform infringing works over the radio without having to get an ASCAP license, which minimized the defendants' expenses. See Boz Scaggs Music v. KND Corp, 491 F. Supp. 908, 913 (D. Conn. 1980); Realsongs v. Gulf Broadcasting Corp., 824 F. Supp. 89, 92 (M.D. La. 1993). Plaintiffs' cases are factually distinguishable. Plaintiffs cannot provide any evidence of a direct financial benefit received by Netcom from Erlich's infringing postings. Unlike *Shapiro, Bernstein*, and like

Fonovisa, Netcom receives a fixed fee. There is no evidence that infringement by Erlich, or any other user of Netcom's services, in any way enhances the value of Netcom's services to subscribers or attracts new subscribers. Plaintiffs argue, however, that Netcom somehow derives a benefit from its purported "policy of refusing to take enforcement actions against its subscribers and others who transmit infringing messages over its computer networks." Plaintiffs point to Netcom's advertisements that, compared to competitors like CompuServe and America Online, Netcom provides easy, regulation-free Internet access. Plaintiffs assert that Netcom's policy attracts copyright infringers to its system, resulting in a direct financial benefit. The court is not convinced that such an argument, if true, would constitute a direct financial benefit to Netcom from Erlich's infringing activities. See *Fonovisa*, 847 F. Supp. at 1496 (finding no direct financial benefit despite argument that lessees included many vendors selling counterfeit goods and that clientele sought "bargain basement prices"). Further, plaintiffs' argument is not supported by probative evidence. The only "evidence" plaintiffs cite for their supposition is the declaration of their counsel, Elliot Abelson, who states that

> on April 7, 1995, in a conversation regarding Netcom's position related to this case, Randolf Rice, attorney for Netcom, informed me that Netcom's executives are happy about the publicity it is receiving in the press as a result of this case. Mr. Rice also told me that Netcom was concerned that it would lose business if it took action against Erlich or Klemesrud in connection with Erlich's infringements.

Netcom objects to this declaration as hearsay and as inadmissible evidence of statements made in compromise negotiations. Fed. R. Ev. 801, 408. Whether or not this declaration is admissible, it does not support plaintiffs' argument that Netcom either has a policy of not enforcing violations of copyright laws by its subscribers or, assuming such a policy exists, that Netcom's policy directly financially benefits Netcom, such as by attracting new subscribers. Because plaintiffs have failed to raise a question of fact on this vital element, their claim of vicarious liability fails. See *Roy Export*, 344 F. Supp. at 1353.

4. First Amendment Argument

Netcom argues that plaintiffs' theory of liability contravenes the first amendment, as it would chill the use of the Internet because every access provider or user would be subject to liability when a user posts an infringing work to a Usenet newsgroup. While the court agrees that an overbroad injunction might implicate the First Amendment, see In re Capital Cities/ABC, Inc., 918 F.2d 140, 144 (11th Cir. 1990), imposing liability for infringement where it is otherwise appropriate does not necessarily raise a First Amendment issue. The copyright concepts of the idea/expression dichotomy and the fair use defense balance the important First Amendment rights with the constitutional authority for "promoting the progress of science and useful arts," U.S. Const. art. I, §8, cl. 8; 1 Nimmer on Copyright §1.10[B], at 1-71 to -83. Netcom argues that liability here would force Usenet servers to perform the impossible—screening all the information that comes through their systems. However, the court is not convinced that Usenet servers are directly liable for causing a copy to be made, and absent evidence of knowledge and participation or control and direct profit, they will not be contributorily or vicariously liable. If Usenet servers were responsible for screening all messages coming through their systems, this could have a serious chilling effect on what some say may turn out to be the best public forum for free speech yet devised. See Jerry Berman & Daniel J. Weitzner, Abundance and User Control: Renewing the Democratic Heart of the First Amendment in the Age of Interactive Media, 104 Yale L.J. 1619, 1624 (1995) (praising decentralized networks for opening access to all with no entity stifling independent sources of speech); Rose, supra, at 4.[25] Finally, Netcom admits that its First Amendment argument is merely a consideration in the fair use argument. . . .

C. Conclusion

The court finds that plaintiffs have raised a genuine issue of fact regarding whether Netcom should have known that Erlich was infringing their copyrights after receiving a letter from plaintiffs, whether Netcom substantially participated in the infringement, and whether Netcom has a valid fair use defense. Accordingly, Netcom is not entitled to summary

---

25. Netcom additionally argues that plaintiffs' theory of liability would have a chilling effect on users, who would be liable for merely browsing infringing works. Browsing technically causes an infringing copy of the digital information to be made in the screen memory. *MAI* holds that such a copy is fixed even when information is temporarily placed in RAM, such as the screen RAM. The temporary copying involved in browsing is only necessary because humans cannot otherwise perceive digital information. It is the functional equivalent of reading, which does not implicate the copyright laws and may be done by anyone in a library without the permission of the copyright owner. However, it can be argued that the effects of digital browsing are different because millions can browse a single copy of a work in cyberspace, while only one can read a library's copy at a time.

Absent a commercial or profit-depriving use, digital browsing is probably a fair use; there could hardly be a market for licensing the temporary copying of digital works onto computer screens to allow browsing. Unless such a use is commercial, such as where someone reads a copyrighted work online and therefore decides not to purchase a copy from the copyright owner, fair use is likely. Until reading a work online becomes as easy and convenient as reading a paperback, copyright owners do not have much to fear from digital browsing and there will not likely be much market effect.

Additionally, unless a user has reason to know, such as from the title of a message, that the message contains copyrighted materials, the browser will be protected by the innocent infringer doctrine, which allows the court to award no damages in appropriate circumstances. In any event, users should hardly worry about a finding of direct infringement; it seems highly unlikely from a practical matter that a copyright owner could prove such infringement or would want to sue such an individual.

judgment on plaintiffs' claim of contributory copyright infringement. However, plaintiffs' claims of direct and vicarious infringement fail.

COMMENTS AND QUESTIONS

1. The issue of ISP liability for passing through messages has been significantly affected by the passage of the Digital Millennium Copyright Act (DMCA), which provides limited safe harbors for ISPs. The DMCA limits the liability of what it terms "online service providers" (OSPs) for messages posted to their systems in a variety of circumstances. "Online service provider" is defined broadly to include not only companies in the business of providing Internet access, but also any entity that provides services "such as Internet access, email, chat room and Web page hosting," even if that is not their primary business. 17 U.S.C. §512(k)(1). Thus universities or companies may fall within the exemption even though the hosting of discussion fora or the provision of email services are incidental to their main mission.

The conditions for exemption are complex. To qualify for the general exemptions, OSPs must accommodate "standard" technological copy protection measures, such as encryption and digital watermarking. 17 U.S.C. §512(i)(2). OSPs must also agree to terminate users who repeatedly infringe copyright rights on the system. However, the OSP need not actively monitor messages on its system in an attempt to identify copyright infringements.

For messages posted to an OSP's system or links provided to infringing material by the OSP, the exemption provides that OSPs generally will not be liable for copyright infringement if they did not know and could not reasonably have known that the material was infringing. However, OSPs that learn of infringement must act expeditiously to remove or block access to the infringing material. In addition, the DMCA creates a "notice and take down" rule. Under this rule, an OSP that receives written notice that material on its system is infringing must remove the material as soon as practicable. The OSP must also notify the poster of that material that it has been taken down and give the poster an opportunity to respond. If the poster responds by giving "counter notification" that the material is not copyrighted or is lawfully used, the OSP must put the material back on its system within 10 to 14 days unless the copyright owner files suit against the poster.

The DMCA also creates exemptions for OSPs who do nothing more than automatically route information through their systems without modifying or redirecting it and also limited exemptions for certain types of caching of information.

2. The first two cases to consider the issue of BBS and ISP liability were Playboy v. Frena and Sega v. MAPHIA, both discussed in the *RTC* decision. In both decisions, the courts concluded that the owners of BBSs

were directly liable for copyright infringement. Thus, the early development of copyright law on the Internet seemed to point in the direction of massive, systemic liability for infringement without regard to fault.

While the Clinton Administration endorsed this position in its White Paper on intellectual property and the National Information Infrastructure (NII), the White Paper approach has been roundly condemned by most commentators. See, e.g., 3 Nimmer on Copyright §12.04[A][2][b], at 12-78 to 12-79 (1995); Henry H. Perritt Jr., Law and the Information Superhighway 430 (1996); Lance Rose, Netlaw 91-92 (1995); Edward A. Cavazos & G. Chin Chao, System Operator Liability for a User's Copyright Infringement, 4 Tex. Intell. Prop. L.J. 13 (1995); Niva Elkin-Koren, Copyright Law and Social Dialogue on the Information Superhighway: The Case Against Copyright Liability of Bulletin Board Operators, 13 Cardozo Arts & Ent. L.J. 346, 390 (1995). The issue was debated (but not resolved) in Congress in 1996, when Congress failed to take action on the government's National Information Infrastructure Copyright Protection Act. A similar provision was introduced before the World Intellectual Property Organization in 1996 and was defeated there. For subsequent developments on the issue, see the Note on the Digital Millennium Copyright Act below.

Since *Netcom*, most courts to consider the issue have rejected the *Frena* approach in favor of *Netcom*'s. The court in Sega v. MAPHIA reversed itself, issuing a permanent injunction based solely on a finding of inducement and contributory, rather than direct, infringement. Sega of America v. MAPHIA, 948 F. Supp. 923 (C.D. Cal. 1996). See also Marobie-FL Inc. v. National Ass'n of Fire Equipment Distributors, 983 F. Supp. 1167 (N.D. Ill. 1997) (following *Netcom*).

On the other hand, district courts in two cases involving copyrighted Playboy images have found direct infringement, even in circumstances where the defendant's role in providing the infringing material was less than clear. See Playboy Ents., Inc. v. Webbworld, 991 F. Supp. 543 (N.D. Tex. 1997) (reprinted above); Playboy Ents., Inc. v. Hardenburgh, 982 F. Supp. 503 (N.D. Ohio 1997). For an excellent treatment of the problems of indirect and contributory infringement in the Internet context, see Elkin-Koren, supra at 345.

3. Consider the breadth of the *Netcom* court's holding on vicarious liability. The court concludes that Netcom had the right and ability to control Erlich's posts but finds that it did not receive a direct financial benefit from the infringement. Suppose that Netcom charged its subscribers per posting they made, or per bit they downloaded. Would the result in the case change? Should it?

4. The *Netcom* court notes that the holding in Playboy v. Frena was based on liability for distribution and public display, while the RTC claimed that Netcom had engaged in reproduction. What difference (if any) does this make? On the interaction between the various rights in section 106 in the context of the Internet, see Mark A. Lemley, Dealing with Overlapping

Copyrights on the Internet, 22 U. Dayton L. Rev. 547 (1997); Jessica Litman, The Exclusive Right to Read, 13 Cardozo Arts & Ent. L.J. 29 (1994). Lemley argues that on the Internet, a single act (say, posting material on a Web page for download) may constitute reproduction, derivation, distribution, performance, display, *and* importation. The fact that the exclusive rights of copyright overlap on the Internet has some troubling consequences. In particular, it means that assignments and licenses of part, rather than all, of a copyright may be ineffective on the Internet and indeed may leave *no* party with the right to post material on the Web. It also means that certain specific copyright defenses, such as the "first sale" doctrine, are rendered ineffective on the Internet because they only apply to one of the exclusive rights, rather than all of them.

Is this a problem with copyright on the Internet? If so, what should be done about it?

5. How does the *Netcom* decision comport with the policies underlying the Copyright Act? On the one hand, it seems grossly unfair to hold Netcom liable for Internet postings that as a practical matter it could never effectively screen for copyright infringement. The case for shielding other parties from liability for direct infringement—such as those who own the routers through which the message passes—is even stronger. On the other hand, the practical effect of the court's holding may be that many copyright owners are unable to recoup their losses from infringement, because the individual who posts the infringing material is either unreachable by court, impecunious, or anonymous.

Which of these competing concerns is stronger? Is your answer affected by the possibility that ISPs could insure against liability? See I. Trotter Hardy, The Proper Legal Regime for Cyberspace, 55 U. Pitt. L. Rev. 993 (1994). Does the objection to holding Netcom liable reflect a more general objection to copyright's rather harsh rule of strict liability for direct infringement?

6. The court leaves open the possibility that Netcom may be liable for not removing the infringing posting after it was notified of the infringement. Consider the incentives this ruling creates for ISPs. What if Netcom was told that the work was an infringement but reasonably believed that Erlich's use of the Scientology materials was fair? Does Netcom have an obligation to take down the work? Does it have some duty to Erlich *not* to take it down? Holding Netcom liable for reasonable mistakes of law may create strong pressure to take down any work about which someone complains, even if the use would turn out to be allowable under copyright law.

7. Copyright infringement in some cases gives rise to criminal as well as civil liability. In United States v. Lamacchia, 871 F. Supp. 535 (D. Mass. 1995), the government prosecuted the operator of a bulletin board who encouraged the posting of copyrighted software without authorization from the copyright owners. The court dismissed the prosecution on the grounds that criminal copyright infringement requires that the copying be both willful and done for purposes of commercial gain. Lamacchia acted without

an intent to profit, and thus could not be liable for either criminal copyright infringement or for a series of related crimes with which he was charged. (Lamacchia could of course be civilly liable.) In 1997, Congress passed the No Electronic Theft Act, which overturned *Lamacchia* by providing that copyright infringement is a felony if the aggregate loss to the copyright owner from infringement exceeds $1,000, regardless of whether the defendant intended to (or did) profit from infringement. 17 U.S.C. §506(a)(2).

Note on the Digital Millennium Copyright Act and Copy Circumvention

In the last days of the 1998 congressional session, Congress passed sweeping changes to the Copyright Act designed specifically to address a variety of Internet-related copyright issues. The Act was nominally intended to bring U.S. law into compliance with the 1996 WIPO treaties on copyright and the Internet, but in fact it went well beyond what those treaties required. The DMCA changed Internet copyright law in three significant ways. One of those, the safe harbor for ISPs, is discussed above.

The second deals with the misuse or destruction of "copyright management information." Section 1202 of the Copyright Act makes it illegal to remove or alter copyright management information conveyed along with a copyrighted work or to provide false copyright management information. Copyright management information includes information that identifies the authors, owners, or performers in a work, and the terms and conditions under which a work may be used. The intent of this section is to punish those who facilitate counterfeiting by stripping identifying information from a work or who falsely identify themselves as the authors of a work. The literal terms of the Act may go further, however, creating a quasi-moral right of attribution and ensuring that "clickwrap licenses" remain embedded in a computer program.

The final (and most controversial) part of the DMCA are its provisions relating to the circumvention of copy protection technologies. The DMCA makes the circumvention of copy protection systems—or the manufacture or distribution of devices with the primary purpose or effect of circumventing copy protection systems—a crime if done without the authority of the copyright owner. 17 U.S.C.§1201(a), (b). Specifically, the statute makes it illegal to "circumvent a technological protection measure" that effectively controls access to a work. "Circumvention" means to "descramble a scrambled work, to decrypt an encrypted work, or otherwise avoid, bypass, remove, deactivate, or impair a technological protection measure." *Id.* §1201(a)(3).

This new statute marks a significant change in the balance between copyright owners and users in at least three respects. First, it reflects a rather striking decision to promote innovation by banning one class of innovations entirely—those that involve decryption technologies. If one thinks in terms of the competition between encryption technologies and decryption technologies as a sort of arms race, it can be said that the DMCA orders unilateral technological disarmament by the decrypters. Second, the statute changes the standard that has traditionally been applied to contributory infringement. The production of devices that facilitate infringement has always been illegal under copyright law, but only if the device produced is not "capable of a substantial noninfringing use." Sony Corp. v. Universal City Studios, 464 U.S. 417 (1984). The DMCA does not adopt this standard; instead, it adopts a broader definition of "illegal conduct," one that is closer to the dissent's "primary purpose or effect" test in *Sony*. The dissent in *Sony* would have applied that test to declare VCRs illegal. It remains to be seen what sorts of commercial devices will be swept into the DMCA's intermediate standard. Third, and perhaps most notable, the statute itself does not condition the illegality of circumvention on proof that the user violated the copyright laws. Indeed, someone who circumvents a copy protection measure in order to make lawful use of a work—to copy the ideas contained therein, for example, or to engage in fair use—has not violated the copyright laws, but has nonetheless committed a crime under the DMCA. Thus, while the statute purports not to affect the rights, remedies, limitations, or defenses of copyright law, 17 U.S.C. §1201(c), the protection provided by that section is illusory.

The power of the DMCA's prohibitions on circumvention is circumscribed by a number of exceptions that were written into the Act. In particular, section 1201(f) allows software developers to engage in reverse engineering of a computer program for the purpose of achieving interoperability between programs as long as copyright law would permit the reverse engineering and there is no other readily available means of obtaining that information. Other sections permit circumvention of copy protection systems for purposes of legitimate law enforcement and government intelligence activity, scientific research into encryption, and testing of the security of devices, and for various other reasons. 17 U.S.C. §1201(e)-(j). Further, the prohibitions on conduct by individuals—as opposed to the creation of circumventing devices—are stayed for two years, pending a report by the Library of Congress. The anticircumvention provisions are explained and criticized by Pamela Samuelson in the excerpt below.

━━━
━━━
━━━
━━━

Pamela Samuelson, Intellectual Property and the Digital Economy: Why the Anti-Circumvention Regulations Need to Be Revised
14 Berkeley Tech. L.J. 519 (1999)

. . . The DMCA ban on the act of circumventing technical protection systems is subject to seven very specific exceptions, as well as being qualified by several other subsections. In addition, it is subject to a two-year moratorium during which the Librarian of Congress is supposed to study the potential impact of the anti-circumvention ban on noninfringing uses of copyrighted works which may lead to further limitations on the act-of-circumvention rule. While several of these exceptions and limitations respond to the gravest of concerns expressed by digital economy firms, they are still too narrowly crafted, as examples given below will reveal. Congress should have adopted a provision enabling courts to exempt acts of circumvention engaged in for other legitimate purposes. Courts interpreting section 1201 may either be forced to find liability in some situations in which it would be inappropriate to impose it or to stretch existing limitations. Congress may eventually need to revise this provision to recognize a broader range of exceptions.

The structure of the final DMCA anti-circumvention provision and its complexity resulted from the maximalist position with which the Administration and its major copyright industry allies began the legislative struggle. Only when IT industry groups were able to identify particularized situations in which circumvention was appropriate was there any legislative "give" on the issue, and then only to the extent of that identified situation. As noted above, Clinton Administration officials initially sought an almost unlimited ban of circumvention activities. The only exception to the circumvention ban in the Administration's favored legislation was an authorization of circumvention of technical protection systems for legitimate law enforcement, intelligence, and other governmental purposes. Without this exception, suspected Mafia bosses and terrorists, oddly enough, might have been able to challenge attempted law enforcement or intelligence agency decryptions of their records or communications under section 1201(a)(1).

The Administration's preferred bill also provided that nothing in section 1201 would "affect rights, remedies, limitations, or defenses to copyright infringement, including fair use, under this title." This seemed to recognize that circumventing a technical protection system for purposes of engaging in fair use or other noninfringing acts would be lawful, although it did not directly say so. Some representatives of major copyright industries who testified at a Congressional hearing on this legislation expressed the view that fair use should not be an acceptable reason to "break" a technical protection system used by copyright owners to protect their works. Allan Adler, testifying on behalf of the Association of American Publishers, for example, stated that "the fair use doctrine has never given anyone a right to break other laws for the stated purpose of exercising the fair use privilege. Fair use doesn't allow you to break into a locked library in order to make 'fair use' copies of the books in it, or steal newspapers from a vending machine in order to copy articles and share them with a friend." The "breaking and entering" metaphor for circumvention activities swayed some influential Congressmen in the debate over anti-circumvention regulations.

Courts should distinguish between circumvention aimed at getting unauthorized access to a work and circumvention aimed at making noninfringing uses of a lawfully obtained copy. Section 1201(a)(1) is aimed at the former, not the latter. Fair use, for example, would provide a poor excuse for breaking into a computer system in order to get access to a work one wished to parody. However, if one had already lawfully acquired a copy of the work, and it was necessary to bypass a technical protection system to make fair use of that copy, this would appear to be lawful under section 1201(a)(1) and (c)(1). Take, for example, an act of circumvention performed by Geoffery Nunberg, a friend of mine who works for Xerox's Palo Alto Research Center. He was an expert witness in a lawsuit which successfully challenged the Washington Redskins' trademark on the ground that the word "redskins" is scandalous or disparaging. Nunberg decided it was necessary to take a clip from an old Western movie to demonstrate derogatory uses of the term in context. It was necessary for him to defeat a technical protection system adopted by the owner of the copyright in this movie in order to make the clip for this purpose. If section 1201(c)(1)'s preservation of fair use and other defenses to infringement are to be given their plain meaning, it would seem that this sort of circumvention should be permissible. Thus, if the clip from the movie qualifies as a fair use, the act of circumvention may be privileged under section 1201(c)(1).

Although this section's apparent preservation of fair use was important, it did not satisfy library and nonprofit groups who expressed substantial concern about the impact that the anti-circumvention provisions would have on public access to information. The only additional concession that the House Subcommittee on Intellectual Property thought should be made to concerns expressed by these groups was to create a special "shopping privilege" for them. This exception, which was included in the final DMCA, enables nonprofit library and educational institutions to circumvent technical protection systems to "make a good faith determination of whether to acquire a copy" of the work. Librarians and educators do not see much value in this provision because vendors of technically protected copyrighted works will generally have incentives to allow librarians and educators to have sufficient access to make acquisition decisions. Their broader concerns about the impact of anti-circumvention regulations on noninfringing uses fell on deaf ears in both the House and Senate Subcommittees on Intellectual Property.

Computer and software industry groups were initially unsuccessful in persuading Congress to create additional exceptions to the anti-circumvention rules and other changes to the anti-circumvention regulations to make them less harmful to legitimate activities in these industries. Not until the full Senate Judiciary Committee and the House Commerce Committee undertook their reviews of the legislation were concerns of these industry groups heeded. Out of the Senate Committee emerged three significant changes to the DMCA. The first was creation of a new exception to enable circumvention of technical protection systems for purposes of enabling a software developer to achieve interoperability among computer programs. The second was a provision clarifying that equipment manufacturers were under no obligation to specially design their products to respond to any particular technical measure used by those providing content for this equipment. The third was a provision indicating that section 1201 was not intended to broaden contributory or vicarious copyright liability.

. . . The Commerce version of the bill added a new exception to enable encryption research and the development of encryption-research tools. It also created two consumer-oriented exceptions, one to enable parents to circumvent access controls when necessary to protect their children from accessing harmful material on the Internet, and the other to enable circumvention to protect personal privacy. It also proposed a moratorium on the anti-circumvention rules so that a study could be conducted about the potential impact of anti-circumvention rules on fair use, the public domain, and other noninfringing uses of copyrighted works.

More clearly than the Judiciary Committees in either branch of Congress, the Commerce Committee recognized the unprecedented nature of the access right that was implicit in the act-of-circumvention provision of section 1201. "If left unqualified," said Congressman Bliley, "this new right . . . could well prove to be the legal foundation for a society in which information becomes available only on a 'pay-per-use' basis." To ensure this would not occur, the legislation was amended to enable librarians and educators to make a showing that the anti-circumvention provision was interfering with noninfringing uses of copyrighted materials and to seek an exemption from the ban. Insofar as such a showing could be made, the Commerce Committee thought that affected classes of works or of users should be exempt from section 1201(a)(1)(A). . . . The Commerce Committee review of the legislation also led to inclusion of a provision indicating that nothing in section 1201 "shall enlarge or diminish any rights of free speech or of the press for activities using consumer electronics, telecommunications, or computing products." This provision recognizes the potential impact of the anti-circumvention rule on free speech and free press interests. . . .

While the final version of the DMCA anti-circumvention provision responded to several significant concerns of the digital economy sector, it did so mainly by adopting specific exceptions. There are, however, many other legitimate reasons for circumventing technical protection systems that are not, strictly speaking, covered by the exceptions in the final bill. Five examples demonstrate that section 1201 should have an "or other legitimate purposes" exception to section 1201(a)(1).

Suppose, for example, that a copyright owner had reason to believe that an encrypted work contained an infringing version of one of its works. The only way to find out whether the copyright owner's suspicion is valid may be to circumvent the technical protection system to get access to the encrypted material. Even if its suspicions proved correct, the copyright owner would have violated section 1201(a)(1)(A) in the course of discovering this. There is no exception in section 1201 to protect this kind of decryption activity.

Or suppose that a content producer had licensed certain software that was essential to the development of its product (e.g., editing software used in the process of making motion pictures). In the course of a dispute about the performance quality of this software, the content producer might withhold payment of a royalty as a way of communicating its displeasure with the licensor's maintenance of the software. The software's licensor might then respond by activating a technical "self-help" system embedded in the software to stop the software from operating. To deal with this development, the licensee might well attempt to circumvent the self-help feature now blocking access to the software because the licensee needed to use the software to finish its movie and because it regarded itself as having a legitimate claim of licensor breach to justify holding back the royalty. However legitimate the claim or this activity, there is no exception to the anti-circumvention rule to protect the licensee in this situation.

Two further examples will illustrate the narrowness of certain existing privileges in the DMCA. Suppose, for example, that a firm circumvented a technical protection system to stop software it had licensed from monitoring certain uses of the software in ways not contemplated in the license agreement and which the licensee regarded as unwarranted and detrimental to its interests. Although there is a "personal privacy" exception in the DMCA, there is no general exception for circumventing to protect other confidentiality interests. Or suppose that a firm was considering making a multi-million dollar acquisition of a computer system whose producer asserted was highly secure. If this firm wished to test the veracity of the producer's assertions, without getting the producer's permission or over the producer's objection, it would seem to violate section 1201. Although there is a computer security testing exception in the Act, it only applies if one is already the owner or operator of the computer system being tested. It should be noted here that many security flaws discovered in widely deployed systems have been found by researchers who tested the system without permission of either the owner or manufacturer of such systems. These activities too are not covered by the computer security exception provided for in the DMCA.

Finally, because the DMCA recognizes that the anti-circumvention rules may have an impact on free speech and free press concerns, it may be worth considering an example of this sort. Suppose that an employee of a major chemical company gave a reporter a disk containing a digital copy of a report and several photographs pertaining to a major chemical spill that the company was trying to cover up. If information on the disk was technically protected and the employee was not authorized by the company to provide the information to the reporter, it would appear that the reporter would violate section 1201(a)(1) if he circumvented the technical protection system to get access to this information, even if consideration of free press and free speech interests might suggest that such a circumvention was justifiable.

One response to these examples might be to assert that copyright owners will generally not sue when these or other legitimate circumvention activities occur. However, in some of the examples given above, the technical protector might well have incentives to sue the circumventor. Given that there are serious criminal penalties for willfully violating section 1201, the overbreadth of this provision and the narrowness of existing exceptions will put many legitimate circumventors at unnecessary risk. If such suits are brought, courts may, of course, and probably will, find other ways to reach just results. They might, for example, decide that the "other defenses" provision of the anti-circumvention rule legitimized the circumvention, that some instances were within the spirit, even if not the letter, of an existing privilege, or that there was insufficient harm to the legitimate interests of the person challenging the circumvention activity to justify imposing liability. However, there should be a general purpose "or other legitimate purposes" provision in section 1201 so that courts will not have to thrash to reach appropriate results. This would add flexibility, adaptability, and fairness to the law. In many other parts of copyright law—with the fair use doctrine, for example, or the distinction between ideas and expressions— Congress has trusted the common law process to distinguish between legitimate and illegitimate activities. It could (and should) have done so with respect to circumvention legislation as well.

It would have been especially appropriate to adopt a general purpose "other legitimate purpose" provision because the anti-circumvention ban is an unprecedented provision for copyright law as to a significant new technology issue with which neither Congress nor the courts have much experience. The lack of a general purpose exception is particularly troubling in view of the harsh criminal and civil provisions in the statute, which may have a chilling effect on legitimate activities, including those affecting free speech. It could also put at risk some legitimate activities in the digital economy that will impede the growth of e-commerce, as will become more apparent in the next section. . . .

If Congress intended for circumvention of technical protection systems to be legal when done for legitimate purposes, it might seem obvious that Congress should be understood to have intended to enable users to effectuate the circumvention privileges it recognized. Although it will not always be necessary for a legitimate circumventor to make or use a circumvention technology to accomplish a privileged circumvention (e.g., enciphered text might be decoded by purely mental activity), most often this will be necessary. The deepest puzzle of section 1201 is whether Congress implicitly intended to allow the development and/or distribution of technologies necessary to accomplish legitimate circumvention activities, or whether, in essence, it created a number of meaningless privileges.

Seemingly relevant to addressing this question are some curious features of section 1201 that close study of this complex provision reveals. First, several exceptions to the anti-circumvention rule specifically authorize the creation of tools necessary to achieving a legitimate circumvention activity (e.g., the encryption research and interoperability privileges), while several others (e.g., the law enforcement privilege and the privacy privilege) do not. Secondly, while the interoperability privilege exempts necessary tools from both device provisions of section 1201, the encryption and security research privileges exempt tools only from the access-device provision, not from the control-device provision. Yet, it would seem that encryption and security research would often require testing both of access and of control components of technical protection systems. Thirdly, section 1201 contains no provision enabling the development or distribution of circumvention tools to enable fair use or other privileged uses in terrain which section 1201(a)(1)(A) doesn't reach (i.e., making fair uses of lawfully acquired copies). If Congress intended to recognize a right to "hack" a technical protection system to make fair uses, this right could be undermined if it could not be exercised without developing a tool to bypass the technical protection system or otherwise getting access to such a tool. Under some interpretations of section 1201(b)(1), development or distribution of such a tool would be unlawful.

Consider, for example, the Xerox PARC [Palo Alto Research Center] researcher who circumvented a movie's technical protection system in order to make a fair use clip for the Washington Redskins' litigation. It was necessary for him to develop a tool to enable him to bypass the technical protection system to make the clip. Suppose that the motion picture copyright owner found out about the circumvention and decided to make an example of this researcher, suing him for statutory damages for violating section 1201(b)(1). On a strict interpretation of this subsection, the researcher might seem to be in trouble. The tool was, after all, "primarily designed . . . for the purpose of circumventing protection afforded by a technological measure that effectively protects a right of the copyright owner under this title in a work or a portion thereof." However, one can easily imagine a court deciding that the researcher's code did not run afoul of section 1201(b)(1). The code might be viewed as a special purpose tool made for the limited purpose of effectuating fair use rights. In view of its lack of commercial significance and the absence of deleterious effects of the sort that the anti-device provisions were intended to reach, a court might decide that this code should not be held to violate this law.

Would the result be different if the researcher asked a co-worker or a friend to develop the tool instead of doing it himself? Or would the result be different if the researcher shared this tool with a co-worker who needed to make a fair use circumvention of a different movie? Even though he might be "provid[ing]" this technology to another person, perhaps he would escape liability because he was not "traffic[king]" in this technology or "offer[ing it] for sale" which are the principal activities Congress meant to curb by enacting this part of DMCA. However, it is fair to observe that courts would have to read some limiting language into section 1201(b)(1) to decide that the researcher would not be liable in all three situations.

An undoubtedly closer question is what courts would do about a technology distributed in the mass-market for purposes of enabling privileged circumventions. Consider, for example, how the 1988 Vault v. Quaid case would fare under the DMCA anti-device provisions. Vault sued Quaid for contributory copyright infringement based on Quaid's development and sale of a program called Ramkey. Quaid's customers could use Ramkey to defeat Vault's Prolok copy-protection software (which Vault sold to other software developers to protect their own software from unauthorized copying). By spoofing Vault's copy-protect system, Quaid's customers could make unauthorized copies of the third-party software protected by Vault's program. Quaid successfully defended against the contributory infringement claim by showing that Ramkey had a substantial noninfringing use, namely, to enable users to effectuate their rights under copyright law to make backup copies.

Quaid would probably not run afoul of the access-device provision of section 1201(a)(2). However, less clear is whether it could successfully defend against a section 1201(b)(1) claim. Suppose that Quaid's president testified that his primary purpose in designing and producing Ramkey was to enable his customers to do legitimate backup copying. Suppose further that the marketing literature for Ramkey emphasized this purpose of the program and even warned potential customers not to use Ramkey to make infringing copies. If a court considered this evidence credible, it would probably save Quaid from criminal prosecution for violating the second anti-device norm, because it would show a lack of wrongful intent. But would it save Quaid from civil liability?

To answer that question, courts would have to grapple with a seeming inconsistency in the statute. On the one hand, the DMCA seems to outlaw technologies if their primary purpose is to circumvent a technical protection measure that effectively protects a right of a copyright owner to control its work (in this case, a right to control illegal copying). On the other hand, the DMCA recognizes that fair use-like circumventions should be lawful. Backup copying is a specially privileged activity in the copyright statute. Because the copyright owner doesn't have a statutory right to control backup copying, perhaps a spoofing technology intended to enable backup copying should be outside the statute. It is important to understand that circumvention for backup copying purposes generally cannot occur without access to such a technology.

So if most lawful users of Prolok-protected software lack the skills to write a Ramkey-equivalent, perhaps it should be lawful to make and distribute a technology to effectuate the backup copy privilege. It is unclear whether Congress intended for the technologically savvy who could "do it themselves" to be the only ones who could engage in privileged acts of circumvention. Yet, as the example of the Xerox researcher illustrates, even the technically sophisticated will often need to develop a tool to accomplish a privileged circumvention; this would seem to put them at risk under a strict reading of section 1201(b)(1).

Potentially relevant to whether the distribution of a tool like Ramkey is lawful is section 1201 (c)(2), which states that nothing in section 1201 "shall enlarge or diminish vicarious or contributory liability for copyright infringement in connection with any technology, product, service, device, component, or part thereof." If what this subsection purports is true, perhaps the result in Vault v. Quaid would be the same after DMCA as before. One can imagine some courts deciding to construe section 1201(b)(1) narrowly so that the honest maker of a Ramkey-equivalent for purposes of enabling backup copying would be able to do so. But they are certainly not constrained to do so.

Moreover, the major copyright industries that supported a broad ban on circumvention technologies would assert that courts should not construe the DMCA so narrowly. They would likely consider Quaid's argument that Ramkey was primarily designed and produced to enable lawful backup copying as a ruse. Moreover, they would likely point out that Ramkey doesn't just enable lawful backup copying; it enables illegal copying as well. They would regard the danger that Ramkey would be used for illegal purposes—regardless of Quaid's intent—as so substantial as to justify banning this technology. The DMCA's anti-device provisions were broadly drafted, they would argue, to address this very danger. They would also consider it an unnecessary burden for copyright owners to have to prove that the primary use of a technology like Ramkey was to engage in infringement. This would be difficult to do, especially for a technology that was about to be introduced into the market. When the dangers of infringement are high, they would argue, the technology ought to be deemed illegal if its purpose is to circumvent a technical protection system copyright owners are using to protect rights granted to them by copyright law. According to this view, Ramkey is illegal under the DMCA. The major copyright industry supporters of the broad anti-device provisions of the DMCA would probably like nothing better than to make Congress' apparent preservation of noninfringing uses into a meaningless promise. . . .

[The author then gives an example of circumvention in order to protect the privacy of the computer user.]

Under a very strict interpretation of section 1201(b)(1), [this] act might be viewed as illegal. It is, however, difficult to believe that most judges would find providing either software or information to enable circumvention of this component of a technical protection system to fall within the DMCA anti-device rules. The DMCA, judges might point out, authorizes circumvention in order to protect personal privacy. While this provision doesn't specifically authorize the development or use of circumvention technologies to accomplish this legitimate act, judges might conclude that Congress must have intended for people to be able to develop or use technology to accomplish the privileged privacy act, or that the Intel identifier was not a component of an effective technical measure. To avert an injustice, judges would likely find an ambiguity in the statute or read in appropriate limiting language. This is clearly not the kind of "black box" circumvention device that Congress had in mind when adopting DMCA. To hold otherwise would, in effect, allow Microsoft to employ the anti-circumvention provisions of DMCA to impose trusted system technology on the public.

It is, of course, an irony that so much of Congressional debate on section 1201 focused on refining the act-of-circumvention provision given that the anti-device provisions are, as a practical matter, by far the more important rules in this section. . . .

When testifying before Congress, proponents of the Administration's anti-device rules repeatedly emphasized that the legislation was needed to stop deliberate and systematic piracy by "black box" providers. Yet, the anti-device provisions adopted by Congress are far broader than this, providing a basis to challenge an unacceptably wide range of technologies that have circumvention-enabling uses. This creates a potential for "strike suits" by nervous or opportunistic copyright owners who might challenge (or threaten to challenge) the deployment of a new information technology tool whose capabilities may include circumvention of some technical protection system. No doubt some expert can be found to say that deployment of a particular technology in the market would meet one of the three conditions in the anti-device provisions, giving plausibility to the suit. Weak as such testimony might be, it may be enough to extract a settlement sum from the information technology firm.

The potential for strike suits becomes stronger if one realizes that it is not necessary (or arguably even relevant) to litigation under the anti-device provisions of DMCA whether any act of underlying infringement (e.g., illegal copying of a protected work) has ever taken place. The mere potentiality for infringement will suffice to confer rich rewards on a successful plaintiff. Consider, for example, a recent lawsuit brought by the maker of a proprietary game console against the maker of emulation software that permits games initially developed for the proprietary console to be played on iMac computers. Relying on the DMCA anti-device provision, the plaintiff is seeking up to $25,000 per unit sold in damages because the emulation software allegedly bypasses an anti-copying feature in the games. The plaintiff did not allege and need not prove any actual illicit copying by users of the defendant's emulation software.

The anti-device provisions of section 1201 are not predictable, minimalist, consistent, or simple, as the Framework principles suggest that they should be. Due to inconsistencies in the statute, it is unclear whether section 1201's anti-device provisions would be interpreted to allow the development and distribution of technologies to enable legitimate uses. Boiled down to its essence, this presents the question of whether Congress should be understood to have made an empty promise of fair use and other privileged circumvention. Unless the anti-device provisions of the DMCA are modified, either by narrow judicial interpretation or by legislative amendments, they are likely to have harmful effects on competition and innovation in the high technology sector. This is not good news for the digital economy.

COMMENTS AND QUESTIONS

1. Should Congress be in the business of regulating what devices can be developed? Is such regulation necessary to combat piracy on the Internet? If Congress did not regulate devices, is there any effective way to stop the spread of pirated information online?

Advocates of the DMCA argued that it was necessary to implement the WIPO treaty the United States entered into in December 1996. In fact, however, it seems quite clear that the treaties could have been ratified without altering U.S. law, which already contained a more limited punishment for those who contribute to an act of copyright infringement. While enacted under the guise of WIPO, the DMCA legislation is in fact significantly more far-reaching. For more detail on the treaty negotiation process and how it relates to the DMCA, see Pamela Samuelson, The U.S. Digital Agenda at WIPO, 37 Va. J. Int'l L. 369 (1997).

2. Is there anything wrong with prohibiting the alteration or misuse of copyright management information (CMI)? This provision seems to serve the laudable purposes of preventing misrepresentations as to ownership and combatting counterfeiting. On the other hand, at least one commentator is concerned that the provision may encourage the development of "smart CMI," systems that not only include terms and conditions but use technological self-help to enforce those terms and conditions. See Julie E. Cohen, A Right to Read Anonymously: A Closer Look at Copyright Management in Cyberspace, 28 Conn. L. Rev. 981 (1996); Julie E. Cohen, Some Reflections on Copyright Management Systems and Laws Designed to Protect Them, 12 Berkeley Tech. L.J. 161 (1997).

3. For a suggestion that the anti-circumvention provisions of the DMCA are unconstitutional because they allow copyright owners to "enclose" and therefore obtain ownership over information in the public domain, see Yochai Benkler, Free as the Air to Common Use: First Amendment Constraints on Enclosure of the Public Domain, 74 N.Y.U. L. Rev. 354 (1999).

4. A related technology to anti-circumvention is serial copy protection technology. Copy protection technology assumes that a consumer will get access to a work but endeavors to limit the copies that can be made from that particular copy. In the music industry, the Audio Home Recording Act of 1992 (AHRA) required the use of copy protection technology in "digital audio recording devices." This act was designed to prevent the exploitation of digital audio tapes (DATs) to make an endless string of perfect digital copies of music. The AHRA was a predecessor to the DMCA in the sense that it made it illegal to circumvent a serial copy management system. The AHRA applies to "digital audio recording devices." The meaning of that phrase in the world of the Internet was at issue in the case that follows.

Recording Industry Association of America v.
Diamond Multimedia Systems, Inc.
United States Court of Appeals for the Ninth Circuit
180 F.3d 1072 (9th Cir. 1999)

O'SCANNLAIN, Circuit Judge:

In this case involving the intersection of computer technology, the Internet, and music listening, we must decide whether the Rio portable music player is a digital audio recording device subject to the restrictions of the Audio Home Recording Act of 1992.

I

This appeal arises from the efforts of the Recording Industry Association of America and the Alliance of Artists and Recording Companies (collectively, "RIAA") to enjoin the manufacture and distribution by Diamond Multimedia Systems ("Diamond") of the Rio portable music player. The Rio is a small device (roughly the size of an audio cassette) with headphones that allows a user to download MP3 audio files from a computer and to listen to them elsewhere. The dispute over the Rio's design and function is difficult to comprehend without an understanding of the revolutionary new method of music distribution made possible by digital recording and the Internet; thus, we will explain in some detail the brave new world of Internet music distribution.

A

The introduction of digital audio recording to the consumer electronics market in the 1980's is at the root of this litigation. Before then, a person wishing to copy an original music recording—e.g., wishing to make a cassette tape of a record or compact disc—was limited to analog, rather than digital, recording technology. With analog recording, each successive generation of copies suffers from an increasingly pronounced degradation in sound quality. For example, when an analog cassette copy of a record or compact disc is itself copied by analog technology, the resulting "second-generation" copy of the original will most likely suffer from the hiss and lack of clarity characteristic of older recordings. With digital recording, by contrast, there is almost no degradation in sound quality, no matter how many generations of copies are made. Digital copying thus allows thousands of perfect or near perfect copies (and copies of copies) to be made from a single original recording. Music "pirates" use digital recording technology to make and to distribute near perfect copies of commercially prepared recordings for which they have not licensed the copyrights.

Until recently, the Internet was of little use for the distribution of music because the average music computer file was simply too big: the digital information on a single compact disc of music required hundreds of computer floppy discs to store, and downloading even a single song from the Internet took hours. However, various compression algorithms (which make an audio file "smaller" by limiting the audio bandwidth) now allow digital audio files to be transferred more quickly and stored more efficiently. MPEG-1 Audio Layer 3 (commonly known as "MP3") is the most popular digital audio compression algorithm in use on the Internet, and the compression it provides makes an audio file "smaller" by a factor of twelve to one without significantly reducing sound quality. MP3's popularity is due in large part to the fact that it is a standard, non-proprietary compression algorithm freely available for use by anyone, unlike various proprietary (and copyright-secure) competitor algorithms. Coupled with the use of cable modems, compression algorithms like MP3 may soon allow an hour of music to be downloaded from the Internet to a personal computer in just a few minutes.

These technological advances have occurred, at least in part, to the traditional music industry's disadvantage. By most accounts, the predominant use of MP3 is the trafficking in illicit audio recordings, presumably because MP3 files do not contain codes identifying whether the compressed audio material is copyright protected. Various pirate websites offer free downloads of copyrighted material, and a single pirate site on the Internet may contain thousands of pirated audio computer files.

RIAA represents the roughly half-dozen major record companies (and the artists on their labels) that control approximately ninety percent of the distribution of recorded music in the United States. RIAA asserts that Internet distribution of serial digital copies of pirated copyrighted material will discourage the purchase of legitimate recordings, and predicts that losses to digital Internet piracy will soon surpass the $300 million that is allegedly lost annually to other more traditional forms of piracy. RIAA fights a well-nigh constant battle against Internet piracy, monitoring the Internet daily, and routinely shutting down pirate websites by sending cease-and-desist letters and bringing lawsuits. There are conflicting views on RIAA's success—RIAA asserts that it can barely keep up with the pirate traffic, while others assert that few, if any, pirate sites remain in operation in the United States and illicit files are difficult to find and download from anywhere online.

In contrast to piracy, the Internet also supports a burgeoning traffic in legitimate audio computer files. Independent and wholly Internet record labels routinely sell and provide free samples of their artists' work online, while many unsigned artists distribute their own material from their own websites. Some free samples are provided for marketing purposes or for simple exposure, while others are teasers intended to entice listeners to purchase either mail order recordings or recordings available for direct download (along with album cover art, lyrics, and artist biographies). Diamond cites a 1998 "Music Industry and the Internet" report by Jupiter Communications which predicts that online sales for pre-recorded music will exceed $1.4 billion by 2002 in the United States alone.

Prior to the invention of devices like the Rio, MP3 users had little option other than to listen to their downloaded digital audio files through headphones or speakers at their computers, playing them from their hard drives. The Rio renders these files portable. More precisely, once an audio file has been downloaded onto a computer hard drive from the Internet or some other source (such as a compact disc player or digital audio tape machine), separate computer software provided with the Rio (called "Rio Manager") allows the user further to download the file to the Rio itself via a parallel port cable that plugs the Rio into the computer. The Rio device is incapable of effecting such a transfer, and is incapable of receiving audio files from anything other than a personal computer equipped with Rio Manager.

Generally, the Rio can store approximately one hour of music, or sixteen hours of spoken material (e.g., downloaded newscasts or books on tape). With the addition of flash memory cards, the Rio can store an additional half-hour or hour of music. The Rio's sole output is an analog audio signal sent to the user via headphones. The Rio cannot make duplicates of any digital audio file it stores, nor can it transfer or upload such a file to a computer, to another device, or to the Internet. However, a flash memory card to which a digital audio file has been downloaded can be removed from one Rio and played back in another.

B

RIAA brought suit to enjoin the manufacture and distribution of the Rio, alleging that the Rio does not meet the requirements for digital audio recording devices under the Audio Home Recording Act of 1992, 17 U.S.C. §1001 et seq. (the "Act"), because it does not employ a Serial Copyright Management System ("SCMS") that sends, receives, and acts upon information about the generation and copyright status of the files that it plays. See *id.* §1002(a)(2). RIAA also sought payment of the royalties owed by Diamond as the manufacturer and distributor of a digital audio recording device. See *id.* §1003.

The district court denied RIAA's motion for a preliminary injunction, holding that RIAA's likelihood of success on the merits was mixed and the balance of hardships did not tip in RIAA's favor. See generally Recording Indus. Ass'n of America, Inc. v. Diamond Multimedia Sys., Inc., 29 F.Supp.2d 624 (C.D.Cal.1998) ("RIAA I"). RIAA brought this appeal.

II

The initial question presented is whether the Rio falls within the ambit of the Act. The Act does not broadly prohibit digital serial copying of copyright protected audio recordings. Instead, the Act places restrictions only upon a specific type of recording device. Most relevant here, the Act provides that "[n]o person shall import, manufacture, or distribute any digital audio recording device . . . that does not conform to the Serial Copy Management System ["SCMS"] [or] a system that has the same functional characteristics." 17 U.S.C. §1002(a)(1), (2). The Act further provides that "[n]o person shall import into and distribute, or manufacture and distribute, any digital audio recording device . . . unless such person records the notice specified by this section and subsequently deposits the statements of account and applicable royalty payments." *Id.* §1003(a). Thus, to fall within the SCMS and royalty requirements in question, the Rio must be a "digital audio recording device," which the Act defines through a set of nested definitions.

The Act defines a "digital audio recording device" as:

> any machine or device of a type commonly distributed to individuals for use by individuals, whether or not included with or as part of some other machine or device, the digital recording function of which is designed or marketed for the primary purpose of, and that is capable of, making a digital audio copied recording for private use. . . .

Id. §1001(3).

A "digital audio copied recording" is defined as:

> a reproduction in a digital recording format of a digital musical recording, whether that reproduction is made directly from another digital musical recording or indirectly from a transmission.

Id. §1001(1).

A "digital musical recording" is defined as:

> a material object —
>   (i) in which are fixed, in a digital recording format, only sounds, and material, statements, or instructions incidental to those fixed sounds, if any, and
>   (ii) from which the sounds and material can be perceived, reproduced, or otherwise communicated, either directly or with the aid of a machine or device.

Id. §1001(5)(A).

In sum, to be a digital audio recording device, the Rio must be able to reproduce, either "directly" or "from a transmission," a "digital music recording."

III

We first consider whether the Rio is able directly to reproduce a digital music recording—which is a specific type of material object in which only sounds are fixed (or material and instructions incidental to those sounds). See *id.*

A

The typical computer hard drive from which a Rio directly records is, of course, a material object. However, hard drives ordinarily contain much more than "only sounds, and material, statements, or instructions incidental to those fixed sounds." *Id.* Indeed, almost all hard drives contain numerous programs (e.g., for word processing, scheduling appointments, etc.) and databases that are not incidental to any sound files that may be stored on the hard drive. Thus, the Rio appears not to make copies from digital music recordings, and thus would not be a digital audio recording device under the Act's basic definition unless it makes copies from transmissions.

Moreover, the Act expressly provides that the term "digital musical recording" does not include:

> a material object —
> (i) in which the fixed sounds consist entirely of spoken word recordings, or
> (ii) in which one or more computer programs are fixed, except that a digital recording may contain statements or instructions constituting the fixed sounds and incidental material, and statements or instructions to be used directly or indirectly in order to bring about the perception, reproduction, or communication of the fixed sounds and incidental material.

Id. §1001(5)(B). As noted previously, a hard drive is a material object in which one or more programs are fixed; thus, a hard drive is excluded from the definition of digital music recordings. This provides confirmation that the Rio does not record "directly" from "digital music recordings," and therefore could not be a digital audio recording device unless it makes copies "from transmissions."

B . . .

2

The district court concluded that the exemption of hard drives from the definition of digital music recording, and the exemption of computers generally from the Act's ambit, "would effectively eviscerate the [Act]" because "[a]ny recording device could evade [ ] regulation simply by passing the music through a computer and ensuring that the MP3 file resided momentarily on the hard drive." RIAA I, 29 F.Supp.2d at 630. While this may be true, the Act seems to have been expressly designed to create this loophole.

a

Under the plain meaning of the Act's definition of digital audio recording devices, computers (and their hard drives) are not digital audio recording devices because their "primary purpose" is not to make digital audio copied recordings. See 17 U.S.C. §1001(3). Unlike digital audio tape machines, for example, whose primary purpose is to make digital audio copied recordings, the primary purpose of a computer is to run various programs and to record the data necessary to run those programs and perform various tasks. The legislative history is consistent with this interpretation of the Act's provisions, stating that "the typical personal computer would not fall within the definition of 'digital audio recording device,'" S. Rep. 102-294, at *122, because a personal computer's "recording function is designed and marketed primarily for the recording of data and computer programs," *id.* at *121. Another portion of the Senate Report states that "[i]f the 'primary purpose' of the recording function is to make objects other than digital audio copied recordings, then the machine or device is not a 'digital audio recording device,' even if the machine or device is technically capable of making such recordings." *Id.* The legislative history thus expressly recognizes that computers (and other devices) have recording functions capable of recording digital musical recordings, and thus implicate the home taping and piracy concerns to which the Act is responsive. Nonetheless, the legislative history is consistent with the Act's plain language—computers are not digital audio recording devices.

b

In turn, because computers are not digital audio recording devices, they are not required to comply with the SCMS requirement and thus need not send, receive, or act upon information regarding copyright and generation status. See 17 U.S.C. §1002(a)(2). And, as the district court found, MP3 files generally do not even carry the codes providing information regarding copyright and generation status. See RIAA I, 29 F.Supp.2d. at 632. Thus, the Act seems designed to allow files to be "laundered" by passage through a computer, because even a device with SCMS would be able to download MP3 files lacking SCMS codes from a computer hard drive, for the simple reason that there would be no codes to prevent the copying.

Again, the legislative history is consistent with the Act's plain meaning. . . .

c

In fact, the Rio's operation is entirely consistent with the Act's main purpose—the facilitation of personal use. As the Senate Report explains, "[t]he purpose of [the Act] is to ensure the right of consumers to make analog or digital audio recordings of copyrighted music for their private, noncommercial use." S. Rep. 102-294, at *86. The Act does so through its home taping exemption, see 17 U.S.C. §1008, which "protects all noncommercial copying by consumers of digital and analog musical recordings," H.R. Rep. 102-873(I), at *59. The Rio merely makes copies in order to render portable, or "space-shift," those files that already reside on a user's hard drive. Cf. Sony Corp. of America v. Universal City Studios, 464 U.S. 417, 455, 104 S.Ct. 774, 78 L.Ed.2d 574 (1984) (holding that "time-shifting" of copyrighted television shows with VCR's constitutes fair use under the Copyright Act, and thus is not an infringement). Such copying is paradigmatic noncommercial personal use entirely consistent with the purposes of the Act.

IV

Even though it cannot directly reproduce a digital music recording, the Rio would nevertheless be a digital audio recording device if it could reproduce a digital music recording "from a transmission." 17 U.S.C. §1001(1).

A

The term "transmission" is not defined in the Act, although the use of the term in the Act implies that a transmission is a communication to the public. See *id.* §1002(e) (placing restrictions upon "[a]ny person who transmits or otherwise communicates to the public any sound recording in digital format"). In the context of copyright law (from which the term appears to have been taken), "[t]o 'transmit' a performance or display is to communicate it by any device or process whereby images or sounds are received beyond the place from which they are sent." 17 U.S.C. §101. The legislative history confirms that the copyright definition of "transmission" is sufficient for our purposes here. The Act originally (and circularly) provided that "[a] 'transmission' is any audio or audiovisual transmission, now known or later developed, whether by a broadcast station, cable system, multipoint distribution service, subscription service, direct broadcast satellite, or other form of analog or digital communication." S. Rep. 102-294, at *10. The Senate Report provides a radio broadcast as an example of a transmission. See *id.*, at *119 (referring to "a transmission (e.g., a radio broadcast of a commercially released audio cassette)."). The parties do not really dispute the definition of transmission, but rather, whether indirect reproduction of a transmission of a digital music recording is covered by the Act.

B

RIAA asserts that indirect reproduction of a transmission is sufficient for the Rio to fall within the Act's ambit as a digital audio recording device. See 17 U.S.C. §1001(1) (digital audio recording devices are those devices that are capable of making "a reproduction in a digital recording format of a digital musical recording, whether that reproduction is made directly from another digital musical recording or indirectly from a transmission"). Diamond asserts that the adverb "indirectly" modifies the recording of the underlying "digital music recording," rather than the recording "from the transmission." Diamond effectively asserts that the statute should be read as covering devices that are capable of making a reproduction of a digital musical recording, "whether that reproduction is made directly[,] from another digital musical recording[,] or indirectly[,] from a transmission."

While the Rio can only directly reproduce files from a computer hard drive via a cable linking the two devices (which is obviously not a transmission), the Rio can indirectly reproduce a transmission. For example, if a radio broadcast of a digital audio recording were recorded on a digital audio tape machine or compact disc recorder and then uploaded to a computer hard drive, the Rio could indirectly reproduce the transmission by downloading a copy from the hard drive. Thus, if indirect reproduction of a transmission falls within the statutory definition, the Rio would be a digital audio recording device.

1

RIAA's interpretation of the statutory language initially seems plausible, but closer analysis reveals that it is contrary to the statutory language and common sense. The focus of the statutory language seems to be on the two means of reproducing the underlying digital music recording—either directly from that recording, or indirectly, by reproducing the recording from a transmission. RIAA's interpretation of the Act's language (in which "indirectly" modifies copying "from a transmission," rather than the copying of the underlying digital music recording) would only cover the indirect recording of transmissions, and would omit restrictions on the direct recording of transmissions (e.g., recording songs from the radio) from the Act's ambit. This interpretation would significantly reduce the protection afforded by the Act to transmissions, and neither the statutory language nor structure provides any reason that the Act's protections should be so limited. Moreover, it makes little sense for the Act to restrict the indirect recording of transmissions, but to allow unrestricted direct recording of transmissions (e.g., to regulate second-hand recording of songs from the radio, but to allow unlimited direct recording of songs from the radio). Thus, the most logical reading of the Act extends protection to direct copying of digital music recordings, and to indirect copying of digital music recordings from transmissions of those recordings.

2

Because of the arguable ambiguity of this passage of the statute, recourse to the legislative history is necessary on this point. Cf. Moyle v. Director, Office of Workers' Compensation Programs, 147 F.3d 1116, 1120 (9th Cir.1998) ("[I]f the statute is ambiguous, [this court] consult[s] the legislative history, to the extent that it is of value, to aid in [its] interpretation."), *cert. denied,* —U.S.—, 119 S.Ct. 1454, —L.Ed.2d— (1999). The Senate Report states that "a digital audio recording made from a commercially released compact disc or audio cassette, or from a radio broadcast of a commercially released compact disc or audio cassette, would be a 'digital audio copied recording.'" S. Rep. 102-294, at *119. This statement indicates that the recording of a transmission need not be indirect to fall within the scope of the Act's restrictions, and thus refutes RIAA's proposed interpretation of the relevant language. Moreover, the statement tracks the statutory definition by providing an example of direct copying of a digital music recording from that recording, and an example of indirect copying of a digital music recording from a transmission of that recording. Thus the legislative history confirms the most logical reading of the statute, which we adopt: "indirectly" modifies the verb "is made"—in other words, modifies the making of the reproduction of the underlying digital music recording. Thus, a device falls within the Act's provisions if it can indirectly copy a digital music recording by making a copy from a transmission of that recording. Because the Rio cannot make copies from transmissions, but instead, can only make copies from a computer hard drive, it is not a digital audio recording device.

V

For the foregoing reasons, the Rio is not a digital audio recording device subject to the restrictions of the Audio Home Recording Act of 1992. The district court properly denied the motion for a preliminary injunction against the Rio's manufacture and distribution. Having so determined, we need not consider whether the balance of hardships or the possibility of irreparable harm supports injunctive relief.

COMMENTS AND QUESTIONS

Behind the controversy surrounding the Rio is a fundamental change in the economics of the music industry: consumers are downloading music directly from the Internet in large numbers. Some of this downloading is illegal copying from pirate sites; much of it, though, is legal. Both new and established bands are releasing their music directly on the Internet, bypassing the traditional distribution mechaism of record companies. Record companies, understandably upset by both piracy and legitimate competition, have sought to ban the devices that enable both. For an overview of this controversy, see Jessica Litman, Free Speech and Electronic Commerce (working paper 1999).

More recently, the music industry has sought to create its own alternative format for downloading music over the Internet while preventing serial copying. So far, the music industry protocol—called Secure Digital Music Initiative (SDMI)—has failed to materialize.

3. Framing, Linking, and Caching

≡≡≡ *Maureen A. O'Rourke, Fencing Cyberspace:*
≡≡≡ *Drawing Borders in a Virtual World*
≡≡≡ 82 Minn. L. Rev. 609 (1998)

. . . The power of the web lies in its ability to link related documents. A particular web site's value is largely determined by how many people access it—the cyberspace equivalent of "foot traffic." Generally, there are two ways for users to access web sites: directly by typing in the site's URL or indirectly by linking from another site or search engine. Until recently, the practice of linking was largely welcomed by web site owners. The more parties that access a site, whether directly or indirectly, the higher the advertising rate the web site's owner may charge and the more revenue the web site's owner may generate from sales of its own products available at the site. Also, until recently, there was not much question that access to a site by linking was impliedly authorized by the owner's placement of material on the web without restriction.

Two recently filed cases have questioned the validity of linking under both copyright and trademark law. In Ticketmaster Corp. v. Microsoft Corp., Ticketmaster sued Microsoft for trademark dilution and unfair competition under the Lanham Act for Microsoft's linking to parts of the Ticketmaster web site without Ticketmaster's permission. In Washington Post Co. v. Total News, Inc., the Washington Post and other news agencies sued Total News for common law misappropriation, copyright and trademark infringement, and trademark dilution for the manner in which Total News linked to their sites.

A brief review of these cases supports the contention that copyright law will become less important as firms turn to both federal actions under the Lanham Act and common law misappropriation claims in attempting to regulate linking conduct. To understand why this is the case, however, first requires an acquaintance with the technical aspects of linking.

A. Types of Linking

The most basic type of link, and the subject of the *Ticketmaster* case, is the Hypertext Reference Link (HREF). An HREF link is usually a bit of text within a web document that is highlighted or otherwise set off from the rest of the text. When a user clicks on the HREF link (or pointer), the computer stops displaying what is currently on-screen, connects to the linked site, and displays the content at that site. Technically, when the user clicks on the pointer, the user's machine sends a request to the server on which the document to be linked resides—the copyright owner's server. That machine then sends a copy of the document to the user's machine where it will be displayed on the screen for the user to browse and perhaps download. The original remains on the copyright owner's server.

A pointer may link to another location on the same page, a different page within the same site, or to a different site remote from the linking site. The web's organization is thus recursive, as a particular web page may contain links to a number of other web pages that in turn contain links to other web pages (or back to the original linking page), and so on. HREF links are "one-at-a-time" links in that the user accesses only one site at a time. When the user leaves the current site by linking to another one, the content of the linked site and its URL replace the content and URL of the linking site on the user's screen.

A second type of link, and the subject of the *Total News* case, is the "frame." Frames function much like the windows that have become familiar to the many users of the Macintosh and Windows operating systems. A site that utilizes framing has the ability to bring up the entire contents or portions of one or more other sites that are "framed" within the linking site. The user remains at the framing site, looking through windows into one or more linked sites. Since framing divides the screen, usually only portions of the framed sites may be seen at any one time, although the user may scroll through the linked site to get a fuller picture of it. Technically, framing is achieved by using certain HTML code in the linking document coupled with enabling code contained in the user's browser software. The linked document is accessed in much the same way as with an HREF link. The user's machine sends a request for the document to be linked to the document owner's server, which makes a copy and sends it back to the user's machine. The contents of the linked site are not altered but their appearance is. The linking site's programming code directs the web browser to display the content in a frame rather than full-screen.

There are some notable differences between HREF links and frames. HREF links end the connection to the linking site and display the URL and entire contents of the new, linked site. In contrast, frames display the URL of the linking site and may incorporate only selected contents of the linked site. It is generally obvious to users that they have changed sites when they access an HREF link while it may not be at all obvious that information has been incorporated from other sites when a frame is activated. The *Ticketmaster* and *Total News* cases provide an ideal means to highlight these differences and assess their legal relevance because each case primarily involves a different type of link.

B.   The Legal Challenges to Linking

1.   *The Ticketmaster v. Microsoft Case: The HREF Link*

The first American case[120] to base its claim on a challenge to an HREF link was filed in the spring of 1997 by Ticketmaster Corp. against Microsoft Corp. Microsoft had recently begun a strategy of setting up advertiser-supported web sites as city guides. For example, its "http://seattle.sidewalk.com" site, the subject of the litigation, contains information on that city, including guides to entertainment and restaurants as well as a menu setting forth events around Seattle, many of which require tickets for admission. These tickets were often available from Ticketmaster at its web site. The companies had negotiated for a mutually beneficial marketing deal involving linking their respective sites. However, no agreement was ever reached. Despite the lack of agreement, Microsoft included a number of links to the Ticketmaster site from Sidewalk. After the agreement with Microsoft failed to materialize, Ticketmaster entered into a licensing agreement with CitySearch, a competitor of Microsoft's.

Ticketmaster's complaint itself was quite brief, alleging six claims for relief. Interestingly, the complaint was based primarily on trademark claims, making no mention of copyright infringement. The complaint alleged that, by using Ticketmaster's trademarks and trade names on its web site, Microsoft was free-riding on Ticketmaster's name and marks and enhancing the value of its seattle.sidewalk.com site at the expense of Ticketmaster's site.

---

120. The first case to involve an HREF link was filed in Scotland. See [Matt Jackson, Linking Copyright to Homepages, 49 Fed. Comm. L.J. 731, 739 (1997)] (describing the Shetland Times suit against the Shetland News for linking to its site). The Shetland News "reproduced verbatim a number of headlines appearing in The Shetland Times. These headlines were hyperlinked to the [Times] Web site. Clicking on the headline took the reader directly to the internal pages on the [Times] site on which the related story was found." Martin H. Samson, Hyperlink at Your Own Risk, N.Y. L.J., June 24, 1997, at 1. The court issued an "interim interdict" pending further litigation. *Id*. The case, however, is of limited usefulness as it primarily turns on English law. But see Jackson, *supra* (noting that, although the case turns on the specifics of English law, it points out that "the concern over links is becoming an increasingly important issue worldwide").

Ticketmaster seemed to object primarily to three Microsoft practices. First, Microsoft linked deeply within Ticketmaster's site rather than to the home page. Ticketmaster alleged that this practice took Ticketmaster's content out of context and diverted advertising dollars from Ticketmaster to Microsoft. Second, in a related complaint, Ticketmaster claimed that the use of the Ticketmaster trademark and trade names generally on Microsoft's site allowed Microsoft to attract advertising dollars: "Microsoft has used Ticketmaster's property and goodwill to sell advertising on its own web site, thereby, in effect, rewriting the rules of commerce for it's [sic] own benefit." According to Ticketmaster, "absent an agreement with the owner for use of a web site, web sites are for personal noncommercial use." Finally, Ticketmaster had agreed with MasterCard to give that credit card prominence in its advertising. The complaint alleged that "Microsoft's use of Ticketmaster's name in connection with MasterCard, which use does not give MasterCard prominence, dilutes the value of that relationship."

[The parties settled early in 1999.]

2. *The Washington Post v. Total News Case: The "Frame"*

The first case to challenge the practice of framing was filed in February, 1997, by a group of plaintiffs operating online news sites. The plaintiffs, led by The Washington Post, sued Total News and others for the operation of a web site that used the plaintiffs' trademarks as pointers and framed the plaintiffs' sites when a user accessed them.

The Total News site is essentially a collection of links, "a one-stop emporium for the news junkie, provid[ing] access to nearly 1,200 media company sites." When the user accesses a link, the contents of the linked site appear in a window, or "frame," surrounded by the contents, including the advertising, of the Total News site. As is characteristic of framing, the Total News URL rather than the URL of the linked site continues to be displayed.

The plaintiffs sued under a number of theories, including copyright and trademark infringement and trademark dilution. The heart of the complaint, however, sounded in misappropriation. The primary basis of the plaintiffs' objection to the defendants' conduct was that Total News was free-riding on the plaintiffs' newsgathering efforts because it sold advertising based on the plaintiffs' content rather than its own:

> Defendants provide little or no content of their own. Instead Defendants have designed a parasitic website that republishes the news and editorial content of others' websites in order to attract both advertisers and users. Specifically, Defendants' website is designed to feature the content of Plaintiffs' and others' websites, inserted within a "frame" on the computer screen that includes Defendants' totalnews.com logo and URL as well as advertising that Defendants have sold. . . . Simply put, Defendants are engaged in the Internet equivalent of pirating copyrighted material from a variety of famous newspa-

pers, magazines, or television news programs; packaging those stories to advertisers as part of a competitive publication or program produced by Defendants' and pocketing the advertising revenue generated by their unauthorized use of that material.

Based on the complaint, the news organizations seemed to object primarily to Total News framing their sites with advertising that Total News had sold. Additionally, the plaintiffs also objected to Total News's use of their logos as the HREF linking symbol.

The parties settled the litigation in June, 1997. . . .

3. Discerning Litigation Trends

Admittedly, two cases, one undecided and the other settled, make a small sample from which to draw inferences about how the law will evolve on-line. However, when those cases are considered against the backdrop of on-line revenue models, one may identify some trends with reasonable certainty.

For example, to a certain extent both cases are a product of building the web revenue model around advertising. Ticketmaster objected to Microsoft's bypassing its home page containing banner ads, while the plaintiffs in *Total News* objected to Total News obscuring their advertising and framing their sites with ads from which Total News profited. As the competition for advertising dollars stiffens, more and more companies are likely to seek legal redress when they can make a tenable claim that other sites are diverting advertising dollars away from them.

Second, the lack of emphasis on copyright is notable. . . .

Third, the gravamen of both complaints was really unfair competition, although stated in different causes of action. Both cases alleged federal trademark dilution and violations of section 43(a) of the Lanham Act for a false implication of association between the plaintiffs and defendants. The plaintiffs in *Total News* also claimed trademark infringement for the use of their trademarks and trade names as pointers on the Total News site and stated a common law misappropriation claim. Disputes over trademarks are likely only to increase because establishing a brand identity is one way to attract users to one's site and thereby generate more advertising dollars. . . .

COMMENTS AND QUESTIONS

1. Most commentators have been critical of any theory of copyright liability for linking. In addition to O'Rourke, see Edward A. Cavazos & Coe F. Miles, Copyright on the WWW: Linking and Liability, 4 Rich. J. L. & Tech. no. 2 (http://www.richmond.edu/~jolt/v4i2/cavazos.html); David Hayes, Advanced Copyright Issues on the Internet, 7 Texas Intell. Prop. L.J. 1 (1998); Mark A. Lemley, The Law and Economics of Internet

Norms, 73 Chi.-Kent L. Rev. 1257 (1998). But see Walter A. Effross, Withdrawal of the Reference: Rights, Rules, and Remedies for Unwelcomed Web-Linking, 49 S.C. L. Rev. 651, 692-693 (1998) (seeming to accept the premise that companies ought to be entitled to prevent unauthorized links to their sites).

Objections to liability for linking take two major forms. First, as a legal matter, a Web site that includes an HREF link has not copied anything. Rather, they have pointed the user to a page, and the user may go there and make a copy. If anyone is copying the page, therefore, it is the end user. But Web site owners generally want to encourage end users to visit their site, even if they object to the particular links that have brought them there. So they are unlikely to sue the end users directly—and without proof that the end user is directly infringing, the linking page cannot be liable for contributing to that infringement.

Second, commentators (and some courts) point to the devastating consequences liability for linking would have on the nature of the Internet, which is built on the idea of links. The one U.S. court to address the issue of liability for linking was Bernstein v. J.C. Penney, Inc., 50 U.S.P.Q.2d 1063 (C.D. Cal. 1998). Rejecting the claim, the court wrote:

> Plaintiff Gary Bernstein sued Elizabeth Arden Co. and Parfums International, Ltd. (collectively "Arden") for copyright infringement based on multiple linking on the Internet. Plaintiff alleges that Arden and JC Penney were liable because Arden's Passion perfume was promoted on a JC Penney website that was "hyperlinked" to a website operated by the Internet Movie Database ("IMDB") that in turn linked to several other websites, one of which—the Swedish University Network ("SUNET")—contained infringing copies of two of plaintiff's photographs of the actress Elizabeth Taylor, the spokesperson for Arden's perfume.
>
> The parent of Arden, Conopco, moved to dismiss the complaint on the ground that it fails to state a claim upon which relief can be granted. Fed. R. Civ. Pro. 12(b)(6).
>
> Arden contends plaintiff's theory of infringement by multiple linking would have a devastating impact on the Internet and argues the claim should be dismissed for three reasons: (1) a company whose product is merely displayed on another entity's website cannot be held liable for any infringement by the author of that website; (2) linking cannot constitute direct infringement because the computer server of the linking website does not copy or otherwise process the content of the linked-to site; and (3) multiple linking cannot constitute contributory infringement because (a) Internet users viewing of the material at issue is not infringing and thus there was no direct infringement in the United States to which Arden could contribute, see Religious Tech. Center v. Netcom On-Line Comm. Servs., 907 F.Supp. 1361, 1378 n.25 (N.D.Cal.1995); (b) linking "is capable of substantial noninfringing uses" and thus cannot support a claim for contributory infringement, Sony Corp. v. Universal City Studios, 464 U.S. 417, 442 (1984); and (c) the Court cannot infer from the facts alleged that Arden knew the photos had been posted to SUNET and multiple linking does not constitute substantial participation in any infringement where the linking website does not mention the fact that Internet

users could, by following the links, find infringing material on another website. Cf. Sega Enterprises, Ltd. v. MAPHIA, 948 F.Supp. 923 (N.D.Cal.1996). [The court accepted this argument and dismissed the case without leave to amend.]

Id. at 1064.

For an argument that linking should be considered fair use, see Pamela Samuelson, Fair Use for Computer Programs and Other Copyrightable Works in Digital Form: The Implications of *Sony, Galoob,* and *Sega,* 1 J. Intell. Prop. L. 49, 112-116 (1993).

2. Should the same arguments protect efforts to "frame" another's site, as in the *Total News* case? As a technical matter, the code that appears on the framer's site is virtually identical to the code that appears on the linker's site. The only difference is a default instruction to the user's browser to display the two pages side by side, or one in a frame around the other. From a copyright perspective, it is hard to see how this changes the result. Indeed, the one U.S. case to have ruled on framing refused to enjoin it pending trial. See Futuredontics v. Applied Anagramics, 152 F.3d 925 (9th Cir. 1998) (unpublished).

Is there reason to be more concerned about framing than about linking? If so, is the concern a copyright concern? Is it a trademark concern — that unsuspecting Internet users will think the two sites are the same, or at least that they are related? Or is there some other theory (misappropriation, say, or unfair competition) that should apply here? Bruce Keller discusses the misappropriation theory in Bruce P. Keller, Condemned to Repeat the Past: The Reemergence of Misappropriation and Other Common Law Theories of Protection for Intellectual Property, 11 Harv. J. L. & Tech. 401 (1997).

3. The plaintiffs in both the *Ticketmaster* and *Total News* cases were able to use technical means to block or redirect the unwanted linking. Ticketmaster simply transferred users linking to its inside page to its home page. The plaintiffs in the *Total News* case blocked the frame either by opening a new browser window containing their page or by rejecting links from Total News altogether.

Should the ability of Web sites to block or deflect unwanted links have any bearing on the legal status of those links?

PROBLEMS

Problem 10-1. BNN, the Washington Dispatch, and USA Total ("the companies") are all mainstream news organizations that provide news information to subscribers in a variety of media (such as newspapers or broadcast television). All have Web sites that provide anyone who uses the Internet with free access to some of their news stories, as well as other features designed specifically for Web users. The companies do not make subscription revenue from their Web pages but do sell some advertising to defray the costs of the pages. However, none of the companies show a net profit on their pages. They maintain the page at least in part for image reasons. None of these organizations register visitors to these Web sites or restrict visits in any way. However, BNN and the Washington Dispatch do make use of a file called "cookies.txt" that appears with modern Web browsers. By reading this file automatically, the companies can tell the server from which the browsing party is visiting, the Web site from which it has come, and the Web site it goes to next.

AlltheNews, Inc. (ANI) is a small start-up company that provides links to each of the major news organization Web pages on the Internet, including those of the companies described above. A link allows the user to jump seamlessly from ANI's site to any of the news organization sites. ANI's particular link uses "framing" technology to permit the linked site to be viewed as if it existed inside ANI's page, with a border provided by ANI. However, ANI has not in fact copied the companies' pages, but has merely sent a command to the user's Web browser instructing it to find the companies' pages and display them inside the frame. ANI sells advertising for its page. Its ads appear inside the border surrounding the frame.

The companies bring suit against ANI for copyright and trademark infringement. Who should prevail on each claim, and why?

Problem 10-2. The University of the Midwest (UM) runs one of the five largest Internet servers in the country. UM provides access to and forwards Usenet newsgroups. However, because of the limitations of server space, the system administrator at UM has decided not to carry all Usenet newsgroups. Instead, the UM server provides access only to about half of the newsgroups available on Usenet.

Playboy sues UM, arguing that it is liable for duplicating, distributing, and displaying numerous Playboy-copyrighted images posted to Usenet on its servers. Is UM a direct infringer? Would it affect the result if the UM sysadmin made a conscious decision to allow the group alt.binaries.erotica.centerfolds (a group that has a large percentage of infringing Playboy material) to be part of the University's Usenet feed?

Problem 10-3. Kat, a law student using her University of Texas account, puts up a home page that includes links to several Web sites. One of those Web sites, run by Bismey Animation Conglomerate, Inc. (BAC), permits copying of its Web information only by those who have joined its "Computer Mouse Club" and have paid a fee to view the information. BAC warns users of its limited distribution policy once they have already accessed its Web page.

Byrd logs in to Kat's Web site from Finland. He follows Kat's link to the BAC Web page, causing a copy of the BAC page to be downloaded to his computer in Finland, even though he is not a member of the Club. He then distributes BAC's images widely in Finland.

Unable to obtain jurisdiction to sue Byrd, BAC files suit for copyright infringement against both Kat and the University of Texas, alleging both direct and contributory copyright infringement. What result?

11 *Content Regulation*

A. DEFAMATION

Zeran v. America Online
United States Court of Appeals for the Fourth Circuit
129 F.3d 327 (4th Cir. 1997)

WILKINSON, Chief Judge:

... On April 25, 1995, an unidentified person posted a message on an AOL bulletin board advertising "Naughty Oklahoma T-Shirts." The posting described the sale of shirts featuring offensive and tasteless slogans related to the April 19, 1995, bombing of the Alfred P. Murrah Federal Building in Oklahoma City. Those interested in purchasing the shirts were instructed to call "Ken" at Zeran's home phone number in Seattle, Washington. As a result of this anonymously perpetrated prank, Zeran received a high volume of calls, comprised primarily of angry and derogatory messages, but also including death threats. Zeran could not change his phone number because he relied on its availability to the public in running his business out of his home. Later that day, Zeran called AOL and informed a company representative of his predicament. The employee assured Zeran that the posting would be removed from AOL's bulletin board but explained that as a matter of policy AOL would not post a retraction. The parties dispute the date that AOL removed this original posting from its bulletin board.

On April 26, the next day, an unknown person posted another message advertising additional shirts with new tasteless slogans related to the Oklahoma City bombing. Again, interested buyers were told to call Zeran's phone number, to ask for "Ken," and to "please call back if busy" due to high demand. The angry, threatening phone calls intensified. Over the next four days, an unidentified party continued to post messages on AOL's bulletin board, advertising additional items including bumper stickers and key chains with still more offensive slogans. During this time period, Zeran called AOL repeatedly and was told by company representatives that the individual account from which the messages were posted would soon be closed. Zeran also reported his case to Seattle FBI agents. By April 30, Zeran was receiving an abusive phone call approximately every two minutes.

Meanwhile, an announcer for Oklahoma City radio station KRXO received a copy of the first AOL posting. On May 1, the announcer related the message's contents on the air, attributed them to "Ken" at Zeran's phone number, and urged the listening audience to call the number. After this radio broadcast, Zeran was inundated with death threats and other violent calls from Oklahoma City residents. Over the next few days, Zeran talked to both KRXO and AOL representatives. He also spoke to his local police, who subsequently surveilled his home to protect his safety. By May 14, after an Oklahoma City newspaper published a story exposing the shirt advertisements as a hoax and after KRXO made an on-air apology, the number of calls to Zeran's residence finally subsided to fifteen per day.

Zeran first filed suit on January 4, 1996, against radio station KRXO in the United States District Court for the Western District of Oklahoma. On April 23, 1996, he filed this separate suit against AOL in the same court. Zeran did not bring any action against the party who posted the offensive messages.[1] After Zeran's suit against AOL was transferred to the Eastern District of Virginia pursuant to 28 U.S.C. §1404(a), AOL answered Zeran's complaint and interposed 47 U.S.C. §230 as an affirmative defense. AOL then moved for judgment on the pleadings pursuant to Fed.R.Civ.P. 12(c). The district court granted AOL's motion, and Zeran filed this appeal.

II.

A.

Because §230 was successfully advanced by AOL in the district court as a defense to Zeran's claims, we shall briefly examine its operation here. Zeran seeks to hold AOL liable for defamatory speech initiated by a third party. He argued to the district court that once he notified AOL of the unidentified third party's hoax, AOL had a duty to remove the defamatory posting promptly, to notify its subscribers of the message's false nature, and

---

1. Zeran maintains that AOL made it impossible to identify the original party by failing to maintain adequate records of its users. The issue of AOL's record keeping practices, however, is not presented by this appeal.

to effectively screen future defamatory material. Section 230 entered this litigation as an affirmative defense pled by AOL. The company claimed that Congress immunized interactive computer service providers from claims based on information posted by a third party.

The relevant portion of §230 states: "No provider or user of an interactive computer service shall be treated as the publisher or speaker of any information provided by another information content provider." 47 U.S.C. §230(c)(1).[2] By its plain language, §230 creates a federal immunity to any cause of action that would make service providers liable for information originating with a third-party user of the service. Specifically, §230 precludes courts from entertaining claims that would place a computer service provider in a publisher's role. Thus, lawsuits seeking to hold a service provider liable for its exercise of a publisher's traditional editorial functions —such as deciding whether to publish, withdraw, postpone or alter content —are barred.

The purpose of this statutory immunity is not difficult to discern. Congress recognized the threat that tort-based lawsuits pose to freedom of speech in the new and burgeoning Internet medium. The imposition of tort liability on service providers for the communications of others represented, for Congress, simply another form of intrusive government regulation of speech. Section 230 was enacted, in part, to maintain the robust nature of Internet communication and, accordingly, to keep government interference in the medium to a minimum. In specific statutory findings, Congress recognized the Internet and interactive computer services as offering "a forum for a true diversity of political discourse, unique opportunities for cultural development, and myriad avenues for intellectual activity." *Id.* §230(a)(3). It also found that the Internet and interactive computer services "have flourished, to the benefit of all Americans, with a minimum of government regulation." *Id.* §230(a)(4). Congress further stated that it is "the policy of the United States . . . to preserve the vibrant and competitive free market that presently exists for the Internet and other interactive computer services, unfettered by Federal or State regulation." *Id.* §230(b)(2).

None of this means, of course, that the original culpable party who posts defamatory messages would escape accountability. While Congress acted to keep government regulation of the Internet to a minimum, it also

---

2. Section 230 defines "interactive computer service" as "any information service, system, or access software provider that provides or enables computer access by multiple users to a computer server, including specifically a service or system that provides access to the Internet and such systems operated or services offered by libraries or educational institutions." 47 U.S.C. §230(e)(2). The term "information content provider" is defined as "any person or entity that is responsible, in whole or in part, for the creation or development of information provided through the Internet or any other interactive computer service." *Id.* §230(e)(3). The parties do not dispute that AOL falls within the CDA's "interactive computer service" definition and that the unidentified third party who posted the offensive messages here fits the definition of an "information content provider."

found it to be the policy of the United States "to ensure vigorous enforcement of Federal criminal laws to deter and punish trafficking in obscenity,
stalking, and harassment by means of computer." *Id.* §230(b)(5). Congress
made a policy choice, however, not to deter harmful online speech through
the separate route of imposing tort liability on companies that serve as
intermediaries for other parties' potentially injurious messages.

Congress' purpose in providing the §230 immunity was thus evident.
Interactive computer services have millions of users. See Reno v. ACLU,
117 S.Ct. at 2334 (noting that at time of district court trial, "commercial
online services had almost 12 million individual subscribers"). The amount
of information communicated via interactive computer services is therefore
staggering. The specter of tort liability in an area of such prolific speech
would have an obvious chilling effect. It would be impossible for service
providers to screen each of their millions of postings for possible problems.
Faced with potential liability for each message republished by their services,
interactive computer service providers might choose to severely restrict the
number and type of messages posted. Congress considered the weight of
the speech interests implicated and chose to immunize service providers to
avoid any such restrictive effect.

Another important purpose of §230 was to encourage service providers to self-regulate the dissemination of offensive material over their services. In this respect, §230 responded to a New York state court decision,
Stratton Oakmont, Inc. v. Prodigy Servs. Co., 1995 WL 323710 (N.Y.
Sup.Ct. May 24, 1995). There, the plaintiffs sued Prodigy—an interactive
computer service like AOL—for defamatory comments made by an
unidentified party on one of Prodigy's bulletin boards. The court held
Prodigy to the strict liability standard normally applied to original publishers of defamatory statements, rejecting Prodigy's claims that it should be
held only to the lower "knowledge" standard usually reserved for distributors. The court reasoned that Prodigy acted more like an original publisher
than a distributor both because it advertised its practice of controlling
content on its service and because it actively screened and edited messages
posted on its bulletin boards.

Congress enacted §230 to remove the disincentives to self-regulation
created by the *Stratton Oakmont* decision. Under that court's holding,
computer service providers who regulated the dissemination of offensive
material on their services risked subjecting themselves to liability, because
such regulation cast the service provider in the role of a publisher. Fearing
that the specter of liability would therefore deter service providers from
blocking and screening offensive material, Congress enacted §230's broad
immunity "to remove disincentives for the development and utilization of
blocking and filtering technologies that empower parents to restrict their
children's access to objectionable or inappropriate online material." 47
U.S.C. §230(b)(4). In line with this purpose, §230 forbids the imposition
of publisher liability on a service provider for the exercise of its editorial and
self-regulatory functions.

B.

Zeran argues, however, that the §230 immunity eliminates only publisher liability, leaving distributor liability intact. Publishers can be held liable for defamatory statements contained in their works even absent proof that they had specific knowledge of the statement's inclusion. W. Page Keeton et al., Prosser and Keeton on the Law of Torts §113, at 810 (5th ed.1984). According to Zeran, interactive computer service providers like AOL are normally considered instead to be distributors, like traditional news vendors or book sellers. Distributors cannot be held liable for defamatory statements contained in the materials they distribute unless it is proven at a minimum that they have actual knowledge of the defamatory statements upon which liability is predicated. *Id.* at 811 (explaining that distributors are not liable "in the absence of proof that they knew or had reason to know of the existence of defamatory matter contained in matter published"). Zeran contends that he provided AOL with sufficient notice of the defamatory statements appearing on the company's bulletin board. This notice is significant, says Zeran, because AOL could be held liable as a distributor only if it acquired knowledge of the defamatory statements' existence.

Because of the difference between these two forms of liability, Zeran contends that the term "distributor" carries a legally distinct meaning from the term "publisher." Accordingly, he asserts that Congress' use of only the term "publisher" in §230 indicates a purpose to immunize service providers only from publisher liability. He argues that distributors are left unprotected by §230 and, therefore, his suit should be permitted to proceed against AOL. We disagree. Assuming arguendo that Zeran has satisfied the requirements for imposition of distributor liability, this theory of liability is merely a subset, or a species, of publisher liability, and is therefore also foreclosed by §230.

The terms "publisher" and "distributor" derive their legal significance from the context of defamation law. Although Zeran attempts to artfully plead his claims as ones of negligence, they are indistinguishable from a garden variety defamation action. Because the publication of a statement is a necessary element in a defamation action, only one who publishes can be subject to this form of tort liability. Restatement (Second) of Torts §558(b) (1977); Keeton et al., supra, §113, at 802. Publication does not only describe the choice by an author to include certain information. In addition, both the negligent communication of a defamatory statement and the failure to remove such a statement when first communicated by another party—each alleged by Zeran here under a negligence label—constitute publication. Restatement (Second) of Torts §577; see also Tacket v. General Motors Corp., 836 F.2d 1042, 1046-47 (7th Cir.1987). In fact, every repetition of a defamatory statement is considered a publication. Keeton et al., supra, §113, at 799.

In this case, AOL is legally considered to be a publisher. "[E]very one who takes part in the publication . . . is charged with publication." *Id.* Even distributors are considered to be publishers for purposes of defamation law:

> Those who are in the business of making their facilities available to disseminate the writings composed, the speeches made, and the information gathered by others may also be regarded as participating to such an extent in making the books, newspapers, magazines, and information available to others as to be regarded as publishers. They are intentionally making the contents available to others, sometimes without knowing all of the contents—including the defamatory content—and sometimes without any opportunity to ascertain, in advance, that any defamatory matter was to be included in the matter published.

Id. at 803. AOL falls squarely within this traditional definition of a publisher and, therefore, is clearly protected by §230's immunity.

Zeran contends that decisions like *Stratton Oakmont* and Cubby, Inc. v. CompuServe Inc., 776 F.Supp. 135 (S.D.N.Y.1991), recognize a legal distinction between publishers and distributors. He misapprehends, however, the significance of that distinction for the legal issue we consider here. It is undoubtedly true that mere conduits, or distributors, are subject to a different standard of liability. As explained above, distributors must at a minimum have knowledge of the existence of a defamatory statement as a prerequisite to liability. But this distinction signifies only that different standards of liability may be applied within the larger publisher category, depending on the specific type of publisher concerned. See Keeton et al., supra, §113, at 799-800 (explaining that every party involved is charged with publication, although degrees of legal responsibility differ). To the extent that decisions like Stratton and Cubby utilize the terms "publisher" and "distributor" separately, the decisions correctly describe two different standards of liability. Stratton and Cubby do not, however, suggest that distributors are not also a type of publisher for purposes of defamation law.

Zeran simply attaches too much importance to the presence of the distinct notice element in distributor liability. The simple fact of notice surely cannot transform one from an original publisher to a distributor in the eyes of the law. To the contrary, once a computer service provider receives notice of a potentially defamatory posting, it is thrust into the role of a traditional publisher. The computer service provider must decide whether to publish, edit, or withdraw the posting. In this respect, Zeran seeks to impose liability on AOL for assuming the role for which §230 specifically proscribes liability—the publisher role.

Our view that Zeran's complaint treats AOL as a publisher is reinforced because AOL is cast in the same position as the party who originally posted the offensive messages. According to Zeran's logic, AOL is legally at fault because it communicated to third parties an allegedly defamatory statement. This is precisely the theory under which the original poster of the offensive messages would be found liable. If the original party is considered a publisher of the offensive messages, Zeran certainly cannot attach liability to AOL under the same theory without conceding that AOL too must be treated as a publisher of the statements.

Zeran next contends that interpreting §230 to impose liability on service providers with knowledge of defamatory content on their services is consistent with the statutory purposes outlined in Part IIA. Zeran fails, however, to understand the practical implications of notice liability in the interactive computer service context. Liability upon notice would defeat the dual purposes advanced by §230 of the CDA. Like the strict liability imposed by the *Stratton Oakmont* court, liability upon notice reinforces service providers' incentives to restrict speech and abstain from self-regulation.

If computer service providers were subject to distributor liability, they would face potential liability each time they receive notice of a potentially defamatory statement—from any party, concerning any message. Each notification would require a careful yet rapid investigation of the circumstances surrounding the posted information, a legal judgment concerning the information's defamatory character, and an on-the-spot editorial decision whether to risk liability by allowing the continued publication of that information. Although this might be feasible for the traditional print publisher, the sheer number of postings on interactive computer services would create an impossible burden in the Internet context. Cf. Auvil v. CBS 60 Minutes, 800 F.Supp. 928, 931 (E.D.Wash.1992) (recognizing that it is unrealistic for network affiliates to "monitor incoming transmissions and exercise on-the-spot discretionary calls"). Because service providers would be subject to liability only for the publication of information, and not for its removal, they would have a natural incentive simply to remove messages upon notification, whether the contents were defamatory or not. See Philadelphia Newspapers, Inc. v. Hepps, 475 U.S. 767, 777, 106 S.Ct. 1558, 1564, 89 L.Ed.2d 783 (1986) (recognizing that fears of unjustified liability produce a chilling effect antithetical to First Amendment's protection of speech). Thus, like strict liability, liability upon notice has a chilling effect on the freedom of Internet speech.

Similarly, notice-based liability would deter service providers from regulating the dissemination of offensive material over their own services. Any efforts by a service provider to investigate and screen material posted on its service would only lead to notice of potentially defamatory material more frequently and thereby create a stronger basis for liability. Instead of subjecting themselves to further possible lawsuits, service providers would likely eschew any attempts at self-regulation.

More generally, notice-based liability for interactive computer service providers would provide third parties with a no-cost means to create the basis for future lawsuits. Whenever one was displeased with the speech of another party conducted over an interactive computer service, the offended party could simply "notify" the relevant service provider, claiming the information to be legally defamatory. In light of the vast amount of speech communicated through interactive computer services, these notices could produce an impossible burden for service providers, who would be faced with ceaseless choices of suppressing controversial speech or sustaining prohibitive liability. Because the probable effects of distributor liability on the vigor of Internet speech and on service provider self-regulation are directly contrary to §230's statutory purposes, we will not assume that Congress intended to leave liability upon notice intact. . . .

=== **Blumenthal v. Drudge**
=== *United States District Court for the District of Columbia*
=== *992 F. Supp. 44 (D.D.C. 1998)*

FRIEDMAN, J.

This is a defamation case revolving around a statement published on the Internet by defendant Matt Drudge. On August 10, 1997, the following was available to all having access to the Internet:

> The DRUDGE REPORT has learned that top GOP operatives who feel there is a double-standard of only reporting republican shame believe they are holding an ace card: New White House recruit Sidney Blumenthal has a spousal abuse past that has been effectively covered up.
>
> The accusations are explosive.
>
> There are court records of Blumenthal's violence against his wife, one influential republican, who demanded anonymity, tells the DRUDGE REPORT.
>
> If they begin to use [Don] Sipple and his problems against us, against the Republican Party . . . to show hypocrisy, Blumenthal would become fair game. Wasn't it Clinton who signed the Violence Against Women Act?
>
> [There goes the budget deal honeymoon.]
>
> One White House source, also requesting anonymity, says the Blumenthal wife-beating allegation is a pure fiction that has been created by Clinton enemies. [The First Lady] would not have brought him in if he had this in his background, assures the wellplaced staffer. This story about Blumenthal has been in circulation for years.
>
> Last month President Clinton named Sidney Blumenthal an Assistant to the President as part of the Communications Team. He's brought in to work on communications strategy, special projects themeing—a newly created position.
>
> Every attempt to reach Blumenthal proved unsuccessful.

Complaint, Ex. 4.

. . . Access to defendant Drudge's world wide web site is available at no cost to anyone who has access to the Internet at the Internet address of "www.drudgereport.com." Drudge Decl. I ¶9. The front page of the web site contains the logo "Drudge Report." Defendant Drudge has also placed a hyperlink on his web site that, when activated, causes the most recently published edition of the Drudge Report to be displayed. *Id.* The web site also contains numerous hyperlinks to other on-line news publications and news articles that may be of interest to readers of the Drudge Report. *Id*. In addition, during the time period relevant to this case, Drudge had developed a list of regular readers or subscribers to whom he e-mailed each new edition of the Drudge Report. Drudge Decl. I ¶¶6-7. By March 1995, the Drudge Report had 1,000 e-mail subscribers, Drudge Decl. I ¶8; and plaintiffs allege that by 1997 Drudge had 85,000 subscribers to his e-mail service. Complaint ¶47.

In late 1996, defendant Drudge entered into a six-month licensing agreement with the publisher of "Wired" magazine. Under the agreement, the publisher of "Wired" had the right to receive and display future editions of the Drudge Report in "Hotwired," a new electronic Internet publication. In exchange, defendant Drudge received a bi-weekly royalty payment. In addition to the publication of the Drudge Report in "Hotwired," defendant Drudge continued to distribute each new edition via e-mail to his subscribers and via his world wide web site. Drudge Decl. I ¶¶11-12.

In late May or early June of 1997, at approximately the time when the "Wired" licensing agreement expired, defendant Drudge entered into a written license agreement with AOL. The agreement made the Drudge Report available to all members of AOL's service for a period of one year. In exchange, defendant Drudge received a flat monthly "royalty payment" of $3,000 from AOL. During the time relevant to this case, defendant Drudge has had no other source of income. Drudge Decl. I ¶¶13-14. Under the licensing agreement, Drudge is to create, edit, update and "otherwise manage" the content of the Drudge Report, and AOL may "remove content that AOL reasonably determine[s] to violate AOL's then standard terms of service." AOL Mem. at 7; see Exhibit C to Licensing Agreement ¶1, Ex. A to Jennings Decl. Drudge transmits new editions of the Drudge Report by e-mailing them to AOL. AOL then posts the new editions on the AOL service. AOL Mem., Declaration of Matt Drudge ("Drudge Decl. II") ¶17; AOL Mem. at 9. Drudge also has continued to distribute each new edition of the Drudge Report via e-mail and his own web site. Drudge Decl. I ¶16; Hearing Tr. at 41-42.

Late at night on the evening of Sunday, August 10, 1997 (Pacific Daylight Time), defendant Drudge wrote and transmitted the edition of the Drudge Report that contained the alleged defamatory statement about the Blumenthals. Drudge transmitted the report from Los Angeles, California by e-mail to his direct subscribers and by posting both a headline and the full text of the Blumenthal story on his world wide web site. He then transmitted the text but not the headline to AOL, which in turn made it available to AOL subscribers. Drudge Decl. I ¶¶15, 16, 19.4.

After receiving a letter from plaintiffs' counsel on Monday, August 11, 1997, Complaint, Ex. 6, defendant Drudge retracted the story through a special edition of the Drudge Report posted on his web site and e-mailed to his subscribers. Drudge Decl. I ¶¶17-19. At approximately 2:00 a.m. on Tuesday, August 12, 1997, Drudge e-mailed the retraction to AOL which

posted it on the AOL service. Drudge Decl. 1 ¶19; AOL Mem. at 12.5
Defendant Drudge later publicly apologized to the Blumenthals. Drudge
Decl. 1120; Complaint, Ex. 6 (Howard Kurtz, Blumenthals Get Apology,
Plan Lawsuit: Web Site Retracts Story on Clinton Aide, Washington Post,
August 11, 1997, at A 11). . . .

Plaintiffs concede that AOL is a "provider . . . of an interactive computer service" for purposes of Section 230, see Complaint ¶94; Pls.' Mem.
at 3, and that if AOL acted exclusively as a provider of an interactive computer service it may not be held liable for making the Drudge Report
available to AOL subscribers. See 47 U.S.C. §230(c)(1).

They also concede that Drudge is an "information content provider"
because he wrote the alleged defamatory material about the Blumenthals
contained in the Drudge Report. Pls.' Mem. at 4. While plaintiffs suggest
that AOL is responsible along with Drudge because it had some role in
writing or editing the material in the Drudge Report, they have provided no
factual support for that assertion. Indeed, plaintiffs affirmatively state that
"no person, other than Drudge himself, edited, checked, verified, or supervised the information that Drudge published in the Drudge Report."
Plaintiffs' Statement of Material Facts ("Pls.' Stmt.") ¶I (ii). It also is
apparent to the Court that there is no evidence to support the view originally taken by plaintiffs that Drudge is or was an employee or agent of
AOL, and plaintiffs seem to have all but abandoned that argument.

AOL acknowledges both that Section 230(c)(1) would not immunize
AOL with respect to any information AOL developed or created entirely by
itself and that there are situations in which there may be two or more
information content providers responsible for material disseminated on the
Internet—joint authors, a lyricist and a composer, for example. Defendant
America Online, Inc.'s Reply Memorandum In Further Support of Its
Motion for Summary Judgment ("AOL Reply Mem.") at 10; Hearing Tr.
at 12. While Section 230 does not preclude joint liability for the joint
development of content, AOL maintains that there simply is no evidence
here that AOL had any role in creating or developing any of the information in the Drudge Report. The Court agrees. It is undisputed that the
Blumenthal story was written by Drudge without any substantive or editorial involvement by AOL. Drudge Decl. II ¶¶46-47. AOL was nothing
more than a provider of an interactive computer service on which the
Drudge Report was carried, and Congress has said quite clearly that such a
provider shall not be treated as a "publisher or speaker" and therefore may
not be held liable in tort. 47 U.S.C. §230(c)(1). . . .

Plaintiffs [argue] that Section 230 of the Communications Decency
Act does not provide immunity to AOL in this case because Drudge was
not just an anonymous person who sent a message over the Internet
through AOL. He is a person with whom AOL contracted, whom AOL
paid $3,000 a month—$36,000 a year, Drudge's sole, consistent source of
income—and whom AOL promoted to its subscribers and potential
subscribers as a reason to subscribe to AOL. Pls.' Mem. at 2, 7. Further-

more, the license agreement between AOL and Drudge by its terms contemplates more than a passive role for AOL; in it, AOL reserves the "right to remove, or direct [Drudge] to remove, any content which, as reasonably determined by AOL . . . violates AOL's then-standard Terms of Service. . . ." Jennings Decl. ¶16 (quoting Exhibit C to Licensing Agreement ¶I, Ex. A to Jennings Decl.). By the terms of the agreement, AOL also is "entitled to require reasonable changes to . . . content, to the extent such content will, in AOL's good faith judgment, adversely affect operations of the AOL network." *Id.*

In addition, shortly after it entered into the licensing agreement with Drudge, AOL issued a press release making clear the kind of material Drudge would provide to AOL subscribers—gossip and rumor—and urged potential subscribers to sign onto AOL in order to get the benefit of the Drudge Report. The press release was captioned: "AOL Hires Runaway Gossip Success Matt Drudge." Complaint, Ex. 1. It noted that "[m]averick gossip columnist Matt Drudge has teamed up with America Online," and stated: "Giving the Drudge Report a home on America Online (keyword: Drudge) opens up the floodgates to an audience ripe for Drudge's brand of reporting. . . . AOL has made Matt Drudge instantly accessible to members who crave instant gossip and news breaks." *Id.*

Why is this different, the Blumenthals suggest, from AOL advertising and promoting a new purveyor of child pornography or other offensive material? Why should AOL be permitted to tout someone as a gossip columnist or rumor monger who will make such rumors and gossip "instantly accessible" to AOL subscribers, and then claim immunity when that person, as might be anticipated, defames another?

If it were writing on a clean slate, this Court would agree with plaintiffs. AOL has certain editorial rights with respect to the content provided by Drudge and disseminated by AOL, including the right to require changes in content and to remove it; and it has affirmatively promoted Drudge as a new source of unverified instant gossip on AOL. Yet it takes no responsibility for any damage he may cause. AOL is not a passive conduit like the telephone company, a common carrier with no control and therefore no responsibility for what is said over the telephone wires. Because it has the right to exercise editorial control over those with whom it contracts and whose words it disseminates, it would seem only fair to hold AOL to the liability standards applied to a publisher or, at least, like a book store owner or library, to the liability standards applied to a distributor. But Congress has made a different policy choice by providing immunity even where the interactive service provider has an active, even aggressive role in making available content prepared by others.

In some sort of tacit quid pro quo arrangement with the service provider community, Congress has conferred immunity from tort liability as an incentive to Internet service providers to self-police the Internet for obscenity and other offensive material, even where the self-policing is unsuccessful or not even attempted. . . .

COMMENTS AND QUESTIONS

1. In *Zeran*, 47 U.S.C. section 230 gave AOL a complete defense to liability for defamatory postings even after Zeran had informed AOL of the offending statements. Congress is not always so kind to Internet service providers (ISPs), however. The safe harbor rules of the Digital Millennium Copyright Act (DMCA), particularly its "notice and take down" rules, discussed in Chapter 10 following the *Netcom* decision, are noticeably different from the exemption in the Communications Decency Act (CDA). The DMCA relieves ISPs from liability for infringing material of which they are unaware, but it also creates a duty to remove such material after they are informed of its existence—a duty that is backed up by the threat of ISP liability. Is there any principled reason for this difference? Is copyright infringement so different from defamation and similar torts that each requires different rules for ISP liability? Does the CDA exemption go too far?

2. Was the anonymous posting in *Zeran* defamatory?

3. Some commentators have suggested that the standard for what is considered defamatory should be different for Internet speech. Mike Godwin, in his book Cyber Rights: Defending Free Speech in the Digital Age 82-100 (1998) argues that defamation liability is unnecessary because the Internet makes it so much easier for people to respond to and cure misstatements or misimpressions made by others about them. A recent California case seemed to agree, although for different reasons than Godwin gave, indicating that the standard should be different because, in the context of a heated debate on the Internet, people expect statements to be hyperbole and emotional outburst, rather than assertions of fact. See Nicosia v. De Rooy, 1999 WL1128892 (N.D. Cal. July 7, 1999).

4. Both Zeran and Blumenthal were upset that AOL did not take defamatory material posted by users down fast enough. In other instances AOL has been criticized for taking down "uncivil" speech too quickly and arbitrarily enforcing the civility rules of its terms of service. See, e.g., Amy Harmon, Worries About Big Brother at America Online, N.Y. Times, Jan. 31, 1999, http://www.nytimes.com/library/tech/99/01/biztech/articles/31aol.html. What, if any, rights should users have to challenge termination of service for "civility" violations?

B. INDECENT OR OBSCENE COMMUNICATIONS

≡ *Reno v. American Civil Liberties Union*
≡ **Supreme Court of the United States**
≡ *521 U.S. 844 (1997)*

Justice STEVENS delivered the opinion of the Court.

At issue is the constitutionality of two statutory provisions enacted to protect minors from "indecent" and "patently offensive" communications on the Internet. Notwithstanding the legitimacy and importance of the congressional goal of protecting children from harmful materials, we agree with the three-judge District Court that the statute abridges "the freedom of speech" protected by the First Amendment. . . .

II

The Telecommunications Act of 1996, Pub.L. 104-104, 110 Stat. 56, was an unusually important legislative enactment. As stated on the first of its 103 pages, its primary purpose was to reduce regulation and encourage the rapid deployment of new telecommunications technologies. The major components of the statute have nothing to do with the Internet; they were designed to promote competition in the local telephone service market, the multichannel video market, and the market for over-the-air broadcasting. The Act includes seven Titles, six of which are the product of extensive committee hearings and the subject of discussion in Reports prepared by Committees of the Senate and the House of Representatives. By contrast, Title V—known as the "Communications Decency Act of 1996" (CDA)—contains provisions that were either added in executive committee after the hearings were concluded or as amendments offered during floor debate on the legislation. An amendment offered in the Senate was the source of the two statutory provisions challenged in this case. They are informally described as the "indecent transmission" provision and the "patently offensive display" provision. . . .

The first, 47 U.S.C.A. §223(a) (Supp.1997), prohibits the knowing transmission of obscene or indecent messages to any recipient under 18 years of age. It provides in pertinent part:

> (a) Whoever—
>> (1) in interstate or foreign communications— . . .
>>> (B) by means of a telecommunications device knowingly—
>>>> (i) makes, creates, or solicits, and
>>>> (ii) initiates the transmission of,
>>> any comment, request, suggestion, proposal, image, or other communication which is obscene or indecent, knowing that the recipient of the communication is under 18 years of age, regardless of whether the maker of such communication placed the call or initiated the communication; . . . .
>> (2) knowingly permits any telecommunications facility under his control to be used for any activity prohibited by paragraph (1) with the intent that it be used for such activity, shall be fined under Title 18, or imprisoned not more than two years, or both.

The second provision, §223(d), prohibits the knowing sending or displaying of patently offensive messages in a manner that is available to a person under 18 years of age. It provides:

> (d) Whoever—
>> (1) in interstate or foreign communications knowingly—
>>> (A) uses an interactive computer service to send to a specific person or persons under 18 years of age, or
>>> (B) uses any interactive computer service to display in a manner available to a person under 18 years of age,
>> any comment, request, suggestion, proposal, image, or other communication that, in context, depicts or describes, in terms patently offensive as measured by contemporary community standards, sexual or excretory activities or organs, regardless of whether the user of such service placed the call or initiated the communication; or
>>> (2) knowingly permits any telecommunications facility under such person's control to be used for an activity prohibited by paragraph (1) with the intent that it be used for such activity,
> shall be fined under Title 18, or imprisoned not more than two years, or both.

The breadth of these prohibitions is qualified by two affirmative defenses. See §223(e)(5). One covers those who take "good faith, reasonable, effective, and appropriate actions" to restrict access by minors to the prohibited communications. §223(e)(5)(A). The other covers those who restrict access to covered material by requiring certain designated forms of age proof, such as a verified credit card or an adult identification number or code. §223(e)(5)(B).

III

On February 8, 1996, immediately after the President signed the statute, 20 plaintiffs filed suit against the Attorney General of the United States and the Department of Justice challenging the constitutionality of §§223(a)(1) and 223(d). A week later, based on his conclusion that the term "indecent" was too vague to provide the basis for a criminal prosecution, District Judge Buckwalter entered a temporary restraining order against enforcement of §223(a)(1)(B)(ii) insofar as it applies to indecent communications. A second suit was then filed by 27 additional plaintiffs, the two cases were consolidated, and a three-judge District Court was convened pursuant to §561 of the Act. After an evidentiary hearing, that Court entered a preliminary injunction against enforcement of both of the challenged provisions. Each of the three judges wrote a separate opinion, but their judgment was unanimous. . . .

The judgment of the District Court enjoins the Government from enforcing the prohibitions in §223(a)(1)(B) insofar as they relate to "indecent" communications, but expressly preserves the Government's right to investigate and prosecute the obscenity or child pornography activities prohibited therein. The injunction against enforcement of §§223(d)(1) and (2) is unqualified because those provisions contain no separate reference to obscenity or child pornography. . . .

IV

In arguing for reversal, the Government contends that the CDA is plainly constitutional under three of our prior decisions: (1) Ginsberg v. New York, 390 U.S. 629, 88 S.Ct. 1274, 20 L.Ed.2d 195 (1968); (2) FCC v. Pacifica Foundation, 438 U.S. 726, 98 S.Ct. 3026, 57 L.Ed.2d 1073 (1978); and (3) Renton v. Playtime Theatres, Inc., 475 U.S. 41, 106 S.Ct. 925, 89 L.Ed.2d 29 (1986). A close look at these cases, however, raises— rather than relieves—doubts concerning the constitutionality of the CDA.

In *Ginsberg*, we upheld the constitutionality of a New York statute that prohibited selling to minors under 17 years of age material that was considered obscene as to them even if not obscene as to adults. We rejected the defendant's broad submission that "the scope of the constitutional freedom of expression secured to a citizen to read or see material concerned with sex cannot be made to depend on whether the citizen is an adult or a minor." 390 U.S., at 636, 88 S.Ct., at 1279. In rejecting that contention, we relied not only on the State's independent interest in the well-being of its youth, but also on our consistent recognition of the principle that "the parents' claim to authority in their own household to direct the rearing of their children is basic in the structure of our society."

In four important respects, the statute upheld in *Ginsberg* was narrower than the CDA. First, we noted in *Ginsberg* that "the prohibition against sales to minors does not bar parents who so desire from purchasing the magazines for their children." *Id.*, at 639, 88 S.Ct., at 1280. Under the CDA, by contrast, neither the parents' consent—nor even their participation—in the communication would avoid the application of the statute. Second, the New York statute applied only to commercial transactions, *id.*, at 647, 88 S.Ct., at 1284-1285, whereas the CDA contains no such limitation. Third, the New York statute cabined its definition of material that is harmful to minors with the requirement that it be "utterly without redeeming social importance for minors." *Id.*, at 646, 88 S.Ct., at 1284. The CDA fails to provide us with any definition of the term "indecent" as used in §223(a)(1) and, importantly, omits any requirement that the "patently offensive" material covered by §223(d) lack serious literary, artistic, political, or scientific value. Fourth, the New York statute defined a minor as a person under the age of 17, whereas the CDA, in applying to all those under 18 years, includes an additional year of those nearest majority.

In *Pacifica*, we upheld a declaratory order of the Federal Communications Commission, holding that the broadcast of a recording of a 12-minute monologue entitled "Filthy Words" that had previously been delivered to a live audience "could have been the subject of administrative sanctions." 438 U.S., at 730, 98 S.Ct., at 3030 (internal quotations omitted). The Commission had found that the repetitive use of certain words referring to excretory or sexual activities or organs "in an afternoon broadcast when children are in the audience was patently offensive" and concluded that the monologue was indecent "as broadcast." *Id.*, at 735, 98 S.Ct., at 3033. The respondent did not quarrel with the finding that the afternoon broadcast was patently offensive, but contended that it was not "indecent" within the meaning of the relevant statutes because it contained no prurient appeal. After rejecting respondent's statutory arguments, we confronted its two constitutional arguments: (1) that the Commission's construction of its authority to ban indecent speech was so broad that its order had to be set aside even if the broadcast at issue was unprotected; and (2) that since the recording was not obscene, the First Amendment forbade any abridgement of the right to broadcast it on the radio.

In the portion of the lead opinion not joined by Justices Powell and Blackmun, the plurality stated that the First Amendment does not prohibit all governmental regulation that depends on the content of speech. *Id.*, at 742-743, 98 S.Ct., at 3036-3037. Accordingly, the availability of constitutional protection for a vulgar and offensive monologue that was not obscene depended on the context of the broadcast. *Id.*, at 744-748, 98 S.Ct., at 3037-3040. Relying on the premise that "of all forms of communication" broadcasting had received the most limited First Amendment protection, *id.*, at 748-749, 98 S.Ct., at 3039-3040, the Court concluded that the ease with which children may obtain access to broadcasts, "coupled with the concerns recognized in Ginsberg," justified special treatment of indecent broadcasting. *Id.*, at 749-750, 98 S.Ct., at 3040-3041.

As with the New York statute at issue in *Ginsberg*, there are significant differences between the order upheld in *Pacifica* and the CDA. First, the order in *Pacifica*, issued by an agency that had been regulating radio stations for decades, targeted a specific broadcast that represented a rather dramatic departure from traditional program content in order to designate when—rather than whether—it would be permissible to air such a program in that particular medium. The CDA's broad categorical prohibitions are not limited to particular times and are not dependent on any evaluation by an agency familiar with the unique characteristics of the Internet. Second, unlike the CDA, the Commission's declaratory order was not punitive; we expressly refused to decide whether the indecent broadcast "would justify a criminal prosecution." *Id.*, at 750, 98 S.Ct., at 3041. Finally, the Commission's order applied to a medium which as a matter of history had "received the most limited First Amendment protection," *id.*, at 748, 98 S.Ct., at 3040, in large part because warnings could not adequately protect the listener from unexpected program content. The Internet, however, has no comparable history. Moreover, the District Court found that the risk of encountering indecent material by accident is remote because a series of affirmative steps is required to access specific material.

In *Renton,* we upheld a zoning ordinance that kept adult movie theatres out of residential neighborhoods. The ordinance was aimed, not at the content of the films shown in the theaters, but rather at the "secondary effects"—such as crime and deteriorating property values—that these theaters fostered: "'It is th[e] secondary effect which these zoning ordinances attempt to avoid, not the dissemination of "offensive" speech.'" 475 U.S., at 49, 106 S.Ct., at 930 (quoting Young v. American Mini Theatres, Inc., 427 U.S. 50, 71, n. 34, 96 S.Ct. 2440, 2453, n. 34, 49 L.Ed.2d 310 (1976)). According to the Government, the CDA is constitutional because it constitutes a sort of "cyberzoning" on the Internet. But the CDA applies broadly to the entire universe of cyberspace. And the purpose of the CDA is to protect children from the primary effects of "indecent" and "patently offensive" speech, rather than any "secondary" effect of such speech. Thus, the CDA is a content-based blanket restriction on speech, and, as such, cannot be "properly analyzed as a form of time, place, and manner regulation." 475 U.S., at 46, 106 S.Ct., at 928. See also Boos v. Barry, 485 U.S. 312, 321, 108 S.Ct. 1157, 1163, 99 L.Ed.2d 333 (1988) ("Regulations that focus on the direct impact of speech on its audience" are not properly analyzed under *Renton*); Forsyth County v. Nationalist Movement, 505 U.S. 123, 134, 112 S.Ct. 2395, 2403, 120 L.Ed.2d 101 (1992) ("Listeners' reaction to speech is not a content-neutral basis for regulation").

These precedents, then, surely do not require us to uphold the CDA and are fully consistent with the application of the most stringent review of its provisions.

V

In Southeastern Promotions, Ltd. v. Conrad, 420 U.S. 546, 557, 95 S.Ct. 1239, 1245-1246, 43 L.Ed.2d 448 (1975), we observed that "[e]ach medium of expression . . . may present its own problems." Thus, some of our cases have recognized special justifications for regulation of the broadcast media that are not applicable to other speakers, see Red Lion Broadcasting Co. v. FCC, 395 U.S. 367, 89 S.Ct. 1794, 23 L.Ed.2d 371 (1969); FCC v. Pacifica Foundation, 438 U.S. 726, 98 S.Ct. 3026, 57 L.Ed.2d 1073 (1978). In these cases, the Court relied on the history of extensive government regulation of the broadcast medium, see, e.g., *Red Lion,* 395 U.S., at 399-400, 89 S.Ct., at 1811-1812; the scarcity of available frequencies at its inception, see, e.g., Turner Broadcasting System, Inc. v. FCC, 512 U.S. 622, 637-638, 114 S.Ct. 2445, 2456-2457, 129 L.Ed.2d 497 (1994); and its "invasive" nature, see Sable Communications of Cal., Inc. v. FCC, 492 U.S. 115, 128, 109 S.Ct. 2829, 2837-2838, 106 L.Ed.2d 93 (1989).

Those factors are not present in cyberspace. Neither before nor after the enactment of the CDA have the vast democratic fora of the Internet been subject to the type of government supervision and regulation that has attended the broadcast industry. Moreover, the Internet is not as "invasive" as radio or television. The District Court specifically found that "[c]ommunications over the Internet do not 'invade' an individual's home or appear on one's computer screen unbidden. Users seldom encounter content 'by accident.'" 929 F.Supp., at 844 (finding 88). It also found that "[a]lmost all sexually explicit images are preceded by warnings as to the content," and cited testimony that "'odds are slim' that a user would come across a sexually explicit sight by accident." *Ibid.*

We distinguished *Pacifica* in *Sable*, 492 U.S., at 128, 109 S.Ct., at 2837-2838, on just this basis. In *Sable*, a company engaged in the business of offering sexually oriented prerecorded telephone messages (popularly known as "dial-a-porn") challenged the constitutionality of an amendment to the Communications Act that imposed a blanket prohibition on indecent as well as obscene interstate commercial telephone messages. We held that the statute was constitutional insofar as it applied to obscene messages but invalid as applied to indecent messages. In attempting to justify the complete ban and criminalization of indecent commercial telephone messages, the Government relied on *Pacifica*, arguing that the ban was necessary to prevent children from gaining access to such messages. We agreed that "there is a compelling interest in protecting the physical and psychological well-being of minors" which extended to shielding them from indecent messages that are not obscene by adult standards, 492 U.S., at 126, 109 S.Ct., at 2836-2837, but distinguished our "emphatically narrow holding" in *Pacifica* because it did not involve a complete ban and because it involved a different medium of communication, *id.*, at 127, 109 S.Ct., at 2837. We explained that "the dial-it medium requires the listener to take affirmative steps to receive the communication." *Id.*, at 127-128, 109 S.Ct., at 2837. "Placing a telephone call," we continued, "is not the same as turning on a radio and being taken by surprise by an indecent message." *Id.*, at 128, 109 S.Ct., at 2837.

Finally, unlike the conditions that prevailed when Congress first authorized regulation of the broadcast spectrum, the Internet can hardly be considered a "scarce" expressive commodity. It provides relatively unlimited, low-cost capacity for communication of all kinds. The Government estimates that "[a]s many as 40 million people use the Internet today, and that figure is expected to grow to 200 million by 1999." This dynamic, multifaceted category of communication includes not only traditional print and news services, but also audio, video, and still images, as well as interactive, real-time dialogue. Through the use of chat rooms, any person with a phone line can become a town crier with a voice that resonates farther than it could from any soapbox. Through the use of Web pages, mail exploders, and newsgroups, the same individual can become a pamphleteer. As the District Court found, "the content on the Internet is as diverse as human thought." 929 F.Supp., at 842 (finding 74). We agree with its conclusion that our cases provide no basis for qualifying the level of First Amendment scrutiny that should be applied to this medium.

VI

Regardless of whether the CDA is so vague that it violates the Fifth Amendment, the many ambiguities concerning the scope of its coverage render it problematic for purposes of the First Amendment. For instance, each of the two parts of the CDA uses a different linguistic form. The first uses the word "indecent," 47 U.S.C.A. §223(a) (Supp.1997), while the second speaks of material that "in context, depicts or describes, in terms patently offensive as measured by contemporary community standards, sexual or excretory activities or organs," §223(d). Given the absence of a definition of either term, this difference in language will provoke uncertainty among speakers about how the two standards relate to each other and just what they mean. Could a speaker confidently assume that a serious discussion about birth control practices, homosexuality, the First Amendment issues raised by the Appendix to our *Pacifica* opinion, or the consequences of prison rape would not violate the CDA? This uncertainty undermines the likelihood that the CDA has been carefully tailored to the congressional goal of protecting minors from potentially harmful materials.

The vagueness of the CDA is a matter of special concern for two reasons. First, the CDA is a content-based regulation of speech. The vagueness of such a regulation raises special First Amendment concerns because of its obvious chilling effect on free speech. See, e.g., Gentile v. State Bar of Nev., 501 U.S. 1030, 1048-1051, 111 S.Ct. 2720, 2731-2733, 115 L.Ed.2d 888 (1991). Second, the CDA is a criminal statute. In addition to the opprobrium and stigma of a criminal conviction, the CDA threatens violators with penalties including up to two years in prison for each act of violation. The severity of criminal sanctions may well cause speakers to remain silent rather than communicate even arguably unlawful words, ideas, and images. See, e.g., Dombrowski v. Pfister, 380 U.S. 479, 494, 85 S.Ct. 1116, 1125, 14 L.Ed.2d 22 (1965). As a practical matter, this increased deterrent effect, coupled with the "risk of discriminatory enforcement" of vague regulations, poses greater First Amendment concerns than those implicated by the civil regulation reviewed in Denver Area Ed. Telecommunications Consortium, Inc. v. FCC, 518 U.S. 727, 116 S.Ct. 2374, 135 L.Ed.2d 888 (1996).

The Government argues that the statute is no more vague than the obscenity standard this Court established in Miller v. California, 413 U.S. 15, 93 S.Ct. 2607, 37 L.Ed.2d 419 (1973). But that is not so. In *Miller*, this Court reviewed a criminal conviction against a commercial vendor who mailed brochures containing pictures of sexually explicit activities to individuals who had not requested such materials. *Id.*, at 18, 93 S.Ct., at 2611-

2612. Having struggled for some time to establish a definition of obscenity, we set forth in *Miller* the test for obscenity that controls to this day:

> (a) whether the average person, applying contemporary community standards would find that the work, taken as a whole, appeals to the prurient interest; (b) whether the work depicts or describes, in a patently offensive way, sexual conduct specifically defined by the applicable state law; and (c) whether the work, taken as a whole, lacks serious literary, artistic, political, or scientific value. *Id.*, at 24, 93 S.Ct., at 2615 (internal quotation marks and citations omitted).

Because the CDA's "patently offensive" standard (and, we assume arguendo, its synonymous "indecent" standard) is one part of the three-prong *Miller* test, the Government reasons, it cannot be unconstitutionally vague.

The Government's assertion is incorrect as a matter of fact. The second prong of the *Miller* test—the purportedly analogous standard—contains a critical requirement that is omitted from the CDA: that the proscribed material be "specifically defined by the applicable state law." This requirement reduces the vagueness inherent in the open-ended term "patently offensive" as used in the CDA. Moreover, the *Miller* definition is limited to "sexual conduct," whereas the CDA extends also to include (1) "excretory activities" as well as (2) "organs" of both a sexual and excretory nature.

The Government's reasoning is also flawed. Just because a definition including three limitations is not vague, it does not follow that one of those limitations, standing by itself, is not vague. Each of *Miller*'s additional two prongs—(1) that, taken as a whole, the material appeal to the "prurient" interest, and (2) that it "lac[k] serious literary, artistic, political, or scientific value"—critically limits the uncertain sweep of the obscenity definition. The second requirement is particularly important because, unlike the "patently offensive" and "prurient interest" criteria, it is not judged by contemporary community standards. See *Pope v. Illinois*, 481 U.S. 497, 500, 107 S.Ct. 1918, 1920-1921, 95 L.Ed.2d 439 (1987). This "societal value" requirement, absent in the CDA, allows appellate courts to impose some limitations and regularity on the definition by setting, as a matter of law, a national floor for socially redeeming value. The Government's contention that courts will be able to give such legal limitations to the CDA's standards is belied by *Miller*'s own rationale for having juries determine whether material is "patently offensive" according to community standards: that such questions are essentially ones of fact.

In contrast to *Miller* and our other previous cases, the CDA thus presents a greater threat of censoring speech that, in fact, falls outside the statute's scope. Given the vague contours of the coverage of the statute, it unquestionably silences some speakers whose messages would be entitled to constitutional protection. That danger provides further reason for insisting that the statute not be overly broad. The CDA's burden on protected speech cannot be justified if it could be avoided by a more carefully drafted statute.

VII

We are persuaded that the CDA lacks the precision that the First Amendment requires when a statute regulates the content of speech. In order to deny minors access to potentially harmful speech, the CDA effectively suppresses a large amount of speech that adults have a constitutional right to receive and to address to one another. That burden on adult speech is unacceptable if less restrictive alternatives would be at least as effective in achieving the legitimate purpose that the statute was enacted to serve.

In evaluating the free speech rights of adults, we have made it perfectly clear that "[s]exual expression which is indecent but not obscene is protected by the First Amendment." *Sable*, 492 U.S., at 126, 109 S.Ct., at 2836. See also Carey v. Population Services Int'l, 431 U.S. 678, 701, 97 S.Ct. 2010, 2024, 52 L.Ed.2d 675 (1977) ("[W]here obscenity is not involved, we have consistently held that the fact that protected speech may be offensive to some does not justify its suppression"). Indeed, *Pacifica* itself admonished that "the fact that society may find speech offensive is not a sufficient reason for suppressing it." 438 U.S., at 745, 98 S.Ct., at 3038.

It is true that we have repeatedly recognized the governmental interest in protecting children from harmful materials. See *Ginsberg*, 390 U.S., at 639, 88 S.Ct., at 1280; *Pacifica*, 438 U.S., at 749, 98 S.Ct., at 3040. But that interest does not justify an unnecessarily broad suppression of speech addressed to adults. As we have explained, the Government may not "reduc[e] the adult population . . . to . . . only what is fit for children." *Denver*, 518 U.S., at —, 116 S.Ct., at 2393 (internal quotation marks omitted) (quoting *Sable*, 492 U.S., at 128, 109 S.Ct., at 2837-2838). "[R]egardless of the strength of the government's interest" in protecting children, "[t]he level of discourse reaching a mailbox simply cannot be limited to that which would be suitable for a sandbox." Bolger v. Youngs Drug Products Corp., 463 U.S. 60, 74-75, 103 S.Ct. 2875, 2884-2885, 77 L.Ed.2d 469 (1983).

The District Court was correct to conclude that the CDA effectively resembles the ban on "dial-a-porn" invalidated in *Sable*. 929 F.Supp., at 854. In *Sable*, 492 U.S., at 129, 109 S.Ct., at 2838, this Court rejected the argument that we should defer to the congressional judgment that nothing less than a total ban would be effective in preventing enterprising youngsters from gaining access to indecent communications. *Sable* thus made clear that the mere fact that a statutory regulation of speech was enacted for the important purpose of protecting children from exposure to sexually explicit material does not foreclose inquiry into its validity. As we pointed out last Term, that inquiry embodies an "over-arching commitment" to make sure that Congress has designed its statute to accomplish its purpose "without imposing an unnecessarily great restriction on speech." *Denver*, 518 U.S., at —, 116 S.Ct., at 2385.

In arguing that the CDA does not so diminish adult communication, the Government relies on the incorrect factual premise that prohibiting a transmission whenever it is known that one of its recipients is a minor would not interfere with adult-to-adult communication. The findings of the District Court make clear that this premise is untenable. Given the size of the potential audience for most messages, in the absence of a viable age verification process, the sender must be charged with knowing that one or more minors will likely view it. Knowledge that, for instance, one or more members of a 100-person chat group will be minor—and therefore that it would be a crime to send the group an indecent message—would surely burden communication among adults.

The District Court found that at the time of trial existing technology did not include any effective method for a sender to prevent minors from obtaining access to its communications on the Internet without also denying access to adults. The Court found no effective way to determine the age of a user who is accessing material through e-mail, mail exploders, newsgroups, or chat rooms. 929 F.Supp., at 845 (findings 90-94). As a practical matter, the Court also found that it would be prohibitively expensive for noncommercial—as well as some commercial—speakers who have Web sites to verify that their users are adults. *Id.*, at 845-848 (findings 95-116). These limitations must inevitably curtail a significant amount of adult communication on the Internet. By contrast, the District Court found that "[d]espite its limitations, currently available user-based software suggests that a reasonably effective method by which parents can prevent their children from accessing sexually explicit and other material which parents may believe is inappropriate for their children will soon be widely available." *Id.*, at 842 (finding 73).

The breadth of the CDA's coverage is wholly unprecedented. Unlike the regulations upheld in *Ginsberg* and *Pacifica*, the scope of the CDA is not limited to commercial speech or commercial entities. Its open-ended prohibitions embrace all nonprofit entities and individuals posting indecent messages or displaying them on their own computers in the presence of minors. The general, undefined terms "indecent" and "patently offensive" cover large amounts of nonpornographic material with serious educational or other value. Moreover, the "community standards" criterion as applied to the Internet means that any communication available to a nation-wide audience will be judged by the standards of the community most likely to be offended by the message. The regulated subject matter includes any of the seven "dirty words" used in the *Pacifica* monologue, the use of which the Government's expert acknowledged could constitute a felony. See Olsen Test., Tr. Vol. V, 53:16-54:10. It may also extend to discussions about prison rape or safe sexual practices, artistic images that include nude subjects, and arguably the card catalogue of the Carnegie Library.

For the purposes of our decision, we need neither accept nor reject the Government's submission that the First Amendment does not forbid a blanket prohibition on all "indecent" and "patently offensive" messages communicated to a 17-year-old—no matter how much value the message may contain and regardless of parental approval. It is at least clear that the strength of the Government's interest in protecting minors is not equally strong throughout the coverage of this broad statute. Under the CDA, a parent allowing her 17-year-old to use the family computer to obtain information on the Internet that she, in her parental judgment, deems appropriate could face a lengthy prison term. See 47 U.S.C.A. §223(a)(2) (Supp.1997). Similarly, a parent who sent his 17-year-old college freshman information on birth control via e-mail could be incarcerated even though neither he, his child, nor anyone in their home community, found the material "indecent" or "patently offensive," if the college town's community thought otherwise.

The breadth of this content-based restriction of speech imposes an especially heavy burden on the Government to explain why a less restrictive provision would not be as effective as the CDA. It has not done so. The arguments in this Court have referred to possible alternatives such as requiring that indecent material be "tagged" in a way that facilitates parental control of material coming into their homes, making exceptions for messages with artistic or educational value, providing some tolerance for parental choice, and regulating some portions of the Internet—such as commercial web sites—differently than others, such as chat rooms. Particularly in the light of the absence of any detailed findings by the Congress, or even hearings addressing the special problems of the CDA, we are persuaded that the CDA is not narrowly tailored if that requirement has any meaning at all.

VIII

In an attempt to curtail the CDA's facial overbreadth, the Government advances three additional arguments for sustaining the Act's affirmative prohibitions: (1) that the CDA is constitutional because it leaves open ample "alternative channels" of communication; (2) that the plain meaning of the Act's "knowledge" and "specific person" requirement significantly restricts its permissible applications; and (3) that the Act's prohibitions are "almost always" limited to material lacking redeeming social value.

The Government first contends that, even though the CDA effectively censors discourse on many of the Internet's modalities—such as chat groups, newsgroups, and mail exploders—it is nonetheless constitutional because it provides a "reasonable opportunity" for speakers to engage in the restricted speech on the World Wide Web. Brief for Appellants 39. This argument is unpersuasive because the CDA regulates speech on the basis of its content. A "time, place, and manner" analysis is therefore inapplicable.

See Consolidated Edison Co. of N.Y. v. Public Serv. Comm'n of N.Y., 447 U.S. 530, 536, 100 S.Ct. 2326, 2332-2333, 65 L.Ed.2d 319 (1980). It is thus immaterial whether such speech would be feasible on the Web (which, as the Government's own expert acknowledged, would cost up to $10,000 if the speaker's interests were not accommodated by an existing Web site, not including costs for database management and age verification). The Government's position is equivalent to arguing that a statute could ban leaflets on certain subjects as long as individuals are free to publish books. In invalidating a number of laws that banned leafletting on the streets regardless of their content—we explained that "one is not to have the exercise of his liberty of expression in appropriate places abridged on the plea that it may be exercised in some other place." Schneider v. State of N.J. (Town of Irvington), 308 U.S. 147, 163, 60 S.Ct. 146, 151-152, 84 L.Ed. 155 (1939).

The Government also asserts that the "knowledge" requirement of both §§223(a) and (d), especially when coupled with the "specific child" element found in §223(d), saves the CDA from overbreadth. Because both sections prohibit the dissemination of indecent messages only to persons known to be under 18, the Government argues, it does not require transmitters to "refrain from communicating indecent material to adults; they need only refrain from disseminating such materials to persons they know to be under 18." Brief for Appellants 24.

This argument ignores the fact that most Internet fora—including chat rooms, newsgroups, mail exploders, and the Web—are open to all comers. The Government's assertion that the knowledge requirement somehow protects the communications of adults is therefore untenable. Even the strongest reading of the "specific person" requirement of §223(d) cannot save the statute. It would confer broad powers of censorship, in the form of a "heckler's veto," upon any opponent of indecent speech who might simply log on and inform the would-be discoursers that his 17-year-old child—a "specific person . . . under 18 years of age," 47 U.S.C.A. §223(d)(1)(A) (Supp.1997)—would be present.

Finally, we find no textual support for the Government's submission that material having scientific, educational, or other redeeming social value will necessarily fall outside the CDA's "patently offensive" and "indecent" prohibitions. See also n. 37, supra. . . .

XI

In this Court, though not in the District Court, the Government asserts that—in addition to its interest in protecting children—its "[e]qually significant" interest in fostering the growth of the Internet provides an independent basis for upholding the constitutionality of the CDA. Brief for Appellants 19. The Government apparently assumes that the unregulated availability of "indecent" and "patently offensive" material on the Internet is driving countless citizens away from the medium because of the risk of exposing themselves or their children to harmful material.

We find this argument singularly unpersuasive. The dramatic expansion of this new marketplace of ideas contradicts the factual basis of this contention. The record demonstrates that the growth of the Internet has been and continues to be phenomenal. As a matter of constitutional tradition, in the absence of evidence to the contrary, we presume that governmental regulation of the content of speech is more likely to interfere with the free exchange of ideas than to encourage it. The interest in encouraging freedom of expression in a democratic society outweighs any theoretical but unproven benefit of censorship.

Justice O'CONNOR, with whom the Chief Justice joins, concurring in the judgment in part and dissenting in part.

I write separately to explain why I view the Communications Decency Act of 1996 (CDA) as little more than an attempt by Congress to create "adult zones" on the Internet. Our precedent indicates that the creation of such zones can be constitutionally sound. Despite the soundness of its purpose, however, portions of the CDA are unconstitutional because they stray from the blueprint our prior cases have developed for constructing a "zoning law" that passes constitutional muster. . . .

I

Our cases make clear that a "zoning" law is valid only if adults are still able to obtain the regulated speech. If they cannot, the law does more than simply keep children away from speech they have no right to obtain—it interferes with the rights of adults to obtain constitutionally protected speech and effectively "reduce[s] the adult population . . . to reading only what is fit for children." Butler v. Michigan, 352 U.S. 380, 383, 77 S.Ct. 524, 526, 1 L.Ed.2d 412 (1957). The First Amendment does not tolerate such interference. See *id.*, at 383, 77 S.Ct., at 526 (striking down a Michigan criminal law banning sale of books—to minors or adults—that contained words or pictures that "'tende[d] to . . . corrup[t] the morals of youth'"); Sable Communications, supra (invalidating federal law that made it a crime to transmit indecent, but nonobscene, commercial telephone messages to minors and adults); Bolger v. Youngs Drug Products Corp., 463 U.S. 60, 74, 103 S.Ct. 2875, 2884, 77 L.Ed.2d 469 (1983) (striking down a federal law prohibiting the mailing of unsolicited advertisements for contraceptives). If the law does not unduly restrict adults' access to constitutionally protected speech, however, it may be valid. In Ginsberg v. New York, 390 U.S. 629, 634, 88 S.Ct. 1274, 1277-1278, 20 L.Ed.2d 195 (1968), for example, the Court sustained a New York law that barred store owners from selling pornographic magazines to minors in part because adults could still buy those magazines.

The Court in *Ginsberg* concluded that the New York law created a constitutionally adequate adult zone simply because, on its face, it denied access only to minors. The Court did not question—and therefore necessarily assumed—that an adult zone, once created, would succeed in preserving adults' access while denying minors' access to the regulated speech. Before today, there was no reason to question this assumption, for the Court has previously only considered laws that operated in the physical world, a world that with two characteristics that make it possible to create "adult zones": geography and identity. See Lessig, Reading the Constitution in Cyberspace, 45 Emory L.J. 869, 886 (1996). A minor can see an adult dance show only if he enters an establishment that provides such entertainment. And should he attempt to do so, the minor will not be able to conceal completely his identity (or, consequently, his age). Thus, the twin characteristics of geography and identity enable the establishment's proprietor to prevent children from entering the establishment, but to let adults inside.

The electronic world is fundamentally different. Because it is no more than the interconnection of electronic pathways, cyberspace allows speakers and listeners to mask their identities. Cyberspace undeniably reflects some form of geography; chat rooms and Web sites, for example, exist at fixed "locations" on the Internet. Since users can transmit and receive messages on the Internet without revealing anything about their identities or ages, see Lessig, supra, at 901, however, it is not currently possible to exclude persons from accessing certain messages on the basis of their identity.

Cyberspace differs from the physical world in another basic way: Cyberspace is malleable. Thus, it is possible to construct barriers in cyberspace and use them to screen for identity, making cyberspace more like the physical world and, consequently, more amenable to zoning laws. This transformation of cyberspace is already underway. Lessig, supra, at 888-889. *Id.*, at 887 (cyberspace "is moving . . . from a relatively unzoned place to a universe that is extraordinarily well zoned"). Internet speakers (users who post material on the Internet) have begun to zone cyberspace itself through the use of "gateway" technology. Such technology requires Internet users to enter information about themselves—perhaps an adult identification number or a credit card number—before they can access certain areas of cyberspace, 929 F.Supp. 824, 845 (E.D.Pa.1996), much like a bouncer checks a person's driver's license before admitting him to a nightclub. Internet users who access information have not attempted to zone cyberspace itself, but have tried to limit their own power to access information in cyberspace, much as a parent controls what her children watch on television by installing a lock box. This user-based zoning is accomplished through the use of screening software (such as Cyber Patrol or SurfWatch) or browsers with screening capabilities, both of which search addresses and text for keywords that are associated with "adult" sites and, if the user wishes, blocks access to such sites. *Id.*, at 839-842. The Platform for Internet Content Selection (PICS) project is designed to facilitate user-based zoning by encouraging Internet speakers to rate the content of their speech using codes recognized by all screening programs. *Id.*, at 838-839.

Despite this progress, the transformation of cyberspace is not complete. Although gateway technology has been available on the World Wide Web for some time now, *id.*, at 845; Shea v. Reno, 930 F.Supp. 916, 933-934 (S.D.N.Y.1996), it is not available to all Web speakers, 929 F.Supp., at 845-846, and is just now becoming technologically feasible for chat rooms and USENET newsgroups, Brief for Federal Parties 37-38. Gateway technology is not ubiquitous in cyberspace, and because without it "there is no means of age verification," cyberspace still remains largely unzoned—and unzoneable. 929 F.Supp., at 846; *Shea*, supra, at 934. User-based zoning is also in its infancy. For it to be effective, (i) an agreed-upon code (or "tag") would have to exist; (ii) screening software or browsers with screening capabilities would have to be able to recognize the "tag"; and (iii) those programs would have to be widely available—and widely used—by Internet users. At present, none of these conditions is true. Screening software "is not in wide use today" and "only a handful of browsers have screening capabilities." *Shea*, supra, at 945-946. There is, moreover, no agreed-upon "tag" for those programs to recognize. 929 F.Supp., at 848; *Shea*, supra, at 945.

Although the prospects for the eventual zoning of the Internet appear promising, I agree with the Court that we must evaluate the constitutionality of the CDA as it applies to the Internet as it exists today. Ante, at 2349. Given the present state of cyberspace, I agree with the Court that the "display" provision cannot pass muster. Until gateway technology is available throughout cyberspace, and it is not in 1997, a speaker cannot be reasonably assured that the speech he displays will reach only adults because it is impossible to confine speech to an "adult zone." Thus, the only way for a speaker to avoid liability under the CDA is to refrain completely from using indecent speech. But this forced silence impinges on the First Amendment right of adults to make and obtain this speech and, for all intents and purposes, "reduce[s] the adult population [on the Internet] to reading only what is fit for children." *Butler*, 352 U.S., at 383, 77 S.Ct., at 526. As a result, the "display" provision cannot withstand scrutiny. Accord, *Sable Communications*, 492 U.S., at 126-131, 109 S.Ct., at 2836-2839; Bolger v. Youngs Drug Products Corp., 463 U.S., at 73-75, 103 S.Ct., at 2883-2885.

The "indecency transmission" and "specific person" provisions present a closer issue, for they are not unconstitutional in all of their applications. As discussed above, the "indecency transmission" provision makes it a crime to transmit knowingly an indecent message to a person the sender knows is under 18 years of age. 47 U.S.C.A. §223(a)(1)(B) (May 1996 Supp.). The "specific person" provision proscribes the same conduct, although it does not as explicitly require the sender to know that the intended recipient of his indecent message is a minor. §223(d)(1)(A). Appellant urges the Court to construe the provision to impose such a knowledge requirement, see

Brief for Federal Parties 25-27, and I would do so. See Edward J. DeBartolo Corp. v. Florida Gulf Coast Building & Constr. Trades Council, 485 U.S. 568, 575, 108 S.Ct. 1392, 1397, 99 L.Ed.2d 645 (1988) ("[W]here an otherwise acceptable construction of a statute would raise serious constitutional problems, the Court will construe the statute to avoid such problems unless such construction is plainly contrary to the intent of Congress").

So construed, both provisions are constitutional as applied to a conversation involving only an adult and one or more minors—e.g., when an adult speaker sends an e-mail knowing the addressee is a minor, or when an adult and minor converse by themselves or with other minors in a chat room. In this context, these provisions are no different from the law we sustained in *Ginsberg*. Restricting what the adult may say to the minors in no way restricts the adult's ability to communicate with other adults. He is not prevented from speaking indecently to other adults in a chat room (because there are no other adults participating in the conversation) and he remains free to send indecent e-mails to other adults. The relevant universe contains only one adult, and the adult in that universe has the power to refrain from using indecent speech and consequently to keep all such speech within the room in an "adult" zone.

The analogy to *Ginsberg* breaks down, however, when more than one adult is a party to the conversation. If a minor enters a chat room otherwise occupied by adults, the CDA effectively requires the adults in the room to stop using indecent speech. If they did not, they could be prosecuted under the "indecency transmission" and "specific person" provisions for any indecent statements they make to the group, since they would be transmitting an indecent message to specific persons, one of whom is a minor. Accord, ante, at 2347. The CDA is therefore akin to a law that makes it a crime for a bookstore owner to sell pornographic magazines to anyone once a minor enters his store. Even assuming such a law might be constitutional in the physical world as a reasonable alternative to excluding minors completely from the store, the absence of any means of excluding minors from chat rooms in cyberspace restricts the rights of adults to engage in indecent speech in those rooms. The "indecency transmission" and "specific person" provisions share this defect.

But these two provisions do not infringe on adults' speech in all situations. And as discussed below, I do not find that the provisions are overbroad in the sense that they restrict minors' access to a substantial amount of speech that minors have the right to read and view. Accordingly, the CDA can be applied constitutionally in some situations. Normally, this fact would require the Court to reject a direct facial challenge. United States v. Salerno, 481 U.S. 739, 745, 107 S.Ct. 2095, 2100, 95 L.Ed.2d 697 (1987) ("A facial challenge to a legislative Act [succeeds only if] the challenger . . . establish[es] that no set of circumstances exists under which the Act would be valid"). Appellees' claim arises under the First Amendment, however, and they argue that the CDA is facially invalid because it is "substantially overbroad"—that is, it "sweeps too broadly . . . [and] penaliz[es] a substantial amount of speech that is constitutionally protected," Forsyth County v. Nationalist Movement, 505 U.S. 123, 130, 112 S.Ct. 2395, 2401, 120 L.Ed.2d 101 (1992). See Brief for Appellees American Library Association et al. 48; Brief for Appellees American Civil Liberties Union et al. 39-41. I agree with the Court that the provisions are overbroad in that they cover any and all communications between adults and minors, regardless of how many adults might be part of the audience to the communication.

This conclusion does not end the matter, however. Where, as here, "the parties challenging the statute are those who desire to engage in protected speech that the overbroad statute purports to punish . . . [t]he statute may forthwith be declared invalid to the extent that it reaches too far, but otherwise left intact." Brockett v. Spokane Arcades, Inc., 472 U.S. 491, 504, 105 S.Ct. 2794, 2802, 86 L.Ed.2d 394 (1985). There is no question that Congress intended to prohibit certain communications between one adult and one or more minors. See 47 U.S.C.A. §223(a)(1)(B) (May 1996 Supp.) (punishing "[w]hoever . . . initiates the transmission of [any indecent communication] knowingly that the recipient of the communication is under 18 years of age"); §223(d)(1)(A) (punishing "[w]hoever . . . send[s] to a specific person or persons under 18 years of age [a patently offensive message]"). There is also no question that Congress would have enacted a narrower version of these provisions had it known a broader version would be declared unconstitutional. 47 U.S.C. §608 ("If . . . the application [of any provision of the CDA] to any person or circumstance is held invalid, . . . the application of such provision to other persons or circumstances shall not be affected thereby"). I would therefore sustain the "indecency transmission" and "specific person" provisions to the extent they apply to the transmission of Internet communications where the party initiating the communication knows that all of the recipients are minors.

II

Whether the CDA substantially interferes with the First Amendment rights of minors, and thereby runs afoul of the second characteristic of valid zoning laws, presents a closer question. In *Ginsberg*, the New York law we sustained prohibited the sale to minors of magazines that were "harmful to minors." Under that law, a magazine was "harmful to minors" only if it was obscene as to minors. 390 U.S., at 632-633, 88 S.Ct., at 1276-1277. Noting that obscene speech is not protected by the First Amendment, Roth v. United States, 354 U.S. 476, 485, 77 S.Ct. 1304, 1309, 1 L.Ed.2d 1498 (1957), and that New York was constitutionally free to adjust the definition of obscenity for minors, 390 U.S., at 638, 88 S.Ct., at 1279-1280, the Court concluded that the law did not "invad[e] the area of freedom of expression constitutionally secured to minors." *Id.*, at 637, 88 S.Ct., at 1279. New York therefore did not infringe upon the First Amendment rights of minors. Cf. Erznoznik v. Jacksonville, 422 U.S. 205, 213, 95 S.Ct. 2268, 2274-2275, 45 L.Ed.2d 125 (1975) (striking down city ordinance that banned nudity that was not "obscene even as to minors").

The Court neither "accept[s] nor reject[s]" the argument that the CDA is facially overbroad because it substantially interferes with the First Amendment rights of minors. Ante, at 2348. I would reject it. Ginsberg established that minors may constitutionally be denied access to material that is obscene as to minors. As *Ginsberg* explained, material is obscene as to minors if it (i) is "patently offensive to prevailing standards in the adult community as a whole with respect to what is suitable . . . for minors"; (ii) appeals to the prurient interest of minors; and (iii) is "utterly without redeeming social importance for minors." 390 U.S., at 633, 88 S.Ct., at 1276. Because the CDA denies minors the right to obtain material that is "patently offensive"—even if it has some redeeming value for minors and even if it does not appeal to their prurient interests—Congress' rejection of the *Ginsberg* "harmful to minors" standard means that the CDA could ban some speech that is "indecent" (i.e., "patently offensive") but that is not obscene as to minors.

I do not deny this possibility, but to prevail in a facial challenge, it is not enough for a plaintiff to show "some" overbreadth. Our cases require a proof of "real" and "substantial" overbreadth, Broadrick v. Oklahoma, 413 U.S. 601, 615, 93 S.Ct. 2908, 2917-2918, 37 L.Ed.2d 830 (1973), and appellees have not carried their burden in this case. In my view, the universe of speech constitutionally protected as to minors but banned by the CDA—i.e., the universe of material that is "patently offensive," but which nonetheless has some redeeming value for minors or does not appeal to their prurient interest—is a very small one. Appellees cite no examples of speech falling within this universe and do not attempt to explain why that universe is substantial "in relation to the statute's plainly legitimate sweep." *Ibid.* That the CDA might deny minors the right to obtain material that has some "value," see ante, at 2347-2348, is largely beside the point. While discussions about prison rape or nude art, see *ibid.*, may have some re-deeming education value for adults, they do not necessarily have any such value for minors, and under *Ginsberg*, minors only have a First Amendment right to obtain patently offensive material that has "redeeming social im-portance for minors," 390 U.S., at 633, 88 S.Ct., at 1276. There is also no evidence in the record to support the contention that "many [e]-mail transmissions from an adult to a minor are conversations between family members," ante, at 2341, n. 32, and no support for the legal proposition that such speech is absolutely immune from regulation. Accordingly, in my view, the CDA does not burden a substantial amount of minors' constitu-tionally protected speech.

Thus, the constitutionality of the CDA as a zoning law hinges on the extent to which it substantially interferes with the First Amendment rights of adults. Because the rights of adults are infringed only by the "display" provision and by the "indecency transmission" and "specific person" provisions as applied to communications involving more than one adult, I would invalidate the CDA only to that extent. Insofar as the "indecency transmission" and "specific person" provisions prohibit the use of indecent speech in communications between an adult and one or more minors, however, they can and should be sustained. The Court reaches a contrary conclusion, and from that holding that I respectfully dissent.

COMMENTS AND QUESTIONS

1. Would it be constitutional for Congress or state legislatures to enact a law that would prohibit minors from engaging in "indecent" speech with other minors? How would the authors of the majority and dissenting opinions in *Reno* answer that question?

2. In the aftermath of the *Reno* decision, Congress enacted the Child Online Protection Act (COPA). Section 1403(a) of this act, which is codified at 47 U.S.C. section 231, provides that

[w]hoever knowingly and with knowledge of the character of the material, in interstate or foreign commerce by means of the World Wide Web, makes any communication for commercial purposes that is available to any minor and that includes any material that is harmful to minors shall be fined not more than $50,000, imprisoned not more than 6 months, or both.

COPA differs from the CDA in a number of respects. For one thing, COPA contains congressional findings about the need to protect children from harmful materials on the Internet. Second, it defines the term "harmful to minors" in a more precise way, as material that is obscene or that

(A) the average person, applying contemporary community standards, would find, taking the material as a whole and with respect to minors, is designed to appeal to, or is designed to pander to, the prurient interest;

(B) depicts, describes, or represents, in a manner patently offensive with respect to minors, an actual or simulated sexual act or sexual contact, an actual or simulated normal or perverted sexual act, or a lewd exhibition of the genitals or post-pubescent female breast; and

(C) taken as a whole, lacks serious literary, artistic, political, or scientific value for minors.

Third, COPA applies only to communications "for commercial purposes," a term that the statute also defines with some precision, apparently in the hope that this too might increase the likelihood that COPA will be adjudged constitutional.

The American Civil Liberties Union has challenged the constitutionality of COPA, arguing that even though this statute is narrower than the

CDA provisions struck down in *Reno*, it nonetheless is not tailored narrowly enough to satisfy First Amendment standards, places unwarranted burdens on free speech, and will substantially chill protected expression. In ACLU v. Reno, 31 F. Supp. 2d 473 (E.D. Pa. 1999), the court issued a preliminary injunction to prohibit enforcement of COPA because of the likely success of the ACLU's First Amendment challenge. This decision is on appeal, however.

3. Another way to prevent children from being exposed to harmful materials on the Internet is for their parents to use filtering software that blocks access to sites that the software's developers rate as unsuitable for children. The World Wide Web Consortium (W3C) has developed a system to enable the tagging of Web sites, known as the Platform for Independent Content Selection (PICS), that can be used to automate filtering. Jonathan Weinberg discusses filtering and PICS in his article Rating the Net, 19 Hastings COMM/ENT L.J. 453 (1997):

> It is easy to understand the acclaim for filtering software. This software can do an impressive job at blocking access to sexually explicit material that a parent does not wish his or her child to see. The PICS standard for describing ratings systems is an important technical achievement, allowing the development and easy use of a variety of sophisticated rating schemes.

Id. at 455. However, Weinberg suggests that filtering and rating systems have their costs:

> It seems likely that a substantial number of adults, in the near future, will view the Internet through filters administered by blocking software. Intermediaries —employers, libraries, and others—will gain greater control over the things these adults read and see. Sites may be stripped out of the filtered universe because of deliberate political choices on the part of rating service administrators, and because of inaccuracies inherent in the ratings process.

Id. at 482.

Lawrence Lessig has also warned that ratings systems such as PICS are troublesome in part because they help to create an infrastructure that could enable censorship. See, e.g., Lawrence Lessig, Code and Other Laws of Cyberspace (forthcoming 2000).

As Weinberg points out, some libraries have decided to use filtering software for the computers through which they provide Internet access to their patrons. An association of library patrons and some individual patrons brought an action under 42 U.S.C. section 1983 to challenge their public library's use of Internet filtering software as an unconstitutional abridgement of freedoms protected by the First Amendment. In particular, they charged that the library's policy was a content-based restriction on access to the Internet and that it impermissibly barred them from accessing protected speech such as the Quaker Home page, the Zero Population Growth Web site, and an American Association of University Women of Maryland site. In Mainstream Loudoun v. Board of Trustees of the Loudoun County Library,

2 F. Supp. 2d 783 (E.D. Va. 1998), the court ruled that the complaint had stated a viable claim against the library. Would the result have been different if the library had allowed adults to gain Internet access without filtering software and insisted on such software only when children wanted to have Internet access?

4. As the *Reno* decision makes clear, the CDA's provisions still apply to obscene communications on the Internet. The *Miller* test for obscenity indicates that whether the content is to be considered as "appealing to prurient" interest should be judged by contemporary community standards. But how should courts determine "community standards" in the context of a global medium like the Internet? One reason the *Thomas* case, below, is interesting is that the material on the bulletin board in that case had been investigated by California officials and was determined not to be obscene under California standards. Tennessee standards, however, are apparently different. As you read the following case, consider whether enough difference exists between the Internet *per se* and Thomas's bulletin board service to warrant different treatment by the law. Should courts reach a different result or employ a different analysis in a case involving pornographic or possibly obscene material posted on the Internet?

≡ *United States v. Thomas*
≡ *United States Court of Appeals for the Sixth Circuit*
≡ *74 F.3d 701 (6th Cir. 1996)*

EDMUNDS, District Judge.

Robert Thomas and his wife Carleen Thomas began operating the Amateur Action Computer Bulletin Board System ("AABBS") from their home in Milpitas, California in February 1991. The AABBS was a computer bulletin board system that operated by using telephones, modems, and personal computers. Its features included e-mail, chat lines, public messages, and files that members could access, transfer, and download to their own computers and printers.

Information loaded onto the bulletin board was first converted into binary code, i.e., 0's and 1's, through the use of a scanning device. After purchasing sexually-explicit magazines from public adult book stores in California, Defendant Robert Thomas used an electronic device called a scanner to convert pictures from the magazines into computer files called Graphic Interchange Format files or "GIF" files. The AABBS contained approximately 14,000 GIF files. Mr. Thomas also purchased, sold, and delivered sexually-explicit videotapes to AABBS members. Customers ordered the tapes by sending Robert Thomas an e-mail message, and Thomas typically delivered them by use of the United Parcel Service ("U.P.S.").

Persons calling the AABBS without a password could view the introductory screens of the system which contained brief, sexually-explicit descriptions of the GIF files and adult videotapes that were offered for sale. Access to the GIF files, however, was limited to members who were given a password after they paid a membership fee and submitted a signed application form that Defendant Robert Thomas reviewed. The application form requested the applicant's age, address, and telephone number and required a signature.

Members accessed the GIF files by using a telephone, modem and personal computer. A modem located in the Defendants' home answered the calls. After they established membership by typing in a password, members could then select, retrieve, and instantly transport GIF files to their own computer. A caller could then view the GIF file on his computer screen and print the image out using his printer. The GIF files contained the AABBS name and access telephone number; many also had "Distribute Freely" printed on the image itself.

In July 1993, a United States Postal Inspector, Agent David Dirmeyer ("Dirmeyer"), received a complaint regarding the AABBS from an individual who resided in the Western District of Tennessee. Dirmeyer dialed the AABBS's telephone number. As a non-member, he viewed a screen that read "Welcome to AABBS, the Nastiest Place On Earth," and was able to select various "menus" and read graphic descriptions of the GIF files and videotapes that were offered for sale.

Subsequently, Dirmeyer used an assumed name and sent in $55 along with an executed application form to the AABBS. Defendant Robert Thomas called Dirmeyer at his undercover telephone number in Memphis, Tennessee, acknowledged receipt of his application, and authorized him to log-on with his personal password. Thereafter, Dirmeyer dialed the AABBS's telephone number, logged-on and, using his computer/modem in Memphis, downloaded the GIF files listed in counts 2-7 of the Defendants' indictments. These GIF files depicted images of bestiality, oral sex, incest, sado-masochistic abuse, and sex scenes involving urination. Dirmeyer also ordered six sexually-explicit videotapes from the AABBS and received them via U.P.S. at a Memphis, Tennessee address. Dirmeyer also had several e-mail and chat-mode conversations with Defendant Robert Thomas.

On January 10, 1994, a search warrant was issued by a U.S. Magistrate Judge for the Northern District of California. The AABBS's location was subsequently searched, and the Defendants' computer system was seized.

On January 25, 1994, a federal grand jury for the Western District of Tennessee returned a twelve-count indictment charging Defendants Robert and Carleen Thomas with the following criminal violations: one count under 18 U.S.C. §371 for conspiracy to violate federal obscenity laws—18 U.S.C. §§1462, 1465 (Count 1), six counts under 18 U.S.C. §1465 for knowingly using and causing to be used a facility and means of interstate commerce—a combined computer/telephone system—for the purpose of transporting obscene, computer-generated materials (the GIF files) in interstate commerce (Counts 2-7), three counts under 18 U.S.C. §1462 for

shipping obscene videotapes via U.P.S. (Counts 8-10), one count of causing the transportation of materials depicting minors engaged in sexually
explicit conduct in violation of 18 U.S.C. §2252(a)(1) as to Mr. Thomas
only (Count 11), and one count of forfeiture under 18 U.S.C. §1467
(Count 12).

. . . Defendant Robert Thomas was found guilty on all counts except
count 11 (child pornography). Defendant Carleen Thomas was found guilty
on counts 1-10. The jury also found that the Defendants' interest in their
computer system should be forfeited to the United States. Robert and
Carleen Thomas were sentenced on December 2, 1994 to 37 and 30
months of incarceration, respectively. They filed their notices of appeal on
December 9, 1994. . . .

Defendants [] argue that their convictions under counts 1-7 of their
indictments violate their First Amendment rights to freedom of speech. As
the Supreme Court noted in *Bose*, when constitutional facts are at issue, this
court has a duty to conduct an independent review of the record "both to
be sure that the speech in question actually falls within the unprotected
category and to confine the perimeters of any unprotected category within
acceptably narrow limits in an effort to ensure that protected expression will
not be inhibited." Bose Corp. v. Consumers Union of United States, Inc.,
466 U.S. 485, 505, 104 S.Ct. 1949, 1962, 80 L.Ed.2d 502 (1984).

1. Defendants' Right to Possess the GIF Files in Their Home

Defendants rely on Stanley v. Georgia, 394 U.S. 557, 89 S.Ct. 1243,
22 L.Ed.2d 542 (1969), and argue they have a constitutionally protected
right to possess obscene materials in the privacy of their home. They insist
that the GIF files containing sexually-explicit material never left their home.
Defendants' reliance on *Stanley* is misplaced.

The Supreme Court has clarified that *Stanley* "depended not on any
First Amendment Right to purchase or possess obscene materials, but on
the right to privacy in the home." United States v. 12 200-Ft. Reels of
Super 8mm. Film, 413 U.S. 123, 126, 93 S.Ct. 2665, 2668, 37 L.Ed.2d
500 (1973). It has also recognized that the right to possess obscene materials in the privacy of one's home does not create "a correlative right to
receive it, transport it, or distribute it" in interstate commerce even if it is
for private use only. Nor does it create "some zone of constitutionally
protected privacy [that] follows such material when it is moved outside the
home area." United States v. Orito, 413 U.S. 139, 141-42, 93 S.Ct. 2674,
2677, 37 L.Ed.2d 513 (1973); see also *12 200-Ft. Reels*, 413 U.S. at 128,
93 S.Ct. at 2669.

Defendants went beyond merely possessing obscene GIF files in their
home. They ran a business that advertised and promised its members the
availability and transportation of the sexually-explicit GIF files they selected.

In light of the overwhelming evidence produced at trial, it is spurious for Defendants to claim now that they did not intend to sell, disseminate, or share the obscene GIF files they advertised on the AABBS with members outside their home and in other states.

2. The Community Standards to Be Applied When Determining Whether the GIF Files Are Obscene

In Miller v. California, 413 U.S. 15, 93 S.Ct. 2607, 37 L.Ed.2d 419 (1973), the Supreme Court set out a three-prong test for obscenity. It inquired whether (1) "'the average person applying contemporary community standards' would find that the work, taken as a whole appeals to the prurient interest"; (2) it "depicts or describes, in a patently offensive way, sexual conduct specifically defined by applicable state law"; and (3) "the work, taken as a whole, lacks serious literary, artistic, political, or scientific value." *Id.* at 24, 93 S.Ct. at 2615.

Under the first prong of the *Miller* obscenity test, the jury is to apply "contemporary community standards." Defendants acknowledge the general principle that, in cases involving interstate transportation of obscene material, juries are properly instructed to apply the community standards of the geographic area where the materials are sent. *Miller*, 413 U.S. at 15, 30-34, 93 S.Ct. at 2610, 2618-20. Nonetheless, Defendants assert that this principle does not apply here for the same reasons they claim venue was improper. As demonstrated above, this argument cannot withstand scrutiny. The computer-generated images described in counts 2-7 were electronically transferred from Defendants' home in California to the Western District of Tennessee. Accordingly, the community standards of that judicial district were properly applied in this case.

Issues regarding which community's standards are to be applied are tied to those involving venue. It is well-established that:

> [v]enue for federal obscenity prosecutions lies "in any district from, through, or into which" the allegedly obscene material moves, according to 18 U.S.C. §3237. This may result in prosecutions of persons in a community to which they have sent materials which is obscene under that community's standards though the community from which it is sent would tolerate the same material.

United States v. Peraino, 645 F.2d 548, 551 (6th Cir.1981). Prosecutions may be brought either in the district of dispatch or the district of receipt, *Bagnell*, 679 F.2d at 830-31, and obscenity is determined by the standards of the community where the trial takes place. See *Miller*, 413 U.S. at 15, 30-34, 93 S.Ct. at 2610, 2618-20; Hamling v. United States, 418 U.S. 87, 105-6, 94 S.Ct. 2887, 2901-02, 41 L.Ed.2d 590 (1974); *Sable*, 492 U.S. at 125, 109 S.Ct. at 2836. Moreover, the federal courts have consistently recognized that it is not unconstitutional to subject interstate distributors of obscenity to varying community standards. *Hamling*, 418 U.S. at 106, 94 S.Ct. at 2901-02; United States v. Sandy, 605 F.2d 210, 217 (6th Cir.), *cert. denied*, 444 U.S. 984, 100 S.Ct. 490, 62 L.Ed.2d 412 (1979).

3. The Implications of Computer Technology on the Definition of "Community"

Defendants and Amicus Curiae appearing on their behalf argue that the computer technology used here requires a new definition of community, i.e., one that is based on the broad-ranging connections among people in cyberspace rather than the geographic locale of the federal judicial district of the criminal trial. Without a more flexible definition, they argue, there will be an impermissible chill on protected speech because BBS operators cannot select who gets the materials they make available on their bulletin boards. Therefore, they contend, BBS operators like Defendants will be forced to censor their materials so as not to run afoul of the standards of the community with the most restrictive standards.

Defendants' First Amendment issue, however, is not implicated by the facts of this case. This is not a situation where the bulletin board operator had no knowledge or control over the jurisdictions where materials were distributed for downloading or printing. Access to the Defendants' AABBS was limited. Membership was necessary and applications were submitted and screened before passwords were issued and materials were distributed. Thus, Defendants had in place methods to limit user access in jurisdictions where the risk of a finding of obscenity was greater than that in California. They knew they had a member in Memphis; the member's address and local phone number were provided on his application form. If Defendants did not wish to subject themselves to liability in jurisdictions with less tolerant standards for determining obscenity, they could have refused to give passwords to members in those districts, thus precluding the risk of liability.

This result is supported by the Supreme Court's decision in Sable Communications of Cal., Inc. v. F.C.C. where the Court rejected Sable's argument that it should not be compelled to tailor its dial-a-porn messages to the standards of the least tolerant community. 492 U.S. 115, 125-26, 109 S.Ct. 2829, 2836-37, 106 L.Ed.2d 93 (1989). The Court recognized that distributors of allegedly obscene materials may be subjected to the standards of the varying communities where they transmit their materials, citing *Hamling*, and further noted that Sable was "free to tailor its messages, on a selective basis, if it so chooses, to the communities it chooses to serve." *Id*. at 125, 109 S.Ct. at 2836. The Court also found no constitutional impediment to forcing Sable to incur some costs in developing and implementing a method for screening a customer's location and "providing messages compatible with community standards." *Id*.

Thus, under the facts of this case, there is no need for this court to adopt a new definition of "community" for use in obscenity prosecutions involving electronic bulletin boards. This court's decision is guided by one of the cardinal rules governing the federal courts, i.e., never reach constitutional questions not squarely presented by the facts of a case. Brockett v. Spokane Arcades, Inc., 472 U.S. 491, 502, 105 S.Ct. 2794, 2801, 86 L.Ed.2d 394 (1985). . . .

COMMENTS AND QUESTIONS

1. Congress has enacted a number of laws to regulate child pornography, three of which were at issue in United States v. Mohrbacher, 182 F.3d 1041 (9th Cir. 1999). Mohrbacher downloaded images of child pornography from a foreign-based electronic bulletin board. He did not challenge his conviction for receiving visual depictions of minors engaging in sexually explicit conduct, nor for possession of three or more items containing such depictions. However, he successfully appealed his conviction on two other counts that required proof that he transported or shipped child pornography in violation of 18 U.S.C. section 2252(a)(1). Did the court get taken in by the virtual nature of the Internet when deciding that Mohrbacher did not "ship" or "transport" images when he used the Internet to get them?

2. Consider the following excerpt from United States v. Hilton, 167 F.3d 61 (1st Cir. 1999):

> In 1996, Congress enacted the Child Pornography Prevention Act (the "CPPA"), 18 U.S.C. §2252A, to attack the rise of computerized or "virtual" child pornography. These images may take many forms—a photograph of a real child may be scanned and replicated, an innocent picture of a child may be manipulated by computer to create a sexually-oriented photo, or a fake child (ranging from a simple cartoon character to a high-resolution image resembling a real child) can be generated wholly by computer graphics. The law prohibits, inter alia, knowing possession of visual images depicting minors or those who "appear to be" minors engaging in sexually explicit conduct. This case presents constitutional issues of first impression in this circuit: whether the CPPA's definition of child pornography is so overbroad as to contravene the First Amendment or so vague as to violate due process.
>
> In resolving defendant David Hilton's motion to dismiss the indictment in his favor, the United States District Court for the District of Maine answered both questions in the affirmative. The court was troubled by a perceived difficulty in determining whether a depicted person appeared to be under 18 years old and by its belief that the statute impermissibly criminalizes possession of adult pornography. We reverse. We hold that the law, properly construed, survives Hilton's facial constitutional challenge. It neither impinges substantially on protected expression nor is so vague as to offend due process.

C. SPAM

CompuServe Incorporated v. Cyber
Promotions, Inc.
United States District Court for the Southern District of Ohio
962 F. Supp. 1015 (S.D. Ohio 1997)

GRAHAM, District Judge.

This case presents novel issues regarding the commercial use of the Internet, specifically the right of an online computer service to prevent a commercial enterprise from sending unsolicited electronic mail advertising to its subscribers.

Plaintiff CompuServe Incorporated ("CompuServe") is one of the major national commercial online computer services. It operates a computer communication service through a proprietary nationwide computer network. In addition to allowing access to the extensive content available within its own proprietary network, CompuServe also provides its subscribers with a link to the much larger resources of the Internet. This allows its subscribers to send and receive electronic messages, known as "e-mail," by the Internet. Defendants Cyber Promotions, Inc. and its president Sanford Wallace are in the business of sending unsolicited e-mail advertisements on behalf of themselves and their clients to hundreds of thousands of Internet users, many of whom are CompuServe subscribers. CompuServe has notified defendants that they are prohibited from using its computer equipment to process and store the unsolicited e-mail and has requested that they terminate the practice. Instead, defendants have sent an increasing volume of e-mail solicitations to CompuServe subscribers. CompuServe has attempted to employ technological means to block the flow of defendants' e-mail transmissions to its computer equipment, but to no avail.

This matter is before the Court on the application of CompuServe for a preliminary injunction which would extend the duration of the temporary restraining order issued by this Court on October 24, 1996 and which would in addition prevent defendants from sending unsolicited advertisements to CompuServe subscribers.

For the reasons which follow, this Court holds that where defendants engaged in a course of conduct of transmitting a substantial volume of electronic data in the form of unsolicited e-mail to plaintiff's proprietary computer equipment, where defendants continued such practice after repeated demands to cease and desist, and where defendants deliberately evaded plaintiff's affirmative efforts to protect its computer equipment from such use, plaintiff has a viable claim for trespass to personal property and is entitled to injunctive relief to protect its property.

I. . . .

Internet users often pay a fee for Internet access. However, there is no per-message charge to send electronic messages over the Internet and such messages usually reach their destination within minutes. Thus electronic mail provides an opportunity to reach a wide audience quickly and at almost no cost to the sender. It is not surprising therefore that some companies, like defendant Cyber Promotions, Inc., have begun using the Internet to distribute advertisements by sending the same unsolicited commercial message to hundreds of thousands of Internet users at once. Defendants refer to this as "bulk e-mail," while plaintiff refers to it as "junk e-mail." In the vernacular of the Internet, unsolicited e-mail advertising is sometimes referred to pejoratively as "spam."

CompuServe subscribers use CompuServe's domain name "Compu-Serve.com" together with their own unique alpha-numeric identifier to form a distinctive e-mail mailing address. That address may be used by the subscriber to exchange electronic mail with any one of tens of millions of other Internet users who have electronic mail capability. E-mail sent to CompuServe subscribers is processed and stored on CompuServe's proprietary computer equipment. Thereafter, it becomes accessible to CompuServe's subscribers, who can access CompuServe's equipment and electronically retrieve those messages.

Over the past several months, CompuServe has received many complaints from subscribers threatening to discontinue their subscription unless CompuServe prohibits electronic mass mailers from using its equipment to send unsolicited advertisements. CompuServe asserts that the volume of messages generated by such mass mailings places a significant burden on its equipment which has finite processing and storage capacity. CompuServe receives no payment from the mass mailers for processing their unsolicited advertising. However, CompuServe's subscribers pay for their access to CompuServe's services in increments of time and thus the process of accessing, reviewing and discarding unsolicited e-mail costs them money, which is one of the reasons for their complaints. CompuServe has notified defendants that they are prohibited from using its proprietary computer equipment to process and store unsolicited e-mail and has requested them to cease and desist from sending unsolicited e-mail to its subscribers. Nonetheless, defendants have sent an increasing volume of e-mail solicitations to CompuServe subscribers.

In an effort to shield its equipment from defendants' bulk e-mail, CompuServe has implemented software programs designed to screen out the messages and block their receipt. In response, defendants have modified their equipment and the messages they send in such a fashion as to circumvent CompuServe's screening software. Allegedly, defendants have been able to conceal the true origin of their messages by falsifying the point-of-origin information contained in the header of the electronic messages. Defendants have removed the "sender" information in the header of their messages and replaced it with another address. Also, defendants have developed the capability of configuring their computer servers to conceal their true domain name and appear on the Internet as another computer, further concealing the true origin of the messages. By manipulating this data, defendants have been able to continue sending messages to Compu-Serve's equipment in spite of CompuServe's protests and protective efforts.

Defendants assert that they possess the right to continue to send these communications to CompuServe subscribers. CompuServe contends that, in doing so, the defendants are trespassing upon its personal property. . . .

The Restatement §217(b) states that a trespass to chattel may be committed by intentionally using or intermeddling with the chattel in possession of another. Restatement §217, Comment e defines physical "intermeddling" as follows:

> . . . intentionally bringing about a physical contact with the chattel. The actor may commit a trespass by an act which brings him into an intended physical contact with a chattel in the possession of another[.]

Electronic signals generated and sent by computer have been held to be sufficiently physically tangible to support a trespass cause of action. Thrifty-Tel, Inc., v. Bezenek, 46 Cal.App.4th 1559, 1567, 54 Cal.Rptr.2d 468 (1996); State v. McGraw, 480 N.E.2d 552, 554 (Ind.1985) (Indiana Supreme Court recognizing in dicta that a hacker's unauthorized access to a computer was more in the nature of trespass than criminal conversion); and State v. Riley, 121 Wash.2d 22, 846 P.2d 1365 (1993) (computer hacking as the criminal offense of "computer trespass" under Washington law). It is undisputed that plaintiff has a possessory interest in its computer systems. Further, defendants' contact with plaintiff's computers is clearly intentional. Although electronic messages may travel through the Internet over various routes, the messages are affirmatively directed to their destination.

Defendants, citing Restatement (Second) of Torts §221, which defines "dispossession", assert that not every interference with the personal property of another is actionable and that physical dispossession or substantial interference with the chattel is required. Defendants then argue that they did not, in this case, physically dispossess plaintiff of its equipment or substantially interfere with it. However, the Restatement (Second) of Torts §218 defines the circumstances under which a trespass to chattels may be actionable:

> One who commits a trespass to a chattel is subject to liability to the possessor of the chattel if, but only if,
>
> (a) he dispossesses the other of the chattel, or
> (b) the chattel is impaired as to its condition, quality, or value, or
> (c) the possessor is deprived of the use of the chattel for a substantial time, or

(d) bodily harm is caused to the possessor, or harm is caused to some person or thing in which the possessor has a legally protected interest.

Therefore, an interference resulting in physical dispossession is just one circumstance under which a defendant can be found liable. Defendants suggest that "[u]nless an alleged trespasser actually takes physical custody of the property or physically damages it, courts will not find the 'substantial interference' required to maintain a trespass to chattel claim." (Defendant's Memorandum at 13). To support this rather broad proposition, defendants cite only two cases which make any reference to the Restatement. In Glidden v. Szybiak, 95 N.H. 318, 63 A.2d 233 (1949), the court simply indicated that an action for trespass to chattels could not be maintained in the absence of some form of damage. The court held that where plaintiff did not contend that defendant's pulling on her pet dog's ears caused any injury, an action in tort could not be maintained. *Id.* 63 A.2d at 235. In contrast, plaintiff in the present action has alleged that it has suffered several types of injury as a result of defendants' conduct. In Koepnick v. Sears Roebuck & Co., 158 Ariz. 322, 762 P.2d 609 (1988) the court held that a two-minute search of an individual's truck did not amount to a "dispossession" of the truck as defined in Restatement §221 or a deprivation of the use of the truck for a substantial time. It is clear from a reading of Restatement §218 that an interference or intermeddling that does not fit the §221 definition of "dispossession" can nonetheless result in defendants' liability for trespass. The *Koepnick* court did not discuss any of the other grounds for liability under Restatement §218.

A plaintiff can sustain an action for trespass to chattels, as opposed to an action for conversion, without showing a substantial interference with its right to possession of that chattel. *Thrifty-Tel, Inc.,* 46 Cal.App.4th at 1567, 54 Cal.Rptr.2d 468 (quoting Zaslow v. Kroenert, 29 Cal.2d 541, 176 P.2d 1 (Cal.1946)). Harm to the personal property or diminution of its quality, condition, or value as a result of defendants' use can also be the predicate for liability. Restatement §218(b).

> An unprivileged use or other intermeddling with a chattel which results in actual impairment of its physical condition, quality or value to the possessor makes the actor liable for the loss thus caused. In the great majority of cases, the actor's intermeddling with the chattel impairs the value of it to the possessor, as distinguished from the mere affront to his dignity as possessor, only by some impairment of the physical condition of the chattel. There may, however, be situations in which the value to the owner of a particular type of chattel may be impaired by dealing with it in a manner that does not affect its physical condition. . . . In such a case, the intermeddling is actionable even though the physical condition of the chattel is not impaired.

The Restatement (Second) of Torts §218, Comment h. In the present case, any value CompuServe realizes from its computer equipment is wholly derived from the extent to which that equipment can serve its subscriber base. Michael Mangino, a software developer for CompuServe who monitors its mail processing computer equipment, states by affidavit that handling the enormous volume of mass mailings that CompuServe receives places a tremendous burden on its equipment. (Mangino Supp. Dec. at ¶12). Defendants' more recent practice of evading CompuServe's filters by disguising the origin of their messages commandeers even more computer resources because CompuServe's computers are forced to store undeliverable e-mail messages and labor in vain to return the messages to an address that does not exist. (Mangino Supp. Dec. at ¶¶7-8). To the extent that defendants' multitudinous electronic mailings demand the disk space and drain the processing power of plaintiff's computer equipment, those resources are not available to serve CompuServe subscribers. Therefore, the value of that equipment to CompuServe is diminished even though it is not physically damaged by defendants' conduct.

Next, plaintiff asserts that it has suffered injury aside from the physical impact of defendants' messages on its equipment. Restatement §218(d) also indicates that recovery may be had for a trespass that causes harm to something in which the possessor has a legally protected interest. Plaintiff asserts that defendants' messages are largely unwanted by its subscribers, who pay incrementally to access their e-mail, read it, and discard it. Also, the receipt of a bundle of unsolicited messages at once can require the subscriber to sift through, at his expense, all of the messages in order to find the ones he wanted or expected to receive. These inconveniences decrease the utility of CompuServe's e-mail service and are the foremost subject in recent complaints from CompuServe subscribers. Patrick Hole, a customer service manager for plaintiff, states by affidavit that in November 1996 CompuServe received approximately 9,970 e-mail complaints from subscribers about junk e-mail, a figure up from approximately two hundred complaints the previous year. (Hole 2d Supp. Dec. at ¶4). Approximately fifty such complaints per day specifically reference defendants. (Hole Supp. Dec. at ¶3). Defendants contend that CompuServe subscribers are provided with a simple procedure to remove themselves from the mailing list. However, the removal procedure must be performed by the e-mail recipient at his expense, and some CompuServe subscribers complain that the procedure is inadequate and ineffectual. (See, e.g., Hole Supp. Dec. at ¶8).

Many subscribers have terminated their accounts specifically because of the unwanted receipt of bulk e-mail messages. (Hole Supp. Dec. at ¶9, Hole 2d Supp. Dec. at ¶6). Defendants' intrusions into CompuServe's computer systems, insofar as they harm plaintiff's business reputation and goodwill with its customers, are actionable under Restatement §218(d).

The reason that the tort of trespass to chattels requires some actual damage as a prima facie element, whereas damage is assumed where there is a trespass to real property, can be explained as follows:

> The interest of a possessor of a chattel in its inviolability, unlike the similar interest of a possessor of land, is not given legal protection by an action

for nominal damages for harmless intermeddlings with the chattel. In order that an actor who interferes with another's chattel may be liable, his conduct must affect some other and more important interest of the possessor. Therefore, one who intentionally intermeddles with another's chattel is subject to liability only if his intermeddling is harmful to the possessor's materially valuable interest in the physical condition, quality, or value of the chattel, or if the possessor is deprived of the use of the chattel for a substantial time, or some other legally protected interest of the possessor is affected as stated in Clause (c). Sufficient legal protection of the possessor's interest in the mere inviolability of his chattel is afforded by his privilege to use reasonable force to protect his possession against even harmless interference.

Restatement (Second) of Torts §218, Comment e. Plaintiff CompuServe has attempted to exercise this privilege to protect its computer systems. However, defendants' persistent affirmative efforts to evade plaintiff's security measures have circumvented any protection those self-help measures might have provided. In this case CompuServe has alleged and supported by affidavit that it has suffered several types of injury as a result of defendants' conduct. The foregoing discussion simply underscores that the damage sustained by plaintiff is sufficient to sustain an action for trespass to chattels. However, this Court also notes that the implementation of technological means of self-help, to the extent that reasonable measures are effective, is particularly appropriate in this type of situation and should be exhausted before legal action is proper. . . .

Defendants argue that plaintiff made the business decision to connect to the Internet and that therefore it cannot now successfully maintain an action for trespass to chattels. Their argument is analogous to the argument that because an establishment invites the public to enter its property for business purposes, it cannot later restrict or revoke access to that property, a proposition which is erroneous under Ohio law. See, e.g., State v. Carriker, 5 Ohio App.2d 255, 214 N.E.2d 809 (1964) (the law in Ohio is that a business invitee's privilege to remain on the premises of another may be revoked upon the reasonable notification to leave by the owner or his agents); Allstate Ins. Co. v. U.S. Associates Realty, Inc., 11 Ohio App.3d 242, 464 N.E.2d 169 (1983) (notice of express restriction or limitation on invitation turns business invitee into trespasser). On or around October 1995, CompuServe notified defendants that it no longer consented to the use of its proprietary computer equipment. Defendants' continued use thereafter was a trespass. Restatement (Second) of Torts §§252 and 892A(5); see also Restatement (Second) of Torts §217, Comment f ("The actor may commit a new trespass by continuing an intermeddling which he has already begun, with or without the consent of the person in possession. Such intermeddling may persist after the other's consent, originally given, has been terminated."); Restatement (Second) of Torts §217, Comment g.

Further, CompuServe expressly limits the consent it grants to Internet users to send e-mail to its proprietary computer systems by denying unauthorized parties the use of CompuServe equipment to send unsolicited electronic mail messages. (Kolehmainen Dec. at ¶2). This policy statement, posted by CompuServe online, states as follows:

> Compuserve is a private online and communications services company. CompuServe does not permit its facilities to be used by unauthorized parties to process and store unsolicited e-mail. If an unauthorized party attempts to send unsolicited messages to e-mail addresses on a CompuServe service, Compuserve will take appropriate action to attempt to prevent those messages from being processed by CompuServe. Violations of CompuServe's policy prohibiting unsolicited e-mail should be reported to . . .

Id. at ¶¶2 and 3. Defendants Cyber Promotions, Inc. and its president Sanford Wallace have used plaintiff's equipment in a fashion that exceeds that consent. The use of personal property exceeding consent is a trespass. City of Amsterdam v. Daniel Goldreyer, Ltd., 882 F.Supp. 1273 (E.D.N.Y.1995); Restatement (Second) of Torts §256. It is arguable that CompuServe's policy statement, insofar as it may serve as a limitation upon the scope of its consent to the use of its computer equipment, may be insufficiently communicated to potential third-party users when it is merely posted at some location on the network. However, in the present case the record indicates that defendants were actually notified that they were using CompuServe's equipment in an unacceptable manner. To prove that a would-be trespasser acted with the intent required to support liability in tort it is crucial that defendant be placed on notice that he is trespassing. . . .

In response to the trespass claim, defendants argue that they have the right to continue to send unsolicited commercial e-mail to plaintiff's computer systems under the First Amendment to the United States Constitution. The First Amendment states that "Congress shall make no law respecting an establishment of religion, or prohibiting the free exercise thereof; or abridging the freedom of speech, or of the press." The United States Supreme Court has recognized that "the constitutional guarantee of free speech is a guarantee only against abridgement by government, federal or state." Hudgens v. NLRB, 424 U.S. 507, 513, 96 S.Ct. 1029, 1033, 47 L.Ed.2d 196 (1976). Indeed, the protection of the First Amendment is not a shield against "merely private conduct." Hurley v. Irish-American Gay Group of Boston, 515 U.S. 557, —, 115 S.Ct. 2338, 2344, 132 L.Ed.2d 487 (1995) (citation omitted).

Very recently, in an action filed by Cyber Promotions, Inc. against America Online, Inc. ("AOL") the United States District Court for the Eastern District of Pennsylvania held that AOL, a company selling services that are similar to those of CompuServe, is private actor [sic]. Cyber Promotions, Inc. v. American Online, Inc., 948 F.Supp. 436, 443-44 (E.D.Pa.1996). That case involved the question of whether Cyber Promotions had the First Amendment right to send unobstructed e-mail to AOL subscribers. The court held that Cyber Promotions had no such right and that, inter alia, AOL was not exercising powers that are traditionally the exclusive prerogative of the state, such as where a private company exercises municipal powers by running a company town. *Id.* at 442-43; Blum v. Yaretsky, 457 U.S. 991, 1004-05, 102 S.Ct. 2777, 2785-86, 73 L.Ed.2d 534 (1982); Marsh v. Alabama, 326 U.S. 501, 66 S.Ct. 276, 90 L.Ed. 265 (1946). This Court agrees with the conclusions reached by the United States District Court for the Eastern District of Pennsylvania.

In the present action, CompuServe is a private company. Moreover, the mere judicial enforcement of neutral trespass laws by the private owner of property does not alone render it a state actor. Rotunda & Nowak, Treatise on Constitutional Law §16.3, 546 (West 1992). Defendants do not argue that CompuServe is anything other than a private actor. Instead, defendants urge that because CompuServe is so intimately involved in this new medium it might be subject to some special form of regulation. Defendants cite Associated Press v. United States, 326 U.S. 1, 65 S.Ct. 1416, 89 L.Ed. 2013 (1945), and Turner Broadcasting Sys., Inc. v. FCC, 512 U.S. 622, 114 S.Ct. 2445, 129 L.Ed.2d 497 (1994), which stand for the proposition that when a private actor has a certain quantum of control over a central avenue of communication, then the First Amendment might not prevent the government from enacting legislation requiring public access to private property. No such legislation yet exists that is applicable to Compu-Serve. Further, defendants' discussion concerning the extent to which the Internet may be regulated (or should be regulated) is irrelevant because no government entity has undertaken to regulate the Internet in a manner that is applicable to this action. Indeed, if there were some applicable statutory scheme in place this Court would not be required to apply paradigms of common law to the case at hand.

In Lloyd Corp. v. Tanner, 407 U.S. 551, 92 S.Ct. 2219, 33 L.Ed.2d 131 (1972), protestors of the Vietnam War sought to pass out written materials in a private shopping center. Even though the customers of the shopping center were the intended recipients of the communication, the Supreme Court held that allowing the First Amendment to trump private property rights is unwarranted where there are adequate alternative avenues of communication. *Id.* at 567, 92 S.Ct. at 2228. The Supreme Court stated that:

> Although . . . the courts properly have shown a special solicitude for the guarantees of the First Amendment, this Court has never held that a trespasser or an uninvited guest may exercise general rights of free speech on property privately owned and used nondiscriminatorily for private purposes only.

Id. at 567-68, 92 S.Ct. at 2228. Defendants in the present action have adequate alternative means of communication available to them. Not only are they free to send e-mail advertisements to those on the Internet who do not use CompuServe accounts, but they can communicate to CompuServe subscribers as well through online bulletin boards, web page advertisements, or facsimile transmissions, as well as through more conventional means such as the U.S. mail or telemarketing. Defendants' contention, referring to the low cost of the electronic mail medium, that there are no adequate alternative means of communication is unpersuasive. There is no constitutional requirement that the incremental cost of sending massive quantities of unsolicited advertisements must be borne by the recipients. The legal concept in *Lloyd* that private citizens are entitled to enforce laws of trespass against would-be communicators is applicable to this case.

Defendants assert that CompuServe has assumed the role of a post-master, to whom all of the strictures of the First Amendment apply, and that to allow it to enjoy a legally protected interest in its computer equipment in this context is to license a form of censorship which violates the First Amendment. However, such an assertion must be accompanied by a showing that CompuServe is a state actor. As earlier mentioned, defendants have neither specifically argued this point nor provided any evidence to support it. CompuServe is entitled to restrict access to its private property.

"The First and Fourteenth Amendments have never been treated as absolutes. Freedom of speech or press does not mean that one can talk or distribute where, when and how one chooses." Breard v. City of Alexandria, 341 U.S. 622, 642, 71 S.Ct. 920, 932, 95 L.Ed. 1233 (1951) (upholding local ordinances banning commercial solicitations over First Amendment objections) (footnote omitted). In Rowan v. U.S. Post Office Dept., 397 U.S. 728, 90 S.Ct. 1484, 25 L.Ed.2d 736 (1970) the United States Supreme Court held that the First Amendment did not forbid federal legislation that allowed addressees to remove themselves from mailing lists and stop all future mailings. The Court stated that the "mailer's right to communicate must stop at the mailbox of an unreceptive addressee . . . [t]o hold less would be to license a form of trespass[.]" *Id.* at 736-37, 90 S.Ct. at 1490.

In Tillman v. Distribution Sys. of America, Inc., 224 A.D.2d 79, 648 N.Y.S.2d 630 (1996) the plaintiff complained that the defendant continued to throw newspapers on his property after being warned not to do so. The court held that the defendant newspaper distributor had no First Amendment right to continue to throw newspapers onto the property of the plaintiff. After discussing the Supreme Court cases of *Rowan* and *Breard*, supra, the court pointed out that:

> The most critical and fundamental distinction between the cases cited above, on the one hand, and the present case, on the other, is based on the fact that here we are not dealing with a government agency which seeks to preempt in some way the ability of a publisher to contact a potential reader; rather, we are dealing with a reader who is familiar with a publisher's product, and who is attempting to prevent the unwanted dumping of this product on his property. None of the cases cited by the defendants stands for the proposition that the Free Speech Clause prohibits such a landowner from resorting to his common-law remedies in order to prevent such unwanted dumping. There is, in our view, nothing in either the Federal or State Constitutions which requires a landowner to tolerate a trespass whenever the trespasser is a speaker, or the distributor of written speech, who is unsatisfied with the fora which may be

available on public property, and who thus attempts to carry his message to
private property against the will of the owner.

Id. 648 N.Y.S.2d at 635. The court concluded, relying on *Lloyd,* supra, that
the property rights of the private owner could not be overwhelmed by the
First Amendment. *Id.* 648 N.Y.S.2d at 636.

In the present case, plaintiff is physically the recipient of the defendants' messages and is the owner of the property upon which the transgres-
sion is occurring. As has been discussed, plaintiff is not a government
agency or state actor which seeks to preempt defendants' ability to communicate but is instead a private actor trying to tailor the nuances of its service
to provide the maximum utility to its customers.

Defendants' intentional use of plaintiff's proprietary computer equipment exceeds plaintiff's consent and, indeed, continued after repeated
demands that defendants cease. Such use is an actionable trespass to plaintiff's chattel. The First Amendment to the United States Constitution
provides no defense for such conduct. . . .

Finally, the public interest is advanced by the Court's protection of the
common law rights of individuals and entities to their personal property.
Defendants raise First Amendment concerns and argue that an injunction
will adversely impact the public interest. High volumes of junk e-mail
devour computer processing and storage capacity, slow down data transfer
between computers over the Internet by congesting the electronic paths
through which the messages travel, and cause recipients to spend time and
money wading through messages that they do not want. It is ironic that if
defendants were to prevail on their First Amendment arguments, the viability of electronic mail as an effective means of communication for the rest of
society would be put at risk. In light of the foregoing discussion, those
arguments are without merit. Further, those subscribing to CompuServe are
not injured by the issuance of this injunction. Plaintiff has made a business
decision to forbid Cyber Promotions and Mr. Wallace from using its computers to transmit messages to CompuServe subscribers. If CompuServe
subscribers are unhappy with that decision, then they may make that
known, perhaps by terminating their accounts and transferring to an Internet service provider which accepts unsolicited e-mail advertisements. That is
a business risk which plaintiff has assumed.

COMMENTS AND QUESTIONS

1. A number of states—Washington, Virginia, and California among
them—have passed laws to regulate "spam." Each state has approached the
problem in a slightly different manner. In Washington, for example, the law
prohibits the falsification of email headers and the creation of misleading
subject lines in commercial electronic mail messages. This prohibition
applies both to messages that are sent *from* computers within the state and

to messages that are sent *to* email addresses that the spammer knows are held by Washington residents. The spammer is imputed with the knowledge that the account is held by a Washington resident if that information would have been available if a request had been made to the registered owner of the domain name contained in the recipient's email address. The California law requires that "opt-out" information be clearly placed in all unsolicited commercial email messages, and further requires that an opt-out request be honored.

The Cyberspace Law Web site on Unsolicited Email of the John Marshall School of Law provides updated information on spam regulation. See http://www.jmls.edu/cyber/statutes/email/state.html. How effective are these laws likely to be? Should Congress pass such legislation? How should "spam" be legally defined?

2. "Netiquette" norms about acceptable and unacceptable behavior on computer networks evolved in an era when these networks were used largely by technically sophisticated researchers at universities and industry laboratories. This included norms against sending chain letters and other unsolicited bulk email over the network. The Internet Engineering Task Force has decided to publish netiquette guidelines to help "newbie" users and network administrators to become acquainted with these norms. See Network Working Group, Netiquette Guidelines, Request for Comments Doc. 1855 (last revised October 1995) http://sunsite.cnlab-switch.ch/ftp/doc/standard/rfc/18xx/1855.

What, if any, deference should be given to netiquette rules in legal disputes? At least one court has decided that netiquette rules against spam may provide an ISP with a justification for terminating service to a spammer even when the ISP's terms of service do not expressly prohibit spam. See, e.g., Carl Kaplan, An Argument for 'Netiquette' Holds Up in Court, N.Y. Times, July 16, 1999, http://www.nytimes.com/library/tech/99/07/cyber/cyberlaw/16law.html. The case discussed in Kaplan's article is 1267623 Ontario Inc. v. Nexx Online Inc. [1999] O.J. No. 2246 (Ont. Sup. Ct.). For an argument that judicial deference to netiquette may not always be appropriate, see Mark A. Lemley, The Law and Economics of Internet Norms, 73 Chi.-Kent L. Rev. 1257 (1999).

3. Some who object to spam believe that netiquette norms, laws, and litigation are inadequate ways to stop spam. One innovative idea for controlling spammers comes from Paul Vixie. He publishes a list of ISPs from which spam emanates and relies on the voluntary actions of ISP subscribers to his list to block mailings from the offending ISPs. Vixie has published a justification for this private action: The Realtime Blackhole List's Rationale, http://maps.vix.com/rbl/rationale.html. An ISP will have the incentive to root out spam in its system if it gets on Vixie's list because suddenly none of its users will be able to send or receive email from other host computers connected to the Internet. Is this laudable private action or vigilantism run amok?

4.   AOL has had a great deal of experience with spammers and has been innovative in the legal claims that it makes against them. Trespass was only one of five causes of action that AOL brought against a spammer who had sent more than 60 million messages to AOL users. It also charged the spammer with a violation of section 43(a) of the Lanham Act because the spammer's mail falsely designated the origin of its spam as aol.com, thus implying that AOL had approved the sending of these messages. In addition, AOL charged the spammer with dilution of the AOL trademark, alleging that its mark had been tarnished by being associated with the defendant's spam. AOL agreed to voluntary dismissal of two other claims in its original complaint—one alleging violation of the federal Computer Fraud and Abuse Act and the other a violation of the Virginia Computer Crimes Act—if the court granted summary judgment in its favor on the other three claims. A federal judge did grant summary judgment on these claims in America Online Inc. v. IMS, 48 U.S.P.Q.2d 1857 (E.D. Va. 1998). The trespass and civil violations of these two criminal statutes raise questions about whether spamming should be criminalized.

Computer Crimes

United States v. Morris
United States Appeals Court for the Second Circuit
928 F.2d 504 (2d Cir. 1991)

JON O. NEWMAN, Circuit Judge:

... In the fall of 1988, Morris was a first-year graduate student in Cornell University's computer science Ph.D. program. Through undergraduate work at Harvard and in various jobs he had acquired significant computer experience and expertise. When Morris entered Cornell, he was given an account on the computer at the Computer Science Division. This account gave him explicit authorization to use computers at Cornell. Morris engaged in various discussions with fellow graduate students about the security of computer networks and his ability to penetrate it.

In October 1988, Morris began work on a computer program, later known as the INTERNET "worm" or "virus." The goal of this program was to demonstrate the inadequacies of current security measures on computer networks by exploiting the security defects that Morris had discovered. The tactic he selected was release of a worm into network computers. Morris designed the program to spread across a national network of computers after being inserted at one computer location connected to the network. Morris released the worm into INTERNET, which is a group of national networks that connect university, governmental, and military computers around the country. The network permits communication and transfer of information between computers on the network.

Morris sought to program the INTERNET worm to spread widely without drawing attention to itself. The worm was supposed to occupy little computer operation time, and thus not interfere with normal use of the

971

computers. Morris programmed the worm to make it difficult to detect and read, so that other programmers would not be able to "kill" the worm easily.

Morris also wanted to ensure that the worm did not copy itself onto a computer that already had a copy. Multiple copies of the worm on a computer would make the worm easier to detect and would bog down the system and ultimately cause the computer to crash. Therefore, Morris designed the worm to "ask" each computer whether it already had a copy of the worm. If it responded "no," then the worm would copy onto the computer; if it responded "yes," the worm would not duplicate. However, Morris was concerned that other programmers could kill the worm by programming their own computers to falsely respond "yes" to the question. To circumvent this protection, Morris programmed the worm to duplicate itself every seventh time it received a "yes" response. As it turned out, Morris underestimated the number of times a computer would be asked the question, and his one-out-of-seven ratio resulted in far more copying than he had anticipated. The worm was also designed so that it would be killed when a computer was shut down, an event that typically occurs once every week or two. This would have prevented the worm from accumulating on one computer, had Morris correctly estimated the likely rate of reinfection.

Morris identified four ways in which the worm could break into computers on the network:

(1)   through a "hole" or "bug" (an error) in SEND MAIL, a computer program that transfers and receives electronic mail on a computer;

(2)   through a bug in the "finger demon" program, a program that permits a person to obtain limited information about the users of another computer;

(3)   through the "trusted hosts" feature, which permits a user with certain privileges on one computer to have equivalent privileges on another computer without using a password; and

(4)   through a program of password guessing, whereby various combinations of letters are tried out in rapid sequence in the hope that one will be an authorized user's password, which is entered to permit whatever level of activity that user is authorized to perform.

On November 2, 1988, Morris released the worm from a computer at the Massachusetts Institute of Technology. MIT was selected to disguise the fact that the worm came from Morris at Cornell. Morris soon discovered that the worm was replicating and reinfecting machines at a much faster rate than he had anticipated. Ultimately, many machines at locations around the country either crashed or became "catatonic." When Morris realized what was happening, he contacted a friend at Harvard to discuss a solution. Eventually, they sent an anonymous message from Harvard over the network, instructing programmers how to kill the worm and prevent reinfection. However, because the network route was clogged, this message did not get through until it was too late. Computers were affected at numerous installations, including leading universities, military sites, and medical research facilities. The estimated cost of dealing with the worm at each installation ranged from $200 to more than $53,000.

Morris was found guilty, following a jury trial, of violating 18 U.S.C. §1030(a)(5)(A). He was sentenced to three years of probation, 400 hours of community service, a fine of $10,050, and the costs of his supervision.

I. The Intent Requirement in Section 1030(a)(5)(A)

Section 1030(a)(5)(A), covers anyone who

(5) intentionally accesses a Federal interest computer without authorization, and by means of one or more instances of such conduct alters, damages, or destroys information in any such Federal interest computer, or prevents authorized use of any such computer or information, and thereby

(A) causes loss to one or more others of a value aggregating $1,000 or more during any one year period; . . .

The District Court concluded that the intent requirement applied only to the accessing and not to the resulting damage. Judge Munson found recourse to legislative history unnecessary because he considered the statute clear and unambiguous. However, the Court observed that the legislative history supported its reading of section 1030(a)(5)(A).

Morris argues that the Government had to prove not only that he intended the unauthorized access of a federal interest computer, but also that he intended to prevent others from using it, and thus cause a loss. . . .

The first federal statute dealing with computer crimes was passed in 1984, Pub.L. No. 98-473 (codified at 18 U.S.C. §1030 (Supp. II 1984)). The specific provision under which Morris was convicted was added in 1986, Pub.L. No. 99-474, along with some other changes. The 1986 amendments made several changes relevant to our analysis.

First, the 1986 amendments changed the scienter requirement in section 1030(a)(2) from "knowingly" to "intentionally." See Pub.L. No. 99-474, section 2(a)(1). The subsection now covers anyone who

(2) intentionally accesses a computer without authorization or exceeds authorized access, and thereby obtains information contained in a financial record of a financial institution, or of a card issuer as defined in section 1602(n) of title 15, or contained in a file of a consumer reporting agency on a consumer, as such terms are defined in the Fair Credit Reporting Act (15 U.S.C. 1681 et seq.).

According to the Senate Judiciary Committee, Congress changed the mental state requirement in section 1030(a)(2) for two reasons. Congress sought only to proscribe intentional acts of unauthorized access, not "mistaken, inadvertent, or careless" acts of unauthorized access. S.Rep. No. 99-432, 99th Cong., 2d Sess. 5 (1986), *reprinted in* 1986 U.S.Code Cong. & Admin.News 2479, 2483 [hereinafter Senate Report].

Also, Congress expressed concern that the "knowingly" standard "might be inappropriate for cases involving computer technology." *Id.* The concern was that a scienter requirement of "knowingly" might encompass the acts of an individual "who inadvertently 'stumble[d] into' someone else's computer file or computer data," especially where such individual was authorized to use a particular computer. *Id.* at 6, 1986 U.S.Code Cong. & Admin.News at 2483. The Senate Report concluded that "[t]he substitution of an 'intentional' standard is designed to focus Federal criminal prosecutions on those whose conduct evinces a clear intent to enter, without proper authorization, computer files or data belonging to another." *Id.*, U.S.Code Cong. & Admin.News at 2484. Congress retained the "knowingly" standard in other subsections of section 1030. See 18 U.S.C. §1030(a)(1), (a)(4).

This use of a mens rea standard to make sure that inadvertent accessing was not covered is also emphasized in the Senate Report's discussion of section 1030(a)(3) and section 1030(a)(5), under which Morris was convicted. Both subsections were designed to target "outsiders," individuals without authorization to access any federal interest computer. Senate Report at 10, U.S.Code Cong. & Admin.News at 2488. The rationale for the mens rea requirement suggests that it modifies only the "accesses" phrase, which was the focus of Congress's concern in strengthening the scienter requirement.

The other relevant change in the 1986 amendments was the introduction of subsection (a)(5) to replace its earlier version, subsection (a)(3) of the 1984 act, 18 U.S.C. §1030(a)(3) (Supp. II 1984). The predecessor subsection covered anyone who

> knowingly accesses a computer without authorization, or having accessed a computer with authorization, uses the opportunity such access provides for purposes to which such authorization does not extend, and by means of such conduct knowingly uses, modifies, destroys, or discloses information in, or prevents authorized use of, such computer, if such computer is operated for or on behalf of the Government of United States and such conduct affects such operation.

The 1986 version changed the mental state requirement from "knowingly" to "intentionally," and did not repeat it after the "accesses" phrase, as had the 1984 version. By contrast, other subsections of section 1030 have retained "dual intent" language, placing the scienter requirement at the beginning of both the "accesses" phrase and the "damages" phrase. See, e.g., 18 U.S.C. §1030(a)(1).

Morris notes the careful attention that Congress gave to selecting the scienter requirement for current subsections (a)(2) and (a)(5). Then, relying primarily on comments in the Senate and House reports, Morris argues that the "intentionally" requirement of section 1030(a)(5)(A) describes both the conduct of accessing and damaging. As he notes, the Senate Report said that "[t]he new subsection 1030(a)(5) to be created by the bill is designed to penalize those who intentionally alter, damage, or destroy certain computerized data belonging to another." Senate Report at 10, U.S.Code Cong. & Admin.News at 2488. The House Judiciary Committee stated that "the bill proposes a new section (18 U.S.C. 1030(a)(5)) which can be characterized as a 'malicious damage' felony violation involving a Federal interest computer. We have included an 'intentional' standard for this felony and coverage is extended only to outside trespassers with a $1,000 threshold damage level." H.R.Rep. No. 99-612, 99th Cong.2d Sess. at 7 (1986). A member of the Judiciary Committee also referred to the section 1030(a)(5) offense as a "malicious damage" felony during the floor debate. 132 Cong.Rec. H3275, 3276 (daily ed. June 3, 1986) (remarks of Rep. Hughes).

The Government's argument that the scienter requirement in section 1030(a)(5)(A) applies only to the "accesses" phrase is premised primarily upon the difference between subsection (a)(5)(A) and its predecessor in the 1984 statute. The decision to state the scienter requirement only once in subsection (a)(5)(A), along with the decision to change it from "knowingly" to "intentionally," are claimed to evince a clear intent upon the part of Congress to apply the scienter requirement only to the "accesses" phrase, though making that requirement more difficult to satisfy. This reading would carry out the Congressional objective of protecting the individual who "inadvertently 'stumble[s] into' someone else's computer file." Senate Report at 6, U.S.Code Cong. & Admin.News at 2483.

The Government also suggests that the fact that other subsections of section 1030 continue to repeat the scienter requirement before both phrases of a subsection is evidence that Congress selectively decided within the various subsections of section 1030 where the scienter requirement was and was not intended to apply. Morris responds with a plausible explanation as to why certain other provisions of section 1030 retain dual intent language. Those subsections use two different mens rea standards; therefore it is necessary to refer to the scienter requirement twice in the subsection. For example, section 1030(a)(1) covers anyone who

(1) knowingly accesses a computer without authorization or exceeds authorized access, and by means of such conduct obtains information that has been determined by the United States Government pursuant to an Executive order or statute to require protection against unauthorized disclosure for reasons of national defense or foreign relations, or any restricted data . . . with the intent or reason to believe that such information so obtained is to be used to the injury of the United States, or to the advantage of any foreign nation.

Since Congress sought in subsection (a)(1) to have the "knowingly" standard govern the "accesses" phrase and the "with intent" standard govern the "results" phrase, it was necessary to state the scienter requirement at the beginning of both phrases. By contrast, Morris argues, where Congress stated the scienter requirement only once, at the beginning of the "accesses" phrase, it was intended to cover both the "accesses" phrase and the phrase that followed it.

There is a problem, however, with applying Morris's explanation to section 1030(a)(5)(A). As noted earlier, the predecessor of subsection (a)(5)(A) explicitly placed the same mental state requirement before both the "accesses" phrase and the "damages" phrase. In relevant part, that predecessor in the 1984 statute covered anyone who "knowingly accesses a computer without authorization, . . . and by means of such conduct knowingly uses, modifies, destroys, or discloses information in, or prevents authorized use of, such computer. . . ." 18 U.S.C. §1030(a)(3) (Supp. II 1984). This earlier provision demonstrates that Congress has on occasion chosen to repeat the same scienter standard in the "accesses" phrase and the subsequent phrase of a subsection of the Computer Fraud Statute. More pertinently, it shows that the 1986 amendments adding subsection (a)(5)(A) placed the scienter requirement adjacent only to the "accesses" phrase in contrast to a predecessor provision that had placed the same standard before both that phrase and the subsequent phrase.

Despite some isolated language in the legislative history that arguably suggests a scienter component for the "damages" phrase of section 1030(a)(5)(A), the wording, structure, and purpose of the subsection, examined in comparison with its departure from the format of its predecessor provision persuade us that the "intentionally" standard applies only to the "accesses" phrase of section 1030(a)(5)(A), and not to its "damages" phrase.

II. The Unauthorized Access Requirement in Section 1030(a)(5)(A)

Section 1030(a)(5)(A) penalizes the conduct of an individual who "intentionally accesses a Federal interest computer without authorization." Morris contends that his conduct constituted, at most, "exceeding authorized access" rather than the "unauthorized access" that the subsection punishes. Morris argues that there was insufficient evidence to convict him of "unauthorized access," and that even if the evidence sufficed, he was entitled to have the jury instructed on his "theory of defense."

We assess the sufficiency of the evidence under the traditional standard. Morris was authorized to use computers at Cornell, Harvard, and Berkeley, all of which were on INTERNET. As a result, Morris was authorized to communicate with other computers on the network to send electronic mail (SEND MAIL), and to find out certain information about the users of other computers (finger demon). The question is whether Morris's transmission of his worm constituted exceeding authorized access or accessing without authorization.

The Senate Report stated that section 1030(a)(5)(A), like the new section 1030(a)(3), would "be aimed at 'outsiders,' i.e., those lacking authorization to access any Federal interest computer." Senate Report at 10, U.S.Code Cong. & Admin.News at 2488. But the Report also stated, in concluding its discussion on the scope of section 1030(a)(3), that it applies "where the offender is completely outside the Government, . . . or where the offender's act of trespass is interdepartmental in nature." *Id.* at 8, U.S.Code Cong. & Admin.News at 2486.

Morris relies on the first quoted portion to argue that his actions can be characterized only as exceeding authorized access, since he had authorized access to a federal interest computer. However, the second quoted portion reveals that Congress was not drawing a bright line between those who have some access to any federal interest computer and those who have none. Congress contemplated that individuals with access to some federal interest computers would be subject to liability under the computer fraud provisions for gaining unauthorized access to other federal interest computers. See, e.g., *id.* (stating that a Labor Department employee who uses Labor's computers to access without authorization an FBI computer can be criminally prosecuted).

The evidence permitted the jury to conclude that Morris's use of the SEND MAIL and finger demon features constituted access without authorization. While a case might arise where the use of SEND MAIL or finger demon falls within a nebulous area in which the line between accessing without authorization and exceeding authorized access may not be clear, Morris's conduct here falls well within the area of unauthorized access. Morris did not use either of those features in any way related to their intended function. He did not send or read mail nor discover information about other users; instead he found holes in both programs that permitted him a special and unauthorized access route into other computers.

Moreover, the jury verdict need not be upheld solely on Morris's use of SEND MAIL and finger demon. As the District Court noted, in denying Morris's motion for acquittal,

> Although the evidence may have shown that defendant's initial insertion of the worm simply exceeded his authorized access, the evidence also demonstrated that the worm was designed to spread to other computers at which he had no account and no authority, express or implied, to unleash the worm program. Moreover, there was also evidence that the worm was designed to gain access to computers at which he had no account by guessing their passwords. Accordingly, the evidence did support the jury's conclusion that defendant accessed without authority as opposed to merely exceeding the scope of his authority.

In light of the reasonable conclusions that the jury could draw from Morris's use of SEND MAIL and finger demon, and from his use of the trusted hosts feature and password guessing, his challenge to the sufficiency of the evidence fails.

Morris endeavors to bolster his sufficiency argument by contending that his conduct was not punishable under subsection (a)(5) but was punishable under subsection (a)(3). That concession belies the validity of his claim that he only exceeded authorization rather than made unauthorized access. Neither subsection (a)(3) nor (a)(5) punishes conduct that exceeds authorization. Both punish a person who "accesses" "without authorization" certain computers. Subsection (a)(3) covers the computers of a department or agency of the United States; subsection (a)(5) more broadly covers any federal interest computers, defined to include, among other computers, those used exclusively by the United States, 18 U.S.C. §1030(e)(2)(A), and adds the element of causing damage or loss of use of a value of $1,000 or more. If Morris violated subsection (a)(3), as he concedes, then his conduct in inserting the worm into the INTERNET must have constituted "unauthorized access" under subsection (a)(5) to the computers of the federal departments the worm reached, for example, those of NASA and military bases.

To extricate himself from the consequence of conceding that he made "unauthorized access" within the meaning of subsection (a)(3), Morris subtly shifts his argument and contends that he is not within the reach of subsection (a)(5) at all. He argues that subsection (a)(5) covers only those who, unlike himself, lack access to any federal interest computer. It is true that a primary concern of Congress in drafting subsection (a)(5) was to reach those unauthorized to access any federal interest computer. The Senate Report stated, "[T]his subsection [(a)(5)] will be aimed at 'outsiders,' i.e., those lacking authorization to access any Federal interest computer." Senate Report at 10, U.S.Code Cong. & Admin.News at 2488. But the fact that the subsection is "aimed" at such "outsiders" does not mean that its coverage is limited to them. Congress understandably thought that the group most likely to damage federal interest computers would be those who lack authorization to use any of them. But it surely did not mean to insulate from liability the person authorized to use computers at the State Department who causes damage to computers at the Defense Department. Congress created the misdemeanor offense of subsection (a)(3) to punish intentional trespassers into computers for which one lacks authorized access; it added the felony offense of subsection (a)(5) to punish such a trespasser who also causes damage or loss in excess of $1,000, not only to computers of the United States but to any computer within the definition of federal interest computers. With both provisions, Congress was punishing those, like Morris, who, with access to some computers that enable them to communicate on a network linking other computers, gain access to other computers to which they lack authorization and either trespass, in violation of subsection (a)(3), or cause damage or loss of $1,000 or more, in violation of subsection (a)(5).

Morris also contends that the District Court should have instructed the jury on his theory that he was only exceeding authorized access. The District Court decided that it was unnecessary to provide the jury with a definition of "authorization." We agree. Since the word is of common usage, without any technical or ambiguous meaning, the Court was not obliged to instruct the jury on its meaning. See, e.g., United States v. Chenault, 844 F.2d 1124, 1131 (5th Cir.1988) ("A trial court need not define specific statutory terms unless they are outside the common understanding of a juror or are so technical or specific as to require a definition.").

An instruction on "exceeding authorized access" would have risked misleading the jury into thinking that Morris could not be convicted if some of his conduct could be viewed as falling within this description. Yet, even if that phrase might have applied to some of his conduct, he could nonetheless be found liable for doing what the statute prohibited, gaining access where he was unauthorized and causing loss.

Additionally, the District Court properly refused to charge the jury with Morris's proposed jury instruction on access without authorization. That instruction stated, "To establish the element of lack of authorization, the government must prove beyond a reasonable doubt that Mr. Morris was an 'outsider,' that is, that he was not authorized to access any Federal interest computer in any manner." As the analysis of the legislative history reveals, Congress did not intend an individual's authorized access to one federal interest computer to protect him from prosecution, no matter what other federal interest computers he accesses.

United States v. Riggs
United States District Court for the Northern District of Illinois
739 F. Supp. 414 (N.D. Ill. 1990)

BUA, District Judge.

. . . In about September 1988, Neidorf and Riggs devised and began implementing a scheme to defraud Bell South Telephone Company ("Bell South"), which provides telephone services to a nine-state region including Alabama, Georgia, Mississippi, Tennessee, Kentucky, Louisiana, North Carolina, South Carolina, and Florida. The objective of the fraud scheme was to steal Bell South's computer text file which contained information regarding its enhanced 911 (E911) system for handling emergency calls to policy, fire, ambulance, and other emergency services in municipalities. The text file which Riggs and Neidorf planned to steal specifically details the procedures for installation, operation, and maintenance of E911 services in the region in which Bell South operates. Bell South considered this file to contain valuable proprietary information and, therefore, closely guarded the information from being disclosed outside of Bell South and its subsidiaries. Riggs and Neidorf wanted to obtain the E911 text file so it could be printed in a computer newsletter known as "PHRACK" which Neidorf edited and published.

In about December 1988, Riggs began the execution of the fraud scheme by using his home computer in Decatur, Georgia, to gain unlawful access to Bell South's computer system located at its corporate headquarters in Atlanta, Georgia. After gaining access to Bell South's system, Riggs "downloaded" the text file, which described in detail the operation of the E911 system in Bell South's operating region. Riggs then disguised and concealed his unauthorized access to the Bell South system by using account codes of persons with legitimate access to the E911 text file.

Pursuant to the scheme he had devised with Neidorf, Riggs then transferred the stolen computer text file to Neidorf by way of an interstate computer data network. Riggs stored the stolen text file on a computer bulletin board system[4] located in Lockport, Illinois, so as to make the file available to Neidorf. The Lockport bulletin board system was used by computer "hackers" as a location for exchanging and developing software tools and other information which could be used for unauthorized intrusion into computer systems. Neidorf, a twenty-year-old student at the University of Missouri in Columbia, Missouri, used a computer located at his school to access the Lockport computer bulletin board and thereby receive the Bell South E911 text file from Riggs. At the request of Riggs, Neidorf then edited and retyped the E911 text file in order to conceal the fact that it had been stolen from Bell South. Neidorf then "uploaded" his revised version of the stolen file back onto the Lockport bulletin board system for Riggs' review. To complete the scheme, in February 1989, Neidorf published his edited edition of Bell South's E911 text file in his PHRACK newsletter.

B. Charges

The current indictment asserts seven counts. Count I charges that Riggs committed wire fraud in violation of 18 U.S.C. §1343 by transferring the E911 text file from his home computer in Decatur, Georgia to the computer bulletin board system in Lockport, Illinois. Count II charges both Riggs and Neidorf with violating §1343 by causing the edited E911 file to be transferred from a computer operated by Neidorf in Columbia,

---

4. A computer bulletin board system is a computer program that simulates an actual bulletin board by allowing computer users who access a particular computer to post messages, read existing messages, and delete messages. The messages exchanged may contain a wide variety of information, including stolen credit card numbers, confidential business information, and information about local community events. See Note, Computer Bulletin Board Operator Liability for User Misuse, 54 Fordham L.Rev. 439, 439-41 & nn. 1-11 (1988); see also Jensen, An Electronic Soap Box: Computer Bulletin Boards and the First Amendment, 39 Fed.Com.L.J. 217 (1987); Morrison, Electronic Bulletin Board System Prover BBS, 13 Legal Econ. 44 (1987); Soma, Smith & Sprague, Legal Analysis of Electronic Bulletin Board Activities, 7 W. New Engl.L.Rev. 571 (1985).

Missouri, to the computer bulletin board system in Lockport, Illinois. Counts III and IV assert that by transferring the E911 text file via an interstate computer network, Riggs and Neidorf violated the National Stolen Property Act, 18 U.S.C. §2314, which prohibits interstate transfer of stolen property. Finally, Counts V-VII charge Riggs and Neidorf with violating §1030(a)(6)(A) of the Computer Fraud and Abuse Act of 1986, 18 U.S.C. §1030(a)(6)(A), which prohibits knowingly, and with intent to defraud, trafficking in information through which a computer may be accessed without authorization.

II. Discussion

A. *Motion to Dismiss Count II*

Neidorf claims that Count II of the indictment is defective because it fails to allege a scheme to defraud, one of the necessary elements for a wire fraud claim under 18 U.S.C. §1343. See Lombardo v. United States, 865 F.2d 155, 157 (7th Cir.) (holding that the two elements of a wire fraud claim under §1343 are a scheme to defraud and the use of wire communications in furtherance of the scheme), *cert. denied*, 491 U.S. 905, 109 S.Ct. 3186, 105 L.Ed.2d 695 (1989). All Count II charges, says Neidorf, is that he received and then transferred a computer text file, not that he participated in any scheme to defraud.

Unsurprisingly, Neidorf's reading of the indictment is self-servingly narrow. The indictment plainly and clearly charges that Neidorf and Riggs concocted a fraud scheme, the object of which was to steal the E911 text file from Bell South and to distribute it to others via the PHRACK newsletter. The indictment also clearly alleges that both Riggs and Neidorf took action in furtherance of the fraud scheme. Riggs allegedly used fraudulent means to access Bell South's computer system and then disguised his unauthorized entry. Neidorf allegedly furthered the scheme by redacting from the E911 text file references to Bell South and other information which would reveal the source of the E911 file, transmitting the redacted file back to the Lockport bulletin board for Riggs review, and publishing the redacted text file in the PHRACK newsletter for others' use. Moreover, both Neidorf and Riggs allegedly used coded language, code names, and other deceptive means to avoid the detection of their fraud by law enforcement officials. These allegations sufficiently set forth the existence of a scheme to defraud, as well as Neidorf's participation in the scheme. See McNally v. United States, 483 U.S. 350, 358, 107 S.Ct. 2875, 2880-81, 97 L.Ed.2d 292 (1987) (where the Court, quoting Hammerschmidt v. United States, 265 U.S. 182, 188, 44 S.Ct. 511, 512, 68 L.Ed. 968 (1924), held that "to defraud" as used in the mail fraud statute simply means "wronging one in his property rights by dishonest methods or schemes" usually by "the deprivation of something of value by trick, deceit, chicane, or overreaching"); see also Carpenter v. United States, 484 U.S. 19, 108 S.Ct. 316, 320-21, 98 L.Ed.2d 275 (1987) (applying *McNally* to the wire fraud statute, the Court held that a Wall Street Journal columnist participated in a scheme to defraud chargeable under §1343 where he executed a plan under which he disclosed confidential financial information to an investor in exchange for a share of the investor's profits from that information).

Neidorf also argues that Count II is deficient because it fails to allege that he had a fiduciary relationship with Bell South. To support this position, Neidorf relies on cases such as United States v. Richter, 610 F.Supp. 480 (N.D.Ill.1985), and United States v. Dorfman, 532 F.Supp. 1118 (N.D.Ill.1981). In each of those cases, as well as other similar cases cited by Neidorf, the court held that where a wire fraud charge is based on the deprivation of an intangible right, such as the right to honest and fair government or the right to the loyal service of an employee, the government must allege the existence of a fiduciary relationship between the defendant and the alleged victim to state a charge under §1343.

In the instant case, however, the wire fraud charge is not based on the deprivation of an intangible right. The government charges Riggs and Neidorf with scheming to defraud Bell South out of property—the confidential information contained in the E911 text file. The indictment specifically alleges that the object of defendants' scheme was the E911 text file, which Bell South considered to be valuable, proprietary, information. The law is clear that such valuable, confidential information is "property," the deprivation of which can form the basis of a wire fraud charge under §1343. See *Carpenter*, 108 S.Ct. at 320; see also United States v. Keane, 852 F.2d 199, 205 (7th Cir.), *cert. denied*, 490 U.S. 1084, 109 S.Ct. 2109, 104 L.Ed.2d 670 (1989). Therefore, Neidorf's argument misconstrues the wire fraud charge against him. Cases such as *Richter* and *Dorfman* are wholly inapposite.[7]

As further support for his argument that fiduciary relationship between himself and Bell South must be alleged to state a wire fraud charge against him, Neidorf analogizes his role in the alleged scheme to that of an "innocent tippee" in the securities context, such as the defendants in Dirks v. Securities Exchange Commission, 463 U.S. 646, 103 S.Ct. 3255, 77 L.Ed.2d 911 (1983), and Chiarella v. United States, 445 U.S. 222, 100 S.Ct. 1108, 63 L.Ed.2d 348 (1980). This analogy, however, is fallacious.

---

7. Moreover, to the extent that prior case law such as *Dorfman* and *Richter* held that a mail fraud or a wire fraud charge can be based on the deprivation of intangible rights so long as a fiduciary relationship exists between the victim and the defendant, those cases are no longer good law. The Supreme Court expressly rejected the notion that such a charge can be based on the deprivation of an intangible right—fiduciary relationship or not—in McNally v. United States, 483 U.S. 350, 107 S.Ct. 2875, 97 L.Ed.2d 292 (1987). See Carpenter v. United States, 484 U.S. 19, 108 S.Ct. 316, 320, 98 L.Ed.2d 275 (1987). The *McNally* Court ruled that a mail fraud charge must be based on the deprivation of property. *Id.* However, the property which forms the basis for a wire fraud or mail fraud charge can be "intangible" property. See Bateman v. United States, 875 F.2d 1304, 1306 & n. 2 (7th Cir.1989); see also United States v. Barber, 881 F.2d 345, 348 (7th Cir.1989), *cert. denied*, 495 U.S. 922, 110 S.Ct. 1956, 109 L.Ed.2d 318 (1990). This distinction between intangible property and intangible rights has somewhat muddled the ruling in *McNally*. *Id.*

Those cases involved individuals who come upon information lawfully; the question in each of those cases was whether, once possessing that information, the individual had a duty to disclose it. In the instant case, in contrast, Neidorf is alleged to have planned and participated in the scheme to defraud Bell South. Although Riggs allegedly was the one who actually stole the E911 text file from Bell South's computer system, the government alleges that Neidorf was completely aware of Riggs' activities and agreed to help Riggs conceal the theft to make the fraud complete. Therefore, in no way can Neidorf be construed as being in a similar situation to the innocent tippees in *Dirks* and *Chiarella*. As a result, the court rejects his argument that Count II is defective for failing to allege a fiduciary duty between himself and Bell South. Neidorf's motion to dismiss Count II is accordingly denied.

B. Motion to Dismiss Counts III and IV

Counts III and IV charge Riggs and Neidorf with violating 18 U.S.C. §2314, which provides, in relevant part:

> Whoever transports, transmits, or transfers in interstate or foreign commerce any goods, wares, merchandise, securities or money, of the value of $5000 or more, knowing the same to have been stolen, converted or taken by fraud . . . [s]hall be fined not more than $10,000 or imprisoned not more than ten years, or both.

The government concedes that charging Neidorf under §2314 plots a course on uncharted waters. No court has ever held that the electronic transfer of confidential, proprietary business information from one computer to another across state lines constitutes a violation of §2314. However, no court has addressed the issue. Surprisingly, despite the prevalence of computer-related crime, this is a case of first impression. The government argues that reading §2314 as covering Neidorf's conduct in this case is a natural adaptation of the statute to modern society. Conversely, Neidorf contends that his conduct does not fall within the purview of §2314 and that the government is seeking an unreasonable expansion of the statute. He urges the court to dismiss the charge on two grounds.

Neidorf's first argument is that the government cannot sustain a §2314 charge in this case because the only thing which he allegedly caused to be transferred across state lines was "electronic impulses." Neidorf maintains that under the plain language of the statute, this conduct does not come within the scope of §2314 since electronic impulses do not constitute "goods, wares, or merchandise."

The court is unpersuaded by Neidorf's disingenuous argument that he merely transferred electronic impulses across state lines. Several courts have upheld §2314 charges based on the wire transfer of fraudulently obtained money, rejecting the arguments of the defendants in those cases that only electronic impulses, not actual money, crossed state lines. For example, in United States v. Gilboe, 684 F.2d 235 (2d Cir.1982), *cert. denied*, 459 U.S. 1201, 103 S.Ct. 1185, 75 L.Ed.2d 432 (1983), the court held, in affirming a §2314 conviction based on the wire transfer of funds:

> The question whether [§2314] covers electronic transfers of funds appears to be one of first impression, but we do not regard it as a difficult one. Electronic signals in this context are the means by which funds are transported. The beginning of the transaction is money in one account and the ending is money in another. The manner in which the funds were moved does not affect the ability to obtain tangible paper dollars or a bank check from the receiving account. If anything, the means of transfer here were essential to the fraudulent scheme.

Id. at 238. Other circuits have followed the reasoning in *Gilboe*. See United States v. Kroh, 896 F.2d 1524, 1528-29 (8th Cir.1990); United States v. Goldberg, 830 F.2d 459, 466-67 (3d Cir.1987); United States v. Wright, 791 F.2d 133, 135-37 (10th Cir.1986); see also United States v. Kenngott, 840 F.2d 375, 380 (7th Cir.1987) (citing *Gilboe* with approval). In all of these cases, the courts held that money was transferred across state lines within the meaning of §2314 because funds were actually accessible in one account prior to the transfer, and those funds were actually accessible in an out-of-state account after the transfer. The courts refused to accept the superficial characterization of the transfers as the mere transmittal of electronic impulses.

Similarly, in the instant case, Neidorf's conduct is not properly characterized as the mere transmission of electronic impulses. Through the use of his computer, Neidorf allegedly transferred proprietary business information—Bell South's E911 text file. Like the money in the case dealing with wire transfers of funds, the information in the E911 text file was accessible at Neidorf's computer terminal in Missouri before he transferred it, and the information was also accessible at the Lockport, Illinois computer bulletin board after Neidorf transferred it. Therefore, under *Gilboe, Kroh, Wright*, and *Goldberg*, the mere fact that the information actually crossed state lines via computer-generated electronic impulses does not defeat a charge under §2314.

The question this case presents, then, is not whether electronic impulses are "goods, wares, or merchandise" within the meaning of §2314, but whether the proprietary information contained in Bell South's E911 text file constitutes a "good, ware, or merchandise" within the purview of the statute. This court answers that question affirmatively. It is well-settled that when proprietary business information is affixed to some tangible medium, such as a piece of paper, it constitutes "goods, wares, or merchandise" within the meaning of §2314. See United States v. Greenwald, 479 F.2d 320, 322 (6th Cir.) (documents containing valuable chemical formulae are "goods, wares, or merchandise" under §2314), *cert. denied*, 414 U.S. 854, 94 S.Ct. 154, 38 L.Ed.2d 104 (1973); United States v. Bottone, 365 F.2d 389, 393 (2d Cir.) (copies of documents describing a manufacturing process of patented drugs constitute a "good" under §2314), *cert. denied*, 385 U.S. 974, 87 S.Ct. 514, 17 L.Ed.2d 437 (1966); United States v. Lester, 282 F.2d 750, 754-55 (3d Cir.1960) (copies of geophysical maps identifying oil deposits come within the purview of §2314), *cert. denied*, 364 U.S. 937, 81 S.Ct. 385, 5 L.Ed.2d 368 (1961); United States v. Seagraves, 265 F.2d 876 (3d Cir.1959) (same facts as in Lester).

Therefore, in the instant case, if the information in Bell South's E911 text file had been affixed to a floppy disk, or printed out on a computer printer, then Neidorf's transfer of that information across state lines would clearly constitute the transfer of "goods, wares, or merchandise" within the meaning of §2314. This court sees no reason to hold differently simply because Neidorf stored the information inside computers instead of printing it out on paper. In either case, the information is in a transferrable, accessible, even salable form.

Neidorf argues in his brief that a §2314 charge cannot survive when the "thing" actually transferred never takes tangible form. A few courts have apparently adopted this position. For example, in United States v. Smith, 686 F.2d 234 (5th Cir.1982), the court held that a copyright does not fit within the definition of "goods, wares, or merchandise" under §2314. The court ruled that in order to come within that definition, "[t]he 'thing' or 'item' must have some sort of tangible existence; it must be in the nature of 'personal property or chattels.'" *Id.* at 241. Similarly, in *Bottone*, supra, where the court held that copies of documents describing a manufacturing process for a patented drug constitute "goods, wares, or merchandise" under §2314, the court opined:

> To be sure, where no tangible objects were ever taken or transported, a court would be hard pressed to conclude that "goods" had been stolen and transported within the meaning of §2314; the statute would presumably not extend to the case where a carefully guarded secret was memorized, carried away in the recesses of a thievish mind and placed in writing only after a [state] boundary had been crossed.

365 F.2d at 393.

Nevertheless, this court is not entirely convinced that tangibility is an absolute requirement of "goods, wares, or merchandise" under §2314. Congress enacted §2314 to extend the National Motor Vehicle Theft Act to cover all stolen property over a certain value ($5000) which is knowingly transported across state lines. See Dowling v. United States, 473 U.S. 207, 218-20, 105 S.Ct. 3127, 3133-35, 87 L.Ed.2d 152 (1985). In line with this broad congressional intent, courts have liberally construed the term "goods, wares, or merchandise" as "a general and comprehensive designation of such personal property and chattels as are ordinarily the subject of commerce." See United States v. Whaley, 788 F.2d 581, 582 (9th Cir.) (quoting *Seagraves*, 265 F.2d at 880), *cert. denied*, 479 U.S. 962, 107 S.Ct. 458, 93 L.Ed.2d 404 (1986). Reading a tangibility requirement into the definition of "goods, wares, or merchandise" might unduly restrict the scope of §2314, especially in this modern technological age. For instance, suppose the existence of a valuable gas, used as an anesthetic, which is colorless, odorless, and tasteless—totally imperceptible to the human senses. If this gas is stored in a tank in Indiana, and a trucker hooks up to the tank, releases the valuable gas into a storage tank on his truck, and then takes the gas to Illinois to sell it for a profit, is there no violation of §2314 simply because the gas is not technically tangible? This court is reluctant to believe that any court would construe §2314 so narrowly.

In any event, this court need not decide that issue to resolve this case, for even if tangibility is a requirement of "goods, wares or merchandise" under §2314, in this court's opinion the computer-stored business information in this case satisfies that requirement. Although not printed out on paper, a more conventional form of tangibility, the information in Bell South's E911 text file was allegedly stored on computer. Thus, by simply pressing a few buttons, Neidorf could recall that information from computer storage and view it on his computer terminal. The information was also accessible to others in the same fashion if they simply pressed the right buttons on their computer. This ability to access the information in viewable form from a reliable storage place differentiates this case from the mere memorization of a formula and makes this case more similar to cases like *Greenwald*, *Bottone*, *Seagraves*, and *Lester*, where proprietary information was also stored, but in a more traditional manner—on paper. The accessibility of the information in readable form from a particular storage place also makes the information tangible, transferable, salable and, in this court's opinion, brings it within the definition of "goods, wares, or merchandise" under §2314.

In order to sustain a charge against Neidorf under §2314, however, the government cannot simply allege that Neidorf transferred "goods, wares, or merchandise" across state boundaries; the government must also allege that Neidorf executed the transfer knowing the goods were "stolen, converted or taken by fraud." This requirement forms the basis for Neidorf's second challenge to Counts III and IV. Relying on Dowling v. United States, 473 U.S. 207, 105 S.Ct. 3127, 87 L.Ed.2d 152 (1985), Neidorf maintains that the §2314 charges should be dismissed because the "things" he allegedly transferred are not the type of property which is capable of being "stolen, converted or taken by fraud."

In *Dowling*, the government charged the defendant with violating §2314 by shipping "bootleg" and "pirated"[10] phonorecords across state lines. *Id.* at 212, 105 S.Ct. at 3130-31. The government argued that the shipments came within §2314 because the phonorecords embodied performances of copyrighted musical compositions which the defendant had no right to distribute. *Id.* at 214-15, 105 S.Ct. at 3131-32. The Court framed the issue in the case as follows:

---

10. A "bootleg" phonorecord is an unauthorized copy of a commercially unreleased performance. A "pirated" phonorecord is an unauthorized copy of a performance already commercially released. *Dowling*, 473 U.S. at 209-10 n. 2, 105 S.Ct. at 3129 n. 2.

> Dowling does not contest that he caused the shipment of goods in interstate commerce, or that the shipments had sufficient value to meet the monetary requirement. He argues, instead, that the goods shipped were not "stolen, converted or taken by fraud."
>
> . . . We must determine, therefore, whether phonorecords that include the performance of copyrighted musical compositions for the use of which no authorization has been sought or royalties paid are consequently "stolen, converted or taken by fraud" for purposes of §2314.

Id. at 214-16, 105 S.Ct. at 3131-32. The Court ruled that while the holder of a copyright possesses certain property rights which are protectible and enforceable under copyright law, he does not own the type of possessory interest in an item of property which may be "stolen, converted or taken by fraud." *Id.* at 216-18, 105 S.Ct. at 3132-34. Thus, the Court held that §2314 does not apply to interstate shipments of "bootleg" and "pirated" phonorecords whose unauthorized distribution infringes on valid copyrights. *Id.* at 228-29, 105 S.Ct. at 3138-39.

Neidorf also cites United States v. Smith, 686 F.2d 234 (5th Cir.1982), to support his argument. Like *Dowling*, *Smith* held that copyright infringement is not the equivalent of theft or conversion under §2314. *Id.* at 241. The instant case, however, is distinguishable from *Dowling* and *Smith*. This case involves the transfer of confidential, proprietary business information, not copyrights. As *Dowling* and *Smith* recognized, the copyright holder owns only a bundle of intangible rights which can be infringed, but not stolen or converted. The owner of confidential, proprietary business information, in contrast, possesses something which has clearly been recognized as an item of property. *Carpenter*, 108 S.Ct. at 320; *Keane*, 852 F.2d at 205. As such, it is certainly capable of being misappropriated, which, according to the indictment, is exactly what happened to the information in Bell South's E911 text file.

In his final gasp, Neidorf points out that in *Dowling*, the Court based its ruling partly on the fact that Congress passed the Copyright Act to deal exclusively with copyright infringements. The Court reasoned that applying §2314 to the infringement of copyrights would result in an unnecessary and unwarranted intrusion into an area already governed by the Copyright Act. 473 U.S. at 221-26, 105 S.Ct. at 3135-38. Neidorf makes a similar argument in this case. He notes that Congress has enacted a statute—the Computer Fraud and Abuse Act ("CFAA"), 18 U.S.C. §1030—which is specifically designed to address computer-related crimes, such as unauthorized computer access. Neidorf claims that the enactment of the CFAA precludes a finding that §2314 reaches his alleged conduct in this case.

The problem with Neidorf's argument, however, is that he does not cite, and this court is unable to find, anything in the legislative history of the CFAA which suggests that the statute was intended to be the exclusive law governing computer-related crimes, or that its enactment precludes the application of other criminal statutes to computer-related conduct. Therefore, the court rejects Neidorf's claim that applying §2314 to the instant case would undermine the Congressional intent behind the CFAA. Similarly, the court rejects Neidorf's bald assertion that the legislative history behind §2314 supports his argument. Nothing in the legislative history of §2314 prevents the court from finding that the information in Bell South's E911 text file was "stolen, converted or taken by fraud" as that term is used in §2314. Accordingly, Neidorf's motion to dismiss Counts III and IV is denied. . . .

COMMENTS AND QUESTIONS

1. The break-in to Bell South computers and subsequent appropriation of E911 information also led to a seizure of computers, files, and equipment from the offices of Steve Jackson Games (SJG). Secret Service agents believed that a copy of the E911 information was being stored on a bulletin board system on the company's computers in an account of the alleged perpetrator. Steve Jackson Games successfully sued the U.S. Secret Service for violating its rights under the Electronic Communications Privacy Act. See Steve Jackson Games v. United States Secret Service, 816 F. Supp. 432 (W.D.Tex. 1993).

Yet, the case was not a total victory for SJG. The trial court had decided that the seizure of the SJG computer that contained the private electronic mail that had been sent to (stored on) the bulletin board but not read (retrieved) by the intended recipients did not constitute an unlawful "intercept" under the Federal Wiretap Act. The judge reasoned that because the Secret Service's acquisition of the contents of the electronic communications was not contemporaneous with the transmission of those communications, it had not "intercepted" them. The Fifth Circuit affirmed the lower court on this issue. See Steve Jackson Games v. United States Secret Service, 36 F.3d 457 (5th Cir. 1994).

2. Two lawyers with considerable experience prosecuting computer crimes have offered an explanation as to why these crimes may be more difficult than traditional crimes for prosecutors to deal with. See Scott Charney & Kent Alexander, Computer Crime, 45 Emory L.J. 931, 940-941 (1996):

> The shift from a corporeal environment—where items are stored in a tangible form that can be physically carried, such as information written on paper—to an intangible, electronic environment means that computer crimes, and the methods used to investigate them, are no longer subject to traditional rules and constraints. Consider, for example, the way the crimes of theft and criminal mischief have changed. Before the advent of computer networks, the ability to steal information or damage property was to some extent determined by physical limitations. A burglar could only break so many windows and burglarize so many homes in a week. During each intrusion, he could take away only what he could carry. While this conduct is by no means trivial, the

amount of property he could steal or the amount of damage he could cause was restricted by physical limitations.

In the information age, these limitations no longer apply. Criminals seeking information stored in networked computers with dial-in access can access that information from virtually anywhere in the world. The quantity of information that can be stolen, or the amount of damage that can be caused by malicious programming code, may be limited only by the speed of the network and the criminal's equipment. Moreover, such conduct can very easily occur across state and national borders.

The lack of physical boundaries not only creates opportunities for criminals, but raises novel issues for law enforcement personnel. For example, when agents seek a search warrant, Rule 41 of the Federal Rules of Criminal Procedure requires that they seek the warrant in the district where the property to be searched is located. In other words, if agents wish to search a file cabinet in lower Manhattan in New York City, they would apply for a warrant in the Southern District of New York.

But suppose an informant indicates that she was working on her computer in lower Manhattan and saw that her company was keeping a second set of books in an effort to defraud shareholders and the Internal Revenue Service. Based upon this information, agents might get a warrant from the Southern District, enter the office, and copy this critical evidence. Although this would appear to be a straightforward case, what if the informant's computer was part of a local area network (LAN) whose server—the computer on which these records were stored—was actually located in New Jersey? Would a warrant issued in New York support such a seizure? Or suppose the offending company was a multinational corporation and the server was located in a foreign country? What would be the international ramifications of executing a search on a foreign computer system without consulting that country's authorities?

The other major impact caused by the shift to intangibles is that many of the existing theft, damage, and extortion laws protect physical property. Thus, new crimes may need to be defined.

3. Computer crimes have given rise to some very interesting and well-written books. Among them are: Katie Hafner & John Markoff, Cyberpunk: Outlaws and Hackers on the Computer Frontier (1995); John Markoff & Tustomu Shimomura, Takedown: The Pursuit and Capture of Kevin Mitnick, America's Most Wanted Computer Outlaw by the Man Who Did It (1996); Bruce Sterling, The Hacker Crackdown: Law and Disorder on the Electronic Frontier (1993); Clifford Stoll, The Cuckoo's Egg: Tracking a Spy Through the Maze of Computer Espionage (1995).

4. Even when miscreants do not intend to commit computer crimes, they may use computers or other information technologies in the course of their endeavors. Because of this, law enforcement officials have sought legislative and voluntary industry adoption of technical infrastructures to enable them to engage in surveillance for law enforcement purposes. These officials have sometimes been successful in these efforts. See Communications Assistance for Law Enforcement Act, 47 U.S.C. §§1002-1005; Federal Communications Commission, Rep. No. ET-98-8, FCC Proposes Rules to Meet Technical Requirements of CALEA (Oct. 22, 1998). Some

commentators express concerns about this and similar developments, in part because of their implications for privacy. See, e.g., Susan A. Friewald, Uncertain Privacy: Communications Attributes After the Digital Telephony Act, 69 S. Cal. L. Rev. 949 (1996).

5. Identity theft—that is, the appropriation of an individual's identity and the use of personal identifying data, such as driver's license and credit card numbers—is becoming easier because so much information about individuals is available in electronic form and is often available even on the Internet. See, e.g., U.S. Government Working Group on Electronic Commerce, First Annual Report, Nov. 1998. With so much information about individuals readily available, the crime of identity theft will continue to be of grave concern.

13

Privacy, Anonymity, and Encryption

A. PRIVACY

In re GeoCities
United States Federal Trade Commission

Complaint

The Federal Trade Commission, having reason to believe that Geo-Cities, a corporation ("respondent"), has violated the provisions of the Federal Trade Commission Act, and it appearing to the Commission that this proceeding is in the public interest, alleges: . . .

2. Respondent has operated a World Wide Web ("Web") site located at http://www.geocities.com. This Web site is a virtual community consisting of consumers' personal home pages that are organized into 40 themed neighborhoods. Respondent "hosts" a personal home page by posting it to an address in the consumer's chosen neighborhood.

3. Respondent has provided numerous services including free and fee-based personal home pages, free e-mail service, contests and children's clubs. Respondent provides personal home pages and e-mail addresses to adults and children who reveal personal identifying and demographic information when they register with the Web site.

4. Respondent has more than 1.8 million members whom it refers to as "homesteaders." As of December 2, 1997, approximately 200,000 GeoCities homesteaders were between the ages of 3 and 15. As of May 18,

1998, approximately 50,000 homesteaders were under age 13. Respondent's site is one of the ten most frequently visited Web sites, and was the sixth top trafficked site in April 1998 with 14.1 million unique visitors ages 12 and up. Among visitors between the ages of 12 and 17, it was the third most frequently visited Web site in March 1998. One out of five U.S. Web users visited respondent's Web site in October 1997.

5. Respondent has created opportunities for third party advertisers to promote products in a targeted manner to its more than 1.8 million members through respondent's collection of personal identifying, demographic, and "special interest" information obtained in the registration process and through the placement of members' personal home pages in themed neighborhoods. . . .

6. Respondent has derived its revenues from: selling third party advertising space on the Web site (including rotated ad banners, pop-up ads, and sponsorships of major areas on the Web site); selling personal identifying, demographic, and/or interest information collected from consumers who register; GeoPlus, an enhanced fee-based service that provides members extra server space for their personal home pages, among other benefits; merchandising in the Web site's GeoStore; and respondent's publishing unit (GeoPress Publishing).

7. Respondent has required consumers, including children, to complete a "New Member Application" form to become a GeoCities member. The form requests certain mandatory information and certain other information that respondent describes as "optional." The form also asks consumers to designate whether they would like to receive "special offers" from a list of topics or from specific companies. The default setting on the form for special offers is for members to receive them unless members choose otherwise.

8. Respondent has promoted on its Web site a children's neighborhood called the "Enchanted Forest." The Enchanted Forest is designated as respondent's "KIDS" area, "[a] community for and by kids." To join the Enchanted Forest neighborhood, children must complete the New Member Application form and post personal home pages. As of May 18, 1998, there were approximately 40,300 homesteads in the Enchanted Forest neighborhood. . . .

9. Respondent has promoted on its Web site a children's club in the Enchanted Forest neighborhood called the "GeoKidz Club." To join the GeoKidz Club, children must complete the "Official GeoCities GeoKidz Club Membership Request Form." This form requires applicants to be GeoCities members and to fill in all information requested, including name, age, e-mail address, GeoCities home page address, and gender. Respondent has also promoted on its Web site contests in the Enchanted Forest neighborhood for which children must complete the "Enchanted Forest Contest Entry Form," by providing their name, personal Web page address, and e-mail address. . . .

11. The acts and practices of respondent alleged in this complaint have been in or affecting commerce, as "commerce" is defined in Section 4 of the Federal Trade Commission Act.

Deceptive Practices in Connection with Respondent's Collection and Use of Personal Identifying Information

Misrepresentations Involving Information Collection by GeoCities

12. Respondent has placed privacy statements on its New Member Application form. This form collects from consumers, including children, certain mandatory information (first and last name, zip code, e-mail address, gender, date of birth, and member name) and certain other information respondent designates as "optional" (education level, income, marital status, occupation, and interests). The form also asks consumers to designate whether they wish to receive "special offers" from advertisers, to select from a list of special offer topics, and to designate whether they wish to receive specific products or services from individual companies. Respondent has also placed privacy statements on its "GeoCities Free Member E-mail Program" Web page and in the September 2, 1997 issue of the World Report newsletter, which refer to consumers' information collected on the New Member Application form. Through the[se] privacy statements . . . respondent has made the following statements about the uses and privacy of the information it collects:

> A. "The following section is completely optional. We will not share this information with anyone without your permission, but will use it to gain a better understanding of who is visiting GeoCities. This information will help us to build a better GeoCities for everyone. . . . [The information requested is] Highest Level of Education Completed . . . Household Income . . . Marital Status . . . Occupation . . . Interests."
>
> B. "When [consumers] apply to GeoCities we ask if they would like to receive information on a variety of topics. . . . Before we send anything out, we deliver an orientation e-mail to explain the program, to ensure that only those people who requested topically-oriented mail receive it and to protect your privacy. . . . We assure you this is a free service provided only to GeoCitizens who request this information, and we will NEVER give your information to anyone without your permission."
>
> C. "[Certain e-mail to members] came from our friends at CMG Direct Corporation. It was only sent to homesteaders who clicked a box in the topic list on the GeoCities application. The letter was meant as a heads-up to those people that information about the interests they selected would be coming from reputable companies. . . . We are sorry about any confusion concerning these e-mails. We assure you that we will NEVER give your personal information to anyone without your permission."

13. Through the means described in Paragraph 12, respondent has represented, expressly or by implication, that the personal identifying information collected through its New Member Application form is used only for the purpose of providing to members the specific e-mail advertising offers and other products or services they request.

14. In truth and in fact, the personal identifying information collected through respondent's New Member Application form is not used only for the purpose of providing to members the specific e-mail advertising offers and other products or services they request. Respondent has also sold, rented, or otherwise marketed or disclosed this information, including information collected from children, to third parties who have used this information for purposes other than those for which members have given permission. For example, third parties have targeted unrequested e-mail advertising offers to individual members based on their chosen GeoCities neighborhoods. Therefore, the representation set forth in Paragraph 13 was, and is, false or misleading.

15. Through the means described in Paragraph 12, respondent has represented, expressly or by implication, that the "optional" information collected through its New Member Application form is not disclosed to third parties without the consumer's permission, and is used only to gain a better understanding of who is visiting GeoCities.

16. In truth and in fact, respondent has disclosed the "optional" information it collects through the New Member Application form to third parties without the consumer's permission, and for purposes other than to gain a better understanding of who is visiting GeoCities. Respondent has disclosed this information, including information collected from children, to third parties who have used this information to target advertising to GeoCities' members. Therefore, the representation set forth in Paragraph 15 was, and is, false or misleading.

Misrepresentations Involving Sponsorship by Geocities Where Information Is Collected by Third Parties . . .

18. . . . . [R]espondent has represented, expressly or by implication, that respondent collects and maintains the children's personal identifying information collected through the Official GeoCities GeoKidz Club Membership Request Form and Enchanted Forest Contest Entry Form.

19. In truth and in fact, respondent does not collect and maintain the children's personal identifying information collected through the Official GeoCities GeoKidz Club Membership Request Form and Enchanted Forest Contest Entry Form. In fact, the Official GeoCities GeoKidz Club and the GeoCities Enchanted Forest contests are run by third parties hosted on the GeoCities Web site, who collect the children's personal identifying information directly and maintain it. Therefore, the representation set forth in Paragraph 18 was, and is, false or misleading.

20. The acts and practices of respondent as alleged in this complaint constitute unfair or deceptive acts or practices in or affecting commerce in violation of Section 5(a) of the Federal Trade Commission Act. . . .

Order

Definitions

For purposes of this order, the following definitions shall apply:

1. "Child" or "children" shall mean a person of age twelve (12) or under. . . .

3. "Personal identifying information" shall include, but is not limited to, first and last name, home or other physical address (e.g., school), e-mail address, telephone number, or any information that identifies a specific individual, or any information which when tied to the above becomes identifiable to a specific individual. . . .

8. "Express parental consent" shall mean a parent's affirmative agreement that is obtained by any of the following means: (1) a signed statement transmitted by postal mail or facsimile; (2) authorizing a charge to a credit card via a secure server; (3) e-mail accompanied by an electronically verifiable signature; (4) a procedure that is specifically authorized by statute, regulation, or guideline issued by the Commission; or (5) such other procedure that ensures verified parental consent and ensures the identity of the parent, such as the use of a reliable certifying authority. . . .

I.

IT IS ORDERED that respondent, directly or through any corporation, subsidiary, division, or other device, in connection with any online collection of personal identifying information from consumers, in or affecting commerce, shall not make any misrepresentation, in any manner, expressly or by implication, about its collection or use of such information from or about consumers, including, but not limited to, what information will be disclosed to third parties and how the information will be used.

II.

IT IS FURTHER ORDERED that respondent, directly or through any corporation, subsidiary, division, or other device, in connection with any online collection of personal identifying information from consumers, in or affecting commerce, shall not misrepresent, in any manner, expressly or by implication, the identity of the party collecting any such information or the sponsorship of any activity on its Web site.

III.

IT IS FURTHER ORDERED that respondent, directly or through any corporation, subsidiary, division, or other device, in connection with the online collection of personal identifying information from children, in or affecting commerce, shall not collect personal identifying information from any child if respondent has actual knowledge that such child does not have his or her parent's permission to provide the information to respondent. Respondent shall not be deemed to have actual knowledge if the child has falsely represented that (s)he is not a child and respondent does not knowingly possess information that such representation is false.

IV.

IT IS FURTHER ORDERED that respondent, directly or through any corporation, subsidiary, division, or other device, in connection with the online collection of personal identifying information, in or affecting commerce, shall provide clear and prominent notice to consumers, including the parents of children, with respect to respondent's practices with regard to its collection and use of personal identifying information. Such notice shall include, but is not limited to, disclosure of:

A. what information is being collected (*e.g.*, "name," "home address," "e-mail address," "age," "interests");
B. its intended use(s);
C. the third parties to whom it will be disclosed (*e.g.*, "advertisers of consumer products," mailing list companies," "the general public");
D. the consumer's ability to obtain access to or directly access such information and the means by which (s)he may do so;
E. the consumer's ability to remove directly or have the information removed from respondent's databases and the means by which (s)he may do so; and
F. the procedures to delete personal identifying information from respondent's databases and any limitations related to such deletion.

Such notice shall appear on the home page of respondent's Web site(s) and at each location on the site(s) at which such information is collected.

Provided that, respondent shall not be required to include the notice at the locations at which information is collected if such information is limited to tracking information and the collection of such information is described in the notice required by this Part.

Provided further that, for purposes of this Part, compliance with all of the following shall be deemed adequate notice: (a) placement of a clear and prominent hyperlink or button labeled **PRIVACY NOTICE** on the home page(s), which directly links to the privacy notice screen(s); (b) placement of the information required in this Part clearly and prominently on the privacy notice screen(s), followed on the same screen(s) with a button that must be clicked on to make it disappear; and (c) at each location on the site at which any personal identifying information is collected, placement of a clear and prominent hyperlink on the initial screen on which the collection takes place, which links directly to the privacy notice and which is accompanied by the following statement in bold typeface:

NOTICE: We collect personal information on this site. To learn more about how we use your information click here.

V.

IT IS FURTHER ORDERED that respondent, directly or through any corporation, subsidiary, division, or other device, in connection with the online collection of personal identifying information from children, in or affecting commerce, shall maintain a procedure by which it obtains express parental consent prior to collecting and using such information.

Provided that, respondent may implement the following screening procedure that shall be deemed to be in compliance with this Part. Respondent shall collect and retain certain personal identifying information from a child, including birth date and the child's and parent's e-mail addresses (hereafter "screening information"), enabling respondent to identify the site visitor as a child and to block the child's attempt to register with respondent without express parental consent. If respondent elects to have the child register with it, respondent shall: (1) give notice to the child to have his/her parent provide express parental consent to register; and/or (2) send a notice to the parent's e-mail address for the purpose of obtaining express parental consent. The notice to the child or parent shall provide instructions for the parent to: (1) go to a specific URL on the Web site to receive information on respondent's practices regarding its collection and use of personal identifying information from children and (2) provide express parental consent for the collection and use of such information. Respondent's collection of screening information shall be by a manner that discourages children from providing personal identifying information in addition to the screening information. All personal identifying information collected from a child shall be held by respondent in a secure manner and shall not be used in any manner other than to effectuate the notice to the child or parent, or to block the child from further attempts to register or otherwise provide personal identifying information to respondent without express parental consent. The personal identifying information collected shall not be disclosed to any third party prior to the receipt of express parental consent. If express parental consent is not received by twenty (20) days after respondent's collection of the information from the child, respondent shall remove all such personal identifying information from its databases, except such screening information necessary to block the child from further attempts to register or otherwise provide personal identifying information to respondent without express parental consent.

VI.

IT IS FURTHER ORDERED that respondent GeoCities, and its successors and assigns, shall provide a reasonable means for consumers, including the parents of children, to obtain removal of their or their children's personal identifying information collected and retained by respondent and/or disclosed to third parties, prior to the date of service of this order, as follows:

A. Respondent shall provide a clear and prominent notice to each consumer over the age of twelve (12) from whom it collected personal identifying information and disclosed that information to CMG Information Services, Inc., describing such consumer's options as stated in Part VI.C and the manner in which (s)he may exercise them.

B. Respondent shall provide a clear and prominent notice to the parent of each child from whom it collected personal identifying information prior to May 20, 1998, describing the parent's options as stated in Part VI.C and the manner in which (s)he may exercise them.

C. Respondent shall provide the notice within thirty (30) days after the date of service of this order by e-mail, postal mail, or facsimile. Notice to the parent of a child may be to the e-mail address of the parent and, if not known by respondent, to the e-mail address of the child. The notice shall include the following information:

1. the information that was collected (*e.g.*, "name," "home address," "e-mail address," "age," "interests"); its use(s) and/or intended use(s); and the third parties to whom it was or will be disclosed (*e.g.*, "advertisers of consumer products," "mailing list companies," "the general public") and with respect to children, that the child's personal identifying information may have been made public through various means, such as by publicly posting on the child's personal home page or disclosure by the child through the use of an e-mail account;

2. the consumer's and child's parents right to obtain access to such information and the means by which (s)he may do so;

3. the consumer's and child's parent's right to have the information removed from respondent's or a third party's databases and the means by which (s)he may do so;

4. a statement that children's information will not be disclosed to third parties, including public posting, without express parental consent to the disclosure or public posting;

5. the means by which express parental consent may be communicated to the respondent permitting disclosure to third parties of a child's information; and

6. a statement that the failure of a consumer over the age of twelve (12) to request removal of the information from respondent's databases will be deemed as approval to its continued retention and/or disclosure to third parties by respondent.

D. Respondent shall provide to consumers, including the parents of children, a reasonable and secure means to request access to or directly access their or their children's personal identifying information. Such means may include direct access through password protected personal profile, return e-mail bearing an electronically verifiable signature, postal mail, or facsimile.

E. Respondent shall provide to consumers, including the parents of children, a reasonable means to request removal of their or their children's personal identifying information from respondent's and/or the applicable third party's databases or an assurance that such information has been removed. Such means may include e-mail, postal mail, or facsimile.

F. The failure of a consumer over the age of twelve (12) to request the actions specified above within twenty (20) days after his/her receipt of the notice required in Part VI.A shall be deemed to be consent to the information's continued retention and use by respondent and any third party.

G. Respondent shall provide to the parent of a child a reasonable means to communicate express parental consent to the retention and/or disclosure to third parties of his/her child's personal identifying information. Respondent shall not use any such information or disclose it to any third party unless and until it receives express parental consent.

H. If, in response to the notice required in Part VI.A, respondent has received a request by a consumer over the age of twelve (12) that respondent should remove from its databases the consumer's personal identifying information or has not received the express consent of a parent of a child to the continued retention and/or disclosure to third parties of a child's personal identifying information by respondent within twenty (20) days after the parent's receipt of the notice required in Part VI.B, respondent shall within ten (10) days:

> 1. Discontinue its retention and/or disclosure to third parties of such information, including but not limited to (a) removing from its databases all such information, (b) removing all personal home pages created by the child, and (c) terminating all e-mail accounts for the child; and
>
> 2. Contact all third parties to whom respondent has disclosed the information, requesting that they discontinue using or disclosing that information to other third parties, and remove the information from their databases.
>
> With respect to any consumer over the age of twelve (12) or any parent of a child who has consented to respondent's continued retention and use of personal identifying information pursuant to this Part, such consumer's or parent's continuing right to obtain access to his/her or a child's personal identifying information or removal of such information from respondent's databases shall be as specified in the notice required by Part IV of this order.

I. Within thirty (30) days after the date of service of this order, respondent shall obtain from a responsible official of each third party to whom it has disclosed personal identifying information and from each GeoCities Community Leader a statement stating that (s)he has been advised of the terms of this order and of respondent's obligations under this Part, and that (s)he agrees, upon notification from respondent, to discontinue using or disclosing a consumer's or child's personal identifying information to other third parties and to remove any such information from its databases.

J. As may be permitted by law, respondent shall cease to do business with any third party that fails within thirty (30) days of the date of service of this order to provide the statement set forth in Part VI.I or whom respondent knows or has reason to know has failed at any time to (a) discontinue using or disclosing a child's personal identifying information to other third parties, or (b) remove any such information from their databases. With respect to any GeoCities Community Leader, the respondent shall cease the Community Leader status of any person who fails to provide the statement set forth in Part VI.I or whom respondent knows or has reason to know has failed at any time to (a) discontinue using or disclosing a child's personal identifying information to other third parties, or (b) remove any such information from their databases.

For purposes of this Part: "third party(ies)" shall mean each GeoCities Community Leader, CMG Information Services, Inc., Surplus Software, Inc. (Surplus Direct/Egghead Computer), Sage Enterprises, Inc. (Geo-Planet/Planetall), Netopia, Inc. (Netopia), and InfoBeat/Mercury Mail (InfoBeat).

VII.

IT IS FURTHER ORDERED that for the purposes of this order, respondent shall not be required to remove personal identifying information from its archived database if such information is retained solely for the purposes of Web site system maintenance, computer file back-up, to block a child's attempt to register with or otherwise provide personal identifying information to respondent without express parental consent, or to respond to requests for such information from law enforcement agencies or pursuant to judicial process. Except as necessary to respond to requests from law enforcement agencies or pursuant to judicial process, respondent shall not disclose to any third party any information retained it its archived database. In any notice required by this order, respondent shall include information, clearly and prominently, about its policies for retaining information in its archived database. . . .

XI.

IT IS FURTHER ORDERED that respondent GeoCities, and its successors and assigns, shall establish an "information practices training program" for any employee or GeoCities Community Leader engaged in the collection or disclosure to third parties of consumers' personal identifying information. The program shall include training about respondent's privacy policies, information security procedures, and disciplinary procedures for violations of its privacy policies. Respondent shall provide each such current employee and GeoCities Community Leader with information practices training materials within thirty (30) days after the date of service of this order, and each such future employee or GeoCities Community Leader such materials and training within thirty (30) days after (s)he assumes his/her position or responsibilities. . . .

COMMENTS AND QUESTIONS

1. The Federal Trade Commission (FTC) has power under its enabling legislation to take action against firms that engage in unfair trade practices. The deceptive nature of Geocities' actions in this case provided ample justification for initiating the complaint in this case. However, the FTC's jurisdiction over privacy matters more generally may be relatively limited and the detailed order in the *Geocities* case may skirt the edges of the Commission's powers. The FTC has, however, been active in reporting to Congress on cyberspace privacy-related issues. See, e.g., Federal Trade Commission, Self-Regulation and Online Privacy: A Report to Congress (July 1999).

Other U.S.-government sponsored reports on privacy in the information age come from agencies that include: Information Policy Committee, National Information Infrastructure Task Force, Options for Promoting Privacy on the National Information Infrastructure (April 1997); Privacy Working Group, Information Infrastructure Task Force, Privacy and the National Information Infrastructure: Principles for Providing and Using Personal Information (1995); U.S. Dept of Commerce, N.T.I.A., Elements of Effective Self-Regulation for Protection of Privacy (Jan. 1998). The literature on cyberspace information privacy is vast. Among the works worth reading are: Fred M. Cate, Privacy in the Information Age (Brookings, 1997); Jerry Kang, Information Privacy in Cyberspace Transactions, 50 Stan. L. Rev. 1193 (1998); Joel R. Reidenberg, Privacy in the Information Economy: A Fortress or a Frontier for Individual Rights?, 44 Fed. Comm. L.J. 195 (1993); Frederick Schauer, Internet Privacy and the Public-Private Distinction, 38 Jurimetrics J. 555 (1998); Paul M. Schwartz, Privacy and the Economics of Personal Health Care Information, 76 Tex. L. Rev. 1 (1997).

2. After the FTC documented Web sites' abusive practices of gathering considerable amounts of information from children about themselves and their families, Congress decided to enact the Children's Online Privacy Protection Act (COPPA). This Act requires Web site owners to get permission from parents before gathering information from children under the age of 13. However, FTC implementation of COPPA may be more difficult than one might expect, particularly as regards formulating an effective, yet practical, definition of "parental permission." See, e.g., Will Rodger, FTC Weighs in on E-Privacy, Inter@ctive Week Online, April 21, 1999, http://www.zdnet.com/zdnn/stories/news/0,4586,2245111,00.html.

3. COPPA is typical of American-style information privacy laws. The Act was adopted only after some documented abuses had occurred and then was narrowly tailored to address those abuses. Similar is the Video Privacy

Act, 18 U.S.C. §§2710-2711. Congress passed this Act to protect video rental records from unauthorized disclosures after information about Robert Bork's video choices were published in an effort to discredit his candidacy for the U.S. Supreme Court. Many other examples of narrowly tailored, sector-based privacy laws can be found in Paul M. Schwartz & Joel R. Reidenberg, Data Privacy Law (1996). This book is a comprehensive study of U.S. information privacy laws, both state and federal.

In contrast to the United States, the European Union (EU) has adopted comprehensive privacy regulations to protect the personal data of its citizens against unauthorized reuse and processing. See Directive 95/46/EC of the European Parliament and the Council, October 25, 1995, on the protection of individuals with regard to the processing of personal data and on the free movement of such data, Official Journal of the European Community, L281 (Nov. 23, 1995). Sympathetic analyses of this Directive can be found in Paul M. Schwartz, European Data Protection Law and Restrictions on International Data Flows, 80 Iowa L. Rev. 471 (1995), and in Spiros Simitis, From the Market to the Polls: The EU Directive on the Protection of Personal Data, 80 Iowa L. Rev. 445 (1995).

The United States has resisted adopting a similarly comprehensive approach, arguing that the EU Directive is unnecessary and overbroad in its regulation. A very American critique of the Directive can be found in Peter P. Swire & Robert E. Litan, None of Your Business: World Data Flows, Electronic Commerce, and the European Privacy Directive, Washington, D.C.: Brookings Institution Press, 1998.

4. Some commentators have proposed giving individuals property rights in personal data as a way to protect privacy. See, e.g., Kenneth C. Laudon, Markets and Privacy, 39 Comm. ACM 92 (Sept. 1996); Richard S. Murphy, Property Rights in Personal Information: An Economic Defense of Privacy, 84 Geo. L.J. 2381 (1996). Would this be a good idea? How would it work?

5. Many opportunities exist for anonymous or pseudonymous communications or activities in cyberspace. While these communications and activities can be enriching, they can also be irresponsible and even illegal. See, e.g., Anne Wells Branscomb, Anonymity, Autonomy, and Accountability: Challenges to the First Amendment in Cyberspace, 104 Yale L.J. 1639 (1995); A. Michael Froomkin, Anonymity and Its Enmities, 1995 J. Online L. art. 4. The State of Georgia passed a law to prohibit anonymous and pseudonymous communications as a preventive measure against abusive uses of anonymity. This legislation was challenged as unconstitutionally vague and overbroad in ACLU v. Miller, 977 F. Supp. 1228 (N.D. Ga. 1997), and the court granted a preliminary injunction against its enforcement. How much support for a right to engage in anonymous or pseudonymous communication can be drawn from decisions such as McIntyre v. Ohio Elections Commission, 514 U.S. 334 (1995) (striking down an Ohio law forbidding the distribution of anonymous campaign literature)?

SPORKIN, District Judge.

. . . The Plaintiff, Senior Chief Timothy R. McVeigh, is a highly decorated seventeen-year veteran of the United States Navy who has served
honorably and continuously since he was nineteen years old. At the time of
the Navy's decision to discharge him, he was the senior-most enlisted man
aboard the United States nuclear submarine U.S.S. Chicago.

On September 2, 1997, Ms. Helen Hajne, a civilian Navy volunteer,
received an electronic mail ("email") message through the America Online
Service ("AOL") regarding the toy-drive that she was coordinating for the
Chicago crew members' children. The message box stated that it came from
the alias "boysrch," but the text of the email was signed by a "Tim."
Administrative Record ("AR") at 110. Through an option available to AOL
subscribers, the volunteer searched through the "member profile directory"
to find the member profile for this sender. The directory specified that
"boysrch" was an AOL subscriber named Tim who lived in Honolulu,
Hawaii, worked in the military, and identified his marital status as "gay."
See AR at 111. Although the profile included some telling interests such as
"collecting pics of other young studs" and "boy watching," it did not
include any further identifying information such as full name, address, or
phone number. . . .

Ms. Hajne proceeded to forward the email and directory profile to her
husband, who, like Plaintiff, was also a noncommissioned officer aboard the
U.S.S. Chicago. . . . [T]he Navy suspected the "Tim" who authored the
email might be Senior Chief Timothy McVeigh. Before she spoke to the
Plaintiff and without a warrant or court order, [the ship's principal legal
adviser] . . . requested a Navy paralegal on her staff, Legalman First Class
Joseph M. Kaiser, to contact AOL and obtain information from the service
that could "connect" the screen name "boysrch" and accompanying user
profile to McVeigh. See AR at 13. Legalman Kaiser called AOL's toll-free
customer service number and talked to a representative at technical services.
Legalman Kaiser did not identify himself as a Naval serviceman. According
to his testimony at the administrative hearing, he stated that he was "a third
party in receipt of a fax sheet and wanted to confirm the profile sheet, [and]
who it belonged to." AR at 14. The AOL representative affirmatively identified Timothy R. McVeigh as the customer in question. See *id.* at 11-15.

Upon verification from AOL, Lieutenant Morean notified Senior Chief
McVeigh that the Navy had obtained "some indication[ ] that he made a
statement of homosexuality" in violation of §654(b)(2) of "Don't Ask,
Don't Tell." AR at 27-28. In light of the Uniform Code of Military Justice
prohibition of sodomy and indecent acts, she then advised him of his right
to remain silent. See *id.* at 28, 30. . . . Shortly thereafter, in a memorandum
dated September 22, 1997, the Navy advised Plaintiff that it was com-

mencing an administrative discharge proceeding (termed by the Navy as an "administrative separation") against him. The reason stated was for "homosexual conduct, as evidenced by your statement that you are a homosexual." AR at 107.

On November 7, 1997, the Navy conducted an administrative discharge hearing before a three-member board. At the hearing, the Plaintiff made an unsworn oral statement that explained the substance of his email to Ms. Hajne, and thus by inference confirmed his authorship of the correspondence. See AR at 84. The Plaintiff presented evidence of a prior engagement to a woman and several other heterosexual relationships to rebut the presumption of homosexuality, pursuant to §654(b)(2). See AR at 82-84. This evidence was rejected by the Board. . . . At the conclusion of the administrative hearing, the board held that the government had sufficiently shown by a preponderance of the evidence that Senior Chief McVeigh had engaged in "homosexual conduct," a dischargeable offense. . . .

[The Court determined that McVeigh's discharge violated the Navy's "Don't Tell, Don't Pursue" policy.]

The . . . steps taken by the Navy in its "pursuit" of the Plaintiff were not only unauthorized under its policy, but likely illegal under the Electronic Communications Privacy Act of 1986 ("ECPA"). The ECPA, enacted by Congress to address privacy concerns on the Internet, allows the government to obtain information from an online service provider—as the Navy did in this instance from AOL—but only if a) it obtains a warrant issued under the Federal Rules of Criminal Procedure or state equivalent; or b) it gives prior notice to the online subscriber and then issues a subpoena or receives a court order authorizing disclosure of the information in question. See 18 U.S.C. §2703(b)(1)(A)-(B), (c)(1)(B).

In soliciting and obtaining over the phone personal information about the Plaintiff from AOL, his private on-line service provider, the government in this case invoked neither of these provisions and thus failed to comply with the ECPA. From the record, it is undisputed that the Navy directly solicited by phone information from AOL. Lieutenant Karin S. Morean, the ship's principal legal counsel and a member of the JAG corp, personally requested Legalman Kaiser to contact AOL and obtain the identity of the subscriber. See AR at 13. Without this information, Plaintiff credibly contends that the Navy could not have made the necessary connection between him and the user profile which was the sole basis on which to commence discharge proceedings.

The government, in its defense, contends that the Plaintiff cannot succeed on his ECPA claim. It argues that the substantive provision of the statute that Plaintiff cites, 18 U.S.C. §2703(c)(1)(B), puts the obligation on the online service provider to withhold information from the government, and not vice versa. In support of its position, Defendants cite to the Fourth Circuit opinion in Tucker v. Waddell, 83 F.3d 688 (4th Cir.1996), which held that §2703(c)(1)(B) only prohibits the actions of online providers, not the government. Accordingly, Defendants allege that Plaintiff has no cause of action against the government on the basis of the ECPA.

Under the circumstances of this case, it is unlikely that the government will prevail on this argument. Section 2703(c)(1)(B) must be read in the context of the statute as a whole. In comparison, §2703(a) and (b) imposes on the government a reciprocal obligation to obtain a warrant or the like before requiring disclosure. It appears from the face of the statute that all of the subsections of §2703 were intended to work in tandem to protect consumer privacy. Even if, however, the government ultimately proves to be right in its assessment of §2703(c)(1)(B), the Plaintiff has plead §2703(a) and (b) as alternative grounds for relief. In his claim that the government, at the least, solicited a violation of the ECPA by AOL, the Court finds that there is likely success on the merits with regard to this issue. The government knew, or should have known, that by turning over the information without a warrant, AOL was breaking the law. Yet the Navy, in this case, directly solicited the information anyway. What is most telling is that the Naval investigator did not identify himself when he made his request. While the government makes much of the fact that §2703(c)(1)(B) does not provide a cause of action against the government, it is elementary that information obtained improperly can be suppressed where an individual's rights have been violated. In these days of "big brother," where through technology and otherwise the privacy interests of individuals from all walks of life are being ignored or marginalized, it is imperative that statutes explicitly protecting these rights be strictly observed.

The government has produced no evidence that would indicate that it would have proceeded without this information from AOL affirmatively linking the email to Senior Chief McVeigh. That the Plaintiff may have made incriminating statements at the subsequent administrative hearing does not bootstrap the Navy out of its legal dilemma of not only violating its own policy, but also a federal statute in its attempt to charge the Plaintiff with homosexuality. . . .

[The Court determined that McVeigh would suffer irreparable harm if his discharge was not halted by a preliminary injunction.]

IV. Public Interest

Certainly, the public has an inherent interest in the preservation of privacy rights as advanced by Plaintiff in this case. With literally the entire world on the world-wide web, enforcement of the ECPA is of great concern to those who bare the most personal information about their lives in private accounts through the Internet. In this case in particular, where the government may well have violated a federal statute in its zeal to brand the Plaintiff a homosexual, the actions of the Navy must be more closely scrutinized by this Court. It is disputed in the record exactly as to how the

Navy represented itself to AOL when it requested information about the Plaintiff. The Defendants contend that Legalman Kaiser merely asked for confirmation of a fax sheet bearing Plaintiff's account. Plaintiff contends, and AOL confirms, however, that the Naval officer "mislead" AOL's representative by "both failing to disclose the identity and purpose [of his request] and by portraying himself as a friend or acquaintance of Senior Chief McVeigh's." See AOL Statement on the Matter of Timothy McVeigh, Ct. Ex. 1. At the final injunction hearing, this issue should be fully explored. . . .

COMMENTS AND QUESTIONS

1. Does McVeigh have a viable cause of action against AOL for revealing his identity to the Navy or against the Navy for the deceptive manner in which it sought his identity from AOL?

2. Networked computer systems make it considerably easier for employers to engage in surveillance of their employees. This may include monitoring electronic mail exchanges to, from, and among employees. Although employees sometimes believe that their electronic communications by email are and should be private, courts have generally been unsympathetic to employees whose email exchanges, once intercepted, provide reasonable grounds for dismissal. Consider, for example, Smyth v. Pillsbury, 914 F. Supp. 97 (E.D. Pa. 1996). Smyth brought a wrongful discharge action against his former employer alleging the discharge violated public policy because Pillsbury had invaded his privacy when it intercepted his email messages after giving assurances that the company would treat email as confidential. The court dismissed Smyth's lawsuit with the following explanation:

> In the first instance, unlike urinalysis and personal property searches, we do not find a reasonable expectation of privacy in e-mail communications voluntarily made by an employee to his supervisor over the company e-mail system notwithstanding any assurances that such communications would not be intercepted by management. Once plaintiff communicated the alleged unprofessional comments to a second person (his supervisor) over an e-mail system which was apparently utilized by the entire company, any reasonable expectation of privacy was lost. Significantly, the defendant did not require plaintiff, as in the case of an urinalysis or personal property search to disclose any personal information about himself. Rather, plaintiff voluntarily communicated the alleged unprofessional comments over the company e-mail system. We find no privacy interests in such communications.
>
> In the second instance, even if we found that an employee had a reasonable expectation of privacy in the contents of his e-mail communications over the company e-mail system, we do not find that a reasonable person would consider the defendant's interception of these communications to be a substantial and highly offensive invasion of his privacy. Again, we note that by in-

tercepting such communications, the company is not, as in the case of urinalysis or personal property searches, requiring the employee to disclose any personal information about himself or invading the employee's person or personal effects. Moreover, the company's interest in preventing inappropriate and unprofessional comments or even illegal activity over its e-mail system outweighs any privacy interest the employee may have in those comments.

3.   Other efforts in the United States to use common law privacy law to get relief against companies for abuses of information privacy have also been largely unsuccessful. Consider, for example, Dwyer v. American Express, 273 Ill. App. 3d 742, 652 N.E.2d 1351, 210 Ill. Dec. 375 (Ill. App. 1st Dist. 1995). Dwyer sued American Express for an unauthorized intrusion or prying into his seclusion after the company compiled various lists of customers having certain spending and shopping habits and then rented these lists to third parties. The court reasoned that

> [b]y using the American Express card, a cardholder is voluntarily, and necessarily, giving information to defendants that, if analyzed, will reveal a cardholder's spending habits and shopping preferences. We cannot hold that a defendant has committed an unauthorized intrusion by compiling the information voluntarily given to it and then renting its compilation.

Is this a reasonable conclusion? Are there any limits on the right of companies like American Express to reuse personal data from their files?

4.   For an insightful discussion of Fourth Amendment-based privacy interests in cyberspace, see Michael Adler, Cyberspace, General Searches, and Digital Contraband: The Fourth Amendment and the Net-Wide Search, 105 Yale L.J. 1093 (1995).

5.   Some technologists are working to develop technological means to protect privacy. See, e.g., Ian Goldberg, David Wagner, & Eric Brewer, Privacy-Enhancing Technologies for the Internet, http://www.cs.berkeley.edu/~daw/papers/privacy-compcon97-www/privacy-html.html. Encryption is among the promising approaches.

B.   ENCRYPTION

≡≡≡
Bernstein v. United States Department of Justice
United States Court of Appeals for the Ninth Circuit
176 F.3d 1132 (9th Cir. 1999)

FLETCHER, Circuit Judge:

The government defendants appeal the grant of summary judgment to the plaintiff, Professor Daniel J. Bernstein ("Bernstein"), enjoining the enforcement of certain Export Administration Regulations ("EAR") that limit Bernstein's ability to distribute encryption software. We find that the EAR regulations (1) operate as a prepublication licensing scheme that burdens scientific expression, (2) vest boundless discretion in government officials, and (3) lack adequate procedural safeguards. Consequently, we hold that the challenged regulations constitute a prior restraint on speech that offends the First Amendment. Although we employ a somewhat narrower rationale than did the district court, its judgment is accordingly affirmed.

Background

A. *Facts and Procedural History*

Bernstein is currently a professor in the Department of Mathematics, Statistics, and Computer Science at the University of Illinois at Chicago. As a doctoral candidate at the University of California, Berkeley, he developed an encryption method—"a zero-delay private-key stream encryptor based upon a one-way hash function"[1]—that he dubbed "Snuffle." Bernstein described his method in two ways: in a paper containing analysis and mathematical equations (the "Paper") and in two computer programs written in "C," a high-level computer programming language ("Source Code"). Bernstein later wrote a set of instructions in English (the "Instructions") explaining how to program a computer to encrypt and decrypt data utilizing a one-way hash function, essentially translating verbatim his Source Code into prose form.

Seeking to present his work on Snuffle within the academic and scientific communities, Bernstein asked the State Department whether he needed a license to publish Snuffle in any of its various forms. The State Department responded that Snuffle was a munition under the International Traffic in Arms Regulations ("ITAR"), and that Bernstein would need a license to "export" the Paper, the Source Code, or the Instructions. There followed a protracted and unproductive series of letter communications between Bernstein and the government, wherein Bernstein unsuccessfully attempted to determine the scope and application of the export regulations to Snuffle.

Bernstein ultimately filed this action, challenging the constitutionality of the ITAR regulations. The district court found that the Source Code was speech protected by the First Amendment, see Bernstein v. U.S. Depart-

---

1. The term "hash function" describes a function that transforms an input into a unique output of fixed (and usually smaller) size that is dependent on the input. For some purposes (e.g. error checking, digital signatures), it is desirable that it be impossible to derive the input data given only the hash function's output—this type of function is known as a "one-way hash function." Hash functions have many uses in cryptography and computer science, and numerous one-way hash functions are widely known. "Zero-delay" means that Snuffle can be used for interactive communications because it encrypts and decrypts on a character-by-character basis—the users need not complete an entire message before encrypting and sending.

ment of State, 922 F.Supp. 1426 (N.D.Cal.1996) ("Bernstein I"), and subsequently granted summary judgment to Bernstein on his First Amendment claims, holding the challenged ITAR regulations facially invalid as a prior restraint on speech, see Bernstein v. U.S. Department of State, 945 F.Supp. 1279 (N.D.Cal.1996) ("Bernstein II"). . . .

B. Overview of Cryptography

Cryptography is the science of secret writing, a science that has roots stretching back hundreds, and perhaps thousands, of years. See generally David Kahn, The Codebreakers (2d ed.1996). For much of its history, cryptography has been the jealously guarded province of governments and militaries. In the past twenty years, however, the science has blossomed in the civilian sphere, driven on the one hand by dramatic theoretical innovations within the field, and on the other by the needs of modern communication and information technologies. As a result, cryptography has become a dynamic academic discipline within applied mathematics. It is the cryptographer's primary task to find secure methods to encrypt messages, making them unintelligible to all except the intended recipients:

> Encryption basically involves running a readable message known as "plaintext" through a computer program that translates the message according to an equation or algorithm into unreadable "ciphertext." Decryption is the translation back to plaintext when the message is received by someone with an appropriate "key."

Bernstein III, 974 F.Supp. at 1292. The applications of encryption, however, are not limited to ensuring secrecy; encryption can also be employed to ensure data integrity, authenticate users, and facilitate nonrepudiation (e.g., linking a specific message to a specific sender). See *id.*

It is, of course, encryption's secrecy applications that concern the government. The interception and deciphering of foreign communications has long played an important part in our nation's national security efforts. In the words of a high-ranking State Department official:

> Policies concerning the export control of cryptographic products are based on the fact that the proliferation of such products will make it easier for foreign intelligence targets to deny the United States Government access to information vital to national security interests. Cryptographic products and software have military and intelligence applications. As demonstrated throughout history, encryption has been used to conceal foreign military communications, on the battlefield, aboard ships and submarines, or in other military settings. Encryption is also used to conceal other foreign communications that have foreign policy and national security significance for the United States. For example, encryption can be used to conceal communications of terrorists, drug smugglers, or others intent on taking hostile action against U.S. facilities, personnel, or security interests.

Lowell Decl. at 4 (reproduced in Appellant's Excerpts of Record at 97). As increasingly sophisticated and secure encryption methods are developed, the government's interest in halting or slowing the proliferation of such methods has grown keen. The EAR regulations at issue in this appeal evidence this interest.

C. The EAR Regulations

The EAR contain specific regulations to control the export of encryption software, expressly including computer source code. Encryption software is treated differently from other software in a number of significant ways. First, the term "export" is specifically broadened[5] with respect to encryption software to preclude the use of the internet and other global mediums if such publication would allow passive or active access by a foreign national within the United States or anyone outside the United States. 15 C.F.R. §734.2(b)(9)(B)(ii).[6] Second, the regulations governing the export of nonencryption software provide for several exceptions that are not applicable to encryption software.[7] In addition, although printed materials containing encryption source code are not subject to EAR regulation, the same materials made available on machine-readable media, such as floppy disk or CD-ROM, are covered. 15 C.F.R. §734.3(b), Note to Paragraphs (b)(2) & (b)(3). The government, moreover, has reserved the right to restrict source code in printed form that may be easily "scanned," thus creating some ambiguity as to whether printed publications are necessarily exempt from licensing. See 61 Fed.Reg. 68,575 (1996).

If encryption software falls within the ambit of the relevant EAR provisions, the "export" of such software requires a prepublication license. When a prepublication license is requested, the relevant agencies undertake a "case-by-case" analysis to determine if the export is "consistent with U.S. national security and foreign policy interests." 15 C.F.R. §742.15(b). All applications must be "resolved or referred to the President no later than 90

---

5. "Export," even as applied to software generally, is defined quite broadly to include any release, including oral exchanges of information and visual inspections, in a foreign country or to a foreign national within the United States. 15 C.F.R. §734.2(b)(2) & (3).

6. Specifically, 15 C.F.R. §734.2(b)(9)(B)(ii) provides that "export" includes:

> downloading or causing the downloading of, such software to locations (including electronic bulletin boards, Internet file transfer protocol, and World Wide Web sites) outside the U.S., or making such software available for transfer outside the United States, over wire, cable, radio, electromagnetic, photo-optical, photoelectric or other comparable communications facilities accessible to persons outside the United States, including transfers from electronic bulletin boards, Internet file transfer protocol and World Wide Web sites, unless the person making the software available takes precautions adequate to prevent unauthorized transfer of such code outside the United States.

7. These exceptions allow for export of software that is publicly available, 15 C.F.R. §734.7(c); results from fundamental research or is educational, 15 C.F.R. §§734.3(b)(3), 734.8, 734.9; is already available from foreign sources, 15 C.F.R. §768.1(b); or contains only a de minimis quantity of domestically-derived content, 15 C.F.R. §734.4(b)(2).

days" from the date an application is entered into the BXA's electronic license processing system. 15 C.F.R. §750.4(a). There is no time limit, however, that applies once an application is referred to the President. Although the regulations do provide for an internal administrative appeal procedure, such appeals are governed only by the exhortation that they be completed "within a reasonable time." 15 C.F.R. §756.2(c)(1). Final administrative decisions are not subject to judicial review. 15 C.F.R. §756.2(c)(2).

Discussion

I. *Prior Restraint*

The parties and amici urge a number of theories on us. We limit our attention here, for the most part, to only one: whether the EAR restrictions on the export of encryption software in source code form constitute a prior restraint in violation of the First Amendment. We review de novo the district court's affirmative answer to this question. See Roulette v. Seattle, 97 F.3d 300, 302 (9th Cir.1996).

It is axiomatic that "prior restraints on speech and publication are the most serious and least tolerable infringement on First Amendment rights." Nebraska Press Ass'n v. Stuart, 427 U.S. 539, 559, 96 S.Ct. 2791, 49 L.Ed.2d 683 (1976). Indeed, the Supreme Court has opined that "it is the chief purpose of the [First Amendment] guaranty to prevent previous restraints upon publication." Near v. Minnesota, 283 U.S. 697, 713, 51 S.Ct. 625, 75 L.Ed. 1357 (1931). Accordingly, "[a]ny prior restraint on expression comes . . . with a 'heavy presumption' against its constitutional validity." Organization for a Better Austin v. Keefe, 402 U.S. 415, 419, 91 S.Ct. 1575, 29 L.Ed.2d 1 (1971). At the same time, the Supreme Court has cautioned that "[t]he phrase 'prior restraint' is not a self-wielding sword. Nor can it serve as a talismanic test." Kingsley Books, Inc. v. Brown, 354 U.S. 436, 441, 77 S.Ct. 1325, 1 L.Ed.2d 1469 (1957). We accordingly turn from "[t]he generalization that prior restraint is particularly obnoxious" to a "more particularistic analysis." *Id.* at 442.

The Supreme Court has treated licensing schemes that act as prior restraints on speech with suspicion because such restraints run the twin risks of encouraging self-censorship and concealing illegitimate abuses of censorial power. See Lakewood v. Plain Dealer Publishing Co., 486 U.S. 750, 759, 108 S.Ct. 2138, 100 L.Ed.2d 771 (1988). As a result, "even if the government may constitutionally impose content-neutral prohibitions on a particular manner of speech, it may not condition that speech on obtaining a license or permit from a government official in that official's boundless discretion." *Id.* at 764. We follow the lead of the Supreme Court and divide the appropriate analysis into two parts. The threshold question is whether Bernstein is entitled to bring a facial challenge against the EAR regulations. See *id*. at 755. If he is so entitled, we proceed to the second question: whether the regulations constitute an impermissible prior restraint on speech. See *id*. at 769.

A. Is Bernstein Entitled To Bring a Facial Attack?

A licensing regime is always subject to facial challenge as a prior restraint where it "gives a government official or agency substantial power to discriminate based on the content or viewpoint of speech by suppressing disfavored speech or disliked speakers," and has "a close enough nexus to expression, or to conduct commonly associated with expression, to pose a real and substantial threat of . . . censorship risks." *Id*. at 759.

The EAR regulations at issue plainly satisfy the first requirement— "the determination of who may speak and who may not is left to the unbridled discretion of a government official." *Id*. at 763. BXA administrators are empowered to deny licenses whenever export might be inconsistent with "U.S. national security and foreign policy interests." 15 C.F.R. §742.15(b). No more specific guidance is provided. Obviously, this constraint on official discretion is little better than no constraint at all. See *Lakewood*, 486 U.S. at 769-70 (a standard requiring that license denial be in the "public interest" is an "illusory" standard that "renders the guarantee against censorship little more than a high-sounding ideal."). The government's assurances that BXA administrators will not, in fact, discriminate on the basis of content are beside the point. See *id*. at 770 (presumption that official will act in good faith "is the very presumption that the doctrine forbidding unbridled discretion disallows."). After all, "the mere existence of the licensor's unfettered discretion, coupled with the power of prior restraint, intimidates parties into censoring their own speech, even if the discretion and power are never actually abused." *Id*. at 757.

The more difficult issue arises in relation to the second requirement— that the challenged regulations exhibit "a close enough nexus to expression." We are called on to determine whether encryption source code is expression for First Amendment purposes.[9]

---

9. As an initial matter, we note that the fact that the regulations reach only "exports" does not reduce the burden on Bernstein's First Amendment rights. It is Bernstein's right to speak, not the rights of foreign listeners to hear, that we are concerned with here. The government does not argue, nor could it, that being cut off from a foreign audience, as distinguished from a domestic one, does not implicate First Amendment concerns. See Bullfrog Films, Inc. v. Wick, 847 F.2d 502, 509 n. 9 (9th Cir.1988). In addition, because the regulations define "export" to include the use of internet fora that may be accessible by foreign nationals, as well as domestic communications with foreign nationals, we think it plain that the regulations potentially limit Bernstein's freedom of speech in a variety of both domestic and foreign contexts. See Reno v. American Civ. Lib. Union, 521 U.S. 844, 117 S.Ct. 2329, 2348-49, 138 L.Ed.2d 874 (1997) (rejecting government argument that restriction of expression on the internet is justified because ample alternative channels of communication exist).

We begin by explaining what source code is. "Source code," at least as currently understood by computer programmers, refers to the text of a program written in a "high-level" programming language, such as "PAS-CAL" or "C." The distinguishing feature of source code is that it is meant to be read and understood by humans and that it can be used to express an idea or a method. A computer, in fact, can make no direct use of source code until it has been translated ("compiled") into a "low-level" or "machine" language, resulting in computer-executable "object code." That source code is meant for human eyes and understanding, however, does not mean that an untutored layperson can understand it. Because source code is destined for the maw of an automated, ruthlessly literal translator—the compiler—a programmer must follow stringent grammatical, syntactical, formatting, and punctuation conventions. As a result, only those trained in programming can easily understand source code.[11]

Also important for our purposes is an understanding of how source code is used in the field of cryptography. Bernstein has submitted numerous declarations from cryptographers and computer programmers explaining that cryptographic ideas and algorithms are conveniently expressed in source code.[12] That this should be so is, on reflection, not surprising. As

---

11. It must be emphasized, however, that source code is merely text, albeit text that conforms to stringent formatting and punctuation requirements. For example, the following is an excerpt from Bernstein's Snuffle source code:

```
for (; ;)
(
uch = gtchr( );
if (!(n & 31))
(
for (i = 0; i<64; i++)
l[ ctr[i] ] = k[i] + h[n - 64 + i]   Hash512 (wm, wl, level, 8);
)
```

As source code goes, Snuffle is quite compact; the entirety of the Snuffle source code occupies fewer than four printed pages.

12. Source code's power to convey algorithmic information is illustrated by the declaration of MIT Professor Harold Abelson:

> The square root of a number X is the number Y such that Y times Y equals X. This is declarative knowledge. It tells us something about square roots. But it doesn't tell us how to find a square root.
>
> In contrast, consider the following ancient algorithm, attributed to Heron of Alexandria, for approximating square roots:
> To approximate the square root of a positive number X,
>
> — Make a guess for the square root of X.
> — Compute an improved guess as the average of the guess and X divided by the guess.
> — Keep improving the guess until it is good enough.
>
> Heron's method doesn't say anything about what square roots are, but it does say how to approximate them. This is a piece of imperative "how to" knowledge.
>
> Computer science is in the business of formalizing imperative knowledge—developing formal notations and ways to reason and talk about methodology. Here is Heron's method formalized as a procedure in the notation of the Lisp computer language:

noted earlier, the chief task for cryptographers is the development of secure methods of encryption. While the articulation of such a system in layman's English or in general mathematical terms may be useful, the devil is, at least for cryptographers, often in the algorithmic details. By utilizing source code, a cryptographer can express algorithmic ideas with precision and methodological rigor that is otherwise difficult to achieve. This has the added benefit of facilitating peer review—by compiling the source code, a cryptographer can create a working model subject to rigorous security tests. The need for precisely articulated hypotheses and formal empirical testing, of course, is not unique to the science of cryptography; it appears, however, that in this field, source code is the preferred means to these ends.

Thus, cryptographers use source code to express their scientific ideas in much the same way that mathematicians use equations or economists use graphs. Of course, both mathematical equations and graphs are used in other fields for many purposes, not all of which are expressive. But mathematicians and economists have adopted these modes of expression in order to facilitate the precise and rigorous expression of complex scientific ideas. Similarly, the undisputed record here makes it clear that cryptographers utilize source code in the same fashion.[14]

In light of these considerations, we conclude that encryption software, in its source code form[15] and as employed by those in the field of cryptography, must be viewed as expressive for First Amendment purposes, and thus is entitled to the protections of the prior restraint doctrine. If the government required that mathematicians obtain a prepublication license prior to publishing material that included mathematical equations, we have no

---

```
(define (sqrtx)    (define (good-enough? guess)
(<(abs (-(square guess) x)) tolerance))
(define (improve guess)
(average guess (/ x guess)))
(define (try guess)
(if (good-enough? guess)
guess
(try (improve guess))))
(try 1))
```

14. Bernstein's Snuffle, in fact, provides an illustration of this point. By developing Snuffle, Bernstein was attempting to demonstrate that a one-way hash function could be employed as the heart of an encryption method. The Snuffle source code, as submitted by Bernstein to the State Department, was meant as an expression of how this might be accomplished. The Source Code was plainly not intended as a completed encryption product, as demonstrated by the fact that it was incomplete and not in a form suitable for final compiling. The Source Code, in fact, omits the hash function entirely—until combined with such a function and compiled, Snuffle is incapable of performing encryption functions at all.

Snuffle was also intended, in part, as political expression. Bernstein discovered that the ITAR regulations controlled encryption exports, but not one-way hash functions. Because he believed that an encryption system could easily be fashioned from any of a number of publicly-available one-way hash functions, he viewed the distinction made by the ITAR regulations as absurd. To illustrate his point, Bernstein developed Snuffle, which is an encryption system built around a one-way hash function.

15. We express no opinion regarding whether object code manifests a "close enough nexus to expression" to warrant application of the prior restraint doctrine. Bernstein's Snuffle did not involve object code, nor does the record contain any information regarding expressive uses of object code in the field of cryptography.

doubt that such a regime would be subject to scrutiny as a prior restraint. The availability of alternate means of expression, moreover, does not diminish the censorial power of such a restraint—that Adam Smith wrote Wealth of Nations without resorting to equations or graphs surely would not justify governmental prepublication review of economics literature that contain these modes of expression.

The government, in fact, does not seriously dispute that source code is used by cryptographers for expressive purposes. Rather, the government maintains that source code is different from other forms of expression (such as blueprints, recipes, and "how-to" manuals) because it can be used to control directly the operation of a computer without conveying information to the user. In the government's view, by targeting this unique functional aspect of source code, rather than the content of the ideas that may be expressed therein, the export regulations manage to skirt entirely the concerns of the First Amendment. This argument is flawed for at least two reasons.

First, it is not at all obvious that the government's view reflects a proper understanding of source code. As noted earlier, the distinguishing feature of source code is that it is meant to be read and understood by humans, and that it cannot be used to control directly the functioning of a computer. While source code, when properly prepared, can be easily compiled into object code by a user, ignoring the distinction between source and object code obscures the important fact that source code is not meant solely for the computer, but is rather written in a language intended also for human analysis and understanding.

Second, and more importantly, the government's argument, distilled to its essence, suggests that even one drop of "direct functionality" overwhelms any constitutional protections that expression might otherwise enjoy. This cannot be so. The distinction urged on us by the government would prove too much in this era of rapidly evolving computer capabilities. The fact that computers will soon be able to respond directly to spoken commands, for example, should not confer on the government the unfettered power to impose prior restraints on speech in an effort to control its "functional" aspects. The First Amendment is concerned with expression, and we reject the notion that the admixture of functionality necessarily puts expression beyond the protections of the Constitution.

The government also contends that the challenged regulations are immune from prior restraint analysis because they are "laws of general application" rather than being "directed narrowly and specifically at expression." *Lakewood*, 486 U.S. at 760-61. We cannot agree. Because we conclude that source code is utilized by those in the cryptography field as a means of expression, and because the regulations apply to encryption source code, it necessarily follows that the regulations burden a particular form of expression directly.

The Supreme Court in *Lakewood* explored what it means to be a "law of general application" for prior restraint purposes. In that case, the Court cited a law requiring building permits as a "law of general application" that would not be subject to a facial attack as a prior restraint, reasoning that such a law carried "little danger of censorship," even if it could be used to retaliate against a disfavored newspaper seeking to build a printing plant. *Id.* at 761. In the Court's view, "such laws provide too blunt a censorship instrument to warrant judicial intervention prior to an allegation of actual misuse." *Id.* Unlike a building permit ordinance, which would afford government officials only intermittent and unpredictable opportunities to exercise unrestrained discretion over expression, the challenged EAR regulations explicitly apply to expression and place scientific expression under the censor's eye on a regular basis. In fact, there is ample evidence in the record establishing that some in the cryptography field have already begun censoring themselves, for fear that their statements might influence the disposition of future licensing applications. See, e.g., National Research Council, Cryptography's Role in Securing the Information Society 158 (1996) ("Vendors contended that since they are effectively at the mercy of the export control regulators, they have considerable incentive to suppress any public expression of dissatisfaction with the current process."). In these circumstances, we cannot conclude that the export control regime at issue is a "law of general application" immune from prior restraint analysis.[17]

Because the prepublication licensing scheme challenged here vests unbridled discretion in government officials, and because it directly jeopardizes scientific expression, we are satisfied that Bernstein may properly bring a facial challenge against the regulations.[18] We accordingly turn to the merits.

---

17. The government also argues that the EAR regulations are "laws of general application" because they are not purposefully aimed at suppressing any particular ideas that may be expressed in source code. With respect to this contention, the panel (including the dissenter) agree that the purpose of the regulations is irrelevant to prior restraint analysis. It is clear that a prior restraint analysis applies equally to content-neutral or content-based enactments. See FW/PBS, Inc. v. Dallas, 493 U.S. 215, 223, 110 S.Ct. 596, 107 L.Ed.2d 603 (1990) (plurality opinion of O'Connor, J.) ("Because we conclude that the city's licensing scheme lacks adequate procedural safeguards, we do not reach . . . whether the ordinance is properly viewed as a content-neutral time, place, and manner restriction. . . ."); *Lakewood*, 486 U.S. at 764 ("[E]ven if the government may constitutionally impose content-neutral prohibitions on a particular manner of speech, it may not condition that speech on obtaining a license or permit from a government official in that official's boundless discretion."). Indeed, where unbridled discretion is vested in a governmental official, it is difficult to know whether a licensing regime is content-based or content-neutral. Accordingly, the government's purpose in censoring encryption source code is, at this stage of our First Amendment inquiry, beside the point. In other words, a prepublication licensing regime that has a chilling and censorial effect on expression is properly subject to facial attack as a prior restraint, whatever the purpose behind its enactment. See *Lakewood*, 486 U.S. at 759 (upholding facial attack against newsrack ordinance because of censorial effects, without discussing governmental purpose for enacting the ordinance).

18. It is at this juncture that we part ways with the dissent. The dissent concedes that source code can be expressive. Nevertheless, the dissent contends that Bernstein is not entitled to bring a facial attack against the EAR regulation. This argument, it seems to us, is based on two foundations. First, the dissent conceives of the exchange of source code among scientists as "conduct." We disagree. The source code at issue here is text intended for human understanding, albeit in a specialized language. To say that the "export" of this text is

B.   Are the Regulations an Impermissible Prior Restraint?

"[T]he protection even as to previous restraint is not absolutely unlimited." *Near*, 283 U.S. at 716. The Supreme Court has suggested that the "heavy presumption" against prior restraints may be overcome where official discretion is bounded by stringent procedural safeguards. See FW/PBS, 493 U.S. at 227 (plurality opinion of O'Connor, J.); Freedman v. Maryland, 380 U.S. 51, 58-59, 85 S.Ct. 734, 13 L.Ed.2d 649 (1965); *Kingsley Books*, 354 U.S. at 442-43; 11126 Baltimore Blvd. v. Prince George's County, 58 F.3d 988, 995 (4th Cir.1995) (en banc). As our analysis above suggests, the challenged regulations do not qualify for this First Amendment safe harbor.[19] In Freedman v. Maryland, the Supreme Court set out three factors for determining the validity of licensing schemes that impose a prior restraint on speech: (1) any restraint must be for a specified brief period of time; (2) there must be expeditious judicial review; and (3) the censor must bear the burden of going to court to suppress the speech in question and must bear the burden of proof. See 380 U.S. at 58-60. The district court found that the procedural protections provided by the

---

"conduct" for First Amendment purposes, rather than straightforward scientific "expression," is to call into question all distribution and circulation of scientific texts that communicate ideas by using specialized languages. Of course, source code may be functional as well as expressive. We are not persuaded, however, that that fact transmogrifies the distribution of scientific texts from "expression" into "conduct" deserving of diminished First Amendment protection.

Having cast the question as one relating to "conduct," the dissent then takes a second step. Drawing from *Lakeside*, the dissent asks whether the "conduct"—the exchange of cryptographic source code—is "commonly associated with expression." This question the dissent answers in the negative; in other words, the dissent concludes that source code is not used expressively often enough. We find this conclusion somewhat perplexing, as there is nothing in the record to support it. Bernstein has introduced extensive expert evidence to support his contention that source code is frequently used for expressive purposes. The government, however, has failed to introduce anything into the record to rebut this evidence. In fact, the government has made it clear that it means to control the export of source code no matter how commonly associated it may be with expression: "Whatever ideas may be reflected in the software, or the intent of the exporter to convey ideas, the NSA recommends that encryption software be controlled for export solely on the basis of what it does. . . ."

19. The Supreme Court has also suggested that the presumption against prior restraints may be overcome where publication would directly and imminently imperil national security. See New York Times Co. v. United States, 403 U.S. 713, 730, 91 S.Ct. 2140, 29 L.Ed.2d 822 (1971) (Stewart, J., joined by White, J., concurring); *Near*, 283 U.S. at 716; see also United States v. The Progressive, Inc., 467 F.Supp. 990, 992 (W.D.Wis.1979). In order to justify a prior restraint on national security grounds, the government must prove the publication would "surely result in direct, immediate, and irreparable damage to our Nation or its people." *New York Times*, 403 U.S. at 730 (Stewart, J., joined by White, J., concurring); see also *id.* at 726-27 (Brennan, J., concurring) (finding that national security is a sufficient interest only where there is "governmental allegation and proof that publication must inevitably, directly, and immediately cause the occurrence of an event kindred to imperiling the safety of a transport already at sea"); Burch v. Barker, 861 F.2d 1149, 1155 (9th Cir.1988) ("Prior restraints are permissible in only the rarest of circumstances, such as imminent threat to national security.").

The government does not argue that the prior restraint at issue here falls within the extremely narrow class of cases where publication would directly and immediately imperil national security.

EAR regulations are "woefully inadequate" when measured against these requirements. *Bernstein III*, 974 F.Supp. at 1308. We agree.

Although the regulations require that license applications be resolved or referred to the President within 90 days, see 15 C.F.R. §750.4(a), there is no time limit once an application is referred to the President. Thus, the 90-day limit can be rendered meaningless by referral. Moreover, if the license application is denied, no firm time limit governs the internal appeals process. See 15 C.F.R. §756.2(c)(1) (Under Secretary "shall decide an appeal within a reasonable time after receipt of the appeal."). Accordingly, the EAR regulations do not satisfy the first *Freedman* requirement that a licensing decision be made within a reasonably short, specified period of time. See *FW/PBS*, 493 U.S. at 226 (finding that "a prior restraint that fails to place time limits on the time within which the decisionmaker must issue the license is impermissible"); Riley v. National Fed. of the Blind, 487 U.S. 781, 802, 108 S.Ct. 2667, 101 L.Ed.2d 669 (1988) (licensing scheme that permits "delay without limit" is impermissible); Vance v. Universal Amusement Co., 445 U.S. 308, 315-17, 100 S.Ct. 1156, 63 L.Ed.2d 413 (1980) (prior restraint of indefinite duration is impermissible). The EAR regulatory regime further offends *Freedman*'s procedural requirements insofar as it denies a disappointed applicant the opportunity for judicial review.[21] See 15 C.F.R. §756.2(c)(2); *FW/PBS*, 493 U.S. at 229 (plurality opinion of O'Connor, J.) (finding failure to provide "prompt" judicial review violates *Freedman*); *Freedman*, 380 U.S. at 59 (licensing procedure must assure a prompt final judicial decision).

We conclude that the challenged regulations allow the government to restrain speech indefinitely with no clear criteria for review. As a result, Bernstein and other scientists have been effectively chilled from engaging in valuable scientific expression. Bernstein's experience itself demonstrates the enormous uncertainty that exists over the scope of the regulations and the potential for the chilling of scientific expression. In short, because the challenged regulations grant boundless discretion to government officials, and because they lack the required procedural protections set forth in *Freedman*, we find that they operate as an unconstitutional prior restraint on speech.[22] See *Lakewood*, 486 U.S. at 769-72 (holding that newsrack licensing ordinance was an impermissible prior restraint because it conferred unbounded discretion and lacked adequate procedural safeguards).

---

21. As noted earlier, the BXA enjoys essentially unbounded discretion under the EAR regulations in administering the license process. Accordingly, even if the challenged regulations provided for judicial review, the lack of explicit limits on the decisionmaker's discretion would likely make such review meaningless. In this sense, the presence of unbounded discretion itself may be considered fatal for purposes of prior restraint review. See *Lakewood*, 486 U.S. at 769-70 (striking down a licensing scheme where the mayor could merely claim that the license " 'is not in the public interest' when denying a permit application").

22. Our conclusion relating to the Source Code also resolves the status of the regulations as applied to the Instructions. Because the Instructions are essentially a translation of the Source Code into English, they are, if anything, nearer the heartland of the First Amendment. Consequently, to the extent the challenged regulations are unconstitutional as applied to the Source Code, they necessarily are unconstitutional as applied to the Instructions.

C. *Concluding Comments*

We emphasize the narrowness of our First Amendment holding. We do not hold that all software is expressive. Much of it surely is not. Nor need we resolve whether the challenged regulations constitute content-based restrictions, subject to the strictest constitutional scrutiny, or whether they are, instead, content-neutral restrictions meriting less exacting scrutiny. We hold merely that because the prepublication licensing regime challenged here applies directly to scientific expression, vests boundless discretion in government officials, and lacks adequate procedural safeguards, it constitutes an impermissible prior restraint on speech.

We will, however, comment on two issues that are entwined with the underlying merits of Bernstein's constitutional claims. First, we note that insofar as the EAR regulations on encryption software were intended to slow the spread of secure encryption methods to foreign nations, the government is intentionally retarding the progress of the flourishing science of cryptography. To the extent the government's efforts are aimed at interdicting the flow of scientific ideas (whether expressed in source code or otherwise), as distinguished from encryption products, these efforts would appear to strike deep into the heartland of the First Amendment. In this regard, the EAR regulations are very different from content-neutral time, place and manner restrictions that may have an incidental effect on expression while aiming at secondary effects.

Second, we note that the government's efforts to regulate and control the spread of knowledge relating to encryption may implicate more than the First Amendment rights of cryptographers. In this increasingly electronic age, we are all required in our everyday lives to rely on modern technology to communicate with one another. This reliance on electronic communication, however, has brought with it a dramatic diminution in our ability to communicate privately. Cellular phones are subject to monitoring, email is easily intercepted, and transactions over the internet are often less than secure. Something as commonplace as furnishing our credit card number, social security number, or bank account number puts each of us at risk. Moreover, when we employ electronic methods of communication, we often leave electronic "fingerprints" behind, fingerprints that can be traced back to us. Whether we are surveilled by our government, by criminals, or by our neighbors, it is fair to say that never has our ability to shield our affairs from prying eyes been at such a low ebb. The availability and use of secure encryption may offer an opportunity to reclaim some portion of the privacy we have lost. Government efforts to control encryption thus may well implicate not only the First Amendment rights of cryptographers intent on pushing the boundaries of their science, but also the constitutional rights of each of us as potential recipients of encryption's bounty. Viewed from this perspective, the government's efforts to retard progress in cryptography may implicate the Fourth Amendment, as well as the right to speak anonymously, see McIntyre v. Ohio Elections Comm'n, 514 U.S.

334, 115 S.Ct. 1511, 1524, 131 L.Ed.2d 426 (1995), the right against compelled speech, see Wooley v. Maynard, 430 U.S. 705, 714, 97 S.Ct. 1428, 51 L.Ed.2d 752 (1977), and the right to informational privacy, see Whalen v. Roe, 429 U.S. 589, 599-600, 97 S.Ct. 869, 51 L.Ed.2d 64 (1977). While we leave for another day the resolution of these difficult issues, it is important to point out that Bernstein's is a suit not merely concerning a small group of scientists laboring in an esoteric field, but also touches on the public interest broadly defined. . . .

Conclusion

Because the prepublication licensing regime challenged by Bernstein applies directly to scientific expression, vests boundless discretion in government officials, and lacks adequate procedural safeguards, we hold that it constitutes an impermissible prior restraint on speech. We decline the invitation to line edit the regulations in an attempt to rescue them from constitutional infirmity, and thus endorse the declaratory relief granted by the district court.

T.G. NELSON, Circuit Judge, Dissenting:

. . . The basic error which sets the majority and the district court adrift is the failure to fully recognize that the basic function of encryption source code is to act as a method of controlling computers. As defined in the EAR regulations, encryption source code is "[a] precise set of operating instructions to a computer, that when compiled, allows for the execution of an encryption function on a computer." 15 C.F.R. pt. 722. Software engineers generally do not create software in object code—the series of binary digits (1's and 0's)—which tells a computer what to do because it would be enormously difficult, cumbersome and time-consuming. Instead, software engineers use high-level computer programming languages such as "C" or "Basic" to create source code as a shorthand method for telling the computer to perform a desired function. In this respect, lines of source code are the building blocks or the tools used to create an encryption machine. See e.g., Patrick Ian Ross, Bernstein v. United States Department of State, 13 Berkeley Tech. L.J. 405, 410-11 (1998) ("[E]lectronic source code that is ready to compile merely needs a few keystrokes to generate object code—the equivalent of flipping an 'on' switch. Code used for this purpose can fairly easily be characterized as 'essentially functional.'"); Pamela Samuelson et al., A Manifesto Concerning Legal Protection of Computer Programs, 94 Colum. L. Rev. 2308, 2315-30 (1994) ("[P]rograms are, in fact, machines (entities that bring about useful results, i.e., behavior) that have been constructed in the medium of text (source code and object code)."). Encryption source code, once compiled, works to make computer communication and transactions secret; it creates a lockbox of sorts around a message that can only be unlocked by someone with a key. It is the function or task that encryption source code performs which creates its value in most cases. This functional aspect of encryption source code contains no expression; it is merely the tool used to build the encryption machine.

This is not to say that this very same source code is not used expressively in some cases. Academics, such as Bernstein, seek to convey and discuss their ideas concerning computer encryption. As noted by the majority, Bernstein must actually use his source code textually in order to discuss or teach cryptology. In such circumstances, source code serves to express Bernstein's scientific methods and ideas.

While it is conceptually difficult to categorize encryption source code under our First Amendment framework, I am still inevitably led to conclude that encryption source code is more like conduct than speech. Encryption source code is a building tool. Academics and computer programmers can convey this source code to each other in order to reveal the encryption machine they have built. But, the ultimate purpose of encryption code is, as its name suggests, to perform the function of encrypting messages. Thus, while encryption source code may occasionally be used in an expressive manner, it is inherently a functional device.

We are not the first to examine the nature of encryption source code in terms of First Amendment protection. Judge Gwin of the United States District Court for the Northern District of Ohio also explored the function versus expression conundrum of encryption source code at some length in *Junger v. Daley*, 8 F.Supp.2d 708 (N.D.Ohio 1998). *Junger*, like Bernstein, is a professor, albeit a law professor, who wished to publish in various forms his work on computers, including a textbook, Computers and the Law. The book was determined by the Government to be subject to export without a license, but his software programs were determined to come within the licensing provisions of the EAR. In the course of rejecting *Junger's* claims, the court said:

> Like much computer software, encryption source code is inherently functional; it is designed to enable a computer to do a designated task. Encryption source code does not merely explain a cryptographic theory or describe how the software functions. More than describing encryption, the software carries out the function of encryption. The software is essential to carry out the function of encryption. In doing this function, the encryption software is indistinguishable from dedicated computer hardware that does encryption.
>
> In the overwhelming majority of circumstances, encryption source code is exported to transfer functions, not to communicate ideas. In exporting functioning capability, encryption source code is like other encryption devices. For the broad majority of persons receiving such source code, the value comes from the function the source code does.

Id. at 716. The *Junger* decision thus adds considerable support for the propositions that encryption source code cannot be categorized as pure speech and that the functional aspects of encryption source code cannot be easily ignored or put aside.

Both the district court and the majority hold that because source code can be used expressively in some circumstances, Bernstein was entitled to bring a facial challenge to the EAR. Such an approach ignores the basic tenet that facial challenges are inappropriate "unless, at a minimum, the challenged statute 'is directed narrowly and specifically at expression or conduct commonly associated with expression.'" Roulette v. City of Seattle, 97 F.3d 300, 305 (9th Cir.1996) (quoting City of Lakewood v. Plain Dealer Publishing Co., 486 U.S. 750, 760, 108 S.Ct. 2138, 100 L.Ed.2d 771 (1988)). That encryption source code may on occasion be used expressively does not mean that its export is "conduct commonly associated with expression" or that the EAR regulations are directed at expressive conduct. See *id.* at 303 ("The fact that sitting can possibly be expressive, however, isn't enough to sustain plaintiffs' facial challenge."); see also *Junger,* 8 F.Supp.2d at 718 ("[T]he prior restraint doctrine is not implicated simply because an activity may on occasion be expressive.").

The activity or conduct at issue here is the export of encryption source code. As I noted above, the basic nature of encryption source code lies in its functional capacity as a method to build an encryption device. Export of encryption source code is not conduct commonly associated with expression. Rather, it is conduct that is normally associated with providing other persons with the means to make their computer messages secret. The overwhelming majority of people do not want to talk about the source code and are not interested in any recondite message that may be contained in encryption source code. Only a few people can actually understand what a line of source code would direct a computer to do. Most people simply want to use the encryption source code to protect their computer communications. Export of encryption source code simply does not fall within the bounds of conduct commonly associated with expression such as picketing or handbilling. See *Roulette,* 97 F.3d at 303-04.

Further, the EAR regulates the export of encryption technology generally, whether it is software or hardware. See 15 C.F.R. §742.15; *Junger,* 8 F.Supp.2d at 718 ("The Export Regulations do not single out encryption software."). These regulations are directed at preventing the functional capacity of any encryption device, including its source code, from being exported without a government license. The EAR is not specifically directed towards stifling the expressive nature of source code or Bernstein's academic discussions about cryptography. This is demonstrated by the fact that the regulations do not object to publication in printed form of learned articles containing source code. See 15 C.F.R. §734.3. Thus, the EAR is generally directed at nonexpressive conduct—the export of source code as a tool to make messages secret and impervious to government eavesdropping capabilities.

Because this is a law of general application focused at conduct, Bernstein is not entitled to bring a facial challenge. The district court's injunction based upon the finding of a facial prior restraint is thus impermissible. This is not to say that Bernstein's activities would not be entitled to First Amendment protection, but that the legal path chosen to get that protection must be the correct one. We should be careful to "entertain [ ] facial freedom-of-expression challenges only against statutes that, 'by their terms,' sought to regulate 'spoken words,' or patently 'expressive or communicative conduct.'" *Roulette*, 97 F.3d at 303 (citing Broadrick v. Oklahoma, 413 U.S. 601, 612-13, 93 S.Ct. 2908, 37 L.Ed.2d 830 (1973)). Bernstein may very well have a claim under an as-applied First Amendment analysis; however, such a claim must be left to the district court's determination in the first instance. Here, the district court did not rule on Bernstein's as-applied claims. I would therefore vacate the district court's injunction and remand for consideration of Bernstein's as-applied challenges to the EAR. Accordingly, I respectfully dissent.

COMMENTS AND QUESTIONS

1. The Ninth Circuit does not emphasize the point, but violations of the export control laws can be prosecuted as crimes. See 22 U.S.C. §2778. Should this affect the court's decision about the First Amendment issues in the case? Another cryptographer, Phil Zimmerman, spent years of his life under threats of criminal prosecution because the pretty good privacy (PGP) software he had written was available on Web sites outside the United States. Although these charges were eventually dropped by the government, Zimmermann continues to risk prosecution through his highly publicized (and unapologetic) distribution of PGP to political dissidents around the globe. See Douglas Hayward, So Arrest Me, Zimmermann Tells Feds, TechWeb News (May 19, 1997) http://www.techweb.com/se/directlink.cgi?WIR1997051915.

2. As the *Bernstein* opinions make clear, other courts have taken less favorable views toward First Amendment challenges to the application of export control laws to encryption software. Is there a sufficient difference between the facts and legal analyses in *Junger* or *Karns* to distinguish them from *Bernstein*? How would you predict the Supreme Court would decide the *Bernstein* case?

3. An interesting observation about export control laws is made in Lawrence Lessig, The Limits in Open Code: Regulatory Standards and the Future of the Net, 14 Berkeley Tech. L.J. 759 (1999). The U.S. government can easily regulate software companies that might wish to distribute products containing strong encryption features because they will be vulnerable to challenge if they export software exceeding current guidelines, or if they post code containing strong encryption on the company Web site. However, if a company posts open-source software on its site, persons outside the United States may be able to add strong encryption features to

the posted code and the U.S. government may be unable to do anything about this.

4. The Clinton Administration has made repeated attempts to employ its commercial clout as a purchaser of computer systems to persuade the marketplace to accept computer chips that complied with certain escrow protocols that would enable the government, presumably upon a proper showing of necessity, to obtain access to encrypted information or communications. Because companies generally do not make one version of their products for the commercial marketplace and another to sell to the government, the Administration hoped that key escrow system technology would become a de facto norm, making it unnecessary for the government to seek legislation from the Congress that would mandate key escrow technologies. Widely known as the "Clipper chip" initiative, this effort met with considerable resistance from the commercial marketplace and from the cryptographic research community. For a narrative on this initiative and an expression of public policy concerns about it, see A. Michael Froomkin, It Came From Planet Clipper: The Battle Over Cryptographic Key "Escrow," 1996 U. Chi. Legal Forum 15 (1996).

5. Froomkin has also analyzed at length the constitutionality of a possible U.S. government mandate that key escrow systems be embedded in all computer systems. See A. Michael Froomkin, The Metaphor Is the Key: Cryptography, The Clipper Chip, and the Constitution, 143 U. Penn. L. Rev. 709 (1995). As the title to his article suggests, the answer to the constitutional question is likely to depend on what metaphor the courts employ to judge the issue.

6. Countries differ in their policies regarding encryption software; yet it is clear that the global nature of the Internet today makes greater commonality in national encryption policies desirable. The Organization for Economic Cooperation and Development has developed guidelines for national policies. See OECD Cryptography Guidelines, http://www.oecd.org/dsti/sti/it/secur/prod/gd97-204.pdf.

7. The National Research Council has published a report entitled Cryptography's Role in Securing the Information Society (Kenneth Dam & Herb Lin eds., 1996), which discusses the multidimensional importance of encryption in achieving a variety of societal objectives. For detailed consideration of the importance of encryption in fostering electronic commerce, see Stewart A. Baker & Paul Hurst, The Limits of Trust (1998); A. Michael Froomkin, Flood Control on the Information Ocean: Living with Anonymity, Digital Cash, and Distributed Databases, 15 J.L. & Comm. 395 (1996); A. Michael Froomkin, The Essential Role of Trusted Third Parties in Electronic Commerce, 75 Or. L. Rev. 49 (1996).

Electronic Commerce

A. BACKGROUND ON ELECTRONIC COMMERCE

Electronic commerce is big business. A few years ago, ecommerce was an interesting concept, but there was not much substance to it. By 1999, it had become the hottest thing around. Not only were consumers buying an enormous volume of goods over the Internet, but business-to-business ecommerce had taken off as well.

The "law of electronic commerce" is a vague and poorly defined thing. In some senses, it is no different from the law of commerce generally. Contract disputes, tax issues, and payment systems each have their own legal infrastructure, and in large part applying law to ecommerce is simply a matter of applying those rules to a new environment. At this writing, there are very few reported ecommerce cases, but that doesn't mean there is no law.

Ecommerce is not all old wine in new bottles, however. Some truly interesting new developments have begun to challenge the law in a variety of ways. In this section, we introduce the reader to a number of these challenges. Because of the embryonic state of development of the law of ecommerce, this section offers more speculation—and less law—than any other part of the book.

We begin with some ideas about how ecommerce might differ from traditional business models.

J. Bradford De Long & A. Michael Froomkin, The Next Economy?

Deborah Hurley et al., eds., Internet Publishing and Beyond: The Economics of Digital Information and Intellectual Property (Cambridge, MIT Press, 1999)

. . . "Technological" Prerequisites of the Market

Modern technologies are beginning to undermine the features that make the Invisible Hand of the market system an effective and efficient system for organizing production and distribution. The case for the market system has always rested on three pillars: call the first excludability, the ability of sellers to force consumers to become buyers and thus to pay for what they use; call the second rivalry, a structure of costs in which two cannot partake as cheaply as one, and in which producing enough for two million people uses up at least twice as many resources as producing enough for one million people; call the third transparency, that individuals can see clearly what they need and what is for sale so that they truly know what they wish to buy.

All three of these pillars fit the economy of Adam Smith's day pretty well. They fit much of today's economy pretty well too—although the fit for the telecommunications and information processing industries is less satisfactory. They will fit tomorrow's economy less well than today's. And there is every indication that they will fit the twenty-first century economy relatively poorly. As we look at developments along the leading technological edge of the economy, we can see what used to be second-order "externality" corrections to the Invisible Hand becoming first-order phenomena. And we can see the Invisible Hand of the competitive market working less and less well in an increasing number of areas. This result is particularly surprising when one considers that most economic theory suggests that things which make information cheaper and more accessible should generally reduce friction in competitive markets, not gum up the works.

Excludability

In information-based sectors of the next economy the owner of a commodity will no longer be able to easily and cheaply exclude others from using or enjoying the commodity. Digital data is cheap and easy to copy. Methods exist to make copying more difficult, but they add expense and complexity. Without excludability the relationship between producer and consumer is much more a gift-exchange than a purchase-and-sale relationship. The appropriate paradigm is then an NPR fund-raising drive. There is no reason to presume that non-excludable commodities will get into the hands of the consumers who value them the most. And—with compensation to the producer determined not by the purchase-and-sale exchange of money for value but by the user's feelings of moral obligation to the producer—there is no reason to expect that production will be as high as it should be to maximize social welfare.

If goods are not excludable then rather than sell things, people simply help themselves. If the taker feels like it, he or she may make a "pledge" to support the producer. Perhaps the average pledge will be large enough that producers cover their costs. Many people seem to feel a moral obligation to tip cabdrivers and waiters and to contribute to National Public Radio. But without excludability it is hard to believe that the (voluntary) payments as a matter of grace from consumers to producers will be large enough to encourage the optimal level of production. Indeed, most of what we call "rule of law" consists of a legal system that enforces excludability—such enforcement of excludability ("protection of my property rights," even when the commodity is simply sitting there unused and idle) is one of the few tasks that the theory of laissez-faire allows the government.

Excludability does not exist in a Hobbesian state of nature: the laws of physics do not prohibit people from sneaking in and taking your things. So the police and the judges exist to enforce it, through penalties for breach of contract and damage awards for theft of intellectual property. The importance of this "artificial" creation of excludability is rarely remarked on: fish are supposed to rarely remark upon the water in which they swim.

We can see how an absence of excludability can warp a market and an industry by taking a brief look at the history of network television. During its three-channel heyday in the 1960s and 1970s, North American network television was available to anyone with an antenna and a receiver because broadcasters lacked the means of preventing the public from getting the signals for free. Free access was, however, accompanied by scarce bandwidth, and by government allocation of the scarce bandwidth to producers.

The absence of excludability for broadcast television did not destroy the television broadcasting industry. Broadcasters couldn't charge for what they were truly producing, but broadcasters worked out that they could charge for something else: the attention of the program-watching consumers during commercials. Rather than paying money directly, the customers of the broadcast industry merely had to endure the commercials (or get up and leave the room; or channel-surf) if they wanted to see the show.

This solution prevented the market for broadcast programs from collapsing: it allowed broadcasters to charge someone for something. But it left its imprint on the industry. Charging-for-advertising does not lead to the same invisible hand guarantee of productive optimum as does charging for product. In the case of network television, audience attention to advertisements was more-or-less unconnected with audience involvement in the program.

This created a bias toward lowest-common-denominator programming. Consider two programs, one of which will fascinate 500,000 people, and the other of which 30 million people will watch as slightly preferable to watching their ceiling. The first might well be better for social welfare: the 500,000 with a high willingness-to-pay might well, if there was a way to charge them, collectively outbid the 30 million apathetic potential watchers. Thus a network able to collect revenues from interested viewers would broadcast the first program, seeking the applause (and the money) of the dedicated and forgoing the eye-glazed semi-attention of the mass.

But the process breaks down when the network obtains revenue by selling commercials to advertisers. The network can offer advertisers either 500,000 or 30 million viewers. How influenced the viewers will be by the commercials depends relatively little on how much they like the program. As a result, charging-for-advertising gives every incentive to broadcast what a mass audience would tolerate. It gives no incentive to broadcast what a niche audience would love.

As bandwidth becomes cheaper, these problems become less important: one particular niche program may well be worth broadcasting when the mass audience has become sufficiently fragmented by the viewability of multiple clones of bland programming. Until then, however, expensive bandwidth combined with the absence of excludability meant that broadcasting revenues depended on the viewer numbers rather than the intensity of demand. Non-excludability helped ensure that broadcast programming would be "a vast wasteland."

In the absence of excludability, there is no reason to presume that industries today and tomorrow will be able to avoid analogous distortions: the absence of excludability leaves potential users with no effective way to make the market system notice how strong their demand is and exactly what their demand is for.

Rivalry

In the information-based sectors of the next economy the use or enjoyment of the information-based commodity will no longer necessarily involve rivalry. With most tangible goods, if Alice is using a particular good, Bob cannot be. Charging the ultimate consumer the good's cost of production or the free market price provides the producer with an ample reward for his or her effort. It also leads to the appropriate level of production: social surplus (measured in money) is not maximized by providing the good to anyone whose final demand for a commodity is too weak to wish to pay the cost for it that a competitive market would require.

But if goods are non-rival—if two can consume as cheaply as one—then charging a per-unit price to users artificially restricts distribution: to truly maximize social welfare you need a system that supplies everyone whose willingness to pay for the good is greater than the marginal cost of producing another copy. And if the marginal cost of reproduction of a digital good is near-zero, that means almost everyone should have it for almost free.

However, charging price equal to marginal cost almost surely leaves the producer bankrupt, with little incentive to maintain the product except the hope of maintenance fees, and no incentive whatsoever to make another one except that warm fuzzy feeling one gets from impoverishing oneself for the general good. . . .

A good economic market is characterized by competition to limit the exercise of private economic power, by price equal to marginal cost, by the return to investors and workers corresponding to the social value added of the industry, and by appropriate incentives for innovation and new product development. These seem impossible to achieve all at once in markets for non-rival goods—and digital goods are certainly non-rival.

Transparency

In the information-based sectors of the next economy—indeed, in many sectors of the economy today—the purchase of a good will no longer be transparent. The Invisible Hand assumed that purchasers know what it is that they want and what they are buying. If purchasers need first to figure out what they want and what they are buying, there is no good reason to presume that their willingness to pay corresponds to its true value to them.

Adam Smith's pinmakers sold a good that was small, fungible, low-maintenance and easily understood. Alice could buy her pins from Gerald today, and from Henry tomorrow. But today's purchaser of, say, a suite of software programs is faced with needs and constraints that a metric designed to explain the market for pins may leave us poorly prepared to understand. The market for software "goods" is almost never a market for today's tangible goods, but rather for a bundle of present goods, future goods, and future services. The initial purchase is not a complete transaction in itself, but rather a down payment on the establishment of a relationship.

Once the relationship is established, both buyer and seller find themselves in different positions. Adam Smith's images are less persuasive in the context of services—especially bespoke services which require deep knowledge of the customer's wants and situation (and of the maker's capabilities) —which are not, by their nature fungible or easily comparable.

When Alice shops for a software suite, she not only wants to know about its current functionality—something notoriously difficult to figure out until one has had days or weeks of hands-on experience—but she also needs to have some idea of the likely support that the manufacturer will provide. Is the line busy at all hours? Is it a toll call? Do the operators have a clue? Will next year's corporate downsizing lead to longer holds on support calls?

Worse, what Alice really needs to know cannot be measured at all before she is committed: learning how to use a software package is an investment she would prefer not to repeat. Since operating systems change frequently, and interoperability needs changes even more often, Alice needs to have a prediction about the likely upgrade path for her suite. This, however, turns on unknowable and barely guessable factors: the health of the corporation, the creativity of the software team, the corporate relationships between the suite seller and other companies.

Some of the things Alice wants to know, such as whether the suite works on quickly enough on her computer, are potentially measurable at least—although one rarely finds a consumer capable of measuring them before purchase, or a marketing system designed to accommodate such a need. You buy the shrink-wrapped box at a store, take it home, unwrap the box—and find that the program is incompatible with your hardware, your operating system, or one of the six programs you bought to cure defects in the hardware or the operating system. . . .

The economics of information is frequently invoked to adjust the traditional neoclassical paradigm to model for the consumer's decision as to whether it pays to attempt to acquire these facts: for example, one can hypothesize that Alice's failure to acquire the necessary information is evidence of the high cost of the investigation compared to the expected value of what it might reveal. So adjusted the basic model retains descriptive power. But its explanatory power is limited. . . .

Out on the Cybernetic Frontier . . .

As a first step toward discerning what new theories of the new markets might look like if new visions do turn out to be necessary, or how old ones should be adjusted, it seems sensible to examine how enterprises and entrepreneurs are already reacting to the fact of widespread market failure. The hope is that experience along the frontiers of electronic commerce will serve as a good guide to what pieces of the theory are likely to be most important, and will suggest areas in which further development might have a high rate of return.

The Market for Software (Shareware, Public Betas and More)

We noted above that the market for modern, complex products is anything but transparent. While one can think of services, such as medicine, which are particularly opaque to the buyer, today it is difficult to imagine a more opaque product than software. Indeed, when one considers the increasing opacity of products in the context of the growing importance of services to the economy, it suggests that transparency is and will become a particularly important issue in the next economy.

Consumers' failure to acquire full information about the software they buy certainly demonstrates that acquiring the information must be expensive. In response to this cost, social institutions have begun to spring up to get around the shrink-wrap dilemma. The first was so-called shareware: you download the program, if you like the program you send its author some money, and maybe in return you get a manual, access to support, or an upgraded version. Shareware dealt with the information acquisition problem by turning the purchase-and-sale of software into a gift-exchange relationship, more akin to an NPR fund raising drive. ("Is this station worth just fifty cents a week to you? Then call . . .") The benefit to try-before-you-buy is precisely that it makes the process more transparent. The cost is that try-before-you-buy often turns out to be try-use-and-don't-pay.

The next stage beyond shareware has been the evolution of the institution of the "public beta." This public beta is a time-limited (or bug-ridden) version of the product: users can investigate the properties of the public beta version to figure out if the product is worthwhile. But to get the permanent (or the less bug-ridden) version, they have to pay.

Yet a third is the "dual track" version: Eudora shareware versus Eudora Professional. Perhaps the hope is that users of the free low-power version will some day become richer, or less patient, or find they have greater needs. At that point they will find it least disruptive to switch to a product that looks and feels familiar, that is compatible with their habits, and their existing files. In effect (and if the sellers are lucky), the free version captures them as future customers before they are even aware they are future buyers.

The developing free-public-beta industry is a way of dealing with the problem of lack of transparency. It is a relatively benign development, in the sense that it involves competition through distribution of lesser versions of the ultimate product. An alternative would be (say) the strategy of constructing barriers to compatibility: the famous examples in the computer industry come from the 1970s when the Digital Equipment Corporation made non-standard cable connectors; from the mid-1980s when IBM attempted to appropriate the entire PC industry through the PS/2 line; and from the late 1980s when Apple Computers used a partly ROM-based operating system to exclude clones. Perhaps the main reason that the free-public-beta strategy is now dominant is the catastrophic failure of both IBM's PS/2 and Apple's ROM-based strategies of exclusion based on non-compatibility—even though they were both near-successes.

ShopBots (BargainFinder)

Predictions abound as to how software will use case- and rule-based thinking to do your shopping for you, advise you on how to spend your leisure time, and in general organize your life for you. But that day is still far in the future. So far we have only the crude prototype of the knowledge-scavenging virtual robot, the automated comparison shopper.

Yet, the online marketplace so far has had an ambiguous reaction to the advent of the automated comparison shopper. BargainFinder is one of the first such—and highly experimental—Internet-based agents. Bargain-Finder does just one thing. Perhaps it does it too well.

The user enters the details of a music compact disk she might like to purchase. BargainFinder interrogates several online music stores that might offer to sell them. It then reports back the prices in a tidy table that makes comparison shopping easy. The system is not completely transparent: it is not always possible to discern the vendor's shipping charges without visiting the vendor's web site. But as BargainFinder's inventors say, "it is still only an experiment."

Most economists, be they Adam Smithian classicists, neo-classical Austrians, or more modern economics of information mavens, would agree with the proposition that a vendor in a competitive market selling a standardized product—for one Tiger Lily CD is as good as another—would want customers to know as much as possible about what the vendor offers for sale, and the prices at which the goods are available.

The reason for this near-consensus is that in a competitive market every sale at the offer price should be welcome: all are made at a markup over marginal cost. Thus all online CD retailers ought to have wanted to be listed by BargainFinder, if only because every sale that went elsewhere when they had the lowest price was lost profit.

Not so. A significant fraction of the merchants regularly visited by BargainFinder were less than ecstatic. They retaliated by blocking the agent's access to their otherwise publicly-available data. Currently (March 1997), one third of the merchants targeted by the BargainFinder (three out of nine) continue to lock out its queries. One, CDNow, did so for frankly competitive reasons. The other two said that the costs of large numbers of "hobbyist" queries were too great for them. Meanwhile, seven additional merchants have asked to be listed.

One possible explanation for the divergence between the economic theorist's prediction that every seller should want to be listed by Bargain-Finder and the apparent outcome is the price gouging story. In this story, stores blocking BargainFinder tend to charge higher than normal prices because they are able to take advantage of consumer ignorance of cheaper alternatives. The stores are gouging buyers by taking advantage of relatively high costs of search.

In this case BargainFinder and its successors are indeed valuable developments. They will make markets more efficient and lower prices. This is entirely possible, although one need not go quite as far as one writer who suggested that the entire world economy is made up of such great pricing inefficiencies that the change to an information economy will drastically reduce inflation.

Another possibility is the kindly service story. Stores blocking Bargain-Finder tend to charge higher than normal prices because they provide additional service or convenience. If commerce becomes increasingly electronic and impersonal (or if "personal" comes to mean "filtered through fiendishly clever software agents"), this sort of humanized attention will become increasingly expensive. To the extent that this additional service or convenience can be provided automatically, things are less clear.

In a sometimes forgotten classic, The Joyless Economy, Tibor Scitovsky noted that the advent of mass production of furniture seemed to cause the price of hand-carved chairs to increase, even as the demand for them shrank. As consumers switched to less costly (and less carefully made, one-size-fits-all) mass-produced furniture, carvers became scarce. Soon only the rich could engage their services. If the kindly service story is right, the rise of the commodity market in turn creates a risk that the economy will become yet more "joyless": mass tastes will be satisfied cheaply as specialty tastes become ever more a luxury.

On the other hand the rise of ShopBots such as BargainFinder offers an opportunity for consumers to aggregate their preferences on worldwide scale. As it becomes increasingly easy for consumers to communicate their individualized preferences to manufacturers and suppliers, and increasingly easy to tailor goods to individual tastes—be it a CD that only has the tracks you like, customized blue jeans, or a car manufactured just in time to your specifications—personalized goods may become the norm, putting the "joy" back into the economy. Some signs of this were visible even before the information revolution: lower costs of customization has already undermined one of Scitovsky's examples, as fresh-baked bread makes its comeback at many supermarkets and specialty stores.

In either the price gouging or kindly service stories, the advent of BargainFinder presents CD retailers with a dilemma: If they join in, they contribute towards turning the market for CDs into a commodity market with competition only on price. If they act "selflessly" and stay out, in order to try to degrade BargainFinder's utility (and preserve their higher average markup), they must hope that their competitors will understand their long-run self-interest in the same way. But overt communication in which all sellers agreed to block BargainFinder would, of course, violate the Sherman Act. And without a means of retaliation to "punish" players who do not pursue the collusive long-run strategy of blocking BargainFinder, the collapse of the market into a commodity market with only price competition appears likely.

Indeed, if the strategy was to undermine BargainFinder by staying away, it appears to be failing. CD retailers are unblocking BargainFinder and more are clamoring to join. Whether or not this is an occasion for joy depends on which explanation above is closer to the truth. The growth of the bookstore chain put the local bookshop out of business, just as the growth of supermarkets killed the corner grocer. Not everyone considers this trend to be a victory, despite the lower prices. A human element has been lost, and a "personal service" element that may have led to a better fit between purchaser and purchase has been lost as well.

So far, the discussion has operated on the basis of the assumption that CD merchants would have an incentive to block BargainFinder if they charge higher than normal prices. Strangely, some merchants may have had an incentive to block it if they charged lower than normal prices. As we all know, merchants sometimes advertise a "loss leader," and offer to sell a particular good at an unprofitable price. Merchants do this in order to lure consumers into the store where they either may be attracted to more profitable versions of the same good (leading, in the extreme case, to "bait and switch"), or in the hope that the consumer will spy other, more profitable goods to round out the market basket.

You can explain this merchant behavior in different ways, either by talking about the economics of information, locational utility, myopic consumers generalizing incorrectly on the basis of a small number of real bargains, or about temporary monopolies caused by the consumer's presence in this store as opposed to another store far away. It may be that merchants blocking BargainFinder did not want consumers to be able to exploit their loss leaders without having to be exposed to the other goods offered simultaneously. Without this exposure the loss leaders would not lure buyers to other, higher-profit items, but would simply be losses. The merchant's ability to monopolize the consumer's attention for a period may be the essence of modern retailing; the reaction to BargainFinder, at least, suggests that this is what merchants believe. The growing popularity of frequent buyer and other loyalty programs also suggests that getting and keeping customer attention is important to sellers.

Interestingly, this explanation works about equally well for the kindly service and loss leader explanations, which are the two stories that are consistent with the assumption that the CD market was relatively efficient before BargainFinder came along.

Browsing Is Our Business (CDNow)

More important and perhaps more likely is the possibility that the BargainFinder and other ShopBots threaten merchants who are in the browsing assistance business. Some online merchants are enthusiastically attempting to fill the role of personal shopping assistant. Indeed, some of the most successful online stores have adapted to the new marketplace by inverting the information equation.

Retail stores in meatspace ("meatspace" being the part of life that is not cyberspace) provide information about available products—browsing and information acquisition services—that consumers find valuable and are willing to pay for either in time and attention or in cash. Certainly meatspace shopping is conducive to unplanned, impulse purchases, as any refrigerator groaning under kitchen magnets will attest. Retail stores in cyberspace may exacerbate this: what, after all, is a store in cyberspace but a collection of information?

CDNow, for example, tailors its virtual storefront to what it knows of a customer's tastes based upon her past purchases. In addition to dynamically altering the storefront on each successive visit, CDNow also offers to send shoppers occasional email information about new releases that fit their past buying patterns.

One can imagine stores tailoring what they present to what they presume to be the customer's desires, based on demographic information available about the customer even before the first purchase. Tailoring might extend beyond showcasing different wares: taken to the logical extreme it would include some form of price discrimination based on facts known about the customer's preferences, or on demographic information thought to be correlated with preferences. (The U.S. and other legal systems impose constraints on the extent to which stores may generalize from demographic information: for example, stores that attempt race-based, sex-based, or other types of invidious price variation usually violate U.S. law.)

A critical microeconomic question in all this is how consumers and manufacturer/sellers exchange information in this market. Both consumers and sellers have an interest in encouraging the exchange of information: in order to provide what the consumer wants, the sellers need to know what is desired and how badly it is wanted; consumers need to know what is on offer where, and at what price. A ShopBot may solve the consumer's problem of price, but it will not tell him about an existing product of which he is unaware. Similarly, CDNow may reconfigure its store to fit customer profiles, but without some external source of information about customers this takes time, and requires repeat visitors.

Indeed, it requires that customers come in through the front door: all the reconfiguration in the world will not help CDNow if customers are either unaware that they would enjoy its products, or if the customers' only relationship with CDNow is via a ShopBot.

The retail outlet in the average mall can plausibly be described as a mechanism for informing consumers about product attributes. The merchant gives away product information in the hopes that consumers will make purchases. Physical stores, however, have fixed displays and thus must provide more or less identical information to every customer. Anyone who looks in the window, anyone who studies the product labels, or even the product catalogs, receives the same sales pitch.

It may be that the dynamic storefront story is the Internet's substitute for the kindly service story. If so, then the rise of agent-based shopping may well be surprisingly destructive. It raises the possibility of a world in which retail shops providing valuable services are destroyed by an economic process that funnels a large percentage of consumer sales into what become commodity markets without middlemen: people use the high-priced premium cyberstore to browse, but then use BargainFinder to purchase.

To appreciate the problem, consider Bob, an online merchant who has invested a substantial amount in a large and easy to use "browsing" database that combines your past purchases, current news, new releases, and other information to present you with a series of choices and possible purchases that greatly increase your chances of coming across something interesting. After all, a customer enters seeking not a particular title, and not a random title, but a product that he or she would like. What is being sold is the process of search and information acquisition that leads to the judgment that this is something to buy. A good online merchant would make the service of "browsing" easy—and would in large part be selling that browsing assistance.

In this browsing is our business story there is a potential problem: browsing assistance is not excludable. Unless Bob charges for his services (which is likely to discourage most customers and especially the impulse purchaser), there is nothing to stop Alice from browsing merchant Bob's website to determining the product she wants, and then using Bargain-Finder to find the cheapest source of supply. BargainFinder will surely find a competitor with lower prices because Bob's competitor will not have to pay for the database and the software underlying the browsing assistance.

If so, then projects like BargainFinder will have a potentially destructive application, for many online stores will be easy to turn into commodity markets once the process of information acquisition and browsing is complete. It would be straightforward to run a market in kitchen gadgets along the lines of the BargainFinder, even if much of the market for gadgets involves finding solutions to problems one was not consciously aware one had: first free-ride off of one of the sites that provides browsing assistance to discover what you want, then open another window and access Bargain-Finder to buy it. Students and other people with more time than money have been using this strategy to purchase stereo components for decades: draw on the sales expertise of the premium store, then buy from the warehouse. But the scope and ease of this strategy is about to become much greater.

To merchants providing helpful shopping advice, the end result will be as if they spent all their time in their competitors' discount warehouse, pointing out goods that the competitors' customers ought to buy. The only people who will pay premium prices for the physical good—and thus pay for browsing and information services—will be those who feel under a gift-exchange moral obligation to do so: the "sponsors" of NPR.

Collaborative Filtering (FireFly)

Collaborative filtering provides part of the answer to the information exchange problem. It also provides another example of how information technology changes the way that consumer markets will operate. In their simplest form, collaborative filters such as FireFly bring together consumers to exchange information about their preferences. The assumption is that if Alice finds that several other readers—each of whom also likes Frisch,

Kafka, Kundera and Klima but gets impatient with James and Joyce—tends to like William Gass, the odds are good that Alice might enjoy Gass's On Being Blue, too.

In the process of entering sufficient information about her tastes to prime the pump, Alice adds to the database of linked preference information. In helping herself, Alice helps others. In this simplest form, the collaborative filter helps Alice find out about new books she might like. The technology is applicable to finding potentially congenial CDs, news, web sites, software, travel, financial services and restaurants—as well as to helping Alice find people who share her interests. Indeed, each of these is a service currently available or soon to be offered via FireFly.

At the next level of complexity, the collaborative filter can be linked to a ShopBot. Once Alice has decided that she will try On Being Blue she can find out who will sell it to her at the best price.

The really interesting development, however, comes when Alice's personal preference data is available to every merchant Alice visits. (Leave aside for a moment who owns this data, and the terms on which it becomes available.) A shop like CDNow becomes able to tailor its virtual storefront to a fairly good model of Alice's likely desires upon her first visit. CDNow may use this information to showcase its most enticing wares, or it may use it to fine tune its prices to charge Alice all that her purse will bear—or both.

Whichever is the case, shopping will not be the same.

Once shops acquire the ability to engage in price discrimination, consumers will of course seek ways of fighting back. One way will be to shop anonymously, and see what price is quoted when no consumer data is proffered. Consumers can either attempt to prevent merchants and others from acquiring the transactional data that could form the basis of a consumer profile, or they can avail themselves of anonymizing intermediaries who will protect the consumer against the merchant's attempt to practice perfect price discrimination by aggregating data about the seller's prices and practices. In this model, a significant fraction of cyber commerce will be conducted by software agents who will carry accreditation demonstrating their credit-worthiness, but will not be traceable back to their progenitors.

Thus potential legal constraints on online anonymity may have more far-reaching consequences than their obvious effect on unconstrained political speech. . . .

COMMENTS AND QUESTIONS

1. DeLong and Froomkin present a rather dystopian vision of electronic commerce, in which economic changes threaten important social values and upset economic assumptions with little clear idea of what will

replace them. By contrast, a more positive view of electronic commerce would focus on the benefits it does offer:

- New opportunities for reducing transactions costs between buyers and sellers. The eBay auction site is a prime example of a site that facilitates transactions that would probably not occur in real space. An even greater reduction in distribution costs is possible when the goods can be distributed electronically over the network itself. And marketing costs may decline—or at least change—because of Internet search technologies.
- A model closer to perfect competition. While deLong and Froomkin worry about the effects of an exclusive focus on price, the Internet can also facilitate better-informed comparison about nonprice attributes like performance, service, reliability, etc. The creation of comparison sites may simply represent the disaggregation of product information from product sales in certain industries.
- The ability to take advantage of economies of scale and scope. In part because they eliminate geography, companies like amazon.com and CDNow can list a range of titles that most Americans would never have access to in a local store. Far from "mainstreaming" product choice, for some products the Internet may support a greater diversity than previous marketing channels ever could.

2.   The background to electronic commerce is not entirely a function of the economics of the goods and services provided. It is also a function of infrastructure—meaning both the bandwidth needed to support a large number of transactions and a secure framework for transactions to take place. On the former, see Jeffrey MacKie-Mason & Hal Varian, Some Economics of the Internet, *in* Networks, Infrastructure and the New Task for Regulation 107 (1997); Howard A. Shelanski, The Speed Gap: Broadband Infrastructure and Electronic Commerce, 14 Berkeley Tech. L.J. 721 (1999). For a variety of perspectives on the subject, see Lee W. McKnight & Joseph P. Bailey, Internet Economics (1997). The latter is discussed in more detail infra.

3.   For a business-oriented look at electronic commerce, see Soon-Yong Choi et al., The Economics of Electronic Commerce (1997).

B.   ONLINE CONTRACTS AND PAYMENTS

Central to the legal challenges posed by electronic commerce is the adaptation of contract and commercial law to the electronic environment.

Jane Kaufman Winn, *The Emerging Law of Electronic Commerce*

1. Introduction

Doing business over the Internet may seem to raise breathtakingly novel issues in business law, but the law of electronic commerce is actually as old as the telegraph. It was not long after the telegraph entered into widespread use that the first case was litigated in which a party tried to avoid liability by claiming that an agreement reached by an exchange of telegrams could not constitute a valid and binding contract. Most courts in the US have risen to the challenge to look beyond form and evaluate the substance of the transaction, whether the new form of agreement was telegram, telex, fax or email. In some instances, however, there are laws that require a specific form be used by the parties in order to give their agreement legal effect, and in other instances, courts have been distracted or confused by new technologies, and refused to validate the parties' agreement. The question how commercial law will adapt to the new business realities of Internet electronic commerce can best be answered by looking at how the law adapted to earlier iterations of electronic commerce—in particular, electronic data interchange electronic contracting conducted over closed, proprietary networks, electronic funds transfer systems used by banks, and electronic settlement and clearing systems used in Wall Street. . . .

While many of the issues raised by Internet electronic commerce closely resemble issues raised by earlier generations of technology such as telexes and faxes, what may be unprecedented is the degree to which electronic commerce is changing some of the basic principles upon which business administration has been based for decades. The volume and magnitude of changes in business practice that are occurring now as a result of adopting electronic commerce systems are putting tremendous pressure on traditional commercial law doctrines to adapt and evolve. Legal institutions can respond to these pressures in a variety of ways, and this chapter will consider the costs and benefits associated with different techniques for adapting law to new business practices. . . .

2. Adapting Commercial Law to New Business Realities

The most elementary way for business parties to adapt commercial law to new circumstances is through the use of contracts. Parties can depart from the terms of current standard form contracts to write new contracts describing new transactions and allocating new risks between the contracting parties. Failed transactions that result in litigation produce reported legal opinions that become case law which in turn helps parties predict how effective in fact their new contract terms are at regulating innovative business practices. The process of building new law through precedent can be slow and problematic, however, as the outcome of litigation is always somewhat uncertain. As contracts become more innovative, their enforceability becomes less predictable as a result.

When the parties are no longer confident that their contracts will produce predictable legal outcomes, they can lobby state legislatures or Congress to enact statutes to resolve the uncertain issues. While statutes may be more comprehensive and coherent than case law, the process of lobbying is also problematic as different interest groups may resist enacting legislation or may counter by offering undesirable alternative legislation. Furthermore, once a law is passed, even if it is found to be inadequate at resolving the matters it was designed to address, getting a statute repealed can be even more difficult than getting one enacted in the first place. . . .

Under ideal circumstances, commercial law statutes should be reformed in response to significant changes in established business practices to reduce uncertainties that arise under existing law. Innovators start the process by using contracts to assign rights and responsibilities among themselves. Having lawyers individually negotiate and draw up contracts can be an expensive proposition, especially if the business party has to educate the lawyer about the basic business model the parties have developed as part of the drafting process, but it may be the only practical way for the parties to reduce some of the legal uncertainties arising out of innovative business practices. As experience grows and business practices that were once considered innovations become routine, parties to commercial transactions can standardize the terms of their contracts, minimizing or eliminating the role of lawyers in individual transactions. When contract terms and business practices become very standard and routine, commercial statutes can be revised to incorporate what can be thought of as default terms based on these standard contract terms. If the parties to a commercial contract fail to specify all the operative terms of their agreements, then commercial law can act as a gap-filler, providing missing terms that should be substantially the same as those the parties would have agreed to if they had thought about the issue. In this manner, commercial law supports routine business practice and eliminates uncertainty among parties to a transaction without requiring lawyers advise the parties on each contract.

Not all commercial law issues can be resolved through the slow accumulation of business custom and practice, however. Some issues, such as consumer protection issues, are generally resolved by legislatures acting to mandate what business parties must do in order to have legally enforceable agreements or to avoid legal sanctions. Regulatory approaches to commercial law may have a shorter incubation time than "freedom of contract" approaches that defer to standards chosen by commercial parties themselves, and often have less predictable outcomes for affected businesses as a result. Regulation often works best when it corrects market failures, such as those caused by information asymmetries or unequal bargaining power in consumer transactions. The success of credit cards as a payment system for Internet retail commerce is a good example of consumer protection regulation helping a market to work better than it would in a pure freedom of contract regime, and is discussed in Section 4 below. Commercial regulation often fails when it tries to anticipate the future development of business practices. Guessing future market developments is hard enough for entrepreneurs, so the odds are generally even worse that legislators will correctly guess the outcome of current business innovations. Once an inaccurate guess about what people in business will want to do in the future is locked into a statute, the law may become simply irrelevant, or worse, may distort the development of business practice into inefficient alternatives. The 1977 revision of Uniform Commercial Code Article 8, the law governing transfers of investment securities, is a good example of failed anticipatory regulation and is discussed in Section 5 below. This analysis may also apply to current efforts to promote the use of digital signatures through legislation, but it is too soon to draw that conclusion yet.

3. Sale of Goods Transactions

A sale of goods is a very basic, very common form of commercial transaction. Under U.S. law, a contract is generally formed by one party making an offer and the other party accepting it. Each party must offer something of value (known as consideration) to the other and there must be a meeting of the minds on what it is will be exchanged under the contract. Once the contract is formed by the exchange of promises, then the parties perform their obligations as defined by the contract. In a contract for the sale of goods, one party might offer goods for sale at a particular price, and the other party might accept the promise to deliver the goods, giving in exchange a promise to pay for the goods. While the theory is clear, the practice may be more ambiguous.

3.1 Signature and Writing Requirements

Contracts for the sale of goods are normally governed by Article 2 of the Uniform Commercial Code. In general, Article 2 seeks to minimize the formalities the parties must follow in order to create a binding contract so that contracts will not become unenforceable just because the parties did not comply with all manner of technical legal requirements. Even so, Article 2 cannot eliminate all uncertainty from the business contracting process about the rights and obligations of the parties. For example, it is common for a sale of goods transaction to involve the exchange of many pieces of paper between the transacting parties. These papers might include a request for a quotation, a price quote for a shipment of goods on particular terms, a purchase order, an acknowledgement of the purchase order, and an invoice. It is unclear at what point in all this exchange of papers the classic offer, acceptance and meeting of the minds occurs, especially if each of paper has boilerplate contract terms printed on it and the preprinted standard terms are mutually inconsistent. Article 2 rejects the notion that actual business practice must match classical contract law principles in order to produce a binding contract, looking instead to whether or not there is an agreement in fact between the parties as the basis for an enforceable contract (Gabriel and Rusch, 1997).

Not all provisions of Article 2 are so flexible. One rule of law governing the sale of goods is referred to as the "statute of frauds" and requires that sales of goods over a specified dollar amount must be evidenced by a writing and signed by the party against whom enforcement is sought in order to be enforceable. This special rule overrides the general rule that oral contracts are just as enforceable as written contracts (although they may be so much harder to prove that the attempt to enforce an oral contract is rendered futile). The policy behind this rule is to prevent fraud such as a party claiming a contract for the sale of goods exists when in fact no such agreement exists. Although other commercial laws exist which require a signed writing for a contract to be enforceable, the UCC Article 2 statute of frauds writing requirement is one of the most commonly encountered.

The statute of frauds raises problems for electronic commerce involving sales of goods. The party seeking to enforce the contract must show that there is a signed writing stating some of the most important terms of the contract. There is no requirement that the writing state all of the terms of the contract, but it must be sufficient to indicate that a contract has in fact been made by the parties. While a court looking at the exchange of email messages between a vendor and a purchaser might find that one of the email messages could be considered a writing signed by the party against whom enforcement is sought, it is far from clear that all courts would come to that conclusion. As long as the parties cannot predict with confidence what interpretation a court would apply to their exchange of email messages, some parties will resist replacing paper forms with electronic messages even though the administrative expenses associated with paper processes are higher. The higher cost of paper-based administrative systems can be thought of as a sort of insurance premium paid to achieve more predictable legal outcomes.

3.2 EDI Trading Partner Agreements

The problem of harmonizing the exchange of email messages with the legal requirement of a signed writing was first presented in the 1980s when parties began adopting electronic data interchange contracting systems. EDI systems set up in the 1980s were often based on the use of "value added networks" (VANs) that were closed, proprietary networks with enhanced security and data integrity features. Before the exchange of electronic quotes, purchase orders, acknowledgements and invoices could begin, the parties normally had to invest considerable time and energy in reengineering their information systems to permit the exchange of messages in standardized formats to take place. In order to draw the maximum benefit from establishing an EDI trading partner relationship, each party needed to take whatever steps were necessary to permit the automated processing of standard messages. Although the parties might reach a complete meeting of the minds with regard to how different messages would be processed as a matter of information system specifications, the issue of how the exchange of messages would be interpreted by a court remained beyond the power of the parties to resolve through technical standards.

A consensus emerged among many EDI trading partners and their attorneys that the best way to reduce uncertainty about the legal status of the EDI messages they planned to exchange would be to sign a traditional contract that would set out the ground rules for interpreting the significance of the electronic messages. This contract, referred to as an EDI trading partner agreement, reduced the uncertainty associated with how a court would treat email messages for statute of frauds purposes, because the trading partner agreement was a writing signed by the party against whom enforcement was sought. Should litigation later arise, the court could look to the trading partner agreement for an explanation of what legal significance the parties expected their electronic messages to have. Provided that what the parties set out in their trading partner agreement was reasonable, a court could be expected to defer to the wishes of the parties. The effectiveness of a trading partner agreement is not entirely without question, however, as a court might nevertheless still expect to see a signed writing for each transaction that takes place within the trading partner relationship, not just for the relationship as a whole.

One strength of the trading partner agreement model for regulating electronic commerce is that it may eliminate the statute of frauds problem at the same time it defines the rights and obligations of the trading partners with regard to other issues as well. One weakness of this model is that it cannot govern the rights and obligations of anyone other than the two parties who signed it, so each electronic contracting relationship must be governed by a separate contract. This administrative expense might not be significant in light of the large investments often required to harmonize the information systems of the trading partners. However, when the Internet made electronic contracting between strangers with no prior relationship a practical reality, the expense of having the parties meet face to face and take pen in hand to sign a paper contract would in many instances more than offset the cost savings associated with using the Internet as a communications medium.

Another weakness of the trading partner agreement model is that it might require a fair amount of work on the part of attorneys to negotiate and draw up, and many EDI trading partners simply never bothered to sign a trading partner agreement as a result. Yet there is no evidence available as to how a court would interpret an EDI trading partner relationship in the absence of a written contract. This is because there are no reported litigated cases involving EDI trading partner disputes, which is an astonishing fact in light of the enormous volume of EDI transactions taking place in the US today. There is no way to be sure why no disputes between EDI trading partners ever reached the point of litigation. It is possible that trading partner agreements provided the parties with such clear guidance as to the rights and obligations of the parties that they felt litigation was unnecessary, although that can hardly have been the case with all the relationships that were not reduced to a written agreement. It seems more likely that the parties were unwilling to write off the large investment in information system reengineering required to establish EDI trading partner relationships, since the underlying business relationship would probably be irretrievably damaged if litigation were initiated. The absence of reported legal cases may indicate that EDI trading partners tend to work hard to find acceptable compromises to keep their relationship going when disputes arise.

3.3 Technology Neutral and Technology Promoting Legislation

For a court trying to determine whether email messages sent through an EDI system can meet the requirements of the statute of frauds, two separate issues must be resolved: whether there is a signature, and whether there is a writing. The standard for what constitutes a signature under the UCC is actually not difficult to meet: any symbol executed or adopted by a party with a present intention to authenticate a writing. This definition is designed to be flexible enough to include documents marked with "X" or signed with a fingerprint, and if approached in the general spirit of flexibility that animates the UCC, can accommodate the identification of the sender on an email message. For example, courts have held that a company's printed letterhead can function as a signature for meeting a statute of frauds requirement.

What constitutes a writing is a harder problem. "Writing" is not a defined term in the UCC, but would seem to indicate that a piece of paper is required. In In re Kaspar, a bankruptcy case in 1997, the court held that a credit card application taken by the credit card issuer in a telephone call with the debtor did not meet the "writing" requirement of one section of the Bankruptcy Code that would have enabled the credit card issuer to prevent the debtor from discharging his obligation to pay the credit card balance in bankruptcy. The court went on to observe that if the statute required a "writing," the court was entitled to insist on a piece of paper, and did not need be concerned by the fact that so holding might prevent businesses taking advantage of more efficient new communications media.

Given that current laws do not generally treat electronic media as a functional substitute for paper documents, and that there is some uncertainty about how flexibly in fact a court will be in interpreting what constitutes a signature in electronic communication contexts, there has been considerable attention focused on the question of law reform in this area. One approach to the problem might be to enact legislation that merely authorizes a court to treat an electronic record as a writing and an electronic authentication as a signature under appropriate circumstances. Another approach might be to enact legislation that requires a court to so hold unless circumstances dictated the contrary. Such legislation, since it focuses on legal outcomes and not technical processes, can be considered "technology neutral."

This is one of the issues that has been considered at length in the context of revising the UCC to take account of new business practices. The outcome of that process will probably be a sort of global "search and replace" throughout the UCC that replaces references to "writing" with references to "record." Record is defined as information that is inscribed on a tangible medium or that is stored in an electronic or other medium and is retrievable in perceivable form. This definition is designed to be broad enough to cover both paper and electronic documents. It is unclear whether the UCC definition of signature is already broad enough to encompass electronic commerce, or whether a new defined term, such as "authenticate" should be introduced to cover both manual signatures and electronic authentication processes. . . .

Even if the UCC is revised along these lines, and these revisions take effect in the near future, many laws relevant to commerce are not included in the UCC. The ULC has appointed a drafting committee to work on a "Uniform Electronic Transaction Act" that is designed to update other state laws in the same manner as the UCC is currently being revised. The UETA, like the UCC revisions, is a technology neutral statute that aims to enable all electronic commerce across the board by giving courts enough flexibility to accept electronic documents and signatures where appropriate.

While the uniform law drafting process grinds on, many states have leapt into the void and enacted laws in this area. The result is a bewildering variety of approaches ranging from technology neutral to technology specific. A technology specific approach identifies one electronic commerce technology and provides that its use will have certain legal consequences. This has the effect of leaving other electronic commerce technologies struggling with the current uncertainty in the law, and focusing the attention of the public on one technology as having been endorsed by the state legislature. Given the current state of rapid innovation in electronic commerce, it is not clear that a technology specific approach to legislation will help or hinder the development of electronic commerce generally. One technology that has been the beneficiary of technology-specific legislation in the US and abroad is asymmetric cryptography, which is used to produce "digital signatures."

3.4   *Digital Signatures and Public Key Infrastructure*

The use of the Internet for commerce changed the landscape of electronic contracting, and raised the statute of frauds problem in a new context. EDI standards and the use of VANs permitted one-to-one electronic contracting, while the Internet opened up the possibility of one-to-many contracting. In order to take advantage of the much wider market access the Internet offered, parties sought an electronic contracting model that did not depend on a written trading partner agreement signed by the transacting parties in a face to face meeting. The flip side of the greater access offered by the Internet was its lack of security infrastructure that the VANs had provided, however. For one party to have confidence that their electronic communications were in fact taking place with the correct counterparty, and that the content of the electronic communications could be trusted, the parties to Internet transactions themselves would have to take responsibility for security. Even if the parties were able to satisfy themselves that their Internet electronic contracting technology was as reliable as paper-based commerce or EDI contracting, until the UCC reforms were finalized and enacted by state legislatures, uncertainty remained as to the legal effect of such commercial practices.

One technology that seems to hold particular promise for resolving the technical problems associated with Internet contracting is asymmetric or public key cryptography. Parties interested in identifying each other over an open network can each generate a pair of matched keys, one to be kept private and one to be distributed publicly. When a message signed with a private key is tested with the associated public key, asymmetric cryptography can be used to determine with high degree of certainty that the message could not have been signed with any other private key than the one associated with that public key. However, merely establishing a strong association between a message signed with a private key with a particular public key is not very helpful for electronic commerce purposes unless the party using the public key is confident of the identity of the person in control of the private key, and confident that person's control over the key has been maintained at all times.

For public key cryptography to support electronic commerce, at a minimum a solution must be found to the problem of how to associate an online identity established through the use cryptographic keys and the identity of an actor in the material world who can be held legally responsible for performing a contract. The simplest solution is to have people meet face to face and exchange keys on floppy disks, but like the trading partner agreement, the costs associated with such a system will negate most of the benefits that the Internet can offer.

Another solution to the problem of binding real world identities with online identities that has been widely discussed is the use of "trusted third parties" to introduce parties to each other, eliminating the need for a face to face meeting between the parties. Such a trusted third party might issue a certificate attesting to the fact that a particular human being was in control of a particular private key at a particular time. The person using a cryptographic key as an online identity card might provide a new acquaintance with a copy of the public key and a certificate indicating that a trusted third party was willing to vouch for the material world identity of the holder of the private key. A trusted third party offering such services might be labeled a certificate authority, and might sell its services to parties wishing to use digital signatures to form electronic contracts with strangers. This particular solution is based on the X.509 certificate standard developed as part of the X.500 directory standard. This standard was established to promote the use of distributed directories over networked computer systems. A system for coordinating the use of digital signature certificates issued by trusted third parties to establish a system of reliable online identities is generally referred to as a public key infrastructure.

The strength of this model is the fact that it can create an environment of trust between parties with no prior relationship online or in the material world. A party considering entering into a contract based on an email communication could ask the counterparty to include an identity certificate from a trusted third party with the signed email in order to establish a reliable association between the digital signature attached to the email and a real human being that can accept legal responsibilities. If the trusted third party has reliably identified the counterparty, and the counterparty has never lost control of the private key used to sign messages, then the party considering the contract can have confidence that the signature is what it appears to be. If the only impediment to the formation of contracts over the Internet was uncertainty among the contracting parties as to their material world identities, then a public key infrastructure that distributes digital signature certificates would permit contracting to take place.

The weakness of this model is its failure to address many of the concerns that a party considering entering into an Internet transaction would have. These concerns include the need to know not simply the material world identity of the sender of a particular email, but the capacity of the sender to enter into a legally binding contract. The sender might be a minor, which creates problems because under US law contracts entered into by minors are generally voidable at the election of the minor. If the party expected to assume responsibility for a contract is a corporation or other legal entity such as a trust, then the other party needs to know whether a particular human being is duly authorized to act for the legal entity. The party considering entering into an Internet transaction also needs information about the ability of the other party to perform his or her promises. This includes the ability to deliver goods that conform to the contract terms, or to pay for the goods as agreed. The party considering whether to go forward might also want to know the jurisdiction in which the other party is located, in order to estimate the risk of being haled into court in a remote location if the transaction goes awry. A simple binding of a human being with a digital signature provides no information about any of these issues.

The most common model of a public key infrastructure and digital signature certificates was actually designed to create online directories of names and addresses equivalent to phonebooks. In the material world, parties do not make the decision whether to enter into contracts based on whether someone can be found in a telephone directory, and it is unlikely that parties will begin to do business online simply based on the proffer of an online ID certificate if there is no easy way to obtain the other information needed to make a business decision about the value of the contract.

It is possible that the basic framework of a public key infrastructure and digital signature certificates can be expanded to include the rest of the information parties need before they would be willing to enter into contracts over the Internet with strangers. Just how the basic framework should be expanded is a topic of considerable debate and what, if any solutions can be found to the problem of adapting the basic model to the complex realities of electronic commerce, will not be apparent for some time.

In addition to these questions surrounding the business model within which digital signatures will be used, there are also substantial unresolved question about the design of large-scale open system public key infrastructures at a technical level. For example, before relying on a digital signature certificate, a party might want to check a certificate revocation list maintained by the certificate authority to make sure that the certificate had not been revoked, but there are many unresolved issues surrounding how a certificate revocation list can be reliably maintained and made accessible in an environment in which large volumes of certificates are in use simultaneously. While digital signature certificate standards permit certificates to be adapted to specific purposes through the use of certificate policies contained in policy extension fields, it is unclear how such policies can be reliably recognized and acted upon in open network systems.

It is possible that the best application of this technology will not be in open environments in which strangers do business with strangers, but within more closed environments in which parties with prior relationships use digital signatures to permit communications to take place over insecure networks and eliminate their reliance on VANs. Many of the thorny business and technical design problems associated with creating a workable open system using digital signatures are not difficult to resolve within a more limited context.

Many entrepreneurs, technologists and lawyers have been distracted from the fact that most current proposals for establishing public key infrastructures do not address basic business issues, and have rushed to embrace the idea of digital signatures as the panacea for Internet electronic commerce. Several states, including Utah, have enacted comprehensive digital signature legislation in advance of any commercial applications of this technology on the assumption that enabling legislation will accelerate adoption of this technology. The debate surrounding how to use digital signature technology to support real commercial transactions has not yet been resolved, and may not be resolved for some time. Until that debate is resolved through actual commercial implementations of the technology, it will not be possible to judge the success of the legislative efforts to promote this technology.

3.5 *Extranets and Trading Partner Agreements*

In 1998, the most successful examples of Internet electronic commerce were Cisco Systems, Inc. and Dell Computer Corporation. Cisco's web revenues for 1998 were projected to be over $6 billion; Dell's web revenues were projected to be in excess of $2 billion, and unlike amazon.com, both companies are profiting from their Internet sales. Both companies use something resembling the old EDI trading partner agreement to minimize the legal uncertainty associated with Internet commerce.

Cisco uses its website to create an extranet, permitting only authorized users to access its web-based "Cisco Connection Online" service. Parties who have entered into a contractual relationship with Cisco are allowed to designate which employees or representatives are authorized to access Cisco's website to place orders. These parties are then assigned user-IDs and passwords that they must use to log into those parts of Cisco website where product availability and prices can be checked and orders placed. These preexisting contractual relationships provide a framework, similar to that created by a trading partner agreement, within which email messages are exchanged that permit contracts to be formed for the sale of Cisco goods and services.

Dell permits credit card holders to make purchases of goods and services directly from its website. The framework of the credit card system determines the rights and obligations of the parties with regard to such possible issues as the ability of the customer to pay for the goods, liability for unauthorized use of the credit card, and the right of the customer to dispute the transaction. The Dell website uses asymmetric cryptography, not as an authentication process, but merely to establish a secure channel of communication between the Dell server and the customer's browser using the Secure SocketsLayer (SSL) protocol. Assuming the customer's browser has the certificate authority's certificate preloaded (which is true for recent releases of standard Internet browser software), then the customer's browser can download a copy of Dell's public key and determine that it has been certified by the certificate authority. The browser and the Dell server share a special cryptographic key, called a "session key" that has been encrypted with Dell's public key for security. The consumer's credit card information travels over the Internet encrypted with the session key, and so is protected from being intercepted in transit. The public key infrastructure merely reduces the risk of certain forms of fraud by third parties, while the contractual and regulatory framework of the credit card system, combined with the terms and conditions of use that Dell attaches to use of its website for electronic commerce, perform similar functions in this system as a trading partner agreement.

4. Payment Transactions

Payment systems were among the first commercial transaction systems to migrate to an electronic environment. In 1957, paper checks were first imprinted with the magnetic ink character recognition line on the bottom that permitted the check processing system to be automated. In the late 1960s, banks began experimenting with automated teller machines and secure systems for wire transfers of funds. At the same time, the use of credit cards rapidly proliferated. In 1970, in response to widespread criticism of aggressive tactics on the part of card issuers to expand rapidly the use of credit cards while at the same time severely limiting card issuer liability, Congress enacted a comprehensive scheme of consumer protections for card holders that remains in effect today. The law governing electronic funds transfers dates from 1978, when consumer protections were passed by Congress that applied to transactions such as ATM withdrawals. Outside the realm of consumer payment systems, in 1989, the ULC formalized a law governing wholesale wire transfers, UCC Article 4A, which has now been adopted in all 50 states.

In the late 1990s, all large-scale payment systems in the US had been adapted to operate within secure networked mainframe computer systems operated by regulated financial institutions. As a result, Internet-based payment systems have faced formidable competition and have not been able to establish any significant market share. Many standard developing organizations and technology vendors are competing to achieve a dominant position in the Internet payment arena, but it is unclear which, if any, of the current competitors will ultimately prevail. First Virtual, the first commercial Internet e-cash system, began operations in 1995 amid great fanfare, but ceased payment system operations in 1998 due to lack of market share. Likewise, Internet micropayment technology seemed very promising in the mid-1990s, but by 1998 commercial products such as Millicent were still not enjoying widespread acceptance. Just as it is hard to predict who will be the winners among these emerging technologies, it is also unclear how the existing large-scale mainframe-based payment systems will adapt to these new competitive forces.

4.1 Credit Card Transactions

Credit cards, used in combination with the SSL protocol supported by the end user's browser, have proven to be the payment system of choice for retail Internet electronic commerce. The SSL protocol works within a very simple public key infrastructure, and provides a secure channel for communication of information between the end user's browser and the e-commerce server. Early concerns over the lack of security for Internet communications led MasterCard and Visa each to begin work on designing a much more complex public key infrastructure that would provide digital signature certificates to card holders, merchants, acquiring banks and issuing banks. These projects later merged into the Secure Electronic Transaction (SET) standard. The SET standard offers a much higher level of security than the SSL standard by adding new safeguards against fraud and unauthorized use of credit card information. In order to do so, however, it will have to place heavy demands on existing credit card transaction processing infrastructure and may require the execution of complex cryptographic algorithms that exceed the processing capacity of the average end user's system. These and other problems have slowed down the rate of adoption of the SET standard and progress in further refining the standard. While work on the more sophisticated and complex SET standard has progressed slowly, the SSL protocol has become the de facto standard for security for retail Internet commerce today.

Although the SSL standard provides only minimal security for payments transactions over the Internet, the existing legal and technical framework of the credit card system supplements those protections to produce an Internet payment system that meets the current minimum requirements of merchants, end users and financial institutions. The only segment of the credit card system that uses the Internet as a medium of communication is the transmission of the cardholder's account number to the Internet merchant. From the merchant's e-commerce server, information about authorized charges are transmitted to the merchant's acquiring bank in the same manner as they would be transmitted by a telephone or mail order merchant. The rights and obligations between the merchant, the merchant's acquiring bank and the cardholder's issuing bank are set by private contracts between the parties.

Consumers considering whether to use the Internet to make purchases can limit their risk of loss due to fraud by using their credit card as a form of payment because federal regulations limit consumer liability for unauthorized charges to $50. This limit applies whether the card is used in a face-to-face transaction, in a telephone or mail order transaction, or in an Internet transaction. The Federal Reserve Board, the federal agency charged with oversight of consumer credit card regulations, has stated that merchants who accept credit card information in transactions in which the merchant does not have the opportunity to inspect the credit card cannot contest a consumer's later claim that a particular charge transaction was unauthorized. This rule was developed in the mail order and telephone order context, and applies equally to the Internet context.

A merchant considering accepting payment by credit card from an Internet retail site must first be satisfied that it has found a way to minimize the risk of fraud and error associated with credit card use, because the merchant will not be allowed to pass those costs on to the consumer, or in most cases, the merchant's acquiring bank. A merchant may decide that it nevertheless makes sense to accept credit cards as a payment device for Internet commerce given the lack of practical alternatives, the increased volume of sales that are likely to result, and the fact that the credit card issuer, not the merchant, assumes the risk of payment default by the card holder.

Consumers also enjoy access to dispute resolution services provided by credit card issuers in the event that the consumer has a dispute with the Internet merchant regarding the goods or services purchased. Under certain circumstances, federal regulations require card issuers to investigate and resolve cardholder complaints about goods and services purchased by credit card. Current business practice among card issuers has considerably expanded the use of this dispute resolution service to include more transactions than are covered by federal regulation. From the consumer perspective, the use of a credit card as a payment mechanism substantially reduces the risk of being forced either to pay for unacceptable goods or services ordered over the Internet, or to submit to the jurisdiction of a remote forum in order to dispute the value of goods and services purchased over the Internet.

4.2 Electronic Funds Transfers

If some of the new technologies for payments under development are ultimately successful, it is possible they will be outside the scope of existing laws, including consumer protection regulations. Unless and until regulators intervene, such systems would be regulated by contracts among the parties. Wholesale funds transfer systems in the US evolved largely outside of any existing regulatory framework for over a decade before a formal body of law was established to govern the rights and obligations of the parties. The law that now addresses wholesale wire transfers is UCC Article 4A. Article 4A is a very significant development in the law of electronic commerce because it was one of the first bodies of law to consider in depth how the use of electronic authentication systems should be regulated.

In the US, financial institutions operate a wholesale wire transfer system for large scale business to business funds transfers. These systems, which include the Fedwire operated by the Federal Reserve system, and the New York Clearing House for Interbank Payment Systems (CHIPS), transfer in excess of one trillion dollars per day. These systems began operations in the early 1970s, and operate largely among banks and their major corporate customers. Before the adoption of Article 4A, the only law that applied to these systems beyond private contracts among the participants were Federal Reserve Board Operating Circulars, for transfers that used the Fedwire, and the operating rules of CHIPS, for transfers that used

CHIPS. Many aspects of these transactions were not covered by any organized body of law, however, and it was possible for disputes to arise between parties which were not clearly governed by any contract or operating system rule.

Banks providing wire transfer services were not particularly concerned about the lack of formal law governing the wholesale funds transfer system until some litigated cases in the 1980s raised issues that the banks found troubling. One such issue that drove the banks to the ULC to support the Article 4A drafting process was a litigated case in which a bank failed to make a funds transfer on the date requested by its customer. The court suggested that a bank making an error in handling a wire transfer might be held liable for the lost profits from any business deal the transferor lost due to the delay. Banks were unwilling to accept liability beyond the time value of the funds while they were delayed due to the error. Because a funds transfer might pass through several banks on the way from transferor to transferee, it was not possible for a bank to be certain that it would always be protected against liability by a preexisting contractual relationship with the disgruntled transferor. The only way to guarantee a limit to the bank's liability would be by statute. After considerable debate in the drafting process, the representatives of the banks' customers agreed to this limitation.

Banks and their customers shared a commitment to keeping the price of funds transfer services low, and expanding liability for the banks would have a necessary consequence of forcing banks to raise the price of funds transfer services or to leave the market. Bank customers agreed that it was more efficient for customers to accept responsibility for monitoring the proper execution of funds transfers when large profits were at stake than to put the banks in the position of insuring all their customers against any risk of bank error in executing transfers. Many bank customers were operating a level of sophistication that was equivalent to the banks themselves, and so in a context in which no consumers were involved, the customer could reasonably be expected to assume some responsibility for the operation of the system in exchange for lower prices.

Another major point of contention between the banks and their customers was how responsibility for unauthorized funds transfers should be allocated. The banks initially took the position that unauthorized funds transfers could only occur as a result of carelessness by their customers because banks had adequate security procedures in place, but their customers were unwilling to accept this analysis. After heated debate, a complex compromise was worked out dividing liability for unauthorized funds transfers between the bank and the customer. The initial allocation of liability was on the bank, but the bank could shift the risk of liability to the customer if the bank and the customer agreed a "commercially reasonable security procedure" that would be used to initiate funds transfers. A "commercially reasonable" security procedure is one that is adapted to the customer's situation, in light of the amount, type and volume of funds transfers the customer makes, the customer's business and other factors. If the bank can prove that it complied with the security procedure agreed upon with the customer, then the bank cannot be held liable for an unauthorized funds transfer executed from the customer's account. The only exception to this rule arises in the unlikely event that the customer can prove that the unauthorized funds transfer did not originate with any person or facility under the customer's control. In that case, which would include funds transfers executed by hackers penetrating the security of the system from outside the customer's facilities, the bank must bear the risk of loss.

Article 4A takes a very different approach to liability issues than the consumer protection regulations that apply to credit card transactions. With credit cards, the consumer is presumed to be incapable of making any significant contribution to reducing the risk of loss due to unauthorized use of the card, and so is exonerated from almost all liability as a result. Card issuers, merchants and acquiring banks bear almost all risk of fraud and error, and as a result have an incentive to invest in the most sophisticated antifraud technology available. In the wholesale funds transfer environment, however, many bank customers are operating at a level of sophistication equivalent to that of the banks, and are required to be active participants in the design and maintenance of the security of the funds transfer system. Even though the loss allocation rules in each system point in opposite directions, Article 4A and the credit card system are each examples of commercial law that has been adapted very successfully to different categories of payment system. . . .

6. Conclusion

Existing commercial law can be adapted to new electronic commerce technologies in a manner that simplifies and supports business practice if changes are made in light of present commercial reality. There are many successful examples of technology neutral commercial law, such as the Article 4A concept of a "security procedure" and the Article 8 concept of a "security entitlement," that are flexible enough to accommodate many different forms of technology. Business practices in Internet commerce may not yet be well enough established for commercial law to capture and reflect the standard default terms the parties might expect to operate in the absence of explicit contract terms. Until a body of business practices develop to guide the direction of legislation, transacting parties should carefully consider how risks are allocated by private agreement.

If Congress and state legislatures leap in too quickly to promote promising technologies, chances are great that the result will be greater inefficiency, not less. Legislators should not be in the business of trying to guess the winners in the current competition among technologies for

Internet commerce. If Congress and state legislatures cannot refrain from acting in this area, however, they should limit their intervention to protecting less sophisticated parties from possible overreaching by more sophisticated parties. The model of credit card consumer protection offers a promising model for legislation that promotes electronic commerce without dictating any technological choices. Credit card consumer protection regulations shelter less sophisticated parties from fraud and error risks they cannot control while forcing more sophisticated parties to invest in security procedures to reduce such risks as much as possible. This type of legislation can help to make the entire system operate more efficiently than it would if transactions were governed simply by standard form contracts drawn up by card issuers.

COMMENTS AND QUESTIONS

1. As Professor Winn notes, many of these issues have been faced before, as the telegraph, the telephone, and other remote means of communication became important conduits for commerce. Given this, do we need to revise contract law at all in the digital environment? If courts could conclude that telegraphs and faxes are "writings" for contract purposes, and that printing a statement on a letterhead was a "signature" where it demonstrated an intent to be bound, couldn't they read contract law expansively enough to solve these problems in the Internet context as well? For a discussion of the existing law regarding the statute of frauds, and how it might apply in the online context, see R.J. Robertson, Electronic Commerce on the Internet and the Statute of Frauds, 49 S.C. L. Rev. 787 (1998).

2. Digital signature legislation has proven very popular: statutes have been passed in a number of states, and are pending in many more. For examples of various sorts of digital signature laws, see Utah Code Ann. §§46-3-101 et seq.; Ga. Code Ann. §§10-12-1 to -5; Kan. Stat. Ann. §60-2616. These laws take a number of different forms. Some, like Utah's, are detailed statements of the rights and responsibilities of digital certificate authorities. Other statutes take a much simpler tack: they permit the use of digital signatures and accept change accepting to (accept) their use as evidence of authenticity without resolving liability issues. The Utah approach has been criticized for allowing certificate authorities to avoid liability merely by using boilerplate forms. Liability for the theft or fraudulent use of a digital signature would presumably fall either on the party accepting the signature or (more likely) on the party whose signature key was stolen.

Credit card laws allocate responsibility for unauthorized charges in a way that is very protective of consumers. Should online payment legislation do the same thing?

For debates over the appropriate rules to be applied to digital signatures and certificate authorities, see, e.g., A. Michael Froomkin, The Essential Role of Trusted Third Parties in Electronic Commerce, 75 Or. L. Rev. 49 (1996); Jane Kaufman Winn, Open Systems, Free Markets, and Regulation of Internet Commerce, 72 Tul. L. Rev. 1177 (1998); Jane Kaufman Winn, Couriers Without Luggage: Negotiable Instruments and Digital Signatures, 49 S.C. L. Rev. 739 (1998).

3. Closely related to the question of digital signatures is the feasibility of new forms of electronic currency such as "electronic cash." A variety of electronic cash systems have been developed. While they differ in technical details, each operates much like a prepaid phone card or "chit" that a consumer buys from a bank or other institution. In this case, though, the "card" is nothing more than an encrypted number. Once credited with a certain sum, the consumer can use that number to pay for goods or services. The key difference between electronic cash and other forms of Internet payments systems is that the merchant can verify that the cash is valid without ever learning the identity of the buyer. Unlike the data trails left by credit cards, therefore, electronic cash can preserve anonymity in commercial transactions—just as paper currency does in the real world. For a discussion of electronic cash, see A. Michael Froomkin, Flood Control on the Information Ocean: Living With Anonymity, Digital Cash, and Distributed Databases, 15 J.L. & Com. 395 (1996).

At this writing, electronic cash has not gained widespread acceptance, for reasons that are not entirely clear. Electronic cash is cumbersome, which may deter many people from using it. Consumers have turned out not to mind paying for goods over the Internet by credit card, perhaps because they value their privacy less than many scholars suppose. And different forms of electronic cash are generally not exchangeable or compatible with each other. Because electronic payment systems have the characteristics of a network market, the absence of either a clear market leader or an open standard may deter the broad acceptance needed to start the ball rolling. See Mark A. Lemley, Standardizing Government Standard-Setting Policy for Electronic Commerce, 14 Berkeley Tech. L.J. 745, 754-756 (1999).

If electronic cash does gain acceptance, it may herald a fundamental change in the way currencies operate. Kerry Macintosh has argued that electronic cash may open a wedge for private (rather than government-issued) currencies. See Kerry Lynn Macintosh, How to Encourage Global Electronic Commerce: The Case for Private Currencies on the Internet, 11 Harv. J.L. & Tech. 733 (1998); Kerry Lynn Macintosh, The New Money, 14 Berkeley Tech. L.J. 659 (1999). For a more skeptical view, see Jane Kaufman Winn, Clash of the Titans: Regulating the Competition Between Established and Emerging Electronic Payment Systems, 14 Berkeley Tech. L.J. 675 (1999).

Is electronic cash a good thing? As in the debates we saw earlier over encryption and anonymity, society must trade off its citizens' interest in privacy against the risk that anonymity can be used to evade the law. For a discussion of financial cryptography and anonymity, see Peter Swire, The Uses and Limits of Financial Cryptography: A Law Professor's Perspective, http://www.osu.edu/units/law/swire.htm.

4. Besides specific digital signature legislation in various states, uniform law groups have drafted a number of model statutes to deal with contracts and commercial law on the Internet. Notable among these are the Uniform Electronic Transactions Act (UETA) and the Uniform Computer Information Transactions Act (UCITA), which has been discussed in detail in Chapter 6. UCITA governs transactions in computer information (a subset of all electronic commerce transactions). By its terms, UETA will govern only where UCITA does not. Thus, if both statutes are enacted, different transactions would be governed by different statutes, depending on the type of goods being sold in electronic commerce.

Both statutes would make it clear that the traditional requirements of a writing and a signature could be satisfied in the course of an ordinary electronic transaction. Beyond that, however, the two diverge in their treatment of various types of electronic transactions. UCITA, for example, has a number of detailed rules validating "agreements" entered into by electronic agents.

While UCITA has received enormous criticism for its contract formation rules and its substantive provisions regarding warranties and self-help, relatively little attention has been devoted to the Act as a rule structure for electronic commerce. For notable exceptions, see Maureen A. O'Rourke, Progressing Towards a Uniform Commercial Code for Electronic Commerce or Racing Towards Nonuniformity?, 14 Berkeley Tech. L.J. 635 (1999); Amelia H. Boss, Commerce and the Symbiotic Relationship Between International and Domestic Law Reform, 72 Tul. L. Rev. 1931 (1998); Amelia H. Boss, Searching for Security in the Law of Electronic Commerce, 23 Nova L. Rev. 585 (1999). Boss's work in particular focuses on how UCITA interacts with UETA and with international efforts to reform commercial law.

For a sharply critical take on UCITA's interaction with digital signature laws, see A. Michael Froomkin, Article 2B as Legal Software for Electronic Contracting: Operating System or Trojan Horse?, 13 Berkeley Tech. L.J. 1023 (1998).

5. As Professor Winn points out in her excerpt, one of the dangers of legislating rules for technologies that don't yet exist is that the technology may not develop in the way you anticipate. Arguably, this has happened with digital signature legislation, which set out a very detailed set of rules for transactions and groups that don't in fact appear to play a very significant role in electronic commerce today. UCITA may suffer the same fate, at least with regard to its rules anticipating contracts entered into by electronic agents.

C. INTERNET TAXATION

Internet Tax Freedom Act

Sec. 1101. Moratorium.

(a) Moratorium.—No State or political subdivision thereof shall impose any of the following taxes during the period beginning on October 1, 1998, and ending 3 years after the date of the enactment of this Act—

(1) taxes on Internet access, unless such tax was generally imposed and actually enforced prior to October 1, 1998; and

(2) multiple or discriminatory taxes on electronic commerce.

(b) Preservation of State and Local Taxing Authority.—Except as provided in this section, nothing in this title shall be construed to modify, impair, or supersede, or authorize the modification, impairment, or superseding of, any State or local law pertaining to taxation that is otherwise permissible by or under the Constitution of the United States or other Federal law and in effect on the date of enactment of this Act.

(c) Liabilities and Pending Cases.—Nothing in this title affects liability for taxes accrued and enforced before the date of enactment of this Act, nor does this title affect ongoing litigation relating to such taxes.

(d) Definition of Generally Imposed and Actually Enforced.—For purposes of this section, a tax has been generally imposed and actually enforced prior to October 1, 1998, if, before that date, the tax was authorized by statute and either—

(1) a provider of Internet access services had a reasonable opportunity to know by virtue of a rule or other public proclamation made by the appropriate administrative agency of the State or political subdivision thereof, that such agency has interpreted and applied such tax to Internet access services; or

(2) a State or political subdivision thereof generally collected such tax on charges for Internet access.

(e) Exception to Moratorium.—

(1) In general.—Subsection (a) shall also not apply in the case of any person or entity who knowingly and with knowledge of the character of the material, in interstate or foreign commerce by means of the World Wide Web, makes any communication for commercial purposes that is available to any minor and that includes any material that is harmful to minors unless such person or entity has restricted access by minors to material that is harmful to minors—

(A) by requiring use of a credit card, debit account, adult access code, or adult personal identification number;

(B) by accepting a digital certificate that verifies age; or

(C) by any other reasonable measures that are feasible under available technology.

(2) Scope of exception.—For purposes of paragraph (1), a person shall not be considered to making a communication for commercial purposes of material to the extent that the person is—

(A) a telecommunications carrier engaged in the provision of a telecommunications service;

(B) a person engaged in the business of providing an Internet access service;

(C) a person engaged in the business of providing an Internet information location tool; or

(D) similarly engaged in the transmission, storage, retrieval, hosting, formatting, or translation (or any combination thereof) of a communication made by another person, without selection or alteration of the communication. . . .

(f) Additional Exception to Moratorium.—

(1) In general.—Subsection (a) shall also not apply with respect to an Internet access provider, unless, at the time of entering into an agreement with a customer for the provision of Internet access services, such provider offers such customer (either for a fee or at no charge) screening software that is designed to permit the customer to limit access to material on the Internet that is harmful to minors.

[Definitions relating specifically to subsections (e) and (f) have been omitted.]

[Sections 1102 and 1103 establish a commission to study the problem and report back to Congress.]

Sec. 1104. Definitions.

For the purposes of this title:

(1) Bit tax.—The term "bit tax" means any tax on electronic commerce expressly imposed on or measured by the volume of digital information transmitted electronically, or the volume of digital information per unit of time transmitted electronically, but does not include taxes imposed on the provision of telecommunications services.

(2) Discriminatory tax.—The term "discriminatory tax" means—

(A) any tax imposed by a State or political subdivision thereof on electronic commerce that—

(i) is not generally imposed and legally collectible by such State or such political subdivision on transactions involving similar property, goods, services, or information accomplished through other means;

(ii) is not generally imposed and legally collectible at the same rate by such State or such political subdivision on transactions involving similar property, goods, services, or information accomplished through other means, unless the rate is lower as part of a phase-out of the tax over not more than a 5-year period;

(iii) imposes an obligation to collect or pay the tax on a different person or entity than in the case of transactions involving similar property, goods, services, or information accomplished through other means;

(iv) establishes a classification of Internet access service providers or online service providers for purposes of establishing a higher tax rate to be imposed on such providers than the tax rate generally applied to providers of similar information services delivered through other means; or

(B) any tax imposed by a State or political subdivision thereof, if—

(i) except with respect to a tax (on Internet access) that was generally imposed and actually enforced prior to October 1, 1998, the sole ability to access a site on a remote seller's out-of-State computer server is considered a factor in determining a remote seller's tax collection obligation; or

(ii) a provider of Internet access service or online services is deemed to be the agent of a remote seller for determining tax collection obligations solely as a result of—

(I) the display of a remote seller's information or content on the out-of-State computer server of a provider of Internet access service or online services; or

(II) the processing of orders through the out-of-State computer server of a provider of Internet access service or online services.

(3) Electronic commerce.—The term "electronic commerce" means any transaction conducted over the Internet or through Internet access, comprising the sale, lease, license, offer, or delivery of property, goods, services, or information, whether or not for consideration, and includes the provision of Internet access.

(4) Internet.—The term "Internet" means collectively the myriad of computer and telecommunications facilities, including equipment and operating software, which comprise the interconnected world-wide network of networks that employ the Transmission Control Protocol/Internet Protocol, or any predecessor or successor protocols to such protocol, to communicate information of all kinds by wire or radio.

(5) Internet access.—The term "Internet access" means a service that enables users to access content, information, electronic mail, or other services offered over the Internet, and may also include access to proprietary content, information, and other services as part of a package of services offered to users. Such term does not include telecommunications services.

(6) Multiple tax.—

(A) In general.—The term "multiple tax" means any tax that is imposed by one State or political subdivision thereof on the same or essentially the same electronic commerce that is also subject to another tax imposed by another State or political subdivision thereof (whether or not at the same rate or on the same basis), without a credit (for example, a resale exemption certificate) for taxes paid in other jurisdictions.

    (B) Exception.—Such term shall not include a sales or use tax imposed by a State and 1 or more political subdivisions thereof on the same electronic commerce or a tax on persons engaged in electronic commerce which also may have been subject to a sales or use tax thereon.

    (C) Sales or use tax.—For purposes of subparagraph (B), the term "sales or use tax" means a tax that is imposed on or incident to the sale, purchase, storage, consumption, distribution, or other use of tangible personal property or services as may be defined by laws imposing such tax and which is measured by the amount of the sales price or other charge for such property or service. . . .

Sec. 1201. Declaration That Internet Should Be Free of New Federal Taxes.

It is the sense of Congress that no new Federal taxes similar to the taxes described in section 1101(a) should be enacted with respect to the Internet and Internet access during the moratorium provided in such section.

Sec. 1203. Declaration That the Internet Should Be Free of Foreign Tariffs, Trade Barriers, and Other Restrictions.

(a) In General.—It is the sense of Congress that the President should seek bilateral, regional, and multilateral agreements to remove barriers to global electronic commerce through the World Trade Organization, the Organization for Economic Cooperation and Development, the Trans-Atlantic Economic Partnership, the Asia Pacific Economic Cooperation forum, the Free Trade Area of the America, the North American Free Trade Agreement, and other appropriate venues.

    (b) Negotiating Objectives.—The negotiating objectives of the United States shall be—

        (1) to assure that electronic commerce is free from—

            (A) tariff and nontariff barriers;

            (B) burdensome and discriminatory regulation and standards; and

            (C) discriminatory taxation; and

        (2) to accelerate the growth of electronic commerce by expanding market access opportunities for—

            (A) the development of telecommunications infrastructure;

            (B) the procurement of telecommunications equipment;

(C) the provision of Internet access and telecommunications services; and

(D) the exchange of goods, services, and digitalized information. . . .

COMMENTS AND QUESTIONS

1. The stated goal of the Internet Tax Freedom Act (ITFA) is to prohibit discriminatory taxation against electronic commerce sellers and multiple or overlapping taxation between different jurisdictions. Such taxation might occur, for example, where a seller located in one jurisdiction sells a product into another jurisdiction, and both jurisdictions seek to impose sales tax on the transaction. It would indeed seem unfair to permit such double taxation. But how likely is that? In the modern world, lots of commerce takes place across borders. Can't we deal with electronic commerce tax issues in the same way we have dealt with other transborder issues?

2. Indeed, the tax law is actually *more* favorable to electronic commerce than to other types of transactions. The Supreme Court has held that interstate commerce is not subject to state sales tax at all by the seller's state. Mail order catalogs, for example, don't charge tax on out-of-state purchases. (In theory, the recipient is supposed to remit local tax to the state of receipt, but that rule is almost never enforced.) Presumably, the ITFA would preserve this state of affairs for electronic commerce. Further, electronic commerce may make it possible for some companies to relocate to tax havens to avoid paying income tax or various other kinds of taxes. Finally, the ITFA provides that no new taxes can be imposed on electronic commerce for a three-year period, even if corresponding taxes are imposed on other sorts of commerce.

3. There is a growing literature on the taxation problems posed by electronic commerce. See, e.g., David Hardesty, Taxation of Electronic Commerce (1999); David L. Forst, Old and New Issues in the Taxation of Electronic Commerce, 14 Berkeley Tech. L.J. 711 (1999); David S. Prebut, State and Local Taxation of Electronic Commerce: The Forging of Cyberspace Tax Policy, 24 Rutgers Computer & Tech. L.J. 345 (1998); Megan E. Groves, Note, Where There's a Will, There's a Way: State Sales and Use Taxation of Electronic Commerce, 74 Ind. L.J. 293 (1998); Matthew G. McLaughlin, Comment, The Internet Tax Freedom Act: Congress Takes a Byte Out of the Net, 48 Cath. U. L. Rev. 209 (1998).

4. While the reach of the ITFA is domestic, much of the electronic commerce tax problem is international in scope. The statute suggests ways to negotiate favorable tax treatment for electronic commerce, but the United States cannot legislate in this area alone. Whether the rest of the world will follow its model remains to be seen.

D. MAKING POLICY FOR ELECTRONIC COMMERCE

In an effort to set the legal and policy framework for the development of electronic commerce, the U.S. government published in 1997 what has become known as the Magaziner Report. That Report sets out a series of areas in which government should—and should not—act to facilitate electronic commerce. We reprint an excerpt below.

≡ *Magaziner Report, A Framework for Global*
≡ *Electronic Commerce, Executive Summary*
≡ *(1997)*

. . . The paper presents five principles to guide government support for the evolution of electronic commerce and makes recommendations about nine key areas where international efforts are needed to preserve the Internet as a non-regulatory medium, one in which competition and consumer choice will shape the marketplace. With respect to these areas, the paper designates lead U.S. government agencies and recommends international fora for consideration of each issue.

Principles

1. The private sector should lead. The Internet should develop as a market driven arena not a regulated industry. Even where collective action is necessary, governments should encourage industry self-regulation and private sector leadership where possible.

2. Governments should avoid undue restrictions on electronic commerce. In general, parties should be able to enter into legitimate agreements to buy and sell products and services across the Internet with minimal government involvement or intervention. Governments should refrain from imposing new and unnecessary regulations, bureaucratic procedures or new taxes and tariffs on commercial activities that take place via the Internet.

3. Where governmental involvement is needed, its aim should be to support and enforce a predictable, minimalist, consistent and simple legal environment for commerce. Where government intervention is necessary, its role should be to ensure competition, protect intellectual property and privacy, prevent fraud, foster transparency, and facilitate dispute resolution, not to regulate.

4. Governments should recognize the unique qualities of the Internet. The genius and explosive success of the Internet can be attributed in part to its decentralized nature and to its tradition of bottom-up governance.

Accordingly, the regulatory frameworks established over the past 60 years for telecommunication, radio and television may not fit the Internet. Existing laws and regulations that may hinder electronic commerce should be reviewed and revised or eliminated to reflect the needs of the new electronic age.

5. Electronic commerce on the Internet should be facilitated on a global basis. The Internet is a global marketplace. The legal framework supporting commercial transactions should be consistent and predictable regardless of the jurisdiction in which a particular buyer and seller reside.

Recommendations

The principles described above guide the following recommendations:

1. Tariffs and Taxation. The Internet should be declared a tariff-free environment whenever it used to deliver products and services. The Internet is a truly global medium, and all nations will benefit from barrier-free trade across it.

No new taxes should be imposed on Internet commerce. Existing taxes that are applied to electronic commerce should be consistent across national and subnational jurisdictions and should be simple to understand and administer. State and local governments should cooperate to develop a uniform, simple approach to the taxation of electronic commerce, based on existing principles of taxation.

2. Electronic Payment Systems. The commercial and technological environment for electronic payments is changing rapidly, making it difficult to develop policy that is both timely and appropriate. For these reasons, inflexible and highly prescriptive regulations and rules are inappropriate and potentially harmful. In the near-term, case-by-case monitoring of electronic payment experiments is preferable to regulation.

3. Uniform Commercial Code for Electronic Commerce. In general, parties should be able to do business with each other on the Internet under the terms and conditions they agree upon. Private enterprise and free markets have typically flourished, however, where there are predictable and widely accepted legal principles supporting commercial transactions.

The U.S. supports the development of an international uniform commercial code to facilitate electronic commerce. Such a code should encourage governmental recognition of electronic contracts; encourage consistent international rules for acceptance of electronic signatures and other authentication procedures; promote the development of alternative dispute resolution mechanisms for international commercial transactions; set predictable ground rules for exposure to liability; and streamline the use of electronic registries.

4. Intellectual Property Protection. Commerce on the Internet will often involve the sale and licensing of intellectual property. To promote electronic commerce, sellers must know that their intellectual property will not be stolen and buyers must know that they are obtaining authentic products. Clear and effective copyright, patent, and trademark protection is therefore necessary to protect against piracy and fraud.

The recently negotiated World Intellectual Property Organization (WIPO) treaties for copyright protection should be ratified. Issues of liability for infringement, application of the fair use doctrine, and limitation of devices to defeat copyright protection mechanisms should be resolved in a balanced way, consistent with international obligations.

The government will study and seek public comment on the need to protect database elements that do not qualify for copyright protection and, if such protection is needed, how to construct it.

The Administration will promote global efforts to provide adequate and effective protection for patentable subject mater important to the development of the Global Information Infrastructure (GII), and establish standards for determining the validity of patent claims.

The Administration also will work globally to resolve conflicts that arise from different national treatments of trademarks as they relate to the Internet. It may be possible to create a contractually based self-regulatory regime that deals with potential conflicts between domain name usage and trademark laws on a global basis.

The Administration will review the system of allocating domain names in order to create a more competitive, market based system and will seek to foster bottom-up governance of the Internet in the process.

5. Privacy. It is essential to assure personal privacy in the networked environment if people are to feel comfortable doing business across this new medium.

Data gatherers should tell consumers what information they are collecting and how they intend to use it. Consumers should have meaningful choice with respect to the use and reuse of their personal information. Parents should be able to choose whether or not personal information is collected from their children. In addition, redress should be available to consumers who are harmed by improper use or disclosure of personal information or if decisions are based on inaccurate, outdated, incomplete or irrelevant personal information.

The Administration supports private sector efforts now underway to implement meaningful, user friendly, self-regulatory privacy regimes. These include mechanisms for facilitating awareness and the exercise of choice online, private sector adoption of and adherence to fair information practices, and dispute resolution. The government will work with industry and privacy advocates to develop appropriate solutions to privacy concerns that may not be fully addressed by industry through self-regulation and technology.

6. Security. The GII must be secure and reliable. If Internet users do not believe that their communications and data are safe from interception and modification, they are unlikely to use the Internet on a routine basis for commerce. The Administration, in partnership with industry, is taking steps to promote the development of a market driven public key infrastructure that will enable trust in encryption and provide the safeguards that users and society will need.

7. Telecommunications Infrastructure and Information Technology. Global electronic commerce depends upon a modern, seamless, global telecommunications network and upon the "information appliances" that connect to it. In too many countries, telecommunications policies are hindering the development of advanced digital networks. The United States will work internationally to remove barriers to competition, customer choice, lower prices, and improved services.

8. Content. The Administration encourages industry self-regulation, the adoption of competitive content rating systems, and the development of effective, user-friendly technology tools (e.g. filtering and blocking technologies) to empower parents, teachers, and others to block content that is inappropriate for children.

The government will seek agreements with our trading partners to eliminate overly burdensome content regulations that create non-tariff trade barriers.

9. Technical Standards. The marketplace, not governments, should determine technical standards and other mechanisms for interoperability on the Internet. Technology is moving rapidly and governments attempts to establish technical standards to govern the Internet would only risk inhibiting technological innovation. . . .

COMMENTS AND QUESTIONS

The Clinton Administration's framework is being updated regularly on its Web site, http://www.ecommerce.gov/. For discussion of counterpart proposals in Europe and Japan, see Francois Bar & Emily Murase, Charting Cyberspace: A U.S.-European-Japanese Blueprint for Electronic Commerce, *in* Transatlantic Trade Cooperation in Asia: Sectors, Issues, and Modalities (1998).

Note on International Harmonization
and Electronic Commerce

With its Framework for Global Electronic Commerce, the Clinton Administration has sought to set the agenda for Internet governance worldwide. The leading user of the Internet, the United States hopes to persuade the rest of the world to adopt the American legal and policy approach to ecommerce so that its rules will become the global norms. Although the European Union (EU) has championed initiatives on personal data protection and on the sui generis law to protect the contents of databases in the international arena, most countries have been in a reactive mode toward U.S. policy initiatives. With the U.S. digital economy growing at a rapid pace, there is a natural tendency among Americans to think that the rest of the world would benefit by adopting American legal and policy initiatives. It is fair for other countries to consider whether this in fact is so.

An obvious fact about the Internet is the global character of its reach. While it is unquestionably true that a great deal of trade is international, the physicality of tangible goods, such as automobiles, vacuum cleaners, and television sets, makes it easy to apply territory-based rules to them. United States law can easily be applied to a transaction based in the United States, but what law applies if unlawful information (e.g., pornography or copyright infringement) is uploaded to a computer in the United States but downloaded in Japan or Belgium? If two electronic agents, one representing a U.S. client and one representing a Japanese client, "meet" in cyberspace and exchange messages, and the U.S. electronic agent thinks a contract has been formed, whose law will determine which jurisdiction's law will be used to judge the validity and terms of the contract? It is readily apparent that laws may vary from nation to nation on such an issue. These variations may interfere with the growth of electronic commerce as well as other desired objectives. The question is: how can nations work together to find enough common ground on the private law of the Internet to promote ecommerce and other beneficial exchanges of information?[1]

Complete harmonization of laws may be desirable to promote Internet commerce, but harmonizing diverse legal rules can be a tediously slow process. Consider, for example, that almost a decade of meetings preceded the diplomatic conference at which the WIPO Copyright Treaty was concluded. An alternative to harmonization may be to form guidelines for countries to employ as they formulate the specifics of their own legal rules on a topic. The Organization for Economic Cooperation and Development (OECD) has been active in promoting this form of international cooperation. Guidelines may not lead to uniformity, however, in part because countries that endorse guidelines sometimes do not actually implement them. Guidelines may also be implemented in inconsistent ways. Yet even inconsistent implementations of rules based on guidelines may be better

---

1. For a discussion of the issues that arise in the international context, see Steven Hoffer, World Cyberspace Law (1999).

than the chaos of complete disharmony. Differences in national culture and legal traditions may make it difficult to attain consensus on the fine details of legal rules on an international basis. Nevertheless, international efforts, such as those undertaken by the United Nations Commission on International Trade Law (UNCITRAL), offer some promise for evolving harmonized rules to promote electronic commerce over the Internet.

Another way to achieve harmony on a global scale may be for one nation to propose legal rules that it urges all nations to adopt. This may be a faster path to harmonization than the laborious consensus process that typifies the treatymaking process. Both the United States and the EU have used this approach to international lawmaking for the Internet, in particular as to global electronic commerce. The U.S. White Paper on Intellectual Property and the National Information Infrastructure, for example, proposed digital copyright rules virtually identical to the treaty proposals the Administration submitted to WIPO at more or less the same time. The United States hoped for, and largely got, a "first mover" advantage by proposing these rules, for the draft treaty considered in 1996 in Geneva largely reflected the U.S. positions. The Clinton Administration's proposed rules became the baseline for discussion, even if they were ultimately transformed in the course of the U.S. legislative and international treatymaking process.

Despite the many initiatives to develop consensus on the law of the Internet, some dangers clearly lurk in the international arena. Some arise from the ability of major multinational firms to engage in what Professor Froomkin describes as "regulatory arbitrage," in which a firm plays some nations off against others as a way to get acceptance of rules that the multinational firm prefers. Also dangerous are potential races to the bottom (that is, contests over which nation will adopt the least restrictive rules and attract the most commercial activity as a result), or races to the top (who can adopt the toughest rules that will become a baseline for applying pressure to get international adoption by others?). Much as countries might like to take some time to think through what laws they think should be used to regulate the Internet, there is a sense of urgency about putting in place a legal and policy infrastructure to promote electronic commerce and other exchanges of information via the Internet. The fear is that those who wait too long will be left behind in the global information economy. Perhaps this fear can have constructive consequences in motivating countries to work together to achieve the minimum level of consensus needed for electronic commerce to flourish. Whether that will happen remains to be seen, however.

15

Internet Governance

The legal problems in regulating the Internet that we have discussed have led a number of commentators to suggest that existing law is ill-suited to solving the problems of Internet governance. Alternative proposals take a variety of forms, from suggesting that the Net be treated as its own jurisdiction to endorsing some sort of international governance structure. Whether the Internet really needs new governance models and what those models might be are disputed questions.

David R. Johnson & David G. Post, And How Shall the Net Be Governed? A Meditation on the Relative Virtues of Decentralized, Emergent Law
Coordinating the Internet 62 (Brian Kahin & James Keller eds., 1997)

Introduction

Now that lots of people use (and plan to use) the internet, many— governments, businesses, techies, users and system operators (the "sysops" who control ID issuance and the servers that hold files)—are asking how we will be able to

(1)   establish and enforce baseline rules of conduct that facilitate reliable communications and trustworthy commerce, and

(2)   define, punish and prevent wrongful actions that trash the electronic commons or impose harm on others.

In other words, how will Cyberspace be governed, and by what right?

By creating a new global, border-disregarding, place that cannot readily be controlled by any existing sovereign . . . the net weakens many of the institutions that we have come to rely on for a solution to the basic problems of collective action—the selection of means by which individuals coordinate and order their interactions so as to achieve what they believe is a greater good. Thus, the very nature and growing importance of the net calls for a fundamental re-examination of the institutional structure within which rulemaking—at least as applicable to the activities conducted solely on the net—takes place. As more fully discussed below, that re-examination might lead us to conclude that the net allows the problem of collective action to be solved by a new, decentralized process that does not closely resemble those we have used in the past to pass laws and enforce behavioral norms.

Questions about whether and how the net shall be governed are now arising most pointedly in connection with the issuance of domain names (like "ibm.com"). Domain names are translated by means of lookup tables distributed across the net into the IP addresses (like "123.45.67.89") that determine how messages are routed over the net. Because domain names are easier to remember than long strings of numbers, and because top level domains are often used in email addresses (like "fred@ibm.com"), they have become a particularly valuable form of "virtual real estate". Yet, despite their value and importance, it is far from clear who (if anyone) has the authority to determine who has the right to use any particular domain name (and on what terms and conditions they have that right), or to establish the basic structure of the domain name system—the combination of technical standards and trade practices pursuant to which domain names are registered and the associated lookup tables are distributed across the net.

As described in RFC 1591 (available at http://ds.internic.net/rfc/rfc1591.txt), the Internet Assigned Numbers Authority (IANA)

is responsible for the overall coordination and management of the Domain Name System (DNS), and especially the delegation of portions of the name space called top-level domains. Most of these top-level domains are two-letter country codes taken from the ISO standard 3166. A central Internet Registry (IR) has been selected and designated to handled the bulk of the day-to-day administration of the Domain Name System. Applications for new top-level domains (for example, country code domains) are handled by the IR with consultation with the IANA. The central IR is INTERNIC.NET. Second level domains in COM, EDU, ORG, NET, and GOV are registered by the Internet Registry at the InterNIC. . . . Currently, the RIPE NCC is the regional registry for Europe and the APNIC is the regional registry for the Asia-Pacific region, while the INTERNIC administers the North America region, and all the as yet undelegated regions.

Although both IANA and InterNIC (which has delegated the DNS administration to Network Solutions, Inc. (NSI), a private company) receive US government funds for their operation, no contract, constitution, or treaty gives either these bodies or the US Government the right to set policy regarding domain names on the global network. Nor do these bodies have any obviously valid claim to make the exclusive delegation of registration duties. The financial support provided by the US Government has not given it ownership of any intellectual property or physical asset essential (other than in the very short term) to the operation of a domain name system. To the contrary, domain name look up tables function because local hosts point their domain name servers at these tables; a form of custom, and not "law," dictates the particular root servers to which local hosts point for this information.

The current uncertainty regarding governance of the domain name system extends to much more than the technical standards governing domain name registration and selection of root servers. Basic economic and policy questions remain unanswered. At present, NSI (with NSF's blessing) demands payment for registration of domain names. But, again, no statute or international convention—nor even a universal acceptance of trade practice—clearly legitimizes NSI's right to charge that fee (or justifies any particular amount that might be charged). Nor is there any obvious source of guidance regarding what other conditions (such as a promise to abide by particular laws, to resolve disputes in a specified manner, or to waive certain claims) may be imposed as a prerequisite to domain name registration. Thus, no one can now say that any given condition must, may, or may not be imposed as a minimum requirement for this particular passport to "netizenship". Nor do any of the many different private and governmental organizations that are currently discussing a range of questions in this area —e.g., how many "top level domains" should be allowed, whether multiple registries should be allowed to compete, and what duties might reasonably be imposed on those who operate registries—have an uncontested or clearly legitimate claim to the authority to decide these matters unilaterally.

These questions are of crucial strategic importance, despite the uncertainty surrounding them, because only through an IP address and an association of that address with a findable reference, whether through a domain name or a directory, can an individual meaningfully enter Cyberspace in the first instance. An IP address block and a Domain Name are necessary to become a sysop offering access to the net. Domain name based email addresses are the essence of online identity for individual users. Dispensers of those virtual addresses thus stand at the border checkpoint between the virtual and the non-virtual world, and the contract pursuant to which one receives a domain name or other online ID can potentially serve as the means—perhaps the most effective means—by which the most basic rights and obligations of all Cyberspace participants can be specified.

Thus, although the current domain name policy debate appears to apply primarily to ministerial duties performed by a registry, for the purpose of avoiding duplicative names, the contracts entered into with such a registry (and any associated subsidiary contracts through which individual users contract with the domain name/address-holder to obtain access to the net) could prove of primary importance in determining both the degree of freedom and the level of order on the net.

Why Must the Net Be "Governed" at All?

Some may ask why the net must be "governed" at all? Even the three judge Federal court in Philadelphia that threw out the Communications Decency Act on First Amendment grounds seemed thrilled by the "chaotic" and seemingly ungovernable character of the net. And the net now prospers precisely because of its decentralized architecture and the absence of centralized rule-making authority. Everyone who can buy a computer and has access to the global telephone network is free to establish a node on the net. Everyone is free to create editorial value by pointing to others' creations. New users connect by agreement with any nearby node or by getting an email address from any commercial or non-commercial supplier. Lots of systems have lots of different rules governing the behavior of users, and users—at least in most countries—are free to leave any system whose rules they find oppressive. Some systems demand full identification from users; some allow or even encourage anonymity. Some impose editorial controls to create "kid friendly" or "lawyer friendly" environments; others act more like common carriers who accept all comers. Some require and enforce promises to abide by traditional copyright laws; others require all participants to waive claims that interfere with redistribution of the materials users post online. And, up until now, access by sysops to domain names and IP addresses that make it possible to settle new territory in Cyberspace has not been conditioned on any required promises to comply with (or to require users to comply with) specific laws or behavioral standards. That has, to be sure, left sysops free to impose their own rules on end users. But the diversity of differing venues on the net, and the ability of users to decide where to visit (and where not to visit) and with whom to communicate, has tended both to keep sysop tyranny in check and to limit the adverse impact of wrongdoing by individual users.

This decentralized decision-making has helped to make it possible for large numbers of people with different goals to get interconnected. But the problem of collective action remains and, indeed, grows more urgent as the net becomes larger and more complex. Anarchy, after all, has costs. It just won't do for packets, for example, to be systematically misrouted. People won't trust their important commercial and private dealings to a network where a domain name might be translated to a different IP address depending on where the message happens to originate. Nor, indeed, will large numbers of users visit online spaces if they encounter systematic fraud or vandalism or other activities they view as harmful or antisocial. There are activities that, when permitted even in only a few online venues, impose costs on all others, and against which individuals may want to protect themselves. Spamming is a form of wrongdoing that may be beyond the capacity (or desire) of a particular local sysop to control but that can make lots of users of lots of other systems miserable. The same could be said of launching destructive code. Some web pages may invade your privacy on contact. Some parts of the electronic forest path may even be conducive to highway robbery. As the global village transforms itself into a complex electronic city, crime cannot be far behind. If the natural result of decentralized activities on the net were the development of unpredictable technical environments and unsafe social spaces, then calls for top down, centralized forms of collective action would become louder and more persuasive. Thus, even with respect to activities that take place solely on the net, we face the questions whether and how to generate and enforce rules to control anti-social users and the sysops who tolerate them.

Moreover, the net can be used to facilitate communications among individuals whose online actions impose harm even on those who only frequent the nonvirtual world. Most real world communities will want to be assured that the net will not be used systematically to undercut their security. Online tax havens could harm the physical infrastructure of local communities that lose tax revenues. Online conspiracies to commit violence in the real world will surely draw a response from the potential victims. Accordingly, both users of the net and all of those affected by their actions will likely demand some form of "governance" or "order" that prevents wrongdoing. The key question now posed, in connection with the domain name system and derivatively with respect to every other aspect of online interaction, is whether that governance must take the traditional form of centralized, top down lawmaking or whether, instead, the nature of the net allows decentralized creation of another, very different, form of public order.

Competing Models

There are four basic competing models for the governance of the global net.

First, existing territorial sovereigns can simply seek to extend their jurisdiction, and to amend their laws as necessary, to attempt to govern all actions on the net that have substantial impacts on their own citizenry.

Second, sovereigns can enter into multi-lateral international agreements to establish new and uniform rules specifically applicable to conduct on the net.

Third, a new international organization can attempt to establish new rules—and new means of enforcing those rules and of holding those who make the rules accountable to appropriate constituencies.

Fourth, de facto rules may emerge as a result of the complex interplay of individual decisions by domain name and IP address registries (regarding what conditions to impose on possession of an online address), by sysops (regarding what local rules to adopt, what filters to install, what users to allow to sign on, and with which other systems to connect) and by users (regarding which personal filters to install and which systems to patronize).

We believe that, in part because of serious problems with the first three, traditional models, and in part because of the surprising ability of decentralized action to address serious problems that might previously have been thought to require "top down" centralized law making by a sovereign with a monopoly on the authorized use of force, the net may well be capable of being "governed" primarily by the fourth method—a mechanism that Tom Bell (following Hayek) calls "polycentric law" and that we will call "decentralized, emergent law." The decentralized, emergent form of collective action involves voluntary acceptance of standards (or, as the Internet Engineering Task Force motto would have it: "rough consensus and working code"). Despite the fears of those who cannot conceive of order as arising from anything other than top down, hierarchical control, this is not a process that necessarily leads to chaos and anarchy. To the contrary, the technical protocols of the net have in effect created a complex adaptive system that produces a type of order that does not rely on lawyers, court decisions, statutes, or votes. We will argue that the same decentralized decisionmaking that created the net at a technical level may be able to create a workable and, indeed, empowering and just form of order even at the highest level of the protocol stack—the realm of rules applicable to the collective social evaluation and governance of human behavior.

Because decentralized action may well be capable of generating responsible self-regulation of the net, those who propose other forms of collective action might be best advised to hold off any efforts to achieve top down control—lest they prematurely preempt the growth of what might be the most efficient and empowering form of net governance. Existing sovereigns need not waive their ultimate power to take action to protect the well-being of their citizens, of course. But they should sensibly defer action to see whether the collective actions of domain name registries, sysops and users produces a set of operational rules that provides reasonable protection for the vital interests they are charged to protect. If the net is allowed to develop a responsible self-regulatory structure, by means of decentralized, emergent law making, and if this new mechanism proves up to the task of building a productive and non-predatory order, then all concerned will have saved the large resources that might otherwise have been spent trying, perhaps without similar success, to impose rules from a centralized source. . . .

Can Net Policies and Rules Be Made and Enforced without Centralized Decision-Making?

We certainly do not mean to suggest that the governance models sketched out above will have, or that they should have, no impact on the net. Merely to suggest that there are "problems" with implementation of any or all of these models, is not to prove that they are inadequate for any of the tasks at hand; after all, proponents of representative democracy are fond of saying that while it is a terrible system, it's better than any known alternative. The fundamental question is whether, at least for the global electronic communications network, the fourth governance model of decentralized and emergent law-making might have significant advantages over the alternative models and should be looked at as the presumptively primary source of online order.

Consider what makes the net work. The net itself solves an immensely difficult collective action problem: how to get large numbers of individual computer networks, running diverse operating systems, to communicate with one another for the common good. And, yet, the net is really nothing more than a set of voluntary standards regarding message transmission, routing, and reception. There is not now and never was a central governmental body that decreed or voted to adopt a law stating that TCP/IP is required to be used by those wishing to communicate electronically on a global scale, or that HTTP is required to be used if you wish to communicate over a particular portion of the global network (the World Wide Web). If you connect to a neighboring host and send out packets of data that conform to the protocol, your messages can be heard by others who have adopted the protocol. All are free to decline to follow the standard and to obey some other protocol, and they will communicate only to those who, literally, speak their language. Many people and groups have, in fact, seceded (or declined to join) the global net, forming local area, or proprietary wide area, networks.

The "rule-making" process for baseline protocols of the net had none of the vices of centralized, top down, bureaucratic or political, governance. The rules instead evolved from the decentralized decisions by individuals to adopt a promising standard because it served their own interests. To be sure, the successful rules were created by individuals and small groups and they spread more quickly as a result of some government funded innovation and communications. But they did not stem from or rely in any way on the law of a geographically defined territory. They did not require any agreement among representatives of sovereign nations. And they did not require the creation of a new policy-making apparatus that required an international bureaucracy or that faced questions regarding the accountability of decisionmakers to particular constituencies. Minorities are protected by their right to propose inconsistent rules and, indeed, to follow those alternative rules if they believe the benefits of doing so outweigh the costs. Enforcement of a predominant rule set stems naturally from uncoordinated, decentralized decisions.

[Johnson and Post respond to a number of possible objections to their scheme and then suggest that some role remains for national law.]

Nevertheless, one might postulate some activities online that threaten most "real world" citizens and that are not even tolerated and protected by any geographic state. Imagine, for example, a host computer based in international waters, using wireless technology to broadcast messages that enable terrorist groups to make chemical weapons and coordinate an attack. In such a case, the small net "community" that patronized that online venue would be, in effect, at war with both the remainder of the online world and the authorities and citizens of the real world as well. Any scheme for responsible self-regulation of the net must deal, conceptually, with this kind of "hard case." The decentralized, emergent form of order deals with this kind of case by conceding that, at this extreme, the national sovereigns may exercise force to defend their interests—just as sysops and users may use their own electronic form of force (their prerogatives to banish users or to leave a particular system) to set boundaries on others' otherwise uncontrollable wrongdoing.

Because the net does have real impacts on the real world, it can best hope to preserve its decentralized, emergent character if it "renders unto Caesar what is Caesar's". If online commercial transactions radically undermine the tax system needed to build the physical infrastructure, territorial governments may be entitled to defend that core interest by shutting down host sites specially designed to facilitate such transactions. Perhaps the sysops who facilitate online transactions should anticipate this problem and create a centralized means for online commerce to pay a fair tax, to a single collector, as a means of discouraging more disruptive and potentially duplicative enforcement proceedings by local authorities. In the face of such responsible action by the net itself, local authorities would be more likely to recognize that they do not possess a writ that automatically runs to all areas of the net, and that they should not seek to set the rules governing online interactions that don't seriously negatively impact the tangible world they govern.

It bears remembering that the users of the net and the policy-setting inhabitants of the "real world" most affected by online activities are, to a first approximation, the same people. As a group, netizens will not want to support activities that threaten core values they share as citizens of the tangible world. There are lots of novel issues that arise from the ability of electronic messages to cross territorial borders—but those issues will be resolved in part by means of the ability of every user and system to filter out unwanted messages, and, in part, by means of the ability of such cross-border communications to bring the world into close agreement about core values. . . .

Domain Name Policy as a Key First Problem for Collective Action—Revisited

To determine whether the combination of decentralized decision-making and better communications between real world authorities and virtual communities could lead to a workable form of governance for the net, let's examine more closely the current core hard case: the policies governing creation of new top level domains. If there is any question on which there at first appears to be a need for strong centralized rule, it's the question of how domain names are issued and how they are translated into IP numbers. The Domain Name System determines where your data packets are sent. If two separate registries both issued a "right" to use "ibm.com", and mapped this domain name to different IP addresses, and if half of the net derived its DNS lookup tables from each of these two incompatible regimes, massive confusion would ensue. If different registries impose differing conditions on access to net real estate or online identity, then there will be no single definition of "netizenship"—and wrongdoers (by someone's definition) could seek out the most tolerant regimes. Because of their mnemonic character, certain domain names and domain name uses are already being challenged as infringing of trademark rights deemed vital by companies who sell branded products. And there are now or soon will be lots of other questions that implicate the potentially intense and conflicting interests of particular communities: Can a registry charge for the use of a domain name? How much? And what decision-making process governs the expenditure of the money? May "indecent" domain names be registered? Must those who use domain names agree to resolve their disputes by arbitration? Agree to abide by copyright laws? Issue email addresses only to identifiable users? The domain name system thus already poses stark questions regarding the relationship between any self-regulatory system for the net and the powers of existing legislatures and courts.

There is reason to believe that even these challenging and contentious issues can be resolved by decentralized, emergent decision-making. For example, even the apparently fatal conflict between inconsistent domain name registration systems seems likely to be avoided without top down controls. Most users and sysops are interested in accurate routing of messages. They will want to connect to the DNS sources that most other people use. The confusing dual and inconsistent system hypothesized above is unstable (or, rather, could never arise in the first place) because the most widely used of the two systems would soon attract virtually all of the traffic (or all of the connections from downstream systems). Thus, the successful deployment of two incompatible versions of a top level domain, or two widely distributed yet incompatible sets of lookup tables, is about as likely as the simultaneous growth in one country of two languages that have the same words mapped onto different meanings. Because people look to reliable sources for their information, good data drive out bad. Network economies, and the creation of order from positive returns to information structure, save the day. Thus, while it is physically possible and currently lawful for system operators to create a mess by pointing their domain name resolving software at multiple incompatible sources, that nightmare scenario probably won't occur and need not be prohibited by legislation of any kind.

Similarly, there is good reason to believe that some combination of domain name registries and domain name holders will impose rules, in connection with issuance of access to the net, that reflect widespread agreement regarding what constitutes wrongful action. And there is reason to think that the actions of users in selecting the online venues they visit and support will in general keep such regulation from becoming either too oppressive or too lax. The online public will band together to electronically shun tyrants and detectable crooks. (We may need to worry more about due process, to protect unpopular minorities from mobs, than law enforcement.) Dens of thieves—and packets of data sent from known dens of thieves—can generally be avoided online. If your concern is privacy, you can avoid web sites that don't post verifiable tokens indicating that they observe rules that you deem satisfactory. If you don't want certain sites to link to your web page, you can use software code to preclude such links. No matter what your policy goal, acting through the filtering power of sysops and users is much more likely to produce rapid and effective results than lobbying for the enactment of some rule by a new transnational legislative body.

To be sure, no decentralized, emergent lawmaking scheme of this kind could be 100% effective. But substantial consensus is, operationally and practically, quite important even when total compliance cannot be achieved (as, by the way, is always the case, even under centralized law enforcement regimes run by non-democratic sovereigns). The reason is, again, that screening applicants for IDs and filtering out known sources of wrongful messages reduces the impact of wrongdoing even when it does not put the wrongdoer totally out of business. Trademark infringement tolerated on web pages in a small corner of the net, and filtered out by most responsible sysops once they are on notice of the problem, simply cannot cause very much confusion.

In contrast, efforts to use traditional top down, centralized lawmaking to solve the problems posed by the domain name system seem very likely to fail in more brittle ways. Take the question whether the establishment of alternative top level domains should be allowed. In the context of decentralized, emergent law, this question is decided in the marketplace—by multiple independent decisions whether to register with a new purported provider of a ".biz" domain or whether to point a local domain name server at another root lookup table. If, in contrast, the US were to purport to exercise its powers to prohibit the establishment of alternative top level domains, it would simply fail to attain jurisdiction over the actions of some host provider operating entirely outside the US. Perhaps the US could effectively prohibit all US hosts from pointing their local domain name servers at that remote root table, but the First Amendment might constrain such restrictions, which in any event would look silly if they contrasted with practices in other countries and the desires of the US market. If the US instead sought to negotiate a new treaty agreement governing the establishment of new top level domains, it would likely still be defining the shape of the bargaining table while the issue was decided, de facto, by engineering decisions. If it sought to delegate decisions on top level domain structure to a new international organization, it would face unanswerable questions about how to compel compliance with that organization's decisions by private actors. And even if most countries agreed to defer to and enforce the decisions of such an organization, there would be a serious question how to assure that its decisions reflected the needs and preferences of all participants in net based commerce. The best indicator of those needs and preferences would be the independent actions by sysops and users to accept a new standard. Traditional law making processes become, in the context, a counterproductive extra loop that at most delays or misdirects decisions otherwise likely to evolve rapidly from a decentralized process. . . .

COMMENTS AND QUESTIONS

1. Is it in fact difficult or impossible to apply existing law to the Internet? Has the development of case law since this article was written (in 1996) offered any more evidence about how well existing law and existing legal systems can handle the challenges posed by the Internet?

Johnson and Post develop their ideas in a number of other articles with similar themes. David Johnson & David Post, Chaos Prevailing on Every Continent: A New Theory of Decentralized Decision-Making in Complex Systems, 73 Chi.-Kent L. Rev. 1055 (1999); David R. Johnson & David Post, Law and Borders—The Rise of Law in Cyberspace, 48 Stan. L. Rev. 1367 (1996); David G. Post, Governing Cyberspace, 43 Wayne L. Rev. 155 (1996); David G. Post, Anarchy, State and the Internet: An Essay on Law-Making in Cyberspace, 1995 J. Online L. art. 3.

For challenges to the Johnson and Post methodology, see Jack Goldsmith, Against Cyberanarchy, 65 U. Chi. L. Rev. 1199 (1998); Jack Goldsmith, Regulation of the Internet: Three Persistent Fallacies, 73 Chi.-Kent L. Rev. 1119 (1999); Neil Weinstock Netanel, Cyberspace Self-Governance; A Skeptical View From Democratic Theory, 89 Cal. L. Rev. (forthcoming 2000). For other takes on how the Internet challenges traditional theories of governance, see, e.g., James Boyle, Foucault in Cyberspace: Surveillance, Sovereignty, and Hard-Wired Censors, 66 U. Cin. L. Rev. 177 (1997); Dan L. Burk, The Market for Digital Piracy, *in* Borders in Cyberspace 205 (Brian Kahin & Charles Nesson eds., 1998); Dan L. Burk, Virtual Exit in the Global Information Economy, 73 Chi.-Kent L. Rev. 943 (1999); A. Michael Froomkin, The Internet as a Source of Regulatory Arbitrage, *in* Borders in Cyberspace 129 (Brian Kahin & Charles Nesson eds., 1998).

2. Internet governance can't be decided only by focusing on the defects of the current system, of course. One must also propose a superior alternative. Does the Johnson/Post model of private ordering work for the Internet? How will it deal with conduct online that has effects offline? With nonconsensual torts online?

One way to explore the limits of the Johnson/Post model is to use the example they chose—the domain name system—as a case study for Internet governance. Johnson and Post suggest that no one need govern the domain name system, because strong network effects mean that everyone will soon coalesce around the same registry. But one might reasonably wonder what would happen to those stranded in the losing registry, and what constrains the power of a single (presumably private) registry once it has been established as an Internet standard. For a very different account of the structure of the domain name system, see the following excerpt adapted from Mark A. Lemley & David McGowan, Legal Implications of Network Economic Effects, 86 Cal. L. Rev. 479 (1998):

> The Internet, like the telephone network, exhibits a strong form of network effects—the network *is* the product in a very real sense. Given the parallels between the two, one might expect the Internet to exhibit the same market structure as the telephone network. But it does not. The Internet looks nothing like the old Bell System, with a single regulated corporation in charge of all the connections. In fact, it doesn't even look like the new, streamlined model of telephone competition, in which various large network owners will be forced to interconnect on government-set (and government-enforced) terms. Rather, the Internet appears (at least at first glance) to be an example of working anarchy—it consists of millions of different entities around the globe, public and private, which connect together in a patchwork network of uncertain provenance.
>
> How can this be? The answer is twofold. First, the Internet is not composed entirely of its own set of lines connecting one Internet user to the next, though some Internet specific "backbone" wires do exist. Rather, the Internet piggybacks on existing communications technology, notably the wire telephone network, using available space to send distributed packets of information from place to place. As a result, no one can fairly be said to have "built" the Internet in the physical sense, though of course a number of people built early pieces of it, and United States government agencies such as the National Science Foundation and the Defense Advanced Research Projects Agency contributed parts of the network backbone.
>
> Second, and more important, the Internet itself is nothing more than a relatively simple set of computer protocols (commonly called TCP/IP today) governing the interchange of data. In other words, what we think of as "the Internet" is really only a published, nonproprietary interface standard. Anyone who uses the standard to transmit data from their computer is "on" the Internet; anyone who doesn't use the standard is not. The success of the Internet is due largely to its spectacularly successful interoperability. It did not drive out its competitors in the "computer networking" market so much as subsume them. In the mid-1980s, one could participate in computer networking by joining one of approximately 50,000 bulletin board systems (or BBS's), or one of the fledgling online service providers like Prodigy or Compuserve, or (depending on where one worked) one of the private networks of military or academic computers. Each of these computer networks was largely incompatible with the others, with the result that joining a bulletin board let you communicate only with other members of that bulletin board. Interconnection protocols beginning with Usenet and SMTP allowed messages to be transferred

between different groups of networked computers. As the communications technology between networks became more seamless, people began to think of themselves as on the Internet itself, rather than connected to a private computer networking group which could itself exchange data with other private groups. From a perspective of network economic effects, the Internet is a tremendous success story because it allows different and often incompatible computer systems to communicate with each other, expanding the size of the network without requiring purchase from the standards owner.

Things are not quite as simple as this, however. TCP/IP does not do everything automatically and without supervision, any more than do the stock exchanges, often cited as the most efficient of "unregulated" markets. Rather, there are a wide variety of rulemaking groups that enforce standards on the Internet. For example, technical standards (including updates or changes to the TCP/IP protocol) are set by the Internet Engineering Task Force (IETF), itself a voluntary body with no "official" authority over the Internet beyond the willingness of Internet users to adopt the changes it proposes. Further "rules" are created by the code written both into the Internet protocols and that written into privately owned programs like Netscape Navigator, Microsoft Internet Explorer, and Sun's Java that operate on the Internet.

For our purposes, though, the best example of the role of network effects in Internet governance has to do with domain names. InterNIC (and the private company Network Solutions, Inc.) set rules for addressing, mapping the "domain names" commonly used to identify people on the Net to the numeric IP address that is actually registered to a particular server. For addressing to work, someone must maintain a list of valid IP addresses and their aliases, and everyone on the Internet must work from that list, so that a user who types in "www.ibm.com" will find the computer identified with that alias. Network Solutions (NSI) has performed this function for several years now with respect to certain of the international top level domains, or iTLDs, like ".com". The list of names and matching IP addresses are entered into a series of "root domain name servers" or DNSs. The servers are themselves updated regularly. If your name is on the list, you can be found on the Internet. If not, anyone who types that name into their browser or mail program will not be able to reach you.

Obviously, therefore, the DNS servers are central to the functioning of the Internet. And if you want your name to have a DNS entry, the only obvious way to get it is to request that NSI put it there. But NSI is a private entity; it is not at all clear what authority they have to "run" the Internet, or indeed who might be able to give them that authority. NSI took over operation of the domain name registration system based on a contract from the U.S. National Science Foundation. That contract will expire in 1998; NSF has already indicated that they do not intend to renew it.

So what happens to the DNS servers? Consider several possible outcomes. First, NSI may decide to keep administering the DNS system, and the courts may decide it has a right to do so. If this occurs, control over the network will effectively have been placed in the hands of a single private entity, which will become the *de facto* standard-setter. In theory, NSI could be displaced from this position by market competition—someone else could set up a competing, incompatible domain name server, and if enough users of the Internet (and therefore of the NSI DNS system) switched to this incompatible system, the owners of the new server would become the new market leader. In practice, network effects make this unlikely, because a "competing Internet" that few people are using will not be attractive to those already on the current Internet. Indeed, some halting efforts toward such an alternate DNS system have so far been unsuccessful. While NSI's control over DNS might also be displaced by hacking, any such unauthorized access to the DNS servers is likely to be illegal.

A second possibility is that NSI will get to keep its control over DNS, but that some legal constraint will be imposed on its discretion in running the DNS system. There have been suggestions that the government should play a fundamental role in compelling access to NSI's domain name servers. Indeed, litigation on this issue has already begun. In a complaint filed in March of 1997 against NSI, a company called PGP Media alleged that NSI's failure to incorporate PGP-registered domains violated the antitrust laws. The claim is that NSI's configuration file "is the central (and essential) technical bottleneck facility for the Domain Name Registration Market," and the plaintiffs seek "extremely limited and narrowly tailored injunctive relief to compel NSI to add reference in the Configuration File on the NSI Root Nameservers so that PGP may compete with NSI in the Domain Name Registration Market for Domain Name registrations." The fact that this claim was even filed pays tribute to the growing confusion over precisely who should have authority to "issue" domain names.

Finally, the government could decide to remove NSI's control over domain name registration entirely, replacing it either with a de novo open system of private registration, or even a system of government registration. In February 1997, the International Ad Hoc Committee (IAHC), a nongovernmental Internet advisory group set up to study the issue, recommended the creation of seven new "generic top-level domains (gTLDs)," to be administered on a global basis by "multiple competing registrars" overseen by a (private) Council of Registrars and a (private) DNS Policy Oversight Committee. The international nature of this approach is an important indication that one cannot merely say "the government" will establish a new policy. While the IAHC report was prepared under the informal auspices of the World Intellectual Property Organization, and the "Memorandum of Understanding" it establishes is deposited with the International Telecommunications Union, there is no governmental or international legal authority behind the proposal, a fact which has upset both the United States and the European Union. Indeed, the Memorandum of Understanding declares that it is agreed to by "The Internet Community," an ethereal entity if ever there was one. NSI probably has no enforceable legal obligation to comply with a dictate from such a body, though of course the body's rules might well end up being incorporated into national or international law. Alternatively, whatever private group claims authority over Internet domain names is undoubtedly subject to existing national laws, at least if the country applying those laws has jurisdiction.

This last alternative seems to have prevailed. The United States, after writing a competing report, merged its proposal with the IAHC's in 1998. Under this revised proposal, administration of the domain name *registry*, and coordination with competing domain name *registrars*, will be managed by a non-profit corporation called ICANN, to be governed by members chosen from a variety of groups interested in the process. While neither the structure of ICANN nor the domain name rules it will create were clear at this writing, it seems likely that the new domain name system will include multiple gTLDs, and that numerous registrars will be licensed to register domain names within these gTLDs (though all the names will be kept in a single registry, under the control of ICANN).

From an economic perspective, there is clearly value to be had in a shared rather than monopolistic top-level domain system. Internet domain names are valuable things; one generic domain name was recently sold for over $100,000. NSI currently charges only [$35] per year per domain name, up from $0 a few years ago. But an NSI freed of governmental constraints on its pricing policy probably has significant power to raise the price of domain names, either across the board or by price discriminating. Competition among domain name registrars would constrain such power, particularly if (as the IAHC report recommends) competing registrars could register names within a single TLD. If IBM can choose to obtain rights to "ibm.com" from either NSI or from a competitor such as PGP, it will be able to shop effectively for the lowest registration price, and price should approach marginal cost.[344]

On the other hand, administering such a competitive system will be more difficult than running the current system. Someone must control access to the DNS root servers; either one of the registrars must be trusted to give nondiscriminatory access to the servers, or some governmental body will have to police interconnections, as is done in the telephone industry. Some provision will also have to be made for preventing conflicting registrations, and the interaction between trademark law and domain name registrations will become more complex. These functions don't necessarily have to be carried out by a government—government regulation of Internet traffic in any form makes a lot of people nervous and would also subject the administrator to constitutional restraints in the US that do not now exist—but they will have to be accomplished somehow if domain name registration is to be competitive rather than proprietary. The existing system—one based on consensus—appears unlikely to survive very long.

3. Since these articles were written, the debate over governance of the domain name system has shifted focus to ICANN—the non-profit corporation organized at the behest of both the "Internet community" and the U.S. government to oversee the transition to competition in the provision of domain names. ICANN has come in for a great deal of public criticism, both for the secrecy of its decision-making processes and for its substantive decision to require alternative dispute resolution in trademark cases. Michael Froomkin, who has participated in this process, wrote about its shortcomings in Of Governments and Governance, 14 Berkeley Tech. L.J. 617 (1999):

The WIPO domain name system/trademark ("DNS/TM") process in which I have been an "Expert" participant is worse still, because the results will never have to be presented to a legislature. WIPO is a body formally composed of its

---

344. By contrast, a competing top-level domain which cannot register ".com" domains might find itself handicapped by the convenience effect of the widespread use of the .com TLD. IBM may be less likely to switch to a competing domain name registrant if the TLD they use is an unfamiliar one, since part of the value of having a name like "ibm.com" is that those who want to visit the site for the first time can easily guess the name.

member states, but blessed with an energetic, intelligent, and surprisingly well-financed Secretariat. In part at the request of the U.S. government, WIPO took on the task of crafting recommendations relating to intellectual property concerns caused by the increasing use of domain names as a marketing tool. The recommendations will be passed on to the fledgling Internet Corporation for Assigned Names and Numbers ("ICANN"), a private not-for-profit California corporation charged by the U.S. government with taking over key coordination functions for the technical management of the Internet. ICANN is not formally obligated to accept WIPO's recommendations, but there is likely to be considerable political pressure for it to take some or all of them, and ICANN currently is not formally accountable to anyone.

There is no denying that the DNS/TM problem is complex. It involves conflicts caused by trying to map a trademark system that is both geographic and sectoral onto a domain name space that is world-wide and has only one .com. In addition, there are conflicts between trademark owners and those with other legitimate interests in a domain name—interests that range from nicknames and surnames to criticism and parody. In addition, there are conflicts caused by speculative behavior and hoarding (sometimes termed "cyber-squatting" or "cyberpiracy"), or outright attempts to deceive by passing off one site as associated with another's brand.

WIPO responded to this challenge by proposing that ICANN use its (arguable) leverage over the bodies that will control the databases of mappings between Internet domain names and IP numbers to impose a series of contractual duties on all users of those databases. Details aside, the key point is that WIPO proposed a series of contracts of adhesion that would result in every registrant in .com, .net, or .org having to agree to a loser-pays arbitration under substantive rules that likely would differ from the laws applied by a competent court. No treaty or legislation would be required. As the arbitrators would be instructed to supplement applicable national law with certain "principles" identified by WIPO, some results likely would differ from what a court would do. At this writing, the final report has not been written, and there remains at least some hope that it will be much changed from an Interim Report that I believe is biased in favor of intellectual property rights holders.

The WIPO process represents an innovative experiment in negotiation between a United Nations body and the private sector. Once having authorized the initial process, the member states have been conspicuous by their absence, at least as a formal matter, except as commentators in response to the various "requests for comments" authored by the Secretariat staff. Regardless of the merits of the WIPO proposals, there can be little debate that the public participation in the process has been dominated by intellectual property rights holders and their lawyers and trade associations. Similarly, the Secretariat staff appear to be very sincerely committed to WIPO's mission of the promotion of intellectual property rights—so much so that to even think about "capture" almost seems besides the point.

The WIPO DNS/TM process has certainly been public in a formal sense, with a series of meetings around the world, and web pages displaying documents and public comments. But public participation has been low for a number of reasons, including poor publicity outside the intellectual property community, and especially the competition for the attention of the relatively small number of people focused on the issue of Internet governance. Most of them understandably have focused on decisions relating to the structure of

ICANN rather than on a merely advisory report, even one likely to be influential. Turnout at the public hearings I have attended has been small—usually under 100 and sometimes about 50, and (with the exception of the Washington D.C. event that followed a publicity campaign I organized) comprised almost entirely of trademark lawyers or Internet service providers. There have also been over 150 e-mailed comments.

The dearth of consumer representatives, public interest groups, and citizens groups participating in the WIPO process should serve to remind us all of the many reasons why we entrust major aspects of social policy making to elected officials. Legislatures and national executives are not paragons of rectitude. But when they are elected, the same political process that may make them over-solicitous to those bearing campaign contributions imposes some form of accountability to the public at large. Equally important, presentation of a matter to an elected official is a way of putting a question onto the public agenda. WIPO has a very nice set of web pages that lay out the issues at stake in the DNS/TM process and lay out the schedule for its public meetings in various world capitals. There is no particular reason, however, to assume that anyone is necessarily going to know that those web pages are there, or would necessarily visit them. In contrast, a hearing in front of a subcommittee, a vote by a house of Congress, or even a publication of a proposed rule in the federal register by an unelected bureaucrat, would serve to put the public (in one country) on notice in a tolerably effective way—at least in a routine and knowable way—of the rules that someone proposes to lay down upon them.

Indeed, it is not obvious that all the relevant portions of governments understood what was going on. WIPO sent notices of its proposals to every one of its member states, but one suspects from the responses received that these were directed at the patent and trademark offices with which WIPO ordinarily corresponds. Whether these notices were then circulated to other departments is hard to ascertain. . . .

The same social process that is making U.S. cryptography policy increasingly irrelevant internationally suggests that top-down regulations of the type proposed in the Magaziner Report may become irrelevant too. If that scenario is at all real, it may be one more reason to balk at processes that do not have a democratic pedigree. If the private sector is poised to lead from the bottom up, perhaps we should celebrate that, not stomp on it, even (especially) if the redistributive effects of this evolution disadvantage large, established parts of the corporate sector at the expense of small companies arising in the new web-based economy. But it is one thing to celebrate market-driven outcomes (corrected for market failures), and to value market-making technical standardization. It is quite another thing to tolerate private sector leadership when it clothes itself in the guise of "bottom-up rulemaking" but actually seeks to use government or government-like power to lock in advantages enjoyed by established firms, often at the expense of consumers or new competitors.

The real challenge comes in telling legitimate processes apart from the others. True "bottom-up" outcomes are entitled to respect. Not every privatized rulemaking procedure carries the same legitimacy, however. The WIPO process in which I participated involved limited consultation, and opaque decision-making as the reports and recommendations were all written by the Secretariat staff in secret. It featured what appeared from my admittedly partisan perspective to be disproportionate input by trademark holders (as opposed to actual and would-be domain name holders without trademarks), especially in the period before I began to kick up a fuss. Rather than be presented to one or more legislatures for ratification, the result will be presented to ICANN, a private non-profit corporation, and if accepted by ICANN will be imposed contractually on all registrants in global top-level domains. This contrasts with the adoption of a technical standard which, at least until the network effects kick in, attracts adherence without the need for any form of external pressure or coercion.

The WIPO process also contrasts with democratic processes. Democratic societies, and especially the U.S., have evolved elaborate techniques for giving notice of upcoming decisions, and making it possible to spot capture in the lawmaking process. Various countervailing advocacy and special interest groups monitor the legislative process seeking to represent the interests of the public or segments of it. Relative to the size of the need, the equivalent public sector is much more attenuated at the international level, and monitoring is in any event much more difficult as institutions are less transparent and much more diverse and spread over the world. As a result, even active citizens and legislators are less able to weigh the results of internationalized rulemaking processes, not least because they cannot have confidence that if the process was seriously deficient someone would blow the whistle. Even the existence of a self-proclaimed whistle-blower is not enough: there is no particular reason to believe that the people claiming a substantive or procedural flaw have a way of getting the attention of relevant auditors, nor for thinking that the auditors have any way of judging the credibility of the source even if they happen to hear the communication.

The difference between the governance procedures endorsed by the Magaziner Report, of which the WIPO process is but one example, and true bottom-up rulemaking can be analogized to the difference between a proprietary standard and Open Source software. Like a manufacturer choosing a proprietary standard, in the WIPO process a single body makes decisions, in relative privacy, after soliciting the degree of input it feels is appropriate. The outcome of the process ought then to be launched on the marketplace of ideas. Instead, the proprietary legal standard threatens to become dominant in its category because ICANN will present consumers with a fait accompli. In its Interim Report, WIPO proposes that ICANN impose WIPO's ideas on registries, who would in turn impose them on registrars who would in turn be required to impose them on domain name registrants. This is more lock-in than is allowed in product markets; even Microsoft's efforts to lock in a large market share by making Windows the required default option on all personal computers sold by a given manufacturer could be reversed by the consumer. It also contrasts with the propagation of open source software, which can freely be copied or modified by anyone so long as the source is open and it is licensed for free. The terms of the open source license are imposed on subsequent designers who choose to incorporate or user of the code, but the decision whether to use the code is left to them.

Undoubtedly it was not the intention of the Magaziner Report to endorse proprietary private lawmaking. We accept proprietary legal solutions when they emanate from a legislature, whatever the source of the original draft. Legal solutions pioneered by judges we often dub "common law" and count on competition between states to produce the best, or a range of acceptable solutions. Other models still must prove themselves.

What does Froomkin's article suggest about Internet governance? Is there any way to create a private body that is representative of the Internet, has legitimacy, and can make decisions in an efficient manner? Or is Froomkin correct that we may fall back in the final analysis on law as the ultimate arbiter of Internet rules?

4. A different strand of legal thought on the Internet has focused not on the choice between existing law and Internet self-determination, but on things outside of law that constrain human behavior online. In particular, an important and growing body of legal scholarship has focused attention on the role of "code" in setting quasi-legal rules on the Net. See, e.g., Lawrence Lessig, Code and Other Laws of Cyberspace (2000); Lawrence Lessig, Reading the Constitution in Cyberspace, 45 Emory L.J. 869 (1996); Lawrence Lessig, Intellectual Property and Code, 11 St. John's J. Legal Commentary 635 (1996); Lawrence Lessig, The Constitution of Code: Limitations on Choice-Based Critiques of Cyberspace Regulation, 5 CommLaw Conspectus 181 (1997); David Post, Bargaining in the Shadow of the Code: File Caching, Copyright, and Contracts Evolving in Cyberspace (working paper 1997); Joel R. Reidenberg, Governing Networks and Rule-Making in Cyberspace, 45 Emory L.J. 911 (1996); Joel R. Reidenberg, Lex Informatica: The Formulation of Information Policy Rules Through Technology, 76 Tex. L. Rev. 553 (1998).

The basic idea here is that the way the architecture of the Internet is constructed both enables and constrains behavior. Because the Internet does not require identification of a person or a location, for example, anonymity and geographical indeterminacy are possible in Internet space. By contrast, if a particular rule or behavior is built into the system, it may foreclose people from certain actions even if the law would otherwise permit them. If the Internet Protocol were set to bar framing another party's Web page, for example, the copyright cases on framing simply wouldn't arise, whether or not framing would be legal under copyright law.

For a concrete example of "code-based regulation," see the Digital Telephony Act of 1994, Pub. L. No. 103-414, 108 Stat. 4279; see also Susan Freiwald, Uncertain Privacy: Communication Attributes After the Digital Telephony Act, 69 S. Cal. L. Rev. 949 (1996). The Digital Telephony Act required telephone companies to modify their network architecture to enable access by law enforcement to the communications of private parties.

5. As Lessig's book notes, law and code are not all that constrain behavior in cyberspace. Behavior is also a function of the market (what I can do is limited by what I can afford), and of social norms, or netiquette. There is significant literature on the sociology of online behavior, and some attention has been given to informal social sanctions like "flaming" that are used to punish or reward behavior. For a skeptical discussion of Internet norms in the legal context, see Mark A. Lemley, The Law and Economics of Internet Norms, 73 Chi.-Kent L. Rev. 1257 (1999). For a discussion of

what constitutes "private" ordering in cyberspace, see Margaret Jane Radin & R. Polk Wagner, The Myth of Private Ordering: Rediscovering Legal Realism in Cyberspace, 73 Chi.-Kent L. Rev. 1295 (1999).

Glossary

For more definitions, the authors of this textbook recommend PHILLIP E. MARGOLIS, COMPUTER & INTERNET DICTIONARY (Random House Webster's 1999).

Algorithm   A procedure for solving a given type of mathematical problem. Most computer programs employ algorithms to calculate the appropriate response to a user request or to locate and manipulate data in memory.

Analog   A method of representing information in a continuous and linear format. For example, the hands of a clock represent the time by moving concentrically instead of as a discrete numeric sum, as a **digital** watch would.

Application Program   A computer program primarily designed for **end users** and made to run on top of an **operating system**. Typical applications include word processors, spreadsheets, database programs, communication programs, and web browsers.

Application Programming Interface (API)   A set of **routines, protocols**, and tools for building software **applications** in order to ensure their compatibility with specific **operating systems** or other **applications**.

Architecture   The overall structure and function of a hardware or software computer system, usually defined by the minimum **standards** a component must meet in order to achieve compatibility with the system.

Arithmetic Logic Unit (ALU)   One of the two main components of the **CPU**, primarily responsible for performing arithmetic and logical operations.

ARPA   The U.S. Defense Department's Advanced Research Project Agency. ARPA was the organization responsible for originally creating the **Internet**.

Backward-compatible   Compatible with earlier models or versions of the same product. Often a key feature for new computers or programs necessary in order to retain user loyalty and perpetuate **network effects**.

Bandwagon Standardization   A process of **standardization** whereby subsequent entrants to the market adopt the standard of an existing firm.

Bandwidth   The amount of data that can be transmitted from one device to another over a given amount of time. For digital devices, bandwidth is usually measured in bits per second (bps) or bytes per second. For analog devices, bandwidth is usually measured in cycles per second, or Hertz (Hz). Bandwidth is the most common way to gauge the speed of a system's **Internet** access.

BBS (Bulletin Board System)   A computer-based message center which allows users to access it remotely and to post text messages for others to read either chronologically and by subject matter.

Berne Convention   An international convention setting minimum standards for copyright protection.

Binary Code   A code based on two unique digits (usually 1s and 0s) used by computers to store data and implement instructions.

BIOS (Basic Input/Output System)   A set of essential software routines that test hardware at startup, start the **operating system**, and support transfer of data among hardware devices. BIOS is typically stored in **ROM**.

Black Box Analysis   A process of **reverse engineering** whereby the analyst tests the software by feeding it instructions or commands and recording the results. While this process does not reveal the actual code of the program, it can often uncover the logical structure of the program.

C++   One of the most popular modern programming languages.

Caching   The process of storing information from an external source (e.g., a disk, the Internet, etc.) in a computer's memory so that it can be accessed repeatedly at a faster pace by the **CPU**.

CDA (Communications Decency Act)   A law passed by Congress in 1996 which attempted, among other things, to protect minors from "indecent" and "patently offensive" communications over the **Internet**. A majority of the content restrictions were subsequently invalidated by the Supreme Court in 1997. The CDA also included provisions which explicitly exempted **OSPs** from liability for online defamation.

Central Processing Unit (CPU)   The main component of a computer system responsible for performing calculations and instructing the system on how to function. A CPU typically consists of (1) an arithmetic logic unit (**ALU**), which performs arithmetic and logical operations and (2) the **control unit**, which gathers instructions from memory and decodes and executes them.

Child Pornography Prevention Act (CPPA)   A law passed by Congress in 1996 to attack the rise of computerized or "virtual" child pornography.

Click-wrap Licenses   Similar to **shrinkwrap licenses**, these licenses often appear during the installation of a program or at the entrance to a web page, requiring the user to click on a button (and thus manifest assent to the license) in order to proceed with use of the program or site.

Compilation   The process of converting **source code** to **object code**. Decompilation converts **object code** back to **source code**.

Computer-Human Interaction (CHI)   An interdisciplinary field combining education, graphic art, industrial design, industrial management, computer science, mechanical engineering, psychology, artificial intelligence, linguistics, information science and sociology to understand how human beings process information so that products can better be designed to enhance useability.

Control Unit   One of the two main components of the **CPU**. The control unit is primarily responsible for gathering instructions from memory and decoding and executing them.

CONTU (Commission on New Technological Uses of Copyright)   A national commission formed by Congress in the late 1970s to recommend the proper application of copyright law to new technologies.

COPA (Child Online Protection Act)   Congress' second attempt to limit the access of minors to offensive content on the **Internet** after major provisions of the **CDA** were struck down by the Supreme Court.

COPPA (Children's Online Privacy Protection Act)   A law passed by Congress requiring website owners to get permission from parents before gathering information from children under the age of 13.

Copyleft   Coined by Richard Stallman of the Free Software Foundation, copyleft licenses are a form of **Open Source License** where all licensees are required to promise not to incorporate the software in a commercial product and to pass it on, even if embedded in a large program, to others free of use restrictions.

Cyberspace   A metaphor for the nonphysical realm created by computer systems. Generally used to refer to the "place" where online interactions and communications occur.

Cybersquatter   An individual who registers a **domain name** in order to deprive the trademark owner of it, or in order to sell it, or confuse customers.

Data Structure   In programming, a scheme used to organize related pieces of information. Examples include data organized as a set of files, lists, arrays, records, trees, or tables.

Database   A collection of information organized so that a computer program can quickly search, retrieve, and sort the data for display.

De Facto Standard   A standard adopted by a majority of users without any effort at coordination from industry groups or the government.

Decryption   The process of translating **encrypted** data into readable data, often utilizing complex **algorithms**.

Digital   A method of representing information as a discrete value. For example, a digital watch represents the time as specific numbers as opposed to **analog** watch hands that represent time through continuous and linear movement.

DMCA (Digital Millennium Copyright Act)   The most recent and comprehensive change to U.S. Copyright law. Passed in 1998, the DMCA extends copyright protection in many areas of technology, including the prevention of **TPM circumvention**.

Domain Name   A name used to identify one or more **IP addresses**. Domain names are most often used in **URLs** to help web browsers find specific sites on the **Internet**. A typical domain name consists of a word or phrase followed by a **TLD** such as <.com>, <.org>, or <.net>.

DOS (Disk Operating System)   A generic term for early PC **operating systems**. The most popular version, MS-DOS, was originally developed by Microsoft for IBM.

Electronic Commerce (E-Commerce)   Using the Internet to sell goods or services.

Emulation Software   A program with the ability to imitate another program or device. For example, some programs allow Apple Macintosh computers to emulate the Windows **Operating System** and run Windows **applications**.

Encryption   The process of translating data into a secret code, often utilizing complex **algorithms** to carry out the translation. To reverse the process and read the data, one must **decrypt** the code.

End User   Customers who purchase finished products from vendors (as opposed to **OEMs**/developers who purchase products in order to modify, improve, bundle, or integrate them with other products).

EPC (European Patent Convention)   The convention which established the **EPO** and set the rules for patentability in the European Union.

EPO (European Patent Office)   The governmental agency in Europe in charge of receiving and processing patent applications and issuing patents.

Filtering   The process of screening incoming content to a computer and eliminating specific selections based on subject matter. Most commonly used to filter out **spam** or offensive sexual, political, or violent material.

Framing   The process of displaying content from different web pages so that it appears to the user to be within the "frame" of the original page.

Freeware   Software distributed for free. Often subject to an **Open Source License**.

Graphical User Interface (GUI)   A method of displaying information about an **operating system** or **application** and receiving commands from users based on visual images, such as **icons**, pointers, a desktop, windows, and menus.

Gray Market   A marketplace where goods are bought internationally and then resold to customers domestically, usually at a price far below the domestic price. Products entering a country from a gray market are also known as parallel imports.

HREF (Hypertext Reference Link)   An **HTML** instruction **linking** text or graphics to another document or website.

HTML (Hyper Text Markup Language)   The programming language used to create documents on the World Wide Web.

HTTP (Hyper Text Transfer Protocol)   The **protocol** used by the World Wide Web to define how data is formatted and transmitted.

I/O (Input/Output) Device   A device whose primary purpose is inputting or extracting data from a computer, such as a floppy disk drive.

ICANN (Internet Corporation for Assigned Names and Numbers)   A non-profit corporation formed in 1998 to administer **IP address** allocation, **protocol** parameter assignment, **domain name** system management, and **root server system** management functions.

Icon   A small picture that represents an object or program on a computer screen. Icons are typically a central feature of **Graphical User Interfaces** (GUIs).

Independent Software Vendors (ISVs)   A company that produces software unaffiliated with a particular hardware product.

Information Technology   Using computers and networks to manage, process, and communicate information.

Infrastructure   The physical **architecture** of a **network**.

Integrated Circuit   Also known as a chip, an integrated circuit is a small device made out of a **semiconductor** material containing transistors and other electronic components.

Internet   A global **network** of millions of computers, originally developed by **ARPA**.

Internet Engineering Task Force (IETF)   The main standards organization for the **Internet**. The IETF is a large international body of network designers, operators, vendors, and researchers working to expand and improve the way the **Internet** functions.

InterNIC (Internet Network Information Center)   A consortium involving the National Science Foundation, AT&T, General Atomics, and Network Solutions, Inc. (**NSI**) whose purpose is to register **domain names**, provide a directory of **Internet** domains to the public, and give general support and information to the Internet community. Until recently, NSI had primary authority as part of InterNIC to register all **domain names**.

Interoperability   Designing a computer component so that it is compatible with (i.e., works with) other components.

IP Address   A numerical identification used to locate a specific computer on the **Internet**. For example, 1.206.40.130.

ISP (Internet Service Provider)   A company that provides access to the **Internet**, usually through local phone lines. For example, America Online (AOL).

Java   An **object-oriented** programming language developed by Sun Microsystems which allows a single **application** to run on any **operating system**. Use of Java programs has become especially common on the **Internet**.

Linking   The process of using **HTML** to allow text or graphics on a web page to refer to another web page or document whereby clicking on the link takes the user to that page or document directly.

Local Area Network (LAN)   A **network** in which all components are located within a relatively small fixed geographic area, often within one building.

Logic Bomb   A "lockout" feature implemented in software programs whereby the program will shut down unless it receives a new "key" from the programmer on a regular basis. Often used to police and enforce license payments from customers.

Market Failure   The inability of a free market to meet the needs of all its consumers and suppliers without generating externalities.

Mass-market Licenses Also known as End User License Agreements. Often found in **shrinkwrap** or **click-wrap** form, these licenses are non-negotiated agreements issued in identical form to all customers without variance in terms.

Metatag A special **HTML** instruction embedded in the code of a web page to provide web browsers with information about who created the page, how often it is updated, what subjects it concerns, and keywords that correspond to its content. **Search engines** often use metatags to properly catalogue web pages.

Microprocessor A synonym for **CPU**.

MP (Madrid Protocol) A recent revision of the **MTA**.

MTA (Madrid Trademark Agreement) An international treaty allowing trademark owners to file a single application in a member country and use that single application to secure rights in all other member countries.

Natural Language Language used by humans to communicate, as opposed to a computer language such as **Java**. Often used to refer to the ability of certain search programs to take human or "natural" language questions and convert them into computer-language inquiries.

NCCUSL (National Conference of Commissioners on Uniform State Laws) A national group of state representatives working to unify state laws.

NDA (Non-disclosure Agreement) A written contract limiting the right of the signatories to discuss or utilize any information they receive that is covered by the agreement. Often used by companies when seeking financing, in forming joint ventures, or entering licensing agreements with other companies. Also used by companies with departing employees in order to maintain trade secrets.

Netiquette A contraction of **Internet** etiquette, netiquette represents an informal set of social norms which define acceptable and unacceptable behavior on computer **networks**.

Network A system connecting two or more compatible points to each other. For example, the telephone network; the **Internet**.

Network Effects See **Network Externalities**.

Network Externalities The increase or decrease in utility or satisfaction that a consumer of a product derives from every additional consumer's use of that product.

Network Market A market for products that exhibit **network externalities**.

Nonexcludability A characteristic of a **public good** whereby the creator of the good is unable to prevent those who do not pay for the good from consuming it.

Nonrivalrous A characteristic of a **public good** whereby additional consumers of the good do not deplete the supply of the good available to others.

NSI (Network Solutions, Inc.) The original company in charge of registering **domain names**.

Object Code Written instructions for a program in a form readable by computers. Usually translated or **"compiled"** from **source code**, the human-readable form most often used by programmers.

Object-Oriented Programming A special type of programming that combines **data structures** with functions to create reusable "objects." Once an object is created, it can be used in several different files or applications (e.g., using an arrow to show the position of a mouse pointer).

OEMs (Original Equipment Manufacturers) Companies that sell customized computers to **end users**, usually packaging or bundling hardware and software components from multiple third-party manufacturers.

Open Source License A license, typically used for software products, that allows anyone to have access to the source code of the product and to use or build on the code in any way they wish as long as they make their results equally available free of charge and under the same Open Source license conditions.

Operating System The main computer program that loads into memory when a computer is first powered up. The operating system serves as the foundation for running other computer programs called **applications**. Operating Systems generally perform basic tasks, such as recognizing input from the keyboard or mouse, sending output to the display screen, keeping track of files and directories, and controlling **peripheral** devices such as disk drives and printers.

OSP (Online Service Provider) See **ISP**.

PCT (Patent Cooperation Treaty) An international treaty signed in 1970 which allows a patent applicant in a member country to delay subsequent member country applications for up to 30 months while still maintaining her original priority date.

Peripheral Any external device attached to a computer, such as a monitor, keyboard, disk drive, mouse, or printer.

PICS (Platform for Independent Content Selection) A system developed by the World Wide Web Consortium to enable the tagging of websites in order to automatically **filter** out objectionable content.

Protocol   An agreed-upon format for transmitting data between two devices.

PTO (Patent and Trademark Office)   The governmental agency in the United States in charge of receiving and processing patent and trademark applications and issuing patents and trademark registrations.

Public Good   A good which benefits all members of society whether they pay for it or not. For example, national military defense. Private markets generally undersupply public goods because producers cannot reap the marginal value of their investment in providing such goods.

Public-key Cryptography   A cryptographic system involving two uniquely correlated **algorithmic** keys—a public key available to any user and a private or secret key available only to select individuals, usually the recipients of confidential messages. By using the public key, the sender of a message can protect its contents by **encrypting** it with the recipient's public key. The recipient can then **decrypt** the message using the corresponding private key, thus ensuring the security of the message.

Random-Access Memory (RAM)   A type of computer memory in which any memory location can be accessed independently (as opposed to sequentially). Unlike **ROM**, RAM memory loses its contents when its power supply is turned off. RAM is most commonly used to store **operating system**, **application**, and data files when loaded into memory from a hard drive or other peripheral.

Read-Only Memory (ROM)   A type of computer memory which can contain pre-recorded data. The data stored in the ROM, unlike **RAM**, cannot normally be reset or erased, even when its power supply is turned off. ROM is most commonly used to store a computer's start up programs and diagnostic applications.

Reverse Engineering   The process of uncovering how a component or **application** functions by analyzing the final product.

Root Server System   A **network** of thirteen servers that supply the world with official domain name information.

Schematic   A model or diagram showing each part of a product.

SDMI (Secure Digital Music Initiative)   An effort by the U.S. recording industry to create a uniform method of distributing music in **digital** format with a security system to prevent unauthorized access or duplication. See also **TPM**.

Search Engine   A website that collects and catalogues the content of web pages, allowing users to input key words or queries and then generating a list of the sites with the highest correlation to the inquiry based on a matching **algorithm**. For example, Alta Vista and Excite are common **Internet** search engines.

Semiconductor A material that acts as both a poor conductor of electricity and a poor insulator, primarily used to manufacture computer chips. For example, silicon or germanium.

Shareware A method of distributing software based on an honor system. Distribution is free, with the author requesting payment from the user if she likes the product and chooses to continue using it regularly. Payment often assures service support and free upgrades.

Shrinkwrap Licenses A **mass-market license** enclosed within the shrink-wrapped box in which a product is sold. A typical shrinkwrap license will declare that by opening the shrinkwrap, the user assents to the terms of the license, even though many consumers are not able to read the license until after they open the box.

Site Licenses Licenses that require payment based on the number of computers in which the program is installed.

Source Code Written instructions for a program in a form readable by humans. Must be translated or **"compiled"** into **object code** in order to be executed by a computer.

Spam Unsolicited commercial communications, originally via Usenet but today usually via electronic mail.

Standards Specific technology that is adopted for use in a particular industry for a particular purpose. Standards can be adopted either by a recognized organization (e.g., **IETF**), by government decree, or **de facto** when a majority of users chooses on their own to employ the technology.

Subroutine The section of a program that performs a particular task.

Switching Costs The cost of converting or replacing a **standard**. For example, the time it takes to learn the features of a new word processing application after having already learned those associated with an old one.

TCP/IP (Transmission Control Protocol/Internet Protocol) The collection of communications **protocols** used to connect computers to the **Internet** and transmit data.

TLD (Top-Level Domain) The suffix attached to **Internet domain names**, such as <.com>, <.net>, or <.org>.

TPM Circumvention The process of either disabling or deceiving a **TPM** in order to access or duplicate the content or program protected.

TPMs (Technological Protection Measures) Security devices that attempt to prevent duplication and unauthorized access to copyrighted works, often some form of **encryption**-based software.

TRIPs (Agreement on Trade-Related Aspects of Intellectual Property Rights) An international treaty, signed in 1994, which relies on national treatment and nondiscrimination principles to set minimum standards for international protection of intellectual property.

UCITA (Uniform Computer Information Transactions Act)   A statute proposed by **NCCUSL** that would expand the role of state contract law in governing transactions in computer information.

URL (Uniform Resource Locator)   The location of a specific web page or document on the **Internet**. URLs begin with the **protocol** they use (e.g., **HTTP**) and are usually listed as a file name within a sub-directory of a **domain name**. For example, http://www.law.berkeley.edu/BCLT

User Friendly   A general term referring to any feature that makes a computer easier to use, especially for novice users. For example, help screens, Graphical User Interfaces (**GUI**s), and menus.

UTSA (Uniform Trade Secrets Act)   A model law promulgated by **NCCUSL** intended to unify state trade secrecy laws throughout the United States. To date, UTSA has been adopted in one form or another by 40 states and the District of Columbia.

Vaporware   A sarcastic term used to describe computer products that have been announced and advertised but are either never released or are not yet under development at the time the announcement is made. Sometimes used to suggest the existence of anti-competitive strategies by large dominant companies, such as Microsoft, where the announcements and advertising are solely meant to intimidate smaller competitors and discourage venture capital investment in competing products.

WIPO (World Intellectual Property Organization)   A specialized agency of the United Nations responsible for the promotion of the protection of intellectual property throughout the world through cooperation among countries, and for the administration of various multilateral treaties dealing with the legal and administrative aspects of intellectual property.

WTO (World Trade Organization)   The international organization responsible for enforcing the provisions of the **TRIPs** agreement.

WYSIWYG (What-You-See-Is-What-You-Get)   A method by which documents appear on the screen exactly as they will look when printed.

Table of Cases

Major cases are in italics.

Table of Statutes

Index